PERSPECTIVES ON DISABILITY

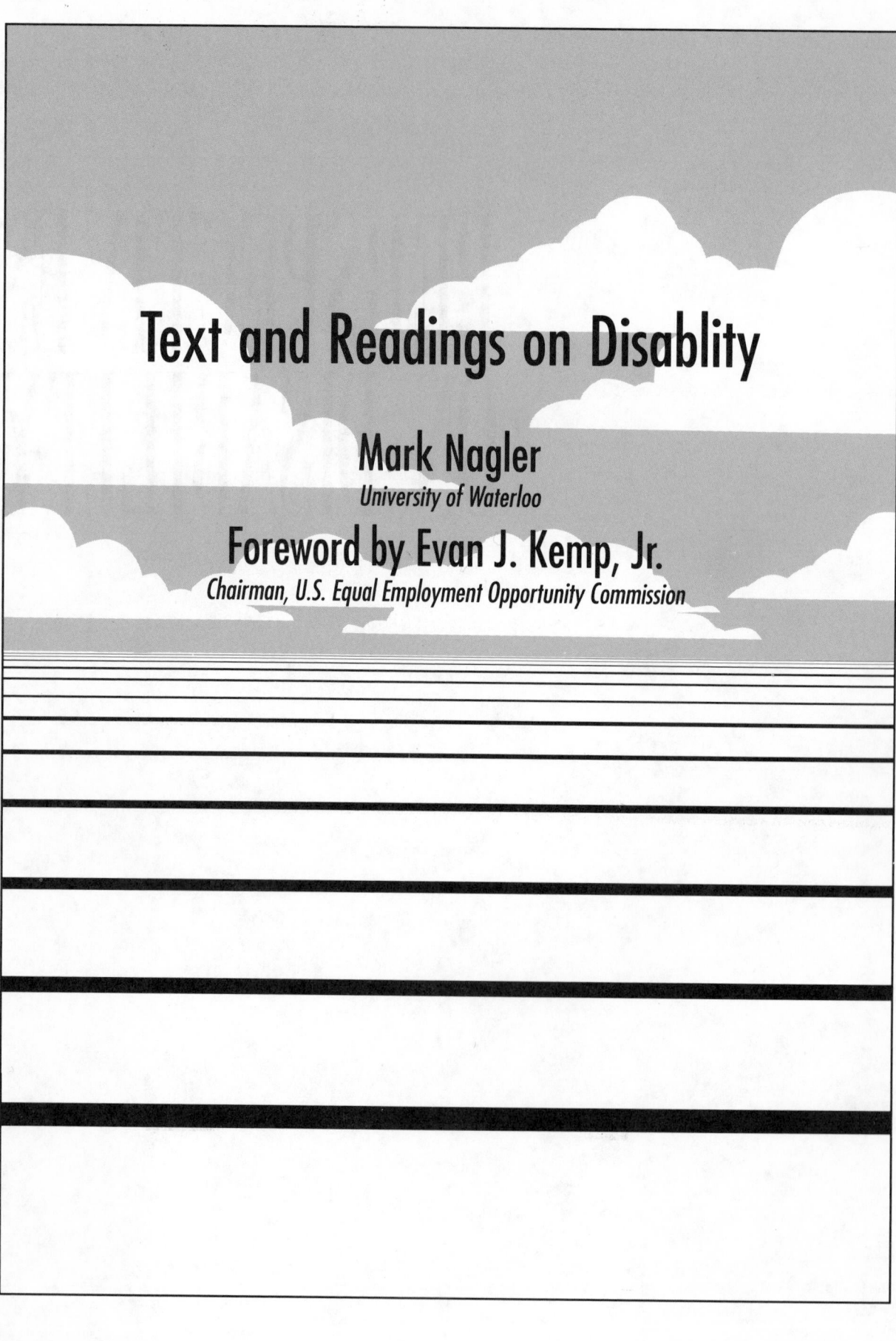

Text and Readings on Disablity

Mark Nagler
University of Waterloo

Foreword by Evan J. Kemp, Jr.
Chairman, U.S. Equal Employment Opportunity Commission

PERSPECTIVES ON DISABILITY

HEALTH MARKETS RESEARCH
PALO ALTO, CALIFORNIA

© 1990 Mark Nagler
Hamilton, Ontario, Canada

Published by HEALTH MARKETS RESEARCH
851 Moana Court
Palo Alto, California, 94306 U.S.A.

Printed in the United States of America

Library of Congress Cataloging-in-Publication Data

Editor, Mark Nagler, Ph.D.

Perspectives on Disability
Text and Readings on Disability

Published in the U.S., Palo Alto, California

Library of Congress Catalog Card Number 90-83832

1. Disability   2. Social Interaction

ISBN 0-9627640-2-7 (hardcover)

ISBN 0-9627640-1-9 (paperback)

INTRODUCTION

Society's attitudes about the disabled are in a process of evolution. The disabled desire to escape from the prejudices and discriminations that have had the effect of casting them into a minority. Since the disabled are a disadvantaged group, they encounter social, physical, psychological, and economic barriers in attempting to maximize their rehabilitative and habilitative potentials. Disability is a condition imposed by physical and/or psychological "problems". Individuals are handicapped in varying degrees by their disabilities while others are able to minimize and in some instances escape the handicapping effects of their disabilities.

Quality of life is central to the living conditions of the disabled as it is to every member of our society. In many instances, the disabled are able to achieve integration; however, many disabled people continue to encounter the barriers which identify them as being different. The process of amalgamation is hindered by the attitudes and values of a society which is often inclined to accept only token integration of those who do not meet the social criteria of normalcy. For instance, in ancient Greece, it was a common practise for those who were born disabled to be identified and eliminated in the bowels of Cata. Those with more serious blemishes were isolated, segregated, institutionalized, and degraded. Although the degradation continues, it is becoming less acceptable to maintain the social, psychological, and legal impediments to integration. The purpose of this text is to identify the significant and paramount concerns of the disabled community and to illuminate the obstacles which are often imposed on this minority. Further, it is the intention of this book to remedy the lack of comprehensive information about the disabled and to present some of the conflicting perspectives which surround many disabled issues.

The following articles will identify and illustrate the major concerns of the disabled community; benefiting not only the disabled person but all those who come into contact with the disabled person, such as family, friends, employers, social workers, medical and para-medical professionals, psychologists, sociologists, clerics, and other academics.

FOREWARD

The Emancipation Proclamation for people with disabilities, the "Americans with Disabilities Act of 1990" (ADA), is at this writing being readied for President Bush's signature. A particular embodiment of the world-wide activism of people with disabilities and their representatives, the ADA proclaims, "the Nation's proper goals regarding individuals with disabilities are to assure equality of opportunity, full participation, independent living, and economic self-sufficiency for such individuals."

While affirming the principle of equality of access and opportunity for millions of disabled Americans, the ADA moreover, represents President Bush's critical shift in Federal policy toward mainstreaming and integration, and away from dependency and segregation. Almost two years ago, Vice President Bush argued: "We must develop programs and policies that promote independence, freedom of choice and productive involvement in the social and economic mainstream. This does not merely mean employment. It also means access to the mainstream educational system, to public accommodation, to public transportation -- in other words, meaningful access to all aspects of society."

The ADA prohibits discrimination in all these areas. The law will thus require that all new non-residential buildings be designed and constructed to be fully accessible. Likewise, new buses and trains, and new transportation facilities will have to be accessible. In addition, the ADA mandates the creation of a national telecommunications relay system so that, at long last, several million speech- and hearing-impaired citizens will be able to use the telephone.

But the crux of the ADA is its employment provisions, for joblessness is the truly disabling condition. A staggering 58% of all men with disabilities and 80% of all women with disabilities are unemployed. So long as two-thirds of disabled Americans are unemployed, we will be unable to break the terrible cycle of dependency and segregation. And, if people with disabilities cannot break the grip of economic dependence, our society is doomed to spend more than $160 billion dollars a year on benefits that most recipients would willingly trade for a good job.

Hence the significance of Title I of the ADA, dealing with employment discrimination -- in particular the question of who is covered and how the law is to be enforced. For the most part, the law adopts the three-part definition of "individual with handicaps" used in the Rehabilitation Act of 1973: an individual with a physical or mental impairment that substantially limits at least one of that person's major life activities; an individual with a record of such an impairment; and an individual regarded as having such an impairment.

The first part of the definition is intended to include only those persons with substantial disabilities "in a major life activity" such as walking, seeing, hearing, speaking, and breathing. Thus, for example, an individual with epilepsy, paralysis, blindness, or a hearing impairment would be covered by exemptions from the definition of disability. The definition of disability does not include: homosexuality, bisexuality, transvestism, transsexualism, pedophilia, exhibitionism, voyeurism, or other gender identity of sexual behavior disorders; nor compulsive gambling, pyromania, kleptomania; and psychoactive substance abuse disorders resulting from current use of illegal drugs. Much concern had been raised about the ADA's application to persons using illegal drugs, but the definition of disability explicitly excludes them. Employers may, if they wish, conduct testing to detect the use of illegal drugs by applicants and employees and may make employment decisions based on the results so long as the test accurately detects the presence of illegal drugs. Moreover, the bill specifically provides that employers may prohibit employees in the workplace from using or being under the influence of illegal drugs or alcohol, as well. And employers may require employees to follow the Drug Free Workplace Act of 1988 as well as applicable government regulations covering sensitive jobs.

An employer's refusal to make a <u>reasonable accommodation</u> that would not impose an undue hardship is also considered discriminatory under the ADA. In brief, a reasonable accommodation is a provision for a person with a disability to perform the essential duties of the position. But an employer's reasonable accommodation responsibility is not limitless. First, the employer must know about the physical or mental limitations of the disabled person. If a disability is hidden and the disabled person does not request an accommodation, an employer is not required by the ADA to intuit whether an accommodation is needed.

Second, the obligation to make a reasonable accommodation only extends to "otherwise qualified" individuals with disabilities. Thus, the ADA does not require an employer looking for someone with a degree or experience in marketing to handle its advertising department to hire or accommodate a disabled person with a degree in philosophy and no experience in advertising.

Third, if an employer can show that the accommodation would impose an undue hardship on the operation of its business, it is relieved of the obligation to provide that accommodation. The ADA defines "undue hardship" as "an action requiring significant difficulty or expense," according to several factors the bill lists to assist EEOC and the courts. EEOC and the courts may look at site-specific resources as well as the resources of the employer as a whole. The site-specific factors require an examination of the relationship between the employer and the site providing the accommodation to determine whether resources from the employer generally are available to the site or not. Exactly when the resources of the employer or the resources of the site alone will be controlling as an undue hardship will be decided on a case by case basis. The guiding principle remains that larger employers have a greater duty to make accommodation than do smaller employers.

In addition to requiring an employer to make a reasonable accommodation, the ADA would make it illegal for an employer to deny an employment opportunity to a disabled applicant or employee if the basis for the denial is the individual's need for reasonable accommodation. This provision is intended to cover a situation in which an eligible and qualified employee is denied a promotion because his new position would require the employer to purchase equipment needed to accommodate his disability. It also responds to instances where employees or applicants themselves offer to provide a necessary accommodation (say, an expensive talking computer) that would otherwise impose an undue hardship on the employer.

With respect to employee selection criteria, the ADA prohibits the use of qualification tests or selection criteria that screen out or tend to screen out a qualified disabled individual or a class of qualified disabled individuals. Employers cannot rely on standards, tests, or criteria that arbitrarily exclude disabled people. An employer may, however, use standards or criteria that are not arbitrary but are job-related and consistent with business necessity. If a disabled applicant cannot meet a job-related standard and there is no accommodation that would enable the applicant to satisfy the standard, the applicant is not qualified for the job. It is not unlawful to refuse to hire him.

In addition, an employer may not make pre-employment inquiries as to the existence, nature, or severity of an applicant's disability, but it may ask questions as to an applicant's ability to perform job-related duties. Also consistent with section 503 regulations, implementing the Rehabilitation Act of 1973, an employer may require a pre-employment medical examination only after a conditional offer of employment and only if a medical examination is required of all applicants for a particular position. Information obtained through such examinations must be kept confidential and must be used in a manner consistent with the requirements of the ADA. This means that if a medical examination reveals that an applicant cannot perform essential job functions, an employer must consider a reasonable accommodation which would permit the applicant to perform the job.

The employment title of the ADA will take effect two years after the date of the law's enactment. During the first year following enactment, the U.S. Equal Employment Opportunity Commission (EEOC) will issue implementing regulations and, working with the Attorney General, develop and implement a plan for technical assistance to employers, employer organizations, persons with disabilities and disability organizations, directly, as well as through grants and contracts. A technical assistance manual shall also be issued. For the two years after the effective date, the law covers only employers with 25 or more employees. Then, two years later (four years after the bill's passage), the law's jurisdiction will extend to employers with 15 or more employees, the same standard currently imposed by Title VII of the Civil Rights Act of 1964. This will likely result in coverage of approximately 15% of all employers and 87% of all employees.

The ADA incorporates Title VII's charge-processing procedures. Thus, an individual claiming employment discrimination on the basis of disability must first file a charge with the EEOC. After 180 days, the individual may request a right-to-sue notice from the EEOC and may then file a lawsuit in court, if he or she wishes to proceed. Alternatively, the individual can await the EEOC administrative process of investigating, determining whether there is cause to believe discrimination has occurred, and, if the cause has been found, conciliating, and when that fails, determining whether the EEOC itself will bring suit.

Hence EEOC has a critical role to play in implementing the ADA. Established by Title VII of the Civil Rights Act of 1964, this agency has 25 years of experience in breaking down barriers to employment opportunity in the private sector caused by race, color, sex, national origin, and religion. Since 1978 the Commission also has been enforcing the Equal Pay Act, the Age Discrimination Act, and section 501 of the Rehabilitation Act of 1973, as amended. The latter law requires that the Federal Government take affirmative action to employ and promote qualified individuals with disabilities. Each Federal agency is required to prepare an affirmative action plan to report to the Commission its progress in hiring and promoting disabled persons. In addition, Federal Government workers and applicants for Federal employment may file complaints of employment discrimination based on disability with their agencies and may make administrative appeals to EEOC if a Federal agency rules against them. In its capacity as an administrative appellate body, EEOC has grappled with many difficult issues under the Rehabilitation Act that will arise under the ADA as well. These include questions concerning the definition of disability as well as the scope of an agency's duty to provide reasonable accommodation. Although this experience with disability discrimination law has been limited to government employment, it provides EEOC with a solid foundation for implementing the ADA employment provisions in the private sector.

EEOC is a small Federal law enforcement agency with approximately 3,000 employees and a fiscal Year 1990 appropriation of $184,926,000. The agency has 50 District, Area and Local offices throughout the United States. During Fiscal Year 1989, EEOC received 55,926 charges of employment discrimination in private sector employment, and it closed 66,209 charges. Approximately 20% of charges result in some positive conclusion, by settlement, an administrative finding of discrimination, or by conciliation and referral for EEOC litigation. During FY 1989, EEOC filed almost 600 lawsuits against private employers.

The enactment of the ADA will result in perhaps an additional 10,000 to 12,000 charges being filed with the Commission alleging discrimination on the basis of disability, an increase of approximately

15 to 20% in the Commission's workload. Thus, the success of its compliance and enforcement programs will depend largely on additional funding from Congress, as civil rights enforcement is a labor-intensive activity, requiring the human capital of investigators and attorneys.

The EEOC is ready to help make the promise of the Americans with Disabilities Act a reality. But government alone, even with the newly-crafted tool of the ADA, cannot make this happen. It will take the persistent efforts of informed people with disabilities to ferret out discrimination, expose it to the light of day, and eradicate it. The contributions to this volume exemplify such educational efforts. We need more efforts like these as the EEOC seeks to inform, conciliate, and litigate, to eradicate barriers and bring persons with disabilities into the mainstream.

Evan J. Kemp, Jr.
Chairman
United States Equal Employment Opportunity Commission
Washington, D.C.

July 4, 1990

CONTENTS

APPENDIX A

Bibliography of Organizations for the Disabled - American and Canadian

ACKNOWLEDGEMENTS

I would like to thank my contemporaries who have disabilities and fellow academics, who motivated me to undertake this project. Their comments and concerns have been most helpful. The articles chosen reflect the spectrum of interests that they have identified. I would also like to acknowledge the strong and continuous support, both emotional and financial, of Ann and Leo Nagler and Sabine Helman. I would also like to thank Craig Bryson and Kelly Hannah for their devotion, hard work, and support. My thanks is also extended to Judy Murdock, who typed the final draft, Lisa Fulford, who completed the formatting and layout, and to Martin Rosner who undertook the publication of this work knowing that past works in disability related studies have not attracted a profitable market interest. Likewise, I am grateful to my colleagues at Renison College and at the University of Waterloo; they have been responsible for creating a rich, intellectual environment where this project originated. I also wish to extend my gratitude to the Social Sciences and Humanities Research Committee for their support and assistance. Most importantly, I want to express my ongoing appreciation to Sharon, Adam, and David for a life that makes everything worthwhile and important. Their observations on a daily basis have been my inspiration.

ABOUT THE AUTHOR

Dr. Nagler was born with Cerebral Palsy which was not diagnosed until he was five years old. His parents, relatives and friends provided him with support which allowed him to progress through the education to receive a Doctoral degree in sociology from the University of Sterling in Scotland. The author specializes in the study of: disability related issues, deviance, and race and ethnic relations. Currently, he is the president of the Advocacy Resource Center for the Handicapped (ARCH), a center embracing forty-one organizations for the disabled in the form of a legal clinic, which defends the rights of people with disabilities. He has also chaired a committee for the disabled on behalf of the Canadian Jewish Congress. Given these experiences and contributions it is evident that Dr. Nagler has a unique understanding of disability related issues, as he has both investigated and experienced many of the concerns raised in this book. Presently, Professor Nagler is teaching at Renison College and in the sociology department at the University of Waterloo, in Waterloo, Ontario, Canada.

1 WHAT IT MEANS TO BE DISABLED

Most disabled people strive for normalization and integration. However they often encounter social, economic, psychological, and political barriers in attempting to achieve this goal. The majority of the disabled endeavour to achieve integration and to participate fully with their able bodied counter parts. However, some segments of our society cannot and will not accept the limitations imposed by disabilities and instead they opt for secondary gains.

When reading the articles in this book it is important to note that there are four basic types of disabilities. The first type of disability prevents the disabled person from ever having the opportunity to experience a normal life. Such people are afflicted with congenital disorders. The second type of disability status is developmental: those who are burdened with hypertension, arthritis, and other related conditions. These individuals must often limit their activities as a consequence of their disabilities. The third category of disability is instantaneous impediments which are usually quite sudden and extremely restrictive. The final disability status is psychological: this group includes those people with mental disorders.

The stress imposed by these four types of disabling conditions can range from mild to severe. In some cases members of the disabled are unable to adjust to their handicap and in other cases they can overcome them completely. However, being able to succeed against the physical challenges of a disability is only a partial victory, since many of the disabled discover that they are impeded by many social, economic, political, and psychological barriers. The disabled often believe that they are members of a victimized minority, who are prevented by the attitudes of society from enjoying the quality of life that they deserve. Being victims of prejudice and discrimination, the disabled often suffer the alienation and isolation experienced by racial, religious, ethnic, and other minority groups.

The authors, Saurez de Balcazar, Bradford, and Fawcett address many of these concerns in their article, "Common Concerns of Disabled Americans: Issues and Options". These authors identify the major anxieties of the disabled in contemporary society. They maintain that "the dissemination of social science research and perspectives relating to the acceptance and advocacy of people with disabilities would seem an important step in any process that is to have the capability of leading to full integration into the larger society."

Lee Meyerson also clearly indicates the evolution experiences of the disabled in his research "The Social Psychology of Physical Disability: 1948 and 1988."

Goffman and Davis[1] address the primary interests of those who possess disabling afflictions and/or those who experience psychiatric illness. In many instances these individuals must re-negotiate their identities with many social groups. The difficulties associated with creating new identities or with re-establishing former identities is analyzed by Hanks and Poplin in their research, "The Sociology of Physical Disability: a review of the literature and some conceptual perspectives." The significance of stigma is further explored by Kaiser, Freeman, and Wingate. Individuals who have had their capacities or appearances altered by accident, surgery, or disease often encounter social, psychological, and physical alienation, if not isolation. The outcome of this exclusion is severe: sociologists have long established that individuals are not often treated in terms of their capacities or abilities, but by their

---

[1]*Stigma* by Goffman and *Passage Through Crisis* by Davis.

imposed labels, which may or may not be legitimate. These effects of labelling are further explored in Grove's analysis of labelling and mental illness.

By contrast, it is evident that not all of the disabled population desires to be integrated, since many of the afflicted are capable of achieving secondary gains through illness. For example, some coronary victims retire early and they confine themselves to sedentary lives while others with the same problem embark on programs of physical fitness and in some cases become marathon participants. Thomas Cutsforth illustrates the idea of personality crippling through disabilities. Many of the physically disabled are unable to cope with the manifestations imposed upon them by their conditions. Cutsforth notes that some disabled individuals attempt to escape and retreat from their situations, and his analysis of the problems of the blind can be transposed into the difficulties experienced by other disadvantaged persons.

The disabled are expected to be law-abiding, submissive human beings, but as Greer points out in his article on substance abuse among the disabled: the disabled are as capable of deviant behaviour as their ablebodied counterparts.

Romeis, in his article on alienation as a consequence of disability, illustrates that there is contradictory evidence on the adaptation and on the subsequent adjustment of individuals who have experienced disabling conditions. Frequently, disabilities are distorted by stereotyping, the implications of this phenomena are examined by Townsend in his research on the "Stereotypes of Mental Illness: a comparison with ethnic stereotypes". "Obviously, individuals who experience 'sudden' disabilities encounter severe interpersonal stress as they discover that in many situations they are victims of differential behaviour. In other words, they are treated not as they wish to be treated, but as 'disabled' and occasionally incompetent. Consequently, many disabled persons express hostility and degradation by the fact that their afflictions are associated with psychiatric manifestations. For example, in many instances the deaf are regarded as stupid, a label often utilized by large segments of the hearing community. The problems associated with this condition are expressed by Jerry Lee "Deafness the Next Ten Years". Disabled groups often band together in order to enjoy a quality of life free from the labels, expectations, and difficulties associated with the 'normal society'.

Adjustment is not a permanent state, but rather an ongoing process. The disabled who experience their conditions for the first time are initially shattered, but physical and mental therapy, as well as the support of significant peers aid the person in adjusting to an altered lifestyle. On the other hand, there are individuals who initially demonstrate positive adjustment to severe physical and psychological limitations imposed on them by their disabled status. Other disabled, on occasion, become discouraged and may relapse, maladjust, and even commit suicide because they are unable to cope with their environment.

Being disabled means many things not only to the disabled person, but also to their associates. The rejection, isolation, and alienation in traditional patterns of treatment have given way to a mainstream orientation. According to the mainstream philosophy, the disabled are to be integrated as much as possible in order to maximize their habilitative potential, thereby ensuring that these individuals will enjoy the highest quality of life achievable for them. However, there are still many citizens in the disabled community who continue to undergo varying degrees of negativism, prejudice, and disassociation because they have been stigmatized and forced into the role of an 'involuntary deviant'.

2

Common Concerns of Disabled Americans: Issues and Options

Yolanda Suarez de Balcazar
Barbara Bradford
Stephen B. Fawcett

The hallmark value of the disabilities rights and independent living movements is the assurance of equal access to all activities society offers, both work- and leisure-related. Over 30 million people with disabilities accept responsibility for their work, family, and individual lives. Their substantial contribution to society can be attributed both to personal competence and to the strengths of those communities that foster and support attempts to live independently. However, there are still many physical and social barriers that limit adequate jobs, housing, accessible transportation, and other needed services. These community problems thwart even the most heroic personal attempts to pursue a full life.

This article outlines the major problems in communities that limit independence. It also provides alternatives for action from the perspective of people with disabilities. It summarizes quantitative data from nearly 13,000 people with disabilities in 319 communities in 10 states and provides qualitative information about the issues and options they identified during local town meetings and public forums. This compendium presents common concerns of people with disabilities and their insights into what actions would help assure equality of opportunity.

Questionnaires were administered to all identified citizens with disabilities in the local community or state. Sponsoring organizations included independent living centers, state vocational rehabilitation agencies, and consumer advisory committees. Average scores for importance and satisfaction were used to identify relative strengths (i.e., items of high importance and high satisfaction) and possible problems (i.e., items of high importance and low satisfaction). Finally, qualitative information was obtained when the results of each survey were discussed in town meetings. Disabled citizens discussed major issues, identifying specific dimensions of issues and generating possible solutions.

Major Problems Identified By Disabled Americans

This section provides a summary of 18 issues identified as major problems, which are organized alphabetically by category headings. Under each category, problematic aspects are noted as well as the total number of participants who responded to surveys in which that issue was chosen as a top problem. The overall average importance and satisfaction ratings for all respondents are also presented.

Assistive Devices: Affordability and Availability

The issue of assistive devices (e.g., wheelchairs) involves aspects such as affordability, availability of financial assistance, cost of services and repair, cost of rental, and price. Six related survey items were chosen by consumers and responded to by 6,355 people with disabilities in 6 different surveys. The issues received consistently high importance ratings, an average of 80 percent, and relatively low satisfaction ratings, an average of 42 percent.

Consumer-Identified Dimensions:

- Assistive devices, such as wheelchairs, are very expensive. Most people with disabilities do not have enough money to purchase devices.
- Rental of assistive devices is almost nonexistent. If rental is possible, consumers don't know where to go or get needed information.
- Medicaid and Medicare do not cover all assistive devices.

Reprinted From: Social Policy, Fall 1988, with permission.

Consumer-Generated Alternatives:
- Change legislation regarding Medicaid and Medicare to cover purchase and repair of assistive devices.

Commercial Services: Accessibility

The issue of accessibility of businesses, particularly public restrooms, has been selected as a problem in three different surveys. Two related survey items were responded to by 299 consumers. The issues were rated with an average importance of 87 percent and an average satisfaction rating of 47 percent.

Consumer-Identified Dimensions:
- In many business and restaurants, the restrooms are inaccessible.
- The restroom doors are too hard to push, and the stalls are too narrow.

Consumer-Generated Alternatives:
- Make a list of accessible and responsive businesses.
- Survey businesses and provide feedback and suggestions.
- Write letters to local businesses about upgrading facilities.
- Consumers should keep informed about and review access plans and permits for new construction in the community.

Commercial Services: Availability of Discounts

A second issue related to commercial services and identified as a problem is the availability of special rates for disabled consumers. This issue was selected in one survey involving 1,185 respondents, with an importance rating of 82 percent and a satisfaction rating of 35 percent.

Consumer-Identified Dimensions:
- Disabled people do not get the same discounts and shopping privileges as senior citizens. Most disabled people are on a very low fixed income.

Consumer-Generated Alternatives:
- Independent living centers can sell discount cards to consumers for use with participating merchants, as was done by Westside CIL in Los Angeles.
- Have a group of disabled people discuss a proposal with local merchants.

Community Support and Responsiveness

This category includes issues related to family, community, and government support in meeting the needs of persons with disabilities. Five somewhat related items were chosen by 1,914 consumers in six surveys. They received consistently high importance ratings, with an average of 86 percent, and relatively low satisfaction ratings, with an average of 46 percent.

Consumer-Identified Dimensions:
- Families and communities do not encourage disabled members to be independent.
- The community does not provide opportunities or assistance for disabled people to live independently.
- There are not enough support groups available for people with disabilities and their families.
- Sexuality counselling for people with disabilities is not available.
- Local governments are unresponsive to disability issues, especially if solutions cost money. For example, disabled citizens are discouraged from registering and voting by inaccessible registration sites, polling places, and lack of transportation.

Consumer-Generated Alternatives:
- Encourage community groups to organize support groups and events to involve disabled people and their families.
- Encourage churches to work with support groups, and include disabled people and their families in church activities.
- Use local media to feature stories about including people with disabilities in com-

munity activities.

- Ask city councils for help in organizing programs that will encourage independence for disabled people and their families.
- Independent living centers should provide training for their staff counsellors in sexuality counselling or bring in professional counsellors for a workshop and provide materials.
- Consumer groups should represent themselves at city council and county court meetings, become familiar with city budgets, and advocate for funds for access improvements and disability programs.
- Consumer groups should encourage and assist disabled citizens to register to vote.
- Use the American Civil Liberties Union to enforce existing access and registration laws.

Disability Rights and Advocacy

Issues related to involving disabled citizens in advocacy activities, increasing their knowledge about their rights, and training in self-advocacy were selected in four different surveys. Three related questions were chosen by 2,430 people with disabilities. They received an average importance rating of 88 percent and an average satisfaction rating of 45 percent.

Consumer-Identified Dimensions:
- People with disabilities are unaware of their legal rights.
- Most people with disabilities are unaware of what pending legislation at state and national levels they should support or oppose.
- People with disabilities need training in forming advocacy organizations.

Consumer-Generated Alternatives:
- Professionals and independent living centers can foster local and state leadership within the disabled community.
- People with disabilities need to inform themselves and attend advocacy meetings at all levels, get on mailing lists for disability groups involved in legislation, and obtain names, addresses, and numbers of elected officials.
- Disabled consumers should organize locally

around identified issues and connect with state and national groups.
- Training in advocacy skills should be provided.

Employment Accommodations, Disincentives, and Training

Five survey items related to job accommodations in the workplace, work disincentives, and quality of job assistance and training programs were identified by 9,118 consumers as relative problems in six surveys. They received an average importance rating of 83 percent and an average satisfaction rating of 42 percent.

Consumer-Identified Dimensions:
- Many businesses do not provide reasonable accommodations in the workplace.
- Work disincentives still exist within the social security system. In addition to loss of economic benefits are losses or reductions in medical benefits, housing subsidies, food stamps, attendant services, etc.
- Disabled job hunters lack basic job-seeking skills and are unaware of incentives to employers and laws prohibiting discrimination.
- Blind people have lost their tax credit; other disability groups were never eligible.
- People with disabilities do not know where to go for job training or assistance in finding a job.

Consumer-Generated Alternatives:
- Consumer groups need to form a coalition to lobby legislators at federal and state levels for tax credits.
- VR could offer training in job-seeking skills.
- Consumer groups should develop guidelines on what constitutes reasonable accommodation in the workplace.
- Disseminate information about where to go for job training skills and job-related assistance.

Employment Discrimination

Two survey items related to job discrimination were identified by 9,314 consumers as top problems in eight surveys. They received an average importance rating of 86 percent and an average satisfaction rating of 41 percent.

Consumer-Identified Dimensions:
- People with disabilities are discriminated against because of their disability.
- Qualified disabled individuals are not given the same opportunity as non-disabled people.

Consumer-Generated Alternatives:
- Consumers need to teach disabled job seekers about proper attitudes and how to develop a businesslike demeanour when dealing with a potential employer. Disabled people must sell an employer on their abilities and not rely on sympathy.
- If a specific employer is perceived as insensitive, invite a representative of that company to speak to a disability group about employment.
- Independent living centers and advocacy groups need to encourage and assist disabled job applicants and employees to enforce laws and regulations prohibiting discrimination.
- Disabled individuals can contact the Job Accommodations Network or similar resources for help in locating jobs and training, marketing themselves to prospective employers, and obtaining reasonable accommodation.

Employment Opportunities

Two survey items related to employment opportunities were identified by 9,412 consumers as relative problems in 11 surveys. They received an average importance rating of 84 percent and an average satisfaction rating of 40 percent.

Consumer-Identified Dimensions:
- Job opportunities for people with disabilities are very limited.
- If there is a nondisabled person and a disabled individual applying for a job, employers prefer to hire the nondisabled person.

Consumer-Generated Alternatives:
- Consumers should educate employers in tax credits, reasonable accommodation, and advantages of hiring disabled employees.

- Disability groups must keep a coalition going at the national level to lobby for reduction of work disincentives.
- Job placement people should know which employers routinely hire disabled applicants.
- Use publicity to inform the community about job needs, interests, and capacities of disabled people, similar to TV spots from Job Service on specific jobs.
- Talk with industries to design programs for people with disabilities similar to programs designed for immigrants.

Handicapped Parking

One survey item related to the issue of enforcement of parking ordinances was identified as a major problem by 8,607 people in 13 surveys. The item received an average importance rating of 83 percent and an average satisfaction rating of 41 percent.

Consumer-Identified Dimensions:
- There are not enough handicapped parking places close to shopping and workplaces.
- Many spaces are not well-marked with an upright sign.
- Police do not ticket violators as often as they should.
- Courts are lax in enforcing handicapped parking laws.

Consumer-Generated Alternatives:
- Review local statutes; seek state uniformity. Include private as well as public zones.
- Ask local mayors to publicize local ordinances.
- Consumer groups can conduct public awareness campaigns and letter-writing campaigns to local officials.
- Develop rapport with several police officers to assure better enforcement.
- Conduct study sessions with police, courts, and consumer groups to promote enforcement.
- Consumers can monitor violations and use data to advocate for compliance.
- Consumers can discuss parking problems with merchants where they shop.

- Consumer groups can distribute stickers to violators.
- Consumers can attend city council meetings and voice concerns to get adequate legislation.
- Consumers can advise businesses about adequate spaces and upright signs.
- Consumer groups can patronize businesses who provide and enforce handicapped spaces.
- Publicize how to get parking Ids.
- Increase fines to over $25 to put teeth into the law.
- Form coalitions among groups needing access and parking.
- Provide consumer consultation in design of spaces.
- Putting parking places on end of row for van lifts. In Anderson, IN, violators get a "candid camera" treatment. In a cooperative effort between local consumers and the town's newspaper, a photo and brief statement by violators appeared on the front of the local section.
- Some police departments have deputized local consumers to ticket handicapped parking violators, paying their salaries from fines.

Health Care: Affordability and Availability

Six survey items were selected relevant to the availability and affordability of health care, including whether hospitals accept Medicaid and Medicare, and sensitivity of health care providers to consumers. Items were identified as relative problems by 3,485 consumers in seven surveys. They received an average importance rating of 88 percent and an average satisfaction rating of 48 percent.

Consumer-Identified Dimensions:
- Increasing numbers of doctors are refusing to take Medicaid or Medicare, because payment is very late and inconsistent.
- There is no respite care for families caring for disabled and elderly family members.
- People with disabilities cannot afford regular, nonemergency medical care and medications.
- Transportation to medical appointments is

difficult, especially regular long-distance transportation, and transportation for rural citizens who go to large cities for dialysis or cancer treatment.
- Medical professionals are often insensitive in dealing with disabled patients, preferring to deal with family members rather than communicate directly with the disabled patient as a responsible adult.
- Medical professionals are often unaware of special medical or physical assistance needs imposed by a disability. Thus, discomfort and temporary setbacks can result or even life-threatening situations.
- The general public is unaware that existing programs do not provide adequate medical care for people with disabilities.
- Disabled consumers are often unaware of medical aspects of their own disabilities or good self-care habits. This occurs because they accept the public's definition of themselves as sick and needing to be cared for rather than healthy human beings responsible for their own well-being.
- Another problem is attendant care. If no state attendant care program is available (Wyoming has no Medicaid waiver or state-funded program), there is no paid attendant care for low-income disabled consumers. They must depend on family and friends or live in nursing homes.

Consumer-Generated Alternatives:
- Use local media to describe health problems of people with disabilities and solicit suggestions to solve these problems.
- Organize local volunteers, church, and civic groups for medical transportation.
- Consumer groups should educate medical professionals about the special needs of disabled patients. The Association for Retarded Citizens does this for people with developmental disabilities.
- Invite medical professionals to speak to meetings of consumers to increase their own sensitivity and educate consumers at the same time.
- Provide inservice training for medical professionals in the dignified, courteous treatment

of persons with disabilities. This should be conducted by consumer groups and consumer-run agencies.

- Provide education to consumers in how they can advocate for themselves with health care providers.
- Form coalitions with other consumer groups to work on common health care objectives.
- Form a protection and advocacy organization to help disabled patients in cases of unfair treatment by health care providers.
- Educate medical professionals about treating different disabilities as part of medical and nursing school curricula.
- Use mutual support groups, counsellors, and self-education to encourage good medical habits, nutrition, exercise, and prevention of illness.
- Locate sources of health care for persons with disabilities; make a directory of these resources.
- Arrange local medical fitness centers for people with disabilities. Provide outreach to commercial fitness centers and provide transportation to them for people with disabilities.
- Place people with disabilities as employees of health care providers (i.e., as social workers and patient advocates).
- Involve independent living centers in training and advocacy.
- Consumer groups at the state level could conduct a survey of health care facilities that covers disabilities served, access to offices and parking, acceptance of Medicaid and Medicare, and sources for financial assistance. This could be conducted through state medical and dental societies and updated periodically.
- Educate consumers about medical aspects of their own disabilities. Train them to advocate for themselves with medical professionals, and teach them to take personal responsibility for educating health care providers about their own appropriate treatment and needs.
- Write government and elected officials about health care issues.
- Attend city council meetings, and petition for city funds to help with medical expenses.
- Seek establishment of adult day care and

home health services. Develop a directory of doctors who accept Medicaid and Medicare payments for treatment of people with disabilities.
- Provide toll-free legal advice about legal matters relating to nonacceptance of Medicaid and Medicare or refusal of treatment to disabled consumers.
- Advocate for program changes to facilitate more timely and consistent payment of Medicaid and Medicare.
- Advocate for cooperative living arrangements with shared attendant care for those who need help.
- Consumer groups need to present need for attendant care and cost effectiveness data to state legislature.
- Support national groups lobbying for national attendant care programs.

Housing Affordability, Availability, and Accessibility

Six survey items related to the affordability, availability, and accessibility of housing have been identified as major problems by 4,127 consumers in 12 surveys. They received an average importance rating of 86 percent and an average satisfaction rating of 37 percent.

Consumer-Identified Dimensions:
- There is an extreme shortage of accessible, affordable housing for people with disabilities.
- Eligibility requirements and regulations keep some disabled consumers, especially the nonelderly who live with family members or attendants, from living in public or subsidized housing.
- Builders do not comply with existing laws, where laws exist, that require a certain percentage of accessible units.
- Builders are unaware of laws, access codes, and modifications necessary for accessibility.
- Managers and directors of public housing are unaware of, and often indifferent to, the needs of disabled tenants.

Consumer-Generated Alternatives:
- Talk to owners if the manager is uncooperative.
- Disabled and low-income people should lobby social service agencies for housing assistance.
- Disabled consumers should educate officials on housing needs of people with disabilities.
- Local consumer groups can bring complaints to local housing authorities.
- Consumers can be educated to be aware of tenant rights and raise money to finance suits when necessary.
- Disabled residents should become familiar with codes, where to file complaints where codes don't exist and how to introduce legislation.
- Groups can obtain 202 and other HUD loans for accessible housing and manage the housing units themselves.
- Examine eligibility requirements for subsidized housing; use net, not gross income.
- A consumer group in Los Angeles located two HUD projects in good neighborhoods; the Telephone Pioneers donated money and labor to upgrade the structure.
- Establish subsidized housing administered by occupants. Provide income subsidy within housing cooperatives.
- Some communities in Minnesota provide vouchers to subsidize rent for housing anywhere in the community.
- Establish a referral network for accessible, affordable housing.
- Enforce existing laws setting aside a certain number of units for people with disabilities.
- Consumers need to educate building professionals and make information available.
- Advocate for statewide legislation to encourage adaptability of units.
- Consumers need to lobby elected officials on lack of accessible housing.
- Disabled community members need to get on housing boards.
- Educate disabled homeowners about programs to help modify their homes for access and safety.

Insurance for Auto, Life, and Liability

This issue refers to the availability and affordability of auto, life, and liability insurance for people with disabilities. This item was selected as a major problem by 2,355 people completing two surveys. It received an average importance rating of 89 percent and an average satisfaction rating of 35 percent.

Consumer-Identified Dimensions:
- Insurance premiums are more expensive for people with disabilities.
- Insurance companies, discriminate based on disability.

Consumer-Generated Alternatives:
- Have a group of disabled people discuss possible solutions with insurance companies regarding adequate prices.

Insurance for Health Care

One survey question related to the affordability of health insurance was identified as a problem by 5,624 consumers in two surveys. It received an average importance rating of 86 percent and an average satisfaction rating of 38 percent.

Consumer-Identified Dimensions:
- Disabled consumers cannot buy health insurance because of their disability and/or pre-existing conditions.
- Disabled consumers cannot afford health insurance.
- Health insurance often does not cover supplies, equipment, regular medications, or therapies used by disabled consumers.
- Inability to purchase individual health insurance and exclusion from some group policies are serious disincentives to individuals with disabilities looking for work.

Consumer-Generated Alternatives:
- Consumer groups can advocate for national health insurance.
- Disabled consumers can set up health insurance cooperatives as they did in Los Angeles.

- Shared risk insurance is an option to consumers with disabilities and pre-existing conditions can get group insurance.
- Educate consumers about supplemental insurance available through groups such as AARP, professional associations, and credit card holders.
- Publicize the fact that laws in some states (such as Missouri and Kansas) prohibit insurance companies from discriminating against persons with disabilities.
- Independent living centers can train and assist consumers in filling out forms, challenge actions and policies of Medicaid, Medicare, and insurance companies, and assist in advocacy, complaints, and appeals processes.
- Get information from and make use of the state insurance commissioner's office.

Media Portrayal and Public Information

Three survey items related to media portrayal of people with disabilities and their access to information about services, benefits, and programs were selected as problems by 7,547 consumers in three surveys. The items received an average importance rating of 81 percent and an average satisfaction rating of 39 percent.

Consumer-Identified Dimensions:
- The media do not provide enough information about what is available for disabled citizens.
- The media portray people with disabilities in a negative and unrealistic way, preferring the sensational or pitiful to the everyday and human side of disability.

Consumer-Generated Alternatives:
- Consumer groups should bring accessibility and independent-living issues to the attention of the press.
- Consumers should monitor coverage of disability issues.
- Consumers should educate the media to correct negative portrayals and terminology.
- Consumer groups should meet with service providers about developing a directory of services and programs for people with disabi-

lities that could be disseminated through the media.

Public Access

Issues related to safe access to public places, including availability of curb cuts, accessible entrances, and snow removal, have been selected as major problems. Two related survey items were chosen by 204 consumers in two different surveys, with an average importance rating of 81 percent and an average satisfaction rating of 48 percent.

Consumer-Identified Dimensions:
- Disabled citizens are forced to stay home or use the street, because curb cuts and sidewalks are absent or inadequate, or in some instances, snow is not removed promptly.
- Many public buildings are totally inaccessible or technically accessible with inadequate or unsafe access.

Consumer-Generated Alternatives:
- Discuss among disabled consumers key areas that need to be made accessible.
- Make up an annual priority list of access and safety issues.
- Describe problems in newsletters and solicit opinions from other disabled community members.
- Offer modification assistance to owners of inaccessible buildings and appropriate government and social agencies.
- Offer assistance to government agencies on ways to increase the safety of streets and sidewalks.

Social Services

Four Survey items related to information social agencies provide to consumers about services and legal issues were selected as major problems in six surveys. A total of 3,581 consumers responded to these questions, with an average importance rating of 88 percent and an average satisfaction rating of 51 percent.

Consumer-Identified Dimensions:
- Social service agencies fail to inform disabled consumers about all services available to them through their own agency, other agencies, or the community.
- Benefits or services from one agency can limit benefits or services from another agency.
- Most social service agencies are unaware of services available at other agencies.
- Disabled people are referred from one agency to another, often encountering agencies unable to serve them or refusing services.
- Forms and policies of social service agencies are confusing.

Consumer-Generated Alternatives:
- Organize a consumer group to review forms used by social service agencies.
- Form a consumer network for information and referral.
- Create more support groups for mutual assistance.
- Provide corrective feedback and information to social service agencies that fail to inform clients about benefits to disabled consumers.
- Provide social service agencies with training on benefits available to disabled consumers.
- Consumers should demand that VR cases be reopened, if they have not been fully informed about all benefits available.
- Independent living centers should train consumers in what benefits are available and how to access them effectively.
- Independent living centers or consumer groups could organize regular cooperative meetings involving representatives of all social service agencies in the community, or if such an organization exists, become active and advocate for services to people with disabilities.
- If consumers are referred to an agency unable to serve the, they should contact the referring agency and tell them the referral was inappropriate and why.
- Educate consumers to use the state CAP agency, Legal Aid, and other available legal help when services are unjustly refused.
- Set up courses in self-reliance that teach

consumers to use social services such as the one used by the CIL in Anaheim, Calif.

Transportation: Availability and Affordability

Three survey items related to the availability and affordability of accessible transportation services were identified as major problems by 4,008 consumers in nine surveys. They received an average importance rating of 83 percent and an average satisfaction rating of 40 percent.

Consumer-Identified Dimensions:
- Disabled citizens are segregated from the rest of the community and forced to remain at home because of lack of transportation.
- In most areas, public transportation is not wheelchair-accessible, and paratransit is expensive or nonexistent. In rural areas, accessible transportation is available infrequently.
- Lack of transportation is the primary barrier to community participation, education, employment, recreation, adequate medical care, and independent living for people with disabilities.
- Weekend and evening transportation is a problem.
- Transportation between neighboring cities and from rural areas to cities is a problem.
- Ideally, a city should have accessible mainline transportation for those who can use it and paratransit for those who need it.
- Recreational events and facilities are sometimes inaccessible. Transportation to recreational events is unavailable.

Consumer-Generated Alternatives:
- Consumer groups need to work with existing community recreational facilities to make them accessible and usable for people with disabilities.
- Contact organizers of recreational events for transportation for disabled participants.
- People with disabilities need to become involved in the planning of community recreational events and active in interest groups.
- Form a local task force on transportation,

decide what local consumers need and want, then fight for it.

- It is against federal law for paratransit to cost more than mainline transportation. Educate consumers about this law, how to make complaints, and how to ensure its enforcement.
- Develop a share-a-fare system as they did in Kansas City, MO, where 900 wheelchair users a month participate.
- Give testimony to state legislatures on transportation funding.
- Have lift buses operate at fixed rates and schedules as they do in Denver, a city with almost 100 percent accessible buses.
- Slow transit schedules to accommodate disabled riders. Drivers should call out stops ahead of time.
- Include disabled drivers in existing driving training programs.
- Develop car pools.
- Conduct public education on varied modes of transportation needed by disabled citizens.
- Submit formal complaints to transportation authorities concerning mainline wheelchair-accessible buses.
- Develop creative rural and small city alternatives. Examples include merging existing systems serving disabled riders (Morgantown, W.V.) ownership of a lift van by a consumer group or cooperative (Cuba, MO) and use of idle church or school lift-equipped buses.

Utility Bills

One survey question related to the affordability of utility bills was identified as a major problem in four surveys. A total of 1,611 consumers answered this survey item, with an average importance rating of 89 percent and an average satisfaction rating of 34 percent.

Consumer-Identified Dimensions:
- Disabled consumers on a fixed income cannot afford inconsistent and high utility bills.

- Because of their medical needs, many disabled consumers cannot survive without water, gas for heat, and electricity to operate their equipment.

Consumer-Generated Alternatives:
- Obtain help to establish programs for weatherization.
- Encourage landlords to weatherize units.
- Educate landlords and disabled homeowners about tax credits for weatherizing and solar installation.
- Encourage consumers to join annualized level payment plans.
- Consumer groups should maintain a list of agencies that help pay utility bills.
- Call local consumer affairs office for help if utilities are shut off.
- Consult local phone company about discounts for disabled consumers.
- Write elected officials describing problems with utility bills and ask for legislative solutions and assistance programs.

This report represents the comments and suggestions of thousands of Americans with disabilities. They have identified specific community features that inhibit independent living, including inadequate job opportunities, job discrimination, insufficient accessible and affordable housing, inaccessible public places, and unavailable and unaffordable service options. These community problems are counterproductive to achieving society's goal of independence.

The common concerns outlined here frame an agenda for public, private, and self-help initiatives. These consumer-generated alternatives feature many practical steps that can be taken at local, state, and national levels. Taken together, these issues and options pose a challenge to all who believe that justice requires equal opportunities to achieve independence.

The Social Psychology of Physical Disability: 1948 and 1988

LEE MEYERSON

The editor of JSI's 1948 special issue on the social psychology of physical disability recalls some of the circumstances associated with its creation. He epitomizes the Zeitgeist in this field in 1948 and 1988, speculates on the influence of the JSI issue in the changes that occurred over those 40 years, and discusses several variables that may influence further developments by the year 2000.

In the mid-1940s, Roger Barker, then at Stanford University, was asked by the Committee on Social Adjustment of the Social Science Research Council to make a review and critical appraisal of the existing research literature on adjustment to physical handicap. World War II had greatly increased the number of people, including veterans of the armed services, who were physically injured. Lives had been saved by remarkable gains in medical and surgical procedures, but many of these individuals now faced the lifelong problems of adjusting to physical handicap. The adjustment process was of primary concern, although the Committee also recognized the scientific importance of increasing our understanding about how a change in physical condition may affect human behavior. It was in this report to the Social Science Research Council (Barker, Wright, & Gonick, 1946) and its later updating (Barker, Wright, Meyerson, & Gonick, 1953) that some parallels between the situations of people with disabilities and the situations of deprived minority groups were identified and presented.

This report developed and applied Lewinian principles, and I believe it was the origin of the now widely accepted belief that underprivileged minority status is a very useful concept in explaining much of the observed behavior of people with atypical physiques. Once put forward, the minority status of "the disabled" turned out to be an intuitively and experientially appealing concept that gained rapid assent not only from psychologists but also from sociologists, educators, anthropologists, political scientists, social workers, lawyers, parents, and other. For some, it offered a radically new and different way of

defining, thinking about, and remedying what could now be understood as a social-psychological problem. For others, it was a useful adjunct or alternative to the existing medical or clinical paradigms.

On the other hand, there was much in the report that has not been well absorbed, implemented, or emulated.

First, the heart of the book was a demonstration that a social psychology of physique -*somatopsychology*-is possible, and that it can unify apparently diverse phenomena. Just as Lewin (1935) emphasized the significance for Galileian physics of the law of gravity ("The same law governs the courses of the stars, the falling of stones, and the flight of birds." p.10), in somatopsychology the same set of principles can account for some important aspects of the seemingly diverse behavior observable in people with normal *and* pathological variations in physical size, strength, motor ability, sensory acuity, health, and appearance (cf. Barker, 1948). Moreover, a field-theoretical analysis-based on the requirements and consequences of new and overlapping psychological situations-permits easy extension of the same principles to some aspects of the behavior of Aristotelian "classes" of people who share the characteristics of race, sex, age, ethnic group, or economic status.

In much disability research reported today, however, the merits of accounting for many different kinds of behavior in terms of a single set of principles are not stressed. Instead, a greater emphasis is placed on a valuative, clinical end product-called *rehabilitation*-that uses multiple principles to account for a multiplicity of discrete behaviors.

Second, further development of basic theory and research method has not been extensive. Although there has been a tremendous increase in the size and output of the scientific community-in number of books, journals, and articles written, and in practical efforts focused on disability phenomena-much of the empirical research reported in the last 40 years remains flawed by the same conceptual limitations and

Reprinted From: *Journal of Social Issues, Vol. 44, No. 1, 1988, pp. 173-188,* with permission.

methodological errors that were identified by Barker et al. (1953, pp. 1-8).

A Little History

For psychologists interested in Lewinian, social-psychological approaches to disability, Stanford University in 1944-1945 was an exciting place to be. Roger Barker, his wife Louise, and his collaborators, Beatrice Wright and Mollie Gonick, were breaking new ground. Gloria Ladieu, Beatrice Wright, Ralph White, Dan Adler, and Eugenia Hanfmann were working with Tamara Dembo on "Adjustment to Misfortune" (Dembo, Leviton, & Wright, 1948/1975) and on some critical components of adjustment to visible injuries such as receiving help (Ladieu, Hanfmann, &Dembo, 1947), curiosity (White, Wright, & Dembo, 1948) and social acceptance (Ladieu, Adler, & Dembo, 1948).

With so many psychologists around who were interested also in the infant *Journal of Social Issues* (*JSI*), it is not surprising that plans were made to organize a *JSI* issue on the social psychology of physical disability (Meyerson, 1948).
The Social Psychology of Disability, 1948

It was Roger Barker, again, who initiated the proposal for a *JSI* disability issue (here referred to as *JSI*-1948), made the arrangements for publication with the *JSI* General Editor, Ron Lippitt, and solicited the papers that anchored the issue: His own, the Ladieu, Adler, and Dembo analysis of "Social Acceptance of the Injured." And the Hanks and Hanks account of "The Physically Handicapped in Certain Non-Occidental Societies, "Roger then asked if I would obtain additional relevant papers and see the manuscripts through to completion--a request that I, as a mere graduate student, interpreted as both generous and challenging.

All of the additional articles were sought for straightforward, objective reasons; but my solicitations of Leo Cain's paper, "The Disabled Child in School," and Spencer Brown's paper, "General Semantics and Physical Disability," were prompted by additional personal motivations.

Sometime earlier at a meeting organized by physicians and educators to raise funds for a school for handicapped children, the official pitch was that these poor children *could not* go to public school because of their incapacitating physical disabilities. I made a speech to the effect that these children *did not* go to school because the school boards, superintendents, principals, and teachers would not let them in. The response to my arguments was glacial. For *JSI*-1948, I hoped that Cain, a professor of education who later became president of San Francisco State College, would put into print a rationale and an implicit demand for the educational entitlement of children with disabilities that would gain assent from the educational establishment.

My motive for requesting a contribution from Spencer Brown was murkier. Part of the doggerel of my childhood was the refrain: "Sticks and stones may break my bones, but names will never hurt me." Yet it was becoming increasingly clear to many that some words, and the thought processes they represented, were hurtful in ways that could be not remedied by cosmetic changes in terminology (e.g., from cripple to orthopedically handicapped, or from defective children to exceptional children). Korzybski's (1941) book *Science and Sanity* was receiving great attention at that time, and his general non-Aristotelian premises ("The map is not the territory, the word is not the object, the word does not symbolize all of the object") were congruent with a somatopsychological approach.

It was typical of the times that Brown, like most of us, concentrated on changing the victim's response processes. To attempt to alter hurtful, but traditional, social language patterns was perceived as a quixotic, insuperable task. It remained for the women's movement to shift the focus to the stimulus: to demand. "Change the language": and to show us how easily some offensive language patterns can be altered.[1]

To epitomize the dominant paradigm in 1948: The locus of disability problems was viewed as being in the bodies of the people categorized as "disabled." In our culture, it was the unfortunate but realistic destiny of most of these people to live deprived, marginal, and devalued lives in a material and social world designed for the able-bodied. The solution to the problem-was to "adjust these people by helping them accept what "fate" and the existing system had consigned to them.

The Influence of *JSI*-1948

Fine and Asch (1988) are most generous in believing that *JSI*-(1948)"fundamentally influenced social policy. . . ." My initial reaction when I read these words was a subvocal, "Don't be silly. We academics tend to write to and for ourselves. Who else pays much attention to what we say?" Then, recalling McGrath's (1980) and Harris, Unger, and Stagner's (1986) historical reviews, Mednick's (1984) presidential address, and SPSSI's influence in *Brown v. Board of Education*, my second thought was "Maybe so, SPSSI and *JSI* do speak out and sometimes are listened to."

The channels of transmission may be indirect, and presently difficult or impossible to document, but they may exist. For example, Madnick (1984) quoted from a news release of the mid-1950s that was signed by SPSSI leaders: "Any decision to use differences in the average achievement of the two racial groups as a basis for classifying *any individual* child, Negro or white, is scientifically unjustified" (p. 167, emphasis in original). Now compare that conclusion with Supreme Court Justice Marshall's opinion in a gender discrimination case: "Even a true generalization about a class cannot justify class-based treatment [of an individual]" (*Arizona Governing Committee for Tax Deferred Annuity v. Norris*, 1983).

The principle advocated by SPSSI 30 years earlier--a foundation plank in the civil rights movement's struggle for equality and equity for all--is now firmly embedded not only in social consciousness but also in the legal system. We do not know with certainty if there is a direct connection between the SPSSI activities and that satisfying outcome. The spirit of the times, other organizations, and other individuals following independent pathways undoubtedly had effect. Without question, however, SPSSI served its stated function: its members made knowledge available; and even though we do not know who

used that knowledge, a SPSSI position somehow became the law of the land.[2]

Academic channels of influence are more easily traceable. McGrath (1980) remarked that *JSI*-1948 articles at several places in his book and mentioned in his first sentence the influence of SPSSI members who have done "good work on stigma--the situation of the individual who is disqualified from full social acceptance" (p.i). He acknowledged sociologist E. Lemert and psychologists K. Lewin, F. Heider, T. Dembo, R. Barker, and B. Wright, and in his sociological treatise he made new and strikingly insightful analyses of some topics and concepts that were discussed in *JSI*-1948.

Goffman's compelling and beautifully written book has been widely disseminated. A hardbound copy of *Stigma* that I obtained from the library (it has been in paperback for years) was labelled "24th printing." Although the date that printing is unknown, there clearly must have been not less than one reprinting a year for the last quarter century. By contrast, *JSI* in 1948 had a circulation of perhaps 1000 copies, and the issue on disability has not been reprinted. Here again, however, *JSI* served its function of making knowledge of social issues available to others, and in turn Goffman passed some of this knowledge to a much larger group of readers. No doubt the information and points of view expressed in *JSI*-1948 articles that have appeared in other scientific periodicals. SSCI did not begin its tabulations until 1966, almost 20 years after *JSI*-1948 appeared, so we will never know who cited that issue during the years immediately following its publication, when the greatest number of citations usually occurs. In addition, some journals such as *Rehabilitation Psychology*, whose contributors might be likely to cite -1948, were not included among the journals searched by SSCI until recent years.

Nonetheless, the data are interesting. Between 1966 and 1985, there was a total of 72 citations to *JSI*-1948, referring to nine different articles. Barker's and Meyerson's articles attracted about half of the citations (23 and 14, respectively), and all but one of the other seven papers were cited at least four times during this period. Contrary to the expectation that citations would decrease over time, only 3 citations to *JSI*-1948 were made in 1966 as compared to 10 citations in 1985. Over the longer term, the difference was weaker but also in the same direction" 13 citations in the four years from 1966 to 1969, 31 citations in the decade 1970-1979, and 28 citations in the six years from 1980 to 1985. Perhaps disability is becoming more visible as a social issue.

To assist in evaluating the citation data a similar citation count was made for another *JSI* issue of the same vintage, "The Consultant role and Organizational leadership" Improving Human Relations in Industry~ (*JSI*, 1948, No. 3, the issue immediately preceding the disability issue). This issue, which contained papers by Douglas McGregor, Irving Knickerbacker, Mason Haire, and Alexander Bavelas, was cited 12 times between 1966 and 1985. The last entry was single citation in 1981 to Bavelas's article.

There are many variables here and several possible interpretations of the data. It should be noted that human relations issue contained fewer papers than the disability issue. In addition, the differences found in the number and time course of citations may reflect, among other possibilities, the larger scope of topics included in the disability issue, greater progress in the study of human relations and therefore greater obsolescence of its older literature, a smaller data base in somatopsychology, or an artifact based on nothing more than changes in the number and kind of journals on which the SSCI count is based.

Nonetheless, from the citation data it is reasonable to believe "someone out there" is interested in the social psychology of disability. Is it SPSSI members? Perhaps. Among 850 responses to a membership survey in 1985 (SPSSI, 1987), in which topics and issues for SPSSI's agenda were requested, 5 members (a little more than half of 1% of those responding) mentioned the "physically impaired" as a social issue. However, until now, no single citation to a *JSI*-1948 article has appeared in *JSI* in the past 40 years, and aside from a few marginally related articles on life-threatening illness, *JSI* has published just one paper on disability (Dembo, 1982) in these four decades.

Of course, SPSSI members have many varied interests that compete for *JSI* expression. It is also possible that members perceive disability as primarily a medical issue (worthy of SPSSI consideration, perhaps, under a category such as equitable distribution of health care) but not as a typical social issue central to their concerns.

Disability as a Social Issue

A typical social issue arises from malfunctioning social system when, by purely social processes, a portion of the population is unfairly and needlessly oppressed. In disability, there is salient *biological* component and a resulting belief by some that the problems of this group arise as much or more from inherent biological inadequacies as from social forces. Similar beliefs of biological inferiority in blacks, women, and certain ethnic groups were common not many years ago, but they are rarely heard today--surely not in SPSSI circles. From time immemorial devalued groups have been presented as inherently inferior people. Repeatedly, however, it has been demonstrated--for racial, gender, religious, and ethnic groups--that the imputed, sometime demontrateable, inferiorities were not due to an immutable minority characteristic but to environments that limited opportunities. Does that generalization hold also for people with disabilities?

A redefinition of the social problem of disability, similar to the redefinition that was so potent for other minority groups, is gaining support among a small but increasing number of investigators, theorists, and activists (Kidder & Fine, 1986; Wright, 1983). This relatively new definition describes and explicates the purely social processes--especially prejudice and discrimination--that create an underprivileged status for people with disabilities, and it denies the centrality or potency of the "loss or impairment of a tool" aspect of disability. Impaired tools can often be improved or replaced with other tools.

Related to the first prong of this definition, for example, is the great reduction in "disability behavior" resulting from some relatively simple changes in the environment--curb cuts on streets, elevators in buildings, and accessible toilets. These changes have made it clear that it was discrimination in providing equally usable facilities to all citizens, and not disability, that in great part limited the past opportunities of people with disabilities. Regarding the second prong of the definition, just as the availability of eye glasses has reduced to insignificance the behavioral limitations imposed by uncorrected refractive errors, an increasing flow of other technology today is reducing many constraints on the behavior of those whose biological tools have been damaged. That reduction has an extent and magnitude hardly imaginable 40 years ago. Today, for example, there are transducing computers that "hear," "speak," and respond to inputs other than touch, and it is predictable that further technological gains will be able to improve or replace every faltering biological tool.

This new redefinition is just now reaching *JSI*. In the past, for example, as in the 1985 membership survey (SPSSI, 1987), and in McGrath's (1980) analysis of *JSI* topics, disability issues were not classified under the rubric "prejudice," "minority rights and discrimination," or other category central to SPSSI concerns, but were isolated or listed as "miscellaneous."

On the other hand, Tamara Dembo (1982) in her Lewin Memorial presentation, "Some Problems of Rehabilitation as Seen by a Lewinian," made a persuasive case for the inclusion of handicap, disability, and rehabilitation as *social* issues, and asserted that the problems of this field "are central for understanding social-psychological issues . . . ." (p. 139). Her assertion should not be dismissed as hyperbole, Dembo's world is the whole universe of human beings. Her concepts of "misfortune" and "devaluation," although they emerged from studies of disability phenomena, are applicable to everyone who has experienced asymmetrical social interactions--and who has not? Dembo has shown us radically new and fruitful ways of thinking about human behavior that, like other Galilean viewpoints, encompass seemingly diverse and unrelated behavior. The breadth and strength of her formulations have yet to be fully appreciated, but they will be drawn upon by many future investigators of social issues.

Despite the phenotypic differences in the populations of interest, students of somatopsychology have benefited greatly over the years from the many *JSI* reviews and analyses on race, gender discrimination, and intergroup contact. SPSSI-sponsored books such as *Redefining Social Problems* (Seidman & Rappaport, 1986) have exposed us to problems and solutions that are similar--sometimes identical--to those encountered in disability research and practice. It is increasingly clear that some central needs and demands of all socially deprived groups--access to education, employment, housing, transportation, empowerment--are the same. More generally, the defining aspirations of the French Revolution for liberty, equality, and fraternity are still with us.

The Social Psychology of Disability, 1988

A number in millions is not easy to comprehend--it can be noted without being understood. Fine and Asch's (1988) number of 36,000,000 people with disabilities in the United States is the most common current estimate (National Council on the Handicapped, 1986). One meaning of that number--and in my experience its significance is always received with astonishment--is that people with disabilities constitute the *largest minority* in the United States. By comparison, blacks in the United States number about 26 or 27 million people, and those with Spanish names a mere 17 million people (*Statistical Abstract of the United States*, 1987).

There are differences between the disabled and other minorities, however. Blacks and Hispanics in the United States are clearly minority *groups*. From birth on, practically all experience the cohesion, the identity, the shared treatment and fate of the group to which they belong. Even if they are adopted in childhood and raised by whites or Anglos, they are usually aware of their heritage and psychologically are members of their racial or ethnic group.

The population of people with disabilities is markedly different. Their parents, siblings, extended family, and associates usually are nondisabled people. A child with a disability may not know for years that other people with similar physiques exist in this world. For adults who are newly disabled by accident or disease, a sense of community with others in similar situations is unlikely to exist.

In the past, most people with disabilities constituted a group only by abstract, statistical classification. They were not members of a sociological or psychological group deriving from their disability status. They were simply relatively isolated, stigmatized individuals. They were treated socially in much the same ways as members of other devalued underprivileged groups, but they functioned largely without group support.[3]

The absence of community appears to have changed in recent years. In a survey of a national sample of people with disabilities (Harris, 1986), 74% of the respondents said they felt at least some sense of common identity with other disabled people, and almost half believed people with disabilities are a minority group in the same sense as blacks and Hispanics.

The strength of this change remains to be seen, and it would be sorely tested if those with different disabilities were required to compete for resources. People with different disabilities or differing degrees of the same disability do not necessarily perceive these differences in a neutral way. It would be surprising if they did not absorb and reflect prevailing cultural attitudes toward different or more severe disabilities.

The Real World

In 1948, people with disabilities were socially invisible, powerless people. Their rise in 1988 to social visibility, social consideration, a modicum of power, and increasing acknowledgement of their rights to equal opportunity has vastly exceeded the wildest hopes of social psychologists and others (Harris, 1986) who were concerned with this issue in 1948. The extent and depth of this unparalleled sea change is a source of wonder, almost disbelief. To be sure, as with other minorities and women, much of the change has been *de jure*--and much more remains to be accomplished--but significant *defacto* gains are undeniable.

On the other hand, in view of other social changes, the improvement in conditions of life for people with disabilities is not surprising.

Barker (1948), 40 years ago, predicted how it would occur:

> The minority status of the physically disabled which is due to the negative attitudes of the physically normal majority . . . would seem to be in almost all respects similar to the problem of racial and religious underprivileged minorities. . . . When and as these problems are solved with respect to these other underprivileged minorities, the solutions may be applied to the physically handicapped also. (p. 36)

Some social scientists have been active in seeking solutions for the social problems of disability, and it would be pleasant to credit their writings and research for the progress made since the 1970s. It is more likely, however, that the salience of the gains achieved by other minority groups, their examples of how to do it, the civil rights Zeitgeist, and the new responsiveness of social gatekeepers to demands for equity for all were more potent forces for change.

The foundation stones of the modern disability rights movement (Scotch, 1988) consist of two laws: The first provides for a free public education in the least restrictive environment. The second prohibits discrimination in employment on the basis of handicap by any organization receiving federal funds. Both laws are based on philosophical conceptions of what is appropriate for a just society, in which "rights of the individual" are a paramount consideration. These conceptions are congruent with SPSSI aspirations for improving the conditions of life for all; but they did not emerge from empirical data demonstrating that instruction in mainstreamed settings produces more or better learning than in segregated settings, or that nondiscrimination in employment maximizes the general productivity of a society. These effects of nondiscrimination may actually exist, but they remain to be demonstrated.

Nevertheless, in American life--at least with respect to law and custom--there has been a perceptible paradigm shift; Bodily impairment is less frequently seen as an obvious "intrinsic inferiority" of the whole person and is more frequently seen as a social issue. The social issue is of the same order, and understandable in the same terms, as prejudice toward other under-privileged minorities. Optimal alleviation is now less frequently perceived as a medical problem or a welfare problem, and more frequently perceived as a problem of extending civil rights to another, previously neglected, underprivileged group.

Academia

A similar paradigm shift has been developing in academia but at a much slower rate.

The number of psychologists interested in disability phenomena has increased vastly over the last 40 years as jobs in health and rehabilitation settings have become more plentiful, and some researchers are both skilled and well informed. However, the number of investigations that are flawed from inception by prejudicial commonsense assumptions, by theoretical bias, or by methodological error remains high.[4] (cf. Fine & Asch, 1988). These errors are functions, in great part, not of psychologists' incompetence in the mechanics of research, but of asking the wrong questions (Seidman, 1986), of incorrect notions of the meaning of disability to those who live with it, and of lack of understanding of the processes by which people come to terms with their own or others' variations in physique. Specific examples of these errors are given below. A particular source of error is the narrowly trained clinician who believes clinical criteria are appropriate measures of problems that arise from systematic social injustice. Psychologists, like others, to the extent that their thinking incorporates cultural myths, become prisoners of plausible but erroneous hypotheses.[5]

The following are ordinary, not particularly egregious, examples of problems seen in academic research on disability.

In a recent dissertation, one of the central criteria for "social adjustment" of adults who had sustained a spinal cord injury was unassisted self-care in the elementary, infantile sense of eating, toileting, personal hygiene, and dressing without assistance. Certainly these are desirable skills, but what do they have to do with adult social adjustment? A practical implication of such a criterion is that no individual with quadriplegia--regardless of skilled, responsible employment, high income, happy marriage, effective parenting, many friends, an active social life, or other manifestations of social adequacy--can possibly be considered "socially adjusted." Yet we know there are quadriplegics and others who have limited self-care skills, but who have escaped the hospital/nursing home ghettos and whose present "social adjustment" is superior. Why is it stigmatizing for such people to employ an aide when it is not discrediting for wealthy individuals to employ a personal maid or valet (cf. Kerr & Meyerson, 1987)?

Another study was an attempt to document a commonsense belief, supported by theoretical trappings, that family disruption occurs when one parent has a disability. The underlying assumptions were that such disruptions inevitably occur, and that the task was simply to document them. When the data for the target group did not show statistically significant differences in family stress, cohesion, adaptability, or satisfaction, as compared to families in which neither parent had a disability, numerous ad hoc and post hoc hypotheses were developed and tested, all aimed at the conclusion that there were, indeed, significant differences between the two groups. The discussion section of the report suggested that, although the differences were subtle and very well concealed, they were real. At no point did the author consider the possibility that some families reorganize when faced with an acute crisis, and thereafter not only function well but thrive (Farber, 1960). A belief that disability has only negative consequences and an evident ban against studying between group commonalities and within-group differences aborted further searches for variables, other than disability, that differentiated families that weakened from families that strengthened when one parent was disabled. The researcher's operating theory specified that disruption had to occur and strengthening could not occur.

Wright (1987) critiqued a study in which interviewees were asked to evaluate interviewers who appeared physically normal or physically disabled. The major *finding* was that raters consistently, on a variety of personality characteristics, evaluated the interviewer with a disability more highly (e.g., "more likeable," "better attitude") than the nondisabled interviewer. The *interpretation* offered by the researchers, however, explained away those positive findings by recourse to an hypothesized "sympathy effect" among interviewees who wished to avoid the appearance of rejection or prejudice toward the handicapped. Maybe so, but this assumption that an underlying, unacknowledged process was operating was not demonstrated. If the data had shown impaired interviewing performance by interviewers who were physically disabled, in all likelihood the result would have been accepted at face value.

The way that biasing beliefs and assumptions are woven into even rigorous scientific efforts is not unique to research on disability. The same kind of biased or "Catch 22" interpretations are made in research on other minorities. McHugh, Koeske, and Frieze's (1986) compilation of the requirements for good research on women holds also for other groups.

Data often are not self-interpreting, and investigators have an obligation to try to make sense out of unexpected or seemingly paradoxical results. In view of the frequency of studies of disability where neutral or positive data turn into negative interpretations, Wright (1987) proposed that some investigators have a "fundamental negative bias" toward disability or people with disabilities. Her insightful account of the conditions under which the fundamental negative bias operates, and what can be done to guard against it, can enlighten not only disability research but also the entire field of social issues.

Recent Progress

On the positive side, there have been some solid gains in knowledge. One of the best summaries of reliable knowledge concerning physique-behavior interactions was made about 10 years ago by Shontz (1977), a field-theoretical psychologist whose contributions to somatopsychology deserve greater attention (e.g., Shontz, 1982). Shontz presented and discussed six propositions that are still tenable today. Two are confuting assertions, stating that a commonly held belief is false, and four were positive assertions. The propositions are as follows:

1. Psychological reactions to the onset or imposition of physical disability are not

uniformly disturbing or distressing, and do not necessarily result in maladjustment. (Corollary: Psychological reactions to the removal of physical disabilities are not uniformly or necessarily pleasant, and do not necessarily lead to improved adjustment.)

2. Reactions (favorable or unfavorable) to disabilities are not related in a simple way to the physical properties of the disabilities.

3. The shorter and less complex the causal linkage between the body structure affected by disability and the behavior in question, the more predictable the latter is from the former.

4. The less direct the linkage between body structure affected by disability and the behavior in question, the more appropriate it is to describe the influence of disability as facilitative, rather than as causal or coercive.

5. Environmental factors are at least as important in determining psychological reactions to disabilities as are the internal states of the persons who have the disabilities.

6. Of all the factors that affect the total life situation of a person with a disability, the disability itself is only one, and often its influence is relatively minor.

We can now epitomize some social aspects of disability in the United States in the 1970s and 1980s: For the first time in history, people with many different kinds of disabilities, their parents, friends--including some social science professionals--organizations, and sensitized legislators joined to demand, "Change the system." They saw the locus of disability problems not primarily in damaged bodies or in other unalterable characteristics of the people who occupy those bodies, but in the political/social/legal system that denies equal protection of the law, equal rights, and equal opportunities. The solutions sought were the same as those that had begun to be achieved by other minority groups and women namely, to remove from the backs of people with disabilities the insufferable burden of depending on the altruism of others, to affirm their constitutional and statutory rights, and to penalize discrimination. In part, the hypothesis was "better attitudes follow better behavior," and although the struggle continues, the data so far are encouraging.

The interpretations above apply primarily to the United States at large. In academia, a small number of academic investigators in somatopsychology joined in. A larger group, however, still ignored commonalities between disabled and nondisabled groups, glossed over or interpreted-away research findings that placed people with disabilities in a favorable light, and determinedly sought only the physique-behavior relationships that confirmed a belief in psychological and social inferiorities of this group. For SPSSI, and other psychologists in the mainstream, clearer recognition of the social issues aspect of disability is only now becoming salient.

Toward the Year 2000

Many variables are likely to affect the social-psychological situation of people with disabilities in the remaining years of the century. At least two factors appear positive, and two may be negative.

On the positive side, once people have been exposed to freedom and opportunities, a return to oppression and denial of opportunity is not easy to accomplish. Some liberating laws and practices are now in place. People with disabilities are not increasingly visible in the streets, educational establishments, and the workplace--sometimes in positions of leadership and authority. Understanding and appreciation is growing that variations in physique do not justify a judgment of inferiority or incompetence, nor do they merit second-class citizenship. Moreover, the fate of people with disabilities is now increasingly tied to the fate of other minorities and women, and it seems reasonable to conclude that if these other groups maintain and increase their gains, so too will people with disabilities.

Also on the positive side is the existence of a small group of investigators who are likely to continue to differentiate the social-psychological from the biological causes of physique-behavior relationships.

On the negative side, a Zeitgeist does not last forever. Already there are voices, including public officials, who complain that certain groups of citizens are consuming too much--or at least more than their fair share--of limited economic resources. In part, that is an empirical question, and investigation will be required to answer it. Whether it is answered in a fair and unbiased way will depend, in part, on whose data are considered relevant.

Clinical psychologists and social psychologists are trained in different ways, to ask different kinds of questions, and to seek different kinds of data. The relatively new but burgeoning fields of health psychology and community psychology, which are likely to be influential in the study and treatment of people with disabilities, draw their students from both areas, but there seems to be a predominance of clinicians. If these clinical psychologists, like their medical counterparts, center their attention on defects, deformities, and disease whose origins and treatment are within the individual, the data that emerge are unlikely to support present trends. If, on the other hand, health and community psychologists, like their counterparts in public health, orient themselves toward person-environment interactions, so central to the Lewinian tradition, a new and even more favorable Zeitgeist for people with disabilities may be in the offing.

Our society has come a long way since the time when infants with disabilities were "monsters" and adults with deviant physiques were "freaks." In the process much has been learned about physique-behavior relationships, but there is still a long way to go.

REFERENCES

American Psychological Association (1984). Final report of the Task Force on Psychology and the Handicapped. *American Psychologist, 39*, 545-550.

Arizona Governing Committee for Tax Deferred Annuity and Deferred Compensation Plans v. Norris, 51 U.S.L.W. 5243, 5245 (July 6, 1983).

Barker, R. G. (1948). The social psychology of physical disability. *Journal of Social Issues*, 4(4), 28-38.

Barker, R. G., Wright, B. A., & Gonick, M. R. (1946). *Adjustment to physical handicap and illness: A survey of the social psychology of physique and disability.* New York, Social Science Research Council.

Barker, R. G., Wright, B. A., Meyerson, L., & Gonick, M. LR. (1953). *Adjustment to physical handicap and illness: A survey of the social psychology of physique and disability* (2nd ed.), New York: Social Science Research Council.

Becker, G. (1980). *Growing old in silence,* Berkeley: University of California Press.

Dembo, T. (1982). Some problems in rehabilitation as seen by a Lewinian, *Journal of Social Issues, 38*(1), 131-139.

Dembo, T., Leviton, G. I., & Wright, B. A. (1975). Adjustment to misfortune--A problem of social psychological rehabilitation, *Rehabilitation Psychology, 22*(1), (Reprinted from *Final report to the Army Medical Research and Development Board,* Office of the Surgeon General, War Department, April 1948, Typescript.)

Farber, B. (1960). Family organization and crisis: Maintenance of integration in the family with a severely mentally retarded child, *Monographs of the Society for Research in Child Development, 25.*

Fine, M., & Asch, A. (1988). Disability beyond stigma: Social interaction, discrimination and activism, *Journal of Social Issues, 44*(1), 3-21.

Goffman, E. (1963). *Stigma: Notes on the management of spoiled identity,* Englewood Cliffs, NJ, Prentice-Hall.

Harris, B., Unger, R. K., & Stagner, R. (1986). 50 years of psychology and social issues, *Journal of Social Issues, 42*(1).

Harris, L., & Associates (1986). *Disabled Americans: Self perceptions--1986,* New York: Author.

Kerr, N., & Meyerson, L. (1987). Independence as a goal and a value of people with physical disabilities: Some caveats. *Rehabilitation Psychology, 32,* 173-180.

Kidder, L. H., & Fine, M. (1986). Making sense of injustice: Social explanations, social action, and the role of the social scientist. In E. Seidman & J. Rappaport (Eds.) *Redefining social problems* (pp. 49-63). New York: Plenum.

Korzybski, A. (1941). *Science and sanity.* Lancaster, PA: Science Press.

Ladieu, G. L., Adler, D. L., & Dembo, T. (1948). Studies in adjustment to visible injuries: Social acceptance of the injured. *Journal of Social Issues, 4*(4), 55-61.

Ladieu, G. L., Hanfmann, E., & Dembo, T. (1947). Studies in adjustment to visible injuries: Evaluation of help by the injured. *Journal of Abnormal and Social Psychology, 42,* 169-192.

Lewin, K. (1935). The conflict between Aristotelian and Galileian modes of thought on contemporary psychology. In K. Lewin, *A dynamic theory of personality.* New York: McGraw-Hill.

McGrath, J. E. (1980),. What are the social issues? Timeliness and treatment of topics in the Journal of Social Issues. *Journal of Social Issues, 36*(4), 98-108.

McHugh, M. C., Loeske, R. D., & Frieze, I. H. (1986). Issues to consider in conducting nonsexist psychological research: A guide for researchers. *American Psychologist, 41,* 878-890.

Mednick, M. T. S. (1984). SPSSI, advocacy for social change, and the future: A historical look. *Journal of Social Issues, 40*(3), 159-177.

Meyerson, L. (Ed.) (1948). The social psychology of physical disability. *Journal of Social Issues, 4*(4).

National Council on the Handicapped (1986). *Toward independence: An assessment of federal laws and programs affecting persons with disabilities--with legislative recommendations* (Stock No. 952-003-01022-4). Washington, DC: U.S. Government Printing Office.

***, R. K., (1988). Disability as the basis for a social movement: Advocacy and the politics of definition. *Journal of Social Issues, 44*(1), 159-172.

Seidman, F. (1986). Justice, values and social science: Unexamined premises. In E. Seidman & J. Rappaport (Eds.). *Redefining social problems* (pp. 235-258). New York: Plenum.

Seidman, E., & Rappaport, J. (Eds.) (1986). *Redefining social problems.* New York: Plenum.

Shontz, F. C. (1977). Six principles relating disability and psychological adjustment. *Rehabilitation Psychology, 24,* 207-210.

Shontz, F. C. (1982). Adaptation to chronic illness and disability. In T. Millon, C. Green, & R. Meagher (Eds.). *Handbook of clinical health psychology* (pp. 153-171). New York: Plenum.

SPSSI (1987, April). Members propose SPSSI's agenda. *SPSSI Newsletter,* No. 175, pp.7-8.

Statistical abstract of the United States, (1987). Washington, DC: U.S. Government Printing Office.

White, R. K., Wright, B. A., & Dembo, T. (1948). Studies in adjustment to visible injuries: Evaluation of curiosity by the injured. *Journal of Abnormal and Social Psychology, 43,* 13-28.

Wright, B. A. (1983). *Physical disability: A psychosocial approach.* New York: Harper & Row.
Wright, B. A. (1987). Attitudes and the fundamental
negative bias. In H. E. Yuker (Ed.). *Attitudes
toward persons with disabilities.* Westport, CT:
Greenwood Press.

Notes

1. Regarding language offensive to people with disabilities, Beatrice Wright (1983) has been among the most sensitive in appreciating the damaging impact of words that devalue: words that make a whole complex person isomorphic with a single characteristic; and words that coerce, or at least foster, negative appraisals.

2. Discrimination against the handicapped has been legally prohibited since 1973. SPSSI members undoubtedly perceive differential treatment of individuals on the basis of age, gender, race, ethnic origin, or sexual preference as unacceptable discrimination. It is less certain whether there is a consensus against generalization from the class to the individual in the case of people who are categorized as "disabled." For some social psychologists, intrinsic classwide inferiority seems much more plausible when attributed to biological "impairment" than when attributed to biological differences in skin color, gender, or appearance.

3. Exceptions to this generalization were people with severe sensory impairments from childhood who were educated in segregated, residential institutions and who did develop a shared culture (Becker, 1980).

4. Barker et al. (1953) identified the location of the most common errors as follows: isolating the somatop-sychological relation between physique and behavior (i.e., as distinguished from genetic, endocrine, neural, psychosomatic, and/or constitutional relations); selecting representative subjects; securing adequate control subjects; securing data on kind and degree of physical variation; securing data on the subject's situation; and describing behavior and personality. Research that avoids or minimizes these sources of error is not easy to design. The most pressing, immediate problem, however, is that so many investigators are still unaware that good design with respect to the variables listed above is essential.

5. One of the goals of the decade-old APA Committee on Psychology and Handicaps is to "educate psychologists and others regarding their own prejudices toward people with handicaps . . ." (American Psychological Association, 1984, p. 546), and that is still an active aspiration. Some psychologists have difficulty in distinguishing "sickness" from "physical disability." For example, one academically respectable chairperson complained in the presence of several graduate students who had disabilities: "This place looks more like a hospital than a university."

Positive Attitudes Toward Disabled People: Disabled and Nondisabled Persons' Perspectives

Elaine Makas

This article addresses the differing perceptions that disabled and nondisabled persons may have of what constitutes "positive" attitudes and behaviors toward people with physical disabilities. Quantitative and qualitative data are presented to suggest that the strain that frequently occurs during interactions between disabled and nondisabled individuals may derive more from misunderstandings of one another's expectations than from negative intentions. Suggestions are made, methodologically, for ways that these areas of misunderstanding can be isolated empirically, and conceptually, for ways that information can be exchanged to correct these misunderstandings.

•Doris goes to her friend's house for a game of Trivial Pursuit. Much to Doris' surprise, she finds that one member of the group, Suzanne, is blind. Determined to show Suzanne that she is not prejudiced against people with disabilities, when Suzanne mistakenly names Portland as the capital of Maine, Doris insists that Suzanne be given another chance. Suzanne responds angrily that she can do well in the game without Doris' help, and that Doris should mind her own business. Doris decides that she will never again try to be polite to people who have disabilities.

•Mike learns that Rick, the new employee hired by his company, has a physical disability. He stops by Rick's office to welcome him. He tells Rick that he is looking forward to getting to know him, since he has always considered disabled to be *easy-going* and very courageous. Rick tells Mike to get out of his office and slams the door behind him. Mike decides that disabled people are not so nice after all.

These scenarios may sound familiar to the nondisabled or the disabled reader. They represent situations in which disabled and nondisabled individuals misunderstand one another. Each interactant may be said to have acted "inappropriately," Suzanne and Rick (disabled) were going about their business of playing a game or working. At the moment of offering "help," Doris and Mike (nondisabled) made disability *salient* and *defining.* They placed the disabled individual in a position of presumed need. They disrupted the "normal scene."

In both cases, the nondisabled persons initiated a special effort to act in ways they considered supportive, to reflect positive attitudes toward persons with disabilities. Their behaviors were, however, received negatively, even though they had the "best intentions." The disabled individuals in the scenarios, however, also behaved in ways that most would consider "inappropriate." They experienced the nondisabled persons' behaviors as patronizing and infantilizing. Their sense of themselves as *ordinary, normal,* and *competent* was attacked.

These negative, if quite typical, behaviors of the "helpers" may have reflected "good intentions," but also displayed erroneous assumptions about how one should behave toward disabled people. Without direct communication, such assumptions will persist, and intergroup tensions will be exacerbated. Angry confrontation, the outcome in both scenarios, will serve simply to increase avoidance, discomfort, and polarization, and it will do nothing to advance the civil rights or integration of persons with disabilities into the social mainstream.

This article was adapted from a paper presented at the 1986 meeting of the American Psychological Association. The author extends special thanks to Suzanne Cook of the George Washington University for allowing the use of extended quotations from the paper that we co-authored: to David Reiss of the Center for Family Research at The George Washington University Medical Center for allowing the use of the IDS raw data; and to the many disabled and nondisabled individuals who participated in this study.

Correspondence regarding this article should be addressed to Elaine Makas, Department of Psychology, The George Washington University, Washington, DC 20052.

Reprinted From: *Journal of Social Issues, Vol. 44, No. 1, 1988, pp.49-61*, with permission.

Empirical research suggests that both disabled people and nondisabled people experience a great deal of stress when interacting with one another. Studies by Kleck and his colleagues (Kleck, 1966, 1968; Kleck, Ono, & Hastorf, 1966) demonstrated that nondisabled subjects report greater emotional distress, exhibit higher physiological arousal, show less motoric activity, display less variability in their verbal behavior, express opinions that are less representative of their previously reported beliefs, and terminate interactions sooner when interacting with a confederate who appears disabled than when interacting with a nondisabled confederate. Comer and Piliavin (1972) found similar indications of discomfort among disabled subjects when interacting with nondisabled confederates, as opposed to confederates who appeared disabled.

Kelley, Hastorf, Jones, Thibaut, and Usdane (1960) and Goffman (1963) have suggested that this tension may result because neither person knows what the other expects. Jones et al. (1984) recommend that clear communication between interactants can reduce interaction strain. Hastorf, Wildfogel, and Cassman (1979) and Belgrave and Mills (1981) have found that simple acknowledgement of the disability by the disabled person can reduce the nondisabled person's discomfort. This line of research, while addressing the significance of breaking down barriers to communication about the disability, does not specify what information must be communicated between the interactants to ease the strain. The focus of this paper is on how each interactant wishes to be treated by the other, in an encounter between a disabled person and a nondisabled one.

An intensive study by Cook and Makas (1979), employing both participant observation and interviews over a two-month period, emphasized the importance of direct communication of *expectations* in the development of successful relationships between disabled and nondisabled individuals. In-depth, repeated interviews were conducted with 11 disabled persons and with 7 nondisabled persons who had extensive professional and personal contact with disabled people.

All 7 nondisabled persons reported seeking advice from disabled friends on how to act in unfamiliar situations with disabled people. This

strategy and its importance in facilitating successful relationships between disabled and nondisabled individuals is clearly expressed in an analysis of responses by three of the nondisabled interviewees:

> Diana told me, "I just talked to lots and lots of disabled people. I asked them what it is about nondisabled people that bugs them." . . . by becoming close to a few disabled people, these three women have been able to more effectively cope with their feelings and have become more competent in their careers. . . . Their primary coping mechanism has now become "clarifying the situation." This strategy has generally replaced the avoidance, catharsis, and other less effective coping strategies used when they were new to the field. (Cook & Makas, 1979, pp. 39-40)

The disabled interviewees in this study also emphasized the importance of direct communication in reducing tension during interactions between disabled persons and nondisabled persons. All 11 disabled interviewees reported situations in which they had developed positive relationships with nondisabled acquaintances after patiently correcting inappropriate behaviors by the nondisabled individuals toward them. For instance, a bus driver told Ralph that he never knew whether or not he should offer help to a wheelchair user. Ralph replied,

> I may not know a whole lot about many things, but the one thing I'm definitely an expert on is my own capabilities. All someone has to do is ask, and I'll be happy to tell them if I need help or not. (p. 52)

Another example involved two other disabled interviewees, who also reported responding to negative behaviors with patient attempts to educate, rather than to avenge:

> They [Sandy and Denise] demonstrate a surprising degree of empathy with the rather confused hostess or waiter, preferring to attribute any slight to a lack of experience with disabled people rather than to intentional malice. This . . . is a tribute to their abilities to understand people who do not necessarily

understand them. (pp. 52-53).

In this study and in later work (Makas, 1985), I have been able to demonstrate the importance of analyzing interactions between disabled people and nondisabled people from dual perspectives. In comparison to a scale developed from responses by nondisabled subjects only, two scales developed from responses by both disabled and nondisabled people were found to be more predictive of behaviors toward a confederate who appeared to have a disability.[1] The present research was designed to identify those attitudinal areas in which clear discrepancies exist between the expectations of disabled people and those of nondisabled people in social interactions--discrepancies that contribute to the kinds of misunderstandings illustrated above.

As Kleck and his colleagues (Kleck, 1968; Kleck et al., 1966) have suggested, most nondisabled people do try to express attitudes and opinions that will be received favorably by disabled persons with whom they interact. If discrepancies exist, however, between disabled and nondisabled respondents' perceptions of what constitutes "positive" attitudes toward disabled people, these discrepancies will exacerbate interaction strain. The nondisabled interactant may express an opinion that he/she believes favorable, but that is received as condescending or false by the disabled interactant. The disabled person may attribute the expressed opinion to a negative intention on the part of the nondisabled person, rather than to differing perceptions of what constitutes a positive attitude.

Method

Respondents

Three distinct samples participated in this study: The *disabled respondents* sample was composed of 92 disabled professionals (48 males and 44 females) from various parts of the United States, ranging in age from 21 to 63 (mean age = 38.2). The sample included 49 persons employed in disability-related professions (e.g., independent living, disability law) and 43 persons employed in fields not directly related to disability (e.g., business, politics). Disabled respon-

dents were individually selected by the experimenter, in consultation with two leaders of the disability rights movement, as people who were professionally successful and who appeared to have positive attitudes toward both disabled people and nondisabled people.

The *"good-attitudes" nondisabled respondents* sample was composed of 69 nondisabled persons (24 males and 45 females) from various parts of the United States, ranging in age from 18 to 63 (mean age = 37.5). Good-attitudes subjects were individually selected by the disabled respondents as nondisabled persons who exhibit "extremely positive attitudes toward people with disabilities." Each disabled respondent was asked to recruit a maximum of two persons, whom he/she knew personally in any capacity, to participate in the study.

The *nondisabled student respondents* sample was composed of 83 nondisabled undergraduate students (38 male and 45 females), ranging in age from 17 to 32 (mean age = 19.2), who were recruited randomly from introductory psychology classes at The George Washington University (GWU).

Questionnaire

All subjects were asked to respond to the Issues in Disability Scale (IDS), a 7-point Likert-type instrument requesting among of agreement/disagreement with 100 items, approximately half of which were adapted from existing measures and half developed by the experimenter. (The 100 items constitute the original item pool used to develop a final 55-item IDS, which is described by Makas, Finnerty-Fried, Sigafoos, & Reiss, 1988.) Items in the IDS address attitudes toward people with disabilities in a variety of settings (e.g., educational, legal/political, intimate social).

Procedure

Disabled respondents were contacted individually by the experimenter and asked to complete the IDS anonymously in a way that they felt reflected "the most positive attitudes toward persons with disabilities." Copies of the IDS were mailed to the disabled respondents after an initial telephone contact.

Good-attitudes nondisabled respondents were given copies of the IDS by the disabled respondents who had selected them. Individuals in this group were asked to complete the questionnaires (honestly) and to return them directly and anonymously to the experimenter. (Disabled respondents were specifically asked by the experimenter to give no further instructions to the good-attitudes subjects, and they were told not to explain to these subjects why they, specifically, were being asked to participate in the study.)

Nondisabled student respondents were administered the IDS in groups of 10-20 people. Each student was asked to complete the questionnaire twice, once "honestly" and once under strong "fake well" instructions. Upon entering the room in which the study was being conducted, subjects were given a copy of the IDS to complete (honestly) and were told that they would be asked to respond to "another questionnaire" upon completion of the first. When they returned the completed IDS to the experimenter, she handed them a second copy of the same form and asked them to respond to it ("faking well") in a way that they felt reflected the most positive attitudes toward persons with disabilities." They were told to imagine that there was someone who had a prize of $10,000 for the GWU student who had the most positive attitudes toward disabled people, and that they should "really try to impress him."

Results

Means were calculated for all IDS items by sample and by condition within the student sample. Using disabled respondents' means to determine the positive direction for each item, 20 items were identified on which student responses were more "negative" in the fake-well condition than in the "honest" condition, and 11 of these differences were found to be significant by repeated-measures *t* tests. One-way analyses of variance were run on all possible pairings among the three groups on these 11 items to determine the significance of differences between means. These 11 items are listed in Table 1. They are called "wrong-direction" items because nondisabled persons' responses were significantly

Table 1. Wrong Direction Items by Category from the Issues in Disability Scale[a]

Give the Disabled Person a Break
5. Most married couples do not get divorced when one of them becomes disabled. (Agree)
10. People who are disabled should have to pay incomes taxes.[b] (Disagree)
19. If a person with a disability breaks the law, he/she should be punished as severely as a nondisabled person who breaks the same law. (Disagree)
25. If a person with epilepsy becomes angry with people over little things, it should be overlooked because of his/her disability.[c] (Agree)
45. Wheelchair users should get special tax credits to pay for the use of accessible transportation. (Agree)
54. Generally, it's a good idea not to try to win a game when competing with a physically disabled person. (Agree)

Disabled Saint
21. Blind people tend to be no more shy than sighted people. (Disagree)
26. Disabled people are generally easier to get along with than nondisabled people. [b] (Agree)
34. Physically disabled people are usually easy-going and seldom get angry.[d] (Agree)
42. Disabled people should be considered courageous for having overcome their disabilities. (Agree)
74. Blind people tend to get a more accurate first impression of others than most people do.[c] (Agree)

---

[a] The responses in parentheses are the "wrong-direction" (negative) responses of the nondisabled group.
[b] Items adapted from Yuker et al. (1970)
[c] Items adapted from Whiteman and Lukoff (1964).
[d] Item adapted from Kastner et al. (1979).

more negative under fake-well instructions than under honest instructions. That is, relying on the standards articulated by the disabled respondents, the nondisabled subjects changed their responses in the "wrong direction" when they were intentionally trying to respond positively.

Table 2 reports the means by sample and by

Table 2.

Means and Significant Differences Between Means on the Wrong-Direction Items

Item No.	Disabled (n = 92)	Good attitudes (n = 69)	Student honest (n = 83)	Student fake (n = 83)
5	4.12	4.06	4.78[ab]	5.40[ab]
10	6.02	5.70	5.25[a]	4.00[ab]
19	6.27	6.29	5.66[ab]	4.58[ab]
21	4.12	3.97	3.83	3.24[ab]
25[c]	6.29	6.17	5.11[ab]	4.41[ab]
26[c]	5.85	5.61	4.77[ab]	3.71[ab]
34[c]	6.05	5.75	4.99[ab]	3.61[ab]
42[c]	5.0	3.96[a]	2.75[ab]	2.04[ab]
45	4.40	4.66	4.78	5.65[ab]
54[c]	6.73	6.41[a]	5.52[ab]	5.07[ab]
74[c]	5.53	5.13	3.73[ab]	3.23[ab]

a   Differs significantly (p < .05) from disabled sample.
b   Differs significantly (p < .05) from good-attitudes sample.
c   These items have had their scores reversed so that a high score reflects a positive attitude toward disability (as determined by responses of the disabled group).

condition within the student sample, and the significant differences among means.   In this table, the scoring of 6 items has been reversed so that a high score always represents positive attitudes toward disability, as determined by the responses of the disabled group. As can be seen, responses to only 2 of these 11 items (item 42: "Disabled people should be considered courageous for having overcome their disabilities"; item 54: "Generally, it's a good idea not to try to win a game when competing with a physically disabled person") discriminated significantly between the disabled respondents and the good-attitudes nondisabled respondents nominated by them. On the other hand, disabled respondents differed significantly from students' honest responses on 9 of the 11 items, and they differed significantly from students' fake-well responses on all 11 items. Not surprisingly, the good-attitudes respondents also differed significantly from students on most items--on 7 of the 11 items in comparison with students' honest responses, and on all 11 items in comparison with students' fake-well responses. It is worth noting that on both items on which the disabled respondents and the good-attitudes respondents differed significantly, the responses by the good-attitudes group remained significantly more positive

(according to disabled respondents) than responses by students in either condition.

Table 3.

Percentages of Agree, Disagree, and Don't Know Responses on the Wrong-Direction Items

Item No.	Response	Disabled (n=92)	Good attitudes (n=69)	Student honest (n=83)	Student fake (n=83)
5	Agree	49	39	60	74
	Disagree	41	30	21	19
	Don't Know	10	30	19	7
10	Agree	89	87	76	53
	Disagree	9	12	12	47
	Don't Know	2	1	12	0
19	Agree	95	94	86	61
	Disagree	5	6	13	37
	Don't Know	0	0	1	1
21	Agree	49	44	33	34
	Disagree	40	46	39	63
	Don't Know	11	10	29	4
25	Agree	3	3	23	42
	Disagree	94	96	75	57
	Don't Know	3	1	2	1
26	Agree	9	7	16	47
	Disagree	82	80	54	39
	Don't Know	10	13	30	15
34	Agree	4	6	10	49
	Disagree	94	83	64	40
	Don't Know	2	12	27	11
42	Agree	23	52	83	89
	Disagree	69	36	12	10
	Don't Know	9	12	5	1
45	Agree	57	63	70	82
	Disagree	34	24	23	16
	Don't Know	10	13	7	2
54	Agree	0	3	10	27
	Disagree	100	97	82	70
	Don't Know	0	0	8	4
74	Agree	12	13	46	60
	Disagree	76	65	25	29
	Don't Know	12	22	29	11

Table 3 presents the percentages of "agree," "disagree," and "don't know" responses by samples and by condition within student samples. (For the purposes of this analysis, the original direction of scoring was used, and the "somewhat agree," "agree," and "strongly agree" responses were collapsed into "agree," while the "somewhat disagree," "disagree," and "strongly disagree" responses were collapsed into "disagree.") As Table 3 shows, consensus among disabled respondents was extremely high (>75%) on 7 of the

11 items. Consensus among good-attitudes respondents was similarly high on 6 of these same items; on the 7th item (item 74: "Blind people tend to be no more shy than sighted people"), a high "don't know" response (22%) among good attitudes respondents precluded higher consensus.

Less consensus was present among the nondisabled students. On the 4 items on which a consensus (≥75%) of positive attitudes was displayed by students in the hones condition, consensus disappeared under "fake well" instructions (Item 10: "People who are disabled should have to pay income taxes"; Item 19: "If a person with a disability breaks the law, he/she should be punished as severely as a nondisabled person who breaks the same law"; Item 25: "If a person with epilepsy becomes angry with people over little things, it should be overlooked because of his/her disability"; Item 54: "Generally, it's a good idea not to try to win a game when competing with a physically disabled person"). On a 5th item (Item 42: "Disabled people should be considered courageous for having overcome their disabilities"), a consensus of negative attitudes was displayed in the honest condition and actually increased under fake-well instructions.

Two items (Item 5: "Most married couples do not get divorced when one of them becomes disabled"; Item 45: "Wheelchair users should get special tax credits to pay for the use of accessible transportation") warrant special attention. Although disabled and good-attitudes respondents tended to agree with these items, no consensus was obtained for either item, and the means for both samples were quite low. Students' responses were significantly higher and demonstrated greater consensus, particularly under fake-well instructions. These items operated in the opposite direction from the usual pattern of means. On all other items, the means were ordered as follows: disabled respondents, good-attitudes nondisabled respondents, nondisabled students' honest responses, and nondisabled students' fake-well responses.

The 11 wrong-direction items were conceptually divided to produce two distinct clusters of items, which are shown in Table 1: The "Give

the Disabled Person a Break" cluster and the "Disabled Saint" cluster. Items that comprise the Give the Disabled Person a Break cluster involve special concessions made for disabled individuals. Disabled respondents rejected this notion. They indicated that they neither want nor expect special treatment because of their disabilities. The good-attitudes nondisabled respondents demonstrated a similar unwillingness to grant special concessions on the basis of a person's disability. Nondisabled student respondents, however, were more likely to argue that disabled people *should* be given special consideration because of their disabilities; this attitude was amplified under fake-well instructions when they were trying to impress disabled individuals!

The first introductory scenario illustrates the differing perceptions that underlie this cluster well. Doris, in her attempts to demonstrate that she carries no prejudice against disabled people, tries to "fake-well" by "giving the disabled person a break." Suzanne perceives Doris' comment as condescending, not merely as an incompetent expression of a positive attitude. Suzanne angrily rejects Doris, as most of us would if we felt patronized. Although Suzanne may certainly be justified in correcting Doris' behavior, her reaction carries much hostility. Such negative affect necessarily limits the likelihood that Doris will be receptive to Suzanne's message.

Items in the Disabled Saint cluster represent positive characteristics frequently attributed to persons with disabilities. Disabled respondents and good-attitudes respondents both rejected these attributes as defining persons with disabilities. Students, on the other hand, significantly more often accepted these distinguishing characteristics when responding "honestly"; their acceptance was amplified when responding under fake-well instructions.

The second introductory scenario illustrates the interaction stress that can result from the differing perceptions represented in the "Disabled Saint" cluster. Mike goes out of his way to let Rick know that he considers disabled people better than average. Rick, reading Mike's intentions as patronizing, terminated the interaction. Rick's extremely negative reaction is not likely to educate Mike about the politics of disability.

Discussion

The results suggest that disabled people and non disabled people differ significantly in their perceptions of what constitutes "the most positive attitudes toward persons with disabilities." For the disabled respondents, "positive attitudes" would mean either dispensing with the special category of disability entirely, or promoting attitudes that defend the civil and social rights of disabled persons. For the nondisabled respondents, "positive attitudes" reflect a desire to be nice, helpful, and ultimately place the disabled person in a needy situation. Nondisabled individuals may actually be perceived by disabled people, therefore, as expressing negative attitudes when, in fact, the nondisabled persons are trying hard to express what they consider to be positive attitudes. Eleven of the 100 items in the IDS indicated areas in which such misunderstandings routinely occur. Students responded more negatively (according to disabled respondents) to these items when instructed to fake well than they did when responding honestly. Thus the paradox of well-intentioned liberalism is that the recipient frequently experiences the interaction as offensive.

If we assume, as research by Kleck (1968; Kleck et al., 1966) suggests, that nondisabled people *do* want to express attitudes that are acceptable to and respectful of disabled persons with whom they come in contact, it is apparent that nondisabled people need to be educated about areas in which their notions of positive attitudes offend disabled people. Nondisabled persons must be educated about disability as a civil rights issue, and made aware that many disabled people reject special treatment on the basis of their disabilities and do not desire to be perceived as different, even if "different" means "better." Nondisabled individuals specifically identified by disabled respondents in this study as having "extremely positive attitudes" did not recommend special treatment for or attribute special characteristics to persons with disabilities.

One important consequence of this research is both methodological and political. Disabled

people themselves need to be involved in identifying attitudes and standards, and in defining social interactions for study. Research in the past has looked at interactions between disabled and nondisabled people primarily, if not exclusively, from the point of view of the nondisabled interactant. Such a methodology reinforces the view that disabled people are passive recipients of social interaction, rather than active social negotiators in interactions with nondisabled people. It is crucial that "real" disabled people, not role-playing experimental confederates, participate in both the design of research and in training that deals with the reduction of interaction strain.

Resolving misunderstandings around disability, however, cannot be confined solely to changing the attitudes of nondisabled people. While nondisabled persons have more power and influence, individuals with disabilities must also become sensitized to the occasional discrepancies between their own perceptions of positive attitudes and those of well-intentioned nondisabled people. A clumsy statement by a nondisabled person may be the result of a misunderstanding rather than evidence of a consciously negative attitude. In situations in which a nondisabled person makes a statement or behaves in a way that demeans or insults, a disabled individual is certainly justified in correcting the error. However, if the correction is accompanied by powerful negative emotions on the part of the disabled person, the *content* of the correction is likely to be lost. Generalized negative reactions to the occasional blunder may discourage the nondisabled person's good intentions and exacerbate the misunderstanding. It is important to remember that, on many of the 100 items in the IDS, student respondents did move in a more positive direction when attempting to fake well.

Interactions between disabled people and nondisabled people may cause a great deal of discomfort for both parties. Communication, particularly the sharing of one another's expectations, can be a valuable tool in breaking down the barriers that contribute to this discomfort. More research needs to be done to clarify the discrepancies in perceptions between people who have disabilities and those who do not.

As demonstrated by Cook and Makas (1979),

one way in which successful relationships between disabled people and nondisabled people can be facilitated is through exchange of information between the two groups to "clarify the situation." It is important to remember that both the disabled and the nondisabled interviewees in the Cook and Makas study were all persons who had had extensive interaction with members of the other group, thus affording them ample opportunity for this sharing of perceptions. For many people, however, particularly for many nondisabled people, *equal-status, personal contact* with disabled persons is not so readily available. Contact across unequal statuses, e.g., in a "helping role," is not likely to reduce strain. Instructional tools are needed to serve as a means of communication between the two groups, and to facilitate this exchange of information. Training materials need to be developed for nondisabled people to help those who are well intentioned to interact in ways that are perceived by disabled people as positive. Training materials also need to be developed for disabled people so that they can become more sensitized to the most prevalent misperceptions about them held by nondisabled people (if they are not already too intensely aware of them), and so that they can learn to respond to these misperceptions firmly but with patience. While this could, unfortunately, become almost a full-time job for a disabled person, only disabled persons can help their well-intentioned nondisabled peers to move into the good-attitudes category.

REFERENCES

Belgrave, F. Z., & Mills, J. (1981). Effect upon desire for social interaction with a physically disabled person of mentioning the disability in different contexts. *Journal of Applied Social Psychology, 11*, 44-57.

Comer, R. J., & Piliavin, J. A. (1972). The effects of physical deviance upon face-to-face interaction: The other side. *Journal of Personality and Social Psychology, 23*, 33-39.

Cook, S., & Makas, E. (1979). *Why some of my best friends are disabled! A study of the interaction between disabled people and nondisabled rehabilitation professionals.* Unpublished manuscript, George Washington University.

Goffman, E. (1963). *Stigma: Notes on the management of spoiled identity.* Englewood Cliffs, NJ: Prentice-Hall.

Hastorf, A. H., Wildfogel, J., & Cassman, T. (1979). Acknowledgement of handicap as a tactic in social interaction. *Journal of Personality and Social Psychology, 37*, 1790-1797.

Jones, E. E., Farina, A., Hastorf, A. H., Markus, H., Miller, D. T., & Scott, R. A. (1984). *Social stigma: The psychology of marked relationships.* New York: Freeman.

Kastner, L. S., Reppucci, N. D., & Pezzoli, J. J. (1979). Assessing community attitudes toward mentally retarded persons. *American Journal of Mental Deficiency, 84*, 137-144.

Kelley, H. H., Hastorf, A. H., Jones, E. E., Thibaut, J. W., & Usdane, W. M. (1960). Some implications of social psychological theory for research on the handicapped. In L. H. Lofquist (Ed.) *Psychological research and rehabilitation* (Miami Conference Report, pp. 172-204). Washington, D.C.: American Psychological Association.

Kleck, R. (1966). Emotional arousal in interactions with stigmatized persons. *Psychological Reports, 19*, 1226.

Kleck, R. (1968). Physical stigma and nonverbal cues emitted in face-to-face interaction. *Human Relations, 21*, 19-28.

Kleck, R., Ono, H., & Hastorf, A. H. (1966). The effects of physical deviance upon face-to-face interaction. *Human Relations, 19*, 425-436.

Makas, E. (1985, August). *The measurement of attitudes toward disabled people: A new approach.* Paper presented at meeting of the American Psychological Association, Los Angeles.

Makas, E., Finnerty-Fried, P., Sigafoos, A., & Reiss, D. (1988). The Issues in Disability Scale: A new cognitive and affective measure of attitudes toward people with physical disabilities. *Journal of Applied Rehabilitation Counselling, 19*(1).

Sigafoos, A., Makas, E., Finnerty-Fried, P., & Reiss, D. (1988). *The Issues in Disability Scale as a predictor of behavior toward disabled persons on three different measures.* Unpublished manuscript.

Whiteman, M., & Lukoff, I. F. (1964). Attitudes toward blindness in two college groups. *Journal of Social Psychology, 63*, 179-191.

Yuker, H. E., Block, J. R., & Younng, J. H. (1970). *The measurement of attitudes toward disabled persons.* Albertson, NY: Human Resources Center.

NOTES

1. Two versions used items selected through analyses of responses by both disabled and nondisabled persons: the items in these versions were selected because they showed low skewness among nondisabled subjects, and high consensus among disabled respondents specifically recruited to help in the development of the scale. (These two versions differed only in the amount of consensus among disabled respondents required for item inclusion.) A third version used items selected through analyses of only nondisabled subjects' responses: the items in this version were selected because they showed low skewness and hight item-to-item correlation within theoretically derived subscales. Using experimental methodology described by Sigafoos, Makas, Finnerty-Fried, and Reiss (1988), attitude scores, as determined by the three versions of the scale, were related to three behaviors toward a confederate who appeared disabled. The two scales developed on the basis of responses by both disabled and nondisabled people, although containing fewer items than the third version, were found to be at least as predictive of behaviors as the scale developed on the basis of only nondisabled subjects' responses.

Stigmata and Negotiated Outcomes: Management of Appearance by Persons with Physical Disabilities

SUSAN B. KAISER
CARLA M. FREEMAN
STACY B. WINGATE

This paper explores the role of clothing in the management of appearances by persons with disabilities. A negotiated outcomes perspective is used to study the clothing choices of disabled persons, rather than viewing them as passive recipients of the labels supplied by perceivers. A two-part study of college students with physical disabilities, including comments from a series of focused group interviews and open-ended responses to a questionnaire with national distribution, resulted in the data presented. The data indicated that most of the students strived to appear as normative as possible through their clothing choices and accordingly used a variety of techniques: "making do" with ingeniously adapted ready-to-wear apparel; using clothes to conceal a disability; deflecting attention from a disability toward more normative but slightly discrediting attributes; compensation through fashionable dress or by emphasizing other social roles and abilities; and social inclusion, i.e., the assertion that all persons very in physical appearance. Some students employed dress to take advantage of their social uniqueness through such techniques as wearing bright or prominent clothing or by displaying humor. Possible directions for future research on the social interactions of disabled persons, particularly involving the implications of normalizing appearance versus emphasizing social uniqueness, are presented.

A physical disability may be used as a cue to categorize a person as abnormal or different (Davis, 1964) and becomes a source of stigmatization when it is used to discredit an individual in a stereotypical manner (Goffman, 1963). The cultural stereotype that "beauty is good" pervades American culture. At the interpersonal level, persons who are physically attractive in the normative sense are evaluated on the basis of implicit "halo effects" involving clusters of positive personal traits (for reviews of the physical attractiveness literature, see Adams, 1977; Adams, 1982; and Berscheid and Walster, 1974). Conversely, a negative stereotype or stigma is associated with persons who deviate from the normal physical appearance. Both the physical attractiveness stereotype (Adams and Crane, 1980; Dion and Berscheid, 1974) and the stigma associated with physical disabilities (Popp et al., 1981) appear to be learned at a relatively young age through socialization processes. Additionally, there is some evidence that adults expect able-bodied children to be involved in more intense best-friend relationships than disabled children (Kleck and DeJong, 1981). Stereotypical traits assigned to people with physical disabilities include dependency, sadness, and isolation; in certain contexts these attributions may reduce perceivers' role expectations and lead to restrictions of behavior and opportunities (Altman, 1981).

The extent to which a physical disability is disruptive to interaction is dependent upon contextual factors. Higgins (1980) has noted that disabilities become disruptive when they present a breach in the taken-for-granted social order. A person with a physical disability may be perceived by nondisabled persons, in certain contexts, as threatening to social interaction (Elliott et al., 1982) due, perhaps, to the inconsistency between a physical disability and the perception that the world is a just place where the innocent do not suffer (Katz, 1981; Lerner, 1970). Davis (1964: 125) reported an account of a strikingly attractive girl in a wheelchair who frequently elicited such comments as, "How strange that someone so pretty should be in a wheelchair."

Funding for the study was provided by a Faculty Research Grant from the University of California at Davis. The authors wish to express their appreciation to Joan L. Chandler and Tami Soler for their assistance in the coding of data, and to the anonymous reviewers who provided constructive and stimulating comments.

Reprinted From: *Deviant Behaviour* 6:205-224, 1985, with permission. Published by Taylor and Francis.

Stigmatization does not necessarily lead to the labelling of an individual as deviant, according to Haber and Smith (1971). They point out that stigmatization becomes a social role which may achieve legitimate status in such contexts as the medical and social helping professions. Labelling theorists are more interested in the contexts in which imputations of deviance are made than in the deviance per se (Kitsuse, 1975). The labelling or societal reaction perspective has increasingly emphasized the processes through which persons come to be perceived, defined, and treated as deviant by others. A major criticism of the traditional labelling approach to deviance is that the reaction of those labelled deviant has been overemphasized, while the perceived persons' abilities to affect the imputation of the deviant label have been undermined (Levitin, 1975; Hanks and Poplin, 1981). In other words, the labelled persons have been depicted as passive recipients of the deviant role rather than as impression-managing persons engaged in social transactions. Levitin (1975) has noted that the self-conceptions of a stigmatized individual should be considered in relation to the strategies used to negotiate identities in different social contexts.

The negotiated outcome perspective provides an alternate view of the labelling process in which persons with disabilities actively participate (c.f., Wright, 1960; Levitin, 1975; Hanks and Poplin, 1981). Hanks and Poplin have pointed out that negative evaluations by others may lead to maladjusted, self-perceived deviance only "if disabled individuals are unable to manipulate and to some extent control the labels that are applied to them by nondisabled individuals" (1981: 317). The manipulation of appearance symbols affords opportunities for individuals to present other aspects of the self and to communicate visually to others that the disability is not the only aspect of the self. Davis (1964) has argued that by definition, the visibly handicapped person cannot control appearance sufficiently so as to reduce the obtrusiveness of the disability. However, through the manipulation of clothing and accessories, persons with disabilities may emphasize other aspects of self if total concealment of the disability is not possible. This role that appear-

ance plays has frequently been ignored and deserves attention if the role of the disabled person in influencing negotiated outcomes is to be fully understood.

Goffman (1963) has pointed out that just as "stigma symbols" draw a perceiver's attention to a debasing identity, "disidentifiers" are signs which serve to disrupt an otherwise coherent picture, thus casting some doubt on the validity of a disqualifying attribution. Persons with disabilities may strive to present appearances which allow them to take the roles of others more readily. Stone (1962) has argued that appearance is a precursory phase to the ability to identify with others and thus facilitate role-taking.

The perceptions of nondisabled persons when observing disabled individuals are affected by clothing cues as well as physical deformities (Miller, 1982). A study by Feather et al. (1979) indicated that university students in wheelchairs held significantly less favorable attitudes towards clothing than did ablebodied students. Other authors have reported that available clothing in the marketplace does not appear to meet the needs of persons with physical disabilities (Hallenbeck, 1966; Kernaleguen, 1978; Shannon and Reic, 1979). Yet specially designed clothing, as available from some mail-order firms, may not be desirable either, due to distinct normative differences. Cuber (1963) noted that ambivalence often results from the conflict between an individual's attitudes based upon unique needs and experiences, and those based upon cultural norms. Such a case is particularly apparent in specially designed clothing for persons with disabilities. Special features of garments designed for people with disabilities, i.e., the of Velcro®, large zippers, and other such features in unconventional places, may be sources of stigma which differentiate the disabled from the nondisabled. This clothing may be both positively and negatively received by disabled persons, in that it may be both functional and different from the norm. As Kernaleguen has noted, "Since the handicapped may have different and specific needs, clothing designed to meet these needs can easily become 'special clothing' which emphasizes, rather than minimizes, a handicap" (1978: 3).

The purpose of the present research was to explore the self-presentations of persons with disabilities, with respect to personal appearance and clothing as factors in social interactions. The qualitative data reported in this paper are part of a larger study on clothing as a social factor in the lives of persons with disabilities. The present study focused primarily on: 1) the forms of social feedback received in everyday encounters with nondisabled persons, and, as the subjects were university students, many of their face-to-face social encounters on a daily basis were fleeting and anonymous, such as during class changes. The second focus of the paper employed a negotiated outcome perspective as applied to the impression management of appearance, considering persons with disabilities as active participants in the labeling process.

Method

The data were obtained in two separate phases. The first of these involved twelve focused group interviews with male and female disabled students (N = 36) attending six different colleges and universities in Northern California. From one to five people attended each interview. Due to the exploratory nature of the investigation and the limited population, no restrictions were placed on either the age or type of disability of the participants. Thus a broad range of disabilities was represented. The students responded to a series of questions related to the following topics: the forms of social feedback received from nondisabled persons, clothing patterns and preferences, attitudes toward specially designed clothing, and suggestions for names of apparel lines or stores catering specifically to the needs of persons with physical disabilities. The latter suggestions were included in order to determine preferred verbal labels that might be assigned to the nonverbal realm of appearance.

The second phase of the study involved the distribution of a self-administered questionnaire to seventy-two colleges and universities across the United States. At least one college or university from each state was represented. One thousand copies of the questionnaire were distributed to the students through handicapped student offices at each university. Of the 1000 question-

naires sent to the schools, 960 were actually distributed to legitimate/current addresses. Of these, 327 questionnaires were returned, representing a 34% response rate.[1] Both males (46%) and females (54%) responded to the questionnaires. As in the interviews, many forms of physical disabilities were represented in the sample.[2] The data reported in this paper are derived from the comments in the focused group interviews as well as from the qualitative component of the questionnaire. There were open-ended questions in the questionnaire in the nature of personally owned clothing which may communicate linguistically (e.g., T-shirts with slogans), attitudes with respect to specially designed clothing, and suggestions for names of stores or clothing designs catering to persons with disabilities. Volunteered general comments at the end of the questionnaire are also included in the present paper. (The remainder of the questionnaire dealt with the students' responses to clothing stimuli and attitudinal statements.) As appropriate, some of the students' responses to selected attitudinal statements in the questionnaire are presented as well, because these statements were derived from students' comments in the group interviews. The extent to which there was agreement with these comments is indicated.[3]

The qualitative data were content-analyzed and categorized on the basis of concepts related to visible disabilities and the importance of dress in social perceptions. Previous work by Davis (1964), Goffman (1963), Elliott et al. (1982), Hanks and Poplin (1981), and Kaiser (1983-84) served to provide a framework for the analysis of the data; however, several novel categories of responses to visible disabilities also arose from the data herein. Because the comments obtained from the group interviews and the questionnaires may have varied as a result of the increased anonymity of the questionnaire responses, throughout the presentation of the results an "(I)" will follow those comments obtained from the interviews, and a "(Q)" will follow those derived from the questionnaires.

Social Feedback

Almost all of the subjects in the focused group interviews felt that clothing and appearance are extremely important in people's responses towards one another when they first meet. And, visible disabilities generally were considered to be conducive to the creation of attitudinal barriers in such cases. Several individuals commented, however, that such effects of disabilities on person perceptions could be at least partially ameliorated by dressing neatly and attractively. There also was some recognition that self-feelings with regard to appearance are related to social feedback.

> If you are well-dressed and you don't look like you spent three days in the same clothes, then you do tend to get a better response. I've been with people in wheelchairs that look real rumpled and it's not that the clothes aren't good enough...It's just that they look unkempt; I'm turned off by that. (I).

> I think that they're more courteous, more social, or smiley if I feel I'm looking nice. I'm more attractive, I'm friendlier, and so they respond differently. (I).

There was almost unaminous agreement in the interviews that when verbal feedback on clothing and appearance is received, it is positive.

> I get a lot of good feedback that makes me feel good. (I).
> I usually get a lot of good comments. (I).

> I get very positive comments about what I wear. (I).

The majority (92%) of the respondents to the questionnaire indicated that they like to receive compliments on their clothes and appearance. Even compliments, however, may be tinged with stigmatization. Some support for the "just world" hypothesis (Lerner, 1970; 1980) was indicated in a response by the wife of a man who had had a stroke that their friends "were astounded that he can look as good as he does or dress as well as he does (I)." Such astonishment seems to suggest that an attractive appearance

seems inconsistent with a disability and thus is the source of some ambivalent perceptions.

With regard to fleeting, relatively anonymous encounters during the course of everyday situations such as changing classes, the respondents in wheelchairs frequently commented that people react initially to the wheelchair, rather than the individual in it. Goffman (1963) would refer to a wheelchair as a stigma symbol, due to its salience in social perceptions.

> A lot of times, I think people look at the chair before they look at who's in it (I).

> I must tell you that the overriding way to characterize them (other's responses) is in relation to my handicap. I suspect that they're noticing my dress...second or third (I).

> Pople I don't know tend to notice my disability first, and my clothing second (I). (Sixty percent of the respondents agreed with this statement in the questionnaire.)

> I think the visual impact of a person, sitting in a chair with wheels on it, is so great as to render all other impressions, such as dress or grooming, virtually insignificant. For example, a nude person seen passing down the street in a wheelchair will be reported as "a person in a wheelchair without clothes on was seen...etc." Rather than, "A person without clothes on was seen in a wheelchair" ".

However, many of the students acknowledged that some of the stigmatizing effects of a physical disability can be ameliorated by dressing neatly or fashionably. Ninety-one percent agreed that the first thing people notice is appearance, and clothes are part of that. Thus clothing is not necessarily seen as a source of secondary impressions only. Moreover, sixty-four percent of the questionnaire respondents agreed with the following statement: "If I'm attractively dressed, people are more likely to notice me rather than my disability."

A conflict may occur between a) a perceiver's desire to attend to a novel stimulus such as a physical disability or related cue and b) social restraints against staring. This conflict leads to uncomfortable, controlled interactions between disabled and nondisabled persons in face-to-face situations (Kleck et al., 1966; Kleck, 1968; Comer and Piliavin, 1972; Safilios-Rothschild, 1970). Several respondents reported their self-feelings based upon the staring behavior of others. One male student with severe burn scars on one arm indicated a preference for overt verbal attention to a stigma symbol, as opposed to staring:

> On a personal basis, for example, if I wear a T-shirt, I get these eyes that are just staring at my arms...I want to tell that person, if you want to sit down we can talk, and I can explain it to you and explain how I got this way. I find it more rewarding when a person will say, "Wow, what happened to you?" Versus somebody who's just looking at you and looking at you. I was in this dance class, and he (a male student) had already seen me for probably three or four weeks, but he was still trying to absorb it. Like trying to look at a picture, and you want to look at it until you finally absorb it. I didn't feel comfortable with that (I).

Smiles were considered to be a desirable form of nonverbal feedback. Seventy-nine percent of the students responding to the questionnaire indicated that they liked for people they did not know to smile at them. However, one female subject in a wheelchair remarked in an interview that one can never be sure why a person is smiling, so a smile is an ambiguous form of feedback for a person with a visible disability.

Management of Appearance Relative to Negotiated Outcomes

As a negotiated outcome perspective would suggest, most of the subjects indicated an interest in using dress or other appearance cues (e.g., hairstyles, overall neatness) to present positive impression to others and thus to supply stimuli to augment or ameliorate the impressions created by a visible disability. The students also seemed to be concerned with their roles in representing the disabled population in general. Eighty-five percent of the questionnaire respondents agreed with the statement, "I want the nondisabled to know that disabled people are concerned with their appearance and clothing."

Only in two instances was there any evidence that individuals were resigned to existing appearances and lacking in motivation to manage the impressions they presented. Such resignation or apathy has been called capitulation (Elliott et al., 1982: 291): "Giving up, the stigmatized accept the stereotype thrust upon them and the concomitant illegitimate status." One subject in an interview indicated that he generally wears pajamas and hospital gowns in public despite the fact that he has received negative feedback on the negative image his appearance presents for disabled persons.

> It (appearance) is only important if you take it to extremes...hospital gowns, etc. Most of the people I know are attendants. They won't freak out if they see me in a hospital gown. That's what I'm wearing right now because it's the most comfortable thing...When I say dressed up I mean anything more formal than a hospital gown (I).

It is important to note that this individual was almost completely paralyzed and was unable to sit up in a wheelchair. He was rolled on a flat bed from class to class by an attendant. One factor in his disinterest in dress may have been his inability to see his body, as he was always in a horizontal position.   he did express some interest in the appearance and function of the blanket used to cover him.

The only other person whose response to appearance might be characterized as capitulation was also severely disabled and was unable to communicate with the group, due to his cerebral palsy. His attendant gave her interpretation of his self-feelings:

You don't like the way you look at all...(he nods). He has a great big closet of clothes that he hates. They are a mess...He has a condom hookup that isn't very convenient with his clothes...They say he's one of the most disabled people in the country...He had problems with the questions about style and fashion. I guess he doesn't get around or pay that much attention to it. And maybe he doesn't care (I).

Facilitation of Normative Identifications

The majority of the students expressed a desire to look like everyone else and considered clothes as a means for such normalization,. The idea that deviance is imputed to a disability because other people consider one's appearance to differ from the norm is fundamental to the application of labeling theory to physical disabilities (Davis, 1964; Safilios-Rothschild, 1970). However, Haber and Smith (1971) have argued that stigmatization is not synonymous with deviance. Disability, in their minds, is a social role which is legitimized in some contexts, i.e., in the worlds of the medical profession or social work. In a college setting, such legitimation may not exist, and persons with visible disabilities may need to strive for normalcy.

Davis' concept of deviance disavowal (1964) involves the stigmatized person's attempts to strive for normalcy. If such a person is able to surpass fictional acceptance by others and then to facilitate reciprocal role-taking, then his/her interactions are likely to be more meaningful. This process of "breaking through" (Davis, 1964: 128) may be facilitated through normative clothing styles. In both the interviews and the questionnaires, normative styles such as jeans, corduroys, and casual sportswear were preferred for wearing on the campus. The students did not want to appear any more conspicuous than they already were, and some indicated that dress was one area in which they could strive for identification with others. Dress, unlike a visible disability, is a reflection of personal choice.

They (disabled people) are so different in so many ways. They are in a wheelchair, walk with a cane or a crutch, that when it comes to clothes they want to be like anybody else (I).

It is very important to me to dress in fashion, like everyone else. It is sometimes difficult to find clothing that is stylish and still practical for my disability (Q).

When the students were questioned with respect to possible outlets for the purchase of specially designed clothing for people with disabilities, the importance of normalization with regard to clothing became apparent. Several students expressed strong feelings that the medical profession (the same profession that legitimizes disability as a social role) should not play a part in the distribution of functional clothing, due to the connotations of essential differentness from the norm.

I'd like to see it away from the medical aspects. Get away from where they sell medical things. The environment--it reminds me of hospitals..I'm going to enjoy shopping, to look at some of the styles of clothing available for disabled people and not to look at braces. They make you sick, whereas if you go to a clothing department you want to buy clothes. It affects you psychologically (I).

Putting clothing into a medical supply store would not be a good idea. It would alter the way the individual felt about herself. It would be too clinical. It would be nice if the 16-year old girl could go to the store with her friends and pick out clothing like any other teenage. Maybe it would help to lessen the "I'm different" attitude and help instill an "I'm a normal" individual concept (Q).

Moreover, there were many comments which indicated that the whole idea of special clothing for people with disabilities reinforces the differences between disabled and nondisabled people, and thus should be avoided.

> I like the idea of clothes that fit everyone. I don't like the idea of having a special category. If I need something special, I will ask somebody to do (make) it. But I don't like the idea of having a special store (I).

> Clothes for the disabled...That can be kind of offensive. You want to be as normal as possible, and you don't want to be tripping into some store...The rich, they do the same thing (buy customized clothes), but it's got a different ring (I).

> No disabled labelling--just a brand name (Q).

> Something normal sounding (Q).

> The biggest drawback I've seen with clothing for the disabled is that there is such a heavy reliance on function, style is almost completely ignored (Q).

With respect to deviance disavowal, or the desire to appear as normative as possible, several appearance-related responses were identified. These responses are discussed in the following section.

Making do. One of the most creative responses to the conflict of function versus style needs with regard to clothing might be referred to as "making do". Goffman (1961) used this phrase to describe the adaptations to clothing made by patients in a mental institution. In the case of persons with disabilities, making do may provide a means for purchasing normative clothing and altering it to suit their own particular physical needs. Many ingenious "make-do's" were reported with a sense of pride by the subjects. In the focused group interviews, the students appeared to enjoy sharing their ideas with one another. For example, one male student dealt with pressure-point problems while seated by having his mother remove the pockets in the back of his blue jeans and sew a patch of sheepskin inside on which to sit. Other make-do's included alterations to shoulders in dresses and shirts for quadriplegic students or alterations to pants to increase their attractiveness in the seated position. One woman who had only one arm wore a prosthesis in the form of an artificial shoulder. She had been provided with a strap to hold the prosthesis, and this strap greatly limited the kinds of clothes she could wear (e.g., high-necked styles and dark colors). She developed the idea of gluing the prosthesis rather than using the straps, and this technique enabled her to wear a greater variety of styles.

Concealment. One obvious way of presenting a normative appearance, when possible, is through concealment of the disability. To conceal a source of stigma, according to Elliott et al. (1982) is to engage in "passing" as normal. Some examples of managing the visual impressions presented through concealment follow:

> I get a different response from people when I wear short sleeves so I very seldom wear short sleeves. It camouflages my disability (missing arm) when I wear long sleeves (I).

> Because of my amputation at the hip, I prefer dresses without a waist or gathering at the bodice of the dress. Dresses that flare out more at the tail are more attractive.

Similarly, Bregman and Hadley (1976) reported that spinal-cord-injured women reported concealing a catheter leg bag through the use of long skirts or dresses and pants. In many cases, Goffman's notion of "covering" (1963), as opposed to "passing" is likely to apply to the concealment of disabilities by persons with disabilities. Covering involves the concealment of a stigma in order to reduce tension, or to make it easier to withdraw overt attention from the stigma, but do not want to be the most salient attribute perceived by observers.

Deflection. When actual concealment is not possible, a stigmatized person may deflect others' attention from the damaging effects of the stigma by presenting the signs of the stigma as signs of a less deeply discrediting attribute (Goffman, 1963; Elliott et al., 1982). For example, a mentally retarded person may pretend to be hard of hearing rather than have others think he/she does not understand a conversation. Although such a guise would not be applicable to the deflection of attention from a visible handicap, other forms of deflection may be possible. A more applicable form of deflection may be to emphasize another aspect of one's identity which may or may not have positive social connotations. Several respondents to the questionnarie indicated that they wore T-shirts with slogans which would serve such a purpose. Some individuals emphasized their drinking habits through the following slogans: "I don't have cerebral palsy; I'm just drunk", "Ten gallon weekend", and "Moosehead beer". Drinking habits, as opposed to the possession of a physical disability, are elected rather than ascribed behaviors. As such, drinking has ambiguous connotations in American society, but nevertheless serves to deflect attention from the disability.

A student may perfer to be known for his/her heavy drinking than for the disability.

A similar example was one student's indication of having a T-shirt saying "Sun your buns". Again, a perceiver might reflect on the questionable taste of a person wearing such a T-shirt, and at least would have an alternate stimulus to attend to in lieu of the disability.

Compensation. One way of gaining legitimacy in social encounters is to compensate for a physical disability by expressing mastery in an area usually closed to disabled persons and/or important to a particular situation in which the stigma is irrelevant (Elliott et al., 1982). For instance, other social roles may be emphasized, as a person communicates, "This isn't all of me" (Levitin, 1975). In this way, the disability does not obscure more positive, socially valued aspects of the self. A strong interest in fashion or dress per se may provide a means of compensation. One male in an interview explained that he emphasizes his ethnic status (Mexican-American) and his flair for style through the wearing of white peasant pants, a white vest, huaraches, a

Panama hat, and a blue handkerchief around the neck. He stated that at times he has enjoyed wearing this outfit to attract attention. Another subject indicated that she spends a lot on her clothes because she feels that she and others respond toward attractive clothing rather than her disability (quadriplegia). Other students indicated on the questionnaires they had T-shirts emphasizing occupational aspirations ("Social workers do it in the field", "Love a nurse today"), social-political orientations ("No nukes", "Nuclear power--No thanks!", "ERA"), or other aspects of the self ("Joe Cool", "I'm a wild and crazy guy", "Short and sexy").

Social inclusion. Another means of disavowing deviance expressed by the students was to include able-bodied persons under the label of disabled, with the assertion that everyone has some form of handicap in certain contexts. In relation to appearance, most people find themselves inappropriately attired for certain situations, for example. And, once attired, persons have little control over the impressions they provide to others. A common comment was that individual differences should be accepted, as they are everywhere.

I don't consider myself especially handicapped. Everyone has a handicap; some are more obvious than others. No one is perfect (Q).

You should really send this (the questionnaire to everyone, because there isn't one person living without some disability (Q).

One subject suggested that "Rainbow fashions" would be a good label for a clothing line for people with disabilities, because "we all have differences but together we make up the world" (Q). Another individual remarked, while viewing pants with a zipper in the side pants leg during the interview, that if such functional features were incorporated into all pants, for disabled and able-bodied persons alike, then functional clothes would lose their negative connotations.[4]

Displays of Social Uniqueness

Wright (1960) has suggested that disabilities

may generate opportunities and positive outcomes as well as grief. Similarly, a review of the literature by Shontz (1977) has provided little support for the assumption that all psychological effects of disability are negative, i.e., disruptive or dissatisfying. There are likely to be situations, at least, in which a physical disability does not lead to a negative outlook on self and society. A physical disability is likely to call attention to a person and to make that person memorable in the eyes of perceivers. Although such remembrances may not always be positive, there are likely to be situations in which they are.

People with disabilites, however, do not appear to desire extra attention. Eighty-two percent of the questionnaire respondents disagreed with the statement, "I like the extra attention I get because of my disability." In contrast, there were more varied responses to the statement, "I like to draw attention to myself through my clothes." Thirty-nine percent of the students disagreed with the statement, while 37% agreed with it, and 24% were undecided. Thus clothing per se may be used to call attention to the self, but attention which is considered to be based upon one's disability is less desirable.

Clothing and a visible disability are likely to work together in presenting impressions to observers. Miller (1982) found that the salience of a disability cue leads to dispositional, rather than situational, attributions about an individual. That is, a perceiver is likely to believe that a person with a disability is more responsible for the outcome of an event than are situational factors. Miller's research suggested that clothing may lessen the impact of physical impairment on some aspects of impression formation. In his research, the appearance cues of a hearing aid and patterned clothing each increased personal attributions, attributions of leadership, and recall.

Since a person with a visible disability is likely to be noticed, he/she may capitalize upon this tendency by further shaping the impression formed through the management of appearance. Some instances of such an attitude were found in the present study, although they were considerably less common than the tendency to emphasize normalcy. A few participants in the focused group interviews indicated that they enjoy the extra attention they receive from others, and they take advantage of this attention by making noticeable clothing choices.

> I like bright colors. I used to think that I didn't like that extra attention, but in the last year I've noticed that I like it. I used to resent all the extra attention I got being in a chair, but I kind-of am finding that I like the extra attention, so I take advantage of it (I).

> Just trying to be sexy. It must be my age. Low cut things that show off my bustline (I).

The desire to draw attention to personal appearance was not a common response, and the other subjects in the interview in which the above attendant made her remarks did not seem especially receptive to them. In contrast to the tendency to draw attention to the self, one subject in the same interview said, "I never dress to draw attention to myself." Thus the desire to emphasize social uniqueness is likely to vary across persons and contexts.

Although few disabled persons appeared to draw attention to themselves through clothing, many had suggestions for clothing labels emphasizing social uniqueness in the questionnaire. Following are some of the typical responses: "Special and spirited", "Special and spicy", "Clothes for special people", "Fashion for the positively unique", "My own style", "Innovations and improvisations", and "Pretty 'n progress". It is possible that official labels stressing the social uniqueness of disability may be perceived as legitimizing it as a social role. Of course, there are likely to be drawbacks even to the latter, as one student pointed out: "I'm sorry, a little realistic, I suppose, but I have learned that 'special' anything costs, and what a racket" (Q).

The expression of humor with respect to personal disabilites also was found in some of the students' responses. Humor may serve as a means of tension release in encounters between disabled and able-bodied persons. During an interview, one male subject in a wheelchair relayed an experience in which his unexpected response to staring disrupted that staring and provided a personal sense of satisfaction. He was in a pizza parlor with his mother when every person in a group at a nearby table stared at him continuously. Finally he started waving and smiling at them; they were so disconcerted that they got up and moved to a new table where they could not see him.

Other examples of the expression of humor in emphasizing social uniqueness were found in the case of T-shirt messages reported in the question-naire: "I'm no quad; I'm just tired of walking" and "Guess which part of me is not bionic". Again, such appearance-related responses were not common among the students, but they do suggest that some individuals tend to emphasize humor or social uniqueness through their dress.

Another variant of the emphasis on social uniqueness involved instances in which there was an expression of minority or in-group power. For instance, several students volunteered that there should be more disabled persons in the media, but only if they have done something which deserves to be there. One student indic-ated that it would be nice to see models with leg braces. There were a number of T-shirt slogans reported which suggest a desire for more recog-nition from society: "Do it in a wheelchair", "High level quads do it with a 'joy stick'", and "If I prove I'm better, will you admit I'm equal?"

A slightly different form of social uniqueness emphasized the importance of mainstreaming in society, rather than emphasizing differentness per se. These responses still, however, would be likely to call attention to the person with a physi-cal disability. T-shirt slogans which indicated a desire for mainstreaming included the following: "Rehabilitatin publicity", "I'm accessible". And, suggestions for store or clothes names indicated a similar emphasis on the ability to mainstream: "No help needed", "Fashions of free life style", "Free me fashions", "Access Fashion", "Access wear", "HAIL fashions (Handicapped Active in Life), and "Freedom fashions". Some comments were made to the effect that nondisabled persons would be more aware of the needs of persons with disabilities if a store catering to their needs were in a mall and were identifiable with respect to its purpose: "It would let them (nondisabled

persons) know that handicapped people are concerned with their appearance (I)."

Safilios-Rothschild (1970) has argued that increased visibility of people with disabilities in society is needed if nondisabled persons are to communicate with them in a more meaningful manner:

> Unless modern societies are successful in altering social and affective prejudices in such a way that the disabled are accepted as "people with a disability", in the same way that people with green eyes or blond hair are accepted, we will not have moved very far from the prejudices and discriminatory practices of the Middle Ages (Safilios-Rothschild, 1970:11).

Conclusions

People with physical disabilities appear to participate actively in the labelling process through the management of aspects of appearance over which they can exert some control. A negotiated outcome perspective encompasses such impression management. Like able-bodied persons, individuals with visible disabilities are likely to present the most positive aspects of the self. Positive feedback from others is received by persons with disabilities, particularly with regard to their clothing. Thus all labels applied to such persons are not stigmatizing.

The most commonly preferred form of dress by the students in this study appeared to be styles which were as normative as possible. Clothes reflect personal choice, unlike a physical disabil-ity; as such, they may be used to express iden-tificaiton with nondisabled persons and thus to facilitate reciprocal role-taking. A variety of normalizing techniques were displayed by the students in this study: "making do" with ready-to-wear apparel through ingenious adaptations, concealment of the disability, deflection of attention towards other aspects of the self which may be perceived as less discrediting, compen-sation by emphasizing other social roles and abilities, and social inclusion (i.e., emphasizing that all persons possess disabilities and physical differences). Linguistic forms of communication, in the form of T-shirt slogans, were used by the students to emphasize other aspects of the self when these aspects could not be displayed through more abstract symbols of dress.

Although they appeared to be in the distinct minority, some students capitalized on their social uniqueness and the resulting attention by drawing further attention to their clothes. Such a technique may provide observers with other aspects of the self to remember. At the same time, the self-attention of the person with a disability may be focused more upon his/her clothing than on the disability. This prospect for impression management is one aspect of the dilemma which appears to confront persons with visible disabilities. Although most persons with disabilities do not want to attract any further attention to themselves and thus dress in styles which blend in with the norm, the effects of such "normalization" may be to neutralize an aspect of appearance--clothing--that might otherwise be used to decrease the salience of the visible disability and to emphasize other aspects of the self.

The possibilities for the inclusion of dress and other appearance cues in future studies on the social interactions of persons with disabilities are extensive. Appearance manipulations provide a novel focus for such studies; the present data may provide a framework for deriving various forms of dress for such manipulations, in order to determine the impact on perceivers' responses. The categories of impression management defined in these data should be refined through research incorporating other populations of persons with disabilities and a contextual varia-tions.[5] In the meantime, an integration of the present categories with existing literature on physical deviance raises several issues which might be addressed in future research.

First, an expectancy/perceptual bias on the part of a person with a physical disability appears to influence the manner in which he/she inter-prets others' responses in interactions, specifical-ly by increasing attention to an observer's gaze behavior and tension (Kleck and Strenta, 1980). In conjunction with the present data, one might hypothesize that clothing could provide an alter-nate stimulus, in lieu of a physical deformity, that might influence both the observed person's

expectations and an observer's forming impres-sions. For example, an observer's gaze behavior might be attributed to the observed person to a dramatic or eye-catching outfit in addition to or instead of a physical disability. Variations in attire (e.g., normative versus socially unique or humorous) might produce diverse foci of atten-tion for both a wearer and a perceiver, as well as provide novel meanings for personal identity.

Second, the self-image of persons with dis-abilities could be explored in relation to preferred mode of dress. In a study by Landon et al. (1980), abnormal patterns of adjustment on the part of males with cystic fibrosis appeared to be attributable to shortness in height rather than to cystic fibrosis per se. It is conceivable that a stigmatized slef-image may be intensified through modes of dress such as those in the category of capitulation or diminshed through normative, deflective, or compensatory styles.

Third, the manner in which perceivers explain situational outcomes for persons with disabilities is likely to be altered by clothing style as well as physical disability. Miller (1982) found some support for this idea; further work with a broader range of apparel styles should be undertaken. Due to the importance of social norms in relation to clothing choices, the social norm of kindness toward persons with disabilities (c.f., Strenta and Kleck, 1982) could be incorporated into studies in which other appearance variables are manipul-ated. For example, normative or compensatory attire may result in a higher degree of kindness from others than more extreme styles (e.g., capitulative or humorous).

Fourth, an examination of social-cognitive processes associated with perceptions of clothing and stigma symbols should consider the improt-ance of social context in relation to emergent meanings, definitions and redefinitions of situat-ions, and attributions (Kaiser, 1983-84). The joint effects of clothing and stigma symbols may be modified as a result of social interactions and fashion changes. Due to the salience of a wheel-chair in person perceptions, as indicated by individuals in this research, this symbol should be considered as a factor in negotiated outcomes. Design researchers might focus upon the develop-ment of novel wheelchair styles which, along with apparel styles, emphasize the aesthetic tastes of users. Design prototypes could be used as stimuli along with various apparel styles in order to determine effects on person perceptions.

Finally, the applicability of the present taxonomy for other persons who are stereotyped in a variety of ways in terms of appearance should be explored. Such persons might include physically attractive females in male-dominated business contexts, gays, or obese persons, to name a few. Some of the impression-managing strategies indicated in the present research may apply to individuals who differ from the contextual norm and respond accordingly through the use of appearance symbols so as to negotiate the desired outcomes in social interactions, either by normalizing appearance or by emphasizing uniqueness.

References

Adams, Gerald R.
1977 "Physical attractiveness research: Toward a developmental social psychology of beauty." Human Development 20:217-239.

Adams, Gerald R.
1982 "Physical attractiveness." Pp. 253-304 in A.G. Miller (ed.), In the Eye of the Beholder: Contemporary Issues in Stereotyping. New York: Praeger.

Adams, Gerald R., and P. Crane.
1980 "An assumption of parents' and teachers' expectations of preschool children's social preference for attractive or unattractive children and adults." Child Development 51:224-231.

Altman, Barbara M.
1981 "Studies of attitudes toward the handicapped: The need for a new direction." Social Problems 28:321-337.

Berscheid, E., and E. Walster.
1974 "Physical attractiveness." Pp. 157-215 in L. Berkowitz (ed.), Advances in Experimental Social Psychology, Volume 7. New York: Academic Press.

Bregman, Sue, and Robert G. Hadley.
1976 "Sexual adjustment and feminine attractiveness among spinal cord injured women." Archives of Physical and Medical Rehabilitation 57: 448-450.

Comer, Ronald J., and Jane A. Piliavin.
1972 "The effects of physical deviance upon face-to-face interaction: The other side." Journal of Personality and Social Psychology 23: 33-39.

Cuber, J.F.
1963 Sociology: A Synopsis of Principles. New York: Appleton-Century-Crofts.

Davis, Fred.
1964 "Deviance disavowal: The management of strained interaction by the visibly handicapped." Pp. 119-137 in H. Becker (ed.), The Other Side: Perspectives on Deviance. New York: The Free Press.

Dion, K.K., and E. Berscheid.
1974 "Physical attractiveness and peer perception among children." Sociometry 37:1-12.

Elliott, Gregory C., Herbert L. Ziegler, Barbara M. Altman, and Deborah R. Scott.
1982 "Understanding stigma: Dimensions of deviance and coping." Deviant Behavior 3:275-300.

Feather, Betty L., Betty B. Martin, and Wilbur R. Miller.
1979 "Attitudes toward clothing and self-concept of physically handicapped and able-bodied university men and women. Home Economics Research Journal 7:234-240.

Goffman, Erving.
1961 Asylums. Chicago: Aldine.

Goffman, Erving.
1963 Stigma. Englewood Cliffs, N.J.: Prentice-Hall.

Haber, Lawrence D., and Richard T. Smith.
1971 "Disability and deviance: Normative adaptations of role behavior." American Sociological Review 36:87-97.

Hallenbeck, Phyllis N.
1966 "Special clothing for the handicapped: Review of research and resources." Rehabilitation Literature 27:34-40.

Hanks, Michael, and Dennis E. Poplin.
1981 "The sociology of physical disability: A review of literature and some conceptual perspectives." Deviant Behavior 2:309-328.

Hansen, Robert A.
1980 "A self-perception interpretation of the effect of monetary and nonmonetary incentives on mail survey respondent behavior." Journal of Marketing Research 17:77-83.

Higgins, Paul C.
1980 "Societal reaction and the physically disabled: Bringing the impairment back in." Symbolic Interaction 3:139156.

Kaiser, Susan B.
1983 "Toward a contextual social psychology of
-84 clothing: A synthesis of symbolic interactionist and cognitive theoretical perspectives." Clothing and Textiles Research Journal 2:1-9.

Katz, Irwin.
1981 Stigma: A Social Psychological Analysis. Hillsdale, N.J.: Lawrence Erlbaum.

Kernaleguen, Anne.
1978 Clothing Designs for the Handicapped. Alberta: University of Alberta Press.

Kitsuse, John I.
1975 "The 'new conception of deviance' and its critics." In W. R. Gove (ed.), the Labelling of Deviance. New York: Wiley.

Kleck, Robert.
1968 "Physical stigma and nonverbal cues emitted in face-to-face interaction." Human Relations 21:19-28.

Kleck, Robert E., and William DeJong.
1981 "Adults' estimates of sociometric status of handicapped and nonhandicapped children." Psychological Reports 49:951-954.

Kleck, Robert, H. Ono, and A.H. Hastorf.
1966 "The effects of physical deviance upon face-to-face interaction." Human Relations 19:425-436.

Kleck, Robert E., and Angelo Strenta.
1980 "Perceptions of the impact of negatively valued physical characteristics on social interaction." Journal of Personality and Social Psychology 39:861-873.

Landon, Christopher, Ronald LRosenfeld, Gregory Northcraft, and Norman Lewiston.
1980 "Self-image of adolescents with cystic fibrosis." Journal of Youth and Adolescence 9:521-528.

Lerner, M.J.
1970 "The desire for justice and reactions to victims." In J. Macauley and L. Berkowitz (eds.), Altruism and Helping Behavior. New York: Academic Press.

Lerner, M.J.
1980 The Belief in a Just World. New York: Plenum Press.

Levitin, T.E.
1975 "Deviants as active participants in the labeling process: The visibly handicapped." Social Problems 22:548-557.

Miller, Franklin G.
1982 "Clothing and physical impairment: Joint effects on person perception." Home Economics Research Journal 10:265-270.

Popp, Rita A., Victoria R. Fu, and Susan E. Warrell.
1981 "Preschool children's recognition and acceptance of three physical disabilities." Child Study Journal 11:99-114.

Safilios-Rothschild, Constantina.
1970 The Sociology and Social Psychology of Disability and Rehabilitation. New York: Random House.

Shannon, E., and Naomi Reich.
1979 "Clothing and related needs of physically handicapped persons." Rehabilitation Literature 40:2-6.

Shontz, Franklin C.
1977 "Physical disability and personality: Theory and recent research." Pp. 333-353 in J. Stubbins (ed.), Social and Psychological Aspects of Disability. Baltimore: University Park Press.

Stone, Gregory.
1962 "Appearance and the self." In A.M. Rose (ed.), Human Behavior and Social Processes. Boston: Houghton Mifflin.

Strenta, Angelo, and Robert E. Kleck.
1982 "Perceptions of task feedback: Investigating 'kind' treatment of the handicapped." Personality and Social Psychology Bulletin 8:706711.

Wright, B.A.
1960 Physical Disability: A Psychological Approach. New York: Harper and Row.

Yu, Julie, and Harris Cooper.
1983 "A quantitative review of research design effects on response rates to questionnaires." Journal of Marketing Research 20:36-44.

Notes

1.   Although the response rate compares favorably with other mail surveys in which the potential subjects receive only one mailing (c.f., Hansen, 1980; Yu and Cooper, 19083), the possibility of a response bias in the questionnaire data should be considered.

2.   The subjects in both phases of the study represented disabilities such as paraplegia, quadriplegia, cerebral palsy, multiple sclerosis, and others. More than half of the respondents used wheelchairs.

3.   Copies of the interview schedules and questionnaires are available upon request from the first author. Additional data derived from the questionnaires are available as well.

4.   The current and innovative style of jogging or tennis shoes with adhesive closures is a good example of the category of social inclusion. This style incorporates both self-help qualities and normative value.

5.   For example, a study of disabled persons within a business context might reveal additional appearance-related responses such as protection or defense. The present sample of college students would be more likely than businesspersons to experience a higher sense of freedom in choices of attire.

Alienation as a Consequence of Disability: Contradictory Evidence and its Interpretations

JAMES C. ROMEIS

Introduction

This study developed from theoretical arguments stating that the social structure of physical disability results in alienation from society. If these arguments are carefully examined, they will be found to be cogent and succinct but empirically inconclusive. Scientific evidence involves making crucial comparisons. If this principle is applied to the thesis that disability results in alienation we see there is no empirical demonstration that the extent of alienation is different between comparable groups of impaired and unimpaired individuals. There may be situations where the social structure of disability is highly alienating. There are probably very vocal individuals who are bitter, angry and quite estranged from society, their families and themselves; and the bases for this estrangement may be directly related to their disability. But, if we look at the generalized long-term experience of disabled individuals, we may find that on the average they are no more alienated from society than their non-disabled counterparts.

If the argument is examined further, there are implications to how social policy and rehabilitation services affect the disabled. Important substantive issues also emerge. For example, the argument implies that alienation resulting from disability is generally undifferentiated from alienation resulting from other situations of social disadvantage. There is not sufficient distinction between socio-psychological and sociological perspectives.

This study does not claim to resolve these issues, rather the results sensitize use to the complexity of them by taking a restricted cooperational approach. We review the disability process and its relationship to alienation described in the sociological literature. The methodology involves comparing physically impaired and unimpaired individuals' responses on a widely used indicator of alienation. Further comparisons are made for the predictors of alienation between each group. The discussion of the results indicates the argument is more complex than described in the literature and requires further critical evaluation.

The disability process

A sociological examination of disability requires that the phenomena be viewed simultaneously from the perspectives both of the individual and of the larger social structure. Within the past decade, disability and rehabilitation have emerged as important substantive areas in sociology with considerable policy potential (Sussman, 1965, 1972). From one policy perspective it is important to know the effect of illness and disability on the labour supply. According to the United States Social Security Administration (Allan, 1976), of the 106.3 million non-institutionalized adults aged 20-64, 15.6 million are limited in their ability to work because of chronic health conditions or impairments, illness and disability rank first as a reason for leaving jobs and applies to 44.9 per cent of prime working-age males at a time when their overall labour-force participation is declining (Deutermann, 1977). Moreover, workmen's compensation insurance in the United States costs employers $4.9 billion annually to cover over 80 per cent of the labour force with benefits extended for approximately 90,000 permanent disability claims, 2 million temporary total claims and over 14,000 occupationally-related deaths per year (National Commission on State Workmen's Compensation Laws, 1973a).

Sociologically, disability may be conceptualized as a social process (Nagi, 1965; 1969; Haber, 1967; Haber and Smith, 1971) with individuals considered impaired relative to some social roles but disabled relative to others. Following Nagi's definition, an impairment refers to the functional loss or physical limitation.

Reprinted From: *Sociology of Health and Illness* Vol. 5 No. 1, 1983, with permission.

Disability refers to role-relevant performance outcomes which are dependent on the interaction between the impairment, social and economic forces. Conceptually an impairment does not necessarily result in being disabled but disability requires being impaired. For example, identically severe work-related impairments for two workers may result in one worker returning to the labour force (impaired) while another withdraws (disabled) and the reasons for these two different outcomes are not clearly understood.

Alienation and the social structure of disability

One problem lacking empirical clarity is the position that disabled individuals experience increased feelings of alienation from society. Safilios-Rothschild (1970:250-78) states that the social structure of the disability process has many alienating dimensions. She argues that: (1) the social system for disabled individuals is complex; (2) high-prestige professionals and others interested in the disabled individual are not organizationally well integrated; (3) there is often conflict over what is 'best' for handicapped individuals; and (4) the ways decisions are made may irreversibly affect the goals of disabled individuals. She argues that the disabled person is 'crushed by too many heterogeneous and warring influences which usually end up dominating the mode and outcome of his disabled life because at a very early point they were successful in taking away his sense of autonomy and self-determination.' (1970:278)

Alienation and social malintegration are related to health status and may be exacerbated by physical incapacity. Bogue (1963) and Bahr's (1970) 'disaffiliated man' research found that physical disability and serious illness are contributory to skidrow populations. Referring to the extent of impairments, Bogue (1963:172-223) found 9 per cent of Chicago's skidrow were severely handicapped, 27 per cent were moderately disabled, and another 25 per cent were classified as slightly handicapped. Only 28 per cent of the skidrow population was estimated to be without handicap. With respect to labour

force re-entry, drinking was a smaller deterrent than illness or physical impairments and age.

Safilios-Rothschild (1970:251-85) argues that attention must be focused on the network of interested others and social situations. Interested others include family members, friends, a vast range of medical and rehabilitation specialists, lawyers, past and future employers, union officials, administrators of public programmes, counsellors and other impaired individuals. The importance of these actors must be seen in the context of how they symbolically and practically encourage the impaired individual to adjust to the impairment in one way or another:

> Some of these decision agents push the disabled toward reintegration within the larger society while others impede him from doing so by encouraging him to stay away from the mainstream of social life, identify primarily with other disabled, avoid living a 'normal' life which includes a productive regular working role. Under the influence of conflicting and powerful points of view, the disabled may at times or even perpetually feel 'alienated' in every way possible.

Through the utilization of Seeman's (1959) typology, interested others encourage the impaired individual to feel: a sense of powerlessness because 'he may realize that he has little control over what is happening to his life'; normlessness, because, 'although there are no clear cut societal norms regulating the behavior of disabled persons, he is expected by different persons to behave in different ways'; meaningless, because 'different interested others may have set goals for him and/or made decisions for him which he considers irrelevant'; self-estrangement, because 'he may be forced according to the occasion and the desired effect to play up the role of the "invalid" who is seriously incapacitated for life or hide his disability and try to pass for "normal". In the end it is difficult to know which of these selves is genuine and the disabled may be feeling inwardly uneasy with his many impersonisations.' (Safilios-Rothschild, 1970:252).

The argument which predicts a high degree of alienation among the severely disabled is not an isolated thesis. Others (Goffman, 1965; Davis, 1961; Freidson, 1965; Gordon, 1966; Krause, 1965; Mechanic, 1976; Sussman, 1972) variously argue that the social structures and processes which are designed to aid the disabled person produce instead an estranged and dehumanized experience. These arguments, however, have not been empirically demonstrated. None of these studies has used recognized measures of alienation and the use of control or comparison groups are needlessly absent. Instead, the argument rests on conclusions and generalizations with inappropriate indicators. In addition, if a study examining the social structure and complex effects of the network of interested others were designed, it would be a quite costly and time-consuming study. The present study is part of a larger study of workers' compensation benefits in the USA (Johnson and Makarushka, 1976) and therefore provides an opportunity to add empirical clarity to the argument that disability results in increased feelings of alienation from society.

Method

Two independent surveys were used to examine this empirical proposition. A sample of unimpaired individuals was constructed by aggregating the 1973 and 1974 General Social Surveys (GSS). These cross-sectional surveys were designed to be representative of the non-institutionalized adult, 18 years of age and older, US population (Davis, 1973, 1974, 1976). The sixty-minute interviews were conducted by National Opinion Research Center (NORC); and resulted in sample sizes of 1,504 and 1,484 for the two respective years. No differences were found on relevant variables between the GSS surveys.

The sample of impaired individuals is taken from the survey of Workers' Compensation Recipients (Johnson and Makarushka, 1976). The sixty-minute interview conducted by NORC

gathered data about three specific periods, relative to claim processing by state WC programmes. The three periods related to the claimant's and his or her household's socio-economic status one year prior to the claim, one year after the claim and the interview period (the latter quarter of 1975 and the first quarter of 1976). Examination of these three periods enabled a reconstruction of the timing and extent of WC and other public programme benefits, as well as how the household adjusted to the impairment, and provides an estimate of how these and other factors may have contributed to work disability among claimants aged 16-64.

The WC data (N=1,495) refer to the jurisdictions of New York, Florida, Wisconsin, and Washington and the impairment year refers to claims initiated in 1970-71. The selected jurisdictions appear representative of state demographic and labour-force criteria. The selection of these jurisdictions was also influenced by the different state benefit structures and operation of computerized record-keeping. The WC programmes in these jurisdictions may rate higher, relative to standards recommended by the Department of Labour (National Commission on State Workmen's Compensation Laws, 1973a:313) than other state's programmes and thus may not be representative of general claimant experience. The impairment year was selected to capture changes associated with the claim within a time-frame during which adjustment was expected to have stabilized (Adams and Jaffe, 1973).[1]

The final sample inclusion criteria was a severity index for all permanent partial claims. Because permanent partial claims may very from a tip of a finger amputation to the total loss of function of an extremity the following severity criteria were established: Jurisdiction records contained information about the location and nature of each claim, e.g. amputation, fracture, sprain, strain to a member of part of the body. A severity threshold involves the problematic assumption that physicians assess functional loss according to reasonably uniform criteria. Using the AMA (1971) guidelines for estimating loss and referencing the sequential conversion tables allows us to estimate a percentage of function loss relative to the whole body and provides a severity index comparable across jurisdictions. The generalized sample inclusion formula for TBI (Total Bodily Impairment.)[2] is: TBI = (loss or loss of use to a member or organ) × (the AMA conversion factor) × 100.

The goal of the WC sampling criteria (TBI > 9% was to select permanent partial cases where the work-related impairment was not a minor event in either the individual's or the household experience, i.e. an industrial accident that will result in a permanent and partial physical loss and will require social adjustments. The inclusion criterion was designed to reflect the sociological and economic distinctions associated with impaired and disabled roles (Nagi, 1965, 1969; Haber, 1967; Haber and Smith, 1971), particularly those related to employment status and alienation. Given a one-to-two year restoration, rehabilitation and settlement period, it is not unreasonable to expect that an additional three years would reflect this goal.

The independent variables in both surveys included nine identically measured structural characteristics (age, sex, employment status, education, gross household income, race, marital status, household size, and number of wage-earners in the household). In addition both surveys included a subjective report of health status. (Would you say your own health, in general, is excellent, good, fair or poor?) This variable was included in an attempt to examine how subjective health status might relate to employment status and alienation.

In both surveys, the dependent variable was Srole's (1956) A9 version of his anomia scale; a nine-item agree-disagree summated rating scale that posits a social psychological continuum of social integration to malintegration, or 'alienation', or 'self-to-others distance'. Srole maintains the measure is a Durkheimian derivative, although Seeman (1972) claims the scale reflects a normlessness variant of alienation. Reliability and validity data have not been reported for the A9 version but the A5 version has been used extensively and found to be acceptable (Robinson and Shaver, 1973:256-9). As used here, the scale is interpreted to represent a general indicator of subjectively experienced alienation from society.

The statistical analysis includes both cross-tabular and regression techniques. Stepwise regression coefficients are used in two ways. Following Schoenberg (1972) and Duncan (1975), unstandardized coefficients are compared between samples. Confidence intervals were set to test for statistical differences between sample equation coefficients. The regression coefficients were also used to define a predictive equation from the GSS data. Applying the GSS coefficients to the WC sample, the predicted results enable us to assess what level of alienation might be expected if the WC recipients were not impaired. The extent to which WC predicted-scale scores differ from the WC observed-scale scores provides an estimate of disability-related alienation.[3]

Findings

On the basis of the National Commission on Workers Compensation (1973) reports, we expected the demographic characteristic differences between the two samples to be greater than we found. The more severely impaired recipients tend to be older men who have fewer years of education and have pre-impairment incomes which are typically low. Table 1 indicates that the WC and GSS samples are fairly comparable. On the average, the WC sample is five years older than the GSS respondents (48.07 v. 43.76), has about one year less formal schooling (10.79 v. 11.70), and for the post-impairment period has about the same amount of gross household income ($9,500 v. $10,000). The WC sample is composed mostly of males (85% v. 47%) and more of the WC sample than the GSS sample were employed (64% v. 51%).

The proportion of WC respondents who had returned to work five years after initiating their claims was also not anticipated. Seventy-two per cent of those who were employed had returned to their former employer and of these slightly over 50 per cent were in the same pre-impairment job. Among the unemployed claimants, 11.5 per cent never returned to work.

These data do not mean the WC respondents were not seriously impaired. Rather the data highlight the problematic relationship between the

Table 1.

Frequency distribution of sample characteristics (%).

	GSS (N=2988)	WC (N=1495)
Work status*		
Employed	51	63
Unemployed	49	37
Gross Household Income		
Less than 3,999	16	7
4,000-6,999	14	17
7,000-9,999	16	23
10,000-14,999	24	33
Over 15,000	29	19
Education		
0-6	6	10
7-12	62	75
13-20	31	15
Sex		
Female	53	15
Male	47	85
Race		
Non-white	13	11
White	87	89
Current age		
Less than 29	26	11
30-49	36	38
50-59	16	24
Over 60	22	25
Marital Status		
Married	72	77
Widowed, divoced, separated	16	15
Never married	13	7
Household size		
1	11	11
2	30	35
3-4	36	34
Over 4	23	20

N's vary because of non-response, refusals, etc. Percentage may not total to one hundred because of rounding.
* Employed refers to working at the time of the interview at a full-time or part-time job. Un employed refers to those not working at the time of the interview.

regarding work disability it is difficult to evaluate what employment percentages mean.

The regression analysis (See Table 2) indicates how alienation, health and employment status are related between the two samples. The two columns represent the unstandardized coefficients for Srole's A9 scale defined by the stepwise procedure. As expected, the best pre-

Table 2.

Regression-defined determinants of Srole's A9 scale for both GSS (N=2,718) and WC (N=13,98) respondents.

	GSS	WC
Variable	$\frac{b}{(\ )}$	$\frac{b}{(\ )}$
Education	-.250*	-.191*
	(.016)	(.023)
Race	-1.237*	-.913*
	(.132)	(.220)
Household Income	-.094*	-.048
	(.017)	(.031)
Health	-.343*	-.213*
	(.051)	(.076)
Age	-.016*	.004
	(.002)	(.005)
No. of Earners	-.078	.192*
in Household	(.047)	(.093)
Employment Status	.170	-.329*
	(.096)	(.168)
Sex	-.140	.057
	(.089)	(.188)
Marital Status	-.049	-.063
	(.101)	(.178)
Household size	-.011	.004
	(.028)	(.044)
Constant	10.82	8.00
MR$_2$	.475	.338
R	.226	.114
Std error	2.15	2.39

b = unstandardized coefficients; ( ) = standard error of b.
* Variables which are statistically significant at the 0.05 level.

nature and type of impairments, work disability, how households adjust and how public programmes function. Moreover, the sample was drawn from legitimate cases in jurisdictions. Jurisdictions did not allow sampling from denied claims, which may or may not be severe and may be largely unemployed. This restriction represents a selection bias and its importance cannot be assessed. Until more controlled research is done dictors of the Srole measure among the GSS respondents are SES characteristics followed by subjective health status and age. Employment status was not found to be a statistically significant determinant of the Srole scale for the GSS respondents.

However, this table obscures the importance of employment status for the alienation and health relationship among the GSS respondents. When employment status was controlled and two subsamples are compared, the health-status coefficient was more than twice the coefficient for those GSS respondents without full-time jobs (b = -0.439) compared to those GSS respondents with full-time jobs (b = -0.208). The importance of these differences are clearer when the average Srole scale scores and health-status measures are compared. GSS respondents with full-time jobs had an average alienation scale score of 3.88 and rated their health slightly above 'good' or 3.23. GSS respondents without full-time employment statuses were more alienated, 4.29, and devalued their health slightly below 'good' or 2.86. The GSS data appear to parallel Cole and LeJeune's (1972) argument where perceived health status and employment vary in a way which may provide legitimation for a failure to perform a work role, which in turn varies directly with alienation from society.

Among the WC respondents, Table 2 indicates that education and race are the best predictors of alienation, followed by health status. Compared to the GSS respondents, gross household income was not statistically significant while the number of household earners and employment status was significant. The significance of the employment-status variable supports the role-relevant criteria differentiating impairment from disability. The lack of importance attributed to the income variable may mean that any income loss by the claimant is absorbed by other household members and is reflected by the number of earners per household variables.

When the employment status for the WC respondents was additionally controlled the health status coefficients varied differently than those described for the GSS respondents above. The coefficients for the employed WC respondents was b = -0.217 compared to b = -0.226 for those

who were not employed. Average WC alienation scale and health-status measures are patterned similar to the GSS findings. Workers' compensation recipients who returned to full-time jobs had average alienation scale scores of 4.30 and rated their health at slightly below 'good', or 2.86. The WC respondents who were not working or retired were on the average more alienated, 5.02, and rated their health slightly above 'fair', or 2.18.

Table 2 is additionally important because of the comparability between the two sets of coefficients. Confidence intervals were established for the coefficients and tested for statistical differences. Except for age none of the coefficients was significantly different between the two samples. The coefficients of determination (R^2) were tested for statistical differences and were found to be significant. These latter two findings suggest the coefficients for the two equations are not statistically different, a large portion of the total variance remains unexplained and additional research should attempt to isolate other explanatory variables.

These data suggest that the degree of general alienation from society may not differ significantly between unimpaired and physically impaired individuals, beyond what would be expected on the basis of key characteristics such as employment status, health status, earnings, education, age, marital status and others. Table 3 provides data for examining this further.

The first and second columns are the average GSS and WC alienation-scale scores that were calculated from the questionnaire. The rows enable employment status and sex subsample comparisons. The third column is the predicted WC average alienation scale score calculated from all the GSS equation independent variables. These three columns enable a comparison of how alienation varies between the two samples from perspectives of what was 'observed' (Columns 1 and 2) and, based on their background characteristics, what degree of alienation might be expected or predicted for the WC sample if their industrial injury had not occurred and thus they might not be impaired (Column 3).

When all variables are considered the first column indicates that the average alienation-scale

Table 3.

The relationships between the observed and predicted mean alienation-scale scores for the GSS and WC samples.

Condition	Observed X Srole GSS (unimpaired)	Observed X Srole WC (impaired)	Observed X Srole WC (impaired)
All variables	4.11	4.55	4.55
Employed	3.88	4.30	4.33
Unemployed	4.29	5.02	4.91
Employed males	3.76	4.31	4.26
Employed females	4.14	4.23	4.70
Unemployed males	4.14	5.05	4.85
Unemployed females	4.23	4.89	4.80

score among the GSS sample was 4.11. As expected, unemployed GSS respondents on the average were more alienated, 4.29, than employed GSS respondents, 3.88. Under the same considerations the second column indicates that the average alienation-scale score among the WC respondents was 4.55. Similar to their unimpaired counterparts, column 2 indicates the unemployed WC respondents were on the average more alienated, 5.02, than employed WC respondents, 4.30.

These two column comparisons would appear to reinforce the notion that disability increases alienation from society, or that physically impaired individuals are more alienated from society than a comparable sample of unimpaired individuals. If simple differences in means tests (t) are calculated, we find that the difference is barely statistically significant (p < 0.05). However, with samples this large, a mean difference of 0.44 is small and an inability simultaneously to control for key structural characteristics makes confidence in a true relationship difficult to maintain.

When the third column is compared to the second column, the notion that disability increases alienation from society is not reinforced. On the average the WC respondents appear no more alienated from society than what we would expect or predict their responses to be if they

were unimpaired. The WC observed average alienation-scale score was 4.55. Based on the GSS structural equation coefficients, what would be predicted for them if they were unimpaired is 4.55. Employed WC respondents had an average alienation-scale score of 4.30 but 4.33 would have been predicted if they had been unimpaired. Unemployed WC respondents had an average alienation-scale score of 5.02, but 4.91 would be predicted if they were unimpaired. These small differences continue when sex and employment status subsamples are compared. These data thus suggest a position counter to the argument that disability produces alienation from society. Rather the pattern and extent to which severely impaired workers' compensation respondents are alienated from society does not appear to differ appreciably from the pattern and extent of alienation that would be predicted if they were unimpaired.

Summary and Conclusions

The study is an empirical examination of the argument that socialstructures and processes are associated with physical disability result in alienation from society. Despite a lack of empirical documentation, the surface validity of the argument appears clear and straightforward. The study should have only had to prove the obvious. The findings do not appear to be straightforward or prove the obvious. Instead the findings were contradictory to what was expected and suggest a position counter to the argument that disability produces alienation. Moreover, the contradictory findings raise several theoretical and policy implications which require further study.

Because empirical studies comparing levels of alienation between impaired and unimpaired individuals were lacking, this study was designed to examine how alienation and its predictors differed between comparable samples of unimpaired individuals and severely impaired workers' compensation recipients in the Untied States. The sample of unimpaired individuals was taken from the 1973 and 1974 General Social Surveys. The workers' compensation-recipient sample was taken from the 1976 Survey of Workers' Compensation, a survey of the adjustment experiences five years after sustaining a severe industrial injury.

Alienation was defined in terms of its subjective properties and measured identically on both surveys using Srole's Anomia (A9) scale. The independent variables were identically measured background characteristics plus a self-reported assessment of health status. The findings indicate that among GSS respondents, SES and self-reported health status were the significant predictors of alienation. Employment status was not a significant predictor of alienation, but when employment status was statistically controlled, alienation increased and self-reported health status decreased for those GSS respondents without full-time jobs. The pattern reversed for those with full-time jobs and suggests a sick role-work role relationship which is linked to alienation in a subtle and complex manner. The significant predictors for the workers' compensation sample were found to be similar to the GSS predictors except employment status was inversely related to alienation and parallels the rehabilitation literature regarding the importance of reintegrating the disabled in society through the work role.

Finally, levels of alienation were compared between the two samples. A simple comparison indicated that the WC respondents had slightly higher average alienation-scale scores than the GSS respondents. When, however, more exacting predictive equation results were compared, the small differences disappeared indicating that on the average the degree of alienation from society may not appreciably differ between unimpaired and severely impaired individuals five years after the impairment was sustained.

These final findings are surprising because they suggest an outcome of the disability process contrary to what would be expected from reviewing the sociological literature. These are reasons to be careful in interpreting these findings. The data refer to one social context in which individuals become permanently and partially impaired. There were sample selection limitations. Interaction terms and injury location were not examined. The small coefficients of determination may distort the predictions, even though beta coefficients between the two samples were statistical-

ly similar. The data do not indicate how alienation as a long-term consequence may differ from a short-term consequence. Nevertheless, there are reasons to believe that the relationship in the literature which argues that disability produces alienation from society is perhaps overstated and requires additional empirical attention. Until these findings are studied further, only initial and speculative interpretations are offered.

For example, the study has applied and theoretical implications. If the sociological literature is re-examined a rehabilitation perspective should be considered which states client motivation, attitude or presentation of self is an important correlate of adjustment to disability (Yuker, 1965; Williams, 1969; Sussman, 1975). The extent to which motivation is low or clients present themselves as being alienated may be misperceived, particularly when pre-impairment levels of alienation are not known. Clients may be alienated, but attributing it to the consequences of disability may be inaccurate. Rehabilitation counsellors may misperceive the source of client alienation and discourage certain employment or other social reintegration activities. Sussman (1975:304) has suggested that counsellor efforts are affected by how they perceive and estimate the client's Gross National Product potential. Whether or not rehabilitation results would differ if alienation were not perceived as a consequence of disability is an empirical question. But when alienation is attributed to the disability process the perception may function to legitimate a decision to invest energies in the client or not.

Another interpretation with larger implications emerges when the findings are seen as contradictory evidence that a disadvantaged group in society which may be considered objectively alienated from society is not found to be subjectively alienated. The data suggest that the usage of alienation as a concept to explain social phenomena requires careful attention. Classical and contemporary usages of the concept indicate that it has considerable scholarly and scientific appeal and is a powerful analytic tool. Because of these qualities Seeman (1972) argues that the concept of alienation has the potential of being used to explain anything and, therefore, may explain nothing. These findings may reinforce Seeman's caution.

Sociology has demonstrated the consequences of labels and how devastating they can be to lives of individuals. We should be particularly cautious in using terms and concepts which can be transformed into clinical tools of exclusion and isolation. The concept of alienation has a rich and enduring humanistic tradition. Those who find its conceptual and empirical properties appealing must also be demanding critics. Otherwise, the understanding of its antecedents and consequences will continue to lack specificity, clarity and empirical proof leading to the promotion of premature obituaries (Lee, 1972).

These interpretations are not the only possible interpretations. There are certainly others including the ones that argue that these findings are anomalous and do not alter the thesis that disability produces alienation from society. In the light of new and surprising findings, the interpretations are logical extensions of the generalized literature. Because the findings are new and contradictory to mainstream understanding, replication of the results are required before a definitive interpretation can be advanced. At best the data are new findings and require careful follow-up. At the least the findings suggest that studying the obvious a worthwhile scientific activity.

Acknowledgements

This study acknowledges the support of the United States Department of Labor, Employment and Training Administration Dissertation Fellowship (Grant No. 91-36-76-13). The discussion does not reflect the position of any government unity but is the sole responsibility of the author.

References

Adams, Walter and A.J. Jaffe (1973), 'Too little too late', *Supplemental Studies for the National Task Force on Workmen's Compensation, 11*. Washington, D.C.: GPO.

Allan, Kathryn H. (1976), 'First findings of the 1972 Survey of Disabled: general characteristics', *Social Security Bulletin* (Oct.): 1-20.

American Medical Association (1971), *Guides to the Evaluation of Permanent Impairments*. Chicago: AMA.

Bahr, Howard M. (1970), *Disaffiliated Man*. Toronto: University of Toronto Press.

Bogue, Donald (1973), *Skid Row in American Cities*. Chicago: University of Chicago Press.

Cole, Stephan and Robert LeJeune (1972), 'Illness and the legitimation of failure', *American Sociological Review* 37:347-56.

Davis, Fred (1961), "Deviance and disavowal: the management of strained interaction by the visibly handicapped', *Social Problems*, 9:120-32.

Davis, James A. (1973), *Codebook: General Social Survey*. Chicago: NORC.

Davis, James A. (1974), *Codebook: General Social Survey*. Chicago: NORC.

Davis, James A. (1976), 'Background characteristics in the U.S. population 1952-1973: a survey metric model', *Social Sciences Research*, 5:349-83.

Deutermann, William V., Jr (1977), 'Another look at working age men who are not in the labor force', *Monthly Labor Review* (June): 9-14.

Duncan, Otis D. (1975), *Introduction to Structural Equation Models*. New York: Academic Press.

Freidson, Elliot (1965), 'Disability as social deviance', in M.B. Sussman (ed.) *Sociology and Rehabilitation*. Washington, D.C.: American Sociological Association.

Goffman, Erving (1965), *Stigma: Notes on the Management of Spoiled Identity*. Englewood Cliffs, New Jersey: Prentice Hall.

Gordon, Gerald (1966), *Role Theory and Illness: A Sociological Perspective*. New Haven, Connecticut: College and University Press.

Haber, Lawrence D. (1967), 'Identifying the disabled: concepts and methods in the measurement of disability', *Social Security Bulletin*, 30:17-34.

Haber, Lawrence D. and Richard T. Smith (1971), 'Disability and deviance: Normative adaptations of role behavior', *American Sociological Review*, 36:87-97.

Jonson, William G. and Julian Loughlin Makarushka (1976), *Closed Case Survey*. Health Studies Program, Syracuse University, Syracuse, New York.

Krause, Elliot A. (1965), 'Structured strain in a marginal profession: rehabilitation counselling', *Journal of Health and Social Behavior*, 6:59-61.

Lee, Alfred McClung (1972), 'An obituary for alienation', *Social Problems*, 20:121-7.

Mechanic, David (1976), *The Growth of Bureaucratic Medicine*. New York: Wiley Interscience.

Nagi, Saad Z. (1965), 'Some conceptual issues in disability and rehabilitation', in M.B. Sussman (ed.), *Sociology and Rehabilitation*. Washington, D.C.: American Sociological Association.

Nagi, Saad Z. (1969), *Disability and Rehabilitation*. Columbus, Ohio: Ohio State University Press.

National Commission on State Workmen's Compensation Laws (1973a), *Compendium on Workmen's Compensation*. Washington: GPO.

Robinson, John P. and Phillip R. Shaver (1973), *Measures of Social Psychological Attitudes* (revised edition). Ann Arbor, Michigan, SRC, Institute for Social Research.

Safilios-Rothschild, Constantina (1970), *The Sociology and Social Psychology of Disability and Rehabilitation*. New York: Random House.

Schoenberg, Ronald (1972), 'Strategies for meaningful comparisons', pp. 1-35 in H. Costner (eds), *Sociological Methodology*. San Francisco: Jossey Bass.

Seeman, Melvin (1972), 'Alienation and engagement', pp. 467-527 in A. Campbell and P. Converse (eds.), *The Human Meaning of Social Change*. New York: Russell Sage.

Smith, Richard T. (1977), 'Disability and the recovery process: role of social networks', Paper presented to the American Sociological Association, Chicago, Illinois.

Srole, Leo (1956), 'Social integration and certain corollaries: an exploratory study', *American Sociological Review*, 21:709-16.

Srole, Leo (1976), 'Measurement and classification sociopsychiatric epidemiology: Midtown Manhattan Study (1954) and Midtown Manhattan restudy (1974)', *Journal of Health and Social Behavior*, 16:347-64.

Sussman, Marvin B. (1972), 'A policy perspective on the United States rehabilitation system', *Journal of Health and Social Behavior*, 13:152-61.

Sussman, Marvin B. (1972), 'Readjustment and rehabilitation of patients', pp. 301-44 in John Kosa and I.K. Zola (eds.), *Pverty and Health* (2nd edn). Cambridge, Mass.: Harvard University Press.

US Department of Health, Education and Welfare (1973), *Work in America*. Cambridge, Mass. MIT Press.

Williams, Ivan (1969), 'Selection factors in the vocational rehabilitation process'. *Social Problems*, 17:110-19.

Yuker, H. (1975), 'Attitudes as determinants of behavior', *Journal of Rehabilitation*, 31:15-16.

Notes

1. The five-year period between impairment year and survey year involves two obvious problems. First, the respondents' reliability to recall should be questioned. Through pretesting we found that the respondents kept detailed records of their claims and would consult them. Work is presently in progress to examine the extent that the respondents recall and state records differ or not. The second problem involves locating claimants since Adams and Jaffe report only a 30 per cent completion rate. Because our time frame and resources were considerably greater, our average completion rate was 67 per cent for the four states.

2. TBI formula calculations are identical across jurisdictions, but the jurisdiction injury location codes are not. Work is underway to develop a comparable across-jurisdiction location code so relationships may be examined for identical locations and severity. Until this work is complete the severity index may not be used as a variable. For a complete explanation of the severity index see Johnson and Makarushka (1976).

3. This method assumes that the two samples are fairly comparable and the independent variables are similarly related to the dependent variable. This method was adopted over conventional dummy variable tests because it allows us to see how the dependent variable compares between samples under predicted or expected contexts. Examination of the intercorrelation matrices indicated that multicolinearity was not a problem and the simple correlating for both the samples were similarly patterned.

Personality Crippling Through Physical Disability

Thomas D. Cutsforth

From a theoretical point of view, it is possible to integrate a physical disability within a healthy, well-rounded personality. However, clinically, a personality so constructed is rarely if ever encountered. It seems to be an inevitable personality growth process to shape the self regarding attitude about the existing disability, with very little realistic evaluation of the actual incapacitation which it entails. For example, a case of acne in an immature individual can produce as much functional disability as complete physical incapacitation does in one who is more mature.

There are many factors within the individual and within the society in which he lives that render him incapable of dealing with his disability in terms of its degree of physical incapacitation alone, and among these are factors which really incapacitate to a much greater extent than the physical defect itself.

From the attitudes of those about him, the disabled person is given a status and a definition which he both accepts and rejects. Within himself, he has a ready made tool for the manipulation of his social world. The manner in which he employs this tool depends both upon his degree of emotional maturity and upon the specific attitudes of the group in which he lives.

It is the purpose of this paper to describe and discuss the personality factors that the condition of blindness induces when an individual so affected attempts to live in a social world unaccustomed to blindness. Any discussion of the personality difficulties and social maladjustments of the blind, within the brief limits of this paper, will appear too generalized, and will suffer much from over-simplification. Many extraneous factors add complexities which too often are not carefully enough differentiated from blindness itself. Thus, even a slight mental defect can become a causal factor in personality difficulties which will not be recognized as distinct from the more obvious physical defect. The effect that congenital syphilis has upon the mentality of the individual, for example, is a much greater factor than blindness.

It is true that blindness makes life more difficult, but blindness alone cannot explain the amount of disability, physical, social and economic, that is found among the blind. The disability and incapacitation so commonly found have their origin not in the physical condition, but in the impact of the individual upon society and its attitudes.

The blind child or adult does not live long in his social world without accepting, in greater or less degree, the attitudes of others towards him. In the case of the child, these attitudes are mostly acquired after sight has been lost. In the case of the adult, the attitudes already have been acquired in large part prior to the loss of sight. They are his own social attitudes inflicted upon himself-- the attitudes he has previously expressed towards others in a similar condition. Hence, in both cases, the effects are deep rooted and extremely persistent.

Regardless whether these attitudes are the result of accretion from society, or whether they are self-inflicted, they have the same result. The individual soon feels himself separate and apart from the group. This feeling of insecurity lays the groundwork for a complex pattern of self regarding attitudes of social inadequacy, a pattern which is increased in width and depth by the individual's attempt to establish security and identity with the group.

There are two reaction patterns of establishing ego-importance in the group and regaining a feeling of security and self-assurance. The first is the pattern of compensation. In following this pattern, the individual attempts to prove to himself and to the group that the inadequacy does not exist. He develops along the line of the compulsive personality. The second pattern is that of retreat, wherein the individual accepts his feelings of inadequacy as a true evaluation of his ego-importance and establishes a false security by failing to meet life aggressively. He develops hysterical responses which only add conviction to his feelings of inadequacy.

Reprinted From: *Journal of Social Issues* Vol. IV, #4, Fall 1948, with permission.

It is impossible to classify blind individuals categorically in either one of these personality groups. While one pattern will dominate in a given personality structure, both tendencies will be in operation. It is this dual pattern which makes the blind individual apparently so erratic, inconsistent and difficult. His social world tends to approve, develop and exploit his compulsive compensations, and at the same time to deplore and be baffled by his hysterical responses. It is obvious that any therapeutic program for the adjustment of the blind personality that concerns itself only with the correction of either or both of these personality malformations is doomed to failure.

Therapeutic or educational emphasis upon compulsive symptoms leads in the dangerous direction of creating lopsided personalities, monstrosities or geniuses, as the case may be. It is the work in this direction that produces the accomplished blind vocalist who is incapable of shining his own shoes or emptying the kitchen garbage can. It is work in this direction that produces the brilliant student whose personality would render him incapable of even giving away papers at a news stand.

Aside from failing of its social purpose, the over-development of compensatory aptitudes achieves little for the stability and emotional security of the blind individual himself. In spite of the approval that educators and social agencies for the blind place upon these compulsive manifestations, and in spite of their tendency to foster and exploit them whenever possible, compensations are as much evidence of personality pathology as are the less approved and more baffling hysterical reactions.

The second pattern, the hysterical tendency to be dependent, to seek protection, to withdraw into blindness, is only another attempt to achieve ego-importance, this time by the regressive route. Such hysterical phenomena are well recognized and much discussed by those who have lived and worked with the blind, and, in the minds of many, they constitute, in themselves, the material of a psychology of the blind.

In spite of their familiarity, these two patterns of behavior in the blind are not too well understood. Essentially, they constitute the disabled person's apparent choice of proceeding "in spite of this disability", or "because of this disability." Outwardly, the individual may appear as though a high degree of integration has taken place, but the clinical picture reveals a personality with full acceptance of an inadequacy pattern. Inwardly, both types of reaction are fundamentally neurotic.

Neurotic Manifestations

There is nothing mystical, unnatural or indecent about a neurosis. Such a condition is the result of the very best efforts of an individual to gain recognition and approval on his level of emotional maturity, with his degree of insight into the social relationships involved. Four important factors are always found in any neurotic condition. *First,* the individual fails to establish himself in his social relationships at his own self-evaluation. *Second,* he meets the situation with inadequate emotional response; that is, he fails to feel the natural, normal irritations, resentments and furies produced by failure of accomplishment. *Third,* he makes an unconscious attempt to resolve the tensions from anger by withdrawing from the objective world and concentrating attention, interest and concern upon the subjective realm. *Fourth,* he employs a substitute problem which gives a false feeling of assurance and importance.

It is not necessary to discuss even briefly the first step of this process, for nearly all the literature on the blind is concerned with it, and all the social attitudes make this situation inevitable. However, it is necessary to point out the fact that the self regarding attitudes of the blind are just as important in creating the conflict as are the attitudes found in others regarding them.

Perhaps the least understood and appreciated aspect of the neurosis involved in blindness centers about the reaction pattern produced by inadequate emotional response. It is a characteristic bio-social mechanism, common to animal and man alike, that docility and compliance are resorted to in attempts to establish ego-importance, and gain approval and security. The domestication and training of animals make use of this neurotic mechanism. It is accomplished by submerging aggressive resentment towards others, and substituting anxiety as to their attitudes toward us.

The blind live in the same social world as does my spaniel. If you must be a dog, at least you can be a nice dog. He is. His ego demands my affection and approval. And he sacrifices his aggressiveness, his normal temper and pugnacity to attain it. With strangers, he is not neurotic. He is a healthy, aggressive, self-assured dog.

The inadequate emotional response of the blind is undoubtedly the greatest factor in their debilitation. The emotional acceptance of any feeling of inadequacy, either real or imaginary, is a preparatory step toward rendering the individual dependent upon those from whom he seeks approval and acceptance. The individual who meets his social world with the ego demand that he be given recognition in spite of this or because of that, becomes a passive recipient rather than an aggressive giver in his social relationships. As has been stated above, this comes about by the conversion of aggressive emotional responses toward the objective world into subjective anxieties regarding security.

This subtle mechanism acts as a two-edged sword in the life of the neurotic. He dare not assume the responsibility of aggressive action, and galls under passive acceptance. The blind, like other frustrated personalities, trade the birthright of self-assurance that goes with aggressive action, the courage that goes with anger, and the audacity that goes with rage for ineffectual action, compliant passivity, and the self-contempt of a dependent.

The egocentric swing of attention and interest that always results from inadequate emotional response takes a variety of forms. Perhaps the most serious and crippling effect of the withdrawal from objectivity and the concentration upon subjectivity is the rigidity that is produced in the personality. This mechanism presents the same problem to the teacher and worker for the blind as it does to the clinical psychologist. This rigidity renders the individual incapable of meeting situations except in terms of his own self-evaluation. In compensatory manifestations of the self regarding attitude, the individual cannot meet a new situation because of his superiority; "I am too proud, too smart, too decent." In the

hysterical manifestation of the same mechanism, the rigidity takes the form of reticence; "I am too sensitive, too inexperienced, too weak, too timid." In the educational and vocational activities of the blind, this rigidity is a more serious disability than among the seeing for, because of the physical limitations, the individual has less choice of alternative action. Many times the condition of blindness itself is blamed for the incapacitation resulting from this very common neurotic trait.

When, in the course of personality conflict, unresolved tensions heighten the physical, emotional and mental awareness of the self, it is not to be expected that these responses to the self will go on without objective expression. Manifestations of this mechanism are common among the blind in the form of day dreaming, fidgeting habits, and various automatisms. It has been the general feeling that somehow these apparently meaningless activities are inherent in the state of blindness. Seldom have they been regarded as an inevitable and inescapable phase of neurosis.

The so-called "blindisms" which comprise a large variety of socially objectionable habits, are only the responses of the individual reacting to his own physical awareness, in an attempt to resolve the tension and gain the satisfaction denied by his own non-aggressiveness. Blindness is no more the cause of this automatism than vision is the cause of nail biting, thumb sucking and autoerotic manifestations in the equally neurotic seeing child. Likewise, day dreams and fantasies are an expression of the heightened emotionality resulting from conflict. They mesh with reality quite as well as the day dreams and fantasies which the clinical psychologist encounters in frustrated seeing persons.

It has long been an accepted concept in psychiatry that the strain of a personality in conflict with itself will either bring about an objective adjustment, or, sooner or later, find some means of resolving the conflict; the new form being known as a conversion mechanism. Conversion mechanism may take many forms, and conversion symptoms can be either real or imaginary; but when real, the symptoms are exaggerated far beyond their intrinsic importance. Some of them are periodic, appearing when strain and conflict become critical, disappearing when the crisis has passed. Apparently, there is a tendency to employ any specific, chronic state or condition as a conversion symptom when one is needed. Since this pattern is a common human reaction, we cannot demand that the blind be a solitary exception. Like the infantile paralytics, they have an avenue of escape already prepared. To those who are acquainted with both the blind and the neurotic personality, it is unnecessary to elaborate the possibilities that blindness offers, and to those who are not so acquainted, it would be futile.

If an accurate clinical survey could be made of the escapes and conversions employed by the blind, undoubtedly the following results would be found. Among those individuals who are employing their physical condition as a successful escape and retreat from reality and objectivity, there would be a marked absence of other forms of symptoms. On the other hand, among those individuals who were most successful, and who were assuming the responsibility for their own adjustment and social relationships, we would expect to find a high frequency of the same sort of psychosomatic disturbances that are found in the neurotic population of the seeing. This clinical concept might be used as an index to the emotional health of blind persons. Those who show psychosomatic disturbances such as nervous indigestion, migraine headache, cardiac symptoms, and the like, might be regarded as emotionally more mature, educable and adaptable than the less nervous who have ceased any attempt to meet the world except on the basis of their major conversion.

Summary

In summary, the following points should be emphasized:

1. Among the blind, and presumably among other physically disabled individuals, the incapacitation of personality is disproportionate to the degree of physical incapacitation.

2. All existing feelings of inadequacy in the personality are drained into the physical disability which, in turn, is made the emotional causal factor for their existence.

3. The acceptance of all the inadequacies of the personality in terms of the disability causes the individual to adopt an overwhelmed attitude towards his world, his responsibilities and his activities. This hysterical reaction serves only to deepen the conviction of deficiency and disability.

4. The attempt to compensate for the feelings of inadequacy drives the individual oftimes to the achievement of successes, but never to personality adjustment.

Much further data on the relationship of physical and emotional disability in the blind is needed. A few such problems are suggested below.

1. Since we have fairly accurate clinical figures on the frequency of psychosomatic disturbances in the seeing, it would be valuable to have similar data for the blind. It would be useful to know how frequent among the blind is the occurrence of gastric ulcers, migraine headaches, asthma, neurodermititis, cardiac symptoms, alcoholism, sex delinquency, and the like.

2. Blindness frequently occurs in the upper age levels as a result of hypertension. It should be ascertained if, and how frequently, blindness is a contributing factor in the creation of a hypertensive condition.

3. It might help define the personality development of the blind if a study were made of the personality structure and social adjustment of the children of blind parents.

Disability Beyond Stigma: Social Interaction, Discrimination, and Activism

MICHELLE FINE
ADRIENNE ASCH

•Between 1981 and 1984, the Eastern Paralysed Veterans Association, Disabled in Action of New York City, and other organizations of people with disabilities fought a court battle with the New York City Metropolitan Transit Authority to gain architectural access to the city's mass transit system. The MTA opposed modifying the system, claiming that the expense would never be made up by rider fares of those mobility-impaired people then denied transit access. The *New York Times* ("Editorial," 1983; "The $2,000 Subway Token," 1984), along with most other sectors of the community, generally favoring progressive social change, supported the Transit Authority in the fight it eventually lost (Katzmann, 1986).

•In 1982 and 1983, the national media described two cases where the parents and doctors of infants with disabilities denied the infants medical treatment based on their impairments. In the first case, an infant with Down syndrome died of starvation six days after birth; in the second case, the parents finally consented to the surgery. The impairments of the infants were used as the basis for denying them treatment that could have alleviated certain of their medical problems but left them with permanent disabilities that no treatment would cure. Virtually the only supports of the infants' right to treatment over parental objections were those commonly associated with the right-wing and right-to-life sectors of society, and perhaps also people with disabilities themselves (*Disability Rag*, 1984). (For a discussion of these cases and their meaning for notions of "community," see Sarason, 1986; and for a civil libertarian supporter of Baby Doe, see Hentoff, 1987).

•In 1983 and 1984, and again in 1986, Elizabeth Bouvia, a young woman whose cerebral palsy made it impossible for her to control any of her limbs save some functions of one hand, sought to get California hospitals to allow her to die by starvation. The American Civil Liberties Union (ACLU), generally regarded as championing the progress of many social causes, wrote a brief in her behalf describing her disability as causing her "pitiful existence," referring to her "affliction" as "incurable and . . . intolerable," and commenting on the "indignity and humiliation of requiring someone to attend to her every bodily need" (ACLU Foundation of Southern California, 1983, pp. 14, 17, 35). The entire tone of the brief implied that it was not at all surprising that someone with her level of disability would wish to end her life. The ACLU was not dissuaded from its line of argument by testimony of the Disability Rights Coordinating Council (DRCC), including a psychologist who was also quadriplegic, suggesting that Ms. Bouvia's situation was complicated by a host of stresses apart form her disability: "death of a sibling, marriage, pregnancy, multiple changes in residence, financial hardship, miscarriage, increased physical pain, terminal illness of a parent, and dissolution of marriage" (DRCC, 1983, p. 3). The DRCC did not dispute that people had the right to take their own lives. It disputed the unquestioned assumption that disability was a reason to end life.

The Superior Court of California, unmoved by those who sought to disentangle Ms. Bouvia's request from the situation of people with disabilities generally, endorsed her request, saying among other things: "She, as the patient, lying helplessly in bed, unable to care for herself, may consider her existence meaningless. She cannot be faulted for so concluding." Later, in describ-

The authors wish to note their equal contributions both to this article and to the editorship of the entire issue.

Correspondence regarding this article should be addressed to Michelle Fine, Graduate School of Education, University of Pennsylvania, 3700 Walnut Street, Philadelphia, Pennsylvania 19104.

Reprinted From: *Journal of Social Issues, Vol. 44, No. 1, 1988, pp. 3-21,* with permission.

ing her, it stated: "Her mind and spirit may be free to take great flights, but she herself is imprisoned, and must lie physically helpless, subject to the ignominy, embarrassment, humiliation, and dehumanizing aspects created by her helplessness" (*Bouvia v. Superior Court of California*, 1986, pp. 19, 21).

In this issue of *JSI*, we wish to resurrect the challenge to social psychology posed by Meyerson, Barker, and others in their 1948 *JSI* issue on disability. In this first article, we review the ways that disability has been viewed by social psychology over the past decades, trying to do for the study of disability what Sampson (1983) has done for the view of justice: namely, to offer some challenges to the assumptions that have guided theory and research, to speculate on the bases for these assumptions, and to suggest how alternative assumptions would alter the study of disability. We conclude by previewing the remaining articles in this issue as they reflect theory and research grounded in both old and new assumptions about the social nature of physical and mental disabilities.

Defining the Population of Interest

Although other articles in this issue elaborate upon the problem of accurately defining and describing the current situation of people with disabilities in 1987, it is essential to specify briefly whom this issue is about. In 1980 Bowe estimated the total population of people with disabilities in the United States to be 36 million, or perhaps 15% of the nation's people. In 1986 ("Census Study"), the *New York Times* reported some 37 million people over 15 years of age with disabling conditions. As Asch (1984) has discussed elsewhere, the mere attempt to define and enumerate the population shows that disability is a social construct. The Rehabilitation Act of 1973, as amended in 1978, defines a handicapped individual as "any person who (i) has a physical or mental impairment which substantially limits one or more of such person's major life activities, (ii) has a record of such an impairment, or (iii) is regarded as having such an impairment" (Section 7B).

We can say the following with assurance: The nation's population includes some 10% of school-aged children classified as handicapped for the purposes of receipt of special educational services (Biklen, this issue); somewhere between 9 and 17% of those between 16 and 64 years of age report disabilities that influence their employment situation (Haber & McNeil, 1983); nearly half of those over 65 indicate having one or more disabilities that interfere with their life activities or are regarded by others as doing so (DeJong & Lifchez, 1983).

Laws governing the provision of educational and rehabilitation services, and prohibiting discrimination in education, employment, and access to public programs, all stress the similarities in needs and in problems of people with a wide variety of physical, psychological, and intellectual impairments. (Scotch, this issue, discusses the benefits to the disability rights movement of such a legislative approach.) In this space, however, it is important to acknowledge the *differences* among disabling conditions and their varied impact on the lives of people in this group.

First, different conditions cause different types of functional impairment. Deafness, mental retardation, paralysis, blindness, congenital limb deficiencies, and epilepsy (all taken up in greater detail in this issue) may pose common social problems of stigma, marginality, and discrimination, but they also produce quite different functional difficulties. Several of these disabilities obviously interfere with functions of daily life, but the last, epilepsy, may not. Some persons with epilepsy have no inherent limitations whatever. Nevertheless, they are likely to be regarded as having an impairment.

Furthermore, people with disabilities have different degrees of impairment: Amounts of hearing and visual loss differ; some people with impairment of mobility can walk in some situations while others cannot. Mental retardation ranges from profound to mild--so mild that many out of school never get the label. In addition, some disabilities are static, while others are progressive. Multiple sclerosis, muscular dystrophy, cystic fibrosis, some vision and hearing impairments, some types of cancer and heart conditions present progressive disabilities that cause ever-changing health and life situations. Some conditions are congenital, others are acquired. All of these factors that distinguish the origin, experience, and effects of disability must be kept in mind in social science research on disability.

Researchers (Davis, 1961; Goffman, 1963; Ladieu, Adler, & Dembo, 1948) have long been aware that the degree of visibility of the impairment or the age at which it was acquired (Barker, 1948; von Hentig, 1948) may influence the psychological consequences and the social situation of people with disabilities. More recently, scholars have addressed the impact of ethnicity, class, and gender upon the experience of disability (Fine & Asch, 1981, 1988). In this issue, Schneider focuses on the social-psychological situation of people with a relatively invisible condition (epilepsy), and Mest analyzes the ways in which living and work contexts affect persons with retardation. Most of the other authors discuss the situations of people whose conditions are manifested by appearance or behavior. Ainlay and Frank (both in this issue) consider the different social-psychological impact of age of onset, and their conclusions contrast with the prevailing clinical and social-psychological views that acquiring a disability later is less damaging to the self and to social interaction than is growing up with an impairment. (See Asch and Rousso, 1985, for a review of psychoanalytic literature on disability.)

Disabled People as a Minority

Having acknowledged differences among these more than 36 million people in terms of their diagnoses, their social contexts, and their experiences of disability, it is important to return to the analysis that informs this article and this issue as a whole: disabled people comprise a minority group and most of their problems can and must be understood in a minority-group framework. This view is neither novel nor exclusively a post-Civil Rights Era position. Roger Barker in 1948 advanced thinking about disability in minority-group terms. Lee Meyerson, in his introduction to the 1948 *JSI*, opened by commenting, "There is general agreement in the literature on physical

disability that the problems of the handicapped are not physical, but social and psychological" (p. 2). Our own analysis owes much to the Lewinian person-in-environment thinking of the 1948 *JSI* contributors, and to the thoughtful work of Wright (1960, 1983), herself a frequent collaborator with Barker, Meyerson, and Dembo. These authors acknowledged that people with disabilities must be understood as having psychological responses to their impairments themselves, but they went on to point out the following: environmental factors posed many barriers of discrimination, marginality, and uncertain social acceptance; people with disabilities faced ambiguous, if not rejecting, social responses; and these people responded psychologically and socially to such situations.

Our analysis expands on this significant work and the 40 intervening years of social and legislative change. In the last 15 years, the movement for disability rights has embraced a minority-group perspective. Scholars of disability outside of social psychology such as Gliedman and Roth (1980), Hahn (1983, this issue), and Scotch (1984, this issue) have attempted to elaborate a minority-group analysis of disability issues and the disability experience. Unfortunately, as seen from the ensuing discussion, much of the frequently cited social-psychological work on disability has not learned all it could from the 1948 *JSI* contributors, nor from others in the emerging field of disability studies.

The minority-group perspective that frames this volume accepts Dworkin and Dworkin's (1976) definition of a minority group, applying it to people with disabilities. The criteria include "identifiability, differential power, differential and pejorative treatment, and group awareness" (p. viii).

While disabled people as a group may fit these criteria, they nevertheless face many obstacles in developing a minority-group consciousness, as Hahn (this issue) and Scotch (this issue) discuss in some detail. Not the least of these obstacles is the inaccessibility of the built environment, rendering transportation and public facilities unusable for people with any impairment, and disrupting potential efforts at organizing. While many people with disabilities have not developed a minority-group consciousness, a recent Louis Harris survey of disabled Americans reported that 74% of people with disabilities do feel some common identity with one another and that 45% see themselves as a minority in the same sense as people who are black or Hispanic (Hill, Mehnert, Taylor, Kagey, Leizhenko et al., 1986). As a footnote to Dworkin and Dworkin, we begin with the premise that a lack of shared consciousness *by some* does not negate the importance of understanding the social, structural, and psychological situation of people with disabilities in minority-group terms. As Hahn (1983, this issue) argues, the consequences of any impairment cannot be understood or appreciated without giving due weight to the environment--physical, structural, social, economic, psychological, and political--of the person with the disability. Just how disabling would deafness be if 20th-century urbanites, like Groce's (1985) rural villagers of Martha's Vineyard in the 19th century, all practice sign language? How disabling would paraplegia be if all cities were barrier free? (See Scheer & Groce, this issue.) How limiting would mental retardation be if nearly all labelled children received their educations in settings with the nonlabelled, as Biklen (this issue) discusses?

Barker (1948) was right when he reminded us that not all of the disabled person's situation can be explained by prejudice and discrimination. It is true that some activities are foreclosed merely because of the biological impairment itself. But the articles in this volume expand upon his thinking by demanding that we cease considering the environment--whether physical or attitudinal--as given. The *JSI* contributors of 1948 and this issue contrast sharply with much of the social-psychological writing about disability in the intervening decades, which assumes that the issues of disability reside in the person and tends to minimize or neglect the environment.

Assumptions About Disability

Considered below are a set of common assumptions about what disability means. For each, there have been important methodological and theoretical consequences:

1. *It is often assumed that disability is located solely in biology, and thus disability is accepted uncritically as an independent variable.* The disability and the person are assumed synonymous, and the cause of others' behaviors and attitudes. Several experimental social psychologists (Katz, 1981; Kleck, 1969; Kleck, Ono, & Hastorf, 1966) have simulated disability in the laboratory to verify Goffman's reports that handicapped people arouse anxiety and discomfort in others and are socially stigmatized. In these experiments, researchers have simulated disability by using a confederate who in one experimental condition appeared disabled and in another appeared nondisabled. The experiments did support the hypothesis that nondisabled people react differently to people with disabilities than they do to people without them. Nevertheless, it should be remembered that the confederate, whose only experience of having a disability may have been simulating it by sitting in a wheelchair, employed none of the strategies commonly used by disabled people to ease the discomfort of strangers in first meetings (David, 1961; Goffman, 1963). By focusing on initial encounters with strangers and by using a confederate whose only experience with disability might be simulating it, these experiments tell us nothing about how disabled people *actually* negotiate meaningful social interactions. Reports by David (1961) and Goffman (1963) acknowledge that obvious disability is generally prominent in initial social encounters. However, the extent to which an experimental confederate's naiveté about living with a disability can contribute to the prominence and the awkwardness of disability has not been recognized as an intervening variable. In these experiments, disability is viewed as an independent variable, much as gender had been considered prior to the early 1970s (Unger & Denmark, 1975). Disability is portrayed as the variable that predicts the outcome of social interaction when, in fact, social contexts shape the meaning of a disability in a person's life.

Most social-psychological work using disability to examine the concept of stigma takes the experience as equivalent regardless of such factors as the disabled person's race, culture, class, and gender. Scheer and Groce (this issue), Becker and Arnold (1986) provide valuable correctives by viewing the situation of disabled people through the disciplines of anthropology and history.

2. *When a disabled person faces problems, it is assumed that the impairment causes them.* In their very thoughtful expansion of Goffman's notion of stigma, Jones et al. (1984) elaborate on the consequences for the "marked" person of being singled out by others. Throughout their discussion of marking and its social-psychological consequences for disabled and nondisabled alike, however, these authors never question the extent to which disability per se poses difficulties in social participation, as contrasted with difficulties caused by the environment--architectural, social, economic, legal, and cultural. For example, in their discussion of changes in the life situations of people who became disabled, the authors never question that *the disability* keeps the person from continuing in employment or from going to restaurants or other recreational facilities. The entire discussion of stigma and marked relationships assumes as "natural" what Hahn aptly terms a *disabling environment;* it views obstacles as being solely the person's biological limitations rather than the human-made barriers of architecture or discriminatory work practices.

Even Barker's (1948) early work went only part way to indicting the environment as an obstacle to the disabled person's participation. Far ahead of his time, he called for antidiscrimination laws in education and employment, although he failed to challenge the architecture, the transportation, and the communication methods that confronted people with disabilities and hampered full participation. Barker's concluding comments took social arrangements as given, urging counselling and psychotherapy for people with disabilities, so that they could come to accept "the fact that the world in which [they live] presents serious restrictions and frustrations." He went on to say that education and antidiscrimination laws cannot "remove all restrictions on the physically deviant in a world constructed for the physically normal. The ultimate adjustment must involve changes in the values of the physically normal. The ultimate adjustment must involve changes in the values of the physically disabled person" (p. 37).

Barker's (1948) view is understandable 25 years before the passage of federal legislation to modify public-sector physical environments. Jones and his colleagues' (1948) obliviousness to environmental issues is not. Their otherwise valuable work on the social-psychological consequences of disability and stigma suffers seriously from such omissions. We can contrast these omissions of attention to environmental effects with Sampson's (1983) work on justice. Sampson urges students of justice and of resource allocation to attend to and be critical of current systems rather than merely to accept them and their consequences. We urge the same for students of disability.

3. *It is assumed that the disabled person is a "victim."* In a great deal of social-psychological research on attribution, the disabled person is seen as a victim who copes with suffering by self-blame (Bulman & Wortman, 1977), by reinterpreting the suffering to find positive meaning (Taylor, Wood, & Lichtman, 1983), or by denying that he or she is really suffering (Taylor et al., 1983). Bulman and Wortman studied 29 people paralysed in accidents. Lerner (1980) describes these people as "young people who had been recently condemned to spend the rest of their lives crippled (p. 161). In order for Lerner to make sense of why Bulman and Wortman's respondents were not displaying a sense of victimization, he posits their belief in a just world and suggests that their interpretations of the disabling events are constructed so as to retain a strong belief that the world is a just place and that bad things only happen to people for reasons. The psychological experiences of the persons with disabilities are thus examined *not* on their own terms, but instead as a form of denial. Disability is used as a synonym for victimization in this theoretical analysis.

Taylor et al.'s (1983) article, "It Could Be Worse," also illustrated the unchecked presumption of disabled-person-as-victim. The researchers examined the responses of people with cancer shortly after the onset of their condition and discovered that the interviewees consistently maintained that their situations "could be worse." To explain this finding, five "strategies" used by these "victims" to make sense of their situations were described. It is disturbing to us that these authors, who were interested in the rich qualitative ways that people describe their coping experiences, minimized informants' consistently expressed view that the trauma was not as severe as it could have been.

As Taylor et al. argued, people diagnosed as having cancer are surely traumatized, and they actively generate coping strategies. However, our concerns arise with respect to the authors' a priori assumptions. First, it should be noted that Bulman and Wortman, and Taylor and her colleagues, studied people quite shortly after the onset of disability, before they had chance to discover what would or would not be problematic about their lives. Their findings that self-blame (Bulman & Wortman, 1977) and making downward comparisons (Taylor et al., 1983) occurred within the first months or years after disability differ dramatically from those of Schulz and Decker (1985) in their study of people with spinal cord injuries 5-20 years after disability. The former authors can be read as suggesting, if inadvertently, that the experience of disability is static in a person's life and that "coping" is the same at any point in time or in one's life situation. The work of Schulz and Decker (1985), and Ainlay (this issue), correct this prevailing assumption and enrich our understanding of disability by demonstrating that responses at a specific time may not be the ones people retain after living with a disability for several years.

There are two more problems with the interpretations of disabled-person-as-victim put forward by Bulman and Wortman (1977), Janoff-Bulman and Frieze (1983), Lerner (1980), and Taylor et al. (1983). First, in contrast to Ladieu et al.'s (1948) report on the reactions of disabled veterans after World War II, these later researchers seem to discount the experiences described by the people they interviewed. Taylor et al., for example, view their respondents as having strategies for managing or camouflaging what must be truly tragic. To the "outsider," the researcher, the "objective situation" is that a diagnosis of cancer is that they had fared better than they

would have expected is not used self-reflectively by the researchers to reframe their notions about how people think about traumatic life events (cf. Frank, this issue). Rather, the statement is interpreted to illustrate psychological defenses that disabled people mobilize in order to manage what researchers feel is not really manageable. What needs to be stated is that disability--while never wished for--may simply not be as wholly disastrous as imagined.

Second, these authors presume that the disability itself constitutes the victimizing experience. None of them emphasize the subsequent reactions or deprivations that people experience because of social responses to their disability or environmentally imposed constraints. While Janoff-Bulman and Frieze (1983) recognize discrimination based on sex or gender to be a societal injustice, disability is assumed a biological injustice and the injustices that lie in its social treatment are ignored.

4.   *It is assumed that disability is central to the disabled person's self-concept, self-definition, social comparison, and reference groups.* Taylor and her colleagues (1983) describe their respondents as having to make downward social comparisons, lest they come face to face with how bad their situations really are. Jones et al. (1984), in their discussion of stigma, assume that the recently disabled paraplegic compares herself to others who are also paralysed. She may, but perhaps only when it comes to assessing her capacity to perform certain activities from a wheelchair. Gibbons (1986) claims that while such severely stigmatized people as those labelled retarded must make only downward social comparisons to preserve self-esteem, more, "mildly stigmatized" people such as those using wheelchairs seek out similarly disabled people with whom to compare themselves, and avoid social interactions and social comparisons with nondisabled people. Because disability is clearly salient for the nondisabled, it is assumed that the marked person incorporates the mark as central to self-definition.

The above authors forget that the woman who is paralysed may be as likely to compare herself with other women her age, others of her occupation, others of her family, class, race, or a host of other people and groups who function as reference groups and social comparison groups for her. Disability may be more salient to the researchers studying it than to the people being studied, who may define themselves as "similar to" or worthy of comparison with people without disabilities. Gurin (1984) reminds researchers in social comparison and relative deprivation to pay more attention to the conditions under which people choose particular groups with whom to compare themselves, and she stresses that social comparison may have nothing to do with gender, race, or disability.

Clearly contrasting with the above discussions of social comparison, Mest (this issue) demonstrates that their "mark" or stigma may be irrelevant to how mentally retarded persons define themselves and each other, particularly if they work and live in supportive contexts.

5. *It is assumed that having a disability is synonymous with needing help and social support.* People with disabilities are perceived to be examples of those ever in need of help and social support (Brickman et al., 1982; Deutsch, 1985; Dunkel-Schetter, 1984; Jones et al., 1984; Katz, 1981; Krebs, 1970; Sarason, 1986). Such an assumption is sustained both by what researchers study and write about those with disabilities and by their omission of disabled people in their discussions as providers of support.

The assumption that disability is synonymous with helplessness is not surprising when we remember that "the handicapped role" in the United States has been seen as one of helplessness, dependence, and passivity (Gliedman & Roth, 1980; Goffman, 1963). Brickman et al. (1982), in their excellent discussion of different models of helping and coping, review the essence of the medical model: The person is responsible for neither the problem encountered nor the solution required. The handicapped role, like the sick role of which it is an extension, compels the occupant to suspend other activities until recovered, to concentrate on getting expert therapy, to follow instructions, to get well, and only then to resume normal life. The nonhandicapped person equates having a disability with a *bad and eternal* flu, toothache, or broken leg. When such conditions are temporary, it may be acceptable to

entrust oneself to helpers and to forgo decision making briefly; but when forced to confront a moment of weakness, unsteadiness, or limitations in the capacity to see, hear, or move, people experience grave difficulty in adjusting. However, it is erroneous to conclude that their difficulties mirror those of the person who has a long-term disability and who has learned to use alternative methods to accomplish tasks of daily living and working.

That disability is assumed tantamount to incompetence and helplessness has been investigated, and supported in laboratory research. Unfortunately, the writing that has been generated *accepts* rather than *challenges* this stereotype, Katz (1981), who found that whites gave more help to competent blacks than to ones they perceived to be less competent and enterprising, expected that the same help-giving pattern would be true for nondisabled subjects when confronting a person with a disability. Contrary to his hypothesis, however, he found that nondisabled people gave *less* help to disabled person perceived as competent and friendly than to those perceived as incompetent and unfriendly. They also gave less help to the "disabled person" (simulated) than to the nondisabled persons. To explain this, Katz relied on Goffman (1963) and Gliedman and Roth (1980) in asserting that nondisabled persons are relatively offended or uncomfortable when confronting a person with an impairment who manages life competently As Jones and his colleagues (1984) remind us, the able-bodied deny the reality of successful adaptation by the disabled person. They perceive it as the disabled person "making the best of a bad job," and this view supports their conviction that their own health and capacities are as important, and infallible, as they think (p. 87).

Even while we wonder whether Katz would have gotten the same finding had he used a person who actually had a disability rather than one who had simulated an impairment, it is valuable to have this experimental support for what Goffman, Gliedman and Roth, and untold numbers of people with disabilities have described. Unfortunately, Jones et al. (1984) fall prey to their own unchallenged assumptions in thinking about ongoing relationships between people with and without disabilities: Throughout their book, and especially in the chapter by French (1984), it is assumed that the person with the disability is in constant need of help and support, rather than being a victim of nondisabled persons' projections or fantasies. Thereby, three problems arise: First, that the person with a disability may need assistance with certain acts is generalized to all aspects of the relationship between a person with a disability and one without. Second, if the person does need assistance, it is assumed that a previous reciprocal relationship will change, rather than that new methods or relationships will develop to provide it. Concurrently, it is assumed that the biological condition rather than the environment and social context makes one-way assistance inevitable. Third, it perpetuates the idea that the impaired person is forever the recipient, rather than ever the provider, of help and support. If disabled people are mentioned, they are mentioned as only on the receiving end of a helping transaction.

In French's (1984) chapter on marriages between disabled and nondisabled people, the assumptions are never challenged that the disability causes marital roles to change fundamentally, that blindness or quadriplegia per se will make resuming a work role difficult or impossible, that recreation will have to be curtailed. The spouse who performs certain amounts of physical caretaking is seen not only as a physical caretaker but as a generous intellectual and emotional caretaker as well. Physical incapacities are perceived as leading inevitably to incapacities in other spheres of life. Wright's (1983) notion that disability "spreads" throughout a relationship is embedded unchallenged in this entire discussion.

Moreover, it is the disability, not the institutional, physical, or attitudinal environment, that is blamed for role changes that may occur. The person with a disability may (initially, or always) need physical caretaking, such as help in dressing, household chores, or reading. It must be asked, however, whether such assistance would be necessary if environments were adapted to the needs of people with disabilities--if, for example, more homes were built to accommodate those who used wheelchairs, if technological aids could

be developed to assist in performing manual tasks, if existing technology to convert the printed word into speech or braille were affordable to all who needed it. Thus, again, the physical environment as an obstruction remains an unchallenged given. In addition, the author is assuming that the role of human assistant for all these tasks will automatically fall to the "significant other" rather than considering whether such activities could be performed by others, including public sector employees, thus permitting the primary relationship to function in its primary spheres of intimacy, sharing, and emotional nurturance for both participants. If the partners reorganize their roles after the impairment of one member, such reorganizations may result from a variety of factors: the way they think about disability, their relational obligations, the way that health care professionals inform them about the implications of disability, or the difficulties faced in affording appropriate assistance in the United States. These are consequences of how people think about disability and of current national disability policy, not of disability per se. As with all too much of this literature, as Wright (1983) points out, researchers who are outsiders make attributions to persons and thus neglect the powerful role of the environment.

The third problem mentioned above--that disabled people are always seen as recipients--may stem not only from distortions about people with disabilities but also from using disability as a metaphor to illustrate theory rather than to reveal more about the lives of people with impairments. Deutsch (1985) may be correct in speculating that, at least temporarily, resources would or should go to a sick child rather than a well one; Dunkel-Schetter (1984) may plausibly learn about the mechanisms of social support by studying what people with cancer find valuable and supportive from others after such a diagnosis; Krebs (1970) makes an important point in discussing how assumptions of legitimacy of others' dependency influence the helping process. Nonetheless, by staying with questions about theories of distributive systems (Deutsch, 1985), social support (Dunkel-Schetter, 1984), or altruism (Krebs, 1970), and by not focusing on ongoing reciprocal transactions, the person with a disability is never imagined or shown to be a provider of support. As Shumaker and Brownell (1984) remind us, those who receive support also commonly seek to provide it, if not to those who gave it to them, then to others. It is regrettable that people with disabilities, when studied or considered at all in most social-psychological literature, are examined only in ways that reinforce and perpetuate existing stereotypes rather than in ways that question and challenge them. In this manner, the literature fails to enrich our understanding of the lives of people with handicapping conditions.

Particularly disturbing, as an illustration of disability-as-metaphor, is Sarason's (1986) discussion of the Baby Jane Doe case. Unfortunately, his laudable effort to call for a renew commitment to the "public interest" and a lessening of individualism is flawed by uncritically accepting the assumption that the infant with a disability can never be expected to make a valuable contribution to family or society. He consistently refers to the existence of the severely disabled child as a problem to both family and society. Sarason's examination of the public interest and of the search for community continues in this "disabled-as-helpless" vein. He refers only to "afflicted children"; finds that families who adopt disabled children were "managing their situations in surprisingly adaptive, stable, and inspiring ways" (p. 903); and describes the child only as a "problem," without any consideration of the possible contributions, benefits, or pleasures the infant born with a disability might bring to its family and society.

The Role of These Assumptions for Society and for Social Science

It is worth speculating on how these assumptions get made, why they persist, and what functions they serve for researchers and society. it remains a task for future research to discover the plausibility of these speculations.

Jones and his colleagues (1984) contend that the thought or awareness of disability evokes feelings of vulnerability and death. They suggest that the nondisabled person almost wants the one with the disability to suffer so as to confirm that the "normal" state is as good and as important as the "normal" thinks it is. Because disability can be equated with vulnerability to the controllable, observing someone with a disability forces all of us to wonder about the consequences of what one cannot control. In a society seeking to control ever more of life, is there a leap to the assumption that one cannot live with the consequences of what one cannot control? Or is there a desire to view disability as a fundamental loss of control, in order to obscure the fact that many aspects of our lives are "out of our control"? Social researchers are in the business of expanding knowledge of the world and trying to optimize prediction and control. As researchers, we highly prize knowledge and the control it can provide. Does such a commitment to control suggest that social scientists may view disability as fearful, unacceptable, and different because the person with the disability is a reminder that we cannot control all life events?

As discussed earlier, perceptions of disability have been the repository and projection of human needs. How much do the social and psychological problems that many people associate with disability actually pervade all of human life? If one can think of a person with a disability as needy, in contrast, one can view those without impairments as strong and as not having needs. By thinking of the disabled person as dependent in a given situation, and the one without disabilities as independent and autonomous, one can avoid considering how extensively people without disabilities too are dependent and sometimes not. Rather than the world being divided into givers and receivers of help, we are all actually interdependent. Attributing neediness and lack of control to people with disabilities permits those who are not disabled to view themselves as having more control and more strength in their lives than may be the case.

Last, perceiving a person with a disability as a suffering victim, as a stimulus object, as in need, or as different and strange, all reinforce what Goffman (1963) describes as perception of the stigmatized as "not quite human" (p. 6). In discussing the scope of justice, Deutsch (1985) comments, "Justice is not involved in relations with others . . . The narrower one's concept of community, the narrower will be the scope of situations in which one's actions will be governed by considerations of justice" (pp. 36-37). Deutsch goes on to contend that it has been a

> too-common assumption of victimizers, even those of good will, as well as of many social scientists, that the social pathology has been in the ghetto rather than in those who have built the walls to surround it, that the disadvantaged are the ones who need to be changed rather than the people and institutions who have kept the disadvantaged in a submerged position. . . . It is more important to change educational institutions and economic and political systems so that they will permit those groups who are now largely excluded from important positions of decision-making to share power than to try to inculcate new attitudes and skills in those who are excluded (p. 61).

These words apply as much to the situation of people with disabilities as to that of people with economic disadvantages whom Deutsch considered. By concentrating on cure or on psychological and physical restoration of the impaired person, society and the discipline of psychology have avoided the need to focus on essential changes in the environmental side of the "person-in-environment" situation. If the person with a disability is "not quite human," then that person can remain outside the community of those who must receive just distributions of rewards and resources (Deutsch, 1985). In contrast, if people with disabilities were perceived as having the same rights to mobility and life's opportunities as people without impairments, we would inevitably be compelled to rethink the view that transportation for people with mobility impairments, or access to treatment for infants or adults with disabilities, are gifts or charities that can be withdrawn when times are tight. Once people with disabilities are admitted inside the human and moral community, the task becomes one of creating an environment where all humans--including those with impairments--can truly flourish.

Aims of This Issue

We conclude by discussing what research might look like without the five assumptions described above and by posing questions for future study.

Although we do not see the influence of the 1948 *JSI* issue on disability in much of contemporary research, we believe it has influenced social policy in the intervening decades and has informed much of the research found in the present volume. Many of the 1948 policy recommendations have been realized: Children with disabilities are now entitled to a free, appropriate public education alongside their nondisabled counterparts (Cain, 1948). Many state civil rights laws now provide people with disabilities the same protection against discrimination in employment, housing, and public accommodations as is afforded to other minority groups. Federal law now mandates that disabled people have equal access to employment and services in all programs that receive federal money (Barker, 1948; Meyerson, 1948b,c). As laws, institutional arrangements, and social relationships begin to change, so too must the social psychology of disability change to reflect the altered experience of people with disabilities--and of persons without disabilities--as members of a common moral community.

Having been critical of the picture of disability portrayed in much of the social-psychological research previously discussed, we must ask what has kept so much research locked into the narrow assumptions about people with disabilities. As Asch (1984) has described, the focus of much social-psychological research on disability has been to determine the impact of contact with disability upon people without impairments. Such a question, particularly when framed by a researcher outside the disability experience, makes the person with the disability the object, not the subject, of study and distances the research from the disabled person's life experience. Furthermore, much of this research was undertaken primarily to bolster particular theoretical notions about stigma, victimization, social comparison processes, justice, altruism, or social support. Not surprisingly, but regrettably, the authors have used notions of disability as a metaphor to advance social theories rather than to advance our knowledge of the experience of disability.

We wonder what keeps researchers from imagining a context in which disability would not be handicapping. Major reasons may be that most research has not focused on the lives and experiences of people with disabilities, and it has often been conducted without substantial contact with people with disabilities. By contrast, the research presented in the following pages, like that of the 1948 *JSI*, stems from the authors' interest in people with disabilities. The articles adopt varying disciplinary perspectives, and they demonstrate that disability often functions as an independent variable, but that reactions to and consequences of disability are dependent upon multiple variables in the social and psychological contexts of disabled and nondisabled persons. (Similarly, several essays in the collection Ainlay, Becker, and Coleman (1986) demonstrate how much historical and cultural variation exists in just who is stigmatized, who becomes a deprive minority.)

In this issue, both Hahn and Biklen examine the ways in which having a disability contributes to minority status. As Dworkin and Dworkin (1976, p. 18) have pointed out, "selection of the relevant characteristics upon which identifiability is based is neither fixed nor self-evident; rather, it is variable and socially defined and interpreted." Hahn looks at what he classifies as nondisabled persons' "existential" and "aesthetic" anxieties as the bases for labelling, and Biklen focuses on educational finances as the primary *raison d'etre* for classifying schoolchildren into categories--disabled or not.

The paper by Ainlay examines the experience of becoming disabled, for elderly men and women, while Schneider discusses the experience of persons with disabilities in their interpersonal relationships over time. These two articles demonstrate how time with an impairment modifies its lived experience. In the spirit of Schulz and Decker (1985), they challenge the notions of Bulman and Wortman (1977) and Taylor et al. (1983).

The articles by Frank and Mest examine interactions among disabled people, and between disabled people and the nondisabled who are in their intimate worlds, to discover how both members of any transaction are influenced by the presence of a known impairment in one or both of them. These reports lead us to question the way disability has been viewed in the stigma and social support literatures. Makas contributes to this analysis by advancing a methodology that distinguishes between "good" and "bad" disability attitudes.

Scheer and Groce, Darling, and Scotch all portray how different cultures and different political climates reshape the experience of having a disability. Impairment may be an ubiquitous "human constant," but response to it is not. Scheer and Groce carry on in the tradition of Hanks and Hanks (1948) to examine how different cultures, eras, institutions, and social structures influence the social integration of people with disabilities in 19th-century rural and 20th century urban U.S. society.

Darling and Scotch each address the political responses generated by persons with disabilities and/or their advocates. Darling traces how families of disabled people have transformed a medical view of disability into a minority-group and political one. Scotch similarly analyzes the disability rights movement of the 1970s, focusing on the experience of disabled people themselves. These papers demonstrate that while the biological fact of disability may be a given, the environment need not be.

As a collection, these articles reframe disability as a minority-group issue in which a set of socially negotiated meanings of the body are played out psychologically, socially, and politically. The force reanalysis along several dimensions, pointing out the following:

1. How the experience of disability is influenced by professionals (Biklen), and how it can be studied by nondisabled researchers (Hahn; Frank; Makas).

2. That disability needs to be studied over time and in context, as a socially transforming and changing process, not a static characteristic of an individual (Ainlay; Becker; Mast; Schneider).

3. That a social-constructivist view of

disability (Gergen, 1985) enables a reassessment of previously taken-for-granted views of the nature and consequences of life with impairment (Darling; Scheer & Groce; Scotch).

4. That accepting a minority-group perspective on disability and attending to all the aspects of the life space that extend beyond the person with the impairment causes social psychologists to raise new questions for research. Examples of such questions include the following: What sustains the belief that having a child with a disability is predominantly burdensome and tragic? What would make possible a different outcome? What does the experience of being close to someone with disability do to broaden one's sense of moral community or to shrink it? What are the consequences and costs, of both disabled and non-disabled people, of an increasingly integrated society? Under what conditions, and with what consequences, does the independent-living movement or the disability-rights movement promote notions of individualism over notions of community? What are the psychological barriers to a person with a disability getting involved in the disability-rights movement? What barriers keep progressives without disabilities from involving themselves in the disability-rights movement?

5. That quality-of-life judgments underpinning public and professional views of individuals like Baby Doe and Elizabeth Bouvia deserve serious reevaluation. Similarly, accepting the powerful role of environment as a mediating variable in outcomes for people with disabilities forces us to reexamine what a just allocation of resources would be.

This *JSI* volume is presented as an interdisciplinary, provocative exploration of an already existing literature on disability and a rapidly emerging transformed perspective on the topic. The 1948 *JSI* issue influenced social policy and the field of rehabilitation psychology. We hope that the ensuing pages will stimulate further development in social psychology and social policy.

References

ACLU Foundation of Southern California. (1983). *Elizabeth Bouvia v. County of Riverside* (Memorandum of points and authorities in support of application for temporary restraining order and permanent injunction). Los Angeles: Author.

Ainlay, S., Becker, G., & Coleman, L. (Eds.) (1986). *The dilemma of difference: A multi-disciplinary view of stigma.* New York: Plenum.

Asch, A. (1984). The experience of disability: A challenge for psychology. *American Psychologist, 39,* 529-536.

Asch, A., & Rousso, H. (1985). Therapists with disabilities: Theoretical and clinical issues. *Psychiatry, 48,* 1-12.

Barker, R. G. (1948). The social psychology of physical disability. *Journal of Social Issues, 4*(4), 28-37.

Becker, G., & Arnold, R. (1986). Stigma as a social and cultural construct. In S. Ainlay, G. Becker, & L. Coleman (Eds.), *The dilemma of difference: A multi-disciplinary view of stigma* (pp. 39-58). New York: Plenum.

Bouvia v. Superior Court of the State of California. Court of Appeal of the State of California. Second Appelate District, Division Two, 2nd Cir. No. B019134 (1986, April 16).

Bowe, F. (1980). *Rehabilitating America.* New York: Harper & Row.

Brickman, P., Rabinowitz, V. C., Karuza, J., Coates, D., Cohn, E., & Kidder, L. (1982). Models of helping and coping. *American Psychologist, 37,* 368-384.

Bulman, R., & Wortman, C. (1977). Attributions of blame and coping the "real world": Severe accident victims react to their lot. *Journal of Personality and Social Psychology, 35,* 351-363.

Cain, L. F. (1948). The disabled child in school. *Journal of Social Issues, 4*(4), 90-93.

Census study reports one in five adults suffers from disability. (1986, December 23). *New York Times.* p. 67.

Davis, F. (1961). Deviance disavowal: The management of strained interaction by the visibly handicapped. *Social Problems, 9,* 120-132.

DeJong, G., & Lifchez, R. (1983). Physical disability and public policy. *Scientific American, 48,* 240-249.

Deutsch, M. (1985). *Distributive justice*. New Haven, CT: Yale University Press.

Disability Rag. (1984, February-March). Entire issue.

Disability Rights Coordinating Council (1983). *Elizabeth Bouvia v. County of Riverside* Declaration of Carol Gill). Los Angeles: Author.

Dunkel-Schetter, C. (1984). Social support and cancer: Findings based on patient interviews and their implications. *Journal of Social Issues, 40*(4), 77-98.

Dworkin, A. & Dworkin, R. (Eds.) (1976). *The minority report*. New York: Praeger.

Editorial. *New York Times*, (1983, June 17).

Fine, M., & Asch, A. (Eds.) (1981). *Women with disabilities: Essays in psychology, culture, and politics*. Philadelphia: Temple University Press.

French, R. De S. (1984). The long-term relationships of marked people. In E. E. Jones et al., *Social stigma: The psychology of marked relationships* (pp. 254-295). New York: Freeman.

Gergen, K. (1985). The social constructivist movement in modern psychology. *American Psychologist, 40*, 266-275.

Gibbons, F. X. (1986). Stigma and interpersonal relations. IN S. Ainlay, G. Becker, & L. Coleman (Eds.), *The dilemma of difference: A multi-disciplinary view of stigma* (pp.123-144). New York: Plenum.

Gliedman, J., & Roth, W. (1980). *The unexpected minority: Handicapped children in America*. New York: Harcourt, Brace, Jovanovich.

Goffman, E. (1963). *Stigma: Notes on the management of spoiled identity*. Englewood Cliffs, NJ: Prentice-Hall.

Groce, N. (1985). *Everyone here spoke sign language: Hereditary deafness on Martha's Vineyard*. Cambridge, MA: Harvard University Press.

Gurin, P. (1984). Review of *Relative deprivation and working women*. *Contemporary Psychology, 29*, 209-210.

Haber, L., & McNeil, J. (1983). *Methodological questions in the estimation of disability prevalence*. Washington, DC: Population Division, U.S. Bureau of the Census.

Hahn, H. (1983, March-April). Paternalism and public policy. *Society*, pp. 36-46.

Hanks, J. Re., & Hanks, L. M. (1948). The physically handicapped in certain non-Occidental societies. *Journal of Social Issues, 4*(4), 11-19.

Hentoff, N. (1987). The awful privacy of Baby Doe. In A. Gardner & T. Joe (Eds.), *Images of the disabled: Disabling images* (pp. 161-80). New York: Praeger.

Hill, N., Mehnert, T., Taylor, T., Kagey, M., Leizhenko, S,. et al. (1986). *The ICD survey of disabled Americans: Bringing disabled Americans into the mainstream*. New York: International Center for the Disabled.

Janoff-Bulman, R., & Frieze, I. H. (1983). A theoretical perspective for understanding reactions to victimization. *Journal of Social Issues, 39*(2), 1-17.

Jones, E. E., Farina, A., Hastorf, A. H., Markus, H., Miller, D. T., Scott, R. A., & French, R. de S. (1984). *Social stigma: The psychology of marked relatinships*. New York: Freeman.

Katz, I. (1981). *Stigma: A social-psychological analysis*. Hillsdale, NJ: Erlbaum.

Katzmann, R. A. (1986). *Institutional disability: The saga of transportation policy fo rthe disabled*. Washington, D.C.: Brookings Institute.

Kleck, R. (1969). Physical stigma and task-oriented interactions. *Human Relations, 22*, 53-59.

Kleck, R., Ono, H., & Hastorf, A. (1966). The effects of physical deviance upon face-to-face interaction. *Human Relatins, 19*, 425-436.

Krebs, D. L. (1970). Altruism: An examination of the concept and review of the literature. *Psychological Bulletin, 73*, 258-302.

Ladieu, G., Adler, D. L., Dembo, T. (1948). Studies in adjustment to visible injuries: Social acceptance of the injured. *Journal of Social Issues, 4*(4), 55-61.

Lerner, M. J. (1980). *The belief in a just world: A fundamental delusion*. New York: Plenum.

Meyerson, L. (1948a). Physical disability as a social psychological problem. *Journal of Social Issues, 4*(4), 107-109.

Rehabilitation Act of 1973, Pub. L. No. 93-112, 87 Stat. 357 (1973).

Roth, W. (1983, March-April). Handicap as a social construct. *Society*. pp. 56-61.

Sampson, E. (1983). *Justice and the critique of pure psychology*. New York: Plenum.

Sarason, S. B. (1986). And what is the public interest? *American Psychologist, 41*, 899-906.

Schultz, R., Decker, S. (1985). Long-term adjustment to physical disability: The role of social support, perceived control, and self-blame. *Journal of Personality and Social Psychology, 48*, 1162-1172.

Scotch, R. K. (1984). *From good will to civil rights: Transforming federal disability policy*. Philadelphia: Temple University Press.

Shumaker, S., & Brownell, A. (1984). Toward a theory of social support: Closing conceptual gaps. *Journal of Social Issues, 40*(4), 11-36.

Solomon, H. M. (1986). Stigma and Western culture: A historical approach. In S. Ainlay, G. Becker, & L Coleman (Eds.), *The dilemma of difference: A multi-disciplinary view of stigma* (pp. 59-76). New York: Plenum.

Taylor, S. E., Wood, J. V., & Lichtman, R. R. (1983). "It could be worse": Selective evaluation as a response to victimization. *Journal of Social Issues, 39*(2), 19-40.

The $2,000 subway token, *New York Times,* (1984, June 23).

Unger, R. K., & Denmark, F. L. (1975). *Woman: Dependent or independent variable?* New York: Psychological Dimensions.

von Hentig, H. (1948). Physical desirability, mental conflict and social crisis. *Journal of Social Issues, 4*(4), 21-27.

Wight, B. A. (1960). *Physical disability: A psychosocial approach.* New York: Harper & Row.

Wright, B. A. (1983). *Physical disability: A psychosocial approach.* New York: Harper & Row.

Labelling Theory's Explanation of Mental Illness: An Update of Recent Evidence

WALTER GOVE

Introduction

According to Horwitz (1979), the conflict between the labelling explanation of mental illness and the psychiatric explanation of mental illness is no closer to being resolved than when Scheff (1966) initially presented the labelling explanation and I presented my rebuttal to his position (Gove, 1970a). Although I agreed (Gove, 1979) with Horwitz that for most *sociologists* the issues seem to be no closer to resolution than when our first work was published, I argued that in the past 25 years there have been so many developments in psychiatry that the issues raised by labelling theory have been largely resolved and that from a pragmatic perspective a *general* labelling explanation of mental illness is no longer tenable. This in no way denies that labelling theory points to real processes; it does. The fact that in the past there were large numbers of chronic mental patients and it is only due to recent innovations that the situation has changed can be interpreted as meaning that in the past labelling theory did provide important insights into the treatment of the mentally ill.

Having asserted that the changes in psychiatric practice and new evidence seriously undermine the tenability of the labelling theory of mental illness I (Gove, 1979) did not go on to indicate in any detail the nature of these changes. The present article is aimed at rectifying that deficiency by providing the sociologist with an overview of (1) the basic changes that have occurred in the practice of psychiatry and (2) the major recent findings that have occurred in the study of labelling theory and mental illness. Because there have been so many developments, I attempt only to highlight what I see as the major changes and I am highly selective in my citations.

Changes in the Rates and Place of Treatment

Given the changes in the setting in which treatment occurs and the brevity of treatment, it is difficult to imagine that most mental patients are in the formal role of the mental patient for long enough to be socialized into the role of the chronically ill. From 1955 to 1971, there was an increase each year in the number of patients admitted to public mental hospitals; after 1971 the admission rate levelled off and then began a slight decline. In spite of a generally increasing admission rate, the resident population has declined every year since 1955. This reduction has largely been brought about by a very sharp decrease in the length of hospitalization. In 1975 the median length of inpatient care in public mental hospitals was 26 days; in private mental hospitals, 20 days; in community mental health centers, 13; in Veterans Administration (VA) hospitals (psychiatric admissions only), 18; and in general hospitals (psychiatric admissions only) 12 days (Klerman and Schecter, 1981).

During this time there also has been a sharp shift away from treatment in public mental hospitals to treatment centers more closely tied to the community. Table 1 presents the number of inpatient and outpatient care episodes by type of psychiatric facility for the United States from 1955 to 1977. As these data show, the rate of inpatient hospitalizations has remained relatively constant, but there has been a marked change in the place of treatment, with fewer persons receiving treatment in public mental hospitals and more persons receiving inpatient treatment in general hospitals, community mental health centers, and to a lesser extent, VA hospitals. The most striking characteristic of the data in Table 1 is the tremendous increase in the number of patients who received care in outpatient psychi-

Reprinted from: *Deviant Behavior: An Interdisciplinary Journal, 3:307-327, 1982*, with permission.
0163-9625/82/030307-21 $2.25 Copyright © 1982 by Hemisphere Publishing Corporation.

atric clinics. Furthermore, many more persons were being treated by general physicians. According to Regier et al. (1978), in 1975 3.1% of the total U.S. population were treated by mental health professionals, .5% received inpatient care for mental illness in nonpsychiatric settings, and 9.0% received treatment as outpatients by physicians. In short, a total of 11.8% of the population received some form of psychiatric treatment from physicians during the year. In 1955 most persons receiving psychiatric treatment were receiving relatively long-term treatment in public mental hospitals; now stays in inpatient hospitals are short, and the vast majority receiving psychiatric treatment receive it as outpatients. Given the short period and the location of treatment, it is difficult to imagine that the stigma of treatment acts as a master status that persists in shaping patients' lives by placing them in the role of the (permanently) mentally ill.

Effectiveness of Treatment

The relationships I reported on treatment (Gove, 1970a, 1975a) have continued to be supported. The literature on the effectiveness of tranquilizers and antidepressants has become extensive and is well reviewed in Berger (1978). In addition, the evidence on the efficacy of psychotherapy continues to be supported (Bergin and Lemert, 1980; Mosher and Keith, 1979; Smith and Glass, 1977; Frank, 1974). As psychiatric practitioners are aware, however, therapy is not without its costs; chemotherapy sometimes produces adverse side effects (Berger, 1978), and not only is psychotherapy not always effective but at least occasionally there can be harmful effects (Strupp et al. 1977).

What is new is that with the deinstitutionalization of mental patients, many persons who had formerly been institutionalized mental patients

Number and Percent Distribution of Care Episodes in Selected U.S. Mental Health Facilities for Selected Years (Per 100,000 Population)

Year	All facilities	All mental services	Inpatient services of					Outpatient psychiatric services of		
			State and county mental hospitals	Private mental hospitals	General hospital psychiatric services (non-VA)	VA Psychiatric inpatient services	Federally assisted community mental health centers	All outpatient services	Federally assisted community mental health centers	Other
1977	2964	842	266	85	265	101	125	2122	808	1314
1971	1977	843	365	62	266	87	64	1134	305	829
1965	1376	817	420	65	271	60	--	559	--	559
1955	1028	795	502	76	163	54	--	233	--	233

Note. In order to present trends on the same set of facilities over this interval, it has been necessary to exclue from this table the following: private psychiatric office practice; psychiatric service modes of all types in hospitals or outpatient clinics of federal agencies other than the VA (e.g., Public Health Service, Indian Health Service, Department of Defense, Bureau of Prisons, etc.); inpatient service modes of multiservice facilities not shown in this table; all partial care episodes, and outpatient episodes of VA hospitals.
Source. Witkin (1980).

are living under very undesirable conditions in the community; in a number of cases these conditions are more undesirable than the conditions in most mental hospitals (e.g., lamb, 1979). Many of these former mental patients cannot function effectively without maintenance therapy, and when they receive such therapy they clearly benefit from it (Davis, 1975; McCrainie and Mizell, 1978; Winston et al., 1977).

Attitudes Toward the Mentally Ill

As Rabkin (1974) shows in her review of public attitudes toward mental illness, on some issues the literature is not clear. In large part this is probably due to methodological problems revolving around what is meant by the term "mental illness." In my earlier work (e.g., Gove and Fain, 1973) I speculate that one reason a substantial number of patients do not view themselves as mentally ill is that the stereotype of mental illness involves such a severe disorder and bizarre behavior that the majority of both mental patients and those with whom they deal recognize that the patient's condition does not conform to the popular conception of mental illness. Thus, although they may realize that the patients need help, many will conclude that they are not mentally ill. There is now strong evidence that this is the case. As the studies by Meile and Whitt (1981), Whitt et al. (1979), Askanasy (1974), Townsend (1976) and Rabkin (1979) indicate, laymen have very stringent criteria for labelling someone mentally ill and they think of the mentally ill as very impaired. To the layman, most persons receiving psychiatric treatment, including a brief hospitalization, are suffering from a "nervous breakdown." Such persons are not perceived as mentally ill, even if they are in treatment, and the evidence indicates that they experience relatively little stigma. Apparently the public stereotype of mental illness is so derogatory and bizarre that the vast majority of persons treated for mental illness do not conform to the stereotype and thus escape the label. This is especially true if the "other" is a long-term acquaintance of the (ex)mental patient or if the other sees the (ex)patient after the most severe symptoms have been brought under control,

which, as noted above, takes only a brief period of treatment.

Regarding stigma the following statements receive clear support from empirical studies:

1. Although being labelled mentally ill may be stigmatizing and produce an exclusionary reaction, being labelled a former mental patient does not (Olmstead and Durham, 1976).

2. Persons who have had experience in dealing with the mentally ill are less rejecting than persons without such experience (Trute and Loewen, 1978).

3. Family members tend not to be particularly rejecting of the mentally ill because close ties override the stigma and enable them to see positive qualities in the individual (Chin-Shong, 1969; Kreisman and Joy, 1974).

4. In general, families experience little fear, shame, anger, or guilt regarding a family member who is mentally ill. If they do experience such feelings, they tend to be reactions to the actual behavior of the mentally ill person, which may be disruptive, frightening, embarrassing, etc. (Kreisman and Joy, 1974; Freeman and Simmons, 1961; Schwartz et al. 1974). The reader should be cautioned that in the relatively few cases where the family members do report feelings of hostility toward the "patient," to some extent they may be rationalizing their feelings of rejection by reporting disruptive behavior.

5. Although employers are apt to express prejudice against the mentally ill, the evidence suggests that employers do not discriminate against former mental patients in their hiring practices (Olshansky et al., 1960; Huffine and Clausen, 1979).

6. A systematic review of quantitative research (18 studies) shows that a substantial majority of hospitalized mental patients have favorable attitudes toward the mental hospital, their treatment, and the staff (Weinstein, 1982).

Patients' Civil Rights

One of the major concerns of labelling theorists is that the civil rights of the prospective patients are violated during the commitment process and subsequently when they are in the hospital. At the time Scheff (1966) was writing his book, a case could be made that such violations frequently occurred; however, because of court rulings, new laws, and changes in procedures, it is very hard to make such a case today. First of all, it should be noted that this issue deals almost entirely with committed patients and such patients are becoming increasingly rare. Virtually all of them are committed to a public mental hospital, and, as noted above, they constitute only a small proportion of all patients receiving psychiatric care. The majority of patients admitted to public mental hospitals are voluntary admissions. In 1972, for the United States as a whole, 41.8% of the admissions involved civil commitments (Meyer, 1974). Moreover, apparently as a consequence of recent legislation and court rulings (see below), the rate appears to have dropped substantially since then. It is interesting to note that among persons who had (a) graduated from grade school, (b) had some high school education, (c) graduated from high school, (d) had some college education, or (e) graduated from college, the national data showed no relationship between being committed and the amount of education (Meyer, 1974), a fact inconsistent with an aspect of labelling theory articulated by Rushing (1978), namely that education is related to avoiding hospitalization.

In 1971, in *Wyatt v. Stickney*, the Federal district court in Alabama held that involuntarily committed patients "unquestionably have a constitutional right to receive such individual treatment as will give each of them a realistic opportunity to be cured or to improve his or her mental condition," and this has become the accepted standard for all hospitals. In 1975, in *O'Connor v. Donaldson*, the U.S. Supreme Court ruled that " a state cannot constitutionally confine a nondangerous individual who is capable of surviving safely in freedom by himself or with the help of willing and responsible family members or friends" (Crain et al., 1977:827). As a consequence of this ruling, the Connecticut Valley Hospital instituted a systematic\ review of all involuntary patients there. Although the review found no other patients like O'Connor, it did find a substantial number of patients who could be cared for in other institutional settings, particularly nursing homes.

The case *Nason v. Bridgewater* confirmed a person's right to an individualized treatment program. A follow-up in the four hospitals against which this suit was filed showed a marked improvement in the hospitals' psychiatric treatment (Kaufman, 1979). Since these court rulings, right-to-treatment suits have become fairly a positive force in improving mental health care, and there is some evidence that institutional psychiatrists will use them to further their own program goals (e.g., Macht, 1978).

On April 30,1979, in *Addington v. Texas*, the Supreme court handed down a ruling that more clearly delineates the nature of the evidence required for commitment. The court ruled the evidence must be "clear and convincing." Although the standard of proof is not as stringent as that required in criminal cases, in which the standard is "beyond a reasonable doubt," the ruling clearly indicates that it is almost as stringent. Moreover, at that time 39 states already had laws requiring the standard used in criminal cases (see *Addington vs. Texas*). The Supreme Court also has imposed stringent limits on how long defendants found incompetent to stand trial can be hospitalized (Steadman, 1979).

The court rulings are complemented by changes in the law. In 1955 the laws affecting the admissions to New York state mental hospitals were reformed and updated. These reforms, characterized at the time as the most revolutionary in the country in the field of mental health in a century (Morrissey, 1982), encouraged the use of voluntary admission procedures and required the conversion of all possible involuntary patients to a voluntary or informal status. The legislation abolished court certification of involuntary hospitalization and established a system of initial admissions based on medical judgement (two-physician certificates) for a two-week period. A number of legal safeguards were introduced. The law established a Mental Health Information Service, which guaranteed that the patient was notified of his or her rights and was automatically provided with legal assistance for a judicial hearing to be held after two weeks in the cases where treatment was still deemed necessary and the patient had not changed to a voluntary or informal status. By 1969 only 7% of the patients requested court a hearing, and of those who requested a court hearing approximately 50% were released. Additional legal safeguards were introduced for involuntary patients hospitalized beyond 60 days (e.g., see Kumasaka et al., 1972; Morrissey, 1982).

In 1967 California passed the Laterman-Petris-Short (LPS) Act, which limited all involuntary hospitalization to 17 days and imposed very strict legal safeguards regarding both the requirements for and the procedures to be used in commitment. Urmer (1978:143) reports that "in the first two years post-LPS the average treatment duration of involuntary patients dropped from 180 days to 15 days while the average duration of voluntary patients dropped from 75 days to 23 days." The California law has received the most careful scrutiny, it has comparatively stringent requirements for involuntary hospitalization, and it has been used as a model for laws in other states (e.g., Sata and Goldenberg, 1977; Bonovitz and Guy, 1979).

There has been no systematic published review of the present laws in the 50 states, but my colleagues and I have recently completed a preliminary review of the laws (Gove et al., 1982). The laws must be considered in light of *Dixon v. Weinberger*, where it was ruled that committed patients have a statutory right to treatment in the least restrictive appropriate facility and that such facilities should be created if they do not exist. In practice this has meant that in considering commitment, courts must conclude that a mental hospital is the least restrictive treatment setting in which the patient can be treated, if it is the case, for example, that the patient cannot be effectively treated in an outpatient facility. Our preliminary review shows that the laws have tightened considerably in recent years. All 50 states specify that the prospective patient has the right to a lawyer. The reasons for commitment are becoming considerably more narrow. In 22 states the law specifies that the patient, in addition to being severely mentally ill, *must be* a danger to him or herself or to others. The legal terms vary but the most common terms are "a clear and present danger" or "poses an immediate danger to self or others." In 25 states, in addition to the dangerousness question, the law specifies that the

patient may also be committed if he or she is gravely disabled, usually with the specification that the patient is unable to care for himself or herself in the community, even with the assistance of others. In the remaining three states, there is also the specification that the patient may be hospitalized if he or she poses a serious threat to property. The law in 43 states specifies either that commitment be for a specified period or that a review be held at a specific time. In most states this is a continuous process; that is, the patient may be recommitted but, again, only for a specific period such as six months. In a few states, however, after the second hearing the commitment may be for an indefinite period. In the remaining seven states the commitment period is unspecified, and there is no periodic review, but in four of these states the hospital must report to the court or review board at specified intervals. Finally, in 43 states the law stipulates that the patient may appeal a ruling that results in hospitalization.

This brief review of the laws does not touch on all of the changes. For example, in Michigan all patients are notified of their rights as specified by the new mental health code, and each institution has a special person designated as a visible advisor who investigates complaints (Coye and Clifford, 1978). In summary, as the law stands at present, in the majority of the states persons can be committed to a mental hospital only if they pose a serious danger to themselves or others. And even in these states, laws often impose stringent standards. For example, in Pennsylvania a "clear and present danger" is limited to the determination that "within the past 30 days the person has inflicted or attempted to inflict serious bodily harm on another or on himself" (Bonovitz and Guy, 1979:1045). This means that in these states the majority of persons whom psychiatrists would see as severely mentally ill (for example, persons who are so severely mentally disabled that they are unable to care for themselves) cannot be committed. As a consequence, many severely mentally ill individuals receive little or no treatment and are found in what Lamb (1979) has referred to as asylums in the community.

With so many severely mentally ill persons in

the community it is not surprising that a number of social control techniques have been developed to contain those who are seriously disturbed (e.g., see the chapter by Morrissey, 1982). Perhaps not surprisingly, jails and prisons appear again to have become places for housing the mentally ill (Gove, 1982).

The recent evidence on involuntary patients clearly suggests that the treatment they are receiving appears to be effective (Sata and Goldenberg, 1977; Gove and Fain, 1977). Although Scheff (1966) argued that the hospital would routinely accept voluntary patients, there is by now a substantial body of evidence that this is not the case (Rose et al., 1977; Feigelson et al., 1978; Morrissey et al., 1979), and on the average a voluntary applicant has about a 50% chance of being admitted. As Morrissey (1982) makes clear, with the recent tightening of procedures, some persons who would benefit from hospitalization apparently cannot get admitted. In summary, the issue of abuse of patient rights raised by the labelling theorists is now only rarely an issue. One should recognize that there usually is a disjunctor between statutes and practice, however, and the fact that psychiatrists now see the practiced institutional psychiatry as being under legal siege (Dietz, 1977; Gove, 1982) strongly suggests that by and large the intent of the law is being met.

Diagnosis

Townsend (1980) has argued that the reliability of psychiatric diagnosis is much lower than the diagnostic reliability in other fields of medicine (a point Spitzer (1976) shows is incorrect and for which he provides no evidence). On the basis of this assumption he argues that presumed low reliability of psychiatric diagnosis argues against the validity of the psychiatric explanation of mental illness. But Townsend does not take into account the fact that although detailed diagnostic categories were often unreliable, the broad categories (psychosis, neurosis, organic disorder, and personality disorder) were fairly reliably diagnosed. A more crucial issue, however, is that Townsend focused on the old diagnostic categories while the American Psychiatric As-

sociation (1980), after five years of effort protest, developed a new *Diagnostic and Statistical Manual of Mental Disorders* (DSM III). The initial work on the reliability of these diagnostic categories shows them to be more than adequate. For example, in the final field trial the Kappa coefficient measuring the reliability of diagnosis was .76 for the organic disorders, .83 for the affective disorders, and .81 for the schizophrenic disorders. (A Kappa of .7 or above is taken as indicating a high degree of reliability). The personality disorders are treated on a separate axis along with specific developmental disorders (American Psychiatric Association, 1980:471-472).

Regarding the present psychiatric conception of mental illness, two passages from the current diagnostic manual are worth quoting:

In DSM-III each of the mental disorders is conceptualized as a clinically significant behavioral or psychological syndrome or pattern that occurs in an individual and that is typically associated with either a painful symptom (distress) or impairment in one or more important areas of functioning (disability). In addition, there is an inference that there is a behavioral, psychological, or biological dysfunction, and that the disturbance is not only in the relationship between the individual and society. *(When the disturbance is limited to a conflict between an individual and society, this may represent social deviance, which may or may not be commendable, but is not by itself a mental disorder.)*

A common misconception is that a classification of mental disorders classifies individuals, when actually what are being classified are disorders that individuals have. For this reason, the text of DSM-III avoids the use of such phrases as "a schizophrenic" or "an alcoholic," and instead uses the more accurate, but admittedly more wordy "an individual with Schizophrenia" or "an individual with Alcohol Dependence" (American Psychiatric Association, 1980:6).

In short, psychiatric diagnosis now appears to have a satisfactory level of reliability. Furthermore, psychiatrists are aware that interpersonal conflicts are not necessarily a sign of mental disorder and they are sensitive to the issues involved in labelling individuals (American Psychiatric Association, 1980:6).

Individual Characteristics and Mental Illness

The relationships of a individual's characteristics to mental illness which I described earlier (Gove, 1970a, 1975a) continue to be supported.

1. Labelling theorists argue that there are no intrinsic differences between those labelled mentally ill and those not so labelled. However, the evidence for a genetic component of schizophrenia and the affective disorders continues to accumulate (e.g., Gershon et al., 1976; Reider and Gershon, 1978; Allen, 1976).

2. Evidence that persons labelled mentally ill differ from other persons is also provided by the fact that persons experiencing a number of changes in their lives are also likely to experience emotional difficulties, and evidence on this also continues to accumulate (e.g., Myers et al., 1975; Rabkin and Struening, 1976; Eaton, 1978; Tennant and Andrews, 1978; Kessler, 1979).

3. Labelling theorists argue that persons in the lower class tend to receive both less treatment and less effective treatment (i.e., organic treatment versus psychotherapy) than higher-status patients, and this is evidence of discrimination. The reason for this pattern of treatment, I contend, is that lower-class patients have much more severe disorders than upper-class patients and that organic treatment is more effective with severe forms of mental disorder (Gove, 1970a, 1975a). The tendency persists for persons in the lower-classes to see professional help as relevant to a much narrower range of problems, which also tend to be more severe, than do persons in the upper classes (Kulka et al., 1979; Stern, 1977).

4. Labelling theorists argue that persons in the lower class are more likely to become mental patients because of discrimination. It is my position (Gove,1970 a and b, 1975 a and b) that the reason lower-class patients have been more likely to receive psychiatric treatment is because they are more likely to be mentally ill. Since that time the finding that persons in the lower classes experience more emotional distress has

continued to be supported (Kulka et al., 1979; Derogatis et al., 1975; Gove and Geerken, 1977; Wheaton, 1978; Kessler and Cleary, 1980; and unreported data in the study described in Gove et al., 1979).

Miscellaneous Issues

In recent years the most popular empirical article that supports labelling theory has been Rosenhan's (1973) "On Being Sane in Insane Places." Labelling theorists have continued to cite it uncritically as an excellent demonstration of whatis wrong with the psychiatric mode. Although that article has received a number of devastating critiques, the being Spitzer's (1976), these critiques have been consistently ignored.

Many of the studies taken to support labelling theory have been shown to be methodologically flawed (see Gove, 1970b, 1975b; Gove and Fain, 1975). However, when labelling theorists have attempted to evaluate the overall evidence in support of labelling theory, these methodological flaws have consistently been ignored and these flawed studies have been taken as supporting the labelling position (e.g., Scheff, 1974,1975; Krohn and Akers, 1977; Conover, 1976; Lemert, 1976; Cullen and Cullen, 1978).

Labelling theorists present a very simplistic and inadequate image of the psychiatric model (Akers, 1977; Scheff, 1974). As Akers (1977) notes, the model they present has been derived from comments made by critics of the medical-psychiatric model. Because considerable attention has been devoted by psychiatrists to clarifying the models they use (e.g., Klerman, 1977; Osmond and Seigler, 1974), one wonders why labelling theorists have not attempted to evaluate the model presented by psychiatrists instead of the straw man presented by psychiatry's critics.

Psychiatry incorporates into its model the idea that social factors play a role both in the etiology and delivery of treatment, and, as I have indicated elsewhere, existing evidence is often consistent with both the labelling and psychiatric explanations of mental illness. Labelling theory, however, tends to apply a double standard when interpreting the implications of societal factors. For example, Lemert (1976) and Tucker (1974) have argued that the data reported in Mendel and Rapport (1969) strongly support labelling theory, but in fact they are open to dual interpretations. Mendel and Rapport studied the factors involved in the decision to admit applicants for psychiatric hospitalization. They found that the hospital studied admitted only 41% of the applicants, but that social factors played a role in the decision to admit. In particular, they found that the hospitalization was strongly associated with a lack of alternative resources, with application for admission at night or on the weekend, and to previous hospitalization; it was weakly related to lack of experience on the part of the decision maker. A psychiatrist would not be surprised that applicants are more likely to be hospitalized if (1) they have few if any alternative to hospitalization, (2) they apply for admission at a time when alternative treatment sources are not available, (3) they have a prolonged history of mental illness, and (4) they have been screened by someone who is inexperienced and cautious (and who is also apt to be working at night or weekends). In fact, from the perspective of medical sociology, the finding that such contingencies affect the treatment of physical disorders would be entirely consistent with what is known about medicine. Krohn and Akers (1977) take a position similar to that of Lemert (1976) and Tucker (1974). In their review article Krohn and Akers (1977:356) state " the findings that extra-psychiatric criteria intrude into psychiatric decisions indicate that the identification of individuals as mentally ill is more control than therapy," while they pay no attention to the nature or type of relationship of these extra-psychiatric factors that affect psychiatric treatment.

In short labelling theorists are prone to assume that societal or other contingencies are ipso facto evidence for labelling theory. The unwillingness of labelling theorists to consider alternative interpretations of the nonpsychiatric contingencies found in these studies helps explain why labelling theory continues to be the dominant perspective among most sociologists who study mental illness.

Conclusion

The evidence reviewed in this paper shows that in the past decade there have been a number of changes in the practice of psychiatry. Furthermore, the literature shows that labelling theory does not provide an adequate general explanation of mental illness. The evidence is now much more substantial than it was a decade ago.

References

Akers, Ronald 1977. Deviant Behavior. Belmont, Calif.: Wadsworth.

Allen, M. 1976. "Twin studies of affective illness." Archives of General Psychiatry 33:1476-1489.

American Psychiatric Association 1980. Diagnostic and Statistical Manual of Mental Disorders (3rd ed.) Washington, D.C.: American Psychiatric Association.

Askanasy, A. 1974. Attitudes Toward Mental Patients: A Study Across Cultures. The Hague, Holland: Mouton.

Berger, P. 1978. "Medical treatment of mental illness: Psychopharmacological therapeutics revolutionize psychiatric care and present scientific and ethical challenges to society." Science 200:974-981.

Bergin, A., and M. Lemert 1980. "The evolution of therapeutic outcomes." In A. Bergin and S. Garfield (eds.), Handbook of Psychotherapy and Behavior Change: An Empirical Analysis. New York: Wiley.

Bonovitz, Jennifer, and Edward Guy 1979. "Impact of restrictive civil commitment procedures on a prison psychiatric service." American Journal of Psychiatry (August): 1045-1048

Chin-Shong, E. 1969. Rejection of the mentally ill: The effects of personal ties versus perception of danger. Paper presented at the annual meeting of the American Sociological Association, San Francisco, September.

Conover, P. 1976. "A reassessment of labelling theory in constructive response to criticism." Pp. 228-243 in L. Coser and O. Larson (eds.), the Uses of Controversy in Sociology. New York: Free Press.

Coye, Janet, and David Clifford 1978. "A one-year report on rights violation under Michigan's New Protection System." Hospital and Community Psychiatry 22:528-533.

Crane, Lansing, Howard Zonana, and Stephen Wiser 1977. "Implications of the Donaldson Decision: A model for periodic review of committed patients." Hospital and Community Psychiatry 28:827-833.

Cullen, Frances, and John Cullen 1978. Toward a Paradigm of Labelling Theory. Lincoln: University of

Nebraska Press.

Davis, John 1975. "Overview: Maintenance therapy in psychiatry: I. Schizophrenia." American Journal of Psychiatry 132:1237-1245.

Derogatis, Leonard, Harriet Yerzeroff, and Bridget Wittelcheng 1975. "Social class, psychological disorder and the nature of the psychopathic indicator." Journal of consulting and Clinical Psychiatry 44:183-191.

Feigelson, E., E. Davis, R. Mackinnon, H. Shands, and C. Schwartz 1978. "The decision to hospitalize." American Journal of Psychiatry 35:354-357

Frank, Jerome 1974. "Psychotherapy and the restoration of morale." American Journal of Psychiatry 131:271-274

Freeman, H., and O. Simmons 1961. "Feelings of stigma among relatives of former mental patients." Social Problems 8:312-331

Gershon, E., W. Bunney, and J. Leckman 1976. "The inheritance of affective disorders: A review of the data and hypotheses." Behavioral Genetics 6:227-261.

Gove, Walter 1970a. "Societal reactions as an explanation of mental illness: An evaluation." American Sociological Review 35:873-884.

-----. 1970b. " Who is hospitalized: A critical evaluation of some sociological studies of mental illness." Journal of Health and Social Behavior 11:294-303

----- 1975a "Labelling and mental illness: A critique." Pp. 42-48 in Walter R. Gove (ed.), The Labelling of Deviance. New York: Sage/Halstead.

----- 1975b "The labelling theory of mental illness: A reply to Scheff." American Sociological Review 40:242-248.

----- 1979. "The labelling versus the psychiatric explanation of mental illness: A debate that has become substantively irrelevant (reply to comment by Horwitz)." Journal of Health and Social behavior 29:301-304.

----- 1982. "The current status of the labelling theory of mental illness." In Walter Gove (ed.), Deviance and Mental Illness. New York: Sage.

Gove, Walter, and Terry Fain 1973. "The stigma of mental hospitalization: An attempt to evaluate its consequences." Archives of General Psychiatry 28 (April): 494-500.

----- 1975. "The length of psychiatric hospitalization." Social Problems 22:407-418.

----- 1977. "A comparison of voluntary and committed psychiatric patients." Archives of General Psychiatry 34:669-676.

Gove, Walter, and Michael Geerken 1977. "Response bias in surveys of mental health: An empirical evaluation." American Journal of Sociology 82:1289-1317.

Gove, Walter, Michael Hughes, and Omer Galle 1979. "Overcrowding in the home: An empirical analysis." American Sociological Review 44 (February):57-81.

Gove, Walter, Michael Hughes, and Maurizia Tovo 1982. Involuntary Hospitalization of the Mentally Ill: A Systematic Review of the Laws in the 50 states. Paper presented at the annual meeting of the southern Sociological Association, April, Memphis.

Hansell, Norris 1978. "Services for schizophrenics: A lifelong approach to treatment." Hospital and Community Psychiatry 29:105-109.

Horwitz, Allen 1979. "Models, modules and mental illness labelling." Journal of Health and Social Behavior 20:296-300.

Huffine, Carol, and John Clausen 1979. "Madness and work: Short and long term effects of mental illness on occupational careers." Social Forces 57:1049-1063.

Kaufman, Edward 1979. "The right to treatment suit as an agent of change." American Journal of Psychiatry 136 (November):1428-1432.

Kerlins, Miriam, and Marilyn Knudsen 1976. "State hospital review boards in Minnesota." Hospital and Community Psychiatry 27:641-643.

Kessler, Ronald 1979. "Stress, social strains and psychological distress." Journal of Health and Social Behavior 20:259-272.

Kessler, Ronald, and Paul Cleary 1980. "Social class and psychological distress." American Sociological Review 45:463-478.

Klerman, Gerald L. 1977. "Mental illness, the medical model and psychiatry." Journal of Medicine and Philosophy 2:220-243.

Klerman, Gerald L., and Gail Schecter 1981. "The impact of psychopharmacology on the Mental Health Service System." In Walter Gove and Russell Carpenter (eds.), Nature and Nurture: The Fundamental connection. Lexington: Lexington Books.

Kreisman, Dolores E., and Virginia D. Joy 1974. "Family response to mental illness of a relative: A review of the literature." Schizophrenia Bulletin 10:34-57.

Krohn, Marvin, and Ronald Akers 1977. "Alternative view of the labelling versus the psychiatric perspectives to mental illness." Social Forces 56:341-361.

Kulka, Richard A., Joseph Veroff, and Elizabeth Douvan 1979. "Social class and the use of professional help for personal problems: 1957 and 1976." Journal of Health and Social Behavior 20:2-17.

Kumasaka, Yorihiko, Janet Stokes, and Raj Gupta 1972. "Criteria for involuntary hospitalization." Archives of General Psychiatry 20:359-404.

Lamb, H. Richard 1979. "The new asylums in the community." Archives of General Psychiatry 36:129-134.

Lemert, Edwin 1976. "Response to critics, feedback and choice." Pp. 244-249 in Lewis Coser and Otto Larson (eds.), The Uses of Controversy in Sociology. New York: Macmillan.

Macht, L.B. 1978. "Commissioner: A special clinical executive." Psychiatric Opinion 15:1133-1135.

McCrainie, Edward, and Terrence Mizell 1978. "After care for psychiatric patients: Does it prevent rehospitalization?" Hospital and Community Psychiatry 29:584-587.

Meile, Richard, and Hugh Whitt 1981. "Cultural consensus and definition of mental illness." Social Science and Medicine 15A:231-242.

Mendel, Werner, and Samuel Rapport 1969. "Determinants of the decision for psychiatric hospitalization." Archives of general Psychiatry 20 (March):321-328.

Meyer, Nessa 1974. "Legal status of inpatient admissions to state and county mental hospitals, United States, 1972." Statistical Note 105, National Institute of Mental Health, Division Biometry, surveys and Reports Branch. Rockville, Md.: NIMH.

Morrissey, J. 1979. "Keeping patients out: Organization and policy implications of emergent state hospital deinstitutionalizating practices." Paper presented at the annual meeting of the Southern Sociological Society, Atlanta, April.

----- 1982. "Deinstitutionalizing the mentally ill: Process, outcomes and new directions." In Walter Gove (ed.), Deviance and Mental Illness. New York: Sage.

Morrissey, J., R. Tessler, and L. Farrin 1979. "Being seen but not admitted: A note on some neglected aspects of state hospital deinstitutionalization." American Journal of Orthopsychiatry 49:153-156.

Mosher, Loren, and Samuel Keith 1979. "research on the psychosocial treatment of schizophrenia: A summary report." American Journal of Psychiatry 136:623-631.

Myers, J., J. Lindenthal, and Max Pepper 1975. "Life events, social integration and psychiatric symptomology." Journal of Health and Social Behavior 16:421-427.

Olmstead, D., and K. Durham 1976 "Stability of mental health attitudes: A semantic differential study." Journal of Health and Social Behavior 17:35-44.

Olshansky, S., S. Brob, and M. K. Dahl 1960. "Survey of employment experiences of patients discharged from three state mental hospitals during the period 1951-1953." Mental Hygiene 44:510-521.

Osmond, Miriam, and Humphry Seigler 1974.

Models of Madness, Models of Medicine. New York: Macmillan.

Rabkin, J. 1974. "Public attitudes toward mental illness: A review of the literature." Schizophrenia Bulletin 19:9-23.

----- 1979. "who is called mentally ill: Public and professional views." Journal of Community Psychiatry 7:253-258.

Rabkin, J., and E. Struening 1976. "Life events, stress and illness." Science 194:1013-1020.

Regier, D., I. D. Goldberg, and C. A. Taube 1978. "The de facto U.S. mental health service: A public health perspective." Archives of General Psychiatry 35:685-693.

Reider, Ronald, and Elliot Gershon 1978. "Genetic strategies in biological psychiatry." Archives of General Psychiatry 35:866-873.

Rose, S., J. Hawkins, and L. Apodaca 1977. "Decision to admit: Criteria for admission and readmission to Veteran's Administration Hospital." Archives of General Psychiatry 34:418-421.

Rosenhan, David 1973. "On being sane in insane places." Science 179:250-258.

Rushing, William 1978. "Status resources, societal reactions and type of mental hospitalization." American Sociological Review 43 (August):521-533.

Sata, L., and E. Goldenberg 1977. "a study of involuntary patients in Seattle." Hospital and Community Psychiatry 27:834-840.

Scheff, Thomas 1966. being Mentally Ill. Chicago: AVC.

----- 1975. "Reply to Clancey and Gove." American Sociological Review 40:252-257.

----- 1979. "Reply to comment by Horwitz." Journal of Health and Social Behavior 20:305.

Schwartz, C., J. Myers, and G. Astrachan

Smith, M., and G. Glass 1977. "Meta-analysis of psychotherapy outcome studies." American Psychologist 31:752-760.

Spitzer, robert 1976. "Move on pseudoscience in science and the case for psychiatric diagnosis." Archives of General Psychiatry 33:459-470.

Steadman, Henry 1979. Beating a Rap? Defendants found Incompetent to Stand Trial. Chicago: University of Chicago Press.

Stern, Maxine 1977. "Social class and psychiatric treatment of adults in the mental health center." Journal of Health and Social Behavior 18:317-325.

Strupp, Hans H., Suzanne W. Hadley, and Beverly Gomes-Schwartz 1977. Psychotherapy for Better or worse: the Problem of Negative Effects. New York: Jascon J. Aronson.

Tennant, Christopher, and Gavin Andrews 1978. "The pathogenic quality of life event stress in neurotic impairment." Archives of General Psychiatry 35:859-863.

Townsend, J. Marshall 1976. "Self concept and the institutionalization of mental patients: An overview and critique." Journal of Health and social Behavior 17:263-271.

----- 1980. "Psychiatry versus societal reaction: A critical analysis." Journal of Health and Social Behavior 21 (September):268-278.

Trute, B., and A. Loewen 1978. "Public attitude toward the mentally ill as a function of prior personal experience." Social Psychiatry 13:79-84.

Tucker, charles 1974. Personal communication.

Urmer, A. H. 1978. "An assessment of California's mental health program: Implications for mental health delivery systems." Pp 137-152 in C. J. Fredrich (ed.), Dangerous Behavior: A Problem in Law and Mental Health. Rockville, Md.: Center for Studies of Crime and Delinquency, National Institute for Mental Health.

Weinstein, Raymond 1979 "Patient attitudes toward mental hospitalization: A review of quantitative research." Journal of Health and Social Behavior 20:232-258.

----- 1982. "The mental hospital from the patient's view: qualitative vs. quantitative data." In Walter Gove (ed.), Deviance and Mental Illness. New York: Sage.

Wheaton, Blair 1978. "The sociogenesis of psychological disorder: Reexamining the causal issues with longitudinal data." American Sociological Review 43:383-403.

Whitt, Hugh, Richard Meile, and Louann Lavson 1979. "Illness role theory, the labelling perspective and the social meanings of mental illness: An empirical test." Social Science and Medicine 13A:655-666.

Winston, Arnold, Herbert Pardes, Daniel Papernik, and Linda Breslin 1977. "After care of psychiatric patients and its relation to rehospitalization." Hospital and Community Psychiatry 28:118-121.

Witkin, Michael 1980. Trends in Patient Care Episodes in Mental Health Facilities 1966-1977. Mental Health Statistical Note No. 154. national Institute of Mental Health. Rockville, Md.: NIMH.

"Mixed Nutters" and "Looney Tuners:" The Emergence, Development, Nature, and Functions of Two Informal, Deviant Subcultures of Chronic, Ex-Psychiatric Patients

Nancy J. Herman

This study systematically examines the rise and nature of two subcultures of discharged, chronic psychiatric patients, and the various positive and negative functions such subcultural formations serve for their members. Participant observation and informal interviewing over a three year period with ninety-seven chronic ex-psychiatric patients provides an ethnographic description of the structural and interactional factors giving rise to the development of, nature of, and consequences of participation in, an informal deviant subculture. The data analysis reveals that, although relatively new, the ex-mental patient subcultures have a clearly-defined set of norms and values, crystallized patterns of behaviour, sharply-defined boundaries within which to carry out their activities, a distinctive vocabulary or argot through which ex-patients communicate to one another, and an ideology or world-view, a set of ideas developed to suit their own interests and justify their behaviours. The ex-psychiatric patient subcultures serve a six-fold function for their members: they provide them with social support, they serve a cathartic function, aid members in dealing with the stigma potential of their "differentness" or "failing", furnish ex-patients with "sound" reasons regarding their deviant attribute, thereby enhancing their self-esteem, provide members with practical stratagems for "making it on the outside", and furnish ex-patients with a self-justifying rationale for engaging in various deviant/illegal acts. The negative consequences of participation in such subcultural forms are also addressed.[1]

Introduction

In the sociological literature on deviant subcultures, much attention has been devoted to the drug subculture (Burr, 1984; Johnson, 1980; Lipton and Johnson, 1980; Ray, 1961), the gay subculture (Humphreys and Miller, 1980; Partridge, 1972), the motorcycle gang subculture (Hooper and Moore, 1980), the delinquent subculture (Cohen, 1979; Demotte, 1984; Yablonsky, 1959), the skid row subculture (Rubington, 1968; Wallace, 1965), the inmate subculture (Webb, 1984); religious subcultures (Lofland, 1966; Melville, 1972), and even the suicide subculture (Platt, 1981) among others.

Despite the preponderance of sociological research on such diverse, deviant groups, and the concomitant theoretical approaches[2] used to explain such phenomena little if any use has been made of such works in the examination of discharged/deinstitutionalized psychiatric patients.[3] Over the past twenty-five years, with the movement toward deinstitutionalization and development of community psychiatry, there has been a marked shift away from the hospital to the community.[4] As a result of the movement toward deinstitutionalization, hundreds of thousands of persons once institutionalized for long periods of time in mental hospitals in the United States, Canada and Great Britain, have been released into the community. Moreover, with this shift in policy and treatment of the mentally ill, newly-diagnosed or defined psychiatric patients, are no longer being sent directly to the government or state institutions, but rather, are being treated primarily on an out-patient basis in community mental health centres or are admitted on a short-term basis to psychiatric wards in general hospital facilities, and are only admitted to mental institutions or "tertiary care facilities" as a last resort.

Since the advent of the movement toward deinstitutionalization and development of community psychiatry, abounding in the literature are studies examining its ideological foundations, background philosophies, treatment programmes, and the medical and psychological consequences of such treatment and aftercare programmes for the ex-psychiatric patients.[5] Although a multitude of research studies exist on various aspects of the deinstitutionalization phenomenon and development of community psychiatry, the majority of such works have been conducted from an objectivist standpoint largely employing medical, psychiatric, psychological or social work models, with only a dearth of ethnographically-based research (Cheadle et al., 1978; Dear et al., 1980; Estroff, 1981; Reynolds and Farberow, 1977) focusing on the effects of deinstitutionalization/discharge from the perspectives of the ex-patients themselves. Moreover, no published work has been located documenting the origins and development of an informal deviant subculture of chronic[6] ex-psychiatric patients.

It is the purpose of this paper then, to explore the effects of deinstitutionalization from the perspectives of chronic discharged psychiatric patients, individuals who are directly affected by this shift in treatment, housing and policies. Adopting a symbolic interactionist perspective, this study seeks to discover the social meanings that the ex-patients define and determine to be important and real. Specifically, this paper examines the ex-patient sub-culture[7] -- one major organizational adaptive response former chronic ex-patients develop and utilize to deal with their "deviantness", the structural and interactional factors giving rise to this formation, its characteristic traits, and the functions it serves for its members.

The Effects of Deinstitutionalization on Chronic Ex-Psychiatric Patients: The Stigma of Mental Illness, Deviant Identities and Adaptive Responses

In other papers, this author (Herman, 1986a, 1986b, 1986c) systematically examined the post-hospital social worlds of 285 non-chronic[8] and chronic ex-psychiatric patients. Specifically, this research examined the relationship among the concepts of stigma, deviant identities, stigma management strategies/adaptive responses, and identity transformation as they related to non-chronic and chronic cases. The data indicated that, in the case of the former group, namely, the non-chronics, upon discharge, such persons actively sought to return to a life of normality. Such persons conceived of their acquired deviant identities as "temporary fixtures", a perception of self influenced not only by the nature, duration and type of psychiatric label bestowed on them, and the minimal numbers and dosages of medications they were taking. Moreover, the data suggested that non-chronic ex-patients employed five major "offensive"strategems or adaptive responses to mitigate the stigma potential of mental illness on their daily rounds: selective concealment, preventive telling, therapeutic telling, normalization and political activism-- strategies having positive implications for identity transformation. By contrast, in the case of the latter group, the chronics, the data indicated that, such persons, upon completion of their hospitalization, made little or no attempt to return to a life of normality. Given that such persons had been hospitalized for a number of years,[9] or on a multitude of occasions,[10] they had fully internalized the role of mental patient and its corresponding status. Such a perception of self as possessing a permanent deviant identity was reinforced by the types of deviant labels bestowed on them while institutionalized, the numbers and dosages of medications they were receiving (and their associated side-effects), and the "disability" cheques they were receiving. In contrast to many non-chronics in the research, who received positive support from family and friends, most chronics interviewed were stigmatized by such persons. The only social ties chronic ex-patients had were with one or two other ex-patients. In an attempt to avoid further or potential stigma from others, such persons adopted the following "defensive" strategems or adaptive responses: "institutional retreatism", "societal retreatism", capitulation and passing-- strategies having negative implications for identity transformation. Just as the chronic ex-patients made use of the above individualized stigma management. It is this stratagem or organizational adaptive response[11] to which this paper will now turn.

Methodology, Sample and Settings

Data were collected from December, 1981 to June, 1984 by means of participant observation and informal interviewing with ninety-seven chronic ex-psychiatric patients living in two cities in Southern Ontario, Canada.

As part of a larger, ongoing study, the researcher initially obtained a disproportionate, stratified random sample[12] of two hundred and eighty-five chronic and non-chronic ex-psychiatric patients living in eight communities in Southern Ontario. Through semi-formal and informal interviewing with the respondents, this researcher came upon, quite by accident, the discovery of two informal ex-psychiatric patient subcultures, referred to here as the "Mixed Nutters" and "Looney Tuners".

In terms of the former, this cultural formation is comprised of forty-nine members (thirty-six males and thirteen females) living in rooming houses, boarding homes and cheap hotels in the southwest section of a large metropolitan city of 2.5 million. Subjects ranged in age from twenty-one to forty-two years of age, were predominantly from working-class backgrounds and were poorly-educated with a mean level of educational attainment being grade seven.

In terms of the latter group, this subculture is comprised of forty-eight members (twenty-six males and twenty-two females) living in boarding homes, rooming houses, in missions, or simply on the streets in the northern section of a smaller of 300,000 in Southern Ontario. Similar to the Mixed Nutters, the Looney Tuners were also poorly-educated with a mean level of educational attainment being grade eight, were from working and middle-class backgrounds and ranged in age from twenty-two to forty-five.

The Emergence of Two Informal Ex-Psychiatric Patient Subcultures

Early subcultural theorists (Gans, 1962; Gillen, 1955; Lewis, 1961) contended that deviant subcultures emerge largely in response to particular problems or social situations. Speaking on the sub-culture of poverty, Lewis (1961:27) argues that:

> Many of the traits of the subculture of poverty can be viewed as attempts at local solutions for problems not met by existing institutions and agencies because the people are not eligible for them, cannot afford them, or are suspicious of them.

In a similar vein, Gans (1962:248) argues:

> Each subculture is an organized set of related responses that has developed out of people's efforts to cope with the opportunities, incentives, and rewards, as well as the deprivations, prohibitions, and pressures which the natural environment and society--that complex of coexisting and competing subcultures--offer to them.

Reacting against this primary emphasis on response to the neglect or secondary role of interaction as having importance for the development of subcultures, other theorists (Becker, 1963; Cohen, 1955: Hughes, 1961; Shibutani, 1955; and Wallace, 1965), proposed an alternative explanation that places equal importance on both factors for subcultural development. Wallace (1965:149); speaking on the emergence of the skid row subculture, for example, states:

> One effect of the self and community imposed isolation [of skid row persons] has been the emergence of skid row subculture. Skid rowers share similar problems of adjustment to their deviance and are in effective interaction with one another.

Cohen (1955), in his systematic attempt to develop a theory of subcultures, states that the following conditions are important in the development of this cultural form: (1) experiencing a problem or set of problems; (2) communicating such problems to others facing the same problems; (3) effectively interacting over an extended period of time with like others on the basis of such problems; and (4) developing solutions to these common problems.

In the case of the Mixed Nutters and Looney Tuners, the data suggest that these ex-psychiatric patient subcultures emerged in 1978 and 1980 respectively.[13] Prior to their formation, chronic ex-psychiatric patients were experiencing a number of post-hospital problems. These problems included: the stigma of mental illness, social isolation, poverty, exploitation, and coping. Speaking on the problems of isolation and poverty, a male ex-patient states:

> It's been the shits ever since I got out [of the hospital]. They plunk you in this here town...you're all alone with no friends in the world, and you get this disability cheque every month most of which goes for rent. You hardly get enough left over to buy a cup of coffee or smokes.

Another ex-patient, speaking of the stigma of mental illness and problems of exploitation says:

> Since I was let out, I've had nothing but heartache. Having mental illness is like having the Black Plague. People who know me have abandoned me--my family and friends. And the people who find out that I was in the mental centre...treat me the same way...And at the boarding home where I was placed, I hardly get enough to eat. For lunch and supper today, all we got was a half a sardine sandwich and a cup of coffee, and they take three-hundred and fifty dollars a month for that kind of meals and lousy, overcrowded, bug-infested rooms to live in.

The ex-psychiatric patient subcultures came into being when the individuals began communicating with one another and realizing that they had a number of problems in common, they shared a common fate of being "in the same boat". speaking on his discovery of others experiencing the same in the community, an ex-patient says:

It was really by accident that I came to realize that I wasn't the only one out there with these horrid problems. For the longest time, I just kept it inside, but then one day when I was so down in the dumps, so low, that I opened up to "Cliff", this patient I met in the park, and we started talking. I took a chance and opened up, and to my surprise, I found that he was also going through the same problems.

Analysis of the data indicates that, subsequent to this initial communication of their problem(s) with others, individuals began interacting with one another over an extended period of time on the basis of their newly-discovered shared fate:

> The four of us girls came clean with each other in October. I mean that this day outside the drop-in centre we opened up and told our true feelings about some of the problems we faced every day since being discharged...From that time on, us girls, and later more people, made a pact to meet every Tuesday and Thursday outside "Lacey's" Department Store where we'd gab and bitch, and just plain listen to each other's problems.

Out of this semi-regular interaction with others of their own kind, chronic ex-psychiatric patients attempt to develop solutionss to the various problems they are collectively experiencing. Speaking of their initial efforts to come up with solution to the problems of the stigma of mental illness, two middle-aged males state:

> At first, we thought that we should buy a gun, load it, and blast anyone who reacted meanly to us because of our sickness. But we knew that we'd only wind up in jail. We also thought about suicide as an answer to our problem, but that's the coward's way out. So we kept thinking and thinking until we figured out something less drastic!

In a similar vein, three young males, discussing their attempts to develop solutions to the problem of poverty, remark:

> We wanted to rob a Brink's truck or some big department store but that would be too risky. We were just tossing around ideas trying to come up with some solution to give us some cash. Eventually, we came up with a better and easier way to make a buck that is a lot less risky, by selling our meds to guys on the streets.

In short then, the data analysis reveals that certain interactional and structural factors contribute to the rise of the ex-mental patient subculture. This subcultural formation arises essentially in response to the various problems and negative post-hospital situations collectively faced by a number of chronic ex-patients, insofar as they are able to effectively communicate and interact with one another over an extended period of time. Given that, upon discharge, these ex-psychiatric patients are "placed" in rooming houses, boarding homes and "approved homes" in specific geographical sections of the city, such concentrated placement in specific neighbourhoods increases the probability of social interaction among ex-patients. When ex-psychiatric patients have the opportunity to interact with one another, they are likely to develop a subculture to deal with such specific problems as poverty, exploitation, stigma, social isolation, and in general, with problems developing out of the discrepancies between their personal perceptions of mental illness and mental patients, and the stereotypical perceptions held by society.

The Social Characteristics of The Mixed Nutters and Looney Tuners

As noted earlier, chronic ex-psychiatric patients have one thing in common: Their deviant attribute (and the problems associated with it). Such things give chronic ex-patients a sense of a common fate. It is from this feeling of a shared fate that the Mixed Nutters and Looney Tuners have developed subcultures consisting of: a set

of perspectives or world-view about the nature of society, its members, and how to deal with them, and a body of activities based on this world-view, some of which are specifically centred on providing solutions to the problems associated with the attribute of mental illness. These deviant subcultures possess five major characteristics to which attention will now turn.

1. Behavioral Patterns

The ex-mental patient subculture centres its attention, interests and activities around their deviant attribute, and the problems associated with it. Specifically, the Mixed Nutters and Looney Tuners participate in three major activities referred to by the subjects as: (1) "Hanging Around"; (2) "Shrink Sessions"; and (3) "Schooling". The data indicate that a major portion of the chronic ex-patient's day is devoted to "hanging around" with a few other ex-patients, usually at a specified location such as a park, shopping centre, street corner, donut shop or hospital canteen:

> Every day, after I get kicked out of the boarding home, I go up town to a bench in front of "Meadville" Shopping Centre and meet a few of the "boys". We're "regulars" you might say. We usually hang around four or five hours watching the people go by, cracking jokes, and rolling our smokes. The day goes by quick when you got someone to share it with.

Similarly, another ex-patient, discussing the activity of "hanging around" remarks:

> There's three, four or sometimes even six of us that meet every day. It's not always the same crowd though. Each day, different faces show up at the "Delicious" Donut Shop...It's our second home and that's why we do our hanging around there. We scrape up our money and drink coffee until we got no more left and Gus, the owner "invites" us to leave.

In order to be allowed to "hang around" in such locations as donut shops or hospital canteens, it is a prerequisite that ex-patients purchase (and continue to purchase) food and/or drink. For those ex-patients unable to purchase items on their own, other group members make contributions, thus enabling them to remain with the others:

> When people don't have enough money to pay for a cup of coffee, or a donut, we chip in to make up the difference. I may give a nickel, another guy may give two cents, but little by little, it all adds up. We give whatever we got. And I know that if I am short of cash next week that the guys would do the same for me!

The activity of "hanging around" or being in the company of other ex-psychiatric patients serves to combat feelings of alienation, social isolation and fear experienced by such persons. As one middle-aged male put it:

> We don't really do anything constructive when hanging around on Elm Street; I mean, we don't have intellectual debates about Reagan or Russia, but meeting with people at a certain place every day and having them just sit next to me helps me not to feel so alone in the world.

Similarly, a second chronic ex-patient adds:

> When we're together, it really boosts me up! We support each other. I feel comfortable with them and they really care about what happens in my life. That makes all the difference in the world. They're my friends.

A second major activity in which chronic ex-psychiatric patients engage are "Shrink Sessions". Shrink sessions or primitive, informal self-help meetings, usually occur (in the case of the Mixed Nutters) at the hospital canteen where ex-patients frequent or at a drop-in centre for discharged patients (in the case of the Looney Tuners). Such meetings vary in duration from a half an hour up to three hours with members coming and going throughout. The data indicate that the sessions begin when an individual initiates the topic of conversation and petitions others for advice. During these sessions, members of the subculture complain about such problems as anxiety, stress, depression and poor follow-up care by psychiatric professionals. So too, do ex-patients frequently complain about the stigma of mental illness on their daily rounds--complaints or concerns to which other ex-patient "experts" supportively respond. Speaking of post-hospital anxiety and stress in his life and the helpful suggestions proposed by the group, one chronic male remarks:

> When we sit down and start "shrinking" each other, I sometimes talk about how tense and nervous I get being out [discharged]. Everything is moving at such a fast pace that it freaks me out. There's too much stress for me...When I talked about it to the other guys, it felt so good to let it all out, and the guys really helped me get a handle on it...They really know about these things, because, after all, they've been through it themselves a hundred times before.

Another ex-patient, speaking of airing, to the group, the problems he was experiencing with stigma, states:

> One day, I brought up the fact that we've all got the mark of Cain on us because of our sickness. I poured my guts out about how my wife and even my parents turned away from me, and how no one wants anything to do with me now...Talking about it made me feel better. They hammered into me the idea that having mental illness isn't nothing to be ashamed of. They made me think more highly of myself, and they showed me how to avoid people who are bigoted about mental illness!

These "shrink sessions" then, serve a three-fold function for the ex-psychiatric patients: disclosure of concerns and complaints in a cathartic fashion, serves to alleviate a portion of the burden of their loads; ex-patients are given social support and helpful suggestions to deal with various problems; and they are presented with an ideology and positive self-image of ex-psychiatric patient that refutes stereotypical beliefs about mental patients held by conventional society, thereby elevating their self-esteem.

Just as chronic ex-psychiatric patients frequently engage in the activities of "hanging around" and "shrink sessions", so too do they participate in one other activity referred to by the subjects as "schooling". Schooling involves ex-patients teaching each other various methods for "making it on the outside" or how to capitalize[14] on their deviant identities. By making it on the outside, ex-patients, through informal interaction with other subcultural members, learn how to make the most of their deviant identities. They are taught such things as where, how, and when they can pick up "quick cash", "free eats", and where to get a "free place to crash". So, for example, the neophyte entering the ex-patient subculture is taught that he/she can pick up "quick cash" by: selling their "meds" for money, and selling their bodies (not only where to sell these commodities, but for how much), and a set of rationalizations justifying such actions:

> When I first started hanging around with those guys, they showed me the ropes. I was pretty green about things, and I never had any money. But they told me that if I ran short of bucks, I could pick up an extra twenty or fifty by selling my meds. They even pointed out this group of young guys who would be willing to but the stuff.

A female chronic ex-patient adds:

> I sell my "wares" when I need to. I'm not a prostitute, don't get me wrong. But when I need money for cigarettes, something important, then I don't mind doing it once in a while. The other patients I know do it too. Kerry and Jean were the ones who taught me to do it and how

much to charge...I make five or ten bucks a shot.

Moreover, in the context of the ex-patient subculture, members learn which religious and social agencies give "hand-outs"--where such agencies are located, how much they may give, and how to approach them:

> Dave and Bill took me to this agency that gives out hand-outs. There's one church down the street. If you ask for the pastor, and tell them this heart-sob story that you've practised before-hand, he's usually good for ten bucks. Then there's the welfare people, and this other community service place. The other guys taught me when's the best time to hit these places, the story to give them which makes things go a lot smoother.

Another chronic ex-patient, discussing the skills and knowledge about various agencies she acquired through interaction with others in the subculture, remarks:

> If is wasn't for my friends, I would be out in the cold. I wouldn't know nothing about where to get a hand-out when I really needed it. They took me by the hand when I met them and pointed out each and every one of them in the area, and not only that, they teached me to dress poorly, muss up my hair and cry a lot when I went to them.

Further, ex-patients learn through participation in their subculture, which agencies, missions and restaurants provide such things as free food, clothing and shelter:

> At first, I didn't know nothing. But my friends taught me where I could get free food whenever I wanted it, like down at the "Lakeside Mission". You gotta put up with their praying and singing, but that's O.K. They also showed me where to go to this church if I needed new

threads and some lady will give you whatever you want.

Speaking on his major source of free food from one fast-food restaurant, a middle-aged male says:

> Moe was the one who wised me up about these free eats from "Burger Town". A couple of times the manager caught us snatching left-overs from the garbage and we told him how hungry we were and really laid it on thick to him. He felt sorry for us, I guess, so he told me to come back near closing and we get a lot of the hamburgs and fries that they don't sell.

Through participation in the Mixed Nutters and Looney Tuners, persons not only learn the "in's and out's" of the system and how to use it to their advantage, but also learn how to capitalize on their deviant identities by becoming "professional crazies":

> I learned that if I want to make some real money, I just have to act pitiful an a certain street where lots of people go by, and hold out my hand and say, "I need money to help with my treatment. I have mental problems. Please help me". Sometimes, I get booed, sometimes I get a quarter. Sometimes, a businessman will throw a dollar or two. On a good day, in a good location, I can make twenty bucks.

A second ex-patient, speaking on the capitalization of his deviant identity says:

> I usually go down the subway at rush hour and act all confused, saying that I'm sick and I'm trying to get back to the hospital but I have no money. Usually someone will give the money to buy a token, but I just pocket the money and start the act all over again. Last night, I made six bucks...This is the one time

when being mental works to my advantage!

In short then, these three behavioral patterns serve to combat the social isolation ex-patients are experiencing, provide a therapeutic function, enhance their self-esteem, provide pragmatic solutions to various problems, and equip ex-patients with important knowledge and skills for "making it on the outside".

2. Subcultural Norms

All cultures and subcultures, for that matter, develop norms, and the ex-psychiatric patient subcultures are no exceptions. In contrast to some subcultures, such as religious sects (Lofland, 1966) and prison inmates (Irwin, 1970) which have fairly elaborate sets of subcultural rules, the ex-mental patient subculture, by contrast, has established a rather simple code specifying beliefs and actions. One such set of norms centres upon the activity of "hanging around". So, for example, in the contest of this activity, ex-patients make and adhere to, rules requiring all participants to share their tobacco, contribute money to buy others' coffee if they are unable to buy it for themselves, and to reciprocate generosity. As one male ex-patient put it:

> When us guys meet at the donut shop, it's expected that if a guy has a whole pack of tobacco and the others have run out that he shares it with everyone. And next time, it he don't have any, and we got some tobacco, we naturally share it with him.

In a similar vein, another adds:

> Last night, we were hanging around at this joint and I run out of dough [money]. But my friends didn't let me down. They pitched in and bought me coffee the rest of the night...Next time, when they're out of dough, I'll buy their coffee. That's how we work it.

Another set of norms centres on the activities in which the chronic ex-patients engage in order to "make it on the outside" or capitalize on their deviant identities. Such norms[15] specify the conditions under which it is appropriate to engage in acts of prostitution, and what type of sexual acts are appropriate. Speaking of necessity as a prime prerequisite for selling her body, one woman states:

> The only time that it's O.K. to screw for money is when I'm absolutely broke. That's the only time that my friends, Sarah and Rhoda-Sue do it...I'm not a whore and neither are they. I'm a decent person and don't do any of those dirty, kinky things, just straight, plain sex.

Similarly, other norms specify the conditions under which it is appropriate to engage in the selling of their maintenance medications and shoplifting. In the case of the former, necessity again being the major prerequisite, ex-patients follow rules regarding to whom they should sell their meds:

> We never sell them to young kids or even teenagers. No way. We have morals too, you know. We only sell the meds if absolutely necessary--like when we're dying for a smoke or we need to buy something. And we only sell it to adults and if they blow their minds, that's their problem. They're old enough to know better.

In the case of shoplifting activities, that data indicates that such behaviour is only deemed appropriate in emergency situations, with only certain articles defined as "acceptable merchandise":

> We only take things from stores when we really need them. Like when we don't have nothing to eat, so we rip off a can of pork and beans. But we don't steal big things like radios or televisions--that would be wrong. We just take food and essential things like that!

One final set of norms have been created in the context of the ex-psychiatric patient subculture, norms centring on the "shrink sessions" in which ex-patients frequently participate. Such norms include not interrupting others disclosing their problems, maintaining confidentiality, and non-ridicule. Speaking of adherence to these rules, one female states:

> When we first began getting together, people used to talk all at once, so we made this rule that when one person is talking, the other shut up. And even if the person is talking stupid, you don't laugh, because laughing can be a deadly weapon--it can hurt someone deeply...Whatever we talk about, nobody goes out and gossips to someone else. It's kept under our hats.

The set of norms to which the mixed Nutters and Looney Tuners have created and adhere function to regulate the conduct of their groups. Their prescriptions contribute to a form of social order and not only protect but dignify their members. In this latter regard, the strict norms regarding the commission of deviant/illegal acts and the concomitant set of justifications, enable members to maintain a positive image of self and high self-esteem.

For those members, who breached a subcultural norm, depending upon the norm, and the circumstances surrounding the breach, they would receive some sort of negative sanctioning. Such sanctioning included verbal abuse, physical abuse, temporary and permanent expulsion from the group. Recounting the negative sanctions he received for violating the rule of non-ridicule during a "shrink session", an ex-patient says:

> Millie was talking about some problem she was having and it sounded so trivial and stupid to me that I blurted out laughing. Everyone got real upset though and told me to get lost. They didn't have nothing to do with me for two months. When I returned, I watched my step; I sure learned my lesson.

For those who breached norms regarding the commission of deviant/illegal acts, the penalties are more severe:

> Joe got himself into a lot of trouble. He knew that it was wrong to sell his meds to little kids on the corner and we called him on it. He didn't like our warning him and he turned on us and went to the cops and gave them our names saying we was the one selling the dope. He caused a lot of trouble for us...But we got even. One night we got him and beat the shit out of him. After that, he towed the line.

3. Argot

The Mixed Nutters and looney Tuners communicate with their respective members by means of an argot (still in its development stage), a distinctive vocabulary that demarcates not only outsiders from insiders, but also, neophytes from veterans. Speaking on the role of argot, one Mixed Nutter remarks:

> The lingo we use is really useful because we can be sitting in a coffee shop talking about some ways to pick up quick cash, and some of these ways are illegal. The people who are sitting right beside us may be eaves-dropping, but they won't be able to understand what we're saying.

In a similar vein, a member of the Looney Tuners adds:

> The words we make up and use describe certain things and they protect us from enemies...It's like we're this club and we share things that no one else understands...The way we speak also lets you know up front who is one of us and who ain't, and who may be a green-horn wanting to be one of us.

Moreover, their argot prescribes symbols for cognition and communication regarding matters of interest to chronic ex-psychiatric patients. So, for example, "plucking the rooster" refers to receiving handouts from clergy or social agency members. "Going to a banquet" refers to individuals discovering a place giving out large amounts of free food. "Doing the groceries" refers to shoplifting various foodstuffs.

All groups make evaluations of its members in an effort to maintain some sense of order and stability. So for example, in the case of the Looney Tuners, at certain times, usually when "hanging around", members will talk about "cheapers", those ex-patients who violated the norm of reciprocity. So too, do they speak about "dozers", those individuals who were caught committing a deviant act. The Mixed Nutters, also refer to members being "turncoats" or "fruitcakes". The former term refers to those ex-patients who have violated norms of trust and confidentiality. The latter term refers to individuals with little common sense. Moreover, they use the terms, "oldies" and "shit-kid" to make the distinction between veterans and novices.

In their demarcation between themselves and outsiders, the Mixed Nutters use such terms as "Nazi", referring to individuals who reject or stigmatize them; the term "moron" refers to unacceptable ex-patients who do not meet the standards for acceptance into the group. Similarly, the Looney Tuners use such terms as "head shrinkers" and "cop patrols" to refer to psychiatric professionals and social workers respectively.

4. Boundaries

Similar to the nudist (Weinberg, 1966) and motorcycle gang (Hopper and Moore, 1980) subcultures, the data indicate that the ex-psychiatric patient subcultures also have sharply-defined territorial boundaries, within which they carry out their activities. In the case of the Looney Tuners, members live and carry out their daily activities in a territorial area of approximately 2.5 - 3.0 square miles. This territory contains a mixture of residential housing, commercial and service-oriented properties. The Mixed Nutters live and carry out their activities in a somewhat larger territorial area of approximately 3.0 - 4.0 square miles. This territory contains a mixture of commercial and service-oriented properties, residential housing, and some light industries.

During the three years this researcher studied these two groups, individuals rarely stepped outside their respective territories. The territories of these two subcultures provide ex-patients with everything they need to "get by on". They bring the world down to size and make life more manageable for the ex-patients. By remaining inside imaginary boundaries, the individuals come to know every inch of their territory--a knowledge that gives them a sense of security:

> In all the time I've been discharged, I've always stayed right here in this area. Most of us do. It's rare to hear that so and so took a bus to Buffalo or Ottawa. You can walk to anywhere you have to. It's like a small town in this neighbourhood. At first I was scared, but now I know every street and store and restaurant. I'm more at ease now.

5. Ideology

Similar to other deviant subcultures, the ex-psychiatric subculture develop an ideology: a perspective on themselves and on their relations with other societal members, a set of ideas repudiating conventional, stereotypical attitudes about their deviant attribute, and a set of justifications for engaging in deviant/illegal activities.

The ideology of the Mixed Nutters and Looney Tuners provides their members with a set of ideas about "normals" in society, and the relations between themselves and such persons. Normals are generally perceived as cruel, untrustworthy, uncaring, dangerous and unknowledgeable about mental illness, an ideology prescribing avoidance on the part of ex-patients. As one ex-patient, speaking on this subject, puts it:

> People out there are just plain mean most of the time. Or they just don't give a damn about us. Some of them wouldn't care if we vanished off the face of this earth. Most are so stupid. They don't have any true idea about what mental

illness is...The best thing we can do is try to avoid them when we can. They don't want us, and we don't want or need them.

Moreover, the ideology of these ex-psychiatric patient subcultures refutes stereotypical perceptions about mental patients and mental illness generally held by conventional society. Members are provided with a set of rationalizations and justifications for their illnesses mitigating their blameworthiness[16], thereby enabling ex-patients to re-define themselves in a more positive, although still deviant light. According to one male ex-patient:

> Since I met these people, they reminded me of the fact that I wasn't some crazy lunatic on the loose--the vision that others seemed to have of me. My fellow patients made me realize that I was a person, someone with psychological problems, an illness that was not my fault. It was all beyond my own control...Since they've been telling me this, I think more highly of myself now.

Similarly, another ex-patient remarks:

> My friends told me that I wasn't responsible for my situation. How could I be? It's not my own fault...They helped me to see that my sickness was caused by others, and that's what I try to convince other [ex-patients] of. It makes them feel less guilt and really picks them up mentally.

Just as the ideology of the subculture provides ex-patients with ideas about normal others and a set of justifications holding others accountable for their deviant attribute, so too, does it function in one final respect: specifically, it provides members with a set of justifications for carrying out deviant/illegal acts. This self-justifying rationale then, furnishes ex-patients with "sound" reasons for engaging in such activities as prostitution, selling their medications, and shoplifting:

We're not doing anything that's really wrong. We don't murder or rob or things like that. We only take a few groceries once in a while from the A & P store. And we only do that when it's absolutely necessary. Other people who have lots of money do it all the time, and they take things much bigger than we do. We do it for medical reasons--our health, but they just do it for greed.

In a similar vein, another ex-patient discussing her rationale for engaging in prostitution, says:

The world is against us patients and we got to get by somehow. And we can't make ends meet on a disability pension. The boarding home takes most of the monthly cheque and we're only left with a few bucks for the whole month. So, what the hell, we "work under the covers" once in a while. It's not that we do it for pleasure, it's necessary. No one will give me a "normal" job because of my sickness, so this is my only option. You look down the big streets and avenues and see lots of girls doing it anyway. It' just another way to make a buck!

In short then, the chronic ex-patients in this study develop and utilize an ideology: a set of ideas that suit their own interests, justify their post-hospital actions, and holds others accountable for their mental illness. Moreover, this ideology contains a set of ideas and judgments about others in society and provides ex-patients with specific prescriptions for action.

Summary and Discussion

This sociological study on the subcultures of chronic ex-psychiatric patients was stimulated by the observation that despite the wealth of sociological research on various deviant subcultures, and the concomitant theoretical approaches utilized to explain such phenomena, little, if any use was made in the examination of discharged/deinstitutionalized chronic psychiatric patients. Moreover, what research had been conducted on ex-patients,

had been done either from a psychiatric, social work or psychological perspective. Little research had focused on the effects of deinstitutionalization from the perspectives of the ex-patients themselves. Further, no published work (at the time of the study) had been located which documented the origins, nature, and functions of deviant subculture of chronic ex-psychiatric patients. Therefore, this paper was concerned with the effects of deinstitutionalization from the subjective standpoints of chronic ex-patients. In specific, this paper has focused on the subcultures that these deviants have developed and utilize, their characteristics, and the role that they serve their members.

According to Simmons (1969:88):

In response to society's disapproval and harassment, deviants usually band together with others in the same plight. Beyond the ties of similar interests and views...deviants find that establishing fairly stable relationships with other deviants does much to ease procurement and coping problems and to provide a more stable and reliable source of direct support and interaction. In these indirect ways, society's condemnation "creates" the deviant subculture.

The results of this study have indicated that his subcultural formation emerged when ex-patients began experiencing a number of problems (created by the deinstitutionalization of mental health services and societal attitudes toward the mentally ill), communicating such problems to other discharged chronic ex-patients, subsequently interacting with like others on the basis of their problems, and attempting to provide solutions to their difficulties. Ex-psychiatric patient subcultures were characterized by: crystallized patterns of behaviour centred around their social plights, a set of clearly-defined norms and values, and an ideology: a set of ideas developed to suit their own interests and justify their actions. Analysis of the data revealed that the ex-psychiatric patient subcultures provided a number of functions for their members. Firstly, through subcultural participation, ex-patients established social relations with understanding others--a relationship that was supportive in nature and served to combat feelings of fear and social isolation. Secondly, group activities, in particular, "Shrink Sessions", allowed members to discuss problems of anxiety, stress, depression, stigma, and alike, and ask fellow group members for advice on how to deal with such problems. Through such "Shrink Sessions" ex-patients were able to disclose various concerns and alleviate a portion of the burden of their loads, thereby elevating actions, in general, and during "Shrink Sessions" specifically, fellow members provided "expert advice" and practical strategies for mitigating the stigma potential of mental illness on their daily rounds. Given that others in the subculture had experienced the stigma of mental illness on numerous occasions during the post-patient phase of their careers, such persons had indeed become "expert managers"--they had a great deal of advice on the "do's and the don'ts" of avoiding stigma associated with their discreditable attribute. In the context of this subcultural formation, various stigma management strategies were imparted upon new charges. Fourthly, in the context of participating in the ex-mental patient subcultures, members were provided with an ideology, a set of justifications or "sound" rationales about their deviant attribute. The ideology of the Mixed Nutters and Looney Tuners provided ex-patients with a set of rationalizations which mitigated their blameworthiness; instead, blame was placed upon various others, ranging from spouses, children, teachers, parents, to society, in general. By placing blame on others for their discreditable attribute, this enabled ex-patients to re-define themselves in a more positive, although still deviant light. Further, the ideology of the subcultures provided members with ideas about "normal others"--that normals were untrustworthy, callous, and uneducated about mental illness--an ideology that prescribed "avoidance of normals" to members of the subculture. Fifthly, the ideology of the ex-patient subcultures furnished members with a self-justifying rationale for engaging in various deviant/-illegal activities. Ex-patients, through subcultural participation, were provided with a set of "sound" reasons for engaging in such activities as selling

drugs, shoplifting and prostitution, enabling them to maintain positive self-images. A final function of the ex-psychiatric patient subcultures was that they provided members with various practical stratagems for "making it on the outside". That is, ex-patients were "educated" in an informal sense, how to capitalize on their deviant identities, specifically, by selling their bodies, selling their medications, locations where to get "free eats" or a "free place to crash". In short, in the context of this subcultural form, individuals were taught how to make the most of their attributes by becoming "professional crazies".

This is not to say, however, that ex-psychiatric patients experienced only positive consequence from participation in the subcultures. In fact, the author observed on a number of occasions, situations of conflict surrounding authority, verbal abuse among members, stolen wallets, tobacco, cigarettes and various articles of clothing. However, the positive consequences of subcultural participation far outweighed the negative effects:

> There is good and bad with everything and this is true of the "Looney Tuners" group. In the last couple of years, there has been a few fist fights over some cigarettes and cash that went missing, but all in all, it's this group that really helped us to make it on the outside. We would have been totally lost without each others help and support.

According to the ideology behind the movement toward deinstitutionalization of mental health services, individuals would be released or discharged from the institution. However, "stone walls do not a prison make, nor iron bars a cage". Many chronic ex-psychiatric patients, even though discharged, remain imprisoned in a metaphorical sense with their guards and wardens being the family, friends, potential employers, and society in general who are unable to tolerate mental illness. The term, "deinstitutionalization" is defined by chronic ex-patients as a form of "social segregation and reinstitutionalization in certain areas in the community". Such persons are in but not of the community. Ex-patients, for the most part, are confined in "institutions without walls, bars or locks" living lives of frustration, disappointment, fear exploitation and poverty. In response to their undesirable social situations, these persons, [similar to other stigmatized deviants in society], have developed and entered into deviant subcultures or "informal self-help groups"--an "expressive group" (cf. Gordon and Babchuk, 1959:25) "exist(ing) primarily to furnish activities for members", including evading stigma.

References

Anspach, Renee. 1975. "From Stigma to Identity Politics: Political Activism among the Physically Disabled and Former Mental Patients". Social Science and Medicine 13A: 765-773.

Bassuk, Ellen. L., and Samuel Gerson. 1978. "Deinstitutionalization of Mental Health Services". Scientific American 238: 46-53.

Becker, Howard S. 1963. Outsiders: Studies in the Sociology of Deviance. New York: Free Press.

Bellak, Leopold. 1964. "Community Psychiatry: The Third Psychiatric Revolution". In L. Bellak, (ed.), Handbook of Community Psychiatry and Community Mental Health. New York: Grune and Stratton.

Brown, Philip. 1979. "The Transfer to Care: U.S. Mental Health Policy Since World War II". International Journal of Health Services 9: 645-662.

Burr, Angela. 1984. "The Illicit Non-Pharmaceutical Heroin Market and Drug Scene in Kensington Market". British Journal of Addiction 79 (3): 337-343.

Cheadle, A.J., H. Freeman and J. Korer. 1978. "Chronic Schizophrenics in the Community". British Journal of Psychiatry 132: 221-227.

Chu, F.D. and S. Trotter. 1974. The Madness Establishment: Ralph Nader's Study Group Report on the National Institute of Mental Health. New York: Grossman.

Cloward, R.A., and L.E. Ohlin. 1964. Delinquency and Opportunity. New Free Press.

Cohen, Albert. 1955. Delinquent boys. Glencoe, Illinois: Free Press.

Cohen, Jere. 1979. "High-School Subcultures an Adult World". Adolescence 14 (55): 491-502.

Dear, Michael, l. Bayne, G. Boyd, E. Callaghan and E. Goldstein. 1980. coping in the Community: The Needs of Ex-Psychiatric Patients. Mental Health Hamilton Project.

Demotte, Charles. 1984. "Conflicting Worlds of Meaning: Juvenile Delinquency in 19th century Manchester". Deviant Behavior 5: 193-215.

Estroff, Sue E. 1981. Making it Crazy: An Ethnography of Psychiatric Clients in an American Community. Berkeley: University of California Press.

Gans, Herbert. 1962. The Urban Villagers. New York: Free Press.

Gillen, John 1955. "National and Regional Cultural Values in the United States". Social forces (Dec.): 110-115.

Goffman, Erving. 1963. Stigma. Englewood Cliffs, New Jersey. Prentice-Hall.

Gordon, C. Wayne and Nicholas Babchuk. 1959. "A Typology of Voluntary Associations". American Sociological Review 24 (February): 22-29.

Gordon, Milton M. 1964. Assimilation in American Life. London: Oxford University press.

Herman, Nancy J. 1986a. Crazies in the Community: An Ethnographic Study of Ex-Psychiatric Clients in Canadian Society--Stigma, management strategies and Identity Transformation. Unpublished Ph.D. Dissertation, McMaster University, Hamilton, Canada.

----- 1986b. "Non-Chronic Ex-Psychiatric Patients: The Stigma of Mental Illness, Information Management Strategies and Implications for Identity Transformation". In submission to the Journal of Contemporary Ethnography.

----- 1986c. "The Chronically Mentally Ill in Canada". In The North American Elders: A Comparison of U.S. and Canadian Issues, B. Havens and E. Rathbone-McCuan. New Hampshire: Greenwood.

Hooper, Columbus and J. Moore. 1980. "Hell on Wheels: The Outlaw Motorcycle Gang". Paper presented at the Mid-South Sociological Association Annual Meeting.

Hughes, Everett Cherington. 1961. Students' Culture and Perspectives: Lectures on Medical and General Education. Lawrence, Kansas: University of Kansas Law School.

Humphreys, L. and B. Miller. 1980. "Identities in the Emerging Gay Culture". In J. Marmor (ed.), Homosexual Behavior: A Modern Reappraisal. New York: Basic Books.

Irwin, John. 1970. The Felon. Englewood Cliffs, New Jersey: Prentice-Hall.

Johnson, Bruce. 1980. "Towards a Theory of Drug Subculture". Paper presented at the annual meetings of the Society for the Study of Social Problems.

Kitsuse, J.I. and D.C. Dietrick. 1959. "Delinquent Boys: A Critique". American Sociological Review 24: 213-215.

Leifer, Rod. 1966. "Community Psychiatry and Social Power". Social Problems 14: 16-22.

Lewis, Oscar. 1961. The Children of Sanchez. New York; Vintage Books.

Landy, David and Sara Singer. 1961. "The Social Organization and Culture of a Club for Former Mental Patients". Human Relations 14: 31-40.

Lipton, D.S. and B.D. Johnson. 1980. "Control at the Subcultural Interface: Heroin vs. Methadone". Paper presented at the annual meeting of the Society for the Study of Social Problems.

Lofland, John. 1966. Doomsday Cult. Englewood Cliffs, New Jersey: Prentice-Hall.

Matza, David. 1964. Delinquency and Drift. New York: Wiley.

Melville, K. 1972. Communes in the Counter culture. New York: Morrow.

Partridge, W.L. 1973. 1973. The Hippi Ghetto. The Natural History of a Subculture. New York: Holt, Rinehart and Winston.

Platt, Stephen D. 1985. "A Subculture of Para-suicide" Human Relations 38 (4): 257-297.

Ralph, Diana. 1980. Where Did Community Psychiatry Come From?: The Labour Theory of Community Psychiatry. Mimeo. University of Regina, Saskatchewan, Canada.

Ray, Marsh B. 1961. "Abstinence Cycles and Heroin Addicts". Social Problems 9: 132-140.

Reynolds, David K. and Norman Farberow. 1977. Endangered Hope: Experiences in Psychiatric Aftercare Facilities. Berkeley: University of California Press.

Rubington, Earl. 1968 "The Bottle Gang:" Quarterly Journal of Studies on Alcohol 29: 943-955.

----- 1982. Deviant Subcultures. In M. Michael Rosenberg, R. Stebbins and A. Turowetz (eds.), The Sociology of Deviance. New York: St. Martin's: 42-70.

Scott, Robert. 1969. The Making of Blind Men: A Study of Adult Socialization. Russell Sage Foundation.

Scull, Andrew. 1977. Decarceration: Community Treatment and the Deviant: A Radical View. New Jersey: Prentice-Hall.

Simmons, J.L. 1969. Deviants. Berkeley: The Glendessary Press.

Shibutani, Tamotsu. 1955. "Reference Groups as Perspectives": American Journal of Sociology (May): 565-566.

Sykes, G.M. and D. Matza. 1957. "Techniques of Neutralization: A Theory of Delinquency". American Sociological Review 22: 124-136.

Wallace, Samuel E. 1965. Skid Row as a Way of Life. New York: Harper Torchbook.

Webb, Gary. 1984. "The Inmate Subculture: A Case Study". Paper presented at the Western Social Science Association Meetings.

Weinberg, Martin S. 1966. "Becoming a Nudist". Psychiatry: Journal for the Study of Interpersonal Processes 29 (1): 15-24.

Wolfgang, Marvin and Franco Ferracuti. 1967. The Subculture of Violence. London: Tavistock.

Yablonsky, Lewis. 1959. "The Delinquent Gang as a Near Group". Social Problems 7 (2): 108-117.

Notes

1. In order to protect the anonymity of the groups, the names of the subcultures used in this paper are pseudonyms. It is important to note, however, that the actual names of the subcultures [chosen by the members themselves] are also negative, stereotypical labels.
2. Cloward and Ohlin (1964); Cohen (1955); Gorden (1964); Kitsuse and Dietrick (1959); Matza (1964); Sykes and Matza (1957); Wallace (1965); and Wolfgang and Ferracuti (1967).
3. See Anspach (1979) and Landy and Singer (1961) for discussions of formal social organizations for ex-mental patients.
4. For detailed discussions concerning the origins and development of the movement toward deinstitutionalization of psychiatric services, consult: Bassuk and Gerson (1978); Bellak (1964); Brown (1979); Chu and Trotter (1974); Herman (1986a); Leifer (1967); Ralph (1980); and Scull (1977).
5. For an extensive review of the literature, consult Herman (1986a).
6. For the purposes of this research, the term "chronic" is defined not in diagnostic terms, i.e., "chronic schizophrenic";rather it is defined in terms of duration, continuity and frequency of hospitalizations. Specifically, this term refers to those individuals institutionalized for time-periods of two years or more, those institutionalized on a continual basis, or those institutionalized on five or more occasions.
7. Following Rubington (1982), the concept of deviant subculture is defined in this paper as: "the shared ways of thinking, feeling, and acting that members of a deviant group have developed for engaging in deviant behavior, organizing relations among themselves, and defending themselves against social punishment".
8. The term "non-chronic" is defined by the researcher in terms of duration, continuity, and frequency of hospitalizations. Specifically, it refers to those hospitalized for time-periods of less than two years, those hospitalized on a discontinuous basis, and those hospitalized on less than five occasions.
9. The mean number of years these respondents were institutionalized was 7.5 years.
10. The mean number of occasions which such persons were institutionalized was six.

11. This response is, by no means, exclusive to ex-patients in light of the movement toward deinstitutionalization. Such a collective response has been well-documented among skid row alcoholics (Rubington, 1968; Wallace, 1965); homosexuals (Humphreys and Miller, 1980); delinquents (Cohen, 1955; Yablonsky, 1959), among countless others.

12. For specific details concerning the sample, consult Herman (1986a).

13. In contrast to the Mixed Nutters who had been in existence for three years prior to the beginning of this research project, the researcher was able to directly follow the development of the Looney Tuners shortly following their inception.

14. See Goffman (1963) and Scott(1969) for discussions on the capitalization of blind persons.

15. These norms have as their underlying assumption the idea of confidentiality.

16. See Sykes and Matza (1957) for a discussion of similar neutralizing techniques employed by juvenile delinquents.

Stereotypes of Mental Illness: A Comparison with Ethnic Stereotypes[1]

JOHN MARSHALL TOWNSEND

In the past decade a number of studies have suggested that attitudes toward the mentally ill have improved since the studies of the late Fifties. The newer studies claim that the public's ability to recognize psychiatric symptoms has increased and their acceptance of mental patients has improved (Crocetti et al., 1974; Halpert 1969; Felix 1967). Some evidence, however, argues that these apparent improvements were research artifacts. Recent restudies of the same populations studied in the Fifties, and controlled comparisons with data from the Sixties suggest that attitudes have not changed much in the last twenty years; the apparent improvements noted by other authors were probably due to variations in sampling and instruments (D'Arcy and Brockman 1976; Olmsted and Durham 1976). Furthermore, comprehensive reviews of the literature suggest that, although some changes may have occurred in recent years, the majority of the population still harbours negative attitudes toward the mentally ill (Rabkin 1972, 1974).

The purpose of this paper is to argue the following: (1) Stereotypes of mental illness persist because they perform definite conative and cognitive functions. (2) They demarcate a qualitative break between normal and abnormal. (3) They help to maintain a high initial recognition threshold for mental illness among lay persons. (4) Psychiatrists also use "stereotyped" categories, but criteria for inclusion in these categories tend to be broad, so that the professionals' recognition threshold is relatively low. Popular and professional categories thus function as complementary components in a system that funnels labelled deviance into social control institutions. I will marshal the evidence for this thesis and then discuss its implications and possible objections to it.

This paper deals primarily with materials from the United States, but some research from Western Europe will be included. For convenience, the terms, "attitude," "conception," and "image," will refer to any statement, depiction, or belief about mental illness or ethnic groups in which no question of truth or falsity is at issue (Nunnally 1961; Brigham 1971). In contrast, the term, "stereotype," will refer to those exaggerated beliefs and images which are popularly depicted in the mass media and folklore and whose inaccuracy can be demonstrated (Brigham 1971; Scheff 1966; Nunnally 1961; Glassner 1979). The term, "function," will be used not in the eufunctional sense but rather in the sense of a phenomenon having reinforcing effects, anticipated or inadvertent, upon other social processes or institutions (Hempel 1959; Davis 1959; Nagel 1961; Spiro 1961). These effects, of course, may have positive *or* negative implications for particular groups, or for society as a whole (Schrag 1978).

In analyzing the stereotypes of mental illness, I will utilize literature on ethnic stereotypes and prejudice. This approach offers several advantages. The literature on ethnic stereotypes is vast, culturally diverse, and derives from behavioral observation as well as psychological testing (Brigham 1971; Ehrlich 1973; Barth 1969; DeVos and Romanucci-Ross 1975). Comparisons of the two sorts of stereotypes can highlight differences as well as similarities and thus give us further insights into the dynamics of the two phenomena. This discussion focuses on labelling by others. Although I do not believe that self-labelling and voluntary treatment are immune to the processes described herein, they do raise special issues.[2]

Stereotypes

In his classic work, *Public Opinion*, Walter Lippmann introduced and explicated the concept of social stereotype. Lippmann (1930) argued that all perception was necessarily selective. The myriad stimuli impinging upon an individual's sensory apparatus are sorted into categories. The

Reprinted From: Journal Culture Medicine and Psychiatry: An Interdisciplinary Journal of Comparative Cross-Cultural Research. 1979, pp. 205-229 categories are to some extent culturally determined and the sorting process itself becomes largely unconscious and automatic. The categories are inevitably "stereotypes" in the sense that they obscure important differences among members of a group and exaggerate the differences between the groups.

Since Lippmann's seminal work, an immense literature on ethnic stereotypes has accumulated. Although generalizing from these studies is difficult (Brigham 1971), several propositions pertinent to our argument can be stated at this time. First, selective perception as described by Lippmann (1930) does seem to be a universal fact of human cognition. People all over the world do seem to group phenomena into categories and to exaggerate the differences between these categories (Levi-Strauss 1965; Needham 1978). Second, when these categories involve human beings they may serve to define the boundaries and relations between groups. The perceived, exaggerated differences between two groups help to justify the behavior of people in one group toward the other group. The exaggeration of stereotypes thus can militate against the in-group perceiving out-group traits in themselves or perceiving in-group traits in outsiders (Shibutani 1970; Ehrlich 1973; Klapp 1972; Barth 1969; Berreman 1972; DeVos and Romanucci-Ross 1975). To be sure, research has shown that a trait praised in the in-group can be used to prejudice against outsiders, e.g., competitiveness and success of Jews in business; but the insiders invariably feel that the outsiders express this trait unfairly or in unseemly ways (Allport 1958; Glassner 1979).

These general statements about ethnic stereotypes suggest two propositions about stereotypes of mental illness: (1) If popular images of mental illness act like ethnic stereotypes in demarcating an in-group-out-group boundary, we should expect these images to be greatly exaggerated. (2) Passing from one group to another occurs in some situations with relative ease, but when the dominant group considers the subordinate group distinctly inferior, crossing over becomes difficult if not impossible (Ehrlich 1973; Goffman 1964; Barth 1969; Eidheim 1969; Glassner 1979; Brigham 1971). Since insanity is by definition

grossly inferior, we should expect the threshold for redefining an in-group person as mentally ill to be very high. In fact, available evidence does suggest that public images of mental illness remain distorted and that crossing the boundary between sanity and insanity is extremely problematic.

Exaggeration

The most consistent elements in our images of the mentally ill are violence and dangerousness. This is true of attitudes measured with abstract instruments as well as content analyses of media images. Contemporary research indicates the situation is similar in West Germany and has changed little in either country in the last twenty years (Nunnally 1961; Olmsted and Durham 1976; Fracchia et al. 1976; Rabkin 1974; Schneider and Wieser 1972; Jaeckel and Wieser 1970; Stumme 1973; Steadman and Cocozza 1977-1978, 1978).

A recent analysis of upstate New York TV Guide program listings (Townsend n.d.) revealed that fifty-four percent of all allusions to mental-health topics for 1976 portrayed the mentally ill as markedly bizarre and/or dangerous. Persons labelled "mentally ill," "psychotic," or "psychopathic," were depicted as appearing and behaving in obviously strange ways: dishevelled or bizarre costume, catatonic stupor, glassy eyes, maniacal laughter, and homicidal tendencies. In Fact, twenty-four percent of all allusions suggested a direct link between mental illness and homicidal behavior.

Empirical data on the behavior of ex-mental patients strongly contradict these images. Extensive studies of dangerousness have recently shown that crime rates among ex-mental patients are no higher than among corresponding persons in the general population. In fact, the reverse may be true. Recently, increases in arrest rates among ex-mental patients are apparently due to the increasing tendency to channel persons with arrest records into the mental health system (Steadman, Cocozza, and Melick 1978).

Another commonly recognized image of mental illness is that of the delusional personality, i.e., people think they are Napoleon, Christ, or some other famous figure (Nunnally 1961; Scheff 1966; Schneider and Wieser 1972). Among 25,000 patients Rokeach (1964) found only a handful of such people: only three patients without brain damage consistently believed they were Christ, and there were no Napoleons, Caesars, Krushchevs or Eisenhowers. The evidence thus suggests that two of the most common stereotypes, violence and delusional personalities, are highly inaccurate. Why stereotypes of mental illness take these particular forms and how they compare to ethnic stereotypes in this regard will be discussed later.

Crossing

Barth (1969:30) has argued that ethnic boundaries only emerge in situations where the categorizations have a self-fulfilling character:

> With such a feedback from people's experiences to the categories they employ, simple ethnic dichotomies can be retained, and their stereotyped behavioral differential reinforced, despite a considerable objective variation. This is so because actors struggle to maintain conventional definitions of the situation in social encounters through selective perception, tact, and sanctions...

Selective perception and self-fulfilling prophecy allow ethnic boundaries to persist despite a flow of personnel across them and despite campaigns to demonstrate their inaccuracy or unfairness (Barth 1969; Ehrlich 1973). I propose that the sanity-insanity boundary is similar. The studies I will examine below suggest that popular *and* professional conception of mental illness share four specific traits with ethnic stereotypes: (1) they are exaggerated and serve to dichotomize between the in-group and the out-group; (2) they are maintained through selective perception; (3) they erect high thresholds for "crossing;" (4) they persist despite the flow of personnel across boundaries and despite campaigns to alter them.

In a now classic study, Star (1955) found that, when presented with textbook examples of mental disorders, the public defined only the most bizarre disorder, paranoid schizophrenia, as mental illness. Thus, it appeared that the public's

exaggerated images of mental illness reflected a cognitive dichotomy between sanity and insanity. A person's behavior had to be "really crazy" for them to earn the title, mental illness.

The Cummings (1957) used the same psychiatric descriptions to study public attitudes. Like Star, the Cummings discovered that the public harboured much narrower and more concrete conceptions than the professionals' more psychological, normative, and continuous criteria. Public images of insanity apparently functioned to dichotomize between sanity and insanity. Because these images performed important cognitive functions, they were not easily altered by campaigns. Indeed, the Cummings' efforts to alter public conceptions were met with heated resistance.

A replication of Cummings' study in the same location (D'Arcy and Brockman 1976) indicated that people's recognition threshold for mental illness has not changed substantially in the last twenty years. These results led the authors to conclude that the apparent "improvements" noted by other authors (e.g., Crocetti et al. 1974) were due to research artifacts and invalid comparisons with previous studies. In any event, the recognition threshold in question here derives not from paper-and-pencil tests but from actual labelling in the community, and the available evidence does suggest that in such cases *the initial recognition threshold is high.* The studies cited below are admittedly dated. To the best of my knowledge, however, they are still the best available because they focus on the actual behaviors precipitating psychiatric treatment rather than dealing with abstractions.

In a study which has remained unexcelled for richness of detail Yarrow et al. (1955) found that husbands had to breach wives' expectations repeatedly before they would finally be recognized as mentally ill. The wives repeatedly rationalized and normalized their husbands' symptomatic behavior because of the unpleasant and threatening consequences of redefining the behavior as symptoms of mental illness. After the "recognition" occurred, the wives tended to redefine past behaviors as symptoms of the incipient disorder. The husband's behavior literally became qualitatively different in their eyes.

More recent studies have produced similar results. Sampson et al. (1962) found that husbands were able to rationalize their wives' increasingly bizarre behavior for months and even years before deciding on hospitalization. Similarly, parents of schizophrenic children repeatedly provide "normalizing" definitions for aberrant behavior (Silver 1955; Bakwin 1963). In an analysis of 100 cases, Smith et al. (1963) found that repeated norm violations were committed before the "last straw" was reached, i.e., the incident which resulted in the family's decision to hospitalize. Apparently the threshold for crossing the sanity-insanity boundary is high for in-group members. When an individual has been designated as "normal", he or she must repeatedly exhibit deviant behavior in order to be reclassified by the family (or other in-group members).

Research on ethnic stereotypes has yielded similar findings. A person's actual appearance or behavior is often less important in how individuals will be perceived than the labels or categories attached to them. For example, when presented with pictures of faces that varied in skin tone from whitest to blackest, subjects attributed stereotypes to the faces according to the (experimenter's) random labelling of them as black or white. Thus, a relatively black face, if labelled white, elicited white stereotypes (Secord 1959). Naturally, there were some limits to this tendency. Most subjects would not attribute white stereotypes to the blackest faces (or the converse), but did follow the suggestion effects of the label on the intermediate faces. It is interesting to note, however, that a small group of subjects were so prejudiced that they sometimes followed the label regardless of the objective appearance of the stimulus. Similar results were achieved by changing the ethnic surnames of faces in the pictures (Razran 1950). Below we will see that mental health professionals exhibit a similar tendency: a label previously attached by another professional or someone in the community appears to be a powerful determinant of how a clinician will perceive a prepatient.

Re-entry

The role of stereotypes after initial labelling is less clear than in the initial process. Smith et al. (191963) found that the incidents preceding re-hospitalization increased in apparent dangerousness and disruptiveness. This suggested a *raised* threshold for re-hospitalization, but it is not clear from the study whether this difference was actually conative or the result of a lowered cognitive threshold, i.e., the second "last straw" was perceived as being more disruptive than the first even though it was not.

Some authors have suggested that labelling lowers the recognition threshold to the point where virtually any behavior could be perceived as a symptom. As we shall see, this seems to be particularly true in the context of the mental hospital (Goldman et al. 1970; Rosenhan 1973). In the community, however, it appears that crossing or recrossing the sanity-insanity boundary is more open to "negotiation" (Edgerton 1966, 1969). Some families may come to see their relative problem as psychiatric, but they evidently do not categorize them as "crazy".

This argument is consistent with evidence indicating that some families resist defining the patient as "mentally ill" even after extensive treatment. Lewis and Zeichner (1960) found that 16% of the families in their sample (N = 109) persisted in such denial, while family attitudes ranged from sympathetic understanding to overt hostility. A recent (and elegant) study of family tolerance and re-hospitalization yielded similar findings. Greenley (1972, and forthcoming) found that re-hospitalization correlated negatively with the family's desire to have the patient at home. Family attitudes that were significantly related to a number of readmissions included: having the patient would be like having a ten-year-old child around, the patient would create a financial burden for the family, and family members do not like the patient. These correlations remained significant even when Greenley controlled for severity of symptoms. Thus, these studies suggest that some families tolerate what others will not. Although existing data do not allow a definite conclusion, it seems plausible to assume that "tolerant" families would not classify the patient as a member of the stereotyped mentally ill. Presumably, they create a new category: someone who has problems or is "sick" but is not really "crazy". How "intolerant" families think of the patient and what role stereotypes play in their decisions also remains an empirical question.

It thus appears that the sanity-insanity boundary is maintained by the same mechanisms as ethnic boundaries: exaggerated stereotypes and selective perception. In both situations people struggle to maintain conventional definitions by selectively perceiving and by rationalizing their categorizations. In this way their stereotypes can exist side by side with their actual experience with a member of the out-group. In ethnic prejudice, this process of rationalization allows the bigot to like some members of an out-group because "they're not like the rest" (Allport 1958; Ehrlich 1973).

A similar process apparently occurs among mental patients. Research has repeatedly indicated that mental patients do not generally perceive themselves or their fellow patients as mentally ill. Mental patients tend to designate only the most "actively ill", e.g., hallucinatory, delusional, severely depressed, as mentally ill (Townsend 1976, 1977; Braginsky et al. 1969; Levinson and Gallagher 1964).

Professional Conceptions

In the preceding section it was argued that the public's initial tendency to diagnose mental illness is conservative. Their initial recognition threshold (at least for family members) is high, partially because they do think of mental illness in stereotyped terms. This high threshold becomes particularly significant when one considers that initial recognition does occur in the community. Representatives of the mental health system usually see the prepatient only after lay persons in the community have brought the prepatient to their attention (Bittner 1967; Yarrow et al. 1955; Mechanic 1962; Smith et al. 1963). This means that the mechanisms of social control are set in motion *before* the professional sees the offender, and the public's high recognition threshold acts as a sort of conservative "filter", repeat-

edly normalizing deviant acts until the "last straw" is reached.

Numerous authors have argued that psychiatrists (and the courts) act as agents of social control once the public's recognition threshold has been exceeded. It is then their task to protect society from further disruption (Mechanic 1962; Scheff 1966, 1975; Szasz 1963, 1970). If this is true, then psychiatrists cannot have the same recognition criteria as the public; otherwise they, like the public, would tend to normalize most of the deviant behavior and send the deviants back to the community. Logically, if psychiatrists are to perform their social control functions, then compared to the public they must have rather loose, broad criteria for recognition. In fact, this seems to be the case.

Broadness

Cross-national studies support the notion that American psychiatrists have relatively broad criteria for the recognition of psychosis. Kendell et al. (1971) had matched groups of British and American psychiatrists view videotapes of patient interviews. Agreement was good in the major diagnoses of patients who exhibit classic, "textbook" symptoms. In contrast, more British than American psychiatrists diagnosed "affective psychosis" in those patients with mixed schizoaffective symptoms, but the authors noted that this was an anticipated and "manageable" difference. Those tapes, however, which were chosen specifically to represent non-psychotic disorders caused serious disagreement. The American audience tended predominantly to diagnose schizophrenia (69 - 85%) while the British shunned this category (2 - 7%). This glaring difference was not due to semantics but rather to *psychiatrists' actually perceiving* different symptoms in the patients' behavior. One patient, for example, was rated by a majority of the Americans as showing delusions, passivity, and thought disorder. Only about seven percent of the British gave similar responses. The authors concluded that the diagnosis "schizophrenia" is used so freely in America as to be virtually meaningless. They noted, however, that diagnosis of "affective disorders" was gaining popularity due to the introduction of lithium salts as an antipsychotic medication.

The results of these comparisons are not merely of academic interest. Such diagnostic differences carry weighty implications. A person labelled "psychotic" is much more likely than a non-psychotic to be: (1) involuntarily committed; (2) treated with major tranquilizers and shock therapy (ECT); (3) have their normal rights and duties suspended. The Americans' response to those tapes representing non-psychotic disorders also raises serious questions as to whether virtually anyone could be perceived as psychotic in America. The following study suggests that this is a possibility.

Temerlin (1968) had a professional actor portray an ideal, normal man in an audiotaped, clinical interview. Before hearing the tape, each group of experimental subjects heard a prestigious confederate remark that the man appeared neurotic but was really psychotic. Control subjects heard that the man was perfectly healthy. Of the experimental subjects 60 percent of the psychiatrists, 28 percent of the psychologists, and 11 percent of the graduate students diagnosed psychosis. In contrast, all control subjects agreed unanimously that the man was not psychotic. Thus, the psychiatrists in particular seemed to have a perceptual set to retain a labelled "out-grouper" in the out-group, and the broadness of their criteria allowed them to do so. Like the experiments in ethnic stereotyping (Secord 1959; Razran 1950), the label attached to a person played a more important role in determining what qualities were attributed to that person's actual appearance or behavior.

Psychiatrists' broad recognition criteria probably sprang from several sources (and not just the suggestion effects of prior labelling). First, family and community members see a prepatient in a social context and are therefore more likely to observe coping strengths and assets as well as disordered behavior. Psychiatrists usually see the prepatient in a clinical context and are thus less likely to observe aspects that militate against a diagnosis of mental illness. Second, psychiatrists are physicians and are trained to look for pathology. Unfortunately, however, no demonstrable organic pathology

exists for the functional mental disorder to validate psychiatric diagnosis. Consequently, there is little objective check on the mental health professional's tendency to look for pathology. This may explain why large-scale psychiatric screening of the public turns up so many unreported "psychotics" (e.g., Strole et al. 1962). Indeed, difficulty in recognizing anybody as "normal" (1971:246): "After the initial surprise, the psychiatrists, upon encountering that rare specimen - the normal man - next began looking for the psychopathology which was felt to "really" underlie the normal facade. This is not unusual behavior for psychiatrists." Beiser remarks that it took several years for the team of psychiatrists to devote an equal number of pages of notes to the respondents' positive functioning. In fact, the team was never able to find enough individuals for their research design who fit the category "almost certainly not a psychiatric case", and subjects from the next category, "doubtful, (but probably not a case)" had to be substituted.

A third reason American psychiatrists may have relatively broad recognition criteria for mental pathology is their basic assumption about "normality". Beiser points out a common assumption is that, in the absence of symptoms, a person will be happy, productive, and competent (1971:254). This assumption ignores the fact that any "normal" life involves some setbacks, some unhappiness, some depression. A comparison (Townsend 1978) of American and German ideology suggests that Americans do tend to assume a more idealistic view of life than Germans, and these basic ideological differences also appeared in American and German mental health professionals' conceptions of mental illness. Thus, harbouring this assumption about normality, American professionals may be particularly prone to perceive pathology in normal people.

Selective Perception

Apparently, both public and professionals maintain their conventional definitions of situations through selective perception and rationalization. But compared to the public's relatively high initial threshold seems low indeed. Compared to the public, psychiatrists are able to perceive their stereotyped images in a much broader range of behavior. The following studies also support the proposition that psychiatrists maintain their definitions of the "out-group" through selective perception, rationalization, and behavioral sanctions.

Rosenhan (1973) and seven confederates had themselves admitted to mental hospitals to conduct concealed participant observation. Upon discovering that virtually nothing they did would be construed by staff as proof of sanity, some of the researchers began to take notes openly. Subsequent inspection of nursing notes revealed that even note-taking was perceived as symptomatic. The pseudo-patients were described as "continuing to engage in writing behavior". Patients who lined up early for meals (presumably because thy had nothing else to do) were seen as exhibiting "oral fixations". Interestingly, although none of the staff perceived the pseudo-patients as normal and discovered their ruse, some of the real patients did.

These examples suggest that professionals maintain their definitions of those who have crossed the boundary not only by selective perception and rationalization but also by behaving in such a way as to "fulfil the prophecy". The case of institutionalized patients may therefore have particular relevance for the study of stereotypes of powerless groups. In both cases the stereotypes held by the dominant group may prescribe not only how they will act toward the subordinate group, but also how they will allow the subordinate group to act (Glassner 1979). Thus, if a white slave-owner thought blacks were lazy, shiftless, and childlike, his own behavior may have contributed to the fulfillment of the prophecy (Elkins 1961). Similarly, if hospital staff expect patients to be docile, unmotivated, and recidivistic, their own treatment of the patients may help to fulfil their prophecy. There is considerable evidence, in fact, that patients become "institutionalized" at least partially because they are often rewarded for adjustment to hospital routine rather than for normal, extra-institutional behaviors (Goldman et al. 1970; Barton 1959; Wing 1962; Braginsky et al. 1969; Townsend 1976).

Selective perception and rationalization also appear influential in the characterization of mental patients as dangerous. Steadman (1972) has shown that psychiatrists tend to be extremely "conservative" in judging the dangerousness of patients. Psychiatrists frequently overestimate this dangerousness and may confine thousands of patients unnecessarily (Steadman and Cocozza 1974, 1977-1978). Moreover, psychiatrists are constantly asked to estimate potential dangerousness in decisions concerning the release of patients even though there is no evidence that their ability to make such predictions exceeds that of lay persons - and may even be inferior to that of police officers (Cocozza and Steadman 1978). Thus, it appears that psychiatrists do use an element of public stereotypes (i.e., dangerousness) in their evaluations; but, unlike the public, the psychiatrist has broad criteria for inclusion. Whereas this stereotype may act as a contrast conception for the laity or cause them to normalize deviant behaviors, the psychiatrist tends to perceive more patients as potentially dangerous. In a sense, he believes the stereotype and uses it to rationalize his decisions.

The preceding studies suggest that groups on either side of the sanity-insanity boundary act like people around ethnic boundaries: actors struggle to maintain their conventional definitions of the situation through selective perception, rationalization, and sanctions. The labelling of people as mental patients or as members of an ethnic group is often a potent determinant of the qualities attributed to them (and of others' behavior toward them).

For the public, these processes function to retain in-group members in the in-group until the "last straw" (recognition threshold) is reached. Professionals generally only see the prepatient after this crucial boundary has been crossed. Selective perception and rationalization then allow them to maintain their definitions of the patient as a member of the out-group. Initial labelling in the community or by other professionals thus tends to lower professional' recognition thresholds. This situation may be changing, however, due to a decline of resources and deinstitutionalization. I will discuss this possibility later.

Several authors have argued that ethnic stereotypes owe their persistence to the fact that they do serve to define social relations and boundaries between groups. The stereotypes only change when the actual social relations change (Ehrlich 1973; Barth 1969; Glassner 1979; DeVos and Romanucci-Ross 1975). If stereotypes of mental illness perform similar functions, we would expect them to exhibit a dogged persistence as well. Numerous studies suggest that this is the case. Popular images of madness apparently have not changed much in the last twenty years, and they have proved largely impervious to attempts to change them (Cumming and Cumming 1957; D'Arcy and Brockman 1976; Nunnally 1961; Townsend n.d.; Olmsted and Durham 1976; Schneider and Wieser 1972; Stumme 1973).

Similarly, psychiatric categories, at least for the major psychoses, have not changed much since Kraepelin's original classification in the late nineteenth century (Robbins 1966; Kendell 1975). Diagnostic procedures have improved: but, as I will show later, these procedures are generally only found in diagnostic research settings. In daily clinical practice psychiatrists continue to use broad criteria for inclusion in these categories despite repeated demonstrations of the pitfalls of these criteria (Kendell et al. 1971; Kendell 1975; Strauss et al. forthcoming).

Discussion

The thesis proposed above is admittedly speculative and impressionistic. Only further research can determine its validity. In this section I will try to answer some of the questions and objections it raises. The first question concerns content: Why do popular and professional conceptions in America take the particular forms they do?

According to our thesis, stereotypes of mental illness must be extremely exaggerated in order to demarcate clearly and qualitatively the boundaries between sanity and insanity. This is probably particularly crucial in pluralistic societies with heterogeneous norms. Some studies suggest that smaller, more homogeneous cultures have more culturally specific conceptions than our popular

stereotypes (Brooks 1971; Foucault 1965; Wallace 1972). In contrast, our common stereotypes, homicidal violence and extreme delusions, contravene universal requirements of human culture: prohibition of murder, and orientation to person, place, and time.

Apparently, one of the reasons stereotypes of mental illness are so exaggerated is precisely because they mark a boundary in a continuum of behavior where few objective markers exist. In contrast, many ethnic stereotypes do contain a "kernel of truth". Statistically, ethnic groups tend to share certain physical and behavioral characteristics more than other groups. These elements are often embodied in the stereotypes of a group, along, of course, with elements that they do not necessarily possess more than other groups (Brigham 1971; Glassner 1979). Thus, when objective physical or behavioral markers exist, they are frequently incorporated in the stereotype. When few markers exist, they can be invented (e.g., the alleged dangerousness of mental patients).[3]

Mass media stereotypes of crime seem to function similarly. The array of actual unlawful acts appears to be continuous, ranging from those which virtually everyone commits occasionally (e.g., speeding) to those which are universally taboo (e.g., mass murder). Moreover, criminals do not necessarily possess distinctive physical characteristics which distinguish them from noncriminals. Mass media treatments of crime are thus greatly exaggerated: they over-represent homicide and violent crime compared to lesser crimes and civil wrongs (Townsend n.d.). In this way, they, like mental illness stereotypes, function to demarcate clearly between what is acceptable and what is not (Erikson 1967).[4]

One objection to the thesis of this paper concerns the discrepancy between cognitive and conative dimensions of attitudes and prejudice. People frequently do not act according to their stated attitudes (LaPiere 1934; Wicker 1969). In this vein, Gove and Fain (1973) have argued that public attitudes toward the mentally ill are only negative when measured with abstract instruments. In real-life situations people purportedly react with humane understanding rather than on the basis of their stereotypes. To support this proposition, the authors offer interview data in which most ex-patients answered "positive" when asked whether the overall effects of their hospitalization had been positive or negative. The authors tell us nothing of the patients' actual experiences before, during, or after hospitalization, e.g., their social relations, work opportunities, financial situations. The authors' data certainly do not justify their conclusion that the public's reaction to mental disorder is *generally* humane and compassionate. Indeed, several lines of evidence indicate that prejudice and discrimination continue to characterize the societal reaction to mental illness.

First, those labelled mentally ill still do not enjoy equal rights under the law (Ennis and Siegel 1973; Dawidoff 1975; German and Siner 1977; Journal of Criminal Law and Criminology 1975; Steadman 1972; Steadman and Cocozza 1974). Even voluntary commitments are frequently not so "voluntary". One study showed that in a majority of voluntary admissions, the individuals were already under some form of official custody and were faced with the threat of involuntary commitment proceedings as the principle alternative. When individuals decide on voluntary commitment, they waive certain constitutional rights, often without full cognizance, and frequently during all these proceedings they are under heavy medication (Gilboy and Schmidt 1971).

Second, while it is certainly true that some people react to mental patients with compassion, it appears that many people do not. Studies of family and community reactions to mental patients show that some people react with fear and hostility to the same behaviors that others tolerate and accept (Greenley 1972, forthcoming; Cumming and Cumming 1972; Handel 1973). Third, many psychiatrists admit (and deplore) the fact that a stigma still surrounds most psychiatric treatment (e.g., Bar-Levav 1976).

Another objection to the proposed scheme concerns the validity of diagnosis. Supporters of psychiatric diagnosis maintain that, although it may be less reliable than some other branches of medicine, it is not so arbitrary as its critics claim (Kety 1974; Spitzer 1975; Millon 1975; Weiner 1975; Murphy 1976; Chauncey 1975; Gove

1975). Actually, this argument is not necessarily incompatible with the present thesis. Previously, we saw that the comparison of British and American psychiatrists demonstrated that those patients with obvious, textbook symptoms could be reliably diagnosed (Kendell et al. 1971). The results of a highly sophisticated statistical analysis of diagnostic validity and reliability pointed to similar conclusions (Strauss et al. forthcoming). These results showed that, although archetypal, textbook symptoms do exist in patient populations, the great majority of symptoms are much less severe and distinctive. Furthermore, in contrast to symptoms, the great majority of first admission patients do not group according to the basic syndromes (and ambulatory patients do even less so). The diagnostician is thus forced to place patients in discrete categories based on severe levels of ambiguous symptoms. The authors conclude that the large discrepancy between the categories and actual symptoms constitutes an important source of diagnostic unreliability.

Presumably, diagnosis of the patients with archetypal symptoms would be less subject to suggestion effects than for those patients with low level and ambiguous symptoms, i.e., the majority, middle-range patients. Available evidence does suggest, at least, that both lay and professional recognition are less problematic with severe, obvious symptomatology (Mendelsohn et al. 1978; Edgerton 1969; Miller 1965, 1967). If so, this would parallel the ethnic stereotyping literature cited previously: suggestion had more effect on subjects' perceptions of faces that were in the intermediate range, i.e., between the blackest and whitest faces. The label was less likely to induce subjects to attribute black stereotypes to the whitest face (or the converse)(Secord 1959).

Logically, the psychiatric perspective finds its best support in the "archetypal" group because socio-cultural factors appear to have less effect on recognition, diagnosis, treatment, and outcome when symptoms are markedly bizarre (Miller 1965; Edgerton 1969; Mendelsohn et al. 1978; Strauss and Carpenter 1972). Markedly bizarre behaviors probably elicit essentially similar reactions throughout the world (Murphy 1976). But most patients exhibit low levels of ambiguous symptoms, and it is this group which best supports the present thesis. To be sure, good diagnostic reliability for a majority of patients can be obtained in research situations through standardization and strict screening procedures (Kety 1974). But these procedures bear little resemblance to the thousands of diagnoses made daily by physicians who are overburdened, have different training backgrounds, and use vague and ambiguous criteria (Kendell 1975: 37-9). In such conditions, it is highly probable that some individuals are "presumed" ill and thus funnelled into the psychiatric system of social control (Rosenhan 1975; Temerlin 1968; Katz et al. 1969). The question remains as to what proportion of patients fall in the "ambiguous" group and whether they should even be treated psychiatrically. These are potentially testable questions.

One could also object that the inaccuracy of popular and professional conception is irrelevant because people nevertheless profit from psychiatric treatment (Gove and Fain 1973). To be sure, some people do seem to profit from their treatment. But clinicians must acknowledge that considerable stigma still surrounds most diagnosis and treatment and that the major modes of treatment may entail serious risks for the patient - both medical and psychosocial (Carpenter et al. 1977; Asnis et al. 1977; Mattes et al. 1977; Friedberg 1975; Aviram and Segal 1973). Since public and professional conceptions do play such crucial roles in inducting people into this system and charting their course through it, these conceptions cannot be considered irrelevant.

The present analysis also has implications for studies of outcome and deinstitutionalization. Researchers have long noted the effects of sociocultural variables in determining case outcome. In particular, people of higher socio economic status and good family connections tend to spend less time in the hospital. Recently, Turner and Gartrell have challenged this view (1978). They argue that this correlation is a selection artifact and that it is really people's social competence that determines their length of stay in the hospital. In their view, social position and resources (allegedly) have no impact on outcome when one controls for social competence. The authors' measure of social competence (derived by means

of some rather dubious statistical procedures) is a person's social mobility (controlling for education and point of origin). Thus, the authors conclude that social status, good family connections, and work performance themselves do not help to determine outcome but rather arise as a consequence of conditions *within* individuals. These conditions are describable as psychopathology on the one hand and social competence on the other (1978:378).

There are several serious problems with this interpretation, but here I will examine only those directly relevant to the present argument. First, only those labelled "schizophrenic" were included in the sample. My analysis would suggest that this label already contains bias introduced by the processes of stereotyping. I argued above that psychiatric recognition criteria in America are broad enough for psychopathology to be perceived virtually anywhere (Beiser 1971; Kendell et al. 1971). We also saw that in psychiatric diagnosis, as in ethnic stereotyping, a previously attached label could greatly influence the qualities attributed to the stimulus (Temerlin 1968; Secord 1959). If this is so, then it is quite possible that this type of bias operates in research as well as clinical settings. Most researchers, including Turner and Gartrell, attempt to control for bias by having a "blind" evaluator rate the psychiatric interview material. But the original interviewers were not blind, nor were the patients' original clinical evaluators. Indeed, it is doubtful whether anyone can ever be totally blind to a respondent's ethnicity or poverty. This suggests that the bias introduced by selective perception may affect not only the makeup of the original population but also the subsequent research procedures.

Several studies of social class and diagnosis tend to support this contention. It appears that people in low status positions are more likely to acquire the diagnosis of schizophrenia (symptoms being equal)(Pasamanick 1963; Fischer 1969). Furthermore, people in higher status positions appear more likely to have their diagnoses changed to a milder syndrome to protect them (Cohen et al. 1975; se also Notes 3 and 4).

A second objection to Turner and Gartrell's conclusion is that some extremely elegant studies have documented the relevance of family desire and social status to patient outcome (Greenley 1972, forthcoming; Steadman and Cocozza 1974). These studies controlled for *various* measures of positive social functioning and found that family desires nevertheless remained a potent determinant. Their broader measures of social competence seem more convincing than Turner and Gartrell's rather narrow, abstruse, and possibly artifactual measure. Furthermore, Rushing (1978) recently demonstrated that, controlling for other significant variables, lower social status correlated with involuntary commitment. People with more resources are able to avoid being committed (symptoms being equal).

A third problem with Turner and Gartrell's argument is their insistence on locating the determinants of outcome exclusively *within* the individual. Earlier I argued that psychiatric diagnosis operates like ethnic stereotypes in defining social relations between groups. This includes relationships of power. The attempt to locate the causes of deviance and social "failure" exclusively *within* individuals preempts an examination of these relationships of power and possible socio-cultural determinants of human misery (Caplan and Nelson 1974). The assumption embodied in such thinking is convenient for those already in power and it is very much in the American grain. The assumption is that a person can "make it" if he really tries, regardless of external circumstances (Arensberg and Niehoff 1975; Hsu 1972; Townsend 1978). A corollary of this assumption, clearly embodied in Turner and Gartrell's definition of social competence, is that people who are not upwardly mobile, i.e., do not have a more prestigious occupation than their fathers, are somehow inferior to those that do. This seems a rather arbitrary (but very American) value judgment. It is quite possible that, viewed from another perspective, some of those behaviors that contribute to upward mobility might be considered selfish, stress-producing, alienating, or otherwise undesirable (Hsu 1972; Henry 1963). The emphasis on self-reliance and upward mobility, however, is deeply entrenched in American ideology and social policies. The comparison of Germany and America mentioned earlier (Townsend 1978) demonstrated that these values

also permeate American popular and professional conceptions of mental health. It is not surprising, therefore, that these values should also crop up in American mental health policy and research.

A final point concerns deinstitutionalization. My analysis of psychiatric conceptions as "inclusive" might prove to be dated because deinstitutionalization has caused some psychiatrists to use evermore strict criteria for psychosis. There is some truth to this proposition. As resources became scarce, an increasing number of patients are being "dumped" on other agencies (Robbins et al. 1977). Agencies frequently manipulate labels and categories to avoid patients with bad prognosis. In fact, there is some evidence to suggest that the penal system (at least in New York state) is increasingly using psychiatric labels to channel "repeaters" into the mental health system (Melick, Steadman and Cocozza forthcoming). For their side, mental health agencies are redefining or more strictly defining certain conditions (e.g., chronic brain syndrome) in order to shift chronic patients to nursing homes and other agencies (Hoyer and Tars 1978). Several officials of mental health facilities have admitted to me privately that such manipulation and "dumping" occurs, but it is difficult to obtain empirical data because of the opprobrium surrounding the topic (Bassuk and Gerson 1978).

We saw earlier that British psychiatrists had much narrower conceptions of psychosis than American psychiatrists (Kendell et al. 1971). One possible explanation for this discrepancy concerns our mental health system's social control function. If this system functions to control (and help) a broad range of deviants, including geriatric cases, indigents, and otherwise helpless people, then American professionals must have extremely broad criteria for psychosis. Insofar as some other countries have better welfare systems, fuller employment, and are less rampantly competitive, they can afford stricter criteria for "mental illness". Some evidence points in this direction (Townsend 1978; Taube and Redick 1973; Braginsky et al. 1969; Stearns and Ullman 1949). However, as deinstitutionalization proceeds and resources evaporate, American clinicians may begin to use different recognition criteria in order to channel patients into alternative agencies.

Conclusion

In his extensive study of prejudice, Ehrlich (1973) concludes that ethnic stereotypes are distinct, exclusive, consensual, persistent and widespread. Because these stereotypes serve as guidelines and boundaries for social relations between groups, they do not change until the actual social relations change. Barth echoes a similar sentiment (1969:30): "Revision only takes place where the category is grossly inadequate - not merely because it is untrue in any objective sense, but because it is consistently unrewarding to act upon, within the domain where the actor makes it relevant".

The evidence we have examined suggests that this is also true of stereotypes of mental illness. These stereotypes will persist until the actual relations between groups, including their relative power, begin to change.

References

Allport, Gordon. 1958. The Nature of Prejudice. New York: Anchor.

Arensberg, C.M. and A.H. Niehoff. 1975. American cultural values. In The Nacirema: Readings on American Culture J. Spradley and M. Rynkiewich, eds. Boston: Little, Brown.

Asnis, B.M., et al. 1977. A survey of tardive dyskinesia in psychiatric out-patients. American Journal of Psychiatry 134:1367-70.

Aviram, U., and S. Segal. 1973. Exclusion of the mentally ill. Archives of General Psychiatry 29:126-131.

Bakwin, R.M. 1963. Attitudes of parents of mentally ill children. Journal of the American Medical women's Association 18:305-8.

Bar-Levav, Reuven. 1976. The stigma of seeing a psychiatrist. American Journal of Psychotherapy 30:473-482.

Barth, Fredrik. 1969. Ethnic Groups and Boundaries. London: Allen and Unwin.

Barton, Russell. 1959. Institutional Neurosis. Bristol: John Wright & Sons.

Bassuk, E.L., and S. Gerson. 1978. Deinstitutionalization and mental health services. Scientific American 238:46-53.

Beiser, M. 1971. A study of personality assets in a rural community. Archives of General Psychiatry 24:244-54.

Berreman, G. 1972. Social categories and social interaction in urban India. American Anthropologist 74:567-586.

Bittner, Egon. 1967. Police discretion in emergency apprehension of mentally ill persons. Social Problems 14:278-292.

Braginsky, B.M., D. Braginsky, and K. Ring. 1969. Methods of Madness: The Mental Hospital as a Last Resort. New York: Holt, Rinehart & Winston.

Brigham, John C. 1971. Ethnic stereotypes. Psychological Bulletin 76:15-38.

Brooks, Garland P. 1971. The behaviourally abnormal in early Irish folklore. Papers in Psychology 5:5-13.

Caplan, N. and S. Nelson. 1974. Who's to blame. Psychology Today 8:99-104.

Carpenter, W.T., T.H. McGlashan, and J. Strauss. 1977. The treatment of acute schizophrenia without drugs: an investigation of some current assumptions. American Journal of Psychiatry 134:14-20.

Chauncey, Robert. 1975. Comment on the labelling theory of mental illness. American Sociological Review 40:248-52

Cocozza, J., and H. Steadman. 1978. Prediction in psychiatry: an example of misplaced confidence in experts. Social Problems 25:253-77.

Cohen, E., H. Harbin, and M. Wright. 1975. Some considerations in the formulation of psychiatric diagnosis. Journal of Nervous and Mental Disease 160:422-27.

Crocetti, G., Herzl Spiro, and Iradj Siassi. 1974. Contemporary Attitudes Toward Mental Illness. University of Pittsburgh Press.

Cumming, E., and J. Cumming. 1957. Closed Ranks: An Experiment in Mental Health Education. Cambridge: Harvard University Press.

----- 1972. On the stigma of mental illness. In Rebellion and Retreat. S. Palmer, ed. pp. 449-61. Columbus, Ohio: Merril.

D'Arcy, Carl, and Joan Brockman. 1976. Changing public recognition of psychiatric symptoms? Blackfoot revisited. Journal of Health and Social Behavior 17:302-310.

Davis, Kingsley. 1959. The myth of functional analysis as a special method in sociology and anthropology. American Sociological Review 24:757-772.

Dawidoff, Donald J. 1975. Commitment of the mentally ill in New York: some comments and suggestions. Journal of Psychiatry and Law 3:79-95.

DeVos. G., and L. Romanucci-Ross. 1975. Ethnicity: vessel of meaning and emblem of contrast. In

Ethnic Identity. G. DeVos and L. Romanucci-Ross, eds. Palo Alto: Mayfield.

Edgerton, Robert B. 1966. Conceptions of psychosis in four East African societies. American Anthropologist 68:408-25.

----- 1969. On the "recognition" of mental illness. "In" Changing Perspectives in Mental Illness. S.C. Plog and R.B. Edgerton, eds. pp. 49-72. New York: Holt, Rinehart & Winston.

Ehrlich, H.J. 1973. The Social Psychology of Prejudice. New York: Wiley.

Eidheim. H. 1969. When ethnic identity is a social stigma. In Ethnic Groups and Boundaries. F. Barth, ed. London: Allen and Unwin.

Elkins. S. 1961. Slavery and Personality. In Studying Personality Cross-Culturally. B. Kaplan, ed. New York: Row, Peterson.

Ennis, B., and L. Siegel. 1973. The Rights of Mental Patients: The Basic ACLU Guide to a Mental Patient's Rights. New York: Avon.

Erikson, Kai. 1967. Notes on the sociology of deviance. In Mental Illness and Social Processes. Thomas J. Scheff, ed. New York: Harper and Row.

Felix, R.H. 1967. Mental Illness: Progress and Prospects. Columbia University Press.

Fischer, J. 1969. Negroes and whites and rates of mental illness: reconsideration of a myth. Psychiatry 32:428-46.

Foucault, M. 1965. Madness and Civilization: A History of Insanity in the Age of Reason. Richard Howard, tr. New York: Pantheon.

Fracchia, J., D. Canale, E. Cambria, E. Ruest, and C. Sheppard. 1976. Public views of ex-mental patients: a note on perceived dangerousness and unpredictability. Psychological Reports 38:495-498.

Friedberg, J. 1975. Let's stop blasting the brain. Psychology Today 9:18-20.

German, J.R., and A.C. Siner. 1977. Punishing the not guilty: hospitalization of persons acquitted by reason of insanity. Psychiatric Quarterly 49:238-54.

Gilboy, J. and J.R. Schmidt. 1971. "Voluntary" hospitalization of the mentally ill. Northwestern University law Review 66:429-53.

Glassner, Barry. 1979. Essential Interactionism. London: Routledge, Kegan Paul.

Goffman, Erving. 1964. Stigma. Englewood Cliffs, New Jersey: Prentice-Hall.

Goldman, A.R., R.H. Bohr, and T.A. Steinberg. 1970. On posing as mental patients: reminiscences and recommendations. Professional Psychology 2:427-34.

Gove, W.R. 1975. The labelling theory of mental illness: a reply to Scheff. American Sociological Review 40:242-48.

Gove, W.R., and T. Fain. 1973. The stigma of mental hospitalization: an attempt to evaluate its consequences. Archives of General Psychiatry 28:495-500.

Greenley, J.R. 1972. The psychiatric patient's family and length of hospitalization. Journal of Health and Social Behavior 13:25-37.

----- Forthcoming: Family symptom Tolerance and rehospitalization experiences of psychiatric patients. In Research in Community and Mental Health. R. Simmons, ed. Greenwich, Connecticut: JAI.

Halpert, H.P. 1969. Public acceptance of the mentally ill. Public Health Reports 84 (January): 59-64.

Handel, Janet. 1973. Breaking fears of mental illness. Journal of Emotional Education 13:133-139.

Hempel, Carl. 1959. Logic of functional analysis. In Symposium on Sociological Theory. Llewellyn Gross, ed. New York: Row, Peterson.

Henry, Jules. 1963. Culture Against Man. New York: Random House.

Hoyer, F.W. and S.E. Tars. 1978. Problems and issues facing the gerontological practitioner in the community mental health center. Paper presented at the 86th Annual Meeting of the American Psychological Association, Toronto, August, 1978.

Hsu, F.L.K. 1972. American core value and national character. In Psychological Anthropology. F. Hsu, ed. San Francisco: Schenkman.

Jaeckel, Martin, and Stefan Wieser. 1970. Das Bild des Geisteskranken in der Öffentlichkeit. Stuttgart: Georg Thieme Verlag.

Journal of Criminal Law and Criminology. 1975. The "crime" of mental illness: extension of "criminal" procedural safeguards to involuntary civil commitments. Journal of Criminal Law and Criminology 66:255-270.

Katz, M.M., J.O. Cole, and H.A. Lowery. 1969. Studies of the diagnostic process: the influence of symptom perception, past experience, and ethnic background on diagnostic decisions. American Journal of Psychiatry 125:109-119.

kendell, R.E. 1975. The Role of Diagnosis in Psychiatry. Oxford: Blackwell.

Kendell, R.E., J. Cooper, A. Gourley, and J. Copeland. 1971. Diagnostic criteria of American and British psychiatrists. Archives of General Psychiatry 25:123-130.

Kety, S.S. 1974. From rationalization to reason. American Journal of Psychiatry 131:957-963.

Klapp, Orrin E. 1972. Heroes, Villains, and Fools. San Diego: Aegis.

LaPiere, R.T. 1934. Attitudes vs. actions. Social Forces 13:230-7.

Levinson, F.J., and E.B. Gallagher. 1964. Patienthood in the Mental Hospital. Boston: Houghton-Mifflin.

Levi-Strauss, Claude. 1965. The Raw and the Cooked. John and Doreen Wightman, tr. New York: Harper and Row.

Lewis, Verl S., and Abraham N. Zeichner. 1960. Impact of admission to a mental hospital on the patient's family. Mental Hygiene 44:503-510.

Lippmann, Walter. 1930. Public Opinion. New York: Macmillan.

Mattes, J., B. Rosen, and D. Klein. 1977. Comparison of the clinical effectiveness of short vs. long stay psychiatric hospitalization. Journal of Nervous and Mental Disease 165:387-94.

Mechanic, David. 1962. Some factors in identifying and defining mental illness. Mental Hygiene 46:66-74.

Melick, M.E., H. Steadman, and J. Cocozza. Forthcoming: The medicalization of criminal behavior among mental patients. Journal of Health and Social Behavior.

Mendelsohn, F., G. Egri, and B. Dohrenwend. 1978. Diagnosis of nonpatients in the general community. American Journal of Psychiatry 135:1163-7.

Miller, Dorothy. 1965. Worlds That Fail: Retrospective Analysis of Mental Patients' Careers, Part I. California mental Health Research Monograph, No. 6. Sacramento: California State Dept. of Mental Hygiene.

----- 1967. Retrospective analysis of posthospital mental patients' worlds. Journal of Health and Social Behavior 8:136-40.

Millon, T. 1975. Reflections on Rosenhan's "On being sane in insane places." Journal of Abnormal Psychology 84:456-61.

Murphy, Jane M. 1976. Psychiatric labelling in cross-cultural perspective. Science 191:1019-28.

nagel, Ernest. 1961. Structure of Science. New York: Harcourt, Brace.

Needham, Rodney, ed. 1978. Right and Left: Essays on dual Symbolic Classification. University of Chicago Press.

Nunnally, Jum C. 1961. Popular Conception of Mental Health. New York: Holt, Rinehart and Winston.

Olmsted, D., and K. Durham. 1976. Stability of mental health attitudes: a semantic differential study. Journal of Health and Social Behavior 17:35-44.

Pasamanick, B. 1963. Some misconceptions concerning differences in the racial prevalence of mental disease. American Journal of Orthopsychiatry 33:72-86.

Rabkin, J.G. 1972. Opinions about mental illness: a review of the literature. Psychological Bulletin 77:153-171.

----- 1974. Public attitudes toward mental illness: a review of the literature. Schizophrenia Bulletin 10:9-33.

Razran, G. 1950. Ethnic dislike in stereotypes. Journal of Abnormal and Social Psychology 45:7-27.

Robbins, E.S., et al. 1977. Transfers to a psychiatric emergency room: a fresh look at the dumping syndrome. Psychiatric Quarterly 49:197-202.

Robbins, Lewis L. 1966. A historical review of the classification of behavior disorders and one current perspective. In The Classification of Behavior Disorders. Leonard D. Eron, ed. Chicago: Aldine.

Rokeach, m. 1964. The Three Christs of Ypsilanti. New York: Knopf.

Rosenhan, D.L. 1973. On being sane in insane places. Science 179:250-258.

----- 1975. The contextual nature of psychiatric diagnosis. Journal of Abnormal Psychology 84:462-474.

Rothman, D.J. 1971. The Discovery of the Asylum: Social Order and Disorder in the New Republic. Boston: Little, Brown.

Rushing, W. 1978. Status resources, societal reactions, and type of mental hospital admission. American Sociological Review 43:521-33.

Sampson, H., S. Messinger, and R. Towne. 1962. Family process and becoming a mental patient. American Journal of Sociology 68:88-96.

Scheff, Thomas. 1966. Being Mentally Ill. Chicago: Aldine.

----- 1975. A reply to Chauncey and Gove. American Sociological Review 40:252-257.

Schneider, U., and S. Wieser. 1972. Der Psychischkranke in den Massenmedien: Ergebnisse einer systematischen Inhaltsanalyse. Fortschritte der Neurologie, Psychiatrie und ihrer Grenzgebiete 40:136-163.

Schrag, Peter. 1978. Mind Control. New York: Pantheon.

Secord, P. 1959. Stereotyping and favorableness in the perception of negro faces. journal of Abnormal and Social Psychology 59:309-15.

Shibutani, Tamotsu. 1970. On the personification of adversaries. In Human nature and Collective Behavior. T. Shibutani, ed. Englewood Cliffs, New Jersey: Prentice Hall.

Silver, A. 1955. The home management of children with schizophrenia. American Journal of Psychotherapy 9:196-215.

Smith, Kathleen, Muriel W. Pumphrey, and Julian C. Hall. 1963. The "last straw": the decisive incident resulting in the request for hospitalization in 100 schizophrenic patients. American Journal of Psychiatry 120:228-233.

Spiro, Melford. 1961. Social systems, personality, and functional analysis. *In* Studying Personality Cross-Culturally. Bert Kaplan, ed. New York: Row, Peterson and Company.

Spitzer, R.L. 1975. On pseudoscience, logic in remission, and psychiatric diagnoses: a critique of Rosenhan's "On being sane in insane places." Journal of Abnormal Psychology 84:442-52.

Strole, L., et al. 1962. Mental Health in the Metropolis: The Midtown Manhattan Study. New York: McGraw-Hill.

Star, S.A. 1955. The public's ideas about mental illness. Paper presented to the Annual Meeting of the National Association for Mental Health. Indianapolis, 5 November 1955.

Steadman, Henry J. 1972. The psychiatrist as a conservative agent of social control. Social Problems 20:263-271.

Steadman, Henry J., and Joseph J. Cocozza. 1974. Careers of the Criminally Insane: Excessive Social Control of Deviance. Lexington, Massachusettes: Lexington Books.

----- 1977-78. Public images of the criminally insane: a case of selective reporting and false perceptions. Public Opinion Quarterly, (Winter) 41:523-33.

----- 1978. Public perceptions of the criminally insane. Hospital and Community Psychiatry 29(7):457-9.

Steadman, Henry J., Joseph J. Cocozza, and Mary Evans Melick. 1978. Explaining the increased crime rate of mental patients: the changing clientele of state hospitals. American journal of Psychiatry 135:816-20.

Stearns, A.W., and A.D. Ullman. 1949. One thousand unsuccessful careers. American Journal of Psychiatry 11:801-9.

Strauss, John S. et al. Forthcoming: Do psychiatric patients fit their diagnoses? Patterns of symptomatology as described with biplot. Journal of Nervous and Mental Disease.

Strauss, J.S., and W.T. Carpenter, Jr. 1972. The prediction of outcome in schizophrenia. I: characteristics of outcome. Archives of General Psychiatry 27:739-46.

Stumme, Wolfgang. 1973. Das Bild vom Psychischgestöten und seinem Therapeuten in den Massendedien. Praxis der Psychotherapie 18:193-199.

Szasz, Thomas. 1963. Law, Liberty, and Psychiatry. New York: Macmillan.

----- 1970. The Manufacture of Madness. New York: Harper and Row.

Taube, C., and R. Redick. 1973. Utilization of Mental Health Resources by Persons Diagnosed with Schizophrenia. Rockville, Md.: Biometry Branch, National Institute of Mental Health.

Temerlin, Maurice K. 1968. Suggestion effects in psychiatric diagnosis. Journal of Nervous and Mental Disease 147:349-353.

Townsend, J.M. n.d. Media images of mental illness: an analysis of T.V. Guide descriptions for 1976. Unpublished manuscript.

----- 1976. Self-concept and the institutionalization of mental patients: an overview and critique. Journal of Health and Social Behavior 17:263-271.

----- 1977. Self-concept and the institutionalization of mental patients: a reply to Henley. Journal of Health and Social Behavior 18:442-4.

----- 1978. Cultural Conceptions and Mental Illness: A Comparison of Germany and America. Chicago: University of Chicago.

Turner, R. Jay and J.W. Gartrell. 1978. social factors in psychiatric outcome: toward the resolution of interpretive controversies. American Sociological Review 43:368-82.

Wallace, Anthony F.C. 1972. Mental illness, biology, and culture. *In* Psychological Anthropology. F.L.K. Hsu, ed. San Francisco: Schenkman.

Weiner, B. 1975. "On being sane in insane places": a process (attributional) analysis and critique. Journal of Abnormal Psychology 84:433-41.

Wicker, A.W. 1969. Attitudes vs. actions: the relationship of verbal and overt behavioral responses to attitude objects. Journal of Social Issues 25:41-78.

Wing, J.K. 1962. Institutionalism in mental hospitals. British Journal of Social and Clinical Psychology 1:38-51.

Yarrow, M.R., C.G. Schwartz, H.S. Murphy, and L.C. Deasy. 1955. The psychological meaning of mental illness in the family. Journal of Social Issues 11:12-24.

Notes

1. Special thanks are due the following scholars for reading and commenting on earlier versions of this paper: Henry J. Steadman, James R. Greenley, and Barry Glassner. A debt of gratitude is also owed Arthur Kleinman, for his helpful editorial comments, and to Patricia J. Waite for her aid in manuscript preparation.

2. One could object that the present argument only applies to involuntary treatment and that self-labelling and

voluntary treatment do not participate in the filtering process described here. The empirical evidence on recognition of mental illness, however, does not support this view. Rather, it appears that self-labelling is subject to essentially the same dynamics and thresholds as labelling by others. In other words, those who do finally recognize they have psychiatric problems have typically resisted this conclusion despite mounting evidence for some time (Yarrow et al. 1955; Lewis and Zeichner 1960). Thus, many patients who appear to be "voluntary" actually began as "involuntary" patients and were under some sort of official custody and/or informal pressure when they were admitted to treatment (Gilboy and Schmidt; Schrag 1978). In fact, it seems that a majority of even long-term institutionalized patients continue to deny they are mentally ill (Townsend 1976, 1977). To summarize, though the question is certainly worth researching, at present there is no good reason to suppose that the stereotypes and processes described in this paper operate significantly differently for patients who voluntarily seek treatment. Note 4 below also pertains to this question.

3.   Interestingly, it seems that stereotypes of mental illness are not only like ethnic stereotypes, at times they actually *are* ethnic stereotypes. For example, Protestant New Englanders frequently labelled Irish immigrants "degenerate" or "mentally ill" and in the mid-nineteenth century the latter became the predominant population in Worcester, Tewksbury, and other state hospitals in the northeast (Rothman 1971). In the same vein, Stearns and Ullman (1949:805) list the characteristics that made recent immigrants particularly vulnerable to such labelling: they have come to this country usually without funds and are only sought as unskilled laborers; they speak a foreign dialect or language; when unemployment increases, they are the first to lose their jobs; they have few resources in family or friends. It should be noted that these same traits characterize urban Blacks and may help to explain the reported correlations between poverty, being Black, and schizophrenia (Fischer 1969; see also "Discussion" in text).

4.   One might also object that American popular culture's tendency to psychologize problems has helped to reduce the actual stigma surrounding mental illness and has therefore increased the public's willingness to enter treatment (Gove and Fain 1973; Crocetti et al. 1974). There are several problems with this argument. First, careful restudies have demonstrated that public attitudes toward mental illness continue to be extremely negative (Olmsted and durham 1976; D'Arcy and Brockman 1976). Second, the present thesis argues that the public's exaggerated stereotypes of mental illness reflect a cognitive and conative dichotomy between what is sane and acceptable and what is not. If this is true, then it is quite possible that psychiatric treatment for certain psychological problems might not be perceived as "mental illness". Consistent with this interpretation is the fact that in some urban upper-class circles it is acceptable, even fashionable, to have a private analyst. It is not fashionable, however, to be hospitalized for schizophrenia. More research is needed, of course, to validate fully the relationships between stereotypes, various mental disorders, and actual public reactions. But it seems reasonable to predict a higher cognitive and conative rejection rate for serious mental disorders (e.g., schizophrenia) than for minor ones (e.g., a visit to a marriage counsellor). Thus, people's actual behavior probably continues to reflect their dichotomous conceptions, and psychologized problems in living are simply perceived as deviations on the "sane" side of the break - as they were before they were psychologized (Szasz 1970; Schrag 1978).

Consistent with this argument is the fact that more serious diagnoses and treatments tend to correlate with lack of status and power: people with the least power tend to receive the diagnoses and treatments which carry the most opprobrium. One of the reasons for this appears to be their inability (due to their relative lack of resources) to avoid those diagnoses and treatments (Rushing 1978; Schrag 1978; Cohen et al. 1975). This suggests that the American middle and upper classes' tendency to psychologize problems in living has not really affected the public's dichotomous conceptions. "Real" mental illness is still perceived in exaggerated and negative terms and as something to be denied and shunned, if at all possible.

The Politics of Physical Differences: Disability and Discrimination

HARLAN HAHN   *University of Southern California*

Although a "minority-group" model has emerged to challenge the traditional dominance of the "functional-limitations" paradigm of the study of disability, research on attitudes toward disabled people has not produced a theoretical orientation that reflects these developments. This paper proposes a new conceptual framework, based on the fundamental values of personal appearance and individual autonomy, for assessing the "aesthetic" and "existential" anxiety aroused by persons with disabilities. Investigations using this perspective might contribute to determining the attitudinal foundations of the competing models that are dividing research on disability.

In recent years, a growing social and political movement of disabled citizens has had a major impact on the study of disability. Inspired in part by the passage of major legislation, such as Section 504 of the Rehabilitation Act of 1973 and P.L. 94-142, the Education of All Handicapped Children Act of 1975, many persons with disabilities have begun to feel that their problems stem primarily from prejudice and discrimination rather than from their functional impairments. This trend has promoted a corresponding interest by researchers in a new theoretical approach to issues confronting this segment of the population—namely, a "minority-group" model of disability, in contrast to the earlier "functional-limitations" model (Hahn, 1985a).

Much of the impetus for this change can be traced to a significant shift in the definition of disability. While disability traditionally has been examined from a *medical* approach that focuses on functional impairments or from an *economic* approach that emphasizes vocational limitations, a new *socio-political* approach has emerged that regards disability as a product of interactions between individual and environment (Hahn, 1982) by recognizing that the fundamental restrictions of a disability may be located in the surroundings that people encounter rather than

within the disabled individual. From a socio-political vantage point, the difficulties confronted by disabled persons are viewed as largely the result of a disabling environment instead of personal defects or deficiencies. The extent to which environmental modifications could ameliorate the functional constraints of a disability may eventually be determined by technology and by the limits of human imagination in designing a world adapted to the needs of everyone. Just as important, this perspective can guide research viewing disabled citizens as an oppressed minority. Whereas the medical and economic definitions have tended to concentrate on methods of improving the disabled individual's capabilities, the socio-political approach indicates the need for strengthened laws to combat discrimination against persons with disabilities.

There are at least two additional corollaries that follow from a socio-political view of the problems of disabled persons. First, this approach emphasizes that the functional demands exerted on human beings by the environment are fundamentally determined by public policy. The present forms of architectural structures and social institutions exist because statutes, ordinances, and codes either required or permitted them to be constructed in that manner. These public policies imply values, expectation, and assumptions about the physical and behavioral attributes that people ought to possess in order to survive or to participate in community life. Many everyday activities, such as the distance people walk, the steps they climb, the materials they read, and the messages they receive, impose stringent requirements on persons with different levels of functional skills. These characteristics of the environment that have a discriminatory effect on disabled citizens cannot be considered simply coincidental. Rather than reflecting immutable aspects of an environment decreed by natural law, they represent the consequences of prior policy decisions.

Reprinted From: *Journal of Social Issues, Volume 44, No.1, 1988 pp. 39-47*, with permission.

Second, awareness that the environment is basically molded by past and present public policy suggests *public attitudes* as a crucial component of the surroundings with which disabled people must contend. From a minority-group perspective, many of their difficulties can be traced to the attitudinal environment of society (Hahn, 1985b). In a culture that places a high premium on the physical and behavioral capabilities for mastering the environment, the effort to disentangle attitudinal factors from functional standards is obviously a complex endeavor. Yet this task seems crucial to the evaluation of people with disabilities as a minority group.

Although many nondisabled observers are reluctant to openly acknowledge their aversion to persons with disabilities, there is a strong possibility that both the prevalent emphasis on disabled people's functional limitations and the pervasive features of an unaccommodating environment disguise widespread feeling of bias or prejudice. As Siller (1976) has noted, "typical 'gut' reactors frequently express queasy feelings aroused by the sight of disability and vehemently resist working or socializing with severely handicapped individuals" (p. 67).

Although many early studies (Barker, Wright, Meyerson, & Gonick, 1953; Safilios-Rothschild, 1970; Wright, 1960) acknowledged that disabled people constituted a minority group, this approach was overshadowed by the predominant focus on functional limitations. The relative lack of a theory identifying disabled persons as an oppressed minority seems to have been perpetuated in studies of attitudes toward disability. Two recent surveys of the literature on this subject (Altman, 1981; Livneh, 1982), for example, offered impressive evidence of burgeoning research on attitudes toward disability, but neither developed a framework that would facilitate investigation of the empirical foundations of the functional-limitations and the minority-group models. Since existing social-psychological theories on attitudes and attributions do not seem clearly adaptable to consideration of the role of disabled citizens in modern society (Hahn, 1985c), there appears a pressing need to develop a new conceptual framework for appraisal of attitudes toward people with disabilities.

Attitudes and Discrimination

Minority groups have been subjected to various forms of exploitation and oppression, and the sources of their treatment may be traced to pervasive social values of the dominant majority. A principal problem in establishing the concept of disabled persons as an oppressed group has been the prevalent assumptions of their biological inferiority. Whereas a major thrust of social science research on other minorities during the past century has been to refute such assumptions and to demonstrate that their unequal status stems primarily from prejudicial attitudes, many professionals as well as popular images of disabled individuals continue to harbor presuppositions of inferiority based on their functional incapacities. Consequently, it has been commonly overlooked that the origins of prejudice are based on widespread perceptions that disabled individuals violate important cultural norms and values, and that this fact permits them to be set apart from the remainder of the population.

Two critical values in 20th-century Western society that especially influence the treatment of disabled people are personal appearance and individual autonomy. The crucial importance of these values is revealed by sources that range from the mundane to the philosophical. Persons who fail to meet prescribed standards of physical attractiveness and functional independence not only are assumed biologically inferior, but they are also exposed to a stigma that depicts them as "not quite human" (Goffman, 1963, p.5).

These ideas can provide the basis for a major reconceptulization of the structure of attitudes about disability. Like other minorities who have been victims of discrimination, disabled persons have characteristics that permit them to be differentiated from the rest of the population. These characteristics, which may be identified by physical or behavioral cues or by verbal labels, are likely to arouse strong feelings in nondisabled observers about their own appearance or autonomy. Moreover, these responses of observers are clearly related to the theoretical underpinnings of the competing models for the study of disability. Whereas responses to disability elicited by worries about individual autonomy are closely related to the functional-limitations model, reactions evoked by concerns about personal appearance are closely associated with the minority-group model. Thus, a new approach to the examination of attitudes toward disabled persons based on the concepts of autonomy and appearance may have important practical as well as theoretical utility for further research on disability.

The need for such a framework is underscored by the relative paucity of studies founded on the minority-group model of disability. Although surveys indicate that 45% of disabled Americans believe people with disabilities are a minority group in the same sense as are Blacks and Hispanics (Harris & Associates, 1986), academic investigations of the problems of disabled persons as a minority group are comparatively recent and rare (Gliedman & Roth, 1980; hahn, 1985c). The purpose of this paper is to propose a new and still speculative conceptual framework for research on attitudes toward disabled persons that encompasses the minority-group as well as the functional-limitations models of disability.

Components of Attitudes Toward Disability

The concepts of "aesthetic" and "existential" anxiety occupied a prominent position in the propositional inventory developed by Livneh (1982), and they seem to constitute a valuable means of assessing the attitudinal foundations of the minority-group and the functional-limitations paradigms for the study of disability (Hahn, 1983). Both of these concepts represent deep and powerful apprehensions.

Existential anxiety refers to the threat of potential loss of functional capabilities by the nondisabled. The existential anxiety triggered by disabilities occasionally may become the subject of conscious attention. Sometimes these concerns are evident in the silent thought that "there, but for the grace of God [or luck or fate or other fundamental beliefs], go I." At other times, these worries may be verbalized in statements such as, "I would rather be dead than live as a paraplegic [or as blind, deaf, or immobilized]." In fact, the threat of a permanent and debilitating disability,

with its resulting problems, can even outrank the fear of death, which is, after all, inevitable.

Existential Anxiety

Probably the most common threat from disabled individuals is summed up in the concept of existential anxiety: the perceived threat that a disability could interfere with functional capacities deemed necessary to the pursuit of a satisfactory life. The expectation that everyone ought to achieve model levels of functional proficiency——or perhaps the fear that many might lose these abilities——seems so strong that, for hundreds of years of modern history, almost no thought was given to the possibility that human capabilities could be increased by altering the environment in which people lived. Individuals who failed to attain the mobility, sensory, or communication skills to master the existing environment were consigned to being recipients of disability benefits from whatever social welfare programs existed in a society. The principal effects of existential anxiety have been to relegate disabled individuals to the role of helpless or dependent nonparticipants in community life, and to exacerbate nondisabled persons' worries about the potential loss of physical or behavioral capabilities that could result from a disability. In a society that appears to prize liberty more than equality, and that tends to equate freedom with personal autonomy rather than with the opportunity to exercise meaningful choice, the apprehensions aroused by functional restrictions resulting from a disability often seem overwhelming.

In general, empirical studies based on the functional-limitations model of disability have not identified existential anxiety as a single component of attitudes toward disabled persons. Jones et al. (1984), for example, described five dimensions of attitudes toward stigmatized groups in addition to aesthetic qualities. Yet all of the specified characteristics of visible human difference including their origin, peril, disruptiveness, and the course or prognosis of the disability, would have little importance unless respondents had some understanding of the personal consequences of these characteristics. In other words, the social stigma of a disability fundamentally derives from the fact that the resulting functional impairments may interfere with important life activities. Hence, there appears ample justification for using existential anxiety as a comprehensive concept to describe unfavorable perceptions of disabled people stemming from the functional-limitations model of disability.

Existential anxiety seems to involve a sense of personal identification with the position of a disabled person. Therefore, the presence or absence of this type of identification could be investigated to determine whether or not a propensity to project existential fears onto disabled people is a primary source of unfavorable perceptions of individuals with disabilities.

Aesthetic Anxiety

The aesthetic anxiety aroused by the appearance of people with visible disabilities has at least two major aspects. First, the discrimination directed at disabled individuals is partly due to their being devalued because they do not present conventional images of human physique or behavior. After an extensive review of research on body images, Fisher (1973) concluded,

> Despite all the efforts invested by our society in an attempt to rally sympathy for the crippled, they still elicit serious discomfort. It is well documented that the disfigured person makes others feel anxious and he becomes an object to be warded off. He is viewed as simultaneously inferior and threatening. He becomes associated with the special class of monster images that haunt each culture. (p.73)

These worries may well reflect a prevalent preoccupation by men and women about their own appearance.

Second, aesthetic anxiety may result in a tendency to place those who are perceived as different or strange in a subordinate role. Throughout history, perceptible features such as racial or ethnic characteristics, gender, and aging have formed an important basis for prejudice toward minority groups. Little research has been conducted on the extent to which people with disabilities are regarded as failing to meet commonly accepted standards of personal appearance. However, studies have shown that perceptions of physical appearance affect the evaluation of writing talent (Landy & Sigall, 1974) and employment decisions (Schuler & Berger, 1979). On the basis of numerous studies, Saxe (1979) concluded that attractiveness

> seems to be more insidious than previously suggested, as it affects and, in some cases, pervades our relationships with others,]. It causes discomfort, both to the unattractive (who are denied justice) and to the attractive (who may be expected to perform at levels higher than they are capable of). (p. 12)

Other research has shown that unattractive physical characteristics can lead to the attribution that their bearer has a disability such as epilepsy (Hansson & Duffield, 1976). By similar logic, there is reason to believe that the perceived unattractiveness of a disability could be a significant source of unfavorable attitudes toward the disabled person, as in the findings of Bull (1979). Also, disabled men and women possess limited choices in the formation of personal relationships as a result of an "aesthetic-sexual aversion" to disability that permeates society (Hahn, 1981; Safilios-Rothschild, 1970). Thus, in a society that places extraordinary stress on beauty and attractiveness, aesthetic anxieties may be an important component of perceptions of disabled people.

Relationship of Existential and Aesthetic Anxiety

One of the major problems that has plagued prior studies of attitudes toward disabled persons can be traced to the traditional ascendancy of the functional-limitations model in research on disability. Most investigators who have defined and understood disability primarily as a problem of physical or behavioral impairments have tended to assume that reactions to disabled individuals can be explained solely in terms of existential concerns. However, both existential anxiety and aesthetic anxiety are involved in unfavorable perceptions of people with disabilities in a wide variety of circumstances.

Given the traditional prevalence of the functional-limitations model, relatively few nondisabled people may be prepared to understand disability as a problem that revolves largely around aesthetic considerations. The effort to disentangle existential and aesthetic elements of attitudes toward disabled people could provide an important contribution to resolving the conflict between the functional-limitations model and the minority-group model for research on disability.

Whereas aesthetic concerns are aroused by the pervasive cultural emphasis on personal attractiveness, existential worries seem based on a process of identification between a disabled individual and the nondisabled observer. Hence, attempts to assess the amount of identification that occurs between disabled and nondisabled persons could provide a means of unravelling responses to disability. If nondisabled individuals were found to have a strong capacity to internalize the threat posed by a disability and to project those feelings onto a disabled individual, such a finding would suggest support for the primacy of existential anxiety in contrast, if most nondisabled observers lack the capability to form a close or accurate identification with the circumstances of a disabled person, their unfavorable perceptions may simply indicate a desire not to associate or interact with others considered alien or strange. The former results would be most consistent with the functional-limitations model, while the latter outcome would highlight the discrimination identified as a major problem by the minority-group paradigm. Some support for the latter interpretation seems indicated by the fact that predominant attitudes toward persons with disabilities reflect aversion rather than more intense manifestations of anxiety (Altman, 1981; Livneh, 1982).

Policy Implications

A socio-political understanding of disability requires that attention must be paid to both existential and aesthetic sources of discrimination. From a functional-limitations perspective, existential anxiety seems primary; that is, nondisabled persons are presumed to focus on the alleged biological inferiority of people with disabilities, thus arousing fears about the potential mutability

and deterioration of their own bodies. Yet policy makers and courts usually have been reluctant to implement the principle of equality by mandating environmental modifications in response to people's clinically demonstrable organic defects or deficiencies. On the other hand, the minority-group model may compel observers to consider the manner in which aesthetic anxieties operate to distance and disparage disabled individuals. Precisely because these worries are relatively trivial and difficult to rationalize, research assessing them could form a firm foundation for constitutional challenges to the unequal treatment of the disabled minority.

The two components of attitudes toward persons with disabilities seem to yield different policy implications. Both types of anxiety can be discriminatory. for example, many job qualifications that bar disabled individuals from employment may reflect existential worries. However, in an environment not yet adapted to the needs of disabled people, aesthetic anxiety is clearly more difficult to justify than existential anxiety. Hence, a finding that aesthetic considerations form a major source of unfavorable assessments of disabled persons could lend strong support to the argument that citizens with disabilities should be considered a "suspect class" within the meaning of the equal protection clause of the Fourteenth Amendment to the U.S. Constitution.

In addition, the results of empirical research utilizing this conceptual framework might have an important impact on strategies for achieving attitude change. For example, the relative lack of success of past efforts to persuade employers to hire disabled workers may be due to the possibility that aesthetic anxiety is less susceptible to influence by cognitive appeals than is existential anxiety. An increased emphasis on the aesthetic component of attitudes toward people with disabilities could fruitfully shift the emphasis in advocacy efforts to the affective dimension of attitude change.

References

Altman, B.M. 1981. Studies of attitudes toward the handicapped: The need for a new direction. *Social Problems*, 28, 321-337.

Barker, R.G., Wright, B.A., Meyerson, L., & Gonick, M.R. 1953. *Adjustment to physical handicap and illness: A survey of the social psychology of physique and disability*. New York: Social Science Research Council.

Bull, R. 1979. The psychological significance of facial deformity. In M. Cook & G. Wilson eds. *Love and attraction: An international conference*. (pp. 21-25). Oxford: Pergamon.

Fisher, S. 1973. *Body consciousness: You are what you feel*. Englewood Cliffs, NJ: Prentice-Hall.

Gliedman, J., & Roth, W. 1980. *The unexpected minority: handicapped children in America*. New York: Harcourt Brace Jovanovich.

Goffman, E. 1963. *Stigma: Notes on the management of spoiled identity*. Englewood Cliffs, NJ: Prentice-Hall.

Hahn, H. 1981. The social component of sexuality and disability: Some problems and proposals. *Sexuality and Disability*, 4, 220-233.

——————— 1982. Disability and rehabilitation policy: Is paternalistic neglect really benign? *Public Administration Review*, 43, 385-389.

——————— 1983 (March-April). Paternalism and public policy. *Society*, pp. 36-46.

——————— 1985a. Changing perceptions of disability and the future of rehabilitation. In L.G. Perlman & G.F. Austin, eds. *Societal influences in rehabilitation planning: A blueprint for the 21st century* (pp. 53-46). Alexandria, VA: National Rehabilitation Association.

——————— 1985b. Disability policy and the problem of discrimination. *American Behavioral Scientist*, 28, 293-318.

——————— 1985c. Toward a politics of disability: Definitions, disciplines, and policies. *Social Science Journal*, 22, 87-105.

Hansson, R.O., & Duffield, B.J. 1976. Physical attractiveness and the attribution of epilepsy. *Journal of Social Psychology*, 99, 233-240.

Harris, L., & Associates. 1986. *The ICD survey of disabled Americans: Bringing disabled Americans into the mainstream*. New York: Author.

Jones, E.E., Farina, A., Hastorf, A.H., Markus, H., Miller, D.T., Scott, R.A., & French, R. 1984. *Social stigma: The psychology of marked relationships*. New York: Freeman.

Landy, D., & Sigall, H. 1974. Beauty is talent: Task evaluation as a function of the performer's physical attractiveness. *Journal of Personality and Social Psychology*, 29, 299-304.

Livneh, H. 1982. On the origins of negative attitudes toward people with disabilities. *Rehabilitation Literature*, 43, 338-347.

Safilios-Rothschild, C. 1970. *The sociology and social psychology of disability and rehabilitation*. New York: Random House.

Saxe, L. 1979. The ubiquity of physical appearance as a determinant of social relationships. In M. Cook & G. Wilson, eds. *Love and attractiveness: An international conference* (pp. 9-13). Oxford: Pergamon.

Schuler, H., & Berger, W. 1979. The impact of physical attractiveness on an employment decision. In M. Cook & G. Wilson, eds. *Love and attraction: An international conference* (pp. 33-36). Oxford: Pergamon.

Siller, J. 1976. Attitudes toward disability. In H. Rusalem & D. Malkin, eds. *Contemporary vocational rehabilitation* (pp. 67-48). New York: New york University Press.

Stubbins, J. 1982. *The clinical attitude in rehabilitation*. New York: World Rehabilitation Fund.

Wright, B. 1960. *Physical disability: A psychological approach*. New York: Harper & Row.

Deafness: The Next Ten Years

JERRY C. LEE

For 120 years Gallaudet College has been——and continues to be——the world's only collegiate institution whose campus, programs, and student body all center around deafness and other degrees of hearing loss. But, what about the next 10 years in deafness?

Recharging for the next decade in deafness——recharging for tomorrow's magatrends——recharging for life is always necessary. There is constantly a need for new energy if we are to accomplish the tasks before us, especially today as we look toward an uncertain future. These are difficult times. We face a difficult future. With the huge federal deficit decreasing federal aid to many of our domestic programs, residential schools for disabled students in jeopardy, and more competition for fewer available dollars, we're in the midst of a turbulent era. And, in some quarters there appears to be a feeling that deaf children, youth, and adults don't need more support——that mainstreaming is the solution.

Gallaudet is prepared and are preparing to handle these situations regardless of how formidable they may be, but there is optimism even though one might become tired of battling what often appears to be cyclical batteries.

Following is an outline of how the future looks in a number of important areas related to deafness based on input from various associates at Gallaudet. These include: 1) Demographics; 2) Legal Issues; 3) Education; 4) Technology; 5) Medical Research; 6) Employment and Rehabilitation; 7) Sign Language and Culture; and 8) Gallaudet.

Demographics

Demographic trends in society at large will be reflected in its hearing impaired segment. For example, the American population is aging, a fact that will profoundly influence the number and percentage of hearing impaired people in this country. The prevalence of hearing loss increases markedly with age and results in dramatically high levels in the oldest age groups. In 1982, the percentage of persons with hearing losses ranged from 2% in the age group of 18 to 30% in the group 75 and over. Because we are living longer, and because the post World War II baby boomers are entering middle age, America is moving toward an older population. In 1982, the median age of the U.S. population was 30.6; by the year 2000 it is projected to be 36.3——a significant change.

We know the proportion of school-age children from minority groups is increasing. The influx of immigrants to the United States will continue to contribute to this trend. There is also a significant movement of the U.S. population toward the South and West. Both of these trends will be reflected in the hearing impaired population.

Over the next decade, the size of the hearing impaired school-age population should remain relatively stable. Today the overwhelming majority of those children deafened in the rubella epidemic of the 1960s have left secondary school programs. During the next several years the sheer magnitude of this group will put an increased strain on the delivery of services related to postsecondary education, vocational rehabilitation, and job placement. In some cases, demands for specific social services will be continuous because many of these individuals have multiple disabilities.

There are no predictable epidemics that would produce the increase in the hearing impaired population that was created by the rubella epidemic of 1963-65. Vaccines and other medical advances may even contribute in the near future to a modest decline in the incidence of hearing impairment caused by early childhood disease. However, improvements in medical care that increase the chances of neo-natal survival may, ironically, also increase the number of hearing impaired or otherwise handicapped infants. In other words, children who can now, through better medical services, survive trauma at birth, premature delivery, or other complications

Reprinted From: Journal of Rehabilitation Oct/Nov/Dec, 1985, with permission.

of pregnancy, end up living with disabilities induced by these conditions.

Legal Issues

During the 1970s, Congress enacted a number of disability-related federal laws which provided a legal base for action against discriminatory practices in employment, education, and public service. These included the Rehabilitation Act of 1973, with Sections 501, 502, 503, and especially 504; the Education of All Handicapped Children Act (Public law 94-142); the Civil Service Reform Act; the Court Interpreters Act; and a number of other lesser laws. State legislation was similarly supportive.

All of this legislative action has resulted in numerous local and state education agency hearings, court cases, appeals, and even Supreme Court cases involving Section 504 and PL 94-142. Over the next decade, we envision further test cases especially related to hearing impairment as this unique handicap becomes more clearly defined and documented by the Architectural and Transportation Barriers Compliance Board. The country and the courts need to face the question of just what is meant by reasonable accommodation in terms of hearing impairment. Accessibility has long been identified solely with mobility concerns; where does communication enter this picture?

Section 504, in particular, will continue to be used to attach stereotyping. Recent court decisions have supported the employment rights of disabled individuals. Last year, the Supreme Court unanimously decided that handicapped people can sue, under Section 504, against employment discrimination in all programs receiving federal aid.

This year, a unanimous Supreme Court decided that Section 504 requires reasonable accommodation to assure meaningful access to programs. The court found support for its view in the federal regulations requiring reasonable accommodation in sections covering employment at colleges and universities. The Court reaffirmed the validity of these regulations. Significantly, the Court also held that a recipient of federal funds may be found guilty of discrimina-

tion from the effect of its actions even if there is no proof the recipient intended to discriminate. These unanimous Supreme Court decisions make it clear that Section 504 is an effective law for disabled people to use to combat employment discrimination.

This year, a concerted legislative effort is underway to reverse a different Supreme Court judgment that narrowed interpretation of federal non-discrimination laws. The decisions, **Grove City College**, vs **Bell**, interprets civil rights law to ban only discrimination in a specific aspect of a program receiving federal aid. If the **Grove City** decision applies to Section 504, it permits discrimination to exist in one part of an institution while prohibiting it in another. This could result in a deaf student having a right to an interpreter for a science course, since that department receives federal funding, but being denied an interpreter for classes taken in the English Department of the same college because that department does not receive direct federal aid. Senators Ted Kennedy (D-Mass.) and Bob Packwood (R-Ore.) have introduced a bill that would prohibit discrimination throughout an institution if any of its programs receive federal aid.

Legislative and judicial actions on the subject of discrimination and accessibility will continue during the next decade. For the future, I also project —— partly but not entirely from wishful thinking —— a federal law requiring no-cost legal interpreting in all 50 states; a tax deduction on technical aids required by disabled Americans; and an adjusted taxable income for retired disabled people.

Education

In his most recent book, futurist Alvin Toffler shares his belief that the entire emphasis in education as we know it will change. He feels more learning will take place outside rather than inside the classroom. He also envisions a reduced period of compulsory education, with schooling becoming interspersed with work and society. In effect, Toffler suggests that education will become a life-long process. This has serious implications for deaf individuals who might be cut off from such a process because of communication barriers.

The past decade has seen an emphasis on integrating hearing impaired students into regular education settings. Presently, about half of the hearing impaired students in special education programs are mainstreamed for a-least a part of their school day or week. This trend toward mainstreaming will continue. As hearing impaired students are thrust into the mainstream, some of them will be asked to meet similar educational requirements as those imposed on hearing students. Many states are beginning to require that students pass minimum achievement tests as a prerequisite for being granted a high school diploma. Because of their lower average of academic performance, deaf students will be disproportionately effected by such requirements.

The recent emphasis in mainstreaming has been on placing deaf students in situations where they are physically located in classes or activities with their hearing peers. Insufficient attention has been given to the social and psychological consequences of this integration. The future will probably see a large number of young deaf people who are academically integrated but socially isolated.

State schools for deaf students and other special institutions face many uncertainties during the next decade. The immediate future may see a continuing decline in enrolment as the rubella student-group moves beyond school age. During this time, there will be a "shake-out" in which these schools will be forced to deal with new realities. Students with profound hearing losses and students who, for whatever reason, cannot be served in their local communities will continue to form a pool from which the special schools draw. In some states, continued political pressures to keep students in local settings and to reduce costs will force many of the schools to re-examine their roles.

On the other hand, there could be a backlash. Some public schools are finding it very expensive to provide special services for only two or three isolated deaf students and may even let them "drift". Once parents become aware of what is happening things may change. Some court decisions, including the Supreme Court ruling on the Amy Rowley case, have observed that Congress did recognize that the regular classroom may not always get the appropriate placement for some handicapped children. The law does provide for separate classes or school settings where necessary.

There is a strong possibility that the residential or enter schools which maintain or increase their enrolment may be those that make arrangements for partial mainstreaming, serve other disabled groups, and interact actively with the state and local public school systems.

Technology

We are caught in an age of rapid technological change. No sooner is a new personal computer placed on the market then it is followed by an even more accelerated and compact model. The newest PC's can be carried in a briefcase and may weigh only eight pounds. The 32-bit microprocessors utilized by these PC's will further revolutionize office work, design shops, factories, printing systems, telephone communications, and much more. We're into a time of voice synthesis, fibre optics, deregulation, and the divestiture of AT&T. All of this technological growth has both positive and negative implications for deaf persons. All too frequently electronics developers move ahead without considering possible adaptations for disabled people. Sometimes hi-tech even decreases accessibility, as with "talking" automobiles and kitchen aids, useless for deaf persons.

The hearing impaired community will benefit, however, from this technology and from the cost decreases in computer-oriented electronics. Specifically, the general market growth will cause a reduction in the unit cost of the next generation telephone. Most of the special telecommunications equipment that meets the needs of hearing impaired individuals will also help to unite them with the general public.

Increasingly, television broadcasts will include closed caption information because of the voice recognition equipment used during television production. Major broadcast studios will generate real-time captions for public events.

Congressional hearing and presidential addresses will be captioned automatically as they happen.

Deaf Americans benefit in several ways from the growth of the cable and satellite delivery systems. Both of these technologies allow for greater program diversity and increased citizen access. There is a potential for deaf Americans to be consumers of materials created for the hearing world, as well as to be producers of television programming that is by and for the members of the deaf community.

At Gallaudet we are encouraging programs that are centered on the daily concerns of deaf citizens and on services provided to these citizens. We are exploring the use and development of educational telecourses. We have begun to produce a monthly magazine program, **Deaf Mosaic**, to bring some of these issues and concerns to deaf people throughout the country. This program is staffed by both deaf and hearing persons. Many of the segments feature interviews with deaf professionals who provide information about the deaf community and who act as role models for deaf people.

Additionally, we have begun work on developing an improved and computerized system for "cueing" in the TV studio. If we are successful in this computerized communication system, studio facilities will be even more accessible to deaf producers, directors, and technicians.

Home life for deaf adults will also be facilitated by technological advances. Advanced television equipment will visually indicate ringing telephones or doorbells, or the crying of young children will control house lighting, and act as alarm-clocks.

The ATBCB will be setting minimum guidelines and requirements regarding accessibility standards (dictated by the Rehabilitation Amendments of 1978) as they relate to communication. This group will also investigate within the next decade alternative approaches to such barriers. We anticipate Congressional hearings concerning the impacts on disabled people of the AT&T divestiture as well as other matters of a technological nature.

Medical Research/Technology

Some 30 years have been added to the life expectancy of men born in this century, and presumably a few more years for women. Many factors are related to this significant evolution which will affect hearing loss. In the old days most ear problems were related to infections——which led to meningitis and acute mastoiditis. Antibiotics changed all this, and mastoid disease has become relatively rare. Progress has also been made in surgery for otosclerosis and chronic infection in the middle ear.

The most exciting frontier today is probably the cochlear implant. The Food and Drug Administration has approved the single channel implant, and centers in Australia, California, and Utah are now investigating three different multichannel implants. It is believed that superior speech discrimination may be possible with these kinds of implants.

Today hundreds of young children have had a cochlear implant, but over the next 10 years we will be researching the long-term implications———whether side effects develop, how it affects their educational programs, and whether a deeper electrode insertion for a multi -channel implant will lead to other complications. It will be some time before the full extent of benefits from the cochlear implant is realized.

A number of people at Gallaudet are and will continue to be actively involved in seeking answers to the above questions. Dr. James Pickett, of the Sensor Communication Research lab, and Dr. William McFarland, chairman of the Department of Audiology, have been involved in a National Institute of Handicapped Research (NIHR) study program in rehabilitation engineering for hearing impaired people involving speech perception through implanted electrodes and tactile aids. They envision continued development and progress over the next 10 years in the utilization of tactile aids for feeling sound. These could help in lipreading, speech development, and in receiving environmental sounds. These aids would also be particularly helpful to persons who are both deaf and blind.

Micro-chip technology will play a significant role in development of hearing aids. These new digital aids will do three things: 1)the aid will be programmed with specific information on the user's hearing loss; 2) the aid will automatically monitor the environment for noise and feedback so that the user does not have to constantly adjust the aid as is the present situation, and 3) the micro-chip will enhance speech sounds to render them more clear.

Rehabilitation/Employment

Over the next 10 years the job market will be shifting from manufacturing, agriculture, and printing to high tech and service industries.

There will be an increasing demand for people in the computer fields; in finance, office work, and personnel; in public services; in food services, and health care; and in light tech manufacturing. A continuing need for trained teachers and other professionals is also anticipated.

Gallaudet College recently received a $25,000 grant from the Leslie and William Seltzer League of New York City to establish a national job data bank for deaf persons. These services will benefit both deaf persons and prospective employers and will, without charge, match deaf persons' careers and career goals with job openings in industry, education, medicine, rehabilitation, government, and other fields. Preliminary work is being handled by the National Information Center on Deafness at the College.

The 1960s were characterized by the miracle of federal infusion of dollars and support into the bloodstream of rehabilitation, education, and other service development for deaf persons. Those were unprecedented times with much excitement. Unfortunately, the excitement (and funding) of those times is past, and , with the current de-emphasis on federal services, it is not likely they will return.

On the employment front, manufacturing plants, as we have known them, are changing. Robotics are in——blue collar workers are no longer in demand. The accent for the future will be on smaller units with more flex-time workers doing individual tasks——a job environment of constant variety and frequent personnel transfers. In this much more mobile working world, deaf workers may find themselves working a great deal more in the hearing mainstream. We will, thus, need to emphasize communication, social, and language skills as we prepare students for the working world,. For such social skills may be as important for work in the future as vocational-technical training for a specific occupation has been in the past.

We also appear to be in the midst of a resurgence of small business operations, a service economy specializing in innovative products for consumers and single-line items to suppliers. With less capital required, fewer labor problems, and reduced plant space and outlay, such small businesses will have improved opportunities for survival. David Birch, economics professor at the Massachusetts Institute of Technology, indicates that employment has dropped three percent in the last 10 years in large manufacturing plants while increasing approximately 20 percent in companies with fewer than 20 employees. Our focus should be on training and placement in "small" industry, and also in directing qualified deaf persons toward the franchise circuit. With training assistance, and minimal capital, deaf operators should be able to move into this area as managers of their own business.

Such occupational trends accentuate the need for a strong liberal arts foundation for the deaf person of tomorrow——both in secondary schools and at postsecondary institutions. What will be required will be the ability to adapt to people, to adjust to change, to accept individual responsibility, to understand how one's work dovetails with the work of others, the see the "big picture", to understand that no man is an island unto himself, to become tuned in —— in the neighborhood, in our changing communities, and in the workplace. At the same time, career preparation will continue to be important. Gallaudet College recognizes the need for short-term training in a variety of emerging occupations. As the College evolves to university status, it will also move toward offering many more training modules in addition to the regular baccalaureate program.

Computer technology will make it possible for more work to be done at home or in a neighborhood satellite office or "electronic cottage". Such optional work places will be dictated by the rising cost of gasoline and other maintenance charges, the stress and complexity of mass transit, and the loss of time going to and from work. The resulting shorter total work day will provide for more family and community interaction, less mobility, and more activity at the local level, including the return of the consumer ethic. More do-it-yourself activities are predicted. We might even become acquainted with our neighbors for a change.

Instead of purchasing services, Toffler predicts, tomorrow's consumers will be fixing their own homes, making some of their own clothing, mending their own fences, doing repairs from self-help manuals, eating at home more, gardening, and the like. Manual labor work will become respectable again.

What are the implications of all this for tomorrow's deaf worker? We apparently will see a continued integration and dispersal into the general hearing community, but will this mean the demise of the deaf community as we know it? I doubt that very much, as community means people, not location. According to Ralph Keyes, one rarely finds a sense of community where one lives. We find community among the people who know us and with whom we feel safe. Community seldom includes our neighbors. It is people, not place.

Today 61% of the graduates of Gallaudet College are employed in deafness-related fields. With the continued demand for special education teachers, media specialists, computer technicians, counsellors, teacher aides, and other education related personnel, it is likely this percentage will remain high. However, we expect to see an increasing number of our graduates and other deaf workers entering non-traditional occupations such as law, business, microbiology, health care, food service, teaching in regular high schools and universities (sign language and deaf studies, as well as regular subjects), and personal and public service industries which already have been penetrated by deaf persons both in this country and overseas.

Sign language and Culture

Since the 1960s sign language has become widely accepted across the United States and making strong impacts all over the rest of the world. The Swedish government has officially recognized sign language as the "first" language of deaf people and has passed a law requiring that it be taught in all schools for hearing impaired students. In our own country, it has been said that as many as 50,000 people are taking sign language classers every day.

American Sign Language (ASL) has been recognized as a legitimate and unique visual language with most of the attributes of a formal language system. The accent today, however, one which I believe will continue in coming years, is on bilingualism, the use of both signed English and ASL in the bicultural world of deaf people.

Even in mainstreamed programs, the prevailing philosophy is that of total communication. All means for communicating——speech, lipreading, auditory training, sign language, mime gestures——are used to impart language and understanding to deaf children. Most interpreting provided in regular public schools for mainstreamed deaf students is manual interpreting, whether in ASL, Signed English, or some other form of manually-coded English.

Although definitely a part of American culture in general, deaf Americans also have a separate culture largely centered around their sign language and their visual perceptions and interpretations of the events of the world, distinct from the "hearing" culture. That is, while hokes, stories, folklore, and "slips-of-the-tongue" for a hearing individual may not be part of the life experience of those who cannot hear, deaf individuals have and share their own stories, folklore, and "slips-of-the-hand".

The problems of declining enrolment in residential schools and the continued emphasis on mainstreaming made it difficult to foresee how such changes will impact on deaf culture as we know it today. However, with increasing numbers of parents and the general public learning some form of manual communication, it would appear that sign language will be around for a long time.

Gallaudet and 1995

My annual report for 1983-1984 as president of Gallaudet College is entitled "A Year of Transition". As we all know, time does not stand still. The college has been undergoing an intensive period of review, self-study, introspection, and analysis in preparation for a new master plan. Our Board of Trustees, program administrators, faculty, outside consultants, alumni, and students will all eventually be involved in fashioning the final product.

The federal government has been sensitive to the needs of the deaf community for a place like Gallaudet and has supported the College generously. Over the coming years Gallaudet intends to become even more cost-effective and provide the American taxpayers with an even greater return on this investment——to increase the credibility of the College as a multi-purpose institution serving hearing impaired Americans in countless ways. As the College moves toward university status its baccalaureate programs will be complemented by new special programs leading to certification and to the associate of arts degree. The college will also develop specific short-term training programs.

I foresee a new school——a College of Management——joining the present three——the College of Arts and Sciences, the School of Education and Human Services, and School of Communication. This will open up new and increased professional horizons for Gallaudet graduates and will create more awareness among business, government, and industry leaders as to the capabilities of deaf persons.

Gallaudet will establish two more extension centers within community or regular colleges to

join our present outreach programs at Northern Essex Community College in Massachusetts, Johnson County Community College in Kansas, and Ohlone College in California. We will see centers in the southeastern and southwestern parts of the country so that deaf persons, their parents, and others will be better served and will not have to travel great distances for training, workshops, information, or contacts.

Over the next 10 years the College will seek increased participants with rehabilitation and deafness education. As I pledged in my inaugural address in October, "My dream is that we will work together, remaining ever conscious of the fact that we share a common mission". Together we will seek more political power in each state and the nation to ensure that the deaf people we serve will receive an equitable share of the attention and funding needed to continue their progress toward self-sufficiency. We shall seek strength in this togetherness.

Our target over the next 10 years and beyond must be the total person. Although deaf people in this country and throughout the world have made wonderful progress, they still live under shadows of misunderstanding, even from some of the very professionals trying to serve them. Deaf people still face communication barriers and discrimination; they still have to pay heavily for TDD's telecaptioners, hearing aids, and other technological aids which make hearing loss an expensive disability; and they continue to have other unmet needs.

We must not lose the momentum that was begun two decades ago, and, important as earning a living may be, we need also to ponder the words of E.F. Schumacher, "What is at stake is not economics, but culture; not the standards of living but the quality of life".

Further Thoughts on a "Sociology of Acceptance" for Disabled People

HOWARD D. SCHWARTZ

Social scientists studying the relationship between people with disabilities and the larger society, in recent years and with increasing intensity, have been waging a frontal assault against the dominant conceptual model of disability as deviance. A central tenet of the critics is that the deviance perspective leads to a predetermined view of people with disabilities as negatively valued by, and socially isolated from, the rest of society.

To be found among the growing number of critical voices are Robert Bogdan and Steven Taylor (1987) who call for the development of a "sociology of acceptance" through which to view people with disabilities. In proposing this, Bogdan and Taylor do not totally reject the deviance approach. Rather, they point to the need for adding a complementary perspective to accommodate those instances when the disabled person is accepted rather than rejected by others. While this contention seems legitimate and important, the informality of their presentation makes their argument less persuasive than it might be.

In the first place, and Bogdan and Taylor recognize this, the supporting data they present are less than satisfactory. Drawn ad hoc from their 15 years of clinical work in human services, the evidence is more suggestive than confirmatory regarding societal acceptance of people with disabilities.

Second, the authors talk about two different accepting public postures without, unfortunately, providing anything more than a preliminary discussion of either posture or the difference between them. On the one hand, they speak of the kind of acceptance found in the seminal work of Nora Groce's *Everyone Here Spoke Sign Language* (1958). Analyzing the position of the deaf in the community of Martha's Vineyard up to the first part of this century, Groce concludes that "they were just like everyone else" (which is, in fact, the title of the first chapter). In a community where everyone was bilingual in English and sign language, the deaf were simply seen as equal to the hearing, no better, no worse.

On the other hand, Bogdan and Taylor consider acceptance in terms of disabled persons being viewed by others as "special, more interesting, more stimulating, more challenging, more appreciative". The example of a caseworker and his mentally retarded client is used to show the disabled person in this favored-status role. After a while, the caseworker came to value as special his disabled friend's candor, which included the ability to express feelings and show emotions.

For conceptual clarity, the *acceptance* will be used here to define relationships between disabled and ablebodied persons in which all participants are viewed as equals. The term *advocacy* will be employed where those with disabilities are given favored status. It thus becomes the positive counterpart of rejection in a continuum of public postures that includes rejection, acceptance, and advocacy.

With these comments about the Bogdan and Taylor argument in mind, what emerges for the recent empirical research, including my own, is admittedly limited, but clear evidence of a change toward a far more favorable public opinion of disabled persons.

Evidence for a "Sociology of Acceptance"

In 1986, in a paper that received considerable attention, Katz, Kravetz, and Karlinsky reported the results of a study comparing the attitudes of high school seniors in Berkeley, Calif., toward disabled and nondisabled people. According to the authors, what was notable about the study results was that they were not consistent with those of many earlier research results, since they seemed "to imply that the disabled person is viewed more positively than the nondisabled one in the United States".

Reprinted Form: *Journal Social Policy*, Fall 1988, with permission.

The students had been presented with video-tapes of a man who was variously identified as being a civilian or in the military, disabled or ablebodied. The respondents rated, on intelligence, vocational (work) competence, morality, and sociability, the individual that they viewed. After an overall rating score was calculated for each student, it was found that the average score for the disabled person was significantly higher than the average score for the able bodied one.

The researchers speculate that an explanation of their results might be found in the unique nature of Berkeley. As an archetypical academic environment, it contains a substantial disabled population affected by mainstreaming and other educational innovations aimed at changing public attitudes toward persons with a disability. Consequently, "the nondisabled population is exposed to persons with disabilities who cope and live within the community" and "get to know them and their abilities beyond the disability."

While Katz and his colleagues are correct in their assessment of the atypical character of their study findings, they are not the only ones to have identified public advocacy of disabled people. Several studies, also using student respondents, have found that, on several key dimensions, disabled people are rated higher than the ablebodied as potential employees.

In one study, Siegfried and Toner (1981) asked college students to rate two target subjects: a potential co-worker and a potential supervisor. One-half of the students thought these people were disabled due to an automobile accident, the other half were presented with the identical description except that there was no mention of a disability. For 11 of the 16 dependent measures, covering a wide range of work-related behaviors (e.g., professional competence, missing work, successful performance, and ability to travel), the disabled and ablebodied target subjects were rated equally. On those five factors for which significant differences were found, the disabled person was rated higher. He or she was seen as more likely to be approached with a personal problem, more likely to be asked a favor of, less likely to upset co-workers, and less likely to need special assistance.

In a similar vein, in a study published earlier by Krefting and Brief (1976), college students rated a disabled person (a paraplegic using a wheelchair) equal to an ablebodied person on most job-related measures, but higher on work motivation and likelihood of being a long-term employee.

The *Playboy* Study

My own research, carried out in the fall of 1987, can now be added to this body of literature (Schwartz, 1988). While similar to the aforementioned studies in its use of student respondents, a wheelchair-user target subject, and the same kind of experimental technique, it differed in an important way. The target subject was neither a military man nor a potential employee, but Ellen Stohl, the first disabled woman to be the subject of a *Playboy* (1987) photo layout.

As explained in the story accompanying the pictures, Ms. Stohl, who had a spinal-cord injury, offered to pose for *Playboy* as a way of demonstrating that people with disabilities can also be sexy. In the letter in which she asked the magazine for the opportunity to pose, she wrote, "Sexuality is the hardest thing for disabled persons to hold onto," and that she wanted to "teach society that being disabled does not make a difference."

Irving Kenneth Zola (1987), a sociologist writing about disability in America, views "the right to be sexy" as a central item on the agenda related to the psychological and social liberation of people with disabilities. Harlan Hahn (1988) has touched on the same issue in his article, "Can Disability Be Beautiful?" Nevertheless, there seem to be limited opportunities for disabled people to assert their claim to sexuality, particularly through the media of popular culture. The *Playboy* article is unique in providing such a forum. It also offered the possibility of research to ascertain how, in a sexual context, the public evaluates the disabled person compared to the ablebodied one, and the disabled versus the ablebodied person's "right to be sexy."

The study was carried out at a medium-sized state university in Virginia, with a total enrolment of about 8,000. The majority of students come from urban centers within a 500-mile radius of the university such as Washington, D.C., with about one-third coming from more rural areas in the general vicinity of the university. Ten percent are from out of state.

The respondents were all of the students taking introductory sociology. Each student was shown one of two pictures of Ellen Stohl that had appeared in *Playboy*: one showed Stohl's face in closeup and shoulder partially bare; the other, providing a higher level of sexual display, had a partially-nude Stohl sitting on a couch with her legs tucked under her and wearing a negligee open in the front exposing a breast and her midriff. An additional aspect for the research design was that each student was given only one of two versions of whichever picture he or she received. An ablebodied version included, along with the picture, a biographical sketch which noted that Stohl was a college student and that the pictures had appeared in a national magazine with a readership of over 3 million. A second, disabled version had the identical biography except that Stohl was identified as spinal-cord injured, and a smaller picture of her fully clothed in a wheelchair was presented along with the larger picture. The analysis centered on comparing, for each picture, the responses of the students receiving the two versions.

The almost 700 respondents (80 students who had seen the pictures in *Playboy* or had heard about them were excluded) were asked to look at the photo of Stohl and rate her on six personal characteristics and on six factors concerned with conjectured success-failure or satisfaction-dissatisfaction in present or future life situations.

Regardless of the picture seen (the specific picture viewed had no effect in any of the comparisons), the disabled Stohl was rated equal to the ablebodied Stohl on sociability, intelligence, physical attractiveness, and the likelihood of having a fulfilling life.

Most interestingly, for five of the eight dependent measures for which a significant difference was found, Stohl was rated higher when presented as disabled than when presented as ablebodied. When identified as spinal-cord injured, she was seen as having greater strength of character, sensitivity to others, and competence at work, more likelihood of being a good parent, and less likelihood of getting divorced. The disabled Stohl's perceived relative superiority on these factors seems to confirm the finding of the previously cited studies which used the same or similar dependent measures that a disabled person is seen as better than one who is not disabled. Put another way, there is the strong hint of the disabled person's being viewed as a "paragon of virtue."

For two of the three measures on which the disabled Stohl was rated lower——the likelihood of getting married and satisfaction with life—— the differences, while statistically significant, were so small as to be negligible. On the third, sexual appeal (the only measure to show a gender difference), the women saw no difference between the disabled and ablebodied Stohl while the men favored the latter. Yet as far as the response of the male students is concerned, this is somewhat misleading. In fact, while both the men and women rated the disabled Stohl's sexual appeal as very high, the men rated it higher than the women did. In absolute terms, the men rated Stohl when disabled as "very sexually appealing," the second highest response on the 6-point Likert item.

Taken together, the ratings on sexual appeal and the equal ratings on physical attractiveness lead us to conclude that disability did very little, if anything, to diminish Stohl's physical appeal in the eyes of respondents.

In addition to rating Stohl on this array of measures, respondents were asked, "In your opinion, was it appropriate for this woman to pose for this picture?" (The respondents could answer "yes," "no," or "undecided".) The results show unequivocally that it was deemed more appropriate for the disabled Stohl to pose.

In all but one group comparison (over 80 percent of the men who viewed Stohl's face in closeup approved of her posing), a significantly higher percentage of those who saw the disabled Stohl approved of her posing. For example, of those shown the partially-nude picture, 55 percent with the disabled version approved compared to 36.4 percent with the ablebodied version. For men alone, the corresponding percentages were

75 percent versus 52.1 percent, and for women, 43.2 percent to 30.6 percent.

The Right to be Sexy

Analysis of the open-ended responses of those who, upon viewing the disabled Stohl, approved of her posing can better help us to understand the distinction between acceptance and advocacy of the disabled person's "right to be sexy." Grouping respondents according to the reasons given for approval allows us to differentiate those reasons in terms of whether they are likely to lead to one or the other positive postures.

Acceptance would seem to be a logical outcome of the responses of two groups. The first group gave what might be called "disabled-blind" explanations ("Why not? An honest way to make a dollar"). The common factor here was the absence of any recognition of the disability. A second group did take account of Stohl's disability, couching their approval in terms of the very basic theme of equal rights ("She has as much right as anyone to pose for this picture").

Advocacy would likely follow from the responses of three other groups. A good number of respondents saw Stohl as an example of role model representing to the public and/or other disabled people the ability of the disabled to succeed in endeavors in which they have not, historically, had the opportunity to participate ("Maybe her doing so will show other handicapped people that they are beautiful and show the general public the same. Good for her"). The responses of a second group expressed admiration for the disabled person having to overcome much more than others to achieve a goal ("With her disability it is a great step and very courageous. She is doing things in her life."). The underlying theme in the responses of the third group was the unique social-psychological benefits that a disabled person would derive from this experience ("If it makes her feel more 'complete' or happier why not?)".

Assuming that the above speculation about the link between response type and the two positive public postures has validity, the difference between acceptance and advocacy is that in the case of advocacy there exists the percep-

tion of a greater urgency, salience, or merit related to the disabled person's "right to be sexy." This is most evident in the statements of those students who held a double standard, resulting in a type of "reverse discrimination" on behalf of the disabled. As one respondent put it, "Normally, I'm *very* against people posing in these pornographic pictures, but in this case I feel she made a statement that she is comfortable with, and I can't but help admire her reasons for it. She's trying to convey that handicapped people can be human, they are sexually attractive, and they are in control of their lives."

Disabled Persons in Society

The data presented provide support, and the beginnings of an empirical database, for social scientists like Bogdan and Taylor, who insist that there is a need to augment the conceptual and theoretical arsenal used in assessing the role of disability and disabled people in society. The finding of overwhelmingly favorable student attitudes toward an individual who uses a wheelchair raises doubts about the relevance of the deviance perspective to specific instances of disability. Maybe most striking is the absence in my research of any evidence of what Hahn has argued is discrimination toward disabled people based on aesthetic criteria. Not only was the disabled Stohl seen as physically attractive as her ablebodied counterpart, but also her disability did not lead to the imputation of "sexlessness," a causal sequence taken as a given in the literature. Quite to the contrary, the disabled Stohl was perceived as a woman with considerable sexual appeal.

Exploration of the origins and implications of the view of the disabled individual as a "paragon of virtue" is called for. Gobdan and Taylor see this perception as arising from the particular character of a specific one-to-one relationship between a disabled and nondisabled individual. While they may be correct on this score, the new research points to the existence of a more generalized notion that may involve a cultural stereotyping of disabled people in this way. Future research can provide important answers as to why they are seen as more likely to fulfill normative-ly-defined role obligations in circumstances ranging from friend to parent, spouse to employee. It is worth cautioning that, although obviously there is nothing inherently wrong with being viewed as a good person, there is always the possibility that this kind of stereotype could lead to unrealistic and unfair expectations concerning what disabled people are like and how they are likely to behave.

The limited purview of the studies presented precludes any grandiose claims about how far society has come in the way it perceives and treats people with disabilities. For example, the target subjects were all physically-disabled wheelchair users. And the literature shows that, in general, the physically disabled evoke more positive reactions from ablebodied people than do those with emotional and cognitive impairments (Bordieri and Drehmer, 1987). Despite this, the data presented do underscore the need to refrain from viewing all disabled people as occupying a unitary social status. One would hope that a new generation of writers will avoid describing all those with disabilities as "stigmatized" (Goffman, 1963) or as "outsiders" inhabiting the "other side" (Becker, 1963, 1964). It is time for works of quality that deal with how the various public —— that is, rejection acceptance, and advocacy —— are distributed over the broad range of disabled persons.

A theoretical perspective that needs to be exploited in the future is one implied by Bogdan and Taylor and explicated most clearly by those taking a "minority group" approach to disabled people. It would replace the focus on disabled versus nondisabled individuals with one on disabling and enabling environments. The research cited here suggests that, as with the contexts of family and friends discussed by Bogdan and Taylor, educational institutions may now constitute enabling environments. This was a position taken by Katz and his colleagues to explain the Berkeley high school Students' favorable perception of disabled people. It is also compatible with my impression of the social milieu at the site of my study. There, over the last decade, disabled people have become an increasingly visible and prominent segment of the campus community.

Student attitudes in the studies discussed may also be a consequence of a more favorable climate toward disabled people in the society at large. In this regard, I cannot help but make mention of the recent, and very striking, events that took place at Gallaudet University in the spring of 1988. The unexpected force of public support —— both immediate and seemingly unanimous —— for the student body seeking deaf leadership may have been the critical factor in the swift capitulation of the powers-that-were. As the board of trustees' choice for the presidency of the university declared when she resigned, "I was swayed by the groundswell across the nation that it is time for a deaf president."

Finally, something must be said about the relevance of what has been discussed to the very practical issue of the employment of the disabled. When *Playboy* decided to publish pictures of Ellen Stohl, the mass media reported that the editorial staff was strongly divided on the wisdom of that decision and that those who held the negative opinion felt that the public was not ready for it. As my data show, they needn't have worried. Moveover, insofar as employers are reluctant to hire disabled people for fear of an unaccepting public, the data from all four studies show that they may be misreading public opinion. The dissemination of social scientific research and perspectives relating to the acceptance and advocacy of people with disabilities would seem an important step in any process that is to have the capability of leading to their full integration into the larger society.

References

Becker, Howard S., *Outsiders: Studies in the Sociology of Deviance* (New York: The Free Press, 1963).
--------. *The Other Side: Perspectives on Deviance* (New York: The Free Press, 1964).
Bogdan, Robert and Steven Taylor, "Toward a Sociology of Acceptance: The Other Side of the Study of Deviance," *Social Policy* (Fall 1987), pp. 34-39.
Bordieri, James W. and David E. Drehmer, "Attribution of Responsibility and Predicted Social Acceptance of Disabled Workers," *Rehabilitation and Counseling Bulletin* (June 1987), pp. 219-26.

Groce, Nora, *Everyone Here Spoke Sign Language: Hereditary Deafness on Martha's Vineyard* (Cambridge: Harvard University Press, 1985).

Goffman, Erving, *Stigma: Notes on the Management of Spoiled Identity* (Englewood Cliffs, NJ: Prentice-Hall, 1963).

Hahn, Harlan, "Can Disability be Beautiful?" *Social Policy* (Winter 1988), pp. 26-31.

Katz, Shiomo, Shlomo Kravetz, and Mickey Karlinsky, "Attitudes of High School Students in the United States Regarding Disability: A Replication of an Israeli Study," *Rehabilitation Counseling Bulletin* (December 1986), pp. 102-9.

Krefting, Linda A. and Arthur P. Brief, "The Impact of Applicant Disability on Evaluative Judgments in the Selection Process." *Academy of Management Journal* (December 1976), pp. 675-80.

"Meet Ellen Stohl," *Playboy* (July 1987), pp. 16-18.

Schwartz, Howard D., "Disability and Sexual Display: Empirical Evidence of Public Advocacy for Disabled People and the Disabled Person's Right to be 'Sexy'." Paper presented at the annual meeting of the American Sociological Association, Atlanta, August 28, 1988.

Siegfried, William D., and Ignatius J. Toner, "Students' Attitudes toward Physical Disability in Prospective Co-Workers and Supervisors." *Rehabilitation Counseling Bulletin* (September 1987). pp. 20-25.

Zola, Irving Kenneth. "Neither Defiant nor Cheering," *Disability Rag* (September/October 1987), pp. 16-18.

2 SOCIETAL ATTITUDES ABOUT DISABILITY

It has been discovered by social scientists that many groups are not treated in terms of what they are, but in terms of their social images. Traditionally, the disabled have been isolated, separated and alienated from larger segments of society through institutionalization and shunning. They have been deemed the "Elephant men" of our society when in fact their humanity, identity, and abilities have been overlooked and ignored in light of their differentness. The leper of biblical times is now the modern "freak" of the mass media, and Bogdan et al. in their article demonstrate how the disabled have become kusimodos of the contemporary media. The unfortunate parallels between disability, revenge, and violence only serves to deprive the disabled of their humanity. For example, the image of Lenn in Steinbeck's classic *Of Mice and Men* has served to damage the mentally retarded in the eyes of the North American public. The disabled are often portrayed and viewed as sick and inept. Ruffner maintains that our goal is to bring disability out of the nineteenth century and into the public eye with the informed help of the mass media. Ruffner maintains that the most common images of the disabled is charity and dependency; he goes further to insist that these attitudes must be replaced by impressions that positively reflect the legitimate status of the disabled.

Brolley and Anderson illustrate that image makers are using advertising campaigns to foster a positive view of many minority groups, including the disabled. Hence advocates for the disabled are now effectively using the media to increase public awareness of the disabled and to enhance positive attitudes towards disabled people. The media is capable of a dual role with respect to the disabled - they are capable of both hindering and complimenting their progress.

Perhaps someday, individuals will be able to accept themselves and be fully accepted by others when they are able to analyse themselves with openness, humility, and humor. Cassel traces disabled humor from the time of Aristotle and Palto to the present, and they indicate that disabled humor has several coping functions. Yet, such humor is also a disparaging form of communication, since humor often disguises real messages.

The work of Morrison and Upsprung illustrates the transitions that often take place in attitudes towards the disabled. They also indicate that self-fulfilling prophecies can have a tremendous effect on the habilitative potential of disabled persons. A stigmatizing illness, be it mental illness, leprosy, cancer, epilepsy, and / or ostomate status, it tends to be an individualizing and privatizing experience. The editor found that there is no illness subculture, and thus, those individuals who experience a stigmatizing illness often feel alienated from themselves and society. Illness, in general, often conveys negative images as far as the public is concerned. Society conceptualizes all minority groups, including the disabled, through pre-existing stereotyped images and in some instances the disabled share these images as part of a self-fulfilling prophecy. Consequently, it is generally difficult for the disabled, especially for those who experience stigmatization, to evolve legitimate self-sustaining reputations in society. The disabled, in Goffman's terminology, are often victimized more by the stigma of disability than by their actual impediment.

The Disabled: Media's Monster

ROBERT BOGDAN, DOUGLAS BIKLEN,
ARTHUR SHAPIRO, AND DAVID SPELKOMAN

The word "monster" is used today to refer to dangerous creatures, but until recently it was the standard medical term for people with abnormalities. The use of this term reveals a blatant association that is lost to most social scientists who try to study attitudes toward people with disabilities. Endless numbers of questionnaires, the most meticulously standardized procedures, and years of research on attitudes toward disabilities have produced unimpressive findings. The literature invariably reports the unremarkable fact that people with disabilities are negatively valued in society. At the same time, researchers generally leave the details of the stereotypes unexamined. The methods by which social scientists measure attitudes toward the handicapped are at once misplaced to some extent surprising, and certainly unfortunate. Social science would do well to examine the monster/disability connection.

What do dangerous people have in common? From the example of movies, television, newspapers, and comics, we might think that most are scarred, maimed, ugly, deformed, physically and mentally handicapped, monstrous. The media present people with disabilities in a variety of stereotypic ways, as objects of pity and as objects of humor and ridicule——but one favorite image is the disabled person as dangerous. By linking ugliness and physical and mental differences with murder, terror, and violence, the media creates, at the same time as it perpetuates, society's prejudices——prejudices that result in fear of the handicapped and, ultimately, in their systematic, intentional exclusion from society. Much of the opposition to group homes for persons labelled "mentally retarded," of course, is based on people's fears of this group.

The association of physical and mental differences with violent crimes did not originate in the modern media. Such portrayals fill age-old folktales and stories. In the early part of the nineteenth century, scientific theories linked the size and contours of the head and other body parts with personality. Writing in the late 1800s, the Italian scientist Lombroso, whom some modern criminologists consider the father of criminology, posited that criminal types could be differentiated by their physical characteristics, by the shapes of their heads and configurations of their body parts. Greatly influenced by Darwin, he saw criminals as a different and lower species than so-called normals. His work was the "science" of discovering criminals through physical examination and measurement. He erroneously concluded that criminals have asymmetrical skulls, flattened noses, large ears, fat lips, enormous jaws, high cheekbones, and narrow eyes.

Some scientists continued to embrace Lombroso-like theories even into the 1930s, '40s, and '50s. While Lombroso's theories are now disfunct——not even neo-social Darwinists adhere to them today——his early theories certainly provide basis for recent media depictions of criminals. And his theories have undoubtedly inspired today's writers, directors, actors, and makeup experts.

Horror Films

Horror films first appeared at the turn of this century. Expositions and fairs featured horror sideshows. Then, as Dennis Gifford, a historian of the horror film, notes, "Early horror movies played off on and incorporated the techniques and effects of the fear produced in so-called freak tents." Horror films began drawing large crowds. They became an institution unto themselves, though they retained their freak show aura.

MGM's 1932 film *Freaks* capitalized on the horror film/freak show link in order to promote the fear of deformity. Tod Browning, the creator of *Freaks*, employed Barnum and Bailey's sideshow attractions——including three people with microphalous, a form of mental retardation——for the film. The Barnum and Bailey characters played sideshow performers. The film

Reprinted from: *Social Policy*, Fall 1982, with permission.

ends with the disabled actors creeping and crawling through the mud on a dark and rainy night to get revenge on a person who has done one of them wrong. They turn her into a "freak" exhibit like themselves.

From the first horror films to modern-day renderings, physical and mental disabilities have been shown to connote murder, violence, and danger. We can see this connection vividly in the transformation scenes so common to these films. Whether from the effect of a full moon or a secret potion, an attractive actor changes before our eyes from a harmless, good citizen to a killer monster. The first American version of *Dr. Jekyll and Mr. Hyde* appeared in 1908. The Incredible Hulk and many other variations parallel the turning of the moral, handsome gentleman scholar Dr. Jekyll into the ferocious, ugly, stooped maniac Mr. Hyde. In the 1931 version of the film, Frederic March played the lead, a role that won him an Academy Award. The basically well-meaning but wildly unpredictable Hulk is counterpart to the Dr. Jekyll-like David Banner. Like Jekyll, Banner is intelligent, even urbane. The Hulk, on the other hand, at least as he is portrayed in comic strips, speaks in half sentences, as if he were mildly retarded.

Horror films have always enjoyed top billing Hollywood. For a long time, actors became stars by playing evil, ugly perpetrators of violence. Lon Chaney, who is best known for his role in the *Phantom of the Opera*, won fame by playing physically deformed, depraved monsters. Known for his ability to distort his body, he spent hours accomplishing his metamorphosis using pounds of makeup and other physically altering devices. In 1923 he played the famous Quasimodo, the frightful, crooked, bugeyed, and in other ways deformed Hunchback of Notre Dame, the classic disabled victim of other's violence.

Often, beauty, usually in the form of a young woman, is the monster's victim. In *Phantom of the Opera*, the protagonist tells his beautiful leading lady, "Feast your eyes, gloat your soul on my accursed ugliness." The erotic overtones behind the-monster-meets-beautiful-woman theme implies an association between certain disabilities and sexual molestation. At the same time, victims, like the Phantom's heroine, are often

people who befriend the murderer. We are told in one movie, for example, "The werewolf instinctively kills the thing it loves the best." The message is clear: keep away from people with physical and mental differences.

Boris Karloff had one of the longest careers ever as a movie monster. He played a variety of roles, but his most famous was Frankenstein. Like Chaney, Karloff spent hours in makeup preparation. he played the role first in 1931. Frankenstein is accompanied by Fritz, a hunchbacked dwarf who steals bodies from cemeteries to supply parts for Dr. Frankenstein's creations. The monster Frankenstein, playing alongside a disabled person, is in most of Karloff's films. In the 1935 *Bride of Frankenstein* the monster teams up with a blind hermit. He played the *Son of Frankenstein* with Bela Lugosi, who played a crazed, deformed shepherd gravedigger who orders the monster to kill. In the 1945 *House of Frankenstein* Karloff played a doctor who is killed by Daniel, a psychopathic, hunchbacked killer.

The pictures Karloff did in the 50 years of his career contained a variety of the roles and most of the themes common in horror movies. Frankenstein was not his only character. In 1932 he was Morgan, the scarred-faced, hulking butler, who became homicidal when drunk. Karloff often played mad scientists. In 1940 he played the title role in *Dr. Adrian and the Ape*, a film in which Frances, a paralysed woman, becomes the object of his concern. In searching for a cure for her polio, he seeks the spinal fluid of apes. Linking lower primates with the handicapped and violence picks up on the Darwinian theme of earlier pictures.

Karloff also played the graverobber in *The Bodysnatcher* who supplies bodies for a doctor's experiments. They unsuccessfully attempt to cure a paralysed child. When they realize their failure, they take up killing. Here, as in *Dr. Adrian and the Ape*, violence is not carried out *by* the person in the wheelchair but *for* them. In 1965 Karloff played a wheelchair-bound scientist who turns his family as well as himself into monsters. As late as 1971 he played a famous blind sculptor, who used human bones for his work.

Revenge in Horror, Gangster, and Adventure Films

Some horror films provide a psychological explanation for disabled people's violence. In the classic *Mystery of the Wax Museum*, the actor Lionel Atwell plays the mad and deformed wheelchair-ridden sculptor who turns to making wax figures for his museum out of real bodies. Early in the movie, a fire leaves him paralysed and full of revenge, in keeping with a prevailing stereotype. The hidden message in this movie, as with many others, is that people with disabilities want to get back at the world. The theme was so well received by the movie-going public that it was used again in the 1950s version entitled *The House of Wax*, starring Vincent Price. Now, after another 30 years, *The House of Wax* has been rereleased for 3-D viewing.

After falling victim to acromegaly, a rare deforming disease, the actor Rondo Hatton was cast in *The Creeper* as a deformed madman who strangled his victims in a rage because they screamed upon seeing his face——the theme of revenge again.

The theme of disability, revenge, and violence is present in gangster and adventure movies as well. Lon Chaney as Buzzard, in *The Penalty*, plays a bitter, cruel master of the underworld, whose legs were unnecessarily amputated when he was ten years old. In one of the scenes, Chaney poses for an artist doing a bust of the devil. In the adventure film *West of Zanzibar*, he plays a similar role. Publicity for the film tells us, "Fate made him a crawling thing, a crippled monster. So he took his revenge out on life." Walter Houston, as Dead Legs Flint in *The Congo*, plays the part of a paralysed tyrant who rules his African kingdom from a wheelchair.

Movies provide endless examples of the line between handicapping conditions and murder. Wilfred Walter, the blind half-wit Jake in *Dark Eyes of London*, is one of many examples. Alfred Hitchcock's *Psycho* and countless other films have contributed to making mental illness synonymous with homicide and insane asylums, the boarding homes of killers. Many films take their plots from famous works of fiction. Lenny, of *Mice and Men*, is the archetypal he-man who,

unable to control his own strength, first kills a newborn puppy and then a young woman. No wonder people who oppose group homes for the developmentally disabled conjure up similar images. In a recent made-for-television version of Steinbeck's classic, the mentally retarded Lenny crushes people's bones with his bare hands, all before an audience of millions——potential neighbors to group homes. Film renditions of Melville's *Moby Dick* depict Ahab, the obsessed one-legged captain, seeking revenge on his crippler. The limb-missing, patched-eyed pirates of *Treasure Island* are cloned again and again in film imitations of this adventure story.

Children's films utilize many of the same disability-as-evil story lines. Disney exploits disabilities as effectively as anyone to create fear. The artificial limb in the form of *Peter Pan's* Captain Hook comes to stand for the evil of the villain, who derives his name from his disability. In Walt Disney's *Snow White*, the beautiful queen must turn into the wart-nosed hunched-over witch to accomplish her dirty deeds. Children learn that disabilities equal evil early in life.

Television

As already mentioned, much of the horror show/disabled-as-evil imagery has found its way into television. In the once popular television series *The Fugitive*, Richard Kimball, the main character, who has been accused of murdering his wife, spends his life on the run. Each week he eludes the authorities as he seeks out the shadowy, one-armed man who really committed the murder. The last show of the series, the one in which the true murderer comes to light, won the highest ever (to date) Nielson rating for an episode of a continuing series by capturing 72 percent of the television-watching audience.

John Townsend, an anthropologist who has studied images of the mentally ill on television, confirms these impressions. He finds that one-quarter of all shows that depict mentally ill people cast them as physically violent. Although there is no substantial evidence that ex-mental patients commit crimes more often than the general population, violent crime and deinstitutionalization go hand and hand in television drama as well as in news broadcasts.

Comics

Disability and physical deformity go together in all media. Nowhere is this more glaring than in Dick Tracy's portrayals of criminals. The rogues gallery of Tracy's villains includes such characters as "Ugly Christine," "Mumbles," "BeeBee Eyes," "Shakey," and "Mrs. Prune Face." Modern-day crime busters promote the same imagery. The great popularity of superheroes, such as Superman, Wonderwoman, and Batman, ensure that the artist's renderings of villains will reach a huge audience of young people. In one recent comic strip, Batman says of a criminal whom he and Robin are chasing, "Perhaps a frontal lobotomy would be the answer. If science could operate on this distorted brain and put it to good use . . . society would reap a great benefit."

The Newspaper

More subtle linking of disability and violence is found in newspaper coverage of murders and other violent crimes. Recently, when a former Metropolitan Opera House stagehand was accused of attempted rape and murder of a Met violinist, headlines for stories on his trial read: SUSPECT HAS LOW IQ, TWO PSYCHOLOGISTS TESTIFY. Across the nation, newspaper coverage linked the disability of retardation with this hideous crime. Yet we know of no scientific evidence to support this assumption.

Similarly, the psychiatric backgrounds of murder suspects are frequently mentioned in news stories as a way of explaining criminal behavior. In especially brutal murders, certainly in mass killings, if the suspect has no record of psychiatric care, the "clean" background is mentioned (e.g., "Authorities could find no evidence of previous psychiatric problems") in such a way as to suggest that it is unusual for someone to commit a crime who doesn't have a psychiatric record. Mental disabilities are not the only handicapping conditions juxtaposed to and presumed causative of violence. Witness these headlines: CRIPPLED MAN CHARGED IN BOMB ATTACK, POLICE ARREST AMPUTEE IN SLAYING OF DOCTOR.

In this context, it was not surprising when The New York *Times* recently announced the New York City police department's new method of dealing with mentally disturbed people in the following way: POLICE WILL USE NETS TO SUBDUE THE DERANGED. The article was accompanied by a picture of police officers holding a net firmly around a person as he struggled violently to escape.

Some films and television shows present people with disabilities in more favorable ways: as multidimensional people with a wide range of human emotions, strengths, and weaknesses. But the image of the handicapped as dangerous dominates cultural media and, ironically, goes almost unnoticed and unchecked, except by people who have disabilities and who are constantly bombarded by these insults. Negative attitudes toward people with disabilities both emanate from and are revealed in such portrayals. Of course, the notion of the disabled as dangerous is false. Rather than being perpetrators of violence, they have, throughout history, been its recipients. Stereotypes of people with disabilities have served to justify such treatment. The great bulk of research on attitudes toward the disabled has consisted of questionnaires and experimental studies that simply miss the point.

Little attempt has been made to examine our culture critically, to see what the mass media display. A few authors have noted the association of ugliness, disability, and violence in literature and have suggested that such imagery is the result of deeprooted psychological fears. They suggest that people with disabilities remind the healthy of death, of their animal ancestry, or of their own imperfections. Such purely psychological explanations, which deny cultural and political contexts, serve no purpose other than to reify further prejudicial associations of disability with evil and fear. We believe the evidence is clear. The association of monsters and disabilities is a social creation. The role of social science, indeed of all of us must be to expose this atrocity.

References

Barbara Altman, "Studies of Attitudes Toward the Handicapped: The Need for New Direction," *Social Problems* (February, 1981), pp. 321-333.

D. Bilken and S. Mlinarcik, "Criminal Justice," *Mental Retardation and Developmental Disabilities,* Vol. X, ed., J. Wortis (New York: Brunner-Mazel, 1978).

R. Bojarski and K. Beale, *The films of Boris Karloff* (Secaucus, N.J.: Citadel Press, 1974).

Leslie Fielder, *Freaks: Myths and Images of the Hidden Self* (New York: Simon and Schuster, 1978).

Denis Gifford, *A Pictorial History of Horror Movies* (New York: The Hamlyn Publishing Group, 1973).

S. Glueck, and E. Glueck, *Physique and Delinquency* (New York: Harper and Row, 1956).

Stephen Gould, *The Mismeasure of Man* (New York: W.W. Norton and Company, 1981).

Hanoch Liuneh, *"Disability and Monstrosity: Further Comments," Rehabilitation Literature* (November/December, 1980).

C. Lombroso, *Criminal Man* (Paris: F. Alcan, 1887).

Thomas Scheff, *Being Mentally Ill: A Sociological Theory* (Chicago: Aldine, 1966).

W.H. Sheldon, *Varieties of Delinquent Youth: An Introduction to Constitutional Psychiatry* (New York: Harper and Row, 1949).

P.S. Strain and M.M. Kerr, *Mainstreaming of Children in Schools* (New York: Academic Press, 1981).

John Townsend, "Stereotypes of Mental Illness: A Comparison with Ethnic Stereotypes," *Culture, Medicine and Psychiatry* (1979), pp. 205-229.

The Invisible Issue: Disability in the Media

ROBERT H. RUFFNER

War. Strife. Angry struggles against oppression. These are daily subjects of the world's mass media: radio, television, newspapers and magazines. The struggles of Iran/Iraq, El Salvador and Northern Ireland are interspersed with the overthrow of governments in Africa and South America.

Communications. People with access to the world's mass media are familiar with the problems of "third world/guest" workers in Europe, the clashes of Hindus, Muslims and Sikhs in India, the unemployed workers of England and the United States, the problems of women's rights in Sweden and Switzerland, and the struggle of Jewish people in the Soviet Union.

We know when the price of bread rises in Poland, when the French franc falls, when an Egyptian leader dies. We have easy access to the problems of the moment. We know of the struggles of minority peoples throughout the world.

The world's mass media provides the information of our daily lives, our daily concerns. It does much more than this, however. It provides the basis for our opinions about what is important and what is not. The most significant aspect of the mass media is its skill in forming public opinion.

In our respective nations, these opinions are the basis of our support for political, social and economic actions. These opinions are the foundations of our present societies and of our national and international understandings and aspirations.

But where do we find our information about ten per cent of the world's population with physical or mental disabilities, who have an unemployment rate of over 60% in developed nations and higher than that in developing ones? For this information, we rely on specialized journals and newsletters, publications with small audiences and little or no impact on people other than those directly concerned with disability.

There are exceptions. The world's mass media does not completely ignore disability; it treats it as a "medical" issue for the most part.

We can learn about diseases and maladies as they strike large numbers of people, technological developments and research that promises "cures." The mass media also devotes attention to "human interest" stories concerning disabled people who are making their way in society "against all odds."

For the most part, though, we depend on select sources for information about disability throughout the world. Professionals and disabled people meet at conferences to exchange ideas and to discuss developments.

We have our own channels of communication. Channels that are separate from the mass media, channels that answer our specific interests and need for information.

But what of the general public in our own countries? They don't have access to our professional channels of information. The public relies on the mass media for its information and, most importantly, for its opinions. For the most part, disabled people are seen as sick, for disability is considered a medical issue; they are seen as dependent on society, for sick people need expert help and care; or they are seen as superachievers, of the calibre of Itzak Perlman. By and large, however, disabled people are not seen. Disability and disabled people are "invisible" and disability is not an issue to be reckoned with.

What a contradiction! If Canadian farmers or Turkish workers in West Germany had a 60% unemployment rate, the mass media would take note. Look at the attention the German worker is receiving today over demands for a 35-hour work-week.

The reasons for this invisibility are many and complex. The central problem is that disability has traditionally been invisible, and traditions linger on.

Disabled people have been their family's

Reprinted from: "Rehabilitation Digest", Winter 1984, Vol 15, No. 4, pub. by CRCD: Toronto, Ontario, with permission.

burden and this has been interpreted in the last 150 years as a burden shared in developed nations by society. The pattern has been to keep disabled people out of sight, in institutions, in separate housing or at home in isolation.

The Professional Bias

There is another reason that disability is invisible as an issue: We, the rehabilitation professionals, project a caring posture towards disabled people, shielding them from the give-and-take, the rough-and-tumble, the risks of competitive life.

We professionals in the disability field also share a bias which affects the information we make available to the mass media. We tend to emphasize need and dependency, pity and charity. In some cultures, the role of the disabled person is that of a beggar, and this role fulfills a religious need: to give alms to the poor. Whatever form it takes, the charity mentality affects all countries, for it is seen as necessary to project disability as a need meriting government and private support.

Disabled people have begun in the past several years to organize their own groups within countries throughout the world; they have pressed for greater attention to their problems and hopes. They are demanding equal time to dispel the invisibility of the disability issue and the stereotype of dependence, need and charity.

Disabled Peoples' International, founded in 1980, grew from the frustration disabled people felt in their dealings with professionals and with the lack of attention society has allotted to the issue of disability. Disabled Peoples' International is a recognition that disability is an important issue throughout the world and that it cannot continue to be ignored by the world's mass media.

For this reason Disabled Peoples' International is a significant development. So too was the United Nations' declared "International Year of Disabled Persons." It conveyed a sense of importance to the media and, through the media, to people everywhere.

With this new sense of organization and recognition, disabled people will have to become competitive. As the world's economy changes and as wealth shifts from developed nations to the burgeoning manufacturing countries of Asia and to the energy-providing nations of the Middle East, Africa and South America, competition for a fair share of a country's wealth is going to become keener than ever. Disabled people are going to be competing for a share of their nation's resources with elderly people, with third-world/guest workers and new immigrants, with women and with racial and religious minority groups.

The struggle for a share of a nation's resources is affecting developed countries in Europe and North America where social programs are being reduced as demands of resources from other sectors grow. Developed nations are assessing the dependency systems that they have established to care for disabled people and professionals regarding their roles in society. The outlook for continued comprehensive, separate programs for disabled people is not promising.

Disabled people will have to compete for support. They will be thrown into a struggle with better-organized, better-known minority groups within their own countries. There will be fierce competition for mass media attention as well as for funding.

Raising the Recognition Level

Never has the need for visibility been greater than it is today. Disabled people throughout the world are making, and have the potential to make, contributions to their societies. Disabled people today need the tools that will allow them to compete effectively: skills, education, training, access to jobs, independent living, a release from dependency, an opportunity to take risks.

Disability needs visibility as a major social, economic and political issue within societies throughout the world. Professionals and disabled people must organize to effectively reach the world's mass media, to ally it with the issue of disability. The once-effective pleas for charity must be replaced by a determined drive towards the recognition that disabled people need not be dependent, that most can participate within their own societies. Disability as an issue means transportation, education, housing, jobs, social opportunities and rights, far more than its traditional focus on medical treatment and rehabilitation. The image of disabled people as "marginal" and "second class" citizens must end.

The world's mass media could transform this invisible issue into one of significance and concern. At least ten per cent of every nation's population is disabled and adding their families who are also primarily affected by disability takes the percentage even higher. No nation can successfully ignore the organized efforts of such a significant group.

Professionals can raise the recognition level of disability. By affirming the rights and dignity of the disabled and, by ridding professional language of insensitive and damaging terms such as "victims," "confined to wheelchairs" and "dependent." Professionals can identify disabled leaders among the people with whom they work, and see that these leaders are known to the mass media within their countries that they are called upon to speak out on issues affecting disabled people. Every nation has leaders among its disabled population, leaders who can have a significant impact upon the opinions of their fellow citizens.

The year 1984 is the second of the United Nations' declared "Decade of Disabled People." Throughout the world, the Decade's significance depends on disabled people and professionals. Will we organize to identify disability as an important issue within our societies: an issue of contribution, not charity; an issue of opportunity, not dependency; a social/economic/political issue, not only a health and welfare one?

My response to this concern has been to establish the American Association of Disability Communicators, a group of professionals in the United States from the private and voluntary sectors, government and disabled consumer organizations. Our goal is to identify disability as a major issue in the United States by improving the management, marketing and public relations skills of disability professionals working with the media. The American Association of Disability Communicators offers a newsletter, training seminars and an opportunity for professionals concerned with disability communications to exchange ideas and tips. Our goal is to

bring disability out of the 19th century and into the public eye with the informed help of the mass media. Disability *is* an issue, it is not something that the Association is creating. Our efforts are to help disabled people and professionals translate this issue into effective treatment by the media, and into serious consideration by the American public.

Disabled people are long overdue for informed public recognition. The prevalent image of disability as charity, dependency and need must be replaced.

Disabled people will gain and grow. Professionals will gain and grow. And societies will gain and grow.

Disability Today

As a means of publicizing disability through the mass media, Robert Ruffner of the President's Committee on Employment of the Handicapped in Washington, C.C., wrote a series of syndicated newspaper columns under the title *Disability Today*. The following article is from that series, and it illustrates clearly how relevant disability issues are to the concerns confronting us daily in the press.

Suicide in the United States is shocking. It's not part of our tradition, as it is in some countries, to use suicide as an expression of religious or social obligation. For us, it is a sad admission of failure.

A young woman in California attracted our attention because she asked the courts to sanction her suicide. What brought her to this low point and how did we respond to her?

As I don't know her, I can only guess that her reasons are many and complex. Apparently, her life has been an uphill battle. According to news reports, she spent years in institutions because her family rejected her as a child. She has had a failed marriage and lost a child through a miscarriage. One of her professors in graduate school told her that she would never find a job.

For Elizabeth Bouvia has cerebral palsy, a birth disorder that left her dependent on other people for such necessities as eating and dressing. Her accomplishments were possible only with the assistance of others. In her court case, she maintained that she needed the assistance of a hospital to help her accomplish her suicide.

And how did we as a society respond to this cry for help? Her court case was decided against her. The hospital refused to risk the liability of helping her kill herself. She reached a stand-off with society.

One of our attitudes towards suicide is that people wishing to kill themselves are usually found to be depressed and not in sound mind. Elizabeth Bouvia, on the other hand, was examined by psychiatrists and determined to be in sound mind. Why this contradiction?

Perhaps the news reports about her case give us a clue as to why she was found in sound mind. She was continually referred to as "hopelessly crippled," "dependent," "confined to a wheelchair." Few news reports even questioned how one so "hopelessly crippled" could have managed to graduate from college, attend graduate school, marry and embody so many other aspects of the American Dream.

As a nation that has welcomed people driven to our shores because of war, famine, racial or religious persecution, we didn't seem to rise to Ms. Bouvia's need. We didn't seem to question why she would want to kill herself when she had accomplished so much in her young life. Was she found to be in sound mind because she has cerebral palsy? Is she truly expendable? These questions have largely been ignored.

Does Elizabeth Bouvia represent the 700,000 Americans with cerebral palsy? As many of them are leading full and accomplished lives in our society, we can only assume that she is not representative.

She is a reminder, however, that people with cerebral palsy run into a lot of painful rejection and thoughtlessness. She has done her country a service if she has made us see that our awareness and acceptance can make a crucial difference in the lives of 700,000 people. While she is not representative in wanting to die, she is in voicing the pain of thousands of others who regularly face pity and discrimination.

Elizabeth Bouvia has given us a lot to think about as a society. She, in turn, has had a chance to do a lot of hard thinking about herself. The last news report I read came from Mexico where Ms. Bouvia was hospitalized. The message was that "she wants to live." We can now do our part to see that her future after the hospital can be one free of discrimination and rejection.

Advertising and Attitudes

DIANNE Y. BROLLEY AND STEPHEN C. ANDERSON

Within the past two decades a rapidly growing interest in the study of disabilities and the role of the disabled person in society has occurred. Research efforts have analyzed a wide variety of attitude characteristics with diverse subjects and interests. However, within this vast collection of data, little has been done to measure the impact of mass media on attitudes toward disabled people. It is only within the last ten years that advocates for disabled persons have recognized the need for effective public awareness campaigns fostering positive attitudes toward disabled people.

Public images of the disabled population are created in many ways, historically and predominantly through fundraising campaigns. Fundraising has tended to produce images of the disabled person that evoke impressions of dependent, needy persons requiring special treatment. To counteract this trend, the image makers of today are using advertising campaigns to foster a positive view of disabled people, as independent and capable. We are only beginning to investigate the impact media have on attitude formation, although researchers have hinted at the probable relationship between the two. We do know, however, that exposure to public relations campaigns designed to improve the image of disabled persons and foster acceptance among non-disabled persons can create strong norms within society.

Mass media consumption has grown to become the number one pastime of the Canadian urban adult population. Exposure to advertising, on television and radio, in magazines and newspapers, rises proportionately with increased media consumption. If we assume that advertising has an effect on the viewer's attitudes and images toward an object or person, we should investigate the stimuli and measure their effects. More importantly, we should determine whether media advertisements directly or indirectly influence the attitudes of the general public toward disabled persons, and subsequently facilitate or impede the acceptance and integration of them in work, social, recreational and educational environments. With the implementation of public policies regarding integrated special education, such as Ontario's Bill 82, there is a need to increase public awareness and recognition of the problems faced by disability groups, and to cultivate positive attitudes toward disabled people.

From 1979 through 1983, the Canadian Rehabilitation Council for the Disabled (CRCD) conducted a public awareness campaign aimed at changing the negative attitudes toward disabled persons. The objective of the campaign was to change society's negative attitude to one that views the disabled individual as a person first, and as a worthwhile contributing member of society. In 1983, the CRCD conducted an evaluation of the magazine component of the awareness campaign. The data indicate that the campaign was successful, both in terms of public acceptance and increased awareness. Ninety-two per cent of the respondents (N=2,063) felt the campaign was performing an important public service.

Also in 1983, the Canadian Mental Health Association (CMHA) initiated a province-wide public education program aimed at dispelling the myths and misconceptions held by the general public with regard to mental health and mental illness. The goals of this program were:
• to increase community understanding of mental health and mental illness.
• to promote the social integration of individuals experiencing mental health problems into an accepting and supportive community.

The results indicated that most respondents (N=92) expressed positive attitudes both toward persons with mental illnesses and toward community-based facilities, and believed that a person who has a serious mental illness can fully recover. The study also emphasized the impact mass media have on the public's perception of persons with mental illness, as 21.4 per cent of the respondents stated newspapers were their major source of information on mental illness.

Reprinted from *Rehabilitation Digest*, Fall 1986 by CRCD: Toronto, Ontario

The data suggest that media do have the potential to influence attitude formation and expression toward disabled persons.

In view of the recent upsurge of interest in public awareness and disability groups, the authors chose to examine the influence mass media have on the attitudes of non-disabled persons toward disabled persons. It is hoped the results of the study will highlight potential deficits in media advertising regarding disabled persons, such that recommendations can be made for future media representations of disabled people.

Subjects were selected from two general psychology courses offered at the University of Waterloo, Ontario. Ninety-one subjects were enroled in Psychology 101 —— Introductory Psychology, and 73 were enroled in Psychology 200 —— Measurement in Psychology. The age range of the subjects was 18-41 years old, with a mean of 22.5 years.

Two treatments were randomly assigned to the two psychology classes. Treatment Group A had 91 Subjects (50 male; 41 female) and Treatment Group B had 73 subjects (13 male; 60 female). Of the total, 124 (75.6 per cent) reported having had previous contact with a disabled person, while 40 (24.4 per cent) reported having had no prior contact with a disabled person.

When asked to rate the extent of their knowledge about disabilities, only seven subjects (4.3 per cent) felt they had an excellent knowledge base. Thirty-eight (23.2 per cent) felt their knowledge level was average; 27 (16.5 per cent) stated they had a fair degree of knowledge about disabilities and six (3.7 per cent) indicated they had a poor knowledge base of the topic.

The questionnaire contained three sections:
PART I   —— Demographic Information
PART II   —— Media Feedback Form
PART III   —— Attitude Toward Disabled
Persons Scale (ATDP)
PARTS I and II were compiled by the investigator. PART III was the Yuker, Block and Young ATDP Scale. Both Form A and Form B of the Scale were utilized to reduce instrumentation bias, and were randomly distributed among the two treatment groups.

Media advertisements depicting various disability groups were obtained from a number of agencies representing disabled people. Ads specifically designed to encourage positive attitudes toward disabled people as well as fund-raising general interest ads were included, for a total of 48. They were presented to five experts who classified the posters as either positively or negatively influencing attitudes toward people with disabilities. Only those posters receiving 80 per cent agreement by the experts were used in the study.

Two slide presentations were then prepared. One contained ten advertisements rated as positively influencing attitudes toward disabled person. The other included eight ads rated as negatively influencing attitudes.

Subjects in Treatment Group A were exposed to the positive ads, and those in Group B were shown the negative ads. The groups viewed each slide for 15 seconds and after that completed the ATDP Scale as well as a short, open-ended questionnaire eliciting feedback on the ads.

Frequencies were calculated to determine the distribution of subjects across the demographic variables, and to indicate group means. A t-test (used to test the difference between the means of two groups) was used to analyze the continuous variables such as age and the ATDP scores. Categorical data were analyzed using Fisher's Exact Test (F Test) for 2 x 2 variable analysis and chi-square analysis. Finally, Yuker and Block's scoring procedure for the ATDP Scale was calculated to determine the range of overall acceptance scores expressed by the subjects toward disabled persons.

The Media Feedback Form of the questionnaire comprised nine open-ended questions designed to elicit information regarding the impact the media advertisements had on the viewers. Twenty questionnaires were randomly sampled from each treatment group and analyzed. The results revealed that subjects in both groups consistently responded to the same set of visual stimuli within their treatment group and had similar attitudes and comments about the ads; however, the nature of the responses differed according to the treatment received. Subjects in Treatment Group A. (positive) were more favourable toward the subject matter than were subjects in Group B (negative).

Comments that were particularly interesting were those in which perceptual contrasts occurred between the two treatment groups. Subjects in the 'positive' treatment group stated that the common element of the advertisements was the focus on attitudes toward disabled persons (70 per cent), as compared to five per cent of subjects in the 'negative' group. Subjects in that group felt the unifying theme inherent in the ads was a request for help (30 per cent). None of the subjects in the positive group listed that point.

Adjectives used to describe the people in the ads also differed between the two groups. Many subjects in the positive group (65 per cent) described the person as *able*, while only five per cent of subjects in the negative group did so. Moreover, 70 per cent of the negative group used the word *sad* to describe disabled persons, as opposed to only 10 per cent of the positive group.

The predominant stimulus evoking emotions also differed between the groups. The positive group favoured the textual stimulus of the ads over the negative group (8:0) while the negative group favoured the pictorial stimulus (10:5).

Differences in the mean scores and range of scores were not found to be significant between the two treatment groups. The ATDP scores were also analyzed according to gender and academic year. Again, non-significant differences were found between the groups for these variables.

In conclusion, the analysis of the ATDP Scale revealed no significant differences between the two treatment groups with respect to attitudes expressed toward disabled persons. The conjecture that positive advertisements would foster more positive attitudes toward disabled persons, while negative advertisements would evoke more negative attitudes toward disabled persons was not supported by the data.

Yuker, Block and Young (1966) concluded that age, gender, education and the amount of prior contact with disabled persons were significantly and positively correlated with expressed attitudes toward disabled persons. These conclusions were not supported by the data

collected in the present study as further analysis revealed no significant correlations for any of the variables or attitudes expressed on the ATDP questionnaire.

The Media Feedback Form presented in Part II of the study questionnaire provided a number of insights into the impact mass media advertising has on attitude formation and the expression of attitudes toward disabled persons. The effectiveness of advertising material representing the disabled is enhanced by the following characteristics:

1. A direct approach with a strong message.
2. An emphasis on pictures and the use of colour in advertisements.
3. The use of children to represent disabled persons.
4. The presentation of concise factual information and demonstration of respect for those represented in the advertisements.

The data indicate that advertising effectiveness is diminished by the manipulation of negative emotions (e.g. guilt and pity), the absence of colour and the presence of detailed explanations of the disability represented. Lengthy paragraphs were largely ignored by the subjects because they required 'too much effort to read.' Negatively oriented ads were rated more often for their shock value and emotional 'guilt trips' than positively oriented ads.

Mass media advertisements are vehicles for public communication whereby knowledge (information, attitudes, ideas and feelings) is made available to society at large, without restricting who may be the viewer. In the past, advocates for disabled persons utilized mass media primarily for the purpose of fundraising. Disabled persons were depicted as weak, dependent individuals in need of care and protection by ablebodied, nonhandicapped persons.

Today the focus is changing. Advocates for disabled people are utilizing media advertising to increase public awareness about disabilities and enhance positive attitudes toward disabled persons. Issues of employment, accessibility, transportation, leisure and acceptance are being challenged through media advertisements, with the ultimate goal of facilitating the mainstreaming of the disabled person in society. Additional research is needed in this area in order to maximize the effectiveness of media advertisements representing disabled persons.

References

Feinburg, L.B. Social desirability and attitudes toward the disabled. *Personnel and Guidance Journal, 46,* 375-81, 1967.

Grand, S.A., Bernier, J.E., and Strohmer, B.C. Attitudes toward disabled persons as a function of social context and specific disability. *Rehabilitation Psychology, 27,* 165-72, 1982.

Stappers, J.G. Mass communication as public communication. *Journal of Communication, 33,* 141-45, 1983.

Tringo, J.L. The hierarchy of preference toward disability groups. *Journal of Special Education, 4,* 295-306, 1970.

Yuker, H.E., Block, J.R., and Young, J.H. *The Measurement of Attitudes Towards Disabled Persons.* Albertson, NY: Human Resources Foudation, 1966.

Zuzanek, J. and Mannell, R. *Life Styles, Mass Media and the Arts in the Lives of Canadians (A Survey Report).* University of Waterloo, in cooperation with D. Durham/J. Bekker, 1983.

Disabled Humor: Origin and Impact

JACK L. CASSELL

Although humor is one of the most pervasive forms of interpersonal exchange, practitioners rarely direct their attention to the humor process and its effects on the behavior of themselves and others. However, responses have been investigated in a variety of therapeutic and research settings (Dworkin & Efran, 1967; Hickson, 1977; Kubie, 1971; Martin & Lefcourt, 1984; Peterson & Pollio, 1982; Poland, 1971; Redlich, Levine, & Sohler, 1951; Scogin & Pollio, 1980; Shurcliff, 1868; Singer, 1968). Further Cassell (1974a) noted that humor responses in rehabilitation settings are important elements in a counsellor's repertoire for understanding and responding to client behaviors. To become comfortable and adept at using the humor process of therapeutic gains, an awareness of the definitional boundaries and the developmental aspects of humor responses is important. This awareness contributes to more effective interpersonal communications in day to day interactions when the counsellor understands the true nature of what is being communicated via the humor response.

Disabled Humor

Many investigators have grouped humor into a variety of categories according to the thematic content. Sexual humor, aggressive humor, and nonsense humor have received the most attention (Donoghue, McCarrey, & Clement, 1983; Dworkin & Efran, 1967; Goldstein, Suls, & Anthony, 1972; Lamb, 1968; Levine & Abelson, 1959; Martin & Lefcourt, 1984; Prerost, 1983a, 1983b; Williams & Cole, 1964). However, another relatively untapped content area can be termed disabled humor (Cassell, 1974b). Disabled humor occurs as a result in an event in which the principal object of the humor response is a disabling condition or some disruption of an individual's body integrity. In designating this area as a disabled humor, the double meaning is purposeful (e.e., the humor is directed toward a disabling condition and the humor itself is disabled). This article traces the origin of disabled humor from its early beginnings and suggests the significance that this type of humor plays in present day interactions.

Historical foundations are significant since they provide a record of how disabled humor has been reinforced over time and enable the reader to understand why disabled humor is viewed as an acceptable mode of communication in present day interactions. With this understanding, insight is gained into the means for reversing negative or maladaptive trends.

Early Beginnings

Disabled humor has been recognized by philosophers and writers as far back as Plato and Aristotle. However, until now, no theorist or researcher has treated disabled humor as a subject worthy of separate investigatory or theoretical exposition.

Plato (1860), in his dialogue, *Philebus* (c.355 B.C.), thought that most laughter was a response to the misfortunes of others, and Aristotle (1898) saw the typical humorous response as stemming from the perception that a situation deviated from an esthetic norm. Worthy of note, is the fact that humor directed at the defects, disabilities, or personal characteristics of others dates back at least 2,300 years. Also, in these early beginnings, Cicero (1903) related that humor could legitimately (i.e., acceptably) focus on one's own personal defects, but not the defects of others. Quintilian (1910) gave renewed emphasis to the deformity theme of Aristotle.

In 1560, Maggi (Piddington, 1933) combined the perception of the "painlessly ugly" (i.e., the ugly condition that is not painful to the person) with a suddenness effect to produce a theory that falls within the purview of disabled humor. For example, when a "painlessly ugly" person is encountered, the perceiving individual initially experiences internal restraints. With the occurrence of a humor response, these internal restraints are suddenly released, and the individual then experiences a relief from this tension

Reprinted From: *Journal Rehabilitation* Oct/Nov/Dec, 1985, with permission.

151

state. The reasons why individuals experience these internal tension states require exacting research.

The part that disabling conditions play in being perceived as "painlessly ugly" becomes apparent when consideration is given to the idolizing of normal standards and the comparative-status value concepts as discussed by Wright (1983). Idolizing standards, according to Wright (1983), "means that the normal standards of behavior are rigidly defined and held forth as the *single* criterion for the desirable or even allowable" (p. 122). The comparative-status value framework suggests that an individual's attributes (e.t., looks, capacities, and background) have status value since these attributes provide the basis for making comparisons with standards along a scale of better and worse. Thus, a person is perceived as "painlessly ugly" when compared against a normal standard of nonugliness, which is assigned a higher value by the perceiver. To encounter ugliness is a dissonant state for the perceiver and there must be a coping outlet. Since the "painlessly ugly" designation suggests that the present condition is causing the "ugly" person no pain, and thus the seriousness seems removed, the repulsion-discomfort (ugliness) is coped with by quickly and effortlessly transposing the experience into a humor response.

Finally, on a positive note, in 1578, Jonson (1904) saw humor (regardless of the type of humor) as serving restorative or rehabilitative functions similar to the then accepted physical therapies such as bleedings and purgings. Thus, in a broad sense, humor can be a rehabilitative, rejuvenating tool. However, the psychological and social impact of humor has definite consequences which cannot be ignored. These consequences are discussed in a later section on the concept of deviance and the humor process.

The greatest misconception held by these and other early theorists was their mistaken insistence that the debasing and degrading forms of humor are directed only at minor defects of others. These authors have implied that humor directed toward more severe defects, which can be interpreted simply as disabling conditions, is of such a condemning nature that its usage would naturally decay with disuse. To the contrary, evidence shows the person with a disability has not been abandoned as the butt of homor in the present century. For example, in a survey of jokes from five different sources, Barker, Wright, Myerson, and Gonick (1953) observed that 4.1% of nearly 7,000 jokes were concerned with persons with disabilities. Of this number, a vast majority (80%) of the jokes clearly placed the person with the disability in a debasing, degrading position.

The Modern Period

In 1649, Descartes (1931) gave a different slant to the flow or directionality of disabled humor. From Descartes' viewpoint, persons with disabilities are prone to use humor to debase, degrade, and deride others. In his view, persons with disabilities appear to desire others to be as "disgraced" as themselves. Descartes valued an intact body integrity and his concept of disability seems to have been reflected as a projection of his own fears. Descartes possibly felt that he would be disgraced by a deformity, and thus gave little thought to the fact that persons with disabilities do not necessarily feel disgraced by their conditions.

For Hobbes (1651), disabled humor again was seen as emerging from the framework of the more physically and mentally average person. Hobbes' theory emphasized that the "infirmities" of others or one's own former "infirmity" are the primary objects of humor. However, Hobbes qualified his position somewhat by affirming that the disabling aspects must be "abstracted from persons" to be objects of humor. The disabling aspects must be of a categorical or class nature to be humorous. The relatively recent jokes, such as "Why did the little moron...," provide examples of this abstracting process.

Hazlitt (1819) contended that humor can result when the anticipation of perceiving customary, normal, standard qualities in the objects of one's perceptions is thwarted by the juxtaposition of deformities on that object. These sudden expectation discrepancies were seen as the basis of humor. For example, humor is elicited by the recent cartoon drawing in which the sequence goes as follows: Two frontier day army officers are talking about waiting for their Indian scout to arrive. The expectation is that a ruggedly handsome, possibly tall, Hollywood figure would appear. One officer then says, "Ug!" The other officer suggests that he stop his poor imitation of an Indian. The first officer says, "No, I mean Ug!" The last frame is a drawing of a dwarfed figure draped in a blanket, wearing an oversized head band with a feather, sporting a huge nose containing a large hairy wart. The earlier discussion on the "painlessly ugly" also can be applied to this example. Or another example of Hazlitt's conceptualizations is the cartoon drawing of a sign over a phone book stating, "Let your fingers do the walking." The scene shows a shredded phone book and a man walking away with a half-pleased, half-bewildered look. The man has hooks for hands.

Bain (1888) introduced the "degradation theory" of humor. While not directed specifically at persons with disabilities, Bain's notions were that one acquires a position of prominence or superiority when the humor debases others. Thus, to degrade the object of the humor (e.g., person with disabilities) is to remind oneself of the high value that he or she holds for having an intact body or whole structure. Thus, for Bain, the idolizing of normal standards and the comparative-values framework get full treatment.

Closer to the 20th century, Hall and Allin (1897) implied that misfortune or exceptionality of some sort provides the basis for humor, and that humor, in general, has a cruel quality. They suggested that disabled humor has continuum properties by noting that the "lame," "cripples without legs," the "hunchback," or the "deaf" are generally attended to with mimicry, while "deformed features" elicit hilarious laughter. Less severely disabling conditions are merely mocked, while conditions involving greater disruptions to body integrity (i.e., severe disabilities) appear to stimulate a much more intense emotional reaction. No satisfactory explanation can be found in the research literature to support this observation of a linear relationship between expression of humor and severity of disability. However, another research question remains as to why disabling conditions should be the object of humor in the first place.

The 20th Century

In a discussion of the various factors that elicit a humor response, Sully (1902) stated, "A special variety of the singular or exceptional which is fitted, within certain limits to excite laughter is *deformity*, or deviation from the typical form" (pp.88-89). Further, Sully (1902) correctly concluded that there is no single uniting principle of humor, but an attempt to arrive at a descriptive heading encompassing the many elements of humor would require one to state:

that they all illustrate a presentation of something in the nature of a defect, a failure to satisfy some standard requirement...our laughter at the odd as opposed to the customary, as the deformed, at failure in good manners and the other observances of social life, at defects in intelligence and of character, at fixes and misfortunes...at the lack of a perception of the fitness of things and at other laughable features, may undoubtedly be regarded as directed to something which fails to comply with a social requirement...(p.139)

Bergson's (1911) "something mechanical encrusted on the living" theory of humor suggested that rigidity, the inability to be chameleonlike, the inability to be fluid in movement or mobile, and the inability to be adaptable to the environment provides the basis for humor. What he termed deformity or disability becomes an object for humor only if the disability can be imitated by a physically normal individual. For example, humor occurs when a stage comedian appears to imitate an individual who has cerebral palsy or some spastic condition. The reason humor occurs in this situation is that the disability has an aura of rigidity about it which was acquired as an habitual exaggeration of a regular feature or characteristics of a nondisabled person. The normal condition has now become encrusted with mechanical properties and, since these mechanical properties constitute restrictions in freedom of movement and expression, this condition must be corrected. According to Bergson, the function of humor is to correct for this lack of freedom. Thus, in this instance, humor becomes possible because the disabling condition is abstracted from reality; it is mechanical and will disappear somehow as soon as the encrusted thing is removed and, what Bergson terms the "living" activity (e.g., freedom of movement), takes over again. Humor, in this case, would appear to function as a denial mechanism for an individual. Bergson (1911) further referred to the humor process as a "ragging" mechanism of society, and considered the object of humor to be humiliated in every instance.

McDougall (1922) maintained that people express humor because they begin to feel displeasure and must thwart that feeling. He asserted that the act of coming into contact with the minor misfortunes of others would tend to excite sympathetic pains, pity, and the like which would be unpleasant. Therefore, laughter occurs and a joyful feeling is placed in juxtaposition to and supersedes the unpleasantness. Thus, according to McDougall, people laugh because they are sad, not because they are happy.

Speaking mostly of the classical period and the 16th century form of humor, Gregory (1924) stressed deformities, physical misfortunes, and infirmities as the recognized objects of humor. However, Gregory revealed his lack of comprehension of the broader aspects of humor and disability when he naively stated, "since deformity is no longer a legitimate object of laughter and among the highly civilized no longer provokes it, it is clear that laughter has been humanized" (p.10). Two criticisms of Gregory's (1924) position should be mentioned. First, by disability not being a "legitimate object" of laughter, there is a tendency to stigmatize disabilities as having unusual, hushed, nonhuman qualities, which are not included among the more "normal" humor themes. Second, disabled humor does exist with great frequency as evidenced by: (a) data mentioned earlier from the survey by Barker et al. (1953); (b) the frequency of such themes in cartoons, popular magazines, and the mass media; (c) the observed frequency that disabled humor is used by physically average children; and (d) the humor evoked by persons with disabilities about their own disability in interpersonal interactions.

In one of the few early studies presenting empirical data on humor responses, Kimmins (1928) showed a curvilinear relationship between the use of misfortune humor and the age of a child. Age 7 was depicted as the peak period for the use of a misfortune theme; a sharp decline occurs at age 9 and 10, with the proportion of usage negligible beyond age 10.

The Concept of Deviance and the Humor Process

Not all writers who can be considered as falling within the purview of the present discussion relied on a specific entity, such as specifiable disability types or deformities, as elicitors of the human response. In another direction, some writers drew upon a general deviance concept to delineate their positions. For example, Klapp (1950) contended that the role of "fool," when ascribed to an individual, serves a definite function in social structure. As the butt of humor, the "fool" serves as a conformity enforcer, as a status adjuster, and/or as a deviance control.

The conflict and control function of humor was espoused by Stephenson (1951), who indicated that the conflict function of humor allows hostile, aggressive material to be expressed without fear of overt retaliatory attacks. The control function serves, among other things, to define group sentiments, to express judgments of group actions, and to initiate and maintain common stereotypes. Thus, Stephenson (1951) provided a plausible explanation for humor that is directed toward, for example, mentally retarded persons (i.e., the "little moron" jokes and the spastic or "klutz" humor).

Pitchford (1960) saw humor as providing a means for the establishment of controls in those social situations that require some movement to be made in the direction of already established norms or normal standards. The implication is simply that one would not want to "do that" or "be like that" because he or she would be laughed at and ridiculed. Kaplan and Boyd (1965) described some of the functions that humor served on an open psychiatric ward. They concluded that one function of humor was to control intragroup deviations from established norms.

Daniels and Daniels (1964) described a case study of an individual in a military setting who served as the butt of the group's humor. The individual's physical awkwardness and obtuseness represented forms of deviance that the group focused upon as objects of humor. By doing so, the group was able to highlight its own values at the expense of the "deviant" individual. Further, Daniels and Daniels emphasized the function of the "fool role." They stated that societies find "the fool 'label' a convenient one for the partly disabled, the weak, those uninterested in the conventional goals, and innovators" (p.228). Thus, those labelled "fool" are incorporated into the social structure with a minimum of conflict, whereas more extreme forms of deviance are punished, expelled, or liquidated.

Finally, the basic theoretical position adopted by La Fave (1972) lends further credence to the deviance control function of humor. La Fave assumed that "a 'joke' is humorous to the extent that it enhances an object of affection and/or disparages an object of repulsion, unhumorous to the extent that it does the opposite" (p. 198). La Fave broke this general proposition down into more specific forms. He substituted "positive identification class" for "object of affection," and "negative identification class" for "object of repulsion" to give a boundary setting function for humor. Since there is a general recognition by lay people, employers, and insurance companies that persons with disabilities represent deviations from established normal standards, the person with a disability is buffered by these same various social and economic forces.

Conclusions

Humor is pervasive, and at times perverse, in society. Disabled humor is a special type of humor, whose linkage extends from Plato and Aristotle to the present day. Disabled humor has, thus, been well conditioned over time to become an acceptable form of social intercourse.

Beyond the conditioning process, disabled humor might well serve as a means for the physically and mentally average person to cope with fears of developing a disabling condition or experiencing a similar disruption in body integrity. Granted, humor can serve as an "ice-breaking" mechanism for persons with disabilities as they interact in the general public. The message from the person with the disability is that his or her condition has humorous qualities; by focusing on the humorous aspects of the disability, the person is stating that "I accept it as no more serious than your own personal frailties, so accept me as being like you." Whether interactions would be more smooth and realistic *without* this form of thrusting the disabilities into social interactions is question for research to answer. A good guess is that a warm-up period, with this type of humorous interlude from persons with disabilities, is unnecessary. Individuals believe that this type of humor is useful only because they have conditioned themselves to rely on humor in meeting the demands of unfamiliar situations.

In the final analysis, disabled humor appears to debase and degrade. Disabled humor clouds reality with an air of nonseriousness or unreality. The positive coping merits of disabled humor are far outweighed by the negative, subliminal effects that it has on one's perceptions of persons with disabilities and the individuals' perceptions of their own condition. The realization should be apparent that disabling conditions establish psychological events in which the individual's perceptions of what is right or best for him or her is thwarted. These events may stem from a set of values (e.g., perceptions surrounding body-whole, body-beautiful values); or they may stem from basic insecurities (e.g., uncertainty as to how one should respond to this new psychological situation, appearing foolish, and loss of control). Or, indeed, some entirely obtuse explanation may be correct. Regardless of the explanation, humor will only serve to sublimate the event, and real coping is unlikely to emerge from the use of disabled humor.

Therefore, a new learning-conditioning process must become socially ingrained so that individuals begin to respond more with *person-accepting* reactions and less with *disability-focused* reactions. Above all, people must realize that humor is not just humorous. There is almost always some underlying message being carried in the humor response. And rehabilitation personnel should become aware of these underlying messages.

References

Aristotle. (1898). **Poetica** (S.H. Butcher, Ed. and Trans.). London: Macmillan (Original work published c.320 B.C.).

Bain, A. (1888). **The emotions and the will.** New York: Longmans, Green.

Barker, R.G., Wright, B.A., Meyerson, L., & Gonick, M. (1953). **Adjustment to physical handicap and illness: A survey of the social psychology of physique and behavior.** New York: Social Science Research Council.

Bergson, H. (1911). **Laughter and the sense of humor.** New York: MacMillan.

Cassell, J.L. (1974a). The functions of humor in the counseling process. **Rehabilitation Counseling Bulletin, 17,** 240-245.

Cassell, J.L. (1974b). **Relation of threat of personal disablement to reactions to humor stimuli and attitudes toward disabled persons.** Unpublished doctoral dissertation, University of Kansas, Lawrence.

Cicero, M.T. (1903). **De oratore** (J.S. Watson, Ed. and Trans.). London: George Bell. (Original work published 55 B.C.).

Daniels, A.K., & Daniels, R.R. (1964). The social function of the career fool. **Psychiatry, 27,** 219-229.

Descartes, R. (1931). The passions of the soul. In E.F. Holdane & G.R.T. Roth (Trans.). **The Philosophical works of Decartes** (pp. 329-428). London: Cambridge University Press. (Original work published 1649).

Donoghue, E.E., McCarrey, M.W., & Clement, R. (1983). Humor appreciation as a function of canned laughter, a mirthful companion, and field dependence: Facilitation and inhibitory effects. **Canadian Journal of Behavioural Science, 15**(2), 150-162.

Dworkin, E.S., & Efran, J.S. (1967). The angered: Their susceptibility to varieties of humor. **Journal of Personality & Social Psychology, 6,** 233-236.

Goldstein, J.H., Suls, J.M., & Anthony S. (1972). Enjoyment of specific types of humor content: Motivation or salience? In J.H. Goldstein & P.E. McGhee (Eds.), **The psychology of humor** (pp.159-171). New York: Academic Press.

Gregory, J.C. (1924). **The nature of laughter.** London: Kegan Paul.

Hall, G.S., & Allin, A. (1897). The psychology of tickling, laughter, and the comic. **American Journal of Psychology, 9,** 1-42.

Hazlitt, W.C. (1819). **Lectures on the English comic writers.** London: Taylor.

Hickson, J. (1977). Humor as an element in the counseling relationship. **Psychology: A Quarterly Journal of Human Behavior, 14,** 60-68.

Hobbes, T. (1651). **Leviathan.** London: Cooke.

Jonson, B. (1904). Dedication to Promos and Cassandra. In G.G. Smith (Ed.), **Elizabethan critical essays** (Vol. 1, pp.58-60). New York: Oxford University Press.

Kaplan, H.B., & Boyd, I.H. (1965). The social functions of humor on an open psychiatric ward. **Psychiatric Quarterly, 39,** 502-515.

Kimmins, C.W. (1928). **The springs of laughter.** London: Methuen.

Klapp, O. (1950). The fool as a social type. **American Journal of Sociology, 55,** 157-162.

Kubie, O. (1971). The destructive potential of humor in psychotherapy. **American Journal of Psychiatry, 127,** 861-866.

La Fave, L. (1972). Humor judgments as a function of reference groups and identification classes. In J.H. Goldstein & P.E. McGhee (Eds.), **The psychology of humor** (pp.195-210). New York: Academic Press.

Lamb, C.W. (1968). Personality correlates of humor enjoyment following motivational arousal. **Journal of Personality and Social Psychology, 9,** 237-241.

Levine, J., & Ableson, R. (1959). Humor as a disturbing stimulus. **Journal of General Psychology, 60,** 191-200.

Martin, R.A., & Lefcourt, H.M. (1984). Situational humor response questionnaire: Quantitive measure of sense of humor. **Journal of Personality and Social Psychology, 1,** 145-155.

McDougall, W. (1922). Why do we laugh? **Scribners, 71,** 359-363.

Peterson, J.P., & Pollio, H.R. (1982). Therapeutic effectiveness of differentially targeted humorous remarks in group psychotherapy. **Group, 6**(4), 39-50.

Piddington, R. (1933). **The psychology of laughter: A study in social adaptation.** London: Figurehead.

Pitchford, H.G. (1960). **The social functions of humor.** Unpublished doctoral dissertation, Emory University.

Plato. (1860). **Philebus** (E. Poste, Ed. and Trans.) Oxford: University Press. (Original work published c.355 B.C.).

Poland, W. (1971). The place of humor in psychotherapy. **American Journal of Psychiatry, 128,** 635-637.

Prerost, F.J. (1983a). Changing patterns in the response to humorous sexual stimuli: Sex roles and expression of sexuality. **Social Behavior & Personality, 11**(1), 150-162.

Prerost, F.J. (1983b). Promoting student adjustment to college: A counseling technique utilizing humor. **Personnel & Guidance Journal, 62,** 222-226.

Quintilian, M.F. (1910). **Institutes of eloquence** (J.S. Watson Ed. and Trans.). London: George Bell.

Redlich, F.C., Levine, J., & Sohler, T.P. (1951). A mirth response test: Preliminary report on a psychodiagnostic technique utilizing dynamics of humor. **American Journal of Orthopsychiatry, 21,** 717-734.

Scogin, F.R., & Pollio, H.R. (1980). Targeting and the humorous episode in group process. **Human Relations, 33,** 831-852.

Shurcliff, A. (1968). Judged humor, arousal, and the relief theory. **Journal of Personality and Social Psychology, 8,** 360-363.

Singer, D.L. (1968). Aggression arousal, hostile humor, catharsis. **Journal of Personality and Social Psychology, 8,** 1-14.

Stephenson, R.M. (1951). Conflict and control functions of humor. **American Journal of Sociology, 56,** 569-574.

Sully, J. (1902). **An essay on laughter.** New York: Longmans, Green.

Williams, C., & Cole, D.L. (1964). The influence of experimentally induced inadequacy feelings upon the appreciation of humor. **Journal of Social Psychology, 53,** 70-85.

Wright, B.A. (1983). **Physical disability: A psychosocial approach.** New York: Harper & Row.

Children's Attitudes Toward People with Disabilities: A Review of the Literature

Joanne M. Morrison and
Alex W. Ursprung

Researchers have consistently documented the existence of negative attitudes toward people with physical disabilities and have claimed that these attitudes develop during childhood (Ryan, 1981; Weinberg, 1978; Wilkins & Velicer, 1980). Consequently, many recent investigations have focused on the formation of children's attitudes toward disabled individuals (Jones, Sowell, Jones, & Butler, 1981; O'Moore, 1980; Westervelt & McKinney, 1980). The popularity of this topic stems, in part, from efforts to provide integrated education for children with disabilities. The authors believe that, by capturing the attention of children at an early age and exposing them to enriching experiences with people who have disabilities, favorable beliefs will be established and remain for a lifetime. Thereford, this article examines the available literature on children's attitudes toward disabled individuals, reviews various methods of promoting positive attitude change, and discusses implications for future research and practice.

Review of the Literature

Ryan (1981) suggested that there is enough consistent research to assume that an age-related acceptance sequence exists with respect to persons who have physical disabilities. Small children may be particularly rejecting because of their subjective role-taking ability. Very young children (4 to 6 years of age) are generally egocentric; they cannot determine another individual's internal state. They may reject people with physical disabilities because they do not understand their subjective perspectives, and may also assume that their own aversive reactions are shared by others (and caused by the person with the disability). Also, for very young children, physical attractiveness has been found to be a large component of social judgment (Ryan, 1981). This could explain some children's

aversive behavior toward individuals who are noticeably disabled. That is, young children may be assuming that a negative physical trait (which induces a negative state within themselves) means a person is bad.

As children get older, they become aware of others' subjective perspectives and are thus more understanding of their feelings and beliefs (Ryan, 1981). This awareness leads to their becoming less rejecting of people with disabilities. It is as though the children tend to adjust their focus and concentrate on what is inside an individual as apposed to interpreting just what they see. In addition, there seems to be a general increase in the complexity and organization of interpersonal judgments as children mature. Ryan felt that older children begin to realize individual variations, they start to understand others' subjective perspective, and they can conceptualize others as having physiques different from their own and yet still being good people.

Ryan (1981) believed that one cannot adequately describe general reactions of children to individuals with physical disabilities because of differing developmental influences, education, and previous experiences with people who are physically disabled. Furthermore, one should not immediately assume that persons who believe one bad thing about a physically disabled individual will generalize this to the total group, or that persons with negative attitudes will behave in a negative way toward people with disabilities.

Finally, Ryan (1981) noted that there are periods during early childhood in which reactions to individuals with disabilities will be favorable or unfavorable. It is necessary to recognize these reactions when considering mainstreaming children with disabilities. Negative results can occur if the effort at integration occurs during an unfavorable time, which could affect the acceptability of the children being mainstreamed. How-ever, integration at early stages, when attitudes

Reprinted From: Journal of Rehabilitation - Jan/Feb/Mar, 1987, with permission.

tend to be positive, may be found to decrease later unfavorable reactions.

O'Moore (1980) studied social acceptance of children with physical disabilities in a school setting, and found that there may be a time when integration is not appropriate. She found that children in the 9 to 11 age group were not as socially accepting of exceptional children as they were of nondisabled controls. The results showed that social acceptability of the exceptional child in an ordinary school was not related to the lack of hand control, or to mobility.

O'Moore (1980) also found that the sex of the subject influenced children's acceptance. Boys, whether physically disabled or not, achieved greater social acceptance with their peers than did girls. Even so, in O'Moores study of 9 to 11 year olds, there were fewer relationships established among physically disabled children when compared to nondisabled children. This suggests that a physical disability can be a powerful component in determining children's preferences. It may cover up a child's better known pattern of social acceptability. O'Moore concluded that children in the schools should be taught to be more readily accepting of their disabled peers.

In contrast to O'Moore's (1980) finding that visibility was not related to social acceptability, Wisely and Morgan (1981) found peer acceptance of children with disabilities to be related to the influence of nondisabled *vs.* physically disabled appearance. They showed slides and tapes to third and sixth graders in which target children were compared as either (a) physically nondisabled and nonretarded, (b) physically disabled only, (c) mentally retarded only, or (d) physically disabled and mentally retarded. The authors found age and sex to be important factors. The third grader rated all stimulus children, regardless of condition, more favorably than did children in the sixth grade. For all the test measurements used, excluding the adjective checklist which is a measure of stereotypic attitudes, boys gave more favorable ratings of the male stimulus child than did girls. The authors also noted a significant relationship between the sex of the rater and the rater and the mental retardation stimulus. Boys rated nonretarded and retarded children

about the same. While girls rated the retarded child approximately the same as boys did, their rating of the nonretarded child was significantly lower. The girls were less accepting of the nonretarded child than were the boys. This finding may be related to the fact that only male children were included in the stimulus conditions.

Wisely and Morgan (1981) also compared behavior and attitude scales. They found that children rated other children who were presented as physically disabled and/or mentally retarded more favorably than children presented as nondisabled and/or nonretarded on behavioral scales. On the stereotypic attitude instrument, this finding was reversed for children presented as retarded and was nonsignificant for children presented as physically disabled. The authors hypothesized that the attitudinal instruments explore the cognitive components of attitudes, and the behavioral intention instruments touch the performance components. More simplistically put, some of the instruments used measured the extent to which children were willing to commit their own behavior toward social acceptance or rejection of the stimulus child. The adjective checklist requires subjects to describe the stimulus child without making any behavioral commitments, and probably measures stereotypic attitudes toward disabled individuals more directly.

In another study of school students, Parish, Baker, Arheart, and Adamchak (1980) used both disabled and nondisabled children and found that students evaluated themselves most favorably, nondisabled children as a group less favorably, and disabled children as a group least favorably of all. This evaluation occurred regardless of whether the respondents were normal or disabled children. Parish et al. (1980) also noted the self-rating of normal males were significantly higher than the ratings of disabled children by both the nondisabled and disabled females. Nondisabled females rated both self and nondisabled children significantly higher than nondisabled males rated disabled children. Both nondisabled and disabled children perceived themselves very positively. Disabled children, though, tended to evaluate other disabled children quite negatively.

Since the data were collected from main-streamed classrooms, it may be that main-streaming has a negative stigma associated with it for both disabled and nondisabled children (Parish et al., 1980). It may be that main-streaming, in its present form, may enhance the social-emotional difficulties encountered by disabled children.

Wilkings and Velicer (1980) also studied children's attitudes toward various stigmatized groups. Specifically, they were testing the assumption that negative attitudes toward these groups are learned in early childhood. Four semantic differential scales were employed to assess children's attitudes toward four groups (nondisabled, physically disabled, retarded, and mentally ill) by both male and female third and sixth graders. People with mental illness were rated most negatively on the evaluation and understandability scales. Both the retarded and the physically disabled were rated less positively than the nondisabled on the evaluation scale, but not as negatively as the mentally ill. This concurs with the findings of Wisely and Morgan (1981), in which people who were either retarded or physically disabled were rated less active and potent than those who were either nondisabled or mentally ill. No differences were found between the third and sixth graders on attitudes toward the three stigmatized groups. This information shows that attitudes toward mentally ill individuals are distinct from attitudes toward nondisabled people, and also distinct from the attitudes toward the other disability grounds in the study. The authors claimed that children's attitudes differed from the attitudes of adults, in that people with mental illness were not viewed by children as less active or potent than normal people.

Weinberg (1978) studied children three to five years old to determine whether they understood the meaning of physical impairment and whether their attitudes differed between disabled and able-bodied children. She conducted two experiments in which children responded to questions concerning pictures. The data from the two studies indicated that a shift does occur between ages three and four——from a lack of knowledge to an understanding about disability,

when depicted as an orthopedic impairment. The results also showed that, when children are forced to choose between a nondisabled child and a disabled child as a playmate, four and five year olds preferred the nondisabled child. Weinberg felt that the discriminatory attitudes tended to follow the understanding of disability. That is, older children who knew about the impairment were less likely to play with the disabled child than the younger children who were lacking knowledge of disability. She found no sex differences in the rating of the disabled child.

Finally, Horn (1982) reviewed a number of studies on attitudes and learning disabilities. She found that peers were most accepting of the normal achieving student and assigned rejectee status to those who had a speech impairment, and amputation, and physical disability or who were low achievers, retarded, and disturbed. The author noted that this sequence of acceptance was also found among teachers and that, perhaps, students actually learned their biases from their instructors. Therefore, she believed that any attitude modification projects should not only be directed at students, but at teachers as well.

From the information found in the literature, it appears that the attitudes of young children toward disabled individuals are flexible and impressionable. Perhaps programs designed to improve attitudes toward people with disabilities will have the most impact when directed toward children who are just beginning to form their perceptions of the disabled. Thus, a review of methods of influencing attitudes is warranted.

Methods for Influencing Change

It is imperative to examine what factors influence the development of attitudes, either positively or negatively, in an individual. Because events that occur in childhood have a lasting impact, young children are a particularly important target group for attitude-enrichment programs. Through such programs, positive experiences introduced early in their lives should be effective in overcoming and preventing further adherence to stereotypes associated with disability. Thus, it is not only important, but also possible, to develop positive reinforcers in the environment that reward valuing people for themselves regardless of race, creed, religious background, or disability.

There are many ways of introducing attitude-enhancing experiences toward disability into the lives of children. Donaldson (1980) suggested the following categories: (a) direct or indirect contact with, or exposure to, disabled persons; (b) information about disabilities; (c) persuasive messages; (d) analysis of the dynamics of prejudice; (e) disability simulation; and (f) group discussions. Further, Donaldson advised those involved in changing attitudes to follow some model which incorporates the ideas that opinion or attitude modification be thought of as a result of either the reduction in restraining forces or an increase in driving forces surrounding an opinion or behavior. For example, when discussing individuals with disabilities, one can seek to reduce the discomfort that occurs when nondisabled persons interact with disabled individuals or by presenting a message sufficiently powerful enough to unfreeze a currently held belief.

Attempting to research the influence that an activity has on children's attitudes, Westervelt and McKinney (1980) measured the effects of a brief film designed to show that the aspirations and interests of children with disabilities are similar to those of their nondisabled classmates. The subjects in the study were 45 boys and 53 girls from the fourth grade. The procedure involved an experimental group who viewed a 13-minute film showing disabled children in wheelchairs participating in physical education and classroom activities with nondisabled children. The focus was on a boy in a wheel chair and the narrator was discussing the fact that the child enjoyed and performed many of the same things a nondisabled child enjoyed. The children then responded to questionnaires while viewing photographs of a child using wheelchair or a child with braces and crutches.

Westervelt and McKinney (1980) concluded that the students who viewed the film were more attracted to the child who used a wheelchair than were the control group children. They found no significant main or interaction effects due to sex or race in attraction to either the child in the wheelchair or the one using crutches. Interestingly, the authors said the effects of the film were

not long term, as they were not apparent on a posttest given nine days later. It appears that a film alone may be useful for exposing children to various disabling conditions, but it must be accompanied by other activities or experiences for them to adequately synthesize the new perceptions.

One intervention that could be used in conjunction with a film is increasing children's knowledge of disabilities. Karniski (1978) designed a study to determine if increased knowledge of persons with physical disabilities would affect the personal-space behavior of sixth grade children on encountering a person who appeared to be disabled. An instructional unit was used to teach nondisabled children about their own bodies and how they function. Comparisons were made to the functioning of disabled bodies. Lessons included discussions, activities, filmstrips, posters, and pictures. After the unit was completed, an experiment was conducted involving personal-spacing behavior. The test examined how close a nondisabled child would sit to a confederate who was in a wheelchair. Significant differences were apparent in personal-space behavior of children who received instruction on the physically disabled and those who did not. An increase in knowledge of physical disability resulted in a decrease in the physical distance exhibited between a child of either sex and a person with a physical disability. The authors concluded that this type of activity may have a lasting influence on attitudes and would be appropriate for inclusion in an educational program.

Miller, Armstrong, and Hagan (1981) conducted a study to measure the effects of teaching on elementary students' attitudes toward disabilities. For six weeks, nondisabled third and fifth grade students were taught about a variety of disabling conditions. At the end of this period, an attitudinal scale developed for children was administered to both the experimental subjects and a control group. The authors hypothesized that increased knowledge about disabilities would positively alter nondisabled students' attitudes toward persons with disabilities. The hypothesis in this instance was not supported. Some positive changes were identified, especially in the younger group of children, but these were not significantly different from the control group's scores on the attitude scale. It seems worthwhile to note that the experiment lasted only six weeks and quite possibly was not long enough to induce significant change. As with the study by Westervelt and McKinney (1980), which involved a film, this technique may also need to be coupled with some other means of behavior change.

Voeltz (1982) examined the effects of structured interactions of nondisabled children with their disabled peers. The authors involved students in grades four, five, and six in a two semester program. The program was a series of orientation activities and direct, structured social interaction experiences conducted during recess and other social event periods. The focus of these activities was on developing peer relationships that resembled friendships more so than helping relationships. In addition to interacting, the nondisabled participants were also asked to write essays, draw pictures, and perform other tasks regarding their experiences. To measure the effects of the program, an attitude survey was administered. Results over the two semesters revealed significantly higher acceptance of individual differences on various attitudinal dimensions by children in the experimental group. Voeltz (1982) found highest acceptance with individuals in the high-contact level group, followed by the low-contact level group, and finally by the no-contact group, which was associated with the lowest responses in relationship to acceptance. The data also represented consistent sex differences in acceptance, with girls significantly more accepting than boys. These results provide support for the use of structured social interactions for promoting acceptance of disabled individuals by their nondisabled peers.

Finally, Lazar, Gensley, and Orpet (1971) examined the effects of an instructional program on attitudes exhibited by gifted children. The subjects were divided into an experimental group which received a special instructional program, and a control group which received no discussions. A four-week workshop was conducted on a college campus for the experimental group.

It focused on creative Americans from every walk of life, some of whom had disabilities. A different individual was studied each day with emphasis on that person's achievements. Personal characteristics, including disabilities, were treated as incidentals. In addition, special guests were invited to tell about their work or experiences with disabled people. The dependent variable was the Attitude Toward Disabled Persons Scale. It was administered the first and last day of the workshop to both groups. The results provide evidence that the special instructional program had some influence on changing the attitudes of these gifted children toward disabled individuals.

Methodological Problems

After completing a review of the literature, a number of methodological problems become evident.   In many of the reports, necessary research controls were missing. Criticisms of the studies in this review include: inappropriate selection of sample groups, lack of a control group, assessment of attitudes with instruments of questionable validity and reliability, and the inability to generalize the findings to a large population.   In examining sample selection methods, it is possible that in some instances convenient or accidental samples were used rather than randomized samples. Certain samples appeared to be nonrepresentative in that volunteers comprised the sample, or the group was too homogeneous in nature (e.g., parochial school children). A second problem involved the use of pencil and paper questionnaires or surveys. Several of the studies relied solely on scales designed by the researcher or used modification of already existing scales. Many of these scales have not been sufficiently tested to determine their reliability and validity. One well known device, the Attitudes Toward Disabled Persons Scale (ATDP), which may have good face validity and consistent reliability, does not reflect the degree to which an attitude is positive or negative. Also, the ATDP was designed for adults, which leads to concerns regarding children's understanding of the instrument. It seems feasible that , with any of the attitudinal scales, individual biases and personality characteristics will influence responses. For the most part, behaviorally oriented measures were not utilized.

In several studies the pretest/postest design was employed. This type of testing design often sensitizes subjects to their own performance, and affects subsequent responses. Therefore, if subjects are tested, treated, and tested again, the experience of being tested the first time may affect responses on subsequent questionnaires.

All of the above mentioned problems are significant enough to generate some scepticism about generalizability to the larger population. Consequently, future research concerns might include examining conflicting findings based on sex differences, studying children's attitudes longitudinally as well as cross-sectionally, looking at various training methods such as individual vs. group session, and considering the lasting impact of training courses with various lengths.

Discussion

The research presented in this review indicates a definite need for educational programs directed at altering children's attitudes toward disabled individuals. There is considerable evidence suggesting that such an undertaking would be beneficial. Classroom teachers, counselors, and other people working to implement such projects know these endeavors must be based on the assumption that the dissemination of accurate information about disabilities will lead to increased positive attitudes and reduction of social rejection, stigmatization, and prejudice. A number of implications are apparent for research and clinical practice.

The first implication is that children would be the most appropriate target population for attitude change or intervention programs. This idea stems from evidence showing age-related differences in reactions to people who are physically disabled (Ryan, 1981). And since there are certain times in the life cycle when individuals are more or less accepting of disabled people, a program geared toward children between seven and nine years of age would have one of the best possibilities of success. Children at this age, according to Ryan (1981), learn to accurately

infer the feelings, thought, and intentions of others; realize that their own states can be the object of another's attention; and are gradually able to consider more than one subjective perspective simultaneously. Thus, education at this early stage is capable of decreasing later unfavorable reactions due to increased knowledge about the abilities and positive qualities of disabled people. There are characteristics of the children that need to be examined and interpreted as they will have an influence upon their reactions toward people with disabilities. These characteristics include: the child's age, social perceptiveness, personality, education, and experiences with disabled persons.

The second implication is that the material developed for any program must be age appropriate and organized for various methods of presentation. The information should be at least geared toward increasing understanding regarding the meaning of physical disability, making nondisabled individuals more aware of their feelings about people with disabilities, and teaching them how to deal with those feelings. It is very important to have some material organized to provide short, structural presentations of, or actual experiences with, disabled persons of equal or valued status and who represent nonstereotypic images of disabilities. These individuals, through their presentations, should convey information about what it is like to be disabled and how they want nondisabled people to relate to them. Exposure to individuals with disabilities who have successfully adjusted to their disability and who can display their confidence and independence would be an enriching experience. lastly, there are a number of ways that information can be presented to keep children's interest. These include simulating a disability, participating in a puppet show, or watching a film

The third implication calls for rehabilitation counselors to take an active role in the attitude changing process. They can be involved in a variety of ways, either directly or indirectly. For example, rehabilitation counselor can assist in the development of materials and in the actual presentation of the programs. Group counseling aimed at information giving can be conducted to gain support and financial backing from parents, teachers, civic organizations, and businesses. Individual counseling may need to be done with students who have had negative experiences with disabled persons and, therefore, fear participation in any activity involving people with disabilities. Finally, counselors can assist disabled students themselves in effectively dealing with the variety of attitudes they encounter. These students can also be helped to be advocates for changing opinions by their positive social interaction and communications with nondisabled people (Goodyear, 1983; Kaplan, 1982; Westwood, Vargo, & Vargo, 1981).

References

Donaldson, J. (1980). Changing attitudes toward handicapped persons: A review and analysis of research. **Exceptional Children, 46,** 504-514.

Goodyear, R.K. (1983). Patterns of counselors' attitudes toward disability groups. **Rehabilitation Counseling Bulletin, 26,** 181-184.

Horne, M. (1982). Attitudes and learning disabilities: A literature review for school psychologists. **Psychology in the Schools, 19**(1), 78-85.

Jones, T., Sowell, V., Jones, J., & Butler, L. (1981). Changing children's perceptions of handicapped people. **Exceptional Children, 47,** 365-368.

Kaplan, S.P. (1982). Rehabilitation counselor's attitudes toward their clients. **Journal of Rehabilitation, 48**(4), 28-30.

Karniski, M. (1978). The effect of increased knowledge of body systems and funcitons on attitudes toward the disabled. **Rehabilitation Counseling Bulletin, 22**(1), 16-20.

Lazar, A., Gensley, J. & Orpet, R. (1971). Changing attitudes of young mentally gifted children toward handicapped persons. **Exceptional Children, 37,** 600-602.

Miller, M., Armstrong, S., & Hagan, M. (1981). Effects of teaching on elementary students' attitudes toward handicaps. **Education and Training of the Mentally Retarded, 16**(2), 110-113.

O'Moore, M. (1980). Social acceptance of the physically handicapped child in the ordinary school. **Child Care, Health & Development, 6**(6), 317-328.

Parish, T., Baker, S., Arheart, K., & Adamchak, P. (1980). Normal and exceptional children's attitudes toward themselves and one another. **Journal of Psychology, 104**(2), 249-253.

Ryan, K. (1981). Developmental differences in reactions to the physically disabled. **Human Development, 24**(4), 240-256.

Voeltz, L.M. (1982). Effects of structured interactions with severely handicapped peers on children's attitudes. **American Journal of Mental Deficiency, 86**(4), 380-390.

Weinberg, N. (1978). Preschool children's perceptions to orthopedic disability. In B. Bolton & M. Jaques (Eds.), **The rehabilitation client** (pp. 49-55). Baltimore: University Park Press.

Westervelt, V., & McKinney, J. (1980). Effects of film on nonhandicapped children's attitudes toward handicapped children. **Exceptional Children, 46,** 294-296.

Westwood, M.J., Vargo, J.W., & Vargo, F. (1981). Methods for promoting attitude change toward and among physically disabled persons. **Journal of Applied Rehabilitation Counseling, 12,** 220-225.

Wilkins, J., & Velicer, W. (1980). A semantic differential investigation of children's attitudes toward three stigmatized groups. **Psychology in the Schools, 17**(3), 364-371.

Wisely, D., & Morgan, S. (1981). Children's rating of peers presented as mentally retarded and physically handicapped. **American Journal of Mental Deficiency, 86**(3), 281-286.

The Effects of Attitudes Upon the Blind: A Reexamination

THOMAS LARGE

Since World War II much has been written about attitudes toward blindness. For the most part this growing literature has focused on negative aspects of attitudes toward blind persons and especially the detrimental effect that attitudes among the sighted can have on the blind person's self-esteem.

At the same time successful blind people continue to publish biographical and inspirational writing which refers to the importance of other people, both blind and sighted, to their own rehabilitation. Furthermore, such positive influences of attitudes toward blindness are a basic part of rehabilitation work. Presumably, the job of the rehabilitation professional, at least in part, is to influence positively his client's self-concept.

Surprisingly little systematic study has been done to synthesize these apparently contradictory phenomena: the negative and positive effects of attitudes upon the blind person's self-esteem. An important question, it would seem, is: Why do some blind people make positive use of the attitudes of others while other blind people do not?

Literature Review

It is tempting to try to answer such a question by emphasizing the clumsy, frightened, denying, sometimes downright sadistic treatment of blind people by a subgroup of the sighted. A review of current literature reveals the universal concern among rehabilitation workers with the blind person's difficult social interactions with the sighted and for preparing the newly handicapped to "manage" such situations (Goffman, 1974; Giarratana-Oehler, 1976; Schulz, 1975; and Scott, 1969). Roberts' (1973) view of the effect of attitudes is typical: "There is the commonly held view of blind people as being helpless, resigned, melancholy, sexually sterile, etc." (p. 52). He goes on to describe the "strong tendency" of most blind people to comply with such social stereotyping.

Such statements, while accurate to a degree, come close to a "good guy vs. bad guy" view of the blind person's social predicament. Whether or not such an antagonistic view is useful in rehabilitation work should remain a separate question from whether it accurately describes social interactions. But the accuracy of this view remained unchallenged until Whiteman and Lukoff (1964) failed to find among a large sighted sample such negative attitudes toward blind people. They concluded that the public at large was simply poorly informed about blindness. Other studies by Whiteman and Lukoff (1965), Lukoff (1972) and Yuker (1977) also have not found a general tendency to attribute socially undesirable characteristics to blind people. Moreover, an interesting study by Peck and Uslan (1980) found a significant discrepancy between rehabilitation workers' view about the public attitudes toward blindness and nonprofessionals' self-report of their attitudes. The 283 professionals "consistently rated the public as having a considerably more negative attitude than members of the sighted public reported having." (Peck & Uslan, 1980, p. 36)

The Problem

If these more recent studies are correct and attitudes of the sighted are more benign than rehabilitation workers and researchers have believed, then perhaps other aspects of the blind person's relationships should be explored. The work reported here was an attempt to learn more precisely what may help and what may hinder adjustment by studying "successful" blind people.

Method

The Maryland State Division of Vocational Rehabilitation supplied the names of people blinded after the age of six who were judged "successful" in their adjustment by their counselors and who had been employed or enroled in

Reprinted from: *Journal of Rehabilitation*, Apr/May/June 1982, with permission.

college for at least one year. Eight men and eight women, ranging in age from 20 to 65, agreed to be interviewed. Interviews which were conducted at job sites or in college dormitories, were tape-recorded.

The interviewer followed a prepared list of 95 questions covering: (a) factual, identifying information, (b) relationships with the blind and sighted and (c) attitudes of subjects and others about blindness. Palacios, Newberry, & Bootzin (1966) demonstrated the usefulness of this recorded interview technique. Some typical questions seeking information about attitude were: Who was the most important person to you during that period right after you lost your sight? How did your parents react to your loss? What will you be doing in five years? After you lost your sight, who was your closest friend? What does your spouse think about your disability? What do you think you would be doing if you had not lost your sight? Did luck play any part in your successful adjustment? Would you do anything differently if you could live that initial adjustment period over again?

The intent of each interview, which was followed up by telephone conversations to check unclear responses, was to encourage candid reports of each subject's experience adjusting to blindness with particular reference to the influence others had on that process. Thus, subjects were asked to elaborate on their initial answers. This led the interviewer to ask unprepared questions and to allow each conversation to linger or stray in areas important to the subjects. It was felt that such a technique would promote greater self-revelations.

Results

To the legally blind interviewer subjects readily provided information about their views of the effect others' attitudes had had upon their adjustment. in addition, the interviewer noted nonverbal signs (laughter, sighs, tearfulness, etc.) within the subjects' conversations about past and present relationships.

Significant common experiences emerged among subjects. First, all subjects reported being deeply influenced in their adjustment by the attitude of at least one family member. This seemed to be as powerful an attitudinal influence for those who lost their sight in middle age as it was for those whose blindness occurred in childhood or in adolescence. For example, Bennett, a 65-year-old factory shop foreman who became legally blind at 40, reported being troubled for at least five years by his father's anxiety over his blindness. The father, himself a vigorous blue collar worker, was highly dependent upon sight to perform a specialized job which he had held full-time until age 75. He viewed his grown son as utterly helpless from the moment he learned Bennett was legally blind.

Second, the power of a relative's attitude upon subjects seemed equally strong regardless of whether it was felt as positive or negative. In other words, some subjects seem to have been as discouraged by a family member's negative attitude as others were encouraged by a family member's positive attitude. For example, Jim, a 30-year-old manager of his own business, reported his parent's view of his blindness as being "a total disaster." He modeled himself after highly independent blind teachers and friends during the 23 years since he lost his sight in a hunting accident. The drive to succeed in his adjustment seems to have come in part from his wish to disprove his parents' negative views about blind people becoming independent.

At the other extreme is Nancy, a 20-year-old college junior, who attributed great importance to her sighted mother's understanding, optimistic attitude toward blindness throughout her daughter's rehabilitation. Nancy lost her sight gradually from congenital glaucoma, which, in contrast to Jim's family, allowed Nancy's parents time to make their own adjustment to their child's loss. Nancy's mother reportedly worked closely with her daughter's ophthalmologist and rehabilitation counselor preparing herself for her daughter's eventual blindness and found ways to aid Nancy's gradual development of independent skills.

Nothing so consistently repeated itself in the interviews as did the powerful influence upon subjects of family members' attitudes. While parental attitudes were most often cited, those of spouses, siblings and even children seemed to have almost equally strong effects. Christine, a 21-year-old senior in college, reported the strong positive influence of her blind and highly independent older bother. Sarah, 52 and blind for 12 years, said she was "stunned" when her son asked that she not come to parents' day activities at his elementary school. His embarrassment about her clumsiness led her to reexamine her denial of loss and consequent reluctance to learn the use of aids that, while they would reveal her blindness to strangers, would also increase her independent mobility. Regardless of whether the influence was positive or negative, similar pivotal experiences involving family members' attitudes about blindness were reported by each subject and apparently had lasting effects.

Discussion

Although reported less frequently, two other common experiences involving attitudes of others may be significant. First, with regard to the use of other blind people as models, half of the subjects made some reference to a series of models during their adjustment. This tendency on the part of blind people in the process of becoming more independent to change their models seems to result from their "outgrowing" early models. As one subject put it: "My first positive images of blindness were created by blind people who I now regard as mostly helpless." If such a progression of modelling relationships is true, it is interesting to wonder whether it continues throughout life or whether such changes in relationships may occur only until each blind person achieves some sort of "fit" within his particular milieu.

Second, nine subjects were highly active members of political or religious organizations. These causes seem to provide a wider context within which the subject's blindness is necessarily secondary to the primary task of the group.

The relegation of blindness to a secondary or nuisance level is a familiar theme in the literature on intrapsychic adjustment. But the possible function of a group identification in accomplishing this relegation rather than merely accompanying it is interesting to contemplate.

Conclusion

The effect of others' attitudes upon the blind person seems to be a highly complex and individual matter. The research of this part of rehabilitation, while it has revealed a great deal about stereotyping and the blind person's problematic interactions with the sighted, has itself been subject to stereotyping. Other aspects of attitudinal influence, specifically family relationships, may influence adjustment as much or more than social stereotyping. This, along with the blind person's changing relationships with other blind people and his or her identification with cause groups, deserves further study if we are to more fully understand the effects of attitudes upon the blind.

References

Giarratana-Oehler, J. Personal and professional reactions to blindness from diabetic retinopathy. **New Outlook for the Blind,** 1976,70, 237-239.

Goffman, E. **Stigma: Notes on the management of spoiled identity.** New York: Jason Aronson, 1974.

Lukoff, I.F. Attitudes toward the blind. In Lukoff I.F., Cohen, O. and others. **Attitudes Toward Blind Persons.** New York: American Foundation for the Blind, 1972.

Palacios, M.H., Newberry, L.A. & Bootzin, R.R. Predictive value of the interview. **Journal of Applied Psychology,** 1966, **50,** 67-72.

Peck, A.F. & Uslan, M.M. Beliefs about public attitudes toward the blind. **Journal of Rehabilitation,** 1980, **46**(2), 36-39.

Roberts, A. **Psychological rehabilitation of the blind.**
    Springfield, IL: Charles Thomas, 1973.

Schulz, P.J. The sight of blindness and the phenom-
    enon of avoidence. **New Outlook for the Blind,**
    1975, **68**, 261-265.

Scott, R.A. **The making of a blind man.** New York:
    Russell Sage, 1969.

Whiteman, M. & Lukoff, I.F. Attitudes toward blind-
    ness and other handicaps. **Journal of Social
    Psychology,** 1965, **66**, 135-145.

Whiteman, M. & Lukoff, I.F. Attitudes toward blind-
    ness in two college groups. **Journal of Social
    Psychology,** 1964, **63**, 179-191.

Yuker, H.E. Attitudes of the general public toward
    handicapped individuals. In **White House
    Conference on Handicapped Individuals.** (Vol.
    1). Washington, D.C., 1977, 89-105.

Ostomates: Negotiating an Involuntary Deviant Identity

This investigation examines, from a symbolic interactionist perspective, a case of spoiled identity. The research examines a segment of the physically disabled who are subject to ostomatic status.

Ostomies are becoming a common operation. Ostomy is a collective and generalized term used to refer to different types of bowel and urinary surgery. Common to all these surgical procedures is the creation of an artificial body opening, located on the abdomen and called a "stoma". The term stoma is derived from two Greek words. *stomoun* meaning "to provide an opening" and *tome* which refers to a "cutting operation". This opening becomes the new body orifice from which body waste elimination occurs, replacing the anus and/or urethra. The waste is then disposed of into a collecting device known as an "appliance" or "bag", which is lightweight and often disposable. It is attached to the body in the frontal stomach region of the abdomen. A few drops of feces or urine flow from the stoma on a regular basis because there is no voluntary muscle in the stoma which can control excretion.

To a layman, explained in this manner, ostomy surgery appears to be relatively "simple". This surgery however, involves many complications, both physical and emotional. The patient in one way or another must come into direct contact with bodily wastes once the operation is performed, and it requires, to some degree, the alteration of one's life patterns. It necessitates major changes in order that a person might live a normal life without rectum or normal bladder function. The common concerns expressed by potential ostomates are: "Will I bulge?"; "Will my sexual functions be interfered with?"; and "Will I be able to resume various activities including sports?"

From a broad sociological perspective this investigation is one which focuses on identity. Identity has been an important sociological concern which had its beginnings with theorists such as Cooley, Mead, Thomas and Zaniecki, and

Blumer. The tradition has been continued in the present by the works of contemporary sociologists such as Becker, Goffman, Davis, Glazer and Strauss. Research on ostomates is part of the sociological tradition which analyses the pattern by which actors victimized by involuntary spoiled identity cope with the physical consequences and the social meaning and reality of being subjected to instantaneous disability. This spoiled identity is often viewed and labelled by others in negative terms. The project investigated the ramifications of being accorded ostomatic status and examined the reactions of patients to their altered physical and social status.

From a conceptual perspective, spoiled identity evolves when an actor has had or believes he has had the attributes which normally define his presence in day to day interactions compromised, so that he is perceived by himself and/or others as possessing attributes which are often negatively defined or labelled deviant. Victims of stigma encounter difficulties in acceptance, maintaining and/or changing their personal identities.

The difficulties for many who are defined as disabled and/or involuntary deviants stem from the fact that they too accept the deviant label applied to them. For the victims, by accepting the self-fulfilling prophecy of ostomy status, the process becomes increasingly insidious. When this is the case, the ostomate is open to attach from within as well as from without.

This project is focused on a basic problem of sociology —— the relationship between an individual's identity, the identity one presents to the world and the reactions, real and imagined of others towards the victim. As a consequence of socialization and one's achieved and ascribed status, one's identity is usually perceived as being continuous, consistent and in an established pattern fitting into an orderly career. The orderly career comprises sets of expectations as to how the actor will be treated in relationships with others. Deviations from established patterns cause spoiled identity.

By focusing on deviations produced by altered physical status as a result of surgery, we can observe how individuals often search for new identities. In viewing the process whereby disabled individuals attempt to regain normalcy or successful rehabilitation, one is able to analyze the patterns illustrated by actors attempting to come to terms with spoiled identity. One can thus ascertain the processes utilized by these actors (involuntary deviants) involved in an identity formation process or in an identity reformation process.

The Sample

Thirty-five patients were intensively investigated over the course of three and one half years. The participants were caucasian and of Canadian citizenship of first to fourth generation, ranging in age from nine to eighty-six. Twenty of the subjects were male and all volunteers except two, one Jew and one agnostic, were from Protestant or Catholic backgrounds. These volunteers were representative of a wide range of socio-economic backgrounds. The sample included ten housewives, two executives, three students, three salesmen, thirteen blue collar workers and three retired subjects.

It was noted that there were no differences displayed in the types of problems and difficulties encountered or in the types of adjustments or adaptations that were subsequently illustrated after surgery. It appears that class backgrounds and education do not influence how actors react to being ostomates.

The patients experience varying degrees of anxiety during the interview. Most patients seemed to be shy and reserved about matters of sexual intimacy.

This study was hampered by its relatively small sample size. The thirty-five patients consented to a series of in-depth interviews which in some instances commenced prior to surgery and extended over the course of the following three years. Their spouses, siblings and peers often contributed valuable data. In addition, ninety-four other people were interviewed which included families of patients, doctors (General Practitioners, Internists and Surgeons), psychiat-

rists, medical social workers, psychiatric social workers, internists, nurses and estmotherapists, who provided valuable insights into the adaptive patterns illustrated by these involuntary deviants.

The limitations were offset by the breadth and intensity of the investigation into the ostomaic career of each individual. This investigation analyzed changes in the perception of self as the patient made the transition through seven stages; 1) minor symptoms phase; 2) major symptoms phase; 3) diagnoses phase; 4) hospital preoperative phase; 5) hospital post operative phase; 6) adjustment phase —— normalcy or disabled and finally an assessment of the patient in terms of normalcy, identity or renegotiated new identity.

Nine of the patients could not recall the signs that led to their eventual surgery. In four instances the patients were born with spina bifida and therefore had never known normal evacuative functions. Seven of the patients had been involved in severe injuries as the result of falls, traffic accidents and other events, during which their bladder and/or kidney had been severely ruptured, necessitating ostomy surgery. In six of these cases the patients had never heard of ostomy status prior to surgery. They literally awoke from surgery with conditions which they never anticipated. Reactions were dramatic: "How could they do this to me?"; "they can't do this to a normal person"; "How can I live with this, my normal life will disappear?" "Marriage will be impossible." "Sex will be impossible."

These concerns afflict those who become ostomates as the result of instantaneous conditions. These are understandable concerns which are usually alleviated as one becomes familiar with the strategies of coping with ostomy status. The major concern for those between the ages of 15 and 30 centre around the acceptability to the opposite sex and sexual activity. There are four normal and solvable problems after surgery, "a) failure (of erection or orgasm) due to attempting intercourse before strength returns following surgery; b) serious anxiety about the ability to perform sexually, or about attractiveness of one's altered body image, about the possibility of odour and the security of the appliance or stoma covering; c) depression which many people suffer following any surgery; d) excessive medication and/or alcohol." For most ostomates, where age is not a factor, these concerns and problems can usually be partially if not totally eliminated.

Eight individuals in the sample who had previously experienced normal sexual relations, encountered difficulties in re-establishing sexual activity. In seven of the eight cases the difficulties were associated with the social and psychological implications of being an ostomate, of wearing a bag, of spillage and of the escaping or possible escaping of urine, feces or gas. For the one patient the ability to have an erection after surgery was apparently a physiological impossibility. "They told me it beats dying, but that is very difficult for someone who is in love and has enjoyed a good sex life. I have never had any problems before but last month my wife moved into another bedroom."

The new ostomate often perceives rejection by family, friends, medical and paramedical personnel during the immediate post operative phase. It is at this stage that the patients are sometimes victimized by escaping gas, spillage, pain and pressure from nurses and/or estomotherapists to manage their own appliances. In other words new patients are forced to take care of themselves. During this time, patients become acutely aware of their spoiled identities. The resulting anxieties often cause severe depression.

Some patients develop a myriad of physical, psychological and social problems. From a physiological perspective, in most cases when age is not a factor, a normal life may be resumed after ostomy surgery. From a medical perspective patients are considered cured. They encounter social stigma because they are "different" and their social adjustment to their spoiled identity is not easily accomplished.

The ostomate is constantly required to be involved in the management of the evacuation of bodily wastes. In many instances the new ostomate is repelled by spillage, escaping gas, skin irritation and accidents which plague most ostomates. The reality of being involved with the disposal of one's waste on a permanent basis, forces many ostomates to radically redefine their images unless surgical resection occurs.

Many ostomates are negatively identified, as a consequence of the physiological effects of ostomy surgery, which hinders sociability and thus produces varying degrees of personal anxiety. Ostomates have become stereotyped and this stereotyping leads to consequences which may be relatively severe. Some ostomates withdraw in varying degrees from societal participation. Many new ostomates are inclined to accept the credibility of folklore, which defines their status as unacceptable. Hence some ostomates are often pressured to disguise their conditions.

The emotional reactions demonstrated by ostomy patients both at the time of the diagnosis and following surgery, are best examined by keeping in mind the importance of body image and North American values of cleanliness.

One of the human organism's earliest accomplishments is the control of waste elimination, a function which is surrounded by strong emotional components as a result of North American cultural values and body perceptions. An individual relinquishes these controls with varying degrees of anxiety. Objectively, having an ostomy appears to be a small price to pay for life itself. Nevertheless, all humans are creatures of their environment, and lack of control of body waste is often perceived as intolerable. Incontinence, through loss of this control, implies a return to infancy, a subsequent loss of self-esteem and resulting depression which may, in extreme cases, result in suicide.

The idea of having to manually expel body wastes is repugnant to most, even to many medical personnel. This pattern of elimination evokes a sense of inadequacy, dirtiness and exposure. To the victims, there is a destruction of masculinity and feminity. Whether one loses a limb, an eye, or a breast, all mutilative surgeries frighten and outrage the patient as he or she faces a compromised physique. No longer are they capable of coming close to society's ideal which is that of the "body beautiful"; their physical appearance has been robbed of integrity. There is a high social premium placed on cleanliness. In mass media there is an emphasis on the ideal body image. Advertisements inform and indeed threaten that we will never find a job, a spouse or friends with the presence of odour or "sensual barriers". Ostomatic defects and other surgically produced conditions create insurmountable barriers to success. At all costs, we are told we must appear and smell attractive.

This symbolic identification of cleanliness and presumed acceptability of the clean individual is taken for granted. Being defined as dirty indicates low status and places the individual in the realm of the "unacceptable". Being seen as "dirty", therefore, has ramifications that are physical, psychological and social in nature.

Many patients solve the physical difficulties associated with being an ostomate, but encounter varying difficulties in establishing and/or maintaining social relationships. One 36-year old insurance salesman who had become an ostomate was subsequently separated and divorced from his wife. One day after having taken his five year old daughter for a birthday dinner he committed suicide. The daughter had accused him of being a "stinker". In this case the individual was able to cope with the physical difficulties but could not adapt to the social stigma produced by ostomy status.

Ostomy status can be conceptualized by stigmatized deviance. The physical impairment imposed by ostomy surgery involves some degree of spoiled identity with regard to the perceived, and usually, the physical performance of sexual and elimination functions. In most, if not all cases, this impairment penetrates the total interactional sphere of the victims. The existence of the physical stigma is a subjective and verbal aspect of one's self concept of identity and one's identity as perceived by many others. Personal cleanliness and sexual prowess are central themes of mass culture. These themes become significant parts of one's total identity.

Ostomates are involuntary deviants in a social milieu where the consequences of the deviance or perceived deviance becomes the central organizing factor in their patterns of social relationships. The ostomates are required to institute a series of strategies that establish, maintain or change many aspects of their relationships with their interacting counterparts.

The extent that these impairments are detectable affects the degree of perceived deviance.

The nature of the impairment is different from other permanent impairments such as blindness, but the consequences for identity renegotiation are similar. Because of this similarity, findings about the renegotiated careers add to our knowledge about the careers of permanently stigmatized involuntary deviants.

With regard to structuring relationships, it is well known that all victims of disability —— be it social or physical —— respond to stigma producing situations differently. Contemporary symbolic interactionists such as Goffman (1963), Roth and Scott have illustrated that affected actors utilize a variety of responses to adapt or maladapt to the contingencies of new conditions. Whenever one examines the roles of ex-mental patients, polio victims, amputees or ostomates, victims of disability exhibit a consistent sequence or career of responses during renegotiation of identity. These responses range from denial, anger, resentment, bargaining, inevitability, and depression. For the stigmatized actors, renegotiation involves three stages; a fictional acceptance of one's new status and acceptance of the disability; the normalization of role taking which included acceptance of self and awareness and understanding of one's limitations; and finally, institutionalization which is a stage where one not only accepts one's self for what he or she is, but where the actor is accepted by others.

The stigma engulfing potential ostomy status is dramatic. Twenty of the adult ostomates interviewed had never heard of the procedures associated with ostomate surgery prior to diagnosis. In eleven of the instances cancer was a precipating factor. The shock associated with diagnosis and the ramifications of ostomy status cannot be underestimated. Physicians have stated, "I'm sorry to tell you this but . . ." or "You will probably have to go through an extremely difficult surgical procedure"; or "Believe me if there were any other way . . ." or perhaps the most destructive of all, "It beats dying." Diagnosis conveyed in this way can hardly be expected to generate positive responses. Assessment of the medical literature indicates that as many as eight percent of various ostomy samples commit suicide as they are unable to contend with the physical and social consequences of their involuntary status.

The majority of patients initially chose not to disclose their anticipated status as they associated it with a deviant identity. Ostomates often encounter difficulty in their attempts to enter the so called ostomate subculture. Establishing an ostomate identity and /or public disclosure is plagued with many difficulties. The majority of patients in their relations with relatives, peers, the medical and paramedical fraternities encountered varying degrees of alienation because all parties are inclined to believe that the status of being an ostomate places one in a devalued group.

Being in a devalued group the motivation to closet one's deviant identity as an ostomate is often profitable. Because of the positive values of cleanliness and sexuality and the negative attribution associated with body waste one can understand why ostomates are inclined to believe that they should hide their spoiled identities.

One patient commented, "I feel like an ex-con with a great intellectual ability at mathematics but being unable to become a bank manager in spite of years of straight behavior. There is no possibility because of the reputation and it does not matter whether the reputation is legitimate." Another patient commented, "I felt like a criminal because for my job I lied and did not disclose that I was an ileostomate. If I had explained my condition I would not have been hired. I was identified two and one half years after I had been working. Although I was not fired the boss told me I should be ashamed because I was a liar and therefore my opportunities would be limited."

This incident illustrates the pressures for concealment. If ostomates desire normalcy many believe that it becomes mandatory to conceal deviant identity. The possibility of coming out of the closet is plagued with many costs —— economic, political, psychological and social. For the majority, after varying degrees of experimentation as an ostomate, it becomes operant to disclose the deviant status. Many patients have no choice as it is difficult if not impossible to camouflage their ostomy condition. For some of those who can camouflage ostomy status there are many positive gains to be achieved.

For the majority of patients the post-operative surgical experience, with experimentation in all realms —— social, psychological, political, allows them to gain the skills needed to manage their new stigmatized identity. They become successful in conveying to others that they are not social and physical "cancers" and are "near normal human beings". A third group of ostomates, mainly those also afflicted with the difficulties of ageism, are significantly disabled as the result of the new deviant status and are forced to relinquish many of their former roles. In some cases the relinquishment of these roles is not voluntary but a direct result of the problems associated with managing the limitations imposed by being an ostomate. A fourth group which is found amongst many other patients who are plagued with stigmatizing conditions, are those who utilize their ostomy status to achieve secondary gains through illness. Two ostomates in the study opted for early retirement when apparently there was no physical need to do so. One subsequently committed suicide.

Ostomates often have similar anxieties to those encountered by homosexuals who contemplate coming out of the closet. The cost of coming out may be substantial even though the identity in and of itself may not be considered deviant in some quarters. The possibility of discrimination, isolation, alienation and honesty create an ambiguous social environment. Many ostomates view the costs and advantages of disclosure but are unwilling to make the choice.

The strategy of disclosure or concealment rests on a complex interaction of factors which the ostomate views as stigma-producing experiences or potentially stigmatizing experiences. This is enhanced by the ambiguity that there are always many who are prepared to accept a deviant identity and to normalize relationships while there are social contacts which are restructured if not destroyed as a consequence of disclosure. The victims find that they can never count on acceptance and thus the personal costs are seen as extreme.

Goffman, Glazer and Strauss, Becker and others have focused on the problems associated with the general sociological problems of how actors utilize strategies to manage what they see as discreditable in their self-concepts. Schneider and Conrad in 1979 maintained "we tried to see how people attempt to maintain favourable or at least neutral definitions of self, given a condition for which no 'new' readily available supportive identity or subculture exists, and which most of the time, except for the occurrence of periodic seizures, is invisible". Ostomate status tends to be invisible, but the possibility of spillage, the odour of escaping gas, skin irritation and the negative reputation furnished by ostomate identity serve to pressure victims to closet their new, undesired, involuntary identities. This identity takes on extremely deviant perceptions because of contemporary values and the bizarre consequences of being an ostomate.

In addition to these difficulties, new ostomates often encounter difficulties in physically looking after themselves, in obtaining employment, in obtaining life insurance policies, in establishing, maintaining and developing relationships. To the teenager or young adult the awareness of ostomy status and its consequences is often severe. As W.C. Fields maintained, "Some things are better than sex, and some things are worse but there is nothing exactly like it." The majority are able to have sex and to bear children.

The stigma associated with ostomy status is somewhat imprecise. In some instances patients encounter little difficulty and in other situations the efforts the patient must make to achieve normalcy may be described as monumental.

A stigmatized illness, be it mental illness, leprosy, cancer, tuberculosis, epilepsy and/or ostomy status tends to be an individualizing and privatizing experience. Persons with stigmatized illnesses are doubly insulated from one another, at least in one very important sense. Because there is no illness subculture they are separated, alone and unconnected with others sharing the same problems.

Although ostomy organizations which are self-help groups exist, the majority of new ostomates seldom have prolonged encounters with these organizations. They are prone to reject the organizations as making unwarranted intrusions into their private lives. Surgeons usually encourage patients to affiliate with ostomy organizations

in order to learn the strategies of coping. Only two of nine surgeons interviewed gave the name of new patients to ostomy associations. Most surgeons felt that it was not their obligation to become involved with the patients' subsequent social and psychological rehabilitative difficulties.

Conclusions

The study was undertaken to analyze the process by which the victims of spoiled identities (ostomates) form new identities. Because of the views of medical and paramedical personnel, patients, peers and society in general it can be said that ostomy status can be perceived as stigmatized deviance.

Whether one examines the roles of ex-mental patients, polio victims, mastectomates or ostomates, victims of disability exhibit a consistent sequence or career of responses during renegotiation of a new identity. These responses range from denial, anger, resentment, bargaining, inevitability, depression and usually renegotiation of a new identity and perhaps even to suicide. For the stigmatized actor renegotiation involves three strategies; a fictional acceptance of one's new status and acceptance of the disability; the normalization of role taking which includes acceptance of the disability; the normalization of role taking which includes acceptance of self, awareness and understanding of one's limitations; and finally institutionalization which is the stage where one not only accepts one's self for what he or she is, but where the actor is accepted by others (Glazer and Strauss). In contrast, for actors afflicted with an illness where recovery is possible, illness involves a non-stigmatizing deviance. There is an eventual return to the status quo as the actor encounters no social barriers as a consequence of illness. This pattern is revealed in Roth's study, Timetables (1963). However, when an individual becomes disabled as the result of becoming blind, or assuming the status of an ostomate, one discovers that one's disability is a stigmatized deviance.

For ostomates the career of renegotiating a new identity begins when an individual realizes that the physical transformation is about to be accomplished or is already accomplished. Before this point patients seldom realize the meaning of ostomatic status and its implications. The ability to build new identities is more or less modified by the severity of the disruption or change required in a new lifestyle and the result of ostomatic status. Older patients generally have more difficulty in addition to the difficulties imposed by becoming an ostomate. Ostomates acquire new identities more easily if they have the advantage of the following situations; 1) they are able to manage or conceal their physical conditions in interactions with significant others; 2) they were born into or acquire this deviant status at an early age so that they are not aware of the terms of their "abnormality"; 3) they are embedded in a familial situation characterized by the existence of strong positive primary relation-ships; 4) their status has already been established by virtue of achieved status in the community; 5) that they are married, past the child-bearing stage and physically able to cope with the consequen-ces of their deviant status; 6) they are not requir-ed to relinquish any previously established roles; 7) they receive adequate counselling from medi-cal and paramedical personnel, both prior to and following surgery (this seldom occurs). The extent to which the above seven sociological preconditions are present usually determines the degree to which ostomates can successfully establish their identities.

Involuntary deviants, be they victims of physical, psychological or social stigma, seldom enjoy the consequences of their compromised identities except perhaps for those who utilize their acquired status to achieve secondary gains. For ostomates and other victims of spoiled identi-ty their capacities for achieving acceptance are often limited by the stigma which the victims accept (self-fulfilling prophecy) or the stigma which is attributed by others to these involuntary deviants. They are the victims of a labelling process. As is known, deviance is viewed not as a property of an act itself, but rather as behavior which violates someone's conception of a rule and is identified as doing so (Becker). Here the distinction between voluntary and involuntary deviance is a useful and theoretically important distinction in the study of spoiled identity. In

this context as Sagarin maintains, in speaking of the physically disabled,

> In the capacity of sociologist, therefore, one is no longer concerned with how people got that way but how and why they are defined in a devalued manner and with what consequences for all parties. (1975:36)

Faced with the accusation that one is some kind of a different person (or not normal) the labelled person has two options; to attempt to fight the imposition of the label or to accept it. Acceptance of the label implies living up to or down to the expectations of the labellers. Osto-mates, especially those who believe they have been seriously mutilated from a physical and social perspective become marginal actors. These marginal patients are seen as fulfilling a devalued position as they possess or are said to possess attributes which are different from the usual. Their life chances are often reduced because of spoiled identity. The problematic nature of their acceptance leads to renegotiation of new identities. The goal in renegotiating identity is to maintain and establish relationships which may otherwise be negatively affected.

The central sociological dimensions upon which the adjustment and the new identity forma-tion of a disabled individual evolve is the fact that societal definitions of the disabled, be they correct, ambivalent or false, are often shared by the victims. Unlike the criminal deviant, the disabled involuntary deviant usually shares the values of the dominant society with regard to the stigma involved in the acquired status. The actor usually values and seeks legitimacy. Legitimacy is obtained most easily through minimizing the visibility and the relevance of the disability in the presence of one's self. The literature on deviant behavior and its utility for understanding the formation of identity, has limitations when applied to the case of the involuntary deviant. The involuntary deviant is like the Mertonian type who shares group norms but is blocked in the access to the means to conformity and either constantly attempts to conform, becomes the ritualist or retreatist, but in any instances it is not the rebel who, by choice, rejects the legitimacy to achieve goals (Merton 1959: p. 131). The majority of ostomates opt for acceptance. When one examines the careers of the instantaneously blind (Scott), the severely burned (McGregor) and ostomates, one generally finds that they pass through a series of stages which are theoretically critical in the subsequent identity formation process. Involuntary deviants illustrate that during the process undertaken in their renegotiation of identity they undergo a series of events where their awareness and patterns of acceptance of self and others are developed as a consequence of their patterns of interaction.

In the immediate post-operative phase, many involuntary deviants initially adapt to their altered conditions because the group that is paramount in determining their legitimacy, to a large extent in the immediate post-operative phase, is medical. However, interaction with others outside the medical realm subsequent to this phase often destroys the legitimate or normal interaction potential of ostomates. As a consequence of stigma their legitimate identity is damaged and perhaps even destroyed. It must be noted that interaction with others can also establish a positive base for the establishment of identity.

By noting the stages which ostomates encounter, we discover the process through which they are assigned a social identity as involuntary deviants by others and subsequently enter upon ongoing careers as deviants. Lemert states:

> The empirical evidence now available makes it doubtful that the emergence of a new morality and procedure for defining deviance can be laid to the creation of any one group, class, or elite. Rather they are products of the interaction of groups. (1967: 457-468)

Once an individual has been a victim of involuntary deviance, problems arise in the managing of this new deviant identity. The involuntary deviant must decide how to integrate his social identity with his personal identity. With medical and paramedical personnel as well as with fellow ostomates, the ostomate is well advised to be open about his difficulties, but with non-ostomates the value of openness is problematic. How the ostomate, as an involuntary deviant, manages his damaged identity affects how he fares in his deviant career. For involuntary deviants the

effects of their careers, their successes and their failures depends on their social, psychological and physiological capacities to manage and adapt to their conditions.

Ostomates, like other involuntary deviants, are required to assume multiple roles with resulting strain on their personal images. For the involuntary deviants, knowledge of the legitimate as well as the illegitimate means of encountering the ramifications of this strain is important in their subsequent adaptations (Cloward 1959:164-176).

Renegotiating one's identity is often difficult because, like some other involuntary deviants, both patients and interacting audiences often possess different sets of expectations. The immediate consequence for all parties may not be as severe as first anticipated. The new ostomate, like the "new ex-mental patient" often discovers that he may not be able to exercise control over the image he wishes to portray to the same degree as was possible before the advent of spoiled identity. Initially exchange between the new ostomate and others can be characterized as strained interaction. As illustrated by Glazer and Strauss the difficulty emanates from the patterns of awareness existing between the ostomate and those who constitute his interacting spheres.

When actors find that they are unable to elicit desired patterns of treatment they encounter the consequences of stigma. Relationships between ostomates and normals often proceed under conditions of anxiety due to embarrassment, concern, pity, shock, revulsion and compassion. These conditions destroy the normal basis of interaction. This leads to the utilization of defence mechanisms amongst those who are subject to disabling conditions. Those subject to spoiled identity often are aware that the core of their being is totally regulated by expectations that subtly govern interaction between normals and those defined as disabled, inadequate or in some other way discredited.

Ostomy status threatens personal esteem as one's body image has been significantly altered. A fairly serious maladjustment rate amongst ostomates and a significant suicide rate indicates a potentially productive area for research in endeavouring to eliminate the difficulties associated with serious cases of maladjustment and involuntary deviance. Ostomates illustrate the dramatic effects of involuntary deviance. Their stigma arises from two fundamental alterations of ability to perform bodily functions which in most societies tend to be strictly regulated —— the sexual and the evacuational.

The renegotiation of new identities as experienced by people with this stigma under such intense social focus can contribute significantly to our understanding of the process of identity formation of those who belong to that segment of society defined as involuntary deviants.

References

Becker, H. 1963. *The Outsiders: Studies in the Sociology of Deviance*. New York, Free Press.

Blumer, 1962. "Symbolic Interaction." A. Rose (ed.), *Human Behavior and Social Process*. Boston, Houghton-Mifflin.

Cloward, R.A. 1959, "Illegitimate Means, Anomie, and Deviant Behavior" *American Sociological Review XXIV*, (April 1959), pp. 164-176.

Cooley, C.H. 1902. "The Looking Glass Self" as quoted in A.R. Lindersmith and A. Strauss, *Social Psychology*. New York, Holt Rinehart, and Winston.

David, Fred, 1963. *Passage through Crisis: Polio Victims and their Families*. New York: Bobbs-Merrill.
1967, "Deviance Disavowal: The Management of Strained Interaction by the Visibly Handicapped." Manis and Meltzer (eds.) *A Reader in Social Psychology*. Boston: Allyn and Bacon.

Goffman, E., 1963. *Stigma: Notes on the Management of Spoiled Identity*. Englewood Cliffs, N.J.: Prentice-Hall.

Glaser, B.G. and A.L. Strauss, 1967. "Awareness Contexts and Social Interaction". *American Sociological Review, XXIX* (October) pp. 669-679.

Lemert, E.M., 1967. *Human Deviance, Social Problems and Social Control*. Englewood Cliffs, N.J.: Prentice-Hall.

McGregor, F.C., 1951. "Some Psychosocial Problems Associated with Facial Deformities." *American Sociological Review* 16:629-38.

Mead, G.H. 1913. "The Social Self" *Journal of Philosophy*.

Merton, R.K., 1959. "Social Structure and Anomie", in R.K. Merton (ed.) *Social Theory and Social Structure*. Glencoe, The Free Press. p. 131-139.

W.C. Fields as quoted by B.D. Mullen and K.A. McGinn, *The Ostomy Book*. Palo Alto. Bull Publishing Company, 1980. p. 139.

Roth, J. 1963. *Timetables*, Indianapolis. Bobbs Merril.

Sagarin, E., 1975. *Deviants and Deviance*. New York: Praeger Publishers, p. 36.

Schneider, J.W. and P. Conrad. 1979. "In the Closet with Illness: Epilepsy, Stigma Potential and Information Control" in Delos Kelly (ed.) *Deviant Behavior*, New York. St. Martins Press. (1984).

Scott, R.A., 1969. *The Making of Blind Men*. New York: Russell Sage Foundation.

 **SOCIAL ENCOUNTERS**

The social sciences often analyse encounters between individuals and groups. In the usual scheme of things, we evaluate strangers by the identities which they present to us. Thus, individuals establish their identities by conveying a series of attributes which they believe legitimately convey their personalities and identity.

For the visibly disabled, these positive attributes are usually overridden by the obvious disability. For the public, disability tends to have a persuasive and stigmatizing effect which causes society to isolate and ignore the disabled. Thus, an individual in a wheelchair is usually viewed in terms of being a quadriplegic rather than as a computer scientist, or artist, as in the case of Christie Brown.

As Hanks and Poplin illustrate, labelling has dominated society's conception of the disabled. These authors point out the key problems with labelling theory when dealing with the disabled, and they further indicate that this theory is not adequate because many of the disabled are beginning to question and rebel against the labels that are unwillingly applied to them. Also in this chapter, Professor Day examines the quality of life and leisure exhibited by individuals who have encountered rehabilitation programs. Likewise, Professor Rumplehart illustrates that successful social integration includes complex activities that occur automatically out of the awareness of the participants during ongoing activities. In doing this, she concludes that it is frequently necessary to interact abnormally, in order to teach normal social interaction to those who have developed psychological abnormalities. Her research carries on an established tradition in sociology, of identity management. Ferguson further maintains that disability is more of a social category than a physical reality when studying mental retardation. Likewise, Link et al. demonstrate that many of the difficulties encountered by former mental patients can be attributed to social response and social interaction.

The disabled are often expected to assume a passive role in society. The disabled who become actively involved in advocacy endeavours are usually perceived as behaving in a non-conforming manner. The role of advocacy is explored by Scotch in his analysis of the disability as a basis for social movement. Indeed we are now in an era where most minorities are actively engaged in advocacy. Large segments of the disabled who have been traditionally institutionalized or confined to their homes in a "total institution" environment are now striving to live in independent living centers free from the regulation and supervision imposed by institutional care-givers. The disabled who are engaged in independent living advocacy maintain that they are minorities who have the right to establish and maintain their own independent living patterns, as illustrated by Williams.

Society tends to define the position of minorities, and historically the disabled have been characterized as weak, poor, and unable to achieve "legitimate integration". Consequently the disabled have often been isolated and alienated from the mainstream of society. Integration and deinstitutionalization conflict with widely held beliefs that state that the disabled ought to accept graciously the traditional care that has been given to them by a "well-meaning society". Unfortunately, this "care" has not been conveyed to the disabled and used to improve the disabled person's quality of life. As a result of this passivity, large segments of our communities are becoming militant in their attempts to achieve integration and meaningful lifestyles, in a society prone to overlook the needs and the barriers facing the disabled.

The Sociology of Physical Disability: A Review of Literature and Some Conceptual Perspectives

MICHAEL HANKS AND DENNIS E. POPLIN

In this paper some of the most significant literature on the sociology of physical disability is examined. Special attention is paid to the labelling perspective because it has dominated thinking about the social and emotional adjustment of disabled individuals during recent years. Much of the empirical research, however, indicates that a key problem in the labelling theory is explaining why many disabled individuals do not passively accept the labels that are applied to them. Hence, two alternative conceptual perspectives, the negotiated outcome perspective and the compensatory perspective, are offered to account for the behavior and emotional adjustment of some physically disabled individuals. In addition, some possible conditioning variables are discussed in terms of their theoretical significance and implications for future research.

Even though our knowledge of the demography of disability is still far from precise, we know that a large number of people in the United States are disabled as a result of some chronic condition or impairment. Depending on how it is measured, official estimates of the prevalence rate for disabling conditions in our society range from 15 million to as high as 50 million--one of the largest minorities in the Unites States today (Bowe, 1978; Social Security Administration, 1967-1974; Allan and Cinsky, 1972; Allan, 1976. Drute and Burdette, 1978). Because of the size of this group it is understandable that the social aspects of disability constitute a problem that has received increased attention from social scientists in the last decade (e.g., Safilios-Rothschild, 1970; Haber and Smith, 1971; Levitin, 1975; Albrecht, 1976). As yet, however, knowledge pertaining to the sociology of physical disability remains fragmentary, tenuous, and theoretically unintegrated. The labelling perspective, which has been central in much research and theory on

social deviance over the last 15 years, has not been sufficiently explored in terms of it application to the area of disability and rehabilitation (Gove, 1976). In this paper we review the concept of disability as deviance and the evidence on the minority status of physically disabled individuals, consider the conceptual framework of labelling for the analysis of physical disability, and finally discuss a number of alternative perspectives for viewing the behavior and adjustment of disabled individuals, as well as some of the variables and issues that must be considered in doing research on disabled individuals.

Disability As Deviance

The idea that physically disabled persons occupy a deviant or stigmatized social role is found throughout the sociological literature on disability (Davis, 1961; Freidson, 1965; Scott, 1969; Safilios-Rothschild, 1970). For example, in his classic paper, "Disability as Deviance," Freidson (1965) suggests that disability is an imputed from of deviance, meaning that the disabled individual is "deviant" because other people consider his or her condition or behavior inappropriate or other than normal. The disability as deviance perspective is also prominent in the work of Fred Davis (1961). Thus, in his article "Deviance Disavowal" Davis (1961) tells us:

> Because the visibly handicapped do not comprise a distinct minority group or subculture, the imputation of generalized deviance that they elicit form many normals are more nearly genuine interactional emergents that conventionalized sequelae to intergroup stereotyping as, for example, might obtain between a Negro and a white. . . . Before discussing how the visibly handicapped cope with

---

The authors shared equally in this work and the ordering of names does not indicate seniority or priority. They are merely listed alphabetically.

Reprinted From *Deviant Behavior: An Interdisciplinary Journal, 2:309-328, 1981*
Copyright © 1981 by Hemisphere Publishing Corporation, with permission.

difficult interaction, it is appropriate to first consider the general nature of the threat posed to the
interactional situation per se as a result of their
being perceived routinely (if not necessarily
according to some prevalent stereotype) as "different," "odd," "estranged from the common run
of humanity," etc.; in short other than normal
(p. 122).

Davis, like Freidson draws his basic definition of
deviant or deviance from labelling theory
(Lemert, 1951. According to his definition, "the
Negro, the career woman, the criminal, the
Communist, the physically handicapped, the
mentally ill, the homosexual, to mention but a
few, are all deviants, albeit in different ways and
with markedly different consequences for their
life careers" (1961:121).

Among the other writers who maintain that
disabled individuals occupy a deviant role are
Thomas (1966:7), who views disability as requiring "resocialization into a deviant social category," and Lorber (1975:278), who indicates
that "some familiar kinds of deviance [are]
socially defined as accidental or illness, foreign-
ness, crippling, or inherited defects." Finally,
even though he has reservations about societal
reaction theory as it applies to disabled individuals, Gove (1976) summarizes the position of
labelling theory well; in his words, "the societal
reaction theorists, who typically see the social
system as oppressing the underdog, view the
societal procedures for processing assisting the
disabled as creating and stabilizing deviant
behavior" (p. 61). There is no question that
Gove himself sees disabled persons as being
stigmatized, that is, "the disabled are typically
stigmatized, and their stigma often appears to act
as a master status which determines the nature of
their interaction with others" (1976:60; see also
Goffman, 1963).

It should be pointed out, however, that the
disability as deviance perspective has been
questioned. For example, Haber and Smith
(1971) view disability not as a form of deviance
but as a social role that becomes legitimized by
diagnostic and helping personnel (medical
specialists, rehabilitation workers, and so on).
According to them, "it is the legitimating evaluation which makes the disability and which

differentiates disability from deviance" (1971:94).
Haber and Smith, of course, recognize that
disabled individuals may be stigmatized, but
following Cohen (1959) and Goffman (1963)
they suggest that "Stigmatization does not imply
nor does it require deviance" (1971:94).

Some Applications of Labelling Theory

The labelling theory approach to the analysis of
deviant behavior has been widely used in the
social science literature. Proponents of this
theory argue that much of what is viewed as
deviance is created by society's reaction to
labelled deviance. When individuals are labelled
deviant, for whatever reason, the societal reaction
to this label reinforces the image of oneself as
being odd, different, or deviant. At this point,
one's deviance may become stabilized. Lowry
(1973) puts it well when he says, "if someone is
continually treated as inferior, dangerous, and
deviant, the chances are great that he will come
to see himself in this way and act accordingly"
(p. 118). In many respects, this is simply an
extension of ideas originally developed by
Cooley (1922) and Mead (1934).

Labelling theory has been applied to a number of different types of deviant behavior. For
example, in his analysis of homosexuality,
Sagarin (1973) tells us that "people become
entrapped in a false consciousness of identifying
themselves as being homosexuals. They believe
that they discover what they are. . . . Learning
their 'identity,' they become involved in it, boxed
into their own biographies. There is no road
back, because they believe there is none" (p. 10).
Presumably, this entrapment occurs at about the
time that other people begin to identify the
individual as a homosexual. Likewise, Scheff
(1966) has applied the labelling perspective to the
mentally ill: "the more the rule-breaker enters
the role of the mentally ill, the more he is defined by others as mentally ill, the more fully he
enters the role, and so on" (pp. 97-98). In a
variation on this same theme MacAndrew and
Edgerton (1969) relate that "over the course of
socialization people learn about drunkenness what
their society 'knows' about drunkenness; and,
accepting and acting upon the understandings

thus imparted to them, they become the living confirmation of their society's teachings" (p. 88). Labelling theory, in one form or another, has also been applied to heroin addition, (Ray, 1964), juvenile delinquency (Piliavan and Briar, 1964), and crime (Schur, 1965).

Some authors have also made use of the labelling perspective in analyzing disabled individuals. In their paper, "The Labelling Perspective and Role Transition," Hanks and Popplin (1979) indicate that "the intent of those who use labelling perspective in analyzing physical disability is to call attention to the fact that observed alterations in the attitudes and behavior of the physically disabled individuals may occur primarily because of societal reactions to the disability rather than because of the disability per se" (p. 3). They furthermore suggest that "once the person adopts being disabled as his or her social role, the disability may *appear* to worsen, both in the individual's own mind and in the minds of other people. . . . In short, being disabled may, in a sense, become a self-fulfilling prophesy" (1979:6). Goffman (1963) has also noted that the person who is stigmatized "tends to hold the same beliefs about identity that we do" (p. 7).

The labelling perspective has also been used by Cahnman (1975) to analyze obesity. Because of its relevance to our concerns here, it would be well to quote Cahnman at some length:

> those who have dealings with the stigmatized person "fail to accord him the respect and regard which the uncontaminated aspects of his social identity have led them to anticipate extending, and have led him to anticipate receiving; he echoes this denial by finding that some of his attributes warrant it" (Goffman, 1963:3-9). The second part of the sentence contains the decisive statement because, no matter what kind of protective cushioning may be interposed by ingenious stigma management, the vicious cycle is completed when the victim agrees with his detractor and considers the discriminatory treatment which is meted out to him deserved and prejudicial attitudes which underlies it justified. The outcome, in whatever form or combination it may manifest itself, is hardly avoidable because our selves are social. In one way or another, we indicate to ourselves

what we are supposed to be and we act accordingly

> The embarrassing and not infrequently harassing treatment which is meted out to obese teenagers by those around them will not elicit sympathy from onlookers, but a sense of gratification; the idea is that they got what was coming to them. The obese teenager is thus doubly and trebly disadvantaged: (1) because he is discriminated against, (2) because he is made to understand that he deserves it, and (3) because he comes to accept his treatment as just. As a result, he is unable to escape his condition and settles down to live with it. He becomes timidly withdrawn, or eager to please, or tolerant of abuse. He may escape intellectual pursuits, assume the role of a funny character, resort to empty boasting, or submit to spells of despondency. Whatever avenue of escape he chooses, he interprets himself in the way that is indicated to him. He accepts dominant values. He responds to expectation (pp. 329-330).

Cahnman's observations are based on open-ended informal interviews with 31 teenagers at an obesity clinic in New York City and on autobiographical accounts prepared by 6 university students. The applicability of Cahnman's observations to people with other disabilities and deformities remains largely unknown.

Although labelling theory has added a great deal to our understanding of disability, it is necessary to point out that the approach still has several limitations (Gove, 1976). First, societal reaction theorists maintain that "primary deviance is unimportant except insofar as it causes one to be labelled as deviant" (Gove, 1976:68). It is, however, obvious that the primary deviance of disabled people, for example, inability to speak clearly, is of crucial importance to the individual and to others in terms of interpersonal relationships, the person's perceived employability, and so on. Secondly, societal relation theorists maintain that official representatives of the larger society, such as mental health personnel, the police, and rehabilitation counsellors, are of primary importance in giving individuals a deviant label (see, for example, Quinney, 1970; Mechanic, 1962; Piliavan and Briar, 1964). In the case of many disabled individuals, however, their deviance is apparent to everyone with whom they come into contact, and they may be labelled as odd, different, or deviant long before they have been officially classified as disabled. Finally, "societal reaction theory has focused almost totally on the negative consequences of labelling" (Gove, 1976:68). Labelling by formal representatives of the larger society may, however, have positive consequences for the disabled individual. Once the disabled individual is recognized and classified as such he or she may become eligible for income maintenance programs, special educational services, job retraining programs, free therapeutic services, and so on. Of course, this world of caution does not mean that labelling theory may not prove useful in the formulation of sociological studies of physical disability. It suggests, however, that subsequent research and analyses that incorporate these more complex propositions are desirable.

Minority Status of Physically Disabled Individuals

It is possible to shed additional light on some of the issues raised above by considering the evidence that disabled persons may constitute a minority group or occupy an inferior status position (Wright, 1960; Tenny, 1953; Sussman, 1969; Kutner, 1971; Roth and Eddy, 1967; Best, 1967; Safilios-Rothschild, 1970, 1976; English, 1977; Bowe, 1978). There are rather consistent data accumulating to indicate that public attitudes toward persons with various types of physical disabilities are substantially negative. Thus, in his review of the relevant research Yuker (1977) reports that "in response to direct questions, more than 50% of the people in the United States express slightly positive attitudes toward disabled people and indicate that they have sympathetic feelings for them" (p. 94). However, Yuker goes on to indicate that "many non-disabled individuals perceive handicapped people as 'different' and in some ways inferior to 'normal' people. . . . Despite the positive attitudes that are expressed in public, handicapped persons are often discriminated against" (1977:94; see also Granofsky, 1956). Similarly, Chesler (1965)

studied attitudes toward persons with various disabilities by administering the Attitudes Toward Disabled Persons (ATDP) Scale and the Intergroup Relations Scale to 77 college and 243 high school students. His conclusion was that "for some purposes the physically disabled can be conceptualized as a minority group subject to many of the same attitudinal and behavioral predispositions as are ethnic minorities" (1965:881).

Employer attitudes toward disabled individuals also tend to be negative. Bowe (1978) reported that employers have more negative attitudes toward disabled persons than they do toward any other potential employees, including elderly persons, minority group members, ex-convicts, and student radicals. Similarly, a 1970 study found that far in excess of 50 percent of the employers surveyed would almost never or never consider blind or mentally disabled persons for any job (Williams, 1972). Findings along this line help explain why "the disabled suffer from the highest unemployment rate of any group. Some estimates place it at 40 percent of those considered employable" (Kleinfield, 1977:90).

Disabled Individuals and Society: A Conceptual Framework

As indicated by the above discussion, physically disabled individuals are often the targets of negative labelling by others. A vital question, however, still remains: "How do physically disabled people react to and manage the labels that are applied to them?" As Shontz (1971) has pointed out, "evidence of consistency in attitudes of others toward people with disabilities does not tell what the attitudes of the disabled themselves are" (p. 333; see also Levitin, 1975). In this paper and in the recent literature, attention has focused on the traditional labelling model of physical disability and, accordingly, the role of society in the process by which disabled individuals become labelled and treated as deviant and the correspondingly *negative* impact that such labelling has on disabled persons' self-concepts and on their ability to adjust to the demands of the social environment. The dominance of this view is perhaps based on the simple fact that to be disabled is to be accorded an inferior social value by our society.

Although there are conditions other than physical disability that lead to social devaluation, certainly a physical disability is one condition that may elicit negative reactions from others. It is generally thought that such reactions may come into play against disabled individuals to distort their conceptualization of self and social reality. What seems to be deficient about this perspective, however, is that it does not give ample consideration to the possibility that being physically disabled may "generate opportunities and gratifications as well as frustrations and grievances" (Shontz, 1971:333; see also Wright, 1960; Safilios-Rothschild, 1970). For this reason, we wish to emphasize that there are times when a physical disability does not lead to negative orientations about self and society. Data reported below do not clearly establish that negative beliefs and attitudes are characteristic of all or most disabled individuals or that such orientations are most likely to occur among the disabled. Rather they show that disabled individuals' responses to social pressures and the evaluations of others are *variable*.

So far in this paper we have emphasized the possibility of a negative response on the part of disabled people to their condition. One reason is that such a view is prominent in the literature. There are, however, at least two other conceptual approaches that may describe the responses of physically disabled individuals equally well and that deserve our attention. These might be called the "negotiated outcome perspective" and the "compensation perspective."

The Negotiated Outcome Perspective

This perspective (c.f., Wright, 1960; Levitin, 1975) assumes the "active participation of the disabled in the labelling process" (Levitin, 1975:555). Moreover, it assumes that the active bargaining for preferred definitions on the part of physically disabled individuals is a technique by which these individuals strive to attain a positive sense of self. In particular, Levitin (1975) has observed that "the definition of self actively presented by the permanently handicapped is one

that states this deviance is not *all* of me" (p. 555). From this perspective, then, negative societal evaluations may lead to problems of social and emotional maladjustment *only* if disabled individuals are unable to manipulate and to some extent control the labels that are applied to them by nondisabled individuals.

There is a major and important way in which the concept of negotiated outcome modifies the traditional labelling perspective on physical disability. Specifically, traditional labelling theory posits that people passively accept the labels that are applied to them (see Schervish, 1973). On the other hand, the negotiated outcome perspective views physically disabled individuals as active participants in shaping and forming the evaluations that other people make of them. For instance, Davis (1961) identifies a three-stage process of sociable interaction between physically disabled and nondisabled individuals in which the disabled individual attempts to move the relationship away from "fictional acceptance" and toward a normalization. Whether the physically disabled individual is able to normalize the relationship and more generally to elicit positive evaluations from nondisabled individuals would seem to depend on a variety of different factors, including the nature and severity of his or her handicap and his or her repertoire of social skills. This list is obviously not exhaustive.

In addition to the interactionist perspective outlined above, there is another view on the negotiated outcome approach that deserves mention here. This view offers a more structural orientation to the problem. Specifically, it sees the negotiation process as taking a collective form, such as when persons with shared traits join together to bargain for improved evaluations on the part of other people (e.g., the women's rights movement). Thus, the formation of the American Coalition of Citizens with Disabilities and the April 1977 demonstration supporting the rigorous enforcement of Section 504 of the Rehabilitation Act of 1973 suggest that some disabled persons now perceive the possibility of negotiating an improved image and status in U.S. society through collective action.

The Compensation Perspective

To a large degree, the concept of compensation comes from the work of psychiatrist Alfred Adler (1917). Adler thought that overcompensation is a typical response to physical deficiency. The prima facie assumption underlying Adler's argument has been stated by Wright (1960): "In order not to be especially bad, the person with a disability (or any minority-group member) must be especially good" (p.50). Other authors (e.g., Myrdal et al., 1944; Atunes and Gaitz, 1975) have used a similar argument in an attempt to explain racial differences in social participation. Specifically, they contend that "blacks compensate for their subordinate status through intense participation in organizations" (London, 1975:275). The advantage in using the compensation approach in the study of physical disability is that it provides for emphasis on discovering instances where labelling may lead to *positive* changes in the lives of physically disabled individuals. Moreover, in conjunction with the labelling approach and the negotiated outcome approach, the compensation approach places no restrictions on the types of comparisons that can be made between disabled and nondisabled individuals. The reader, however, should recognize from the careful consideration of the compensation perspective that determining when compensation actually occurs may be highly subjective. In particular, we know of no examination quantifying the influence of compensation on disabled people's accomplishments. This, of course, does not rule out the possibility that compensation is a behavioral alternative for *some* physically disabled individuals. However, if the compensation perspective is to prove fruitful in research on physically disabled individuals, future investigators must resolve the problems of defining and indexing compensation and specifying those dimensions of the social situation under which compensation is likely to occur.

EMPIRICAL EVIDENCE

Research on physically disabled persons is not abundant, and as far as we know there has been no sociological study of a large sample of disabled individuals. What little evidence that is available seems to cast doubt on the idea that physically disabled persons are entirely at the mercy of their social environments. For example, after reviewing a great deal of the pre-1960 literature dealing with the psychological and social impact of physical disability on the individual, Wright (1960) states that:

> Our position must be further clarified on one point. It does not assert that physical disability plays no role at all in the development of inferiority feelings or other problems. It does imply, however, that the objective fact of disability is an extraordinarily poor criterion for judging which individual is unduly beset by self-abnegation and which individual is not, and that the common association between inferiority feelings and atypical physique is a gross oversimplification unwarranted by the facts (p. 55).

Similarly, Zunich and Ledwith (1965) found little difference between visually handicapped and sighted fourth graders in terms of their self-concepts, and Pringle (1964) found no clear evidence that being physically handicapped leads to emotional and social maladjustments in children.

There have also been doctoral dissertations that have focused on the social relationships of physically disabled students and on their levels of social participation. In one such study (Dunn, 1967) "men and women college students with severe disabilities reported greater satisfaction with social relationships than did college students without disabilities" (quoted in Shontz, 1971:46). Likewise, in her study of 139 disabled adolescents (73 with orthopedic disabilities and 66 with cardiac impairments), Glovannoni (1967), found that "in terms of their social participation, the disabled reported lower social participation only in membership in formal groups, but not in informal socializing with peers nor in their social relationships with the opposite sex" (p. 3933).

We must stress again, however, that there is a paucity of empirical data and an abundance of untested theory pertaining to physically disabled individuals. The empirical research that has been done on disabled individuals has almost always been based on very small and homogeneous samples and in most cases has involved the use of cross-sectional data. These studies do not validate (or invalidate) one of the views described above or another. In fact, they suggest that regardless of the findings, research along the lines discussed in this paper should yield a high payoff.

CONDITIONING VARIABLES

The existing evidence indicates that responses to the experience of physical disability are variable. This, of course, suggests that analyses of how physically disabled individuals react to and manage their disability may involve complex interrelationships among variables at different levels (physiological, psychological, social-psychological, and structural). Research workers have generally failed to incorporate such contingencies into their models. Therefore, we can make only a tentative effort to specify some conditioning variables that may increase or decrease the ability of disabled individuals to cope with their disability.

CHARACTERISTICS OF THE DISABLING CONDITION

Two variables that surely influence how physically disabled persons feel about themselves and how other people react to the disabled person are the nature and the severity of the disability. Seemingly, these two variables would operate independently of one another. For example, Yuker (1977) reports that public attitudes are more favorable toward people with sensory handicaps than toward people who sometimes exhibit uncoordinated and unpredictable behavior, such as some cerebral palsied individuals, but this finding may be a gross oversimplification. It may well be that societal reactions toward a mildly afflicted cerebral palsied individual tend to be more positive than toward a deaf mute. There are almost no data on this problem, but it raises a question for future researchers to consider whether different types and degrees of disability are associated with distinctive social and emotional responses.

DEMOGRAPHIC COMPARISONS: CLASS, SEXUAL STATUS, AND RACE

Another variable that is thought to condition the impact that societal reactions have on physically disabled persons is that of social status. In specific, several authors (Wright, 1960; Scott, 1969; Safilios-Rothschild, 1976) have suggested that high social status is a resource that is useful to physically disabled individuals in resisting the deviant label. As Safilios-Rothschild (1976) has noted "high social status is an overriding characteristic whose desirability can outweigh the undesirability of several other characteristics, including disability" (p. 43). Thus, we may expect to find that physically disabled individuals from higher SES backgrounds have greater coping ability than those from lower SES backgrounds with the same disability. One reason for this may be that higher status persons are more skilled at negotiating the outcomes of their interactions with other people. They may also possess more of the resources that are necessary to compensate for their disability.

There are relatively few clues in the literature pertaining to how the sex of physically disabled persons influences the way in which they and others respond to their condition. Nonetheless, a variety of evidence indicates that cultural pressures and expectations may differ between the sexes. Several studies have suggested that females, as they progress through the educational system, undergo a socially induced change in priorities in which qualities such as independence, aggressiveness, and competitive achievement are largely given up (Bardwick and Douvan, 1972; Kamarovsky, 1946; Horner, 1972). If this is true, then physically disabled females may be more inclined than others to passively accept the labels that are applied to them. This distinction is important and is clearly an area for more systematic investigation.

We know almost nothing about how the physically disabled person's race might influence the way in which he or she is evaluated by other people. A strong impression, however, is that because of generally low social status and inferior educational opportunities the racial minority group member may be especially lacking in the skills and resources required to negotiate and compensate successfully. In effect such a person has the double burden of being a member of not one but two groups that are sometimes negatively evaluated.

CONDITIONING SOCIAL CHARACTERISTICS

A somewhat different set of variables that may well influence how a physically disabled person handles societal evaluations are found in the family itself. If the disabled person's family is strongly supportive and encouraging, the reactions of other people to the individual may be of relatively little consequence. The case would seemingly be much different if family support is weak and if the family members themselves are overtly pessimistic about the individual's ability to function normally. Although this formulation is admittedly speculative, there is accumulating evidence that social support from peers and family members may improve the ability of individuals to cope with stress effects in a variety of situations (cf., House, 1974). It is, of course, tempting to suggest that the disabled person's significant others are of overwhelming importance in determining how the disabled individual fares. This, however, may not be the case. Even though the individual's spouse, parents, siblings and other close acquaintances may be motivated to provide support and encouragement, they may lack the skills, insight, and information that is necessary to do so. Richardson (1969) puts it very well in the following:

> It is unlikely that the child born with a handicap will have parents, neighbors, sibs, and peers who have the same handicap and from whom he can gain experience in dealing with others. Generally, he will be surrounded by nonhandicapped people who share the general negative values of the culture toward the handicap (p. 1059).

CONCLUSION

Sociological research pertaining to disabling conditions in our society has most often focused on nondisabled rather than disabled persons (see Cameron et al., 1973; Davis and Heyl, 1978). Most typically, these studies have involved the investigation of public reactions to persons with various types of disabilities. This research generally shows that physically disabled individuals are stigmatized by the rest of society. Yet, almost nothing is known about how physically disabled individuals react to their stigmatized social status and about how stigmatization influences their self-concept, academic and occupational performance, interpersonal relationships, and so on. Much research needs to be done in this general area and the data must be gathered directly from disabled persons themselves.

This paper develops the rudiments of a framework that specifies some of the concepts, types of variables, and hypotheses necessary to increase our understanding of the nature and consequences of physical disability. This framework, we believe, presents a more realistic picture of the disability experience and appropriately cautions against uncritical acceptance of the commonsensical view of disability as a negative experience. In addition, it argues strongly for research conducted at multivariate levels of analysis. Underlying our interest in this problem is the assumption that efforts directed toward integrating physically disabled people into the mainstream would benefit from an understanding of those socially induced conditions that help or hinder disabled persons in adjusting to the demands that are placed on them.

References

Adler, Alfred
    1917   "Study of organ inferiority and its physical compensations. Nervous and Mental Disease, Monograph, No. 24.
Albrecht, Gary L. (Ed.)
    1976   The Sociology of Physical Disability and Rehabilitation. Pittsburgh: University of Pittsburgh Press.
Allan, Kathryn
    1976   "First findings of the 1972 survey of the disabled: General characteristics." Social Security Bulletin 39:18-37.
Allan, Kathryn H. and Mildred E. Cinsky

1972 "General characteristics of the disabled population." Social Security Bulletin 35:24-37.

Altman, Barbara M.
1978 "Critique of studies of attitudes toward the handicapped: What do they really tell us?" Paper presented at the Annual Meeting of the American Sociological Association.

Atunes, G., and C.M. Gaitz
1975 "Ethnicity and participation: A study of Mexican-Americans, blacks and whites." American Journal of Sociology 80:1192-1211.

Bardwick, Judith M., and Elizabeth Douvan
1972 "Ambivalence: The socialization of women." In Judith M. Bardwick (ed.), Readings on the Psychology of Women. New York: Harper & Row.

Becker, Howard S.
1963 "Outsiders: Studies in the Sociology of Deviance. New York: Free Press.

Best, Gary A.
1967 "The minority status of the handicapped." Cerebral Palsy Journal 28:3-4, 8.

Blyth, Dale A., and Roberta G. Simmons
1978 "The transition into early adolescence: A longitudinal comparison of youth in two educational contexts." Sociology of Education (July):149-162.

Bowe, Frank
1978 Handicapping America: Barriers to Disabled People. New York: Harper & Row.

Cahnman, Werner J.
1968 "The stigma of obesity." The Sociological Quarterly, 9:283-299.

Cameron, Paul, Donna G. Titus, John Kostin, and Marilyn Kostin
1973 "The life satisfaction of nonnormal persons." Journal of Consulting and Clinical Psychology 41:207-214.

Campbell, Ernest Q.
1969 "Adolescent socialization." Pp. 821-859 in David A. Goslin (ed.), Handbook of Socialization Theory and Research. Chicago: Rand-McNally.

Chesler, Mark A.
1965 "Ethnocentrism and attitudes toward the physically disabled." Journal of Personality and Social Psychology 2:877-882.

Cohen, Albert K.
1959 "The study of social disorganization and deviant behavior." Pp. 461-484 in Robert K. Merton et al., Sociology Today. New York: Basic Books.

Cooley, Charles Horton
1922 Human Nature and the Social Order. New York: Scribner's.

Davis, F. James, and Barbara Heyl
1978 "Approaches to needed sociological research on the physically disabled." Paper presented at annual meeting of American Sociological Association.

Davis, Fred
1961 "Deviance disavowal: The management of strained interaction by the visibly handicapped." Social Problems 9:20-32.

Dunn, M.A.
1967 Satisfaction with social relationship of college students who are physically disabled. Unpublished doctoral dissertation, University of Illinois.

Elder, Glen H., Jr.
1968 Adolescent Socialization and Personality Development. Chicago: Rand-McNally.

English, R. William
1977 "Correlates of stigma towards physically disabled persons." Pp. 207-224 in Joseph Stubbins (ed.), Social and Psychological Aspects of Disability. Baltimore: University Park Press.

Erikson, Kai T.
1964 "Notes on the sociology of deviance." Pp. 9-21 in Howard S. Becker (ed.), The Other Side: Perspectives on Deviance. New York: Free Press.

Freidson, E.
1965 "Disability as social deviance." Pp. 71-99 in Marvin B. Sussman (ed.), Sociology and Rehabilitation. New York: American Sociological Association.

Giovannoni, Jeane Marie
1967 "Social role behavior and extent of social participation in disabled and nondisabled adolescents." Dissertation Abstracts 27:3933-3934.

Goffman, Erving
1963 Stigma: Notes on the Management of Spoiled Identity. Englewood Cliffs, NJ: Prentice-Hall.

Gove, Walter R.
1976 "Societal reaction theory and disability." Pp. 57-71 in Gary L. Albrecht (ed.), The Sociology of Physical Disability and Rehabilitation. Pittsburgh: University of Pittsburgh Press.

Granofsky, J.
1956   "Modification of attitudes toward the physically disabled." Dissertation Abstracts 16:1182-1183.

Haber, Lawrence D., and Richard T. Smith
1971   "Disability and deviance: Normative adaptations of role behavior." American Sociological Review 36:87-97.

Hanks, Michael, and Dennis E. Poplin
1979   "The labeling perspective and role transition: The case of the visibly disabled." Paper presented at the Annual Meetings of the Southern Sociological Society.

Hare, Bruce R.
1977   "Black and white child self-esteem in social science: an overview." Journal of Negro Education 46:141-156.

Horner, Matina
1972   "The motive to avoid success and changing aspirations of college women." In Judith M. Bardwick (ed.), Readings on the Psychology of Women. New York: Harper & Row.

House, James S.
1974   "Occupational stress and coronary heart disease: A review and theoretical integration." Journal of Health and Social Behavior. 15:12-27.

Kerr, Nancy
1970   "Self-expectations for disabled persons: Helpful or harmful?: Rehabilitation Couseling Bulletin 14:85-94.

Kleinfield, Sonny
1977   "The handicapped: Hidden no longer." The Atlantic 240:86-96.

Komarovsky, Mirra
1946   "Cultural contradictions and sex roles." American Journal of Sociology. 52:184-189.

Krute, Aaron, and Mary E. Burdette
1978   "1972 Survey of disabled and nondisabled adults. Chronic disease, injury and work disability." Social Security Bulletin 41:3-17.

Kutner, Bernard
1971   "The social psychology of disability." Pp. 143-167 in Walter S. Neff (ed.), Rehabilitation Psychology. Washington, D.C.: American Psychological Association.

Lemert, Edwin M.
1951   Social Pathology. New York: McGraw-Hill.

Levitin, Teresa E.
1975   "Deviants as active participants in the labeling process: The case of the visibly handicapped." Social Problems 24:548-557.

London, Bruce
1975   "Racial differences in social and political participation: It's not simply a matter of black and white." Social Science Quarterly 56:274-286.

Lorber, Judith
1975   "Deviance as performance: The case of illness." Pp. 277-285 in Frank R. Scarpitti and Paul T. McFarlane (eds.), Deviance: Action, Reaction, Interaction. Reading, Mass.: Addison Wesley.

Lowry, Richie P.
1973   Social Problems: A Critical Analysis of Theories and Public Policy. Lexington, Mass.: D.C. Health.

MacAndrew, Craig, and Robert B. Edgerton
1969   Drunken Comportment: A Social Explanation. Chicago: Aldine.

Mead, George Herbert
1934   Mind, Self, and Society. Chicago: University of Chicago Press.

Mechanic, David
1962   "Some factors in identifying and defining mental illness." Mental Hygiene 46:66-74.

Myrdal, Gunnar, Richard Stenner, and Arnold Rose
1944   An American Dilemma. New York: Harper and Bros.

Piliavin, Irving, and Scott Briar
1964   "Police encounters with juveniles." American Journal of Sociology. 70:206-214.

Pringle, M.L.K.
1964   "The emotional and social readjustment of physically handicapped children: A review of the literature between 1928 and 1962." Educational Research 6:207-215.

Quinney, Richard
1970   The Social Reality of Crime. Boston: Little Brown.

Ray, Marsh B.
1964   "The cycle of abstinence and relapse among heroin addicts." Pp. 163-177 in Howard S. Becker (ed.), The Other Side: Perspectives on Deviance. New York: Free Press.

Richardson, Stephen A.
1969   "The effects of disability on the socialization of the child." Pp. 1047-1064 in David A. Goslin (ed.), Handbook of

Socialization Theory and Research. Chicago: Rand-McNally.

Roth, Julius A., and Elizabeth M. Eddy
1967   Rehabilitation for the Unwanted. New York: Atherton Press.

Rusk, H.A., and E.J. Taylor
1946   New Hope for the Handicapped. New York: Harper & Row.

Safilios-Rothschild, Constatina
1970   The Sociology and Social Psychology of Disability and Rehabilitation. New York: Random House.

1976   "Disabled persons' self-definitions and their implications for rehabilitation." Pp. 39-56 in Gary L. Albrecht (ed.), The Sociology of Physical Disability and Rehabilitation. Pittsburgh: University of Pittsburgh Press.

1977   "Prejudice against the disabled and some means to combat it." Pp. 261-267 in Joseph Stubbins (ed.), Social and Psychological Aspects of Disability: A Handbook for Practitioners. Baltimore, Md.: University Park Press.

Sagarin, Edward
1973   "The good guys, the bad guys, and the gay guys." Contemporary Sociology 2:1973.

Scheff, Thomas J.
1966   Being Mentally Ill: A sociological Theory: Chicago: Adline

Scheruish, Paul G.
1973   "The labeling perspective: Its biases and potential in the study of political science." The American Sociologist 8:47-57.

Schur, Edwin M.
1965   Crimes without victims: Deviant Behavior and Public Policy. Englewood Cliffs, NJ: Prentice-Hall.

Scott, Robert A.
1969   The Making of Blind Men. New York: Russell Sage Foundation.

Shontz, Franklin C.
1971   "Physical disability and personality.: Pp. 33-73 in Walter S. Neff (ed.), Rehabilitation Psychology. Washington, D.C.: American Psychological Association.

Social Security Administration Reports Nos. 1-24
1967-1974. Social Security Survey of The Disabled: 1966, Office of Research and Statistics.

Stiller, J.
1964   "Personality determinants of reaction to the physically disabled." American Foundation for the Blind Bulletin 7:37-52.

Sussman, Marvin B.
1969   Dependent disabled and dependent poor: Similarity of conceptual issues and research needs." The Social Service Review 43:383-395.

Tenny, John W.
1953   "The minority status of the handicapped." Exceptional Children 19:260-264.

Thomas, E.J.
1966   "Problems of disability from the perspective of role theory." Journal of Health and Social Behavior 7:2-14.

Titley, Robert W., and W. Wayne Viney
1969   "Expression of aggression toward the physically handicapped." Perceptual and Motor Skills 29:51-56.

Williams, C. Arthur
1972   "Is hiring the handicapped good business?" Journal of Rehabilitation (March-April):30-34.

Wolff, I.S.
1972   "Acceptance." American Journal of Nursing 72:1412-1415.

Wright, Beatrice A.
1960   Physical Disability: A Psychological Approach. New York: Harper & Row.

Yuker, H.E., J.R. Block, and W.J. Campbell
1960   "A scale to measure attitudes toward disabled persons." Human Resources Study Number 5. Albertson, N.Y: Human Resources, Inc.

Yuker, Harold E.
1977   "Attitudes of the general public toward handicapped individuals." In White House Conference on Handicapped Individuals, Vol. 1, Awareness Papers, Washington, D.C.: U.S. Government Printing Office.

Zunich, M., and B.E. Ledwith
1965   "Self-concepts of visually handicapped and sighted children." Perceptual and Motor Skills 21:771-774.

A Study of Quality of Life and Leisure

HY DAY

A large number of studies have examined the leisure behaviour of people from different geographical locations, and of different ages, marital statuses and income levels. Few have looked at how people feel about what they do in their leisure time, what they would rather be doing and why they don't do it. It might be assumed that since one characteristic of leisure activity is that it is voluntary, one would not choose activities that are not satisfying, and so the study of satisfaction in leisure activities is meaningless. However, the opposite is true: people do not always do the things that they would like to do, and sometimes substitute less satisfying activities, even in leisure time.

In 1981, a study was conducted with men and women aged 18 and up who had been through the rehabilitation process in the previous two years. Its concern was the manner in which they spent their leisure time and how they felt about it. The extent to which people yearn to do things other than those in which they are engaged is the way we measured the quality of leisure in this study. Although we were determined to avoid value judgements on their choice of leisure activities, we could not avoid reflecting on the kinds of activities performed by them. Is there a difference in the quality of leisure activities experienced by people with disabilities? If so, is it due to choice of the opportunities offered by society? These were questions to which we hoped to find some answers. Finally, the study reported on the verbal responses to a lengthy questionnaire by rehabilitation consumers, and comparisons, whenever possible, have been made with a normative sample, hereafter referred to as the control group.

The sample in this study consisted of 151 adults in Metro Toronto and its environs who had, in the previous two years, been through a rehabilitation program, successfully or not. The sample could not have been drawn in a random fashion, for not all rehabilitation 'consumers' were available from which to choose. In fact,

provincial and federal agencies did not cooperate in the study, and the sample was drawn from the closed files of four community agencies in Toronto. The agencies had different philosophies and included both vocationally-oriented and broadly-based rehabilitation programs. All individuals were approached by mail or by telephone and their participation was solicited, with a promise of anonymity. A large proportion of the consumers could not be contacted as they did not return the stamped, self-addressed, willingness-to-participate response cards, and could not be contacted by telephone. When approached personally, only two alumni were unwilling to participate in the study.

Demographic Information

Of the 151 respondents, 107 (70.9%) were male and 44 female. They ranged in age from 18 to 58, with a mean of 32.

Four types of disabilities were identified and respondents were allowed to classify themselves under more than one category. However, for purposes of the analysis, each respondent was placed in only one group and it was arbitrarily determined that physical disability was the primary one, with emotional handicap second. Thus, in the final placement 78 were identified as primarily physically disabled, 37 as emotionally handicapped, 35 as developmentally disadvantaged and one as socially disadvantaged. This last participant had to be dropped from some of the analyses where group comparisons were made.

No significant differences were found between the sexes in their distribution among the three groups. But even more interesting is that significant differences were rarely found across the three disability groups and so most comparisons were made between a single group of 151 respondents and the control group. The control group participants also lived within commuting distance of Metropolitan Toronto.

Reprinted from: Rehabilitation Digest, Summer 1985, Vol. 16 #2, published by CRCD, Toronto, Ontario, with permission.

Table 1

A Comparison of Quality of Life of Rehabilitation Consumers with a Control Sample

	Rehab Consumers	Control Group	X²
1 Generally speaking, how happy would you say you are now?			
Very happy	44	263	
Fairly happy	70	327	
Not too happy	37	41	
	151	631	45.2*
2 How often do you feel that you are really enjoying life?			
All the time	25	123	
Fairly often	56	373	
Now and then	37	269	
Rarely	24	22	
	151	633	52.2*
3 How often do you feel in low spirits or depressed?			
Fairly often	28	68	
Now and then	72	248	
Rarely	37	269	
Never	14	47	
	151	632	38.3*
4 During the past year would you say that your life has			
Become better	92	315	
Become worse	11	70	
Stayed the same	48	247	
	151	632	45.2*
5 Right now, would you say your own life is			
Getting better	72	302	
Getting worse	11	45	
Staying about the same	68	285	
	151	632	.005

*Statisticlly significant difference between the two groups exists.

Twenty-one of 151 respondents in the sample lived alone, and 23 lived in boarding homes. Nineteen lived with one other person, 63 with parents and 25 with their own families. Thus 44, or 29%, lived alone or with strangers. Only 20% of the sample were married, compared to 61% in the control group.

Quality of Life

The next section of the questionnaire required the respondents to indicate how happy they were, whether life had improved for them and what they anticipated for the future. The results are presented in Table 1.

The results clearly indicate optimism. While the respondents were far less happy, enjoyed life less and became depressed more often, a larger proportion felt that life had become better for them in the previous year, and they looked to the future with the same degree of hope as the control sample.

The respondents were then asked to indicate on ten-point scale their perceptions of themselves along a continuum of 'quality' of life, ranging from the worst to the ideal.

A test comparing the distribution of the two groups showed that the respondents in the consumer sample viewed themselves as far less satisfied with their lives than the control group. When asked where on the continuum they expect to be in two years, the difference between the two groups had decreased somewhat but was still significant.

Finally, when asked to indicate the best life they would ever expect to have, the differences between the two groups continued to decrease, though remaining significant.

It should be noted that 53% of the respondents, despite the fact that at the time of the interview they were no longer involved in any rehabilitation services, believed that life would improve until it became ideal.

Leisure Activities

The rehabilitation consumers felt that they had more time on their hands significantly more often than the control group.

This is not surprising considering the fact that many do not work. A breakdown of the way an average 24-hour day spent is presented in Table 2.

The average time spent working is 3.4 hours on weekdays and less than one hour on weekends. Leisure time available after all other activities are subtracted is 10 hours on weekdays and 12 hours on Saturdays, rising to 13 hours on Sundays.

Table 2
How the Rehabilitation Consumers Spend the Day

	Weekday	Saturday	Sunday
Working hours	3.4	0.8	0.3
Eating	1.1	1.1	1.1
Sleeping	7.8	8.2	8.3
Grooming	0.6	0.7	0.6
Preparing Food	0.4	0.4	0.4
Laundry, dishes, etc.	0.5	0.6	0.5
Leisure hours	10.1	12.2	12.8

The average amount of leisure time spent watching T.V. by the rehabilitation consumer sample is 2.7 hours per weekday compared to 2.1 hours for the control group; the difference is, in fact, statistically significant. On weekends this group spends 4.8 hours watching T.V. compared with 3.1 hours for the control group, which is an even more significant difference.

When asked about their preferred activity, 15% of the rehabilitation group chose T.V. watching. Table 3 indicates the top ten choices of both the rehabilitation group and the control group. It should be noted that the choices ranged widely (39 different choices for the rehabilitation group and 62 for the control sample), and therefore the number selecting any one activity seems relatively small.

The first two activities (reading and watching television) are similar, though in reversed order, for both groups and the other activities occur in numbers that are really too small to compare. Grouping the activities into classes of activities gives a somewhat better basis for comparison.

The largest differences seem to be in the active-passive split; the rehabilitation group generally chose a more passive type of activity. Forty-five percent of the rehabilitation consumers chose active things to do and 45% passive, while 62% of the control group chose to do active things as compared with 31% who chose passive activities.

Quality of Leisure

The next question was designed to determine the degree of satisfaction that rehabilitation consumers feel about their free time. Asking them to rate their satisfaction with the way they spend their free time on a ten-point scale yielded a mean of 5.44, compared with the control group mean of 7.70.

What the respondents would prefer to be doing is an important question. Of the 151 rehabilitation consumers, 66% felt that there were other things that they would like to do but weren't doing, compared to 59% in the control group. The first choice of 16% of the respondents was travelling, the next most popular choice (15%) was working; and the third choice was dating and going out with friends (11%). The control sample also chose travelling as its first preference and its second most popular choice was reading. The main reasons for not performing these activities seemed to be lack of money, motivation and poor health for the consumer group, but mainly a lack of time for the control group.

Table 3
Distribution of First Choices of Leisure Activities

Consumer Sample	Percent	Toronto Sample	Percent
1 T.V.	15	Reading	17
2 Reading	13	T.V.	7
3 Walking	8	Knitting, etc.	6
4 Relaxing	6	Gardening	5
5 Listening to Records	5	Visiting friends	5
6 Movies	5	Sewing, etc.	4
7 Visiting friends	5	Tennis	3
8 Knitting	3	Family activities	3
9 Sports	3	Sports, general	3
10 Work in the house	3	Shopping	3
11 Socializing	3	Golf	3
12 Playing board games	3		

Respondents were then asked to indicate the average amount of time spent at a variety of activities. A list of activities was offered because when the first respondents were asked to recall those activities they performed, they tended to name only one or two. When the categories were read to them, they seemed to recall more. There is no doubt that error is built into both of these methods.

Listing the average time spent at each activity is meaningless since many were not performed at all and the variability for those that were performed was great. For example, 21 respondents said that they did not watch television at all during an average weekday and the other 130 watched it anywhere from one-half hour per day to 15.5 hours per day. The most common activity was reading, yet 74% indicated that they did not read at all during the weekday. The range of time spent reading by the other 77 respondents was from one-half to six hours per day.

Looking at the results from another perspective, it is clear that most of the time is spent at home alone and with activities that are free and passive.

The purpose of this study was to examine leisure activities of people who had recently been through a rehabilitation program and to compare their activities and satisfactions with a control group. While few people will be surprised at the results, a study of the situation is a better basis upon which to plan programs and conduct further research, rather than preconceived notions.

Summary

Acknowledging that the sample interviewed in this study was not a random sample and may not be fully representative of disabled people as a group, the differences between it and the control group are enormous. Generally, the rehabilitation consumers were less stable in income and living accommodations. Fewer worked, and those that did were mainly unskilled or semi-skilled. A larger proportion indicated unhappiness with their quality of life and were generally more often depressed and enjoyed life less. They rated their lives as poorer than the control group, but believed that their lives were getting better; 53% believed that someday their lives would become "ideal."

Meanwhile, a great deal of leisure time was spent in ways that we, with our work ethic orientation, consider to be of poor quality and low value. The activities are usually passive, unplanned, solitary and require no financial investment. Society, on the other hand, values activities that are active, preplanned, done in a group and require organization, equipment and rules.

If we wish people who have terminated rehabilitation programs to be integrated into our society, we must look to the rehabilitation programs to provide training in skills for, and attitudes towards, those leisure activities that we value and deem more acceptable. This is not being done today, judging from the results of this study. Only 28% of the sample acknowledged receiving any training in leisure activity skills, as compared with 92% who received training in vocational skills. Until interest in developing leisure skills is raised to the same level as vocational activities, we will have failed.

The Normalization of Social Interaction: When Shared Assumptions Cannot Be Assumed

Marilyn A. Rumelhart

Among human service professionals who work with the developmentally disabled, the term *normalization* refers to the "the idea that mentally retarded persons would live in a manner as nearly 'normal' as possible" (Edgerton and Dercovici, 1976: 485). As a principle, it has had important consequences of social policy (Dybwad, 1982; Jones, 1975). Many of its proponents believe, however, that a mentally retarded person can "live normally" only insofar as he or she is taught to "maintain behaviors and appearances that come as close to being normative as circumstances and the person's behavioral potential permit" (Wolfensberger, 1972:28). Therefore, many special education and re-socialization programs have been designed to help retarded people seem more normal.[1]

This paper reports on research conducted in one of these programs. Although the term *normalization* has been used in other ways by some sociologists (cf. Davis, 1964), in this paper, it will refer to the training process advocated by Wolfensberger and others in the field of mental retardation. This process is a far more subtle and complex undertaking than might be assumed, and the difficulties inherent in it have important implications for the study of social interaction. The purpose of this paper is to examine these implications.

In order to be perceived as normal during a social interaction, a person must appear and act in a way which is not discordant with the expectations of the other participants. Therefore, teaching someone to seem normal (normalization) involves sensitizing him or her to those expectations. The difficulty of this task is frequently underestimated because both theoretician and human service professionals fail to recognize the huge reservoir of tacit knowledge upon which people depend during most of their ordinary

social activities. The extent and subtlety of this knowledge is graphically described by Polanyi (1967). He points out that, although we are able to recognize most actions and events which do not seem normal to us, we are usually much harder pressed to specify the perceptual bases for such observations. We rely for our understanding on a set of tacit assumptions about the nature of social reality.

As will be demonstrated in this paper, retarded individuals frequently appear deviant in their social interactions because they have not acquired many of these assumptions and do not know how to compensate for their difference in perspective. The normalization of such a person requires a detailed assessment of his or her perspective on the aspect of social behavior for which re-socialization is being attempted. The goal is to help the individual learn which of his or her usual reactions to situation need to be modified in order to minimize identification as a deviant member of society.

It is the labelling theory of deviance (cf. Becker, 1963; Schur, 1971) which provides the rationale for normalization. Wolfensberger and the other proponents of this approach to re-socialization maintain that being identified (i.e., labelled) as deviant by the people whom he or she encounters in the community prevents a retarded person from having a normal life. Of course, in order to be enroled in a normalization program, a person must already have been identified as retarded through some educational or medical process. Therefore, he or she has not really escaped the public or personal identity transformation which the labelling process entails (Lemert, 1951). Instead, the retarded have what Goffman calls "discreditable" social identities. Their disability is highly stigmatizing, but in most cases, it is not "immediately perceivable"

I wish to thank Professors Aaron Cicourel and Hugh Mehan for their comments concerning an earlier draft of this paper. For reprint requests write: Marilyn A. Rumelhart, School of Social Work, San Diego State University, San Diego, CA.

Reprinted form: Qualitative Sociology 6(2), Summer 83 ©1983 Human Sciences Press, with permission.

(Goffman, 1963:4). Although this permits them the possibility of passing as normal, the retarded are an exception to what Goffman and most other writers on the subject (cf. Edgerton, 1967) assume about potential passers: "...one can assume that the stigmatized and the normal have the same mental make-up and that this necessarily is the standard one in our society" (Goffman, 1963:131).

In addition to the cognitive disabilities associated with low intelligence, the ability of mentally retarded individuals to engage in what Goffman calls "identity management" is often limited by their atypical life experiences. Most retarded children develop mentally at a slower rate than do their chronological peers. This automatically makes the circumstances of their socialization different from those of most other children. A retarded child of eight is not the same as a non-retarded one of three, even if their levels of cognitive development are similar. The eight-year old does not look like a three-year old and therefore elicits different expectations from others. Even if the two children gain the capacity to learn something at the same time, the social knowledge which they acquire will usually differ because their social environments differ. Therefore, anyone seeking to normalize mentally retarded individuals should expect some unusual features in their social knowledge base. Discovering these differences is an inherently difficult task, however, because the verbal exchange which would ordinarily be the basis for an assessment of someone else's perspective on a matter is itself the problematic issue (cf. Cicourel, 1974a; Mehan, 1974). Two identical sentences or sentence fragments can have entirely different meanings depending on such factors as the identities and relationship of the speaker and hearer, the context of the conversation and the gestures used. What is necessary in order to interact "normally" is not the mastery of a set of facts or rules but rather a vast array of contingencies which govern when one is expected to say what to whom.

Furthermore, there is a seemingly endless fund of social knowledge which is required in order to understand the statements of other people. Successful social interaction is possible because the participants assume that they all share this knowledge base and set of expectations. Even when searching for what went awry in a misunderstanding, the cause is virtually never sought among these fundamental (and generally tacit) assumptions. They need to be examined by anyone who seeks to normalize the social interaction of individuals whose socialization is markedly atypical. In other words, successful normalizers must themselves behave nonnormally by making problematic matters which are ordinarily never questioned. It is this unusual process which makes normalization interesting for students of social interaction.

Three major types of knowledge appear to be required for successful social interaction. The first is knowledge about the sorts of things that are likely to be of interest to the persons with whom one is interacting (what people want to know). The second is an adequate assessment of the necessary background or explanatory information needed to render one's statements intelligible to another person (what other people need to know). The third is the large body of information and associations with which members of our society are assumed to be familiar (what other people expect you to know). Following a description of the research process on which these conclusions are based, each of these types of knowledge will be discussed.

Research Setting and Process

I conducted a two year participant-observation study while serving as a volunteer social worker at a facility which I will call Alpha Center. The program was located in an urban area of Southern California and was funded as part of the local public education system. (Elsewhere, I have discussed some of the implications of this organizational arrangement [Rumelhart, 1978]). All of the clients served at Alpha had been defined as functionally mentally retarded (regardless of the source of the disability). Their IQ scores varied from about 50 to the normal range. Most were in their middle 20s, but some were much older. They lived either with their families, in board-and-care homes, or in a semi-supervised apartment complex and could (at least potentially) care for their own personal needs, use public transportation, and attend recreational events such as movies without supervision.

Normalization was the explicit purpose of the Alpha program. Its staff members tried to help the clients live as normal a life as possible in terms of residential situation, finances, and other personal matters. They agreed with Wolfensberger that a retarded person's chances for a normal life vary directly with the extent to which he or she is perceived as normal by other people. Therefore, the Alpha program was designed to teach its clients how to appear normal.

What Other People Want to Know

During the course of my study, I frequently observed Alpha clients being punished for engaging in "inappropriate verbalizations". This was a sincere attempt at normalization, but although the staff members usually agreed on what constituted an instance of "inappropriate verbalization", they were singularly unsuccessful in conveying to the client exactly what had been wrong with the comment in question.

Occasionally, there are social rules which can be applied in a rote manner without the risk of too much contextual difficulty (e.g., "Never say hello to the same person more than once in the same day."). Most are much more problematic.

For example, I saw a client punished (denied certain privileges because he told the two staff members with whom he worked the closest that, "I have a new bank account". They did not try to explain his infraction to him or to understand the reason for it beyond the assessment that he was being "manipulative". They could not have told him that they were uninterested in his bank account because such moves toward independence were encouraged by staff and praised in other contexts. The problem was that the two staff members had just been having a serious discussion with this young man concerning some of his behaviors which were disruptive to other clients. His bank account comment occurred at the conclusion of this, as he was leaving the room. It did not seem appropriate to them because it was not in keeping with the tone of

what had gone on before. While interacting with this client, they assumed that he shared their understanding of the situation (teacher scolding student) and, therefore, interpreted comments not in keeping with this scenario as deliberate attempts to sabotage their disciplinary efforts. In making this assumption, the teachers were behaving normally. As re-socializers, however, they failed because they did not suspend their normal assumptions and assess the actual perspective of the client before responding to him.

My observations of another client, whom I will refer to as Nancy, yielded numerous examples of the need for explicit instruction in what other people want to know. Nancy came to Alpha after spending most of her adolescence in a state hospital. While there, she was befriended by a safety officer whose proscriptions she took very seriously. Nancy had definite intellectual and emotional problems, but she also had life experiences which caused her to expect helping professionals to be interested in matters of personal safety. Nancy brought up current events related to this topic in every possible context. She talked about the need for paramedics, new types of alarm systems, and crimes and accidents which had been in the news. She soon got a reputation for this. During the course of my study, however, no one ever explained to her what she was doing that upset people.

Since she did not usually bring them up out of context, it was really the frequency of Nancy's comments that bothered others. I am sure she could have learned that most people do not like to think too much about sad and frightening things. She could have been encouraged to watch for and mention happy and inspiring news stories at least as often as she did distressing ones. The crucial thing, however, would have been to alert her to the reactions of others (what they wanted to hear). Nancy herself might remain unusually interested in problems of violence. Normalizing her, however, would involve helping her to make this characteristic less socially intrusive. Simply training her never to mention such matters (i.e., penalizing her each time she did so) would probably have produced additional odd behaviors.

An example of the results such simplistic training can have was an Alpha client whose mother had taught her to be pleasant under any circumstances. Her smiles, light comments, and avoidance of complaint about obviously distressful circumstances frequently made her seem quite peculiar. The rote learning of a behavioral rule had not been normalizing. Under many circumstances, people need and want to hear unpleasant matters, but except for the most extreme cases (e.g., dangerous emergencies), specifying these circumstances in advance is an extremely difficult task. Participants in normal social interaction decide such issues of appropriateness as they come up, based on factors such as who is present, their relationships with one another, their past interactions and their probable future contacts as well as features of the immediate context. Few of us could explain how we evaluate such information. Teaching someone else how to do so seems virtually impossible, but this is what normalization requires.

In focusing on the failure of mentally retarded individuals to ascertain what they are expected to say, we may inadvertently overlook the abilities they do have in this area. Some of these were evident in the "role-playing" which occurred as part of the counseling groups at Alpha. The scenes which the clients frequently chose to act out included: going to a restaurant, being on a date, discussion between husband and wife, applying for a job, and riding in a bus, taxi, airplane or train.

Although they were often unable to carry the role-played conversations very far, the clients knew that a wife is supposed to ask her husband about his day at the office, a gentleman is supposed to ask his date how she feels about seeing a particular movie, and seat mates on a bus invariably inquire about each other's destinations. None of these clients were married, and few of them dated. Therefore, they must have relied on something other than direct personal experience in ascertaining what someone else would want to know in those particular situations. Although their role-played scenes were somewhat stereotypical, they demonstrated that these individuals had the capacity to take the probable interest of the other person into account when deciding what to say to him or her.

Theoreticians of social interaction have identified this capacity as crucial to the interactional process (cf. Mead, 1934; Piaget, 1965; Schutz, 1962). From a developmental perspective, Piaget points to the abandonment of what he calls "egocentric speech" as the critical step toward interactive competence. Most of the Alpha clients had the cognitive capacity to put themselves into the place of another person, and yet they failed to do so a significant proportion of the time. It is probable that their real difficulty lay in the area of context clarification. A useful way of conceptualizing this problem is provided by Nelson and Gruendel in their study of dialogues between preschool (and therefore presumably egocentric) children.

> We would like to suggest, in fact, that what has been generally termed egocentrism in the young child is a misplace assumption of shared context by either or both participants in a dialogue. By "misplaced" we mean an assumption made either without a check on validity or without sufficient direct experience in different contexts to adjust it automatically. A misplaced assumption of shared context also may result if the child lacks the conversational strategies which enable a context adjustment, such as repetition, questioning for clarification, or disagreement. (Nelson & Gruendel, 1979: 77)

The youngsters studied by Nelson and Gruendel will presumably learn these strategies with little or no direct instruction. The clients at Alpha have been only partially successful at doing so. I observed numerous examples of conversations which went awry because clients were either unable or unassertive enough to clarity the context. The one transcribed below occurred just after a group of clients had been given copies of the Center's calendar for the coming academic year.

(1) Tom: We don't get Good Friday [off].
(2) Teacher: Yes, Good Friday——that's the one that says Easter——March.

(3) Bill: How come sometimes they call "Bad Friday"?——sometimes, you know——
(4) Teacher: Black Friday?
(5) Bill: Bad Friday.
(6) Jim: The thirteenth time——
(7) Teacher: Friday the thirteenth?
(8) Bill: How come they call it that?
(9) Teacher: It's superstition.

It is possible that Bill was talking about Friday the thirteenth. At the time, however, I assumed that he was referring to the comment some Christians make about Good Friday being bad because it commemorates Christ's death. If I was correct, then Jim confused the issue (line 6). Either way, however, Bill was unable to clarify the context in which he intended his question to be understood. If his social interaction were to be normalized, this problem would need to be addressed.

Even when an Alpha client (or anyone else) is able to clarify the context and ascertain what the other person in an interaction wants to know, communicating that information usually requires an assessment of what the person already knows about the subject. A man's wife can be expected to know what sorts of tasks he generally performs in his work. Therefore, he can describe his day to her without giving as much background information as would be necessary when talking to someone he just met on a bus (cf. Garfinkel, 1967: 35-75). Individuals who significantly over or underestimate what other people need to know appear incompetent at social interaction. Therefore, this too must be a target of normalization.

What Other People Need to Know

On several occasions, I observed the Alpha staff explicitly trying to teach clients how to assess what other people needed to know in order to understand what the clients were trying to say. A few times, they practised giving each other directions to their homes. Differences in familiarity with particular bus routes, landmarks, etc. were noted and the reasons for them discussed. Alpha's social worker also tried to teach this assessment skill during a discussion of specific tasks which the clients had been performing in

the Center's workshop. She used the topic to encourage both curiosity about the purpose of the task and sensitivity to the need for background knowledge in understanding descriptions.

(1) Social Worker: Ok, what would you like to talk about today? Let's make a list of things. What's been happening since last week?
(2) Lyle: We have a good job putting those things in there and——you know what those things are called? You know you put those things
(3) Ray: Tri-coronector
(4) Diane: Tri-connectors.
(5) Lyle: Tri-connectors?
(6) Social Worker: I'm ignorant. Please let me know what you're talking about. What are you talking about? Where are you talking about?

Since the social worker was not too often in the workshop, her ignorance about this relatively new task seemed quite believable to me. By asking the question (line 6), she was attempting to demonstrate to the clients that different amounts of detail about a subject are required when conversing with different people.

(7) Ray: We're trying to help him when he wanted to know what those
(8) Social Worker: But what are you talking about?

Although the context would seem to make it obvious that the social worker's question (line 6), was directed at Lyle, line 7 shows that Ray misunderstood its intent. He thought that she was asking what he and Diane had been saying to Lyle, and the social worker did not directly address his misunderstanding (line 8). Although she was deliberately trying to teach assessment of what other people need to know, she failed to consider as problematic her basic assumption about the nature of the interaction. She assumed that all of the participants understood that she was trying to secure information from them which they had but she lacked.

Ray's failure to perceive the context in this way (line 7) becomes more explicable in view of his probable life experiences. People who are considered mentally retarded are not often asked serious information questions (as opposed to known information questions, cf. Mehan 1974). Ray thought he was helping his friend to pass a kind of test (line 1). It evidently did not occur to him that they were actually being asked to educate an "ignorant" teacher.

By not explicitly discussing this difference in perspective, the social worker probably lost an opportunity to normalize Ray's interaction. I found that it is difficult to have such discussions, however, even when the differences in perspective were clearly defined. For example, the Alpha social worker and I read the following sentences to another group of clients.

> Mary heard the ice cream truck coming down the street. She remembered her birthday money and ran into the house.

Since these sentences had been part of a psychological experiment conducted with many people, we knew that they usually conjured up an image of a six or seven or year old girl. The fact the members of our group described Mary as between 17 and 35 was a clue to us concerning their atypical perceptions of the life-cycle. Further discussion confirmed that these developmentally disabled individuals had not been permitted independent use of money until they were physiologically adults. The insight concerning the perspectives of the group members could have enabled the social worker and me to help them avoid a variety of misunderstanding.

The fact that we did not follow through on this opportunity to teach reflects the great hesitance which I observed in Alpha staff members (and in myself) to confront clients directly with the fact of their "goals and objectives" in the program, but I never heard anyone say straight out, "You are different from most other people, and this is why". If the thesis of this paper is correct, normalization in the sense of minimizing the probability of a deviant label requires awareness of what it is that makes one liable to such identification. To have followed through on this process, the social worker and I should have told the members of this client group that we had imagined Mary to be six or seven years old and

that we ourselves had had small amounts of money to spend by that age. The difference in perspective as well as experience would thereby have been highlighted.

In order to communicate effectively, participants in a social interaction usually need to know whether they are talking about an adult, a young child or a senior citizen. These clients might always have had a rather atypical conception of the life-cycle. This difference would be less likely to present a social problem for them, however, if they learned to be explicit about the age group to which they were referring and asked others to do likewise. As Nelson and Gruendel (1979) point out, failure to clarify features of the context often leads to very non-normal interactions. On the other hand, in order not to have his or her competence questioned, an individual must not betray ignorance of matters about which knowledge is expected for members of our society. Therefore, normalization also involves a seemingly endless process of teaching social knowledge.

What Other People Expect You to Know

Probably because they lacked the interactional skills being discussed in this paper, most Alpha clients either did not know how or were fearful about asking questions. As a result, staff members had to assess what the clients already knew and what they needed to know before proceeding to teach social knowledge. Their standard procedure for doing this was to ask the clients to define something or to state another word or idea which was associated with it. They almost always had a specific correct response in mind. The clients were right or wrong in their answers. This was unfortunate because it usually failed to elicit (or at least disregarded the associations which the client did have with the topic being discussed.

A counter example to this occurred following a chance reference to the Salk Institute during one of the group sessions.

(1) Social Worker: What about the Salk Institute? What's it famous for?

(2) Sam: Research——cure——find a cure
(3) Social Worker: For what? What did they find a cure for?
(4) Karen: People
(5) Social Worker: What's the most important thing that——you have it [motioning to Paul]
(6) Paul: [unintelligible on the tape]
(7) Social Worker: No.
(8) Sam: Cancer?
(9) Social Worker: No——polio vaccine. Dr. Salk discovered the polio vaccine. Do you know what polio is?
(10) Sam: Yah, its some kind of disease.
(11) Karen: You're in wheel chairs.
(12) Sam: Cripples you. Its a disease that cripples you.

Before the subject came up, I would not have been able to predict whether these clients knew anything about polio. All but one of the ones in this group were born after the vaccine had been discovered so their confusion about Dr. Salk was not surprising, but giving them an opportunity to connect what they knew about polio's symptoms with his name was probably a useful expansion of their social knowledge. Conversations in which the name Salk comes up normally have polio as an implicit association.

Expected social knowledge, however, is obviously not a static body of information. On another occasion, a staff member spent several minutes trying to get the response "sweet sixteen" to a question about special birthdays. She evidently thought that this was part of what everyone knows and therefore essential for normalization. However, her point was not immediately obvious to me, and no one in the group gave a sign of recognition even after she gave the answer. Time, place and social circumstances significantly alter what one is expected to know, but attempts at normalization such as these illustrate how difficult it is to specify these changing expectations.

One effective (albeit pragmatically limited) way of identifying gaps in a person's social knowledge is to observe him or her in a variety of naturally occurring situations. For example, one of the Alpha teachers told me that while enroute to the library, a group of clients had passed through the skid row region of the city.

Their reactions revealed that this group of urban adults had not previously known of the existence, let alone the significance, of skid row. The teacher pointed out to me that this innocence itself made them seem deviant.

Although exposure is clearly an important factor in the learning of social knowledge, one cannot assume that a mentally retarded person will derive the same meaning from the exposure as do most other members of our society. Both the disability itself and the atypical prior experiences which he or she is likely to have had mitigate against a "normal" reaction. When passing through the skid row area of the city, one frequently sees people who appear to be unconscious lying on benches or even sidewalks. These individuals are usually assumed to have passed out from over-use of alcohol and not to desire assistance, despite the inherent danger in their situation. Someone lying unconscious on the sidewalk of a middle-class residential district, however, would normally arouse much more concern and activity (especially if the person were well-dress). We may bemoan such stereotyped reactions, but an adult (e.g., an Alpha client) who revealed that he or she did not relate the skid row scene to chronic alcoholism or recognize the anomaly in the suburban equivalent would seem socially incompetent. Therefore, the normalization of such an individual must include attention to issues of interpretation such as this.

One of the basic tenets of this paper is that it is maladaptive to teach social interaction skills as a set of rules or invariant association. What must be learned is the ability to assess social contexts, including the perspective of those with whom one is interacting. One aspect of this interpretive ability is knowing what other people expect you to know and think about topics and situations which come up in the course of everyday life. Actually having some particular attitude or bit of knowledge is usually not essential. What is required is an awareness of when, in the absence of information to the contrary, other people will assume that you have it.

Conclusion

Successful social interaction entails complex activities which occur automatically and out of the awareness of the participants during ordinary discourse. One of these activities is the utilization of a very large body of knowledge about the world and the perspectives other people have on it. Individuals engaged in social interaction ordinarily assume that all of the other participants share this knowledge base. In other words, they assume that thy share the same set of assumptions about whatever is occurring.

Because it is made tacitly, this assumption is rarely questioned. The interactional difficulties of many mentally retarded individuals are interesting because analyzing them does make this assumption problematic. The clients at Alpha often appeared deviant when interacting with others because they were unable to take into account the expectations of them and of the situation which the other people had. For this reason, attempts to make retarded people appear less deviant (normalization) needs to include instruction on how to assess these expectations, including those discussed in this paper: what other people want to know, what other people need to know, and what other people expect you to know.

It is exceedingly difficult to carry out such instruction. In this paper, I have described how Alpha staff members failed to accomplish their goal of normalization because they were unable to suspend the assumption that they and the client with whom they were interacting shared a common definition of the situation at hand. If the client's comments were not in keeping with that presumed context, he or she was called "inappropriate" or "manipulative". These were bad behaviors to be eliminated rather than misunderstanding to be straightened out and avoided in the future. A similar process of explaining away the contextually untoward remarks of others undoubtedly goes on during all sorts of social interactions (cf. Cicourel, 1974b). Mentally retarded people are especially vulnerable to this process, however, because they are frequently deficient in the skills of context assessment and clarification.

In order to be successful at normalization, a re-socializer must make explicit and comment upon aspects of social knowledge which are not normally discussed (except among students of social interaction). Hence, it is necessary to interact abnormally in order to teach normal social interaction. This paper has focused primarily on the failure of the Alpha staff to do this. It would be very interesting to observe professionals who are successful at carrying out this seemingly contradictory process. From their strategies of "identity management" we could learn more about the effects of naturally occurring breaches of expectation on social interaction (cf. Garfinkel, 1967; Goffman, 1967; Mehan and Wood, 1975). I hope that a setting for such study can be found.

References

Becker, Howard S.
1963   Outsiders: Studies in the Sociology of Deviance. New York: The Free Press.
Cicourel, Aaron V.
1974a   "Some Basic Theoretical Issues in the Assessment of the Child's Performance in Testing and Classroom Settings." Pp. 300-349 in A. Cicourel (ed.). Language Use and School Performance. New York: Academic Press.
Cicourel, Aaron V.
1974b   Cognitive Sociology: Language and Meaning in Social Interaction. New York: Free Press.
Davis, Fred
1964   "Deviance Disavowal: The Management of Strained Interaction by the Visibly Handicapped." Pp. 119-137 in H. Becker (ed.), Perspectives on Deviance: The Other Side. New York: Free Press.
Dybwad, Gunnar
1982   "Normalization and Its Impact on Social and Public Policy." Pp.1-7 in G. Foss (ed.), Advancing Your Citizenship: Normalization Re-examined. Eugene, OR: Rehabilitation Research and Training Center in Mental Retardation.
Edgerton, Robert B.
1967   The Cloak of Competence: Stigma in the Lives of the Mentally Retarded. Los Angeles: University of California Press.

Edgerton, Robert B. and Syliva M. Bercovici
    1976   "The Cloak of Competence: Years Later." American Journal on Mental Deficiency 80:485-497.
Garfinkel, Harold
    1967   Studies in Ethnomethodolgy. Englewood Cliffs, NJ: Prentice-Hall.
Goffman, Erving
    1963   Stigma: Notes on the Management of Spoiled Identity. Englewood Cliffs, NJ: Prentice Hall.
Goffman, Erving
    1967   Interaction Ritual. Garden City, NY: Doubleday.
Jones, Kathleen
    1975   Opening the Door: A Study of New Policies for the Mentally Handicapped. Boston: Routledge & Kegan Paul.
Lemert, Edwin M.
    1951   Social Pathology. New York: McGraw-Hill.
Mead, George Herbert
    1934   Mind, Self and Society. Chicago: University of Chicago Press.
Mehan, Hugh
    1979   "What Time Is It, Denise? Asking Known Information Questions in Classroom Discourse." Theory Into Practice 18:285-294.
Mehan, Hugh
    1974   "Accomplishing Classroom Lessons." Pp. 76-142 in A. Cicourel (ed.), Language Use in School Performance. New York: Academic Press.

Mehan, Hugh and Huston Wood
    1975   The Reality of Ethnomethodology. New York: Wiley.
Nelson, Katherine and Janice M. Gruendel
    1979   "At Morning It's Lunchtime: A Scriptal View of Children's Dialogues." Discourse Processes 2:73-94.
Piaget, Jean
    1965   The Moral Judgement of the Child. New York: Free Press.
Polanyi, Michael
    1967   The Tacit Dimension. Garden City: Anchor Books.
Rumelhart, Marilyn A.
    1978   The Pursuit of Normalization: A Study of an Organization with an Illusory Goal. Unpublished doctoral dissertation, University of California, San Diego.
Shur, Edwin M.
    1971   Labeling Deviant Behavior: Its Sociological Consequences. New York: Harper & Row.
Schutz, Alfred
    1962   Collected Papers, Volume 2. The Hague: Martinus Nijhoff.
Wolfensberger, Wolf
    1972   Normalization. Toronto: [Canadian] National Institute on Mental Retardation.

Notes

1. Some advocates of the normalization principle disagree with the re-socialization version of it because they believe that "it is normal to be different" (Dybwad, 1982:1).

The Social Construction of Mental Retardation

PHILIP M. FERGUSON

When we first met, Peter was 17 years old. For the last 16 of those years, he had lived in large state institutions. The labels used to describe Peter range from the laughably euphemistic to egregious slurs on his very humanity: medically fragile, vegetable, severely/profoundly retarded, idiot, multiply handicapped, custodial. Some of the terms are official argot; some used to be but are now colloquial. Tomorrow's playground insults are always foretold by today's professional diagnoses.

As for Peter, he could not walk or talk—either officially or colloquially. He could not sit up unsupported. He was fed through a tube that plugged into his stomach. His frequent seizures were powerful enough to knock him out of his specially adapted wheelchair if he was not strapped in. Peter's eyes seldom stopped flicking about long enough to focus on you. His hands seldom moved at all. He had a spindly body twisted by muscles that never relaxed. He was shaped like a human question mark. For me, though, Peter began the questions, he did not mark their end.

The questions evoked by Peter are all related to how relatively unaffected he has been by all of the reform efforts of the past two decades under the broad heading of disability rights. Despite 20 years of deinstitutionalization in mental retardation, Peter and over 125,000 other people with similar labels of retardation remain incarcerated in large, segregated public institutions.[1] For 11 years now, school systems across the country have been required to teach all children, regardless of handicaps, in the "least restrictive environment" commensurate with optimal educational progress. For Peter, that has meant that he gets on an elevator in the morning and goes down two floors below the ward where he lives. Once there, he spends the day much as he would had he stayed on the ward: sitting or lying in a corner, perhaps with a mirror placed in front of him, some Fisher-Price toys arrayed before him, a radio or TV nearby, and large amounts of time with no human contact at all.

Even if Peter lived in the community, in most states he would still be likely to attend school in a self-contained segregated building rather than the neighborhood high school. For all of the anti-discrimination in hiring regulations and supported work initiatives, there is still a 50 to 80 percent unemployment rate for all people with disabilities.[2] Between 800,000 and 900,000 mentally retarded adults are either not working or making less than $300 per month.[3] Indeed, it is difficult to imagine how Peter would fit into a job market governed by productivity, even if it were barrier free.

The Independent Living Movement has made great strides in demonstrating the potential of people with disabilities to "make it" on their own in society. However, independence and self-help groups seem far removed from Peter's future. The notion of what would be a fulfilling life for Peter, much less achieving it, remains unclear. The reality always falls short of the best reform efforts. In Peter's case, however, even the vision of reform has left his future largely out of sight.

This article will explore why disability policy has failed at the conceptual level to elaborate a theory of social inclusion for even those who are severely retarded. First, some brief historical considerations will illustrate how reform efforts in the field of social welfare have repeatedly followed a pattern of de facto exclusion similar to that which is currently leaving people with profound retardation and multiple disabilities beyond the pale of the disability rights movement. Second, the theoretical components of social constructionism as the conceptual foundation for much of the current emphasis of disability reformers will be examined. It is a position that has fostered the increased social awareness that much——if not all—— of what we mean by terms such as "disability" and "handicap" is cultural artifact rather than physiological inevitability. This section will argue, however, that this same perspective of social construction unintentionally justifies the continued exclusion of people with the most

Reprinted From: Social Policy - Summer 1987, with permission.

severe levels of retardation. Finally, the article will identify the advantages of "critical theory" as a conceptual perspective for disability studies in general, and as the frame for a more inclusive agenda of social reform within the disability community.

The History of Reform and Mental Retardation

We tend to identify each generation of reform by emphasizing its difference from earlier efforts. Such attention to details of specific issues often clouds our ability to recognize the patterns that recur through all reforms. While specific issues may differ, some conceptual categories continue unchanged and unchallenged. One such consistent, though often unstated, category comprises those people who fall beyond the pale of the particular reform. Thus, despite a reform movement's optimism, the nature of an incremental approach means that at least in practice, if not in theory, some will remain unhelped because they are thought helpless, untaught because thought unteachable, and unemployed because work seems to have no meaning for them. Membership in this group has varied from reform era to reform era. However, it has always included the Peters of this world: those we would today call severely retarded and multiply disabled.

Certainly, part of the problem in improving Peter's life is technological. Instructional technology in special education has made great strides over the past two decades in demonstrating that even severely retarded students can learn complicated tasks in the vocational, social, and personal domains of life. However, the best instruction can not yet give people with the most profound degrees of retardation and physical disabilities the skills needed to function at more than the most minimal levels of performance.

There have also been impressive advances in medical treatment and rehabilitation technology that allow many people with the most severe physical disabilities to achieve a degree of functional independence that would have been almost unimaginable 20 or 30 years ago. Once again, these habilitative advances, while certainly valuable, have a much more limited utility for in-dividuals whose physical disabilities are combined with severe cognitive limitations.

The limitations of technology, however, do not fully explain why the reforms in disability policies and programs have so effectively ignored people like Peter. The problems go beyond the technical obstacles. To borrow the phrase of the historian E.P. Thompson,[4] there is also a "poverty of theory" that has increasingly shortchanged those people with the most profound combinations of mental retardation and physical impairment. It is this failure of reform at the level of social theory that this article will examine.

Modern special education is usually said to have begun in France at the beginning of the nineteenth century and the efforts of Jean-Marc-Gaspard Itard to educate the feral child known as "The Wild Boy of Aveyron".[5] For more than five years, Itard worked with the boy he named Victor, using techniques of operant conditioning and task analysis that are still at the heart of special education today. At the end of the period, however, Itard believed his famous experiment a failure, not because he could not teach Victor anything, but because he could not teach him enough. In the end, Itard decided his Parisian counterpart Pinel was right. Victor was an "incurable idiot", rather than a noble savage: essentially helpless, hopeless, and useless. As Itard himself explained, Victor's development was "the slow and laborious result of a very active education in which the most powerful methods are used to obtain most insignificant results".[6] The move was on to educate people with all types of disabilities, all except retardation.

In later generations the excluded population narrowed, but the concept remained. For Seguin, Howe, Wilbur, and other leaders of the early institutionalization movement in America, the new version of reform was that not all retarded people were Victors, or unteachable idiots. These men discovered that many retarded people could learn if nurtured in the small, school-like asylums that would save these children from the wretched almshouses. The new measure of success for this generation of reformers was that a student would become a "useful laborer", trained to "such habits of industry as to support himself". Still, even in this golden age of optimism in the history of institutions for retarded people, some remained beyond help, if not pity. The have-nots of this era were the more narrow group described by Howe as "idiots of the lowest class...mere organisms, masses of flesh and bone in human shape".[7] These hopeless cases were specifically excluded from the new asylums in Massachusetts and New York precisely when those asylums were the location of reformative zeal to help disabled people.

In our own century, the content of reform changes once again, but the category of exclusion persists and the economic definition of success remains. H.H. Goddard, one of the early advocates of I.Q. testing and a leading light of the eugenics movement, thought it possible that social reform and improved training could finally "find use for all these people of moderate intelligence", [i.e., "morons" and some "imbeciles"]. Moreover, the entry of these people into the economy as productive workers would provide society a steady supply of people "who are able and willing to do much of the drudgery of the world, which other people will not do".[8] A new century's optimism required (as noted reformer testified without a trace of irony) that "no child should be excluded from school as untrainable or ineducable...except idiots and the lowest grade imbeciles".[9] Thus continued in the language of reform a reliance on a smaller, but conceptually consistent group of unteachables.

Two points emerge from this cursory review of some past reform movements that are relevant to the current push for disability rights. First, over the last two centuries at least, service reforms and policy initiatives for people with disabilities have been explicitly justified on economic grounds. The aim of reform has always been stated as the achievement of economic productivity and self-reliance for people who otherwise would be dependent on society's handouts and production. Without examining the more complicated social forces at work, one can remain at the level of stated intentions of reformers and see a consistent endorsement of what

each has termed the Industrial Age's "single standard of honor": self-reliance and self-support through selling one's labor in the marketplace.[10] Disabled people could "earn their own way" only by becoming productive wage earners.

The second point, however, is that the reformers consistently defined their claims of new success by maintaining a contrasting class of continued failures. There is always a new version of Itard's Victor, those continuing exceptions used to prove the rule of our good intentions. If the criterion of success is economic utility and productivity, then some will unavoidably remain economically useless and unproductive. What remains constant is the category of exclusion, not the individuals barred from pratication in society.

Members of the excluded category are always identified, when even mentioned, by their failure to meet the varying requirements of reform, rather than by some immutable set of individual traits and abilities. Increasingly in the recent past, however, this residual population has meant those defined as severely mentally retarded. As the introductory comments about Peter mentioned, normalization and deinstitutionalization have not avoided the continuation of institutional ghettos for the most severely disabled. Indeed, even the most progressive representatives of adult services still have only a vague notion of what an adult life of meaningful community participation might encompass for severely retarded individuals.

The Disability Rights Movement and Severe Retardation

Given the historical pattern of reform initiatives in the area of disability policy to exclude all or some of the people labelled retarded, it should come as no surprise that the various reforms of the past two decades collectively referred to as the disability rights movement have made little difference in the life of my friend Peter, or even many people less profoundly retarded than he. Once again, it appears that an array of promising reforms in education, housing, leisure activities, vocational services, and health care has maintained=ed a de facto segregation of neglect for the most handicapped segment of our population.

However, the continued exclusion is surprising in some respects because the motive force of the disability rights movement seemed less economically based than previous reforms. To borrow Harlan Hahn's typology, there was a move beyond both the medical and the economic perspectives to a socio-political one.[11] Surely, the disability rights movement is based on the notion that those very economic barriers that seemed unavoidable for disabled people, and certainly for retarded people, were socially created and culturally relative. The focus of the movement seems to be society itself and the barriers needlessly created through prejudice and stigma based on cultural stereotypes analogous to those experienced by racial and ethnic minorities.

One indication of the overall influence of the disability rights movement is how commonplace its key conceptual tenet now seems. The notion that disability in general is more a social category than a physical "reality" is at least familiar to most people, if not universally accepted. The negotiation meaning of our social world is an increasingly popular alternative to the more traditional, "medical" paradigm of objective, individual deficits.[12] Whether phrased in terms of symbolic interaction, labelling theory, or the language games of Wittgenteinian philosophy, this new combination of hermeneutics and social policy in the approach to disability has provided the conceptual basis for much of the progress in the disability rights movement.

Despite this shift in perspective, the extension of the sociopolitical perspective to mental retardation has created some theoretical difficulties that help explain the relative lack of success in including the most severely retarded people in the reform effort. Some adherents of the sociopolitical perspective have been explicit about these difficulties and openly excluded severely retarded people from their consideration. Gliedman and Roth have written one of the best extended examinations of the social construction of disability as a civil rights issue they are quick to limit the scope of their critique:

Not all handicapped children fit the minority-group model. Perhaps 10 percent of all handicapped children possess a disability so limiting mentally or emotionally that they would not be able to lead normal lives even if prejudice against them melted away.[13]

An earlier, and even blunter, example of this overt exclusion of severely and profoundly retarded people from a sociopolitical understanding occurs in an otherwise excellent examination of retarded children in institutions. After stating the criteria used for the selection of subjects for study from the population of two state training schools, the authors admit that these meant no profoundly retarded people were included. Their explanation is worth repeating in full, not particularly to criticize the authors' sensitivity some 15 years after the fact, but rather to illustrate a line of reasoning that still persists today even among progressive social critics——only now it is usually left unstated.

There are few sights more pitiful than the children who live in institutions for the mentally retarded. The feeling is inescapable when one sees the profoundly retarded inmates, incapacitated, needing almost total care. That it is, perhaps, more acute at the sight of the mildly retarded child. One's pity for the profoundly retarded is tempered somehow by the obvious nature of their defects, and one is relieved that institutions exist which assume this human burden. When one, however, encounters thousands and thousands of mildly retarded children living in the same institutions, children who in many ways so much resemble children on the outside, the pity is confounded with confusion. It is this group of mentally retarded children...rather than the profoundly and severely brain-damaged or genetically impaired persons, with whom this book is concerned.[14]

Such explicit examples of exclusion are rare in discussions of the sociopolitical perspective.

More often the topic is simply not mentioned. "Disability" becomes, in effect, a synonym for "physical disability" in much of the writing about the disability rights movement. It is as though some writers decide that the way to avoid the difficulty of fitting severely and profoundly retarded people under the umbrella concept of social construction, is to decide arbitrarily that they are no longer even disabled. However, there are certainly scholars within the field of mental retardation who have forcefully argued the social construction thesis.[15] Finally, then, whether explicitly considered or not, the conceptual adequacy of the minority group perspective must be assessed directly as a way of understanding severe retardation.

In most aspects, the sociopolitical perspective is one I share and value for the focus on rights and dignity that it has encouraged. The shift in focus from the medical model has certainly allowed a more obvious connection with the struggles of other minority groups such as Blacks, native Americans, elderly people, and gays, just to name a few. Moreover, the situational emphasis of the perspective encourages a historical awareness of how the socially created definitions of disability and dependence have changed over the years. Finally, the sociopolitical perspective captures well the power of language to shape our thoughts and not merely to express them. It is more than delicacy that encourages the use of "Down's Syndrome" or "Trisomy 21" rather than "Mongolism". All of these are undeniable strengths of the social constructivist position.

The weakness of the constructivist position in disability studies emerges at those examples where culture seems beside the point; where physiology has gone so far awry that it threatens to overwhelm the social context. The very epistemology of the minority group paradigm assumes that humans are agents in the social interpretation of their world, rather than reactors to our confrontations with an unchanging world of facts that are "out there", in the "real world". The challenge of profound retardation, however, is precisely how close it seems to come to the absence of agency. It is not just that the passivity is often enforced by limbs that do not move or environmental barriers that trap the individual physically. One reason for the almost total absence of qualitative research with profoundly retarded and multiply handicapped individuals is the difficulty in conceiving the social world of someone whose experience of concepts and communication is so uncertain for us. The relativity of language seems inadequate explanation.

Many people are labelled "retarded" who should not be. Some people are labelled "retarded", who have real, severe, cognitive limitations. All who are labelled "retarded" are saddled with socially created valuations that are discriminatory, demeaning, and unnecessary. But to be severely cognitively impaired is not a difference just like skin color or gender. It is not even a difference in the same way that getting around in a wheelchair instead of walking is a difference. There is nothing inherent in being a woman that is necessarily undesirable. There is nothing innately unfortunate about being a Black, a native American, or homosexual. There is something profoundly unfortunate about severe cognitive limitations.

It is easy to imagine a society where gender, skin color, age, nationality, and sexual preference have no social inequities attached. It seems much harder to imagine a world where it would not be preferable to be capable of abstract thought. Indeed, the very act of imagination required therein contradicts the world we would have to conceive. All of this has nothing to do with the rights, the intrinsic value, of people who happen to be severely and profoundly retarded. It has a lot to do, however, with how those rights and values should be secured.

The exclusion of people with severe retardation from the disability rights movement is not simply an oversight or an understandable delay in fully implementing the theoretical guidelines. The exclusion is also a logical concomitant of the conceptual base.

The Socioeconomic Perspective and Future Reform Efforts

The analysis so far has shown a pattern of exclusion in the major reform movements affecting people with disabilities. Retarded people in general, and severely retarded people especially, have always served as those falling beyond the pale of serious consideration. The current disability rights movement reframes but does not remove the tendency to exclude categorically those with severe cognitive limitations. The economic basis of social inequity in the treatment of disabled people continues to rest on the demand for economic "usefulness" and productivity. The minority group perspective is conceptually ill-equipped to challenge the structural denial of full community participation in a way that does not reinforce the continued neglect of those most severely disabled.

Given that analysis, this section will suggest three directions for future reform efforts and scholarly research that would be more inclusive of all disabilities. Briefly, the need is to combine progressive economic reform with broadened historical understanding, and add a renewed attention to the implications of our language.

First, there must be increased historical research into the social history of disability and of mental retardation in particular. The pattern of exclusion from reform movements can at this time only be drawn in broad strokes. Yet that pattern would seem to have great relevance to the continuing efforts for reform of disability policy. It is ironic that this pattern of exclusion extends even into the very historiography of the general topic. The neglect of people labelled severely retarded by the reform movements of the last two centuries is equalled by the absence of mental retardation as an area of research within social history. It is difficult to account for this absence.

Social history has at least two differences from conventional history in its choice of topics. First it attempts to deal with ordinary people rather than the elite classes dominant within traditional intellectual history. The overused phrase "history from the bottom up" attempts to imply this perspective. Second, social history examines the institutions, customs, and behavior relevant to these ordinary people. Instead of wars, elections, and philosophical fashions, the social historian will analyze "sexual behavior, social mobility, family roles and functions, attitudes and practices relating to death, popular

health and medicine including mental illness, crime and law enforcement".[16] Mental retardation would seem a natural topic, given these criteria. Yet, with only a few exceptions, it has not been studied by professional historians.[17]

The contrast with mental illness is striking. Closely attached throughout history, the two areas have been curiously separated in historians' research. Speculation about academic preferences for research topics perhaps reveals the limitations of a methodology still governed by cultural stereotypes. Madness (to use the nineteenth century label) has always been the malady of choice for genius. The sensitive spirit driven insane by a heartless world; the tortured philosopher whose flashes of insight betray a mind burning up; the amusing eccentric whose oddball perspective underlines for all the non sequiturs of life; all of these are powerful cultural archetypes of how the distracted intellect can show us some hidden part of ourselves, the dark side of our psychological moon.

Retardation possesses no such revelatory cachet to attract an academic embrace for research. An invidious intellectual pecking order seems to operate that subtly assigns worth to objects of knowledge. Some things are more worth knowing about than others. Even some deviancies, some stigmas, are more intellectually acceptable than others. Within this caste system of knowledge, mental retardation as a field of study has remained part of the great unwashed.

Of course, there is an opportunity in all of this. Absence should always make the researcher's heart grow fonder. Historical research into the concept of severe retardation and the daily lives of people affected by it offers fertile ground for the growth of an interdisciplinary approach to the topic of retardation in general. Even with mental retardation, professionals have historically given little attention to severe retardation. As a field, mental retardation is ignorant of its own past or convinced of the truth of superficial generalities that obscure as much as they reveal. If the disability rights movement is ever to achieve an inclusive vision of the future for all people with disabilities, then it must first open its eyes to the mistakes and triumphs of the past.

Besides historical research, there is also a need to refocus the interactionist approach to disability studies in such a way as to reintegrate a social and economic critique. The point is not to abandon the current disability rights movement altogether. Indeed, the attractiveness of the minority group approach does encourage the search for analogous struggles among the other groups striving for equality and social justice.

The question can be asked if any other minority group can be compared to the social needs of disabled people in such a way as to suggest a conceptual redirection of reform efforts that would finally include all people with disabilities, no matter how severe. The single group that seems most useful returns us to the economic analysts that the sociopolitical perspective too easily avoids. As a group, people with disabilities should align their struggle with that of poor people in general. The basic inequities in adult services are based in matters of class: not race, not individual abilities, and not the prejudices derived from that class hierarchy.

Poverty, like severe disability, is an undesirable category that we should move to eliminate. There is something inherently undesirable about being poor, but there is certainly nothing undesirable about poor people themselves. Obviously, there is significant overlap between poverty and race, poverty and gender, and most of the other minority groups already mentioned. The point is that social and economic concerns must be seen as indivisible if our reform efforts are to escape the historic cycle of good intentions gone awry.

There is a "commonality of deprivation" among all disadvantaged groups whether handicapped, unemployed, underpaid, or unsupported.[18] Policy reforms for people with severe handicaps will never be secure until there is a coalition of policy advocates for all devalued workers——women, minorities, and migrant labor, for example——not just a dozen or so separate policy agendas.[19] Moving people from one segment of the deprived population to another will never finally alter the social mechanisms demanding that some deprivation must always persist. Disability advocates must look to those others, from whatever background, who are

asking and answering these questions. The economics of integration into adult life must be addressed simultaneously with the attitudinal stereotypes emphasized by Hahn and others. The policy connections were summarized well by Miller:

> Those concerned about social policy must also be concerned about economic policy. Social policy cannot undo what economic policy harms. ...A pro-employment, pro-poor economic policy is the basic social policy....The goals of social policy must become the goals of economic policy.[20]

Hahn dismisses the economic perspective as a whole because the limited uses of it in past policy and reform had implicitly endorsed the individual income supports and vocational rehabilitation. What Hahn and others ignore is the possibility of a sociopolitical perspective that questions the very emphasis of the marketplace on personal productivity as the price of full community participation. The disability rights movement must expand its vision of social justice beyond the opportunity to join the ranks of the working poor, and unquestioning consumerism.[21] Only by an economic vision that refuses to accept the participation of most at the cost of the continued exclusion of an unproductive few will the disability rights movement have a secure base of advocacy.

Finally, there is a need for renewed attention to the slogans that try to encapsulate the social agenda of disability activists. Too often, the very language of the disability rights movement threatens unintentionally to exclude those people already at greatest risk of failure by society's standards: people with severe and profound mental retardation. Indeed, too often the word "disability" itself is used as a synonym for "physical disability", excluding by name as well as by deed those retarded people who are deemed unworthy to even share in a stigma.

To be optimistic, many progressive advocates are trying to include people with even the most severe retardation and multiple disabilities in the reform of adult services and larger society. That struggle might be eased if we stopped talking of "competitive work" and began talking of "cooperative work"; if we talked less of "independent living" and more of "interdependent living". A new standard of participation and contri bution for very severely handicapped people that values mere presence as much as productivity is needed. Giving voice to the conception of that standard might very well hasten its actual achievement.

Notes

1. Florence A. Hauber, Robert H. Bruininks, Bradley K. Hill et al., "National Census of Residential Facilties: A 1982 Profile of Facilities and Residents," *American Journal of Mental Deficiency* (November, 1984), pp.236-245.

2. Paul Wehman, M. Sherril Moon, and Pat McCarthy, "Transition from School to Adulthood for Youth with Severe Handicaps," *Focus on Exceptional Children* (January, 1986), pp.1-12.

3. Jean K. Elder, Ronald W. Conley, and John H. Noble, Jr., "The Service System," in William Kiernan and Jack Stark (eds.), *Pathways to Employment for Developmentally Disabled Adults* (Baltimore: Paul H. Brookes, 1986), pp.53-66.

4. E.P. Thompson, *The Poverty of Theory and Other Essays* (New York: Monthly Review Press, 1979).

5. Harlan Lane, *The Wild Boy of Aveyron* (Cambridge: Harvard University Press, 1976).

6. Jean-Marc G. Itard, *The Wild Boy of Aveyron,* trans. G. Humphrey and M. Humphrey (New York: Appleton-Century-Crofts [1806], 1962), p.100.

7. Samuel G. Howe, *On the Causes of Idiocy* (New York: Arno Press [1852], 1972), pp.xi,7.

8. Henry H. Goddard, *Feeblemindedness: Its Causes and Consequences,* (New York: MacMillan, 1920), p.588.

9. New York State, *Report of the State Commission to Investigate Provision for the Mentally Deficient* (Albany: J.B. Lyon, 1915), p.12.

10. Christopher Lasch, *The World of Nations: Reflections on American History, Politics, and Culture* (New York: Alfred A. Knopf, 1973), p.17.

11. Harlan Hahn, "Toward a Politics of Disability: Definitions, Disciplines, and Policies," *Social Science Journal* (October, 1985), pp.87-105.

12. Robert Bogdan and Steven Taylor, *Inside Out: The Social Meaning of Mental Retardation,* (Toronto: University of Toronto, 1982); John Gliedman and William Roth, *The Unexpected Minority: Handicapped Children in America* (New York: Harcourt Brace Jovanovich, 1980); Harlan Hahn, *The Issue of Equality: European Perceptions of Employment Policy for Disabled Persons* (New York: World Rehabilitation Fund, 1984).

13. Gliedman and Roth, p.4.

14. Dorothea Braginsky and Benjamin Braginsky, *Hansels and Gretels: Studies of Children in Institutions for the Mentally Retarded* (New York: Holt, Rinehart and Winston, 1971), pp.11-12.

15. Bogdan and Taylor; J.R. Dudley, *Living with Stigmas; The Plight of the People Who We Label Mentally Retarded* (Springfield, IL: Charles C. Thomas, 1983); Seymour Sarason and John Doris, *Educational Handicap, Public Policy and Social History: A Broadened Perspective* (New York: The Free Press, 1979).

16. Peter Stearns, "The New Social History: An Overview," in James B. Gardner and George R. Adams (eds.,), *Ordinary People and Everyday Life: Perspectives on New Social History* (Nashville: The American Association for State and Local History, 1983), pp.4-5.

17. See, for example, Mark Friedberger, "The Decision to Institutionalize: Families with Exceptional Children in 1900," *Journal of Family History* (Winter, 1981), pp.396-409; Michael B. Katz, *Poverty and Policy in American History* (New York: Academic Press); B. Luckin, "Towards a Social History of Institutionalization," *Social History* (Spring, 1983), pp.87-94.

18. Gareth H. Williams, "The Movement for Independent Living: An Evaluation and Critique," *Social Science and Medicine* (August, 1983), pp.1003-1010.

19. See, for example, Barbara Ehrenreich and Frances F. Piven, "Women and the Welfare State," in Irving Howe (ed.), *Alternatives: Proposals for American from the Democratic Left* (New York: Pantheon, 1984), pp.41-60; Theresa Funicello, "Welfare Mothers Earn their Way," *Christianity and Crisis* (December 10, 1984), pp.469-473.

20. S.M. Miller, "Reformulating the Welfare State," *Social Policy* (Winter, 1985), pp.62-63.

21. Dianne L. Ferguson and Philip M. Ferguson, "The New Victors: A Progressive Policy Analysis of Work Reform for People with Very Severe Handicaps, *Mental Retardation* (December, 1986), pp.331-338.

The Social Rejection of Former Mental Patients: Understanding Why Labels Matter[1]

BRUCE G. LINK, FRANCIS T. CULLEN,
JAMES FRANK AND JOHN F. WOZNIAK

Recent research shows that the crucial factor determining the rejection of former mental patients is their behavior rather than their stigmatized status. The study reported here, based on a vignette experiment (with a design that varies patient status with the nature of behavior), challenges this conclusion. Like previous research, it indicates that a simple assessment of labelling shows little effect on a social distance scale. However, when a measure of perceived dangerousness of mental patients is introduced, strong labelling effects emerge. Specifically, the data reveal that the label of "previous hospitalization" fosters high social distance among those who perceive mental patients to be dangerous and low social distance among those who do not see patients as a threat. It appears that past investigators have missed these effects because they have averaged excessively lenient responses with excessively rejecting ones. This suggests that labels play an important role in how former mental patients are perceived and that labelling theory should not be dismissed as a framework for understanding social factors in mental illness.

Since its inception in the exchanges between Scheff (1966, 1974) and Gove (1970, 1975, 1982), the debate over the importance of labelling in mental illness has focused on various questions. As Gove (1975, 1980a; cf. Cullen and Cullen 1978) has indicated, these questions can be grouped in two broad categories. The first deals with "who gets labelled" and involves questions about whether individuals with varying status characteristics (male vs. female, black vs. white, etc.) are exposed to different societal reactions and thus to very different labelling experiences (e.g., Horwitz 1982; Rosenfield 1982, 1984; Ruching 1978, 1979; Tudor, Tudor, and Gove 1977).[2] The second category considers the consequences of labelling and includes such issues as whether institutionalization is harmful (e.g., Gove and Fain 1973; Gruenberg 1967; Townsend 1976; Wing and Brown 1970), whether patients are rejected on the basis of labelling information (e.g., Bord 1971; Farina and Felner 1973; Huffine and Clausen 1979; Phillips 1963, 1964; Schwartz, Myers, and Astrachan 1974), whether patients themselves feel stigmatized (e.g., Cumming and Cumming 1965; Weinstein 1983), and whether the ex-patient status limits an individual's ability to function effectively in social and economic roles (Huffine and Clausen 1979; Link 1982).

In addressing questions about the significance of the labelling in either category, a salient consideration has been how much the mentally distrubed behavior of a labelled individual influences societal reaction. The critics of labelling theory have charged that it incorrectly assumes (1) that societal reactions are largely unaffected by the behaviors people manifest and (2) that, once the "reality" of a mental illness label is socially constructed, it will act as a master status determining the subsequent reactions of others regardless of the labelled person's behavior. In

[1]This research was supported in part by NIMH grants 5-T32 MH13043 and 1RO1 MH38773. We would like to thank Serena Deutsch, Paula Dubeck, Jill Goldstein, Michael Hubbard, Dolores Dreisman, and Judith Rabkin for comments on an earlier draft of this paper. Requests for reprints should be sent to Bruce G. Link, Psychiatric Epidemiology, 100 Haven Avenue, Apt. 20E, New York, New York 10032.

contrast to what are seen as the inappropriate assumptions of labelling theory, critics assert that there is a close connection between the nature of disturbed behavior and both the activation of labelling and any negative social consequences that might be suffered after a label is affixed. As Clausen has cautioned: "By whatever name they are referred to, psychotic persons tend to be hard to live with. They are frenquently unreasonable. Even when they pose no threat to self or others, they mey be exquisitely sensitive to slights from others, and they often rage furiously against those who love them most. Severe mental disorder evokes negative responses in those who must live with the affected person, whatever the label applied to that person" (1981, p. 287).

To support the conclusion that the rejection former psychiatric patients face is far more likely to be caused by their aberrant behavior than by stereotypes associated with the label "former mental patient", labelling theory's critics have marshaled a growing body of empirical research. It is noteworthy, however, that there is also evidence on this issue that is favorable to labelling theory. Particularly relevant is that many, though not all current and former psychiatric patients report that they are unjustly "stigmatized" and suffer consequences unrelated to their behavior.

In an attempt to reconcile and clarify these discrepant views, we reconsider the relative importance of labelling and behavior as determinants of social rejection. Theoretically, we propose that a more complete understanding of the issue must incorporate an assessment of what a label means to members of the public. Consistent with this idea, our empirical analysis includes a measure of how dangerous mental patients are believed to be and then investigates whether labelling information activates these beliefs, allowing them to play a potent role in determining levels of rejection. We begin our development with a detailed examination of the discrepant views of researchers and psychiatric patients.

Perspectives On Social Rejection

The "Behavior Causes Rejection" Perspective of Researchers

A core aspect of Scheff's (1966, 1974) labelling theory is that former patients will face stigmatization and rejection, that they will be "punished when they attempt to return to conventional roles" (proposition 7, p. 87). Apparent support for this propostion comes from Phillips's influential experimental study, which showed that rejection varied as a function of treatment source (1963). An individual described in a vignette was rejected more strenuously if a help source involved psychiatric contact (mental hospital, psychiatrist) as opposed to contact with a physician, contact with a clergyman, or no help whatsoever.

Shortly after these findings were published, however, further evidence led to a growing consensus that behavior, not labels, is the crucial factor determining rejection. The first step was Phillip's own research published one year after his earlier study (1964). Phillips noted that, in determining rejection, behavior as indexed by four Star (1955) vignettes and his own "normal" vignette was more important than the previously emphasized "help source" variable. Phillips commented; "Probably the most important source of information that is considered in defining any social situation is the behavior of the persons involved. In general, the more closely a person's behavior conforms to institutionalized expectations, the more favorabley he will be evaluated by other members of the system."

Since Phillips's (1964) study, published labelling experiments or quasi experiments assessing the relative effect of behavior is the most important factor determining social distancing responses. Table 1 presents 12 studies published since 1963, all of which involve experimental or quasi-experimental designs assessing the relative effects of a mental illness label versus some variation of behavior. Studies were excluded from the table if they involved only a manipulation of labelling (e.g., Farina and Felner 1973; Foster, Ysseldyke, and Reese 1975; Langer and Abelson 1974; Page 1977; Pollack et al. 1976) or examined the effect of a label on the basis of a respondent's subjective labelling of a behavior description (Bentz and Edgerton 1971; Phillips 1967; Spiro, Siassi, and Crocetti (1973).[3]

TABLE 1

EXPERIMENTAL AND QUASI-EXPERIMENTAL STUDIES ASSESSING THE ROLE OF OBJECTIONABLE BEHAVIOR AND A
MENTAL ILLNESS LABEL IN DETERMINING ACCEPTANCE-REJECTION

Authors and Publication Date	Sample	Nature of Experiment	Outcome Measure	Effect of Behavior	Effect of Label	Behavior Stronger than Label
Phillips (1963, 1964)	300 married white women from a small New England town	Four Star vignettes describing disturbed behavior and Phillips's normal individual vignette were each read to a respondent. Labeling was varied by mention of help source - no help, clergy, physician, psychiatrist, mental hospital	Five-item social distance scale	Significant	Significant - rejection increases as help source approaches mental health content	Yes
Schroder and Erlich (1968)	80 psychiatric nurses employed at a state psychiatric institute	Identical to Phillips above	Identical to Phillips	Significant	Significant - but the pattern is inconsistent with more severe labels leading to more severe rejection	Yes
Loman and Larkin (1976)	204 college students in a general sociology class	Two versions of a videotape of an attractive female college student. In one, she showed evidence of paranoia; in the other, she did not. Label was varied by describing the woman as normal or as having a psychiatric problem. The account the actor gave (no account, situational stress, mental disorder) was varied as well	Five-item social distance scale and a five-item social competence scale	Significant for social distance but not competence	Significant	No - label stronger across both outcome variables
Lehman, Joy, Kreisman, and Simmens (1976)	90 undergraduate introductory psychology students	Three videotaped persons (female) acted either anxious and agitated, depressed and withdrawn, or normal. Labeling was varied by reference to a three month hospitalization for psychiatric problems	11-item social distance scale, three adjective check list measures (unpredictable, dangerous, and/or irresponsible)	Significant across all four outcomes	Not significant - for social distance, dangerous, and irresponsible. Significant for unpredictable	Yes

TABLE 1

Experimental and Quasi-Experimental Studies Assessing the Role of Objectionable Behavior and a Mental Illness Label In Determining Acceptance-Rejection

Authors and Publication Date	Sample	Nature of Experiment	Outcome Measure	Effect of Behavior	Effect of Label	Behavior Stronger than Label
Farina, Murray, and Groh (1978)	48 male employees in a physical plant of a university	A female college student confederate behaved either normally or tensely and was described as a mental patient or as a normal applicant	15-item checklist	Significant for six of the 15 items - tense condition worse for get along with, assets, liabilities, reliability, adjustment, and value	Significant - for one of 15 items - mental patient condition led to a rating of fewer assets	Yes
Link and Cullen (1983)	153 community respondents from a midwestern city	A Star vignette and Phillip's normal individual vignette were administered by questionnaire. Labeling was manipulated by reference to a mental hospitalization	Five-item social distance scale	Significant	Significant - for "normal" vignette. Not significant - for "depressive neurotic" vignette	Yes
Bord (1971)	350 introductory sociology students	Replicated procedure used by Phillips but administered material by questionnaire	Identical to Phillips	Significant	Significant-but the pattern is inconsistent with more severe labels leading to more severe rejection	Yes
Farina, Felner, and Boudreau (1973) study I	48 female employees of a department store in Hartford, Connecticut	A 22-year-old female confederate behaved either normally or tensely in an interview situation. Half the respondents were told the confederate was a mental patient	Asked how they would "get along" with and whether confederate should be hired	Significant	Not significant - trend toward being more accepting of mental patient	Yes
Farina, Felner, and Boudreau (1973) study II	48 male employees of a veterans administration hospital in Providence, Rhode Island	A 25-year old male confederate behaved either normally or tensely and was described as either an ex-mental patient or an ex-surgical patient	Same as Farina et al. 1973 study I, above	Significant	Significant	Mixed - behavior stronger for "get along" question, label stronger for "should be hired" question

TABLE 1

Experimental and Quasi-Experimental Studies Assessing the Role of Objectionable Behavior and a
Mental Illness Label In Determining Acceptance-Rejection

Authors and Publication Date	Sample	Nature of Experiment	Outcome Measure	Effect of Behavior	Effect of Label	Behavior Stronger than Label
Farina, Felner, and Boudreau (1973) study III	44 female employees of a veterans hospital in Providence, Rhode Island	A 27-year old female confederate behaved either normally or tensely and was described as either an ex-mental patient or an ex-surgical patient	Same as Farina et al. 1973 study I, above	Significant	Not Significant	Yes
Kirk (1974)	864 community college students in San Francisco area	Two Star vignette cases and Phillip's normal vignette are labeled mentally ill, wicked, or under stress in a questionnaire. Source of labeling is also varied - self, family, same people, and psychiatrist	Nine-item social rejection index	Significant	Not significant - neither the label nor the source of the label was significant	Yes
Farina and Hagelauer (1975)	60 female employees of a department store in Hartford, Connecticut	A male confederate behaved either normally of tensely and was described as either a mental patient or a normal job applicant	Same as Farina et al. (1973) study I	Significant	Not significant	Yes

et al. 1976) or examined the effect of a label on the basis of a respondent's subjective labelling of a behavior description (Bentz and Edgerton 1971; Phillips 1967; Spiro, Siassi, and Crocetti 1973).

Ten of the 12 studies reported that behavior had an effect that was statistically significant and more potent than that of labels. The only exceptions are Loman and Larkin's (1976) quasi-experimental study of college students, which found labelling to have more influence and Farina, Felner, and Boudreau's (1973) study, in which mixed results occurred. In addition, since Phillips's (1963) initial study, the research has demonstrated consistent labelling effects. Although most studies found some evidence of labelling effects, these effects have either not been significant across all the outcomes assessed (Lehman et al. 1976; Faring, Murray, and Groh 1978; Link and Cullen 1983) or have not been in

the direction of more severe labels leading to more severe rejection (Schroder and Erlich 1968; Bors 1971).[4]

The effect of the studies discussed above has been pervasive. For example, Rabkin, a frequent reviewer of the literature on attitudes toward mental illness, has reported that a 1980 National Institute of Mental Health Workshop of experts in the field decided not to use the term "stigma" in the title of its proceedings (1974, 1975, 1980). Apparently, stigma was not viewed as an appropriate designation if "one is referring to negative attitudes induced by manifestations of psychiatric illness" (Rabkin 1984, p. 327). Consistent with this position, Cockerham's text on the sociology of mental disorders concludes a section on community responses to former mental patients by echoing these views: "If former mental patients can act relatively normal, they probably can shed their label and live a normal life" (Cockerham 1981, p. 303). Similarly, writing in *Social Work*——the official journal of a profession with considerable responsibility for the care of the mentally ill——Segal (1978) has used the research literature to derive five major statements concerning attitudes toward the mentally ill. One of these states that "The behavior itself or the pattern of behavior is the major determinant of the positive or negative character of the public's attitude toward mental illness." Accoridng to Segal, this brings into question "the impact of the labelof mental illness itself" (1978, p. 213).

The Views of Psychiatric Patients: Evidence That Labels Matter?

In contrast to the strong and definitive statements that have emerged from research on the relative importance of labels and behavior, the views expressed by psychiatric patients vary considerably. Many current and former patients remark that they have suffered or will suffer greatly because of labelling, while others indicate that they have not or will not be harmed. This wide range in their views argues against a simplistic interpretation of the effects of labels. Below, we examine more generally the literature on former patients' feelings about stigma and then focus on information from patients that is relevant to the specific issue of behavior versus labelling as determinants of rejecting responses.[5]

Evidence from Studies Assessing the Attitudes of Former Patients

Systematically collected evidence concerning patients' views of stigma reflects considerable variability in their opinions. This is evident in Weinstein's (1983) review of patient attitude studies. He found 12 studies assessing former patients' attitudes about two issues: (1) the degree of stigma they feel and (2) their views of the quality and effectiveness of mental hospital treatment. When these two domains of patient attitude were considered together, Weinstein reported that five studies tended to show that have labelling experience was seen as unfavor-

able, while six tended to show that it was seen as favorable, and another study revealed ambivalent results (Weinstein 1983, pp. 77-79).[6] If attention is restricted solely to the studies that deal explicitly with patients' feelings about whether they feel stigmatized or have faced stigmatization, the results from counting studies continue to reflect variability.[7] Weinstein classified three of these studies (Miller and Dawson 1965; Nuehring 1979; Spiegel and younger 1972) as indicating unfavorable attitudes (i.e., patients tend to feel stigmatized or report rejection) and two as indicating favorable attitudes (Cumming and Cumming 1965; Rosenblatt and Mayer 1974).

In addition to using counts of studies as indicators of patient opinion, it is important to examine the distribution of patient attitudes within studies. As Weinstein has pointed out, a study classified as favorable or unfavorable suggests "a tendency——not a unanimity" (1983, p. 78). Thus, it is instructive that, in the two stigma studies Weinstein classified as favorable (Cumming and Cumming 1965; Rosenblatt and Mayer 1974), there is nevertheless substantial evidence that stigma is a difficulty for some patients. In one of these (Rosenblatt and Mayer 1974), an exact quantitative estimate of how many of the 30 patients interviewed reported feelings of shame is not available. However, the authors characterized their respondents as differing on whether successive hospitalizations increase feelings of stigma. Further, they furnished the following verbatim comments, which suggest that at least some patients have (or have had) acute feelings of being stigmatized: "I don't think that it makes any difference how often you come in. I think once you've been there (in the hospital) and they know you've been there, they call you crazy or sick" (p. 76). "The first time I went to a hopsital I felt ashamed. I was ashamed in the neighborhood when I got out of the hospital. I figured everybody knew I was there and they would think I was. . . . I really don't care so much now. I still care about what people think of me, but not as much as I did . . ." (p. 76).

The Cumming and Cumming (1965) investigation, a second "favorable" study, was conducted on two independent samples and used two very different methods for gathering data about stigma. In the first, no direct questions about stigma were asked of the 22 former patients sampled. Instead, general questions about problems in the posthospital period were the basis of the interview. Still, 41% of the patients volunteered information that constituted evidence that psychiatric hospitalization contributed to either expectations of inferior treatment or feelings of shame and inferiority. In the second study, a nine-point agree-disagree stigma scale that directly measured these two aspects of stigma was administered to 87 former patients. Cumming and Cumming reported that 54% (47) of the patients endorsed four or more of these nine items.[8]

Thus, while it is difficult to use this literature to assess precisely how many former patients feel stigmatized, it seems reasonable to conclude (1) that there is considerable variability in patients' sentiments and (2) that many, if not most, patients feel some shame and believe that others will respond negatively to the fact of their hospitalization. It is notable that this assessment of the patient attudinal data is difficult to reconcile with the research claiming that a label per se matters little. This disagreement becomes even sharper, however, when one considers sources of evidence on former patients' opinions that directly address the behavior versus labels issue.

Patients Views on Behavior versus Labelling

Experiential accounts reported anonymously in the National Institute of Mental Health's *Schizophrenia Bulletin* constitute one source of evidence on former patient views of a label's importance, when behavior is held constant. An author, who is both a former patient and a mental health professional working at NIMH, has written, "If my own research and experiences are representative, public attitudes have not changed. Families continue to treat mental illness as a silent, shameful disease. Clergymen continue to preach that mental illness is a result of satanic influence. The barriers remain. They are real" (Anonymous 1980, p. 545). Another former patient, who lost a job because of a history of mental illness and

needed to hide a gap in his employment record to secure another one, concluded, "There is much descrimination against people who seek or have obtained psychiatric treatment (inpatient or outpatient). No matter how productive and functioning they are, the stigma is still there" (Anonymous 1981, p. 737). Although they are highly selected instances of patient opinion, these statements reflect the view that prejudice and discrimination are present regardless of how normal the patients' behavior has been.

Second, in a recent study conducted in the Washington Heights section of New York City, Lind (1985) asked patients about their perceptions of how most people would treat a former mental patient. A majority of these patients indicated that they agreed that an ex-patient would be devalued (e.g., seen as less intelligent, less trustworthy) and discriminated against (e.g., excluded from jobs and close relationships). Because they specify full recovery and thus explicitly address the behavior issue, two particularly relevant questions read, "Most people would accept a fully recovered former mental patient as a teacher of young children in a public school" and "Most people would not hire a former mental patient to take care of their children even if he or she had been well for some time." Fifty-six percent of the patients queried disagreed with the first item, while 57% agreed with the second. These results indicate that a majority of patients believe they will be rejected even if their behavior is entirely normal.[9]

Finally, there is evidence indicating that patients will forgo insurance benefits in order to maintain privacy concerning their treatment for a mental disorder. While it is difficult to quantify the number of individuals involved, National Institute of Mental Health psychiatrist Steven Sharfstein has estimated that as many as 150,000 people, 15% of those with insurance, forgo benefits to avoid the possibility of mental health treatment becoming part of their records (*New York Times* 1981). This information is particularly feeling because patients are obviously concerned about people's reactions to the fact of treatment per se. Furthermore, the considerable amount of money that patients forfeit suggests that their convictions are deeply felt.

Understanding the Discrepancy Between the Views of Patients and Views Emanating from Research: A Theoretical Elaboration

Why would many, if not most, former patients believe that a label matters, and apparently believe that it matters regardless of the normality of their behavior, even though considerable research appears to have demonstrated just the opposite? Although this question has rarely been confronted systematically in past research, one explanation has been offered. This explanation implicitly accepts the notion that research data are objective and valid and that patients' beliefs are subjective and therefore are not trustworthy. The most extreme position along these lines asserts that the views of former patients are distortions of reality and simply a consequence of their enduring psychopathology. According to Crocetti, Spiro, and Siassi, major disorders such as depression and schizophrenia involve symptomatology that would cause those afflicted to perceive rejection from others inaccurately (1974, p. 130). The gap between patients' beliefs and research findings is a consequence of these inaccurate perceptions. We offer a very different explanation.

If a label has an effect, it would make little sense to claim that the consequences emerge directly from the fact of labelling. Instead, a label is a starting point that activates an array of beliefs about the designated person that may ultimately affect the level of acceptance or rejection such a person experiences. Thus, when a person learns that someone has been in a mental hospital, a set of preexisting conceptions about what this means is activated. Expectations emerge about how friendly, competent, or dangerous such a person is likely to be. These expectations are then applied to the labelled person and can affect how he or she is perceived and, eventually, is treated. If the person is not labelled, such beliefs are, of course, irrelevant and play no role whatsoever in evaluations.

One source of the idea that labels evoke preexisting beliefs is Scheff's original labelling theory formulation. Commenting on responses to labelled individuals, he indicated that stereotypes of mental illness, learned early in childhood, become the "guiding imagery for action" in dealing with the "deviant" (Scheff 1966, p. 82). That is, preexisting beliefs are activated by a label and have consequences for the subsequent treatment of the designated person. Scheff's idea about these preexisting beliefs is that they are strongly and rather uniformly negative. As a result, when labelling occurs, and these beliefs become salient in interpreting the labelled person's behavior, the consequences are strongly negative. Although we accept Scheff's insight that labels activate preexisting beliefs, we suggest that the negative or positive nature of these preexisting beliefs remains an empirical question. Thus, in our analysis, instead of assuming that all people are fearful of former patients, we assess the extent to which members of the public find the mentally ill dangerous.

Interestingly, there is some evidence in the literature suggesting that preexisting beliefs are important in understanding labelling effects. Phillips, for example, showed that reactions to a label varied considerably according to whether his respondents had a relative or friend who had sought help for emotional problems. Those with closer relations to a help seeker were considerably less rejecting than those with more distant relations, perhaps because the label had come to take on new meaning as a consequence of their greater familiarity (1963). In addition, Schroder and Erlich's sample of psychiatric nurses showed a distinctly different pattern of responses to a label than Phillips's community sample (1968). This could be due to the different meaning a label tends to have for psychiatric nurses. As Schroder and Erlich emphasized, nurses are likely to examine the behavior described in a vignette and to use a label to judge whether appropriate treatment (no help, clergy, physician, psychiatrist, mental hospital) is being sought (1968). For nurses, rejection is more likely if the individual seeks appropriate care. Together, these two examples suggest that labels have different meanings for members of different groups. In turn, this indicates that, to reach a more adequate understanding of labelling effects, we need to ask people what a label means to them.

Despite the importance of the idea that a label activates preexisting beliefs, this phenomenon has not been addressed directly by any of the studies reported in table 1. Phillips (1963, 1964) and Schroder and Erlich (1968) present group comparisons that suggest that this would be useful. However, none of these studies examines the meaning a label has for an individual or uses this information in uderstanding the relative effects of behavior and labelling. Instead, a label is placed in competition with descriptions of behavior without any exploration of what the label might mean to respondents, that is, without assessing how friendly, competent, or dangerous they believe mental patients and former mental patients to be.[10] This approach is problematic for two reasons. To begin with, it obscures the relevance of labels by omitting their potential role in evoking preexisting beliefs. In addition, it may lead researchers and the public to conclude mistakenly that those patients who feel rejected are incorrect, or worse, sick, because of their beliefs.

In this paper, we replicate the work of previous investigators by experimentally manipulating behavior and labelling. We use a 3 × 3 factorial design, randomly assigning respondents to one of six vignettes formed by the three levels of behavior (no objectionable behavior vs. mild vs. severe) and two levels of labelling (mental hospitalization vs. hospitalization for back problems). Unlike previous work, however, our study also measures an important set of beliefs that the label "mental patient" might activate. We focus on the concept of how dangerous the mentally ill are preceived to be, generating a reliable measure of our respondents' beliefs about this. With this addition, we are able to test whether a label activates such beliefs by examining whether preceptions of dangerousness are important determinants of rejection in the labelled condition but not in the unlabelled. In other words, we test whether there is an interaction between beliefs about how dangerous the mentally ill are and labelling, on the level of expressed rejection of the person described in the vignette.

If a label has no meaningful influence, as many have claimed, there should be no interacting effect. Such a result would be consistent with a formulation that claims either that labels do not call out more general beliefs about mental patients or that these beliefs, once called out, do not affect acceptance or rejection. If an interaction is present, however, there will be support for the notion that a label activates a set of beliefs about a social category and allows these beliefs to be salient in the evaluation of the labelled person. Furthermore, an interaction finding would indicate the possibility that those former patients who perceive rejection are not simply distorting their assessment of others' responses. While previous work has shown that, overall, a label has little effect on rejection, an interaction of labelling and perceptions of dangerousness would suggest that some people——those who fear that the mentally ill are dangerous——do reject on the basis of labelling information. If this group is sizable, say more than 20% of the population, it is understandable why some former mental patients fear rejection——a large subgroup of the population freely expresses negative sentiments and endorses distancing responses. With these issues in mind, we will describe the experiment conducted to test the ideas involved.

Methods

Sample

A simple random sample of 240 Ohio residents was selected from the telephone directory for the Cincinnati area. The chosen individuals were sent a letter, written on university letterhead and signed by one of the investigators, explaining the study. In order to ensure the respondents' confidentiality, they all were provided woth postcards with their names written on them. Respondents were able to return the postcards to the study's offices, separately from their questionnaires. This allowed investigators to know who had responded while preserving the respondents' confidentiality. One week after the initial mailing, all respondents were sent a second letter thanking them for having returned the questionnaire if they had done so or reminding them of the importance of their response if they had not. Finally, eight weeks after the initial mailing, a follow-up letter and a replacement survey were sent to nonresponders along with a $1.00 token of appreciation. These steps resulted in a response rate of 63.3% (N = 152).

Of the 152 individuals who responded, 53% were female. The mean number of years of education was 13.5 and the mean age 47.6. Sixty-five percent of the sample was married, whereas 16% were single and 19% either separated, widowed, or divorced. By choosing our respondents from a telephone directory, we unavoidably missed individuals with unlisted numbers and people without phones. Because of this, we compared the sociodemographic characteristcs of our respondents with the 1980 census for the area from which the sample was drawn. We found that our sample was much like the county as a whole in terms of sex and age but different in educational level. Fifty-three percent of the county is female, as is 53% of our sample, for age, we compared the proportions in various age groups over 25 years old and found that 46% of our sample was between 25 and 44, whereas 45% of the census population was in this age range. Similarly, 32% of our sample was between 45 and 64, wehreas 35% of the census population fell in this age group. In contrast to these correspondences on age and sex, we found that our sample was more highly educated than the county population. Thirty-three percent of the county population, as opposed to 53% of our sample, pursued at least some education beyond high school.

The implications of this difference between our sample and the population on educational level will be considered more fully when we evaluate our results. At this point, however, it is important to note that previous studies (for a review, see Rabkin [1980]) suggest that stereotyped images of mental patients are more pronounced among those with less education. Thus, we are likely to have underrepresented individuals with negative views of the mentally ill, thereby biasing against a finding that would suggest that the mentally ill face rejection.

Procedures

The vignette employed was written to provide more information about the person involved than

is typically supplied in vignette studies. The "Normal man" vignette, Phillips [1963]). The vignette includes specific information about income, grooming, and work behavior as well as more general information on aspirations such as a desire to meet young women and find a better paying job. Incorporating information of this sort is important because some inviestigators have claimed that labelling has an effect only when there is little other information to use in evaluation (Crocetti et al. 1974). As such, if labelling is shown to have an effect, it will be more convincing in the context of a vignette that provides relatively extensive information about the individual involved. The basic vignette presented to the respondents read as follows:

Here is a description of a 27-year-old man, let's call him Jim Johnson. About two years ago, he was hospitalized in a mental hospital because of problems he was having at the time. Now he appears to be recovered and is doing pretty well.

Jim works at a job in a local business. He earns $20,000 a year before taxes and is doing well enough. He is well groomed and known for dressing neatly.

At his job, he gets along well with his co-workers and is on friendly terms with them. He begins his days chatting briefly with the people he works with and then gets down to business. He takes coffee and lunch breaks during the day, just like everyone else, and returns to work when his co-workers do.

While on the job, Jim checks his work carefully and doesn't pass it along until it is correct. This might slow Jim down a little, but he is never critized for the quality of the work he completes.

Jim is interested in meeting and dating young women in the community. He is considering joining a local church group to meet them. He is also looking for a job that gives him more responsibility and pays better than his current one.

Labelling was manipulated by changing the sentence about mental hospitalization to indicate the fictitious Jim Johnson had been hospitalized for a back problem. The levels of behavior were manipulated by adding material after the third paragraph of the vignette. The mild and severe conditions formed in this way appear below.

> *Mild.*——Every once in a while Jim becomes frustrated with all the demands at work and says he feels anxious about them. Once when he felt this way, he got red in the face, went to a back room, and began pacing and complaining to a co-worker in an angry tone of voice. Later, he talked to some of the people he works with about the pressures he is sometimes under.

> *Severe.*——Jim has a tendency to get upset about demands at work. He often bangs his fist on a table and storms away shouting that other people "aren't fair to him." Sometimes he gets so angry that he begins throwing things and threatening the people he works with.

The condition of "no objectionable behavior" is simply the vignette without either of these two conditions added.

The value of vignettes such as that presented above is that they allow random assignment of respondents to experimental conditions. The internal validity (Cook and Campbell 1979) of the study is therefore greatly enhanced. At the same time, vignette studies such as this one (and those in table 1) expose respondents to specific experimental interventions. As a result, a great deal rests on whether the particular vignette material presented is believable. In addition, the way the material is presented might allow respondents to guess the nature of the experiment and, if so, to react in such a way as to support the hypothesis inappropriately (Orne 1962).[11] In order to assess whether the vignette we constructed involved these kinds of difficulties, we administered a postexperimental "funnel questionnaire" (Page 1973; Page and Kahle 1976) to a group of 43 students enrolled in an introductory sociology class.[12] Our results showed that a majority found the vignette believable, noting nothing out of place in the description provided to them. The minority who did report something out of place did not consistently mention the same factor and were not clustered in any one cell of the experiment. Moreover, only two individuals indicated that they could guess the

hypothesis. Thus, we conclude that there is evidence that some respondents found some of the vignette out of place and that some may even have guessed our hypothesis. Our assessment also shows, however, that neither of these issues represented an extensive or systematic problem in the experiment.

Measures

After reading the vignette, the respondents were asked to answer each of seven social distance questions referring to the target person, Jim Johnson (see App. A for the questions used) by employing a four-point Likert format (definitely unwilling, probably unwilling, probably willing, and definitely willing). These responses were scored from 0 = definitely willing to 3 = definitely unwilling. They were then added together and divided by seven to form a composite social distance measure varying from 0 to 3. The internal consistency reliability (Cronbach's α) of this measure was .92.

The placement of the perceived-dangerous questions with respect to the vignette posed a dilemma for us in the conduct of our community mail survey. Ideally, the order would be randomized, but, in a mail survey, it is difficult to keep strict control of the order of presentation because respondents can easily move back and forth through the questionnaire. Our decision to place the vignette and the social distance questions first in our questionnaire was based on the assumption that, in this position, the experimental portion would be least contaminated by other aspects of the questionnaire. However, the issue of order effects is an important one that we address in a supplementary study below.

The scale measuring perceived dangerousness included eight items (see App. B) designed to tap respondents' beliefs about whether a person who is, or has been mentally ill, is likely to be a threat. While the items in the perceived-dangerousness scale appear initially to be similar to some of the social distance items, it is important to recognize that the target they specify is very different. The social distance items are about the individual in the vignette, Jim Johnson, whereas the perceived-dangerousness items are about the mentally ill and former mental patients in general. The difference in the targets specified, coupled with the randomization of the labelling factor, will provide a test for the possibility that the constructs are correlated simply because their content is similar. Under the assumption that similar item content is not a problem, we should find a nonsignificant correlation between social distance responses and perceived dangerousness of mental patients in the unlabelled condition in which Jim Johnson is identified as having a back problem. Alternatively, if the similar item content is troublesome, we should find a correlation of considerable magnitude. Because this test of possible overlap in item content involves central substantive results of the paper, we will postpone our conclusion about the issue until we have presented our findings.

Each of the items measuring perceived dangerousness was answered using a six-point, strongly agree——strongly disagree Likert format. We scored the six response categories from 0 to 5, summed the items using unit weighting and divided by eight to create a scale varying form 0 to 5. The scoring was done so that a high score reflects the belief that the mentally ill are dangerous. The internal consistency (Cronbach's α) of the scale is .85.[13]

Results

In presenting our results, we begin by showing that our findings are consistent with those of past investigators (see table 1). We then proceed to a more refined analysis which incorporates the idea that one way a label has an effect is in activating beliefs about the dangerousness of mental patients and former mental patients.

Consistency with Past Research

Table 2 presents the means and standard deviations of the social distance measure within each of the six cells formed by the labelling and behavior factors. As is evident from these mean values, the levels of behavior make a considerable difference in how much social distance is desired; labelling does not. This is tested more formally in table 3, which presents an analysis of

variance. The results show that, while the behavior variable is highly significant, labelling and behavior by labelling are not.

Given this evidence, one may be tempted simply to reaffirm past work and declare, once again, that a label has little or no effect on responses to the mentally ill. As we have pointed out, however, a theoretically more appropriate assessment of labelling effects is possible. Therefore, we turn to an expanded set of findings that, by bringing our measure of perceived dangerousness of mental patients into the analysis, incorporates the notion that labels activate beliefs.

Table 2

MEANS OF THE SOCIAL DISTANCE SCALE IN THE SIX CELLS FORMED BY LABELING AND BEHAVIOR CONDITIONS (N = 151)

	No Objectionable Behavior	Mildly Objectionable Behavior	Severely Objectionable Behavior
Label	.98 (.51) N = 25	1.16 (.69) N = 27	1.76 (.59) N = 24
No Label	.92 (.55) N = 26	1.40 (.58) N = 24	1.92 (.53) N = 25

NOTE: -- The number of cases for this table is 151 instead of 152. Because of a missing value, we could not generate a score on social distance for one respondent. Numbers in parentheses are standard deviations.

Evidence Concerning the Activation of Beliefs About the Dangerousness of Mental Patients

Recall that the crucial test is concerned with whether there is an interaction between perceived dangerousness and labelling on social distance. In order to assess this hypothesis, we concluded a multiple-regression analysis using dummy variables to capture the behavior and labelling factors.[14] We tested for interactions between the behavior levels and perceived dangerousness, and between behavior and labelling, were not significant, and we excluded them from the analysis.

Table 3

ANALYSIS OF VARIANCE SHOWING THE EFFECT OF
LABELING BEHAVIOR AND LABELING X BEHAVIOR ON
SOCIAL DISTANCE (N = 151)

Variable	Sum of Squares	Degrees of Freedom	Mean Square	F value	Signif-icance
Label	.51	1	.51	1.53	n.s
Behavior	20.20	2	10.10	30.12	$P < .001$
Label x behav-ior	.59	2	.30	.88	n.s.
Residual	48.63	145	.34		

Table 4

MULTIPLE-REGRESSION ANALYSIS SHOWING EFFECTS OF
BEHAVIOR LABELING, PERCEIVED DANDGEROUSNESS OF
MENTAL PATIENTS AND THE INTERACTION OF LABELING
AND PERCEIVED DANGEROUSNESS OF SOCIAL DISTANCE
IN THE COMMUNITY SAMPLE (N = 150)

Variable	Unstandard-ized Regression Coefficient	Standard Error	t-value	P-value
Label (1=present,0=absent)	-.686	.228	-3.006	.003
Mild behavior (1=present, 0=absent)	.309	.107	2.877	.005
Severe behavior (1=present, 0=absent)	.747	.111	6.707	.000
Perceived dangerousness	.055	.068	.817	.415
Labeling X perceived dangerousness	.283	.094	3.000	.003
Constant	.935			
	R^2 = .412			

NOTE. Number of cases for this table is 150. One respondent had a missing value on
the social distance measure while another was missing on perceived dangerousness.

As can be seen in table 4, the interaction between labelling and perceived dangerousness is highly significant.[15] The coeeficients indicate that the slope of perceived dangerousness is .338 (.005 + .283) in the labelled condition and .055 in the unlabelled condition. Labelling does indeed appear to evoke beliefs about dangerousness of mental patients and to make them applicable to the individual described in the vignette.

Figure 1 presents this interaction effect in the form of a diagram showing a steep slope of perceptions of dangerousness in the labelled condition and a relatively flat slope in the unlabelled condition. The figure as presented is for the no-objectionable-behavior condition. However, since there are no significant interactions between labelling and behavior or between dangerousness and behavior, the same picture would simply be shifted upward ——indicating higher levels of social distance ——to portray either the mild (.31 units up) or severe (.75 units up) conditions. As the figure shows, respondents are likely to be more rejecting of the labelled vignette than of the unlabeled one. If respondents believe mental patients are relatively harmless, however, they are actually more adcepting of the labelled than of the unlabelled vignette. This is why the coefficient for labelling is negative. (-.686) in table 4. It tells us the difference (in units of social distance) between the two slopes at the zero point of the perceived dangerousness scale (Cleary and Kessler 1982). When perceived dangerousness is zero, as the figure shows graphically, labelling does have a negative

effect——that is, on average, labelling reduces social distance (-.686 units). For those who score high on perceived dangerousness, the estimate of the labelling effect becomes positive; that is, more social distance is desired from the labelled individual. For example, for those scoring as high as possible (5), labelling increases social distance by 1.00 unit [5 × .338) - .686]).[16] Because previous research averaged effects like these together, many investigators have been led to the conclusion that labelling is unimportant or trivial. By contrast, it appears that labelling evokes potent beliefs that are strong determinants of levels of attitudinal rejection.

Figure 1 is also useful for addressing the methodological issue raised earlier concerning the potential overlap of the content of the social distance and perceived dangerousness items. As the figure shows, the slope in the unlabelled condition (N = 75) is close to being flat and is not significantly different from zero (see table 4), indicating that the similarity in item content does not automatically produce correlatin between the two variables (r = .106, P = .367). The hypothetical Jim Johnson must have the label "former

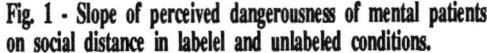

Fig. 1 - Slope of perceived dangerousness of mental patients on social distance in labelel and unlabeled conditions.

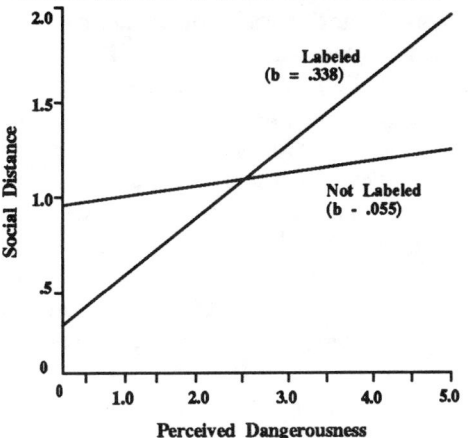

mental hospital patient" (N = 75) for a strong association between social distance responses and perceptions of dangerousness of mental patients to emerge (r = .657, P < .001).

Finally, the results also bear on whether the expectations of rejection that many former patients feel as a consequence of labelling have a factual basis. Referring once again to figure 1, if we draw a perpendicular line from the point at which the two slopes intersect, we can get a crude estimate of an interesting point on the perceptions-of-dangerous scale. On the average, those individuals who score above this point are likely to be more rejecting of the former mental patient than of the person with a back problem. The point turns out to be 2.42, and using the frequency distribution of our sample, we can see that 39.1% of the respondents score above this point. This means that a sizable minority of people are likely to reject on the basis of labelling information. The expectations of rejection that many former patients report, when reviewed from this different angle, are far more understandable than past work would have had us believe.

Our results also indicate that, where there is labelling, 60.9% of the individuals sampled are likely to reject the individual less because of it. This kind of result has been termed the "extra break" effect by Rosen, Cowan, and Grandison (1982) and has arisen in other studies as well (Farina et al. 1973). We will return to its interpretation in the discussion of our results.

Patients' Behavior versus Public Attitudes as Predictors of Social Distance

Another aspect of the results of this study should be highlighted. Previous research has juxtaposed labels and behavior, essentially asking which is the strongest predictor of rejection. Given that the label of former "mental hospital patient" activates beliefs about dangerousness, we can restate the question with a different twist: which is more important in determining attitudinal rejection——behavior or attitudes about dangerousness that are activated by labelling information?

In order to answer, we restrict attention to subjects in the labelled condition (N = 75) where beliefs about the dangerousness of mental patients are relevant to the individual being evaluated and then examine the predictive power of the behavioral conditons versus the perceived dangerousness measure. If we first enter the two dummy variables reflecting the behavior dimension in an equation explaining social distance and allow them to explain all the variance they can, we obtain a substantial R^2 of 23.8%. Then if we add the perceived-dangerousness measure, the R^2 more than doubles to 49.4%. Clearly, perceived dangerousness is an important, or slightly more important, than the behavior factor in this analysis. Further, these results suggest that characteristics of respondents, in this case, their beliefs about the dangerousness of the mentally ill, affect how they react to a labelled person above and beyond that person's described behavior. The conclusion that reactions to a former patient are a simple function of his or her behavior appears to need revision.

Evaluation of the Results Considerations Concerning the Generalizability of the Results

In evaluating the results presented above, we return to the issue we raised in describing our sample, our concern with the higher-than-expected educational level of the respondents. We have already mentioned the observation that the underrepresentation of lower-educated respondents is likely to bias against finding evidence that the mentally ill face rejection. In addition, now that it is clear that the predicted interaction effect is both strong and highly significant, we can see that, to reduce the effect to near zero, the missing lower-educated respondents would have to be radically different from the respondents forming our sample. Finally, we tested whether the hypothesized interaction of labelling and perceived dangerousness was relatively constant across gender, age, and education. Cook and Campbell call evidence suggesting a constant effect in different groups, "generalizing across" and point out that it increases confidence that an effect is generalizable (1979).

In this regard, we ran our analyses separately for (1) men and women, (2) those both below and above the median age, and (3) most important, among those with a high school education or less, as well as among those with more schooling. In every case, the coefficient of the cross-product term reflecting the interaction was in the expected direction, and in no case was there evidence that this coefficient was significantly different in one half of the sample (e.g., high education) as opposed to the other (e.g., low education). To the extent that there was a difference by education, our results showed that the interaction of labelling and perceived dangerousness was stronger in the less educated group. Thus, while the less than perfect response rate (63%) and the tendency to have sampled more highly educated respondents would lead us to question the exact magnitude of the estimates reported here, there is considerable reason to be confident that the key interaction we have emphasized occurs in the direction suggested by our analysis.

Potential Bias Owing to the Ordering of the Vignette and the Perceived-Dangerousness Question

The vignette was placed before the perceived-dangerousness questions in our community survey. Unfortunately, this means that the experiment could affect any of the respondents' subsequent responses, including their beliefs about the dangerousness of the mentally ill. For

example, it is possible that the vignettes we presented may affect responses to questions about the perceived dangerousness of mental patients only when the vignette is labelled. If so, this could lead to the kind of interaction effect we have predicted but through different causal processes. We believe that this alternative explanation is weak because it seems unlikely that the very brief intervention posed by the vignette would dramatically influence the general beliefs encompassed by the measure of perceptions of dangerousness of mental patients. Nevertheless, we decided to conduct the same experiment on a sample of college students where the order of presentation could be randomized and strictly controlled. Thus, college student subjects were randomly assigned to receive either the vignette and social distance questions followed by the perceived-dangerousness questions or the same questions in reverse order. Further, the students returned each portion of the questionnaire immediately after they completed it, thereby ensuring that they could not move back and forth between the survey's different sections.

The student sample consists of 140 members of three introductory sociology classes at Western Illinois University in Macomb, Illinois.[17] In table 5, we report two multiple-regression analyses based on the student sample. The first is a replication of the analysis reported in table 4 concerning the community residents. Despite the dissimilarity between the two samples, the coefficients show the same pattern. The dummy variables for behavior are both significant, as in the community sample, and, most important, perceptions of dangerousness and labelling interact in the same way.

The second analysis in table 5 controls for the order in which the social distance and perceived-dangerousness questions are asked. If order mattered a great deal, one would expect the coefficients expressing the effect of perceived dangerousness on social distance to vary considerably depending on which questions were asked first. In terms of a regression model, this would be evident in interaction terms involving order and perceived dangerousness. As table 4 shows, however, none of the coefficients

Table 5

MULTIPLE-REGRESSION ANALYSIS SHOWING DETERMINANTS OF SOCIAL DISTANCE
CONTROLLING FOR POTENTIAL ORDER OF PRESENTATION EFFECTS IN THE STUDENT
SAMPLE ($N = 140$)

Variable	REGRESSION ANALYSIS WITHOUT CONTROLS FOR ORDER EFFECTS		REGRESSION ANALYSIS WITH CONTROLS FOR ORDER OF PRESENTATION	
	Unstandardized Regression Coefficient	P-value	Unstandardized Regression Coefficient	P-value
Label (1=present,0=absent)	-.295	.147	-.332	.134
Mild behavior (1=present,0=absent)	.233	.024	.237	.028
Severe behavior (1=present, 0=absent)	.760	.000	.755	.000
Perceived dangerousness	.080	.226	.021	.806
Labeling x perceived dangerousness	.212	.020	.263	.024
Order (1-vignette first, 0=vignette second)			-.321	.311
Order x labeling			.269	.532
Order x perceived dangerousness			.147	.290
Order x labeling x perceived dangerousness			-.120	.548
	$R^2 = .410$		$R^2 = .415$	

reflecting the effect of order even approaches statistical significance, and together they add only one half of 1% to the explained variance. These results support our interpretation of the interaction as arising from a process in which the label calls out preexisting beliefs about mental patients and former mental patients and makes them applicable to the labelled individual.

Advantages and Disadvantages of the Experimental Vignette Approach

In conducting an experiment of any kind in the social sciences, one creates interventions and then evaluates their effects. One potential problem in doing this involves the extent to which the intervention reflects social processes outside of a constructed situation. In our study, for example, the vignettes present relatively concrete, specific

information. In daily interaction, information is likely to come from different, perhaps contradictory sources, thereby providing a more ambiguous picture of events than our vignettes offer. The effects of labelling may be different, perhaps even more important, under such conditions of uncertainty.

Given the possible lack of congruence between our experimental manipulation and common everyday social processes, we believe that an evaluation of the effects of labels should involve different methodologies, each of which has different strengths and weaknesses. On the one hand, a significant strength of both nonexperimental survey research and participant observation is that they provide data about people outside of contrived experimental conditions. On the other, the strength of the experimental approach is that randomization helps rule out alternative explanations with far more certainty than is allowed by nonexperimental techniques. Clearly, the best assessment of the effects of labels would come from a series of studies that used different methodologies. With this in mind, the current research should be seen as contributing to the relatively extensive body of experimental work (see table 1) by extending that approach and thereby challenging the conclusion that labels matter little.

Discussion

Since the emergence of labelling theory as a major deviance paradigm (Cole 1975), the question of whether former mental patients suffer stigmatization and social rejection as a consequence of labelling has been a central issue. A large number of studies have focused on whether people react to former patients primarily on the basis of their acquired labels or on the basis of their everyday behavior. The weight of recent research (see table 1), when assessed in experimental or quasi-experimental designs, has decidedly favored behavior over labelling as the prime determinant of acceptance or rejection. Understandably, this research has led some investigators to conclude that labels are relatively unimportant, a conclulsion that puts them in sharp disagreement with those patients and former patients who believe that they will be rejected if the fact of their mental hospitalization is known.

This disagreement and the related conclusion that labels matter little stems, we believe, from the fact that none of the experimental or quasi-experimental research employed a sufficiently complex assessment of the labelling process in determining the effect a label may have. People who interact with former mental hospital patients do not simply form evaluations on the basis of behavior or a label per se but instead react in a manner consistent with their understanding of what the label of former patient means. Thus, by demonstrating that a label evokes potent beliefs about the dangerousness of mental patients and former mental patients, this study suggests that an adequate perspective concerning this phenomenon cannot overlook potential labelling processes and effects. Further, showing that a subgroup——those who believe patients and former patients are dangerous——bases its rejection on labelling information gives us a better understanding than previous research does of why many patients fear rejection.

Below, we first explore the meaning of our findings in more depth and then consider their possible consequences for the adjusment of former mental hospital patients to community life.

Understanding the Interaction between Labelling and Perceptions of Dangerousness on Social Distance

The finding that individuals who believe that mental patients and former mental patients are dangerous and are likely to reject a labelled person can be interpreted realtively straightforwardly. Such individuals find former patients threatening (Chin-Shong 1968) and prefer to maintain a safe social distance from them. Recall, however, that individuals who are substantially less threatened by mental patients and former patients accord a labelled person an extra break, allowing him closer association than a similarly described "back patient."[18] The meaning of this effect is not as straightforward.

Ideally, from a public health point of view, labelling and the proper identification of "cases" would have positive consequences. A label would evoke helping responses and lead to swift, effective treatment. Some of the effects of labelling have been shown to be positive in just this way. Considerable evidence (Smith, Glass, and Miller, 1980) has suggested that psychotherapy has beneficial effects, particularly on the nonspecific (across diagnoses) condition of "demoraliztion" (Frank 1973; Klein and Rabkin 1984). Similarly, an increasing amount of research has revealed the effectiveness of drugs in treating major mental disorders. For example, phenothiazines have been demonstrated to be effective for schizophrenia (Davis 1975), tricyclics and lithium for affective disorder (Davis 1976) and tricyclics and monoamine oxidase inhibitors for anxiety disorders (Liebowitz 1984).[19] In these cases, labelling leads to differential treatment aimed at helping a person with a severe problem. This suggests one interpretation of our finding concerning those respondents who give an extra break to individuals labelled by mental hospitalization: the label evokes sentiments of concern, and the labelled individuals are treated differentially in order to facilitate their adjustments to community life. Thus, one potential interpretation of our extra-break result is that labelling leads to positive effects among a specific group of community residents.

A second potential interpretation of the extra-break finding is that it is a form of stigma. Here one might draw on what are generally considered stigmatizing responses to handicapped people that appear to be based on "benevolent intentions." Katz (1981, pp. 50-56) has experimentally demonstrated such effects for paraplegics and blacks, and Goffman (1963) has provided pithy examples of the phenomenon from the point of view of the stigmatized. As described, this form of stigma can involve attributing great capacitites to a handicapped person for achieving normal human functions, such as when a blind man is praised for being able to move about his apartment. It can also take the form of "helping" based on an inappropriate assumption about the stigmatizing condition. Goffman has furnished the example of a one-legged woman who recalls some of her childhood roller-skating experiences in a book entitled *Out on a Limb:* "Whenever I fell, out swarmed the women in droves, clucking and fretting like a bunch of bereft mother hens. It was kind of them and in retrospect I appreciate their solicitude, but at the time I resented and was greatly embarrassed by their interference. For they assumed that no routine hazard to skating——no stick or stone——upset my flying wheels. It was a foregone conclusion that I fell because I was a poor, helpless cripple" (1963, pp. 15-16). Such instances of special kindness seem to be resented because one is being defined in terms of one's stigma instead of more relevant characteristics. The consequence is that an individual receives inappropriate (albeit well-intentioned) treatment. This literature suggests an interpretation of our extra-break effects as an inappropriately benevolent response that is likely to be resented by those exposed to it. In this regard, Ellsworth has shown that hospital staff who endorse items measuring "protective benevolence," on Cohen and Struening's (1962) Opinions about Mental Illness scale are rated as more aloof, distant, and dishonest by hospitalized mental patients (1965).

There are, then, at least two ways of interpreting the extra-break effect suggested by our data. Making a definitive choice between these two interpretations requires further data about the unmeasured attitudes and behaviors of those inclined to give an extra break as well as data about the responses of patients who are exposed to such incidences of benevolence. At this point, however, we are more inclined to interpret our result as a form of stigma.

Our reasoning comes from contrasting the extra-break effect in our study to those instances mentioned earlier in which labelling has positive consequences by exposing patients to helpful treatments. In both cases, the labelled individual receives special treatment. However, when a patient is provided with psychotherapy or drug treatment, it can often be conceived as an appropriate response. Frequently, the labelled individual is in psychic pain or has had difficult functioning in social roles, and the treatment administered is one that has been demonstrated to be effective in improving these conditions. In sharp contrast, the extra-break effect in our study seems strikingly inappropriate. The described individual was hospitalized two years ago, has a good job ($20,000 a year), and appears to have recovered. Particularly in the no-objectionable-behavior condition, there is little reason to suggest that an extra break is needed. Further, since there were no interactions between behavior and labelling in our study, the extra break clearly did not emanate from a strong tendency to excuse the labelled individual for objectionable behavior. Instead, it seems more likely to have emerged from inferences about former mental hospital patients that go beyond the evidence provided and lead to inappropriately benevolent responses. Again, our data cannot tell us whether this benevolent response will have positive or negative consequences for former mental patients. However, evidence concerning the physically handicapped, and Ellsworth's study (1965) showing that hospitalized mental patients tend to view benevolent staff as problematic, lead us to suspect that most patients will resent manifestations of inappropriate benevolence.

This is not to say that the public is incapable of a nonstigmatizing response to former patients. In our view, a nonstigmatizing response, given the nature of the vignette we presented to them, is one that reflects no differential treatment of the labelled individual. It is important to note that many of our respondents can be classified as having just such a response. Figure 1, for example, suggests that such individuals are most common near the 2.42 point of the dangerousness scale. However, since the slope of perceived dangerousness on social distance represents a trend only, it is also true that some, though considerably fewer, individuals who are near to the extremes of the dangerousness scale, respond to a former mental patient as they would to a back patient. Thus, our data suggest that a label can lead to freely expressed attitudinal rejection among some community residents, can precipitate well-intentioned but perhaps inappropriate benevolence among others, and finally, among still others, have little if any effect.

Potential Consequences for Patients

Our research has implications for the reason why the status of former patient can prove problematic for those who are labelled. As we have noted, a label can induce a wide range of sentiments among members of the public. What becomes difficult in interaction is that the former patient cannot readily or fully predict the responses of others. Inability to predict may lead to protective withdrawal and defensiveness as the studies of Farina, Allen, and Saul (1968) and Farina et al. (1971) have shown. Further, the responses one receives may be hard to interpret. Is a decrease in the frequency of phone calls from a friend related to one's mental hospitalization, or is it fully attributable to some other factor? Is the increased kindness of another's genuine affection, or is it a manifestation of that person's religious or moral belief that one is obliged to do right by the unfortunate? Fundamental information required to guide and then interpret social interactions can be upset. Such ambiguity, particularly in new social situations or in secondary relationships, may intensify stress or lead to coping mechanisms that induce former patients to conceal their history of treatment or to withdraw from social interactions. In any event, it would appear that the label is salient for former patients and holds the continuing potential to diminish the quality of social interactions (see Farinal et al. 1968, 1971) and the quality of role performance (see Link 1982).

Conclusion

In conclusion we stress two major points. First, our results suggest that the fears of stigmatization and rejection expressed by some former patients should not be viewed as mere symptoms of their underlying pathologies. Although it would be too much to assert that those who have suffered emotional difficulties are immune to misperception, the evidence here indicates that a meaningful segment of the public sees former patients as dangerous and expresses a reluctance to interact with them. Further, since the variability in patients' views is matched by variability in the public's response, it seems that researchers would be wise to treat the feedback of former patients as important data that contain clues regarding both the societal reactions to psychiatric patients and the ramifications of these for their personal and social adjustment.

Second, it is becoming more and more of an accepted social "fact" that empirical data have revealed that labels do not matter and that the field should move on to more fruitful and less ideologically inspired research topics. As Gove concludes, "Briefly put, labelling theory points to processes that exist but their overall impact is small," (1980b, p. 268). The value of our study is that it offers an empirical challenge to this conclusion and indicates that it may well be premature to accept the demise of labelling theory as a paradigm for directing research endeavors.

Appendix A
Social Distance Items[20]

1. How would you feel about renting a room in your home to someone like Jim Johnson?
2. How about as a worker on the same job as someone like Jim Johnson?
3. How would you feel having someone like Jim Johnson as a neighbor?
4. How about as the caretaker of your children for a couple of hours?
5. How about having your children marry someone like Jim Johnson?

6. How would you feel about introducing Jim Johnson to a young woman you are friendly with?

7. How would you feel about recommending someone like Jim Johnson for a job working for a friend of yours?

Appendix B
Perceived Dangerousness of Mental Patients Items[21]

1. If a group of former mental patients lived nearby, I would not allow my children to go to the movie theater alone. (Reversed Scoring)

2. If a former mental patient applied for a teaching position at a grade school and was qualified for the job I would recommend hiring him or her.

3. One important thing about mental patients is that you cannot tell what they will do from one minute to the next. (Reversed Scoring)

4. If I know a person has been a mental patient, I will be less likely to trust him. (Reversed Scoring)

5. The main purpose of mental hospitals should be to protect the public from mentally ill people. (Reversed Scoring)

6. If a former mental patient lived nearby I would not hesitate to allow young children under my care to play on the sidewalk.

7. Although some mental patients may seem all right it is dangerous to forget for a moment that they are menatlly ill. (Reversed Scoring)

8. There should be a law forbidding a former mental patient the right to obtain a hunting license. (Reversed Scoring)

Table C1

CORRELATION MATRIX OF THE MAIN STUDY VARIABLES AND CROSS PRODUCT TERMS USED TO TEST FOR INTERACTION ($N = 150$, COMMUNITY SAMPLE)

	Social Distance	Label	Behavior Mild	Behavior Severe	Perceived Danger	Label x Mild	Label x Severe	Danger x Mild	Danger x Severe	Label x Danger
Label (1=mental hospital; 0=back patient	-.089									
Behavior mild (1 vs. all others = 0	-.079	.042								
Behavior severe (1 vs. all others = 0)	.504	-.029	-.492							
Perceived danger	.397	-.146	-.001	.195						
Label x mild	-.129	.469	.653	-.321	-.188					
Label x severe	.264	.426	-3.05	.620	.204	-.199				
Danger x mild	.052	-.078	.856	-.422	.337	.411	-.262			
Danger x severe	.487	.019	-.453	.919	.382	-.295	.633	-.388		
Label x danger	.184	.829	-.040	.135	.282	.296	.559	.000	.247	
Mean	1.352	.500	.340	.320	2.217	.180	.153	.753	.797	1.037
Standard Deviation	.685	.502	.475	.468	.970	.385	.362	1.230	1.269	1.255

References

Anonymous. 1980. "First Person Account: After the Funny Farm." *Schizophrenia Bulletin* 6:544-46.

------. 1981. "First Person Account: The Quiet Discrimination." *Schizophrenia Bulletin* 7:736-38.

Bentz, W. Kenneth, and J. Wilbert Edgerton. 1971. "The Consequences of Labeling a Person Mentally Ill." *Social Psychiatry* 6:29-33.

Berger, Joseph, Bernard P. Cohen, and Morris Zelditch, Jr. 1972. "Status Characteristics and Expectation States." *American Sociological Review* 37:241-55.

Berger, Joseph, M. Hamit Fisek, Robert Norman, and Morris Zelditch, Jr. 1977. *Status Characteristics and Social Interaction.* New York: Elsevier.

Bord, Richard. 1971. "Rejection of the Mentally Ill: Continuities and Further Developments." *Social Problems* 18:496-509.

Chin-Shong, Edwin. 1968. *Rejection of the Mentally Ill: A Comparison with the Findings of Ethnic Prejudice.* Ph.D. diss., Columbia University.

Clausen, John. 1981. "Stigma and Mental Disorder: Phenomena and Terminology." *Psychiatry* 44:287-96.

Cleary, Paul, and Ronald Kessler. 1982. "The Estimation and Interpretation of Modifier Effects." *Journal of Health and Social Behavior* 23:159-69.

Cockerham, William. 1981. *Sociology of Mental Disorder.* Englewood Cliffs, NJ: Prentice-Hall.

Cohen, Jacob. 1968 "Multiple Regression as a General Data-Analytic System." *Psychological Bulletin* 70:426-33.

Cohen, Jacob, and Elmer Struening. 1962. "Opinions about Mental Illness in the Personnel of Two Large Mental Hospitals." *Journal of Abnormal and Social Psychology* 5:349-60.

Cole, Steven. 1975. "The Growth of Scientific Knowledge: Theories of Deviance as a Case Study." Pp. 175-220 in *The Idea of Social Structure: Papers in Honor of Robert K. Merton,* edited by Lewis A. Coser. New York: Harcourt Brace Jovanovich.

Cook, Thomas, and Donald Campbell. 1979. *Quasi-Experimentation: Design and Analysis Issues.* Chicago: Rand McNally.

Crocetti, Guido, Herzl Spiro, and Irad Siassi. 1974. *Contemporary Attitudes towards Mental Illness.* Pittsburgh: University of Pittsburgh Press.

Cronbach, Lee, and Paul Meehl. 1955. "Construct Validity in Psychological Tests." *Psychological Bulletin* 52:281-302.

Cullen, Francis, and John Cullen. 1978. *Toward a Paradigm of Labeling Theory.* Monograph no. 58. Lincoln: University of Nebraska Press.

Cumming, John, and Elaine Cumming. 1965. "On the Stigma of Mental Illness." *Community Mental Health Journal* 1:135-43.

Davis, John. 1975. "Overview: Maintenance Therapy in Psychiatry. I. Schizophrenia." *American Journal of Psychiatry* 132:1237-45.

--------. 1976. "Overview: Maintenance Therapy in Psychiatry. II. Affective Disorders." *American Journal of Psychiatry* 133:1-13.

Ellsworth, Robert. 1965. "A Behavioral Study of Staff Attitudes toward Mental Illness." *Journal of Abnormal Psychology* 70:194-200.

Farina, Amerigo, Jon Allen, and Brigid Saul. 1968. "The Role of the Stigmatized Person in Effecting Social Relationships." *Journal of Personality* 36:169-82.

Farina, Amerigo, and Robert D. Felner. 1973. "Employment Interviewer Reactions to Former Mental Patients." *Journal of Abnormal Psychology* 82:268-72.

Farina, Amerigo, Robert Felner, and Louis Boudreau. 1973. "Reactions of Workers to Male and Female Mental Patient Job Applicants." *Journal of Consulting and Clinical Psychology* 41:363-72.

Farina, Amerigo, Donald Gliha, Louis Boudreau, John Allen, and Mark Sherman. 1971. "Mental Illness and the Impact of Believing Others Know About It. *Journal of Abnormal Psychology* 77:1-5.

Farina, Amerigo, and Henry Hagelauer. 1975. "Sex and Mental Illness: The Generosity of Females." *Journal of Consulting and Clinical Psychology* 43:122.

Farina, Amerigo, Pauline Murray, and Thomas Groh. 1978. "Sex and Worker Acceptance of a Former Mental Patient." *Journal of Consulting and Clinical Psychology* 46:887-91.

Foster, Glen, James Ysseldyke, and James Reese. 1975. "I Wouldn't Have Seen It If I Hadn't Believed It." *Exceptional Children* 41:469-73.

Frank, Jerome. 1973. *Persuasion and Healing.* Baltimore: The Johns Hopkins Press.

Goffman, Irving. 1963. *Stigma: Notes on the Management of Spoiled Identity.* Englewood Cliffs, NJ: Prentice-Hall.

Gove, Walter. 1970. "Societal Reaction as an Explanation of Mental Illness: An Evaluation." *American Sociological Review* 35:873-84.

--------. 1975. *The Labeling of Deviance: Evaluating a Perspective.* New York: Sage.

--------. 1980a. "Labeling and Mental Illness: A Critique." Pp. 53-109 in *The Labeling of Deviance: Evaluating a Perspective,* 2d ed. Edited by Walter Gove. Beverly Hills: Sage.

-------. 1980b. "Postscript to Labeling and Crime." Pp. 264-70 in *The Labeling of Deviance: Evaluating a Perspective,* 2d ed. Edited by Walter Gove. Beverly Hills: Sage.

-------. 1982. "The Current Status of the Labeling Theory of Mental Illness." Pp. 273-300 in *Deviance and Mental Illness,* edited by Walter Gove. Beverly Hills: Sage

Gove, Walter, and Terry Fain. 1973. "The Stigma of Mental Hospitalization: An Attempt to Evaluate Its Consequences." *Archives of General Psychiatry* 29:494-500.

Gruenberg, Ernest. 1967. "The Social Breakdown Syndrome - Some Origins." *American Journal of Psychiatry* 123:12-20.

Horwitz, Alan. 1982. *The Social Control of Mental Illness.* New York: Academic.

Huffine, Carol, and John Clausen. 1979. "Madness and Work: Short- and Long-Term Effects of Mental Illness on Occupational Careers." *Social Forces* 57:1049-62.

Katz, Irwin. 1981. *Stigma: A Social Psychological Analysis.* Hillsdale, NJ: Erlbaum.

Kirk, Stuart. 1974. "The Impact of Labeling on the Rejection of the Mentally Ill: An Experimental Study." *Journal of Health and Social Behavior* 15:108-17.

Klein, Donald, Rachel Gittelman, Frederic Quitkin, and Arthur Rifkin. 1980. "Side Effects of Antipsychotic Drugs and Their Treatment." Pp. 174-214 in *Diagnosis and Drug Treatement of Psychiatric Disorders: Adults and Children,* edited by Donald Klein, Rachel Gittelman, Frederic Quitkin, and Arthur Rifkin. Baltimore: Williams & Wilkins.

Klein, Donald, and Judith Rabkin. 1984. "Specificity and Strategy in Psychotherapy Research." Pp. 306-29 in *Psychotherapy Research: Where We Are and Where We Should Go,* edited by Robert Spitzer and Janet Williams. New York: Guilford.

Langer, Ellen, and Robert Abelson. 1974. "A Patient By Any Other Name ...: Clinician Group Difference in Labeling Bias." *Journal of Consulting and Clinical Psychology* 42:4-9.

Lehman, Stanley, Virginia Joy, Dolores Kreisman, and Samuel Simmens. 1976. "Responses to Viewing Symptomatic Behaviors and Labeling of Prior Mental Illness." *Journal of Community Psychology* 4:327-34.

Liebowitz, Michael. 1984. "The Efficacy of Antidepressants in Anxiety Disorders." In *Psychiatry Update,* Vol. 3, edited by Lester Grinspoon. Washington: American Psychiatric Association Press.

Link, Bruce. 1982. "Mental Patient Status, Work and Income: An Examination of the Effects of a Pyschiatric Label." *American Sociological Review* 47:202-15.

--------. 1985. "The Labelling Perspective and Its Critics: A Reformulation in the Area of Mental Disorder." Paper presented at the Eastern Sociological Association Meetings, Philadelphia, March 15.

Link, Bruce, and Francis Cullen. 1983. "Reconsidering the Social Rejection of Ex-Mental Patients: Levels of Attitudinal Response." *American Journal of Community Psychology* 11:261-73.

Loman, L. Anthony, and William E. Larkin. 1976. "Rejection of the Mentally Ill: An Experiment in Labeling." *Sociological Quarterly* 17:555-60.

Miller, Dorothy, and William Dawson. 1965. "Effects of Stigma on Re-employment of Ex-mental Patients." *Mental Hygiene* 49:281-87.

New York Times. 1981. (August 4): sec. 3, p.1.

Nuehring, Elane. 1979. "Stigma and State Hospital Patients." *American Journal of Orthopsychiatry* 49:626-33.

Orne, M.T. 1962. "On the Social Psychology of the Psychological Experiment: With Particular Reference to Demand Characteristics and Their Implications." *American Psychologist* 17:776-83.

Page, Monte. 1973. "On Detecting Demand Awareness by Post Experimental Questionnaire." *Journal of Socila Psychology* 91:305-23.

Page, Monte, and Lynn Kahle. 1976. "Demand Characteristics in the Satiation-Deprivation Effect of Attitude Conditioning." *Journal of Personality and Social Psychology* 33:553-62.

Page, Stewart. 1977. "Effects of the Mental Illness Label in Attempts to Obtain Accommodation." *Canadian Journal of Behavioral Science* 9:85-90.

Phillips, Derek. 1963. "Rejection: A Possible Consequence of Seeking Help for Mental Disorders." *American Sociological Review* 28:963-72.

--------. 1964. "Rejection of the Mentally Ill: The Influence of Behavior and Sex." *American Sociological Review* 29:679-87.

--------. 1967. "Identification of Mental Illness: Its Consequences for Rejection." *Community Mental Health Journal* 3:262-66.

Pollack, Stephen, Deborah Huntley, John Allen, and Steven Schwartz. 1976. "The Dimensions of

Stigma: The Social Situation of the Mentally Ill Person and the Male Homosexual." *Journal of Abnormal Psychology* 85:105-12.

Rabkin, Judith. 1974. "Public Attitudes about Mental Illness: A Review of the Literature." *Schizophrenia Bulletin* 10:9-33.

--------. 1975. "The Role of Attitudes toward Mental Illness in Evaluation of Mental Health Programs." Pp. 431-82 in *Handbook of Evaluation Research*, vol. 2. Edited by Marcia Guttentag and Elmer Struening. Beverly Hills, Calif.: Sage.

--------. 1980. "Determinants of Public Attitudes about Mental Illness: Summary of the Research Literature." Pp. 15-26 in *Attitudes Toward the Mentally Ill: Research Perspectives,* edited by Judith Rabkin, Lenore Gelb, and Joyce Lazar. Washington: DHHS Publication No. (ADM) 80-1031.

--------. 1984. "Community Attitudes and Local Psychiatric Facilities." Pp. 325-35 in *The Chronic Mental Patient: Five Years Later,* edited by John Talbott. New York: Grune and Stratton.

Rosen, Catherine, Claudia Cowan, and Richard Grandison. 1982. "The Stigma of Patienthood." Pp. 59-82 in *Psychiatric Patient Rights and Patient Advocacy,* edited by Bernard Bloom and Shirley Asher. New York: Human Sciences.

Rosenblatt, Aaron, and John Mayer. 1974. "Patients Who Return: A Consideration of Some Neglected Influences." *Journal of the Bronx State Hospital* 2:71-81.

Rosenfield, Sarah. 1982. "Sex Roles and Societal Reactions to Mental Illness: The Labeling of 'Deviant' Deviance." *Journal of Health and Social Behavior* 23:18-24.

--------. 1984. "Race Differences in Involuntary Hospitalization: Psychiatric vs. Labeling Perspectives." *Journal of Health and Social Behavior* 25:14-23.

Rushing, William. 1978. "Status Resources, Societal Reactions, and Type of Hospital Admission." *American Sociological Review* 43:521-33.

--------. 1979. "The Functional Importance of Sex Roles and Sex Related Behavior in Societal Reactions to Residual Deviants." *Journal of Health and Social Behavior* 20:208-17.

Scheff, Thomas. 1966. *Being Mentally Ill: A Sociological Theory*. Chicago: Aldine.

--------. 1974. "The Labeling Theory of Mental Illness." *American Sociological Review* 39:444-52.

Schroder, David, and Danuta Ehrlich. 1968. "Rejection by Mental Health Professionals: A Possible Consequence of Not Seeking Appropriate Help for Emotional Disorders." *Journal of Health and Social Behavior* 9:222-32.

Schwartz, Carol, Jerome Myers, and Boris Astrachan. 1974. "Psychiatric Labeling and the Rehabilitation of Mental Patients." *Archives of General Psychiatry* 329-34.

Segal, Steven. 1978. "Attitudes toward the Mentally Ill: A Review." *Social Work* 23:211-17.

Smith, Mary Lee, Gene Glass, and Thomas Miller. 1980. *The Benefits of Psychotherapy*. Baltimore: Johns Hopkins University Press.

Spiegel, Donald, and Jennifer Younger. 1972. "Life Outside the Hospital: A View from Patients and Relatives." *Mental Hygiene* 56:9-20.

Spiro, Herzl, Iradj Siassi, and Guido Crocetti. 1973. "Ability of the Public to Recognize Mental Illness: An Issue of Substance and An Issue of Meaning." *Social Psychiatry* 8:32-36.

Star, Shirley. 1955. *The Public's Ideas about Mental Illness*. Chicago: National Opinion Research Center (mimeographed).

Swanson, Robert M., and Stephen P. Spitzer. 1970. "Stigma and the Psychiatric Patient Career." *Journal of Health and Social Behavior* 11:44-51.

Thoits, Peggy. 1985. "Self-labeling Processes in Mental Illness. The Role of Emotional Deviance." *American Journal of Sociology* 91:221-49.

Townsend, J. Marshall. 1976. "Self Concept and the Institutionalization of Mental Patients: An Overview and Critique." *Journal of Health and Social Behavior* 17:263-71.

Tudor, William, Jeanette Tudor, and Walter Gove. 1977. "The Effect of Sex Role Differences on the Social Control of Mental Illness." *Journal of Health and Social Behavior* 18:98-112.

Weinstein, Raymond. 1983. "Labeling Theory and the Attitudes of Mental Patients: A Review". *Journal of Health and Social Behavior* 24:70-84.

Wing, John, and George Brown. 1970. *Institutionalism and Schizophrenia*. Cambridge: Cambridge University Press.

Notes

2. Thoits (1985) has recently developed a theory of self-labelling. Since most treatment seeking is vouluntary rather than imposed, such theorizing is necessary in order to formulate a more complete answer to questions about who gets labelled.

3. Although most of the studies that experimentally manipulate labelling but not behavior show significant mentall illness labelling effects, not all do (Pollack et al. 1976). The studies that rely on the respondents' subjective labelling presented Star vignettes to respondents, asked them whether the cases were mentally ill, and then assessed whether those who labelled teh cases were more rejecting than those who did not. These studies are excluded because in them, the labelling variable is not manipulated by the investigator, which dispualifies them as experimental or quasi-experimental studies. In these studies, Phillips (1967) reported negative effects of labelling, whereas Bentz and Edgerton (1971) and Spiro, Siassi, adn Crocetti (1973) found no significant labelling effect and a strong behavior effect.

4. A number of observational studies have supported the conclusion of these experimental and quasi-experimental studies. Hiffine and Clausen investigated the occupational careers of 36 male patients followed for over 20 years after an index mental hospitalization. They concluded that these "data provide strong evidence that, in and of itself, being labelled mentally ill does not determine the course of a man's career event though he may be confined for months in a public mental hospital. Those men whose symptoms abated have not suffered gross occupational setbacks" (Huffine and Clausen 1979, p. 1050). Similarly, basing their results on an examination of the determinants of social distancing responses among relatives of hospitalized patients, Schwartz et al. reported that "psychiatric treatment per se is of lesser importance in determining rejection of the mentally ill than the ex-patient's level of impaired mental status" (1974, p. 333).

5. For the most part, the literature we examined focused on patients' feelings of shame and expectations of rejection. Such feelings and beliefs are probably more common than reports of actual incidents of rejection would be (Clausen 1981). This descrepancy may be due to the fact that patients wisely hide their history of treatment or effectively avoid those who may reject them. The rejection may also be subtle, occurring through processes such as those suggested by the expectations state tradition (Berger, Cohen, and Zelditch 1972; Berger et al. 1977), so that it is difficult to articulate concrete incidents. Finally, it is possible that patients' fears are unfounded and that the public is really far more accepting than they believe it to be (see below for further evidence on this last initial explanation).

6. In most cases, Weinstein classified a study as "favorable" if the mean of the responses to a question or a scale was on the favorable side of the midpoint of the response options available to the respondents. "Unfavorable" studies were on the unfavorable side of the midpoint. For more detail see Weinstein (1983, pp. 76-78).

7. Most of the studies could be clearly classified into the two domains of felt stigma and views of hospitalization. Swanson and Spitzer's (1970) research is an exception. In this study, former patients were asked how much social distance they would maintain from a former patient. We excluded this study because it asked the patients whether they would reject, instead of whether they thought they would be rejected by others.

8. Weinstein (1983) used the first of the Cummings's studies to classify the article as favorable. The second study may have been excluded because it is impossible to determine from the Cumming and Cumming article whether more patients were above or below (the midpoint) on the 9-point scale.

9. The results of the Link (1985) study are, in general terms, consistent with the Weinsten (1983) review. As is true of about half of the studies in Weinstein's review, the Link study would be classified as an unfavorable study. Further, while the Link study shows that a majority believe they will be rejected, a large majority never *** believe they will not be.

10. It must be pointed out that some of the studies in table 1 were motivated by ideas other than the behavior vs. labelling issue. As a result, it would be inappropriate to fault them for not including the elaboration we advocate. The problem comes when these studies are interpreted as unqualified evidence that labels do not matter or matter very little.

11. We are grateful to an anonymous reviewer of an earlier version of this paper for having pointed out these potential problems.

12. After the experiment was administered, the student respondents were asked to answer a series of questions starting with general open-ended questions like, What did you think the purpose of this study was? Subsequent questions became more and more specific (thus, the term "funnel") until the study hypothesis was presented and respondents were asked to report whether they knew it. Each question was answered on a separate page, and the student respondents were told to answer the questions in order, turning each page over as they completed it. The students were watched by one of the authors and a research assistant to be sure that they followed instructions and did not return to questions they had already answered. This strict procedure helps the investigator understand the answers to the specific questions, in that the respondent should have shown his insight into the purpose of the study in the earlier open-ended questions. Using this technique, we found that most respondents (63%) reported nothing "out of place" or discrepant in the vignette. We also checked to see whether the minority (37%) who did report something out of place were clustered in one cell of the experiment or reported the same material as discrepant. Here we found no evidence that a particular cell was unusual since at least two individuals in each cell found something discrepant and in no cell did more than four individuals indicate that something was out of place, Furthermore, the open ended reports of precisely what was discrepant varied widely, suggesting that no one dominant factor is likely to have influenced responses in an undesigned way. With respect to guessing our hypothesis, we found that two of the 43 indicated that they knew with certainty that we were comparing a former mental patient with a nonpatient and that the acceptant, Jim Johnson, the former mental patient, would depend on how dangerous former patients are in general were perceived to be. Even with these two individuals, there was some question about whether they had really guessed the hypothesis, since this was not evident in the open-ended comments.

13. Since the scale of perceived dangerousness has not been widely used, a consideration of its validity is in order. As a first step, we believe that the items show considerable face validity. They tap components of the unpredictability of the mentally ill, the inability to trust a former patient, and the safety of children if former patients are present in the community. Also involved is the need to protect the community through the use of mental hospitals and to prohibit former patients' access to dangerous objects such as guns. Further evidence of validity comes from an independent sample that shows that the scale behaves in a reasonable fashion in relation to other variables such as a respondent's age and years of education (Link and Cullen 1983). In addition it was found that a variety of indicators of contact with the mentally ill, ranging from knowing someone with a mental disorder to having a friend who works in a mental health facility, were associated with lower levels of perceived dangerousness. Furthermore, the same questions about contact were asked in this study, and the same consistent pattern emerged. When a scale consistently behaves in a

predictable fashion, we claim some demonstration of "construct validity" (Cronbach and
***, 1955) and feel more confident we are measuring what we intend to measure.

14. As Cohen (1968) has demonstrated, this shift from analysis of variance to multiple
regression has no implications for statistical inference because both procedures involve the
general linear model. We present our initial results in analysis-of-variance terms to show
correspondence to past work and then shift to multiple regression to take advantage of the
flexibility of this system.

15. Appendix C. contains a correlatin matrix of the main variables in the analysis and the
cross-product terms used to test for interaction.

16. *** perceived dangerousness could potentially vary from a low of 0 to a high of 5.
Empirically, we found that respondents fully covered this potential range. Thus, the
examples of 0 and 5, which we have used to illulstrate the meaning of our results, represent
the range of values our respondents actually had on the perceived-dnagerousness scale.

17. Eight questionnaires were removed from the analysis either because there was missing
data on a key variable ($N = 4$) or because the questionnaires were obviously not completed
in a serious vein ($N = 4$). Of the 140 remaining respondents, 57.9% were female. The
ages ranged from 17 to 28, with a mean of 19.6. In terms of socioeconomic origins the
student sample showed considerable variability, with 18.6% coming from homes where the
father had not completed high school and 27.9% coming from homes where the father had
a college education or more. The rest (53.5%) came from homes where the father had
completed high school or had some college.

18. As Katz (1981) has argued, the strength of an extra break is likely to vary according to
situational factors. In our study, for example, it costs respondents very little to give the
hypothetical Jim Johnson a break when he is described as a former patient. If there were
immediate consequences to one's responses, such as actual association with the labelled
person, the extra break might be attenuated. That is, in the absence of costs, respondents
may report something closer to what they feel to be the ideal response, which *** and
Cullen (1983) have shown, is greater acceptance.

19. This is not to say that treatment interventions are always effective or that they have no
harmful side effects. Serious side effects such as tardive dyskinesia (which involved, e.g.,
uncontrolled grimacing) can result from the overuse of phenothiazines, for example (Klein
et al. 1980).

20. Response format was 0 = defintely willing, 1 = probably willing, 2 = probably
unwilling, 3 = definitely unwilling.

21. Response format 0 = strongly agree, 1 = agree, 2 = not sure but probably agree, 3 =
not sure but probably disagree, 4 = disagree, 5 = strongly disagree.

Disability as the Basis for a Social Movement: Advocacy and the Politics of Definition

RICHARD K. SCOTCH

Many people with disabilities do not identify themselves as disabled or choose not to be part of a politically active community of disabled persons. This paper discusses both the barriers to the formation of a social movement of disabled people and the ways in which these barriers have been overcome. The role of public policy in the evolution of this movement is discussed, as are the current status and prospects of the disability rights movement.

Although 1 in 11 Americans of working age identify themselves as having a disability (McNeil, 1983), for most of them such self-identification does not translate into group consciousness or political action. Disabled individuals face many barriers to full participation in American society, but until recently there has not been a significant social movement of disabled people dedicated to removal of those barriers. Disabled individuals in noninstitutional settings are geographically and socially dispersed, and this fact constitutes a barrier to collective political action.

Nevertheless, in the past quarter century, a small but growing number of disabled people have formed a community, both through informal interaction and the establishment of formal organizations. Following in the wake of the racial, gender, and other civil rights movements of the 1960s, increasing numbers of disabled people embraced activism and political action, and demanded integration into the mainstream of American society. Groups first formed among individuals with similar disabling conditions, such as blind people and deaf people, and among disabled war veterans. By the 1970s, organizations had been formed that crossed disability lines and encompass individuals with a wide range of physical and mental impairments.

This paper discusses the barriers disabled people face in forming a social movement and how such barriers have been overcome. In addition, the relationship between the disability rights movement and public policies of the past two decades is explored, together with the current status and prospects of the disability rights movement.

This paper builds on research on the growth of the disability rights movement since the 1960s, and the relationship between that developing movement and the passage and implementation of federal civil rights legislation affecting disabled people (Scotch, 1984). Drawing on archival materials and a series of interviews with advocates and public officials, this research traced organizational histories and the development of linkages among movement organizations and between such groups and government agencies. While this previous work focused on a particular statute, Section 504 of the Rehabilitation Act, the current paper concerns the more general topic of the formation and mobilization of the disability rights movement.

Barriers to Organization

As the study of social movements and collective behavior indicates, exclusion and discriminatory treatment alone do not inherently generate collective identity or collective political action. For the estimated 36 million Americans with disabilities (Bowe, 1980), the creation of an effective social movement may be even more problematic than for other excluded groups. With the exception of a few organizations based in particular geograph-

An earlier version of this paper was presented at the meeting of the Society for the Study of Chronic Illness, Impairment, and Disability in Fort Worth, Texas in April 1985. The author is grateful to Adrienne Asch and Michelle Fine for their comments on earlier drafts.

Correspondence regarding this paper should be addressed to Richard K. Scotch, School of Social Sciences, The University of Texas at Dallas, Box 830688, Richardson, TX 75083-0688.

Reprinted from: *Journal of Social Issues*, Vol. 44, No. 1, 1988, pp. 159-172, with permission.

ical locations or on particular physical impairments, people with disabilities do not constitute a group that acts politically "for itself." Nondisabled excluded groups such as racial and ethnic minorities may share geographical communities, workplaces, or religious and other voluntary associations. Many groups develop their own subcultures based on their collective history or social position. For the most part, this has not been true for disabled people.

The social and political isolation of the vast majority of the disabled population is reinforced by a number of factors. Disability is concentrated among the least powerful members of American society——those with low incomes, low education, and low work-force participation (Asch, 1984a). Individuals with physical impairments may face major barriers to obtaining education and entering the work force; furthermore, there are many risk factors associated with working-class and lower-class life in the United States that may contribute to the onset of disability.

While those lacking economic and political resources are more likely to be disabled, disability is nonetheless spread across the various social classes and status groups in our society. If a disabled person's impairment does not result in institutionalization, that person may spend nearly all of his or her time in the company of nondisabled individuals. Parents, neighborhood friends, school classmates, fellow employees——most of the people with whom a disabled person associates are likely to be nondisabled. Even where circumstances lead to interaction with other individuals with disabilities, the physical or mental impairments involved may be so disparate as to discourage mutual recognition of a shared social status. Thus, disability is an individualized experience for most people.

Of course, there are exceptions. People with disabilities stemming from a single cause may already have a great deal in common, particularly if they already share occupational or other ties, as in the case of disabled war veterans or miners with black lung disease. In cases such as these, perceptions of relatedness may lead to joint activities ranging from mutual support to political action. Even so, the medicalization of these

disabilities has often forced individuals to give up control over their lives and to experience undertones of moral stigma, which make political identification and action problematic (Zola, 1983).

Another exception is the shared subculture that may develop among disabled residents of institutions. Individuals being treated in long-term-care facilities may construct a patient culture as a means of coping with common impairments or in response to the indignities of life in a total institution (Goffman, 1961a). However, only in rare instances have such bonds led to activism upon departure from institutional confines. (One notable exception is the case of association of ex-mental patients——Anspach, 1979.)

In most circumstances, it may be more accurate to characterize people with disabilities as members of a social category rather than as an identifiable social or political group (Goffman, 1963). Disabled people not only lack the common demographic conditions to foster group awareness and activism, but the social status of being disabled can create serious disincentives for many to identify themselves as disabled and act collectively on that basis. To be perceived as disabled is typically to be seen as helpless and incompetent, and many individuals with physical impairments seek to disassociate themselves from disability, exercising what Goffman (1961b) calls "role distance." Such disassociation may or may not be successful, since disabling images are reinforced by the proliferation of architectural barriers, by providers of services to disabled individuals (Gartner, 1984), and by the very language used to characterize disability (Longmore, 1985). In either case, however, the unattractiveness of the role of disabled persons can serve to discourage both self-identifications as a member of an excluded group and the likelihood of political action flowing from that identification.

This lack of disability consciousness has been noted by Hahn, who wrote, "Persons with disabilities often are understandably reluctant to focus on that aspect of their identity that is most negatively stigmatized by the rest of society and to mobilize politically around it" (1985, p. 310).

Boyte (1984), in discussing research on blind men and women, noted,

> Escape out of the ghetto created by pervasive social expectations and assigned roles has almost always meant individual attempts to deny or render irrelevant one's disability——not to challenge the expectations themselves. . . . Thus the story of how a movement of self-assertion among the disabled emerged in the 1970s and continues today involves an exploration into changing self-perceptions as well as dominant social attitudes. (p. 116)

Interaction among disabled people may reflect and even exaggerate the stigmatization of disability practiced by the rest of society. In such instances, disabled individuals can deliberately distance themselves from each other or make invidious distinctions between good and bad impairments, rather than seek to develop social ties on the basis of common experiences and similar social positions.

The stigmatization of disabled persons is reinforced and even created by the attitudes of providers of rehabilitation services (Krause, 1976). Limitations and dependency are attributed to disability and the disabled person is encouraged to accept these as part of the rehabilitation process (Anspach, 1979; Scott, 1969;). By promoting the image of disabled people as dependent and in need of professional help, medical and rehabilitation professionals retain control over program beneficiaries at the cost of severely constraining the disabled person (Zola, 1983). Those who seek to avoid such constraint may choose to present themselves and to conceive of themselves as nondisabled.

Even to accept one's disability while rejecting ascriptions of dependency is in itself no guarantee of participation in collective political activity. Those people who are most severely impaired, and thus perhaps most likely to identify themselves as disabled, may face the greatest handicaps to effective political action.

Perhaps more importantly, the rejection of prejudicial stereotypes can often be an act of individual self-assertion against personal troubles, rather than an attempt to correct public problems

(Mills, 1959). In a society that celebrates the individual (Bellah, Madsen, Sullivan, Swidler, & Tipton, 1985), it is all too natural to seek solutions to our problems as individuals rather than as members of an excluded class. Those individuals best able to reject the disabled role may refuse to identify themselves as disabled, thus avoiding political involvement as a disabled person. On the other hand, those individuals who accept the role are at risk of accepting its handicapping connotations of dependency and thus also avoiding political involvement.

Who, then, is left as potential organizers and participants in a social movement of disabled people? Those who accept an identity as disabled while denying the associations of incapacity that our society attempts to impose. In order to do this, it may be necessary to conceive of a world in which physical impairment need not be disabling and in which prejudicial exclusion is proscribed.

However, "disability" as a unifying concept that includes people with a wide range of physical and mental impairments is by no means an obvious category. Blind people, people with orthopedic impairments, and people with epilepsy may not inherently see themselves or be seen by others as occupying common ground. Even greater divisions may exist between individuals with physical impairments and those with mental disabilities. Thus, another prerequisite for collective action may be the social construction and promulgation of an inclusive definition of disability.

Anspach (1979) has termed the efforts by disability rights activists to redefine disability "identity politics," an attempt to create a new public perception of disabled people as independent. In such politics, she writes, "political goals and strategies often become a vehicle for the symbolic manipulation of persons and the public presentation of self" (p. 766). Anspach describes identity politics as "a sort of phenomenological warfare, a struggle over the social meanings attached to attributes" (p. 773). However, while redefining disability may be an important prerequisite for the emergence of a social movement of disabled persons, redefinition has not been the only aim of that movement. Disability rights activists have also sought a number of policy goals, from changes in admissions and hiring practices to the literally concrete changes involved in increased architectural accessibility. Nevertheless, in order for an active and broadly based social movement of disabled people to come about, a redefinition of disability was required——one that treated disability as a label for a group of people who had the potential for political action and who were unfairly excluded from mainstream social institutions on the basis of their physical or mental impairments. The next section of this paper briefly reviews the history of political organizations among disabled people and discusses how disability rights activists attempted to promote new definitions of disability through political action.

Growth of the Social Movement of Disabled People

Some of the earliest formal associations of disabled people in the United States were organized between the two world wars (Lenihan, 1976-77). These included the Disabled American Veterans (DAV) and the National Federation of the Blind (NFB). Each stressed the needs of its own constituency rather than more universal disability issues. While the DAV focused essentially on expanding government benefits for disabled veterans, the NFB challenged the paternalistic practices of rehabilitation agencies and was often a militant supporter of equal rights for blind people. The NFB promoted some of the earliest civil rights laws guaranteeing access regardless of disability, the white cane and guide dog laws. It is not surprising that blind people, because their disability allows a relatively high degree of participation in the mainstream of everyday life, were particularly active in claiming full participation as their due.

Other organizations of disabled persons were established in the 20 years following World War II, including the Paralyzed Veterans of America, the National Association of the Deaf, and the American Council of the Blind. These groups had varying degrees of political involvement, but none were oriented toward the general issue of civil rights for all disabled people (Asch, 1984c).

For the most part, each sought to advance the position of its particular constituency group.

This situation changed dramatically in the late 1960s. At that time, important changes were affecting those who identified themselves as disabled. Medical technology was extending the lives of those with the variety of medical problems or injuries who previously would not have survived, and thus the number of active disabled adults increased. Medical and rehabilitative advances were giving those who in earlier times would have been totally incapacitated the potential to function in society——for instance, many who had contracted polio in the final epidemics of the 1950s. For growing numbers of disabled people, physical impairment was becoming less handicapping than the barriers of stereotyped attitudes and architectural constraints.

Another development was the increase in the number of people who remained socially active despite disabling injuries in childhood, adolescence, and young adulthood. Most individuals who experienced disability as the result of polio, teenage automobile or diving accidents, or the Vietnam War had clear memories of themselves as nondisabled, and many retained expectations of full economic and social participation. They had not incorporated a self-image of dependency and sought to live as normal young adults, which was increasingly technologically possible.

Even for children whose disabilities came at birth and who grew up in the 1950s and 1960s, individual potential was stressed by the Spock-influenced middle-class parents of that affluent era, who promoted self-confidence and achievement in their children. This "new generation" of disabled people was encouraged to think of themselves as capable of participation. As Asch has written, "many activists, then, are not people who were kept out of the mainstream as children; they had been in the mainstream and had never questioned their right to be there. So, when others questioned it, they were ready with armor and anger to fight to preserve their sense of themselves that the adult world was trying to shatter" (1984b, p. 551).

These aspirations of participation were promoted by the politics of the times. In the communities and colleges there were many other groups seeking greater participation in social institutions, and more autonomy and control in their lives. Demands for full access by disabled people occurred in the wake of the widespread and highly visible social conflicts of the 1960s: the struggle for civil rights by black people and other racial minorities, the antiwar and student movements, and a revitalized feminist movement. A number of disabled people who had been active participants in these movements came to see their disability in the same political sense as blacks viewed their race or women their gender.

Along with this new consciousness came an appreciation of how change strategies used by other movements could be adopted: While models of change-oriented advocacy did not guarantee success, they did suggest a method for stirring up latent support among a constituency and among the general public, and for channeling that support toward influencing governmental and institutional decision makers. The potential of integration into the societal mainstream motivated disabled people to form new organizations included individuals with a variety of disabilities——e.g., the Centers for Independent Living organized in Berkeley and a number of other communities, and Disabled in Action in several East Coast cities.

The growing potential for political activism, however, was not sufficient to ensure the growth of a broadly based and effective social movement. By the early 1970s, many grass-roots groups had been formed, but there had been little or no attempt made by these local organizations to join in influencing public policy. Contacts among the various organizations had begun, however, through the networking opportunities provided by the annual meetings of the President's Committee on the Employment of the Handicapped (PCEH). PCEH had been founded after World War II in order to promote the employment of disabled veterans. While PCEH was, for the most part, dominated by service providers and traditional emphases on education, rehabilitation, and incrementalist approaches to change, it did sponsor annual meetings that attracted people concerned with disability issues from around the country. These meetings became a forum for communication among the

younger, more militant disability rights activists. Several remained in contact between meetings, and this evolving network helped organize demonstrations against President Nixon's vetoes of the Rehabilitation Act in 1972 and 1973. The demonstrations, in turn, helped strengthen personal and organizational ties among disabled activists.

This loose network evolved into a formal organization at the 1974 PCEH meeting. Alternative workshop sessions were held in the conference hotel lobby, bringing together about 150 people to discuss discrimination issues not included in the formal program. This group became the first national coalition of disability activists when it organized itself as the American Coalition of Citizens with Disabilities (ACCD), linking several local and single-disability organizations while retaining the autonomy of each constituent organization.

A steering committee was formed, and ACCD held its first formal meetings at the 1975 PCEH conference. Bylaws were adopted, a board of directors chosen, offices opened in New York and Washington, and in 1976 a grant was obtained from the federal Rehabilitation Services Administration to permit the hiring of staff. ACCD was to become a major coordinating network of disability rights groups through the 1970s, and a major advocate for incorporating civil rights guarantees for disabled people into federal laws and regulations.

ACCD was not the only cross-disability organization to develop in the mid-1970s. One of its major constituent groups, Disabled in Action, developed affiliates in a number of states, while in many localities and states, coalitions of existing groups were organized. Several non-membership organizations that claimed national constituencies were formed as well, including the National Center for Law and the Handicapped in South Bend, Indiana, and the Disability Rights Center in Washington, D.C., one of the Ralph Nader advocacy centers. Some advocacy groups not exclusively oriented toward disability issues, such as the Children's Defense Fund, became heavily involved in disability advocacy efforts. Furthermore, a number of established single-disability organizations built up their advocacy components, including the American Council of the Blind, the National Association of the Deaf, and the Paralyzed Veterans of America.

Increasingly, the attention of the evolving disability rights movement became focused on events in Washington, D.C., as the federal government considered and enacted policies prohibiting discrimination on the basis of disability in a number of institutional spheres. A community had grown up among the Washington-based advocates for disability rights, who met regularly to compare notes, develop strategies, and divide up the various lobbying tasks. Positions on issues were debated and agreements were reached on public stances. Although frequently consensus was not obtained, a viable movement had been constructed. Changes in public policy by the federal government had been critical elements in the growth of this movement.

The Role of the State in Redefining Disability

The above discussion of barriers to political activism by disabled people suggested that a prerequisite to such activism was a redefinition of disabilities as impairments that are limiting only to the extent that constraints are imposed by the physical and social environment. The activists who created the various disability rights organizations redefined disability in this way and sought to have this redefinition institutionalized and accepted in public policy and by the general public.

However, the political and financial resources of most of the disability rights organizations were extremely limited. A major proportion of their budgets in the late 1970s was provided by the federal government in the form of grants and contracts, and substantial amounts of this federal funding were used for newly initiated political activity. (Several organizations were major exceptions, such as the NFB.) The political impact of many disability rights organizations in the late 1970s was extremely dependent on the support of agencies of the federal government.

The contribution of the federal government to the growth of the disability rights movement, however, extended far beyond financial support.

The social movement of disabled people became better organized and more broadly based as the result of federal civil rights activities. Contracts for training and technical assistance to local groups were received by a wide range of disability organizations. Disability rights leaders were often sought out by federal policy makers, thus making lobbying even easier to pursue. Activists were routinely asked to review draft policies and to testify at congressional hearings. These contacts served the further function of reinforcing the visibility of disability rights activists and of legitimating their leadership role, both within the disability community and outside it.

The consultations and meetings organized by federal officials seeking policy input had another important impact on the disability rights movement by fostering a network among locally based activists around the country. This network was also furthered by a number of federal agencies that created advisory committees on disability rights issues, as well as by the annual PCEH conferences.

More important still, the government contributed to the redefinition of disability. Through such legislation as Section 504 of the Rehabilitation Act of 1973 and the Education for All Handicapped Children Act of 1975 (P.L. 94-142), federal policy makers established disabled people as a class to be protected from discrimination by federal law, and made it illegal to exclude them from publicly supported programs and activities. The programmatic effects of these statutes were far-reaching: They dramatically increased the accessibility of public education, employment, government services, and public facilities to disabled people. Of equal or greater importance, however, were the definitions included in the new laws, which focused on a broad group of people in a way that aided the formation of a social movement.

There are two types of statutory definitions of disability, both extremely broad. The first, employed in P.L. 94-142, was categorical. Section 121a.5 of the law defined handicapped children as those evaluated as being mentally retarded, hard of hearing, deaf, speech impaired, visually handicapped, seriously emotionally disturbed, orthopedically impaired, other health impaired, deaf-blind, multihandicapped, or as having specific learning disabilities. P.L. 94-142 guaranteed these children a free and appropriate public education and related services in the least restrictive possible environment. Schools were mandated to provide individually appropriate services to children defined as handicapped, but procedurally all disabled children were accorded the same rights.

The second type of statutory definition was more functional in nature. Section 504, for example, defined a handicapped individual as any person who has a physical or mental impairment that substantially limits one or more major life activities, has a record of such an impairment, or is regarded as having such an impairment. Disabled people falling within this broad group were protected from discrimination in all federally supported programs and activities.

The centrality of government-sponsored definitions is emphasized by Hahn and Longmore (no date), who state that "the definition of disability is essentially determined by public policy. In other words, disability is whatever laws and implementing regulations say it is" (p. 5). They point out that government definitions of disability have historically been influenced by rehabilitation and medical professionals. However, in the 1970s, federal definitions of disability were specified with the assistance of disability rights advocates, and in several cases they were actually written by representatives of movement organizations (see Scotch, 1984).

Conventional interest-group explanations of policy changes characterize advocacy groups as shaping the development and implementation of public policies. In the case of disability rights legislation in the 1970s, this process was largely reversed. Advocates for the disability rights movement did not apply political pressure that resulted in the passage of these laws. Rather, the adoption and implementation of the laws contributed to the growth of national advocacy organizations representing disabled people and reinforced their involvement with civil rights issues. Civil-rights-oriented statutes such as Section 504 and P.L. 94-142 became focal points for organizing among disabled people and provided a good opportunity for establishing policy-oriented coalitions of the new generation of grass-roots disability organizations.

The emphasis in this paper on the role of the state in providing resources and creating networks is consistent with the evolving literature on resource mobilization in social movements (Freeman, 1982; McCarthy & Zald, 1977). The importance of network linkages and resource availability, however, has sometimes been stressed to the exclusion of any emphasis on the role of ideas and symbolic categories in framing issues——e.g., in attempts to argue for structural over social-psychological modes of analysis. As Snow, Rochford, Worden, & Benford (1986) have recently pointed out, however, social-psychological and resource-mobilization models are not mutually exclusive. The disability rights movement is one in which the way an issue was framed had serious effects on both movement participation and the ability of the movement to influence public policies (as was also the case with the problem of drunk driving——Gusfield, 1981).

Ensuring access to public buildings or public services may be viewed as a social welfare benefit or a civil right. The former connotes dependency by the disabled person and largess on the part of society. It suggests that we must approve of disabled people, their attitudes and behavior, in order to help them, and that they must earn our approval by conforming to our expectations, however handicapping those expectations may be. Within this conception, helping disabled people is analogous to helping single mothers with dependent children——a qualified and rather grudging form of assistance. Further, providing access as a welfare benefit invites the rationing of accessibility, for welfare is typically given and withdrawn based on the limits of generosity of the giver rather than according to the needs of the recipient.

Alternatively, when access to societal institutions is defined as a right, it becomes virtually unconditional. Removing architectural barriers to public buildings becomes analogous to abolishing the poll tax, a necessary guarantee of equity in our society. Cost, inconvenience, or disapproval of the deprived group's behavior become far less relevant to whether their lack of access should be remedied.

Of course definitions and perceptions are not independent of social structure and political power——the efficacy of definitions typically depends on structural factors, not the least of which is the power held by their proponents. Nevertheless, as the tradition of scholarship dating back to Max Weber has demonstrated, ideas can influence social structure, just as social structures can generate ideas.

The Politics of Disability in the 1980s

While disability has been less visible as a public issue in the 1980s, the growth of grass-roots organizations has continued around the country. The establishment of independent living programs, access to mass transit systems, architectural accessibility, and other civil-rights-oriented issues have been passed, along with attempts to maintain a number of benefit programs in the face of federal cutbacks. One particularly visible issue has been public transportation, for the Reagan administration has substantially weakened federal requirements for accessibility, thus leading to many local debates over what services should be provided by financially besieged transit operators. While national organizations such as the Denver-based ADAPT have been more active in this arena, much of the impetus for activism has been at the local level. However, conflict has continued between proponents of total access to transit systems and those supporting paratransit and other special services.

Nationally, organizations such as the Disability Rights Education and Defense Fund and ACCD have continued to lobby Congress and federal agencies. However, many observers of the disability rights movement have perceived a decline in its effectiveness and national influence. The Reagan administration has removed a number of advocacy-oriented individuals with ties to established movement organizations from administrative and advisory positions in federal agencies. Lowered expectations have dimmed the hopefulness of the late 1970s about promoting vigorous enforcement of civil rights protections such as Section 504 and enacting new legislation prohibiting discrimination in private-sector employment. Optimism about further advances has been replaced by concerns about court decisions and administrative rulings that circumscribe the effectiveness of existing laws. A successful effort was made to prevent weakening P.L. 94-142, yet many local school districts have been accused of less than full compliance with the provisions of that statute. Clearly, the federal government has retreated from its activist role in promoting the rights of disabled persons, and the growth of organizations seeking to support and extend those rights.

While during the 1970s disability advocates were often in a collaborative relationship with many federal officials, the relationship between disability rights organizations and the federal government is now much more adversarial in nature. Similar tensions have been experienced by other advocates involved with issues ranging from environmental protection to occupational safety to human services. Thus, the crucial change has been in the political environment rather than in the disability rights movement itself.

On the positive side, although the disability rights movement may have lost some of its political efficacy, its relationships with other "progressive" movements may have been enhanced. Common opposition to Reagan administration policies may have helped to institutionalize the participation of disability rights activists in the broad coalition of Washington liberal-left advocacy groups. Similar partnerships have formed in a number of states and local communities, as social program budgets have experienced severe fiscal constraints in the wake of federal reductions.

However, quite a different alliance has been formed around one important issue. Right-to-life advocates within and outside the Reagan administration have joined disability rights organizations in seeking federal intervention in cases where medical treatment had been withheld from newborn infants with physical disabilities, i.e., the "Baby Doe" cases. Section 504 has been cited as the legal basis for intervention in these cases, since it prohibits discrimination on the basis of disability in all federally supported programs, including hospitals. On the other side of these cases, feminist groups, civil libertarians, and health care providers have opposed government intervention. The Supreme Court has ruled that the federal government may not intervene in such cases, but there is likely to be continuing public debate over the appropriateness of medical treatment for severely disabled newborn. Advances in medical technology are likely to generate other such debates involving the quality of life for disabled persons, the personal choice of parents and other family members, and the ability of health care professionals to make informed decisions about sustaining life.

The disability rights movement will have a great deal to say on ethical and policy issues involving abortion, care for disabled newborns, the right to treatment, and the right to refuse treatment (e.g., Asch, 1986). It remains unclear to what extent spokesmen for the disabled will be accepted as legitimate contributors in these debates by policy makers, as experts rather than as unfortunate and axe-grinding victims. Having reconstructed their own definition of self, disability rights activists must continue to influence the definitions of others, through reasoned debate and through political activity. The ability of movement leaders and grass-roots disabled advocates to be full participants will depend on both their organizing ability and their acumen as issue entrepreneurs.

Equally unclear, due to its current political unpopularity, is the future of further extensions of government-guaranteed rights in the United States. Diminished funding for programs that promote independence for disabled people, such as attendant care, independent living centers, and facility modification to remove architectural barriers, may inhibit the political participation of many people with disabilities and thus limit their ability to mobilize politically. Political conservatism within government and the general public may mean that the catalytic role of public officials in promoting the growth of the disability rights movement is over, at least for the present. Also unclear is the long-term impact of the policy gains of the 1970s. The large-scale entry of disabled Americans into schools, jobs, and public life may have taken on a momentum of its own, or it may merely have reached a plateau of tokenism.

Progress should continue, even in the absence of government support, if disability rights groups can raise the consciousness of the vast majority of disabled people who have not been involved politically and who may not share the political definition of disability promoted by the movement. However, redefinition of disability can no longer be expected to flow from court rulings and government policies. Community organizing will be essential——to broaden participation in the movement, to build acceptance of a positive image of people with disabilities, and to sustain and expand the organizational infrastructure created by the movement in the 1970s. Organization at the community level can create the resources necessary for the movement to be effective and continue the extension of conceptions of disability that promote social and political participation.

Clearly, the emergence of a social movement of disabled people is no guarantee of major institutional changes. If the movement continues to grow at the local level, however, its power may be expected to accumulate. The more that people with disabilities become integrated into mainstream social institutions, the more their presence may lead to further institutional changes. And to the extent that more political definitions of disability become widespread, the disability rights movement may be expected to continue to play an active role in American political social life.

References

Anspach, R.R. (1979). From stigma to identity politics: Political activism among the physically disabled and former mental patients. *Social Science and Medicine 13A*, 765-773.

Asch, A. (1984a). The experience of disability. *American Psychologist, 39*, 529-536.

Asch, A. (1984b). Personal reflections. *American Psychologist, 39*, 551-552.

Asch, A. (1984c). Understanding and working with disability rights groups. In H. McCarthy (Ed.). *Complete guide to employing persons with disabilities* (pp. 170-194.). Albertson, NY: National

Center on Employment of the Handicapped, Human Resources Center.

Asch, A. (1986). Real moral dilemmas. *Christianity and Crisis, 46*, 237-240.

Bellah, R.N., Madsen, R., Sullivan, W.M., Swidler, A., & Tipton, S.M. (1985) *Habits of the heart*. Berkeley: University of California Press.

Bowe, F. (1980). *Rehabilitating America*. New York: Harper & Row.

Boyle, H.C. (1984). *Community is possible: Repairing America's roots*. New York: Harper & Row.

Elder, C.D., & Cobb, R.W. (1983). *The political uses of symbols*. New York: Longman.

Freeman, J. (Ed.) (1982) *Social movements of the sixties and seventies*. New York: Longman.

Gartner, A. (1984, August). Disabling images. *The Disability Rag*. pp. 3-4.

Goffman, E. (1961a). *Asylums*. Garden City, NY: Anchor Books.

Goffman, E. (1961b). *Encounters*. Indianapolis, IN: Bobbs-Merrill.

Goffman, E. (1963). *Stigma*. Englewood Cliffs, NJ: Prentice-Hall.

Gusfield, J.R. (1981). *The culture of public problems: Drinking-driving and the symbolic order*. Chicago: University of Chicago Press.

Hahn, H. (1985). Introduction: Disability policy and the problem of discrimination. *American Behavioral Scientist, 28*, 293-318.

Hahn, H., & Longmore, P.K. (no date). *The emergence of the study of disability and society at the University of Southern California*. Unpublished paper, University of Southern California.

Krause, E.A. (1976). The political sociology of rehabilitation. In G.L. Albrecht (Ed.), *The sociology of physical disability and rehabilitation* (pp. 201-221). Pittsburgh, PA: University of Pittsburgh Press.

Lenihan, J. (1976-77). Disabled Americans: A history. *Performance, 27* (5-7), 1-72.

Longmore, P.K. (1985). A note on language and the social identity of disabled people. *American Behavioral Scientist, 28*, 419-423.

McCarthy, J.D., & Zald, M.N. (1977). Resource mobilization and social movements: A partial theory. *American Journal of Sociology, 82*, 1212-1241.

McNeil, J.M. (1983). *Labor force and other characteristics of persons with a work disability: 1982* (Series P-23, No. 127). Washington, D.C.: U.S. Bureau of the Census.

Mills, C.W. (1959). *The sociological imagination*. New York: Oxford University Press.

Scotch, R.K. (1984). *From good will to civil rights*. Philadelphia, PA: Temple University Press.

Scott, R.A. (1969). *The making of blind men*. New York: Russell Sage Foundation.

Snow, D.A., Rochford, E.B., Worden, S.K., & Benford, R.B. (1986). Frame alignment processes, micromobilization, and movement participation. *American Sociological Review, 51*, 464-481.

Zola, I.K. (1983). Medicine as an institution of social control. In I.K. Zola (Ed.), *Socio-medical inquiries* (pp.247-268). Philadelphia, PA: Temple University Press.

The Movement For Independent Living: An Evaluation and Critique

GARETH H. WILLIAMS

Introduction

In two quite recent reports [1,2] Gerben De Jong has attempted to elucidate and explain the manifold nature of the movement for independent living (ILM) in the United States. This movement is one of the most recent and vocal manifestations of a growing radicalism amongst people with disabilities and the sentiments it represents, although not peculiar to American society [3], are nonetheless peculiarly symbolic of that society.

The central tenet of De Jong's thesis taken as a whole is that environmental factors should be seen as at least as important as disability-related factors in determining the degree to which a person with given disabilities is able to live independently. In arguing thus, De Jong claims to be establishing a new 'paradigm' (in Thomas Kuhn's sense [4]) in contradistinction to traditional individualistic rehabilitation research, where the importance of environmental barriers and social settings has tended to be overlooked or played down.

Now, although I welcome these publications and support many of the author's stated aims, I sense some ambiguity in his approach: an ambiguity deriving from ideological assumptions which, in the final analysis, renders unconvincing and inconclusive many of the empirical findings. I would contend that in spite of the explicit orientation to issues of environmental constraint and accessibility, the underlying image of society to which De Jong claims attachment and which informs his definition and specification of concepts for research, leads him to a position which is as reductionist as much of the work in rehabilitation of which he is critical. If this is so, it casts doubt on De Jong's suggestion that independent living provides a new paradigm for disability research and policy.

Independent Living: History and Political Economy

The 1979 report [1] provides a sketch of what the movement is about in terms of its origins, influences and projected destinations. This entails chapters devoted to a description of the movement's constituency: its indigenous and professional origins and the legislative background: the historical and ideological relationship to other social movements and an analysis of their shared properties: an outline of the theory of economy and society upon which the movement's advocates rest their case: the way in which their ideas have found expression (or not) in disability services; an examination of the 'paradigmatic' status of independent living; and finally, a glance towards what the future may hold.

The movement originated in the campus culture of American universities in the 1970s and in the contemporaneous efforts of enlightened rehabilitation professionals to influence the formulation of national legislation. It is from these origins that the movement's 'core constituency' of young disabled has developed. The bias towards the young within the movement is, in part, a function of its campus origins, but it is also due to the nature of the major disabling conditions represented - spinal cord injury, muscular dystrophy, cerebral palsy, multiple sclerosis and post-polio disablement. De Jong notes however that, as is generally the case with broad social movements, independent living advocacy touches upon and engages the interests of other groups who do not form part of the core constituency. On this reading, ILM may be characterized as a vanguard of reform, asserting ideals and values deemed significant also for the silent majority of people whose disabilities have started later in life.

Reprinted from: *Soc. Sci. Med.* Vol. 17, No. 15. pp.1003-1010, with permission. Printed in Great Britain, Perganson Press Ltd.

The political agitation of the movement has, from its inception, been directed towards enhancing disabled persons' participation in the world whether or not that participation included a vocational component. The first independent living centres in Berkeley and Boston provided a wide range of related services such as peer counselling, transportation, attended care referral and so on. These local initiatives burgeoned and then linked with allied organizations such as the American Coalition of Citizens with Disabilities in helping to co-ordinate coast-to-coast demonstrations.

The outcome of all this activity, and a major political triumph for the movement, was the Rehabilitation Act of 1973 which, following a struggle, included a clause to provide independent living services for those people for whom vocational training was not a realistic option. The Rehabilitation Act also mandated priority in provision to those "most severely handicapped", affirmative action and anti-discrimination programmes and corporate compliance in matters of architecture and transportation.

The activities of the movement are located within a political philosophy and political tradition which De Jong goes to some lengths to explain and, indeed, to justify. It is a tradition of radical voluntarism which has also stimulated other movements of reform and revolt such as civil rights, consumerism, self-help, demedicalization/self-care, and deinstitutional-ization/norm-alization/mainstreaming. The author suggests that while these trends and movements have arisen in response to different social problems, each has influenced independent living, notably with regard to its emphasis on independence and control. In this regard, the movement has sought to reject the assumptions entailed in the medical model, the sick role and the impaired role.

In spite of their historical diversity, De Jong argues that there are three principled assumptions common to all these social movements: consumer sovereignty, self-reliance and political and economic rights. These assumptions, however, although radical, nonetheless entail a basic commitment to the American capitalist system with its free-market pluralist ideology - a commitment which the movement, or at least De Jong, con-

dones.

The definition of the situation is one where the central constraints are conceived as bureaucratic inertia and professional dominance and where the overriding goal is that people with disabilities should reclaim their own lives through reasserting their autonomy in opposition to state-controlled monopolies (in the American federalist sense). Given this definition, De Jong suggests that the best way to achieve their goals is through the rational and competitive pursuit of personal interests in the political and economic market place. In this utilitarian model, aggregate social well-being is assured by the equilibrating tendencies of full economic competition and multiple pressure-group bargaining.

De Jong argues, somewhat disarmingly, that:

"Some may find it difficult to view the movement for independent living as an apologist for a free-market pluralist ideology. After all, many disabled persons are hardly in the mainstream of this nation's economic and political system. They have been excluded."

Apparently, however, this is to miss the point because:

"While disabled persons have been excluded from full participation in the American economic-political system, they still subscribe to the system's most cherished values and assumptions. They still want to become a part of the system." [5]

(We are given no evidence for this confident assertion.)

This acceptance of the major assumptions of the capitalist system, then, is founded on the notion that the market allows the consumer to exert more control over disability services, thus helping to break "the monopolistic stranglehold of state-controlled human service organizations such as public welfare departments or vocational rehabilitation agencies" [6].

De Jong admits the potentially damaging tendencies to ignore the economic basis of political power, to conserve existing power relations and to encourage a situation where one group will simply outbid and out-bargain other worthy groups in the skilled pursuit of scarce resources in the market-place. He argues that it is against such tendencies that the movement "must be on its guard". As an indication that the movement is on its guard, De Jong points to features of the movement which mitigate the destructive effects of economic competition - mutual aid, community action and support, a focus on environmental pathology as opposed to victim-blaming and the development of coalitions with other vulnerable groups.

All this, then, is the crux of the 1979 report, and before considering research issues and the question of paradigms, it is necessary to give critical consideration to the issues of politics and ideology which I have outlined.

A Critique of Ideology

Confusion arises in assessing De Jong's position because he appears to use the market image both prescriptively and descriptively. On the one hand, the simple contractual relationships of the free-market are seen as a *modus operandi* to which we *ought* to return. On the other hand, he also uses the image as a working description of the essential mechanisms of modern capitalist America, where bureaucracy and "welfarism" are incidental aberrations in what is basically a market system.

If you take the prescriptive level, it suggests a lack of historical memory. The socialist response to the liberal dilemma grew out of a recognition that the "equilibrium" of polity and economy left some more equal than others. As Plant *et al.* [7] suggest, the social service and public welfare "monopoly" in Great Britain was a response to the accurate observation that in the free expression of preferences in the market, people's basic needs were not being met and through no fault of their own. Their powerlessness was but an aspect of their relationship to a pre-existing economic system, because where resources are scarce the power needed to obtain those resources itself becomes a scarce resource [8] - freedom for some means death for others. This perception is not a prerogative of Marxist thinkers:

"Freedom for the wolves has often meant death to the sheep. The bloodstained story of economic individualism and unrestrained capitalist competition does not, I should have thought, today need stressing" [9].

De Jong, as I note, also appears to use the free-market pluralist model as a working analytic description of modern America, while acknowledging the historical changes brought about by cartels and bureaucracies. The market still provides the mechanism for the expression of preferences and for the equitable distribution of social goods, and it is this that needs to be reasserted in the form of consumer choice against the bureaucratic monopoly of public welfare. In De Jong's terms professional and welfare control exacerbates dependence, and independence is best achieved through challenging this monopolistic control in the marketplace.

On this view, the role of government needs to be reduced to an essentially "negative" function, removing economic and environmental disincentives and constraints, rather than expanding ever more "positively" into the realms of welfare provision. Provisions that entail dependence in the satisfaction of basic needs - such as care attendants - should be "controlled" by the disabled person who hires, pays, and fires them. Such consumer control is put forward as an important way of creating greater possibilities for independence. In this manner:

"... the attendant care market is largely deregulated. The disabled consumer is sovereign. The role of government is mainly that of financial intermediary" [10].

It is not difficult to see the attractions of the market/pluralist model for members of the movement. It is a child of the doctrine originally elaborated by Thomas Hobbes and John Locke in seventeenth century England, which as since been characterised as "possessive individualism", where:

"The individual, it was thought, is free inasmuch as he is proprietor of his person and capacities. The human essence is freedom from dependence on the wills of others, and freedom is a function of possession...society consists of relations of exchange between proprietors. Political society becomes a calculated device for the protection of this property and for the maintenance of an orderly relation of exchange" [11].

The trouble with using this model as a means for understanding capitalist society in its later phases is not that it is wrong. It is just that it leaves too much out; it is partial. To be impartial, it would have to account also for the perpetuation of poverty, inequity and class divisions, in spite of the "free and equal" access to market-place opportunities. Long ago C. Wright Mills took a hard look at the magical "free market" and it accompanying "political balance" as assumptions used by liberal theorists in descriptions of American society and concluded:

"Such are the images of democracy which are still used as working justifications of power in America. We must now recognize this description as more a fairy tale than a useful approximation" [12].

De Jong recognizes that changes have occurred and argues that it is precisely because of the development of monopolies, corporations, professional organizations, welfare agencies and a general enlargement of state capitalist enterprise that the small groups need to reassert themselves - in pressure group activities to influence legislation and consumer involvement to offset the dead weight of bureaucratic organization.

There is much to be said for De Jong's concern with enhancing self-reliance through consumer power, but in the context of current concerns with shrinking national budgets, only a limited amount is going to be available for an increasing number of "dependency groups" [13]. It is this recognition, of course, that makes the statutory enactment of particular wants and needs as rights particularly important to the movement. Although they reject the paternalistic encroachment of government and welfare agencies, they do support government action to eliminate barriers and disincentives. They are concerned primarily with the enactment of the opportunity to live freely and independently and to satisfy

wants and preferences, rather than with the elimination of poverty and deprivation.

The consumer approach is growing in popularity at the moment, partly because of genuine disaffection amongst *some* health consumers with what is seen as the bureaucratic unresponsiveness of health care systems - both in U.S.A. and Britain. This search for more sensitive and sensible alternatives has found its main support in the young and affluent [14]. Its popularity is given strength by the way in which it happens to fit in with the prevalent ideology of robust conservative individualism. Gerben De Jong has friends in high places:

"Interest in the ... 'consumer choice' approach has been on the ascendancy for the past two years, stimulated by a small but influential cadre of senators, congressmen, and academics. Advocates see a revitalized medical market place in which health care providers and insurers actively compete for consumers' business on the basis of price, quality and service" [15].

The attractions of this approach are dependent upon the kind of political theory to which De Jong adheres, where free and equal persons compete for resources. However, as I have suggested, the market model of society, with its possessive individualist assumptions, is only partially accurate because it does not adequately recognize power differentials and class divisions. The market model conceptualizes atomised individuals competing for scarce resources in a context of equal natural rights. It fails, however, to adequately account for the fact that in spite of the postulate of equal natural rights and rationality market societies *generate* class differences in effective rights and rationality [11].

In Britain, where health care is free at point of contact, there is plenty of evidence to suggest that those who most need help and services are least effective in claiming and using them [16, 17]. Where the supply depends on effective market-place shopping these people are likely to find themselves especially disadvantaged. In this regard, it is important to question the extent to which the movement for independent living may be said to represent "the disabled". The core constituency of the independent living movement is young, male and "fit" as opposed to "frail" [18], whereas a major feature of the social reality of disablement is the elderly female, lacking in robustness and living far from the supportive confines of university campuses. It may well be that the disadvantages and needs of an elderly arthritic in an urban slum have more similarity to the problems of her able-bodied neighbours than to the values of the movement for independent living.

The notion of distributive justice through consumer choice arouses nostalgic sympathy because it evokes the lost contexts of a simple market society [19]. In the midst of concern over the allocation of scarce resources, the idea of allowing preferences expressed in the market to form the basis of distributive justice is particularly attractive because it avoids consideration of the problem of power as something more than individual exchange and because it circumvents the very real dilemmas associated with developing adequate criteria of need [20, 21, 7].

The difficulties in developing government-directed redistribution according to need have strengthened the individualistic wants-based strategies of movements such as self-help and independent living and have led to a resurgence of individualist philosophies in modern thinking on justice [22, 23].

Commenting on Nozick's [23] work, Lukes suggests:

"Nozick's world not only excludes the ever-growing role of the state within contemporary capitalism; it is also radically pre-sociological, without social structure, or social and cultural determinants of, and constraints upon, the voluntary acts and exchanges of its component individuals" [24].

Nozick's belief that an "alert citizenry" can mitigate the potential savagery of economic individualism is naive, as in the same way is De Jong's stricture that the movement for independent living should guard against tendencies to selfishness, avarice and so on.

The problem with consumer choice, self reliance and related principles, is that their use often dodges the issues of power and structure in social life. The consumer cannot be sovereign within a world in which the mechanics of power are located elsewhere - in corporations and industrial/financial conglomerates, which have the power to control price-cost relationships, levels and composition of investment, the intervention of governments and "the physical and socio-physiological environment of the consumer public" [25].

Inequality between social classes is a pervasive feature of the historical development of capitalist society, and within the dominant ideology of this society the concomitant principle of justice implied is one of people getting what they deserve. As Miller puts it:

"What the market achieves is distribution according to desert (where desert is measured by the creation of exchange value) rather than economic equality" [26].

Consumer choice and self-reliance are worthy principles, but outside the context of a comprehensive political strategy they can, especially in the present context, become an excuse for public neglect to pass itself off as benevolent minimal government, leaving the mechanics of social and economic disadvantage undisturbed [14].

Independent Living: Research and Methodology

At the end of the 1979 report, De Jong began to suggest ways in which disability research could be framed in order to operationalize the ideas and concepts of independent living. He argues:

"As a paradigm of research independent living offers us an opportunity to steer away from unalterable individual characteristics that divert our attention from the larger institutional and environmental context in which disabled people live" [27].

In the later report De Jong conducts an empirical examination of independent living 'theory', attempting to discover how and why people with disabilities fail to realise their potential in society. What are the determinants of dependence in a society that offers such rewards to self-directed independence? The paradigm of independent living leads De Jong to suggest:

"The locus of the problem is not the individual but the environment that includes not only the rehabilitation process but also the physical environment and the social control mechanisms in society at large" [28].

Given this identification, the hypothesised solutions will include advocacy, peer counselling, self-help, consumer control and barrier removal. Their theory of (or belief about) causation suggests that "environmental variables are as critical as, if not more so than, personal characteristics in determining disability outcomes" [29].

In this regard, it departs from the traditional concerns of rehabilitation research and practice which have focused on the retraining of people with disabilities in basic skills such as eating, washing and other activities of daily living, while overlooking the extent to which levels of dependence may be increased, both by the rehabilitation process itself and broader aspects of the environment in which the individual lives. In fairness, thought, it should be pointed out that many rehabilitation professionals are becoming more aware of the ambiguities in their role [30, 31].

In a chapter devoted to a review of the literature on spinal cord injury (SCI) (the impairment group on which the author has chosen to concentrate), De Jong shows how particular 'paradigms' as well as professional roles within paradigms determine the choice of variables for analysis. I sympathise completely with his criticism of the way in which rehabilitation psychologists, for example, employ concepts of 'denial' and 'motivation' in such a way that the individual can find himself in a 'no-win' position. I feel less sympathy, however, with the 'behavioural ecology' paradigm which, in a 'value-free', 'non-assumptive' way, simply observes all 'patient behaviour' in different environments. Firstly, such value-freedom in social science is a myth and secondly, the human actor and agent is here reduced to a cultural dope. Social action, insofar as it is meaningful, involves more than patterns of behaviour in response to environmental contingency.

However, with his aims in view, De Jong goes on to detail the features of his own study. Four chapters comprise the meat of the report; chapters on research model and methodology, characteristics of the study group, outcomes of the study group and the specification and evaluation of predictors of independent living. The description and analysis is complex and indeed, I would suggest that much of the detail of statistical analysis could happily have been relegated to an appendix. Would policy-makers *want* to wrestle with the ins and outs of principal component analysis and interaction terms? Moreover, tables which one would expect to enlighten are often themselves too detailed and crowded.

In order to translate the diffuse concerns of the ideology into a mathematical model geared to influence policy-makers, a great deal of space is given over to the specification and delineation of relevant variables. The outcome measures they chose as dependent variables were 'living arrangements' and 'productivity', which they thought would be most relevant to policy concerns. These were ranked and weighted in terms of their 'desirability' by the 42 member Massachusetts Interagency Council on Independent Living, consisting of "a large cross-section of individuals concerned with, and knowledgeable about IL issues" [32]. The tricky evaluative basis of ranking and weighting of outcomes was recognised, but as some judgement had to be made this was reckoned to be as reasonable a way as any of accomplishing it.

The independent variables were selected according to three considerations: the IL 'paradigm' and its 'theory of causation', the research literature on spinal cord injury outcomes, and the investigator's own experience in addressing IL issues. Four sets of independent variables were conceptualised: socio-demographic characteristics, disability-related variables (severity and duration of disability), environmental variables (including 'settings' and 'barriers') and interface variables (assistive devices of various descriptions). These cover quite a large chunk of the world and so, with relation to environmental factors for example, they only gave in-depth consideration to attendant care, housing, transportation, economic disincentives, the patient role and services received or needed.

The main data source was 111 SCI persons from 10 comprehensive medical rehabilitation centers around the U.S.A. and the data were collected with six instruments, the most important of which was an 'interview questionnaire' (a dubious juxtaposition).

This, then, constitutes the framework of the study. Subsequent chapters go into more detail on the selection of the study group and on the weighting of outcome variables. The study group was predominantly male and youthful, containing both traumatic and non-traumatic SCI and 75% of the group required or used a wheelchair for getting around. In the weighting of outcome variables, a vast number of factors were identified and then collapsed for purposes of analysis. The main point to come out of all this was that those scoring high on 'productivity' may not score high on 'living arrangement', suggesting that they may be very different dimensions determined by different predictive factors.

The analysis of predictors of independent living outcomes was a complex exercise in multivariate analysis. The goal was to find out which independent variables (both environmental and individual) were most predictive of independent living outcome. Perhaps the data analysis was *too* complex. The stepwise multiple regression analysis appeared to create more problems than it resolved, especially with regard to the interactive effects involved in conjoint factor influence. Functional variables (severity of disability) and environmental variables (transportation barriers) for example, were found to explain equal proportions of variance depending on which was stepped into the regression analysis first.

One of the most important results of the analysis was the discovery of a strong interaction between personal (disability-related) and environmental factors, such as transportation barriers and economic disincentives. The relative effects proved very difficult to separate out. The attempted use of 'interaction terms' (cross products of two independent variables) was dropped because the strong association between the interaction term itself and the component variables generated a multicollinearity problem

which produced unstable regression coefficients, thus reducing the statistical significance of the results.

The author concluded that the study offers a beginning - the start of a new perspective on the analysis of disability issues and outcomes. The movement for independent living provides the clearest statement on how people with disabilities wish to be viewed in modern America: "not as passive victims needing constant professional intervention but as self-directed individuals seeking to remove environmental barriers that preclude their full participation in the life of the community" [33].

A Critique of Method

The statistical and methodological procedures employed by De Jong are complex, but beneath that complexity some highly shaky judgements were made - as in the process of weighting and ranking the dependent variables in such a way that objective features of the person's world were treated as offering *prima facie* evidence on the basis of which the property of dependence could then be inferred. This is alright as long as the *prima facie* case is only treated as preliminary. In order to make any meaningful judgement with regard to dependence, intensive studies of the specific contexts and dynamics of social action would have to be developed.

The criteria for developing accounts of cause and effect with predictive validity are strict [34]. In spite of De Jong' explanatory footnote [35] there is clearly more than a degree of tautology underlying the predictive power of marital status in relation to a 'desirable' living arrangement where that arrangement's desirability has already been specified as 'living with a spouse'. Moreover, De Jong himself appears uncertain as to the methodological specification of marital status. It starts off life as a socio-demographic factor - presumably because this is the standard convention in this type of research - but when its predictive capacity is revealed, it is transformed into an environmental surrogate for in-home care. In the end, I suppose it does not really matter much what name you give it, but it still needs to be clearly separated from the dependent variable it seeks to explain.

This type of arbitrariness creeps in elsewhere. Why are special equipment needs 'interface variables' while care attendant needs are 'environmental variables'? Both types of social resources required "to bridge the gap between physical limitations of the individual and the shortcomings of the environment". I would have thought that within De Jong's research design, these would both be 'intervening variables' modifying the relationship between the environment and the individual.

If you are going to do the type of research which requires a detailed discrimination of independent and dependent variables then this must be done well. If there are unclear distinctions in the original conceptual specification, no amount of complex statistical procedure is going to cover them up. The problem of multicollinearity occurs in the use of interaction terms when the procedures for data reduction have been inadequate. In this sense, either De Jong has failed to do a proper analysis of principal components or his original summing and separating of different variables has been misguided. And again, to discover a strong relationship between 'interaction terms' and the composite variables is not an invitation to ignore it. It may well be evidence that the two independent variables have not been adequately separated out in conceptual definition and that the independent effects of the two independent variables are not as important as the regression analysis suggests. Perhaps this type of mathematical muddle should be taken to mean that multiple regression analysis is not the best procedure to be using unless more rigorous conceptual analysis and specification has been carried out first.

At a higher level, there lies the whole question of the viability of the use of quasi-experimental techniques in the analysis of social structure and social action. Such an approach presupposes that different factors can be meaningfully extracted from their context and separated into variables standing in external relations to each other which can then be varied independently. But, a classic dilemma for those attempting to develop social theory is that many of the phenomena you seek to elucidate and explain are internally related and mutually constitutive. To separate out such phenomena is to violate the very relationships your are trying to explain [36]. In considering aspects of life with disabilities, the 'environment' is not simply given, but is both constitutive of and constituted by, the symbolic performances and practical engagements of social actors.

De Jong's quasi-experimental research only attains plausibility on an assumption of linear relationships existing between environmental factors and ways of living where alteration of independent variables fractures the linear sequence and alters the dependent variable. But, as one commentator points out, there is no simple deterministic relationship between the built environment and, for example, the productivity of people with disabilities [37]. While adhering to an individualist pre-sociological image of society, De Jong then tries to bring society back in. His individualism, political and methodological, prevents him from doing this in a convincing way. In the absence of a more certain theoretical foundation, De Jong's assumptions are an unsound basis for policy.

A New Paradigm?

De Jong refers to independent living as providing a new paradigm, but to claim a view of the world as a new paradigm is a pretty grand claim to make. The concepts of 'paradigm', paradigm shift' and 'anomaly' employed by De Jong are taken from Thomas Kuhn's [4] major treatise in the philosophy of science which attempted to explain how and why, in the history of scientific endeavour, revolutionary transitions or paradigm-shifts occur in the fundamental axioms of practising scientists.

In sociological theory, the use of Kuhnian concepts has been noticeably undisciplined [38]. Thus, sociologists have been eager to point out the 'multi-paradigmatic' nature of their discipline in spite of the fact that this violated Kuhn's principle that only one paradigm could be ascendant at a given time, and that each paradigm succeeds and absorbs previous ones. In this regard De Jong's identification of independent living and behavioural ecology as potentially converging paradigms makes no sense, especially as he has anyway indicated the atheoretical nature of behavioural ecology, an approach which sounds rather reminiscent of Francis Bacon and would not, I am sure, prove acceptable as a new paradigm.

All this should not be taken to imply that the concept of paradigm is, *de facto*, useless in understanding developments in social science, but simply that it means something different and cannot be legitimised by reference to Kuhn [38]. If some philosophical legitimation is necessary to those engaged in disability research, a far more persuasive case could be made for using Lakatos' [39] concept of a 'research programme'. This allows for the existence of two or more equally powerful but distinct explanations for the existence of, and variance in, the same phenomenon [40].

If, for sake of argument, we were to overlook De Jong's terminological laxity and simply assume that when he says new paradigm, he just means a new orientation or approach, can even such a watered-down assertion be sustained? De Jong argues that independent living has arisen in response to a paradigm shift forced by the existence of an anomaly - a problem insoluble within the existing paradigm. He identifies this anomaly as the fact that many chronically physically disabled" ... were achieved independence without the benefit of, or in spite of, professional rehabilitation" [41]. There are a number of points to be made here. Firstly, the existence of an anomaly does not necessarily lead to the demise of a paradigm, it may simply mean that existing theories within the paradigm need to be refined. Secondly, De Jong's anomalous 'core constituency' represents only a small part of the overall field encompassed by rehabilitation professions. Thirdly, De Jong's *a priori* identification of 'severity' of disablement in biophysical terms prejudges the issues and reproduces the individualist ontology and reductionist epistemology of traditional rehabilitation research. Finally, all the foregoing implies that those involved in independent living, rehabilitation or whatever are developing explanatory theory. I see little evidence for this. Certainly, there are clinical descriptions and statistical associations, but to talk of theory

implies a profound grasp of the generative mechanisms involved in the production of particular effects. This cannot be derived simply on the basis of regression analysis, where that analysis lacks any tie to a theory of social structure and human agency.

The bundle of methods used by De Jong does not (yet) constitute a theory, and in the absence of a theory (as distinct from a model), it is difficult to take seriously his assertions about the paradigmatic significance of independent living.

Conclusion: A Way Forward

Disablement is a feature of human life in social contexts and in order to understand it as something more than an individual problem for rehabilitation, you need a sociological perspective that recognises the complex relationships between people as social beings and the wider world. This is what the World Health Organization has attempted to do in its definition of handicap as social disadvantage, distinct from the 'individual' problems of disability and dependence:

"There is a distinct cleavage between disability and handicap, both conceptually and in the means for intervention and methodological obstacles need not compel social action on disadvantage to be determined by measures of disability alone" [42].

De Jong may argue that this is precisely what his emphasis on the 'environment' is designed to accomplish. But his epistemology tends towards a behaviourism which assumes a one-way causal relationship between environmental contingencies and individual states, and ignores the mediating effects of the symbols and contexts of social life. Thus, he mentions the difficulties involved in deciding whether 'living alone' should be seen as a desirable outcome or not. It all depends on the context and on the meaning attributable to an absence of social relationships. If living alone means 'social disintegration', then it is undesirable. If, on the other hand, it is read as a measure of 'self-willed independence' then it is desirable *if*, in the particular society in question, independence is a central value.

In order to begin to appreciate the responses

of people to disablement you need to go beyond the aggregated, statistically standardized individual, simply moulded by circumstance, to a perspective that treats individuals and social worlds as mutually constitutive. In this Kantian world, in contrast the De Jong's Skinnerian world [36], social actor and agents appraise, create and respond actively to a world that is both enabling and constraining. In this world, too, autonomy is eminently desirable but it is recognised to be relative and relational, depending on norms, mores and values in society and on the complex motives, intentions, projects and plans of actors working with a more *or* less open-ended script. From such a perspective, it would simply be nonsense to infer 'dependency' from a simple observation of living arrangement.

Again though, De Jong might argue that in pushing ideas of consumer involvement and participation and self reliance, he *is* using an image of rational and competent actors expressing preferences and making decisions in the context of the market place. What, after all, could be more 'active' than the image of man maximising his utility through rational choice. In a sense this is so, but:

> "... on the other hand, there is a marked tendency to behaviourism in which revealed preference is sufficient evidence of desire and rationality assumptions are used to eliminate all actual differences between men placed in economically similar settings" [43].

A political understanding of handicap as disadvantage would define handicap in sociological terms thus emphasising the commonality of deprivation and allowing a way into the ascertainment of social need required for government and effective pressure group action. The environment is part of the social structure, and features of the environment need to be seen in the context of the power relationships from which they come. If we are to move toward a more equitable and rational procedure for thinking about and responding to handicap, it is essential to move from an individualist to a relational model that posits an autonomous but social being in a political context rather than an abstract individual battling against a sanitised environment. Such a shift would add strength the disability pressure groups and it would provide a more comprehensive picture of the problems for policy-makers obsessed by fiscal constraints. It might even provide the beginnings of a new 'paradigm'. If we remain entrapped by images of individual consumers and clients, divorced from any sense of power and social structure, we will only replicate the current weaknesses of research in rehabilitation.

Acknowledgements - The author is grateful to Steve Cooper, Orin Smith, Sue Wagstaff and Philip Wood for their helpful comments and suggestions.

References

1. De Jong G. *The Movement for Independent Living: Origins, Ideology and Implications for Disability Research.* University Centre for International Rehabilitation, U.S.A./Michigan State University, 1979.
2. De Jong G. *Environmental Accessibility and Independent Living Outcomes: Directions for Disability Policy and Research.* University Centre for International Rehabilitation, U.S.A./Michigan State University, 1981.
3. Frieden, L. *et al. Living Independently: Three Views of European Experience with Implications for the U.S.* Monograph No. 10, World Rehabilitation Fund, New York, 1981.
4. Kuhn T.S. *The Structure of Scientific Revolutions.* University of Chicago Press, Chicago, 1962.
5. De Jong G. *op cit.* p.46, 1979.
6. De Jong G. *ibid.* p.47.
7. Plant R. *et al. Political Philosophy and Social Welfare.* Routledge, London, 1980.
8. Giddens A. *Central Problems in Social Theory: Action, Structure and Contradiction in Social Analysis.* Macmillan, London, 1979.
9. Berlin I. Introduction to: *Four Essays on Liberty,* p.xlv. Oxford University Press, New York, 1969.
10. De Jong G. *op cit.* p.56, 1979.
11. MacPherson C.B. *The Political Theory of Possessive Individualism: Hobbes to Locke* p.3. Oxford University Press, Oxford, 1962.
12. Mills, C.W. The Structure of Power in American Society. In *Power, Politics, and People: The Collected Essays of C. Wright Mills* (Edited by Horowitz I.L.), pp.36-37. Oxford University Press, New York, 1967.

13. Illsely R. Problems of dependency groups: the care of the elderly, the handicapped, and the chronically ill. *Soc. Sci. Med.* **15A**, 327-332, 1981.

14. Allegrante, J.P. and Green L.W. When healthy policy becomes victim blaming. *New Engl. J Med.* **305**, 1528-1529, 1981.

15. Winsten J. Competition in health care: is 'consumer choice' in the consumer's interest? *New Engl. J. Med.* **305**, 1280, 1981.

16. Hart J.T. The inverse care law. *The Lancet* **1**, 405-412, 1971.

17. DHSS. *Inequalities in Health: Report of a Research Working Group,* HMSO, London, 1980.

18. Wood P.H.N. and Badley E.M. *People with Disabilities: Towards Acquiring Information which Reflects more Sensitively their Problems and Needs.* Monograph No. 12, World Rehabilitation Fund, New York, 1980.

19. O'Neill J. *Sociology as a Skin Trade: Essays towards A Reflexive Sociology.* Heinemann, London, 1972.

20. Miller D. *Social Justice.* Clarendon Press. Oxford, 1976.

21. Culyer A.J. and Wright K.G. *Economic Aspects of Health Services.* Martin Robertson, London, 1976.

22. Rawls J.A. *A Theory of Justice.* Clarendon Press, Oxford, 1972.

23. Nozick R. *Anarchy, State, and Utopia.* Blackwell, Oxford, 1974.

24. Lukes S. *Essays in Social Theory.* p.194. Macmillan London, 1977.

25. O'Neill J. *op. cit.* p.29.

26. Miller D. *op. cit.* p.296.

27. De Jong G. *op. cit.* p.66, 1979.

28. De Jong G. *op. cit.* p.29, 1981.

29. De Jong G. *ibid.* p.2 and 32.

30. Ben-Sira Z. The structure of readjustment of the disabled: an additional perspective on rehabilitation. *Soc. Sci. Med.* **15A**, 565-580, 1981.

31. Cochrane G.M. Hidden resources for rehabilitation and care of the disabled. *Jl. R. Soc. Med.* **75**, 89-95, 1982.

32. De Jong G. *op. cit.* p.65, 1981.

33. De Jong G. *ibid* p.33.

34. Hirschi T. and Selvin H. *Principles of Survey Analysis.* Free Press. New York, 1973.

35. De Jong G. *op. cit.* p.129, 1981.

36. Harré R. *Social Being: A Theory for Social Psychology.* Blackwell, Oxford, 1979.

37. Goldsmith S. *Designing for the Disabled.* 3rd Edition. RIBA, London, 1976.

38. Harvey L. The use and abuse of Kuhnian paradigms in the sociology of knowledge. *Sociology* **16**, 85-101, 1982.

39. Lakatos I. and Musgrave F.W. *Criticism and the Growth of Knowledge.* Cambridge University Press, London, 1970.

40. Marmot M. Facts, opinions and affaires du coeur. *Am. J. Epid.* **103**, 519-526, 1976.

41. De Jong G. *op. cit.* p.59, 1979.

42. WHO. *International Classification of Impairments, Disabilities and Handicaps: A Manual Relating to the Consequences of Disease.* WHO, Geneva, 1980.

43. Hollis M. *Models of Man.* Cambridge University Press. London, 1977.

 # 4 FAMILY EXPERIENCES

The family has been defined as the most important institution in society. This is particularly apparent for the disabled as their patterns of development, self identity, and ability are often influenced and determined by the family environment. However, some families do choose to closet their disabled members, while some others spare no effort in attempting to integrate the disabled person in all activities.

Joanne Shapiro demonstrates the coping process of individuals in the family, particularly in response to a serious illness or disability in a child or family member. In many instances, parents and other family members must become advocates for their disabled counterparts in attempting to solicit the most positive patterns of care and involvement available. In many cases, the disabled encounter economic, educational, and social constraints which inhibit if not prevent them from achieving acceptance and integration into society. Thus, "normal" parents, friends, and spouses must often resort to entrepreneurship as a way of life to ensure that their disabled counterparts will have a "normal life". Marlett enhances this perspective in her work on the family and rehabilitation.

Disability in any aura often leads to family crisis. Frequently, families are reluctant to be totally involved with the care of disabled family members. In the Hollywood classic "Rain Man", it was illustrated that those who are traditionally institutionalized due to so-called psychological problems are able to *participate and enjoy normal activities beyond the walls of the* institutional environment. However, there is a societal bias which still dictates that those who are afflicted with severe psychological disorders ought to remain in institutions. The above-mentioned Hollywood extravaganza received a great deal of justified and widespread criticism among disabled groups because its message signified that psychologically impaired individuals are probably better off in institutions. Deinstitutionalization, as demonstrated by Ursprung, often precipitates family crisis, as a result of economic, social, psychological, and political concerns. Indeed, tradition dictates that people who are different should be isolated from the mainstream of society, when in fact their accomplishments and quality of life may be significantly in an atmosphere free of institutional barriers.

Family concerns are crucial since families like individuals have different coping capacities. The image of the family is often in marked contrast with the difficulties that emerge when a person encounters the barriers imposed by a disabling condition. In many cases, the intervention of a medical practitioner, the clergy, or the legal profession may be required to serve the best interests of the victims in the family environment, where all members need to adjust to the new situation. However, most families maintain a state of normalcy with the support, and understanding of skilled people who are trained to cope with the difficulties associated with disability status.

Family Reactions and Coping Strategies in Response to the Physically Ill or Handicapped Child: A Review

JOHANNA SHAPIRO

Introduction

This article will examine different forms of family reactions and coping strategies activated by a significant physical illness or handicapping condition in a child family member. The literature is replete with articles stressing the importance of family variables in considering issues of treatment, rehabilitation, and outcome. What is the rationale for this emphasis? This article briefly reviews evidence that there exists a powerful interactive effect between family and illness. It then explores the concepts of individual and family coping. Finally, it attempts to summarize what is known about family response to illness and handicapping conditions in children.

This review is necessarily restricted within certain limits: (1) Its focus is on the child as the identified patient. Available evidence suggests that while illness in one family member affects the entire family unit, which individual is ill also influences the nature of family responses [1,2]. By restricting the focus to the ill child and a responsive family, a fairly consistent frame of reference is created. It is also, at this point, the situation which has been shown to illustrate most clearly principles of family/illness interaction. (2) The review examines only two major interrelated issues: (a) the impact of the illness on the family and (b) the nature of coping strategies generated by the family in response to the illness. This emphasis was selected because it is at once of great potential clinical relevance and simultaneously extremely elusive in terms of concrete clinical implications.

A Relationship Between Family and Illness

It has been argued for many years that the family is an appropriate unit for health care intervention [3-10]: and it has been observed that a common physician error is overtreatment of the child and undertreatment of the family [11]. Simultaneously, there has been interest generated in family ramifications of various chronic and life-threatening disease entities [12,13] and several review articles exist in the literature [3, 14, 15].

It is by now clear that an undeniable relationship exists between family and illness, and that a specific illness both affects and is affected by the family context. Important implications for the nature of health care derive from this statement. If the response of the family to an illness has an ability to influence the outcome of that illness, or to influence secondary complications of the patient's illness (e.g. psychological sequelae), then we are justified in understanding and studying this response. Similarly, if the illness of one member produces effects on the family which reverberate in the health care system (e.g. development of physical symptomatology, affective disorders, alcoholism, etc.), then this also is worthy of attention. It is well-documented, for example, that uncontrolled events and events with long-term threat of loss and disappointment (such as physical illness) are more linked to psychiatric disorders (e.g. depression) than are controllable events (e.g. marriage) [16, 17].

In order to understand the nature of the interaction between family and illness, it is important to review briefly how the family functions as a system, for it is this property which allows for the interaction effects observed in the literature. The family system has been defined as a network of interpersonal relationships characterized by a continuous interchange between members and by reciprocal causal effects [18]. In this conceptualization, the family is viewed as an organic unit, a dynamic system in which every part is simultaneously organizing and being organized by other parts [19]. A systems approach to understanding the

Reprinted From: Soc. Sci. Med. Vol. 17, No. 14, pp. 913, 931, 1983. Printed in Great Britain. All rights reserved. Pergamon Press Ltd., with permission.

family [20] may be contrasted to a linear approach in that the latter identifies the individual as the patient and primary focus of treatment, and assumes that responses and behavior of the individual are determined by antecedent and consequent environmental forces [21], while the former emphasizes feedback loops [22] among all members of a family and distributes responsibility for dysfunction throughout the family system.

Some characteristics of a family system are as follows [20, 21]: (1) It is an open, rather than a closed system, and has continuous interchange with the external social and physical environment. Thus, it is affected by and responds to outside input, for example, from the physician. (2) It is complex, with an intricate organizational structure. Thus, simplistic interpretations of effects of illness on the family are often inappropriate. (3) It is self-regulating, in the sense of containing homeostatic mechanisms to restore balance and equilibrium. (4) It is capable of transformation. The family system, confronted with continuous internal and external demands for change, may be able to respond with growth, flexibility and structural evolution.

The assumptions of a family approach to health care that are the course and outcome of a given illness are influenced by the way family members behave with each other: that the psychosocial and environmental context affects individuals' responses to disease process; and that the change in context can produce positive change in the individual's adaptation to disease [25].

Impressive evidence exists to support the contention that the family should be considered a basic unit of health and medical care [26]. This came to the attention of health care professionals perhaps most strikingly in the case of the hospitalized child. It was observed time and again that many physical and psychological aspects of the child's experience in the hospital were related to the child's reaction to separation from the family [27]; and that in this situation of extreme stress, families needed as much psychotherapeutic attention as did the identified patient [28, 29]. Thus, the adjustment of both parent and hospitalized child became of concern [30,31],

and family centered care of the hospitalized child emerged as a widespread trend [32-34]. Of special interest is that recent anecdotal reports appearing the in the literature have documented that even minor inpatient procedures can be extremely distressing for parents [35], and can result in the cycle of guilt, blame, denial and depression [36] which characterizes more stressful hospitalization conditions.

Looking beyond the experience of hospitalization, researchers and clinicians established that the family exhibits characteristic patterns of morbidity, transmission [37], susceptibility to infections agents [38] and utilization of medical services [39]. For example, it has been shown that some families have a high frequency of disease, while others over the course of time experience very little disease [40]. One author [41] points out that illness in some families is characterized by clusters of simultaneously occurring symptoms in several family members, while in other families, only the identified patient becomes ill. Another study of family illness patterns [42] concluded that symptoms of one family member influenced clinic attendance of other family members, and that the presence of chronic illness in the family was associated with increased clinic attendance in other family members. Other studies have also related family patterns of illness to medical care, identifying a relationship between different family variables (e.g. rigidity), frequency of illness and frequency of physician consultation [43].

In addition, the family is perhaps the major health/illness defining unit [44]. Children learn illness attitudes and behaviors from their parents, and parental behavior is important in reducing psychological sequelae of any major disease episode [11]. There is also some evidence to suggest that differences in parenting behavior toward children are associated with differences frequency of symptom reporting [45, 46]. In another study, health beliefs in mothers appeared to be related to patterns of office visits for children [47]. Mothers with an active, interventionist approach to health care, who attributed good health to low illness susceptibility to their children were high users of preventive services and generated few illness accident visits. By contrast, mothers with a more passive attitude, who perceived their children to be in poor health and susceptible to illness, generated fewer well-child and more illness visits.

Cross-culturally, variations in family child-rearing practices have an important influence on child health [48]. Families rooted in different cultural and socio-economic milieus also have differing interpretations of the meaning and significance of a particular illness [49], which in turn may either facilitate or hinder the physician's therapeutic efforts. Family members are frequent sources of information about home remedies and self-medication. Further, the family can be important in terms of preventive health care practices [3].

A relationship has been observed for several decades between physical disease and family function [50, 51]. A family system may influence the course and outcome of disease; it may constitute the conditions sufficient to precipitate illness; or it may act as a predisposing influence, by increasing susceptibility to disease. It is widely accepted that patient disease may derive from or be compounded by family stresses, especially marital and sexual problems, housing problems, and serious illness in other family members [52]. Family development crises also influence the frequency of illness [1].

Families tend to experience illness as a unit [53]. From a common cold to a major life-threatening illness, other family members are affected to a greater or lesser degree by the symptomatology of the identified patient, and in turn their responses also have an effect on that patient [54]. The family often responds as an organic entity to the stressor of illness in a family members. For example, reference is made to the concept of 'family pain' in response to terminal illness in the child [55]. It has been pointed out that the family is usually thrown into a state of disequilibrium by the stress of illness. The initial psychosocial effects of illness and handicap are almost inevitably family disruption and disorganization [56]. Resolution of this crisis will be related to family coping patterns [57, 58]. The stress of illness may also accentuate potential problems in family adjustment and social relationships [59-61].

The famous Newcastle-upon-Tyne study indicated a significantly higher incidence of many forms of physical disease, as well as a higher incidence of mortality, in poorer-functioning families and highlighted for the first time in a well-documented, systematic fashion that the health of children and the outcome of disease were closely related to physical and psychological dimensions of family environment [62]. Other investigators have observed that children with chronic illness appear to do better in well-functioning than in poorer functioning families [7]. Other studies have documented that children coming from dysfunctional families were seen more frequently in physician's offices for minor illness [63]. By contrast, in another study, 50 child nonattenders at a well-child clinic were compared to 50 regular attenders [64]. The former were characterized by multiple factors, including chronic, longstanding, multiple problems affecting the whole family.

Disorganization of the family also often leads to failure to provide basic adequate health care [15]. Parental deprivation has been associated with a number of psychosomatic and psychiatric diseases, notably suicide, tuberculosis and accidents. The relationship of marital status to overall mortality is especially striking with respect to tuberculosis, suicide, influenza, pneumonia, syphilis and cirrhosis. Family attitudes have also been shown to be significant in rheumatoid arthritis, mental illness, addiction and cardiovascular disease [65]. Further, the death of a spouse or the serious illness of one family member raises the statistical likelihood that other family members will also develop signs of illness [66].

On the other hand, there is little evidence that perceived family solidarity, marital happiness or close family ties 'protect' the family against the disruptive impact of a member's illness on family relations. In fact, in one study, just the opposite appeared to be true, and those with disparate family ties often reported being more drawn together by illness [67]. There was also little evidence to support the idea that egalitarian families were less likely to be adversely affected by a member's illness than were their more maternally dominated counterparts.

Of course, the interaction between family and illness is reciprocal, and illness can also change a family's dynamics. However, even this impact is mediated by the family's interpretation of the illness crisis. If the family interprets the illness as a threat, the crisis will produce anxiety; if it is interpreted as a loss, it will produce depression; and if it is interpreted as a challenge, both anxiety and hope will create problem-solving energy and promote motivation and growth within the family [68].

Models for Understanding Individual and Family Coping

It is clear that some relationship exists between the family unit, the nature of family functioning, and various aspects of how an illness expresses itself. That being the case, it becomes particularly important to understand how the family copes with the child's ill health: how it reacts and what proactive strategies it employs to deal with this stressor.

Individual coping processes

Coping may be defined as all responses made by the individual who encounters a potentially harmful outcome, including overt behaviors, cognitions, physiological responses and emotional reactions [69]. Lazarus [70] has defined coping as "efforts, both action-oriented and intrapsychic, to manage environmental and internal demands, and conflicts among them, which tax or exceed a person's resources". According to his formulation, coping efforts can be directed toward the threat itself, or toward efforts to regulate the emotional distress caused by the threat. The former style is instrumental or problem-solving, the latter labelled palliative [71].

It is important to make a distinction between coping resources and coping responses.[1] According to this formulation, a *coping response* is an action, thought, verbalization or feeling elicited by the stressor of illness [73], thus having a direct and identifiable link to this particular stressor. *Coping resources* [74], on the other hand, may be considered as aspects of the individual's external and/or internal environment

which are either not directly or completely under the individual's control; they exist in a quiescent state, ready to mediate in a positive or negative direction the individual's response to the advent of a stressor. Clearly, the nature and type of coping responses generated by the individual will be determined to some extent by the coping resources available in that person's environment. While the exact nature of this relationship has not been specified, both theoretical and research efforts indicate that the presence of coping resources increases the range and effectiveness of the coping response [75, 76] while their absence would have the opposite effect.

Coping resources in the individual's internal environment might include stable, cross-situational personality attributes, such as self-concept [77] and psychological hardiness [78, 79]. They might also include the person's previous experience with other stressful situations [80]. In the external environment, such disease-specific factors as susceptibility, diagnosis and prognosis might also be categorized as coping resources (or deficits) [81]. Other coping resources might include demographic and socioeconomic variables (social class, marital status, educational attainment, financial status, religious affiliation) [82, 83]. Finally, both formal and informal support systems (group membership, friendship networks) [84, 85] also are resources available to the individual, although utilization of such systems by the individual would constitute a coping response.

Although it is generally agreed that coping responses act as a buffer between life stress and illness, judgments of positive versus negative coping are subjective and vague. Early work on coping tended to evaluate coping behavior as 'good' or 'bad' in and of themselves; i.e. individuals who engaged in emotional expression were coping well, while individuals characterized by intransigent denial were coping poorly [87]. Other researchers have identified different 'positive' coping responses, such as information-seeking, emotional control, maintaining a positive self-image and a sense of mastery [88]. Effective coping may also be inferred based on the relative maturity of the individual [89-91]. Finally, the good coping may be defined with some circularity by the patients' own perceived success of their coping [92].

It may be said that positive coping alleviates the problem and reduces individual distress, while negative coping exacerbates the problem and may become a problem in itself (e.g. drinking). Successful coping is often associated with specific outcome criteria in the anecdotal literature. For example, one author [93] judges that a family is coping successfully if (a) the family unit remains intact, (b) the family is able to accept the affected child, (c) there are normal sexual relations in the marital dyad, (d) siblings in the family have an age-appropriate awareness of the situation, (e) the family has retained their original primary care doctor, (f) the family has made concrete and realistic plans for the affected child, (g) safe passage through the different stages of coping has occurred, (h) parents express satisfaction with the management of their child, and (i) parents have a willingness to help in the management of other families facing a similar situation. Successful parental adaptation also has been said to be characterized by the enforcement of only necessary and realistic restrictions for the affected child; the promotion of peer interactions, self-care and school attendance; a tendency to isolate and deny anxious and helpless emotion, especially during a medical crisis.

Positive coping often depends on the support, through parent groups, of other families in similar situations [94, 95]. Good coping is also associated with such factors as good communication and assistance between parents; adequate financial resources and a willingness to use them in coping with the affected child; and functioning support systems [96]. Good adjustment to illness is found in families in which (a) there is a clear separation of the generations, (b) a satisfying of each other's emotional and psychological needs, (c) flexibility within roles, (d) toleration of individuation and (e) communication with is direct and consistent, and tends to confirm the self-esteem of the other [59].

Adaptive patient responses have been identified [97] as including realistic self-reliance; acceptance of physical limitations, but with the development of compensatory activities; the ability to express anxious, sad and angry feelings;

guarded optimism during periods of clinical quiescence; denial and isolation of affect to cope with emotional distress; a focus on the here an now; and the effective use of support individuals. Positive coping in the affected child has also been associated with independence, contact with peers, achievement in school and participation in other normalization activities.

Several coping strategies have been clearly identified as maladaptive or dysfunctional in the literature, although these conclusions are based on anecdotal evidence more than on research findings [97, 98]. Prolonged poor adjustment in the identified patient is characterized by fearfulness, inactivity, dependency; or, in contrast, an overly independent attitude, engaging in prohibited, risk-taking behaviors; or finally, resentful hostile attitudes toward non-disabled or healthy individuals. Negative child coping has been labelled as centering around fear, withdrawal, regression, neurotic utilization of organic symptoms, clowning and low self-esteem.

On the family level, it has been noted that severe and unchanging denial of the reality of illness tends to impede successful adaptation. Isolation of the ill member while the rest of the family attempts to survive also is dysfunctional both for patient and family. Hypochondriasis in other family members may be an indication that the family is not coping well with the identified patient's illness. The continued projection of angry feelings onto other family members, with no efforts at resolution or movement, also is considered dysfunctional. Extreme regression on the part of siblings, and extreme rigidity on the part of the family system in the face of life-threatening illness are further danger signs of poor coping. Finally, a significant withdrawal from accustomed social interactions tends to be associated with dysfunctional coping. Other maladaptive coping strategies include flights into activity; unremitting hostility to health personnel; and feelings of being overwhelmed by the child's care.

However, despite such value judgements about positive and negative coping, other authors have emphasized that coping is an extremely person- and situation-specific phenomenon [17, 69]. Thus, it may not be useful to talk about successful coping independent of identifying the particular stressor(s) being confronted, and the particular internal and external resources of the person or family doing the confronting.

Illness may be viewed in several ways [69], all of which mediate the nature of the coping response elicited. It may be seen as a challenge, an enemy, a punishment, weakness, a relief, a strategy, an irreparable loss, a positive value (opportunity for growth and development). The adaptive tasks of illness, to which coping must address itself, include: (1) to reduce harmful environmental conditions and enhance prospects of recovery; (2) to tolerate or adjust to negative events and reality; (3) to maintain a positive self-image and to construct a new self concept, a new mode of self-being; (4) to maintain emotional equilibrium; and (5) to continue satisfying relationships with others.

Illness is most often perceived as a threat [99], and coping processes are activated to reduce, deflect or eliminate anticipated harm. Several coping styles may be employed. *Cognitive* coping styles may be divided into minimization, or a tendency to selective inattention, ignoring, denial, rationalizing of facts or significance of illness; or vigilant focusing; an obsessional hypervigilance, rigidity, and compulsivity about details of therapeutic management. *Affective* coping responses include fear, panic, anxiety, depression, anger resentment, shame, disgust, helplessness. *Behavioral* coping strategies include tackling, characterized by active energetic engagement; capitulating, characterized by passivity, inactivity and helpless dependency; and avoidance, or the active effort to free oneself from the constraints implicitly in the acceptance of illness or injury. Other important concepts in considering the coping process are the roles of courage, will, and personal growth.

Several theories of coping have been proposed [100]. Klinger's incentive-disengagement theory states that the encounter of an obstacle or threatened loss increases the vigor of the initial response: but if unsuccessful, there will first be frustration and anger, then depression and subsequent disengagement form the goal. Wortman and Brehm have proposed an interactive coping model in which the nature of the individual's response to a potentially aversive outcome depends on (1) the expectation of control over the outcome and (2) the outcome's importance. Seligman's learned helplessness model suggests that depression and a sense of victimization stem from the subject's interpretation that individual behavior will have no effect on outcome. Haan [89] distinguishes coping mechanisms, which are healthy, reality-oriented and conscious, from defense mechanisms which are rigid, distorting and unconscious.

Lazarus [71] groups coping into problem-solving vs. palliative responses, and identifies information-seeking, direct action, inhibition of action and intra-psychic modes. Lazarus has emphasized that a person's cognitive appraisal of a stressful situation will significantly influence the coping strategies elicited and the ultimate success of a person's adjustment. Potentially harmful situations may be conceptualized either as a threat or as a challenge (with the implied potential for mastery or gain). Lazarus suggests that the coping elicited in response to a stressor may be more important than the stressful event itself [17, 71]. Thus, coping may be considered both as changing one's appraisal of the threatening event or some combination of the two. It is both problem-solving and regulation of emotional distress.

Four models of coping have been generated based on the distinction between attribution of responsibility for a problem and attribution of responsibility for a solution [101]. In the *moral model*, the individual holds himself responsible for both problems and solutions: effective coping (resolution of problems) is based on proper motivation. The *compensatory model* argues that the individual is not responsible for the problem, but *is* responsible for the solution, and needs power to accomplish this. The *medical model* is based on the assumption that individuals are responsible neither of problems nor solution, and should be the passive recipients of treatment. In this case, 'coping' would consist of adaptive adjustment to the patient role. Finally, in the *enlightenment model*, individuals are seen as responsible for problems, but unwilling to provide solutions; in this view, they require discipline to move to the problem-solving level.

The models are all based on a balance between blame (attribution of problems) and control (attribution of solutions).

Another model for understanding coping strategies is derived from Shapiro's work on control theory [102]. Basically, Shapiro posits a need for control as a fundamental human drive. A significant consequence of the illness experience is to render the individual helpless and out of control. The sick person becomes an object manipulated by forces beyond comprehension and regulation. Illness raises issues of vulnerability, and the fragility and transitoriness of life as well. Thus, an important coping task is to regain a sense of mastery and control at some level of existence. Many coping strategies seemed to be directed at the patient's (or parents') need to control the uncontrollable. This phenomenon has been posited as an alternative explanation to psychodynamic interpretations of guilt; i.e. parents prefer to blame themselves than to confront the helplessness of having nowhere specific to lay blame [103].

Thus, many coping strategies may be understood as an attempt to maintain a sense of control, whether over life in general, or over the outcomes of the illness in particular. In this regard, work on locus of control becomes relevant, as individuals may maintain a sense of control through a belief in personal efficacy (active participation in the recovery process): or, through a belief in chance, or through a belief in powerful others [104].

	Active	Passive
+	1 Active-Positive	2 Passive-Positive
-	3 Active-Negative	4 Passive-Negative

Figure 1. A control model of coping

Shapiro posits a four quadrant model of control, which is divided into dimensions of active and passive control, as well as adaptive and dysfunctional control (see Fig. 1). In this model, quadrants 1 and 3 are active; 2 and 4 are passive; 1 and 2 are adaptive; 3 and 4 are dysfunctional. Using this model as a theoretical framework, we may examine further some of the commonly identified coping strategies. This conceptualization cuts across other coping models, in that adaptive strategies of active control may be either cognitive or behavioral, instrumental or palliative.

Adaptive, active control coping strategies would clearly include the following: information-seeking, direction action (or inhibition of action) regarding the illness: tackling strategies; mastery of specific illness-related procedures; and goal-setting, in the sense of mastery over the illness. It might also include making life changes in the hopes of positively affecting the outcome of the illness; and escaping or distracting behaviors to avoid, for a time, the reality of the illness.

One of the most commonly employed cognitive coping strategies is denial, or minimizing and avoiding. This can occur with reference to actual facts, to the meaning of those facts, or to one's own emotional state. Denial may also be interpreted as an active control coping strategy in the following sense. Active control coping strategies take as their basic premise that the disease is the enemy, and all efforts must be directed toward conquering or excising it. This is a typically Western mode of controlling the environment, through conquering and active mastery. In this sense, denial becomes a cognitive mechanism for rejecting the reality of the illness, or the limits it imposes. It is rooted in the effort to keep the individual intact by rejecting the intrusion of illness or its implications. Isolation of affect, or denial of the emotional effect of an illness crisis on the individual, may also be conceptualized in this manner. Similarly, mental imagery such as that used by the Simontons [105] with cancer patients is based on the idea of combatting and vanquishing cancer cells, and as such may be considered an adaptive active control strategy.

Coping strategies falling into quadrant 3 might include the following: obsessional hyper-vigilance, or the effort to be in active control of all aspects of the disease and its treatment: dysfunctional denial and avoidance; and control through thinking [106], in the sense of accumulating information and other forms of cognitive mastery in an attempt to obviate one's essential helplessness in the face of an overwhelming stressor; intellectualization and denial of affect [107]. In this respect, more typically active outward-turning emotions such as anger might also be considered as falling in this quadrant 3, as they are based on a rejection of the illness.

Passive control coping strategies, on the other hand, appear to be organized around an acceptance of the disease, of essential helplessness, and of realistic limitations. Quadrant 2 adaptive passive coping strategies might be characterized by 'insight', or acceptance in the positive sense: continuing to live as fully as possible given the constraints of the illness. Other quadrant 2 strategies might include turning to others for support and encouragement, acceptance of and ability to express one's own feelings in this situation, and finding a general pattern or meaning in the experience. Rationalization, or focusing on the enriching aspects of the experience, might also be considered to fall within this quadrant. Rehearsing possible outcomes with the aim of gaining acceptance both of recovery and death also might be included in this category. Humor and laughter would also be considered adaptive passive coping strategies, in that they challenge not the outcome itself, but the interpretatin of the seriousness of the outcome. Similarly, prayer in the sense of the accomplishment of God's will would be included in this quadrant, while praying specifically for the recovery of the patient would be a quadrant I coping behavior. Stress reduction behaviors, such as meditation, positive imagery, and relaxation would also fall in this quadrant if their object was the increased centeredness and tranquility of the participant. Dysfunctional quadrant 4 strategies would include capitulating, focus on helplessness, hopelessness, and pervasive dependency, feelings of depression and low self-esteem (self-blame), and negative acceptance in the sense of resignation and giving-up.

Coping in children

Very little has been written specifically on child patterns of coping with stress. Rutter [16] examines mediating mechanisms of stress in children and points out that first, stress has a cumulative effect; and second, that (1) favorable home environment, (2) self-esteem, (3) availability of environmental options, (4) structure and control in the family and (5) stable relstionships with adults were protective factors associated with better social adjustment in children. Rutter identified positive self-esteem, ability to derive pleasure in life, adaptability and malleability as coping skills which protected against psychiatric disorder in childhood under conditions of chronic stress.

Family coping

Family health has been defined as its capacity to effectively cope with illness events. An effectively coping family is able to attain a new adaptive equilibrium around a particular illness. Thus, the healthy family is not one that does not experience illness, but one that is able to cope with the demands of illness [6]. Little has been examined in the way of family coping *per se*. The most extensive work done in this area [108-110] has identified several family coping responses to stressful separations, including seeking resolution and expressing feelings, reducing anxiety, maintaining family integrity, religion and faith, establishing independence and self-sufficiency, building and utilizing interpersonal relationships. At this point, however, it is unclear in what sense it is possible to talk about family coping in more than an aggregate of the coping strategies of individual family members.

The goals of family coping strategies in response to major illness may be summarized as follows: (1) Responding to the challenge of family adaptation. Does the family have a sufficiently large capacity for tranformation to include this development and encompass it? (2) Maintaining a sense of membership in the family, for the ill person. (3) Reorganizing the family and reassigning roles. (4) Reestablishing an emotional baseline——and the mastery of resentful, self-accusatory and other negative feelings [111]. Another family coping goal has been conceptualized as maintaining relationships with the child which afford some parental gratification and at the same time fulfill the child's physical and psychological needs. Other family tasks when confronted with a chronically ill child include an effort to contain the impact of the child's illness and to develop expertise about their child's condition [112]. The family's overall coping style is influenced by (a) the characteristics of the event, (b) the perceived threat to family relationships, status and goals, (c) the resources available to the family and (d) past experience with crisis situations.

Stage models of family coping
The most prevalent approach to understanding and conceptualizing family response to physical illness in the child has been through use of the stage model [93, 113-116]. Most of these models are derived from observations of family response to the chronically ill, the physically handicapped or patients suffering form cancer. In their progression, they are generally quite similar to Kubler-Ross' classic stages of death and dying [117]——grief, denial, anger, bargaining, depression and acceptance. In general, they are not explanatory models, in the sense that they offer no insights as to why particular processes occur. They attempt to define a normal course of development for the psychosocial aspects of the family's reaction to the patient's disease. Their stated goal is to allow the physician to predict, anticipate, and deal with the family's response to illness, and to help discriminate between normal and pathological responses. Although there is considerable variability among models, all have certain elements in common. Acute coping reactions tend to reflect denial, overprotection, anger, guilt and blame; while chronic coping reactions have been categorized as masochistic, overprotective, withdrawal, doctor-shopping, denial and hope [97]. Stage theory has been collapsed temporarily and applied to situations of short duration, such as the child in the ICU [118]. However, these stages also closely parallel those identified in coping over time: (1) shock, disbelief, helplessness; (2)search for etiology and self-blame; (3) once the child is stable, anticipatory waiting, concern for the future; and (4) elation or mourning, depending on the outcome.

In most of these models, there is universal agreement that the initial response of family members to the child's diagnosis consists of shock, disbelief, anxiety, denial and helplessness.

This is then followed by guilt, self-blame, depression and a generalized grief reaction [94], often including anticipatory mourning and/or chronic sorrow. There may also be an interval of searching for meaning, questioning reasons and values [119]. This stage may be followed by anger. Often, a stabilization is achieved after resolution of the initial crisis, only to be destroyed by second-order crises (relapse, entering school) [120]. Finally, the family comes to a point of chronic deterioration and disorganization, or reintegration. Adams, in an exhaustive work on childhood malignancy and its psycho-social ramifications [121], interprets family response in terms of anticipatory mourning and anticipatory grieving. He identifies the employment by the family of: (1) defense mechanisms; denial, repression, isolation of affect and avoidance; (2) affective responses: sorrow, anger, guilt, anxiety; and (3) adaptational responses: information-seeking, invoking emotional support, partialization or compartmentalization (focus on the moment) and rehearsing death. This is similar, although more detailed, to other family models of coping with cancer [113, 122].

One important and comprehensive stage model for understanding family response to illness is that of the family-illness trajectory [123]: Stage I raises legitimacy issues, and examines the nature of response to the onset of illness. Stage II deals with the reaction to diagnosis, including common phenomena of shock, anxiety, denial, disbelief and anticipatory grief. Stage III, the therapeutic intervention, emphasizes the importance of creating consistency between the family's belief system and the mode of therapeutic intervention, dealing with guilt/anger over helplessness, and dealing with assumption of responsibility for health care. Stage IV deals with early adjustment to outcome (recovery) and emphasizes issues such as regression in the child, delayed reactions of depression in the family, the reassignment of familial roles, the heightened sense of vulnerability, and what kind of relabelling occurs in the family. Stage V is the adjustment to the permanency of outcome and acceptance of death or permanent disability.

Despite its neat conceptual appeal, the stage model suffers from several deficits. For example, at present there is little research evidence to suggest the validity of this developmental approach, and it may be an example of shared, consensual thinking rather than reality. Secondly, it severely restricts the amount of options available to individuals in terms of coping. Because of the theoretical nature of the terms employed, it is difficult to know on a more concrete, behavioral level how the various stages are mainfest. In all these models, it is unclear as to whether these stages are necessarily sequential. Perhaps stages may be omitted entirely, or conversely repeated or reverted to. Finally, and most complex, different family members may experience different stages at different times.

Family coping in psychosomatogenic families
One model for family coping with disease in the child which deserves special mention is Minuchin's psychosomatogenic family [124-126]. Psychosomatogenic (or psychosomatic) families are fascinating examples of the potentially endless interactive effects of family and illness. In these situations, the family is not only responding to a particular type of illness (e.g. some cases of childhood asthma, brittle juvenile diabetes and anorexia nervosa), but in fact their method of 'coping' with the disease exacerbates and perhaps precipitates illness episodes.

Minuchin identifies the psychosomatic family as characterized by four components [127-129]: (1) enmeshment, or an overinvolvement of family members with a lack of boundaries between familiar subsystems (groupings of certain family members——siblings, grandmother/-granddaughter, all males——within the family; (2) overprotectiveness, especially where physical signs and symptoms are concerned; (3) rigidity, or a lack of ability to accommodate change and growth within the family system; and (4) inability to deal overtly with conflict, leading to the sublimation of conflict through symptoms of the identified patient. In one study [130], psychosomatic families were significantly worse than controls in that they failed totally to cope with experimentally induced conflict, and had vague and unclear communication patterns characterized by avoidance of conflict and pseudo-agreement. In families of patients with duodenal ulcers, the

mothers exerted obsessional control and banned direct expression of aggression, while fathers were mild-mannered and distant [131]. In psychosomatic families, concern and preoccupation with the patient is used to avoid family conflicts [132, 133], but has the result of reinforcing symptomatology. Thus, illness in the child [134] may stabilize the family unit, resulting in a pattern of chronic illness. If the symptoms are alleviated, other family members may exhibit psychosomatic outbreak or other dysfunction. In these families, a clear relationship between emotional conflict and onset of symptoms tends to emerge [135]. The patient is externalizing by his/her symptoms the pathology inherent in the family system and therapeutic treatment modalities are generally undermined unless change also occurs in the family system.

Issues in family coping
Most models of coping have focused primarily on the indiviudal. Even the stage models enumerated above do not specify precisely how the family experiences these different stages. Family coping is a new concept in need of further theoretical formulation. For example, does family coping mean simply the aggregate of individual family members' styles of coping? Does it refer to the discrepancies of stage coping between family members? Can the family unit function as a whole in such a way as to produce 'family coping' at a structural and/or process level? There are insufficient literature and research to adequately answer these questions. However, some speculation on these topics is appropriate, if only as a stimulation to further investigation.

Family members' coping response can be categorized in a variety of ways. An important dimension to consider is intentionality: i.e. whether the individual family member (or the family group as a whole) is consciously selecting a strategy as a means of dealing with the stressor; or whether the individuals of the family group simply respnd, and those behaviors, thoughts, and emotions are labelled by an outside observer as 'coping' with the stressor. This is an important dimension because future investigation may show that intentional strategies are more effective in terms of various outcome measures than nonintentional strategies.

The most obvious intentional strategies are related to problem-solving. These may involve information-seeking, decisions to take (or not take) action, participation in treatment process, etc. Intentional cognitive strategies may also be categorized under this heading: for example, if a conscious effort is made to think positively, or to make encouraging self-statements. Less frequently, but theoretically possible, we see as examples of intentionailty positive acceptance, where an individual or family group consciously selects a particular acceptance strategy to practice (meditation exercises, relaxation techniques).

Clearly, the 'problem' confronting the family is not unidimensional; thus, it may be appropriate to identify the various adaptive tasks generated by a single illness stressor. As various aspects of the illness are delineated, different coping mechanisms may be called into play. For example, one task to be addressed in the child cancer patient is that he/she receive the best possible and most appropriate medical treatment. Therefore, parents may devise strategies to allow them an active influence on this aspect of the stressor. However, another task to arise might be the child's quality of life. To deal with this issue, parents might problem-solve by spending more time with the affected child, engaging in more pleasurable activities together.

Thus, there are several different aspects of the stressor of illness. One has to do with the physical health of the affected child, and how that can be optimized. A second has to do with the emotional health of the affected child, and how that can be optimized. A third has to do with managing the emotional (and to a less extent, the physical) impact on parents of the child's illness. The fourth involves managing the emotional and physical impact on siblings.

Clearly, these areas are highly interrelated, and the coping strategy selected may alternatively (a) be helpful in one area and irrelevant to other ares of concern, (b) be helpful simultaneously in two or more areas, (c) be harmful simultaneously in two or more areas, and (d) be helpful in one area and harmful in another area. An example of (c) would be a parent's denial of a diagnosis of

ALL, which would negatively affect the physical health of the affected child, and in an extreme form also negatively affect the parent's own emotional health. An example of (b) would be increasing the number of mutually perceived enjoyable activities that parent and child engaged in, which would have a positive impact on the psychological health of both parent and child. An example of (d) would be a parent who, to deal with her own level of stress, would physically leave her child at a point close to the child's death. While such an action might be necessary to reduce parental stress, it would have a deleterious emotional effect on the child.

Much of the thinking on coping becomes quickly circular. For example, is 'feeling guilty' a coping response to diagnosis? From a psychoanalytic point of view, the answer would be yes. This raises the possibility that coping strategies in themselves, which families employ either consciously or nonconsciously, may engender further coping strategies, required to deal with the consequences of the initial coping strategies. In this case, attending a support group might be a positive way to deal with guilt feelings.

There is also considerable confusion about how to evaluate coping strategies: i.e. what outcome measures are appropriate? Quick judgements in this area are clearly risky, for example, pejoratively labelling a parental response as denial, a word with definite negative connotations. Perhaps definitions of functionality are most useful. For example, any strategy which decreases the emotional or physical wellbeing of its user might be considered negative. Of course, these things are not easy to measure. But clearly-excessive use of drugs or alcohol: eating disorders, significant and prolonged depression, phobic response are all negative in the sense that they negatively affect the health of the individual engaging in them. The individual's subjective perception is also of importance. For example, an individual who says, "I feel better when I try to look on the bright side", may be employing a strategy which is personally useful.

Another important idea is the concept of relating different coping stratgies to different stages of a disease. It may be more 'appropriate' to feel shock and disbelief on the day of diagnosis than on the day of the child's death. Similarly, active problem-solving strategies may be better suited to the early phases of a disease, while nonjudgmental, acceptance strategies may be more appropriate during a terminal phase.

Several as yet unanswered questions emerge from the coping literature as a whole. For example, what are the factors which reduce a person's subjective distress when an aversive event is encountered? What are the conditions under which exposure to unpleasant events results in undesirable outcomes? Perhaps flexibility, and the range of coping behaviors are the most critical determinants. Perhaps the avoidance of obviously negative strategies is more important than which good strategies have been selected. When does exposure to negative outcomes produce renewed determination to overcome obstacles, and when does it result in feelings of helplessness and passivity? Of particular interest is the question of individual differences in responses to stressful events. For example, why, when confronted by equally stressful situations, do certain individuals appear to cope better than others? What is the phenomenon of resiliency and how can it be applied to the concept of family coping? Are there universal reactions to aversive life events (e.g. shock, anger, depression)? Is there an orderly progression through a sequence or stages of coping through which everyone proceeds? Finally, and most complex, what really is successful adjustment to an aversive life event?

Family Coping with Minor Illness

As one might expect, little has been written about the response of the family to minor illness. It is often assumed that because minor illness is, after all, minor, any impact or challenges it presents also will be minor. However, there is evidence to suggest that the child's negative response to minor illness is related to later hypochondriasis, persistent dependence, and excessive fear of physical hurt. Thus, a family's and patient's responses to minor illness are significant if only because of the potential chronic anxiety engendered [136].

Responses to minor illness of the child-patient have been noted most frequently [68, 137, 138]. The affected child often experiences reactions of guilt, fear, anger, depression, apathy, loss of normal social contacts, restrictions and a changed relationship with parents (either in the form of increased indulgence or hostility). This response in some ways parallels the commonly reported reactions of the child to major illness and even to death and dying. Behavioral changes, particularly in the age range 1-4 years, have also been documented, including clinging, fear of being alone, fear of going to bed, feeding problems, enuresis, general anxieties, nightmares, jealousy of other children, being more babyish and loving the mother more. Younger children tend to become regressive and dependent, while 3-4 year olds tend to be irritable and to withdraw.

Parents are also affected by the minor illnesses of their child and it is interesting to note that mother's reaction to the illness is the most important etiological factor in any subsequent behavioral disturbances in the child. Parents respond with fears, guilt, anxiety, fatigue, depression and may have misconceptions about the illness. Marital discord often increases. Depending on the nature of the experience itself, parents emerge from the illness either frightened and confused or with a feeling of mastery and accomplishment [136]. It has also been noted that siblings may exhibit behavioral problems during the minor illness of another child in the family.

Virtually nothing has been written about how parents and child cope with the stress of minor illness. It has been observed, in terms of dysfunctional coping, that physicians may be pressured to either overmanage or undermanage minor illness because of intrafamilial dynamics.

Family Coping with Chronic Illness

The family is affected in profound ways by the occurrence of a chronic and/or life-threatening illness. The family has the responsibility for mediating stress for its members [139]. However, great or prolonged stress can destroy the role of the family as buffer for its members. Both individual and family reactions to such threats as prolonged illness are formed from one to four weeks after the diagnosis is confirmed; both maladaptive and adaptive coping responses become evident then, and these responses persist throughout the course of the illness. The depth of the family response may be seen in the vulnerable child syndrome, or children mistakenly identified to be at risk for or suffering from some serious physical condition. In one study [140], it was found that years afterwards the misdiagnosed child was still perceived differently and treated differently by the mother. (For an opposite finding see [141]). The most important variable in this situation was the maternal reaction to the baby's illness, rather than the physician's opinion or the objective severity of the disease.

We are beginning to be able to generalize about the responses of families to serious illness in the child. Dysfunctional responses seem to have received the greatest attention in the literature. This list is a lengthy one [142-145]. Initial responses of shock, denial, guilt, inadequacy and helplessness are commonly reported [94]. Resolution of these feelings is apparently quite variable. Resentment, irritation at the unexpected burden and anger are also possible reactions [146], yielding either punishment, rejection or ignoring the ill member. Mothers may develop unrealistically low expectations for their child to protect themselves from disappointment and adopt a custodial rather than a parental role [96]. Even more common are feelings of anxiety and uncertainty, often producing overprotectiveness and overindulgence toward the patient. Anxiety may focus initially on the appearance and/or care of the child, and later may be direct to questions of future function and/or survival. Depression and unersolved grief or anticipatory mourning are also frequently repoted consequences. There exists some research evidence to support the belief that higher levels of depression and anxiety exist in mothers of handicapped children than in the general population [147]. The frequently reported phenomenon of 'chronic sorrow' [119] refers to parental emotional response to their child's handicap or chronic illness, where, because the child does not die, parents must deal with issues of loss and disappointment on an ongoing, often unresolved basis.

Further, parents' sense of competence appears to be severely challenged by the presence of a chronic health condition in their child, especially for fathers. Fathers also seem to derive less satisfaction and gratification from these children than do fathers of normal controls [148]. At times, parents become so preoccupied with their own feelings that they are unable to contribute adequate emotional support to the child. Marital dysfunction is frequently mentioned, and it has been pointed out that the stress of dealing with a chronically ill or handicapped child can destroy family life [115]. However, it is not clear that a significantly higher divorce rate is characteristic of families coping with a major illness [149-153].

Parents of affected children often display both psychosomatic and psychiatric illnesses, especially depressive disorders [154]. Parents may also experience sleep disturbances, nightmares, increase in smoking, anorexia and a need for tranquilizers and sedation [155]. They may report themselves to be tired, worried and generally unwell [156].

Frequently, overconcentration of attention on the sick member is reported, and child-rearing practices are distorted, influenced by parental guilt, ambivalence, depression or rejection [157]. Often, mother becomes overinvolved in an intense dyadic relationship with the identified patient, while father, and to some extent other siblings [158-160] are isolated outside the 'magic circle'. Even more generally, there is an overall distortion of family life, as the ill child becomes the center of attention, and the hub of the family for whom considerable lifestyle and financial sacrifices are made [161].

Very often, a chronic stress syndrome is identified in the family, where the main goal of the family becomes physical survival, with little hope of accomplishing or identifying goals. Often, in long-term adaptation, the family fluctuates between feelings of mourning and denial. Sometimes, lethal dyads emerge [145] characterized by a see-saw of symptoms between family members. Families with a chronically ill or dying member are frequently characterized by a web of silence [162], a notable lack of communication in the household about the disease, and the consequent isolation of the patient.

Communication within the family also can be a major problem because family members may be at different stages of the grief process [119], and are threatened by the perceptions of other family members. In response to chronic or fatal illness, parental communication often ceases altogether as a result of psychological processes of guilt, blame, denial and depression [163]. Parents also seem to lose touch affectively with their children, and to be unaware of the child's fears and fantasies concerning the illness.

Another kind of isolation occurs for the family itself. Families struggling with chronic disabling or life-threatening conditions may become isolated from the large society, and often view themselves in a we-they relationship with the outside world [164]. Because of this feeling, a family may at times postpone or avoid seeking help. Finally, there are significant infringements on family's leisure and work time, as well as on time with spouse and time for self [165].

Initially, during the first episodes of serious illness, family members still maintain a spirit of hopefulness and helpfulness. In relapse, a process of disintegration sets in, and splits appear within the family group. Family members begin to drift apart. In the 'pseudo-narcotic' syndrome [166], family members walk about in a dazed state, there is a sense of profound apathy, a loss of feeling, impoverished interaction between family members, diminution of sexual desire and loss of contact with the outside world. Where there is past evidence of family strength, this disintegrative process may be halted and reversed. Attempts are made at denial of deviance, and rationalization of symptoms. Then an effort is made to localize the disturbance by isolating the patient. This may be followed by a turning to outside connections and social affiliations. Eventually the patient's perspective is understood and viewed with compassion. Often, this regeneration is charcterized by outbursts of creativity in family members.

Coping responses specific to the affected child have also been noted. It has been observed [167] that in terms of the psychological effect on the child, the illness itself is less menacing than familial response to that illness. About 10% of all children will be affected by chronic illness by age 15, and one third of these will develop secondary psychological complications [168]. These secondary psychological and behavioral pathologies are an attempt to cope with the stress of meeting the demands of daily living. Maladaptive responses in the pre-adolescent include demoralization, self-denigration, denial and depression. Interestingly, in a study of 100 7-12 year old children hospitalized for orthopedic procedures, of the 23 diagnosed as clinically depressed, significantly more had parents with adjustment or emotional problems (problems in adjusting to the child's handicap).

Of course, there is at times the effect of secondary gain for the child, in the sense of increased attention, special treatment and privileges, etc. However, this does ot compensate for the negative feelings of low self-esteem, moodiness, withdrawal, depression, over-sensitivity, denial, rebellion, overdependence, immaturity and passive resignation which often affect the chronically ill child. Like his or her parents, the child also experiences anxiety, shame, deviance, a sense of doom and failure, a sense of 'badness', fears of death, denial, guilt and anger [169]. The child may either internalize his/her predicament as a punishment, or project blame onto the parents for causing him/her to be defective. The child may also become isolated from peers. Behavioral problems are often an issue [157, 170]. The combined presence of chronic illness and a low level of family functioning serves to increase the probability that a child will be described as having three or more deviant behavioral symptoms.

Just as family relationships and communication patterns are critical in determining the affected child's response to serious illness, so these are often more important in determining siblings' reactions than the type and severity of the illness itself [171]. Siblings particularly at risk for maladaptive responses are undergoing other, concurrent streses, have poor relationships with parents and/or with the ill child, poor support systems, and limited communication skills. They may themselves develop physical symptoms, school problems, anti-social or attention-seeking behaviors, changes in mood, regressive behaviors, or anxiety-related habits (nightmares, fears, accident-proneness, nailbiting, stuttering, eating problems) and poor self-esteem. Sibling effects also reported prevalent include feelings of being deprived of emotional or material support, behavior problems [94], excessive involvement with the sick child, and some degree of social isolation and alienation. Other studies report that siblings fear they themselves may become ill or have caused the patient's condition [118]. Other sibling problems in cases of chronic illness include jealousy, enuresis, encopresis and fire-setting [172]. Often the sibling suffers even more psychological distress than the affected child.

However, there appear to be some positive responses as well in the family confronted with major and life-threatening illness. These appear to be reported more commonly in the popular literature, or in anecdotal form. Several anecdotal reports stress the feelings of happiness and growth that come from sharing the experience with their child [174]. Indeed, some researchers have dismissed these positive consequences as rationalizations on the part of parents attempting to keep their defenses intact. On the other hand, parents sometimes report that professionals put too much emphasis on the negative aspects of the experience, and underestimate their capacity to make adjustments after the initial shock has dissipated. It seems valid to consider these responses for what we can learn about making life-threatening illness a major growth experience for the family.

Families often report becoming closer as a unit, developing a true sense of family for perhaps the first time [175]. Family members also sometimes feel they have grown on a variety of personal and interpersonal dimensions as a result of the experience [176]. Specifically, the development of a more positive and humorous worldview is sometimes reported, as is an increased compassion and tolerance [177]. Also reported is the development of unusually deep and meaningful friendships, both with other parents and at times with hospital personnel. These families often report a basic normalcy and independence, as well as an unusual maturity, in their affected child [178]. One research study of adolescent illness in relation to parental relationships found that when chronically ill adolescents were overtly ill, there were noticeably positive changes in the reactins of family members [179]. Perhaps reality lies somewhere between these findings. One study indicated that in terms of coping, parents raising a physically handicapped child fell between normal and poorly-adjusted parents [180]. There was lower parental confidence, understanding and less acceptance of the child than in a normal population, but greater than in poorly functioning families. Similarly, the children themselves had more behavior problems than normal children, but less than emotionally disturbed children.

Coping in Families with a Handicapped Child

Both anecdotal observation and survey methodology have been used to report on the effect of a handicapping condition on the family and on the family's coping response to such a condition. Existing summaries [157, 181, 182], based primarily on opinion and case studies, stress the high morbidity of parents and/or children due to (1) lack of acceptance of such a child and (2) severity of stress imposed on the family. Several studies [119, 183, 184], refer to identifiable phases which families undergo as a result of their child's disability, similar to the stages identified in the death and dying literature. For parents of a handicapped child, these include initial shock and disbelief, often followed by rage, guilt, denial and adjustment or acceptance. Reference is also made to the phenomenon of chronic sorrow [115]. Another important theoretical concept is that of marginality, in which both parents and child must come to terms simultaneously with the child's normal and deviant aspects [185].

Several articles attempt to distinguish between successful and unsuccessful coping in parents and families of the disabled child. Denhoff [186] concludes that good coping on the part of parents consists of (1) acceptance, (2) developmental understanding, (3) warm and secure family relationships, (4) encouragement of self-help, (5) initiative and stamina in the area of therapy and rehabilitation and (6) professional trust. Another article, examining the adaptive patterns of parents of amputee children [187], mentions as indices of good coping the importance of love and acceptance, communication within the family, limit setting for the affected child, and flexibility in managing daily crises. An English study [188] gathered survey material on the problems of 50 handicapped children and their families. This study identified widespread emotional difficulties in the parents, such as over-anxiety, depression, over-protection, rejection, friction and aggression. Among siblings, poor coping was marked by jealousy, a negative effect on their social life, and a negative effect on family leisure time. For the affected child, poor coping was associated with withdrawal, behavior problems, anxiety, depression, temper tantrums, enuresis and aggression.

A study of 25 children and families [164] emphasized the importance of realistic acceptance of the child's condition and prognosis, and the importance of effective information-seeking and help-seeking. According to parents surveyed in this study, successful coping meant achieving a quality of life as close to normalcy as possible. This study, as do others [95, 189], also emphasized communication efforts and utilization of support systems as positive coping strategies. The study previously cited which concluded that coping styles of parents raising a handicapped child fell somewhere between normal and poorly-adjusted parents [180], emphasized that the presence of the ill child was the primary contributor to these patterns. Several articles [94, 171, 190-194] specifically discuss the user of family groups as part of a coping strategem. Most of these groups were led either by physicians, psychiatrists, or social workers. Most were nondirective , emphasizing group discussion and the disclosure of feelings. The goals of such programs were to minimize individual feelings of isolation and difference, demonstrate universality of feelings thereby diluting their intensity, provide information, emotional expression and support, encourage the formation of friendships and participation in group activities. These groups generally seemed to be effective in channeling parental hostility and diffusing parental guilt, but measures are rarely reported and no control procedures were utilized. These programs rarely derive from an empirical or theoretical base, and

are rarely systematically evaluated. Thus, it becomes diffult to assess whether significant improvement has occurred in the family, and if so, why.

One article of particular interest cross-culturally dealt with factors interfereng with the successful implementation of intervention programs aimed at physically handicapped Mexican-American children and their families [195]. These included (1) strong family pride, rejecting the help of 'outsiders', (2) the need for approval of any treatment plan by the priest or other religious leader, (3) the machismo ethic, which often interpreted disruptive, maladaptive behavior in male children as normal 'masculine' behavior and thus not in need of treatment, (4) family values encouraging child passivity, which reduced the affected child to an inappropriately dependent state, (5) superstition and lack of knowledge about medical and rehabilitation technology and (6) the potential negativism of extended family and friends. The article stressed the importance of a home-centered approach.

Family Coping with Childhood Cancer

The initial parental reaction reported is one of shock and disbelief. The period after diagnosis is characterized by confusion, anxiety and realistic fear: insomnia, sleep disturbances and anorexia. The period of remission appears to be characterized by ongoing strains in daily living, as well as behavioral and academic problems of siblings [196]. In the initial phase, other parental responses include loss of control, physical distress, depression, inability to function, anger and hostility. Blame and gult are other common reactions, although guilt was not characteristically manifested by prolonged and exaggerated feelings of wrongdoing but was more usually a transient phenomenon. Anticipatory grief reaction occurs, characterized by intellectualization, irritability, depression, somatization, denial, frenzied activity and worry about the circumstances in which the child will die. After the child's death, there was no unusual incidence of somatic complaints or minor illnesses in the parents reported [197, 198].

In a University of Kansas Medical Center Study [199]. it was found that while families of child cancer patients had extremely high marital stress levels (higher than hemophilia parents, for example, and approaching couples in marital counseling) the incidence of person-year divorce rates was actually less in the study gorup than in the general population. Death of the sick child did not seem to be associated either with divorce or elevated marital stress scores. Couples in the study group were characterized by feelings of low self-esteem, helplessness and strong dependency needs. Also noted were discomfort on the part of one spouse and conflict between marital partners over social contacts.

Several parental reports claimed that the child's illness either improved the marital relationship or did not have any effect [200]. In only a few cases did subjects report any serious marital friction resulting from the illness. Subjects also reported no change in their attitudes toward religion. They did acknowledge a more protective attitude toward remaining children. During the terminal phase of the chil'd illness, sleep difficulties and loss of appetite were common, as was a preoccupation with the sick child. Somatic complaints were infrequent, but 33% reported some difficulty in performing their routine duties during this period. During this phase, some parents felt ambivalence and in implicit ways rejected their child. Signs of an incomplete grief process included: (1) refusal to dispose of personal effects; (2) severe, unremitting feelings of depression; and (3) fear of the mourning process by refusing to think of the loss and/or attempts to replace the lost loved one. Many parents looked forward to their child's death, and experienced relief as well as grief at the actual death. Thirty-three percent of this sample reported the time of diagnosis most difficult, while 33% reported the death as the most difficult time and another third felt these two periods were equally difficult [201].

The family dimension in childhood cancer has been treated with increasing importance [202]. There is awareness of the child as part of a complex biopsychologic system, and an acknowledgement that the entire family system requires treatment, not only the child. Predictors of successful familycoping include the stability of the marital unit and the family's ways of dealing with recent crises.

Various coping responses in the child triggered by cancer have been identified [163]. These include quietude, withdrawal, denial of seriousness, aggressiveness, acting-out. It has been pointed out that the child's response is generally influenced by the family's reaction. There appears to be a maturational aspect to the fear child cancer patients experience [203]. Younger children were most threatened by maternal separation. Children aged 6-10 were most fearful of physical injury, while those aged over 10 were most fearful of death itself. One survey reported no noticeably rebellious behaviors in affected children. Similarly, no noticeable effect on school performance was noted. Parents felt that, except for relapse periods, their children behaved the same as they had prior to contracting the disease. However, other studies observed the child to be openly rejecting of parents, partly because the parents had been unable to protect the child from pain, and partly because the parents were a safer target for aggression than the hospital staff.

Numerous effects on siblings of cancer patients also have been noted, including resentment at extra attention and restricitons on family life. At the death of the affected child, many siblings displayed what has been labelled a 'short sadness span', resuming apparently normal behavior in a relatively brief amount of time. During the illness itself, siblings manifested physical and behavioral problems, enuresis, headaches, poor school performance, depression, tearfulness, separation anxieties, disturbed eating habits and persistent abdominal pains. Several felt jealousy toward the affected child due to parental attention. Siblings often felt responsible for the death, or feared they would also die of leukemia. One study showed that after the death of the affected child, more than one-half of the siblings required some sort of medical consultation lasting longer than one year [200]. Another study of childhood cancer [204] showed that siblings experienced even more psychological distress than patients in terms of perceived social isolation, perception of parents as overindulgent toward and overprotective of the sick child, concern with failure and fear of confronting parents with negative feelings. In terms of general anxiety and perceived vulnerability to illness, siblings and patients reported similar levels. However, another study based on parentla report indicated 70% of siblings were 'back to normal' within one week of the child's death [205].

Coping with cancer may take a variety of forms. In one study, close and intimate support from friends was associated with longer than predicted survival rates [122]. Many parents also reported the helpfulness of discussion groups to ease guilt and to clarify the normalcy of their feelings. Parents most appreciated discussing their feelings about the lukemic child, as well as financial advice [200]. Several articles emphasized the importance of coping through information accumulation and processing. Coping often took the form of focusing on details, rather than on the more general (and tragic) picture, denial and motor activity. Coping after the death of the child included an opportunity to relive the experience over and over, until finally acceptance occurred [196]. Often, fathers coped by absenting themselves from families. Parents sometimes turned to each other for support, but sometimes were too overwhelmed by their indivdual grief to give much support to their partner. Persistent denial seemed to characterize the outer circle of relatives, rather than the inner circle of the family itself, with the phenomenon of "concentric circles of disbelief" being noted [197]. Parents tried to treat the child normally, and to live day-by-day. Coping with a sense of guilt came from contact with other mothers of the ward, also through rational learning, and ventilation of guilt feelings. It was felt that the mother's participation in the care of her child facilitated resolution of guilt and denial [203].

A study by Kaplan [139] estimated that 87% of the families they studied failed to cope successfully with the diagnosis of a leukemic child. School difficulites among healthy siblings, divorce and illness occurred frequently. Adaptive coping in this situation seemed to be charact4erized by an understanding of leukemia as a serious, ultimately fatal illness involving remissions and exacerbations: an acceptance of the child as chronically sick instead of normal; and a period of shared family mourning and mutual consolidation. Maladaptive coping, on the other hand, was characterized by a persistent denial of the reality of the diagnosis, a lack of open communication in the family, and the feeling that knowing will lead to disaster, an inhibition of emotion out of fear of the consequences of emotional expression, flights into activity, which only increased the family's burdens, hostile reactions to members of the health center staff, and inappropriate feelings of being unable to cope with the child's care. Another phenomenon, which Kaplan labelled discrepant coping, was identified, in which parents took opposing positions in terms of their emotional responses, decisions about treatment, and decisions about whom to tell and how. Discrepant coping produced dishonest communication or prevented communication, prohibited or interrupted individual and collective grieving, and overall, tended to weaken family relationslhips. Finally, Kaplan stressed the importance of phase-related coping tasks, tied to diagnosis, remission, relapse, and the terminal phase, which must be resolved in proper sequence to enhance the success of the overall coping process.

Family Coping with Death

Families respond to death of a child based on their own dynamics and homeostatic mechanisms, the assignment of family roles, the need to maintain secrecy around sensitive information, defense mechanisms and affective reactions [206]. It has become increasingly clear that, in the case of a dying child, the family's emotional pain must be attended to [207]. Families respond to death with a combination of guilt, anger, hostility, shock, and a period of grieving [208]. Bowlby has identified three stages of mourning[209]——(1) protest and denial, (2) despair, and disorganization and (3) reorganization——which families experience. Other common reactions include confusions, depression, despair and overly controlled behavior. Sudden death prolongs feelings of shock and disbelief, as the family does not have the opportunity to work through other stages of the grief reaction. However, with a chronically ill child, two losses are involved, one at the time of diagnosis, and the other at the time of actual death [210]. Fathers tend to maintain more overt calm, yet feel dazed, preoccupied, heartsick and cry when alone. Parents often exhibit a surface control, in an effort to produce appropriate behaviors [206]. They may act warmly and supportively toward the dying child, or may withdraw or may engage in inconsistent indulgence. This inconsistency may frighten the child, who reacts by testing parents, which in turn provokes parental anger, then guilt. Parents sometimes manifest phobic reactions to death. They tend to be overly restrictive, protective and to infantilize siblings. Parents also may attempt to replace the lost child with another sibling. Severe anxiety states, insomnia, nightmares and incessant talk about death and the dead child, auditory hallucinations of the dead child and rage-filled agitation are not uncommon [211]. The death of a child can be disastrous if the function of the child was to camouflage existing conflicts in the family.

Siblings also need attention at this time; otherwise they may regress, experience somatic symptoms, develop fears of death, isolate their feelings, or express anxiety in other ways. A study of siblings under psychiatric care for pathologies related to the death of their brother or sister [212] emphasized a feeling of responsibility, whether objectively justifiable or not. (Many of these deaths were related to accidents which did in fact involve the siblings.) Siblings can acquire distorted concepts of illness and death, which exaggerate their vulnerability in the real world. Like parents, siblings may also develop death phobias and an associaton of physicians and hospitals with death.

In terms of coping, there is some evidence that families able to deal with death openly and personally may experience less physical illness than those who do not. Families that coped well with death were found to have more open internal communicaiton, discuss and make realistic plans, express feelings of sadness and loss as well as anger, guilt, and relief and basically attempt to deal with stress rather than deny it [213].

The inability to cope with death may be characteristic of an entire family. Death may become a family pattern in which members collude to avoid confrontation. Family functions of the deceased individual must be redistributed among other family members. In incomplete adaptation, some families may encourage a particular member to assume the role of the deceased as though he were still alive. Unresolved grief reactions have a deep influence on the personality, and may result in later marital discord, behavior problems in children, irrational behavior in parents and mental illness.

Implications for Health Care

The clear interaction between family and illness, the potentially devastating impact of serious illness in the child on the entire family unit, and the power of family coping to positively or negatively influence eventual outcome of the illness episode all point to significant implications for the delivery of health care to child patients. These implications may be conceptualized as occurring on an awareness level and on an implementation level; on an individual level and on a systems level. Figure 2 illustrates the interactive nature of this model.

	Awareness	Implementation
Individual	Personal Consciousness	Personal Action
System	Systematic Attitudes	Systematic Change

Figure 2. Individual and systems implications of a family-oriented approach to health care.

For the individual health care provider (physician, nurse, health, psychologist, social worker, health educator, etc.) an important implication has to do with developing a family-focused way of viewing concepts of health and illness. Once it is understood that the family plays such a critical role in a variety of health care outcomes, adopting an attitude of attention to and inclusion of the family in the provision of health services becomes much easier and more natural.

Attitudinal changes, however, also need an action outlet. Again considering only the indiviudal health care provider, several action implications become evident. One aspect of implementation would be developing the tools and skills to assess family coping resources and responses. Several attempts have already been made at family assessment schema [214-219]. Patient charting could also be arranged to reflect a family orientation. From a preventive medicine standpoint, physicians and other health care providers could be more sensitive to anticipating psychological and physical problems in family members other than the identified patient, to anticipating interactions between family members know to be statistically or clinically associated with increased family distress and dysfunction, and to anticpating points of particularly high stress during the developmental family life cycle. The physician should also have basic skills to intervene therapeutically with families in the sense of educating them to increase the range and flexibility of their adaptive coping responses.

It is obvious that, in order to produce physicians and other health care providers skilled in these areas, major systemic changes would also have to occur. One major area of change might be in the field of medical education, which currently pays scant attention to instruction about family process, structure, and function. A family-oriented approach to health care is not simply an attiude of mind, but requires a specialized knowledge base, which is at present neglected in most areas of medical education.

In addition to education changes, other systemic changes might include (1) structural changes in hospitals and other in-patient facilities encouraging the current trend toward family involvement with the hospitalized child, (2) attitudinal and procedural changes among staff and hospital personnel to allow the family more of a traditional caretaking, rather than a guest role in such facilities, (3) recognition among the medical profession of the importance of the family doctor as the coordinator and supervisor of all aspects of medical care concerning the family unit and (4) changes in insurance policies to make treatment (preventive or non-pharmaco-logical) of family members less of a family financial burden.

Clearly, the above represent only a few brief illustrations of the wide-ranging implications of family ramifications of illness in a child. In particular, a concept deserving greater attention is that physicians have at their disposal a largely underutilized resource, the patient's family, which often works at cross purposes to therapeutic medical aims, and yet, with increased knowledge, could be mobilized efficiently and productively as a crucial support system for medical intervention. Many experienced, and all good doctors intuitively know this already, and are able to involve the family in their treatment approach with beneficial results for both patient and family. What is still needed is additional research and clinical investigation to clarify concepts such as 'family' coping, 'adaptive and dysfunctional' coping, and to tie these to specific behavioral and cognitive skills which the physician can integrate into medical practice. In this way, a critical dimension of the art of medicine, the awareness of the family as patient, will begin to move into the realm of science.

References

1. Hadley T.R., Jacob T., Milliones J., Caplan J., and Spitz D. The relationship between family developmental crisis and the appearance of symptoms in a family member. *Fam. Process* **13**, 207-214, 1974.
2. Worby C.M. The family life cycle: an orienting concept for the family practice specialist. *J. med. Educ.* **46**, 198-203, 1971.
3. Litman T.J. The family as a basic unit in health and medical care: a social behavioral overview. *Soc. Sci. Med.* **8**, 459-519, 1974.
4. Alpert J.J., Kosa J. and Haggerty R.J. A month of illness and health care among low-income families. *Publ. Hlth Rep.* **82**, 705-713, 1967.
5. Curry H.B. The family as our patient. *J. Fam. Pract.* **1**, 70-71, 1974.
6. Pattison E.M. and Anderson R.C. Family health care with special emphasis on the U.S.A. Technostar Ltd. International Scientific Publications, Israel, pp. 83-134, 1978.

7. Pless I.B. and Satterwhite B. A measure of family functioning and its application. *Soc. Sci. Med.* **7**, 613-621, 1973.

8. Geyman J. *Family Practice: Foundation of Changing Health Care.* Appleton-Century-Crofts. New York, 1980.

9. Carmichael L.P. The family in medicine, process or entity? *J. Fam. Pract.* **3**, 562, 1976.

10. Courant I. The patient does not come alone. A systems-oriented approach by the general practitioner. *Huisarts en Wetenschap* **24**, 92-96, 1981.

11. Illingsworth R.S. Paediatrics: some related psychological trends of the last thirty years. *Acta paedopsychiat,* **43**, 253-259, 1978.

12. Grant W.W. What parents of a chronically ill or dysfunctioning child always want to know but may be afraid to ask. *Clin. Pediat.* **17**, 915-917, 1978.

13. Lewis J.M., Beavers, W.R., Gossett J.T., Phillips V.A. *No Single Thread: Psychological Health in Family Systems.* Brunner/Mazel, New York, 1976.

14. Geyman J.P. The family as the object of care in family practice. *J. Fam. Pract.* **5**, 571-575, 1977.

15. Chen E.J. and Cobb S. Family structure in relation to health and disease: A review of the literature. *J. chron. Dis.* **12**, 544-567, 1960.

16. Rutter M. Protective factors in children's response to stress and disadvantage. *Annl Acad. Med.* **8**, 324-338, 1979.

17. Rutter M. Stress, coping and development: Some issues and some questions. *J. Child Psychol. Psychiat.* **22**, 323-356, 1981.

18. Miller J.G. and Miller J.L. The family as a system. In *The Family: Evaluation and Treatment* (Edited by Hofling, C.K. and Lewis J.M.). Brunner Mazel, New York, 1980.

19. Ackerman N.W. *Treating the Troubled Family.* Basic Books, New York, 1966.

20. Jackson D.D. *Communications, Family, and Marriage.* Science and Behavior Books, Palo Alto, CA, 1974.

21. Kerr M.E. Family systems theory and therapy. In *Handbook of Family Therapy* (Edited by Gurman A.S. and Kniskern D.P.), pp. 226-266. Brunner/Mazel, New York, 1981.

22. Kanton D. and Lehr W. *Inside the Family.* Jossey Bass, San Francisco, 1977.

23. Andolfi M. *Family Therapy: An International Approach.* Plenum Press, New York, 1979.

24. Jones S.L. *Family Therapy: A Comparison of Approaches.* Robert J. Brady Co., Bowie, MD, 1980.

25. Goldenberg I. and Goldenberg H. *Family Therapy: An Overview.* Brooks/Cole Publishing Co., Monterey, CA, 1980.

26. McWhinney I.R. *An Introduction to Family Medicine.* Oxford University Press, London, 1981.

27. Okane K. *et al.* Behavior characteristics of children in extended hospitalization. *Jap. J. Nurs. Art* **24**, 105-119, 1978.

28. Henningsen F. *et al.* Psychotherapeutic care of dying and critically ill children and their relatives. *Munchener medsch. Wschr.* **123**, 247-250, 1981.

29. Henningsen F. *et al.* Psychotherapeutic support for critically ill children. *Munchener medsch. Wschr.* **123**, 251-254, 1981.

30. Van der Schyff G. The role of parents during their child's hospitalization. *Aust. Nurs. J.* **8**, 57-61, 1979.

31. Veeneklaas G.M. Child, parents, sickness and hospitalization. *Acta paedopsychiat.* **42**, 91-100, 1979.

32. Tonkin P. Parent care for the low risk and terminally ill child. *Dimens Hlth Serv.* **56**, 42-43, 1979.

33. McCawley C. Report on observation visits to pediatric hospitals. *Lamp N.S.W. Nurs. Ass.* **38**, 33-38, 1981.

34. McCawley C. Family-centered care: A transatlantica study. *Aust. Nurs J.* **11**, 49-50, 1981.

35. Harris P.J. Children in the hospital: How parents feel. *Nurs. Times* **77**, 1803-1804, 14 October, 1981.

36. Nahigian E.E. Minor procedure becomes major for child, mother. *AORN J.* **30**, 630-634, 1979.

37. Medalie J.H. The development and transmission of health and disease with particular emphasis on the family. In *Testbook of Preventative Medicine* (Edited by Leavill H.R. and Clark A.), pp. 67-77, McGraw-Hill, New York, 1980.

38. Meyer R.J. and Haggerty R.J. Streptococcal infections in families: Factors altering individual susceptibility. *Pediatrics* **29**, 539-549, 1962.

39. Bursten B. Family dynamics and illness behavior. *GP* **29**, 142-145, 1964.

40. Lewis J.M. *How's Your Family?* Brunner Mazel, New York, 1979.

41. Peachy R. Family patterns of illness. *GP* **27**, 82-89, 1963.

42. Kellner B.R. *Family Ill Health*. Tavistock, London, 1963.

43. Jackson D.D. Family Practice: A comprehensive medical approach. *Compreh. Psychia.* **7**, 338-344, 1966.

44. Potash S. and Migenes J. The family. In *Family Medicine, Principles and Practice* (Edited by Taylor R.B.), pp. 212-215. Springer-Verlag, New York, 1978.

45. Mechanic D. The experience and reporting of common physical complaints. *J. Hlth soc. Behav.* **21**, 146-155, 1980.

46. Buck C.W. and Laughton K.B. Family patterns of illness: The effect of psychoneurosis in the parent upon illness in the child. *Acta Psychol. Neurol. Scand.* **34**, 165-175, 1959.

47. Becker M.H., Nathanson C.A., Drachman R.H. and Kirscht J. P. Mother's health beliefs and children's clinic visits: A prospective study. *J. Communit. Hlth* **3**, 125-135, 1977.

48. Gupta M.L. *et al.* A review of child-rearing practices prevalent in the families of hospitalized children at Gwalior. *Indian Pediat.* **17**, 261-265, 1980.

49. Mumford E. Culture: life perspectives and the social meaning of illness. In *Understanding Human Behavior in Health and Illness* (Edited by Simons R.C. and Pardes H.), pp. 173-183. Williams & Wilkins, Baltimore, MD, 1978.

50. Parsons T. and Fox R. Illness therapy and the modern urban American family. *J. Soc. Issues* **8**, 31-44, 1952.

51. Steidl J.H., Finkelstein F.O., Wexler J.P. *et al.* Medical condition, adherence to treatment regimens, and family functioning. *Arch. gen. Psychiat.* **37**, 1025-1027, 1980.

52. Metcalfe D.H. The recognition of family and social problems by general practitioners: Toward developing a taxonomy. *Jl. R. Coll. gen. Pract.* **28**, 46-52, 1978.

53. Craven R.F. and Sharp B.H. The effects of illness on family functions. *Nurs. Forum* **11**, 187-193, 1927.

54. Huth, C.M. Illness and the family. *Annls intern. Med.* **89**, 132-133, 1978.

55. Chapman J.A. and Goodall J. Helping a child to live whilst dying. *The Lancet* **1**, 753-756, 5 April, 1980.

56. Goldson E. The family care center: Transitional care for the sick infant and his family. *Children Today* 15-20, July-August, 1981.

57. Glaser H.H., Harrison G.S. and Lynn D.B. Emotional implications of congenital heart disease in children. *Pediatrics* **33**, 367-379, 1964.

58. Smilkstein G. The family in trouble -- How to tell. *J. Fam. Pract.* **2**, 19-25, 1975.

59. Olsen E.H. The impact of serious illness on the family system. *Postgrad. Med.* **47**, 169-174, 1970.

60. Korsch B.M., Fine R.N., Gruskin C.M. and Megrete V.F. Experiences with children and their families during extended hemodialysis and kidney transplantation. *Peds. Clin. N. Am.* **18**, 625-637, 1971.

61. Haggerty R.J. and Alpert J.J. The child, his family and illness. *Postgrad. Med.* **34**, 228-233, 1963.

62. Miller F.J.W., Court W.D.M., Walton W.S. and Knox E.G. *Growing up in Newcastle-on-Tyne*. Oxford University Press, London, 1960.

63. Christie-Seely J. Preventive medicine and the family. *Can. Fam. Phys.* **27**, 449-455, 1981.

64. Cooper N.A. and Lynch M.A. Last to follow-up: A study of non-attendance at a general pediatric outpatient clinic. *Archs Dis. Childh.* **55**, 765-769, 1979.

65. Fleck S. Unified health services and family-focused primary care. *Int. J. Psychiat. Med.* **6**, 501-513, 1975.

66. Holmes, T. and Masuda M. Life change and illness susceptibility. In *Separation and Depression, Clinical and Research Aspects,* Publication No. 94, American Association for the Advancement of Science, Washington, DC, 1973.

67. Haggerty R.J. The management of episodic disorders. In *Ambulatory Pediatrics* (Edited by Green J.J. and Haggerty R.J.), pp. 771-773. W.B. Saunders, New York, 1968.

68. Shrand H. Behavior changes in sick children nursed at home. *Pediatrics* **36**, 604-607, 1965.

69. Cohen F. and Lazarus R.S. Coping with the stresses of illness. In *Health Psychology* (Edited by Stone G.C., Cohen F. and Adler N.E.), pp. 217-155. Jossey Bass, San Francisco, 1979.

70. Lazarus R.S. The stress and coping paradigm. In *Theoretical Bases for Psychopathology* (Edited by Eisdorfer C., Cohen D., Cleinman A. and Maxim P.). Spectrum, New York, 1981.

71. Lazarus R.S. Psychological stress and coping in adaptation and illness. *Int. J. Psychiat. Med.* **5**, 321-333, 1974.

72. Revenson T.A. Stressful life events, coping and illness course in middle-aged and elderly diabetics: a prospective study. Unpublished Doctoral Dissertation. New York University, 1982.

73. Pearlin L.I., Leiberman M.A., Menaghan E.A. and Mullan J.T. The stress process. *J. Hlth soc. Behav.* **22**, 337-356, 1981.

74. Kohn M.L. Class, family and schizophrenia. *Soc. Forces* **50**, 295-302, 1972.

75. Ben-Sira Z. The interrelationship and dynamics of the symptoms of psychological distress: An additional approach to the theory of readjustment and breakdown. In *Research in Psychology and Medicine* (Edited by Oborne D.J., Gruneberg M.M. and Eiser J.R.) Vol. 1, Academic Press, New York, 1979.

76. Felton B.J., Brown P., Lehmann S. and Liberatos P. The coping function of sex-role attitudes during marital disruption. *J. Hlth soc. Behav.* **21**, 240-247, 1980.

77. Jenkins, C.D. Psychosocial modifiers of response to stress. *J. Hum. Stress* **5**, 3-15, 1979.

78. Kobasa S.C. Stressful life events, personality, and health: An inquiry into hardiness. *J. Personal. soc. Psychol.* **37**, 1-11, 1979.

79. Kobasa S.C., Maddi S.R. and Courington S. Personality and constitution as mediators in the stress-illness relationship. *J. Hlth soc. Behav.* **22**, 368-378, 1981.

80. Murphy L.B. Coping, vulnerability, and resilience in childhood. In *Coping and Adaptation* (Edited by Coelho C.V., Hamburg D.A. and Adams J.E.). Basic Books, New York, 1974.

81. Antonovsky A. Conceptual and methodological problems in the study of resistance resources and stressful life events. In *Stressful Life Events: Their Nature and Effects* (Edited by Dohrenwend B.S. and Dohrenwend B.P.). Wiley, New York, 1974.

82. Myers J.K., Lindenthal J.J. and Pepper M.P. Social life events and psychiatric symptoms: a longitudinal study. In *Stressful Life Events: Their Nature and Effects* (Edited by Dohrenwend B.S. and Dorhrenwend B.P.). Wiley, New York, 1974.

83. Liem R. and Liem J. Social class and mental illness reconsidered: the role of economic stress and social support. *J. Hlth soc. Behav.* **19**, 139-156, 1978.

84. Cobb S. Social support as a moderator of life stress. *Psychosomat. Med.* **38**, 300-314, 1976.

85. Dean A. and Lin N. The stress-buffering role of social support. *J. nerv. ment. Dis.* **165**, 403-417, 1977.

86. Hamburg D.A. and Adams J.E. A perspective on coping: Seeking and utilizing information in major transitions. *Archs gen. Psychiat.* **17**, 277-284, 1967.

87. White R.W. Strategies of adaptation: an attempt at systematic description. In *Coping and Adaptation* (Edited by Coelho G.V., Hamburg D.A. and Adams J.E.). Basic Books, New York, 1974.

88. Moos R.H. and Tsu V.D. The crisis of physical illness: an overview. In *Coping with Physical Illness* (Edited by Moos R.). Plenum Press, New York, 1977.

89. Haan N. *Coping and Defending.* Academic Press, New York, 1977.

90. Meichenbaum D., Turk D. and Burstein S. The nature of coping with stress. In *Stress and Anxiety* (Edited by Sarason I.G. and Speilberger C.D.). Vol. 2, Wiley, New York, 1975.

91. Vaillant G. *Adaptations to Life.* Little Brown, Boston, 1977.

92. Weisman A.D. and Worden J.W. The existential plight in cancer: significance of the first 100 days. *Int. J. Psychiat. Med.* **7**, 1-15, 1976-1977.

93. Shokeir M.H.K. Managing the family of the abnormal newborn. In *Risk, Communication and Decision Making in Genetic Counseling* (Edited by Epstein C.J., Curry C.J.R., Packman S., Sherman S. and Hall B.D.). Allen R. Liss, New York, 1979.

94. Valman H.B. The handicapped child. *Br. med. J.* **283**, 1166-1169, 1981.

95. Morgan M. Counseling parents who have a handicapped child. *Jl R. Coll. Physns* **13**, 245-247, 1979.

96. Strand E. Living with a handicapped child: How can we face the strain. *New Zealand Nurs. J.* 30-32, April, 1979.

97. Mattson A. Long-term physical illness in childhood: a challenge to psycho-social adaptation. *Pediatrics* **5**, 801-811, 1972.

98. Gardner R.A. Psychogenic problems of brain-injured children and their parents. *J. Am. Acad. Child Psychiat.* **7**, 471-491, 1968.

99. Kiely W.F. Coping with severe illness. In *Role of the Family in the Rehabilitation of the Physically Disabled* (Edited by Power P.W. and Dell Orto A.E.), pp. 94-105. University Park Press, Baltimore, MD, 1908.

100. Silver R.L. and Wortman C.B. Coping with undesirable life events. In *Human Helplessness* (Edited by Garber J. and Seligman M.E.P.). Academic Press, New York, 1980.

101. Brickman P., Rabinowitz U.C., Karvza J., Coates D. et al. Models of helping and coping. *Am. Psychol.* **37**, 368-384, 1982.

102. Shapiro D. and Shapiro J. Areas of self control for men and women. *J. Clin. Psychol.* In press.
103. Gardner R.A. The guilt reaction of parents of children with severe physical disease. *Am. J. Psychiat.* **124**, 638-644, 1969.
104. Wallston B.S., Wallston K.A., Kaplan G.D. and Maides S.A. Development and validation of the Health Locus of Control (HLC) Scale. *J. consult. clin. Psychol.* **44**, 580-585, 1976.
105. Simonton O.C. and Simonton S.S. Belief systems and management of the emotional aspects of malignancy. *J. Transpersonal Psychol.* **7**, 29-47, 1975.
106. Mattson A. and Agle D.P. Group therapy with parents of hemophiliacs: therapeutic process and observations of parental adaptation to chronic illness in children. *J. Am. Acad. Child Psychiat.* **11**, 558-571, 1972.
107. Galdston R. and Gamble W.J. On borrowed time: observations on children with implanted cardiac pacemakers and their families. *Am. J. Psychiat.* **126**, 142-150, 1968.
108. McCubbin H.I. Integrating coping behavior in family stress theory. *J. Marr. Fam.* **41**, 237-244, 1979.
109. McCubbin H.I., Dahl B., Boss P. and Lester G. Spouse's coping inventory. Family Studies Branch, Naval Health Research Center, San Diego, CA, 1976.
110. McCubbin H., Dahl B. *et al.* Coping repertoires of families adapting to prolonged war-induced separation. *J. Marr. Fam.* **38**, 461-471, 1976.
111. Shellhase J.J. and Shellhase F.E. Role of the family in rehabilitation. *Soc. Casew* **53**, 544-550, 1972.
112. Kodadek, S. Family-centered care of the chronically ill child. *AORN Jl* **30**, 635-638, 1979.
113. Power P.W. and Dell Orto A.E. (Eds) Impact of disability/illness on the child. In *Role of the Family in the Rehabilitation of the Physically Disabled*, pp. 111-117. University Park Press, Baltimore, MD, 1980.
114. Jacobson A. The child in the hospital, illness and death: a psychological process in four phases. *Sygeplejersken* **79**, 16-18, 1979.
115. Green C. Handicapped children: Let's be more positive and practical. *Med. S. Aust.* **1**, 402-404, 1981.
116. Wong D.L. The child w/a life-threatening illness. *New Jersey Nurs.* **10**, 1-9, 1980.
117. Huberty D.J. Adapting to illness through family group. *Int. J. Psychiat. Med.* **5**, 231-242, 1974.
118. Rothstein P. Psychological stress in families of children in a pediatric intensive care unit. *Pediat. Clin. N. Am.* **27**, 613-620, 1980.
119. Gruppo P. Helping the handicapped child. *J. Pract. Nurs.* 30-37, September, 1978.
120. McNair F.L. At-home rehabilitation of pediatric cancer patients: a team approach. *Hlth soc. Wk* **5**, 50-55, 1980.
121. Adams D.W. *Childhood Malignancy: The Psycho-social care of the Child and His Family.* Charles C. Thomas, Springfield, IL, 1979.
122. Parkes C.M. The emotional impact of cancer on patients and their families. *J. Laryngol. Otol.* **89**, 1271-1279, 1975.
123. Burr B.D., Good J.B. and Del Vecchio-Good M. The impact of illness on the family. In *Family Medicine: Principles and Practice* (Edited by Taylor R.B.). Springer-Verlag, New York, 1978.
124. Minuchin S. *Families and Family Therapy.* Harvard University Press, Cambridge, MA, 1974.
125. Minuchin S., Rosman B.L. and Baker L. *Psychosomatic Families: Anorexia Nervosa in Context.* Harvard University Press, Cambridge, MA, 1978.
126. Minuchin S. and Fishman H.C. *Family Therapy Techniques.* Harvard University Press, Cambridge, MA, 1981.
127. Liebman R., Minuchin S., Baker L. and Rosman B.L. The treatment of anorexia nervosa. *Curr. Psychiat. Thr.* 51-57, 1975.
128. Bruch H. Family transactions in eating disorders. *Comprehen. Psychiat.* **12**, 238-248, 1971.
129. Minuchin S., Baker L., Rosman B.L., Leibman R., Milman L. and Todd T.C. A conceptual model of psychosomatic illness in children: family organization and family therapy. *Archs gen. Psychiat.* **32**, 1031-1038, 1975.
130. Wikran R., Faleide A. and Blaker R.M. Communication in the family of the asthmatic child: an experimental approach. *Acta psych. scand.* **57**, 11-26, 1978.
131. Grolnick L. A family perspective of psychosomatic factors in illness: a review of the literature. *Fam. Process* **11**, 457-486, 1972.
132. Block J., Harvey E., Jennings P.H. and Simpson E. Clinicians' conceptions of the asthmatogenic mother. *Archs gen. Psychiat.* **15**, 610-618, 1966.
133. Levenstein S. Psychosomatic families and the general practitioner. *J. Afr. Med. S.* **59**, 289-291, 1981.
134. Bacari A. Acute episodic psychophysiological decompensation (AEPPD). *Br. J. med. Psychol.* **47**, 173-180, 1974.

135. Meissner W.W. Family dynamics and psychosomatic processes. *Fam. Process* **5**, 142-161, 1966.

136. Carey W.B. and Sibinga M.S. Avoiding pediatric pathogenesis in the management of acute minor illness. *Pediatrics* **49**, 553-562, 1972.

137. Platou R.V. and Woody N.C. A psychological approach to pediatric practice. In *The Psychological Basis of Medical Practice* (Edited by Leif H.I., Leif V.P. and Leif N.R.), pp. 347-361. Harper & Row, New York, 1963.

138. Mattson A. and Weisberg I. Behavioral reactions to minor illness in pre-school children. *Pediatrics* **46**, 604-610, 1970.

139. Kaplan D.M., Smith A., Grobstein R. and Fischman S. Family mediation of stress. In *Role of the Family in the Rehabilitation of the Physically Disabled* (Edited by Power P.W. and Dell Orto A.E.), pp. 475-488. University Park Press, Baltimore, MD, 1980.

140. Carey W.B. Psychologic sequelae of early infancy health crisis. *Clin. Pediat.* **8**, 459-463, 1969.

141. Costanza M., Lipsitch I. and Charney E. The vulnerable children revisited: a follow-up study of children three to six years after acute illness in infancy. *Clin. Pediat.* **7**, 680-683, 1968.

142. Green M. The management of long-term nonlife-threatening illness. In *Ambulatory Pediatrics* (Edited by Green M. and Haggerty R.J.), pp. 443-450. W.B. Saunders, New York, 1968.

143. Green M. The care of the child with a long-term life-threatening illness. In *Ambulatory Pediatrics* (Edited by Green M. and Haggerty R.J.), pp. 659-665. W.B. Saunders, New York, 1968.

144. Garrard S.D. and Richmond J.B. Psychological aspects of the management of chronic diseases and handicapping conditions in childhood. In *The Psychological Basis of Medical Practice* (Edited by Leif H.L., Leif V.F. and Leif N.R.), pp. 370-403. Harper & Row, New York, 1963.

145. Bruhn J.G. Effects of chronic illness on the family. *J. Fam. Pract.* **4**, 1057-1060, 1977.

146. Shapiro R. and Harris R.I. Family therapy in treatment of the deaf: a case report. *Fam. Proc.* **15**, 83-96 1976.

147. Burden R.L. Measuring the effects of stress on the mothers of handicapped infants: Must depression always follow? *Child: Care, Hlth Dev.* **6**, 111-125, 1980.

148. Cummings S.T. The impact of the child's deficiency on the father: a study of fathers of mentally retarded and of chronically ill children. *Postgrad. Med.* 173-177, June 1970.

149. Begleiter M.L., Burry V.F. and Harris D.J. Prevalence of divorce among parents of children with cystic fibrosis and other chronic diseases. *Soc. Biol.* **23**, 260-264, 1976.

150. Freeston B.M. An enquiry into the effect of a spina bifida child upon family life. *Dev. Med. Child Neuro.* **13**, 456-461, 1971.

151. Hare E.H., Laurence K.M., Paynes H. and Ransley K. Spina bifida cystica and family stress. *Br. med. J.* **2**, 757-760, 1966.

152. Field B. The child with spina bifida: medical and social aspects of the problems of a child with multiple handicaps and his family. *Med. J. Aust.* **2**, 1284-1287, 1972.

153. Cynes S. The physically handicapped child--is active management justified? *S. Afr. med. J.* **58**, 647-651, 1980.

154. Lawler T.H., Nakielny W. and Wright N.A. Psychological implications of cystic fibrosis. *Can. Med. Ass. J.* **94**, 1043-1046, 1966.

155. Kanof A., Kutner B. and Gordon N.B. The impact of infantile amaurotic familial idiocy (Tay-Sachs disease) on the family. *Pediatrics* **49**, 37-45, 1972.

156. Walker J.H., Thomas M. and Russell I.T. Spina bifida and the parents. *Dev. Med. Child Neurol.* **13**, 462-476, 1971.

157. Wright L. Counseling with parents of chronically ill children. *Postgrad. Med.* 173-176, June 1970.

158. Browne W.J., Malley M.A. and Kane R.P. Psychosocial aspects of hemophilia: A study of twenty-eight hemophilic children and their families. *Am. J. Ortho-psychiat.* **30**, 730-740, 1960.

159. Martin H. Parents' and children's reactions to burns and scalds in children. *Br. J. med. Psychol.* **43**, 183-191, 1970.

160. Larcombe E.S. A handicapped child means a handicapped family. *Jl R. Coll. Gen. Pract.* **28**, 46-52, 1978.

161. Dubo S., McLean J.A., Ching A.Y. *et al.* A study of the relationships between family situations, bronchial asthma, and personal adjustment in children. *J. Peds.* **59**, 402-414, 1961.

162. Turk J. Impact of cystic fibrosis on family functioning. *Pediatrics* **34**, 67-71, 1964.

163. Fomufod A.K. Chronically ill institutionalized children: psychosocial effects of prolonged hospitalization of the terminally sick child. *Soc. Sci. Med.* **14A**, 239-242, 1980.

164. Darling R.B. *Families Against Society*. Sage, Beverly Hills, CA, 1979.

165. Salk L., Hilgartner M., and Granich B. The psychosocial impact of hemophilia on the patient and his family. *Soc. Sci. Med.* **6**, 491-505, 1972.

166. Anthony E.J. The impact of mental and physical illness on family life. *Am. J. Psychiat.* **127**, 138-145, 1970.

167. Gutton P. Psychopathology of the physically sick child. *Revue Neuropsychiat. infant.* **26**, 471-476, 1978.

168. Kashani J.H., Venzke R. and Millar E.A. Depression in children admitted to hospital for orthopedic procedures. *Br. J. Psychiat.* **138**, 21-25, 1981.

169. Raimbault G. and Royer P. How do mother and child react to a child's illness? *Clin. Peds.* **8**, 255-256, 1969.

170. Burnette B.A. Family adjustments to cystic fibrosis. *Am. J. Nurs.* **75**, 1986-1989, 1975.

171. Taylor S.C. Siblings need a plan of care too. *Pediat. Nurs.* 9-13, November-December, 1980.

172. Allan J.L., Townley R.W. and Phelan P.D. Family response to cystic fibrosis. *Aust. Pediat. J.* **10**, 136, 1974.

173. Lademann A. The neurologically handicapped child. *Scand. audiol. Suppl.* **10**, 23-26, 1980.

174. Motohashi S. A record of a mother of a handicapped child. *Jap. J. Nurs.* **42**, 968-970, 1978.

175. Valens E.G. *The Other Side of the Mountain.* Warner Books, New York, 1975.

176. Massie R. and Massie S. *Journey.* Warner Books, New York, 1976.

177. Craig M. *Blessings.* Bantam Books, New York, 1979.

178. Mattson S. and Gross S. Social and behavioral studies on hemophilic children and their families. *J. Pediat.* **68**, 952-964, 1966.

179. Peterson E.T. The impact of adolescent illness on parental relationships. *J. Hlth soc. Behav.* **13**, 429-437, 1972.

180. Tavormina S.B., Boll T.S., Dunn N.S. *et al.* Psychosocial effects on parents of raising a handicapped child. *J. abnorm. Child Psychol.* **9**, 121-131, 1981.

181. Neff W.S. and Weiss S.A. *Handbook of Clinical Psychology* (Edited by Wolman B.B.), p. 785. McGraw-Hill, New York, 1965.

182. McDaniel J.W. *Physical Disability and Human Behavior.* Pergamon Press, New York, 1969.

183. Minde K., Hackett J.D., Killou D. and Silver S. How they grow up: 41 handicapped children and their families. *Am. J. Psychat.* **128**, 1554-1560, 1972.

184. Heisler V. *A Handicapped Child in the Family.* Grune & Stratton, New York, 1972.

185. Minde K. Coping styles of 34 adolescents with cerebral palsy. *Am. J. Psychiat.* **135**, 1344-1349, 1978.

186. Denhoff E. and Holden R.H. Understanding parents: One need in cerebral palsy. In *Counseling Parents of the Ill and the Handicapped* (Edited by Noland R.L.), p. 225. Charles C. Thomas, Springfield, IL, 1971.

187. Daniels L.L. and Berg C.M. The crisis of birth and adaptive patterns in parents of amputee children. *Clinical Proceedings/Childrens Hospital* **108**, 1967.

188. McMicheal J.D. *Handicap: A Study of Physically Handicapped Children and their Families.* Fletcher, Great Britain, 1971.

189. Edelstein S. and Styrdom L.M. The doctor's dilemma--how and when to tell parents that their child is handicapped. *S. Afr. med. J.* **59**, 534-536, 1981.

190. Milman D.H. Group therapy with parents: An approach to the rehabilitation of physically disabled children. In *Counseling Parents of the Ill and the Handicapped* (Edited by Noland R.L.), p. 227. Charles C. Thomas, Springfield IL, 1971.

191. Katz A.H. Therapeutic aspects of parent associations for the handicapped. In *Counseling parents of the Ill and the Handicapped* (Edited by Noland R.L.), p. 248. Charles C. Thomas, Springfield, IL, 1972.

192. Jordan T.E. Physical disability in children and family adjustment. In *Counseling Parents of the Ill and the Handicapped* (Edited by Noland R.L.), p. 10. Charles C. Thomas, Springfield, IL, 1972.

193. Forstenzer F. and Curry B. Support groups for parents of physically handicapped children. *Publ. Hlth Curr.* **20**, 9-12, 1980.

194. Field B. The child with spina bifida. *Med. J. Aust.* **2**, 1284-1287, 1972.

195. Adkins P. and Young R.G. Cultural perceptions in the treatment of handicapped school children of Mexican-American heritage. *Res. Dev. Educ.* **9**, 83-90, 1976.

196. Koch C.R., Hermann J. and Donaldson M.H. Supportive care of the child with cancer and his family. *Seminars Oncol.* **1**, 81-86, 1974.

197. Friedman S.B., Chodoff P., Mason J.W. and Hamburg D.A. Behavioral observations on parents anticipating the death of a child. *Pediatrics* **32**, 610-625, 1963.

198. Chodoff P., Friedman S.B. and Hamburg D.A. Stress, defenses and coping behavior: Obser-

vations in parents of children with malignant disease. *Am. J. Psychiat.* **120**, 743-749, 1964.

199. Lansky S.B., Cairns N.V., Wehr J., Hassanein R. and Lwoman T. Childhood cancer: Parental discord and divorce. *Peds* **62**, 184-188, 1968.

200. Lewis I.C. Leukemia in childhood: Its effects on the family. *Aust. Pediat. J.* **3**, 244-247, 1967.

201. Lascari A.D. and Stebbens J.A. The reactions of families to childhood leukemia--an evaluation of a program of emotional management. *Clin. Pediat.* **12**, 210-214, 1973.

202. Nir Y. Psychologic support for children with soft tissue and bone sarcomas. *Natl Cancer Inst. Monogr.* **56**, 145-148, 1981.

203. Knudson A.G. and Natterson J.M. Participation of parents in the hospital care of fatally ill children. *Pediatrics* **26**, 555-564, 1969.

204. Cairns N.V., Clark G.M., Smith S.D. and Lansky S.B. Adaptation of siblings to childhood malignancy. *J. Pediat.* **95**, 484-487, 1979.

205 Stehbens J.A. and Lascari A.D. Psychological follow-up of families with childhood leukemia. *J. clin. Psychol.* **30**, 394-397, 1974.

206. Taubman R.E. The physician and the dying patient and his family. In *Psychosocial Care of the Dying Patient* (Edited by Garfield C.A.), pp. 276-287. McGraw-Hill, New York, 1978.

207. Chapman J.A. and Goodall S. Dying children need help too. *Aust. Fam. Physn* **8**, 1236-1237, 1979.

208. Verwoerdt A. Death and the family. *Med. Opin. Rev.* **1**, 38-43, 1966.

209. Krupp G. Maladaptive reactions to the death of a family member. *Social Casework* **53**, 425-434, 1972.

210. Koop, C.E. The seriously ill or dying child: Suppporting the patient and the family. *Ped. Clin. N. Am.* **16**, 555-564, 1969.

211. Smith A.G. and Schneider L.T. The dying child: Helping the family cope with impending death. *Clin. Peds* **8**, 131-134, 1969.

212. Cain A.C., Fast I.F. and Erikson M.E. Children's disturbed reactions to the death of a sibling. *Am. J. Orthopsychiat.* **34**, 741-752, 1964.

213. Vollman R.R., Ganzert A., Picher L., Williams W.V. The reactions of family systems to sudden and unexpected death. *Omega* **2**, 101-106, 1971.

214. Arbogast R.C., Scratton J.M. and Krick J.P. The family as patient: Preliminary experience with a recorded assessment schema. *J. Fam. Pract.* **7**, 1151-1157, 1978.

215. MacVicar M.G. and Archbold P. A framework for family assessment in chronic illness. *Nurs. Forum* **15**, 180-194, 1976.

216. Reiss D. Pathways to assessing the family: Some choice points and a sample route. *The Family: Evaluation and Treatment* (Edited by Hofling C.K. and Lewis J.M.), 1980.

217. Smilkstein G. The family APGAR: A proposal for a family function test and its use by physicians. *J. Fam. Pract.* **6**, 1231-1239, 1978.

218. Moos R.H. and Moos B. A typology of family social environments. *Fam. Process* 357-371, 1976.

219. Moos R.H. Evaluating family and work settings. In *New Directions in Health* (Edited by Ahmed P. and Coelho G.). Plenum Press, New York, 1979.

Notes

1. For a more complete discussion of coping processes in serious illness, the reader is referred to Revenson [72].

Parental Entrepreneurship: A Consumerist Response to Professional Dominance

ROSALYN BENJAMIN DARLING

The symbolic interactionist perspective in social psychology suggests that parent's roles are learned by children in a continuing process of interaction with their own parents, the patents of other children, various media models, and later their own and other people's children. How people play their role continues to develop and change as they encounter new interaction situations, with both new and familiar significant others. Although parents of children with disabilities begin their socialization for the parent role in the same way as parents of typical children, that role diverges form the norm when preexisting definitions become inadequate to meet the special challenges of their "deviant" situation.

In response to their need for supportive services, information, and advocacy (Ayer, 1984), parents of disabled children have often adopted the role of *parental entrepreneur* (darling, 1979). These parents seek and/or create novel solutions to special problems. As with other social roles, this role is learned through interaction with others. It includes both expressive and instrumental components, and its behaviors differ more in quantity than in quality from the behaviors of parents of nondisabled children.

The major defining behaviors of the parental entrepreneur include (1) seeking information, (2) seeking control, and (3) challenging authority in order to secure services to meet the needs of the disabled child. The role involves action to bring about change in social and service arrangements, rather than passive acceptance of a child's condition. The process through which this role is learned parallels the process of conversion that operates in other areas of life. In particular, these parents must overcome learned dispositions to be submissive and to accept the authority of professional experts. This article explores the development of the entrepreneurial role using a "career" perspective, and examines the changes in parental orientations and behaviors that occur over time, as well as the forces that drive ill-prepared parents to become advocates for their own and other people's disabled children.

Background Research

Research that gave rise to the concept of parental entrepreneurship was conducted in the late 1970s. The original research involved in-depth interviews with mothers and fathers of 25 children with serious birth defects (see Darling, 1979, for a further description of this study). Additional information about the role and its evolution as disabled children move toward adulthood was gathered in 1980 from in-depth interviews with the families of 10 children with Down syndrome, spina bifida, and other disabilities. The original research involved a random sample drawn from the files of a genetic counselling service; the later interviews involved families who were members of local disability organizations. In addition, I have informally gathered a large amount of information as the director of a program that has served over 500 infants and preschool children with various disabilities during the past eight years. Because of the descriptive nature of this article, a large random sample was not deemed necessary. The following discussion describes a common parental behavior pattern. However, the reader should not assume that the pattern is descriptive of all, or even most, parents of disabled children in the population today.

The Emergence of Entrepreneurship

Anticipatory Socialization
Lack of experience with disability. Prior to their children's birth, most parents have had little direct personal contact with individuals known to have disabilities. Most exposure has been limited to stereotypes, to stigmatizing images in the media, or to distant strangers who looked or acted "different." As a result, most expectant parents report dreading the thought of giving

Reprinted From: Journal of Social Issues, Vol. 44, No. 1, 1988, pp. 141-158, with permission.

birth to a child who is disabled. As one mother of a Down syndrome child said, "I remember thinking before I got married, it would be the worst thing that could ever happen to me" (Darling, 1979, p. 124).

In addition to this fear of having a disabled child, most expectant parents lack factual information about various disabilities. The following quotes are illustrative:

> I knew nothing about mental retardation——just the vague stories one hears when growing up....I was ignorant of any factual knowledge. (Father of a moderately retarded child)

> I'd heard of from a book. It was just a terrible picture on a certain page of an abnormal psych book that I can still sort of picture. (Mother of a Down syndrome child; Darling, 1979, pp. 124, 125)

Lack of prior knowledge about disability accompanies a lack of appropriate treatment skills, such as positioning and handling (e.g., children with motoric disabilities may need to be held and carried in special ways or placed in atypical positions to encourage normal development), feeding, and infant stimulation. Parenting courses and informal instruction from friends and relatives usually focus on typical child development. Unless they are professionals in the field, few parents know how to evoke responses from a baby who cannot hear or see. Without appropriate instruction and support, such parents are likely to feel helpless.

Submission to professional dominance. Although exposure to consumerism is increasing, most lay persons remain intimidated by the "professional dominance" of physicians and other professionals. Describing physicians, Freidson (1970, p. 42) wrote that the patient is believed "too ignorant to be able to comprehend what information he [sic] gets and ... is, in any case, too upset at being ill to use the information he does get in a manner that is rational and responsible." Patients are often treated in a paternalistic manner and usually submit to the authority of the expert. Haug and Lavin (1983) reported that less

than half of the respondents in their general population sample wanted the right to make decisions about their own medical care. A large majority (72%) reported never having challenged their physicians in any way.

The discussion of professionals in this article is based on ideal-type descriptions of Freidson, Parsons, and others. Although the professional role in general can be characterized by these description, individual physicians and other professionals adopt this role in all of its manifestations to greater or lesser degrees, and play their role in different ways. Certainly, many physicians have warm, personalized, nonauthoritarian relationships with their patients. However, social structure imposes certain constraints on these relationships, which frequently result in problematic interactions.

Although submission to professional dominance is widespread, more and more people are becoming familiar with a movement of consumerism. An outgrowth of a rise in public expectations concerning rights and benefits, the consumerist trend has been growing since the 1960s but has more recently entered the realm of health care. Polls by Gallup and Harris (reported in Betz & O'Connell, 1983) indicate a marked decline in the public's confidence in and respect for physicians since 1950. For instance, 72% of the public expressed confidence in physicians in 1966, but only 43% in 1975. Betz and O'Connell suggested that the sense of trust is diminished as the doctor-patient relationship becomes more specialized, impersonal, and short-lived as a result of population mobility, professionalization, bureaucratization, and specialization.

Prior to the birth of their child, then, most parents have been socialized to respect the authority of the professional and have not had occasion or encouragement to challenge that authority. However, most have also been exposed to consumerist values through the mass media, if not through personal experience. They may be reluctant to challenge the social system, but today they are aware of the possibility of doing so.

Values and expectations about parenting. Prior to their child's birth, prospective parents expect to play a normative parental role. Among all societal subgroups, parents are expected to be nurturant and protective of their infants and young children. While parents expect and want to do "good" things for their children, most also envision being able to continue to participate in occupational or leisure activities after a child is born.

Like other parents in society, parents of children with disabilities hope to maintain a "normal" lifestyle (Birenbaum, 1970, 1971). They believe, at least initially, that their children will enjoy the same access to medical care and educational opportunities as children without disabilities. They expect to continue pursuing their careers, participating in recreational and social activities with family and friends, and having as much financial security as others in their social class. When these expectations are not met, parents are likely to feel cheated.

The Birth Situation and Beyond

Anomie and Meaninglessness
Parents learn about the existence of their children's disabilities in a variety of ways, sometimes immediately after birth, sometimes later. Because parents have, and are given, so little information about disabling conditions prior to their child's birth, they are often left with many unanswered questions:

> When the baby was born, they said, "Oh my God, put her out." That's the first thing they said, "Oh my God, put her out"...and the next thing I remember was waking up in the recovery room....I had my priest on my left hand and by paediatrician on my right hand...and they were trying to get me to sign a piece of paper....I just couldn't believe that this was happening to me and I said to my priest, "Father, what's the matter?," and he said, "Your have to sign this release. Your daughter is very sick." And I said to the paediatrician, "What's the matter with her?," and he said "Don't worry honey, she'll be dead before morning"....He said she had something that was too much to talk about, that I shouldn't worry myself....It was a very traumatic time...Nobody was telling me what this was...I was very depressed. (Darling, 1979, p.130)

In other cases, medical professionals may issue various clues about a baby's condition before they offer a complete diagnosis. Such behavior tends to increase parents' anxiety and can result in a protracted period of *anomie*—— i.e., a state of normlessness and lack of definitional clarity (cg. McHugh, 1968). During such periods, patents' feelings of meaninglessness can become overwhelming, as the following case illustrates:

> The mother was concerned from the beginning because her baby would not suck...After she got home from the hospital the baby was "crying all the time" from hunger... The paediatrician prescribed a sedative, and "the baby stopped crying altogether."

> When the child was brought to the paediatrician for his first check-up at 6 weeks, he was immediately hospitalized for "failure to thrive." During the entire 6 weeks while the mother was struggling to feed her child, both her husband and mother had insisted that nothing was wrong.

> During his hospitalization, the child was incorrectly diagnosed as microcephalic [having a small brain]...the parents took their son to a neurologist. Although he assured the parents that their son was not microcephalic, the neurologist would not give them another diagnosis. The mother reports: "The neurologist said, 'I think I know what's wrong with your son but I don't want to frighten you.' Well, I think that's about the worst thing anyone could say...We didn't go back to him...We insisted that our doctor refer us to ... Children's Hospital, but the doctor said, 'He's little. Why don't you wait? You don't need to take him there yet'...Every time we went, they told us something else. It's my feeling that you can't really cope unless you know the whole truth...You can't cope in stages... Everyone was pablum-feeding us, and we wanted the truth."

> Finally the child was diagnosed as having cerebral palsy ... the parents were more relieved than upset by the diagnosis (Darling & Darling, 1982, pp. 121-122)

In some cases, parents can see their baby has a problem by "the look on the doctor's face" or atypical behavior by delivery room staff. Such clues are inadvertent. In other cases, physicians deliberately delay telling the truth, as these comment by pediatricians indicate:

> You start thinking in your mind as you're examining this child month after month. Here you try to hint. You say, "I'm not really sure. We'll watch it a little longer"...When you finally tell them they react pretty well.

> The first visit I make a note on the chart. Maybe I make a suggestion to the parent by listening longer to the baby's heart or whatever. By the next visit, parents start to ask...You can't tell them all you know. the specialist can slap them with the facts. (Darling, 1979, p. 207)

By avoiding a diagnostic confrontation, the professional can prolong parents' uncertainty, avoid an emotion-laden encounter, and maintain control over the situation. Information control, then, is a management technique. As Sosnowitz (1984) noted about a neonatal intensive care nursery, "The staff wanted a chance to observe how the parents would react to the crisis. When the staff was unable to predict the parents' reactions, they usually gave just enough information to keep the parents involved" (p. 396).

As studies have shown (e.g., D'Arcy, 1968; Darling, 1979) such techniques seem to increase the parents' feelings of anomie and, paradoxically, make them more ready to question professional authority. Some parents who have previously submitted to professional dominance willingly may be disillusioned by these experiences, as this parent's report indicates:

> I asked what was wrong with her ears, and they said not to worry about...*I always thought they told you the truth in the hospital* and if you wanted to know anything you should ask. I really thought her ears looked funny and I had this funny feeling, so I asked the doctor, "Is there anything wrong?," and he looked right at me and said, "No." So I assumed she was OK...I was very bitter about it....I had had the same paediatrician for 6 years, and he had always been truthful. *I trusted him.* (Darling, 1979, pp. 131-132; emphasis added)

Powerlessness: A Second Response to Professional Dominance

Anomie has been classically defined to consist of both meaninglessness and powerlessness (McHugh, 1968). Even after parents have obtained a diagnosis, many continue to experience powerlessness as a result of two kinds of experiences: (1) getting information about *diagnosis* without any information about *treatment*, and (2) seeing their child's treatment as totally in the hands of professionals, thus obscuring their parental role.

All parents expect to "do things" for their children, and parents of children with disabilities are no exception. As a result, most feel uncomfortable when they are given no concrete suggestions about techniques for aiding their children's developmental progress. These parents usually use whatever research skills they possess to find help, but such efforts are often inadequate:

> When you're told something like this, you can't go and look it up in the encyclopedia. My encyclopedia doesn't even mention it. The encyclopedia at the library mentioned it in a paragraph. Nobody had any information at all.

> I was looking for a door at that point—somebody who could give us any help at all. Dr. _____ didn't even tell us there was a state agency that dealt with mental retardation. (Darling, 1979, pp. 140-149)

Such parents usually continue their search for help, sometimes even against the advice of their physicians:

> Because nothing was happening, and I was just sitting there with this baby, we got involved with the patterning program... Up to that time he had done nothing. My paediatrician said, "You're just looking for hopes." I said, "No, I'm just looking to *do* something for him. I'm sitting at home doing nothing." (Darling, 1979, p. 153)

When parents are denied the opportunity to be "good parents," they ripen for activism and advocacy. As Pizzo (1983, p. 19) has written,

The most universal shared experience we have as parents is the struggle to protect children and to get them the resources they need to develop well. Listening to parent activists describe their work, one soon learns that their organizational activities are not radically different from the basic task we undertake as parents. In self-help and advocacy, parents take the intimate, nurturing vigilance needed for effective childrearing into a social and political domain.

Powerlessness and advocacy may also be engendered in the hospital or clinic, where the professional is in control. Many parents come to resent their own role as "helpless bystanders":

> We were always going back and forth to _____ Children's Hospital... It was a constantly pulling away. We could never be a family...It was always. "We have to go to the hospital." We had to go to doctors, doctors, doctors... We never could get to know our child... We got to the point where we hated doctors, we hated _____ Children's Hospital. (Darling, 1979, p. 154)

Although parents' feelings of powerlessness usually develop as a by-product of the controlled medical setting, sometimes they result from more deliberate management practices, as this example from a neonatal intensive care nursery indicates:

> The staff wanted parents to cooperate and be flexible; to trust that the staff had their infant's best interests at heart——even though these may not be identical; and not to restrain their work by questioning every test. Often this fear of restraint limited the kind of information which the staff shared with parents. For example, parents were rarely told about the pain involved in spinal taps or laborious eye examinations. These tests were ordered regularly, performed when the parents were not on the unit, and only mentioned to them after the fact.... This handling of parents contributed even more to their feeling of helplessness and cultivated their compliance with the role expected of them. (Sosnowitz, 1984, p. 395)

Such parents typically come to resent professional control over their lives and grow more receptive to consumerist activities as a result.

The literature also contains a few examples of professionals who willingly share information with and sought advice from parents as shown by this parent's story (Stotland, 1984, p. 72, emphasis added):

> The most important aspect of the doctor's presentation was that he involved us as equals in the decision-making process...by involving us in the process and by giving us his professional opinion as an opinion, he returned to us our parental rights of making the important decision that would affect our child's life. _We were in control_, but we were no longer alone.

An encounter with such a professional could be a turning point that would _end_ a career of entrepreneurship.

Both meaninglessness and powerlessness can encourage parents to enter a state of _seekership_ (Lofland & Stark, 1965), in which they begin "shopping" for answers. Ripe for contact with all sources of help in order to ease their anomie, "seekers" are further impelled by repeated negative interactions with professionals and others, as the child ages and develops new needs.

The Growth of Seekership

The Parent-Child Bond: Increasing Commitment
When their children are first diagnosed, most parents feel shock and anger. Many even reject their infants or wish they would die. This negative reaction is usually short-lived, however. Studies (e.g., Darling, 1979; Irvin, Kennell, & Klaus, 1982) have shown that the more they interact with their child, the more parents become committed to the child's welfare, regardless of his or her disability. The mother of a Down syndrome baby reported her first reaction to her child: "I was kind of turned off. I didn't want to catch it." After feeding and caring for the baby in the hospital, her attitude changed: "By the time she came home I loved her. When I held her for the first time I felt love and I worried if she'd live." (Darling, 1979, pp. 135, 136)

The emotional bond that develops between parent and child is a strong catalyst to parental activism. Pizzo (1983) has suggested that the bond "energizes" parent advocacy. Parents who are totally committed to their children come to resent the lack of commitment by professionals and others. While professional responses to disabled children are generally characterized by affective neutrality, universalism and functional specificity, parental responses are affective, particularistic, and functionally diffuse——terms explained below (Darling, 1983).

As Freidson (1961) and others have shown, most patients *want* their physicians to satisfy their emotional needs. Parents of disabled children similarly want professionals to take a personal interest in their children. One mother (reported in Darling, 1979) complained because her paediatrician never talked directly to her severely retarded son or called him by name. Unsatisfied emotional needs can provoke parental activism.

The professional role is also characterized by universalism, that is, a belief that all cases are to be treated equally. But to the parent, the *particular* child is important. This mother's experience at a cerebral palsy clinic is typical:

> We saw a different doctor every time and we always had to wait a long time. One time, Kathy was so fussy by the time they got around to examining her, they couldn't even examine her... The doctors treated her like a "thing". (Darling, 1979, p. 152)

Parents who repeatedly encounter such impersonal treatment may be more likely to challenge professional authority.

Finally, the professional's task is functionally specific. To the parent, however, the child's roles as son or daughter, sibling, grandchild, student, playmate, or church member may supersede his or her disability. Conflicts may arise when the professional focuses exclusively on a part. Indeed, a disabled part. Featherstone (1980, p. 57) quotes a professional who became a parent:

> Before I had Peter I gave out (physical therapy) programs that would gave taken all day.

> I don't know when I expected mothers to change diapers, sort laundry, or buy groceries.

Just as the child with a disability is more than a "disabled child," the parent of such a child also has multiple roles. Parents may come to resent professionals who do not take all of these roles or those of their children into account.

Data from a large-scale study of visits to a paediatric outpatient clinic (Francis, Korsch, & Morris, 1968) support the relationship between lack of professional responsiveness to parent needs and parental dissatisfaction. Non-compliance, too, correlates with unmet expectations, lack of warmth in the doctor-patient relationship, and failure to receive an explanation of the diagnosis. Non-compliance may become a form of activism, or resistance against professional authority.

Lack of Societal Resources: New Barriers to Normalization

As their children grow, many parents continue to encounter unresponsive professionals, in the medical and educational fields during early and middle childhood, and later in the worlds of employment and independent living when children approach their adult years.

Meeting medical needs. Parents of all children, both disabled and nondisabled, expect appropriate medical care for their children. Although they may have to do some "shopping," parents of nondisabled children usually find a satisfactory clinic or family doctor. Parents of children with disabilities often have a longer search. Many physicians do not enjoy serving children who can not be fully cured. As one paediatrician said,

> I don't enjoy it...I don't really enjoy a really handicapped child who comes in drooling, can't walk and so forth...Medicine is geared to the perfect human body. Something you can't do anything about challenges the doctor and reminds him of his own inabilities. (darling, 1979, p. 215)

The mother of a child with cerebral palsy said, "[Our paediatrician] didn't take my complaints seriously...I feel that Brian's sore throat is just as important as [my normal daughter's] sore throat" (Darling, 1979, p. 152).

Meeting educational needs. Parents of disabled children often encounter a delay in referral to appropriate infant and preschool education programs, and because the educational system primarily serves nondisabled children, they may continue to encounter problems in finding appropriate educational programs for older children. The following situation was described by the mother of a child with spina bifida:

> When Ellen entered kindergarten, she was in a special needs class in the morning and mainstreamed in the afternoon...[In the special needs class], she was with children whose needs were much more demanding than Ellen's...Some were retarded...At the end of the year we had a meeting. The first grade was on the second floor...[Ellen was in a wheelchair]. They said we should keep he in the special needs class. I was furious...She had done so well in the mainstreaming class...I wanted her in a regular first grade and I suggested moving the class downstairs...They wanted Ellen in the special needs class because it was easier for *them*, not for any other reason. (Darling & Darling, 1982, p. 140)

while inappropriate placements may be the most common educational problem for parents of disabled children, difficulties in obtaining "related services," such as clean intermittent catheterization or physical therapy, are also fairly widespread.

Meeting other needs. In addition to the frustrations parents encounter in meeting their children's medical and educational needs, they may discover limits on their access to other resources. In the United States, the financial burden associated with raising a disabled child may be overwhelming. Medical equipment can be very expensive, and adaptive seating aids or computerized communication devices, which may be needed by more severely involved children, typically cost far beyond the means of the average family.

In the area of respite care, finding babysitters capable of caring for children with special needs may be quite difficult, particularly for older,

heavier, nonambulatory children and children with seizures.

More severely disabled children continue to require special services as they approach adulthood, e.g., special living arrangements, sheltered employment, or help with activities of daily living. In some communities, these services are readily available. In others, parents of adult dependent children are faced with a continuing burden and fears about their children's futures after they are no longer able to care for them.

When parents continue to encounter needs that cannot be met by existing societal resources, they may embark on a prolonged career of seekership. The goal of seekership is *normalization*, or the establishment of a lifestyle that approximates that of families with only nondisabled children. Seekership results in advocacy and activism when certain situational contingencies, or *turning points*, occur.

Turning Points

In their study of social movement members, Lofland and Stark (1965, p. 870) note that conversions usually occur in "situations in which old obligations and lines of action were diminished, and new involvements became desirable and possible." In the case of parents of disabled children, turning points include interactions that push parents away from complacency and others that pull them toward increasing involvement in movements for social change. "Push" factors include (1) both supportive and unsupportive interactions with familiar significant others, and (2) media experiences. Each of these is discussed in turn.

Interactions with Familiar Significant Others
When they look for support from relatives and friends, many parents initially encounter negative or unhelpful attitudes:

> [My in-laws] to this day will not accept her as retarded. They will not say the word. They don't like us to talk about retardation...She's their only grandchild.
>
> the neighbors just ignore our kids. Nobody ever offers to help lift a wheelchair. (Darling, 1979, pp. 145, 160)

These parents must often look beyond their existing social networks in order to find support and help.

Even in positive cases, friends and relatives may encourage parents to seek help elsewhere. In one case, a friend called the mother of a Down syndrome child to tell her that she had seen a former mutual friend at a doctor's office with "a little girl that looked like Michelle." The mother, who until that time had had no contact with other parents of disabled children, discovered that "the little girl" did have Down syndrome, and thus learned about and became active in the Association for the Retarded (Darling, 1979, p. 148). In other cases, grandparents, aunts, uncles, or other relatives of the disabled child may accompany parents to support group meeting and became involved, along with the parents, in association activities. Both positive and negative experiences with significant others may provoke parental entrepreneurship.

Acute, Painful Experiences
Pizzo (1983) has noted that parent advocacy often derives for "acute, painful experiences," whereas Haug and Lavin (1983) found the most important predictor of consumerist challenges to medical authority was the *experience of medical error:*

> Reports of medical error... make a considerable difference that is statistically significant both in attitudes and behavior. In fact, almost two-thirds of those who charge they have suffered from a physician's mistakes claimed to have taken a consumerist action...Most people who offered a reason for challenge alluded to a real or potential event that they would consider a medical error. (Haug & Lavin, 1983, p. 106)

Such an experience erodes trust in professional authority and may serve as the turning point to launch parents' activism.

Parents of disabled children are of course relatively more likely than other parents to encounter medical or professional error because of the frequency and intensity of their professional contacts. Over time they may also come to realize and trust that *they* know more about

their children than the experts do. As one mother of a multiply handicapped child said,

> In all of her hospitalizations I've been very frustrated by residents who think they know everything. They've given us so much misinformation and details we didn't want to hear... Now I tell them....I find that other parents are too accepting. They don't question their doctors. (Darling, 1979, p. 153)

The following incident served as one of a series of turning points that led the parents of four multiply handicapped children to take the initiative in managing their children's treatment:

> Our doctor sent us to _____ Teaching Hospital [about 250 miles away]. She was supposed to be a research patient there. We went down twice. The first time they didn't have her admission papers... [After the second time], when we finally brought her home, the doctor there said, "Frankly, Mrs. Jones, with the hospitals you have in [your state], I don't know why you brought her here." It turned out that she was just an ordinary admission, not a research patient...We were furious. When we got home, I sent an 8 page letter to the administrator of the hospital...I said I wouldn't pay the ...bill....We were broke. Up until that time we had always struggled to pay even though we didn't have the money. We were dumb. (Darling, 1979, pp. 153-154)

Turning points both redefine the past and set a course for the future.

Interaction with New Significant Others
Through their children's medical treatment or educational programs, most parents meet other parents of disabled children. Exchanging stories, they learn about shared and systemic problems. This experience of meeting other parents often provides a powerful turning point:

> I met other parents of the retarded after we moved here. I felt that made the biggest difference in my life...Down there (where we lived before) with my husband working so much and no other families with retarded children, I felt that I was just singled out for something, that I was weird. I felt a lot of

isolation and bitterness. (Darling, 1979, pp. 162-163)

Parents' groups provide an opportunity to learn about effective techniques, to realize that authority can be successfully challenged, and to mobilize for collective action. The parent who hesitates to act alone may willingly participate in group action. The mother of a young adult with spina bifida described her increasing involvement in such a movement as follows:

> Michael started first grade at the Oakmont School [a facility that served all handicapped children within the region]. It was an old, noisy building...and it seemed that each year he did the same thing as the year before... There was no separation by age. They just didn't know what to do with the kids...Parents didn't get together. It was an unpopular thing to do at that time, and who wants to be unpopular? After a while it didn't matter... Parents got together. We went to meeting...We decided we wanted our kids in our own school district...
>
> Several parents got together and went to [our school district]. They were building a new elementary school...They weren't going to put in an elevator...They didn't want to provide transportation...Your eventually get what you need...if you're very persistent. (Darling & Darling, 1982, pp. 137-138)

Although most interactions that encourage activism involve peers, occasionally meeting with helpful professionals or advocates can also provoke a move to action. Many states now have developmental disabilities' advocates who engage in outreach activities to train parents to be effective advocates for their own children. Groups like the Federation for Children with Special Needs in Massachusetts, for example, have received grants to train parents and professionals in strategies of social change.

Media Experiences
Pizze (1983) notes that many parents become involved in self-help groups after exposure to the media. Both general and specialized newspapers, magazines, and television programs may report on the activities of disability advocacy or support groups. *The Exceptional Parent* magazine, for example, contains a pen pals column in which a parent might see a letter from another whose child has the same disability. Such magazines also print "success stories" about and by parents who have found solutions to their children's problems. When Mary Tatro received *The Exceptional Parent* Award of 1984, her merits were described as follows:

> Mrs. Tatro was able to persist more than five years to get the services necessary for her child, although this meant sustaining personal hardship, a prolonged struggle, and an eventual confrontation at the United States Supreme Court. ("Related Services," 1984, p. 36)

One recently formed national group of parents of children who suffered neonatal intraventricular haemorrhages (I.V.H.——bleeding in the brain) and subsequent brain damage got started through an article in a "baby magazine" about the mother of an I.V.H. child. Other parents wrote, the group expanded, and it now distributes a newsletter (*I.V.H. Parents Newsletter*, 1984).

Negative media reports can also trigger entrepreneurial activities. Recent attention to nontreatment of disabled newborns and the "Baby Doe" cases have incited some parents of disabled children to activism. These parents are apt to imagine themselves and their own child in a similar situation and to become alarmed at the thought of the child's being allowed to die. Organized groups of parents, such as the Spina Bifida Association of America and the National Down's Syndrome Society, have actively responded to these publicized cases.

After a turning point has occurred and a parent's interest in advocacy has been awakened, that interest must be nurtured and socialized if the parent is to continue the career of entrepreneurship.

Socialization

Socialization to the entrepreneurial role occurs through formal and informal techniques that are used by parents individually and collectively.

Many parents become increasingly committed to entrepreneurship as a way of life, devoting significant amounts of time to activities intended to meet their child's needs and to demand change from previously unresponsive structures.

Intensive Interaction
After a turning point has occurred, parents continue to interact both with their own child, and with old and new significant others. New role models emerge at parent meetings or elsewhere, and parents' commitments increase with time. The frequency, duration, and intensity of parent-child interactions sustain parents' involvement and activism. Later children may confront unresponsive school systems and inaccessible or discriminatory labor markets. Children's continuing unmet needs motivate these parents to remain involved in demanding changes in opportunity structures.

Lofland and Stark (1965) note that total conversion to the social movement they studied occurred only after a period of intensive interaction between the new convert and old members of the movement. Similarly, parents of disabled children become increasingly committed to activist goals after frequent, intense, and long exposure to parents who already have internalized these goals.

Trial and Error: Learning from Experience
Most parents learn from their own experiences. After talking to many professionals, they discover who will be responsive. After successfully challenging an authority, they are more likely to try again.

The parents in the following example watched their children move through a series of inappropriate educational placements before they successfully intervened. Now they are actively involved in an entrepreneurial lifestyle:

> At Children's Hospital, Tony was in a class with active, bright kids. . . .He just sat in the corner and played in the sandbox. . . Then he went to the School for the Blind. . . .Finally, Tony and Jean had to leave the school. They said they were retarded. . . [Then]they started in the [city] Public School System, but they had no appropriate program either. . . .After 3

years, we started fighting. . . . The Board of Education said, "We've got all kinds of retarded programs. We'll just put them in one of those". . . I visited the programs, and there wasn't one child in a wheelchair. . . .I said, "How are my children going to get around? How are they going to go on the stairs?" . . - They kept saying "No" to us. . .

We were lucky at this time because [my husband changed jobs and] was in the school system and knew a lot of people. And they were guiding us and telling us where to write, each step of the way. We went right to the top. . . A program was established within 2 weeks. (Darling, 1979, pp. 176-177)

Formal Training
The growth of the consumer movement in various areas of life has given rise to the establishment of formal courses in advocacy. Parents can receive training in demonstrating, letter writing, lobbying, and community education. In addition to courses offered through self-help organizations and disability rights' groups, a number of books and manuals have also been published in recent years to familiarize parents with their legal rights, and to teach assertiveness and other strategies (e.g., Biklen, 1974; DesJardins, 1971; Lurie, 1970; Market & Greenbaum, no date).

Through both informal interaction and formal training, parents learn to be advocates for their children. For some, advocacy becomes a way of life. For others, advocacy is only a means to the end of normalization. When that end is achieved, the parents' commitment to entrepreneurship may diminish.

The End of Entrepreneurship

For most parents, active entrepreneurship ends after they reach what they consider to be normalization. Once they have obtained satisfactory medical care, secured appropriate school placements, and won the support of family and friends, most parents decrease their attendance at parents' association meetings and encourage their children's friendship with nondisabled peers. As one mother explained:

We went to the Association pretty regularly for 2 years. But after a while we felt that they did not have that much to offer. . .Karen went to their nursery school, but we just got too busy to go to the meetings. Karen didn't have a lot of problems. (Darling, 1979, pp. 161-162)

This child was also well accepted in the family and the neighbourhood, and as the father stated, "Retardation is not number one around here. It's just something Karen has."

Birenbaum (1970, 1971) has argued that true normalization may be difficult to attain but that families often maintain a "normal-appearing round of life" nonetheless. Such families create the impression that their daily routine approximates that of families with nondisabled children. However, these families who "suffer in silence" may be declining in number as activism becomes a more accepted alterative in society.

A few families choose a more *altruistic* adaptation and remain active in disability rights organizations even after their own problems have been solved. Parents of children with the most severe disabilities and for whom societal resources are least available may also remain active in disability associations. These parents often adopt a *crusadership* mode of adaptation. They continue to work toward changing their children's opportunity structure. Entrepreneurship becomes a way of life.

Finally, some parents abandon the entrepreneurial role even though they have not achieved normalization. These parents assume a *retreatist* adaptation. Doubly isolated, they lack access both to opportunities for normalization and to involvement in advocacy groups. They may live in isolated rural areas, have other, overriding problems such as extreme poverty or illness, or they may have language or cultural barriers that prevent their integration in either normative or consumerist social groups. As one parent who became a successful entrepreneur remarked:

The search for excellence for David was done by parents fortunate enough to have funds to explore resources and a healthy disrespect for professional authority. We also were lucky to have a bright, energetic child to reward our efforts. What can parents with fewer resources do? (Stotland, 1984, p. 74)

Retreatist parents have not generally been included in studies because, by definition, their isolation makes them difficult to find.

The career paths followed by parents of disabled children are summarized by the model in Fig. 1. Parents are predisposed toward entrepreneurial careers by their expectations prior to their children's birth and by the failure of society to meet those expectations after their children are born. This predisposition is a necessary but not a sufficient condition for activism. Some parents are rewarded fairly soon in their search for solutions by the discovery of good medical care, appropriate educational opportunities, and sources of financial help and social support. For others, such opportunities are not readily available and seekership continues.

Actual challenges to professional authority and the social order come about as a result of situational contingencies in the form of turning points. Turning points help parents reframe their situations to include the possibility of social change.

Fig. 1 Career paths of parents of disabled children.

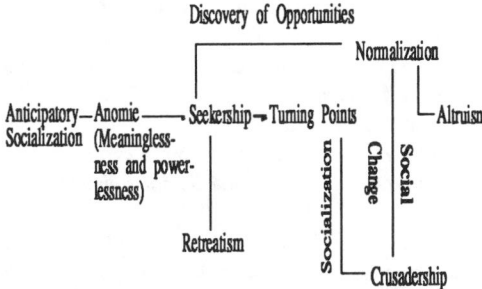

Once parents become aware of the possibilities for change, their increasing commitment to the entrepreneurial role must be nurtured by informal and formal agencies of socialization, including training courses and/or intensive interaction in parent associations. Parents who have successfully challenged authority are more likely to do it again. As long as opportunities for access to "normal" society remain limited, these parents are likely to sustain their crusadership.

When crusadership is successful and opportunities for social integration become more accessible, parents are likely to choose normalization and to abandon activism.

The model is by no means static. Modes of adaptation change continually as life situations change, and as a result, normalization is always precarious in a society that refuses full integration to persons with disabilities. A family that has attained normalization during a child's school years, for example, may move back into a crusadership mode once the child finishes school and encounters inadequate vocational opportunities. New illness, life crisis, or the consequences of aging can reinitiate the entrepreneurial process. As the parent consumerist movement becomes increasingly successful, opportunities for normalization will continue to increase. However, until society provides equal opportunities for all its members, crusadership will continue to be a way of life for many parents of children with disabilities.

References

Ayer, S. (1984). Community care: Failure of professionals to meet family needs. *Child: Care Health and Development, 10,* 127-139.

Betz, M., & O'Connell, L. (1983). Changing doctor-patient relationships and the rise in concern for accountability. *Social Problems, 31,* 84-95.

Biklen, D. (1974). *Let our children go: An organizing manual for advocates and parents.* Syracuse, NY: Human Policy Press.

Birenbaum, A. (1970). On managing a courtesy stigma. *Journal of Health and Social Behavior, 11,* 196-206.

Birenbaum, A. (1971). The mentally retarded child in the home and the family cycle. *Journal of Health and Social Behavior, 11,* 196-206.

D'Arcy, E. (1968). Congenital defects: Mothers' reactions to first information. *British Medical Journal, 3,* 796-798.

Darling, R.B. (1979). *Families against society: A study of reactions to children with birth defects.* Beverly Hills, CA: Sage.

Darling, R.B., (1983). Parent-professional interaction: The roots of misunderstanding. In M. Seligman (Ed.), *The family with a handicapped child: Understanding and treatment* (pp.95-121). New York: Grune & Stratton.

Darling, R.B., & Darling, J. (1982). *Children who are different: Meeting the challenges of birth defects in society.* St. Louis, MO: Mosby.

DesJardins, C. (1971). *How to organize an effective parent group and move bureaucracies: For parents of handicapped children and their helpers.* Chicago: Coordinating Council for Handicapped Children.

Featherstone, H. (1980). *A difference in the family: Life with a disabled child.* New York: Basic Books.

Francis, V., Korsch, B.M., & Morris, M.J. (1968). Gaps in doctor-patient communication: Patients' response to medical advice. *New England Journal of Medicine, 280,* 535-540.

Freidson, E. (1961). *Patients' views of medical practice.* New York: Russell Sage Foundation.

Freidson, E. (1970) *Professional dominance.* Chicago: Aldine.

Haug, M., & Lavin, B. (1983). *Consumerism in medicine: Challenging physician authority.* Beverly Hills, CA: Sage.

Irwin, N.A., Kennell, J.H., & Klaus, M.H. (1982) Caring for the parents of an infant with a congenital malformation. In H.H. Klaus & J.H. Kennell (Eds.) *Parent-infant bonding* (pp.227-258). St. Louis, MO: Mosby.

I.V.H. *Parents Newsletter.* (1984, September). 2.

Latland, J., & Stark, R. (1965). Becoming a world saver. A theory of conversion to a deviant perspective. *American Sociological Review, 30,* 862-875.

Lorie, E. (1970). *How to change the schools: A parent's action handbook on how to fight the system.* New York: Vintage.

Markel, G.P. & Greenbaum, J. (no date). *Parent are to be seen and heard: Assertiveness and educational planning for handicapped children.* San Luis Obispo, CA: Impact.

McHugh, P. (1968). *Defining the situation.* Indianapolis: Bobbs-Merrill.

Pizzo, P. (1983). *Parent to parent: Working together for ourselves and our children.* Boston: Beacon Press.

Related services and the Supreme Court: A family's story. (1984, October). *The Exceptional Parent,* pp. 36-41.

Sosnowitz, B.G. (1984). Managing parents on neonatal intensive care units. *Social Problems, 31,* 390-402.

Scotland, J. (1984). Relationship of parents to professionals: A challenge to professionals. *Journal of Visual Impairment & Blindness,* 69-74.

The Role of the Family in Rehabilitation

Jean Marlatt

When I was 52 years old, I went back to college to finish a degree I had begun 34 years earlier.

One of the plays I studied was "The Trojan Women" by Euripides. There was line in the play that puzzled me. The Trojan Queen announced her daughter's arrival by saying, "It is my daughter, Cassandra. She is mad."

I wondered why those simple words held so much impact. I didn't realize in four years I would share with Cassandra's mother the kind of experience which make a matter-of-fact statement high drama.

Now I understand those words are the result of acceptance, not resignation——but acceptance.

I want to share experiences and observations as the parent of a young woman who has a disability. My daughter, Ruth, became schizophrenic with a sudden onset at age 16.

We don't usually anticipate or prepare ourselves for the probability of a major mental illness. We felt guilt, despair and confusion and floundered for months——years——trying to restore family functioning and personal equilibrium.

During these first "awful" months, our family's entire efforts were to stabilize our daughter and to become knowledgeable about the illness. We looked for an effective therapist, who in turn, searched for the right anti-psychotic drugs. All our energies, as well as insurance and savings, went in this direction. And while there were wider directions, eventually, we initially thought only of restoration, not rehabilitation.

The process we experienced at that time was much like the stages of recovery when someone we love dies. But this time, the process did not lead to the acceptance of a death, but to the acceptance of a life——a life and a person who was far different from the daughter we knew before the illness.

One day Ruth said to me, "Am I handicapped?" I dreaded that question. I was afraid she was too vulnerable to handle the answer—— afraid my answer would be clumsy, depress her, or cause a relapse. But she told me she was hearing about schizophrenia at the drop-in center where she went. She wanted to know if schizophrenia was what she had. "If I do, am I handicapped?"

So we discussed handicaps. We talked about my handicap as an amputee, which she had grown up with and knows of first hand. Ruth knew that having one leg made it extra hard to raise a large family.

The we discussed her disability. "On bad days," she said "messages come in like tangled wires." Such problems certainly made her life more difficult and constituted a handicap for her. As we talked, her eyes lit up, which is very rare for her, and she said, "I see. I have two good legs and you have a good head on your shoulders!" That day I think Ruth found a measure of acceptance for which she was ready, or she probably would not have asked the question, "Am I handicapped?"

Acceptance was the turning point for our family. Amazingly, when we accepted the reality of the illness, that it was not going to go away, we regained ability for constructive action. We found renewed vitality and purpose.

That was the beginning of our family's search for ways to rehabilitate and not to focus solely on a cure. We broke out of the isolation and united with other families in support groups such as the National Alliance for the Mentally Ill, or N.A.M.I.

Before deinstitutionalization, families were told at the hospital doors "to pretend as though their children were already dead." But now, the powers-that-be have said, in effect, "Those with mental disabilities must live in the community." However, to live in the community requires skills our family members have lost or never had the opportunity to acquire.

The largest percentage of people with mental illnesses live with their families. Among N.A.M.I. members, and this may not be representative of the whole population, two-thirds live with their families. Nationally, one estimate is that about 67 percent live in the family home. One-third or so of persons with psychiatric

Reprinted from: Journal of Rehabilitation Jan/Feb/March 1983, with permission.

disabilities are homeless, unconnected with a support system, in hospitals and jails, or living in other housing.

There are the small but increasing numbers who fortunately are part of psycho-social clubhouses such as Thresholds or Fountain House. And through the country, many are striving to expand the number of rehabilitation centers such as these.

As new skills, better coping methods and family management are taught and learned, the family home can, up to a point, be part of an effective rehabilitation resource.

But families in general, parents in particular, may not be long-termed. We have built in obsolescence. Among N.A.M.I. members for instance, the average age of the parent is 59 years old, while many of our sons and daughters are still in the 20's and 30's (since severe mental illnesses, such as schizophrenia, frequently occur in early adulthood).

Nevertheless, whether still intact as "a family," middle-aged, retired, in marginal health, widowed or divorced, parents usually return to functioning as full-time parents and caretakers when our adult children become ill. Therefore, the word "home" based on the American ideal of a nuclear family unit is deceptive. The "home" risks the possibility of becoming a small, albeit attractive, mini-institution, fostering isolation guised as protection and safety but unable, in spite of good intentions, to foster optimum development and growth.

What about our daughter now? Ruth is living at home or set up in an apartment. She has a regular weekly session with a good therapist. Anti-psychotic drugs are taken without too much resistance. An SSI check comes the first of every month. Estimating it should take about four hours of time to pick up the medication and go to the therapy session, the person with the disability now has left approximately 162 hours of the week. Enough time to tangle the therapy, to decide compliance with medication serves no useful purpose, and to smoke 442 cigarettes.

The work ethic of our culture does not tolerate 162 free hours a week. It is easy to stigmatize a person who has 162 empty hours a week. Establishing self-respect or self-esteem as a therapeutic goal is akin to a delusional idea when 162 hours are available for coffee and cigarettes. Even successful therapy crumbles and dissolves in 162 free hours without creative rehabilitation.

Imperative as they are, successful psychiatric intervention and medication are not substitutes for rehabilitation. Hopeful studies indicate, "A chronic or severe impairment does not mean total or life long disability. It only increases the risk." One hundred and sixty-two idle free hours a week guarantees that risk.

Looking back over the past 35 years that I have been a person with a handicap, I wonder how emotionally disabled I would be, if those years were spent in aimless activity and without adequate and appropriate rehabilitation.

Those of us who live closest to a person with a severe mental illness must consider the long-range outlook for their lives, especially at their needs for independent living skills and their natural life-task of development and growth.

Families in so-called normal circumstances have the task of disentangling themselves from their children's lives. This changing of roles seems to become impossible when a son or daughter in early adulthood is struck with a severe mental disability.

In the beginning of the illness, the resumption of strong parental ties may be necessary. Families develop an apprehension of relinquishing this role due to the vulnerability of the family member and the unavailability of programs for the rehabilitation of persons with psychiatric disabilities.

Because of the unique problems our family had with our mentally ill relative, we are both encouraged and discouraged by what we understand are a few basic tenets of rehabilitation philosophy and practice as these apply to persons with psychiatric disabilities.

For example, it is encouraging to know a fundamental practice of rehabilitation is to "assess strengths." I have never heard the word strengths applied to Ruth since she became ill at 16. "Strengths," present or potential, are so rarely alluded to, it is as though none exist in our family member any more.

The concepts of "closure" or "time in status" are, on the other hand, discouraging——like constituting a "barrier" such as a staircase to an amputee. Impatiently, we expect recovery to be affirmed by a full-time, 40-hour-a-week job or vocation.

Our society helps the physically disabled person to cope by making certain concessions to the disability. As an amputee, I am not expected to walk on scaffolding or deliver mail from door to door.

Concessions for the psychiatrically disabled person are often in the allocation of "time." For instance, a person who must screen out excessive distractions expends large amounts of energy in order to concentrate. It is logical that a job working three or four hours a day rather than the traditional nine to five is an achievement. What is most important is getting to a stage where they can do something constructive with their lives.

Our communities and businesses modify the environment for those of us with physical handicaps by providing ramps. Persons with psychiatric handicaps need "ramps" built which enable them to perceive the living, teaching or work place as supportive.

Finally, not until we families learn to adopt an "open-ended" expectation, does a valid and realistic hope materialize that "recovery is possible"——as Ken Turkleson says——"not recovery form the illness, but recovery of a life."

Sometimes I wonder which condition influences the progress of the disability the most——the illness itself or society's response to the illness. Until we react more in the manner we do with physically disable persons, I don't see how we can realistically evaluate the potential for productivity of person with psychiatric disabilities.

I believe the family and the professional are natural allies in our mutual concern for persons who have psychiatric disabilities. Families want to be allies in treatment with the mental health professionals and allies in rehabilitation with your profession. It has been for us an educational process. Many families are just beginning to be fully aware of the elements necessary to complete the circle of supports and services that expand the quality of life for our sons and daughters. It is a circle which equally includes the person who has the disability, the mental health professions, the rehabilitation professions, and the natural support stems such as the family.

A parent cannot say the words, "This is my daughter. She is mad," or hear the words, "Your son has schizophrenia. At this time we don't know the cause or the cure," without making the promise to ourselves that we will encourage and work with those who can take away some of their pain and help reconstruct some of their life.

Toward that ongoing goal, I have written a statement of my own mission:
To offer continuing emotional support for my daughter, Ruth. To find and cooperate with the professionals and programs which increase her functioning and growth. To advocate for all persons with severe mental illnesses with the government and society to provide the necessary laws and funds for basic and rehabilitation research and for the training of skillful and nurturing professionals. To never allow the community to resign itself to the mere custodial care of my daughter. And to do this with the least amount of restrictive parenting.

Family Crisis Related to the Deinstitutionalization of a Mentally Retarded Child

Alex W. Ursprung

Large scale deinstitutionalization of mentally retarded citizens is a relatively recent development which is gaining momentum. The philosophical and clinical bases for this trend can be traced to the normalization principle (Wolfensberger, 1972) and to the growing number of legal actions brought against states and large institutions by groups of residents and their advocates (Halderman v. Pennhurst, 1977; N.Y.A.R.C. v. Rockefeller, 1972; Wyatt v. Hardin, 1971). As a result of these legal actions, several states have been mandated by the courts to phase out large congregate facilities and to replace them with community based services.

In addition to the growing number of legal suit pertaining to deinstitutionalization, a considerable amount of writing has appeared in professional journals concerning the strengths and weaknesses of this trend. A review of the issues associated with deinstitutionalization is contained in a document by the Center on Human Policy (1979). Numerous methods of arriving at deinstitutionalization have been implemented, and these methods are reviewed by Flynn and Nitsch (1980). Blatt, Bogdan, Biklen, and Taylor (1977) also provided a critical summary of many of these approaches.

A review of the literature on deinstitutionalization indicates a preoccupation with administrative and theoretical implications (Hatcher & Rasch, 1980; Messina & Davis, 1981). What is strikingly absent is a body of literature concerning the impact that deinstitutionalization has upon family members, and the corresponding impact that family resistance or acceptance have on a retarded person's ability to make a successful adjustment to community placement. For example, the author found only one study (Meyer, 1980) pertaining to family adjustment to deinstitutionalization. This lack of information should be particularly surprising to those individuals who have been clinically involved with deinstitutionalization projects, since family resistance and crisis are often the major issues that workers have to address. Working with families can be more difficult and time consuming than finding community placement resources or educational and vocational services.

The purpose of this article is to describe a framework (developed by the author) that might assist in understanding the type of crisis that a family experiences dealing with deinstitutionalization. This framework is timely and highly relevant to the success of deinstitutionalization since it focuses on both the mentally retarded person and the family. From the perspective of the mentally retarded person and his or her advocates, gaining parental approval and support is important legally, especially if the person is a minor or if the parents have retained guardianship. In addition, family support must be a critical concern of clinicians, regardless of the legal implications. Family support is essential in motivating the client, in attempting to reintegrate the child with the family, or in restoring family ties when the child is going to live outside the family but within the neighboring community. Furthermore, family members must understand their own attitudes toward the child, the institution, retardation, and community services. They may be in need of therapeutic interventions in what can be a potentially painful adjustment, and may also need educational intervention and advocacy.

Due to the complexity of the deinstitutionalization issue, and the lack of literature on the topic, this article will attempt to provide some initial understanding of the problem. The related literature that will be reviewed is concerned with the initial adjustment of the family to a disabled child and the family's adjustment to institutionalization. In addition, based on the author's experiences, a compilation of contextual variables will be presented which supplement and extend the usefulness of the existing literature.

Reprinted from: Journal of Rehabilitation Oct/Nov/Dec 1984, with permission.

Related Literature

Family variables related to the birth of a disabled child and his or her subsequent institutionalization have been studied by a number of authors, notably Downey (1963); Farber (1960, 1964, 1975); Farber, Jenne, and Toigo (1960); Hersh (1970); and Saenger (1960). A variety of conclusions have been advanced by these authors.

Farber (1960, 1964) originally defined two types of family crises; namely, role reorganization and tragic crisis. Retarded boys were found to be more destructive to family unity than were retarded girls, especially in lower class families. Families with a "marital strategy" functioned better than those without one. The initial impact of the birth was reported to be greater on the father, but the long-range impact was found to be greater on the mother. Willingness to institutionalize a child was greater among upper class fathers and lower class mothers, and generally greater in large upper class families.

Downey (1963) found that parents of high status tended to institutionalize their disabled children early and then failed to visit them, while lower status parents delayed placement and continued contact with the child once he or she was placed. Saenger (1960) found that institutionalization was likely when (a) the degree of retardation was great, (b) secondary or physical handicaps were involved, (c) the child was from a lower class home, and (d) a severely retarded child with adjustment problems was in a middle class home. Hersh (1970) noted the following five variables which inclined parents to institutionalize: (a) high regard for the institutional staff as experts, (b) viewing the child as disruptive to family life, (c) in the face of failing home management, seeing the child as threatening family stability, (d) former knowledge of institutions, and (e) physical or emotional weariness of the parents.

Wolfensberger (1967) pointed out several shortcomings with these types of studies. Samples tended to be biased toward white, middle class families who were members of parent groups or who were on institutional waiting lists. Measures tended to lack validity or were often based on researcher intuition, not empirical

findings. One could also argue that this entire line of inquiry may not be fruitful since institutionalization is an overdetermined event, attributable to the various reasons posited above, but compounded by factors such as the amount of extended family support, the influence of professionals such as paediatricians, and the time of diagnosis (i.e., early or late). A broader view, focusing on family systems theory, would seem more applicable.

In a more recent article, Farber (1975) developed a view of family adaptation to mental retardation which includes several stages. In the first stage, referred to as *labeling*, the family realizes that social roles will have to be renegotiated. In the second stage, *normalization*, the pretence of former roles is maintained, especially in family interactions with the outside world. In the third stage, *mobilization*, family members intensify the amount of effort and time devoted to family demands, but cling to the concept of normalcy. In the fourth stage, *revisionist*, the family has become isolated from the community and can no longer maintain the normalcy pretext. Roles are changed, as are expectations, in order for the family unit to remain cohesive in an environment perceived as hostile. In the fifth stage of *polarization*, the family begins to turn its attention to the hostility that is perceived within the family system. The sixth and final stage, referred to as *elimination*, is characterized by efforts to block interactions with the person within the system who is seen as offensive. An attempt is made to renegotiate roles regarded as normal.

This model of Farber's is quite relevant to the deinstitutionalization issue, and the sixth phase (elimination) is most applicable since it presumably leads to institutionalization, thus providing the family with a final solution. Farber, however, indicated that it may not be necessarily be the retarded child who is eliminated, but could just as easily be a spouse who is viewed as responsible, or another sibling who develops adjustment problems. When the retarded child is placed in an institution, a family may return to the normalization phase, and come to some decision as to the future role of the eliminated child. Farber claimed that middle class families are apt to depersonalize the child or to consider the child as dead, never visiting the institution, while working class families are apt to see the child as "living away from home." They may retain contact, holding onto the possibility of future reintegration.

Two related points fit in very well with the elimination phase. Wolfensberger (1967) cited a 1955 article by Beddie and Osmond which compared institutionalization to child loss and drew on Lindmann's (1944) theory of grief work. If the grief work is not done at the time of institutionalization it will have to be done at a later date. Since there is no socially acceptable ritual for grief related to institutionalization, the process may be delayed and prolonged. According to Wolfensberger (1967), "institutionalization is a death without proper rite." (p.333).

Another useful perspective on parental adaptation to a retarded child is Olshansky's (1962) concept of chronic sorrow. Both Olshansky and Wolfensberger have pointed to the limitations of discussing "adjusting to" or "accepting" retardation. Perhaps professionals are expecting parents to perceive and accept retardation from their own perspective. It may be more realistic to view chronic sorrow as a natural reaction to a tragic fact, rather than a neurotic denial or a problem of adjustment or acceptance. Olshansky claimed that chronic sorrow will persist whether or not the child is institutionalized, will vary in intensity from person to person in the family over time, and will only be eliminated through death.

These ideas are compelling, and their credibility can be enhanced by considering other situations where they might apply, and where we may see them as reasonable reactions. Family adjustment to a soldier missing in action or to a missing child come readily to mind.

Keeping in mind the concept of chronic sorrow and Farber's elimination phase, the initial reaction of a family faced with the deinstitutionalization of a retarded child can now be considered. When families do institutionalize a child, it is often assumed that this is a final solution. Institutions have a history of over 100 years in this country, giving them a sense of permanence. Furthermore, professionals at institutions often assure parents that the arrangement

is lifelong. With the placement made, the family can attempt to return to a state of normalcy. Chronic sorrow may be maintained at a fairly constant level depending on circumstances and the amount of continued contact with the child. Plans to deinstitutionalize the child, when suggested by professionals, can be seen as forcing the family to return to the beginning of Farber's stages. One would expect the labeling phase to begin again. Although the child is not living with the family, and community placement plans may not call for home placement, family roles may still need to be renegotiated. If the family depersonalized the child, tried to forget the child, or greatly minimized the child's potential, the incongruent views of current professional thought and practice can have a shocking effect. As a result, chronic sorrow can be intensified, and guilt for having made an "improper" decision years ago may have to be dealt with by family members. If the initial decision to institutionalize a child was not entirely mutual on the parents' part, it is likely that conflicts between the parents will be rekindled.

Tracing a crisis through Farber's six phases a second time may not be the appropriate means of addressing a crisis related to deinstitutionalization, despite the suggestions made above. Farber's phases focus on negative adaptation culminating in the elimination of the offending family member. It would seem more logical and useful to try to conceptualize a new series of stages, and to consider the possibility of positive, as well as negative, family adjustment. In order to attempt this conceptualization, consideration will be given to a new set of variables that may be more relevant to the issue than traditional socio-familial approaches.

Contextual Variables to Consider in Deinstitutionalization

The material presented in this section is based on several years of clinical experience on the part of the author with community services that were primarily concerned with deinstitutionalizing mentally retarded children and adults. The families encountered had children ranging in age from 5 to 50 years. Positive and negative reactions to deinstitutionalization and a variety of crisis reactions appeared in families in ways that were not always consistent with the literature reviewed in the previous portion of this article.

From clinical experience and from the review of the literature it is possible to make some assumptions about the variables that will have the most impact on family reaction to deinstitutionalization. These variables include: (a) the context in which the child was originally institutionalized, (b) the role that the institution plays in current family life, (c) the context in which deinstitutionalization is planned, (d) the context in which human services are provided, and (e) the situation of the family at the time that deinstitutionalization is planned.

The Context of Institutionalization

The decision to institutionalize a child is usually made on the basis of advice from significant others. Wolfensberger (1967) reported several studies from the 1960's which indicated that physicians recommended institutionalization immediately after birth in 50% to 80% of the cases of severe mental retardation. The social status of the physician makes this advice seem imperative, and carries considerable weight in the family's thinking for years to come. Advice also comes from extended family members, neighbors, friends, the clergy and lawyers.

Families often assumed or were advised that their retarded children should require special services (educational and medical) which a family of lay people could not provide. The ability of institutions to effectively provide these services has been greatly exaggerated, but none the less accepted. The inability of institutions to deliver needed services has been well documented in recent years (Center on Human Policy, 1979), but it is often difficult to convey this to parents.

Many parents have institutionalized their children because of lack of community services when the child was born, or because of their lack of knowledge of such services. This reason may have been valid 10 or 20 years ago, but generally is no longer true. However, families may act *as if* it were still true out of denial or ignorance.

The family context at the time of institutionalization must also be taken into account. Parents may react with shame or guilt when they feel that they have produced a less than perfect infant, and may react by attempting to hide the child, especially if it was an unwanted pregnancy. It is not uncommon to encounter families where younger siblings are not aware of the existence of a first-born institutionalized sibling.

When parents are having personal difficulties at the time of birth, it is often easy for them to attribute their problems to the disabled child. Subsequent institutionalization can be the resulting solution. Similarly, divorce (related or not to the presence of the child) can leave a single parent who does not have the ability to cope with the retarded child alone. Single parents who choose to keep their child at home may remarry and at this point, disabled children are often placed outside of the home as new family roles are negotiated. A new marriage may take priority over the needs of the child.

The Institutional Context as Perceived by Parents

Parents may view the institution as a lifelong service provider, which guarantees a home for their children. Some parents have been told that it is best to place the child in the institution, to resume life as normal, and to forget the child.

Parents may also feel secure in the institution's medical base, since such facilities have traditionally been administered by physicians. Parents are generally unaware that many institutions are medically understaffed, or that many institutional physicians are not licensed. Wolfensberger (1975) provided a detailed critique of the medical model in institutional settings.

Parents may also have distorted views of the institution as a safe, clean, pleasant place. This viewpoint is the result of the family having no access to certain areas of the facility or having only limited access on visiting days, and by not having another model of services against which to compare the institution. Thus, the selected institution is seen as an ideal setting.

The Deinstitutionalization Context

Families may perceive several alternatives to large congregate institutions as relatively unthreatening. These alternatives include placement in nursing homes or smaller institutions, such as regional centers. These facilities are essentially smaller institutions, may have a medical model of operation, and appear to be more of a transfer than a sudden shift in type of service provision.

Group homes or apartment programs represent a sharp break with the institutional service model, and families may perceive them negatively. Family resistance and family crisis can be intensified by the location of the facility (in a slum for example), by negative media coverage, by attitudes in the community, or by attitudes within the social circle of the family.

Foster care probably represents the most threatening alternative to institutionalization, yet in some cases it is the most positive alternative for the retarded individual. The family's sense of adequacy may be called into question if another family appears willing to care for the child when they appear unwilling or unable. Occasional media coverage of exceptionally good or exceptionally poor services in foster care can alter family perceptions. For families who can externalize reasons for not being able to care for their own child, foster care may be an attractive alternative.

The Human Service Context

The nature and frequency of parent contact with human service professionals will have an effect on their receptivity to further interventions. When parents institutionalize their children, many if not most of their dealings with professional personnel center around early diagnostic concerns and admission issues. Since medical doctors have often been involved with these concerns and issues, contact with human service workers often stops when the child is institutionalized. Although institutions may develop extensive treatment plans, parents are often not consulted in the formulation of these plans, and are usually not involved in an ongoing role with their child's

life. The result is that they are not used to dealing with professionals. Having initially dealt with medical doctors, the credibility of other human service professionals may be called into question.

Parents may also be overwhelmed and confused by changes in human services over the years. Many parents institutionalized their children 20 or more years ago. In the intervening years our society's technology, manpower, and philosophical approaches to treating mentally retarded people have changed dramatically. Treatments and approaches such as psychotropic drugs, behavior modification, and the application of normalization principles are relatively new innovations. Large numbers of professionals have been trained in the *specialty* of mental retardation, a specialty with a very limited membership not too many years ago. In this respect, parents of older institutionalized children have been living in a time warp.

In addition to an increase in professionals and treatments, there has been a corresponding increase in the number and extent of community services available to mentally retarded persons. When deinstitutionalization is discussed with parents, they may suddenly find themselves dealing with workers from the institution, community residential programs, workshops, schools, hospital outpatient departments and clinics, local mental health centers, and representatives of various parent groups. These contacts may or may not be organized and coordinated; the results can be confusing and overwhelming, especially after years of silence about their child.

The Family Context when Deinstitutionalization is Suggested

Having placed a child away from home, and having made some level of adaptation to that fact, family life goes on. Naturally, other developmental and situational crises will occur over the course of the family life cycle. If deinstitutionalization decisions are forced on a family at a critical time, the result can be a crisis. On the other hand, suggesting a community placement at the right time can result in a favorable reaction, and can perhaps help lessen the level of chronic sorrow or guilt among family members.

Workers need to be aware of several predictable and unpredictable types of family crises. There are a number of normal developmental events in families that can be stressful in and of themselves, and these events can lead to a crisis situation if additional stressors are imposed on the family. Such events include new births, adolescent adjustment problems, death of a spouse or child, and retirement. Unpredictable stressors that workers need to keep in mind include marital problems not related to the institutionalized child, illness or disability, alcoholism, and unemployment.

A number of predictable family developmental events may enhance the likelihood of a positive family reaction to deinstitutionalization. These events include retirement, other children leaving the home as they mature, increased income, and increased leisure time.

Counseling Parents During Deinstitutionalization

A large body of information on counseling parents of retarded individuals exists, and this information is generally useful to professionals involved in resolving a deinstitutionalization crisis. However, this material may have limited applicability since much of it was developed in the context of counseling parents of young retarded children, where the issues were initial diagnostic concerns and adjustment problems. In addition, virtually all of the material is directed at parents who have kept their children at home. There has never been a well-documented systematic effort to counsel parents on an ongoing basis once a child has been institutionalized. Social service departments at institutions have historically been small, and have been primarily concerned with the admission and management of persons at the facility. The recent expansion of institutional social services is the direct result of legal actions.

When services are rendered to parents whose child has been institutionalized and who may not have had any contact with professionals for many years, the difficulty of providing adequate coun-

seling or casework services is compounded. The core difficulties seem to relate to needs of parents for information about retardation and service models, as well as the provision of therapeutic or supportive services. Many parents may become overwhelmed or angry when deinstitutionalization is suggested, placing the counselor in an identity conflict between the roles of client advocate, parent educator, and parent counselor. Most parents believe that they followed the best alternative when they institutionalized their child. That decision may have been a reasonable response at the time of institutionalization and, in fact, may have been the only available option. However, it is one thing to understand this situation as a counselor and quite another to be able to convey to parents a sense that what was right is no longer so, and that the parents are not being blamed for their earlier decision. Sternlicht and Merritt (1977) aptly pointed out that all too often parents are "viewed as necessary evils obstructing care for the child, and with varying degrees of resentment and distaste by child welfare workers and community" (p. 278).

Conclusion

Very little literature exists on family response to the deinstitutionalization of a retarded child. This article has presented a review of related literature, and described a number of contextual variables that might give human service workers insight into the various dynamics at work within families when faced with deinstitutionalization. Awareness of these variables should enable workers to avoid unnecessary crises and resistance in families of institutionalized retarded people.

A model of family adaption which, unlike Farber's, allows for the possibility of a health-based positive response to deinstitutionalization needs to be developed. The effectiveness of human service interventions and the direction toward normalization will continue to be circumscribed if professionals continue to rely on a pathology-based model, especially when that model conceptualizes deinstitutionalization in negative terms. Examining contextual variables, which include both the positive and negative impact of interventional strategies on families, is one step in the movement toward normalization.

References

Beddie, A. & Osmond, H. (1955). Mothers, mongols and mores. **Canadian Medical Association Journal. 73,** 167-170.

Blatt, B., Bogdan, R., Biklen, D., & Taylor, S. (1977). From institution to community: A conversion model. **Educational programming for the severely handicapped.** Reston, VA: Council for Exceptional Children.

Center on Human Policy. (1979). **The community imperative: A refutation of all arguments in support of institutionalizing anyone because of mental retardation.** Syracuse, NY: Center on Human Policy Press.

Downey, K.J. (1963). Parents' interest in the institutionalized severely mentally retarded child. **Social Problems, 11,** 185-193.

Farber, B. (1960). Perception of crisis and related variables on the impact of a retarded child on the mother. **Journal of Human Behavior, 1,** 108-118.

Farber, B. (1964). **Family: Organization and Interaction.** San Francisco: Chandler Publishing.

Farber, B. (1975). Family adaptions to severely mentally retarded children. In M.J. Begab & S.A. Richardson (Eds.), **The mentally retarded and society: A social science perspective.** (pp.247-266). Baltimore: University Park Press.

Farber, B., Jenne, W., & Toigo, R. (1960). Family crisis and decision to institutionalize the retarded child. **Council for Exceptional Children, National Education Association,** (Research Series A - No.1), 1-66.

Flynn, R., & Nitsch, K. (1980). **Normalization, social integration, and community services.** Baltimore: University Park Press.

Halderman v. Pennhurst, No. 74-1345 (E.D. PA 1977).

Hatcher, M., & Rasch, J. (1980). Deinstitutionalization and community based treatment alternatives. **Journal of Rehabilitation, 46**(3), 64-67.

Hersh, A. (1970). Changes in family functioning following placement of a retarded child. **Social Work, 15,** 93-96.

Lindmann, E. (1944). Sympotomotology and management of acute grief. **American Journal of Psychiatry, 101,** 141-149.

Messina, J., & Davis, J. (1981). Deinstitutionalization: Myth or reality. **Journal of Rehabilitation, 47**(1), 36-39.

Meyer, F.J. (1980). Attitudes of parents of institutionalized mentally retarded individuals toward deinstitutionalization. **American Journal of Mental Deficiency, 85**(2), 184-187.

N.Y.A.R.C. et al v. Rockefeller. (1975) . (Nos.73-C-55-C-113).

Olshanasky, S. (1962). Chronic sorrow: A response to having a mentally defective child. **Social Casework, 43,** 190-193.

Saenger, G. (1960). **Factors influencing the institutionalization of mentally retarded individuals in New York City.** Albany, NY: State Interdepartmental Health Resources Board.

Sternlicht, M., & Merritt, J. (1977). Variables related to obtaining natural parents' consent for family care placement. In P. Mittler (Ed.), **Research to practice in mental retardation: Care and intervention** Vol.1 (pp.87-91). Baltimore: University Park Press.

Wolfensberger, W. (1967). Counseling the parents of the retarded. In A. Baumeister (Ed.) **Mental retardation appraisal, education and rehabilitation.** (pp. 329-386). Chicago: Aldine Publishing Co.

Wolfensberger, W. (1972). **The principle of normalization in human services.** Toronto: National Institute on Mental Retardation.

Wolfensberger, W. (1975). **The origin and nature of our institutional models.** Syracuse, NY: Human Policy Press.

Wyatt v. Hardin (1971). (LA No. 3195-N).

 # 5 SEXUALITY AND DISABILITY

The image of the disabled is in transition; prior to the 1960's a general orientation prevailed that those with severe disabilities ought to be institutionalized and hence, the deaf, blind and others were segregated. Recently, deinstitutionalization has been practised since it is now believed by some that the disabled are entitled to enjoy all of the benefits of contemporary lifestyles. The disabled have come out of the closet, so to speak, and social support for this change can be obtained. Likewise, the mass media is no longer representing the disabled as the leper of society; instead these attitudes have changed and the disabled person is now being portrayed as a legitimate person with desires, needs and capability for successful integration. The disabled are now trying to participate in all aspects of society and movies such as "Mask", "Elephant Man", and "My Left Foot" are attempts to counter some of the widespread negative images and portrayals of the disabled. These changes are illustrated by Hahn; he demonstrates that disabled individuals have had many varied experiences including isolation, alienation, and rejection. Yet, they have still been able to partake in positive pursuits which increase the quality of their lives and the lives of others. Thus, Buchanan, Barrett, Cushman, Hahn, Miller, and Morgan indicate that through sexual, vocational, educational, and social participation in society the disabled can be active and productive members of the community.

Further, it is important to note that the disabled, like all individuals, have sexual desires and needs which must be satisfied; the disabled are by no means sexless eunuchs. The disabled are quite capable of enjoying the pleasures of marriage and other intimate relationships such as becoming a parent. Unfortunately, beliefs still exist which bar the disabled person's access to these relationships. The belief that the disabled person should remain concealed in the institutions is strong. The perception of the disabled as sexual beings is an alien one. However, the disabled do, in fact, encounter the same problems as do non-disabled people in their sexual and social encounters.

Tragically, it has also been revealed that the disabled are also exposed to tragic events and they can also be victims of psychological, physical, economic, and sexual abuses. Cole presents a lucid explanation of sexual abuses experienced by the disabled. Unfortunately, when people become integrated into a community, they not only experience the benefits of that community, but they also encounter its excesses. Additional concerns about the disabled and sexuality are outlined in the research presentations of Miller et al., Hahn, Westgate, and Snow. Image, identity, self-assurance, and experimentation are all vital issues to the establishment and maintenance of healthy and satisfactory sexual relationships.

This book has attempted to illustrate through the eyes of experts, the issues which confront the disabled in social interactions. During the last three decades this minority has been able to overcome many of the social, psychological, economic, and political restraints. Yet, this population often experiences the ramifications of prejudice and discrimination, factors which negatively influence the lives of most minority groups. The disabled have formed many groups in order to promote integration and to motivate society to accept them on equal terms in all realms of society. With the support of medical and para-medical professionals, the helping professions, and the political arena, disabled citizens can overcome many of the impediments that have confined them to minority status.

Can Disability Be Beautiful?

HARLAN HAHN

In a decade that has often turned its back on the political aspirations of Black, Hispanic, feminist, gay, aging, and other disadvantaged groups, there is an increasingly urgent need to develop a means by which the disability rights movement can mobilize a potential 27 to 36 million[1] disabled citizens to join the ranks of a powerful progressive coalition. This process could enable persons with disabilities to gain a new kind of political identity and non-disabled groups to develop an innovative basis for forging electoral alliances. Both goals represent admittedly difficult tasks, but I believe they can be achieved through an enhanced awareness of the significance of discrimination based on perceptible physical differences.

The foundation for these developments has already been established by research that recognizes disabled Americans as a minority group and by a sociopolitical definition of disability that identifies their problems primarily as the product of a disabling environment rather than of personal deficiencies.[2] In the present human-made milieu, which was not designed to accommodate the interests or needs of this minority, people with disabilities have experienced one of the highest rates of unemployment, poverty, and welfare dependency in the country. They have usually been sent to separate, or segregated schools, and they have been prevented from interacting, or integrating, with their nondisabled peers in transportation, housing, and public accommodations by barriers and policies as rigid as the most restrictive practice of apartheid. By contrast, in an environment adapted to the needs of everyone, which appears to be both technologically and economically possible, disabled and nondisabled persons could become functionally equal; the only remaining distinction between them would be the presence of irreducible physical differences that result form labelling or visible characteristics.[3]

The most salient features of many disabled person are bodily traits similar to skin color, gender, and other attributes that have been used as a basis for differentiating people for centuries and without which discrimination probably could not occur. In fact, in a recent survey, 45 percent of disabled Americans said they considered themselves "a minority group in the same sense as . . . Blacks and Hispanics."[4] Unlike other minorities, however, disabled men and women have not been able to refute implicit or direct accusations of biological inferiority that have often been invoked to rationalize the oppression of groups whose appearance differs from the standards of the dominant majority. Since most disabled children and adults have been raised by nondisabled parents or guardians, they also lack a sense of generational continuity that might otherwise allow the legacy of their experience to become an important solace in an uncaring and inhospitable world. Perhaps even more significantly, people with disabilities have been forced to bear a stigma that virtually defines them as "not quite human."[5]

The sources of aversive and unfavorable attitudes toward disabled women and men seem to be deeply rooted in the psychic and social structure of the nondisabled majority. Recently, however, I have suggested that such views may reflect "existential" anxiety (the projected threat of the loss of physical capabilities) or "aesthetic" anxiety (the fear of others whose traits are perceived as disturbing or unpleasant).[6] Both worries can result in discriminatory behavior.

Employers who refuse to hire a disabled applicant for a job because they are reminded of their own physical vulnerability are no less guilty of prejudice than those who would consider the presence of a disabled employee unsightly or upsetting to customers. Yet, government leaders and courts may be more likely to outlaw discrimination based on the simple fear of others who are regarded as alien or strange than to prohibit prejudicial acts founded on

Reprinted From Social Policy, Winter 1988, with permission.

310

apprehensions concerning clinically demonstrable physiological defects. Hence, there is a pressing need to focus increased attention on the "aesthetic" dimension of perceptions of disabled individuals.

Ironically, however, many persons with disabilities have been reluctant to acknowledge the existence of discrimination based on aesthetic criteria. Although a recent note in the *Harvard Law Review* indicates that the prejudicial treatment of people with so-called unattractive attributes might already be illegal under Section 504 of the Rehabilitation Act of 1973,[7] this aspect of the stigma imposed on disabled citizens probably has been the major obstacle to the development of a political identity that would allow them to emerge as a strong and cohesive voting bloc. Disabled Americans, thus, are forced to confront an awkward dilemma. Certainly, no one wants to be considered unattractive. Epithets that characterize another persona as ugly or unappealing may be the most vicious insults that can be hurled at a human being. And yet the failure to examine candidly the extent to which unfavorable assessments of people with disabilities are determined by feelings that might not be encompassed by "existential" anxiety could impede the efforts of the disability rights movement to achieve equal rights.

Prior researchers have tended to ignore the aesthetics of disability; if they mentioned the subject at all, they have cast disability almost exclusively in negative terms. Fisher, for example, states:

> Despite all the efforts invested by our society in an attempt to rally sympathy for the crippled, they still elicit serious discomfort. It is well documented that the disfigured person makes others feel anxious and becomes an object to be warded off. He is viewed as simultaneously inferior and threatening. He becomes associated with the special class of monster images that haunts each culture.[8]

Kern even seems to imply that the exclusion of disabled men and women from the ranks of the aesthetically pleasing may be desirable:

As long as physical beauty determines sexual choices, human relations will be guided by fortuitous, pleasing compositions of bone, muscle, and skin. Elites of the beautiful will continue to live privileged lives, and character and "inner" beauty will continue to take second place in the contests for sexual partners. It is tempting to condemn this rewarding of physical beauty by pointing to the riches and fame we shower on fashion models and athletes while the aged and the deformed are hidden away in poverty and neglect. But perhaps our condemnations are in bad faith and even a bit silly...It is, after all, the physical expression of sexual desire that produces offspring. Though erotic stimuli vary from one age to another, they are always based on physical attraction, and as long as that is the case, we will remain dominated by the mysterious and enduring power of the body to generate sexual tension and release sexual pleasure.[9]

The subject of disability probably represents one of those issues in which politics and sexuality are juxtaposed in unexpected ways. In view of the overwhelming failure of prior investigations to discover any positive features of the aesthetics of disability, it is not surprising that many persons with disabilities have tended to deny this aspect of their oppression. Most relevant studies have imposed an unacknowledged taboo or censorship in the discussion of this topic, and even the burgeoning literature on sexuality and disability has not provided a means of transcending the supposedly unattractive qualities of obvious physical differences. In fact, the effort to persuade disabled citizens to adopt a social and political identity based on a recognition of this type of discrimination might even be construed as a request that they sacrifice their personal lives for the sake of their public agenda.

Clearly, what is needed is an equivalent to the "Black is beautiful" phenomenon of the 1960s that would allow disabled persons to redefine their identity in a positive manner. Even though the phrase "disability is beautiful" hardly flows trippingly from the tongue; history discloses abundant proof that images of beauty have changed continually and that physical differences or disabilities sometimes have been considered attractive and appealing. By examining this evidence, disabled men and women might gain both an enhanced appreciation of their history and a new basis for developing a political identity. And, in this process, nondisabled observers also may acquire valuable insights about varying concepts of physical appearance as well as a firm foundation for working cooperatively with the disability rights movement.

The History of a Subversive Sensualism

In many respects, the history of perceptions of disability has appeared to reflect two contrasting tendencies. On the one hand, disability sometimes has been associated with what might be termed a "subversive sensualism" reflecting a curiosity and fascination that is frequently infused with erotic impulses. On the other hand, views of physical differences or disabilities also have been shaped by a supposedly more civilized tradition of charity and help that has seemed to transform disabled adults into sexless beings. In order to unravel these conflicting and often overlapping trends, I intend to develop a brief and somewhat revisionist interpretation of the limited but significant historical evidence available concerning people with disabilities from antiquity to the modern era.

Perhaps the oldest known disabled individual was the Neanderthal "Nandy," whose bones, excavated in the Shanidar cave in Iraq, not only disclosed congenital deformity but also "show that even in death this person was an object of some esteem, if not respect, born out of close association with a hostile outside."[10] Several thousand years seemed to elapse before definitive information about the social role of people with disabilities reappears, although it does seem significant that many artifacts from ancient fertility cults resemble men and women who——in modern eyes——might be regarded as grotesque, distorted, or deformed rather than as aesthetically pleasing.[11]

Folk tales transmitted by oral traditions include a disproportionately large cast of disabled characters who appear to denote a persistent fascination——perhaps of both attraction and repulsion——with physical differences and disabilities.[12] In the fairy tales collected by the Grimm brothers, for example, there are several figures such as the stepsisters of Cinderella who disable themselves in order to enhance their attractiveness.[13]

Perhaps the first evidence that disabilities could be perceived as valued characteristics, paradoxically, may be found in competitive bidding for impaired Roman slaves, who, like their counterparts in Aztec civilizations and in later medieval courts, were often entertainers at intemperate and uninhibited banquets or festivals.[14] In fact, the appearance of disability often has been especially conspicuous at festive celebrations associated with a relaxation of personal restraints and a heightened sense of eroticism.

Early records concerning the role of disabled people in many societies indicate that, although they have generally been oppressed and exploited, the physical differences represented by disabilities also have been perceived as socially and sexually desirable. In many cultures, humans continue to disable themselves through techniques ranging from scarification and mutilation to tattooing, resculpting, and painting in order to achieve commonly accepted standards of physical beauty.[15]

There are also indications that, in some societies, persons with distinctive physical differences have been especially prized as sexual partners. Among the Hopis, for example, the sexual activity of a tiny proportion of the population has perpetuated an unexpectedly high rate of albinism.[16] Ironically, persons of short stature, who appeared to be favorites of many royal courts of Europe until the seventeenth century,[17] have encountered rejection in modern times that has perhaps been partially responsible for placing an unusual reliance on their own organizational resources to facilitate processes of family formation.[18]

From the decline of the Roman Empire to the end of the Middle Ages, the careers of many disabled adults who survived as comedians or entertainers appeared to follow different paths. Some, including several famous individuals of short stature and other seemingly retarded adults, managed to attach themselves to royal courts, as jesters or "fools," a role in which they were granted more satirical freedom and other privileges than were available to most members of the entourage.[19] The highly eroticized nature of their status is underscored by the fact that, in the thirteenth century, many of them apparently were naked when they performed.[20]

In addition, groups "of wandering minstrels who were blind, deaf, and lame travelled from manor to manor, carrying information and providing entertainment in exchange for food and shelter."[21] Less is known about these bands, but they seemed to play not only an important role in the life of medieval society but also in festivities such as the Feast of Fools, an occasion for gaiety, mirth, and heightened feelings of sexuality. Hence, physical disabilities during the Middle Ages, both in feudal courts and among the general populace, appeared to be related to revelry, debauchery, and laughter rather than to inferiority, ugliness, and tragedy.

All of these activities were strongly condemned by the medieval church that sought to control the social and sexual conduct of its members. And yet, for hundreds of years, neither religious nor secular authorities seemed capable of suppressing the popular excitement that was associated at least symbolically with physical difference or disability.

The explanation of this phenomenon can only be sought in speculation based on the fragmentary information available about public emotions and behavior in the pre-modern era. In a legacy extending from ancient rites and Roman civilization into the Middle Ages, perhaps persistent human curiosity and fascination about physical differences connected with fertility, along with the dialectical reversals that permeate uninhibited conduct, have been stimulated as often by physical traits that modern observers would consider unattractive as by attributes that would be perceived as aesthetically beautiful by contemporary viewers.

This propensity has been most clearly described by Bakhtin in his interpretation of the work of Rabelais: "The acute awareness of victory over fear is an essential element of medieval laughter. . . .All that was terrifying becomes grotesque. . . . The people play with terror and laugh at it; the awesome becomes a 'comic monster.'" Perhaps Bakhtin's most penetrating comment, however, was: "Various deformities such as protruding bellies, enormous noses, or humps are symptoms of pregnancy or of procreative power."[22]This sentence implies the interesting and significant possibility that both the process of pre-modern thinking and its symbolic content might betray an undercurrent of dialectical or dialogical images.

Such perceptions also are infused with political implications that manifest themselves most clearly on festive occasions. "Carnival masks, costumes, and grotesque distortions of the body served to destabilize fixed identities and role differentiations."[23] The prominence of physical differences or disabilities at festivals, therefore, posed a threat that the established order of bodily images might be overthrown by unleashing repressed instincts that could exceed the repressive capacitates of civil or religious leaders. While some visible impairments have been interpreted as implying that their bearers were unlovable and aesthetically unlovely,[24] the physical symptoms of other disabilities such as tuberculosis continued to evoke erotic connotations throughout the nineteenth century.[25] The sexual feelings triggered by atypical physiques have exerted consistent and disturbing effects on the social and political perceptions of the nondisabled majority.

The revolutionary potential of eroticized images of physical differences or disabilities, however, was overwhelmed and defused by economic forces. In the Middle Ages, men and women with disabilities were the heirs to two contrasting and ambiguous legacies. In one tradition emanating from the early treatment of disabled persons as parasites, mascots, or scapegoats who might bring good fortune to those who responded to their plight with compassion and generosity, some people with disabilities were beggars who wandered through the countryside until they became the first group to receive outdoor relief under the English Poor Law of 1601 and subsequent legislation.[26] Others became entertainers and minstrels, and court jesters. The relative status of disabled citizens in medieval society is indicated by the fact that many individuals during this era intentionally disabled themselves in order to join either group.[27]

Even though the intensely curious and intriguing nature of physical disabilities continued to find expression at exhibitions in carnivals throughout the nineteenth century,[28] historical trends depicting human differences both as an inverted antidote to the prospect of increasing debility and as sensually provocative traits finally succumbed to legacies that have portrayed disabled women and men as the aesthetically neutered objects of benevolence and assistance.

The Moral Order of the Body

The human body is a powerful symbol conveying messages that have massive social, economic, and political implications. In order to perpetuate their hegemony, ruling elites have attempted to impose what might be termed a moral order of the body, providing images that subjects are encouraged to emulate. By manipulating prescribed forms of appearance, they also have been able to maintain control of a significant aspect of human behavior. Since physical disabilities during the Middle Ages commonly had been linked with relatively unrestrained social and sexual conduct, officials sought to establish a standard that would stress similarities rather than differences among human beings.

Instead of exalting the visible differences that had long been associated with uninhibited sensuality, the medieval church and secular leaders turned to another disability as a source for images of a new moral order of the human body. As evidence of their intense commitment to denial of the flesh, mortals——especially women——with anorexia nervosa, were widely promoted as a physical model that the laity ought to imitate.[29] This look was later endorsed by Protestant leaders such as John Wesley who invoked nutritional as well as moral arguments in urging parishioners to strive for the slender and svelte figure that has, ironically, become the idealized symbol of modern hedonism.[30] These comparatively restricted bodily contours, of course, not only have excluded persons with a

wide range of so-called deformities or disfigurements such as visible scars, scoliosis, amputated limbs, and readily identifiable orthopedic or sensory impairments, but they also have eliminated others perceived as too short, too fat, or too old from the category of those who might be considered aesthetically attractive.

Perhaps the most influential modern agent promoting images of the moral order of the body inherited form the Middle Ages has been the mass media, which emerged after the Industrial Revolution as a potent ally of capitalists seeking to promote mass consumption as a natural corollary of mass production. In fact, advertisers probably have been less successful in selling their products to consumers than they have been in persuading the public to seek to mimic virtually unattainable standards of physical appearance that, of course, have reinforced the social and economic unacceptability of individuals with disabilities or other so-called deviant characteristics.[31]

Visual depictions of disability have continued to serve as a focal point of film and television drams, but these traits usually are employed as a vehicle to portray malevolence or maladjustment.[32] The reinterpretation of disability from a sensually stimulating attribute to a socially and aesthetically devalued characteristic has advanced to a point where even venerable fairy tales such as Cinderella have been transformed from a story about women who mutilate themselves In order to win male approval to a legend that teaches the rewards of hard work and incomparable beauty. And, Snow White could never have retained her purity or her reputation by living with seven adult males if they had not been described as harmless "dwarfs."

Another explanation for the increasing devaluation of physical differences and disabilities probably can be traced to the growing proclivity of modern civilization to study and discuss human sexuality to a far greater extent than any prior epoch.[33] Contemporary men and women have a vast wealth of statistical data with which to compare their private fantasies and desires. Hence, although sexual feelings might conceivably be elicited more by atypical physiques than by convention or ordinary appearances, they are also more likely to be suppressed by men and women who fear that such emotions are unusual or "abnormal." in order to preserve a belief in the "normality" of their behavior, many may be willing to sacrifice their own satisfaction and fulfillment. The use of this research as a benchmark for asserting personal conduct, therefore, probably has contributed to the perceived unattractiveness of physically disabled persons who are not ordinarily included in such studies.

Perhaps the most significant facet of the pervasive effect of mass media on aesthetic perceptions is exemplified by the fact that, for the first time in history, women and men are inundated with physical images of others who can only be found outside the confines of their immediate vicinity. Modern individuals have been taught to compare the appearance of those they encounter in their everyday lives with the idealized models they see in the media instead of appreciating the heterogeneity that surrounds them.

The ubiquitous views of a restricted range of physical characteristics disseminated by the media seem to encourage observers to focus on the similarities between these pictures and their personal acquaintances rather than on the enduring fascination of human differences. As a result, most men and women who attempt to approximate these images not only have been doomed to disappointment, but they also have deprived themselves of the rich experience to be gained from recognizing the value of physical diversity——a world in which, fortunately, everyone does not look alike. And, of course, conventional viewpoints seem automatically to eliminate most people with obvious disabilities from the ranks of the aesthetically desirable. While treatment as "sexual objects" has been a major grievance of the women's movement, many disabled adults have been perceived in modern society as "asexual objects."

Toward a New Understanding of Disability

There is an alternative means of resolving the complex issues of disability, sexuality, stigma, and political identity. Basically, physical attrac-

tiveness can be defined as a multi-dimensional dialectical phenomenon encompassing traits that the culture defines as unattractive as well as characteristics that are popularly perceived as attractive or appealing. The multi-dimensional component involves perceptions focused less on the total composition of the body than on a diverse range of physical details that the viewer finds exciting or pleasurable. The fascination of personal attraction is based less on the gestalt, or unified whole, of the body than on its separate and discrete parts. The phenomenon is also dialectical because it encompasses a shifting kaleidoscopic series of intriguing images rather than static or unidirectional observations contributing to a definitive impression.

This unfolding of sensual emotions is molded by cultural expectations, but, contrary to modern beliefs, attraction is not stirred exclusively by attributes that society designates as aesthetically pleasing. Nor, of course, can such feelings be aroused solely by opposite characteristics. Instead, true attractiveness emanates from the tension produced by these contrasting elements. It is, after all, the unique convergence of these features that comprises individuality and that stamps one person as the special object of admiration and affection.

Rather than stressing the similarity between idealized media images and the physiological traits of a specific woman or man, this approach to physical appearance focuses on the intrinsic appeal of the differences that are embodied in a particular individual. By reclaiming an aesthetic tradition that originated in one of the earliest eras of human history and by overturning the moral order of the human body imposed by authorities such as the organized church and the mass media, it is possible to assert proudly that "disability is beautiful." The capacity to affirm this statement with dignity and pride has profound social, political, and aesthetic implications for nondisabled as well as disabled people.

Ironically, perhaps the major advantages of a renewed appreciation of the value and appeal of visible differences might eventually be conferred on the nondisabled community. For decades, nondisabled viewers have been bombarded with almost unattainable media images of physical "perfection" that most of them could never possibly approximate. Magazine, billboard, and television advertisements are basically designed to trigger anxiety in the minds of viewers about their own appearance, and a multi-billion dollar industry has been created to assuage these worries by peddling an awesome range of products that promise to improve attractiveness. But the ultimate futility of these efforts has even been recognized by sex symbols such as Brigitte Bardot who said:

I don't want to die, so I have to accept old age, right? It is horrible; you rot; you fall to pieces; you stink. It scares me more than anything else. There's a beach not far away, but I never go during the day. I'm 48 and not so pretty. I wouldn't inflict this sight on anyone anymore.[34]

By developing awareness of the beauty to be discovered in the physical differences that distinguish human beings rather than the similarities between them and idolized media images, everyone could be liberated form the conformity perpetuated by these depictions and acquire a heightened aesthetic appreciation of anatomical variations. Perhaps even more importantly, by accepting alternative standards for assessing the aesthetic pleasure of bodily attributes, the nondisabled might uncover a reciprocal advantage that could sustain an enduring coalition with the disabled minority.

Eventually, every person must confront the inescapable reality that most are not likely to resemble the models of youth and beauty promulgated by the mass media, and that their chances of receiving the rewards bestowed on the physically desirable are almost certain to diminish as they grow older. Hence, both nondisabled and disabled individuals have a vested interest in expanding the restrictive confines of physical models that, though they seem deeply implanted through media socialization, are not necessarily irreversible. As the history of physical differences demonstrates, humans have always exercised the right to make choices about the anatomical features that they consider desirable or interes-

ting, and, at times, these options have included rather than excluded women and men with disabilities.

Perhaps the most significant effects of the realization that attraction can be elicited by a visible disability, however, are apt to be experienced by disabled people themselves. Saddled with a stigma that appears to render them unlovable as well as unacceptable, the personal lives of many disabled people have been plagued by reduced odds, options, and opportunities, the increased risk of rejection, "settling" for less desirable partners, isolation, and, perhaps worst of all, a denial of their identity as people with disabilities.

Private concerns previously have seemed to exert disastrous consequences on the public status of the disabled minority. Since many have been understandably reluctant to confront candidly the dire impact that disability might have on personal lives, we have been equally reticent about embracing an identity that may otherwise have permitted us to organize a potentially large segment of the electorate. As a result of this unusual conjunction of private and public considerations, disabled persons have been trapped by the discriminatory effects of the stigma that we have also identified as our greatest enemy.

Just as other disadvantaged groups have sometimes uncovered solutions to their problems by reexamining their own history, research on people with disabilities seemingly provides a solid foundation for the development of a positive sense of personal and political identity. For thousands of years, in a legacy that appeared to emerge from ancient fertility rites that persisted until religious and economic interests managed to impose another order of the human body, the appearance of physical differences seemed to be associated with festiveness, sensuality, and entertainment rather than with loss, repugnance, or personal tragedy. These trends seem to forma sufficient basis for the redefinition of the identity of persons with disabilities.

I believe that this revitalization of personal and political identity can be most effectively achieved by three means. First, disabled people could play a significant role as the critics of a culture that places inordinate stress on a rather conformist vision of external attractiveness and on a vain search for "the body beautiful." In a society that often seems to have gone berserk in a futile quest to achieve unattainable physical standards, women and men with disabilities may need to offer an alternative model of attraction that would permit both disabled and nondisabled persons to discover enhanced aesthetic satisfaction in the appearance of the ordinary men and women whom they encounter in everyday life.

Second, disabled individuals might appropriately stress the innate appeal of physical differences that contribute richness and diversity to human perceptions. In a fundamental sense, disability demonstrates the superficiality of physical standards in modern society. In a world that can be adapted to accommodate the needs of everyone, the presence of people with disabilities may also signify the dangers of an otherwise drab environment in which everyone begins to appear increasingly alike.

Finally, all persons may need to realize that the occurrence of disability is not necessarily a tragic fate. In many respects, it is also an opportunity to play a significant role in a major process of social change. In the immediate aftermath of a disability, an individual is compelled to answer two of the most difficult metaphysical questions that can be posed to any human being: why? and why me? In the past, they have been given little assistance in their efforts to grapple with such imponderables. Increasingly, however, disabled Americans are beginning to recognize that they have a unique chance to become involved in an historic struggle to extend and expand the definition of human rights. And there are perhaps few other activities that can provide greater meaning and purpose in life. In this sense, therefore, disability can also become an important source of empowerment and a major potential for promoting the increased acceptance

of human differences in modern civilization.

In addition, efforts to reduce prejudice based on aesthetic considerations can be facilitated by changes in public policy. One scientist has even proposed that sharply increased taxes should be imposed on products solely designed to improve personal attractiveness.[35] Educational institutions, from elementary and secondary schools to universities, also might focus increased attention on teaching about the salience of physical appearance and alternative means of perceiving individual attraction. For a generation that has been exposed to supposedly ideal physical models via television and films, at least some instruction might be appropriately offered to allow students to evaluate the impact of these forms on their own perceptions of other people.

A method must be found to affect policies that govern the presentation of visual images to the general public. Perhaps the major initiative in this field might be taken in the private sector by television and film producers, who might rediscover the interest and fascination of human characteristics that represent a departure from——rather than conformity with——idealized notions of physical appearance.

Eventually, policy makers also need to become aware that visual displays of physical features convey messages that are just as political as the content of verbal declarations. In the past, such communications have had an effect upon the disabled minority and other groups that have been subjected to discrimination on aesthetic grounds. By regaining appreciation of the historical legacies that have shaped earlier perceptions of human differences and by promoting the development of alternative standards of physical attractiveness, however, disabled people themselves can play a major role in combatting this form of prejudice.

Notes

1. Estimates of the number of disabled persons in the United States vary considerably, depending on the definitions and methods used to identify them. The 27 million figure is reported in *The ICD Survey of Disabled Americans: Bringing Disabled Americans into the Mainstream* (New York: Louis Harris and Associates, 1986), p. iii. Thirty-six million is described as "the most widely quoted estimate" by Frank Bowe, *Handicapping America: Barriers to Disabled People* (New York: Harper & Row, 1978), p. 17.

2.   See, for example, Harlan Hahn, "Civil Rights for Disabled Americans: The Foundation of a Political Agenda," in Alan Gartner and Tom Joe (eds.), *Images of the Disabled, Disabling Images* (New York: Praeger, 1987), pp. 181-203.

3.   See Harlan Hahn, "Disability and the Urban Environment: A Perspective on Los Angeles," *Society and Space* (1986), pp. 273-288.

4.   *The ICD Survey of Disabled Americans*, p. 114.

5.   Erving Goffman, *Stigma: Notes on the Management of Spoiled Identity* (Englewood Cliffs, N.J.: Prentice-Hall, 1963), p. 5.

6.   Harlan Hahn, "The Politics of Human Differences: Disability and Discrimination," *Journal of Social Issues* (forthcoming).

7.   "Facial Discrimination: Extending Handicapped Law to Employment Discrimination on the Basis of Physical Appearance," *Harvard Law Review* (June, 1987), pp. 2035-2052.

8.   Seymour Fisher, *Body Consciousness: You Are What You Feel* (Englewood Cliffs, N.J.: Prentice-Hall, 1973), p.73.

9.   Stephen Kern, *Anatomy and Destiny: A Cultural History of the Human Body* (Indianapolis: Bobbs-Merrill, 1978), p.256.

10. Ralph S. Solecki, *Shanidar, the First Flower People* (New York: Alfred A. Knopf, 1971), p. 196; Eric Trinkaus, *The Shanidar Neanderthals* (New York: Academic Press, 1983), pp.401-413.

11. Janet and Colin Bord, *Earth Rites: Fertility Practices in Pre-Industrial Britain* (London: Granada, 1982), pp.69-80; Reay Tannahill, *Sex in History* (New York: Stein and Day, 1980), pp.33-35.

12. Shari Thurer, "Disability and Monstrosity: A Look at Literary Distortions of Handicapping Conditions," *Rehabilitation Literature* (January/February, 1980), pp.12-15.

13. Alan Dundes (ed.), *Cinderella: A Folklore Casebook* (New York: Garland, 1982).

14. Dr. Doran, *The History of Court Fools* (New York: Haskell House, 1966, originally published in 1855), pp.32-40, 79-80, 41-61.

15. Robert Brain, *The Decorated Body* (New York: Harper & Row, 1979); Bernard Rudofsky, *The Unfashionable Body* (Garden City, NY: Doubleday, 1971).

16. Charles M. Woolf and Frank C. Dukepoo, "Hopi Indians, Inbreeding, and Albinism", *Science* (April 4, 1969), pp. 30-37.

17. Leslie Fiedler, *Freak: Myths and Images of the Secret Self* (New York: Simon and Schuster, 1978), especially pp.47-63.

18. Joan Albon, *Little People in America: The Social Dimensions of Dwarfism* (New York: Praeger, 1984).

19. Enid Welsford, *The Fool: His Social and Literary History* (New York: Farrar and Rinehart, n.d.), pp. 113-127.

20. Sandra Billington, *A Social History of the Fool* (New York: St. Martin's Press, 1984), pp.4-5.

21. Debra Connors, "Disability, Sexism, and the Social Order," in Susan E. Browne, Debra Connors, and Nanci Stern (eds.), *With the Power of Each Breath: A Disabled Women's Anthology* (Pittsburgh: Cleis Press, 1985), p.95.

22. Mikhail Bakhtin, trans. by Helen Iswolsky, *Rabelais and His World* (Cambridge: MIT Press, 1968), p.91.

23. Robert Anchor, "Bakhtin's Truths of Laughter," *Clio* (Spring, 1985), p.240.

24. See Douglas Biklen and Lee Bailey (eds.) *Rudely Stamp'd: Imaginal Disability and Prejudice* (Washington, D.C.: University Press of America, 1981).

25. Susan Sontag, *Illness as Metaphor* (New York: Farrar, Straus, and Giroux, 1978).

26. Deborah A. Stone, *The Disabled State* (Philadelphia: Temple University Press, 1984), pp.51-55.

27. C. Esco Obermann, *A History of Vocational Rehabilitation in America* (Minneapolis: T.S. Denison, 1965), pp.58-59; Victor Finkelstein, *Attitudes and Disabled People* (New York: World Rehabilitation Fund, 1980), pp.8-9.

28. Robert Bogdan, "The Exhibition of Humans with Differences for Amusement and Profit," *Policy Studies Journal* (March, 1987), pp.537-550.

29. Rudolph M. Bell, *Holy Anorexia* (Chicago: The University of Chicago Press, 1985); Caroline Walker Bynum, *Holy Feast and Holy Fast: The Religious Significance of Food to Medieval Women* (Berkeley: University of California Press, 1987).

30. Bryan S. Turner, *The Body and Society: Exploration in Social Theory* (Oxford, England: Basil Blackwell, 1984).

31. Harlan Hahn, "Advertising the Acceptably Employable Image: Disability and Capitalism," *Policy Studies Journal* (March, 1987), pp.551-570.

32. Paul K. Longmore, "Screening Stereotypes: Images of Disabled People," *Social Policy* (Summer, 1985), pp.31-37.

33. Michel Foucault, trans. by Robert Hurley, *The History of Sexuality* (New York: Pantheon, 1978).

34. quoted in Alexandra Dundas Todd, "Women and the Disabled in Contemporary Society", *Social Policy* (Spring, 1984), pp.44-45.

35. Don B. Giddon, "Through the Looking Glasses of Physicians, Dentists, and Patients," *Perspectives in Biology and Medicine* (1983), pp.451-458.

Sexuality and Disability: An Overview

Sandra Keller, Ph.D. and
Denton C. Buchanan, Ph.D.

Sexuality is psychological and physiological. From a psychological perspective, sexuality is an expression of intimacy, affection, and love. When one acquires a disability, the subsequent worries and outright emotional disruptions and anxiety cloud the ability to express and perceive such tender emotions. Injury or disease often produces a lowered self-confidence, self-esteem, and self-worth. The ability to see oneself as attractive, masculine or feminine is threatened. It is difficult to either express or feel love and affection when one loses respect for one's own body.

Similarly, able-bodied partners can experience difficulty in the expression of intimacy. A decrease in sexual performance can become an early symptom of the stresses and strains within the partnership as both adjust to the disability. The non-disabled partner may fear making the disorder worse through sex, for example by increasing blood pressure and thus risking another heart attack or stroke. Some fear contagion or genetically impaired offspring as a result of the disease. Muscular dystrophy and multiple sclerosis are occasionally thought of in these terms. Unfortunately, these false beliefs and needless concerns are often unspoken yet produce an atmosphere that perpetuates sexual problems.

From a physiological standpoint, experimental research with animals has given us some understanding of brain function in relation to sexuality. Animals appear to be primarily dependent upon hormonal influences. Specifically, the release of hormones initiates sexual behaviour in almost all species that have been studied. Males, for example, are stimulated by a pheromone or odour emitted from the female during estrus. Similarly, an inhibitory system in the brain serves to decrease sexual drive. In contrast, the cortex appears to play only a minimal role in animals. For example, female rats can mate, become pregnant and deliver pups with the majority of their cortex removed while male rats, which require more neuromotor involvement, can complete sexual behaviour with as much as 60 percent of the cortex removed.

However, the pattern for humans does not appear to be the same as for animals. Human female sexual behaviour is not dependent upon the estrus cycle, and sexual arousal in the male can occur independent of any changes in sex hormones. In man, sexual arousal and behaviour are functions of personality and emotion, which depend upon the cerebral cortex.

This article will introduce many aspects of sexuality and disability. Psychological and physical aspects of a number of disabilities are discussed with an emphasis on practical solutions to common problems, and the illumination of current research and perspectives within the domain of sexuality.

Multiple Sclerosis

Multiple sclerosis (MS) has a significant effect on an individual's sexuality since it is a disorder of the nervous system that most commonly strikes young adults at an age when sexual performance and attractiveness are paramount. As its name implies, MS can occur in multiple areas of the body and consequently has varying effects on different individuals. In general, however, MS affects sensory and motor neurons, causing impairments in the individual's ability to perceive or enjoy sexual stimulation and the muscular ability to sustain sexual behaviour. The most common physical symptoms in men are fatigue, weakness, and a loss of the ability to attain and sustain erections. Women report reduced numbers of orgasms, numbness, decreased vaginal lubrication resulting in pain or discomfort during sex, and muscle spasms that interfere with sexual performance. One survey of

Reprinted from "Rehabilitation Digest", Spring 1984, Vol. 15, #1, with permission. Published by CRCD: Toronto, Ontario

MS individuals reported that 91 percent of men and 72 percent of women experienced changes in their sexual performance ranging from mild loss of sensation to severe impairment. For example, between 20 percent and 40 percent of MS males report total failure to attain an erection.

It is important to realize that despite the physical symptoms, people with MS have a normal interest in sex. Their symptoms, therefore, cause frustration and embarrassment. It is common to develop significant feelings of inadequacy and lack of confidence because of their difficulty in expressing attitudes of affection and intimacy.

Although MS is a progressive disease, it is common for symptoms to wax and wane, being absent for long periods of time then reappearing without any apparent cause. Therefore, both patient and partner must continually readjust. This creates uncertainty about one's ability to perform sexually each time an attempt is made and can produce a total avoidance of sex to escape the embarrassment of failed performance. Jealousy and suspicion that the spouse is seeking affection elsewhere can be an offshoot of this lack of confidence.

Pregnancy is another concern. MS strikes at an age when couples are planning children. Males worry about their ability to father a child. Females are concerned about the impact of pregnancy upon the course of the disease.

Women with MS usually continue to menstruate and ovulate, and therefore have a normal chance of becoming pregnant. However, pregnancy may make the symptoms worse. These difficulties appear to be transient, related to the hormonal changes that occur during the 9-month gestation period. A larger problem appears to be the early post-partum period when the hormonal fluctuations are at their peak.

Questions of heredity and of contagion often arise in the topic of sexuality and MS. MS is not contagious and sexual contact produces no risk. Similarly, breast-feeding causes no risk for the infant. There is, however, an increased risk of contracting MS in the offspring of MS parents. A child has approximately one percent chance of getting MS if one parent has the disease. The complicated interaction between genetics and environment is not totally understood.

Many recommendations can be made to increase the MS patient's enjoyment of sex. Open communication between the partners is essential. Emptying the bladder before love-making removes the fear of loss of bladder control. Women can use water soluble lubricant jellies, such as KY Jelly. Recognizing that fatigue is a major obstacle, couples can often overcome this problem by experimenting with different positions and different times of the day to increase strength. There are several surgical procedures that have been tried, such as implants into the penis to provide an erection.

For the reader interested in the topic of sexuality and MS, a comprehensive booklet is available through the Multiple Sclerosis Society: *Sexuality and Multiple Sclerosis* by Michael Barrett.

Spinal Cord Injury

The spinal cord injured (SCI) male may experience erections in response to external stimulation to the body below the level of the cord lesion (reflex erection), or as a result of internal stimulation such as bladder distension (spontaneous erection). Research has also shown that while a small percentage of men report the sensation of ejaculation, the seminal fluid backs up into the bladder rather than being expelled (retrograde ejaculation). Thus, the male's reproductive capacity is greatly reduced or eradicated.

In contrast, the female's reproductive capacity is virtually unimpaired. Although the menstrual cycle may be temporarily interrupted, it is restored in almost all women within a year. Pregnancy is as possible as it was prior to the injury. Not only are women capable of carrying a fetus to term without serious medical problems, but most are capable of vaginal deliveries. In fact, caesarian sections are no more common among SCI women than they are among ablebodied women.

Because of the loss of sensation to the genital region, the utilization of fantasy can enhance sexual experience. A large number of spinal cord injured people, both male and female, report that they can achieve fantasized orgasms that seem similar to those experienced by neurologically unimpaired individuals. By concentrating on sensations being received form innervated ares of their body and transposing that stimulation to the genitals, some SCI men and women report multiple orgasms during a single sexual encounter. Thus, portions of the body that retain feeling may become more highly eroticized than they were before injury.

Many of the problems of SCI are similar to those of MS. Spinal injured people have normal libidos while experiencing changes in sensation and muscle strength. The major difference is that the disorder is sudden rather than gradual, thereby requiring an immediate adjustment by both spouse and patient. Although it is not uncommon for marital difficulties to develop from feelings of frustration and inadequacy, once adjustment is achieved the SCI patient does not have to cope with progressive deterioration.

Several group programs and literature exist for counselling and education. Training in social skills for young SCI people is as essential as sexuality counselling. With the sudden switch to a wheelchair, confidence in social relationships is often lost, and routine activities such as dating can become frightening.

Brain Dysfunction

There are many social myths concerning the sexuality of individuals with brain dysfunction. A stereotype of sexual deviance resulting from brain damage exists, yet there has been little research done on brain damage and sexual behaviour.

We know that sexual behaviour results from an interaction between two major areas of cerebral cortex: the frontal and temporal lobes, and the underlying limbic system. Damage to the top areal of the frontal lobes (which is beneath the forehead) causes a general loss of initiative and of the ordering of sexual behaviour. Damage to the orbital frontal cortex (underneath the brain above the eye orbits), in contrast, appears to cause a loss of inhibition, or moral and ethical restraint. This can result in sexual misconduct and inappropriate behaviour.

When the temporal lobes of the brain (located above the ears) are damaged, either an increase in inappropriate sexual behaviour or a reduction in sexual interest and performance can result. Although the precise areas within the temporal lobes affecting sexual behaviour are not as well understood as the frontal lobes, the primary area appears to be the anterior temporal lobe.

It is important to recognize that these two large areas of the brain, the frontal lobes and the temporal lobes, are the most prone to damage in closed head injury. Thus, it is not only possible, but likely to experience changes in sexual functioning following a blow to the head. However, it is much more difficult to predict the nature of the change.

Several studies have looked at the impact of cerebral vascular accident or stroke upon sexual functioning. Bray, deFrank and Wolfe studied the sexual interest, function, and attitude of thirty-five patients before and after stroke. They found that there was a significant reduction in sexual ability following the stroke. Only 46 percent of the men could maintain an erection and only 29 percent could experience an ejaculation. Similarly, only 9 percent of the women could achieve orgasm and only 27 percent continued to menstruate after the stroke.

Allsup-Jackson conducted a telephone survey in 1981 of fifty stroke patients between the ages of 45 and 60. She found that 60 percent of the men had a reduction in sexual contact and 70 percent of the females reported a decrease in sexual behaviour following the stroke. Of these, 20 percent reported that sexual contact had stopped completely.

There are a number of reasons for reduced sexual behaviour after stroke. Hemiplegia and the resulting neglect of one side of the body and visual field cause patients to have less sensory enjoyment and to notice fewer sexual cues from their partner. Muscle weakness and awkwardness impair sexual performance. Speech difficulties also impair sexual communication. However, the major cause for the lack of performance when interest remains the same is emotional in nature.

In temporal lobe epilepsy, more than in any other disorder, there exists a folklore and stigma of bizarre sexual behaviour. However, several recent studies have clearly shown that the most common sexual change in temporal lobe epilepsy is a reduction in sexual interest and behaviour (hyposexuality).

It is important to distinguish between behaviour that occurs during a seizure and behaviour that occurs at other times. Seizures can produce sexually deviant behaviour that cannot be controlled by the person at that moment. Such behaviour may include automatic acts as undressing, verbal utterances, and even public masturbation. These events are rare and do not represent the most common experience of epileptics. quite the opposite, temporal lobe epileptics generally have lower than normal interest in sex.

Coronary Dysfunction Disease

Patients who have suffered a myocardial infarction (MI) have been shown to reduce the frequency of sexual activity. One study reported a 58 percent decrease in sexual activity in post-infarct patients. This finding has been confirmed more recently with the reports of MI patients.

Another study demonstrated that the frequency of orgasm declined as well. Furthermore, this decrease in sexual activity or even outright abstinence from sexual intercourse has been found as late as forty-seven months after MI. When interviewed, males reported that the most common cause is impotence and decrease of sexual desire. Ten percent of post-infarct males reported permanent impotence. The incidence of additional sexual difficulties has been reported as premature ejaculation in 37 percent of the patients, retarded ejaculation in 54 percent, and 60 percent manifested erectile difficulties at least half the time.

Although the majority of the studies have evaluated the various aspects of the sexual life of males, study of the female coronary patient appears to have been neglected. Abromov compared the sexual activity of 100 female patients with acute MI to that of a control group of 100 female general medical patients. Sexual frigidity and dissatisfaction were found among 65 percent of the coronary patients as compared with 24 percent of the controls. The coronary patients were also found to have a significantly earlier

menopausal age than the patients hospitalized for other diseases.

Little attention has been paid to the concerns of the spouse. Spouses have been found to contribute to the difficulties by being over-protective, overly solicitous, afraid to make demands or to induce emotional upset. Ambiguous instructions from physicians often add to their confusion and accentuate their concern.

Extensive work by Hellerstein and colleagues has determined that there are few, if any, physiological reasons for the cardiac patient to suffer sexual dysfunction. A "sexercise" tolerance test, using electrocardiographic tape-recordings during sexual activity, showed that the energy expended during sexual intercourse is significantly lower than the energy expended in most everyday tasks. Furthermore, they found that the mean maximal heart rate achieved during orgasm was 117.4 beats per minute, while the mean maximal heart rate during the performance of the usual occupational activity was 120.1 beats per minute.

The prescription of a physical conditioning program may increase the cardiac patient's cardiovascular and respiratory fitness. Indeed, patients in one study indicated that both the frequency and quality of sexual activity improved significantly as a result of a physical fitness program. Moreover, 67 percent of the patients reported much fewer, or complete absence of cardiac symptoms during sexual activity. However, a conditioning program must be highly individualized, and personal limiting factors such as angina, dyspnea, and body weight must be considered before advising a patient to resume physical activity——sexual or otherwise. Another means of gradually returning a post-coronary patient to sexual activity is to recommend masturbation, not only to allay fears, but also to allow time for experimentation of one's limits and to gain confidence.

Chronic Obstructive Lung Disease

Chronic obstructive lung disease (COLD) refers to a group of chronic respiratory disorders including asthma, emphysema, and chronic bronchitis. It has been reported that COLD can precipitate diverse sexual difficulties such as impotence and frigidity, loss of spontaneity in sexual contact, premature ejaculation, sexual inhibitions, and reduced libido. However, the extent to which these difficulties occur has not been settled. One study of 100 male respiratory patients found that only 17 were impotent. Details from the case histories led the authors to speculate that these dysfunctions were due to lifelong patterns of behaviour and not due to the disease. In contrast, two studies contended that COLD was detrimental to sexual physical expression in as many as 74 percent of the patients.

Individuals suffering from lung disease are chronically short of breath and it is not uncommon for some to develop anxiety about participating in physical activity of any kind. Given the increased depth and rate of respiration during sexual excitement, it is easily understood why many patients are afraid that they may suffocate during sexual activity. The patient and partner should be educated and reassured by the research findings which show that effort required for intercourse does not jeopardize blood pressure, heart rate or respiratory rate.

Chronic coughing and phlegm production may be a source of embarrassment and patients may suffer form a poor self-image because of physical alterations such as a caved-in or barrel-shaped chest. Regular physiotherapy could increase not only exercise tolerance, but could also add to the patient's self-confidence. The able-bodied partner could also be advised to assume a more active role in lovemaking.

Assessment

Sexuality counselling is a vital component in the rehabilitation of disabled people. Since some patients will feel uncomfortable discussing the topic of sex, and indeed will never initiate such a discussion, it is often incumbent upon the therapist to introduce the subject, preferably as a matter of routine. The person's religious and sexual attitudes must be considered. A sexual history should include prior sexual activity and address such variables as frequency of coitus, level of sexual desire, capacity for arousal, and orgasmic experience. A program can then be designed that will take all of this information into account. Whether sexual counselling is delivered individually or in a group, it should be supportive and reassuring, striving to facilitate communication between the patient and partner.

A number of assessment inventories have been devised to help the clinician in determining a treatment program. In fact, since Masters and Johnson published *Human Sexual Inadequacy* in 1970, mental health professionals have exhibited a widespread interest in the treatment of sexual dysfunction. Research on the clinical treatment of sexual dysfunction has been greatly impeded by lack of objective, valid, and reliable testing methods. There are a number of simple behavioural checklists which are used to assess the range of sexual behaviours a person engages in, heterosexual - homosexual orientation, and masculinity - feminity. However, there are relatively few assessment devices that focus on actual sexual functioning and satisfaction.

The Sexual Interaction Inventory is a paper and pencil self-report inventory that assesses the nature of a couple's sexual relationship in terms of sexual functioning and sexual satisfaction. It is valuable both as a measure of the effectiveness of treatment and as a diagnostic tool. As a descriptive system for sexual dysfunctions, it examines the desire, arousal, and orgasm phases of the sexual response. The Sex History Form, to be used before the initial intake interview. helps the clinician become aware of the areas of sexual functioning requiring a closer assessment.

The Sex Knowledge Attitude Test (SKAT) is a self-administered multiple choice test which measures sexual attitudes, knowledge, and a degree of experience in a variety of sexual activities. The attitude section of this test comprises a heterosexual relations scale that deals with an individual's general attitude toward pre- and extramarital heterosexual behaviour, a sexual myths scale that is concerned with the individual's acceptance or rejection of commonly held sexual misconceptions about sex education, homosexuality, etc., an abortion scale, and a masturbation scale. The knowledge section of the SKAT yields a score based on the respondent's general store of factual information concerning the physiological and social aspects of sexual functioning.

The Minnesota Sexual Attitude Scales require respondents to give their emotional reaction to the notion of different persons (e.g. mid-adolescents, unmarried adults, married adults) engaging in certain categories of sexual activities. On the Sexual Attitude and Behaviour Survey, respondents indicate under what circumstances they would find different sexual behaviour or thoughts to be permissible.

Intervention Strategies

There are many articles and studies on intervention techniques to improve sexuality in physically disabled people. Space does not permit a review of these reports. However, there are two conceptual frameworks that can be of assistance to rehabilitation professionals and clients alike. These are the Plissit Model outlined by Jack Annon and the Developmental Skill-Based Approach described by Shrey, Kiefer and Anthony.

The Plissit Model is a conceptual scheme for behavioural treatment of sexual problems in general and not specifically for the disabled. The title "Plissit" is an acronym derived from the four stages: permission (P), limited information (LI), specific suggestions (SS), intensive therapy (IT). Each stage is a more advanced approach than the one preceding it.

Permission implies that many patients merely need to have the reassurance that their behaviour, coping strategies, fantasies, and ideas are normal and acceptable. Such permission often removes sexual anxieties and barriers to sexual expression.

Limited information is seen as providing clients with specific factual information directly relevant to their particular sexual concerns. This imparting of information needs to be directed at a specific sexual concern and at dispelling sexual myths. It is not intended as a broad-based session on all of human sexual behaviour.

Clinical experience has shown that the majority of sexual obstacles are met during the first two stages, of relieving anxieties and providing limited information.

The third level of treatment, specific suggestions, involves direct attempts to help the client change his behaviour in order to overcome specific sexual problems. For the problem to be clearly understood by both the patient and the therapist, a clear sexual history is needed. The necessary treatment approach becomes obvious with a clear understanding of the problem.

In the fourth stage, intensive therapy, the patient is referred to a specialist in sexual problems and treatment approaches to develop a specific program.

The second model to be discussed here, the Development Skill-Based Approach, falls within the specific suggestion and intensive therapy stages of the Plissit Model. This approach provides the clinician with a three-phase strategy in interviewing clints and developing treatment plans for change.

The first phase is called exploration. Through discussions, both therapist and client gain insight into the sexual needs and capabilities of the client. Physical impairments and capabilities as they relate to sexuality are discussed. Information concerning physical capacity is also obtained from the patient's partner, physicians, and other health care professionals, with care being taken to observe the rule of confidentiality. Similarly, psychological assets and disadvantages are explored. Areas of concern may include feelings of unattractiveness, lack of motivation, or fears regarding sexuality, interpersonal and social skills, and satisfaction with current sexual behaviour. The clients' sexual values are also discussed. Religious beliefs concerning birth control and sexual freedom, cultural beliefs, and the clients' attitudes towards sexual activities such as masturbation and body positions are important sources of information.

The second phase is called understanding. It helps the client to acquire the knowledge and skills necessary for sexual adjustment. During this phase, the client develops methods to overcome sexual barriers and sets priorities on the various concerns he or she may have. The therapists and client determine the steps needed to establish a behaviour change program. This may involve community resources, physical aids, etc.

The third phase in this model is the action phase in which a step by step plan to overcome sexual adjustment problems is developed by the client and the therapist. Each step identifies specific behavioural goals and completion dates.

This overview is not meant to be a definitive study of all aspects of sexuality and disability. It is simply intended to be an introduction to the experience and current research which has contributed to our knowledge of this long neglected yet vital subject.

How to Find Help

If you have concerns or problems with sexual functioning, you can improve your chances of finding a qualified therapist by seeking sex therapy at centres that are affiliated with universities, medical schools or hospitals, or by contacting reputable professional associations for referral.

In Canada, referrals can be obtained by contacting the Sex Information and Education Council of Canada (SIECCAN) at 423 Castlefield Avenue, Toronto, Ontario M5N 1L4, or by calling Michael Barrett, SIECCAN Chairperson, (416) 978-3488. For Ontario only, contact BESTCO, The Board of Examiners in Sexual Therapy and Counselling in Ontario, c/o OAMFT, 271 Russell Hill Road, Toronto, Ontario M4V 2T5, (416) 968-7779.

In the United States, AASECT publishes listings of qualified therapists including certified Canadians. Contact:
American Association of Sex Educators,
Counsellors and Therapists
5010 Wisconsin Avenue N.W.,
Suite 304
Washington, D.C. 20016
(Cost $2.00)

The telephone directory yellow pages may list Sex Therapists under Marriage and Family Therapy. Be certain to check out qualifications: request names of physicians or health clinics who refer patients to this therapist; ask the therapist for information about their education and training in Sex Therapy; avoid therapists who make unrealistic promises or guarantees of cure; request treatment costs, whether medical insurance coverage is available, and the particular therapy approach used by the therapist.

In many centres, well-trained and qualified sex therapists are few in number or non-existent. Careful shopping and perhaps a willingness to travel to a city where there is a clinic or a number of qualified therapists will result in a greater chance of success and prove both a financial and emotional saving.

Professional Training in Sex Therapy

Training and certification in Sex Therapy are difficult to obtain in Canada. Since there is no English University sexology degree program available, completion of a Master's or Doctorate Degree in a discipline such as psychology, sociology, social work or medicine is usually a prelude to subsequent specialization in sex counselling and therapy. It is necessary to search out programs, courses, workshops, and clinical supervision in sex therapy. This may mean going to the United States.

Two professional organizations, the Society for Sex Therapy and Research, New York (SSTAR) and the American Association of Sex Educators, Counsellors and Therapists, Washington D.C. (AASECT) publish national directories. AASECT has a sex therapist certification process and also sponsors courses and programs which are credited towards certification. SSTAR has stricter membership requirements which it believes are equivalent to certification. SIECCAN (address above) also provides information on professional education programs.

—— Marg Jacobs
Professor of Human Sexuality
Algonquin College

There is a Master of Science (M.Sc.) degree in family studies offering the opportunity to specialize in the field of human sexuality. For more information, contact the Chairman, Department of Family Studies, University of Guelph, Guelph, Ontario N1G 2W1 (519) 824-4120 Ext. 3968.
Humber College in Toronto offers a multi-disciplinary advance certification program in human sexuality to professionals already working in institutional and community settings. For more information on the *Human Sexuality: Counselling*

and Teaching Program contact Paul Pieper, Coordinator, Community Health Education Programs, Health Sciences Division, Humber College, 105 Humber College Blvd., Rexdale, Ontario M9W 5L7. (416) 675-3111 Ext. 587.

Resources on Sexuality and Physical Disability

MICHAEL BARRETT, PH.D.
Chairperson, Sex Information and Education Council of Canada (SIECCAN) and Associate Professor, University of Toronto.

A severely handicapped young woman writes for "any information you have" on sexuality and cerebral palsy. She also wants to know about sexual assaults on disabled women. An occupational therapist writes for suggestions on sexual counselling with men and women disabled through spinal cord injuries. A 55-year-old man, left hemiplegic by a stroke six years ago, writes to ask for literature on the sexual implications of his condition. He adds that although his body has changed, he "still has needs and feelings like anyone else." The mother of a 13-year-old with spina bifida wonders what kind of sex education material is available for her son. Requests of this type, particularly from health care professionals, have been a regular feature of the Sex Information and Education Council of Canada's correspondence over the past ten years.

Although SIECCAN is dedicated to improved public and professional education about all aspects of human sexuality, the issues surrounding sexuality and disability have attracted particular professional interest. This may be, in part, a reflection of greater societal awareness and discussion about sexuality in general, but I think it is also the result of specific demands by disabled people that they be treated as whole persons with sexual and relational aspirations. Indeed, much of the growing literature in the field now deals with the sexual implications of specific disabilities or conditions. My intention here is to share some of that literature with you and to offer some admittedly subjective observations on the "state of the art." The reflections come first.

• The sexual concerns faced by disabled people may differ in degree but not in kind, from those experienced by others in society. Much helpful literature for both professionals and the general public is now available. It deals with varied aspects of sex education, counselling, therapy, research, ethics, etc. and treats human sexuality in a positive manner that informs without creating unrealistic expectations or performance demands. Suggested reading on specific topics can be obtained by writing SIECCAN, 423 Castlefield Ave., Toronto, M5N 1L4.

• Much of the literature pertaining to sexuality and disability has been written for a professional audience. While some associations now distribute nontechnical material on the sexual implications of specific disabilities, much remains to be done. To my knowledge there is no single "clearinghouse" in Canada through which people can obtain access to this growing body of literature. Books for professionals are expensive and journal articles appear in such a wide variety of publications that it is difficult for all but the most ardent bibliophile to keep up.

• Much remains to be learned about the effect of different conditions on the physiological aspects of sexual arousal and response (see "The physiology of the sex response in the disabled: Discovery wanted," by Dr. George Szasz (SIECCAN Newsletter 16 [No. 2]: 5-8, 1981). This can make some of the literature necessarily vague about questions for which we would like precise answers.

• In a "needs assessment" of sexuality related services for disabled people in the United States, Sophia Chipouras found that 39.4 percent of the disabled people surveyed said they wanted access to reading materials but only 18.6 percent had such access; 35.1 percent wanted access to audiovisual materials but only 9.3 percent had experienced such assess (*Sexuality and Disability: Personal Perspectives*, 1981). While reading material is an important route to self-discovery, it is also important to have a chance to discuss concerns with others. For example, 48.9 percent said they would take a sexuality and disability course if it were offered but only 2.1 percent had found such a course. Other differences included: group discussion (47.9 percent would take vs

Reprinted From: "Rehabilitation Digest", Spring 1984, Vol 15, #1, with permission. Published by CRCD: Toronto, Ont.

14.4 percent had them) and individual counselling (40.4 percent would use vs 6.2 percent had been counselled). Discrepancies between perceived needs and available services were also noted in relation to availability of sex therapy, group counselling, couples counselling, contraceptive/genetic counselling, and obstetric/gynecological/urological care. These findings should not be taken to imply that disabled people are generally in need of intensive counselling or therapy. However, having the opportunity to seek out information and advice from a variety of sources as needed is vital.

• The literature appears to be heavily weighted toward the concerns of adults with acquired disabilities. There is less on congenital disabilities and very little on the sexual development and education of physically handicapped children and teenagers. In contrast, there is a sizeable body of literature on sex education for mentally handicapped children. Some curricula for sex education of visually impaired and hearing impaired children are also available.

• I suspect that many hospitals or rehabilitation centres have handouts on specific sex-related topics which are given to patients locally but are otherwise unpublished and unknown in the field. I would be pleased to learn about such resources.

• Textbooks on human sexuality written expressly for health care professionals may provide comprehensive information on sexuality and disability but this does not appear to be the case for university-level human sexuality texts in general. In a content review of twenty-five recent texts, Deryck Calderwood and Martha Calderwood reported that none were ranked as exceptional and only one as thorough in its treatment of sexuality and disability. Six had superficial treatment of the topic, fourteen did not cover it, and the remainder were considered inadequate (basic information only or limited perspective). This topic area may be considered too specialized for most general texts.

The following resources are listed according to their relevance to specific disabilities: spinal cord injury, arthritis, spina bifida, ostomy, cerebral palsy, multiple sclerosis, stroke, and heart attack. Books on sexual assault or abuse and

medication are also discussed. I have indicated which are intended specifically for professionals. To begin, I'll suggest some good general sources of information.

General Reading

David Bullard and Susan Knight eds, 1981. *Sexuality and Physical Disability: Personal Perspectives*. C.V. Mosby Company, 318 pp.

This is a wonderful resource because of the diversity of its content and the range of audience it is likely to satisfy. Disabled people will learn from the self-described experiences of others with similar disabilities. Professionals will gain from these accounts and from a variety of practical and informative papers, many written by health care professionals who are also disabled.

Task Force on the Concerns of Physically Disabled Women, 1978. *Toward Intimacy: Family Planning and Sexuality Concerns of Physically Disabled Women*. Human Sciences Press, 72 Fifth Avenue, New York, NY 10011 (US $2.50).

This 63-page booklet is a gold-mine of quotes, suggestions, and information including a 5-page table listing the contraceptive implications of eleven different disabling conditions.

Yvonne Duffy, 1981. *All Things are Possible*. A.J. Garvin and Associates, P.O. Box 7525, Ann Arbor, MI 48107 (US $8.95), 179 pp.

The author refers to herself as "differently abled" as a result of polio. She recounts here, through extensive use of verbatim quotes, the reflections of disabled women who responded to her written and verbal questionnaires on such topics as menstruation, sex education, parental attitudes, self-image, relationships, marriage, sexual feelings, sexual intercourse, birth control, childbirth and child-rearing, masturbation, and lesbianism.

Susan Ferreyra and Katrine Hughes, 1982. *Table Manners: A guide to the pelvic examination for disabled women and health care providers*. Sex Education for Disabled People, 477 Fifteenth St., Oakland CA 94612.

This 16-page booklet does precisely what the title suggests, packing a remarkable amount of information into a few pages, with insights for women with a variety of disabilities. It should be required reading for health care providers.

For Professionals
W.F.R. Steward, 1979. *The Sexual Side of Handicap: A guide for caring professionals.* Woodhead-Faulkner Publishers, 8 Market Passage, Cambridge, England CB2 3PF.

A good introductory overview of the sexual implications of a variety of disabling conditions is presented in terms of direct and indirect effects on sexual functioning.
Alex Comfort, ed., 1978. *Sexual Consequences of Disability.* George F. Stickley Company, 210 West Washington Square Philadelphia PA 19106.

This publication presents articles on a wide variety of disabling conditions and related issues including three papers on counselling and psychosexual adjustment following mastectomy.
Sydney Siemens and Rose C. Brandzel, 1982. *Sexuality: Nursing intervention and assessment.* J.B. Lippincott and Company, 481 pp., (US $14.95).
Harold I. Lief, 1981. *Sexual Problems in Medical Practice.* American Medical Association, 419 pp., (US $24).

Spinal Cord Injury

Elle Friedman Becker, 1978. *Female Sexuality following Spinal Cord Injury.* Cheever Publishing, P.O. Box 700, Bloomington Il 61701 (US $10.95).

The author is a paraplegic whose horseback-riding accident in 1975 led her to interview other cord-injured women about their own sexual adjustments and experiences. The book was an early contribution to the extremely limited literature on female sexuality following spinal cord injury that existed at that time. The interviews cover the range of physical, psychological, and social changes and adaptations in the sexual lives and self-images of the women involved.
M.G. Eisenberg and L.C. Rustad, 1975. *Sex and the Spinal Cord Injured: Some questions and answers.* Superintendent Documents, U.S. Government Printing Office, Washington DC 20402 (US $2.50).

Although there have been a number of developments in the field since this booklet was published, it remains a helpful and easily understood guide to sexual adjustment following spinal cord injury.
Thomas O. Mooney, Theodore M. Cole and Richard A. Chilgren, 1975. *Sexual Options for Paraplegics and Quadriplegics.* Little Brown and Co., 34 Beacon St., Boston MA 02106 (US $9.95).

The combination of practical suggestions and positive acceptance of sexual expression for disabled people makes this highly readable book an excellent, nontechnical resource for cord-injured people, their partners, and health care professionals. The explicit, black-and-white photographs illustrate the issues surrounding preparation for sexual activity (e.g. catheters, appliances, means of arousal, etc.), intercourse, and oral-genital activity. The focus is on cord-injured men and their partners and gains authenticity from the personal insights of Thomas Mooney, who is disabled.
Joanne M. Taggie and M. Scott Manley, 1978. *A Handbook on Sexuality after Spinal Cord Injury.* M. Scott Manley, 3425 South Clarkson, Englewood CO 80110 (US$5.00).

This loose-bound workbook encourages active participation of cord-injured people and their partners in the exercises of self-discovery that it presents. It explores some of the feelings and experiences associated with sexual adjustment following cord injury. One couple who reviewed the book indicated that books such as this seldom discuss the issued faced when both partners are disabled.

For Professionals
Sherrill Miller, George Szasz and Leslie Anderson, 1981. "Sexual health clinician in an acute spinal cord injury unit." *Arch. Phys. Med. Rehabil..* 62:315-320.

It describes the role of the sexual health care clinician as "a nonphysician specialist trained to diagnose and treat sexual dysfunctions of disabled persons" and explains the role of such clinicians in the Acute Spinal Cord Injury Unit at Shaughnessy Hospital and at the G.F. Strong

Rehabilitation Centre, both of which are located in Vancouver, British Columbia.

George Szasz, Sherrill Miller and Leslie Anderson, 1979. "Guidelines to birth control and counselling of the physically handicapped." *CMA Journal* 120:1353-1358.

This article details seven steps in effective birth control counselling for physically handicapped men and women with an emphasis on those with spinal cord injuries.

Carla Thornton, 1981. "Sexuality counselling of women with spinal cord injuries." In *Sexuality and Physical Disability: Personal Perspectives,* edited by David Bullard and Susan Knight, C.V. Mosby Company, pp. 156-165.

Arthritis
(Rheumatic Diseases)

Arthritis Information Clearinghouse, 1983. *Sexuality and the Rheumatic Diseases: An annotated bibliography, 1970-1982.* Arthritis Information Clearhinghouse, P.O. Box 9782, Arlington VA 22209.

A 20-page listing of resources on the topic, classified according to their usefulness for professionals and people with arthritis.

For Professionals
Kristi Ferguson and Barbara Figley, 1979. "Sexuality and rheumatic diseases: A prospective study." *Sexuality and Disability* 1:130-138.

Jan Onder, Donna Lachniet and Marjorie Becker, 1973. "Sexual counselling, arthritis and women." Arthritis Foundation. *Allied Health Professionals Section Newsletter*, Vol 7: Nos. 3 and 4 (December 1973).

Kathleen Buckwalter, Theodore Wernimont and Joseph Buckwalter, 1982. "Musculo-skeletal conditions and sexuality (Part II)." *Sexuality and Disability* 5:195-207.

J. Scott Richards, 1980. "Sex and arthritis." *Sexuality and Disability 3:97-104.*

Spina Bifida

M.C. Treadwell and R.L. Patrias, 1981. *Growing Up with Spina Bifida: A book about puberty, independence and caring.* Available from Dr.

Mason Barr, University Hospital, K2027 Holden, Box 07 Ann Arbor, MI 48109 (US $1).

This 27-page booklet was written for puberty-aged children with spina bifida. It contains a discussion of a variety of issues pertaining to sexuality, and includes a glossary and bibliography.

For Professionals
S. Dorner, 1977, "Sexual interest and activity in adolescents with spina bifida." *J. Child Psychol. Psychiat.* 18:229-237.

A research study on sex education and concerns of young people with spina bifida done in London, England is described, but the conclusions and recommendations are probably applicable elsewhere.

Alan Wabrek, Carolyn Wabrek and Clay Burchell, 1978. "The human tragedy of spina bifida: spinal myelomeningocele." *Sexuality and Disability* 1:210-217.

The sexual experience, concerns, and adjustment of twenty-six males and twenty-six females ranging in age from 12 to 31 are surveyed.

I. McAndrew, 1979. "Adolescents and young people with spina bifida." *Develop. Med. Child Neural.* 21:619-629.

Semi-structured interviews provide insight into sociosexual adjustment and self-image of young people with spina bifida.

Ostomy

Ed Gambrell, 1982, *Sex and the Male Ostomate.* Gordon L. Dickman and Carolyn A. Livingston, 1982. *Sex and the Female Ostomate.* Donald Binder, 1981. *Sex, Courtship, and the Single Ostomate.* All are publications of the United Ostomy Association and are available from U.O.A. (Canadian office) 5 Hamilton Ave., Hamilton, Ontario L8V 2S3 (CAN $1.25).

For Professionals
Ellen A. Shipes and Sally T. Lehr, 1980. *Sexual Counselling for Ostomates.* Charles C. Thomas, 301-327 East Lawrence Avenue, Springfield IL 62717 (US $8.50).

Victor Alterescu, 1981. "Sexual functioning following creation of an abdominal stoma." *Sexuality and Physical Disability: Personal Perspectives*, edited by David Bullard and Susan Knight, C.V. Mosby Company, pp. 194-201.

This is an excellent brief overview of the questions and concerns encountered by enterostomal therapists and other counsellors and rehabilitation personnel.

Katherine Jeter, 1982. "Sex and the cystectomized male: A lack of communication, a need for education." *Sexuality and Disability* 5:89-97.

This retrospective study on seventy-one men illustrates the potential role of counsellors and enterostomal therapists in correcting misconceptions, misinformation, and misinterpretations that cause problems and concern.

Cerebral Palsy

Carla Thornton, 1981. "Growing up with cerebral palsy." *Sexuality and Physical Disability: Personal Perspectives*, edited by David Bullard and Susan Knight, C.V. Mosby Company.

For Professionals

Sex and Disability Project, 1979. "Cerebral palsy: A review of the literature." *Who Cares? A Handbook on Sex Education and Counselling Services for Disabled People*. RRRI-ALLB, 1828 L Street NW, Suite 704, Washington DC 20036.

The organizations listed are in the United States but the article contains a good review of the issues associated with sexuality and cerebral palsy plus an extensive annotated bibliography.

Harilyn Ruosso, 1982. "Special considerations in counselling clients with cerebral palsy." *Sexuality and Disability* 5:78-88.

R.C. Geiger and D.E. Knight, 1975. "Sexuality of people with cerebral palsy." *Medical Aspects of Human Sexuality*, March 1975, pp. 70-83.

Multiple Sclerosis

Michael Barrett, 1982. *Sexuality and Multiple Sclerosis*. Multiple Sclerosis Society of Canada, Suite 700, 130 Bloor St. West, Toronto M5S 1N5.

Although this booklet is directed specifically to people with MS, their partners, and those who interact with them, it addresses a sufficiently wide range of issues that can be helpful to others as well. The extensive discussion on the physical aspects of sexual response and the possible effects of MS will enable readers to better understand and cope with some of the common sexual implications of the condition. It contains an extensive bibliography.

Michael Carrera and Simi Kelley, 1979. "MS: The right to a sexual life." Available from The Foundation for Care and Research, Education and Planning in Chronic Diseases, 432 Park Avenue South, New York NY 10016.

This 7-page article takes a nontechnical, personalized look at sexual adjustments with MS, presented in a sensitive, supportive, and realistic manner.

Stroke

For Professionals

Domeena Renshaw, 1978, "Stroke and sex." *Sexual Consequences of Disability*, edited by Alex Comfort, George F. Stickley Company, pp. 121-132.

Michael Humphrey and Glynda Kinsella, 1980. "Sexual life after stroke." *Sexuality and Disability* 3:150-153.

Gail Allsup-Jackson, 1981. "Sexual dysfunction of stroke patients." *Sexuality and Disability* 4:161-168.

Heart Attack

For Professionals

Harry Krop, David Hall and Jawahar Mehta, 1979. "Sexual concerns after myocardial infarction." *Sexuality and Disability* 2:91-97.

Frank T. Masur, 1979. "Resumption of sexual activity following myocardial infarction." *Sexuality and Disability* 2:98-114.

Jawahar Mehta and Harry Drop, 1979. "The effect of myocardial infarction on sexual functioning." *Sexuality and Disability* 2:115-121.

Collier M. Cole, 1979. "A treatment strategy for postmyocardial sexual dysfunction." *Sexuality and Disability* 2:130-138.

R.L. Clancy and Mary Quinlan, 1978. "Sex for the cardiac patient." *Human Sexuality for Health Professionals*, edited by M.U. Barnard, B.J. Clancy and K.E. Krantz, W.B. Saunders Company, pp. 249-258.

Sexual Assault or Abuse

For Professionals
Ellen Ryerson, 1981. "Sexual abuse of disabled persons and prevention alternatives." *Sexuality and Physical Disability: personal perspectives*, edited by David Bullard and Susan Knight, C.V. Mosby Company, pp. 235-241.
Charles K. Stuart and Virginia W. Stuart, 1981. "Sexual assault: disabled perspective." *Sexuality and Disability* 4:246-253.

The article lists ten myths about sexual assault, suggests strategies for self-defense, and identifies issues of importance to counsellors working with victims of sexual assault who have various disabilities.

Homosexuality

George P. Zakarewski, 1979. "Patterns of support among gay/lesbian deaf persons." *Sexuality and Disability* 2:178-191.

This paper describes some issues related to homosexuality and deaf people, and raises many concerns that other gay disabled people may have.
Gerald Hannon, 1980, "No sorrow, no pity." *Body Politic*, Number 60, pp. 19-22.

For Professionals
Laura C. Schlessinger, 1982. "Counselling families with homosexual children." *The Journal of Sex Education and Therapy*, Volume 8, pp. 25-28.

While this article does not refer specifically to gay disabled people, issues such as counselling and self-awareness are discussed.

Sexual and Sensual Aids

R.E. Goodman, 1980. "Sex aids and the disabled." *Sexuality and Disability* 3:232-235.
For more information on aids, contact Mary Sutherland, Lovecraft Ltd., 63 Yorkville Avenue, Toronto, Ontario M5R 1B7 (416) 923-7331.

Surgical Treatment (Penile Implants) for Erectile Dysfunction

Paul H. Lang and Arthur Smith, 1978. "A comparison of the two types of penile prosthesis used in the surgical treatment of male impotence." *Sexuality and Disability* 1:307-311.

This issue is devoted to surgical management of erectile dysfunction, including diagnostic procedures.

Sexual Counseling in a Rehabilitation Program: A Patient Perspective

Laura A. Cushman

The need for formal sexual counselling as part of spinal cord injury (SCI) rehabilitation programs has often been discussed in the literature. Less information is available regarding the role of sexual counselling in other rehabilitation programs. The present study represents a survey of both SCI and non-SCI patient groups regarding satisfaction with staff efforts to address their sexual concerns. Results indicated that there were few overall differences between SCI and non-SCI groups. Most patients felt that adequate information was available to them, even though no formal counselling was conducted. The study also found that many patients did not view sexual concerns as of primary importance during their rehabilitation stay; this was more true of non-SCI patients. Nonetheless, the results do suggest the need for efforts to provide additional information to a subgroup of patients, particularly those who are not SCI and who may not feel comfortable in asking for such information.

The need for sexual counselling and information giving as part of a rehabilitation program for spinal cord injured (SCI) persons has been emphasized in the literature since at least the early 1970's. Several programs that utilize a group format for sexual counselling of patients have been described (Romano, 1973; Eisenberg and Rustad, 1976). However, as Trieschmann (1980) notes, little data exists to suggest that any such program results in increased sexual satisfaction and adjustment.

Other approaches to incorporating sexual counselling in rehabilitation programs have included group training sessions designed to assist staff in becoming more comfortable and open in discussing sexual issues (Cole, Chilgren and Rosenberg, 1973), including the provision of private rooms which enable patients to have opportunities for sexual intimacy while hospitalized (Griffith and Trieschmann, 1977, 1988). The former type of program is based on the assumption that increased staff comfort in dealing with sexuality would result in their improved ability to serve as facilitators for sexual counselling. Although the vast majority of participants in such programs rate them as worthwhile (Held, Cole, Held, Anderson & Chilgren, 1975), it is difficult to assess the impact of such training on existing sexual counselling programs.

Some approaches focus on active behavior change versus attitude readjustment, such as those which encourage mutual re-learning by individual spinal cord injured persons and their partners (e.g. Griffith and Trieschmann, 1977).

All of the staff or patient counselling approaches described share the assumption that some form of sexual counselling is vital to a complete rehabilitation program; Trieschmann (1980) has stated that "if health care professionals are going to be receptive to the needs of persons with spinal injury, sexual functioning must be part of a rehabilitation program" (p. 142). It is possible to extrapolate this thinking to include other forms of disability which are represented in comprehensive rehabilitation programs. Although other forms of disability may not as directly affect physiological aspects of sexual functioning, changes in body image and self-perception which occur may well influence persons' views regarding their sexuality, and thereby their willingness and ability to participate in sexual activity. For example, Allsup (1981) reported that diminished sexual activity in post-stroke individuals was primarily related to feeling of inadequacy and other attitudinal factors. Thus, the rehabilitation staff's responsiveness to the sexual concerns of all patients, can be viewed as an important and integral feature of treatment programs.

Reprinted from: Journal of Rehabilitation, Apr/May/June 1980, with permission.

The approaches described in the literature derive largely from theoretical assumptions regarding, for example, the relative advantages of group versus individual approaches, or of primary attitudinal versus behavior change, rather than from patient-requested programs. On the general hospital rehabilitation unit represented in this study, educational information regarding sexuality was typically given to SCI patients by nurses in one-to-one discussions. Nurses were thought to be trained and qualified for this program. Prior to assessing whether information-sharing, counselling or both would be more effective in a group format, it was decided to first assess the effectiveness of current educational efforts by asking the consumers (i.e., patients) themselves what they thought. It was hypothesized that if SCI patients were satisfied with the current nursing education efforts, it would be most profitable to improve this program rather than implement a new type of counselling program.

The present study thus represents a survey of patients' satisfaction with available information about sexual functioning, level of concern with sexual issues, perception of staff attitudes, and preferred types of service delivery regarding sexuality-related information. To assess potential generalization of program efforts to a broad rehabilitation population, spinal cord injured as well as other disability groups were included. It was anticipated that the results would provide a basis for developing potentially more effective intervention programs in inpatient rehabilitation settings of this kind, and act as a potential impetus for those with educational and counselling programs to evaluate patient satisfaction along similar dimensions.

Method

Subjects

Subjects in the study were patients who participated in an inpatient rehabilitation program located within a university hospital. Over a 14 month period, consecutive patients who were about to be discharged were invited to participate (N=118). (Forty-two patients were not approached regarding participation in the study due to severe aphasia (or other cognitive disturbances),

or a stay of less than 8 days). Fifty-eight patients approached (49 percent) declined to participate or failed to give informed consent; 10 others failed to return the questionnaire. Only one SCI patient approached declined to participate; the rest were non-spinal cord injured. A total of 50 patients completed and returned the questionnaire.

There were 25 SCI subjects, 16 male and 9 female. Their ages ranged from 16 to 74, with mean age of 41.8 (SD=20.8) and a median age of 45. There were 25 non-spinal cord injured patients; of this group, 14 were male and 11 were female. Ages ranged from 23 to 82, with a mean age of 51 years (SD=17.5) and a median of 52 years. The two groups did thus significantly differ with respect to age (t(1,48)=8.06, p<.01).

Fifty-five percent of subjects (N=22) in the non-spinal cord injured group had suffered a stroke. Ten percent were diagnosed as suffering spinal stenosis and eight percent as having multiple trauma. Subjects with brain tumor and amputation each represented 5 percent of this group; the remaining 17 percent was comprised of seven individuals with assorted diagnoses.

The SCI subjects in the study spent an average of 85.5 days on the Rehabilitation unit; non-spinal cord injured subjects spend an average of 34 days. By the time of discharge (when the questionnaire was given), SCI subjects were an average of 126.1 days after injury, whereas other subjects were an average of 84.33 days after onset of their illness. Thus, SCI subjects spent significantly more time both on the Rehabilitation unit and in the hospital overall (z = 5.07, p .01; z = 2.24, p < .025), and were therefore further from the onset of injury or illness than were other subjects at the time the questionnaire was administered.

Procedure

The questionnaire used was developed for use in the study setting. It was designed to survey, in a broad manner, patient perceptions of how issues related to sexuality had been addressed. (Many of the questions are illustrated in Table 1). No effort was made via this instrument to ascertain whether patient had been given specific bits of information.

Subjects were given the questionnaire during the week preceding their discharge. They were given the option of returning the questionnaire before they left the hospital, or of mailing it back in a postage- paid envelope. Subjects who were unable to write were asked if they would allow someone of their choice (e.g., nurse, family member, research assistant) to record their responses. Two SCI subjects and 4 other subjects required such assistance.

Questionnaires were returned anonymously. When the period of data collection had ended, responses were tabulated. The responses of subjects who indicated they were spinal cord injured (SCI) were tabulated separately.

As previously indicated, this study was conducted at a time in which no individual or group sexual adjustment counselling was routinely available for all patients. SCI patients were involved in nursing education programs which included a group-oriented information sharing session, and written information as part of a self-instruction program. The information presented centered on physiological aspects of sexual functioning, but also included body image and attitudes regarding sexuality. For non SCI patients, staff or patient-initiated discussions likely formed the single source of any sexual counselling or education.

Results

Subjects were asked to indicate whether they felt that concerns about sexual functioning were an important issue during their stay on the rehabilitation unit. Forty percent of spinal cord injured (SCI) patients and twenty percent of the non-spinal cord injured (NSCI) answered yes; four and eight percent of each group (respectively) did not respond (Table 1).

In terms of access to information about sexuality, eighty and eighty-four percent of the SCI and NSCI groups, respectively, indicated that they felt such access was available to them. Eighty percent of the SCI group and 88 percent of the NSCI group indicated that there was someone present with whom they felt free to talk about sexual matters. The frequencies with which various sources were cited as being such

a confidant are listed in Table 2; the most frequent choices were "nurse" and "doctor," respectively.

When asked to consider whether the amount of information or discussion about sexuality they received was sufficient, 72 percent of the SCI group and 76 percent of the NSCI answered affirmatively. Thirty-six percent of the SCI group and 20 percent of the NSCI group indicated that they had received or reviewed written materials regarding sexuality. Fifty-two percent of the SCI group indicated that they had received or reviewed written materials regarding sexuality. Fifty-two percent of the SCI group and 32 percent of the NSCI group indicated that someone had volunteered information regarding sexuality to them.

With respect to their initiation of information sharing, subjects were asked to indicate whether, during their stay on the rehabilitation unit, they had ever asked a question about sexual functioning. Thirty-six percent of the SCI group and 8 percent of the NSCI group answered "yes." Of those who answered "no," 52 percent of the SCI group and 92 percent of the NSCI group indicated that they had felt "free to ask" such a question.

Subjects were asked to indicate which of three educational formats (private discussion, group discussion or printed booklet) they would most prefer for further sharing of information by staff. The preferences of each group are shown in Table 3. Most subjects (in both the SCI and NSCI groups) preferred either a private talk with staff or printed booklet.

Subjects were also asked to indicate which of five attitudes listed best described that of most staff on the unit. The five attitudes were comprised of one positive statement and four negatively-oriented statements (Table 4). The majority of patients selected a positive staff attitude. ("It is natural for you to wonder or ask about sexual matters").

Discussion

The results of this study must be interpreted cautiously, in light of the low rate of participation. It is not clear what factors led to a reluctance to participate on the part of more than half the subjects approached. It may be speculated that the lack of a formal program in sexual counselling left potential subjects more generally uncomfortable with the topic area. This hypothesis is given some support by the fact that the vast majority of those who declined to participate were NSCI, those patients for whom no intervention (such as the nursing education program) was designated. The age difference between the SCI and NSCI groups may also have been a factor. Further research is needed to evaluate these hypotheses.

It is interesting to note that the majority of patients in both SCI and NSCI groups indicated that concerns about sexual functioning were not an important issue during the course of their rehabilitation. This would appear to be counter-intuitive to reports which highlight this area as one of chief significance to be addressed, particularly in rehabilitation of SCI patients. A recent report one interventions in SCI, for example, cites the sexual dysfunction that SCI patients face as on of "mankind's greatest fears" (Friedman-Campbell and Hart, 1985). Apparently, the patients who participated in the present study felt other areas to have priority. Alternatively, the response that concerns about sexual functioning were not important may represent a general reluctance to further discuss this area. The former interpretation may be viewed as consistent with Hanson and Franklin's (1976) finding that SCI males ranked sexual functioning as the third most important functional loss (out of three major areas of loss) which they experienced. Subjects in Hanson, et. al.'s, study were extremely heterogeneous in terms of time since injury, however. The present study does not, unfortunately, allow examination of changes in patient attitudes following discharge. One might well assume that concerns about sexual functioning would become more important after individuals return home. The present study also does not allow examination of the specific behaviors and attitudes included under the category of "sexual functioning" to which patients responded. Further research to pinpoint interindividual differences in this area will help clarify this finding.

In terms of general consumer satisfaction with access to information regarding sexuality, a majority of patients in both groups indicated hat they had access to necessary information, and that the amount of information was adequate. Likewise, most patients felt that there was another individual available with whom they would feel comfortable discussing sexual concerns.

Doctors (there was no differentiation between resident and attending physicians) and nurses were most frequently cited as individuals to whom patients would presumably turn. It is noteworthy, however, that the full range of staff represented on the unit was able to serve in this capacity, at least for some patients.

In examining how information was actually conveyed to patients, it is striking that less than half the patients in either the SCI or NSCI groups reported that anyone volunteered any information to them. Likewise, less than half reported having reviewed or received any written material. Given this, it is surprising that the majority still described the "amount of information or discussion available" as adequate. It does not appear that patients were obtaining information due to requests which they initiated, as only a minority of patients reported doing so.

Although, as noted above, less than half the patients surveyed reported having been given written materials or been given unsolicited information, these approaches emerged as the preferred sources of information sharing. A minority of patients in both groups selected group discussion as a preferred mode of information sharing. This would appear to contrast the emphasis on group educational programs which have been implemented at many centers. Of course, this questionnaire did not distinguish presentation of factual information and more personal, feeling-oriented group discussion. Further, the question of the efficacy of various educational approaches in helping patients achieve some criterion of knowledge was not addressed.

Table 1
Summary of Patient Responses to Several Questionnaire Items
(SCI = Spinal Cord Injured; NSCI = Non Spinal Cord Injured)

	SCI N = 25) N(%)			NSCI (N = 25) N(%)		
	Yes	No	No Response	Yes	No	No Response
Were concerns about sexual functioning an important issue to you while here?	9(36)	15(60)	1(4)	5(20)	18(72)	2(8)
Did you ever ask a question about sexual functioning or sexuality while you were here on the rehabilitation unit?	9(36)	16(64)	0(0)	2(8)	23(92)	0(0)
Did you feel you could get access to information about sexuality if needed?	20(80)	3(12)	2(8)	21(84)	3(12)	1(4)
Was there anyone that you felt free and comfortable to talk to about sexual matters?	20(80)	5(20)	0(0)	22(88)	3(12)	0(0)
Did anyone volunteer information to you?	13(52)	12(48)	0(0)	8(32)	17(68)	0(0)
Did you receive and/or review any written materials regarding sexuality and disability while here?	9(36)	16(64)	0(0)	5(20)	20(80)	0(0)
Overall, was the amount of information or discussion about sexuality available to you: enough (yes) or not enough (no)?	18(72)	4(16)	3(12)	19(76)	3(12)	3(12)

The questionnaire attempted to assess patient perceptions of staff attitudes regarding sexuality. The fact that a vast majority of patients indicated that they felt free to ask questions about sexual functioning (even if they did not do so) provides indirect evidence that staff were perceived as open to such discussion. And, in fact, the statement describing staff attitude that was most frequently chosen suggested that staff did convey the sense that concern about sexual functioning is a natural response. This finding must be viewed very cautiously, however, due to the confound of social desirability in selecting the positive response.

Some patients did indicate that staff were conveying the message that it was unusual for patients to ask about sexual matters, that sex was not an important issue, and that only family members should discuss these concerns. It is interesting to speculate as to the extent that patients' statements regarding the current importance of sexual functioning were influenced by staff attitudes regarding the same.

A general overview of the SCI and NSCI groups reveals few striking differences in the pattern of responses. One exception is that four times as many patients in the SCI group as in the NSCI group indicated that they had asked a question about sexual functioning, and twice as many indicated that sexual functioning was an important issue while on the rehabilitation unit. Patients in the SCI group reported having received verbal or written information with greater frequency. The latter is expected given that provision of information regarding sexual functioning is a goal of the SCI rehabilitation nursing program. However, given this objective, it is surprising that less than half of the SCI patients reported having received such information. One possible factor is that educational efforts have, in the past, typically been aimed at traumatically injured SCI patients; older patients with spinal cord dysfunction secondary to other illnesses may not have been targeted in the same manner.

Some differences were noted between the SCI and NSCI groups in terms of perceived staff attitudes. The NSCI group more frequently described staff as conveying the idea that "it is unusual to wonder about sex here", or that "sex is not important now." The attitude that "disabled persons shouldn't worry about sex" was cited by some member of the NSCI group, but not at all by the SCI group. These findings may reflect a possible bias to de-emphasize sexuality with an older group, as the NSCI group had a higher mean age. These findings may also suggest that interventions aimed at conveying sexual information were effective primarily in that group (i.e., SCI) for which such interventions had been targeted.

Conclusion

This study was designed as a descriptive review of patient perceptions of and satisfaction with staff effort to address sexual concerns. Results indicated that most patients found existing resources adequate to meet their needs, although most stated that they received no formal educational material, either written or verbal. Most patients indicated that sexual concerns were not an important issue for them during their stay on the

rehabilitation unit, although a greater proportion of those in the SCI group indicated such concerns were, in fact, important to them.

Most respondents indicated a desire for either more private discussions with staff or written material to supplement provision of information. Only a minority of patients indicated that they felt a group-oriented approach to be most desirable.

These results imply that written educational material, consistently provided to all patients, as well as staff-initiated discussions, may create the most effective routes to creating a higher level of consumer satisfaction in this setting. It remains a question for future program development and to research to determine whether such interventions would be effective in reducing the number of patients who feel that current information sharing is inadequate, or who do not feel comfortable in seeking such information on their own.

The results of this study would also seem to suggest that facilities which use group counselling approaches might profitably make this an option only for those patients who show a preference for this approach.

Perhaps the primary implication of this study for other general rehabilitation units is that patients of all ages and diagnostic groups should be considered for participation in sexual education or counselling programs. This does not mean that identical approaches would be applicable to all patients, but rather that there is evidence that some patients (e.g., older stroke patients) to whom such information is relevant may currently be overlooked.

Is There A Difference?

Four years ago I dived into a swimming pool and broke my fifth vertebra. I am now a C-5 quadriplegic. I'll probably be confined to a wheelchair for the rest of my life. I was then nineteen years old, working as an ambulance attendant and attending Western University hoping one day to become a dentist. I was socially active. Today my life differs but is basically the same: I am still socially active.

After having been hospitalized for more than a month, I was sent to a rehabilitation centre where I spent the next thirteen months. I was then transferred to another rehabilitation centre for three weeks to make arrangements to attend university the following September.

At the first rehabilitation centre the subject of sexuality was rarely discussed between staff and patients. Jokes among patients about sex were often made. Quadriplegics, in particular, laughed at jokes about how strong the girl had to be to transfer her partner. Inventing sentences such as "I would like to have sex with you, but would you put me to bed and take off my clothes first?" got a laugh, especially when a female visitor was nearby. A staff member would sometimes mention that paralysis should not interfere with sex, that even though feeling was gone there were different ways that sexual satisfaction could be achieved. It was up to us to find the way from future sexual encounters. During my thirteen months at the centre, I was never aware that sexual education was available to patients who suffered from paralysis, nor did I ask. There seemed to be some shyness on the part of both staff and patients. Orderlies warned us to make sure our bladder was empty before any sexual encounter. Several quadriplegics viewed catheterization as an extra burden to having sex. We had to learn about sex from personal experiences.

The second rehabilitation centre was quite different. We saw a psychologist on a regular basis as part of the program during my three week stay. Sexuality was one of the topics before I left. Films, books, and discussions were available to us when needed. When films were viewed with the psychologist we could express opinions, doubts, and fears about what was happening in the films, and about sexuality in general. This was new to me because at first rehabilitation centre I only saw the psychologist once and sexuality was not one of the topics discussed. However much counselling one gets, there are still loose ends that have to be tied up. Fears can only be overcome by facing them and trying to work them out with your partner. At the second rehabilitation centre we greatly appreciated that sexuality was discussed with us without having to ask. At the first rehabilitation centre you had to rely on your personal experiences. To a certain extent that feeling of uncertainty remained.

One of the main barriers for disabled people is the attitude of society. Able-bodied people should appreciate disabled people and try to better understand their needs. They should realize that disabled people are equally capable of making important contributions to society. The attitude of the able-bodied towards the disabled is important, especially when dealing with sexuality. Today more people confined to wheelchairs are leading active social lives. Sex is therefore a need that has to be met.

Some able-bodied people think that people confined to wheelchairs are incapable of having sex with someone other than another person in a chair. Some feel uncertain when they meet a disabled person; it is hard for them to be themselves. They are hard to approach and sexual encounters rarely result. Several contacts are usually needed for a sexual relationship to develop. Pick-up bars are usually avoided and a one-night stand is a rarity.

The quality of the relationship between an able-bodied and a disabled person must grow for a sexual relationship to occur. One must explain to his or her partner that lovemaking will be done in a different way. Explaining your physical

Reprinted from: "Rehabilitation Digest", Spring 1984, Vol 15 #1, with permission. Published by CRCD: Toronto, Ont.

condition can be embarrassing for both parties. This is where the attitude of the able-bodied person must change. Your partner will have to come to know you for your personality and interests, aspects often forgotten in this physically-oriented world of ours. Several meetings will centre on the character of both partners and their attitude of the able-bodied becomes such that he or she understands the limitations involved in a sexual relationship with a disabled person and is aware of the opportunities that exist, then both parties can enjoy a sexual relationship. It is a matter of adjusting to the situation so that the disability will not be seen as an inconvenience. This is not easy to achieve because it depends on a person's beliefs and norms and the disabled know better than anyone how hard it is to change them.

Communication between able-bodied and disabled people can be hampered by the attitudes disabled people have towards the able-bodied. Our life changes in one split second, the time it takes to sever a spinal cord. It is therefore normal for us to assume that shortly after the injury people will see us through our disability rather than as a person. As we become more socially involved, this belief remains or fades away, depending on our experiences. We must first find the security and confidence in ourselves that we may have lost because of an injury. This is complicated by the barriers that we must face due to the paralysis. Bladder and bowels have to be trained. We must learn how to transfer ourselves. As we adjust to this, we gradually become more socially active.

Sexual adjustment should not be an exception to the rule. After facts on sexual matters have been given, it is up to the individual to do what he or she wants with them. He may stay socially active and develop a relationship or he may drop back into seclusion. Interfration is then based on two important points: the opportunity to make contacts and the ability to maintain them.

This is where the attitude we hold towards the able-bodied is important. Some might be satisfied to talk to people, others will want more. If a strong and sexual relationship develops, the disabled partner must explain the help that will be needed to continue the sexual relationship.

This may not be an easy task; here again personality is an asset. Some people will gladly explain their limitations, while others will find their shyness stands in the way. We must realized that a refusal of sexual activity by a person may leave us cold. Every situation is different. What was refused at one time might be accepted at another. But all in all, sexual adjustment depends on the individual. He is the only person who can make the decision about his sexual life.

Therefore, information and counselling should be available in, and part of, any rehabilitation program. Films, books and discussions should be readily available when needed. The disabled must also be given the opportunity to live the sexual life desired, even though it means educating the able-bodied about the needs of disabled people. Finally, the disabled should give themselves the chance to meet people, which provides the opportunity for future relationships. Able-bodied and disabled people should try to establish communication to develop a relationship based on mutual understanding, friendship, and love in order to enjoy a satisfactory sexual life.

The author is a 23-year-old man currently living independently in a university residence and attending classes full time.

Disabled Youngsters Face Sexual Pressure Too

As a species, we humans have been maturing physically earlier over recent generations. Social pressures and expectations, and adjustments to new body functions, are facing younger and younger people. And it is the same for disabled youngsters.

This was a background consideration presented by Heather Davey, education officer for the Family Planning Association in Auckland, New Zealand, in a three-evening series on human relationships and sexuality.

One evening was for parents only one for disabled young adults, and the third was for both, with a panel discussion of questions from the first two.

"Society tends to regard disabled people as 'Peter Pans' who never grow up," Ms. Davey said, explaining the general reluctance to face up to the reality of sexual development and maturing of disabled children into adults.

Sex education includes thinking of the social, cultural, and ethical aspects of human relationships, as well as the biological, she said. The FPA analyzed some current uses of sex in the media aimed at young people: records, record covers, television commercials, magazine advertisements. They presented, she said, "a clear message of 'Go out and have sex.'"——she gave examples——"So let's make it cleaner for them, and respect their finer feelings and need for modesty and privacy."

But she added that this had to be backed up with information on human relationships and sexual maturity, which disabled youngsters reach like everyone else.

Source: AID Magazine, December 1983.

The Social Component of Sexuality and Disability: Some Problems and Proposals

HARLAN HAHN, PhD

Perhaps one of the major difficulties facing the study of sexuality and disability has emerged from the common tendency to view disability strictly from a clinical or biological rather than from a social perspective. In general, research on most aspects of physical disability has been guided by a medical etiology which tends to focus on separate diagnostic categories and by the specific concerns of various professions which work with disabled persons. Although there has been much discussion of social issues in the literature on sex and disability, most of these issues have been considered only within the context of particular physical impairments. In many respects, this approach seems to be somewhat incongruous with the commonly accepted contemporary definition of disability as "a form of inability or limitation in performing roles and tasks expected of an individual within a social environment." Since the concept of disability encompasses important social as well as physical components, there appears to be a need to devote increased attention to the social problems which may affect sexual relationships involving disabled persons.

This shift might have several research advantages. An emphasis on the social dimensions of sexuality and disability, for example, could enable researchers to develop generalizations that transcend the limitations of specific physical conditions or diseases. In addition, it might facilitate the emergence of new research questions and priorities which are of special concern to disabled persons. By focusing on this perspective, a growing interest could develop in the study of problems which may be precluded or neglected by prior theoretical orientations.

Perhaps one important reason for the relative neglect of the social aspects of sexuality and disability can be attributed to the lack of studies which have been conducted or prepared by physically disabled persons. Although an editorial in the initial issue contained a special invitation to disabled readers "to submit relevant manuscripts," only a few articles in the first three volumes of *Sexuality and Disability* have been written specifically from the viewpoint of disabled individuals. Since physically disabled persons may have more experience and awareness of the social dimensions of this subject than their nondisabled counterparts, the comparative absence of significant input from disabled persons might be sociological as well as psychological or physiological. Even more importantly, the neglect of the social problems encountered by disabled persons in the sexual realm of life may prevent researchers from recognizing their personal vulnerability. While there may be important similarities in the difficulties faced by disabled and nondisabled persons, disabled men and women often confront special or distinctive obstacles in their efforts to form satisfactory marital or sexual relationships. Such problems deserve increased recognition by physicians, lawyers, psychologists, social workers, sex educators, rehabilitation counsellors, and others who assist disabled persons. As a result of their unique position in a society which is often hostile or resistant to their physical characteristics, physically disabled persons may be especially vulnerable to psychological, legal, and economic exploitation in their personal relationships with nondisabled individuals.

The purpose of this study, therefore, is to identify several social problems regarding the sexual relationships of disabled persons which may require further research. In examining this subject, particular attention will be devoted to visible physical disabilities and to the implications of sexual relationships between disabled and nondisabled partners.

Reprinted from: *Sexuality and Disability, Volume 4, Number 4, Fall 1981* 0146-1044/81/1600-0220 $00.95 © 1981 Human Sciences Press, with permission.

Methods

The impetus for this study was derived primarily from two sources. Initially, as a professional social scientist, I have conducted a broad survey of the literature on the social aspects of sexuality and disability in an effort not only to gather available data but also to discover insights, ideas, and suggestions which may be helpful in the development of future hypotheses. Insofar as possible, I have confined the use of materials obtained in this search to those studies which discuss the social problems of visible physical disabilities generally rather than to research on specific types of physical conditions or impairments.

Secondly, and perhaps more importantly, I have been a "participant-observer" concerning this subject for more than thirty-five years. As a result of polio, I have walked with crutches and braces since the age of six. In some respects, I have found my life as a disabled person to be a more useful source of concepts and propositions regarding physical disability than much of the published literature on the subject. Many aspects of behavioral research——ranging from the selection of a topic to the interpretation or acceptance of empirical findings——are related to personal values; hence, most of the ideas expressed in the following discussion also are based upon my own experience.

Obstacles to Marriage and Sexual Relationships for Visibly Disabled Persons

There is, unfortunately, little existing information on the extent of sexual problems confronting persons with visible physical disabilities. Even such basic data as the proportion of visibly disabled people who marry seem to be generally unavailable. In part, this deficiency can be attributed to the common tendency of public surveys and other sources of data to define "disabilities" as either work impairments or functional limitations, which prevents researchers from examining the personal or demographic characteristics of the visibly disabled segment of the populations. While most of these studies have indicated that disabled persons are less likely to marry than nondisabled individuals, this pattern also may be related to the economic loss suffered by persons with work disabilities which may prevent them from supporting a family.

There are, however, strong theoretical reasons to believe that an obvious or visible physical disability may reduce the opportunities of achieving a marital or sexual relationship. In his classic study of *stigma*, Goffman not only notes that a physical disability is a discrediting attribute which may induce others to believe that such a person "is not quite human," but he also concludes by pointing out that "the devaluation of those with bodily disfigurements can perhaps be interpreted as contributing to a needed narrowing of courtship decisions." The perceptibility of a stigmatized physical characteristic may vary along a continuum which reflects the severity of a disability and which may be enhanced by increasing degrees of intimacy. But, for some disabled men and women, the effects of stigmatization may be so powerful that they may pose a seemingly insurmountable obstacle to love or marriage.

Some support for this proposition can be derived from studies of visibly disabled persons. One study of veterans with spinal cord injuries, for example, found that one-half did not expect to be married, and an earlier study of 437 former polio patients disclosed that only 27.7 percent of the men and 41.1 percent of the women had either married or contemplated marriage after their release from the hospital. Another study revealed that, even in countries such as Columbia where strong social traditions support the institution of marriage and the family, more than 85 percent of the physically disabled women and 69 percent of the disabled men were single. The published autobiographies of disabled persons also display an intense concern about sexual problems; and they indicate that many visibly disabled persons have, for a variety of reasons, reached a reluctant decision to remain celibate. Although some of the reservations of disabled persons about sexual relations may be based upon psychological considerations, their reticence also may reflect barriers which are imposed upon them by society.

Another source of data concerning this subject can be found in studies of the attitudes of nondisabled persons. Such research not only has demonstrated a correlation between the visibility of physical disabilities and the disruption of conjugal and family relationships, but it also has revealed the existence of widespread and deeply rooted attitudes of aversion and prejudice which effect the personal or social acceptability of disabled persons. Studies utilizing social distance measures have discovered an unwillingness to accept visibly disabled partners in a close personal or intimate relationship. As a result, several writers have observed that the disabled frequently are regarded as "asexual objects" and as unacceptable candidates for marriage. Safilios-Rothschild, for example, in suggesting that "the main type of aversion (to disabled persons) is 'esthetic-sexual,'"concluded that the likelihood of intermarriage between visibly disabled and nondisabled individuals is "very small" and that "while the nondisabled tend to be cooperative and understanding when it comes to the occupational world, they close their ears to the disabled's attempts to gain social acceptance and marriage eligibility." This, of course, does not imply an absolute prohibition on relationships between disabled and nondisabled individuals; but it does suggest the possibility that, among many nondisabled people, the mere thought of an intimate relationship with a disabled person may be an offensive idea which conjures up feelings of disgust or repugnance. For some undetermined portion of the nondisabled population, the barriers against sexual relationships with disabled persons almost amount to a taboo which few are willing to defy. Just as there has been a virtual ban on serious consideration of the reduced marriage potential of visibly disabled persons both in popular discussions and in the professional literature, similar taboos may impede the acceptance of disabled persons in intimate relationships.

Social Conventions

Taboos against sexual contact with disabled persons often are reinforced by pervasive social norms or conventions. Although the explanation for the widespread aversion to visibly disabled persons is beyond the preview of this study, there are many social customs which regulate the formation of intimate relationships and which impose a significant disadvantage upon disabled persons. Physical attractiveness, for example, often has been considered of paramount importance in the development of such relationships. This emphasis may reflect traditional values which were attached to physical strength and power as well as to physical beauty or grace, the contemporary significance of the "the whole body" or "the body beautiful," and the narcistic anxiety which is easily aroused in many people who are plagued by doubts about supposed flaws or defects in their own physical images. While each of these historical, social, and psychological influences may have an effect upon nondisabled as well as disabled individuals, they seem to have a special impact upon the visibly disabled segment of the population. There is a chemistry in sexual relationships which can be traced primarily to physical characteristics and which may pose exceptional difficulties for disabled persons.

Visibly disabled persons also may confront unique problems in their efforts to initiate social interactions with nondisabled people. As a result of the so-called "spread" phenomenon, the symbols of a physical disability may be so prominent that they overshadow a disabled person's personality or intellectual traits. Such factors may affect both those with communications impairments such as blindness or deafness and persons with orthopedic disabilities which may restrict their movements. According to Davis, informal encounters between disabled and nondisabled individuals usually are characterized by a stage of "fictional acceptance," in which no reference is made to an obvious physical disability, and by a subsequent attempt of the disabled person to "break through" the initial perception of the disability and to demonstrate other aspects of her or his personal characteristics. In many respects, this effort may reflect the desire to overcome conventional patterns of "paternalism" which place disabled people in a child-like (asexual) position of defencelessness, dependency, and inferiority and which often permeates interactions between disabled and nondisabled persons. Since superficial considerations seldom can sustain a personal relationship, the ability to "break through" may be an especially crucial concern of visibly disabled persons. (Although there are great risks in making such an estimate, in my own experience I would guess that I have been able to "break through" and to suggest the basis for a closer relationship only with about one-in-twenty of the eligible members of the opposite sex whom I have met. There are, of course, significant variations in psychological, social, mental, emotional, as well as physical abilities; but among the remaining eighty percent, there is a suspicion that many may have been influenced by a social or cultural taboo, standards of physical attractiveness, and similar considerations. Thus, in a "case study" of one visibly disabled person, it is possible that only about five percent of the eligible population might be willing to entertain, even briefly, the possibility of a closer relationship between a disabled and a nondisabled individual.) Despite the obvious difficulties of such an effort, similar studies, which could be of great potential significance to research on sexuality and disability, might be conducted by persons with different degrees of visible disabilities.

Even if a visibly disabled person succeeds in "breaking through" to allow another individual to perceive human qualities that are unrelated to the disability, (s)he may confront unusual obstacles in attempting to determine whether or not the possible interest of the other party might extend to a physical or a sexual relationship. The language of sexuality often is conveyed by subtle unspoken clues such as eye contact, gestures, seemingly casual movement, and physical contact. While the interpretation of such ambiguous cues also is a concern of nondisabled people, they present particular problems both for disabled individuals who must not misperceive the nature of the encounter and for others who may find the mannerisms of disabled persons both awkward and difficult to translate. As a result, a disproportionate number of contacts between disabled and nondisabled individuals are terminated without explanation before they have an opportunity to explore the potential of the interaction.

For a variety of reasons, relations between disabled and nondisabled persons frequently are confined to a platonic realm. Disabled young people often serve as "good friends," "valued confidants," or even as "mascots" to their non-disabled peers. Many disabled adults also have found it easier to form viable relationships when the threat of physical contact is absent. In a society dominated by physical standards and conventions which visibly disabled persons seldom can hope to approximate, they are frequently compelled to assume a role that denies the sexual aspect of their being.

If a disabled person should attempt to venture beyond a simple friendship by suggesting the possibility of a close or intimate relationship, (s)he may be forced to confront an increased likelihood of rejection. Although this too is an issue for the nondisabled, the risk of rejection may have special consequences for visibly disabled men and women. In accordance with commonly accepted social customs, such refusals usually are shrouded in mystery; and many disabled persons may find it difficult to determine if the response of a nondisabled individual reflects a genuine excuse, an emotional conflict, a polite rebuff, or a reaction to the disability itself. Since each of these replies may have different implications for the formation of both specific and other relationships, their interpretation often is an important concern of disabled individuals; but, just as there is uncertainty in the assessment of social cues, there may be even greater ambiguity in responses to a proposal to enter a personal relationship. As a result, some disabled persons might make the mistake either of attempting to avoid the prolonged frustrations of ultimate rejection by suggesting a physical relationship prematurely or of assuming incorrectly that intimacy is not possible with a nondisabled partner. Perhaps most importantly, the cumulative effects of repeated rejections of visibly disabled individuals may result in a lowering of their sense of self esteem and in an unfavorable perception of their bodily images. Although some writers have urged disabled persons to become more assertive in their efforts to initiate personal relationships, there might also be a need for an awareness that they face increased probabilities of rejection.

If a disabled man or woman should succeed in forming a social or personal relationship with a nondisabled person, (s)he still may face major pitfalls in the courtship process. Most interactions between disabled and nondisabled individuals are conducted "as if" the disability were not present; and they may be severely tested by unanticipated architectural or other obstacles. Many common social or recreational patterns in courtship involve physical skills or activities which are beyond the capacity of the disabled person. Disabled and nondisabled persons also may face intensive resistance from others, including parents and friends of both parties as well as casual onlookers, who often regard the relationship as inappropriate or inadvisable. As a result, dating between disabled and nondisabled individuals might be subjected to unique or unusual stress.

Visibly disabled men and women, therefore, may face significantly reduced probabilities in their efforts to form marital or sexual relationships. Those who are able to overcome the effects of adverse attitudes or a taboo against physical contact between disabled and non-disabled persons still must confront the "handicaps" of ambiguous social cues, repeated rejection, and the strains of courtship. (For readers who are keeping score, I would hazard the estimate that, among five percent of the women who were able to see beyond the physical disability of one disabled male, the proportion who might actually enter into a relationship was reduced to an indeterminate number well below the .001 level of probability). Thus, social customs may be an even more powerful deterrent to relationships between disabled and nondisabled persons than physical appearances or stigma.

Although many professionals may be implicitly or explicitly aware of the social problems which restrict the sexuality of visibly disabled persons, perhaps less attention is devoted to the fact that those problems produce an increased vulnerability among people in this segment of the population. The reduced prospect of forming a marital or sexual relationship poses a serious threat to the natural instinct of all human beings to find a mate, to establish a home, or to raise a family. Very few disabled persons seek sexual conquests, but they are interested in securing the companionship and love enjoyed by most other members of society. The traits which limit the opportunities for marital or sexual relationships involve unalterable physical characteristics rather than mental or emotional attributes that can be changed, and they are the product of events or circumstances over which a person has no choice and no control. Hence, many disabled individuals experience a strong sense of frustration and anger in their personal lives. Perhaps a primary source of these feelings, however, can be attributed to the widespread reticence to discuss or to examine the social factors which may inhibit the development of sexual relations between disabled and nondisabled people. Both disabled persons and the professionals who work with them may be cognizant of the reduced probabilities which confront the former in their efforts to achieve marital or sexual satisfaction, but the latter often appear reluctant to acknowledge or to admit such facts. As a result, many disabled individuals may believe that they are given little guidance or assistance concerning one of the most significant difficulties in their lives; and they may feel exposed and defenceless in their efforts to cope with these problems.

Suitability of Marriage or Sexual Partners

The personal vulnerability of visibly disabled persons also may have a strong effect upon the types of individuals with whom they might engage in sexual relationships. Hicks, for example, has pointed out, "All types of handicap restrict one's range of potential partners." Although the task of identifying an appropriate mate among those who might be willing to enter a relationship with a disabled person is a critical problem, relatively little attention has been devoted to this subject. DeLoach and Greer, in noting that "lack of available sexual partners doesn't always concern the disabled as much as lack of suitable sexual partners," offered a typology of "persons unusually attracted to the disabled" which includes the "walking wounded," the "would-be dictators," the "unsolicited missionaries," and the "gallant gestures." Similarly, Odgers described "five types of men disabled women should avoid." Another examination of the nondisabled partners of men with spinal cord injuries observed that these women tended to be "sexually inexperienced" and that they perceived "beauty where others might not." While such studies reflect the paternalism and the emphasis on physical standards which shape most interactions between the disabled and the nondisabled, they do not exhaust the problems which may confront visibly disabled persons after a relationship has been established.

Unfortunately there is little available data on the dissolution of relationships between disabled and nondisabled persons. One study suggested that the divorce rate among a group of disabled subjects was lower than the national average, but other research has indicated that the possibility of divorce may depend upon the age at which a person becomes disabled and/or the degree of marital satisfaction prior to the disability. Similarly, while some early analyses implied that a disability may produce role strains within the home or family, subsequent investigations have concluded that he physical mobility of a disabled spouse is not significantly related to marital satisfaction.

Yet, there are strong reasons to believe that relationships between disabled and nondisabled partners are exceptionally fragile and tenuous. Many of the factors which may form an initial basis of attraction——including curiosity, pity, paternalism, and even sexual fetishes directed at some types of disabled persons such as amputees-——obviously cannot sustain a relationship. As a result, there seems to be a need for increased research on the social and psychological characteristics of nondisabled individuals who may be willing to accept visibly disabled persons in a sexual relationship.

Perhaps one important social factor that often disrupts relationships between disabled and nondisabled persons can be traced to the well-known principle of "selective perception," which allows human beings to obliterate stimuli that are distasteful or inconsistent with previously held images or beliefs. Many disabled people are startled by the comments of others who have said, after many years of close association, that they "did not see" their disabilities or that they "did not think of them in that way." This orientation may be especially prevalent during an

intimate relationship in which an individual tends to "idealize" physical and other attributes of his or her lover. Of course, the danger is that when a nondisabled person is suddenly confronted with the inescapable fact of disability, (s)he may react by attempting to withdraw or to flee from the situation. Nondisabled persons may seek to escape their disabled mates (often for another nondisabled partner) because of the inundating effects of a disability which can destroy prior favorable perceptions.

Disabled individuals, therefore, may confront significantly reduced probabilities in forming and in maintaining relationships with the nondisabled. Both the personal motives of others who are attracted to disabled persons and social or situational pressures create peculiar tensions which may threaten to terminate such a relationship. (For more visibly disabled persons, this reduces the potential of maintaining a satisfactory relationship to a level below the finite range of probability. Although nondisabled people may claim that their ability to find a compatible partner also is a "one in a million" experience, I believe that this analogy seriously distorts reality because it underestimates the vast discrepancy between the social and sexual problems faced by disabled and nondisabled individuals). Since most of life's significant and sustaining relationships encompass a level of intimate or physical involvement, the inability to maintain such a relationship not only poses a major threat to the personal and vocational goals of a disabled man or woman; but it also may create doubts, uncertainties, and insecurities about future relationships. If disabled men or women lose their lovers, they may be forced to search for another mate in a ritual which places them at a disadvantage in every step of the process. Although some commentators have urged that disabled persons should be especially cautious in the choice of their mates, this advice may fail to take adequate account of the needs or the problems of this portion of the population.

Perhaps the greatest danger, however, is that the unique difficulties of visibly disabled persons could subject them to psychological, economic, and legal exploitation in their relationships with nondisabled individuals. Many people who enter relationships with disabled persons may be motivated not only by particular psychological needs but also by a desire for personal or material gain. The unique vulnerability of visibly disabled people can be transformed into a form of victimization. It might also be difficult to achieve genuine equality between disabled and nondisabled couples because of both the innate social advantages enjoyed by the nondisabled and the desire of many disabled individuals to pursue or to maintain a relationship in the face of overwhelming odds. Although there has been relatively little discussion of this subject in prior studies of sexuality and disability, the potential for exploitation is a serious problem which might receive increased attention from the professionals who work with visibly disabled persons.

Summary and Discussion

This examination of the social dimension of sexual relations between disabled and nondisabled persons has attempted to raise several issues and problems which have been neglected or avoided in prior research. In particular, a candid investigation of the reduced probabilities for marriage or sexual relationships, the possible vulnerability, and the potential of exploitation confronted by visibly disabled persons has seemed to suggest some important implications for future studies. While the full ramifications of these subjects cannot be foreseen as yet, this analysis has appeared to indicate a need for extended research on the social aspect of sexuality and disability, an expanded discussion of this topic, a reexamination of personal values, and increased efforts to eliminate the vulnerability and exploitation of the visibly disabled in personal relationships.

Perhaps the most pressing priority is the need for increased research. Although hopefully this study also has suggested some specific hypotheses which are worthy of further explanation, there seems to be three broad areas in which subsequent investigations might be conducted. Initially, extended attempts might be made to examine the range of acceptance of different types of visible disabilities, particularly in intimate relationships. This research could utilize

both direct indicators of accepting attitudes and subtle measures of covert emotions. Since many nondisabled people may be genuinely unaware of their feeling about such matters, the experience of visibly disabled persons also would be a useful resource in this research effort. Secondly, increased studies might be conducted concerning the characteristics of non-disabled people who have accepted visibly disabled partners in a marital or sexual relationship. Finally, growing efforts could be made to examine the reasons for the success or failure of relationships between disabled and nondisabled persons.

The increased discussion of social issues affecting sex and disability could also have a salutary effect upon various segments of society. Many people may find that taboos and prejudicial attitudes tend to dissolve when they are exposed to rational scrutiny. By seeking to diminish ambiguities in social encounters, visibly disabled persons might be better equipped to cope with the possibility of rejection or acceptance by others. Greater honesty in personal relationships not only might reduce the frustration or anger which is sometimes experienced by disabled individuals, but it also could have an important value for the nondisabled as well.

In addition, a candid investigation of the social and sexual problems of visible disability might lead to an increased recognition that there is value and attractiveness in physical differences. An obvious disability need not necessarily detract from an individual's desirability. In fact, a disability might even enhance a person's appeal because it is a feature which may contribute to his or her character and distinctiveness. Physical differences provide much of the richness and diversity that adds vitality to life. Although people often tend to think of themselves *as* their bodies, society also is beginning to recognize that there may be great beauty in a human being who resides *within* a body.

The realization that physical differences or disabilities can be attractive may represent a distant goal, but there is some immediate action which might be taken to reduce the vulnerability and potential exploitation of visibly disabled persons in personal relationships. An increased recognition of the social problems confronting disabled persons, for example, might lead to some mitigation of the effects of laws concerning divorce, paternity, and other official policies which ordinarily regulate marital or sexual relationships between the members of a society. Similarly, an increased cognizance of the importance of personal relationships to occupational goals might produce some changes in the process of vocational rehabilitation. Perhaps most importantly, however, an enhanced awareness of the social dimensions of sexuality and disability could result in valuable improvements in the counselling activities of many professionals who are engaged in careers of service to disabled persons.

References

1. Gliedman, J., Roth W.: *The Unexpected Minority: Handicapped Children in America.* New York, Harcourt Brace Jovanovich, 1980.
2. Fink, SL, Skiopper, JK Jr., Hallenbeck PN: Physical disability and problems in marriage. *Marriage and the Family* 30:64-73, 1968.
3. Howards, I. Brehm, HP. Nagi, SZ.: *Disability: From Social Problem to Federal Program.* New York, Praeger, 1980.
4. Nagi, SZ.: The concept and measurement of disability. In ED Berkowitz (ed): *Disability Policies and Government Programs.* New York, Praeger, 1979. pp.1-15.
5. Sha'ked, A: Editorial. *Sexuality and Disability* 1:3-5, 1978.
6. Becker, EF.: Sexuality and the spinal-cord-injured woman in an interview. *Sexuality and Disability* 2:278-286, 1976.
7. Davidson, A. Venditti, V: Two clients views. *Sexuality and Disability* 2:23-27, 1979.
8. Ellis, RG: The corona-Frenulum trigger. *Sexuality and Disability* 3:50-56, 1980.
9. Berkowitz, M., Johnson, WG, Murphy, EH: *Public Policy Toward Disability.* New York, Praeger, 1976.
10. US Bureau of the Census. Census of the Population of 1970. Persons with work disability. Final report PC (2)-6c, Washington, D.C., U.S. Gov't Print Off. 1973.
11. Barron, E: The survey of low-income aged and disabled: Survey design and data system. In *Policy Analysis with Social Security Research Files.* Washington, DC, US Gov't Print Off, 1978, pp.433-446.
12. Goffman, E: *Stigma: Notes on the Management of Spoiled Identity.* Englewood Cliffs, NJ, Prentice-Hall, 1963.
13. Morgan, ED, Hohman, GW, Davis, JE Jr: Psychosocial rehabilitation in VA spinal cord injury centers. *Rehab Psych* 21:3-33, 1974.
14. Barker, RG, Wright, BA, Meyerson, L, Gonick, MR: *Adjustment to Physcial Handicap and Illness: A Survey of the Social Psychology of Physique and Disability.* New York, Social Science Research Council, 1953.
15. Schlesinger, HA: Living at home in Latin America. In *Models of Service for the Multi-Handicapped Adult.* New York, United Cerebral Palsy of New York City, 1973, pp.41-55.
16. Wright, BA: *Physical Disability: A Psychological Approach.* New York, Harper and Row, 1960.
17. Battge L: The Chatterley syndrome. In P. Hunt (ed): *Stigma: The Experience of Disability.* London, Geoffrey Chapman, 1966, pp.1-16.
18. Eareckson, J: *Joni.* Grand Rapids, Michigan, Zondervan, 1976.
19. McKee, JD: *Two Legs to Stand On: My Battle with Cerebral Palsy.* New York, Appleton-Century, Crofts, 1955.
20. Zahn, MA: Incapacity, impotence and invisible impairment: Their effects upon interpersonal relations. *Health and Social Behavior* 14:115-123, 1973.
21. English RW: Correlates of stigma toward physically disabled persons, *Rehab Research and Practice Rev* 2:1-17, 1971.
22. Yuker, HE, Block, JR, Young, JH: *The Measurement of Attitudes Toward Disabled Persons.* Albertson, New York, 1970.
23. Ingwell, RH, Thoreson, RW, Smits, SJ: Accuracy of social perceptions of physically handicapped and non-handicapped persons. *Social Psych* 72:107-116, 1967.
24. Richardson, SA, Goodman, N, Hastrof, AH, Dornbusch, SM: Cultural uniformity in reactions to physical disabilities. *Am Sociological Rev* 26:241-247, 1961.
25. Goodman, N, Richardson, SA, Dornbusch, SM, Hastrof, AH: Varient reactions to physical disabilities. *Am Sociological Rev* 28:429-435, 1963.
26. Shim, N, Dole, AA: Components of social distance among college students and their parents in Hawaii. *Social Psych* 73:111-124, 1967.

27. Siller, J: Reactions to physical disability. *Rehab Counsel Bulletin* 7:2-16, 1963.

28. Nigro, G: Sexuality and the handicapped: Some observations on human needs and attitudes. *Rehab Lit* 36:202-205, 1975.

29. Safilios-Rothschild, C: *The Sociology and Social Psychology of Disability and Rehabilitation.* New York, Random House, 1970.

30. Wright, BA: Spread in adjustment to disability. *Bulletin Menninger Clinic* 28:198-208, 1964.

31. Davis F: Deviance disavowal: The management of strained interaction by the visibly handicapped. *Social Problems* 9:121-132, 1961.

32. Bennett, JW: Paternalism. In DL Sills (ed): *International Encyclopedia of the Social Sciences.* New York, Macmillan Co., 11:472-477, 1968.

33. Dunn, M, Lloyd EE, Phelps, GH: Sexual assertiveness in spinal cord injury. *Sexuality and Disability* 2:293-300, 1979.

34. Hicks, S: Relationship and sexual problems of the visually handicapped. *Sexuality and Disability* 3:165-176, 1980.

35. DeLoach, C, Greer, BG: *Adjustment to Severe Physical Disability: A Metamorphosis.* New York, McGraw-Hill, 1981.

36. Odgers, S: Five types of men disabled women should avoid. *Accent on Living* 24:72-76, 1979.

37. Neumann, RJ: The forgotten other: Women partners of spinal cord injured men, a preliminary report. *Sexuality and Disability* 2:287-292, 1979.

38. El Ghatit, AE, Hanson, RW: Marriage and divorce after spinal cord injury. *Arch Phys Med Rehab* 57:470-472, 1976.

39. Safilios-Rothschild, C: Prejudice against the disabled and some means to combat it. *International Rehab Rev.* 19:8-10, 15, 1968.

40. Deutsch, CP, Goldston, JA: Family factors in home adjustment of the severely disabled. *Marriage and Family Living* 22:312-316, 1960.

41. Skipper, JK, Jr, Fink, SL, Hallenbeck, PN: Physical disability among married women: Problems in the husband-wife relationship. *J Rehab* 34:16-19, 1968.

42. Hohmann, GW: Considerations in management of psychosexual readjustment in the cord injured male. *Rehab Psych* 19:50-58, 1972.

Marriage Matters: For People with Disabilities Too

SUSAN MILLER, B.SC. AND
MARGARET MORGAN, MBE.

Ten years ago, almost to the day, Margaret Morgan presented a paper on "Marriage and the Handicapped" to an audience of approximately 250 people with cerebral palsy at an annual conference of the 62 Clubs. These social clubs, run by and for disabled people, were first inaugurated in 1962 and they have a very important bearing on the topic of this paper.

Through the 62 Clubs a wide variety of people with cerebral palsy were able to extend the sphere of their contacts and friendships and to learn to make relationships with other people in new ways. Because the clubs were run by disabled people who had rarely, or never, had the opportunity to take responsibility or to organize activities for others, many learned new skills through serving on committees, arranging meetings and social activities, and caring for each other. The acquiring of these new skills and the enhanced self-confidence enabled many younger——and older——people with cerebral palsy to extend their relationships and interests well beyond the immediate field of other people with disabilities and those who saw themselves as helpers. It also soon became clear that within an enlarged social group, many disabled people were attracted to others with similar disabilities (and why shouldn't they be?) and many more real friendships and deeper relationships were formed.

Before 1969 there were, of course, a number of people with cerebral palsy who were married, but those who had found a partner were usually relatively mild in their degree of physical handicap and were of good intelligence. Where two disabled people had married each other, this was often in the face of great opposition. Marriage, or any sexual relationship or activity, was generally considered to be quite out of the question for the majority of people with cerebral palsy, who were conditioned from an early age to accept a non-sexual role in life. Since 1969, the number of marriages, both of and between people with cerebral palsy, has substantially increased and the

range and degree of handicaps of those involved is much wider.

Public opinion has changed too, and is continuing to change, to the extent that professional people, or even families, may suggest that people with a severe physical handicap or with a mental handicap do not need to——or even should not——marry. These people are quite prepared to allow or even encourage a sexual relationship without either the personal or legal commitments of marriage vows——and I am not taking any particular moral or religious line when saying this. Our experience is that marriage still matters to many people with disabilities, perhaps even more than to many other young people of their own generation. This is probably partly due to the need to be "like other people," and many people still *do* get married, and partly due to the need for the security of a long-term and mutually supportive relationship with another person.

In order to learn more about the outcome of some of these marriages, The Spastics Society has recently been engaged in a follow-up study which looked at the experiences of a sample of people with cerebral palsy who are or have been married. The group included a wide age range and covered people whose cerebral palsy had resulted in a wide range of disabilities.

The sample was drawn from people who were known to The Spastics Society through their Personal Social Services. The contact with the Society was varied in degree and it was, therefore, hoped that there would be little bias in using this population. Without a very complex and expensive screening process it would have been impossible to obtain a sample from other sources. In the end, 72 couples were interviewed using a mainly pre-coded schedule.

The most important limitation of the data is a high loss from the selected sample. The actual refusal rate was low, but it was found that many potential respondents had moved from their last known addresses. There is some evidence that

Reprinted from: *Sexuality and Disability, Volume 3, Number 3, Fall 1980*, 0146-1044/80/1500-0203 $00.95 © 1980 Human Sciences Press, with permission.

this was most often true of people who had married able-bodied partners. They may have themselves been less disabled and with an able-bodied partner not tied to the adaptations of a particular dwelling, and so be more geographically mobile. Of the actual refusals to take part in the survey there is, unfortunately, some indication that people who had recent marital problems were understandably unwilling to take part.

It is important, therefore, to treat the data with some caution. It should not be generalized too freely to other populations of congenitally disabled people. However, it does give a picture of the lives of a substantial number of these people with a wide variety of degree of disability and from a variety of social milieux. The people who are least accurately represented are those who are or have been married to an abled-bodied person.

In this paper we shall concentrate on the data concerned with the sexual relationships of the couples and the children of the marriages. However, the whole study was of marriage, not sex. As one young wife said:

Marriage is not all sex——there's the work——the ironing and the cooking.

Marriage is not the same as expression of sexuality; neither is sex necessarily the most important or interesting aspect of marriage. However, whatever other cultural differences there are between the institution of marriage in different societies, sexual intercourse is always permitted and expected between a married pair. Where there is a physical disability, there is the possibility that this social expectation will not be fulfilled. People who are physically disabled usually share the same norms and social expectation as others; therefore, a couple may find if they are physically quite happy with a purely companionate marriage, the inability to fulfill their own social expectations in this respect may create difficulties between them. Some couples are, however, happy with a marriage without sex. To quote a severely disabled man with a progressive condition married to a woman with cerebral palsy, also severely disabled:

We don't have any sex life, I think we almost took it for granted. We both had a problem of loneliness and this is the way we solved it. I don't think sex really came into it.

People disabled or otherwise have very different sexual needs; every married couple needs to work out their own mutual sexual adaptations. An individual or a couple experience sexual problems when they are unable to fulfill their own personal sexual needs. For some people warmth, affection and physical proximity may be sufficient; for others, frequent genital intercourse and orgasm are essential. Because people with severe disabilities are physically dependent on others, they are open to many subtle pressures and influences. It is important that people who care for them respect their relationships as they are and, while offering an open social environment in which physical sexual difficulties can be dealt with, do not impose standards of sexual expression which may be unwanted.

Attitudes towards marriage of people with disabilities have changed considerably in the last 10 years. Problems are now almost as likely to arise for a young couple because of over-enthusiasm for their marriage from residential staff as they were in the past from obstruction.

As one young husband said, "Don't let other people be involved in your marriage; they try to help but really they always get in the way."

Emotional privacy is as important as physical privacy for a couple who are severely disabled and physically dependent, and probably more difficult to ensure.

while it is obviously true that attitudes have changed towards marriage of people with disabilities, an explanation of this seems necessary. Certainly this change in attitude is in line with a general liberalization of attitudes towards sexual expression. The availability of efficient contraception has obviously been of some importance in allowing the separation of the roles of married adult and parent. One might suggest that the role expectations associated with a married adult are now almost entirely concerned with the emotional content of the marriage; other agencies are now seen as properly concerned with the old family functions of maintenance of the extended family, child rearing and education. Disabled people, while unable to fulfill the old role expectations and therefore subject to sanctions against their marriage, are no less able than others to fulfill the emotional demands effectively. These social sanctions of negative attitudes to their marriage are no longer valid.

This is not to say that couples who are disabled do not find problems with the attitudes of others, particularly parents. A third of both men and women reported that their parents had had a generally positive attitude to their proposed marriage, but almost as many reported that their parents did not approve of their marriage. However, most couples reported positive responses from their wider social circle.

Wives were generally more upset by the negative attitude of their parents than husbands, but very few were seriously affected by opposition; most were made more determined to marry.

In the study undertaken by Bill Stewart for SPOD a very high proportion of the couples indicated that they had quite severe unhappiness connected with their sex lives. These couples were very mixed in disability, including many who had acquired their physical disability in later life. This sample differed substantially from the SPOD group in this respect.

It is often assumed that people with disability are likely to be prone to periods of severe sexual frustration. Several people commented that other forms of frustration were more prominent in their awareness than those of a sexual nature. As would be expected, men reported sexual frustration more often than women (25 percent versus 18 percent). It should be noted that 20 men and six women did not answer this question for a variety of reasons. Two women pointed out that their sexual frustration occurred within marriage because their husbands were frequently too tired to want to have intercourse. In fact, the reported frequency of intercourse of these couples is lower than in other studies of sexual behavior, perhaps indicating the considerable extra effort required by cerebral palsied people to deal with the other daily activities of their marriages.

About a quarter of both men and women said that they had had some experience of sexual intercourse before marriage. These figures are, of course, open to considerable error, but several couples mentioned that their past experiences had helped them to reach a satisfactory technique in their current marriage. These figures include those who had been previously married.

When it comes to premarital intercourse with their current partner, a third of the couples had had sexual intercourse but 44 percent had had only very little physical contact with each other. The main reason given by the couples for not having premarital intercourse was for moral or religious reasons. lack of opportunity was reported very little. It seems likely that for those who wish for privacy before marriage this is available, when the social climate in which the couple lives is conducive to marriage in the first place.

Although 80 percent of the couples were eventually able to consummate their marriages, 45 percent reported that when they first tried to have intercourse, they had some difficulties. It should be said that cerebral palsy does not effect the functions of the genital organs. The sexual difficulties of the cerebral palsied are related to their inability to position and move the body appropriately. The "missionary position", judging from the couples who talked about their problems in this area, seems to be one of the most difficult positions for a couple with cerebral palsy. Some initial problems were not connected with the couples's disability but rather with those factors encountered frequently when a virgin couple attempt intercourse after a long period of restraint, following the excitement and exhaustion of a wedding. The duration of these initial sexual problems was generally short: 20 percent were resolved in a week and almost another 50 percent within a month. However, about 20 percent continued to have problems after a year.

Of those who had longer-term sexual difficulties, 15 couples answered the question concerning alternative methods of sexual gratification. Seven of these couples used some method, usually manual or oral stimulation. Although the number is so small, several of these couples had some problems achieving mutual gratification; often one partner seemed more satisfied than the other. Mechanical aids were generally not used. Their limitations when set in a social context are obvious. One couple was referred to a counselling service by sensitive care staff in their residential home. The counselling was seen as very helpful by the couple concerned but they found it impossible to use the device suggested by the counselor because neither partner was able to secret the device away from the view of the staff and the wife just could not face the staff seeing it. Several women reported lubrication problems with the use of vibrators.

Congenitally disabled people do not expect that physical activities in which they engage are likely to be without problems. Sexual intercourse is, therefore, not expected to be without its problems.

In view of the tendency towards late marriage in this group a comment by one couple about their sexual relationship seems opposite:

> If you're young you expect it all at once, but if you are a little older you have more respect for each other and you know a relationship can have time to grow.

Couples were rather varied in their response to books as a source of information to solve sexual difficulties. Some had found these helpful, but others pointed out that there is no readily available literature specifically designed for the disabled, and the suggestions in some of the manuals aimed at the able-bodied couple served only to enhance the feeling of inadequacy of the couple. For one man this was quite a problem. He was only able to have intercourse in one position and because of reading books on the subject, he felt that he was failing his wife in some way because of this.

The overwhelming message from the couples who were interviewed was:

> Talk to each other, then do your own thing and don't try to compete.

In fact, of the 70 couples answering the question about the use of books, two-thirds had not used them for information about sex compared to a third who had. Of course, it must be said that in general this group had only low average educational attainments and, as they

would probably not have look to books for information about other topics, they might not be expected to do so for sexual information.

Very few of the couples had taken any advice about their sexual difficulties. Doctors were generally seen as the most appropriate people to talk to: 10 to 15 percent of both men and women had discussed sex with a doctor.

The use and efficiency of contraceptives is obviously very important to married couples where one or other or both is disabled. The presence of a child may upset a delicate balance of complementary caring. A residential center is not, at the present time, an adequate place to bring up a child. However, just over a third of the couples used no contraceptive. These included one couple who said that they did not wish to have further children and had sexual intercourse, on average, twice a week.

One woman in five was taking the contraceptive pill. Those currently on the pill were happy with it but, as would be expected in any sample of women, some had experienced side effects. Some wheelchair bound women were very positive about the effects of the pill in reducing their periods and so increasing their comfort.

About 10 percent of men and 20 percent of women had been sterilized. Men seemed able to see vasectomy in a positive light. One man said, "I was sterilized. I saw it as a creative act of love to enable us to have a full sex life." The women, however, had much greater difficulties in accepting the long-term implications of sterilization. This is an area fraught with difficulties. We are quite sure that from the viewpoint of professional people, many of these women had received detailed counseling before their sterilization operations, but it is also true that most reported unhappiness and a feeling of having been manipulated into sterilization. In some cases, the women had been quite unable to accept their sexuality in isolation from their capacity to have children and had ceased to have intercourse. Even young women with severe disabilities who intellectually accept the necessity for sterilization seem to need to express some mourning for their loss of child-bearing capacity. This is true even of those women who decided to be sterilized rather than their husbands because they felt that in the future he might be in a position to have children by another woman. This is obviously an area where great care and sensitivity are needed.

Although marriage no longer necessarily entails parenthood, the bearing and upbringing of children is an option available to couples. There are role expectations connected with the status of parent which it may be difficult for people with disabilities to fulfill. Attitudes towards the disabled as parents are perceived by people with disabilities as often very negative. Parents of people with disabilities, while accepting marriage for their children, often express greater concern when parenthood is suggested.

Forty-one percent of the couples had a child, but few had more than one child. This is obviously a somewhat lower birth rate than in the general population when length of marriage is taken into account.

The couples studied varied considerably in degree of disability they had to contend with. The difficulties which parents experienced in rearing children were varied, but two peak periods of problems seemed to be the general pattern. Usually the care of the tiny baby and toddler can be very difficult, although some problems were solved quite simply, for example, by the daily provision of a home helper to bath a small baby. The myth that all children of parents who are disabled come to appreciate their parents' problems and cooperate with operations such as diaper changing should be dispelled. It does happen but should never be relied on.

The second peak of problems occurs in the teenage years. Here children are beginning to identify with the peer group and often have a strong desire to conform to the norms of its culture. They look to the family for status and may find the disability of parents very difficult to accept at this time.

One must, of course, place the problems of parents with disabilities in the context of all parental problems. Very few child-rearing experiences are likely to be without stress or anxiety at some time. Even so, it is probably true to say that parents with disabilities will have to face some extra heartache in their relationship with their children at some stage. This may not be

until adulthood, when (as in one case) a marriage partner was unable to accept the mother's now more severe disability.

Until disability has no implication of lower status, but is seen merely as a physical incapacity, relationships with a child who may be looking to the family to enhance his own status are likely to be difficult.

In conclusion, the picture that emerges of these married couples is that they lead very similar lives to other married couples of similar age and social class. The standard of the households in which they live show a generally high degree of social competence, 50 percent being at least average and 30 percent being well above average in household care. Most of the marital relationships appeared harmonious, although no validated test of marital harmony was used and it is possible (as mentioned earlier) that those who refused to take part in the survey had had particularly difficult experiences. Although those married to able-bodied people were underrepresented in the final sample, there is some evidence to suggest that these relationships, especially between an able-bodied man and a disabled woman, are more difficult. However, this is not always so, as one husband of a now retired couple made clear: "She's a woman, not a bit of furniture. We have our up's and down's but I married her because I though the world of her."

From most of the couples there was an overwhelming sense of achievement of mutual caring and belonging. People with disabilities are not necessarily saints and are no easier, one may assume, to live with then others, but we shall finish with some quotations from these couples which serve to illustrate their overall philosophy towards marriage:

"Give it time——things do work out but not necessarily to plan, live each day as it comes and make the most of it."
"Be together——face up to the fact you're disabled and live within it."
"If two people love each other enough to get married, material and physical difficulties can be overcome."

Sexual and Personal Relationships of the Mastectomee

Betty Westgate, M.B.E.

Initially it may be helpful to define a mastectomy. It is the surgical removal of the breast. There are three main types of operations; a radical mastectomy, when the breast tissue, under arm glands and the muscle of the upper part of the chest are removed. The modified radical——often referred to as a radical today——when the breast and under arm glands are removed, and the simple mastectomy when the surgeon removes the breast tissue, and one or two glands for investigation. Modern surgical techniques have enabled many surgeons to make a horizontal incision (the bikini incision) and carry out the mastectomy. When final healing takes place the chest wall is flat - with a single line scar, but with the nipple and the natural curved contour on the opposite side of the chest wall. Often a woman does not know exactly what is involved prior to a mastectomy, and her imagination can run riot, causing additional distress. This can be overcome, quite simply, by pre-op counselling.

The Women's Problems: As well as facing the fact that she has had breast cancer, a woman wonders whether her emotional feelings will be similar to those when she was physically complete. Will she feel and remain sexually attractive? Will her partner accept or reject her changed appearance? Will she too be able to accept this change?

The Man's Problems: What will the physical appearance be like?——without previous knowledge his imagination can be equally as distorted as that of his partner. He too should receive pre- and post-op counseling.

The man wonders when he should 'approach' his partner——consideration and common sense are necessary. Too soon and he's afraid of causing physical discomfort, to delay may be misinterpreted and give a false impression of his feelings toward her.

Do Problems Really Exist? With the right partner, far less than anticipated. Many have expected problems——only to find that the mastectomy brought them closer.

Sexual emotions spring from within and are the expression of sexual needs, also love.

The lowering of one's self esteem can so easily be passed on to others. To hold one's head up high gains respect.

Many areas of the body are involved in sexual satisfaction. Initially, gentle fondling and caressing, and taking a lead from the woman——often, she guides his hands——can lead to sexual fulfillment.

Adopting a different position——even something as simple as changing sides of the bed can be helpful and make the situation easier to cope with.

When a mastectomee is asked "If your man had a disfiguring operation would you be repelled by his appearance?"——the answer is so often "of course not." Then why expect his attitude toward you to change?——it shows little real confidence in the strength of the partnership.

In most cases, a mastectomy not only brings partners closer, but a greater appreciation of each other develops, but if the partnership is already unsatisfactory, a mastectomy can be used, by either partner, as an excuse to terminate the relationship.

One woman found that her boyfriend "vanished in a cloud of dust" when he realized what had occurred. Later, she met a man who wanted her for herself regardless of the situation——as she said, "it separates the men from the boys and who wants a boy?" When the first hurdle was reached in marriage, the first man would probably have failed to cope anyway. Very few men seem concerned for themselves, but for the lives and well being of their partners. Few of us are physically perfect.

Problems of the Woman Alone: The single woman——the widow——the divorcee and the woman whose marriage exists in name alone have their own particular problems, especially the unsatisfactory marriage. The husband may deliberately taunt and so hurt his wife.

Reprinted from: *Sexuality and Disability, Volume 3, Number 3, Fall 1980, 0146-1044/80/1500-0162 $00.95 ©
1980 Human Sciences Press,* with permission.

The love and understanding and support of family and friends help tremendously, but when it comes to reality, it is up to the woman herself to come to terms with the situation in her own personal way.

Boyfriends play an important part in restoring confidence in the existence of sexual adequacy.

Individuals vary greatly. One widow was relieved that her husband had not lived to see her "disfigurement; "another wished that "he had lived to support her at her time of great need."

Involving the Family. Children of the family need to be told of the situation; explanations should be expressed according to the age of the children——in simple, unemotional explanations, remembering that children are logical, but can easily "pick up" adult emotion. Parents know their own children and must act accordingly, but for a child to be informed of its mother's mastectomy by others can shatter family confidence.

A mother sought advice regarding telling her 11-year-old son of her mastectomy, and was advised against this. But "little pigs have long ears," and children of her friends heard discussions and during a playground argument he was told "Your mother only has one tit"——playground language is very basic——this he hotly denied; when he taxed his mother with this she had to tell him of her mastectomy, so the next day he had to admit that his friends were right. This incident caused a rift in family confidence which took a very long time to heal. His mother regretted her decision to avoid telling her son the truth very much.

Another woman showed her young daughter her prosthesis and explained that it took the palace of her breast which the doctor had removed because it "was bad." She let the child feel the flat area through her nightdress——later the child asked to see it and was pleased and surprised to find that the scar wasn't round——like the prothesis.

Another mastectomee, the mother of four young children, waited until the scar was less obvious, then resumed her normal practice of leaving the bathroom door open. Her four year old son wandered into the bathroom and said, "You are a Mummy side but a Daddy the other". The family gathered, and she explained that when a tooth is bad the dentist takes it away and if tonsils or appendix are troublesome the doctor takes them away, and that Mummy's breast had been troublesome so the doctor had decided to take it away, and in a flash of inspiration added, "Wasn't it wonderful to think that the surgeon was able to do this and leave a single line scar?"———leaving the children with a feeling of wonder——not fear. She had rehearsed what would be said many times——expecting tears from all including herself——but had forgotten that children are essentially practical and can see reason when well presented. Teenagers need extra help to enable them to accept the situation———they are emotionally involved——both as developing adults and with their mother's loss.

The Ostomist——Self Image and Sexual Problems

BRIDGET SNOW

To be told that you must live the rest of your life with a piece of intestine protruding from your abdomen, continually voiding waste matter into a bag, is extremely distressing, to say the least. Although there can be no true concept beforehand of what it will be like, the reality after the operation can be more daunting than the mind had envisaged, and an over-riding fear is of how your partner is going to react. Your previous self-image is badly shaken. Will you smell? Will the bag show? Are people going to shun you? Will you still be loved? Will you still be wanted sexually or should you insist on your partner being "released" to find sexual pleasure elsewhere, because how can anyone overlook such an unnatural mutilation?

And if you are single, how do you explain to someone who wishes literally to get to grips with you? What do you say and when? Do you tell them before the affair becomes serious, or do you wait and allow the involvement to grow, in order that there might be a better chance of acceptance?

These are the constant thoughts and fears of the new ostomist, but on the whole, these problems do vanish with time and experience. A large part of the remedy is to see and meet other ostomists, who are obviously living normal lives with their partners and who are not clothed in baggy garments, or smelling furtively in lonely corners. The mechanical problems have straightforward solutions, in that the right appliance to suit individual needs is found; sore skin is coped with and prevented, and so on.

During lovemaking, as long as the bag is empty and flat, it will neither become dislodged nor get in the way and the stoma will not be damaged. A bag cover can be worn if wished, or the bag can be rolled up and taped down.

The enormity of the situation dwindles, the constant over-awareness fades and life with a stoma takes on its correct perspective. You begin to feel with relief, and a certain gladness of heart, that you are still the person you want to be. The stoma becomes a triviality and when you, the ostomist, see it and treat it as such, others will take the cue from you and see it in a similar light. If you are casual about being an ostomist, others will be; if you see yourself as second-rate, others will conclude that you are. Of course, there are people who reject anyone with a blemish because they are seeking perfection, but this is life and they will have very few friends.

Unfortunately, although the majority of ostomists do regain their self-esteem and continue their lives as before and in better health, there are those who perhaps have never had the chance. They may have been sent home from hospital with unsuitable appliances which they dare not trust, or which smell; their skin may have become badly excoriated and they become isolated or, understandably, choose to withdrew from society. Recent publicity about the Ileostomy Association in a magazine brought in hundreds of enquiries from such ostomists who have been suffering needlessly.

Apart from the problems of self-image which affect most ostomists initially to some extent, a minority do have more serious problems of sexual dysfunction. The most common are those of men who are unable to get any erection at all, or only partial erection. During surgery in the rectal area, the nerves governing erection and ejaculation may be unavoidably damaged, leaving the man without an erection but able to ejaculate, or capable of erection but no ejaculation or orgasm. That there has been damage may not be apparent until the man has returned home and tried to resume his sexual relationship. The nerves may regenerate for up to two and a half years after the operation, but if there has been no improvement in that time, the damage is permanent. Sometimes the man is told of the risk or the likelihood beforehand, or the surgeon may explain afterwards. Sometimes he is left to find out for himself.

Reprinted From: *Sexuality and Disability, Volume 3, Number 3, Fall 1980, 0146-1044/80/1500-0156 $00.95* ©*1980, Human Sciences Press*, with permission.

The important thing for such ostomists is to reassure them that although intercourse is difficult or impossible, this does not mean that their sex-lives have come to an end. They and their partners can still give and receive pleasure and satisfaction by making love with their hands, or by using their mouth, lips and tongues. There is a variety of sex-aids available, and it is also becoming increasingly possible for suitable candidates to have a penile implant inserted surgically.

Women seem to have fewer problems, and the remedy is very often simply to change positions for intercourse. For both, but especially for the male ostomist, if they can accept that the usual form of intercourse is no longer possible and make the most of the alternatives, it can be the start of a new and very good relationship.

1982 Literary Award Winning Paper
Sexual Counseling in Cardiac Rehabilitation

MARY ELLEN MITCHELL

You have just experienced one of the most frightening medical conditions in modern society——a heart attack. After you realize you are going to survive——this time——you begin to consider other concerns precipitated by this crisis——medical, vocational, financial, social, and interpersonal. Your mind turns to that special area of pleasure and intimacy, sexual relations. Fears emerge. Can I ever have sex again? Will sexual exertion kill me or cause another heart attack? Will sex cause pain? Will my partner reject me now that I am weak and dependent? Will I lose my desire for sex? Will I lose my ability to experience sexual pleasure and give pleasure to my partner? What are the facts? Who can answer these questions?

Unfortunately, research has shown that physicians do not usually address the sexual issues of heart patients effectively and that this leads to an adjustment often significantly below what patients are capable of achieving. Current literature supports the concept that sexual counseling for cardiac patients is a necessary part of the rehabilitation process, and that sexual activity can be resumed by most people following myocardial infarctions.

Research

Masters and Johnson (1966) commented briefly on problems associated with advising coronary patients about the resumption of sexual activity, identifying questions which needed to be researched. How much strain does sexual tension put on the heart? How do coitus and masturbation compare in cardiac stress? What sexual techniques are effective with the least strain on the heart?

In a landmark study, Hellerstein and Friedman (1969, 1970) reported that a review of 33 cardiology textbooks revealed almost no information concerning the subject. A summary of available research confirms that little research on the sexual activity of coronary patients was done prior to their study. Only two articles are important enough to mention.

One was done in Japan by Ueno (cited in Hellerstein & Friedman, 1970), who reported that only 34 out of 5,559 cases (.6%) of sudden deaths occurred as a result of coitus. Only half (.3% overall) were due to heart disease, and they occurred most often in extramarital sexual encounters. In research and reports within the past decade, numerous authors (Abbott & McWhirter, 1978; Friedman, 1978; Green, 1975; Gulledge, 1975; Masur, 1979; Wagner, 1975) have cited as evidence that the chances of a heart attack as the result of coitus, particularly within a marital unit, are very small, thereby dispelling part of a myth that has limited physicians' advice and patients' activity.

In the second study, Tuttle, Cook, and Fitch (1964) interviewed men attending a cardiac work evaluation unit about their sexual activity. All had experienced myocardial infarctions one to nine years before the interview. Two thirds reported receiving no advice about sex from their physicians, and one third reported receiving advice that was "vague and unspecific" (p. 140). Only one third of the subjects had resumed their precoronary pattern of sexual activity, while two thirds experienced a significant and lasting reduction in frequency and 10% reported impotence. Tuttle et al. concluded:

> Having received little or no advice from their physicians, these patients set their own patterns which represented a considerable deviation from their previous sexual activity. Our interviews suggested that this change in behavior was based on misinformation and fear. (1964, p. 140)

The authors admonished physicians to address the issue more specifically.

However, it was not until after the changes in sexual attitudes in the late 1960s and the pioneering work of Master and Johnson in sex research

Reprinted from: Journal of Rehabilitation, Oct/Nov/Dec 1982, with permission.

that Hellerstein and Friedman (1969, 1970) conducted their study of the amount of stress put on the post myocardial infarction heart during sexual intercourse. Masters and Johnson (1966) documented physical changes during the sexual act that might contraindicate sexual activities for heart patients, including high heart rates (170-180 beats per minute). Hellerstein and Friedman speculated that these rates might be lower for older male patients with heart disease who had intercourse in the privacy of their bedrooms with their wives of 20 or more years. A total of 48 subjects with heart disease were participants in a physical reconditioning program. The mean number of orgasms per week for these subjects had declined from 2.1 before the coronary event to 1.6 after the event. Reasons for this decline included lessening of desire, wife's decision, depression, fear, and coronary symptoms. None of the participants reported impotence.

The subjects were fitted with portable ECG devices and monitored for 24 to 48 hours. Of the 48 subjects, 14 engaged in intercourse during the monitoring period. For these men, the mean maximal heart rate was 117.4 beats per minute (range 90-144). The heart rate rose rapidly before orgasm and fell rapidly afterwards, and the time of maximum heart stress was 10 to 15 seconds at most. The authors compared the cardiac cost of this sexual activity with other activities of the subjects and found that the mean maximal heart rate at work (120.1 beats per minute) slightly exceeded that of sexual activity. The authors conclude that sex is similar in cost to "climbing a flight of stairs, walking briskly, or performing ordinary tasks in many occupations" (Hellerstein & Friedman, 1970, p. 997). They suggest that sexual activity can be resumed if the patient can engage in "exercise at 6 to 8 calories per minute...without symptoms, abnormal pulse rate, or blood pressure or ECG changes" (p. 998). They recommend prophylactic drugs and exercise for symptomatic patients.

Four articles completed after Hellerstein and Friedman's report address the evaluation of sexual activity after a myocardial infarction, the concerns of the patients, and the attitudes of their physicians.

Bloch et al. (1975) surveyed 88 males and 12 females (mean age 58 years) on their pre- and postcoronary activity at an average of 11 months after an acute myocardial infarction. Mean frequency of intercourse was reduced from 5.2 to 2.7 per month, although most patients had returned to normal levels of activity in other areas. Reasons for the decline in frequency include "decrease in sexual desire, anxiety, wife's decision, fear of relapse or of sudden death, fatigue, angina, and impotence" (p. 536).

Of 107 male myocardial infarction patients interviewed by Amsterdam et al. (1977), 53% had resumed previous levels of intercourse, 43% had decreased frequency or were abstaining, and only 4% had increased frequency. Problems during intercourse included angina (16%), dyspnea (32%), and impotence (49%). Only 40% of the patients had discussed with their physicians return to sexual activity. Physicians initiated discussions with only 21%, although 65*5 of the patients expressed a desire for such information. Fear of resuming sexual activity was reported by 43%. The authors stress that patients' needs for sexual counselling were not being adequately met.

Similarly, Krop et al. (1979) interviewed 100 married male patients, at a Veterans Administration hospital, who had suffered myocardial infarctions. The interviews took place before discharge from the hospital. Some 49% feared sexual activity would harm them, and 51% were worried about their marital relations. Discussion of sexual activity was initiated by the physician in only 16% of the cases, while in 20% discussion was initiated by the patient. No discussion was held with 64% of the patients, although 66% expressed concerns about resuming sexual activity, including pain or discomfort (43%), impotency (41%), more difficulty for patient or partner (34%), decreased desire (28%), premature ejaculation (24%), retarded ejaculation (23%), partner's decreased desire (17%), and partner's feeling guilty (18%).

Mehta and Krop (1979) interviewed the same population six months after discharge. At that point, 30% had not resumed intercourse, including 24% who had not resumed any shared sexual activity. Those who had intercourse at least once a week dropped from 72% before their myocardical infarctions to 29%. Reasons for this decrease were inability to maintain or obtain an erection(39%), chest pain (28%), lack of physical fitness (28%), lack of desire (19%), fear of another heart attack (16%), boredom (15%), depression (14%), change in opportunity (10%), physician's advice (10%), self-advice (5%), and partner's decision (2%).

These four articles have been reported in detail to emphasize the fact that , despite Hellerstein's and Friedman's (1969, 1970) encouraging report, the problems reported by Tuttle et al. in 1964 are still being reported in the most recent surveys. This is surprising and disturbing since several textbooks and numerous journal articles appeared in the 1970s describing sexual counselling for postcoronary patients. Friedman (1978) examines the possible reasons behind this lack of communication. These include a conservative bias until more research information is reported, the physician's own discomfort with sexuality, constraints on the time a physician has to talk to the patient about sexual concerns, and ineffective communication due to discomfort of physician and patient. Friedman emphasizes that

> it remains the responsibility of the physician to take the initiative and begin sexual counseling when needed. This requires time, openness, empathy, sexual knowledge, and an acceptance of the importance of sex. (1978, p. 376)

He recommends referrals to other professionals when the physician is unable to satisfy these requirements.

Sexual Counselling

Cohen, Wallston, and Wallston (1976) interviewed 17 former cardiac patients and their spouses. They found that questions about sexual activity resolve themselves in some way (positively or negatively) about three to four months after hospitalization; therefore sexual counselling and information should be initiated either during hospitalization or immediately thereafter.

Before initiating sexual counselling, a number of authors recommend assessment of the client's status. Factors to be assessed include:

1. Pre-illness level of sexual activity (Abbott & McWhirter, 1978; Friedman, 1978; Green, 1975; Hellerstein & Friedman, 1970; Koller, Kennedy, Butler, & Wagner, 1972; Wagner, 1975).
2. Effects of aging (Friedman, 1978; Hellerstein & Friedman, 1970).
3. Spouse's health and attitudes (Green, 1975; Hellerstein & Friedman, 1970).
4. Psychologic factors like depression or anxiety (Friedman, 1978; Green, 1975; Gulledge, 1975; Hellerstein & Friedman, 1970).
5. Psysiologic functions including cardiovascular response to treatment, general health, extent of recovery, severity of damage, and frequency of pain or arrhythmias (Abbott & McWhirter, 1978; Friedman, 1978; Green, 1975; Hellerstein & Friedman, 1970; Koller et al., 1972; Wagner, 1975).

Since Hellerstein and Friedman (1970) suggested that sex was similar to climbing stairs, walking briskly, or many work tasks, some authors have tried to establish simple tests of cardiovascular fitness for sexual activity. Friedman (1978) fears that walking up a flight of stairs may be too generalized. Abbott and McWhirter (1978), Koller et al. (1972), and Wagner (1975) adopt Hellerstein and Friedman's (1970) criteria. Eliot and Miles (1975) recommend a tape recording of the electrocardiogram during sex. Semmler and Semmler (1974) set the limits at expenditures of six to eight calories per minute without abnormal pulse rate, blood pressure, or ECG but do not specify how this information can be obtained. Elster and Mansfield (1977) researched a two-flight step test and determined that the climbing activity did not reach the levels exerted during sex. They concluded, therefore, that the test was not an accurate predictor of cardiovascular function but could still be used to make a rough estimate.

In specifying the conditions under which sexual activity should be undertaken, Eliot and Miles (1975), Hellerstein and Friedman (1970), and Wagner (1975) recommend that sex with new partners be avoided. Griffith (1973) recommends avoiding secretive or anxiety-producing situations. Many others suggest avoiding temperature extremes and waiting three hours following a meal or alcohol consumption (Abbott & Mcwhirter, 1978; Griffith, 1973; Masur, 1979; Semmler & Semmler, 1974). Griffith (1973) and Masur (1979) recommend sex in the morning with rest periods before and after. Masur (1979) and Semmler and Semmler (1974) suggest avoiding emotional stress, and Masut (1979) adds fatigue to the list.

Contraindications to sexual activity include congestive heart failure and general debilitation (Friedman, 1978; Wagner, 1975). Abbott and Mcwhirter (1978) and Semmler and Semmler (1974) suggest reporting the following signs to the physician: (a) anginal pain during or after intercourse, (b) palpitation continuing more than 15 minutes after intercourse, (c) sleeplessness following sex, and (d) extreme fatigue the next day.

Hellerstein and Friedman's (1970) subjects were participating in an exercise program and may thus have benefited from improved tolerance. Eliot and Miles (1975) and Gulledge (1975) recommend a conditioning program when appropriate. Stein (1877) reports increased aerobic capacity and consequent reduction in peak coital heart rate in 16 men (ages 46-54) who participated in a 16 week bicycle ergometer training program 12 to 15 weeks after myocardial infarction. He suggests the use of such training to reduce the incidence of angina during intercourse.

There is some discrepancy in the positions recommended for intercourse. Masur (1979) suggests that the counselor must assess the precoronary style before making recommendations. Some evidence indicates that the male-on-top position is to be avoided because increased heart pressure is caused by the isometric exercise of the man supporting his weight with his arms (Eliot & Miles, 1975; Masur, 1979; Wagner, 1975). However, Griffith (1973) and Semmler and Semmler (1974) still recommend this position. Other positions suggested include female on top (Abbott & McWhirter, 1978; Wagner, 1975), side by side (Abbott & McWhirter, 1978; Griffith, 1973; Semmler &

Semmler, 1974; Wagner, 1975), and sitting in a low, wide chair (Abbott & McWhirter, 1978; Griffith, 1973; Semmler & Semmler, 1974). Abbott and McWhirter (1978) recommend that, if tension develops, the patient should breathe deeply to relax.

The use of medication, especially the prophylactic use of nitroglycerin for angina pain during intercourse, is widely accepted (Abbott & McWhirter, 1978; Eliot & Miles, 1975; Friedman, 1978; Koller et al., 1972; Semmler & Semmler, 1974; Wagner, 1975). However, Gulledge (1975) reports that impotence, diminished libido, and impaired ejaculation are possible side effects of antihypertensives, tranquilizers, ganglion block agents, depressants, and hypnotics. Should sexual dysfunction occur, the effects of these medications should be investigated.

Wagner (1975) reports a pilot study in progress to determine whether masturbation as an alternative to intercourse, particularly in the hospital, is within the acceptable range of heart activity. Preliminary finding indicate that, if the heart can tolerate a rate of up to 130 beats per minute, then it is within the limits required for masturbation. Abbott and Mcwhirter (1978) recommend sensate focus exercises——extensive caressing without demand for intercourse——as an alternative for the couple.

Several authors strongly feel that the counsellor or physician should work with the spouse as well as the patient (cohen et al., 1976; Koller et al., 1972; Wagner, 1975). Friedman (1978) warns of signs of stress, anxiety, and depression in the spouse. Green (1975) feels that the shift of "sexual aggressiveness" to the female may be traumatic and may lead to the avoidance of sex, overprotection, or resentment. If these occur, they may be dealt with in counselling.

Cole describes a method for providing sexual counselling for coronary patients. He recommends that the counselling begin before discharge from the hospital. Couples are followed by a counselling team (two psychologists, a social worker, and a minister) for approximately eight sessions, including those in the hospital and monthly outpatient visits. Two underlying principles guide the team. First, plans for resuming sexual intimacy are explored with the couple together and, second, the counsellor's goal is to assist couples in achieving their pre-illness level of activities. Three basic steps are recommended in the counselling process:

1. Providing accurate information on the effects of heart disease on sexual functioning, including written material.
2. Providing support for the marital relationship by encouraging couples to openly share their feelings and fears about the traumatic illness they are experiencing.
3. Describing permisible sexual behaviors, including touching, caressing, body massage, and holding hands.

Cole (1979) suggests an exercise tolerance test at eight weeks following discharge to determine if return to sexual and other activities is permissible. Having the spouse present helps assure a realistic understanding of the limits of acceptable activity. Resumption of sexual activities, if complications do not occur, can generally begin eight to 12 weeks following hospitalization.

Two articles of recent research need to be mentioned because of their impact on sexual counselling in general and the possible implications for the study and prevention of heart disease in particular. Wabrek and Burchell (1980) and Abramov (1976), in separate studies of men and women, respectively, found that significant levels of sexual dysfunction existed in their populations before the myocardial infarction. Wabrek and Burchell (1980), after interviewing 131 male patients (ages 31-86), discovered that two-thirds reported significant sexual dysfunction before their heart attacks. Among those reporting problems, 64% were impotent, 28% had significantly decreased sexual frequency, and 8% had premature ejaculations. In a survey of 100 female myocardial infarction patients, Abramov (1976) found sexual frigidity and dissatisfaction among 64%, compared with 24% of the control group. Although the relationship between sexual stress and cardiac problems is not conclusive, the implication can be drawn that increased stress in the sexual aspects of living, as well as in other areas, without appropriate release of this stress, may well by unhealthy.

Healthy sexual functioning is an appropriate goal for any individual who desires to share mutual physical pleasure and intimacy with another person. Wabrek and Burchell (1980) hypothesize that counselling to help patients achieve the levels of functioning they had before their myocardial infarctions may not be enough. Participation in sexual activity that relieves stress and produces relaxation and comfort may be an appropriate therapeutic goal for the prevention of the first or subsequent myocardial infarctions.

Conclusion

Research has shown that, even with more recent information regarding the limits of activity which can be tolerated, physicians are as unprepared or as unwilling today to be involved in sexual counselling with cardiac patients as they were in 1964. Although research into the area is still sketchy, enough reliable information exists to make cautious recommendations for a return to sexual activity, with specific recommendations for determining readiness for such activity, methods of reducing cardiac stress during intercourse, and problems which might occur. As in all counselling with couples, it is imperative to see the cardiac patient and spouse as a functioning sexual unit and to accept their own values and preferences as right for them. However, a benefit of the sexual counselling may be more closeness and increased sharing as a result of more open communication by the couple. Appropriate sexual counselling should be an integral part of any rehabilitation program for the cardiac patient.

References

Abbott, M.A., & McWhirter, D.P. Resuming sexual activity after myocardial infarction. **Medical Aspects of Human Sexuality,** 1978, **12**(6), 18-28.
Abramov, L.A. Sexual life and sexual frigidity among women developing acute myocardial infarction. **Psychosomatic Medicine,** 1976, **38**, 418-425.
Amsterdam, E.A., Amsterdam, G.L., Riggs, K., DeMaria, A.N., & Mason, D.T. Sexual counseling and sexual activity after myocardial infarction: Patient attitudes and physician response. **Clinical Research,** 1977, **25**, 86A.

Bloch, A., Maeder, J.P., & Haissly, J.C. Sexual problems after myocardial infarction. **American Heart Journal,** 1975, **90,** 536-537.

Cohen, B.D., Wallston, B.S. & Wallston, K.A. Sex counseling in cardiac rehabilitation. **Archives of Physical Medicine and Rehabilitation,** 1976, **57,** 473-474.

Cole, C.M. A treatment strategy for postmyocardial sexual dysfunction. **Sexuality and Disability,** 1979, **2,** 122-129.

Eliot, R.S., & Miles, R.R. Advising the cardiac patient about sexual intercourse. **Medical Aspects of Human Sexuality,** 1975, **9**(6), 49-50.

Elster, S.E., & Mansfield, L.W. Stair climbing as a test of readiness for resumption of sexual activity after heart attack (abstracted). **Circulation,** 1977, Vols. 55 and 56, Supp. III, p.102.

Friedman, J.M. Sexual adjustment of the postcoronary male. In J. LoPiccolo & L. LoPiccolo (Eds.), **Handbook of sex therapy.** New York: Plenum Press, 1978.

Green, A.W. Sexual activity and the postmyocardial infarction patient. **American Heart Journal,** 1975, **89,** 246-252.

Griffith, G.C. Sexuality and the cardiac patient. **Heart and Lung,** 1973, **2,** 70-73.

Gulledge, A.D. The psychological aftermath of a myocardial infarction. In W.D. Gentry & R.B. Williams, Jr. (Eds.), **Psychological aspects of myocardial infarction and coronary care.** St. Louis: C.V. Mosby, 1975.

Hellerstein, H.K., & Friedman, E.H. Sexual activity and the postcoronary patient. **Medical Aspects of Human Sexuality,** 1969, **3**(3), 70-96.

Hellerstein, H.K. & Friedman, E.H. Sexual activity and the postcoronary patient. **Archives of Internal Medicine,** 1970, **125,** 987-999.

Koller, R., Kennedy, K.W., Butler, J.C., & Wagner, N.N. Counseling the coronary patient on sexual activity. **Postgraduate Medicine,** 1972, **51**(4), 133-136.

Krop, H., Hall, D., & Mehta, J. Sexual concerns after myocardial infarction. **Sexuality and Disability,** 1979, **2,** 91-97.

Masters, W.H., & Johnson, V.E. **Human sexual response.** Boston: Little, Brown and Co., 1966.

Masur, F.T. Resumption of sexual activity following myocardial infarction. **Sexuality and Disability,** 1979, **2,** 98-114.

Mehta, J. & Krop, H. The effect of myocardial infarction on sexual functioning. **Sexuality and Disability,** 1979, **2,** 115-121.

Semmler, C., & Semmler, M. Counseling the coronary patient. **American Journal of Occupational Therapy,** 1974, **28,** 609-614.

Stein, R.A. The effect of exercise training on heart rate during coitus in the post myocardial infarction patient. **Circulation,** 1977, **55,** 738-740.

Tuttle, W.B., Cook, W.L., & Fitch, E. Sexual behavior in postmyocardial infarction patients. **American Journal of Cardiology,** 1964, **13,** 140.

Wabrek, A.J., & Burchell, R.C. Male sexual dysfunction associated with coronary heart disease. **Archives of Sexual Behavior,** 1980, **9,** 69-75.

Wagner, N.N. Sexual activity and the cardiac patient. In R. Green (Ed.), **Human sexuality: A health practitioner's text.** Baltimore: William & Wilkins, 1975.

Mary Ellen Mitchell is a doctoral student in counseling and human development at the University of Georgia where she received her masters degree in rehabilitation counseling in 1978. She obtained her bachelors degree in English from Duke University in 1971. Her experience in rehabilitation includes two years at a private nonprofit facility for visually handicapped persons and three years as director of vocational evaluation and rehabilitation director at Chattanooga Goodwill Industries.

Facing the Challenges of Sexual Abuse in Persons with Disabilities

SANDRA S. COLE, AASECT,CSE,CSC

Definition

Child abuse has been defined in the literature to include any act of commission or omission that endangers or impairs a child's physical or emotional health and development. It may be evidenced by an injury or series of injuries appearing to be non-accidental in nature and which cannot reasonably be explained. The most frequently recognized forms of child abuse are physical abuse (including neglect or lack of adequate supervision) emotional abuse or deprivation and sexual abuse.

All children, unfortunately, are candidates to experience sexual abuse. This includes children who were born with or have acquired a disability. They may be living in foster homes or institutions or with their families.

Sexual abuse can consist of visual, physical or verbal aggression which can be perceived as unwanted sexual activity. This is particularly true about the victim who is less than the age of consent. Sexual assault or abuse includes any form of unwanted sexual touching, nonconsensual sexual intercourse, other ongoing sexual exploitation, or perhaps isolated incidences of physical harassment which is experienced as sexual intent.

The Illusion Theatre in Minneapolis, Minnesota defines sexual abuse as occurring when a person is "manipulated, tricked or forced into touch or sexual contact." A helpful definition of sexual abuse to use with children is: forced or tricked touch or sex. This touch can begin anywhere on your body and may mean the person touches your breasts, buttocks, the vagina or penis. Sexual abuse can also involve oral, anal or vaginal penetration. Rape is sexual abuse with penetration. For children, a way to discuss penetration is to say that one part of a person's body (finger, tongue or penis) goes into a part of another person's body (vagina, anus, mouth).

Penetration may occur with an object or a body part.

There is also sexual abuse without touch as when someone forces or tricks another person to look at their genitals or forces or tricks an individual into exposing his or her own genitals. Another type of sexual abuse without touch is an obscene phone call, as when a person calls and talks about sex (ways he/she wants to touch a person's body or be touched him/herself).

Sexual abuse of children involves someone too young to give informed consent but who has been involved in a sexual act. The exploitation of an individual who lacks adequate information to recognize such a situation or who is unable to understand or communicate is also labelled sexual abuse (i.e., the mentally or physically disabled children).

Sexual abuse or assault is a violation of the whole person and is not restricted to "just a sexual act." It results in indignation and an overwhelming sense of violation and invasion which can affect the victim in a physical, psychological and social way. Frequently, the aftermath of the assault or abuse is more severe than the actual event. This is particularly true of disabled individuals who cannot (or do not) access support systems and services that may be available.

It is a crime committed by adults who have forgotten or not adequately learned that it is their responsibility to protect children or to respect the privacy and integrity of another person. These adults instead force or coerce their victims into sexual encounters, the specifics and ramifications of which are beyond their comprehension. For many reasons, these victims cannot resist what they perceive as the authority of the offender.

The effects of these crimes may be short-term, but in many cases there is virtually irreparable psychological harm done to the victim. Sexual exploitation, molestation and incest are

Reprinted from: *Sexuality and Disability, Volume 7, Numbers 3/4, Fall/Winter 1984-86,* © *1986 Human Sciences Press*, with permission.

devastating types of abuse. Some explanation will clarify here that victims include children but also frequently include women, adolescents, the disabled (physically or intellectually) and the female sexual partners of aggressive dominant men, especially if fear of abandonment because of children is involved. The societal taboos surrounding this type of abuse have kept it from widespread exposure. Until recently, it has received very little publicity, helping to keep it a hidden form of abuse. The media is now daily recording such events and demanding our attention.

The nature of sexual abuse also makes it difficult to observe and therefore more threatening to report. The guidelines given for its detection are by no means comprehensive. Several publications are now available in the literature to assist and guide the public and professionals in recognizing signs and symptoms of sexual abuse. These symptoms may exist singly or in various combinations of behavior and attitude as well as physical manifestations.

Illusion Theatre reminds us that it is important to remember that this form of abuse can make a child or individual both a victim and a prisoner. Those who seek help are often accused of lying. This results in embarrassment, fear, shame and confusion. Society particularly does not want to accept the fact that disabled persons have become victims of abuse, assault or rape. The assumption that this is unthinkable creates even more difficulty for persons with disabilities to receive specific services which could help to protect them. Many people perceive the disabled as asexual or not eligible to receive the attention of others in a sexual way. These resistant attitudes are pervasive and also exist in agencies, facilities, courts, homes and police stations. This disbelief can result in unnecessary questioning and pressure on the victim, adding yet another burden of victimization.

A Perspective

As children, we are taught to obey adults and persons in authority. In addition, victims of sexual abuse are often pressured into secrecy about sexual activity by the abuser, leaving the victim feeling helpless and guilty about the behavior. Victims often perceive that they have no place to turn for help and no acceptable way out. Frequently, they have been coerced, manipulated, bribed or threatened. Frequently they are filled with feelings of self-blame, fear and, for the physically disabled, increased concerns about being repulsive to others.

Children, adults with disabilities, intellectually impaired individuals and those in institutions can experience feelings of social powerlessness which make them particularly vulnerable to exploitation and they may not be able to exert their will against the will of the offender. In some cases, the victim does not fully understand what is happening because of intellectual limitations, a lack of experience, or a lack of knowledge. It is also recognized that powerlessness of children, disabled or otherwise limited individuals is socially legitimized and even supported. Isolation from society is a major contributor to this feeling of powerlessness. Inability to be viewed as adult or credible because of societal myths about their abilities and rights further contributes to potential exploitation.

It is dehumanizing to be omitted or disbelieved as ever being a candidate for molestation, exploitation, or assault. In some cases, sexual abuse is not viewed as a serious crime because it occurred to someone who is considered "different" or lacking in power and dignity. The perceived damage won't affect society as a whole or in general; therefore, it won't get the full attention of society.

In the last few years, there has been an increase in the media reporting of sexual abuse. Statistics have been presented which speculate that a child is molested every two minutes in the United States. The majority are between the ages of eight and thirteen. Some estimated that for every victim revealed, none are hidden from authorities. Because of recent events, we now are forced to recognize that thousands of youngsters fall prey to deviant day care workers, teachers, coaches and others entrusted with their care. Recent television programs have devoted extensive attention to this topic. The parallel here is that the disabled or institutionalized who are dependent on others fall prey to their care providers in the same way as do children to their assailants. At present, society does not really recognize these parallels.

Characteristics

Finkelhor, in his recent studies, indicates that a quarter of all abuse occurs before the age of seven. Others suggest that over a third of all those who suffer sexual abuse are victimized before the age of nine. These statistics vary depending on different reference sources, and it is difficult to know the exact numbers which occur because each study has its own limitations. But it is important to recognize the fact that probably most assaults and molestation events are not reported or reflected in the statistics at all. A general estimation is that 20% of cases are reported, the rest are silenced. One of the most uncomfortable facts is that perhaps as much as 50% of sexual abuse occurs within the family (again statistics vary depending on the study).

Sexual abuse is a crime almost always suffered in silence, shrouded in such fear that the offenders are able to continue for years or perhaps a lifetime without being apprehended. It is recognized that the average molester may have abused as many as an appalling total of 70 victims. Many speculations estimate that a typical offender within the family may have committed as many as 80 acts of incest with female children. It is recognized that child molesters also reveal far more sexual assaults than the number for which they were originally charged. Sex offenders can be sentenced ranging from dismissal and forgiveness to forty years in prison.

Facts about family sexual abuse can be disturbing and confusing. Families differ in values surrounding touch and behavior. A distinction must be made between *normal* family practices of affection, touching and interaction and that which is defined as incest. Touching, communication patterns, behavior and play patterns may change from culture to culture and family to family. Families will react in different ways to hugging, cuddling and snuggling of children, to levels of nudity permitted in the family and permissible topics of conversation. Families of disabled children frequently are on either extreme——avoidance of touch (affectional deprivation) or excessive touch (overcompensating, especially touch). This can confuse both child and adult and appropriate boundaries are crossed or blurred.

The Illusion Theatre has created a "touch continuum"——the difference between good touch and bad touch and what you do when the touch is confusing. "Most touch is good: that means it feels good, warm, fun or playful. Good touches may include a kiss, hug or handshake. Some types of touch are bad: that means the touch hurts our feelings or our bodies. Bad touches may include a slap, kick or punch. Bad touch also includes sexual abuse——where the touch is tricked or forced sexual contact. Some types of touch are confusing: that means we are mixed up about whether the touch is good or bad, but we do know that something doesn't make sense or feel right. The good or fun touches, including tickling, wrestling, or 'touch games' can become confusing if it doesn't feel like a game anymore or we begin to feel uncomfortable, mixed up or hurt by the touch. Sometimes people are not used to touch, or don't like to be touched. We need to respect people's right not to be touched if they don't want to be. We also need to understand that severe deprivation of touch has some of the same effects on children as abusive touch and leaves them very vulnerable to being manipulated by what seems to be affectionate contact." We need to consider the importance of teaching these principles, particularly to persons with disabilities and their families.

Special Considerations

Exploitive situations become more complicated when individuals have a developmental or physical disability. In some cases involving sexual abuse, when the offender is identified as a family member or perhaps care provider, the victim may be unaware of being victimized and may lack the information to recognize exploitation or may be confused about what the activity really means or what the intent of the offender is. In fact, frequently the victim is told that this activity is "special," and in return for compliance and secrecy will be given rewards. Of paramount importance in these situations is recognizing that frequently the individual who is dependent on relatives and care providers for personal care (i.e. hygiene, dressing, grooming) can become very confused and unable to distinguish appropriate affectionate behavior and touch from exploitative touch which is expressly designed for the sexual gratification of the offender——*not* the victim.

This inability to differentiate basic assistance with personal care activities of daily living (ADL) from sexual exploitation renders them ultimately vulnerable. In a recent NIMH study by the Institute for the Study of Sexual Assault (ISSA) which was designed to identify patterns of sexual abuse of patients in psychiatric settings, it was discovered that orderly psychiatric aides, technicians, and nurses (predominantly male staff) were the most frequent offenders. Their victims were patients, mostly female, who were most dependent and needing constant physical contact. "Testing" of the patient which involved gradual escalation of physical contact wherein the victim was assessed for cooperation resulted in staff perpetrator assaults which included the full range of sexual acts: intercourse, oral copulation, masturbation and/or sexual battery. The study also reports that, although staff assailants often did not directly force patients, they simply took advantage of them because many were completely helpless, in restraints, medicated or in some cases physically limited.

The physical affects of sexual abuse may range from almost nonexistent to venereal disease or pregnancy. Violent attacks often result in bruises and lacerations. Although relatively few instances of sexual molestation are rape or committed with intended violence, it is very easy for the larger, more powerful person to cause serious injury to the child or to the physically limited individual whether or not they resist or try to defend themselves.

Emotional Impact of Abuse

It is well recognized that the two factors of shame and guilt (either one or the other or both in tandem) are the prime psychological injuries. Both of these devastating repercussions are the result of the internalization of the offense. Victimized individuals frequently view themselves as the cause and as responsible and perhaps ultimately "bad."

Shame is the emotion most experienced out of feelings of defeat and weakness in such situations. There is a sensed loss of self-control with accompanying loss of self-esteem. Victims may be pressured, forced or tricked and still feel themselves to be accessories to the sexual activity even though they do not truly consent and/or perhaps do not fully understand. The adult can completely dominate and manipulate the victim. Following these experiences is a loss of self-esteem. The main dilemma of shame is that it becomes a part of the individual's personality. When this happens, shame manifests itself in the feeling that the individual has no worth to self or society. Thus, another "disability" is added to the existing physical or intellectual disability of victims.

One of the more common fears of victims is that of being abandoned. Children and dependent or limited individuals particularly can feel at risk if they are unsafe in their environment. When adults do not believe them, or if disclosure threatens their safety, they are further victimized. In some cases, this can lead to the belief that they are deserving of this punishment and they begin to experience not only a loss of self-esteem but a general discounting from family members or society.

The victim can also feel the devastating psychological effects of guilt. The individual may have enjoyed the attention and "love" given to some degree and may believe they have created the situation or been responsible for the problem. Children and others who are vulnerable are told they will be doing a misdeed if they do not agree to the pressures of the offender, and they are put into the difficult position of having to agree or go against that which they have been taught is authority and must be obeyed. In most cases, the offender lets the victim know that there is something wrong about the act itself by the mere fact that the child or individual is sworn to secrecy. In essence, the victim can feel caught in a double bind. This process is also commonly recognized in the workplace and is called "sexual harassment." There is now legislation to protect the victim from molestation and exploitation, including verbal harassment. Those who are not in the workplace deserve the same protection.

Feelings of guilt are further created by offenders in incest situations when they tell the child/victim that to reveal the sexual abuse would be to destroy the family. This sense of culpability can be reinforced by the management of abuse cases when the child, not the parent, is removed from the home. This guilt becomes part of the person as much as does shame and is incorporated into the individual's development. When these incidences remain unidentified and are not appropriately dealt with, the psychological impact of the sexual trauma is carried exclusively and alone.

Recognition and Prevention

There is a direct correlation between the results of training professionals to understand and identify sexual abuse and the number of cases reported. However, low statistics of reported cases do not necessarily mean that the situations do not exist. It is generally recognized in our society that the topics of sexual abuse, exploitation and molestation are difficult to discuss, and many people are not comfortable and/or will not believe it occurs. In spite of all this reluctance, it does. David Finklehor reports in his book *Sexually Victimized Children* that one in every five female children and one in every ten male children will be sexually abused before the age of eighteen. There is indication that over 80% of the sexual abuse of children is by someone the child knows, not a stranger. However, in a study conducted by the Seattle Rape Relief and Sexual Assault Center over a seven year period, it was revealed that 99% of developmentally disabled reported victims were sexually abused by relatives and caretakers (residential staff, bus drivers, recreation workers, volunteers, work supervisors and others serving in care-provider capacities). Only one percent were strangers to the victim. These are dramatic statistics and serve to alert all of us working in the area of rehabilitation health care. As a first step toward prevention, we must begin to realize that sexual abuse is common.

The most recent statistics and general unpublished reports reflect that the number and incidence is higher than has been previously documented in the literature. Some therapists and mental health workers with sex offenders report or discuss among themselves the possibility that perhaps as many as one in three girls experiences molestation by the time she is fourteen and that perhaps as much as 50% of the victimization occurs within the family.

Prevention of sexual abuse starts with recognition and acknowledgment that it is happening. Many victims of sexual abuse suffer long-term and permanent effects not only of shame, guilt, fear and lowered self-esteem, but also health disorders, learning problems, delinquent behavior and chemical abuse. Efforts aimed at prevention must necessarily involve an intention to stop assaults before they occur. It is essential to identify and change societal beliefs and norms which permit sexual abuse and exploitation to continue. The power structure in our society sets up males as more powerful than females, able-bodied persons as more powerful than the physically disabled, white persons as more powerful than those of other color, the wealthy as more powerful than the poor, and adults as more powerful than children. The child or disabled individual is particularly a candidate to be victimized since there is an imbalance of age, size, power, self-control or knowledge.

Children have the right to grow in a safe environment. Because they are vulnerable, they look to adults for protection. As previously mentioned, victims of sexual abuse are often tricked, not forced, by the offender who is likely to be someone the child knows and trusts. It is easy to understand that the child may not believe or even perceive that this person could/would possibly ever hurt him/her. The same rationale can be applied to adult individuals with intellectual or physical disabilities, those who are institutionalized, the elderly.

Prevention efforts must include programs for individuals which inform them of their right to trust their feelings, to say "no," to tell someone, to live in a safe environment, to not permit any touch or behavior which frightens, confuses or hurts them.

The media in the recent five years has make great strides toward publicizing this problem which is reaching national health hazard proportions. General information, highly publicized public service events and announcements, docudramas, talk shows, special news reports help increase public awareness and reporting. In an effort to teach individuals some prevention techniques, the books, media, theater companies, and instructions include basic guidelines:

- say "no" if touch or situation is uncomfortable
- tell someone if help is needed
- do not keep secrets if it feels uncomfortable
- ask questions if confused or frightened by touch behavior
- right to privacy and to not permit anyone else to touch their body in any way without permission
- right to be taught appropriate touch behavior
- right to learn alternative ways of expressing affection without intimate or inappropriate touch

Indications of Sexual Abuse

Suspicion of sexual abuse is indicated if:

- clothing appears stained or bloody
- there are reports of injury or neglect by the parents
- the child (victim) has a diagnosis of venereal disease of eyes, mouth, anus, genitalia
- the child (victim) reports pain or itching, bruises or bleeding in the genital area
- overadaptive behaviors that meet the parents' needs rather than the child's (victim's)
- there is extreme fearfulness, withdrawal or fantasy
- the child (victim) exhibits behavior extremes (passive, overly compliant to rageful and extremely aggressive), stealing or hoarding, habit disorders or neurotic traits, hyperactivity, running away, lagging in development

- there is severe emotional conflict at home
- the child (victim) shows fear of intervention
- there is past history of abuse by the parent or parents
- there is an unwanted pregnancy
- there is inappropriate dress
- there is seductive behavior
- sleep disturbances are being manifested
- there are mood swings, feelings of humiliation, anger, nightmares, eating pattern disturbances, fear of sex, development of phobias about the attack

Specialists who work in the field of sexual abuse consistently state that when an individual does take the risk to identify the abuse and report information related to sexual exploitation or activities, it is crucial that he or she is believed. It may be the only time they risk revealing the taboo and may be the only cry for help which will be given.

There is relatively little written on the topic of sexual abuse and individuals with physical disabilities. However, with the statistics which are available, combined with the knowledge of the personal and societal pressures generally experienced by an individual with a disability, it is not difficult to understand that physically disabled persons are potentially at higher risk that the general population. The mere fact that they are in many ways more dependent on the care-providers to assist them in activities of daily living creates multiple opportunities for them to be vulnerable in ways that the able-bodied are not. Not only do they lack privacy, but also they may lack the ability to be spontaneous in protecting themselves. Many individuals are without speech or language abilities and limited in or without mobility. Some may be so totally dependent on others for health care needs for daily living survival that to consider resisting anything from a care-provider or family member may seem too frightening for their own existence. They may also not know in whom to confide for assistance were they to try to identify abusive behavior. They may already have experienced a disenfranchisement from society and would not be willing to risk a further separation. It is understandable that handicappers may predict that their stories might not be believed because their credibility would be pitted against that of an able-bodied person. It is commonly recognized that many sex offenders are viewed as pillars of the community——respected and trusted. Offenders themselves often state that they are aware of the vulnerability of their victims and deliberately plan this abuse since the likelihood of its being reported is minimal.

The emotional reactions and adjustments of someone who has been denied his or her personal integrity by being assaulted are the same as those of someone who has been denied personal integrity by being institutionalized. Because of the denial of freedom, personal decision-making, privacy, economics, independence, and decreased feeling of personal strength, many persons who have been institutionalized share outward characteristics which indicate a history of abuse. This makes recognition somewhat difficult at times.

An obvious preventive measure is to encourage and assist parents and families in being comfortable with discussing sex and sexuality and in having the skills and information necessary to provide sex education and prevention techniques. Often parents have difficulty doing so. They may not have received any particular education in sexual health and may find themselves limited and perhaps confused in their own knowledge and skills. This leads many families to avoid the issue and to cloak it in further silence. Individuals who live in institutions may experience the same kind of silence from the institutional staff for the same reasons.

Sexual abuse is not restricted to any social or economic class and, contrary to some popular belief, parents with higher levels of education or income are not providing better sex education and abuse-prevention techniques than parents who have less education and a lower income. A family containing a physically disabled member, particularly a child, is often seen closing around that individual in a self-containing way in an effort to protect itself from the community and society. Not only might a family be naturally more protective of a child with a disability but also it might isolate itself in a cautious way from society and its insensitivities. Although it is

subtle, it creates yet another barrier for the sexually abused, disabled child who might otherwise reach out. Frequently, the only community the disabled child knows is that of the family and the care-providers upon whom she or he is dependent.

Although evidence indicates that most children don't reveal their victimization and, even when they do, that many families try to shroud the incident in silence lest they call attention to themselves and sexually inappropriate behavior or make a false accusation, increased numbers of treatment programs are needed to respond to victims. All children, particularly the disabled, must be taught personal safety lessons preventing sexual abuse, and protecting the right and dignity of their well-being. Books have been written for children helping them to identify "good" and "bad" touch. Audio-visual materials are being created regularly, materials are being written for families to use together and efforts are being taken to train professionals to recognize and identify the events surrounding sexual exploitation. However, in an effort to adequately prepare children to recognize sexually exploitive situations they must understand that a normal looking person, or even someone they know, could molest them. Most importantly, they must be given the message that they can tell anything to the parent or a trusted adult and that they will be believed and loved. If we can teach the children to say "no" and to yell for safety, even if a family member, the local school coach or teacher, attendant, scout leader, transporter or the next door neighbour are the abusers, we will participate in enabling safety for the vulnerable individual.

Reporting is also directly proportional to the number of education programs operating in the community, and although children often know the difference between touch which is given in love and exploitive touch, they are generally reluctant to acknowledge this unless asked *directly* by a trusted individual and in what they perceive to be a safe setting, free from harm.

Linda Sanford, in her brochure for parents entitled "Come Tell Me Right Away," emphasizes that we must tell the children that we believe them, that the offender did something wrong and that it is not the child's fault. We must report to the authorities (professionals are obligated by law to report suspected sexual exploitation within twenty-four hours.) She instructs that we not confront the offender in the child's presence and that we be sure that the child has a physical examination to reassure him/her that his/her body has not been harmed or changed. Most importantly, she stresses that we allow the child to talk about the incident at his or her own pace, that counselling is helpful and that covering up the incident will not make it go away. The same criteria is applicable for other vulnerable persons.

Myths

Some of the more common myths about sexual exploitation, particularly as it relates to disability, are that nice girls don't get raped, that society feels compassion toward disabled individuals and therefore would not think to do such a thing, that people who are handicapped are not really sexual or attractive and are therefore not eligible to be sexually assaulted, that rapists/abusers are strangers to their victims; that someone who can't speak or doesn't have full mental capabilities wouldn't really understand what happened to them anyway and also probably can't be believed. Other myths are that the mentally retarded or physically disabled lie about assault or are promiscuous and "ask for what they get." Many disabled individuals may participate in sexual acting out behavior which is then labelled as offensive or inappropriate by takers. Usually in these circumstances, no effort is made to modify the negative behavior. These same individuals are also candidates to be treated in a trivial manner and kept socially isolated, reinforcing their sexual ignorance and ultimate vulnerability.

Recovery

The most difficult step in recovery from sexual exploitation is actually identifying the sexual abuse. Most therapists acknowledge that "telling the secret" is threatening and traumatizing in and of itself and creates feelings of isolation and further vulnerability. When an individual's life

has been violated by a parent or adult who has forced himself or herself as a lover, it results in a loss not unlike that which is experienced with an acquired or traumatic disability. It can be extremely disruptive and create enormous vulnerability. It is common for victims to say "He robbed me of my childhood . . . of my dignity," and "I am broken."

Incest continues to be perceived as the most damaging form of sexual abuse because of the ambivalence created between hating and living with the offender-family member. Frequently, the offender may have been the more nurturing of the family members, and the victim experiences further isolation and loss by severing this tie.

A recognized common response to sexual abuse of families and of accused offenders is denial, followed by anger toward the victim. This can result in further shame, increased vulnerability and at times panic, retreat, and even rescinding the accusation. When support groups, networks, counselling and therapy can be provided, the therapeutic process can result in reduced suffering and positive, although difficult recovery. The emotional scarring can be pervasive and can affect a person's feelings of safety and well-being for the rest of his/her life.

At times of crisis intervention, it is important to determine what the victim needs: to assess his/her immediate health needs, to be assured that he or she is not at fault and to validate the feelings of fear, anxiety and revulsion being felt. We must stand by and assist the victim with problem solving skills for further situations and we must let the individual know that he or she has a right to be safe. These simple guidelines are essential to the healing process.

Responses

Reluctance to talk about sexual assault and exploitation, particularly of children and those with disabilities, is common. The reasons tend to be consistent throughout our society. Parents are afraid of unnecessarily frightening the child by giving them information about abuse. They are often reluctant to talk about sex eduction mainly for feelings of inadequacy and discomfort of their own.

It is generally regarded as inadequate to discuss sexual abuse in isolation from sex education. Without the context and perspective of sexual health, it is difficult and very frightening for an individual to understand abuse.

Common community resistance often appears in the form of denial that the issue is really a problem in "our neighbourhood". Communities are reluctant to inform the individuals about sexual abuse and sexual information for fear that they will try out all of the sexual activities, act inappropriately, make up false reports or be terrorized. Although most parents support sex education and preventive education for their children, they are most critical of *who* provides it. Interestingly, Finklehor reports that "only 29% of the parents give their children information about sexual abuse despite their awareness of the prevalence of child sexual abuse." Generally, communities struggle over who should teach prevention programs and how much they should contain and cost. Some community groups suggest task forces or child protection teams should do the training, others say the schools, others the police, clergy, rape centers, parents, etc. It is generally acknowledged that specific, professional training needs to be provided to those who teach these topics.

Another common concern of communities is limited financial resources. Particularly in times when some conservative elements in the community are against sex education, communities are concerned that talking about anything sexual (healthy or otherwise) is inappropriate and will not be supported financially. There are no easy answers to the dilemma of persuading communities to invest in educational programs, but clearly the intervention techniques are necessary if we are to continue to provide all individuals, able-bodied and disabled, with the right to sexual health.

It is also timely and appropriate to routinely provide sex education, including the area of sexual exploitation, to professionals working in the health care and rehabilitation milieu. It is time for us to aggressively address these unacceptable situations and establish clear directions which mandate respect, dignity, and integrity.

References

1. Children's Village U.S.A.: Child Abuse and You, National Headquarters Woodland Hills, California.

2. Anderson, Cordelia: No Easy Answers, Secondary Curriculum on Sexual Abuse, Illusion Theatre, Minneapolis, MN. Available from Network Publications, Santa Cruz, CA, 1983.

3. Aiello, Denise, Capkin, Lee, Catania, Holly: Strategies and Techniques for Serving the Disabled Assault Victim: A Pilot Training Program for Providers and Consumers, *Sexuality and Disability*, Volume 6, Number 3/4, Fall/Winter 1983.

4. Life Magazine: Special Report on Childhood Sexual Assault, December 1984.

5. Finklehor, D.: Child Sexual Abuse: Theory and Research, New York Free Press, New York, 1984.

6. Ryerson, Ellen: Sexual Abuse and Self-Protection Education for Developmentally Disabled Youth: A Priority Need, SIECUS, *Where The Action Is*, Developmental Disabilities Project, Seattle Rape Relief, 1825 South Jackson, Suite 102, Seattle, WA 98144.

7. Musick, Judith: Patterns of Institutional Sexual Assault, *Response to Violence in the Family and Sexual Assault*, Volume 7, Number 3, May/June 1984.

8. Finklehor, D.: Sexually Victimized Children, New York Free Press, New York, 1979.

9. Seattle Rape Relief: The Developmental Disabilities Project, 1825 South Jackson, Suite 102, Seattle, WA 98144.

10. Assault Prevention Training Project: Women Against Rape, P.O. Box 82024, Columbus, Ohio 43202.

11. Sanford, Linda Tschirhart: Come Tell Me Right Away, Ed-U-Press Inc., P.O. Box 583, Fayetteville, NY 13066, 1982.

12. O'Day, Bonnie -- Minnesota Program for Victims of Sexual Assault: Preventing Sexual Abuse of Persons with Disabilities: A Curriculum for Hearing Impaired, Physically Disabled, Blind and Mentally Retarded Students, Network Publications, Santa Cruz, CA, 1983.

13. Finklehor, D.: Public Knowledge and Attitudes about Child Sexual Abuse: A Boston Survey, Paper presented to the National Conference on Child Sexual Abuse, Washington, D.C., 1982.

 **EDUCATIONAL OPPORTUNITIES AND BARRIERS**

Often the key to acceptance is education; without knowing the culture and the facts of society, any minority will be left on the fringes of society. The disabled have often experienced difficulties in achieving an education, and where education has been available, it was only accessible in a sheltered and segregated environment. Bill 82, which mandates that all individuals with exceptionalities (a current polite term for the disabled), wherever possible ought to be educated within the Ontario public school system. Similar bills are now in place in the other jurisdictions, both Canadian and American, as a part of the mainstream process. Yet, the disabled still encounter many problems in attempting to be educated. Many of these difficulties involve acceptance, as illustrated by Donovan. The disabled, especially disabled women, as outlined by Holcomb, have traditionally encountered barriers which have directed them to residential schools where they are trapped in a traditional and stereotyped curriculum. Indeed the curriculum of separate education facilities for the disabled seldom, if ever, prepares students adequately to participate in the pursuits of higher learning and subsequent employment. Those with a disabled status are often typed and defined well before they have been legitimately assessed. Thus, individuals with learning disabilities and other impediments are often victimized by a series of factors which inhibit, if not prevent, them from enjoying the benefits of education. Cruickshank, Buchanan, and Weller focus on the difficulties traditionally experienced by those defined "learning disabled". Greber further illustrates the problems that this group experiences in university admissions testing, as it is known these tests may be inconclusive for all students, not just the disabled student. Emotional stress, economic factors, and social factors are but a few of the elements that effect the scores of all students. Therefore, all tests must be constructed and evaluated with the knowledge that they are, at best, only general tools for assessing potential academic ability.

Individuals who experience disability statuses are often able to overcome their conditions through the use of new technological devices such as the computer, as demonstrated by Irons. Indeed through technology, legislation, and intervention of third parties, provisions can be employed and developed which allow the disabled community to enjoy the benefits of education in an integrated environment.

376

How Accessible is an Education?

Maura Donovan

How accessible is a university education for someone with a disability? Providing services in the university setting for an increasingly vocal and ambitious population of adults with disabilities is a relatively new challenge for universities. Until recently, many adults with disabilities hadn't received proper high school education, had never been encouraged to attend university, or didn't have the funds to make a university education possible. There were also attitudinal and prejudicial barriers that kept people out of the higher education system.

But recently this has changed. Better special education in public schools, legislation, government programs, and increased awareness have put many young adults in a frustrating position: they are capable of, and ready for university, but the universities can't or won't take them.

Attitudes Must Change

According to Gladys Loewen, a founder of the Adult Special Education Network in British Columbia, there are "still a lot of problems with accessibility." When asked what needed to be done, she stated, "Everything...we need to do a lot of work on attitudes. Until you get administrators who are supportive of increased programs, altered facilities, and better funding, all the other changes won't amount to enough to change the whole picture. Attitudes need to be changed before the elevators, ramps, talking books, support personnel, and other services can really be effective."

Loewen stressed that accessibility varies depending on the school, the province, and the individual's disability. Some universities are highly accessible and have made huge efforts to provide for people with special needs. Other schools put it on the back burner.

Such was the recent case with McGill University, in Montreal. The university administration said that the funds were not available to increase services and facilities to students with disabilities. Early in March, Access McGill, the

organization of disabled students at McGill, took the issue to the student body in the form of a referendum. The referendum passed by an overwhelming majority, as the students voted to give approximately $160,000 over two years in support of students with special needs. The students are now attempting to get the university faculty and staff to give matching funds.

If this seems like a lot of money, consider the circumstances. Wheelchair vans, tutors, interpreter services for students who have impaired hearing, photo enlarging machines, scholarships, and building renovations are costly...and needed.

For example, special buses or vans are needed for students who have a mobility impairment. Stairs, doors, washrooms, telephones, laboratory tables, and theatres must be altered to accommodate wheelchairs.

Planning Ahead

Students who are visually impaired often need talking textbooks. These cassette tapes must be requested four months prior to the date they will be needed! Some universities don't allow students to plan this far ahead. Computers with braille, photo enlarging machines, and other equipment are also extremely expensive and not available at most schools.

Agencies that fund students with special needs sometimes insist that students go to school full-time. many can't do this because of other commitments or because their disability limits their course load.

it is difficult enough to find a university which offers the services a student needs, to get the funding, and then to adjust to the new environment and the routine of the school. Students with disabilities also meet prejudice and ignorance. Getting professors to believe in the existence of a hidden disability——such as a learning disability or an allergy to the environment——is an additional challenge.

Building codes, according to loewen, need upgrading. "We agree that buildings have to

Reprinted from: "Rehabilitation Digest", Fall 1988, Vol. 19, #3., with permission. Pub. by CRCD, Toronto, Ontario have ramps and wide doors, but often the doors are big heavy wooden doors."

Awareness is also a key issue. Many people see disabled students as being different. Instead of thinking, "We're both biology majors," or "We're both on the orientation committee," people tend to think, "she's in a wheelchair and I'm not." People are afraid of the disability and often find it hard to see past the disability to the student.

Changes in building renovations, policies, program accessibility, and funding can all come about if there is increased awareness and a better attitude toward disabilities. The most rewarding part of this change will be that society can be given back just as much as it gives to these students...and maybe more.

The most important change all of us——professors, staff, administrators, and students——need to make doesn't cost a dime. It's a change in attitude...and it's priceless.

Carleton University Wins Minister's Award

Carleton University was the winner of an award presented by the Ontario provincial government for creating an innovative and comprehensive support program for disabled students. Carleton, the first Canadian university to initiate a 24- hour attendant care program for disabled students who live in residence, received its award March 1st during the annual Premier's Awards for Accessibility ceremony.

In the following testimonial, Luc Polnicky, Carleton graduate of the Masters of Social work program, provides his perspective.

Testimonial

Equal Access to Education
Luc Polnicky

Eight years ago I dove into a swimming pool and broke my fifth vertebra. I am now a C-5 quadriplegic. I will probably spend the rest of my life in a wheelchair. I was then nineteen years old, working as an ambulance attendant and studying

at the University of Western Ontario. It was my hope one day to become a practising dentist.

Today my life is different. My conscious thinking processes determine my emotions, motivations and behaviour. The difficulties that I encounter because of my disability are largely a problem of consciousness. A change in my perceptions has altered my emotions, goals, and behaviour. Also, a change in my goals has influenced my behaviour. Finally, the new activities and new kinds of behaviour engendered by my disability have transformed my perceptions.

In order for a person to survive a traumatic spinal cord injury, it is necessary to reorganize one's life pattern. This has significant effects on the course and outcome of the rehabilitation process. In this article I will discuss my post-secondary education at Carleton University, and the adaptations and accommodations within the educational system that were a consequence of my disability.

A higher education has always been of great importance to me. And yet, despite my wish for unhindered access to a university program of choice, education is an aspect of my life that has required tremendous adjustments——both physical and emotional. Every day, for the past three years, I have boarded my own van, equipped with special hand controls and a hydraulic life, and driven to Carleton University where I recently completed the Masters program in Social Work. I hope that this degree, combined with the four previous years of undergraduate study in psychology/sociology, will provide me with the opportunity to be employed and become a contributing citizen in our society.

Carleton U. Provides Support

I was able to achieve these goals with the help of an exceptional support group at Carleton university. This group of people provided me with the necessary technical and financial assistance in order to ensure that I had an equal chance to access my education. Carleton has an underground tunnel system which links all buildings on campus. A fully-interconnected campus makes access to classrooms possible for disabled students with physical impairments.

Larry McCloskey, the full-time co-ordinator for disabled Students, provides assistance and information to the students that he serves, while promoting the availability of post-secondary education——in the broad sense——for disabled persons. During my stay at Carleton, Larry provided me with a referral service and acted as an advocate, researcher and friend. I've discussed with him on numerous occasions ways in which I could realize my potential. He has encouraged me to take responsibility for my education in a variety of ways, including providing hints on how to approach teachers for help and assistance with the acquiring of technical aids.

Over the seven years that I attended Carleton, I was assisted by various specialized support services, which include a vocational rehabilitation counsellor to help me with educational funding and career choice decisions, and attendants to aid my morning and evening tasks. Secondly, Carleton University has an impressive assortment of technical aids, electronic door openers, mobility aids of various types, recording and transcription devices, and audit amplification equipment. Support services, technical aids and devices made it possible for me to use the resources of both the university community and the Ottawa community at large. Such opportunities have allowed me to concentrate efforts on school work, rather than expending my energy advocating within the system.

As a small community of students and educators, Carleton University has provided its disabled members with equal access on many levels. The Co-ordinator for Disabled Students has, over the years, challenged the physical plant planners with various modifications of service delivery systems. Carleton has consistently provided for the removal of physical barriers to education and ensures that its institution is physically accessible to the disabled population. Several structural changes have been made over the years. Some changes, such as altering ramps and curb cuts to ensure easy access to building for the physically disabled, accessibility of washrooms, as well as elevators with braille to assist the visually im-

paired, are areas where money has been spent to advantage.

Attitudes, One of the Greatest Handicaps

In pursuing my education over the years, I had to cope with many mistaken and handicapping assumptions made by others. Seven years ago, when services for the disabled on campus were not as developed as they are today, I had to form a sense of self-confidence and assertiveness and demand my right to equal access to amenities and services at Carleton. Some people still think that because disabled students are not able to perform certain tasks, they are not suited for university education. When confronted with this view, I have had to accentuate my efforts to prove the contrary.

Rehabilitation Digest

On the other hand, while at Carleton, people were often coming up to me and displaying a patronizing attitude to compensate, in their view, for my disability. I think this attitude is as harmful as the first one because it may lead to the failure on the part of the disabled student to develop a sense of self-worth and independence. In the final analysis, if one is to succeed, he/she must overcome physical and attitudinal limitations to go to school and develop interpersonal skills in the acquisition of practical knowledge in a chosen field.

The key to Academic Success

During my stay at Carleton I discovered that a successful academic outcome requires actions from both the students and the teachers. Teachers must be flexible in allowing certain modifications to disabled students. This may include extra time for a quadriplegic to complete the written part of an exam, giving an advanced reading list to a blind student so that he/she can have taped text books, or providing a special seating arrangement for a deaf student to allow lip reading of the lecture.

On the other hand, disabled students must realize that sometimes certain academic tasks will require a little more patience and effort from them. For example, a blind student might require the help of a friend to complete library research. He or she must establish a network of volunteers who are willing to read the printed material available on a subject.

A significant amount of time and energy might be spent in order to establish such a system, but it is a worthwhile effort.

All in all, disabled students who decide to pursue an education are faced with a challenge to break down socially- imposed barriers, and should realize that they are equally capable of making an important contribution to the academic world, the working community and society at large.

Disabled Women: A New Issue in Education

LILLIAN P. HOLCOMB

This paper presents a review of the literature that describes the problems encountered by females with disabilities in the educational system. Since this is a new area of inquiry, few research studies have been conducted. In much of the rehabilitation literature, it has been assumed that what applies to men or boys with disabilities also applies to disabled women or girls. Most of the available statistics are based upon the "disabled in general" without regard to gender, and most definitions of disabling or handicapping conditions relate to the more visible male (Corbett & Weeks, 1981; Deegan, 1981; Fitting, Salisbury, Davies, & Mayclin, 1978). Only within recent years, have disabled women come to be viewed as a separate minority group, with personality characteristics and needs that set them apart from disabled men or from women and men who are not disabled.

Handicapped women are doubly discriminated against as a result of being both disabled and female. Saviola (1982) described this situation as "double jeopardy" since the stereotypes ascribed to both disabled people and women consist of passivity, dependence, helplessness, and failure. Disabled females may be considered members of a multiple minority group (Deegan, 1981) since they are the recipients of discrimination and prejudicial attitudes from several groups simultaneously. They are the victims of a "less than whole" attitude held by able-bodied women and men, as well as a "sexist" attitude held, not only by able-bodied persons, but also by disabled men in their own subculture.

Early Education Experience of Disabled Girls

Disabled girls have experienced particular isolation and trauma when exposed to the educational system, and the law requiring that children receive some kind of education has been differentially applied to disabled boys and girls. One factor contributing to greater discrimination against female school children is that, in certain areas of exceptionality, boys outnumber girls and, therefore, tend to be a more visible group for potential financial support. Mumpower (1970), for example, reported that, at a Special Education Center in Louisiana, there were two or three times as many boys as girls. Boys constituted 61.9% of those with physical handicaps, 77.1% of those with mental retardation, and 93.7% of those with non-fluent speech articulation; in some cases (such as heart condition and trainable mentally retarded), girls constituted about half of the population. Because more boys have been found to be deviant from the norm, Mumpower (1970) concluded that "it seems almost essential that something be done to equalize opportunities for boys," and that "changes in the total educational program need to be made in order to help the more deviant sex make a better adjustment to school" (p. 621).

Gillespie and Fink (1974) found that, because boys generally initiate aggressive behaviors, their behavior problems become more noticeable to teachers, who refer them in greater numbers to helping agencies. Kaplan and Kinsbourne (1974) found this to be true for learning disabled boys as well. Learning disabled boys were viewed as more hostile and antisocial, while learning disabled girls were perceived as having the option of trying to please the teacher; the boys saw this desire to please as "unmacho." Furthermore, the Chapman and Boersma (1979) study on learning disability included twice as many third to sixth grade boys as girls. Singer and Osborn (1970) offered additional findings that boys were admitted more frequently to treatment centers for retardates, although their IQ's were higher than those of the girls who were referred. Society in general has been more concerned with male achievement and male activity, with the result that girls do not become visible to society until their IQ's are so low that they too are perceived as having behavior problems. It is possible that society has accepted less activity, less achievement, and lower IQ's for girls than for boys.

Reprinted from: Journal of Rehabilitation, Jan/Feb/Mar 1984, with permission.

The personal experience of disabled girls in school tends to be frustrating, isolating, conservative, and traditional. In their study of 100 physically disabled women, Landis and Bolles (1942) discovered that their subjects had been hindered in school attendance as young girls due to constant problems with transportation, illness and hospitalization. In cases where disabilities permitted fairly regular attendance, school resources were frequently inadequate. Large print materials and accessible chalkboards needed by the partially blind, for example, were often lacking. Because they have often been perceived as mentally retarded, disabled students have tended to work longer and harder than other students to keep their grades high (Cerello, 1981). In the public schools, wheelchair-bound girls have had little access to physical education programs (Casey,1981). In the literature, the author was unable to find evidence of existing wheelchair sports for girls or support groups for girls who wished to express their anger about the situation. In addition, the girls may not have had access to bathroom facilities even if they had been able to participate in the classes (Savitz, 1979). The personal experience of deaf girls in school has been laden with problems of frustration and isolation, as illustrated by Peterson's (1974) example of a deaf girl who reported that "they would stare at me, whisper to each other . . . talk to me just to find out how 'dumb' I was . . . pushed me into a receptacle of wet cement . . . boarded me up in a big dog house and set fire to it. This nearly destroyed my self-confidence and made an introvert of me" (p. 21).

With regard to sex role stereotyping in career planning, Egelstno and Kovolchuck (1975) found a potentially constraining situation when junior high school deaf girls classified occupations according to traditional expectations more rigidly than did deaf boys or hearing girls. And on the issue of new social roles for deaf women, Doctors (1977) observed that, like those persons without disabilities, deaf boys felt uncomfortable about the prospect of deaf girls taking on nontraditional careers if it meant the girls would abandon homemaking. Cook and Rossett (1975) studied the reactions of 20 teenage deaf girls toward vocational/curriculum preparation. Compared to a group of 42 hearing girls, 55% of the deaf group agreed that if a woman had a baby she should stay home, while only 23% of the hearing group had the same value. Harslem (1974) discussed the conflicting values of a deaf girl, and indicated that,as in the nondisabled population, the deaf girl receives the message that it is important to go to college to find a husband, but it's a waste of money since all she will do with it is get married. Smith (1974), however, has reported more encouraging data, which revealed that while deaf girls do tend to stop their education to marry, the number of older women returning to school is on the rise in the deaf population, as well as in the hearing population.

Earlier, this author noted a reaction of fear and anxiety on the part of the nondisabled population when first exposed to disabled girls in the early academic years. Simon and *** (1979) discussed what might happen when administrators decide to mainstream handicapped children without giving the teachers of nondisabled children any warning or training beforehand. When sighted school children with no prior exposure to blind children were suddenly confronted with "mainstreamed" blind children, they became anxious and frightened, and the blind children were made fun of and rejected. Henderson (1979) reported that, throughout her public school years, she was treated cruelly by other children who chanted, "you're blind, you're blind;" they also pointed fingers and made shrieking noises in an attempt to get her away from them.

Even high school nondisabled adolescents have negative attitudes toward disabled students, and these attitudes seem to relate to the low levels of prior exposure or contact (Higgs, 1972). Thurman and Lewis (19179) noted that handicapped children are rejected by nonhandicapped children at very early ages. To counteract the problem, they suggested that direct confrontation begin very early. Despite the Thurman and Lewis (1979) finding that young children tend to reject that which is different from themselves, experimental exposure and social contact efforts suggest that exposure can reduce rejection. Storey (1980) exposed children between the ages of 8 and 12 to a television series, and followed that exposure with a post-TV group discussion on handicapped children. As a result of that experience, both able boys and girls were observed to be more accepting, more aware of handicapped children's feelings, and more likely to have perceived them as potential friends. Beardsley (1980) had more disappointing result, with the use of bibliotherapy. Third grade children who listened for 15 days to stories about handicapped children did not become more positive on the retest. However, pretest attitudes were already fairly favourable toward the disabled in this study. Westervelt and McKinney (1980) discovered that when fourth grade children's attitudes toward handicapped children improved after watching a film about an active wheelchair child, the effects wore off within several days. The authors suggested that such a method (use of a film) be introduced immediately before the entry of a handicapped child into the class. It seems that the more "live" the exposure is, the better the results, and that the actual contact with disabled guest speakers is quite effective. This finding is reminiscent of the work of Bandura, Ross, and Ross (1963), in which life and filmed aggression models were more effective than cartoons in eliciting aggressive imitative responses from children.

Much can be done to improve the attitudes of those in the educational system in which disabled girls are placed. One problem that has not been adequately addressed is the placement of disabled girls into traditional sex role programs that emphasize laundry service, clerical duties, and housekeeping; on the other hand, boys are exposed to occupational information and preparation that lead to higher-paid careers than girls usually enter (Gillespie & Fink, 1974). Gillespie and Fink found that, as with nondisabled children, the reading materials and textbooks distributed to handicapped girls and boys depicted girls as mothers' helpers, performing cooking tasks, making curtains, and making recipe boxes; they were pictured as pretty and small. Boys were depicted as strong and tall, and shown as participants in action-packed stories, farming, repairing furniture, and excelling in athletics. Dodd (1977) discussed the need to include more nontraditional books and to provide counsellors with

nonsexist career-related material. O'Toole and Weeks (1978) suggested bringing disabled women to the classroom and conducting field trips to visit disabled women who are professionals. McNett and Merchant (1981) emphasized the need for handicapped educators to adopt a leadership role in the teaching profession. Research might be undertaken to illustrate the impact that such competent and successful role models have on disabled girls.

Residential Education

Up to this point, the focus of the literature discussed has been on handicapped girls in the *Public* education system. While a number of advantages have been offered for the placement of disabled girls into the "mainstream" of public education, certain disadvantages have been noted. For example, disabled students have needs for socialization and friendship that nondisabled teachers and children cannot or will not meet. Many handicapped girls, therefore, enter private and public specialized programs at "residential schools," where they live and study together with other similarly disabled youngsters. But, due to their limited subculture, disadvantages are also found in residential schools. For example, in residential schools for the deaf, deaf girls have tended to socialize among themselves and have been exposed only to Ameslan (American Sign Language), the language of "their people" (Pugin, 1981). Some schools for the deaf have not encouraged pride in the language of the deaf and have focused on the "oral method" of teaching children to read lips of hearing people with perfection, and often wind up apologizing for their speech and signing "me dummy" (Becker & Jauregui, 1981)

Problems have also emerged with the sex role stereotypic nature of vocational and occupational training in residential school. Rosenstein and Lerman (1963) reported that the school may train girls for certain types of jobs, but these jobs are usually of the low paying variety. The schools place female students into programs leading to keypunch and seamstress work, while male students have been pointed to printing and carpentry occupations (Becker & Jauregui, 1981).

This author, who was a student at Perkins School for the Blind, remembers that the expected program for girls was that of typing and dictaphone usage, while boys studied piano-tuning.

A number of advantages have been found for disabled students who enter residential schools, including the opportunity to associate with peers who have similar problems, to participate in sports, to engage in support-rap groups, and to use disability-appropriate equipment. MacFarland (1966) suggested that the temporary segregation of disabled students into peer units actually trains them, in an atmosphere of acceptance, to gain the skills needed to function independently in an able-bodied world. Similarly, O'Toole and Weeks (1978) contended that the isolation, frustration and feelings of ugliness and awkwardness of girls with handicapping conditions can be alleviated in a residential school atmosphere, where the friendship of disabled peers, wheelchair sports, support-rap groups, and necessary equipment (reading machines, braille,ramps, Ameslan) were available to provide essential learning experiences. It would be difficult to find a public school that "mainstreams" to this degree.

Disabled Women in College: Public Education in Adulthood

Disabled women desiring a college education have been confronted with a more intellectual world than in the residential school or the public elementary and secondary school system, but many barriers have continued to exist (O'Toole & Weeks, 1978). Disabled women have confronted negative attitudes of able-bodied students and professors and have spent more time working and studying while able-bodied students play and socialize. Further, disabled women have taken course work preparing them for traditional careers and have battled accessibility problems such as the need to maintain the appearance of lovely old historic buildings that would be "ruined" if modified to accommodate the disabled student. After all this, a handicapped woman may complete a master's degree, perhaps even a doctorate, only to find no positions open to her. According to Kutza (1981), only the most fortunate of severely physically disabled persons

have been able to finish high school; over 40% did to complete high school and very few have attended college. Those who attend college must plan to become overachievers in order to overcome the hardships that are imposed on them. (McNett & Merchant, 1981).

Attitudes Toward Disabled College Women

According to McNett and Merchant (1981), "the most serious barriers to careers and education are not physical but attitudinal. Those who are not disabled often hold stereotypes of challenged people that are especially destructive because they become embedded in policy" (p. 36 GS). These authors presented a case of a young woman who was not admitted to a college that had already agreed to accept her. She received a letter stating that they had changed their minds after she had sought out officials to investigate the accessibility of the campus. Admittance to higher education has been problematic because the criteria have tended to be discriminatory. A blind woman, for example, appeared at a university for the entrance examination only to discover it was in fine print and no reader had been provided. No braille or recorded versions were available. Myers and Witt (1979) have written that Myers, who is deaf, was not welcome in law school because it was felt that he should be spared the misfortune of "flunking" because of an inability to hear his professors. He later graduated second in the class and became an attorney. Newman (1976) studied the University of Pittsburgh's faculty, with respect to admission preferences. Although 78% of the respondent faculty members favoured an open admission policy, when it came to their admission of students into their own departments, favorability toward disabled students fell to 60 percent. Blindness seemed to bother the respondents most; deafness was viewed as less problematic, perhaps because of its "invisibility" (i.e., the deaf students appear to be more "normal" than those who are blind).

Researchers have found disabled college students who were willing to discuss a myriad of problems. Klemesrud (1981) cited an instance in which one blind woman had found professors who would not let her use the tape recorder for lectures, and professors who would constantly write on the board and refer to their notations without discussing the significance of the writing. O'Toole and Weeks (1978) described a woman who solved the problem of not being allowed to tape record lecture material by threatening to call her lawyer because of a violation of Section 504 of the Rehabilitation Act of 1973, which makes it unlawful to forbid classroom access. McNett and Merchant (1981) reported that one disabled woman's assignments were not accepted because the professor demanded that they be in writing, not on tape.

With regard to college admission problems, the classic Davis case should be addressed. Francis B. Davis, a deaf Licensed Practical Nurse, desiring to upgrade her skills and further educate herself, applied to Southeastern Community College for the Registered Nurse training program. She was rejected on the basis that she might jeopardize the safety of patients and might not grasp directions from surgeons when their masks were worn. She sued on the basis that the college had violated Section 504 of the Rehabilitation Act of 1973 and had evaluated her, not on the basis of her academic performance, but on a stereotypic predictive fear of what *might* happen *if* after receiving her degree she *later* applied for and was granted a license. She claimed that it was the school's duty to train and educate. A typical fear of able-bodied people has been that if disabled individuals were educated for certain careers they may endanger society. Frances Davis lost in Federal District Court, won in the Court of Appeals, but then lost in the Supreme Court. Perhaps the case of Frances Davis and David Hartman never said they would demand licensures in surgery; like others in the field who specialize, they wanted the opportunity to train for the areas of specialization in which auditory and visual impairments did not handicap their ability to perform (Gavin, 1979; Gill, 1981; Gliedman, 1979; Supreme Court, 1979).

Access to the Campus

The attempt to admit disabled women into college is of little value if they cannot get to and from campus, and, once on campus, cannot gain access to buildings, classrooms, and facilities. Under the 504 regulations, any university accepting federal monies must structure itself to be accessible (O'Toole & Weeks, 1978). A few years ago, no college in the nation was fully accessible (President's Committee on Employment of the Handicapped, 1968-1969). Polio quadriplegic Bev Baer (1977) wrote that "I went to ... college in the fifties, long before the word 'accessible' became popular. My classmates carried my wheelchair and me up and down two and three flights of stairs to class," (p. 6). Milner (1980) presented the issue of "reasonable accommodation," and mentioned that, according to the 504 regulations, steps, high thresholds, narrow doors, small toilet stalls and unreachable telephones, drinking fountains, and light switches in and about campus buildings must be modified to be usable by individuals who are blind, paraplegic, or quadriplegic. One of the problems Milner noted related to the desire to preserve historic structures. There has been considerable resistance, both emotionally and financially, by able-bodied administrators to modify these structures. They attempt to switch classes to newer buildings and contend that the 504 regulations have been obeyed since programs and courses have been made accessible to disabled students.

This author is reminded of a recent talk with a rehabilitation counsellor who claimed that the world could never be accessible to all handicapped people because of their individual needs. It seems logical to suggest that ramps for paraplegic students have also been useful to the elderly, who have returned to campus in increased numbers. Nearly everyone could appreciate the colorful signs which give important information and are visible at a distance (Milner, 1980). A study cited by Harris and Harris (1977) at the University of Kansas showed that when curb cuts were designed for wheelchairs to get from the sidewalk to street and vice versa, the able-bodied students thought the nice administrators had done it for *them* so they could get their bikes around more easily. Furthermore, the buildings and grounds workers thought the nice administrators had it for *them*, so they could slide their garden and snow equipment from place to place more efficiently. Freedom for the disabled has become freedom for everyone. When people in wheelchairs, on crutches, or with white canes, have been provided additional security in crossing campus alone, the able-bodied also have profited.

People inevitably must become more important then "charming" old buildings. Akamu (1975) has claimed that the University of Hawaii's campus is very accessible, but this author (employed previously at the University) had often been unable to get into her office, barred by several flight of dangerous, dark steps when the elevator didn't work or when the administrator would no turn it on. On one of the university's campuses, a program has been established that the administrators claim to be accessible to all students because they have been willing to switch some of the classes to buildings equipped with ramps and elevators. However, a mobility-impaired friend of this author was barred form seminars and regular meetings held in the inaccessible building housing the program itself. An offer was made by a professor to carry her up the flight of crumbling steps at the entrance, but she declined, fearing what would happen should he drop her or injure himself. Indeed, "program accessibility" in such cases has become a mockery of "barrier-free design."

Conclusion

It has been noted that girls and women with physical impairments face a number of difficulties in both early and postsecondary education. Because boys have tended to out number girls in several disability categories and have been more highly visible, both in activity and achievement efforts, they have been more successful than girls in competing for financial support. Girls have experienced frustration in their schooling via the traditional sex role stereotypes to which they have been exposed in course work and career planning, in both public schools which "mainstream" and in residential schools. One possible solution to this problem has been suggested by the results of the DWEP (Disabled Women's Education Project) research (Corbett & Weeks, 1981). Attitudes toward disabled women need to become less rejecting and more inclusive of opportunities for college courses and materials, recreational programs, and access to campus buildings.

One of the problems underlying the education of disabled girls and women has been the lack of role models, especially in normal contexts. It seems critical for women with disabilities to become visible role models for younger students enroled in both residential and public early education programs, as well as the university system (Neel & Pedro, 1981). Disabled adolescent girls need to see disabled women as professors, scientists, counsellors, businesswomen, and data processors. Furthermore, it is important for them to work with people with whom they can directly identify——as women who are disabled.

Much work needs to be done in the research on disabled women. Deegan (1981) noted that, in a computer search of *Psychological Abstract* of both women's issues and rehabilitation (concerns of the disabled population), 17,500 entries were discovered specifically on handicapped people (gender unspecified); 3,300 entries were found on women without regard to disability; while in combination (women who are disabled), only 31 articles existed. Of these 31 articles, 19 dealt with cancer, especially breast cancer. On the specific topic of the education of disabled girls and women (regardless of type of disability), the related literature is indeed small. Issues such as the impact of the women's movement on residential schools, sex education for pre-teen handicapped girls, and marriage and childbearing for disabled women in college have been rarely explored. As an increasing number of disabled girls enter the public school "mainstream" and disabled women enter colleges and universities, research responses will be much in demand.

References

Akamu, T. (1975). Facilities and services for handicapped students at colleges in Hawaii. **Rehabilitation Literature, 36,** 134-138.

Baer, B. (1977). Social worker/doctoral candidate in art education. In G. Laurie (Ed.) A compendium of employment experiences of 25 disabled women (p.6) **Rehabilitation Gazette, 20,** 6.

Bandura, A., Ross, D., & Ross, S.A. (1963). Imitation of film-medicated aggressive models. **Journal of Abnormal and Social Psychology, 66,** 3-11.

Beardsley, D.A. (1980). The effects of using fiction in bibiliotherapy to alter the attitudes of regular third grade students toward their handicapped peers (Doctoral dissertation, University of Missouri-Columbia, 1979). **Dissertation Abstracts International, 40,** 4869A.

Becker, F., & Jauregui, J. (1981). The invisible isolation of deaf women: Its effect on social awareness. **Journal of Sociology and Social Welfare, 8,** 249-261.

Caplan, P.J., & Kinsbourne, M. (1974). Sex differences in response to school failure. **Journal of Learning Disabilities, 7,** 232-235.

Casey, S. (1981). Wheelchair marathoning: Susan Schapiro tells how it's done. **Women Sports, 3,** 38-39.

Cerello, V. (1981). Life in between: Partially sighted. **Off Our Backs, 11,** 24-25.

Chapman, J.W., & Boersma, F.J. (1979). Learning disabilities, locus of control, and mother attitudes. **Journal of Educational Psychology, 71,** 250-258.

Cook, L. & Rossett, A.R. (1975). The sex role attitudes of deaf adolescent women and their implications for vocational choice. **American Annals of the Deaf, 120,** 341-345.

Corbett, K.J., & Weeks, C., (1981). Invisible women. **Off Our Backs, 11,** 6-7.

Deegan, M.J. (1981). Multiple minority groups: A case study of physically disabled women. **Journal of Sociology and Social Welfare, 8,** 274-297.

Doctors, S. (1977). (Ed.) Report of the National Deaf Women's Conference, Washington, D.C.: Gallaudet College.

Dodd, J.E. (1977). Overcoming occupational stereotypes related to sex and deafness. **American Annals of the Deaf, 122,** 489-491.

Egelston, J.C. & Kovolchuk, L. (1975). Deaf women - A double handicap in career development. **Social Science Record, 12,** 25-26.

Fitting, M.D., Salisbury, S., Davies, N.H., & Maychlin, D.K. (1978). Self concept and sexuality of spinal cord injured women. **Archives of Sexual Behavior, 7,** 143-156.

Gavin, J.J. (1979). Judicial reasoning or attitudinal barriers? **America,** December 8, 366-369.

Gill, F. (1981). To and fro: The federal judiciary and section 504 of the 1973 Rehabilitation Act. **Disability Rights Review,** July, 10-12.

Gillespie, P.H., & Fink, A.H. (1974). The influence of sexism on the education of handicapped children. **Exceptional Children, 41,** 155-161.

Gliedman, J. (1979). The wheelchair rebellion. **Psychology Today,** August, 59-60, 63-64, 99.

Harris, R.M., & Harris, A.C. (1977). A new perspective on the psychological effects of environmental barriers. **Rehabilitation Literature, 38,** 75-78.

Harslem, B.P. (1974). Women are too emotional **Gallaudet Today,** Spring, 30-33.

Henderson, L.T. (1979). Mama and the miracle. **Good Housekeeping.** June, 50-54, 57-58.

Higgs, R.W. (1972). Attitudes toward persons with physical disabilities as a function of information level and degree of contact (Doctoral dissertation, University of Minnesota, 1971). **Dissertation Abstracts International, 32,** 4450A.

Kutza, E.A. (1981). Benefits for the disabled: How beneficial for women? **Journal of Sociology and Social Welfare, 8,** 298-318.

Landis, C., & Bolles, M.M. (1942). **Personality and sexuality of the physically handicapped woman.** New York: Paul B. Hoeber.

MacFarland, D.C. (1966). Social isolation of the blind; An underrated aspect of disability and dependency. **Journal of Rehabilitation, 32,** 32, 49.

McNett, I., & Merchant, D. (1981). Disabled educators: assets - not handicaps - to good teaching. **Today's Education,** February-March, 34GS-37GS.

Milner, M. **Adapting historic structures for accessibility.** Washington, D.C.: Association of Physical Plant Administrators of Universities and Colleges.

Mumpower, D.L. (1970). Sex ratios found in various types of referred exceptional children. **Exceptional Children, 36,** 621-622.

Myers, L., & Witt, L. (1979). "Dummy" lawyer Lowell Myers takes aim at rights for the deaf. **People,** June 4, 83-84, 87-88.

Neel, C.E., & Pedro, L. (1981). Surviving our society with its limitations. **Off Our Backs, 11,** 12-13.

Newman, J. (1976). Faculty attitudes toward handicapped students. **Rehabilitation Literature, 37,** 194-197.

O'Toole, J.C., & Weeks, C. (1978). **What happens after school? A study of disabled women and education.** San Francisco: Far West Laboratory for Educational Reserach and Development.

Peterson, R. (1974). The deaf woman as wife and mother, two views. **Gallaudet Today,** Spring, 21-22.

President's Committee on Employment of the Handicapped. (1968-69). **To every man his chance.** Washington, D.C.: Author.

Pugin, M.A. (1981). Deafness and deaf women. **Off Our Backs, 11,** 31.

Rosenstein, J., & Lerman, A. (1963). **Vocational status and adjustment of deaf women.** New York: Lexington School for the Deaf.

Saviola, M.E. (1981). Personal reflections of physically disabled women and dependency. **Professional Psychology, 12,** 112-117.

Savitz, H.M. (1979). **Run, don't walk.** New York: New American Library.

Simon, E.P., & Gillman, A.E. (1979). Mainstreaming visually handicapped preschoolers. **Exceptional Children, 45,** 463-464.

Singer, B.D., & Osborn, R.W. (1970). Social class and sex differences in admission patterns of the mentally retarded. **American Journal of Mental Deficiency, 75,** 160-162.

Smith, D. (1974). Being deaf being a woman. **Gallaudet Today,** Spring, 7.

Storey, K.S. (1980). **The effects of the television series "Feeling Free" on children's attitudes toward handicapped people (Doctoral dissertation, Harvard University, 1979). Dissertation Abstracts Internationa, 40,** 6119A.

Supreme Court to hear case of deaf nurse. (1979). **Science, 204,** 158-159.

Thurman, S.K., & Lewis, M. (1979). Children's response to differences: Some possible implications for mainstreaming. **Exceptional Children, 45,** 468-470.

Westervelt, V.D., & McKinney, J.D. (1980). Effects of a film on nonhandicapped children's attitudes toward handicapped children. **Exceptional Children, 46,** 294-296.

Definition: A Major Issue in the Field of Learning Disabilities

WILLIAM M. CRUICKSHANK

Introduction and Background

Learning Disabilities as a term can be defined, although a perusal of the literature would leave the unsophisticated reader in a state of confusion. The term is used in the plural in this paper, since (a) that is the customary manner in which it is popularly used, and because (b) it is a phenomenon which rarely is singular in its characteristics as these are observed in a given child or adolescent.

There is a variety of types of definitions possible, i.e., (a) diagnostic and etiological definitions, (b) educational, pedagogical, paediatric or biochemical definitions, and (c) legislative definitions. In this chapter, the author has chosen to pursue the first strand, i.e., diagnostic and etiological, from which other definitions can ultimately flow. In the paragraph which follows, a logical, step-by-step procedure will be offered, ultimately resulting in a definition which will hopefully achieve some common understanding of a very complex issue.

It is appropriate to consider some background information basic to a definitional statement of learning disabilities. The term learning disabilities itself is one of the interesting accidents of our professional times. It was never used prior to 1963, at least with the connotation which it presently has. Several parent organizations had been brought together at that time in Chicago, Illinois, in an attempt on the part of their members to organize themselves in an effective manner to represent their children on a national basis. Dr. Samuel A. Kirk had been invited to address the group at an evening dinner meeting. During his prepared, but informal remarks, he ruled out several clinical problems, such as *primary* mental retardation, as not being issues germane to the problem which the parents were considering. He did approach the matter positively, however, and indicated that these were children who showed "problems of learning," "learning difficulties," "learning disabilities," or other problems related (in Kirk's remarks) essen-

tially to school learning (Hallahan and Cruickshank, 1973, Chapter 1).

Prior to this time, a great variety of terms had been used to delineate essentially the same population as those which Kirk was considering. Kephart spoke of the child who was "perceptually handicapped"; Myklebust and often Kirk and Bateman, the child with "language disorders"; Cruickshank, the "brain injured child"; Clements, Payne and others, "children with minimal cerebral dysfunction" or "minimal brain damage." Still others referred to this population under the terms of hyperactive, organic, strephosymbolic and dyslexia (Orton), clumsy child syndrome, Strauss syndrome, or any one of more than forty terms which have been reported in the literature (Cruickshank and Paul 1971).

Immediately following the 1963 dinner, to which reference has been made, the parents on a national level in the United States organized themselves under the banner of Association for Children with Learning Disabilities, an organization which soon spread widely throughout Canada and the United States and in modified forms to other countries as well (see also Stott 1972).

The term learning disabilities was adopted as a functional term without precedents to guide those who attempted to define it, and without research or common usage which would assist in its appropriate formulation as a functional term. Although a small group of professional personnel met in 1964 to consider the term and its use (Kirk, Lehitnen, Barsch, Kephart, Strothers, Frostig, Cruickshank, Myklebust, among a few others), it was seen then as a term which could not satisfy both the professionals and the parents, and one which would lend itself to innumerable definitions depending upon the orientation of the author. On the positive side it was a term which emphasized the primary problems of the child and adolescent, i.e., learning, and focused these problems directly on the school's responsibility to solve them. It is a term which in general has positive connotations, and places the child in the

Reprinted from: Journal of Rehabilitation, April/May/June 1984, with permission.

best possible light. It is, however, a term which lends itself to misinterpretation, misdefinition, and misunderstanding. In this paper, the paper will be approached from two points of view, namely, (a) historical accuracy, and (b) neuropsychological accuracy. Out of these two strands comes an accurate concept of learning disabilities per se.

Learning Disabilities and Environmentally Determined Learning Problems

Much of the confusion regarding learning disabilities, when not accurately conceptualized, comes from a failure on the part of many persons to differentiate between learning disabilities in children and those educational problems in children and youth which are primarily related to environmental causes.

Special Needs

The total school population of a province or local school authority is the base for planning. A second smaller population is identified as including *children with environmentally determined problems* and those with *special needs* (psycho-educational, medical, nutritional, or others). For the purpose of this chapter, but within the generally accepted construct, *this population refers essentially to problems of learning in children and youth which are environmentally produced.* There are some exceptions to this statement which will be mentioned later. These are children who may have had a difficult mother-child separation at the time of initial school entrance. These are children whose parents may have been undergoing a divorce when the child was in Grade One or Grade Two at a time of initial school entrance. These are children whose parents may have been undergoing a divorce when the child was in Grade One or Grade Two at a time when basic skills should have been acquired. For each of these there may have developed deficiencies in school achievement, learning problems, and often emotional disturbances related to school and to school activities. The size of this population is actually unknown,

although varying estimates and figures are available. In this group, the deficits are not chronic, but respond to education or treatment regimens.

All children with learning disabilities have chronic special needs, but they present a very special type of school, home, and community learning problem. These are the specific and central elements of this paper.

Learning Disabilities and Neurological Dysfunction

The relationship between learning disabilities and environmentally determined learning problems must be kept in focus in order to understand fully the issues of learning disabilities as a clinical entity.

The definition of learning disabilities is a three-step process. (1) Learning disabilities, whether in singular or in complex forms, are the end result of other factors. (2) As the problem is being defined here in terms of its historical and neuropsychological accuracy, learning disabilities are the result of perceptual processing deficits of an extremely diverse nature. The moment one mentions "perception," however, one must account for still another level basic to the learning disability. (3) As is all learning, perception is neurological. Perception is an inherent function of the neurology of the organism. Perception is not something separate and apart from the organism, but is the direct reflection of the capacity of the neurological system to receive stimuli, to transform them into neuro-electrical energy, to transport this energy to appropriate portions of the central nervous system, to provide a mechanism or mechanisms whereby experience, judgment, symbolization, the organization of symbols in linguistic structure, intelligence and other forms of higher intellectual function can be related to the energizing forces, and ultimately to achieve efferent nerves (output) so that appropriate motor responses in the form of movement, speech, listening, viewing, or feeling can be experienced. Perception is a process through which the steps we have just delineated are accomplished and by which the individual accommodates or adjusts to its environment. Socially acceptable responses are those which are perceived and processed within the standards recognized by society. Reading, writing, acquisition of number concepts, as well as overt forms of more gross behavior, constitute such responses.

The neurological processes of the human organism are well documented (Gaddes, 1966, 1975, 1980; Critchley, 1953; Luria, 1966), and will not be discussed here in any detail. The neurological aspect of learning disabilities is mentioned here only to indicate the specific base of the handicaps and to *differentiate learning disabilities from the environmentally determined problems of learning.* When this differentiation and the respective characteristics are kept in mind, it is easy to obtain clarity with respect to learning disabilities as an educational and social set of problems.

To paraphrase and slightly modify Wepman and his associates (in Hobbs, 1975), *learning disabilities are the result of neurologically based perceptual processing deficits.*

It must be pointed out that, since the sciences of neurology and neuropsychology are of relatively recent development, it is not always possible in the current state of the arts to make a specific diagnosis of neurological dysfunction in a given individual. We reiterate, if perceptual processing deficits are observed in a child, neurological dysfunction in some degree must be present whether or not it can be accurately identified or described through neurological examination, electroencephalography, or pneumoencephalography——common techniques available to the neurologist. The future may indeed provide for greater accuracy and definitive diagnosis in these cases through the future development and refinements of the radio microscope, Computerized Axial Tomography (CAT scan), Positron Emission Tomography (PET scan), or Nuclear Molecular Resonance (NMR) techniques, and possibly even holography when the latter science is perfected. No one of the techniques commonly used at present or suggested for the future provides fully accurate information today, but each contributes something and may be developed on a much more sophisticated basis for later diagnostic use. Certainly, the brain scan and NmR hold much promise in this regard.

Another investigator whose work has yet to be corroborated, but is related, is Julio deQuiros (Argentian) who stated that vestibular dysfunction in infants may prove to be a significant diagnostic due to the future presence or absence of learning disabilities (1976). Amniocentesis and the still newer *chorionic villi* techniques may hold predictive value of significance. While fuller discussion of these matters is more appropriate elsewhere, it is essential to this paper to state that learning disabilities, the result of perceptual processing deficits, are based on diagnosed or assumed malfunctions of the neurological system of the organism. This is historically the point of view of those whose research and clinical studies gave form to the problems of children now called learning disabilities. It is since 1963, and the widespread use of the less-than-satisfactory term "learning disabilities," that other inaccurate connotations have been given to it. If clarity regarding the essential problem is to be achieved, and if children and youth with perceptual processing deficits are to be helped, it is essential that clarity of understanding regarding the fundamental nature of learning disabilities be achieved. The needs of youth with accurately defined learning disabilities are not being met, because of the confusion related to definition which is observed in many countries, and because classrooms are characterized by heterogeneity of learning disorders rather than a maximum of homogeneity. Educators are thus faced with insurmountable tasks, all essentially based on the absence of an accurate definition of the clinical problem for education purposes.

In the sections which follow there will appear (a) a discussion and examples of perceptual processing deficits, (b) issues inherently related to learning disabilities and some tangential to it, and finally (c) other elements which lead ultimately to a definitional statement.

Example of Perceptual Processing Deficits

Perceptual processing deficits are of an unusual variety as they are observed in children and youth. Terminology commonly used is not always accurate either, so that the problem becomes confused for the parent or teacher. *The aspects of processing deficits which are included here are those which relate essentially to school learning and home and vocational adjustment. They are also defined here in terms of their psychoeducational realities,* since it is in this phase of adjustment that the greatest amount of attention is required. *It must be emphasized that,* although many examples are taken from the area of visual processing, *all sensory modalities are or may be involved:* auditory, haptic, olfactory, or gustatory as well as visual. Perceptual processing deficits may result in a variety of learning disabilities in children which, if unattended, in turn, will result in serious academic retardation. The Wepman Committee, the CELDIC Report and Australian Select Committee (1976) have emphasized numerous of the deficits as have others which will be mentioned. Since the issue of perceptual processing deficits is the result of neurological dysfunction and subsequently the cause of the learning disabilities, considerable attention will be given to the manifestations of these problems. It is clear delineation of the processing deficits which is the responsibility of the psychoeducational diagnosticians. Children and youth with perceptual processing deficits demonstrate inadequate abilities in a number of both overlapping and discrete functions. Some of these problem areas are delineated in the paragraphs which follow. The reader must keep in mind that all of the examples provided below may affect interactional learning which thus requires that those who work with learning disabilities children maintain a constant concern for social adaptation and development, effective emotional development, as well as the specific implications of the psychomotor match between perceptual deficits and educational management planning.

1. Discrimination. Children and youth with learning disabilities frequently show an inadequate ability in the recognition of "fine differences between auditory and visual" and tactual "discriminating features underlying the sounds used in speech and the orthographic forms used in reading" (Wepman et al., 1975, p. 309). Golick speaks of this same characteristic under

the heading of inadequate "visual efficiency" (1970, p. 8). She emphasizes an important dimension which others have often overlooked, namely, that "With some, the problems seem to be poor perception of the three-dimensional world; yet, two-dimensional vision——for written material, pictures——is intact." Seventeen year-old Dale, when blindfolded, is unable to discriminate between a quarter and a nickel and sometimes between a dime and a quarter. Twenty year-old Steve is confused with sounds which appear different, i.e., "tall" and "call." Phonemes such as "pf" and the sound of "f" cannot be distinguished as separates in oral reading. "Two," "too," and "to" are literally impossible to differentiate by this learning disabled dyslexic young adult.

The Wepman Committee stressed discriminatory malfunction in terms of auditory and visual modalities. To these we have added tactual (haptic) discrimination in some children. Although the visual and auditory modalities are undoubtedly the most significant in terms of learning, some research of a minimal nature exists to indicate that the processing deficits here under consideration are probably to be observed in all of the sensory modalities. This fact, although not firmly authenticated, should be kept in mind as subsequent characteristics of perceptual processing deficits are briefly discussed.

2. Memory. Children and adolescents with learning disabilities often show an inadequate ability in "retaining and recalling those discriminated sounds and forms in both short- and long-term memory" (Wepman et al., ibid.). Although failure to remember is an often-heard complaint of teachers and parents, it may not be a discrete processing deficit, but may be the result of other factors which will be mentioned later. However, the inability to recall constitutes a tremendous hazard to successful achievement, is a characteristic noted by most authors, and indeed was stressed in what is perhaps the first published description of these children under the heading of a "Composite of a Child" (Cruickshank et al., 1961, p. 55). Until a Grade 10 math teacher agreed to permit Tracy to utilize a ten dollar calculator in his algebra class, Tracy failed. When the calculator was admitted to class on all occasions, Tracy could compete with the best of his class. The youth knew concepts, but he was unable to recall the multiplication tables and therefore, was either too slow in his operations on tests, for example, or completely failed because he could not remember number facts.

3. Sequencing. Many youth with learning disabilities show an inadequate ability and a "poor grasp of sequence" (Golick, p. 9). The Wepman Committee likewise call attention to this disability area in stating that learning disabled children often are characterized by difficulties in "ordering the sounds and forms (referred to in par. 1 above) sequentially, both in sensory and motor acts" (ibid, Wepman, 1975).

Sequencing and memory functions are undoubtedly closely interrelated. Sequencing requires an efficient memory by which to order things, events, or commands in a proper relationship. Irrespective of its independent or dependent status, the lack of ability to sequence is a fundamental characteristic of many children with learning disabilities, and is a significant hurdle to their school achievement and general adjustment.

The same Tracy had extreme problems with sequencing——extreme to the point that his mother or older brother nightly had to lay out on the floor in a correct sequence form window to door (left to right) at the foot of his bed the clothing he was to wear the following morning to school. Starting with jockey shorts and ending with an outside jacket, Tracy followed a path of clothing and ended up appropriately dressed. Without this aid, his sequencing problem was greater than he could encompass. Starting an automobile in driver-training class involved learning a sequence of steps which took all summer in daily lessons to accomplish. He did accomplish, however, but with much effort and with many "crutches."

4. Figure-background relationship. Individuals with learning disabilities frequently have an inadequate ability to distinguish visual, auditory, and/or tactile figure-background relationships (Wepman et al., ibid.; Frostig, lefever, Wittelsey, 1961). This factor may also be related to attentiveness to be discussed below, but in isolation it is, in itself, a serious processing impediment for learning. Undoubtedly the most

extensive studies of this problem have been carried out with cooperation of cerebral palsy children of the athetoid and spastic subtypes (Cruickshan, Bice et al., 1965). However, studies of the figure-background pathology were completed by Werner and Strauss as early as 1941 with exogenous mentally retarded children, and numerous other investigators have studied this phenomenon in relation to populations of children and youth with varying neurophysiological diagnoses. In practically every study which has examined the psychological characteristics of children with learning disabilities, the element of figure-ground pathology have been observed. Irrespective of its etiology, it is a serious impediment to appropriate development of reading skills, and its presence seriously impairs achievement in all forms of school-oriented learning situations.

Figure-ground pathology is a hurdle to elementary and secondary school students in reading, math, and in all tasks involving printed words or numerals. Tom, aged twenty failed his driver examination when he attempted to read it by himself, but passed with no errors when the examination was read to him by an agent in the State office. Davey, aged 8, was accused of being sexually precocious when he continually "felt up" his teacher. This behavior stopped completely when the teacher wore solid colored dresses instead of clothing which involved prints or polka dots. Figure-ground and attention disturbances were problems here.

5. Time and space orientation. The Wepman Committee (ibid, p. 306) stresses that children with learning disabilities often have an inadequate ability in "recognizing spatial and temporal orientations." Problems of directionality, recognition of body parts, inadequate spatial and temporal orientation have been commented upon many times by clinical investigators (Hallahan and Kauffman, 1975) who work with the learning disabilities population. The interrelationship of these factors with others which are included in this section is obvious, but, as with some of the others, these problems stand out in such a manner as to isolate them. It is undoubtedly the failure to function well in these areas in which many children with learning disabilities contributes to the development of inadequate body-image concepts and poor self-concepts, other characteristics of a secondary order which are frequently commented upon by writers in this field (Kronick, 1973; Golick, 1970; Cruickshank, 1977; and others).

In demonstrating before a group of teachers, Ted, aged 12 years of age broke down and cried when he was asked to walk over a maze placed on the floor with masking tape and at each corner to tell whether he was going to turn right or left. Concepts of directionality were simply not within his ability to handle. One has to consider the number of times daily a learning disabled child or youth is expected to respond to direction. Billy, a youth with time disorientation, used to ask his teacher about the time as many as fifty times a day until someone bought for him a digital watch with the numbers clearly visible on the face. However, this complicated his understanding of how to "tell time" when this involved the half-hour, quarter hour, or number of minutes before or after the hour.

6. Closure. Children and adolescents with learning disabilities have an inadequate "ability to obtain closure" on either an ideational or more concrete form. For example, a child asked to draw a square or a circle may produce something in the form of a letter "U." A child who starts to relate an event of the previous day may find that he cannot continue to the close of the story or idea (Wepman, et al., ibid., Gyr, 1975).

7. Sensory integration. Individuals with learning disabilities have an inadequate capacity in "integrating intersensory information" (Birch and Leford, 1964). Golick (1970) states that "some children seem to be able to handle tasks that are purely visual or tasks that are purely auditory, but seem to have difficulty in combining the information that comes to them through separate sense organs. For example, they may be able to see and recognize the letter, *a*, and hear and repeat the vowel sound, *a*, but seem to be unable to learn to associate the two." Frostig (1975) writes of this aspect of processing deficits as "one of the most significant hurdles to learning and adjustment which faces the child with learning disabilities." How often does the following situation occur in the classroom?

"*Listen,* boys and girls," calls the teacher, "listen to me. *Look* at the blackboard. *See* what I have written there. *Copy* what you see on paper." "Listen" (auditory), "look" (visual), "copy" (motor) involve three neurological systems. For children who have difficulty in associating activities which involved two or more systems, a failure experience is certain to take place. Intersensory integration is another aspect of processing which demands research at all levels of child growth and development. (See also Koupernik, MacKeith and Francis-Williams, 1975; Ayres, 1975).

8. Perceptual-motor function. Children and adolescents with learning disabilities have an inadequate ability in "relating what is perceived to specific motor functions" (Wepman et al., ibid., Kephart, 1975). In part, this function is related to the poor grasp of sequence to which reference was earlier made (Golick, 1970), to an inadequate judgment of the amount of energy required to initiate and accomplish a given motor task, and to the inability to refrain from reacting to motor-eliciting stimuli until a task analysis of the required operation is completed by the child.

9. Dissociation. Persons with learning disabilities very often have an inadequate ability to associate. To state it negatively, these children are characterized by dissociation. Dissociation is the inability to see parts in relationship to the whole. These persons have difficulty in conceptualizing new concepts which are built upon previously learned or recognized elements. Dissociation contributes to the problems in sequencing and to figure-ground pathology. On a functional basis, these individuals have difficulty with pegboard designs, block designs, parquetry blocks, lacing shoes, as well as with more abstract wholes which must be developed form related parts (Strauss and Werner,1942; Cruickshank, 1977). The individual parts appear to have greater significance for the child than does the ultimate whole concept, probably some of the other characteristics mentioned earlier, are closely related to the attention problems which these persons often demonstrate.

10. Attention. Children and adolescents with learning disabilities are often characterized by attention disturbances (Cruickshank, 1977;

Werner and Strauss, 1942; and many others). Hagan and Keil (1975) and Lewis (1975) have made excellent analyses of the problems of attention and attention disturbances in children with learning disabilities. At least one point of view holds that the attention disturbances of the learning disabilities child are the result of being unable to refrain from reacting to extraneous environmental stimuli which may include those of a visual, auditory tactual or other modalities. The extraneous stimuli may be internal as well as external to the organism (Rappaport, 1969). Kinaesthetic stimuli resulting from clothing which bind (tactual stimuli) may be the source of real, but unconscious disturbances for the child. Extraneous stimuli may be of two major types: sensory or motor. Whereas the neurologically intact normal child or youth can negatively adapt to the unessential, the unusual, or the extraneous, the child with perceptual processing deficits at times appears almost driven to respond to them. Kurt Goldstein, in a classic paper, speaks of this characteristic in terms of "driveness" (1941). Homberger (1926) refers to the phenomenon as "being stimulus bound," i.e., tied to stimuli. Strauss and Werner (1941) and Cruickshank have referred to this behavior as forced responsiveness to stimuli (1966, 1977).

If the child is driven to respond to stimuli of whatsoever nature, the attention span will be significantly shortened (Kronick, p. 143). A short attention span is directly related to the amount of time the child has to learn. It is not unusual to see children in a clinical situation where the attention span is of two or three minutes duration, and children with attention spans as short as fifteen to thirty seconds have been observed on many occasions. But even longer attention spans, yet short by normal standards, will produce learning and adjustment problems for the child in school or home learning situations.

Although little if any quantitative data is available, clinicians often also report that these children make deviant or unusual responses to reinforcement. While the etiology of this observed behavior may not be clear, it is possible that this also is directly related to short attention span or to attention disturbances of other natures.

Likewise, these children may process stimuli at a different rate than normal children. If left alone, these children are observed to have an erratic rate of processing, slower rates, or sometimes appear to be overwhelmed by the task of processing that they function behaviorally on almost totally a trial-and-error basis.

Previously, it was stated that the lack of attention or forced responsiveness to stimuli probably is related to dissociation and to figure-ground disturbance, among other characteristics, e.g., closure. The backgrounds of most visual situations and of many auditory and tactual representations contain much more stimuli than does the figure itself. Cruickshank, Bice, et al. (1965) have shown that it takes a relatively large increase in the value of a figure (through size, color, and commonness of concept) before a child with visual perceptual processing deficits can perceive it adequately on a routine basis. Grube has demonstrated that this capacity is developmental in normal children (at least during the chronological years of four through seven). The neurologically handicapped subjects in the Cruickshank and Bice study were between the ages of six and sixteen years.

The normal auditory climate of a classroom, home, or playground contains a great amount of stimuli. The visual environment of a printed page in a child's reading or arithmetic book contains hundreds, if not thousands of background stimuli in comparison to the few stimuli contained in the specific word or set of numerals which the child is attempting to respond to at the moment. Learning disabilities children are often characterized as having poor table manners. This may in part be due to the excessive number of background stimuli (many of which are motoric in nature) surrounding the child at meal time in comparison to the specific piece of food which is being put by him or her onto a fork or spoon. The psychologist often sees this characteristic of overreaction to stimuli defeating the child when the latter is asked to perform on marble boards, Rorschach cards, or other types of psychological testing material.

These comments are written by way of stating that the factor of stimuli attraction (a) reduces the child's attention span, and (b) may well be a significant deterrent to appropriate processing in other related areas, i.e., increasing chances of dissociation, hindering closure, producing figure-background confusions, and, among others interfering with the capacity to make fine discriminations (par. 1 above) which are so much a part of good initial reading and speaking.

11. Rate of processing. Rate of processing has been mentioned above. However, it warrants special stress. Marjorie Golick writes: "There are some children whose difficulties in learning language are related to their inability to process the stream of speech quickly enough to identify (and therefore remember) the component stimuli. This is evident at the beginning stages of speech development in their mispronunciation and mis-identification of those parts of words (consonants articulated in clusters and unstressed syllables) which demand rapid temporal judgments. Later on, it is apparent in their inability to repeat accurately polysyllabic words where several consonants follow in rapid succession; in their spelling errors (where sounds and syllables are omitted); in their difficulty in learning exceptions to linguistic rules (irregular parts and plurals which must be individually noticed and remembered); and in their difficulty in using and understanding those sentence structures which depend on precise tracking of unstressed elements whose forms of placements are unpredictable."

12. Perseveration. Some children and adolescents with learning disabilities demonstrate varying degrees of perseveration which interfere with learning and adjustment processes. Perseveration is a characteristic which is not reserved to learning disabilities children and youth alone. Furthermore there appears to be more than one way in which perseveration is manifested. In the psychotic or the neurotic patient one frequently observes conceptual perseveration. This type of adjustment may or may not be a matter of perceptual processing deficit, but is the result of other dynamics not pertinent to this paper.

Perseveration in the child with learning disabilities has been described (Werner and Strauss, 1942; Cruickshank, 1977) as (a) the prolonged after-effect of a stimulus, or (b) as the

inertia of the organism preventing easy movement from one stimulus situation to the other. Whether perseveration is a genuine processing deficit or a learned emotional response serving to protect the individual is not clear and need not be argued here. It is, however, a very significant deterrent to learning and to appropriate adjustment in the child with learning disabilities when it does occur. It is probably one of the more difficult characteristics to deal with on either a psychological or an educational level.

13. Language and communication. Language and communication are learned behaviors based on essential neurological functions involving adequate reception of auditory stimuli, their transmission and translation into appropriate expressive behavior. These functions are basic examples of perceptual processing, and when undamaged systems convey stimuli appropriately, good normal speech, language as well as non-vocal speech is the result. When the system does not function adequately, as in the case of children with learning disabilities, then the commonly-observed characteristics of faulty understanding of language and its use, poor speech per se, and their often-reported absence of "inner conversation" or subliminal language is reported.

14. Other characteristics. Numerous authors have listed other characteristics of processing deficits, some of which are overlapping with those which have been mentioned above. Chief among these, however, are:

a. deficits in size discrimination (Australian report);

b. deficits in judgment of time (Australian report; Hallahan, 1975);

c. deficits in judgment of distance (Australian report);

d. deficits in abstract reasoning (Goldstein, Strauss, Cruickshank, Australian report, others_;

e. inadequate concept formation (Strauss, Werner, Australian report, Crichton er al., Golick and others); and

f. poor sense of rhythm (Golick).

Learning Disabilities: Multifaceted
Before the discussion of learning disabilities per se is concluded, it is important to note a number

of subsets which fully or partially overlap within this population. The size of the learning disability population is unknown. There are many estimates, often guesses, which have been repeated so often that unfortunately they have become accepted as fact. The actual situation, however, is that there is not one adequate epidemiological or demographic study of learning disabilities in the world's literature as of the time this paper is written. There have been studies, very limited in size of populations of children with learning disabilities, but there have been no studies of total school populations to determine, with even rough screening devices, the number of children who accurately could be termed those with learning disabilities. This is a reflection of the newness of the field, the sudden use of the categorical term, the lack of adequate research, and the pressure to provide services in the absence of adequately prepared general educators and administrators, to say nothing of the almost total absence of qualified clinical teachers able to meet the needs of children with specific learning disabilities. It is this lack of accurate epidemiological data which makes the application of statistical definitions of learning disabilities unsatisfactory, although this problem will be discussed later in this chapter. With this in mind, it is possible to consider some of the elements central and closely related to learning disabilities.

Intelligence

Many definitions of learning disabilities include a cut-off point insofar as intelligence quotient is concerned. This is an historical slip which was permitted to occur in 1963, when the initial use of the term learning disabilities took place following Kirk's speech. Although it was stated earlier by Kirk that these were not children with *primary mental retardation*, his audience chose to hear that these were *not primarily mentally retarded children*. Therein developed a situation which is without fact, and which has served to deprive thousands of children of their educational birthright. Parents wanted to put their child's best foot forward, and this is understandable. There were enough problems to be faced without the added one of mental retardation. And some of them had heard that these were children

without primary retardation. To drop the word primary was a very easy thing for some parents to do, just as it was with some educators who did not understand the essential issues of learning disabilities. Thus early on the ACLD (USA) defined this problem in terms of intellectual normality. This led to numerous educational authorities defining the problem as being one reserved to children with intelligence quotients above 80, 85, or 90! Obviously any educational authority can define the problem as the citizens of the authority wish, but in terms of accuracy and child need, to equate learning disabilities with intellectual normalcy in all cases is to perpetuate inaccurate statements and to ignore much of what little research there is.

The basis for this statement lies in the early work of Werner, Strauss (as reported in Strauss and Lehtinen 1947), and their associates, studies which appeared for the first time in the literature between 1935 and 1945. All of these research studies, vigorously critiqued by Sarason (1946), were completed on endogenous and exogenous, educable mentally retarded boys between the ages of 12 and 16 years. Although their statistical sophistication accuracy may be criticized, as Sarason has done, the studies of Werner and Strauss demonstrate without a doubt the clinical presence of learning of record much which was known about children later to be called learning disabled in 1963, came from research done originally on mentally retarded youth. It is thus inaccurate to speak of learning disabilities, as we shall presently define the problem, as being restricted to children and youth of average or above-average intellectual ability. It is accurate to state that the issues of "*perceptual processing deficits are respectors of no single intellectual level, but are to be found throughout the intellectual spectrum*" (a phrase used by Dr. John McLeod, University of Saskatchewan and Mrs. Barbara McElgunn, Toronto). Indeed, to perpetuate the inaccuracy regarding the relationship of intelligence to learning disabilities is not only to fail to serve many children in need, but to perpetuate an insidious form of racial discrimination as well. In some communities classes for the mentally retarded are essentially composed of minority group learners: those for the learning disabled, white learners.

The terms *endogenous* and *exogenous* may require definition. In this paper and in general usage in the study of mental retardation, endogenous children are those in whose history there is no evidence of brain injury, neurological signs, accident, illness, or injury which could account for the intellectual retardation, but in whose history there is evidence of genetic, familial, or hereditary factors which could account for it. Exogenous children, on the other hand, are those in whose history there is no evidence of genetic or familial entities, but where there is evidence of some adventitious factors (e.g., neurological signs, brain injury, accident, illness or injury) which occurred at some point during the fetal through the postnatal developmental period and which might or do account for the abnormal perceptual responses, the lowered functional intelligence, or both. It is the latter group to which reference is made here, and it is those who are indicated to have learning disabilities comparable to their intellectually more normal peers.

It must also be added that many learning disabilities children of whatsoever level of intelligence function may "test low" on initial psychological testing, but who with appropriate instructional regimens may later function more ***arly or fully normal. There are, of course, many learning disabilities children and youth who are fully functional at traditional levels of normal intellect, and some who are functioning well above "normal" insofar as measured intelligence is concerned. Irrespective of these latter comments, there is the person who can be differentially diagnosed as an exogenous mentally retarded learning disabilities child or youth. The careful differentiation required here to insure the appropriate therapeutic or educational regimens requires diagnosticians of excellent preparation and highly developed skills.

Cerebral Palsy

Illustrative of one of the more complex aspects of child growth and development is the relationship of cerebral palsy, mental retardation, and learning disabilities. Although a relatively small popula-tion, it is a significant one on whom longstanding research data are available on this topic. The initial studies of Dolphin and Cruickshank (1951) illustrate the similarities between the perceptual pathology in cerebral palsy and in the exogenous mentally retarded populations of Werner and Strauss. As a matter of fact, the emphasis on intellectual normalcy which was seized upon by the parent groups may have come in part from the Dolphin-Cruickshank studies which were the first to be done on groups of intellectually normal children who had definite diagnosis of neurological impairment. Following these, a comprehensive study of intellectually normal cerebral palsy children (Cruickshank, Bice, Walled, and Lynch, 1965) was completed which corroborated in a much more definitive manner many perceptual similarities between exogenous mentally retarded youth and the cerebral palsy population. Four hundred children between the ages of 6 and 16 years were included in the latter study. However, the study was restricted to athetoid and spastic type cerebral palsy subjects only. The similarities between the mentally retarded and cerebral palsy subjects insofar as perceptual processing was concerned formed the first link between these neurophysiological disability groups and the population later to become known as learning disability, a fact corroborated by Wedell (1961) and Critchley (1953). In terms of certain aspects of perceptual processing, more than 80 percent of the two subtypes of cerebral palsy which were studied are so characterized.

A second characteristic of major significance pertaining to the cerebral palsy subset should be noted, namely, the high incidence of mental retardation in cerebral palsy. This fact has been known for many years through the research of Asher and Schonel (1950) Heilman (1952), Miller and Rosenfeld (1952), Bice and Cruickshank (1955), and others. The incidence of retarded mental development in cerebral palsy is variously reported by these authors, each working independently, to be overall in the vicinity of 70-80 percent. A high incidence of cerebral palsy-mental retardation-learning disability overlap is easily demonstrated, producing indeed a most complex psychoeducational diagnostic and teaching problem.

Aphasia and Dyslexia

Two subjects of aphasia and dyslexia are suggested to fall completely within the learning disability population. There are many popular concepts regarding these two clinical problems, but if they are accurately defined, they are seen to be very specific types of neurophysiological dysfunction involving severe forms of perceptual-motor input and output functions. McGinnis, (1963) in her classic work on aphasia, describes this population in almost exact terms comparable to the description of exogenous mentally retarded subjects of Werner and Strauss, the cerebral palsy subjects of Cruickshank and Bice, and the populations of children later to be called learning disabled as described by M.S. Rabinovitch, Gaddes, Kephart, Golick, Knonick, and many others. Similarly, R. Rabinovitch and others describe the dyslexic population, when accurately defined, from the same orientation, although each clinical subtype involves different central nervous system tracts.

Hyperactive and/or Emotionally Impaired

There is reason to believe that many hyperactive and/or emotionally disturbed children are actually learning disabled children who, on a motoric basis, are unable to refrain from reacting to stimuli which produce a motor response. Admittedly this forms a theoretical position. However, when some hyperactive and "brain injured" children were submitted to a similar education model specifically designed for learning disabilities, and the teachers not informed regarding the diagnostic categories of their pupils, those with a diagnosis of hyperactivity performed equally well as those with a more definitive neurological diagnosis. This fact has been observed on frequent occasions in clinical teaching situations. Although there is no epidemiological data available, it is hypothesized that a significant number of hyperactive and/or emotionally disturbed children are learning disabled children, the latter with severe emotional overlay which is probably the result of continued failure experiences. This, as with most aspects of learning disability,

provides an important area of needed future research.

Other

Other clinical subtypes exist, some members of which undoubtedly demonstrate characteristics similar to the learning disabilities population. Some children with organic types of deafness have been shown to have many of the same characteristics of learning disabilities (McKay, 1952). Some blind children are observed clinically to have poor tactual perceptual precessing and thus have great difficulties in learning Braille, for example. Some children with epilepsy and others who have experienced encephalitis, meningitis, or other forms of central nervous system diseases, are often left with problems of perceptual processing among other handicaps. Autism, accurately defined, may well be considered here also.

The number of subsets which could be mentioned might be much larger. The point here, however, is not to make a complete inventory, but to suggest that there is a variety of clinical categories in each of which there is an identifiable percentage of children whose learning disabilities are due to the same basic neurophysiological dysfunction as are those of the larger group whose name identifies the problem per se. There is, of course, the learning disabilities child who does not have other complicating problems such as have been described thus far.

The skills of the neuropsychologist, the clinical or school psychologist, and the educational diagnosticians are crucial here, not only to identify the levels of intellectual functioning in these multiply-handicapped children and youth, but to provide a differential diagnosis which will indicate the nature of the perceptual problem and the type of educational planning which is required (see also Crichton, Kendall, Cutterson and Dunn, 1972). Unfortunately, not all of these professional groups are being prepared at the present time to be able to address adequately these complex problems of growth and development.

To this point in this paper learning disabilities have been identified as being:

1. a large subset of the population of children with special needs which is an identifiable population within any total school community;
2. characterized by numerous overlapping subsets, e.g., exogenous mental retardation, aphasia, dyslexia, among others, each of which has been demonstrated to have many common neuropsychological characteristics;
3. often present without multiple characteristics;
4. characterized as a condition to be found at all intellectual levels and frequently in relationship with numerous physical and emotional manifestations; and
5. the end result of perceptual processing problems which are inherent manifestation of the neurological and physiological systems of the human organism.

Other Definitional Factors
Etiology

As learning disabilities are being defined in this paper, they may be the result of a wide variety of etiological factors each of which may have a deleterious impact on the developing central nervous system. These may occur at prenatal, perinatal, or postnatal periods of development.

Typical of factors which may cause central nervous system impairment in the fetus (and subsequent processing deficits) are such things as rubella, maternal toxaemia, phenylketonuria (PKU), so-called "hard drugs," narcotics, such as heroin and methadone, and a wide variety of prenatal accidents and injuries. Injuries during the birth process constitute one possible perinatal etiological factor, but this may also be related to the failure of the bones and ligaments of the pelvic arch to give sufficiently to permit easy passage of the fetus, breach birth, abnormal position of the umbilical cord, and the failure to establish breathing immediately. Examples of postnatal etiological factors could be almost endless involving a wide variety of childhood illnesses, accidents, and injuries. It would appear, however, in terms of the present knowledge that most processing deficits are coincident with prenatal and perinatal etiological factors. Thus definitionaly it is possible to state that *the central nervous system impairment with its subsequent processing deficits and learning disabilities may be related to almost any etiological factor.*

Age

Although most learning disabilities occur, it is thought, during the prenatal and early postnatal years, they *may occur at any age* in the developmental span of childhood and youth. In addition to chronological age, the age of the brain and the recency of trauma will be factors of significance in the ability of the individual to respond to treatment and educational regimens.

In recent years, a number of studies have appeared in the literature which of necessity focused attention on the possibility of learning disabilities in some cases being related to genetic factors. Under no circumstances do these studies indicate this to be the sole source of perceptual processing deficits, but the matter must now be considered as another possible etiological factor. While admittedly more research is required, clinical observations alone would give one cause to wonder about the familial, if not the genetic, factors. The presence of nearly identical learning disabilities in a mother (age 43 years), for example, and in her daughter (age 25 years), her son (age 19 years), her second daughter (age 16 years), and her second son (age 10 years), is a convincing bit of evidence. Learning disabilities have been found in numerous sets of fraternal twins. Sons with learning disabilities quite frequently are reported to have nearly identical problems as those experienced by their fathers a school generation earlier. The familial incidence of learning disabilities is certainly recognized clinically. Whether or not the issue is genetic in the sense of a chromosomal abnormality remains one for further research. The relationship at this time appears sufficient so that both familial and genetic factors may tentatively be included as etiological factors, and as such should be evaluated carefully in all complete assessments of children and youth suspected of having learning disabilities.

Biochemical Imbalances

Although there is inadequate information available as yet, some evidence is accruing which relates biochemical imbalances to learning disabilities. Not enough is known about either normality or deviance in biochemical balance or imbalance to generalize. However, it can be postulated that this may be found as an etiological factor of significance. Abnormal retention or excretion of proteins, zinc, magnesium, among other items, must be viewed as having a potential impact on the developing central nervous system, perception and learning.

Definition

Out of the structure which has been provided her, definitions which are applicable to any discipline can be drawn. Disciplines differ in the vocabulary which is used. Members of each discipline related to learning disabilities can utilize effectively the concepts contained herein for their appropriate disciplinary adaptation. The example which follows, while applicable in the final analysis to any discipline, focuses on the psychoeducational reality of learning disabilities. The elements which have been described in the preceding paragraphs and sections can be brought together to form a meaningful and historically accurate definition of learning disabilities. Two assumptions must be kept in mind, namely (a) there is an inherent dysfunction in the learning process which is manifested in deficiencies in one or more academic skill subjects, language or communication problems and/or social adaptation problems; and (b) there is a significant discrepancy between measured potential and measured performance of both an academic and social nature.

Based therefore on these psychoeducational realities, it can be stated that (1) *learning disabilities are problems in the acquisition of developmental skilled, academic achievement, social adjustment, and secondarily emotional growth and development, which are the result of perceptual and linguistic processing deficits.* Further defined, learning disabilities (2) *may be of any etiological origin,* (3) *may be observed in child-*ren and youth of any age* and (4) *of any level of intellectual function,* (5) *are the result of perceptual processing deficits which, in turn,* (6) *are or may be the result of a (diagnosed or inferred) neurophysiological dysfunction occurring at prenatal, perinatal, or (in the case of linguistic dysfunction) at the postnatal periods of development.*

Quantitative Application of the Definition

The development of a definition of learning disabilities is a logical process. Unfortunately, when a definition is reached, professional personnel are faced with a blind alley of unknowns. The lack of epidemiological data of a definitive nature, to which reference was made much earlier, leaves many perplexing problems. The clinical entity is known and relatively well understood. Knowledge regarding the size of the population is not available. This means a number of questions cannot be accurately addressed, *vis-a-vis:* (1) How many children should an area board of education and a director of education expect to find in a given school authority? (2) How many will need self-contained classrooms and how many could normally be expected to be included in the ordinary grades of the public school system? (3) What kind of in-service training is required for teachers of ordinary classrooms so they will be able to meet the needs of the learning disabilities children who are integrated? (4) How many teachers should be prepared by colleges and universities in given state or province? (5) How much grant money should be requested by ministers of education from legislatures to support local programs? These questions among others can now be answered only with guesses and estimates in spite of the fact, as has been stated, that some estimates have been used so widely and for such a long period of time that the figures often have become accepted as fact. Such cannot be permitted for the future. There is an immediate need for a carefully conducted epidemiological study in a large school system which contains urban and suburban elements and which contains a sufficiently multiracial population to be able also to reach firm conclusions regarding the demography of the problem of learning disabilities. Such a study should include school population in order that the problem as it affects the secondary schools can be ascertained, an issue which is even more subject to the guess estimate approach than it is in the elementary school level. When this matter is concluded, then the efficacy of the approaches to be discussed below can be determined.

Often quantitative applications and regulations of an administrative nature are confused with definition. In this paper, there has been a serious attempt to keep these two matters separate. A definition has been presented. How that definition is applied may vary from one school to another. The problem of learning disabilities has become very confused over the years, confused essentially by those who have failed to recognize the historical antecedents to the problem. As a result, attempts at quantitative applications have likewise sometimes become cumbersome. It is difficult to establish education guidelines for anything when officials do not hold in mind a clear-cut idea of the size of the problem and qualified personnel to teach the child if and when they are accurately defined and diagnosed. This is a field of education which has grown with less than the best of logic and thought. It is obvious that *once a definition is agreed upon or accepted in principle, rules, regulations or guidelines for its implementation are required.*

Learning Disabilities or the Learning Disabled?

It must be apparent to the reader that the term learning disabilities is one which is inefficient, and lends itself to much misunderstanding and misinterpretation. It is a poor set of words which has been used to describe a very technical problem of human growth and development. For the individual coming onto the term without a background of experience with it, the concept of learning disabilities provides a convenient niche into which a heterogeneous series of childhood problems can be placed. For the teacher with little or no specialized training in the area of perceptual processing, the term learning disabil-

ities can easily become synonymous with concepts of remediation, lack of motivation, or behavior problems. For the parent who is confronted with the problem for the first time, the term learning disabilities can easily be translated to mean a problem for the schools to solve, since one of the chief aspects of the business of the schools is to deal with problems of learning and achievement.

Although we are not urging the adoption of another term, clarity and specificity of the problem would be much more quickly achieved if the pupils involved were termed children with perceptual processing deficits (PPD children). That is hardly an acceptable label, and it would only serve to create another category, the very thing which the few leaders who were active with this problem prior to 1963 tried hard to avoid. Their efforts were in vain, and a term——learning disabilities——was created which not only added to the classification nomenclature, but provided a term which produced extremes in misunderstanding and confusion when it was accepted and utilized by novices in the field. Rather than to create yet another term, it is perhaps wiser to thoroughly understand the parameters of the present term learning disabilities, and to conceive it in the technical sense in which it has been described in this paper.

One further consideration regarding the term learning disabilities needs attention. These clients being served, and indeed the names of the organizations purporting to represent them, place an emphasis on *children* with learning disabilities.

It is with children, of course, where it all started, but over time these children have grown up. The seven-year old children in 1963 about whom parents were concerned are at the date of this writing adults of twenty-one years, often married, and sometimes with their own children, but regardless, they are all coping with the responsibilities of adulthood. Just how many children with learning disabilities approach Grade Seven or Grade Ten still with functional characteristics or perceptual processing deficits is not known. The fact of the matter is, however, that many of them do. When their needs as youth with learning disabilities are not served by the secondary schools, the community often receives the brunt of their frustrations and maladjustment. The close relationship between the unsolved problems of youth with learning disabilities and delinquency has been demonstrated (Murray, 1975).

It is essential that these youth be served by the schools, a problem which has not been conceptualized by school personnel at this time to any significant extent. The question is raised: can a problem which emphasizes children be accepted by secondary schools as typical of the youth they purport to serve? Should the issue become one of the problems of *learning disabled*? Should formal associations functioning in behalf of these pupils be called "association for the learning disabled"? The New York Association for the learning Disabled, attempting to be an organization which speaks for those with learning disabilities of any age, may be the forerunner of change in emphasis.

References

Asher, P., & Schonel, E.E. (1950). "A survey of 400 cases of cerebral palsy." **Archives of Disease in Childhood, 25,** 360-379.

(Australia)   *)

Learning Disabilities in Children and Adults. (1976). Report of the House of Representatives Select Committee on Specific Learning Difficulties. Canberra: Australian Government Publishing Service.

Ayres, A.J. (1955). "Sensorimotor Foundations of Academic Ability; in William M. Cruickshank and D.P. Hallahan, **Perceptual and Learning Disabilities in Children,"** 2. Syracuse: Syracuse University Press.

Bice, H., & Cruickshank, W.M. (1955). "Evaluation of intelligence," in W.M. Cruickshank and G.M. Raus (Eds.), **Cerebral Palsy: Its Individual and Community Problems.** Syracuse: Syracuse University Press.

Birch, H.G., & Leford, A. (1964). "Two strategies for studying perception in 'Brain-Damaged' children," in H.G. Birch (Ed.), **Brain Damage in Children.** Baltimore: Williams & Wilkins, 46-60.

Crichton, J., Kendall, D., Cutterson, J., & Dunn, H. (1972). **Learning Disabilities: A Practical Office Manual.** (Victoria, B.C.: Canadian Pediatric Society, Norris Printing Co.

Critchley, M. (1953). **The Parietal Lobes.** Lond: Edward Arnold, Ltd.

Cruickshank, W.M. (1977). **The Brain Injured Child in Home, School and Community,** 1966 revised as **Learning Disabilities in Home, School and Community.** Syracuse: Syracuse University Press.

Cruickshank, W.M., & Bice, H.V. (1955). "Personality characteristics," in Cruickshank, W.M., & Raus, G.M., **Cerebral Palsy: Its Individual and Community Problems.** Syracuse: Syracuse University Press.

Cruickshank, W.M., Bice, H.V., Wallen, H.E., & Lynch, K.S. (1965). **Perception and Cerebral Palsy.** Syracuse: Syracuse University Press, revised edition.

Cruickshank, W.M., & Paul, J.L. (1971). "Psychological Characteristics of Brain-Injured Children," in Cruickshank, W.M. (Ed.), **Psychology of Exceptional Children and Youth.** Englewood Cliffs, NJ, Prentice-Hall, Inc.

Cruickshank, W., Bentzen, F., Ratzberg, F., & Tannhauser, M. (1961). **A Teaching Method for Brain-Injured and Hyperactive Children.** Syracuse: Syracuse University Press.

Dolphin, J.E., & Cruickshank. W.M. (1951). "The Figure-Background Relationship in Children with Cerebral Palsy," **American Journal of Mental Deficiency,** 41, 336-392.

Frostig, M., Lefever, D.W., & Wittelsey, R.B. (1961). "A Developmental Test of Visual Perception for Evaluating Normal and Neurologically Handicapped Children," **Perceptual Motor Skills, 12,** 383-394.

Gaddes, W.H. (1966). "The Needs of Teachers for Specialized Information on Handedness, Finger Localization, and Cerebral Dominance," in W.M. Cruickshank (Ed.), **The Teacher of Brain-Injured Children.** Syracuse: Syracuse University Press.

Gaddes, W.H. (1975). "Neurological Implications for Learning," in W.M. Cruickshank and D.P. Hallahan (Eds.), **Perceptual and Learning Disabilities in Children, I.** Syracuse: Syracuse University Press.

Gaddes, W.H., & Spellacy, F.J. (1977). **Serial Order Perceptual and Motor Performances in Children and their Relation to Academic Achievement.** Victoria, B.C.: Department of Psychology, University of Victoria, Reserach Monograph 31.

Goldstein, K., & Scheerer, M. (1941). "**Abstract and Concrete Behavior: An Experimental Study with Special Tests,**" Psychological Monographs. **53,** 1-151.

Golick, M. (1970). **A Parent's Guide to Learning Problems.** Montreal: Quebec Association for Children with Learning Disabilities.

Golick, M. (1970). **She Thought I was Dumb But I Told Her I had a Learning Disability.** Toronto: The Bryand Press, Ltd.

Grube, M.M. (1978). A doctoral dissertation in preparation at the University of Michigan, Rackham School of Graduate Study.

Gyr, J.W. (1975). "The Relationship Between Motor and Visual-Sensory Processes in Perception," in Cruickshank, W.M., and Hallahan, D.P. (Eds.), **Perceptual and Learning Disabilities in Children, II.** Syracuse: Syracuse University Press.

Hagan, J., & Kail, R.V. (1975). "The Role of Attention in Perceptual and Cognitive Development" in Cruickshank, W.M., and Hallahan, D.P. (Eds., **Perceptual and Learning Disabilities in Children, II.** Syracuse: Syracuse University Press.

Hallahan, D.P., & Cruickshank, W.M. (1973). **Psychoeducational Foundation of Learning Disabilities.** Englewood Cliffs, NJ: Prentice-Hall, Inc.

Hallahan, D.P. & Kauffman, J.M. (1975). "Research on the Education of Distractible and Hyperactive Children," in Cruickshank, W.M., and Hallahan, D.P. (Eds.), **Perceptual and Learning Disabilties in Children.** Syracuse: Syracuse University Press.

Hallahan, D.P. (1975). "Distractibility in the Leaning Disabled Child," in Cruickshank, W.M., and Hallahan, D.P. (Eds.), **Perceptual and Learning Disabilities in Children.** Syracuse: Syracuse University Press.

Heilman, A. (1952). "Intelligence in Cerebral Palsy," **The Cripppled Child, 30,** 11-13.

Kephart, N.C. (1975). "The Perceptual Motor Match," in Cruickshank, W.M., and Hallahan, D.P. (Eds.). **Perceptual and Learning Disabilities in Children. 1,** Syracuse: Syracuse University Press.

Kephart, N.C. (1960). **The Slower Learner in the Classroom.** Columbus, OH: Charles Merrill Publishers.

Koupernik, C., MacKeith, R., & Francis-Williams, J. (1975). "Neurological Correlates of Motor and Perceptual Development," in Cruickshank, W.M., and Hallahan, D.P. (Eds.). **Perceptual and Learning Disabilities in Children, 2.** Syracuse: Syracuse University Press.

Kronick, D. (1973). **A Word or Two About Learning Disabilities.** San Rafael, CA: Academic Therapy Publications.

Lewis, M. (1975). "The Development of Attention and Perception in the Infant and Young Child" in Cruickshank, W.M. and Hallahan D.P. , (Eds.),

Perceptual and Learning Disabilities in Children. Syracuse: Syracuse University Press.

Luria, A. (1966). **The Higher Cortical Functions in Man.** New York, Basic Books, Inc.

McGinnis, M. (1963). **Aphasic Children.** Washington, DC: Alexander Graham Bell Association for the Deaf, Inc.

McKay, E. (1952). **An Exploratory Study of the Psychological Effect of a Severe Hearing Loss.** Unpublished doctoral dissertation, Syracuse University.

Miller, E.A., & Rosenfeld, G. (1952). "Psychological Evaluation of Children with Cerebral Palsy and its Implications for Treatment," **Journal of Pediatrics, 41,** 613-621.

Murray, C. (1976). **The Link Between Learning Disabilities and Juvenile Delinquency: Current Theory and Knowledge.** Washington, U.S. Department of Justicw Law Enforcement Assistance Administration, National Insititute for Juvenile Justice and Delinquency Prevention.

Quiros, J. (1976). "Diagnosis of Vestibular Disorders in the Learning Disabled," **Journal of Learning Disabilities, 9.**

Rappaport, S. (1969). **Education for Children with Brain Dysfunction.** Syracuse: Syracuse University Press.

Sarason, S. (1953). **Psychological Problems in Mental Deficiency.** New York, Harper and Row.

Shaw, M.E. (1955). **A Study of Some Aspects of perception and Conceptual Thinking in Idiopathic Epileptic Children.** Unpublished doctoral dissertation, Syracuse University.

Stott, D.J. (1972). **The Parent as a Teacher.** Toronto: New Press.

Strauss, A., and Lehtinen, L. (1947). **The Psychopathology and Education of the Brain Injured Child.** New York: Grune and Stratton.

Wepman, J.M. (1975). "Auditory Perception and Imperception," in Cruickshank, W.M., and Hallahan, D.P. (Eds.), **Perceptual and Learning Disabilities in Children, 2.** Syracuse: Syracuse University Press.

Wepman, J.M. et al. (1975). "Learning disabilities," in Hobbs, N., (Ed.), **Issues in the Classification of Children, 1.** San Francisco: Jossey-Bass Publishers.

Weiderholt, J.L. (1975). "Historical perspectives on the education of the learning disabled," in L. Mann and D. Sabatino (Eds.), **The Second Review of Special Education.** Philadelphia, JSE Press, 103-152.

Selected Additional References

Prepared from a Selected Bibliography
Provided by Dr. Robert Knights,
Carleton University, Ottawa, Ontario

Campbell, S.B. Douglas, V.I., and Morgenstern, G. (1971), Cognitive styles in hyperactive children and the effect of methylphenidate. **Journal of Child Psychology and Psychiatry, 12,** 55-67.

CELDIC, (1970). **One Million Children.** Toronto, Ontario: Crainford.

Cohen, N.J., Douglas, V.I., and Morgenstern, G. (1971), The effect of methylphenidate in attention behavior and autonomic activity in hyperactive children. **Psychopharmacologia, 22,** 282-294.

Crockett, D. Klonoff, H., & Bjerring, J., (1969), Factor analysis of neuropsychological tests. **Perceptual and Motor Skills, 29,** 791-802.

Czunder, G., & Rourke, B.P. (1972). Age differences in visual reaction time of "brain-damaged" and normal children under regular and irregular preparatory interval conditions. **Journal of Experimental Child Psychology, 13,** 516-526.

Doehring, D.G. (1968). **Patterns of Impairment in Specific Reading Disabilities.** Bloomington, IN: Indiana University Press.

Doehring, D.G., & Rabinovitch, M.S. (1969), Auditory abilities of children with learning problems. **Journal of Learning Disabilities, 2,** 467-474.

Douglas, V.I. (1974), in press, Sustained attention and impulse control: Implications for the handicapped child. In J.A. Swets and L.L. Elliott (Eds.), **Psychology and the Handicapped Child.** United States Government Publications Office.

Freibergs, V., & Douglas, V.I. (1969), Concept learning in hyperactive and normal children. **Journal of Abnormal Psychology, 74,** 388-395.

Freibergs, V., Douglas, V.I., & Weiss, G. (1968), The effect of chlorpromazine on concept learning in hyperactive children under two conditions of reinforcement. **Psychopharmacologia, 13,** 299-310.

Gaddes, W.H. (1966). The performance of normal and brain-damaged subjects on a new Dynamic Visual Retention Test. **The Canadian Psychologist, 7(a),** 313-323.

Gaddes, W.H. (1967). A new test of Dynamic Visual Retention. **Perceptual and Motor Skills, 25,** 393-396.

Gaddes, W.H. (1968). A neurophsychological approach to learning disorders. **Journal of Learning Disabilities, 1,** 523-534.

Gaddes, W.H. (1969). Can educational psychology be neurologized? **Canadian Journal of Behavioral Science, 1,** 38-49.

Hardy, M.I., McLeod, J., Minto, H., Perkins, S., & Quance, W.R. (1971). **Standards for Educators of Exceptional Children in Canada.** Toronto, Ontario: Crainford.

Hinton, G.G., & Knights, R.M. (1971). Neurological and pyschological test characteristics of 100 children with seizures. In B.W. Richards (Ed.), **First Congress of the International Association of the Scientific Study of Mental Deficiency.** Surrey, England: Michael Jackson Company.

Klonoff, H. (1971). Factor analysis of a neurophyschological battery for children aged 9 to 15. **Perceptual and Motor Skills, 32,** 603-616.

Klonoff, H. (1971). Head injuries in children: Predisposing factors, accident conditions, accident proneness and sequelae. **American Journal of Public Health, 61,** 2405-2417.

Klonoff, H., Robinson, G.C., & Thompson, G. (1969). Acute and chronic brain syndromes in children. **Development Medicine and Child Neurology, 11,** 198-213.

Knights, R.M. (1966). Normative data on tests for evaluating brain damage in children 5 to 14 years. University of Western Ontario, **Research Bulletin No. 20,** mimeo.

Knights, R.M. (1973). A problem of criteria in diagnosis: A profile similarity approach. **Annals of the New York Academy of Sciences, 205,** 124-131.

Knights, R.M. (1974). Psychometric assessment of drug-induced behavior change. In Proceedings of Abbott Laboratories symposium on **The Clinical Use of Stimulant Drugs in Children.** Chicago, Illinois, North Chicago.

Knights, R.M., & Hinton, G.G. (1969). Minimal brain dysfunction: clinical and psychological test characteristics. **Academic Therapy Quarterly, 4,** 265-273.

Knights, R.M., & Hinton, G.G. (1948). The effects of methylphenidate (Ritalin) on the motor skills and behavior of children with learning problems. **Journal of Nervous and Mental Disease,** 643-653.

Knights, R.M., & Moule, A.O. (1967). Normative and reliability data on finger and foot tapping in children. **Perceptual and Motor Skills, 25,** 717-720.

Knights, R.M., & Moule, A.O. (1968). Normative data on the Motor Steadiness Battery for Children. **Perceptual and Motor Skills, 26,** 643-650.

Knights, R.M., & Richardson, D.H. (1974). Automated assessment and training of retarded and disadvantaged children. Department of Psychology, Carleton University, **Research Bulletin** No. 10, mimeo.

Knights, R.M., & Tymchuk, A.J. (1968). An evaluation of the Halstead-Reitan Category Tests for Children, **Cortex, 4,** 403-414.

Knights, R.M., & Viets, C.A. (1973). The effects of pemoline on hyperactive boys. Paper presented at the American Psychological Association, Montreal.

Knights, R.M., & Watson P. (1968). The use of computerized test profiles in neuropsychological assessment. **Journal of Learning Disabilities, 1,** 696-710.

Kronick, D. (Ed.), (1969). **Learning Disabilities: Its Implications to a Responsible Society.** Chicago, IL: Developmental Learning Materials.

Kronick, D. (1970). Directory of learning disabilities help across Canada. **Chatelaine Magazine.** 43(10), Toronto, 100-104.

Meichenbaum, D.H., & Goodman, J. (1969). Reflection -- impulsivity and verbal control of motor behavior. **Child Development, 40,** 785-797.

Meichenbaum, D.H., & Goodman, J. (1971). Training impulsive children to talk to themselves: A means of developing self-control. **Journal of Abnormal Psychology, 77,** 115-126.

Minde, K., Webb, G., & Sykes, D. (1968). Studies on the hyperactive child. VI: Prenatal and perinatal factors associated with hyperactivity. **Developmental Medicine and Child Neurology, 10,** 355-363.

Rourke, B.P., & Czunder, G. (1972). Age differences in auditory reaction time of "brain damaged" normal children under regular and irregular preparatory interval conditions. **Journal of Experimental Child Psychology, 14,** 372-378.

Rourke, B.P., Dietrich, B.M., & Young, G.C. (1973). Significance of WISC verbal-performance discrepancies for younger children with learning disabilities. **Perceptual and Motor Skills, 36,** 275-282.

Rourke, B.P., Young, G.C. & Flewelling, R.W. (1971). The relationships between WISC verbal-performance discrepancies and selected verbal, auditory-perceptual and problem solving abilities in children with learning disabilities. **Journal of Clinical Psychology, 27,** 474-479.

Spreen, O., & Gaddes, W.H. (1969). Developmental norms for 15 neuropsychological tests age 6 to 15. **Cortex, 5,** 171-191.

Stott, D.H., Flying Start Learning-to-Learn Kit (Toronto: Gage) 1972.

Sykes, D.H., Douglas, V.I., Weiss, G., & Minde, K. (1971). Attention in hyperactive children and the effect of methylphenidate (Ritalin). **Journal of Child Psychology and Child Psychiatry, 12,** 129-139.

Tymchuk, A.J., Knights, R.M., & Hinton, G.G. (1970a), Neuropsychological test results of children with brain lesions, abnormal EEGs and normal EEGs, **Canadian Journal of Behavioral Science, 2,** 322-329.

Tymchuk, A.J., Knights, R.M., & Hinton, G.G. (1970b). The behavioral significance of differing EEF abnormalities in children with learning and/or behavior problems. **Journal of Learning Disabilities, 3,** 548-552.

Weinstein, R., & Rabinovitch, M.S. (1971). Sentence structure and retention in good and poor readers. **Journal of Educational Psychology, 62,** 25-30.

Weiss, C., Werry, J. Minde, E., Douglas, V.I., & Sykes, D. (1968). Studies on the hyperactive child - V: The effects of destroamphetamine and chlorpromzine on behavior and intellectual functioning. **Journal of Child Psychology and Psychiatry, 9,** 145-156.

Wiener, J., Barnsely, R.H. & Rabinovitch, M.S. (1970). Serial order ability in good and poor readers. **Canadian Journal of Behavioral Science, 2,** 116-123.

Witelson, S.F, & Rabinovitch, M.S. (1972). Hemispheric speed laterization in children with auditory-linguistic deficits. **Cortex, 8,** 412-426.

The Learning Disabled Young Adult in Transition from School to Career

MARY BUCHANAN AND CAROL WELLER

The various environmental experiences that an individual must cope with during the late adolescent and young adult years consist of those social, adaptive, problem-solving, and learning experiences necessary for positive movement from the environment of high school into the environment of career, self-support, and community involvement. Those transitional experiences that relate to the career selection and training of learning disabled young adults are the focus of this article.

Little is known about the quality of the transition experience for learning disabled individuals. Frequently these individuals leave high school with little or no career counselling and are unaware of the skills needed for seeking employment or "making it" in the community. Sometimes, with the help of parents or relatives, learning disabled young adults move into a job or career within a family business. Some learning disabled individuals enroll in postsecondary education programs, and achieve varying degrees of success in these programs. But many remain unemployed and dependent upon their families far into adulthood (Chesler, 1982).

The provision of transitional services to learning disabled adolescents and young adults is a relatively recent mission of vocational rehabilitation. The purpose of this paper is to describe the nature of the client pool, the diagnostic processes that have been used with these clients, and the unique career preparation and planning needs of these individuals. Such factors must be understood if vocational rehabilitation is to provide the most appropriate services to learning disabled young adults during the transition years.

Orientation to the Learning Disabled Population

Client Pool

Potential learning disabled clients who are in transition from high school to vocational rehabilitation fall into several categories. These clients approach vocational rehabilitation with different diagnostic and job preparation needs because of the specific nature of their learning disabilities. The client pool is comprised of the following general categories:

1. Recent high school graduates who have received services from learning disabled classes. Many transition clients of vocational rehabilitation will be recent high school graduates who have been diagnosed as learning disabled and have received educational services in classes for the learning disabled. These individuals will have extensive diagnostic histories and academic records which describe their individual strengths and weaknesses. The extent and type of remediation procedures that have been employed will be a matter of record. In many cases, information relative to career exploration, vocational training, and work experience will be documented.

2. Recent high school graduates who have received services form special education, but not learning disabled classes. Some transition clients of vocational rehabilitation will be recent high school graduates who have been misdiagnosed as behavior disordered or mentally retarded rather than as learning disabled. Severe language disorders, improper diagnostic decisions, and inadequate classroom experiences for learning disabled individuals may have led to these diagnoses. These individuals may have extensive diagnostic histories that describe behavioral problems or intellectual deficits, but that do not attend to the presence of a learning disability strength and weakness profile. Academic records of these individuals may include information relative to career exploration, vocational training, or work experience, but such information should not be expected.

3. Recent high school graduates whose condition has been remediated or undiagnosed. Often learning disabled individuals have developed compensatory mechanisms that enable them to meet the academic requirements of high

Reprinted from: Journal of Rehabilitation, Oct/Nov/Dec 1984, with permission.

school. These mechanisms may have been developed either through early remediation of academic difficulties or through coping strategies that the individual acquires unaided. Although these coping mechanisms have been sufficient to meet the academic requirements of the educational system, they are often insufficient to meet the demands of a career. Consequently, when these recent high school graduates approach vocational rehabilitation for assistance, counsellors must be aware of their unique social, interpersonal, and adaptive needs.

Young adults who are self-diagnosed as learning disabled. Another potential transition client is the older unidentified young adult who hears about learning disabilities through the media and popular press and, through self-analysis, pinpoints a possible answer to a long standing problem. These individuals may pose problems similar to those of the preceding group, but such problems may be compounded due to extensive job jumping behavior and intermittent unemployment. They may have become frustrated at their lack of ability to achieve vocational goals and often relate a history of many false starts at unsatisfying low level jobs.

5. Young adults who recognize that a problem exists, but do not know it is a learning disability problem. Another potential group of learning disabled clients consists of older undiagnosed individuals who have adjustment problems, but do not suspect that a learning disability is contributing to their problems. These individuals are characterized by persistent difficulty in learning, an inability to make adjustment in life, and difficulty in reaching goals. These multiple problems are intensified because the individual does not suspect the presence of a learning disability and cannot pinpoint the cause of his or her difficulties.

6. Learning disabled students in high school. Although the preceding groups will comprise the majority of vocational rehabilitation's learning disabled transition clientele, other individuals should be considered a part of the potential client pool. These are the identified learning disabled students who have not yet graduated from high school. Early assistance from vocational rehabilitation during the high

school years can help young learning disabled students avoid later transition difficulties. Through early assistance, a multitude of concomitant problems that intensify the learning disability can be solved before life adjustment becomes extremely difficult. The ideal time for such assistance is prior to graduation from high school. At this time, rehabilitation services should focus on goal setting so that it will be unnecessary to rectify the consequences of negative experience at a later date.

Diagnostic History

Since the diagnostic histories of learning disabled transition clients vary greatly, vocational counsellors need to evaluate the diagnostic, as well as the vocational, needs of individual clients. A good argument can be made for utilizing past diagnostic information if available. First, many individuals with specific learning disabilities have received extensive testing, and their problem remains unresolved. For them testing serves to build anxiety and has negative connotations. Second, retesting often provides only information that is already known and that is a matter of record. If more testing were to be done, the learning disabled individual has a right to know how its results will augment existing testing, and why it is needed.

For transition clients who do not have a diagnostic record or for those who carry another diagnosis, a valid argument can be made for the use of a full diagnostic battery. Since these individuals do not have an accurate picture of their problems and do not understand the cause of their difficulties, neither they nor their records will be able to provide information sufficient for vocational counsellors to render adequate vocational assistance.

The results of a diagnostic battery, that has been either administered to an individual or obtained from his or her file, should allow counsellors to consider the broadest options for the client's transition into career areas. A fundamental objective underlying the diagnostic process is to determine the functional strength and limitations that might affect transition experiences. There should be an assessment of adaptive skills, learning patterns, speed of learning, problem solving ability, and intellectual functioning. Medical and psychological assessment results can augment this information by providing diagnostic data concerning the existence of emotional problems, physical limitations, and attentional deficits.

Measures of adaptive behavior and social skills provide critical information about learning disabled individuals in transition. Adaptive and social behavior data, if gained in naturalistic settings, can describe the individual's strengths and deficits in interpersonal interaction, relationships with others, social coping strategies, problem solving strategies, and interpersonal communication (Weller & Buchanan, 1983).

Adaptive behavior and social skills are an integral part of an individual's functional ability. Factors such as pragmatic language, social coping, quality of relationships, and level of productivity are important indicators of adaptive behaviors needed for success in employment (Weller & Strawser, 1982). Appropriate social/adaptive behaviors can be a major strength for a learning disabled individual and may be used to great advantage in career selection. For example, an individual with excellent conversational and interpersonal interaction skills, who is well liked by colleagues, can be an asset in a public relations occupation. Although this individual may have functional deficits that inhibit performance in written language or mathematics, training for a career in sales might be appropriate.

Information on learning strengths and weaknesses should be included in a diagnostic history. Actual performance levels in reading, writing, mathematics, and other basic skills, as well as intellectual functioning, are needed to facilitate career decision making. Assessment of learning processes in the areas of listening and speaking, visual reception, spatial perception, visual organization, and gross motor and fine motor skills can also provide valuable information to counsellors about potential vocational options (Weller & Buchanan, 1983).

Achievement tests in basic skills can provide useful information in planning for careers that require postsecondary schooling or in determining functional literacy. The results of achievement tests may provide answers to the following questions: (a) What are the individual's academic strengths and limitations?, (b) What functional skills are present?, (c) Should remediation be tried?, and (d) Is compensation a more viable option?. Strengths in selected academic areas are not uncommon among learning disabled individuals. Some will read well and write poorly; some will be proficient in mathematics to the exclusion of other basic skills. As in the example given previously, some will excel in oral language. Other learning disabled individuals may lack sufficient basic skills in all areas, but evidence strengths in areas such as motor control, physical strength, or endurance.

One final factor that relates to functional skills is the intellectual functioning level of the individual. While caution must be exercised in using intelligence as a single factor in determining a career option, the level of intellectual functioning is an important consideration.

Interest inventories are a necessary means of eliciting from learning disabled individuals their personal career preferences. Although personal interests may not interface with functional strengths, interest inventories can provide useful information. If interests are not compatible with abilities, career counselling and self-awareness education may be needed. If compatibility is evident, directions for career selection will evolve. Motivation, self-direction, independence, and perseverance can be significantly tied to the information gained through an interest inventory. Many learning disabled individuals are willing to invest inordinate amounts of time and energy in attaining their goals (Weller & Buchanan, 1983).

Another important component of a diagnostic battery is the career aptitudes derived form work samples and other activities that closely approximate the job environment. Use of career aptitude tests provides learning disabled individuals with the opportunity to demonstrate ability, while pinpointing the extent to which the disability inhibits maximum performance on various tasks. When information from these tests is compiled with data from the remainder of a diagnostic battery, the transition needs of the learning disabled individual will become evident.

Career Preparation and Planning

After diagnostic information has been compiled and analyzed to yield a personal profile of a client, goal planning can begin. In all cases, goal planning involves the integration of diagnostic information into a total career preparation scheme. Medical, therapeutic, and psychological services, in addition to educational or training programs, must be integrated into the individual's rehabilitation plan by the vocational counsellor.

Counsellors must carefully scrutinize the educational components of goal planning. The issue of remediation versus compensation must be addressed. For many learning disabled adults under age 30, remediation has been tried throughout the school career. Academically, they have run out of time and further remediation is unrealistic given their immediate basic needs, motivations, and goals.

Studies related to the effectiveness of basic skill remediation are discouraging. Remediation in adult education programs that focus on the specific skills needed for a job is seldom undertaken, but rather these programs rely on a general approach to academic achievement. The U.S. army recently suspended its basic skills program, stating dissatisfaction with its inadequate linkage to job performance. They concluded that the short-term remedial programs were working for only a few, and that the programs were not designed in such a way to meet the needs of jobs in this technological age ("Army Program," 1983).

Academic disabilities may not be as important to job success as most people have been led to believe. Many success stories have been documented in spite of academic problems. However, there may be instances when remediation of academic deficits is a viable option. But each instance should be considered in light of the individual's motivation to improve his or her academic skills. Additional considerations include:

1. Is the remediation specifically focused toward job-related skills?
2. Is a program available that employs teachers trained in teaching academic skills to adults?
3. Does the individual have a strong support system (such as family, friends, or counsellor) that will be of assistance in the pursuit of this high risk experience?
4. Does the individual understand the commitment involved in remediation in terms of time and energy requirements, and that progress is likely to be slow?

Areas that may be suitable to remediation are social skills and adaptive behaviors. Problems with self-concept, peer appeal, interpersonal communication, and coping with the environment often interfere significantly with career success. These are behaviors for which accommodation in job setting may be difficult or impossible unless careers are selected that minimize social interactions. Remediation in the form of group counselling, role-playing with feedback, or video taping of social interactions may be beneficial remedial strategies.

Often, functional limitations for learning disabled young adults in transition (whether academic, behavioral, motoric, or cognitive) need to be viewed as controlled annoyances that require compensation. If the individual has a long-term understanding of the disability, he or she may have developed many accommodations to minimize the problems. However, if the individual has just become aware of the learning disability or if current accommodation strategies are inefficient, he or she may need special help in understanding how the disability inhibits performance and the kind of compensatory procedures needed to achieve goals.

Several questions should be posed prior to determining the most appropriate compensatory mechanism for an individual. These questions include:

1. How highly motivated is the individual to circumvent the problem?
2. Why does the individual wish to circumvent the problem?
3. Is the individual aware of techniques that can be used to circumvent the problem?

Many learning disabled individuals insist upon remediation when compensation is the better alternative. These individuals may be responding to the demands of schools and society to read, write, and compute rather than to intrinsic forces or job demands. If this is the case, individuals may need to contemplate the idea that there are innovative ways to circumvent these skills. They may need information about compensatory mechanisms such as tape recorders, readers, taped books, oral presentations, computers, and calculators.

The use of compensation in career planning, training, and job performance has potential pitfalls for which the learning disabled individual must be prepared. For a learning disabled individual to apply compensation techniques fully, cooperation and education of all involved parties are required. If career preparation is to be successful, models need to be conceptualized that reflect the inherent need for system accommodation, as well as compensation on the part of the learning disabled individual.

Transitional Model

Currently, tested models for serving learning disabled individuals in transition are lacking. Prototypes are borrowed from existing literature related to other handicapping conditions such as mental retardation, but these prototypes may not be appropriate. If the career models for mentally retarded individuals are used without sufficient modification, the career potential of learning disabled individuals may be underestimated. Additionally, reaction to a model designed for mentally retarded persons may be negative on the part of learning disabled clients and their parents.

Creative thinking is needed to reconceptualize a working model for serving learning disabled young adults in the rehabilitation system. The data base is small, but the literature suggests that nearly all learning disabled individuals end up in competitive employment. Currently, most are employed in unskilled and semiskilled jobs; many are dissatisfied and underemployed (Chester, 1982). This dilemma indicates that the present system may not be the most advantageous and that community resources should be tapped to build more adequate models. These resources can blend harmoniously to produce transition models based on the interdependence of the roles of counsellor, instructor and /or employer, and the learning disabled individual. In an interdependence model, counsellor, instructor/employer, and the learning disabled individual

have both shared and personal roles and responsibilities. Such a model is illustrated in Figure 1 and described below.

FIGURE 1.   TRANSITION MODEL

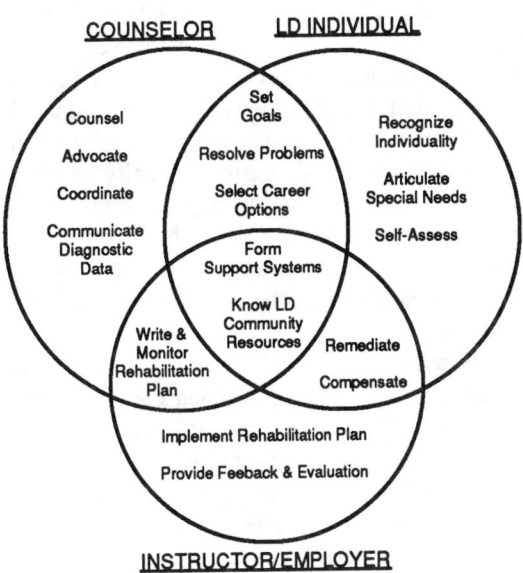

Counsellor Role

The role of the counsellor in this model includes advocacy, communication, counselling, coordination, and prescription. Initial success of the transition process will depend on how effectively the counsellor conveys diagnostic information and its career relevance to the learning disabled individual. Through counselling about diagnosed learning strengths and weaknesses, the individual should develop an understanding of his or her career potential in relation to the learning disability. Extensive counselling may be required if the client denies the disability or fails to understand how the disability is interfering with goal attainment. Sometimes learning disabled individuals persist in unrealistic goals because their learning disabilities interfere with understanding or communication. The need for persistence on the part of the counsellor cannot be minimized in these instances.

Learning disabled individuals in transition need a type of advocacy from a counsellor that is somewhat unique. For example, a brief letter certifying the nature of the disability based on diagnostic findings is often needed. Such a letter should specify the effect of the learning disability on performance in an academic pursuit or employment. Such advocacy may be essential for gaining special assistance or compensation when they are needed. Further, a certifying letter lends credibility to the learning disabled individual's verbal contention that a handicap exists. As an advocate, the counsellor is often able to describe the nature of the disability more clearly than the individual.

If remediation is chosen as a part of the career preparation plan, the counsellor will need to provide several resources to assure success. For example, educational prescriptions must be established on the basis of specific career choices, and competent teachers must be provided. In some instances, an actual teaching sequence may need to be written. Such a sequence may entail a detailed analysis of each step required for completing a job-related task.

Instructor/Employer Role

The employer or instructor is a vital link in the interdependent transition model. The employer's or instructor's primary role lies in the implementation of accommodation procedures, and they must understand the need for such compensation. If an individual is placed in either an academic setting or a training site, the professionals in charge need to have knowledge about how the disability might affect performance and the types of accommodations that must be made. In an academic setting, courses may need to be waived or substituted. When information is being presented, notetakers or tape recorders may need to be allowed and encouraged. Assignments may need to be altered, shortened, or reduced in scope. Orally presented assignments may be accepted in lieu of written ones, and teaching techniques may need to be modified. Demonstra-

tions, oral instructions accompanied by visual diagrams, development of step-by-step learning sequences, and provisions for practice may be required.

Employers will need to make many modifications similar to those required of instructors. When on-the-job training is being conducted, modification of training strategies will usually be required. Special assignments and projects may be necessary to teach about the day-to-day operation of the setting where the individual will be working, and tasks may require sequential analysis and step-by-step training.

Instructors and employers can assist learning disabled individuals in transition in several other ways. Tests of licensure, accreditation, or demonstration of competency may be read to the individual and responses transcribed by the examiner. Extra time is often needed in a training program or an apprenticeship. For example, a two-year nursing course may be extended to three or more years. Periodic evaluations that assess progress and redefine short-term goals for improvement of performance are usually needed.

If an individual is in an apprenticeship or technical school program, caution should be taken not to close that individual out of a career requiring performance in an area affected by the disability that has little relationship to job performance. for example, it may not be as necessary to pass a written examination on the history of house painting as it is to read instructions and labels on equipment used for painting. Quite often, prescribed curricula have been developed for an individual whose overall skills are equal, rather than one with a strength and weakness profile such as that evidenced by a learning disabled individual.

Client's Role

For individuals with years of failure and low self-esteem, articulation of a learning disability may be very difficult and very risky. Often individuals are embarrassed at their inability to perform basic tasks such as reading, writing, recalling phone numbers, and following simple directions. They have no convincing way of explaining their deficiencies to themselves or others.

With guidance from the rehabilitation counsellor, learning disabled individuals in transition must develop an understanding of their learning patterns and ways to articulate compensatory strategies needed for success in assigned tasks. They must recognize their equality of rights and responsibilities in the academic system, the community, and the work force.

The ability to project into the future and set realistic short and long term goals is often lacking in learning disabled young adults (Kronick, 1978; White, Schumacker, Warner, Alley & Deshler, 1980). Initial responsibility for defining goal-setting and problem-solving strategies may fall on the counsellor who teaches problem-solving strategies. As soon as possible, goal-setting should become a shared responsibility with the client. Otherwise, when independent goal-setting is required, individuals may become immobilized and dissatisfied because they lack the skills to plan, organize, and reach even short-term goals or because they set goals so far out of reach that inaction results. The sensitive counsellor can point out the history of "false starts" displayed by learning disabled individuals and assist them with problem-solving strategies early in the counselling process.

Learning disabled individuals need to find and maintain a support system that encompasses family, friends, and professionals. Furthermore, they need to know how to use such a system without overreliance. If assisted by counsellors, they can become acquainted with organizations for learning disabled adults. The support received from these organizations is often sufficient to keep the individual involved.

Organizations for learning disabled adults are helpful for a variety of reasons. They can provide insights into learning problems, compensatory procedures that may be beneficial, and the motivation to pursue goals vigorously. The other learning disabled adults in these organizations can serve as sounding boards to test the reality of goals and aspirations, and may serve as models whose personal experiences can be useful to others. Groups of learning disabled adults are forming on college and university campuses and as arms of existing organizations such as the Association for Children and Adults with learning

Disabilities. These organizations provide excellent models for the formation of other community groups. Learning disabled clients in transition need to avail themselves of other support as well. After clients are placed on a job, they often become locked in at an entry level because they have a fear of being promoted to inappropriate positions that capitalize on deficits rather than strengths. Clients would benefit from information about agencies that provide ongoing career counselling before release from vocational rehabilitaiton is finalized. Follow up with these agencies and community resources should be strongly encouraged (Weller & Sipherd, 1982).

Summary

To establish successful linkages between counsellor, client, and instructor or employer during transition, close cooperation is essential. An understanding of learning disabilities is a beginning step; beyond that, communication links between all parties are vital. Flexibility within the system, shared responsibility in a variety of situations, and accommodation are key features for success.

Vocational rehabilitation has the mandate and opportunity to develop successful transition experiences for learning disabled individuals. However, it is not alone in its efforts. Through the media and popular press, public awareness has been raised and many individuals are speaking out on behalf of learning disabled adults. A significant number of these speakers are learning disabled individuals who are experiencing success in a variety of professions and occupations. Many of these persons own their own businesses, practice skilled trades, have completed college, and are active in professions such as medicine, engineering, and architecture. Some have learning disabled children and are concerned about their education and future careers. They are most anxious to see systems develop that accommodate learning disabled individuals, and their personal experiences in coping with transition could be a wealthy resource to personnel in the rehabilitation system.

References

Army basic-skills program said failing. (1983, July 27). **Education Week,** p.7.

Chesler, B. (1982). On realistic expectations. **ACLD Newsleter, 146,** 3.

Kronick, D. (1978). An examination of psychosocial aspects of learning disabled adolsescents. **Learning Disability Quarterly, 1**(4), 86-93.

Weller, C., & Buchanan, M.B. (1983). **Career inventories for the learning disabled.** Novato, CA: Academic Therapy.

Weller, C., & Sipherd, C. (1982). The learning disabled woman: Implications for the work force. **Journal of Rehabilitation, 48**(4), 67-69, 80.

Weller, C., & Strawser, S. (1982). **Weller-Strawser Scales of Adaptive Behavior,** Novato, CA: Academic Therapy.

White, W., Schumacker, J., Warner, M., Alley, G., & Deshler, D. (1980). **The current status of young adults identified as learning disabled during their school career** (Research Report No. 21). Lawrence, KS: University of Kansas, Institute for Research on Learning Disabilities.

University Admissions Testing For Learning Disabled Applicants

PAUL JAY GERBER

While the focus of the field of learning disabilities in past years has been on the school-age learning disabled student, in recent years increased attention has been directed toward the learning disabled adult. Interest in adults with learning disabilities has been generated by (a) professionals who are concerned with the lifelong learning and adjustment of learning disabled individuals (Patton & Polloway, 1982) and (b) learning disabled individuals themselves who are now advocating for their own needs and rights.

Professionals in the field of learning disabilities have generally acknowledged that the learning disabled population is diverse in its psychological, learning, social, and behavioral characteristics. However, one common characteristic of this group is that they possess an intelligence quotient that approximates or surpasses normality. Thus, upon reaching adulthood many options are available to individuals who have a learning disability. This variety of potential options has been emphasized in the developing literature on the learning disabled adult (Cronin & Gerber, 1982).

Background Perspective: The College Bound Learning Disabled Adult

As learning disabled individuals attain adulthood, numerous vocational options are available to them. A large number of learning disabled adults enter the workforce, enrol in vocational training programs, or join the armed forces. Moreover, many learning disabled adults aspire to careers that require undergraduate and graduate degrees. Sedita (1980) suggested that learning disabled adults make up a large body of potential college students.

Furthermore, in their longitudinal study of learning disabled adults, Lehtinen-Rogan and Hartman (1976) indicated that 40% of their sample attended college, while 11% attended graduate or professional schools. Many learning disabled individuals are reaching adulthood after having received quality special education and support services during their school-age years, and are demanding access to a wide array of university degree programs.

Postsecondary Institutions' Accommodations for learning Disabled Individuals

Because of the influx of learning disabled adults who have entered or demanded entry into colleges and universities, many institutions of higher education have become concerned with the development of procedures that would enable them to comply with Section 504 of the Rehabilitation Act of 1973 (P.L. 93-112). The provisions of Section 504 have an impact on every post-secondary institution in the nation since these provisions state that:

> *No otherwise qualified handicapped individual in the United States shall solely by reason of handicap, be excluded from the participation in, be denied the benefit of, or be subjected to discrimination under any program or activity receiving federal financial assistance (p. 49).*

Subpart E of Section 504 applies to all postsecondary programs and activities that receive federal financial assistance. In colleges and universities, the recruitment, admission, and treatment of students must be free of discriminatory practices, and a quota may not be placed on the number of disabled persons admitted. Also, admissions testing must be as non-discriminatory as possible, and the tests must measure what they are purported to measure rather than being indicative of the disability of the person tested. This compliance factor of Section 504 is one of the most controversial, and when applied to the

Reprinted form Journal of Rehabilitation Apr/May/June 1985, with permission.

learning disabled population, it becomes extremely complex.

Controversy in definition and identification procedures and variation in the characteristics endemic to the field of learning disabilities have been superimposed on postsecondary institutions with the provisions of Section 504. Generally, universities have begun to accommodate their programs to the instructional and counselling needs of learning disabled students. Some universities have specially designed *bona fide* programs for learning disabled students (Fielding, 1977). Yet with all this progress, an area of concern still persists——how to accommodate admission procedures to the learning disabled individual. More specifically, within the area of admission procedures, standardized testing for learning disabled individuals is a pressing issue that must be addressed.

Fielding (1977) identified two common admission policies that learning disabled persons may encounter when applying to undergraduate programs within universities. First is the open admission policy option, which typically requires only a high school diploma or equivalent. The second policy option is regular admission, which typically requires the individual to possess a high school diploma or equivalent, to attain a particular rank or grade point average in high school, and receive *acceptable scores on a designated standardized test.*

At the graduate level, admission policies become more program-specific, and criteria for admission are more rigorously applied because of the limited number of students that can be trained for their respective fields. Thus, the criteria for graduate level admission focuses on grade point average earned in undergraduate school, letters of recommendation, and possibly the results of an interview and *standardized tests which are designed to measure aptitude for the applicant's aspiring field.*

Although no single criterion can theoretically preclude an applicant from entrance into an undergraduate or graduate program, standardized admission tests are often used to select students for such programs. The reliance on standardized tests to determine admission feasibility creates problems for institutions of higher education

when considering the applications of disabled individuals in general and learning disabled applicants in particular. Great strides have been made by universities to comply with Section 504 through the use of nonstandardized testing procedures. However, many problems exist with the the application of nonstandardized tests and with the interpretation of their results. These problems are affecting a greater number of individuals and universities each year. For example, Rogosta & Nemceff (1982) reported that requests for special testing on the Standardized Achievement Test (SAT) from learning disabled individuals were 1,779 in 1979-80 and 2,762 in 1980-81 (a 55% increase).

Need for the Study

Recently, a report entitled *Ability Testing of Handicapped People: Dilemma for Government, Science, and the Public* was prepared by Sherman (1981) for the Office of Civil Rights in the United States Department of Education. The report concluded that current psychometric theory and practice does not allow full compliance with Section 504 regulations. Moreover, the report recommended actions to improve the administration and use of tests, to disseminate information regarding the availability of modified tests, and to solve known problems with specific tests or types of tests.

In view of the growing number of learning disabled individuals who are applying to take university admission tests, the author of this article analyzed the current policies of those admissions testing programs that are commonly used by undergraduate, graduate, and professional schools in order to determine how those policies relate to the learning disabled university applicant.

Methodology

Recent announcement bulletins of various university admission testing programs were obtained in order to analyze the policy statements for accommodation to disabled test-takers. The admission tests were broken down into three areas; namely, undergraduate, graduate, and professional (graduate) school.

Policy statements were analyzed via numerous criteria that might provide evidence of the testing programs' accommodation to handicapping conditions. These criteria were: (a) how to request nonstandard testing, (b) whether documentation was needed to verify the existence of a handicapping condition, (c) whether learning disability was specifically stated as a handicapping condition, (d) type of testing material available to accommodate disabled applicants, (e) whether special testing conditions were allowed, and (f) how scores from nonstandard testing were reported.

Results
Undergraduate Admission Tests[1]

Scholastic Aptitude Test. According to the College Entrance Examination Board (1982), special arrangements can be made to accommodate the testing of disabled students on the Scholastic Aptitude Test (SAT). In discussing the SAT, the Educational Testing Service (1983b) indicated that learning disabilities are specifically considered a handicapped condition. The special materials available for testing disabled applicants include a large type edition of the test (printed in five separate test books), a braille edition (verbal section in regular grade 2 braille and math in 1972 Nemeth Code), and an audio edition. All of these materials may be administered with extended time; additional time is also available to disabled students who take the regular standard edition of the SAT. Practice materials are made available for disabled persons as well. For example, practice audio cassettes may be ordered by a counsellor for learning disabled students and other disabled persons if necessary. Scores on SATs are reported to indicate that they were obtained through nonstandard conditions; universities are also informed that candidates took the exam under nonstandard conditions in order to minimize any adverse effect of their disability on test performance. There is no documentation needed to verify the existence of a handicapping condition and no special testing conditions are

outlined for disabled persons beyond special materials.

American College Testing Program. The American College Testing Program (ACT) makes provisions for physical disability in its publication *Taking the Act Assessment* (1983). It is suggested that if a disability is an issue for examinees, a letter is to be written and enclosed in the registration form. The letter should explain the disabled person's special needs. The ACT program will make special arrangements if it can arrange for necessary facilities and/or personnel. Special arrangements do not include extended time or the use of an edition of the ACT other than standard test booklets.

Other accommodations for testing are available but seem to be stated unclearly. If a disability prevents an examinee from attending a national test center or if a special edition of the ACT is available, then one may qualify with documentation of a professional diagnosis of the disability. From the above statements it is uncertain whether learning disabled individuals can have access to these special testing materials. There is no documentation needed to verify the existence of a handicapping condition, nor is learning disabilities specifically listed as a handicap. Also, there are no stated special test taking conditions and the procedure for reporting scores is not explained.

Test of English as a Foreign Language (TOEFL). The TOEFL, which test English language proficiency for undergraduate and graduate university students, addresses the needs of disabled individuals in various ways. According to the Educational Testing Service (1982) bulletin, entitled *TOEFL International and Special Center Testing Programs* (1982), nonstandard testing arrangements will be made whenever possible, but procedures for qualifications are not stated.

Accommodations for nonstandard testing include: extending time, a reader, amanuensis if necessary, specific accommodations (not stated) for aural impairment, and adjustments in physical arrangements or a reader/amanuensis for motor impairment. Some local testing conditions may make special testing procedures impossible.

The TOEFL bulletin indicates a concern for the effect that nonstandard testing conditions will have on the assessment of language proficiency. For example, the bulletin states that, if a disability is a confounding variable in assessment, institutions may consider other ways of evaluating English language proficiency. The following statement suggests that there is a problem in reporting scores obtained under nonstandard testing conditions:

> Scores obtained under different, nonstandard testing conditions cannot be compared to scores obtained under regular conditions; therefore it is difficult to evaluate the English proficiency of an examinee under nonstandard testing conditions (p. 14).

Logically then, such scores on the TOEFL are reported with the notation that nonstandard testing procedures were used, and that normative data is not available for comparison. No documentation is needed to verify that an examinee has a disability, and the TOEFL bulletin does not specifically mention learning disability when discussing disabled students.

Graduate and Professional School Admission

Graduate Record Examination. The Graduate Record Examination (GRE) provides the most comprehensive effort to accommodate the needs of disabled persons. The Educational Testing Service (1983a) states in its publication, *GRE 1982-1983 Information Bulletin,* that special provisions will be made for persons with visual, physical, or learning disabilities. For some cases, registrants may be asked to document their disability in order to determine whether testing under special conditions is appropriate. However, the kind or form of documentation is not described.

Individuals who need nonstandard testing conditions must describe these accommodations in a letter. The letter should accompany the application and must include a description of the nature of the disability, the special testing arrangements that are needed, and whether extra time is needed. A wide array of accommodations are available for testing disabled persons. Special materials include braille (1972 Nemeth Code), large print edition, cassette recording, and large print answer sheets. Options are well outlined in the *GRE Information Bulletin* (1983a):

> The cassette edition is accompanied by a set of illustrative materials——diagrams, charts, drawings——in either large type or braille, depending on the choice of the person taking the test. The illustrations are also described on tape by the reader. Large print answer sheets are also described on the tape by the reader. Large print answer sheets are available on the Subject (Advanced) Tests, but test books are available only in regular print (p. 60).

Other accommodations are provided as well. These include a reader, a recorder of answers, separate testing area, and extra time to complete the tests (up to six hours testing time per test).

When reporting scores, the GRE includes a statement that scores were obtained under nonstandard testing conditions. Normative data on which to compare nonstandard test scores are not available. Furthermore, the GRE bulletin states that admissions decisions should be based on multiple criteria (i.e., academic achievement). There may be cases in which handicapping conditions create such complicated problems that taking the GRE may not be appropriate. In these cases, the GRE bulletin advises the applicant to request a waiver of this requirement.

The Law School Admissions Test (LSAT). The LSAT states in its publication, *1983-1984 Law School Admission Services: LSAT Preparation Materials* (1983), that whenever possible they will make special accommodations for disabled persons. There is no mention of any specific handicapping condition, including learning disability. All examinees who need special testing arrangements are asked to request them on their registration form, but no further documentation is needed.

The LSAT bulletin outlines all of the accommodations which are possible. These include: amanuensis, use of a separate testing room, large type 18 point edition of test (readers not permitted), and extra rest time. There will be no extra time for the test itself.

The LSAT bulletin also proffers its position concerning the predictive validity of the LSAT. The bulletin questions whether the LSAT, given under nonstandard conditions, is a reliable predictor of an applicant's ability. Moreover, the bulletin raises the issue of a waiver of this admission criteria altogether. Currently , many law schools will waive the LSAT requirement and the LSAT staff will offer advice on this matter.

Medical College Admission Test (MCAT). The MCAT is administered by the American College Testing Program (ACT) which has already shown good faith in trying to accommodate the special needs of disabled persons at the undergraduate admission level. The Association of American medical Colleges (1982) states in its information bulletin, entitled *MCAT 1982 Announcement*, that it will provide reasonable accommodation to specific handicapping conditions wherever and whenever possible, but specific handicapping conditions are not stated in the MCAT bulletin. Yet, the Association of American Medical Colleges may ask for medical documentation of any disability and may refuse the request for special accommodation.

The MCAT bulletin does not suggest any types of accommodations for the testing situation, but specifies how scores will be recorded. All scores obtained by nonstandard conditions will be identified by an asterisk. However, neither the accommodation nor reasons for special testing conditions will be reported.

Pharmacy College Admissions Test (PCAT). The PCAT, which administered under the auspices of the American Association of Colleges of Pharmacy, does not state anything, in its information bulletin, entitled *1982-83 Announcement Pharmacy Admission Test* (1982), about special testing conditions for disabled populations. At this writing, there does not seem to be any policy related to this issue. Therefore, there is no information on requesting special testing arrangements, whether documentation is needed,

whether special testing conditions and special materials are allowable, and how scores are reported. In addition, there is no mention of learning disability in their document.

Dental Admission Testing Program (DAR). The American Association of Dental Schools Application Service (1983) does not describe any accommodations for disabled populations in its information bulletin called *Instructions for Applicants to the 1983 Entering Class*. There are several statements in its bulletin which leads one to believe that learning disabled individuals might have problems with the DAT. In their description of the purpose of the testing program it is stated that, the DAT is designed to measure general academic ability, comprehensive scientific information and perceptual ability. Moreover, one is left with the impression that there is little room for consideration of a nonstandardized format since the DAT Bulletin states:

Since 1972,...has met the needs of dental schools and prospective dental students by providing participating schools with uniform information in a standard format...(p. 5).
In cases of handicapping condition, there is no information on how to request nonstandardized testing, how one can document disability, whether learning disability is viewed as a handicapping condition, what special material and accommodations are possible, and how nonstandard score (if generated would be reported to the admission committees of dental schools.

Graduate Management Admission Test (GMAT). The GMAT is administered under nonstandard conditions to candidates with visual, physical, and learning disabilities (specifically stated). According to the Graduate Management Admission Council (1982) information bulletin, *GMAT 1982-83 Bulletin of Information*, an examinee can be tested under special conditions with a letter indicating disability, specifying the accommodations needed, and what version of the test is needed. There is no statement regarding the documentation of a learning disability, however, the GMAT bulletin states that some persons may be asked to verify disabilities in order to determine whether testing under nonstandard conditions is appropriate.

The GMAT cites many possible accommodations for disabled applicants, including the use of braille, cassette, and large print editions (large print may be given under standard time conditions if warranted). The cassette edition is accompanied by a set of illustrative materials (diagrams, charts, and drawings, either in large print or braille). The illustrations are also described by the reader on tape. The test center will provide a reader or an amanuensis, extra time to complete the test, additional rest time between sections, or a separate testing room.

Scores are reported with a statement which denotes that the test was taken under nonstandard conditions. This is done with the following GMAT consideration:

> *Our intent is to remind graduate school admissions officers that handicapped persons are usually at a disadvantage when taking standard tests such as GMAT and therefore need to be considered individually (p. 11).*

Table 1 provides a summary of the accommodations that are available for the testing of disabled individuals on each admission test discussed above.

Discussion

Nonstandard testing on university admissions examinations is an issue that currently is having an impact on the learning disabled population and will have an even greater impact as more learning disabled individuals aspire to college training. It is encouraging to know that some of the most frequently administered tests, such as the SAT at the undergraduate level and the GRE at the graduate level, specifically address the needs of the learning disabled candidate. Likewise, 37.5% of the university admission tests analyzed acknowledge the needs of learning disabled examinees, and 75% of all entrance examinations address the needs of disabled applicants. Learning disabled individuals can find comfort in the special testing accommodations specifically outlined for them; what remains unclear is the extent to which learning disabled individuals may gain access to the potential accommodations provided for disabled persons in a generic sense. However, there has been an apparent lack of attempt by the DAT and PCAT admissions tests to comply with the provisions of Section 504.

Another issue that needs immediate clarification is how learning disabled applicants may become eligible for special testing conditions on many of these tests. While most tests ask for a request for special testing conditions when the application is submitted, eligibility is easier to document for visually impaired, hearing impaired, and related populations. What is not clear is the type of documentation needed for learning disabled individuals. The MCAT specifies medical documentation, but the type of documentation required of other entrance examinations is not specific.

Many questions arise when special testing conditions are requested by learning disabled individuals. Will examination authorities accept the assessment of a physician (if so, what kind), a psychologist, or an educational consultant? Is there a severity level that must be demonstrated in order to warrant special testing conditions? Finally, can a learning disability diagnosis at any time during school-age years qualify one for special testing accommodations?

Presently, it would seem that there is ample opportunity to abuse the eligibility requirement for nonstandard testing. Since there is a growing trend for nonstandard testing of learning disabled university applicants (Ragosta, 1980), the issue will need immediate attention by those responsible for overseeing the development and administration of university admissions tests and testing procedures. Any delay might lay open a system of abuse where those who are learning disabled will suffer in the long run. Furthermore, widespread abuse will no doubt have a significant

Table 1								
SUMMARY OF ACCOMMODATIONS FOR UNIVERSITY ADMISSIONS TEST								
Test	Request	Documentation Initially Required	LD Specifically Stated	Materials		Special Conditions		Reporting
SAT*	letter at registration	no	yes	1. 2.	braille audio cassette			statement of nonstandard testing
ACT*	letter at registration	no	no	1. 2. 3.	braille large print audio cassette	1. 2.	no extended time standard booklet only	
GRE	letter at registration	yes on a request basis from GRE	yes	1. 2. 3. 4. 5. 6. 7. 8. 9.	braille large print cassette recording (accompanied illustrative materials) large print answer sheets Advanced part test books in regular print only reader recorder of answers separate testing area extra time to complete test	1. 2.	extra time proximity seating	statement of nonstandard testing
LSAT	letter at registration	no	no	1. 2.	amanuensis large print edition	1. 2. 3.	separate testing room extra rest time no extra test time	statement of nonstandard testing
MCAT	letter at registration	may ask for medical documentation	no	not stated		not stated		statement of nonstandard testing
PCAT	not stated	not stated	no	not stated		not stated		not stated
DAT	not stated	not stated	no	standard format		standard format		not stated
TOEFL	letter at registration	no	no	amanuensis		adjustments in physical conditions		statement of nonstandard testing
GMAT	letter at registration	no	yes	1. 2.	braille cassette editions (accompanied illustrative materials)	1. 2. 3.	extra time for test extra rest time separate testing room	statement of nonstandard testing
* Check note at beginning of results section								

impact on how reported scores are perceived by university admission officers.

Another vital concern to the learning disabled candidate is the impact that the disclaimer about nonstandard testing conditions might have on the ultimate admission decision. Without question, these disclaimers are necessary because of the lack of comparative normative data. In examining each of the disclaimer statements, one can be readily assured that there is a strong beneficent tone. Moreover, admissions decisions are made on multiple criteria. Yet, what is not known is how these nonstandard scores are perceived by admission officers of colleges, universities, and professional schools. Since a learning disability is more difficult to define than a visual impairment, hearing impairment, or orthopaedic handicap a distinct possibility exists for widespread misinterpretation of ability and potential. It remains to be seen how the part of the disclaimer, that accompanies score reports, will affect admissions decisions.

The issue of admissions testing for learning disabled university applicants is in its infancy. Presently, some admission tests are doing remarkably well in accommodating learning disabled candidates. Conversely, some admission tests seem to be in direct conflict with federal law. There is much more work to be done on this issue, especially since learning disabled individuals will soon gain greater access to graduate and professional programs.

This article is an initial attempt to expose some of the critical issues surrounding university admission testing for undergraduate, graduate, and professional schools. Since a myriad of issues are intertwined in this area of study, a research agenda has been set to tackle some of these difficult questions. But the focus of this agenda is on handicapping conditions in a generic sense (Ragosta & Nemceff, 1982). Most important, however, learning disabled individuals have a better chance than ever before to compete fairly for admission to university programs. But the issue is closed since much more work needs to be done in order to reach the philosophical goals and fulfil the legal mandates of Section 504 of the Rehabilitation Act of 1973.

References

The American College Testing Program. (1983). **Taking the ACT assessment** (1983-84 edition). Iowa City: The American College Testing Program.

American Association of Dental Schools Application Service. (1983). **Instructions for applicants to the 1983 entering class.** Iowa City: The American College Testing Program.

Association of American Medical Colleges. (1982). **MCAT 1982 announcement.**

College Entrance Examination Board. (1983). **Student bulletin for the SAT and achievement tests, 1983-1984.** Princeton: College Entrance Examination Board.

College Entrance Examination Board. (1982). **Taking the SAT: A guide to the Scholastic Aptitude Test and the Test of Standard Written English.** Princeton: Educational Testing Service.

Cronin, M.E., & Gerber, P.J. (1982). Preparing the learning disabled adolescent for adulthood. **Topics in Learning and Learning Disabilities, 2**(3). 55-68.

Educational Testing Service. (1983a). **GRE 1982-1983 information bulletin.** Princeton: Educational Testing Service.

Educational Testing Service. (1983b). **Information for students with special needs.** Princeton: Educational Testing Service.

Educational Testing Service (1982). **TOEFL international and special center testing programs, 1982-83 bulletin.** Princeton: Education Testing Service.

Fielding, P.M. (Ed.). (1977). **A national directory of 4 year colleges, 2 year colleges and post high school training programs for young adults with learning disabilities.** Tulsa, OK: Partners in Publishing.

Graduate Management Admission Council. (1982). **GMAT 82-83 bulletin of information.** Princeton: Educational Testing Service.

Law School Admissions Services (1983). **1983-84 law school admission services: LSAT preparation materials.** Princeton: Law School Admissions Services.

Lehtinen-Rogan, L.L., & Hartman, L.D. (1976). **A follow-up study of learning disabled children as adults.** Washington, DC: U.S. Department of Health, Welfare, Office of Education. Final report grant number DEG-0-74-7453.

Patton, J., & Polloway, E. (1982). The learning disabled: The adult years. **Topics in Learning and Learning Disabilities, 2**(3), 79-88.

Pharmacy College Admission Tests. (1982). **1982-1983 announcement pharmacy college admission test.** New York: The Psychological Corporation.

Ragosta, M. (1980). **Handicapped students and the SAT.** (Research Report 80-12). Princeton: Educational Testing Service.

Ragosta, M., & Nemceff, W.P. (1982). **Research memorandum: A research and development program on testing handicapped people.** Princeton: Educational Testing Service.

Rehabilitation Act of 1973. (1973). Section 504.

Sedita, J. (1980). **Help for the learning disabled college student.** Prides Crossing, MA: Landmark School.

Sherman, S.W. (1981). **Ability testing of handicapped people: Dilemma for government, science, and the public.** Washington: Panel on Testing of Handicapped People, National Academy of Sciences, Executive Summary.

Notes

1. Since the initial research was done the SAT and ACT have tightened up their procedures for requesting nonstandard testing and doucmenting a learning disability.

Microcomputer Usage For the Person With a Disability

Thomas R. Irons

Legislation in the 1970's has mandated that there should be a national focus on meeting the independent living needs of the person with a severe disability. These needs include an appropriate education in the least restrictive environment, solutions for activities of daily living, and independent functioning to the fullest extent possible. One remedy advocated has been the use of microcomputers in the educational environment and in other spheres of daily living. If microcomputer usage is demonstrated to be a feasible solution, it will then require special educators and rehabilitation specialists as well as those who train these professionals to become aware of the advantages and disadvantages of computer usage by persons with disabilities.

Benefits to the Person with a Disability

In becoming productive, independent, and able to merge into society, the person with a disability must overcome numerous obstacles. Their survival is initially dependent on the ability to overcome a life-threatening situation, and is directly related to the provision of appropriate medical care and the acquisition of medical self-management skills. The next obstacle, and perhaps the greatest in regards to living independently, is the person's ability to perform everyday tasks, thereby increasing their chances of merging into society (DeLoach & Greer, 1981). An obvious problem encountered by persons with a severe disability concerns energy expenditure. Whether severe disability has occurred due to traumatic injury or is the result of a congenital anomaly, energy expenditure is of the utmost importance in the person's education or rehabilitation. Energy expenditure is an important concern because the nature of the disability often limits the tasks that a person can and cannot do effectively. The use of a microcomputer could enhance a disabled person's lifestyle by enabling the person to engage in tasks that would otherwise be impossible or difficult to perform.

The person with a severe disability might use a microcomputer to meet two basic needs. The first need is specific to the disability. For example, a person who cannot speak could use a microcomputer's voice output system to communicate. The second need that can be fulfilled through the use of a microcomputer relates to the conservation of time and energy. This application is the same for disabled and nondisabled persons. That is, the microcomputer can be used to file and access information, to do budgets, to do word processing, and to control systems in the home and work environment.

The specific benefits of microcomputer utilization for the person with a severe disability fall into five basic categories; namely, (a) communication, (b) education, (c) environmental control, (d) recreation, and (e) vocation. In each category it is essential that the professional know what is available and consider the potential impact of the microcomputer on the person's life.

Communication

Microcomputers are of value to the person who is both nonverbal and has limited skills. A person who cannot communicate in a conventional manner (by speaking, writing, signing, or typing) could learn to communicate through the use of a microcomputer and appropriate interface equipment. The interface is usually a switch or sensor which can be operated reliably by the person. The problem lies in assessing the individual to identify the most appropriate switch or sensor. The device selected must allow for ease of functioning by the individual, and yet take into consideration the individual's highest level of functioning. Assessments kits, with a variety of switches and sensors, are available to determine the most appropriate one for a specific individual.

Some switches are designed for attachment to eyebrows, tongues or fingers. Almost any body part that is under the voluntary control of the individual can be used for this purpose. Sensors

Reprinted from: Journal of Rehabilitation, Jan/Feb/Mar 1985, with permission.

can be used that detect the slightest movement if the individual lacks the strength to operate a switch. A point of caution in selecting a switch or sensor device is that the user's skill level and /or physical capabilities may change with time, and thereby require the installation of a new interface device.

Many persons with severe disabilities can effectively use a standard keyboard with a finger, mouthstick, or head pointer. The keyboard may have to be repositioned or require a keyguard to prevent simultaneous selection of keys.

Selection of keys on a standard keyboard can be made by voice. Cerebral palsied speech can be programmed, as only a unique acoustical signal must be identified for such programming. Computer keyboards can be replaced by enlarged keyboards or surfaces that require little or no force for key activation. A system that will allow eye-gazing to be sufficient for keyboard activation is under development (Foulds, 1982).

The next consideration is the choice of an appropriate selection system technique. Two such techniques are (a) direct selection and (b) scanning. In direct selection, a body part that the individual can control is used to select, by means of the switch or sensor, the desired item directly. This type of selection can be accomplished by pointing a headstick or focusing a beam of light on the switch or sensor, and would be the preferred method of microcomputer operation for the individual who has motor capability. In those instances where the individual has a jerky motoric motion and cannot select a desired item directly, there can be specific selection of the desired item by averaging all items (typical alphanumeric characters) focused on selecting the item with the highest average hit. In scanning, the individual can make a choice by controlling only a single motion. The motion can be with the hand, head, tongue, or eyebrow. In group item scanning, groups of possible choices are successively narrowed. Other types of scanning are row-column scanning and frequency grouping. In the former, rows and columns are scanned rather than individual items, making the process faster. In frequency grouping, the most frequently selected items are scanned first.

In the majority of instances, it is preferable to allow the person with a disability to access regular microcomputer software than to develop special software for each individual. Through careful selection of the microcomputer and the appropriate sensors, switches, and selection techniques, available commercial software can be used by most individuals.

The possibilities for the use of microcomputers in teaching communication to the person with a severe disability are just now being explored (Brinker & Lewis, 1982). For example, a microcomputer can be used as a monitoring and intervening teaching device. Many individuals who do not have a consistent means of communicating have developed a learned helplessness. Either they never learned that they can control the environment or the ability to exercise such control has been lost due to injury. For these individuals, the first step to independent living and self-sufficiency is learning that they can control the environment. A microcomputer can be programmed to monitor the occurrence of a selected number of inputs from the individual; it can also monitor input from a teacher. The microcomputer can be programmed to provide output on a preselected reinforcement schedule. Responses can be counted, graphed, and the microcomputer can then be programmed to change reinforcement schedules, or the output reinforcer.

A number of modifications enhance the use of microcomputers in the area of communication. Some general types are:

1. Those where abbreviation-expansion is used——an abbreviated word is the input, the whole word is the output.
2. Those using anticipation——the computer anticipates the whole word before it is spelled out.
3. Those where the user indicates picture, and words are printed out.
4. Those where the user indicates a symbol, and words are printed out.
5. Those where the user indicates a word, and a sentence is printed out.
6. Those giving a visual display of speech as a feedback mechanism for the deaf.
7. Those giving voice output.

8. Those activated by voice control.

It should be noted that many programs use either a preselected vocabulary or a programmed one. Also, many programs are programmed for either adults or children. Another option is to select a program that has vocabulary for a specific area (biology, for example).

A thorough listing of available commercial products may be found in the *Trace Center International Software/Hardware Registry* (Vanderheiden & Walstead, 1976). This registry is frequently updated. Catalogues can also be obtained from the manufacturers listed in this registry.

The ability to communicate with others has a great impact on the social life of the individual. Self-esteem is likely to improve, while possibilities for independent living and vocational placement are greatly expanded.

Education

The microcomputer provides disabled individuals with many opportunities in an educational setting. Disabled students can use a microcomputer to communicate in class, join in social interactions with peers, take notes, and participate in homework and in-class assignments. On a more direct educational level, a microcomputer can be used to interact with the student at his or her own rate of progress while taking into account: (a) repetition (which is often necessary for lower intellectually functioning individuals), (b) latency of response (for the person with a severe physical disability who may require a slow rate of responding), (c) the need for education to be nonthreatening (for the student with an emotional or autistic problem who might be fearful of people or failure). The microcomputer can present the stimulus, accept a response, evaluate the response, present appropriate feedback, reinforce, and move to the next appropriate instructional segment (Hannaford & Taber, 1982). An additional positive aspect of a microcomputer is its motivational value. For the individual with lower intellectual functioning, the microcomputer provides interesting and challenging types of drill. For the person with a physical disability, it can make adjustments for high level thinking and

low level motor abilities, which few teaching aids can do. The microcomputer can be used in an educational setting to teach the basics of computer usage; tasks that have independent living and vocational significance for the individual can then be readily learned at a later date. Also, in the vocational sphere, production rate skills and independence in working can be taught through the use of a microcomputer (Vanderheiden, 1981). Finally, for individuals with disabilities who reside in rural areas, educational service delivery in the home via a microcomputer would be a timesaving educational tool (Aeschleman & Tawney, 1978).

Again, it is preferred that regular commercial software be used in the area of education. Furthermore, use should be made of commercially available programs that are designed to teach the student to use various switches, to determine the most appropriate switch and its placement, and to teach the student to use various selection techniques.

For the individual with a severe disability the use of microcomputers in education might assist in determining whether the individual could function in a less restrictive setting. Such usage would also have implications for the older individual in a prevocational/vocational training setting. A primary focus of past legislation has been on least restrictive placement, the acquisition of functional living skills, and the development of self-sufficiency in order for the individual to attain the maximum possible degree of independent living. The microcomputer could be an effective vehicle for assisting the individual in achieving these goals.

Environmental Control

A third area in which microcomputers may benefit the person with a disability is in gaining control over his or her environment. Although an individual with a severe physical disability might not be able to attain full independence, he or she should have the opportunity to become as fully functioning as possible. Two related areas of concern are the individual's inability to achieve success in activities of daily living and to conserve energy and time in performing daily tasks. Problems in these areas can impede adequate adjustment in the community and vocational spheres.

Activities of daily living are those tasks and skills that the person must be able to accomplish to the fullest extent possible. Such tasks might include dressing, feeding, toileting, mobility, safety, and communication. The greater the quantity and quality of task performance that the person can achieve, the better are his or her chances of adequately adjusting in the community and vocational areas of life and, therefore, the greater the degree of independence.

The second area of concern pertains to two obstacles in a disabled individual's life that are of dire importance; namely time management and energy expenditure. By the very nature of a severe physical disability, the individual must take every opportunity to effectively manage time and actively seek means to conserve energy for priority tasks. Closely related to the concepts of "time and energy expenditures" is speed, which involves how fast one can transfer information or complete a task. Speed in performing tasks is important in other areas of daily living, but is of utmost importance in the vocational realm. Included are tasks such as communicating and writing, which are important both at home and in the employment setting.

Microcomputer usage can have a dramatic effect on an individual's ability to achieve independent living by diminishing some of the problems noted. Several aids and programs are available to meet these needs.

At present, a use for the computer is in the area of security/monitoring systems (Vanderheiden, 1981). Through microcomputer adaptations, the individual can control locks and windows, turn appliances on and off, and gain access to an emergency call system. Monitoring systems can check the individual to see if all is well, and a medication reminder system can be adapted for the individual (Vanderheiden, 1981). These kinds of applications could be of benefit, not only to the person with a disability, but also to older individuals. It should be noted, however, that technological problems with the microcomputer exist at this time since it is not possible to handle multiple tasks at the same time, nor switch from one program to another as the need arises. For example, a person cannot use the computer to answer the telephone and at the same time gain access to information from the computer for the caller. Once technology has advanced to the level that multiple tasks can be performed with a microcomputer then more sophisticated uses will be possible.

The aids and programs that are available can be used in a variety of settings (educational, home, and vocational), and are designed specifically for the person who is nonverbal and severely physically disabled. An example is the use of voice entry terminal capabilities. Some programs that are available are designed to meet specific educational/training, home, and vocational needs. For example, programs are available for budgeting, money management, banking, and comparative buying. Application of this nature would certainly lead to improved self-esteem, socialization, and self sufficiency, as well as a greater degree of independence for the person with a severe disability.

Recreation

Recreationally, microcomputers have given the person with a severe disability an opportunity to compete in the very fashionable arena of computer games. Computer games are a popular recreational activity among nondisabled persons, as evidenced by increased sales and the number of new programs appearing in numerous commercial locations and homes. The skill used in these games might be very important to the socialization and well being of the person with a disability, who is often unable to compete in many recreational games. Younger users can learn many social concepts from game playing with microcomputers. They learn to have consideration for others, be fair in competition, take turns, share, lose, and win. The student with a physical disability can learn special concepts on the screen that he or she might be unable to learn in real life due to limited ability to move in space. Artistic skills can be developed with the drawing and musical game programs. Finally, educational games can be used to allow for recreational and educational development.

Vocational

The microcomputer can have a great impact vocationally on the employability of the person with a severe disability. Many commercially available adaptations may help make persons employable (Vanderheiden & Walstead, 1976).

Many of these vocationally-related programs are the communication tools discussed earlier. Not to be forgotten, however, is that instructing an individual to use a microcomputer system for whatever reason, provides that person with a vocational skill in the field of computers (Vanderheiden, 1981). Therefore, the individual has acquired a skill that can be used in daily living, that has increased employability in several vocational settings, and that may enable the person to enter the field of computers as an employee.

Numerous microcomputer programs and aids are available in the areas of job awareness, career guidance, vocational assessment, job readiness, job seeking skills, basic educational skills, consumer skills, banking, job development and placement, and work adjustment, as well as technology to monitor and analyze work performance on the job. Programs are also available which deal with comprehensive vocational assessment pertaining to the use of different interfaces and the best system for a particular person.

An additional use of computers involves the employment of job restructuring and modifications that can be done in conjunction with the microcomputer. In the past several years, an increasing number of business concerns have incorporated modifications for persons with disabilities into the work setting and have increased their recruitment and training of employees with disabilities.

It would appear that the use of the microcomputer in a vocational setting can greatly enhance the employability of the person with a disability. The ability to be vocationally independent has many positive effects such as increased self-esteem and independence. As an added factor, the vocationally independent person who is disabled can serve as a model for other persons with disabilities.

Precautions

In exploring the impact of the microcomputer on the person with a disability one would be remiss not to mention the following precautions:

1. Microcomputers are still expensive, though less expensive than ever before. Therefore, selection of an appropriate computer for the individual is very important. It should also be noted that there are other expenses for switches, programs, printer, and related devices.

2. Many microcomputers, although transportable, still require access to 110 volt AC. This is especially important in the selection of a system by or for a disabled person. Does the truly "portable" model meet the needs of the individual? Can it only be used three feet from a wall?

3. Maintenance must be kept in mind. Who can do it? How fast can it be done? How much does it cost?

4. Educational and vocational personnel must be taught to use the system and support it, or it will probably not be successfully used by the disabled person.

5. Family training and followup must be accomplished.

6. Some individuals feel that allowing a developing child to use an artificial aid might hinder normal development (Vanderheiden & Walstead, 1976).

7. Time involved in training the person may be lengthy.

8. Consider whether the learner's expected capacity warrants the effort and expense involved (Hannaford & Taber, 1982).

9. The teacher's or trainer's teaching style will greatly influence the use of a microcomputer in an educational or training setting (Hannaford & Taber, 1982).

10. The curriculum must fit the capabilities of the microcomputer (Hannaford & Taber, 1982).

11. Can the system be further modified to allow for future growth and needs of the individual?

The use of microcomputers in the fields of special education and rehabilitation holds great promise. Numerous applications have been noted in this article. The challenge to those professionals serving the person with a severe disability and to those who train those professionals is to acquire sufficient knowledge of microcomputer usage to continue performing adequately in the field of special education and rehabilitation.

References

Aeschleman, S.R., & Tawney, J.W. (1978). Interacting: A computer based telecommunications system for educating severely handicapped preschoolers in their homes. **Educational Technology, 18**(10), 30-35.

Brinker, R.P., & Lewis, M. (1982). Making the world work with microcomputers: A learning prosthesis for handicapped infants. **Exceptional Children. 49,** 163-170.

DeLoach, C., & Greer, B.G. (1981). **Adjustment to severe physical disability. A metamorphosis.** New York: McGraw Hill, Inc.

Foulds, R.A. (1982). Applications of microcomputers in the education of the physically disabled child. **Exceptional Children, 49,** 155-162.

Hannford, A.E., & Taber, F.M. (1982). Microcomputer software for handicapped: Development and evaluation. **Exceptional Children, 49,** 137-142.

Vanderheiden, G.C., & Walstead, L.M. (1976) **International software/hardware registry.** Trace Research & Development Center for the Severely Physically Handicapped, University of Wisconsin-Madison, 314 Waisman Center, 1500 Highland Ave., Madison, WI.

Vanderheiden, G.C. (1981). Practical application of microcomputers to aid the handicapped. **Computer, 14**(1), 54-61.

7 EMPLOYMENT AND DISABLED WORKERS

The disabled are often victims of prejudice and discrimination, even when not impaired by their disabling conditions. The traditional axiom, "last to be hired and first to be fired" is tragically, most applicable to the disabled worker. Likewise, it has been verified that victims of disabilities are the most unlikely to be accepted to graduate studies and employment if their condition is known. Thus, if a disabled person views education and employment as an important goal, then it is a positive strategy to attempt to conceal the disability status. Therefore, it can be stated that many disabled people, such as diabetics, and heart patients, find it necessary to camouflage their imperfect identities. However, large segments of the disabled population are unable and unwilling to disguise their conditions from society's "gate keepers". As illustrated by Matkin, employers continue to be extremely reluctant to hire the disabled, in spite of the fact that current data illustrates most disabled workers among the most reliable individuals in the labour market.

Being a disabled worker often pressures the victim to accept lower wages and inferior working conditions. These disadvantages are apparent in Weller and Siphered's analysis. They demonstrate that low self-esteem, impulsivity, inability to cope with stress, and learning disorders which affect learning disabled women in school, create difficulties for them in job seeking, in employment, and social situations.

Even the most severely disabled psychiatric patients, as illustrated by McCue et al., can become self-sufficient and reliable workers. The authors admit, however, that the work adjustment of a severely disordered psychiatric patient has an uneven record. Yet, we can agree that like all other minority groups, the disabled ought to be given opportunities by a society that is becoming more aware of the dilemmas facing minority groups.

430

Educating Employers to Hire Disabled Workers

RALPH E. MATKIN

Employment development for, and job placement of, disabled clients are perhaps the most unique characteristics that set the rehabilitation field apart from other human service professions. Indeed, locating job openings may be the most important phase within the vocational rehabilitation process after client's abilities have been identified. Nevertheless, job development probably has received the least attention from rehabilitation personnel in terms of technological advances and practice (Ugland, 1977). This general lack of perceived importance and subsequent reluctance to engage in employment development activities is apparent particularly when examining role and function studies of rehabilitation counsellors: the single largest professional group in the field (Emener & Rubin, 1980; Matkin, 1982; Muthard & Salomone, 1969; Rubin, Matkin, Ashler, Beardsley, May, Onstott, & Punkett, in press). It is surprising to note, however, that rehabilitation administrators, supervisors, and especially rehabilitation educators attribute significantly higher importance to these activities than do rehabilitation counsellors as being part of the counsellor's job (Emener & Rubin, 1980; Muthard & Salomone, 1969; Rubin et al., Note 1).

The apparent reluctance among rehabilitation counsellors to engage in job development tasks may arise from "many counsellors feeling that talking to employers about hiring disabled people is comparable to being door-to-door salesmen and, as such, is somewhat 'unprofessional'" (Minton, 1977, p. 144). For whatever the reason(s) offered by practising rehabilitation counsellors to minimize their involvement in the job development and placement processes, the question of whose responsibility these duties are remains unanswered. Regardless of who performs these activities, it is clear that effective job placement process, the question of whose responsibility these duties are remains unanswered. Regardless of who performs these activities, it is clear that effective job placement must begin with strategies designed to educate employers about the benefits of hiring disabled workers. The purpose of this article is to suggest a method whereby rehabilitation personnel, particularly counsellors, can communicate more effectively with employers; thereby, increasing the likelihood of locating job openings and improving job placement activities for disabled workers in spite of a depressed labor market.

Economics: A Recurring Theme

Employer Concerns

Florian (1978) indicated that rehabilitation personnel can encourage employers to hire disabled persons by designing and implementing specific information campaigns that focus on employers as a group, rather than as individuals. Yet, forming an alliance between rehabilitation and industry requires addressing the concerns expressed by employers relative to such issues as productivity and costs. The rehabilitation literature is replete with examples of employer attitudes toward disabled workers. Most notably, these opinions are expressed generally in the following manner: (a) increased costs are a barrier to hiring disabled workers, especially when architectural changes are believed by the employer to be necessary; (b) insurance rates for employee coverage will increase when disabled clients are hired; (c) attendance among disabled workers will be substandard, job turnover will be higher, and productivity will be negatively affected; and (d) disabled employees will be less flexible in their ability to perform a variety of jobs, thereby increasing the associated manpower needs (and costs) of the employer (e.g., Randles, 1976; Reagles, 1981; Williams, 1972).

Not only have these concerns (based primarily on stereotypic misunderstanding and/or misinterpretation) been perpetuated among employers, evidence suggests that these misconceptions are the principal reasons disabled persons are received less than enthusiastically by private employment agency counsellors (Johnson & Heal, 1976). Needless to say, attempts by rehabilitation

Reprinted from: *Journal of Rehabilitation, July/Aug/Sept 1983*, with permission.

personnel to dispel inaccurate employer beliefs about disabled persons' work capabilities have been numerous. On the other hand, the net effect of these attempts on changing employer attitudes seems to have been minimal, despite their focus on cost and productivity issues.

Assorted Research Findings

Studies of National Scope. large scale research addressing the effects of disabled employees on productivity rates and other economic issues have been few and date back to a period shortly after World War II. In 1948 the United States Bureau of Labor Statistics found that disabled workers were as efficient as non-disabled employees; they also had no more injuries and a lesser number of severe injuries than their able-bodied peers (President's Committee on Employment of the Handicapped, 1948). Furthermore, this report indicated that no disabling injury suffered by a disabled worker could be traced to the original impairment, but rather injuries sustained on the job were related to job hazards, not to the presence of disabilities. These findings were significant in that they were generated from 109 different industrial plants employing over 11,000 disabled workers and over 18,000 unimpaired workers (President's Committee on Employment of the Handicapped, 1948).

About the same time as the Bureau of labor Statistics was conducting its investigations, the Dupont Corporation began studying the effects of its 1,452 severely disabled employees on safety, absenteeism, work performance, and related variables. When compared to able-bodied employees, the Dupont Corporation found that 96% of its disabled workers were rated average or better in safety, both on and off the job, 79% had average or better attendance; 93% had less job turnover; 91% were rated as average or better in job performance; and few modifications were required to alter the physical operation of the different job activities (Sears, 1975). Certainly, the large number of disabled persons included in these two studies lends increased credibility to their findings. Unfortunately, these results and their implications are over 30 years old and may not accurately reflect the present employment

situation among handicapped workers. Therefore, more recent information about the effects on productivity and costs associated with hiring disabled workers must be communicated to employers.

Small Scale Studies. Investigations conducted more recently among local employers support the earlier national findings that there is little difference between disabled and non-disabled workers with regard to job performance, and often times less of a tendency toward absenteeism and injury (Wessman, 1965; Wright & Trotter, 1968). Moreover, in a study conducted in the Fresno, California Internal Revenue Service Center between disabled and non-disabled employees, no significant differences were found in overall job performance when measured by starting and current salary levels, length of employment, overall supervisory ratings, and self-rating of employee satisfaction (Goodyear & Stude, 1975). Nevertheless, in spite of evidence that shows that disabled employees are less likely to be injured and are more reliable workers than their able-bodied counterparts, barriers to employment continue to be expressed in other forms, such as, perceived problems of job transfer, suitability, and difficulty in supervision once a disabled person is employed (Survey of Attitudes, 1974).

Since economic issues appear to be the focal point of concern among many employers, it would seem most beneficial to approach employment development from that perspective. Consequently, to be effective in employment development, rehabilitation personnel must either possess or acquire the knowledge and language skills associated with business and economics in order to communicate effectively with employers. However, developing a comprehensive understanding of business and economic issues in a reasonably short time is not realistic. Therefore, it would be more advantageous for rehabilitation personnel to initially become familiar with basic terminology, while simultaneously utilizing the expertise of intermediaries who are familiar with the concerns and daily activities of employers from a business perspective.

Alternative Employer Contact Sources

Private Industry Councils
Congress soon will begin the process of diverting billions of dollars from programs funded under the expired Comprehensive Employment and Training Act (CETA) into 460 private industry councils (Business Tackles Hard-Core Unemployment, 1982). Private Industry Councils (PICs) were created in 1978 to determine whether input by business into training programs would improve the chances of reducing unemployment among the so-called "hard-core" unemployed worker. Interviews with job training experts in 15 cities have revealed that PICs have been useful particularly when matching training to existing jobs; especially when voluntary PIC boards meet regularly to help design training for specific job classifications (Business Tackles Hard-Core Unemployment, 1982).

Initially, PICs were established on $400 million-a-year pilot programs to find solutions to CETA's weaknesses (Business Tackles Hard-Core Unemployment, 1982). The idea was that councils were to be formed which were composed primarily of business representatives rather than government officials or designees. The rationale for the predominant business orientation of PICs was that training programs could be designed that are more applicable to the job market and which lead to permanent job positions, rather than the temporary 18-month jobs of CETA. How well PICs use Congressionally appropriated monies certainly will have an impact on disadvantaged workers and public policy. If PICs can make federal training programs work, thousands of the nation's estimated three to four million "hard-core" unemployed could become productive members of society. PICs could also help employers meet their needs for skilled workers relatively inexpensively. On the other hand, if PICs fail, such groups as the National Alliance of business, which helped organize and lobby for PIC legislation, may lose future support for federal manpower programs.

Rehabilitation personnel responsible for conducting employment development activities have an opportunity to educate employers to hire disabled workers by contacting and working closely with PICs. Needless to say, the dominant business representation on these councils can serve as substantial leverage for influencing employers to seriously consider hiring disabled persons. Moreover, involvement with PICs can assist rehabilitation personnel in becoming more familiar with the fiscal issues affecting employers, can serve as a demonstration of rehabilitation's interest in employers' concerns, and can probably lead to the development of more job openings for qualified disabled persons.

Employment Agencies
It has been estimated that approximately 7,500 private placement firms with nearly 12,000 offices exist in the United States and Canada (How to Put an Employment Agency to Work for You, 1980). An effective employment agency has a sizable and varied inventory of job orders (i.e., notice of position vacancies) from employers, as well as a steady flow of job seekers representing a wide range of work skills and career experiences. By using a placement firm, employers are thereby relieved of the costs of advertising job openings and the time it takes to screen out unqualified applicants. However, employers with federal contracts are required by law to list all job openings (up to the $25,000 salary level) with local Job Service Offices (Matkin, 1982a). Generally speaking, private employment agencies differ from other similar service agencies by charging a fee for activities that result in a client being hired for a job. The placement fee is paid to the employment agency either by the hiring employer or the newly hired job seeker. *Changing Times,* a monthly business magazine, reported that approximately two-thirds of the jobs listed with private placement firms are fee-paid by the employer at a cost ranging from 7% to 15% of the employee's first year income (How to Put an Employment Agency to Work for You, 1980).

Despite the fact that employment counsellors working in private placement agencies attempt to match persons to available jobs, much in the same manner as rehabilitation personnel perform selective job placement with disabled clients, Johnson and Heal (1976) noted that private employment counsellors are reluctant to serve disabled clients. Indeed, Zadny and James (1978) found that the use of employment agencies account for less than 5% of the jobs obtained by disabled persons. On the other hand, when vocational rehabilitation personnel used the "job order" techniques mandated within private placement firms, not only were more job placements obtained, but the number of rehabilitated clients increased while the number of cases closed as "not rehabilitated" decreased (Zadny & James, 1979). In spite of this finding being significant in and of itself, it was equally applicable for *severely* disabled clients as well; leading to the conclusion that increases in the number of placements obtained through third-parties were tied to increases in total rehabilitation (Zadny & James, 1979).

Rehabilitation personnel appear to have at least two options available as methods of increase employment development and job placement relative to using private employment agencies. First, it has been demonstrated that using *job orders* is perhaps the most effective method for determining both the availability of job openings and the securing of job placements. A job order generally consists of information provided by the employer which includes the name and address of the employer, the name of the job position and a brief description of the duties and skills required in that specific employment situation, salary/wage range, starting date, and the date that the job order was initiated (Matkin, 1982a). Job orders also identify the contact person authorizing the employment request, as well as the person within the employment agency who receives the job information. Obtaining job orders from employers would then require rehabilitation personnel to personally contact employers/-personnel managers on a continuing basis to solicit job referrals.

A second method would be for rehabilitation personnel to work in concert with private employment agencies. This technique may take any number of forms, such as, providing consultation to employment agencies about rehabilit-

ation issues and the needs of disabled persons, offering time and space within the rehabilitation agency for a private employment counsellor to work part-time, or having a rehabilitation person working part-time, or having a rehabilitation person working part-time within a private employment agency to serve the needs of disabled job applicants. Regardless of the employment development and job placement techniques used when working with a private placement agency, it is important to remember that the clients sent to prospective employers must be capable of performing the specified job in terms of the prerequisite knowledge and skill requirements. Referral of individuals without these abilities, under the hope that the employer will have compassion for, and be understanding of, a disability that interferes with the job performance, will not only jeopardize future relations with the employer, but can serve to reinforce any negative beliefs held by the employer about disabled persons in general.

Insurance Representatives

Contrary to the popularly held belief that hiring disabled workers increases insurance premiums, workers' compensation rates are determined by the relative hazards of the industrial occupation and the employing company's accident record (Alliance of American Insurers, 1982; Baker & Karol, 1979; Illinois Governor's Committee, 1982; President's Committee on Employment of the Handicapped, 1982; Reagles, 1981). When determining workers' compensation insurance rates, different occupations are classified separately so that the cost of accidents can be assessed proportionately to the accident risks involved. In other words, hazardous occupations, such as window cleaning, will command a higher insurance rate than a more sedentary occupation such as accounting. Similarly, some employers have better safety programs than do others. Thus, workers' compensation pricing structure recognizes and encourages accident prevention programs and safety consciousness by reducing the rate for those employers having better-than-average safety experiences and, conversely, increasing the rate for those who have lower-than-average safety records. Furthermore, workers' compensation rates are established for each basic occupation in terms of $100 of direct labor cost (payroll). For example, if the rate for "machine assembly" is $1.50 per $100 of payroll, an employer having $100,000 in payroll cost associated with machine assembly will pay $1,500 in workers' compensation premiums. Finally, each $100 of payroll for the other major occupational groups in an employer's workforce (e.g., secretaries, administrators, etc.) is then multiplied by the corresponding rate for each group in order to derive an overall premium cost (Wallace, Note 1).

Compensation payments for work deaths and injuries in the United States in 1975 amounted to over $6.5 billion according to the Alliance of American Insurers (1978). This figure included over $3.4 billion *paid by* private insurance carriers under standard workers' compensation policies, nearly $2.3 billion paid by state funds, and over $8.15 million paid by self-insured employers. Analyzed differently, payments consisted of over $2 billion paid for medical and hospitalization expenses and over $4.49 billion in compensating payments (Alliance of American Insurers, 1978).

Employers may provide employee group insurance in any of five different forms: life, accidental death and dismemberment, short-term disability, long-term disability, and health (Baker & Karol, 1979). The basic principle behind these forms is one of reducing risk and spreading the loss. Risk relates to the degree of probability that a loss will be incurred. Spreading the loss is then accomplished by extending insurance coverage to a sufficient number of persons so that the distribution of losses can be predicted with a higher degree of certainty. With regard to this issue, employers have expressed the belief that disabled workers will suffer more severe injuries than non-disabled employees, thus compounding the pre-existing disability and the associated costs (President's Committee on Employment of the Handicapped, 1982). All states, however, provide second-injury funds financed by insurance carriers and self-insured employers to relieve the employer of liability of preexisting disabilities (United States Chamber of Commerce, 1983). The second-injury funds generally

pay the difference between the employer's responsibility of the new injury and the total benefits payable to a disabled worker. Most states require knowledge by an employer prior to the accident, or prior notification by the employer to the state administrative agency that a disabled applicant has been hired, in order for benefits from these second-injury funds to be made available (United States Chamber of Commerce, 1983).

Given the assumption that rehabilitation personnel generally possess insufficient knowledge of insurance issues, especially as they relate to disabled employees, a viable method for educating employers about the benefits of rehabilitation is by educating personnel who market insurance policies becomes a viable method for indirectly educating employers. Private insurers market their products two major ways: (1) through independent agents or brokers, or (2) directly through their own sales employees (Alliance of American Insurers, 1981). Insurance representatives can be most beneficial to rehabilitation personnel who are responsible for job development and placement in the following manner:

(a) *They have direct access to the employer.*

(b) *They explain how employers are affected by workers' compensation law in business language.*

(c) *They arrange the required coverage best suited to the employer's needs.*

(d) *They distribute safety literature and emphasize the benefits of loss control measures.*

(e) *In the event that accidents occur, they assist employers in the important aspects of contacting the insurer and working with the injured worker.*

When rehabilitation personnel become able to convince the insurance industry of the cost benefits to policyholders that ultimately reduce compensatory payments paid by insurers for medical and rehabilitation services, the rehabilitation field will have developed perhaps its most influential ally for educating employers to hire disabled workers.

Conclusions

Most people with handicaps demand state and private rehabilitation agencies to be more effective, imaginative, and assertive in performing employment services (Galvin, 1975). Yet, in spite of the abundance of data suggesting that hiring disabled persons is "good business," employment development and job placement activities continue to be infrequently and generally ineffectively practised among rehabilitation personnel. The reluctance of rehabilitation personnel (particularly counsellors) to engage in job marketing activities is understandable if training and preparation for those activities is minimal or nonexistent in graduate rehabilitation programs or in on-the-job training situations. Although educating employers to hire disabled workers certainly should enhance employer attitudes in a positive direction, the mechanisms used to educate employers have not produced the results to the degree desired. Therefore, it is suggested that rehabilitation personnel attempt to educate employers in a more indirect manner by consulting with Private Industry Councils, Private Employment Agencies, and Private Insurance Carriers. Indeed, each of these groups is more familiar with employer needs and concerns in terms of manpower and its associated costs than are rehabilitation personnel. Furthermore, by speaking the language of business to business persons and incorporating the benefits of rehabilitation into these discussions, employment development and job placement of disabled persons can be improved.

Project Transition: Competitive Employment Service for the Severely Handicapped Mentally Retarded

W. Grant Revell, Jr., Sue Arnold,
Brenda Taylor, Sheri Zaitz-Blotner

Project Transition is a competitive employment program designed to provide services to both severely handicapped mentally retarded individuals and their employers. The project provides a means for mentally retarded individuals capable of productive, competitive-level job performance to make the transition from sheltered training and subsidized employment programs, such as activity centers and sheltered workshops, into competitive employment. It also provides substantial services to employers. These services include the identification and training of dependable workers at the employment site, the matching of qualified prospective employees to jobs which frequently have a higher turnover rate, and the Federal Targeted Job Tax Credit for hiring handicapped workers.

Project Transition is a cooperative effort of the Virginia Department of Rehabilitative Services and the Fairfax-Falls Church Community Mental Health and Mental Retardation Services Board. It is funded through a local CETA grant. Its original first-year goal was to place and maintain 16 severely handicapped mentally retarded individuals in unsubsidized competitive employment. This goal was expanded during the grant year to 20 successful placements. This expanded goal was fully met as 20 individuals were successfully placed and fully maintained in community-based competitive employment through Project Transition during its first year. In addition, six other project trainees at year end were working in the community under the supervision of project staff.

Project Transition was initiated as a part of an interagency state and local effort to strengthen community-based habilitation services for mentally retarded individuals. The predominant client-group served in the project are former and potential sheltered workshop/activity center clients. The 20 first-year successful placements range in age from 18 to 37. All have a primary handicap of mental retardation; some also have significant physical handicaps; and the initial group of placements includes individuals who recently returned to the community from state training centers for the mentally retarded.

Sheltered employment and work activity centers are needed and necessary placements for many severely handicapped mentally retarded individuals. However, with the return to the community of many formerly institutionalized individuals and the increased vocational emphasis of special education programs for this population, the demand for workshop training and employment slots frequently exceed available opportunities. Project Transition staff emphasize full competitive employment for its clients as a means to provide both greater opportunities to the mentally retarded workers as well as to provide workshop openings for clients who are appropriate for these settings. This competitive employment rationale is based on a number of factors which include wages, earnings, and benefits available in competitive employment as compared to sheltered employment and also community integration and community perception of this mentally retarded population.

Wages, Earnings and Benefits

The U.S. Department of Labor (DOL) funded a comprehensive study of the operation of sheltered workshops. As a part of this study, a survey was completed of the wages and earnings in 1976 of work activity center and sheltered workshop clients.

The average monthly wage as noted in Table 1 earned in regular work, work activity, and training/evaluation programs was below the monthly income poverty level of $239 for 1976. The average monthly income for all clients in each of the three programs when supplemental income is included remains at or significantly below the poverty level.

Reprinted from: *Journal of Rehabilitation* Jan/Feb/March 1982, with permission.

A second consideration regarding the wage income for clientele of sheltered programs is the potential for earnings growth. Table 2 is a brief comparison of client earnings between 1973 and 1976.

Table 1
Average Monthly Income

Income Source	Regular Program Workshops	Work Activities Centers	Training/ Evaluation Programs
All Clients	$243	$102	$134
Clients with no supplemental income (wages)	204	31	63
Clients with wages and supplemental income	282	176	201

Source: U.S. DOL Sheltered Workshop Study, Volume II, Appendix Table 37, 1979.

It is noted that client hourly earnings did not keep pace with increases in minimum hourly wage from $1.60 to $2.30. In summary, the average earnings and earnings growth generated through sheltered work programs, including regular work programs, leave their clients financially dependent on government, community, and family income supplement. The DOL study also noted that only a small percentage of workshop employees received benefits usually provided to competitively employed individuals. These benefits, where available, were mostly restricted to vacation and sick leave.

Community Integration

Participation in a sheltered workshop program provides limited community integration opportunities for the more severely handicapped mentally retarded individual. The findings of Phase I of the DOL-funded sheltered workshop programs during the reporting year (1972-1973) were placed in competitive employment (DOL,

Table 2
Client Average Hourly Earnings

Type of Client	1973	1976	% Increase
Work activities center clients	$.34	$.43	26%
Trainees & Evaluees	.63	.82	30%
Regular program clients	1.40	1.54	10%
Minimum hourly wage	1.60	2.30	44%

Source: U.S. DOL Sheltered Workshop Study, Volume II, Appendix Table 30, 1979.

1979, p. 39). The placement figure for the different types of workshop programs ranged from a high of 19% for training and evaluation programs to a low of 7% for work activity centers. The majority of clients placed competitively from regular workshops or training and evaluation programs had been in the program for six months or less.

The findings of the DOL study are consistent with the competitive placement rates identified by other workshop studies. The Greenleigh study reported that a total of 13% of clients enroled in 400 sampled workshops were placed in competitive employment in a one-year (1974) period (Greenleigh, 1975). The National Industries for the Severely Handicapped (NISH) **Job Placement Study** reported that a total of 15.11% of clients enroled in 82 sampled workshops during the fiscal year 1977 were placed in competitive employment (Perlman, 1978). It can be concluded from these studies that participation in a sheltered workshop program provides an individual very guarded opportunities to advance to the level of competitive employment. This limited opportunity is especially apparent for individuals who remain in workshop programs longer than six months.

The community integration component of Project Transition's competitive employment rationale emphasizes the opportunity for both job-related advancement and also for participation in mainstream society alongside nonhandicapped individuals. Handicapped individuals are the predominant labor force in workshop programs. It is difficult, as evidenced by the productivity reflected through average wages paid to workshop clients, to develop competitive level work speed and job skills when the peer models available are mainly other handicapped workers below standard. The lack within many workshop programs of both competitively-oriented work experience and a competitive job placement emphasis severely restricts the integration into the community work force of competitively employable mentally retarded individuals.

Community Perception of the Mentally Retarded

Both self-contained special education and adult workshop programs isolate the severely handicapped mentally retarded from the nonhandicapped mainstream of society. This isolation reinforces the perception that these individuals cannot learn to work productively on the competitive level. This isolation causes a continued reliance on federal, state and local monetary subsidy for long-term placements and for the income available to this population.

The average amount of supplemental income other than wages reported by the 1979 DOL study for workshop clients receiving such income was $150 per month (DOL, 1979). This income came mainly form SSI and SSDI payments. The DOL study also reported that the average annual fee paid to workshops during the Phase I reporting years was $1,348 per mentally retarded workshop client (DOL, 1979). For calendar year 1979, the range of annual fees charged by regular workshops in Virginia for sheltered employment was approximately $1,200 to $4,300 per client.

This monetary subsidy in terms of supplemental income and fees paid to workshop programs required to maintain a mentally retarded individuals in sheltered employment is substantial. This on-going monetary cost reinforces the community perception that the severely handicapped mentally retarded are a marginally productive or nonproductive population. Successful competitive placements of individuals who have a history of sheltered training and employment turn these individuals from tax users into tax payers. Competitive level employment establishes these individuals as having a potential level of productivity and independence not previously perceived by their families and the community.

Job Training and Employment Model

The Project Transition training and employment model makes use of a professional job site coordinator who provides training and education services on the job for the mentally retarded worker. The primary components of the model are adapted from the work of Dr. Paul Wehman and his staff in Project Employability (Wehman & Hill, 1979 Wehman, 1981). The model is consistent with the training approach used in significantly increasing the productivity of mentally retarded individual in sheltered employment (Bellamy, 1979).

The features of this employment model which differentiate it from traditional transitional training services such as work experience and on-the-job training are as follows: (a) project funds are used to provide professional staff support in the areas of job development, job placement and job maintenance; (b) project funds are not used to subsidize client wages; (c) the project coordinator serves also as the job developer, the point of client referral within the project, and coordinator of support services needed to prepare clients for employment; (d) the project job site coordinators, in cooperation with the project coordinator, match available jobs to job-ready clients; and (e) the job site coordinators assure both the employer and the trainee that the job requirements are fulfilled during the training period and that the skills needed to maintain the job are attained. In the beginning, project staff will supervise the trainee at the job site to assure that these requirements are met and will gradually decrease supervision as necessary over the training period. However, continued follow-up services are provided on a weekly basis or as often as necessary to ensure the continued success of the training.

The job coordinator is the most important component of the project, and the relationship between the coordinator and the client is the key to the project's success. The job coordinators are role models and advocates for the clients. They also provide a means to constructive change and growth by providing a new set of expectations and goals for the client, the client's family, employers and habilitation professionals.

A unique component of Project Transition is its approach to preplacement orientation. Most project clients have a background of workshop training with little non-sheltered work experience. A most difficult aspect of placing individuals with this type of background into competitive employment is providing support for the abrupt change in the work and interpersonal demands they will encounter. To provide an opportunity to reduce this placement handicap facing project clients, the management of the Eisenhower Avenue Holiday Inn in Alexandria agreed to the use of their kitchen, housekeeping, and janitorial areas as preplacement orientation sites.

Preplacement orientation lasts for up to two weeks at the Holiday Inn. The opportunity to interact with nonhandicapped coworkers during the training period is an important transitional experience for the trainees. Job-client match in specific trade areas can be checked by the project staff. The chance for the trainee to keep a regular work schedule, including mobility to and from work, within a competitive setting gives the project staff a realistic opportunity to observe and, where possible, reduce job-related problems prior to the actual job placement.

An important component of the job-client match is transportation to and from work. The job site coordinators teach clients how to transport themselves through a systematic approach to bus training. Individualized training aids are developed based on the needs and learning skills of each trainee. At first, staff accompany trainees on the bus rides. As the trainee demonstrates an ability to make correct decisions independent of a staff person, mobility assistance is reduced and eventually removed. Once employed, efforts are made to include the client in car pools and other alternative transportation arrangements. However, employers are assured the project clientele will have the skills and support needed to transport themselves independently.

Another important component of the Project Transition model is job analysis. Before a client is referred to a job opening, a job coordinator performs a job analysis of the actual tasks of a position, the work environment, job benefits and any other variables at the work site that will have an impact on an employee's job performance.

This component is well like by employers and has often led to identifying jobs within an organization that are considered nontraditional for the mentally retarded persons. It provides valuable placement information but more importantly allows the employer to build a trusting relationship with the project staff.

Completing the job analysis has led us to new employment opportunities for the retarded population, especially in the clerical field. The metropolitan Washington area abounds in clerical jobs, many of which do not require typing or shorthand skills. The job analysis technique has allowed us to identify these jobs and has led to the establishment of a clerical training site with a federal agency.

The final component of the job training and employment model is the role of the job coordinator as a client advocate. Just as severely handicapped mentally retarded individuals frequently enter the project with minimal exposure to the demands of competitive level performance, many handicapped employees and potential coworkers have limited experience with these handicapped individuals. The advocacy role of the job site coordinators includes assisting clients in learning how to socialize with the people at work, teaching employers and co-workers training methods that are effective with mentally retarded individuals, and easing the transition into the work demands unique to each job. The job site coordinators combine preplacement preparation, mobility training, on-site development of competitive level speed and skills, and assistance with interpersonal skills through an advocacy approach into an effective job placement methodology for use with severely handicapped mentally retarded individuals.

Benefits to the Employer

The job site coordinator, during the client training period, also provides significant services to employers. All employers are assisted in making use of the Target Job Tax Credit program which allows employers a credit of 50% of first-year wages up to $6,000, and 25% of the second year wages up to $6,000 for each handicapped individual certified by the Department of Rehabilitative Services, the state vocational rehabilitation agency. All clients served in the project are DRS certified as handicapped.

Project Transition provides a number of additional services to employers including:

1. **An identified pool of qualified workers to fill, on a long-term basis, jobs which are frequently difficult to fill.**
2. **A means of systematizing job development through a central source.**
3. **A job site training resource which significantly reduces the time spent by the employer in training the disabled employee.**
4. **An on-site educational resource to assist the employer and fellow employees in learning the many positive, productive qualities of individuals who happen to have experienced an employment handicap.**
5. **Reduction of the demand for increased tax support of subsidized employment programs.**

Bruce Summer, food and beverage manager at the Holiday Inn used as an orientation site, serves as a member of the Project Transition advisory committee. He is strongly supportive of Project Transition's efforts, and he emphasizes that offering jobs to people who are mentally retarded is a beneficial hiring practice.

"It's very difficult in this business to get dependable help," Summer says. "There's a lot of mentally retarded people capable of working and they're good workers."

Don Gates, a Holiday Inn vice president, states he is also highly sportive of the work skills of the project clientele.

"There is a place in any business for these people," he stresses. "They have a sense of achievement and pride. Achievement is the greatest thing. Whether you want to own up to it or not, everyone is seeking achievement. To a lot of people that might mean making a million dollars. To others, achievement is the ability to hold down a job when you've never been able to."

Cost Effectiveness

The first year expenditures for Project Transition were $77,694. This budge figure consisted primarily of administrative and personnel costs; project money was not used to subsidize client wages. The average cost per placement in the first year of Project Transition for the 20 successful terminations was $3,885.

In discussing cost effectiveness, it is important to note a number of factors:

1. **The clients placed in this project were all either former or potential sheltered workshop employees. Placement in competitive employment removes the project trainees from the list of individuals requiring community or government monetary support for sheltered employment. With the waiting list that existed in the project area for sheltered employment services, competitive placement also reduces the pressure on the community to expand its current level of sheltered employment subsidy.**
2. **The primary alternative source of income other than wages gained from sheltered employment for project trainees prior to their placement in competitive employment was SSI. All individuals placed through Project Transition were placed at minimum wage or above and receive the fringe benefits associated with competitive level employment. Most of the 20 individuals successfully terminated are no longer SSI recipients.**
3. **Many traditional approaches to job placement for the type of population served by Project Transition make use of fee for service and/or wage subsidy programs. Two primary examples are on-the-job training programs and public service employment placement, both of which require substantial government funded**

wages subsidy. **Wages paid to the Project Transition trainees were paid fully by the employers from the first day of employment. Once individuals began receiving job preparation and placement assistance through Project Transition, project monies were not used to subsidize client salaries or pay fees for training services.**

In summary, the per-placement cost of $3,885 during the first year of Project Transition compares very favourably to the tax and subsidy savings generated by these placements. Individuals who previously had been subsidized in terms of sheltered employment opportunities, supplemental income, numerous other disability benefits, and family financial support have become unsubsidized tax payers. As these individuals continue to work competitively, the actual real cost of their placement will continue to decline. And excellent example maintained on a longitudinal basis of the cost-return ration for the job placement model adopted by Project Transition can be found in the second year monograph of Project Employability (Wehman & Hill, 1980).

Summary

The first-year success of Project Transition has resulted in significant expansion efforts in terms of individuals served and services provided. The project's second year goal is to place an maintain in full competitive employment 38 severely handicapped mentally retarded individuals. Also, a second CETA prime sponsor is providing funding support for initiation of the project in the city of Alexandria, and the project is being continued in the Fairfax-Falls Church area with expanded prime sponsor support.

The food service, kitchen utility, and general housekeeping job areas were heavily used during the first year of Project Transition. The preplacement orientation in these job areas offered at the Alexandria Holiday Inn has provided an invaluable client assessment and job preparation opportunity. At present, a preplacement orientation site is being developed at the Naval Operation Center at the Pentagon. This site will emphasize certain clerical duties for which project clientele

can be trained. For example, clerical job areas are filing, microfiche, and quality control. In addition, job opportunities are being identified in certain maintenance areas at the Pentagon. Another preplacement orientation site is planned at a local hospital for development during this second year.

The expanded number of preplacement orientation sites and the varied job areas being developed by Project Transition have led to an increasing emphasis on providing services to individuals with multiple handicaps. At present, individuals with mental as well as physical handicaps such as hearing impairments or functional limitation, usually resulting from cerebral palsy, are being served through the project. Continued expansion of both the client groups and targeted job areas are planned.

A final support service on which increasing emphasis is being placed by project staff is the development of volunteer advocates to assist severely handicapped mentally retarded individuals integrate themselves on a long-term basis into the community. An excellent example of volunteer advocacy arranged through Project Transition involves a 30-year-old deaf client. This individual is now working successfully in competitive employment through the project. However, he requires additional help with his own communication skills, those of his parents, and his independent living skills (especially community orientation). This help is being provided through a volunteer advocate.

The first-year results of Project Transition are very encouraging. The expansion efforts initiated during the early stages of the second year, in terms of increased placement goals, services to larger geographic area, and a focus on a more varied number of job opportunities represent the project's commitment to the job placement needs of severely handicapped mentally retarded individuals. The project's overall goal continues to be the full integration of its trainees into competitive level, unsubsidized employment.

References

Bellamy, G.T., Horner, R., & Inman, D. **Vocational Training of Severely Retarded Adults.** Baltimore, MD: University Park Press, 1979.

Greenleigh Associates, Inc. **The Role of Sheltered Workshops in the Rehabilitation of the Severely Handicapped.** New York: May, 1975.

Perlman, L.G. **Job Placement Study.** National Industries for the Severely Handicapped. Washington, D.C., August, 1978.

U.S. Department of Labor. **Sheltered Workshop Study: Volume I.** Washington, D.C., June, 1977.

U.S. Department of Labor. **Sheltered Workshop Study, Volume II.** Washington, D.C., March, 1979.

Wehman, P. & Hill, J. (Eds.) **Vocational Training and Placement, Volume I.** Richmond, VA: School of Education, Virginia Commonwealth University, 1979.

Wehman, P. & Hill, M. (Eds.) **Vocational Training and Placement, Volume II.** Richmond, VA: Virginia Commonwealth University, 1980.

Wehman, P. **Competitive Employment: New Horizons for Severely Disabled Individuals.** Baltimore, MD: Paul H. Brookes Publishers, 1981.

Alternative Employment Schemes for Developmentally Handicapped People: Some Observations

ROBIN JACKSON

Self Help Equals No Help

The decline in employment opportunities for developmentally handicapped people and adults in Britain has been both precipitate and precipitous. The rapidity of the decline has occasioned a range of responses from fatalistic acceptance, to paralytic bewilderment, to knee-jerk remediation. This decline is symptomatic of a fundamental change that has taken place in the British economy - namely, an accelerating collapse of our industrial base. A railway journey taken from the south to the north of England in 1985 would provide clear confirmation of the transformation in the industrial landscape. The traveller would see decaying, derelict and deserted factories, mills, steelworks and coal mines interspersed with dusty and desolate urban wastelands, where industrial buildings formerly stood but have since been razed to the ground.

It is a matter for political debate whether this collapse need have been so rapid. What is of more general concern is the future of the British economy once it is no longer protected by the wealth generated from North Sea oil and gas. Whilst any discussion about alternatives to open employment must be set against this economic backdrop, it is equally necessary to highlight certain political factors. Since 1979 with the election of a Conservative government Britain has seen the single-minded and determined pursuit of a clearly articulated political philosophy. Central to this philosophy is the open and undisguised reaffirmation by Prime Minister Thatcher of the Victorian value of 'self help'. Less apparent is the acceptance of the doctrine of utilitarianism. Some observers of the present political scene have taken comfort from La Rochefoucauld's maxim that 'Single-minded people do not please for long'.

It is perhaps instructive and salutary to examine the historical context in which the value of self help was born. Victorian Britain felt no sense of societal responsibility for mentally handicapped people. On the contrary, they were seen as a parasitic and predatory population responsible for most of the social ills that ravaged the cities —— poverty, crime, alcoholism, drug addiction, prostitution and vagrancy. Mentally handicapped people were also seen as a threat to social order and the genetic purity of the race. The impact of Charles Darwin's theory of evolution, when translated into Social Darwinism by Herbert Spense, encouraged acceptance of the belief that mentally handicapped people were biologically 'unfit'. Acceptance of the Malthusian doctrine that there was an optimal population size for every society led many to believe that the apparently higher reproductive capacity of mentally handicapped people constituted a threat to the nation's stability and welfare. The Benthamite principle of self help which was popularized by Samuel Smiles ('Heaven helps those who help themselves') laid the onus squarely on the individual to make good. Thus, mentally handicapped people who were perceived as constitutionally incapable of helping themselves, gained little sympathy.

A further characteristic feature of the Victorian Age to which some contemporary politicians nostalgically allude was the crucial role played by the entrepreneur. The fact that the commercial success of these entrepreneurs rested on economic exploitation and the existence of a subservient work-force is forgotten. However, encouragement of entrepreneurial enterprise is a key element in the government's present economic strategy. A disturbing aspect of this strategy is the evident eagerness of the government to extend its policy of privatisation (free enterprise) beyond state industries (e.g. British Airways) to embrace state services (e.g. National Health Service). The pursuit of this policy, it is feared, will lead to the eventual disintegration of the

Reprinted by - permission of author - taken from Journal of Practical Approaches To Developmental Handicap Vol. 9, no. 1, 1985. Pub. by Vocational "Rehabilitation Research Institute" Calgary, Alberta.

welfare state and to the exposure of those economically and socially disadvantaged groups currently protected and supported by our health and social services.

The moral bankruptcy implicit in the doctrine of utilitarianism was clearly identified by Charles Dickens, an eminent Victorian and perceptive social commentator in his novel 'Hard Times'. The sole end of public action, this doctrine proclaimed, should be securing the greatest happiness of the greatest number. The resurrection of this discredited doctrine does not bode well for members of minority groups.

Critics of the present government are concerned that this reaffirmation of Victorian values, where they are translated into policy and practice, will serve to re-create the acute social problems which were endemic in Victorian Britain. Lord Stockton —— formerly Conservative Prime Minister Harold MacMillan —— in an emotional maiden speech in the House of Lords in the Fall of 1984 expressed his profound sadness at the social divisions that were being created in British society. In a landmark speech which spoke for and touched the nation's conscience, he reminded politicians —— particularly Conservative ones —— that politics in Britain had traditionally been characterized by moderation not confrontation. Lord Stockton was clearly concerned at the long-term effect of these newly formed social divisions and the growing intolerance shown to individuals and groups expressing critical points of view. In a society lacking compassion, the views of minority groups are unlikely to be heard, or if heard, not given serious and sympathetic consideration.

It is against this harsh and inimical economic, political and social background that any discussion of future policy, provision and practice for developmentally handicapped people has to be set. If it so wished, the government could introduce measures to alleviate the problems confronting developmentally handicapped people in obtaining employment —— measures which have been adapted successfully in other European countries. It could provide subsidies or tax reliefs to employers to encourage them to engage handicapped workers. It could more rigorously enforce the present quota scheme. It could create

more special employment arrangements (e.g. enclaves). It could, partially or totally, reserve certain economic activities for handicapped persons through the establishment of cooperatives. But such interventionist measures fly in the face of the principle of self help! So, on ideological as well as practical grounds, the government is unlikely to act.

What are the consequences of governmental inaction? The last five years have seen an increasing number of training, workshop and residential facilities provided by voluntary organizations. This is a development that the government obviously welcomes for both philosophic and pragmatic reasons. The danger in the present situation is the rapid growth of fringe enterprises, which claim to offer workshop or training provision but which in reality are no more than crude exploitative enterprises governed by commercial and not habilitative considerations. A proliferation of such facilities without some form of regulation and monitoring could set back the significant advances that have been made in rehabilitation practice over the course of the last decade.

But the establishment of a licensing or accreditation system would require government intervention. Herein lies a dilemma for government. If there is a genuine concern by a government for greater public accountability, then facilities purporting to provide a public service should be exposed to regular and systematic checks. Failure by the state to monitor the operation of a burgeoning private welfare industry would not only be costly in economic terms but also in human terms. However, the introduction of a code of practice and an accreditation system for all such facilities would require from the government a commitment to centralis direction and control which runs counter to its instinct and will.

Alternative Employment Schemes: A Cautionary Note

The kind of problems experienced by those who establish alternative employment schemes for handicapped workers was one of the main topics for discussion at a recent seminar sponsored by the International Cerebral Palsy Society (ICPS, 1984). One particular paper, which described the setting up of a small reprographics/printing company in a West German city to serve physically and mentally handicapped workers clearly exemplifies the nature of some of these problems. Closer inspection of this paper is merited for two reasons. First, it was one of the few papers at the seminar that actually described an alternative employment scheme! Second, whilst some of the problems experienced by the company were recognized, serious weaknesses in the scheme's concept and operation were overlooked.

It was made clear by the company's managing director who presented the paper that it was the goal of the company to be completely self supporting. Full exploitation of the technical assets of the company could, it was claimed, yield a monthly turnover in excess of £7000 or c $13,000 which would be sufficient to pay twelve workers (six non-handicapped and six handicapped) a normal wage. It was conceded that this target had not yet been reached.

The first observation to make is that whilst it is important that such enterprises should operate on sound commercial principles, it is unrealistic to expect economic viability. Where any company employs a significant proportion of handicapped workers and where it also provides on-the-job training, that company is unlikely to achieve levels of productivity comparable to its commercial competitors. Proximate viability (i.e. 80-85%) is the nearest that can be achieved. It therefore follows that those who propose to establish employment schemes should neither state nor imply that economic viability is their goal. Whilst this may make the task of securing support from governmental and non-governmental agencies more difficult, it is necessary to educate professional and lay people to economic realities.

A further problem facing the German company was the extent to which it was in debt even before it was fully operational. Over one third of the capital raised to launch the company took the form of loans on which interest had immediately to be paid. The purchase of expensive and complex equipment in a commercial field where innovation is rapid also brings problems. Only firms linked to the multinational companies (e.g.

Xerox, Sharp, etc.) or firms that generate sufficient profit can afford to counter the effects of obsolescence. In other words, considerable care has to be exercised in one's choice of commercial activity. The managing director acknowledged that the company was finding it difficult to compete. But this difficulty will increase, for customers will expect reprographic firms to keep abreast of technological developments.

Further, insurance premiums on expensive capital items are likely to be high. Paper and electricity —— the two crucial elements in the reprographic/printing process —— are also high cost items. Depreciation on reprographic machinery is likely to be rapid. If it is used heavily, it will require frequent and careful maintenance, which is costly. A failure to maintain machinery adequately increases the likelihood of expensive breakdowns, which in turn loses customers and reduces even further the 'viability' of the enterprise.

The location of the company in a downtown area of a major commercial city would seem ill-advised. Such a location can only make sense for a genuinely commercial enterprise. One of the major items on an expenditure sheet, which can be subject to dramatic and unpredictable increases, is rent. Only where a company is offered a guaranteed fixed level rent over a specified time period or a subsidized rent, should the location in the expensive heart of an urban centre be contemplated.

In his paper, the director acknowledged that competition in the copying and printing market is strong; and competition poses its own problems. There are temptations to lower prices to a point that income falls far short of costs. It is difficult to think of any other form of commercial activity in which firms are so frequently required to respond to tight dead-lines. In a highly competitive situation, a company must have the capacity for flexible and fast response. However, organizations which employ a high proportion of handicapped workers are at a disadvantage. Whilst some handicapped workers may have the ability to achieve high productivity rates, difficulty is often experienced in achieving the very high levels needed to meet critical dead-lines.

Whilst one applauds the good intentions of those who initiated the German repro project, it is difficult to see it ever reaching its goal of financial independence. Indeed, for the reasons which are briefly summarized below, it is doubtful whether it will even achieve proximate viability:

(a) the company's dependence on expensive, fast depreciating and quickly obsolescent capital equipment makes it very vulnerable;

(b) unlike normal commercial firms, the company does not possess resources for re-investment. Neither governmental nor non-governmental agencies are likely to provide regular grants to update or replace costly machinery.

(c) the high ratio of handicapped to non-handicapped workers reduces the company's flexibility to respond to critical dead-lines in a fiercely competitive business field;

(d) its location in a downtown commercial district imposes a heavy rent burden;

(e) the high loan to grant ratio means that interest payments will delay the attainment of proximate viability;

(f) reprographics and printing are wholly dependent on a high cost commodity (paper) and a high cost form of energy (electricity); and

(g) downtown location and expensive capital equipment involves high insurance premiums.

In an area of commercial activity where the profit margins of conventional repro/printing businesses tend to be low, a company working under the kind of financial, operational and commercial constraints identified must have a very uncertain future.

The failure of alternative employment schemes for handicapped people may have consequences which go far beyond those immediately involved. It makes the task for those who follow with better conceived proposals more difficult. In short, those seeking funding from governmental or non-governmental agencies bear a heavy responsibility for the future development of alternative employment schemes. One conspicuous failure can create a long-lasting and hostile psychological climate which is not conducive to the acceptance of innovative employment schemes.

Employment Development Centre

Successful rehabilitation programmes generally occur when organized groups have been able to sensitize local and national governments, their communities and relevant professionals that a need exists. One possible approach might be through the establishment of a network of employment development centres (EDC) by a new or an existing voluntary organization. The concept of the EDC was first advanced, in general terms, by Soloyanis (1978). The precise functions that an EDC might fulfil have been sketched in by this author:

(a) to identify, within a defined catchment area, possible areas for development; (*project identification*)

(b) to formulate project proposals for submission to potential funding agencies; (*project formulation*)

(c) to have responsibility for the administration and development of all EDC-linked projects; (*project administration*)

(d) to be directly accountable for the financial integrity of the projects administered; (*financial accountability*)

(e) to monitor at regular intervals the effectiveness of projects administered; (*evaluative role*)

(f) to prepare progress reports on projects administered; (*report preparation*)

(g) to disseminate information about the purpose and operation of the EDC to all relevant groups in the community (e.g. trade unions, chambers of commerce, etc.); (*information dissemination*)

(h) to maintain close contact with employers in the EDC's catchment area to determine whether any significant changes in skill demands and/or occupational patterns have occurred; (*employer contact*)

(i) to offer advice and guidance to employers considering employing developmentally handicapped people; (*advisory role*)

(j) to encourage employers by all appropriate means to discuss and examine ways to employ developmentally handicapped people; (*catalytic role*)

(k) to provide a consultancy service for employers running non-EDC linked programmes for developmentally handicapped workers; (*consultancy role*)

(l) to exercise a leadership role in this field within the community (*leadership role*).

An essential feature of EDC projects would be that they were not oriented exclusively to meet the needs of handicapped people. Such a policy of exclusivity would run counter to the normalization principle and would be morally and ethically unacceptable at a time of high mass unemployment.

Conclusion

This paper has sought to identify certain features int he present economic, political and social climate in Britain which militate against the development of effective rehabilitation services for developmentally handicapped people. Critical attention has been given to one alternative employment scheme in order to highlight some of the difficulties in establishing alternatives to open employment. The concept of the employment development centre has been tentatively advanced not because it offers the best or only solution in the current crisis but because it may be an alternative strategy worth further and more detailed consideration.

But we do not have the luxury of unlimited time in which to engage in protracted and academic discussion about possible strategies. With the passage of each day the predicament facing developmentally handicapped people worsens. This situation represents a challenge to those working in the rehabilitation field who profess a commitment to the creation and maintenance of services that recognize and uphold the human rights and dignity of handicapped persons. Professional workers in Britain have shown little signs of recognizing the magnitude and immediacy of that challenge.

References

INTERNATIONAL CEREBRAL PALSY SOCIETY (1984) Alternatives for Daily Living for People with a Severe Disability. **ICPS Bulletin,** October.

SOLOYANIS, G. (1978) Employment development centres. In **Vocational Rehabilitation of the Mentally Retarded.** International Labour Office, Geneva.

The Learning Disabled Woman: Implications for the Work Force

Carol Weller, Carolyn Sipherd

In the past two decades, the increase of women joining the work force has been dramatic. The labor market now contains more and more women who have been thrust into work for any number of reasons; among them the increased divorce rate, the unexpected death or incapacitation of a spouse, and double digit inflation. The latter of those mentioned has forced many families to have both parents act as "bread winners" just to break even. Not only are more women joining the work force, but an increased number of women are occupying new areas of employment previously thought to be inappropriate for women. Thoroman (1968) observed that the large number of women flooding the labor force has as its underlying cause the basic need to survive, not just in terms of existence, but in regard to social acceptance, status, and prestige.

This paper will deal with a unique group of this vast body of women: the learning disabled woman. To address the status, needs, acceptance, and prestige of this group of women through the literature is difficult, since there is, at present, limited specific literature on the subject. Therefore, this paper will focus on some characteristics of the learning disabled woman, how these characteristics could affect her performance and goals in the work force, and the services available to learning disabled women to help them enhance their work experience.

Characteristics of the Learning Disabled Woman

There are many factors that may come into play when a learning disabled woman joins the work force. The factors may be related to those characteristics of learning disabilities that have been present in the school years. If these characteristics have been present over the academic careers of the learning disabled girl, it would seem logical that they would still be present during the employment careers of the learning disabled woman. Although some of these characteristics are both sex and learning disability related, their effect on the work performance of the learning disabled woman could be profound.

One characteristic of the learning disabled which may have an effect on work performance is that of impulsivity. Keogh and Donion (1972) have proposed that impulsivity and the inability to reflectively organize information may be a characteristic which can limit the performance of many learning disabled children and youth. The learning disabled woman, who has experienced a lack of organization and planning skills as a young child and adolescent, may lack sufficient reflectivity to choose an occupation based on careful study and evaluation of the situation. Instead she may choose an occupation on the basis of irrelevant influences or disorganized information. Rather than narrowing down possible choices in a logical and systematic manner, the learning disabled woman may either randomly choose a career opportunity, take the first opportunity available, or take a career option that a friend or family has encouraged her to take. Otte and Sharpe (1979) have found that knowledge of a variety of possible choices increases the probability of an individual choosing a realistic and rewarding occupation. When learning disabled women do not receive the knowledge or do not organize the knowledge they have into usable forms, they often select career opportunities on the basis of immediate need gratification rather than on the basis of insightful, logical choosing.

The learning disabled woman is often forced to find work rapidly and on the heels of a divorce or some other traumatic event in her life. She must then contend with her own emotions concerning the stressful cause of her employment plus an unusual lack of preparation in work related skills. In 1976, Cagelka reported the status of vocational preparation in the high school

Reprinted from: *Journal of Rehabilitation* Oct/Nov/Dec 1982, with permission.

work-study programs for female students. In her investigation, she found that fewer girls than boys received prevocational and vocational training; that girls who did receive training did not receive equal training opportunities or equal remuneration for their training; and girls who were trained in vocational settings were expected to use behavior and skills suitable for non-specific careers such as homemaker or housekeeper. While there have been positive exchanges in the way society views sex-role discrimination of late, these changes may have come too late for the learning disabled adult woman who graduated from a regular education or a special education program five, ten, or more years ago.

A second characteristic of the learning disabled woman which may influence her success in the job market is her self image and self-esteem. Kirk and Elkins (1975) have reported that often the learning disabled student feels less than positive about him or herself. Often these students are plagued with feelings of self-degradation, worthlessness, or insecurity about their abilities to perform. The added stress and pressure that these once learning disabled children, now learning disabled adults, encounter in the job market occasion a psychodynamic overlay which can affect not only their performance in their job, but also their abilities to cope with their emotional lives. In his forward of the **Handbook on Learning Disabilities**, Senator Mike Gravel of Alaska (1974) observed that we must try harder to let others know that children with learning disabilities are not "lazy", "retards", or "stupid". Learning disabled children, having average to above average intelligence, probably begin life with little or no emotional difficulties or obvious handicapping conditions. It is often the constant failure and ridicule encountered over the years that results in hostility, poor self-concept, and serious emotional problems.

The learning disabled woman needs a positive self-image, because it may be her self-concept and esteem which allows her to choose and plan her behavior on job related tasks. If poor self-image causes her to view herself as an object in life rather than a dynamic, growing member of a career community, she will be in a poor position

for job enhancing, job security or advancement. Field, Kehas, and Tiedeman (1970) postulated that individuals choose courses of action which fit their current notions about themselves. These notions involved what they were like, what they could be like, what they wanted to be like, what their situations were like, what their situations might become, and their viewpoint of self in relation to situation. Learning disabled women who are unable to view themselves as worthy, productive, and dynamic individuals could tend to see themselves as fragmented from the situation in which they were involved. This fragmentation could lead only to worsened opinions about themselves and their ability to function in a career role.

Self image can affect the career choices a learning disabled woman makes as well as the decisions she makes while on a job. Learning disabled women, often endowed with a poor appraisal capacity, may allow their poor appraisal of themselves to interfere with the selection of job avenues which are open to them. Consequently, they may take jobs below their ability levels, jobs which hold no future for them, or jobs which hold no possibility other than that of discontinuance. Coopersmith (1967) noted that individuals with low esteem tend to be less realistic in evaluating themselves and their abilities. Therefore, they were theoretically less likely to choose occupations needed to achieve a strong sense of well being. Being a woman and learning disabled, the learning disabled female adult could be more likely to experience role conflict involving self-esteem in career selection. She may feel the lack of esteem necessary to confront the occupational role configurations that traditionally have been held by men. She may also feel the lack of esteem necessary to confront roles typically held by women if she feels those women to be more capable than she.

A third characteristic of the learning disabled woman that may result in lowered job potential is that of an inability to facilely handle stress. The adaptive behavior of learning disabled children and adolescents shows that many exhibit non-productive performance under stress (Mercer, 1979; Weller & Strawser, 1081). Behaviors such as avoidance, off-task performance, and escape are often the result. When these behaviors carry over from the child performance in school to the adult performance in work, the learning disabled individual cannot expect a smooth and unstressful employment career. Learning disabled women, encountering the stress of their own emotional upsets which may have triggered the search for the job, the stress of trying to produce in a job that is ill suited to them, and the stress of family, wage, and home obligations, may turn to a number of avoidance and escape patterns including alcohol, drugs, or psychosomatic illnesses. They frequently are plagued with allergies and digestive problems which they may accentuate through faulty nutrition, rest, and exercise. As the escape mechanisms increase, the health of the woman may deteriorate, leaving her unable to function on the job or care for her home and family. As she neglects, so may she be neglected, leading to a lowered image in the eyes of others, her own lowered self-esteem, and a lowered capacity to deal with the stress which began her difficulties in the first place.

Stress for the learning disabled woman can be more pervasive than that encountered by the learning disabled student. In school, compensatory behaviors of quitting, avoiding, and blaming others for failure are learned in order to assist the student in manipulating stressful situations (Mercer, 1979). While these behaviors may make teachers and parents uncomfortable, they do not afford the opportunity to "fire" the student from the school or home. In the social and vocational world of the adult, similar behavior would inevitably lead to social rejection, job termination, and loss of income. Employers value punctuality, responsibility, production, and hard work (Clark & White, 1980), not compensatory avoidance behaviors. If the learning disabled student has spent the school career learning these avoidance of stress techniques, the behaviors can not be expected to instantly change when the learning disabled adult enters the world of work.

A final characteristic of the learning disabled woman that can greatly affect her performance in a career, is the disability which has caused her to be called learning disabled. The seemingly obvious continuity between the disability of the child and the disability in the adult does not occur in the minds of many learning disabled women and employers alike. Often the older woman who possessed learning difficulties as a child, does not perceive the presence of these disabilities in her adult life. She may know that something is wrong with her ability to perform, but is not aware of the exact nature of the problem. She may tend to be so frightened that someone will find out that she is not capable of doing her job in the same manner as everyone else, she may attempt to hide her problems from those who would help or deny that her problems exist. Whatever her method of avoiding the problem, its avoidance will not minimize its impact on her career.

As in the learning disable student, there are many patterns of strengths and weakness in abilities which can occur in the learning disabled adult. Academic discrepancies such as the act of reading, writing, and spelling may become less pronounced, but the application of these skills in the vocational endeavour increases in importance. When learning disabled women whose academic difficulties predominated in these areas are relegated by choice or chance to traditional female positions requiring these skills, their hope for survival in the job market is minimal. These roles, including secretaries, typists, nurses, or teachers, are particularly unsuited for their deficit/strength pattern. Learning disabled women require astute and insightful counselling services to prevent them from traditionalising their job selections and dooming themselves to repeated psychological insult.

Guidance and Counselling Services for L.D. Women:

The lack of adequate adult services for career counselling and guidance has been documented in the literature (Carnegie Commission, 1973; Comly, 1975; Commission on Non-Traditional Study, 1973; Ironsides & Jacobs, 1977). When the delivery system is examined from an overall view, it becomes apparent that programs concerned with counselling and guidance related functions do not hold a high priority. Libraries, some military institutions, industrial training departments and some agencies provide a measure of services, usually conducted on an informal basis. While there are exceptions, most adult educational providers do not have the financial resources to provide these services. Where they are provided, they are frequently restricted to a particular clientele and limited only to exploration of the various types of jobs available.

In public adult education settings, guidance and/or counselling is mainly provided for those working toward completion of high school, technical, or vocational career preparation. Limited services are available for the disadvantaged and undereducated, and these have been seen as far from adequate (Mezerow, Darkenwald, and Knox, 1975). Guidance and counselling for the handicapped may be provided for those individuals with obvious handicaps, but less available for those with the subtle handicap of learning disabilities. Learning disabilities, recognized under P.L. 94-142 as a handicapping condition during the school years, may be denied as a handicap by a State's interpretation of Section 504 of the Vocational Rehabilitation Act of 1973. Consequently, the avenues of guidance and counselling most easily open to the learning disabled woman through vocational rehabilitation may be inaccessible. In order to receive services through a vocational rehabilitation agency, the learning disabled woman may be labelled as emotionally disturbed, psychotic, or developmentally disabled. These labels may provide needed guidance services but can do little to enhance the acquisition of a positive self image.

Services specifically for the learning disabled woman are practically non-existent (Sitlington, 1981). Although service is being provided through some university programs (Bireley & Manley, 1980), learning disabled women are often forced to seek counselling at women's centers, women's network organizations, or from other women. Here, counsellors tend to see non-stereotyped roles for women in the job market, however these counsellors are usually unprepared to offer guidance to a woman whose employment strengths are complicated with learning deficits. Learning disabled women, plagued by a feeling

that someone will find out about their problem, yet, not fully aware of what their problem is, are often too guilt ridden and stressful to give an honest evaluation of their abilities. Consequently, the honest relationship that is so vital to the counsellor/counsellee roles are never established.

Counsellors who provide services to learning disabled women must often provide more than mere vocational guidance. They must become builders of self-esteem for the woman, must offer suggestions on how organization can be initiated and maintained in the woman's life, and must provide suggestions to help the woman cope with the inevitable stress she will encounter. They must deal with the lack of adaptive behavior skills encountered by the learning disabled woman as with the successful matching of individual to job. Somehow they must take over where the school left off or failed and become vocational, social, family, and life management counsellors for the woman. If counsellors choose to reject such a role, who could blame them. The task is overwhelming, tenuous, and one for which they are not often trained.

The Implications for the Future

Clearly the task to suitably involve the learning disabled woman in the job market is enormous and extremely complex. Much research is needed especially in the areas of assessment, programming, and counselling options. While schools will be unable to assist the learning disabled woman who never received special instruction for her disability they can help those young learning disabled children and adolescent women who will soon enter the world of work. Assessment of social/vocational and adaptive behaviors are required, as are programs which prepare learning disabled females for a variety of vocational possibilities. Training designed to assist the female students in handling the stresses they will encounter in home, vocational, family, and social life should be incorporated into prevocational and vocational programs. Measures to enhance the self esteem of these young women are a necessity. Traditional academically oriented secondary programs may not be providing the needed services. Specialized vocational training, designed specifically for the needs of these students may be in order.

Guidance and counselling options for learning disabled women who have left the school environment are also needed. Special educators must become an active member of the team involving vocational and guidance specialists, employers, and learning disabled women. Educators involved with the mentally retarded or physically handicapped have long provided assistance to businesses who hire the handicapped into their work force. Educators involved with the learning disabled would be well advised to provide such assistance as well.

Although this paper in no way minimizes the vocational and social difficulties of the learning disabled male, it does attempt to bring to light some of the often overlooked problems of the learning disabled woman. Learning disability does not seem to minimize as a woman reaches maturity. Instead, it appears to become more complex and more debilitating as demands of employment and social status increase. The resolution of the problems of the adult learning disabled woman will require knowledge, sensitivity, and tenacity on the part of those who assist her in the quest for a career.

References

Bireley, M., & Manley, E. The learning disabled student in a college environment: A report of Wright State University's program. **Journal of Learning Disabilities**, 1980, **13**, 7-10.

Carnegie Commission in Higher Education **Towards a learning society.** New York: McGraw Hill, 1973.

Cegelka, P.T. Sex role stereotyping in special education: A look at secondary work-study programs. **Exceptional Children**, 1976, **42**, 323-328.

Clark, G.M., & White, W.M. **Career education for the handicapped: Current perspectives for teachers.** Boothwyn, Pa.: Educational Resources Center, 1980.

Comly, R. **Community based educational and career information and counselling services for the adult public: Draft report.** Albany, N.Y.: New York State Education Department, 1975.

Commission on Non-Traditional Study. **Diversity by design.** San Francisco: Jossey-Bass, 1973.

Coopersmith, C. **The antecedents of self-esteem.** San Francisco: Freeman, 1967.

Field, F.L., Kehas, C.D., & Tiedeman, D.V. The self concept in career development: A construct in transition. In R.M. Roth, D.B. Hershenson, & T. Hilliard, **The psychology of vocational development: Readings in theory and research.** Boston: Allyn & Bacon, 1970.

Gravel M. Forward. In R.E. Wever, **The handbook on learning disabilities: The prognosis for the child, the adolescent, the adult.** Englewood Cliffs, N.J.: Prentice Hall, 1974.

Ironsides, D., & Jacobs, D. **Trends in counseling and information services for the adult learner.** Toronto, Canada: Ontario Institute for Studies in Education, 1977.

Keogh, B.K., & Donion, G. Field dependence, impulsivity, and learning disabilities. **Journal of Learning Disabilities,** 1972, **5**, 331-336.

Kirk, S., & Elkins, J. Learning disabilities: Characteristics of children enrolled in the Child Service Demonstration Center. **Journal of Learning Disabilities,** 1975, **8**, 630-647.

Mercer, C.D. **Children and adolescents with learning disabilities.** Columbus, Ohio: Charles E. Merrill, 1979.

Mezerow, J., Darkenwald, G., & Knox, A. **Last gamble on education: Dynamics of adult basic education.** Washington, D.C.: Adult Education Association, 1975.

Otte, F.L., & Sharpe, D.L. The effects of career exploration on self-esteem: Achievement, motivation and occupational knowledge. **The Vocational Guidance Quarterly,** 1979, **28**, 63-70.

Sitlington, P.L. Vocational and special education in career programming for the mildly handicapped adolescent. **Exceptional Children,** 1981, **47**, 592-598.

Thoroman, E.C. **The vocational counseling of adults and young adults.** Boston: Houghton Mifflin, 1968.

Weller, C., & Strawser, S. **The Weller-Strawser scales of adaptive behavior for the learning disabled.** Novato, Calif.: Academic Therapy, 1981.

The Severely Disabled Psychiatric Patient and the Adjustment to Work

MICHAEL MCCUE AND LYNDA KATZ-GARRIS

Relatively few articles dealing with the importance of work and, more specifically, the work adjustment of psychiatric patients are present in the mental health literature (Anthony, 1979). Aside from the "work therapy" movement (Black, 1970), which appeared to flourish and then die out in the 1960s, attention to the vocational functioning of psychiatrically disabled individuals has been minimal. While the provision of vocational rehabilitation services to the psychiatrically disabled person began with the 1943 Rehabilitation Legislation, the vocational rehabilitation aspects of psychiatric treatment have only recently begun to receive attention. For example, the emphasis on community interventions, increased concern with patient behaviors and functioning (as opposed to internal dynamic processes), the concept of a more holistic approach to treatment, and federal mandates which require state vocational rehabilitation agencies to serve the severely disabled, have led to an increased concern for the occupational functioning of individuals with severe psychiatric disorders. From the perspective of the vocational rehabilitation field, there is recognition of the need to broaden existing services. Likewise, the mental health field has begun to expand its services and include a concern for the vocational needs of psychiatric patients (OVR/OMH Agreement of Cooperation, 1982).

A primary treatment modality for dealing with the work difficulties of a disabled population is work adjustment training. Work adjustment training programs are designed for those clients who lack the basic work and social skills needed to maintain a job (Neff, 1968). The major component of a work adjustment training program is work, whether it be simulated work in a sheltered environment or real work in a natural environment. Although certain aspects of work adjustment are common to individuals with and without a psychiatric disability, there is reason to believe that the presence of mental illness further complicates the work adjustment process (Gunn, 1973). Severely psychiatrically disabled clients appear to experience more problems in adjusting to work than do clients in the general rehabilitation population.

It is, therefore, important to recognize the specific problems of individuals who are psychiatrically disabled since many of these individuals are potential consumers of vocational rehabilitation services. After identifying the unique features of this population, efforts can then be directed to specifying their work adjustment problems, many of which may also be uniquely related to this disabling condition. Knowledge of the personal and work adjustment problems of this population should serve to enhance the process and outcome of vocational rehabilitation services for clients with severe psychiatric disabilities.

Defining the Population

The individual with a severe psychiatric disability experiences some severe and/or chronic psychiatric problem which significantly interferes with the performance of ordinary life functions. Individuals who experience psychiatric disorders are more specifically defined by using diagnostic labels. Although the utility, validity, and reliability of psychiatric diagnosis in the field of psychiatric rehabilitation has been questioned (Anthony, 1979; Lamb, 1971; Rogan, 1980), diagnostic labels remain the primary means of describing and classifying mental illness, both for treatment and research purposes. The American Psychiatric Association's **Diagnostic and Statistical Manual of Mental Disorder, Third Edition** (DSM - III), (1980) provides "a common language with which to communicate about the disorders for which they (clinicians and research investigators) have professional responsibility" (p. 1). In the DSM-III, each mental disorder is conceptualized as a clinically significant behavioral

Reprinted From: *Journal of Rehabilitation* Oct/Nov/Dec 1983, with permission.

or psychological syndrome or pattern occurring in an individual and typically associated with a painful symptom or impairment in one or more important areas of functioning.

The primary diagnostic categories which will be addressed in this paper are schizophrenic disorders, the affective disorders, and personality disorders. A discussion of other diagnostic categories (e.g., organic mental disorders, substance use disorders, anxiety disorders, and somatoform disorders) will not be included for several reasons. While it is possible that an individual who experiences difficulties associated with these other syndromes may be considered "chronically psychiatrically disabled", it is generally agreed that individuals with chronic, debilitating psychiatric difficulties fall within the schizophrenic, affective, and personality disorders diagnostic categories. Neurotic disorders, classified as a separate diagnostic category in the **Diagnostic and Statistical Manual (2nd Ed.)** are found in a number of categories in the DSM-III, including the category of affective disorders. For the purpose of this discussion, neurotic disorders are not considered chronic and severe. An analysis of the Rehabilitation Service Administration's 1979 caseload statistics for Region III (Katz-Garris & McCue, 1980) reveals a 38% rehabilitation success rate for neurotic disorders while psychotic and personality disorders average only a 16% success rate. These statistics are indicative of the lack of evidence to support the chronic, disabling effective or neurotic disorders on individuals. On the other hand, according to legislation defining severe handicap, mental illness is considered severe if "...the disability requires multiple services over an extended period of time..." (Public Law 93-112, Sec. 7(12)). Thus, while various types of mental disorders may meet the federal criteria for severe handicap, only those disorders which most frequently result in a severe psychiatric impairment will be described below.

Schizophrenic Disorders

Schizophrenia is a broad descriptive label that is applied to persons who experience gross personality disorganization and a severe impairment in psychosocial function. The disorder is quite prevalent, with estimates of over one percent of the world's population experiencing deficits associated with the disorder at some time during their lives (Page, 1971).

Included in this diagnostic category are schizophrenia, paranoid disorders, and other psychotic disorders such as atypical psychosis and schizoaffective disorder. In order for a diagnosis of schizophrenia to be made, the following criteria must be met:

(a) at least one of the following during a phase of the illness: bizarre delusions...; somatic, grandiose, religious, nihilistic, or other delusions without persecutory or jealous content; delusions with persecutory or jealous content if accompanied by hallucinations of any type; auditory hallucinations in which either a voice keeps up a running commentary on the individual's behavior or thoughts, or two or more voices conversing with each other; auditory hallucinations on several occasions with content of more than one or two words, having no apparent relation to depression or elation; incoherence, marked lessening of association, markedly illogical thinking or marked poverty of content of speech...;

(b) deterioration from a previous level of functioning in such areas as work, social relations and self-care;

(c) continuous signs of the illness for at least six months at some time during the person's life, with some signs of the illness at present...; the full depressive or manic syndrome, if present, developed after any psychotic symptoms, or was brief in duration relative to the duration of the psychotic symptoms listed under "a";

(d) onset...before age 45; and

(e) not due to any Organic Mental Disorder or Mental Retardation (American Psychiatric Association, 1980, pp. 188-190).

There are four types of schizophrenic disorders; namely, disorganized, paranoid, undifferentiated, and residual. Other psychotic disorders that are defined in the DSM III and which might be considered chronic and severe include: atypicalpsychosis, a category for cases in which there are psychotic symptoms that do not meet the criteria for any specific disorder, and schizoaffective disorder (used when it is unclear whether the patient is experiencing an affective disorder or a schizophrenic disorder).

Affective Disorders

Some authorities have estimated that at least 12% of the adult population have had or will have an episode of depression of sufficient clinical severity to warrant treatment (Schuyler & Katz, 1973). In a special report on depressive disorders (Secunda, Katz, Friedman, & Schuyler, 1973), the authors reported that depression accounts for 75% of all psychiatric hospitalizations and that during any given year, 15% of all adults between 18 and 74 may suffer significant depressive symptoms. Affective psychoses are distinguished by extreme disturbances of mood, either elation or depression, which dominate an individual's existence to the extent that feelings, ideas and attitudes are relatively unaffected by rationality.

> *The essential feature of this group of disorders is a disturbance of mood, accompanied by a full or partial manic or depressive syndrome, that is not due to any other physical or mental disorder. Mood refers to a prolonged emotion that colours the whole psychic life; it generally involves either depression or elation. The manic and depressive syndromes each consist of characteristic symptoms that tend to occur together (American Psychiatric Association, 1980, p. 210).*

Major affective disorders are a subclassification of affective disorders which are considered severe. Major affective disorders include bipolar disorders, distinguished by whether there has been a manic episode, and major depression, where "the essential feature is either a dysphoric mood, usually depression, or loss of interest or pleasure in all or almost all usual activities and pastimes" (American Psychiatric Association, 1980, p. 210). Other features associated with major depression included feelings of hopelessness, worthlessness, sleep disturbance, appetite disturbance, and difficulty in concentration. Thoughts of death and suicide are also common.

Personality Disorders

Some individuals develop enduring patterns of perceiving and dealing both with their environment and themselves. These patterns may be thought of as personality traits. It is when these traits "are inflexible and maladaptive and cause either significant impairment in social or occupational functioning or subjective distress that they constitute Personality Disorders" (American Psychiatric Association, 1980, p. 305). Difficulties associated with personality disorders usually appear in adolescence and persist throughout adult life, significantly limiting overall functioning. Disorders that fall under the category of personality disorders in the DSM-III include:

1) **Paranoid Personality Disorder,** characterized by suspiciousness and mistrust, hypersensitivity and restricted affect;

2) **Schizoid Personality Disorder,** characterized by emotional aloofness, indifference and few social contacts;

3) **Schizotypal Personality Disorder,** which may include magical thinking, ideas of reference, social isolation, recurrent illusions, odd speech, inadequate rapport, suspiciousness and/or undue social anxiety;

4) **Histrionic Personality Disorder,** characterized by overly dramatic behavior and disturbances of interpersonal relationships;

5) **Narcissistic Personality Disorder,** which involves a grandiose sense of self-importance;

6) **Antisocial Personality Disorder,** characterized by a history of continuous and chronic antisocial behavior in which the rights of others are violated.

7) **Borderline Personality Disorder,** in which there is instability in a variety of areas, including, mood, interpersonal behavior and self-image.

8) **Avoidant Personality Disorder,** in which there are hypersensitivity to rejection, unwillingness to enter to interper-

sonal relationships, social withdrawal and low self-esteem;

9) **Dependent Personality Disorder,** in which an individual allows others to assume responsibility for major life area;

10) **Compulsive Personality Disorder,** characterized by emotional restriction, perfectionism, dominance and indecisiveness; and

11) **Passive Aggressive Personality Disorder,** in which there is indirect resistance to demands for adequate performance in occupational or social functioning (DSM-III, pp. 328-329)

The prevalence of personality disorders is much lower than that of schizophrenic or affective disorders, but these disorders are typically so debilitating that they negatively influence functioning throughout an individual's life.

Specific Work Problems of the Severely Disabled Psychiatric Client

Olshansky, Grob, and Malamud (1958) classified the work adjustment problems of the psychiatrically disabled in a two-fold manner: (1) limitations imposed upon the degree of employability of the individual by his or her own personality difficulties and (2) limitations imposed by employer attitudes and practices. As shown below, Neff (1968) added a third category which appears to render his conceptualization of the work adjustment problems of the psychiatrically disabled individual more comprehensive.

First, a disability may impair or limit certain functional abilities and aptitudes which are required by the specific kinds of work. Second, the disabled person may have to cope with the many kinds of negative and aversive feelings which some disabilities arouse in other persons, both employers and co-workers. Third, a disability may, under certain conditions, arrest, distort, or block the development of...the work personality (pp. 233-234).

In Neff's first category, impairment or functional limitations are results of the specific nature of the illness. For example, in the visually impaired individual, limitations incurred by the lack of sight would be classified here. The second category deals with environmental concerns. Using the previous example of the visually impaired individual, these limitations arise out of negative stereotypes attached to being blind. The third category deals with the effect of the disability upon an individual which may not be directly related to the disability itself. Again, in the example of the visually impaired individual, institutionalization or overprotective parenting may have resulted in poor social skills or a lack of independence. Several applications of Neff's three categories of work adjustment problems with the severely disabled psychiatric population are presented below.

Direct Effects Upon Functioning

Research on the vocational functioning of psychiatric patients has been limited. Gunn (1973), in discussing the reported results of a Psychiatric Evaluation Project (PEP) designed to follow-up mentally ill persons over a four-year period, reported that "The factor which was judged to be most significant in understanding why patients did not work...was, pure and simple, their shaky emotional integration" (p.171).

Neff (1968) stated that, "Certain broad patterns of work behavior can be observed, suggesting the possibility that there are types or kinds of work psychopathology" (p. 207). Through clinical impressions derived from studying clients in a sheltered workshop and through an empirical validation procedure, Neff was able to observe characterological types or patterns of qualities that appeared to lead to failure in work. Seven categories of maladaptive behavior were identified and rated by judges, whose ratings were then statistically tied to work performance. These characteristic patterns of behavior were categorized as: fearful, dependent, impulsive, socially naive, withdrawn, apathetic, self-deprecatory, and hostile. Results of Neff's study with 100 psychiatrically disabled clients indicated that an individual's general style of relating to demanding social situations was crucial to work success. Individuals who had the greatest difficulties were marked by certain specific personality styles such as poor impulse control, excessive fearfulness and timidity, dependence, and immaturity.

Although Neff's study attempted to empirically describe and define the work problems of the severely emotionally disturbed, approaching the problem from a "trait" approach had obvious limitations. Work problems are typically thought of in terms of specific behaviors which are not conducive to acceptable work performance. An attempt to identify personality traits associated with success or failure at work contributes little to objective identification of specific problems which can then be treated. A further limitation of Neff's study was that it observed workers in a simulated environment. Because of the vastly different values, expectations, and pressures associated with a "real" work setting as opposed to a sheltered setting, generalization of the results is, therefore, questionable.

Work problems associated with physically disabled populations or general populations have been objectively identified through observation using behavioral rating scales (Fifth Institute of Rehabilitation Issues, 1978; Matthews, Whang, & Fawcett, 1980). In order to define the specific work problems of the psychiatrically disabled client, similar procedures need to be undertaken. Van Allen and Loeber (1972) reviewed seven existing scales for assessing work behavior of psychiatric patients. Their summary, which points out many methodological weaknesses and deficiencies, concludes "that the development of work rating scales for psychiatric patients was as yet at an embryonic stage" (p. 113). Existing work rating scales focus upon job behavior but none attempt to objectively define work problems. Expanded assessment tools need to be developed. Behavioral definitions of symptomology need to be established and validated along with validated instruments so that identification of work problems "in vivo" can then be undertaken.

Attitudinal Barriers Influencing the Work Adjustment of the Psychiatrically Disabled Client

The second category of employment difficulties noted by Neff (1968) deals with "the many kinds of negative and aversive feelings which some disabilities arouse in other persons —— both employers and co-workers" (p. 233). The nature of this specific work problem is not limited to those individuals with psychiatric disabilities, but is experienced by all disabled person. Olshansky, et al. (1958) surveyed employers, co-workers, industrial physicians, public and private employment agencies, and labor unions in order to "inquire into the basic attitudes underlying the practices, policies and thoughts of employing groups with respect to the ex-mental hospital patient as a job applicant or employee" (p. 392). Employers reported concern with violence, recurrence of illness, limited tolerance for pressure and speed, incompatibility, bizarre behavior, immorality, and mental deficiency. Olshansky, et al. (1958) indicated that the most significant finding of the study was that employers reported very limited experience with ex-mental patients and while a large majority of employers said that they were willing to hire, few employers actually did.

Another study by Margolin (1961) surveyed employers who, with full knowledge, hired ex-mental patients. In addition to generating an extensive list of strengths and weaknesses of ex-mental patients on the job, the study elicited a number of suggestions and recommendations by employers. Suggestions implied "...that there was an iron curtain between hospital and industry. Communication barriers exist because hospital personnel tend to be unrealistic, while business and industry are hardheaded and practical" (p. 114). The author suggested that negative attitudes toward the ex-mental patient could be minimized or avoided by adequate preparation, training, and follow-up by the hospital.

A third study, by Whatley (1964), attempted to determine the effect of employer attitudes upon the duration of employment of discharged mental patients. Whatley hypothesized that "intolerant, unfavourable attitudes toward mental illness and its associated, residual manifestations among ex-patients will tend toward early dismissal or resignation" (p. 121). Results of his study indicated that ex-patient status not only hampered the applicant's chances for initial employment, but continued to operate in the employers' evaluation of job performance after hiring the former patient. Thus, attitudinal barriers pose further obstacles to the potential adjustment by the psychiatrically disabled to a work situation. When the stressors associated with mistrust, misunderstanding, and prejudice are added to difficulties in work performance due to symptomatology, work adjustment becomes even more tenuous.

Employment Difficulties Indirectly Related to the Psychiatric Disability

The final category of work problems of the disabled proposed by Neff (1968) included those effects of disability which are unrelated to the specifics of the disability, but which interfere with the normal development and/or learning process. Because individuals experience severe psychiatric difficulties, institutionalization becomes the external reality with which they learn to relate. Individuals "...have either not experienced or have had limited exposure to a working environment. They may have been overprotected and shielded from the realities of life..." (Stone, 1975, p. 32). Bertram Brown, former Director of the National Institute of Mental Health, commented that "Persons emerging from years in a mental hospital face serious difficulties in obtaining employment. How could it be otherwise? They bear the marks of long institutionalization" (1977, p. 3).

Seligman's (1972) concept of "learned helplessness" has particular relevance in the instance of chronic psychiatric patients leaving the hospital and attempting to work. The reality in which they previously functioned adequately (the psychiatric hospital) is no longer available, replaced by the new reality of the community and its accompanying pressure and stress. Coping methods learned in the hospital do not apply to the new environment and thus result in adjustment difficulties. Growick (1976) illustrated the problem:

Although the client has been discharged from a mental hospital, suggesting a certain degree of improvement, the client is usually still unable to utilize normal restorative services...This condition can be attributed to residual symptoms such as the desocializing effects of hospitalization and atrophied vocationally-related skills (p. 119).

Psychiatric rehabilitation treatment, therefore, must take into consideration problems that extend beyond specific symptomatology to broader deficits resulting from institutionalization and identification with the patient role.

Work Adjustment Differences Between the Severely Psychiatrically Disabled and the General Rehabilitation Client Population

Although no evidence exists to provide empirical proof, there is overwhelming agreement that the nature of the vocational rehabilitation problems for the severely psychiatrically disabled client are quite different than those which face the general rehabilitation client. A major reason for this difference is the lack of objectivity in problem determination with a psychiatrically disabled population. Disorders that have a physical or biological bases are much more easily evaluated through current assessment technology for diagnosis, prognosis, and functional abilities and handicaps. Because of the lack of objectivity in the diagnostic process and the difficulties in the assessment of the functional deficits related to mental illness, few attempts have been made to objectively define problems. Because of the lack of sound problem definition, treatment attempts have not been geared toward specific problems as is the case with physical disabilities (physical restoration services), but rather toward general ideas or hypotheses of what specific problems psychiatrically disabled clients experience.

Jacks (1975) documented the lack of effectiveness of traditional rehabilitation services with psychiatrically disabled clients:

> The rehabilitation client with severe emotional problems has continued to be a challenging task to vocational rehabilitation. Traditional approaches serving this population have resulted in a low level of success as far as restoration to normal functioning in interpersonal relations, adjustment in the community, and productivity in work are concerned (p. 3).

Five years later Rogan (1980) was to write:

> For physically disabled clients, the methodology of the state vocational rehabilitation agency is usually effective..This mode of operation, however, is either too structured or too sketchy to achieve rehabilitation with...our clientele who have psychiatric disabilities (p. 49).

Although this problem was recognized in the 1960s, the Rehabilitation Services Administration caseload statistics for 1979 continued to document the lack of effectiveness of current vocational rehabilitation services. Data on rehabilitation rates for various disability categories indicate that the lowest success rate exists for those individuals who fall within the general category of "mental illness" (5XX disability codes). No single disability has a lower rehabilitation success rate than psychotic disorders (Katz-Garris & McCue, 1980).

In pointing out the differences in work adjustment problems between severely psychiatrically disabled clients and rehabilitation clients in general, it is important to note that emotional and interpersonal problems are not limited to psychiatrically disabled individuals. Many rehabilitation clients experience emotional difficulties as direct or indirect results of their primary disability. Martin (1959) pointed out the difference:

> ...Vocational rehabilitation with the psychiatric patient presents a very different set of problems which must be approached with a different orientation (than with the physically handicapped). Although the physically disabled frequently have emotional problems, they are usually secondary to their physical disability, and as such are self-limited and respond to a direct approach to overcome the physical problem. With such an orientation, one may be tempted to work with the psychiatric patient primarily by supplying services, which is frequently contra-indicated since such an approach is likely to immobilize rather than stimulate the use of his assets (p. 52).

Ethridge (1968), further supported Martin's contentions by pointing out the differences in work adjustment problems between severely psychiatrically disabled clients and rehabilitation clients in general. Ethridge (1968) indicated that: "...Work skills or job performance are not the major questions as they are with the physically handicapped. Of more import is the patient's attitude toward work, co-workers, supervisors, etc." (p. 167). Therefore, rehabilitation treatment must go beyond traditional approaches to client problems and address the specific symptomatology which produces deficit performance. Rubin and Roessler (1978) stressed the increased need for counselling and education with this population, while Anthony (1979) proposed a skills training approach which focuses upon client strengths and assets.

A final factor differentially affecting the psychiatrically disabled rehabilitation client is attitude. Research by Tringo (1970) using the Attitude Toward Disabled Persons (ATDP) scale to identify a hierarchy of preference toward major disabled groups, suggested that the least preferred groups was the mentally ill. This attitude prevails not only in the community but also in the rehabilitation environment where, as Olshansky (1960) pointed out, policies of exclusion or limited acceptance in rehabilitation workshops exist because of preexisting ideas and feelings about persons with a psychiatric disability.

The Differential Impact of Symptomatology

Symptomatology which characterizes the various types of illness often directly interferes with vocational performance. Barriers to employment may occur in the pre-vocational stage of employment acquisition (application and interviewing), as well as in on-the-job performance (Bean & Beard, 1975). In this final section, a number of behavioral symptoms associated with mental illness and how each symptom might directly inhibit job acquisition and/or work adjustment will be discussed.

Delusions, hallucinations, and fantasies are found most frequently in individuals experiencing a schizophrenic disorder. These symptoms directly interfere with the performance of work tasks by blocking or detracting focus of attention from the task to the interfering internal stimuli. These symptoms may also interfere with interpersonal relations on the job. Difficulty concentrating and general distractibility are found in many classifications of mental disorders. As with the symptomatology mentioned above, the ability to attend to a task is inhibited, thus resulting in performance deficits. Gelfund (1966) reported that the high degree of distractibility seen in mentally disabled clients "can be directly related to numerous errors on...work samples" (p. 27).

Social isolation and withdrawal also exist across diagnostic categories. This particular symptomatology negatively affects necessary interpersonal relationships which exist in employment in that it is particularly difficult for psychiatrically disabled individuals experiencing these symptoms to place themselves in an environment which requires social intercourse. The individual will either avoid or withdraw from work or will experience distractibility and performance deficits resulting from focusing upon his or her level of interpersonal discomfort.

Peculiar or bizarre behaviors, such as those found in schizophrenic disorders, may present significant problems in relationships with co-workers or consumers in an employment situation. Peculiar or bizarre behaviors, when displayed in an employment interview, are devastating to chances of being hired. Suspiciousness, which again is seen in schizophrenia and certain of the personality disorders, significantly interferes with an individual's ability to perceive and integrate praise and/or criticism about his work performance and may ultimately lead to more serious work difficulties. The gross disorganization found in a severe psychotic episode, marked by incoherence, loose association, illogical thinking, or catatonia is incompatible with tasks in even the most restrictive work situation. Decreased concern with personal hygiene typically found in severe schizophrenic disorders and also, to a lesser degree, in affective and personality disorders, obviously interferes with job acquisition and may have a detrimental effect on performance and interpersonal relationships on a job.

Restlessness, pressured speech, flight of ideas, and distractibility associated with mania are significant obstacles to steady, consistent performance. Also associated with mania, inflated self-esteem may inhibit job acquisition and interpersonal relationships in an employment situation. Symptoms of a depressive disorder may result in physical performance limitations. Decreased appetite, sleep disturbance, and psycho-motor agitation or retardation may present physiological barriers to performing optimally on a job. In addition, the lack of energy, interest, and motivation coupled with feelings of hopelessness and worthlessness significantly limit an individual's desire to work.

Factors associated with personality disorders may not totally preclude the possibility of employment but, either singularly or in combination, create work difficulties which have the potential to significantly disrupt performance. Symptomology includes: emotional coldness and aloofness; indifference; isolation and withdrawal; overly dramatic behavior; disturbances in interpersonal relationships; preoccupation; anti-social behaviors; impulsivity; lack of control; identity disturbances; mood shifts; self destructive urges and behaviours; hypersensitivity; decreased self-esteem; dominance or submission; and active or passive resistance.

A final symptom to note which is frequently observed across mental diagnostic categories is impairment of insight and judgment. Whether the result of a cognitive disorder or irrationality resulting from a disorder characterized by a negative view of self, judgment problems are common. Judgment difficulties may be manifested in a number of ways. The ability to problem solve on a job is frequently impaired by deficits in this area. Insight into cues, whether verbal of non-verbal, which has an impact on job acquisition or retention may be completely absent. McGuffie (1974) pointed out that "the person who deals with his environment successfully possesses the ability to read cues, and acts within reasonable boundaries of acceptable behavior for that setting. However, the person who does not possess this ability possesses a great deal of frustration" (p. 122). Finally, setting occupational goals which are realistic and consistent with aptitudes, interests, and emotional needs may be affected by poor judgment and insight (Durie, Gardner, & Matthews, 1972). The reality of performance deficits due to psychiatric symptoms may not be readily apparent to patients who are this hesitant to accept the reality of their deficits (Gelfund, 1966). "They (psychiatrically disabled clients) may set goals commensurate with their intellectual abilities (or with previous levels of functioning) while ignoring the impact of their psychiatric disability" (Rogan, 1980, p. 50).

Summary and Recommendations

Work adjustment, as process and outcome, in the rehabilitation of persons with severe psychiatric disabilities has, at best, an uneven track record. After the work therapy movement died out in the 1960's, relatively few, if any, active interventive strategies were employed with this group of disabled individuals. Studies that did exist, were focused on differentiating and defining the work adjustment problems of psychiatrically disabled individuals, both intrinsically and in terms of ecological variables. It was not until 1979 that Anthony set out to prescribe a specific approach

to the vocational adjustment of such persons. His approach, while concerned with identifying client strengths, specific counselling techniques, and community resources, does not address the residual and, at times, incapacitating sequelae of a psychiatric disorder, particularly as it is manifest in the work environment.

It is therefore proposed that, while there is considerable impetus in psychiatric rehabilitation to emphasize patient assets and strengths in the rehabilitation process, there is need to integrate information on diagnosis, symptoms, and weakness as well. With the severely psychiatrically disabled, to do otherwise would be counterproductive. To ignore significant behavioral difficulties which present numerous and, at times, insurmountable obstacles to functioning in favour of working with assets and strengths appears irresponsible, unfair to clients, and potentially dangerous. It is not suggested that psychiatric rehabilitation adopt the disease model and focus upon sickness, but rather, it is important to acknowledge symptomatology and deficits and work to overcome them. It is only through such an educated approach which recognizes, understands, and develops coping strategies to deal with psychiatric symptomatology that effective, lasting rehabilitation will occur with severely psychiatrically disabled individuals.

References

American Psychiatric Association. **Diagnostic and statistical manual of mental disorders (3rd Ed.).** Washington, D.C.: American Psychiatric Association, 1980.

American Psychiatric Association. **Diagnostic and statistical manual of mental disorders (2nd Ed.).** Washington, D.C.: American Psychiatric Association, 1968.

Anthony, W.A. **The principles of psychiatric rehabilitation.** Amherst, MA: Human Resource Development Press, Inc., 1979.

Bean, B., & Beard, J.H. Placement for persons with psychiatric disability. **Rehabilitation Counseling Bulletin,** 1975, **18,** 253-258.

Black, B.J. **Principles of industrial therapy for the mentally ill.** New York: Grune & Stratton, 1970.

Brown, B.S. Responsible community care of mental hospital patients. **New dimensions in mental**

health. Rockville, MD: National Institute of Mental Health, 1977.

Durie, M., Gardner, R.V., & Matthews, C.J. Spinning straw into gold. **Mental Hygiene, 1972, 56**(2), 39-42.

Ethridge, D. Prevocational assessment of rehabilitation potential of psychiatric patients. **The American Journal of Occupational Therapy, 1968, 22,** 161-167.

Fifth Institute on Rehabilitation Issues. **The vocational rehabilitation of persons with mental disorders.** Dunbar, WV: West Virginia University Research and Training Center, 1978.

Gelfund, B. The concept of reality as used in work evaluation and work adjustment. **Journal of Rehabilitation,** 1966, **32**(6), 26-28.

Growick, B. Effects of a work adjustment program on emotionally handicapped individuals. **The Journal of Applied Rehabilitation Counseling,** 1976, **7,** 119-123.

Gunn, R.L. Special problems in work adjustment of the mentally ill. In J.G. Cull & R.E. Hardy (Eds.) **Adjustment to work.** Springfield, IL: Charles C. Thomas, 1973.

Jacks, J. Psychiatric rehabilitation. In B. Schumacher (Ed.) **Rehabilitation of the mentally ill.** Carbondale, IL: Rehabilitation Institute, Southern Illinois University, 1975.

Katz-Garris, L., & McCue, M. Training of vocational rehabilitation counselors in psychiatric rehabilitation. Federal training grant application No. 13-629, February 5, 1980, 27-33.

Lamb, H.R. **Rehabilitation in community mental Health.** San Francisco: Jossey-Bass, 1971.

Margolin, R.J. A survey of employer reactions to known former mental patients working in their firms. **Mental Hygiene,** 1961, **45,** 110-115.

Martin, H.R. A philosophy of rehabilitation. In M. Greenblatt & B. Simon (Eds) **Rehabilitation of the mentally ill.** Washington, D.C. American Association for the Advancement of Science, 1959.

Matthews, R.M., Whang, P.L., & Fawcett, S.B. Development and validation of an occupational skills assessment instrument. **Behavioral Assessment,** 1980, **2,** 71-86.

McGuffie, R.A. Rehabilitation of the mentally ill. In R.E. Hardy & J.G. Cull (Eds.) **Severe disabilities: Social and rehabilitation approaches.** Springfield, IL: Charles C. Thomas, 1974.

Neff, W. **Work and human behavior.** New York: Atherton Press, 1968.

Olshansky, S. The transitional sheltered workshop: A survey. **Journal of Social Issues,** 1960, **16**(2), 33-39.

Olshansky, S., Grob, S., & Malamud, I. Employers' attitudes and practices in the hiring of ex-mental patients. **Mental Hygiene,** 1958, **42,** 391-401.

OVR-OMH Agreement of Cooperation. Commonwealth of Pennsylvania. February 1, 1982.

Page, J.D. **Psychopathology.** Chicago: Aldine-Atherton, Inc., 1971.

The Rehabilitation Act of 1973, P.L. 93-112, 29 U.S.C. 794, 45 C.F.R., § 84, **et seq.**

Rogan, D. Implementing the rehabilitation approach in a state rehabilitation agency. **Rehabilitation Counseling Bulletin,** 1980, **24,** 49.

Rubin, S.E., & Roessler, R.T. Guidelines for successful vocational rehabilitation of the psychiatrically disabled. **Rehabilitation Literature,** 1978, **39,** 70-74.

Schuyler, D., & Katz, M.M. **The depressive illness: A major public health problem.** Washington, D.C.: US. Government Printing Office, 1973.

Secunda, S.K., Katz, M.M., Friedman, R.J., & Schuyler, D. **Special Report: 1973, the depressive disorders.** Washington, D.C.:U.S. Government Printing Office, 1973.

Sigman, M.E. Learned helplessness. **Annual Review of Medicine,** 1972, **23,** 407-417.

Stone, M.A. The evolution of activity therapies in transition from long-term psychoanalytic to a community mental health approach. **National Association of Private Psychiatric Hospitals Journal,** 1975, **7**(1), 30-35.

Tringo, J.L. The hierarchy of preference toward disabled groups, **The Journal of Special Education,** 1970, **4,** 295-306.

VanAllen, R., & Loeber, R. Work assessment of psychiatric patients: A critical review of published scales. **Canadian Journal of Behavioral Sciences,** 1972, **4,** 101-115.

Whatley, C.D. Employers' attitudes, discharged patients and job durability. **Mental Hygiene,** 1964, **48,** 121-131.

⑧ LEGAL ISSUES

The disabled are beginning to recognize that they are entitled to the same qualities of life as the able-bodied community. This recognition has been relatively slow to evolve in many jurisdictions. Traditionally, the disabled have been isolated, alienated and perhaps even institutionalized. As such, they have experienced totalitarian impositions in their "legal" relations with society.

Prior to the 1970's, advocacy was not in the nature of contemporary society so far as the disabled were concerned. Therefore, large segments of the disabled expected little if any protection in their relationship with the institutions which they encountered on a regular basis. They were therefore victimized by compromised civil rights and inadequate representation and protection in the fields of education, employment, housing and access.

With the dawn of the mainstreaming movement, the disabled, like the able-bodied are expecting protection in all societal pursuits. In most jurisdictions they are demanding and receiving excellent legal representation in their efforts to obtain fair housing, accessible transportation, basic human rights and indeed protection from physical abuse which tragically has affected many segments of society. Deborah Dean, in her article "Fair Housing for the Disabled," illustrates the basic needs for housing the disabled in an accessible integrated society. Factors such as: segregation, isolation and prejudice have in the past prevented or inhibited the blind, the hearing and mobility impaired amongst others from obtaining satisfactory living accommodations. New housing regulations, government support systems and advocacy groups are now engaged in a process of evolving satisfactory living conditions for both the disabled and non-disabled communities.

Traditionally, as illustrated by Smith and Riggar, accessible transportation and indeed accessibility in general, has served to isolate large segments of the disabled community. In many instances, communities desire to achieve accessibility for the disabled but tend to be reluctant to incorporate accessibility as a general provision because of the very large financial outlays that would be required to make existing facilities accessible to the disabled. The issue is one of human rights versus so-called economic realities. In 1990, the Toronto Ontario Transit Commission agreed to spend over 20 million dollars in an effort to make Toronto's subway system accessible to the mobile impaired. This is reflective of a general trend toward accessibility in the disabled community. However, this community continues to experience barriers and "traditional mind sets" with regard to the cost necessary to increase accessibility.

In his article "Human Rights For The Disabled," David Baker illustrates the difficulties encountered by the disabled in achieving equality as their civil rights are often compromised. Being at the lower socioeconomic level and constituting a relatively small segment of society, at least as far as the public is concerned, the disabled often encounter a series of barriers which inhibit if not prevent the achievement of their rights in society. In Canada, as Baker illustrates, the Charter of Rights and Freedoms provides security for this group but Charters and other codes are often required to ensure that the disabled community enjoys the same civil rights available to most other groups in North American society. There is a trend away from exclusion to equality and hopefully this trend will allow the disabled to enjoy the civil rights available to most other groups.

Finally and tragically, like most other minorities, the disabled are often victimized by all forms of family violence, being more disfranchised in comparison to other groups, being victims of poverty and often being institutionalized. Many segments of the disabled have traditionally been victimized by the most insidious forms of abuse. Catherine MacPherson in her article "Abuse of People with Disabilities," illustrates how society must indeed respond to the needs of abused people with disabilities. Like the elderly and children, the disabled encounter extreme difficulties in obtaining protection and security when they become abused victims. Tragically, this area of sociology has only recently emerged.

Fair Housing For The Disabled

DEBORAH GORE DEAN

Everyone is aware of the many difficulties and frustrations involved in the search for a home. Finding housing that meets and individual's needs, budget and taste requirements and is situated in an area offering ready access to schools, jobs, shopping and transportation is almost becoming the "impossible" American dream.

For our disabled citizens, however, the same search can be an almost hopeless one due to a severe lack of accessible housing in a compatible range of styles choice and price. To make matters even worse, they often have to deal with discriminatory treatment as well.

Many disabled people know how it feels to be told they will be denied the housing of their choice because they are considered to be a "hazard;" or because owners' "insurance rates will go up;" or, perhaps for no real reason at all. The sad truth of the matter is that the disabled——unlike other minorities who have been discriminated against usually have no recourse to such injustice.

In order to remedy this situation, both President Reagan and HUD Secretary Samuel R. Pierce, Jr. have proposed legislation which would finally give a disabled person the means to fight back. If Congress acts to include the disabled as a protected class under the Federal Fair Housing Law, we are going to finally ensure the removal of "dead end" signs for those who need housing as badly, if not even more so, than anyone else in this country.

New legislation to discourage old prejudices will certainly lessen the housing problems of the disabled, but it cannot even begin to solve them. The major barrier to real progress is that homebuilders and realtors continue to neglect the growing market for accessible housing. The situation can only change when they recognize that this market is both a substantial and profitable one; and that it is not so complicated and full of red tape as they might suppose.

In real terms, the market for housing which is accessible has greatly increased in the past few years due to the independent living movement and recent laws providing for the protection of the disabled in education, employment, and transportation. More and more disabled people are working. Their buying power has increased. At the same time, a parallel demand for housing meeting their specifications has grown. To begin meeting this demand, both realtors and homebuilders need to know the answers to certain questions.

For example:

- Who are disabled people and what are their needs?
- Does it cost more to build an accessible home?
- Can a person without disabilities benefit from increased accessibility as well?
- What is a Group Home?
- Will disabled people bring down property values?

It is of primary importance to educate the real estate industry about the various kinds of disabilities and the related needs of each. When most people think of access or of disabled people, they usually focus upon wheelchairs and ramps for wheelchair users. But the issue of access is much broader. They need to be reminded that, in addition to ensuring housing itself is accessible and in adequate supply, the issue demands that interior facilities also be accessible for use by a disabled person.

It is important to promote the overall utility and wisdom of Universal Design——design that meets the needs of all people, disabled or not. Everyone can benefit from design features that promote access. A smooth running access ramp, for example, is also much easier than a flight of steps for an elderly person or even a younger person carrying a heavy load.

Accessibility features do not have to be unattractive. Builders today are coming up with a multitude of ideas for increasing the appeal and attractiveness of accessibility——so that it blends into the decor or style of a home.

Reprinted from: *Journal of Rehabilitation,* Apr/May/June 1987, with permission.

New developments in housing design help to assure universal accessibility of most facilities. Accessible design also has the potential to be widely marketable. Vanity mirrors in bathrooms for example, are now large enough to accommodate anyone, whether standing or sitting in a wheelchair. Another development that assists both disabled and nondisabled persons is the inclusion of lazy-susan cabinets in kitchens. Most of us can recall the struggle to find something hidden at the rear of a floor-level cabinet. The lazy-susan design allows ease of access to persons in wheelchairs, and certainly benefits the elderly as well as able-bodied persons. What about cost?

Most persons seek housing that is already accessible because they lack the financial capability necessary to renovate, or adapt an inaccessible residence. But, the difference in the cost of building in access features from the ground up, such as providing doorways that are at least 32 inches wide, is minimal or nonexistent. Electrical wiring or other building elements are designed so that access features can be made with minimum labor and cost.

It is of key importance to point out that allowing greater ease of movement for the disabled also benefits non-disabled persons. One builder was asked to promote accessibility by putting a bathroom door on the right side instead of the left in all the units of an entire development. Realizing immediately that this change would facilitate use of the bathroom for all home-buyers, the builder changed the blueprints for all the homes.

There is still much work to be done to finally weed out use of terms that are negative——the "handicapped," or even worse, terms like "crippled, wheelchair-bound, deaf and dumb," and so on.

We can also learn to deal with the fact that the issue of group homes for mentally disabled raises fears that locating such facilities in residential neighbourhoods will affect property value.

This is not true. In fact, studies show that the presence of these group homes has little or no effect on property values. In some declining areas, group homes have even had a stabilizing effect. This is attributable to the promise of assured supervision of residents and the requirement that these facilities be well-maintained.

If disabled people are promoted as a viable housing market with many of the same concerns as non-disabled homebuyers, local businessmen should be made aware that they can profit by enlightening their views. HUD wants to help. If you need help starting an effective outreach program, contact the Department's Office of Fair Housing and Equal Opportunity. The Section 504 Division of FHEO can provide a range of technical assistance services.

We know that the goal of the independent living movement is to gain for disabled people the right to a choice of lifestyle and the ability to direct their own lives.

When disabled people are given the opportunity to enter the economic mainstream, to live and to prosper in a community, they will soon be in a position to contribute back to that community. Their contribution can be a great national resource, a resource which can be used so that everyone in our society may benefit.

Accessible Transportation:
Human Rights ... Versus ... Costs

EDWARD R. SMITH AND T.F. RIGGAR

Introduction

Proponents of accessible regular transit services and the transportation industry have been locked in an intense political struggle for the last 10 to 15 years. Both groups have consistently disagreed on the type and kind of accessible transportation services that should be offered. The disabled demand equal access to all transit facilities, while the transit industry, and many elected officials, demand equal mobility through some combination of separate specialized services (Fielding, 1982). This disagreement over "human rights versus costs" represents a classic illustration of clashing ideologies and policy conflicts. This paper will summarize the development and progression of federal legislative and regulatory action relative to the creation of accessible transportation for disabled persons. The costs associated with making public transportation accessible, as well as the number of disabled persons who may benefit, will also be examined.

Legislative History of "Full Accessibility"

The history of federal regulations that govern programs with transportation elements for disabled persons dates back to the 1944 Amendments to the Social Security Act. This Amendment sought to provide transportation assistance to elderly, blind, and disabled persons. Since the 1944 Amendment, federal policy making has consistently sought to provide transportation services to the aforementioned target groups.

In 1964 the Urban Mass Transportation Act (UMTA) was passed. This Act provided federal financial assistance to preserve the nation's decaying transit systems. In its original form the UMTA Act provided no funding relative to public transportation of disabled persons. However, in 1970, New York Congressman Mario Biaggi introduced an important amendment,

Section 16(a), to the UMTA Act of 1964 (Fielding, 1982). The immediate result of the Biaggi Amendment [Section 16(a)], was to set forth as national policy that persons who were elderly or disabled would be able to utilize mass transit facilities and services just as other Americans (Fielding, 1982). However, the amendment did not specify how disabled populations were to be served. That omission ultimately caused considerable debate between the proponents of accessible regular transit services, and those who support separate, specialized services.

In some instances federal regulations that have ultimately aided disabled persons were not always grounded in legislation relative to transportation. One example is the amended section [165(b) of the Federal-Aid Highway Act of 1973 (41 Fed. Reg. 18,234, 1976). While Section 165 required that federally assisted public transit systems be accessible to disabled patrons, Section 165(b) required that projects funded under this act be planned, designed, constructed, and operated to allow effective use by persons using wheelchairs. The immediate impact of Section 165(b) resulted in the provision of funding for accessibility measures for Washington D.C.'s Metropolitan Rapid Transit System (METRO). Thus, by attaching funding for METRO's accessibility onto the 1973 Federal-Aid to Highways Act, Congress established a federal obligation to cover the capital costs of accessibility for both highways and public transit (Fielding, 1982).

In terms of the rights of disabled persons, the Rehabilitation Act of 1973 proved to be more important than any specific transportation legislation. Section 504 of the Rehabilitation Act of 1973 led to revolutionary changes in policy making and in the lives of many disabled persons (Clark, 1978; Donnelly, 1980; Stanfield, 1978; Stanfield, 1982; Fielding, 1982). Section 504 provided that:

Reprinted from: *Journal of Rehabilitaiton*, April/May/June 1988, with permission.

"no otherwise qualified handicapped individual ...shall ...be excluded from participation in ...any program or activity receiving federal financial assistance."

Ironically, even the sponsor of the Section 504 Amendment, Congressman Charles A. Vanick, suggested that "he had no idea that his amendment would become the most far reaching and costly civil rights law for the disabled ever enacted" (Clark, 1980).

From 1973 until 1976, hospitals, universities, colleges, transit authorities, and state and local governmental units successfully resisted implementation of Section 504. In fact, it was not until 1976, when the Carter Administration issued an executive order compelling the Department of Health, Education, and Welfare (HEW) to comply with Section 504's accessibility standards. As a result of the executive order, HEW was then faced with the task of developing guidelines for itself and other agencies to provide equal access.

Closely following Section 504 was the National Mass Transportation Assistance Act of 1974, which mandated half-fare policies for persons who were elderly or disabled on urban transit systems during off-peak hours. The Act further authorized grants under UMTA's Section 16(b)2 to private, non-profit organizations providing transportation services to this clientele. Congress subsequently amended Section 16(b)2 a second time in 1975. This subsequent amendment required that all new buses be accessible to disabled and elderly persons. In addition, the Secretary of Transportation was authorized to grant exceptions to the second amendment if a local area was presently offering alternative specialized transportation services to disabled persons. Thus, the authority to grant exceptions resulted in giving the U.S. Department of Transportation (DOT) discretionary authority over what type of service(s) to require.

Clark (1978) and Clark (1980) argue that because of DOT's perhaps ambiguous legislative mandate, the agency issued conflicting policy directives toward transportation for disabled persons. For example, in April, 1976, the Department of Transportation (DOT) issued

performance standards which required bus manufacturers to offer accessibility options (40 Fed. Reg. 39). These accessibility options included wheelchairs lifts or ramps, slip-resistant floor surfaces, passageway clearance and at least one tiedown device (i.e., wheelchair securement device) for all buses. At the time of the rule issuance, however, accessible buses were not available on the market. Thus, DOT's policy directives seemed confusing (Stanfield, 1979).

In 1976, DOT issued a final regulation with a unique criteria under the heading of "special efforts" (41 Federal Register, 85). The regulation required that all special efforts projects on behalf of disabled riders be made by localities that operate public transit in order to receive regular capital grants and operating subsidies. The special effort regulation required that transportation plans submitted for funding had to demonstrate satisfactory "special efforts" in planning accessible services and facilities. In addition, these plans had to demonstrate that all project designs would benefit disabled persons. Furthermore, the "special efforts" regulation required that "reasonable progress" be made implementing accessibility standards in previously planned transportation projects. However, DOT did not provide standards which clarified "reasonable progress."

Later that year, DOT issued regulations which proposed design specifications for urban transit buses (41 Fed. Reg. 202). The proposed specifications were tied to a design prototype called "Transbus" (40 Fed. Reg. 39). Transbus was a low-floor bus which featured a front end which could drop or kneel by four to five inches (Stanfield, 1979). Unfortunately, the two potential manufacturers of Transbuses did not agree on a contract to build these buses which would have served disabled persons (Stanfield, 1979).

Cannon (1980) suggests that the decision not to bid was due to efforts by both companies to persuade UMTA to write Transbus specifications that only each specifically could build. By then, however, the DOT had paid up to 30 million dollars to the transit industry to develop Transbus (Stanfield, 1979). The end result of the Transbus project was the virtual elimination of the "special efforts" clause that required local transit authorities to provide transportation alternatives such as specialized small vehicles. Thus, the practical effect of Transbus action and DOT's policy reversal was to limit local transit authorities' efforts to retrofit existing buses with unreliable wheelchair lifts.

In 1979, DOT issued a second regulation which embraced full accessibility or "mainstreaming" (44 Red. Reg. 106). Mainstreaming referred to the physical integration of disabled persons with other non-disabled persons who use mass transportation. This regulation set time frames for full accessibility for various types of transportation. Unfortunately the legality of the 1979 regulation was questioned by subsequent litigation brought by the transit industry represented by the American Public Transit Association (APTA).

In **American Public Transit Association v. Lewiss**, 655 F.2d 1272 (1981), the court held that the 1979 DOT regulations, based upon Section 504, required modifications that were "too massive and too costly." As a result of the ruling, DOT issued a third regulation on July 21, 1981 (46 Fed. Reg. 138). This third set of regulations essentially returned to the 1976 "special efforts" approach, thereby superseding the 1979 mainstreaming regulations.

Finally, the DOT issued yet another set of proposed regulations which established a "service criteria", and set limitations on the costs to transit providers (48 Red. Reg. 175). The proposed service criteria required that special transit services be available to both disabled persons and the general public over the same general service area, and that special transit services be available on the same day, and during the same hours as the general service. Additionally, fares for disabled persons using special transit services must be comparable to fares for the general public that use regular services. The service criteria prohibited the use of waiting lists, as well as limiting waiting periods for disabled persons using special services. Finally, the proposed regulation also prohibited restrictions on trip purposes and service priorities, based on trip purpose. Interestingly enough, while comments on the service criteria regulations were due on November 7, 1983, to date the final regulations do not appear to have been released.

But How Much Will It Cost and How Many Will It Benefit?

Faced with the above history, DOT in 1979 issued what it thought was its final rule implementing Section 504. Under the 1979 rules, transit authorities who accepted federal money had to make their systems "fully accessible" to disabled persons by equipping buses with wheelchair lifts and subways with elevators. The immense cost and complexity of the DOT rule caused immediate controversy because it affected every mode of public transportation (Clark, 1980). The DOT estimated that it would take 1.8 billion dollars to retrofit the older rapid transit systems of New York City, Philadelphia, Chicago, Boston, and Cleveland. Transportation officials contended that the estimate was far too low (Clark, 1980). The APTA, which represents the transit industry, estimated that retrofitting mass transit systems in the above five cities would cost between three and five billion dollars spread over 30 years (Clark, 1980). Their estimates differed substantially from DOT's estimates. Due to these disagreements DOT commissioned a second and third study to re-examine earlier estimates. DOT finally raised its estimate to a cost of more than five billion dollars over a 50 year implementation period.

While accurate costs for compliance remain a controversy, the question of the number of disabled persons who would benefit from transportation expenditures also remains. Additional questions included: (a) the percentage of the target population who would be able to make additional trips with a new or retrofitted transportation system, and (b) the number of additional trips they would make.

To answer the above questions, several studies by UMTA and the Congressional Budgeting Office (CBO) were undertaken and the results were disappointing for advocates of full transportation access for disabled persons (Clark, 1978; Clark, 1980; Donnelly, 1980; Fielding, 1982). According to UMTA's survey, there would be 143,900 new users of accessible (i.e., new/retrofitted) transit systems, while the separate specialized demand service (i.e., small vans) would generate 1,639,700) new users. When comparing the total number of persons benefitting from either alternative 1,344,200 more persons would benefit from the specialized service option, or nearly double the figure for accessible transit. Furthermore, the additional trips per year for a separate, specialized service show an additional 177.6 million trips per year for a margin of better than 3:1 over accessible transit trip-making projections.

In general, the impact projections for the Congressional Budgeting Office (CBO) study were lower than the UMTA estimates. Although CBO's estimates between the two alternatives were similar, the CBO study made an interesting observation. CBO's estimates point out that for the severely disabled population, only seven percent would use accessible transit as compared to the 26 percent that would use the specialized service alternative. Accordingly, the results of both the UMTA and CBO estimates seem to indicate that the separate specialized service alternative would have a greater impact on those disabled persons who desire public transportation (UMTA Summary Report, 1978).

Underutilization

Using the experience of existing accessible transit systems, the transit lobby argues that few disabled people would actually use mass transit even if all physical barriers were removed (Donnelly, 1980). For example, the St. Louis transit system which has had the most extensive experience with wheelchair lifts on approximately 157 buses, state that they average only one wheelchair trip per 320 scheduled accessible bus runs (Casey, 1979). In addition, 40 percent of the St. Louis transit system accessible buses were inoperable at any given time (Clark, 1978). Similar transit system experiences reinforce the fact that ridership on lift-equipped buses is exceedingly low (Stanfield, 1982).

The St. Louis transit system experience is often cited as a failure (Casey, 1979). However, there are a number of reasons which may explain its failure to provide an accessible fixed route

service and generate ridership. One basic problem stems from the lack of consumer involvement during the planning process (Booz-Allen & Hamilton, 1980). By not establishing a citizen advisory committee, disabled consumers had little impact on the resulting service. Another problem resulted from the selection of routes (Booz-Allen & Hamilton, 1980). Transit planners decided to offer a "geographically dispersed service" instead of concentrating its lift-equipped buses on a few heavily travelled routes. A third problem involved the inadequate training bus drivers received on how to use wheelchair-lift equipment. Bus drivers received only one hour of training, with driver's training limited to 45 minutes on the operational aspects of wheelchair lifts, accompanied by a 15 minute slide show (Booz-Allen & Hamilton, 1980). Therefore, one may argue that the negative St. Louis transit experience may not stand for the proposition that an accessible fixed route service cannot be provided.

While authors Casey (1978), Donnelly (1980), and Stanfield (1982) argue that the initial underutilization of newly accessible services should be seen as an inefficient use of public resources, they seem to ignore certain facts. The problem of underutilization of accessible service may actually be the by-product of the isolation of disabled persons from the mainstream of society. Disabled persons have often been unable to participate in many fundamental democratic processes, such as the right to vote, due to their lack of mobility. Integrating disabled persons into society will take time, great expense, and will to occur overnight. Thus, as the physical environment becomes more accessible, disabled persons will begin to utilize mass transit more and more.

Accessibility vs. Costs ... or ... Separate but Equal?

The organized movement of disabled people has grown along with the enforcement of Section 504 (Bowe, 1978; Clar, 1978; Donnelly, 1980; Stanfield, 1978; Wallin, 1982). Through vigorous lobbying efforts, advocates have successfully brought the issue of transportation barriers to the American people and Congress. This lobby is morally and philosophically committed to barrier free, accessible transportation (Fielding , 1982). As a result of their commitment, disabled persons have consistently rejected alternative specialized services because to them, it merely represents "separate but equal" treatment (Clark, 1980; Donnelly, 1980; Fielding, 1982). Disabled persons also argue that alternative specialized services reinforce negative images of disabled persons as dependent, burdensome individuals, rather than as functioning productive persons (Eastern PVA Position Paper, 1977). The disability lobby also seems opposed to specialized services from a social as well as a psychological need to enter buses from the front. They simply prefer to enter buses the same as everyone else. The APTA is against any regulations that require accessible buses on all systems. The APT contends that it should provide alternative specialized services (i.e., small vans), whereas disabled persons prefer regular modes of transportation (Stanfield, 1978). While disabled persons argue that access to regular modes of transportation is a right that is established by Section 504, one cannot determine what Congress actually intended (Clark, 1978; Donnelly, 1980; Clark, 1980).

Conclusion

The clash between advocates and the transit industry can be viewed as an issue of human rights, one of equal access and the equality of disabled persons, versus costs——the transit industry's concern for cost efficiency and fiscal responsibility. Both sides specifically disagree whether fixed-route buses ought to be made accessible for disabled persons, or whether some separate special service (paratransit, e.g., small vans) should be developed instead.

The human rights position of the advocates is a familiar one. It says that all persons, as well as disabled persons, possess an equal right to use public transportation. Furthermore, this unalienable right is guaranteed by the Unites States Constitution, as well as federal and state law. Arguably, the transit industry's position of fiscal responsibility which embodies the concept of a separate transportation system will not satisfy the disabled person's equal right to use public transportation.

While in theory, the concept of separate but equal has been rejected by the courts, in practice separate special transportation services have been developed and implemented. For example, separate special services often provided door-to-door and curb-to-curb service throughout the country. These services eliminate the need for disabled persons to travel to some distant bus stop, or to venture out in inclement weather. But, while separate special service may have been seen in some ways as a better approach, it is also restrictive and often fails to provide equal service. For example, these separate special systems often require long reservation times, thereby eliminating emergency or spontaneous trips. This inherent restriction removes some degree of flexibility in taking trips and causes a loss of control over one's life. For one who is disabled, this additional loss of control can be devastating.

It must be recognized that the transportation needs of disabled persons cost more on the average than the transportation needs of the able-bodied (United States General Accounting Office, 1982). However, after recognizing this fact, one must face the complex and difficult task of reconciling the responsibility to provide accessible transportation and the best method of providing a cost efficient system. Given the potentially devastating fiscal cutbacks to transit assistance demanded by the Gramm-Rudman-Hollings bill, advocates of a totally accessible transportation system face an almost monumental task.

The decision of which approach, an accessible fixed-route service or the separate special service, as the most efficient and effective method has proven to be an extremely difficult one to make. This difficulty translates into an exercise of estimating the costs of planning, developing, supplying and implementing these systems, and the demand for them. while the differences between urban and rural services can be determined, the problem of ascertaining the projected level of total demand has proven to be an inexact science.

Policy makers have found it much more difficult to determine the costs of accessible fixed-route service than for separate special services because of the small numbers of accessible transit systems which currently exist. Also, the costs associated with these systems vary dramatically. Even more discouraging is the difficulty in calculating demand because for comparative purposes there are too few similar existing systems. In most instances ridership for both systems have not yet stabilized to being an analysis and comparison. Therefore, the process of determining the most effective and efficient accessible transportation alternative is such a complex task that additional research and demonstration projects are necessary.

Rehabilitation professionals can impact both the rehabilitation and public policy systems with regard to this important transportation issue. Working with clients, their families and other professionals to further assess the needs, issues, barriers and incentives involved with transportation systems through established rehabilitation systems, can advance the accessibility of transportation. At the public policy level rehabilitationists can have a great impact by analyzing and translating pertinent data to use in developing accessible facilities. Often an appropriate role, especially at the local level, is to encourage clients to "mainstream", to use what systems do exist, and to consult and assist policy makers in developing appropriate accessible systems. Given the history and data examined herein allows those concerned to more accurately and effectively initiate a forum to address and redress these needs.

Responding to the Abuse of People with Disabilities

This publication was written and produced by Cathy McPherson for the Advocacy Resource Centre for the Handicapped (ARCH) with the advice and assistance of the following people:

- Harry Beatty, Barrister and Solicitor, ARCH
- Liz Stimpson, DisAbled Women's Network (DAWN)
- Scott McArthur, Ontario Federation for the Cerebral Palsied, CREED Project
- Professor Nathalie Des Rosiers, Faculty of Law, University of Western Ontario
- Christine McGoey, Ontario Ministry of the Attorney General
- Joan Hurley, Ontario Ministry of the Solicitor General
- Kapri Rabin, CONNECT Counselling Services, Canadian Hearing Society
- Flossie Enman, Ontario Association of the Deaf
- Joyce Main, Blind Organization of Ontario with Self-Help Tactics (BOOST)
- Metro Toronto Association for Community Living
- Marcia Rioux, G. Allan Roeher Institute
- Jim Docherty, Consultant
- The Institute for the Prevention of Child Abuse
- Toronto Rape Crisis Centre
- Department of Justice Canada

Cover design by Andrea Johnston; photo by James Blake

Publication of this manual was made possible through funding from the Department of Justice Canada, Health and Welfare Canada, and the Secretary of State.

Printed in Canada

Introduction

It has been estimated that people with disabilities are more than twice as likely to be assaulted and sexually assaulted as non-disabled people. Although most abuse happens to women, children and elderly persons, anyone can become a victim, whether they are disabled or not disabled, female or male. This manual is designed to help those who have contact with people with disabilities respond to situations of abuse. While we refer specifically to people with disabilities throughout the manual, the information can be applied to most victims of abuse. It is our hope that this manual will assist those in contact with disabled victims to help them deal with the abuse and overcome the experience to become a "survivor". Abuse must be stopped. We hope this manual will help.
We have attempted to summarize the law and related systems, to reflect what generally exists

across the country, with special emphasis on the criminal justice system. We advise disabled people and their advocates to become aware of the variations in their areas. This document is not meant to replace legal advice which should be obtained as soon as possible after a situation of abuse has been identified.

Who are "the disabled"?

They are the people you work with, members of your family, neighbours and school chums. "They" could be you and me. People with disabilities may have a mobility disability which requires them to use crutches or a wheelchair; they may be blind or have low vision; or they may have a hearing disability. They may be "invisibly" disabled with epilepsy, a heart condition, diabetes or a learning disability. Or they may be labelled as being "developmentally disabled", "mentally retarded", or "mentally handicapped" or having "psychiatric problems".

Affection and Physical Assistance in the Lives of People with Disabilities:

People with disabilities have the same desire - and right - to enjoy affection as do other members of our communities.

They may also experience forms of touching which enable them to live as independently as possible. Some of these "daily living activities" involve getting help to eat, get dressed, go to the toilet, and get washed. They may involve having someone assist them in communicating more effectively, helping them in travel, learning or counselling. All of these activities put the individual(s) carrying out these tasks in a position of trust with respect to the person with a disability.

What is "Abuse"?

Depending on the nature of the incident, abuse may be an offence under the Criminal Code or a violation under provincial or federal human rights legislation.

Abuse can take many forms. It can include criminal acts such as assault and sexual assault or negligence (not washing, feeding, or toileting an individual); human rights violations (such as sexual harassment); verbal taunting; degrading, humiliating behaviour; rough handling; or isolation through silence. Abuse can take place once, or it can happen on an on-going basis.

The physical and emotional contact people with disabilities have with a large number of caregivers, puts them at greater risk for abuse than the majority of the population. Knowing the difference between normal/necessary forms of touching, and abuse, and learning how to protect themselves from inappropriate behaviour or unwanted touch, is essential to their survival.

Can People with Disabilities Legally Consent to Sexual Activity?

Yes. The law says that adults are able to give their consent to sexual activity.

However, sexual activity without consent with anyone, including people with disabilities, is a crime. If a person with a disability agrees to sexual activity with someone upon whom she or he is dependent, it is questionable whether true legal consent has taken place. When someone has consented or submits to sexual activity because a person with authority over them has used that authority to obtain her or his consent, a crime has been committed.

The Criminal Code says: children under 12 years of age can never give legal consent to sexual activity. Children between 12 and 14 are not considered old enough to consent to sexual activity except when two young people consent to the sexual activity and the older teenager is less than 16. As well, there must be less than two years age difference between the two. Furthermore, consent is not legal where one teenager is in a position of trust or authority over another.

Children 14 and over are protected against sexual exploitation by adults who are in a position of trust or authority over them, or is a person upon whom the young person is dependent. The fact that the young person consented is not a defence in these circumstances.

If You Suspect or Are Aware of Abuse

As with the non-disabled population, in most cases of abuse the offender is someone the victim knows: a caregiver, a parent or relative, a friend, or a neighbour. The guilt and shame over the incident(s), experienced by many victims, is compounded in many cases by the disabled individual's isolation and their level of self-esteem. People with disabilities also have a legitimate fear that they will lose the daily living assistance, supported housing and accommodation that the abuser may provide, leaving them with no place to go other than an institution or a situation of reduced independence.

The isolation and dependence which many disabled people experience, not only makes them vulnerable to abuse, but also makes it more difficult for them to report it. Many people who are abused, including those with disabilities, are told to keep the abuse a secret. They may be bribed, intimidated or threatened. The perpetrator may even use physical force to keep the individual from telling.
Never presume that because individuals have disabilities they are incapable of understanding or explaining what happened to them. All allegations should be taken seriously. In a minority of cases, disabled individuals may not understand that they have been victims of abuse (in the absence of sex education, or where an individual may lack the capacity or experience to explain).

Keep What You Learn Confidential

Discretion is always important. If the allegation is made public prematurely, a great deal of harm can be done: the abuser may be alerted, the investigation undermined or an innocent person defamed. The disabled victim could end up in serious difficulty. Where a report is made it should be made to the proper authorities immediately.

Your Legal and Ethical Responsibility to Report Abuse

In all provinces and territories, **professionals or volunteers** who believe that children are being abused or may be in need of protection, **must** report the situation to child protection agencies. Additionally, many professionals have an obligation to report abuse in accordance with the law or their professional standards. In some provinces there is a duty to report abuse of residents in certain facilities. In Ontario, for example, there is a duty under the Nursing Homes Act.

Individuals, programs, facilities, or agencies which fail to take reasonable steps to protect clients with disabilities (children and adults) against persons who have abused them may be liable to civil action (i.e. a lawsuit) by the individual or even the family of the individual who has been abused and be required to pay damages. They may also be investigated by government authorities and run the risk of having their license to operate the program or facility revoked.

If you have any concerns or suspicions at all about abuse, report it.

Changes in a Child or Adult's Behaviour Which Can Signify Abuse

If you suspect a disabled individual may be a victim of abuse, listen carefully to what the child or adult has to say. In addition, pay attention to their behaviour - it is sometimes an indicator that abuse is taking place. Although the following are not conclusive indicators of abuse and vary in importance, the

existence of one or more may indicate that an individual is in need of assistance (this is not an exhaustive list):

Indicators of Physical Abuse (received from being shaken, hit, burned or restrained)

- signs of new injuries when old injuries have not yet healed;
- unexplained and unusual burns, cuts, bites, blisters/bruises, broken bones or bald spots on head
  (in unusual or clustered patterns);
- unusual imprints on the skin from the instrument used to inflict abuse
  (such as the round pattern of a stove burner, etc.);
- injuries inconsistent with description of cause.

Indicators of Neglect

- poor hygiene;
- dirty, torn clothes worn every day;
- insufficient clothing;
- bug infestation in the individual's clothes or body;
- unattended medical or dental needs;
- underweight or overweight (when not associated with the primary disability).

Indicators of Sexual Abuse

- the existence of sexually transmitted diseases (especially in young children) or pregnancy;
- stained, torn and/or bloody underclothes;
- bruised or swollen genitalia/anal area;
- sore throat (which may be due to pressure applied to the throat through choking or forced oral sex);
- pain while walking or sitting (with evasive or illogical explanation);
- semen about the mouth, genitals, or on clothing;
- unusual or offensive odour;
- a significant change in sexual behaviour or attitude.

Emotional Indicators of Abuse

- extreme, unusual behaviour (aggression, compliance, withdrawal);
- high level of anxiety/fear of returning to a particular place;
- attempted suicide;
- delayed emotional or physical development;
- lack of attachment to parents or other caregiver.

What should you do if you become aware of a situation of abuse?

If a Person with a Disability Chooses to Tell You About Abuse, or You have Evidence that Abuse has Taken Place:

talk to the individual privately	It is important that any discussion take place in a **private**, comfortable place of **the disabled person's choosing**. It is essential that the conversation cannot be overheard. No one should be present unless the disabled person wants them there.
listen to the individual tell the story in their own words	Get a clear understanding of what happened. You may say,"I'm here to listen, if you want to talk about it." Make sure that you let the person tell you what happened. Don't put words in the victim's mouth. Asking leading questions (questions which may suggest a particular answer) may mean the individual's testimony could be discounted should the situation go to court. You **can** reassure and offer a refreshment or other small courtesies to relax the individual. Make sure you tell the individual disclosing the abuse that they are not bad or responsible for what happened. Find out what they want and need. But do not promise to keep it a secret. You may have a responsibility to inform the proper authorities.
help the individual to communicate	Where a disabled individual has difficulty communicating, be patient and let her or him tell the story through their own method of communication such as bliss board, gestures, etc. Do not interrupt and fill in the silences with your own words. Allow the individual to use **her or his own words** to describe body parts or experiences. If the individual cannot easily speak, encourage her or him to write their experiences down, type them on a computer, or draw where appropriate.
don't panic or make assumptions	**Take it seriously.** Accept what the individual is telling you. Don't make value judgements about the individual disclosing the abuse or the suspected abuser. Don't assume that it was or was not a frightening experience; that the victim did or did not enjoy the experience; or that the victim likes or dislikes the alleged abuser. People who have been abused often experience many conflicting emotions about the experience and the perpetrator.

Reporting Abuse

Try to get the name of the suspected abuser but do not **confront him or her.** Let the police or the responsible agency take care of the investigation. Revealing details of a disclosure to a person accused of abuse could undermine any future investigation or legal action that might take place.

If an individual does not tell you of abuse, but you have evidence that it is taking place, you should take action. At the same time respect the individual's right to make decisions about options where they are available.

write it down   <u>After</u> the interview make notes of the disclosure for future reference.

The Response - Assisting the Victim

. **If the individual is in danger, problem-solve on how to get the individual out of danger.**

. **Be aware of the physical and emotional needs of the person with a disability, before, during and after reporting the incident.**

. **If you are a staff person in an institutional setting, follow your facility's protocol or report the incident, where appropriate, to your supervisor, the administrator, or police. Under no circumstances should you report to the abuser.**

Some organizations have established protocols (procedures) to deal with suspected abuse. If you are a worker in these organizations, however, reporting an abuse to someone within your organization **does not absolve you of your professional responsibility.** You must ensure that the police or child protection authorities are notified as soon as possible.

explain the options available

Both children and adults should be told what could take place following their disclosure and what the possible outcome might be. Ask if there is someone that they would like to have to support them through the process. Explain who will be told and what action can be taken to protect them from further abuse. Explain the avenues open to them for follow-up such as: contacting the police to lay charges; getting a lawyer or legal advocate; receiving counselling and post-trial support. These will be different for children and adults and will vary depending on the nature of the abuse and the resources in your community.

If you don't know what options are available, contact someone who does know (**see list of resource groups attached on page 19**).

**get assistance as
soon as possible**

If there has been a sexual or physical assault, victims should be taken to a hospital emergency department, sexual assault unit, or their family doctor for an examination and treatment of any injuries. This is important for the individual's health as well as to help gather/provide evidence of the assault. Discourage the individual from showering, bathing, combing hair, or changing clothes if the assault is recent. In some jurisdictions you may be legally required to report the incident immediately. Photos of injuries close to the day of the injury and a week later, when bruising appears, may also be useful as evidence. This may be done by the police.

The victim should be asked who should accompany her or him to the hospital. Where an adult lacks the capacity to consent, or where a child is under the age of 16, the legal guardian who can give consent to treatment must be contacted. But if the guardian or near relative is the suspected abuser, or is someone who may inform the abuser, **they should not be contacted.**

**remove the
individual from
the situation
of risk**

Regardless of where the individual lives, the most important consideration is to ensure the individual is safe and is not vulnerable to further victimization. Removing the suspected abuser from the environment of abuse is preferable to moving the victim. In most provinces where a child is being abused, child abuse services have the authority to remove her or him from the abuse setting.

Once criminal charges have been laid, the accused may be kept in jail or released on bail (this is where a court may ask that money be deposited to ensure that the accused will come back for trial). A judge can also issue a "bail order" which puts a condition on the bail to ensure that the suspected abuser does not have contact with the victim.

Removing an adult victim from a home when the suspected abuse has occurred within a family setting, is usually only possible where the individual is able to give his or her consent to the move and is willing to do so. **The laying of criminal charges, or even a conviction, does not necessarily give anyone authority to remove the person from the home.** Where appropriate advocate that the alleged perpetrator be removed and the victim be allowed to remain at home.

Call the Authorities As Soon as Possible!

a) Children:

Throughout Canada, it is mandatory to report where there are reasonable grounds to suspect a child is being abused or is in "need of protection". In most jurisdictions, there is an extra onus on professionals and volunteers to report abuse. While reports to child abuse authorities may be kept confidential during the investigation, the name of the person reporting may be revealed if the case goes to court.

b) Adults:

With disabled adults who are able to give their own consent, it is advisable to get their permission to proceed with any investigation. In some cases, however, the severity of the abuse may mean overriding the wishes of the individual with a disability. The disabled individual and her or his family also has the option of calling the police themselves for an investigation.

How the Criminal Justice System Deals with Assault

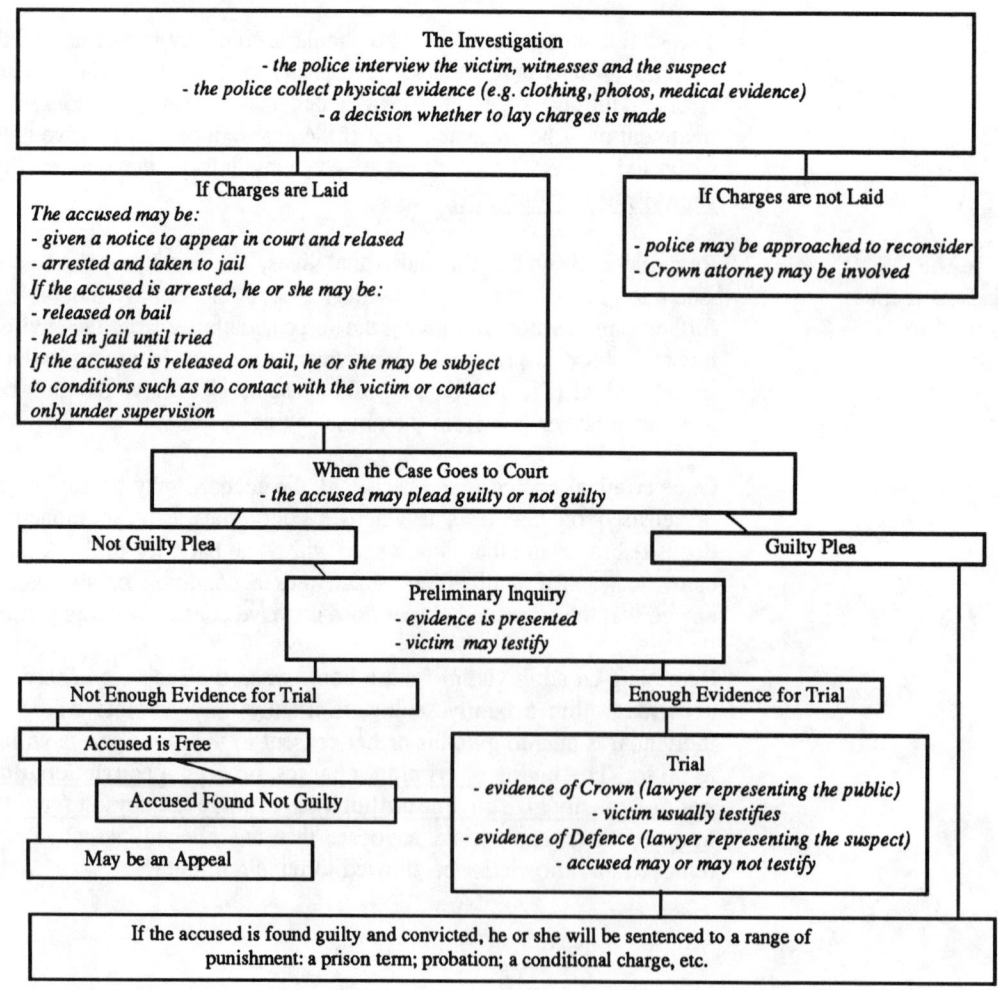

The Investigation
- *the police interview the victim, witnesses and the suspect*
- *the police collect physical evidence (e.g. clothing, photos, medical evidence)*
- *a decision whether to lay charges is made*

If Charges are Laid
The accused may be:
- *given a notice to appear in court and relased*
- *arrested and taken to jail*
If the accused is arrested, he or she may be:
- *released on bail*
- *held in jail until tried*
If the accused is released on bail, he or she may be subject to conditions such as no contact with the victim or contact only under supervision

If Charges are not Laid
- *police may be approached to reconsider*
- *Crown attorney may be involved*

When the Case Goes to Court
- *the accused may plead guilty or not guilty*

Not Guilty Plea

Guilty Plea

Preliminary Inquiry
- *evidence is presented*
- *victim may testify*

Not Enough Evidence for Trial

Enough Evidence for Trial

Accused is Free

Accused Found Not Guilty

Trial
- *evidence of Crown (lawyer representing the public)*
- *victim usually testifies*
- *evidence of Defence (lawyer representing the suspect)*
- *accused may or may not testify*

May be an Appeal

If the accused is found guilty and convicted, he or she will be sentenced to a range of punishment: a prison term; probation; a conditional charge, etc.

The Investigation

Calls to report abuse may be investigated by either the police or a child protection agency or both. As part of the investigation the police may also examine physical evidence (such as clothing, photos, sperm and blood samples). The length of time taken to investigate the case will vary depending on its complexity. Investigators will talk to the child or adult, to family members and to the individual who reported the incident. The accused abuser may also be interviewed. Where a disabled individual cannot communicate without assistance (e.g. is deaf or has cerebral palsy), she or he should have someone of his or her choice available to help facilitate communication with the police (such as a sign or oral interpreter). An advocate may also be helpful.

If Charges are Laid

If the police are satisfied that there is enough evidence against a person they will lay charges. In some cases, the police will consult with the Crown attorney (a lawyer who represents the state), during the investigation, about laying charges. If charges are laid, the accused may plead guilty or not guilty. If the accused pleads guilty, the court will review the circumstances of the offence and the offender and decide on a sentence. If the accused pleads not guilty, there will be a trial.

> **What happens if the police do not lay charges?**
>
> - In some cases, the police may decide not to lay charges. If disabled people, their families and their advocates do not agree with this decision, they can:
> - try to find out if other individuals have been abused by the same perpetrator and see if they will get involved in the case;
> - call the Chief of Police and ask that the decision be reviewed;
> - lay charges themselves by appearing before a Justice of the Peace. This is a difficult process, however. Without police involvement, it is harder to prepare for these cases, and proceeding with the case is up to the discretion of the Justice of the Peace.

The Case Goes to Court

Our criminal justice system is based on the presumption that an individual is innocent until proven guilty. This means that the police, Crown and judge must treat the accused as an innocent person until a judge (or jury) hears the evidence and concludes that the accused is guilty "beyond a reasonable doubt". Not every trial results in a conviction. An acquittal means there was not enough proof to find the accused guilty. Victims should be reassured by their advocates that an acquittal does not mean that no one believes them.

At the Trial

**preparing
disabled adults
and children
for court**

It is essential that the victim meet with the Crown attorney before the court appearance to discuss the case and make arrangements to accommodate the disabilities of the victim and other witnesses. Before the court appearance the Crown attorney and advocates may find it useful to take the victim into the courtroom to familiarize her or him with the set-up and to help her or him understand what to expect.

It is important that the child or adult with a disability be familiar with the vocabulary that will be used in court and the questions she or he are likely to be asked. Being introduced to the Judge and defence on the day of the court appearance can make the victim feel more comfortable with the process. A reassuring phone call by the night before the court appearance by an advocate of the victim can also be useful.

**ensuring that
the court has accom-
modated the disabilities
of the participants**

People with disabilities are entitled to accommodation in the legal system under the <u>Charter of Rights and Freedoms</u> and the federal, provincial and territorial human rights legislation.

Where a disabled individual has difficulty communicating, it is essential that the court make arrangements ahead of time to ensure that someone with expertise be there to assist and translate. A sign or oral interpreter, someone to assist with blissboard or deaf/blind communications, or an advocate to explain the proceedings to someone labelled "mentally handicapped", can help facilitate communication.

Courtrooms and adjoining washrooms should be wheelchair accessible. Attendant care arrangements may be necessary for people with physical disabilities.

Anxiety or excitement can aggravate some disabilities. People with epilepsy, for example, can have more seizures; people with cerebral palsy can experience more muscle spasms or involuntary laughter; some people may have more difficulty communicating.

When arrangements are made ahead of time to accommodate these and other special needs, the disabled victim has a better chance of a fair hearing in court.

Documents which the victim needs to be aware of must be made available in a form accessible to the person with a disability prior to the court appearance. Written material may not be appropriate for blind and low vision people or for people who are illiterate or have learning disabilities.

Special arrangements should be made for the disabled person's comfort such as allowances for toilet breaks, eating and taking of medication.

It may be useful for the victim, in preparing for a trial, to refer to her or his diary, any notes she or he may have taken, or pictures she or he drew (when the abuse was first revealed).

**keeping names
out of the media**

In cases of sexual assault, the judge can be asked to make an order prohibiting the media from reporting the victim's name or any identifying information. In other cases of assault, the individual's name can appear in the media. In some cases the Crown can also ask the judge that the courtroom be cleared of public spectators in some circumstances, if that is the wish of the victim.

videotaped evidence

A police videotape of a child's report of sexual abuse made at the beginning of the investigation can be used as evidence in court. The child must, however, be available to confirm the information on the video and to be cross-examined by the lawyer of the accused.

When the equipment is available a sexually assaulted child may be protected from testifying in front of the accused. Closed-circuit television or room-divider screens can be used. The evidence of adults may not be given through videotaped statements.

giving evidence

A person who is 14 or older is presumed to be competent to give evidence under oath or solemn affirmation. (A solemn affirmation is like an oath except there is no reference to God).
Where a person is under 14, or the person's capacity to understand the nature of an oath is challenged, there is an inquiry (a **voir dire** or "trial-within-a trial").

At this voir dire, the judge will decide if the person is able to understand the nature of an oath or a solemn affirmation, and is able to communicate the evidence. If so, the person can testify under oath or solemn affirmation. If the person is not able to understand the nature of an oath or a solemn affirmation, but is able to communicate the evidence, the person may testify on "promising to tell the truth".

A person who is not able to communicate the evidence cannot testify.

alternatives

Whether or not charges are laid and the case goes to court, the victim may be entitled to financial compensation from the government as a victim of crime. They may also start a civil action (lawsuit) to ask for financial compensation from the abuser or others who are responsible. There are limitations on the period of time civil suits may be started after the incident has taken place (this time period may be extended if a person is considered to be "incompetent"). In some circumstances this period may be very short, so legal advice should be sought as soon as possible.

Where sexual harassment or discrimination can be proven, a victim may be eligible to receive compensation through federal, provincial or territorial Human Rights Commissions.

Working to End Abuse

Victims with disabilities should be supported and encouraged to use the justice system. Using the law can help to empower people with disabilities who have been victimized and give them the opportunity to feel validated and vindicated. It can lead to the punishment of abusers and may deter them from abusing others. It indicates to abusers and the community that "we mean business" and helps to educate courts and the public that the abuse of people with disabilities is a problem which must be taken seriously.

Resources - Publications

...after sexual assault ... Your guide to the criminal justice system, Department of Justice Canada, Communications and Public Affairs, Ottawa, Ont. K1A 0H8 1988

Beating the "Odds": Violence and Women with Disabilities, DAWN Canada: DisAbled Women's Network Canada, 776 E. Georgia St., Vancouver, B.C. V6A 2A3 1989

Choices: A Sexual Assault Prevention Workbook for Persons with: Visual Impairments; Physical Disabilities; Deaf and Hard of Hearing, Seattle Rape Relief, 1825 So. Jackson, Suite 102, Seattle, Washington USA 98144

Escape! A Handbook for Battered Women who have Disabilities, FINEX HOUSE, P.O. Box 1154, Jamaica Plain, Massachusetts, USA02130

Investigating Child Abuse in Residential Care Settings, Jim Docherty, The Institute for the Prevention of Child Abuse, 25 Spadina Rd., Toronto, Ont. M5R 2S9 1989

Myths about the Sexual Assault of Persons Labeled Mentally Retarded/Developmentally Disabled/Chronically Mentally Ill, Assault Prevent Training Project, Women Against Rape, P.O. Box 02084, Columbus, Ohio USA 43202

911 is for Everyone: Residential Security for People with Disabilities
Abuse: Physical, Verbal, Sexual. Ontario Federation for the Cerebral Palsied, Crime Risk Education is Essential for the Disabled (CREED) Project, Suite 303, 1020 Lawrence Ave. W., Toronto, Ont. M6A 1C8 1988

Put the Child First, a training program to help voluntary organizations deal with child abuse, The Canadian Council on Children and Youth, 2211 Riverside, Suite 14, Ottawa, Ont. K1H 7X5. 1989

Sexual Abuse and Exploitation of People with Disabilities, Dick Sobsey and Connie Varnhagen, University of Alberta Developmental Disabilities Centre 1988

Sexual Assault: It happens to blind women too. BOOST, 597 Parliament St., Suite B3, Toronto, Ont. M4X 1W3

Sexual Assault Manual for the Dependent Adult, Vocational Rehabilitation & Research Institute, Calgary, Alta. 1987

Sexual Abuse and Self Protection: Handicapped Students have a Right to Know. A Curriculum for Development of Awareness of Sexual Abuse and Teaching of Self- Protection, Comprehensive Health Education Foundation, 20832 Pacific Highway South, Seattle, Washington USA 98198

Vulnerable: Sexual Abuse and People with an Intellectual Handicap. The G. Allan Roeher Institute, Kinsmen Building, 4700 Keele St., Downsview, Ont. M3J 1P3 1988

Victim Justice for Disabled Persons: A Resource Manual, Victim Witness Project for the Handicapped, Gallaudet College, Washington, D.C.

What to do if a child tells you of sexual abuse - Understanding the Law, Department of Justice Canada, Communications and Public Affairs, Ottawa, Ont. K1A 0H8

How to Find Support Services

Alberta

The Alberta Committee of Disabled
Citizens (ACDC),
10010 - 105 St.,
Edmonton, Alta. T5J 1C8
(403) 425-8833

Alberta Council of Women's Shelters
34-9912 106 St.,
Edmonton, Alta. T5K 1C5
(403) 429-2689

Alberta Human Rights Commission,
1333 8th Street S.W., Room 102,
Calgary, Alberta T2R 1M6
(403) 297-6571

Crime Compensation Board,
7th Floor, 10365-97 St.,
Edmonton, Alta. T5J 3W7
(403) 427-7217

Office for the Prevention
of Family Violence,
11th Floor, South Tower,
7th Street Plaza, 10030-107 Street,
Edmonton, Alta. T5J 3E4
(403) 427-7599

Severe Disabilities Program,
6-102 Education North,
University of Alberta,
Edmonton, Alta. T6G 2G5
(403) 492-3755

Western Canadian Centre of
Specialization in Deafness,
6-102 Education North,
University of Alberta,
Edmonton, Alta. T6G 2G5
(403) 492-5213

British Columbia/Yukon

B.C. Coalition of the Disabled,
211-456 W. Broadway,
Vancouver, B.C. V5Y 1R3
(604) 875-0188

B.C. Council of Human Rights,
Parliament Building,
Victoria, B.C. V8V 1X4
(604) 387-3710

BC/Yukon Society of Transition Houses,
Room 315, 119 West Pender St.,
Vancouver, B.C. V6B 1S5
(604) 669-6943

Battered Women's Support Services,
Suite 203, 1847 West Broadway,
Vancouver, B.C. V6J 1Y6
(604) 734-1574

Criminal Injuries Compensation Board,
c/o Workers' Compensation Board,
6951 Westminster Highway,
Richmond, B.C. V7C 1C6
(604) 276-3129 or 1-800-972-9972

Child Abuse Resource Centre,
Society for Children and Youth of B.C.
3644 Slocan Street,
Vancouver, B.C. V5M 3E8
(604) 433-4180

Protection Services,
Family and Children's Services Division,
Ministry of Social Services and Housing,
6th Floor, 614 Humboldt St.,
Victoria, B.C. V8W 3A2
(604) 387-7074

Family and Children's Services,
Dept. of Health and Human Resources,
P.O. Box 2703 - H10,
Whitehorse, Yukon Y1A 2C6
(403) 667-3002

Resource Committee for Child
Sexual Abuse Prevention,
P.O. Box 267,
Duncan, B.C. V9L 3X3
(604) 746-4121

Territorial Compensation for
Victims of Crime Authority,
Yukon Workers' Compensation Board,
Suite 300 - 4114 - 4th Avenue,
Whitehorse, Yukon Y1A 4N7
(403) 667-5645

Victim's Information Line,
Room 202 -3102 Main St.,
Vancouver, B.C. V5T 3G7
(604) 875-6381 or 1-800-VICTIMS

Yukon Human Rights Commission,
205 Rogers Street,
Whitehorse, Yukon Y1A 1X1
(403) 667-6226

Manitoba

Child Abuse Program,
Child and Family Support,
Dept. of Community Services,
2nd Floor, 114 Garry St.,
Winnipeg, Man. R3C 1G1
(204) 945-6948

Consulting Committee on the
Status of Women with Disabilities,
929-294 Portage Ave.,
Winnipeg, Man. R3C 0B9
(204) 947-2742

Criminal Injuries Compensation Board,
763 Portage Ave.,
Winnipeg, Man. R3G 3N2
(204) 774-3565

Family Dispute Services,
Dept. of Family Services,
2-210 Osborne St. N.,
Winnipeg, Man. R3C 1V4
(204) 945-1705

Manitoba Human Rights Commission,
301 - 259 Portage Ave.,
Winnipeg, Manitoba R3B 2A9
(204) 945-3007

Manitoba League for the
Physically Handicapped (MPLH),
200 - 294 Portage Ave.,
Winnipeg, Man. R3C 0B9
(204) 943-6099

New Brunswick

Child Protection Services,
Dept. of Health and Community
Services, P.O. Box 5100,
520 King St., Carlton Place,
Fredericton, N.B. E3B 5G8
(506) 453-2040

Crime Victim Compensation,
Office of the Attorney General,
P.O. Box 6000, Room 444,
Centennial Building,
Fredericton, New Brunswick E3B 5Hl
(506) 453-3606

New Brunswick Human Rights Commission,
P.O. Box 6000,
Fredericton, New Brunswick E3B 5H1

Women in Transition Inc.
P.O. Box 1143,
Fredericton, N.B. E3E 5C2
(506) 455-1498

Newfoundland/Labrador

Child Care and Protection,
Dept. of Social Services,
3rd Floor, Confederation Bldg.,
P.O. Box 4750,
St. John's, Nfld. AlC 5T7
(709) 576-2493

Consumer Organization of
Disabled People of Newfoundland
and Labrador (COD),
P.O. Box 422, Station "C",
St. John's, Nfld. AlC 5K5
(709) 722-7011

Crime Compensation Board,
Dept. of Justice,
P.O. Box 8700,
319 Duckworth Street,
St. John's, Newfoundland AlB 4J6
(709) 576-6183

Newfoundland Human Rights Commission,
345 Duckworth Street, 4th Floor,
P.O. Box 4750,
St. John's, Nfld. AlC 5T7
(709) 576-2709

Prov. Assoc. Against Family
Violence,
P.O. Box 221, Station C,
St. John's, Nfld. AlC 5J2
(709) 739-6759

Northwest Territories

Family Life Education,
Department of Health,
Gov't of the NWT, P.O. Box 1320,
Yellowknife, Northwest Territories
XlA 2L9
(403) 920-8758

Family Violence Prevention
Programs, Family and Children's
Services, Dept. of Social Services,
Box 1320, Yellowknife, N.W.T. XlA 2L9
(403) 920-6254

Dept. of Justice, Legal Division,
Government of Northwest Territories,
Box 1320, Yellowknife, N.W.T. X1A 2L9
(403) 873-7466

NWT Council for Disabled Persons,
P.O. Box 1387, NWT, XlA 2Pl
(403) 873-8230

Spousal Assault Network,
Culture and Communications,
Gov't of the NWT, P.O. Box 1320,
Yellowknife, N.W.T. XlA 2L9
(403) 873-7615

Nova Scotia

Criminal Injuries Compensation Board,
Box 985, Suite 402, 1660 Hollis Street,
Halifax, Nova Scotia B3J 2V9
(902) 424-4651

Disabled Victims of Violence
Program, c/o Jim and Barb Campbell,
R.R. 1, Ingonish Beach,
Cape Breton, Nova Scotia B0C IL0
(902) 285-2494

Halifax Transition House Assoc.
P.O. Box 3453, Halifax, N.S. B3J 3J1
(902) 423-7183

Nova Scotia League for Equal
Opportunity (LEO),
Box 8204,
Halifax, N.S. B3K 5L9
(902) 455-6942

Nova Scotia Human Rights Commission,
5675 Spring Garden Road, 7th Floor,
P.O. Box 2221, Lord Nelson Arcade,
Halifax, Nova Scotia B3J 3C4

Ontario

Advocacy Resource Centre
for the Handicapped,
40 Orchard View Blvd., Suite 255,
Toronto, Ont. M4R 1B9
(416) 482-8255

Criminal Injuries Compensation Board,
17th Floor, 439 University Ave.,
Toronto, Ont. M5G IY8
(416) 965-4788

Behavior Management Services,
York Central Hospital, 10 Trench Street,
Richmond Hill, Ontario L4C 4Z3
(416) 883-2270

Blind Organization of Ontario
with Self-Help Tactics,
597 Parliament St., Suite B3,
Toronto, Ont. M4X IW3
(416) 964-6838

Institute for the Prevention
of Child Abuse,
25 Spadina Rd.,
Toronto, Ont. M5R 2S9
(416) 965-1900

Ontario Human Rights Commission,
400 University Ave., 12th Floor,
Toronto, Ont. M7A 1T7
(416) 965-6841

Ontario Native Women's Assoc.,
ll7 North May St., Suite 101,
Thunder Bay, Ont. P7B IR8
(807) 623-1310

Ontario Assoc. of Interval
and Transition Houses,
229 College St., Room 202,
Toronto, Ont. M5T IR4
(416) 977-6619

Ontario Prevention Clearinghouse,
984 Bay Street, Suite 603,
Toronto, Ont. M5S 2S5
(416) 928-1838

Ontario Federation for the Cerebral
Palsied - Crime Risk Education is
Essential for the Disabled (CREED),
1020 Lawrence Ave. W., Suite 303,
Toronto, Ont. M6A IC8
(416) 878-4595

People United for Self-Help
in Ontario (PUSH),
4B - 597 Parliament St.,
Toronto, Ont. M4X IW3
(416) 923-6725

Prince Edward Island

Anderson House,
P.O. Box 964,
Charlottetown, P.E.I.
C1A 7M5
(902) 368-7337

Division of Child and Family
Services, Dept. of Health
and Social Services,
P.O. Box 2000,
Charlottetown, P.E.I. C1A 7N8
(902) 368-4928

Island Information Service,
P.O. Box 2000,
Charlottetown, P.E.I.C1A 7N8
(902) 368-4000

P.E.I. Council of the Disabled,
P.O. Box 2128,
Charlottetown, P.E.I. C1A 7N7
(902) 892-9149

P.E.I. Human Rights Commission,
3 Queen Street, Box 2000,
Charlottetown, P.E.I. C1A 7N8
(902) 368-4180

Quebec

Commission Des Droits de la Personne
due Quebec,
360 rue Saint-Jacques, 8 étage,
Montréal, (Québec) H2Y IP5
(514) 873-5146

Confédération des Organismes
Provinciaux de Personnes
Handicapées du Québec (COPHAN),
4545, Pierre-de-Coubertin,
Montréal (Québec) HlV 3N7
(514) 251-1383

Indemnisation des victimes d'actes criminels,
1199, rue Bleury, 9 ieme étage,
C.P. 6056, succursale A,
Montréal (Québec) H3G 4E1
(514) 873-6019

Multi-Ethnic Assoc. for the Integration
of Handicapped People of Quebec,
91, rue Saint-Zotique Est,
Montréal (Québec) H2S 1K7
(514) 272-0680

Regroupement provincial des
maisons d'hebérgement et de transition
pour femmes victimes de violence,
907, rue Rachel est,
Montréal (Québec) H2J 2J2
(514) 596-0693

Saskatchewan

Child Protection Inquiry,
Central Intake/Child Abuse Unit,
Dept. of Community Services
2240 Albert St.,
Regina, Sask. S4P 3V7
(306) 787-3760

Criminal Injuries Compensation Board
Sturdy Stone Centre,
122 - 3rd Ave. North, 10th Floor,
Saskatoon, Sask. S7K 2H6
(306) 933-5153

Prov. Assoc. of Transition
Houses of Saskatchewan,
#307, 135-21st St. E.,
Saskatoon, Sask. S7K 0B4
(306) 652-6175

Saskatchewan Human Rights Commission,
Room 802, Canterbury Towers,
224- 4th Ave. South,
Saskatoon, Saskatchewan S7K 2H6
(306) 933-5952

Saskatchewan Voice of the Handicapped,
112 - 514 Victoria Ave. E.,
Regina, Sask. S4N 0N7
(306) 569-3111

National Groups

Canadian Advisory Council on
the Status of Women,
110 O'Connor St., 9th Floor,
Box 1541, Station "B",
Ottawa K1P 5R5
(613) 992-4975

Canadian Assoc. for Community
Living, Kinsmen Building,
York University, 4700 Keele St.,
Downsview, Ont. M3J 1P3
(416) 661-9611

Canadian Assoc. of the Deaf/
Canadian Assoc. of the Hard of Hearing,
2435 Holly Lane, Suite 205,
Ottawa, Ont. K1V 7P2
T.D.D. (613) 235-7880

Canadian Assoc. of Independent
Living Centres,
905-150 Kent St.,
Ottawa, Ont. K1P 5P4
(613) 563-2581

Canadian Assoc. of Sexual
Assault Centres,
77 E. 20th Ave.,
Vancouver, B.C. V5V 1L7
(604) 876-8819

Canadian Hearing Society,
Connect Program,
271 Spadina Rd.,
Toronto, Ont. M5R 2V3
(416) 964-9595

Canadian Human Rights Commission,
320 Queen Street, Place de Ville,
Tower A, 13th Floor,
Ottawa, Ont. K1A 1E1
(613) 943-9000

Coalition of Provincial
Organizations of the Handicapped,
926-294 Portage Ave.,
Winnipeg, Man. R3C 0B9
(204) 947-0303

Canadian Council on Children
and Youth,
2211 Riverside Drive, Suite 14,
Ottawa K1H 7X5
(613) 738-0200

DisAbled Women's Network - Canada,
5 Warner Ave.
Toronto, Ont. M4A 1Z3
(416) 755-6060

Family Violence Program,
Canadian Council on Social Development,
55 Parkdale Ave., Ottawa K1Y 4G4
(613) 728-1865

The National Clearinghouse
on Family Violence,
7th Floor, Brooke Claxton Bldg.,
Health and Welfare Canada,
Ottawa K1A 1B5
(613) 957-2938 or 1-800-267-1291

National Victims Resource Centre,
Law Information Section,
Department of Justice Canada,
239 Wellington St.,
Ottawa K1A 0H8
(613) 957-1526 or 1-800-267-0454

People First - National,
Kinsmen Building, York University,
4700 Keele St.,
Downsview, Ont. M3J 1P3
(416) 661-9611

Victims of Violence Society,
B150-151 Slater St.,
Ottawa, Ont. K1P 5H3
(613) 233-0052

*Please note: many of these organizations have
provincial and regional affiliates.*

APPENDIX
Laws Pertaining to Assault and Sexual Assault
(<u>Criminal Code</u> of Canada)

ASSAULT

265. (1) A person commits an assault when
a) without the consent of another person, he applies force intentionally
to that other person, directly or indirectly;
b) he attempts or threatens, by an act or gesture, to apply force to
another person, if he has, or causes that other person to believe upon
reasonable grounds that he has, present ability to effect his purpose; or
c) while openly wearing or carrying a weapon or an imitation thereof,
he accosts or impedes another person or begs.

(2) Application:
This section applies to all forms of assault, including sexual assault,
sexual assault with a weapon, threats to a third party or causing bodily
harm and aggravated sexual assault.

(3) Consent:
For the purposes of this section, no consent is obtained where the
complainant submits or does not resist by reason of
a) the application of force to the complainant or to a person other than
the complainant;
b) threats or fear of the application of force to the complainant or to a
person other than the complainant;
c) fraud; or
d) the exercise of authority.

(4) Accused's belief as to consent:
Where an accused alleges that he believed that the complainant
consented to the conduct that is the subject-matter of the charge, a
judge, if satisfied that there is sufficient evidence and that, if believed
by the jury, the evidence would constitute a defence, shall instruct the
jury, when reviewing all the evidence relating to the determination of
the honesty of the accused's belief, to consider the presence or absence
of reasonable grounds for that belief.

SEXUAL ASSAULT

271. (1) Every one who commits a sexual assault is guilty of
(a) an indictable offence and is liable to imprisonment for a term not exceeding ten years; or
(b) an offence punishable on summary conviction.

SEXUAL ASSAULT WITH A DEADLY WEAPON, THREATS TO A THIRD PARTY OR CAUSING BODILY HARM

272. Every one who, in committing a sexual assault,
(a) carries, uses or threatens to use a weapon or an imitation thereof,
(b) threatens to cause bodily harm to a person other than the complainant,
(c) causes bodily harm to the complainant, or
(d) is a party to the offence with any other person, and is guilty also of an indictable offence and liable to imprisonment for a term not exceeding fourteen years.

AGGRAVATED SEXUAL ASSAULT

273.(1) Every one commits an aggravated sexual assault who, in committing a sexual assault, wounds, maims, disfigures or endangers the life of the complainant.
2) Every one who commits an aggravated sexual assault is guilty of an indictable offence and is liable to imprisonment for life.

CORROBORATION REQUIRED

274. Where an accused is charged with an offence under section 151 (Sexual Interference), 152 (Invitation to Sexual Touching), 153 (Sexual Exploitation), 155 (Incest), 159 (Anal Intercourse), 160 (Bestiality), 170 (Parent or Guardian Procuring Sexual Activity), 171 (Householder Permitting Sexual Activity), 172 (Corrupting Children), 173 (Indecent Acts), 212 (Procuring), 272 (Sexual Assault with a Deadly Weapon ...), or 273 (Aggravated Sexual Assault), no corroboration is required for a conviction and the judge shall not instruct the jury that it is unsafe to find the accused guilty in the absence of corroboration.

NO EVIDENCE CONCERNING SEXUAL ACTIVITY

276. (1) In proceedings in respect of an offence under section 151, 152, 153, 155 or 159, subsection 160(2) or (3), or section 170, 171, 172, 173, 271, 272 or 273, no evidence shall be adduced by or on behalf of the accused concerning the sexual activity of the complainant with any person other than the accused unless

(a) it is evidence that rebuts evidence of the complainant's sexual activity or absence thereof that was previously adduced by the prosecution;
(b) it is evidence of specific instances of the complainant's sexual activity tending to establish the identity of the person who had sexual contact with the complainant on the occasion set out in the charge; or
(c) it is evidence of sexual activity that took place on the same occasion as the sexual activity that forms the subject-matter of the charge, where that evidence relates to the consent that the accused alleges he believed was given by the complainant.

(2) No evidence is admissible under paragraph (1)(c) unless

(a) reasonable notice in writing has been given to the prosecutor by or on behalf of the accused of his intention to adduce the evidence together with particulars of the evidence sought to be adduced; and (b) a copy of the notice has been filed with the clerk of the court.

(3) No evidence is admissible under subsection (1) unless the judge, provincial court judge or justice, after holding a hearing in which the jury and the members of the public are excluded and in which the complainant is not a compellable witness, is satisfied that the requirements of this section are met.

(4) The notice given under subsection (2) and the evidence taken, the information given or the representations made at a hearing referred to in subsection (3) shall not be published in any newspaper or broadcast.

(5) Every one who, without lawful excuse the proof of which lies on him, contravenes subsection (4) is guilty of an offence punishable on summary conviction.

(6) In this section, "newspaper" has the same meaning as in section 297.

REPUTATION EVIDENCE

277. In proceedings in respect of an offence under section 271, 272 or 273, evidence of sexual reputation, whether general or specific, is not admissible for the purpose of challenging or supporting the credibility of the complainant.

SPOUSE MAY BE CHARGED

278. A husband or wife may be charged with an offence under section 271, 272 or 273 in respect of his or her spouse whether or not the spouses were living together at the time the activity that forms the subject-matter of the charge occurred.

Child Sexual Abuse Legislation
(Criminal Code of Canada)

CONSENT NO DEFENCE

150.1(1) Where an accused is charged with an offence under section 151 or 152 or subsection 153(1), 160(3) or 173(2) or is charged with an offence under section 271, 272 or 273 in respect of a complainant under the age of fourteen years, it is not a defence that the complainant consented to the activity that forms the subject-matter of the charge.

(2) Notwithstanding subsection (1), where an accused is charged with an offence under Section 151 or 152, subsection 173(2) or section 271 in respect of a complainant who is twelve years of age or more but under the age of fourteen years, it is not a defence that the

complainant consented to the activity that forms the subject-matter of the charge unless the accused

(a) is twelve years of age or more but under the age of sixteen years;

(b) is less than two years older than the complainant; and

(c) is neither in a position of trust or authority towards the complainant or is a person with whom the complainant is in a relationship of dependency.

(3) No person aged twelve or thirteen years shall be tried for an offence under section 151 or 152 or subsection 173(2) unless the person is in a position of trust or authority towards the complainant is in a relationship of dependency.

(4) It is not a defence to a charge under section 151 or 152, subsection 160(3) or 173(2), or section 271, 272 or 273 that the accused believed that the complainant was fourteen years of age or more at the time the offence is alleged to have been committed unless the accused took all reasonable steps to ascertain the age of the complainant.

(5) It is not a defence to a charge under section 153, 159, 170, 171 or 172 or subsection 212(2) or (4) that the accused believed that the complainant was eighteen years of age or more at the time the offence is alleged to have been committed unless the accused took all reasonable steps to ascertain the age of the complainant.

SEXUAL INTERFERENCE

151. Every person who, for a sexual purpose, touches, directly or indirectly, with a part of the body or with an object, any part of the body of a person under the age of fourteen years is guilty of an indictable offence and liable to imprisonment for a term not exceeding ten years or is guilty of an offence punishable on summary conviction.

INVITATION TO SEXUAL TOUCHING

152. Every person who, for a sexual purpose, invites, counsels or incites a person under the age of fourteen years to touch, directly or indirectly, with a part of the body or with an object, the body of any person, including the body of the person who so invites, counsels or incites and the body of the person under the age of fourteen years, is guilty of an indictable office and liable to imprisonment for a term not exceeding ten years or is guilty of an offence punishable on summary conviction.

SEXUAL EXPLOITATION

153.(1) Every person who is in a position of trust or authority towards a young person or is a person with whom the young person is in a relationship of dependency and who

(a) for a sexual purpose, touches, directly or indirectly, with a part of the body or with an object, any part of the body of the young person, or

(b) for a sexual purpose, invites, counsels or incites a young person to touch, directly or indirectly, with a part of the body or with an object, the body of any person, including the body of the person who so invites, counsels or incites and the body of the young person, is guilty of an indictable offence and liable to imprisonment for a term not exceeding five years or is guilty of an offence punishment on summary conviction.

(2) In this section, "young person" means a person fourteen years of age or more but under the age of eighteen years.

INCEST

155.(1) Every one commits incest who, knowing that another person is by blood relationship his or her parent, child, brother, sister, grandparent or grandchild, as the case may be, has sexual intercourse with that person.

(2) Every one who commits incest is guilty of an indictable offence and liable to imprisonment for a term not exceeding fourteen years.

(3) No accused shall be determined by a court to be guilty of an offence under this section if the accused was under restraint, duress or fear of the person with whom the accused had the sexual intercourse at the time the sexual intercourse occurred.

(4) In this section, "brother" and "sister", respectively, include half-brother and half-sister.

ANAL INTERCOURSE

159.(1) Every person who engages in an act of anal intercourse is guilty of an indictable offence and liable to imprisonment for a term not exceeding ten years or is guilty of an offence punishable on summary conviction.

(2) Subsection (1) does not apply to any act engaged in, in private, between

(a) husband and wife, or

(b) any two persons, each of whom is eighteen years of age or more, both of whom consent to the act.

(3) For the purposes of subsection (2),

(a) an act shall be deemed not to have been engaged in in private if it is engaged in in a public place or if more than two persons take part or are present; and

(b) a person shall be deemed not to consent to an act

(i) if the consent is extorted by force, threats or fear of bodily harm or is obtained by false and fraudulent misrepresentations respecting the nature and quality of the act, or

(ii) if the court is satisfied beyond a reasonable doubt that that person could not have consented to the act by reason of mental disability.

BESTIALITY

160.(1) Every person who commits bestiality is guilty of an indictable offence and liable to imprisonment for a term not exceeding ten years or is guilty of an offence punishable on summary conviction.

(2) Every person who compels another to commit bestiality is guilty of an indictable offence and liable to imprisonment for a term not exceeding ten years or is guilty of an offence punishable on summary conviction.

(3) Notwithstanding subsection (1), every person who, in the presence of a person under the age of fourteen years, commits bestiality or who incites a person under the age of fourteen years to

commit bestiality is guilty of an indictable offence and liable to imprisonment for a term not exceeding ten years or is guilty of an offence punishable on summary conviction.

PARENT OR GUAR-DIAN PROCURING SEXUAL ACTIVITY

170. Every parent or guardian of a person under the age of eighteen years who procures that person for the purpose of engaging in any sexual activity prohibited by this Act with a person other than the parent or guardian is guilty of an indictable offence and liable to imprisonment for a term not exceeding five years, if the person procured for that person is under the age of fourteen years, or to imprisonment for a term not exceeding two years if the person so procured is fourteen years of age or more but under the age of eighteen years.

HOUSEHOLDER PER-MITTING SEXUAL ACTIVITY

171. Every owner, occupier or manager of premises or other person who has control of premises or assists in the management or control of premises who knowingly permits a person under the age of eighteen years to resort to or to be in or on the premises for the purpose of engaging in any sexual activity prohibited by this Act is guilty of an indictable offence and liable to imprisonment for a term not exceeding five years, if the person in question is under the age of fourteen years, or to imprisonment for a term not exceeding two years if the person in question is fourteen years of age or more but under the age of eighteen years.

CORRUPTING CHILDREN

172. (1) Every one who, in the home of a child, participates in adultery or sexual immorality or indulges in habitual drunkenness or any other form of vice, and thereby endangers the morals of the child or renders the home an unfit place for the child to be in, is guilty of an indictable offence and liable to imprisonment.

INDECENT ACTS

173.(1) Every one who wilfully does an indecent act
(a) in a public place in the presence of one or more persons, or
(b) in any place, with intent thereby to insult or offend any person, is guilty of an offence punishable on summary conviction.
(2) Every person who, in any place, for a sexual purpose, exposes his or her genital organs to a person who is under the age of fourteen years is guilty of an offence punishable on summary conviction.

PROCURING

212.(1) Every one who
(a) procures, attempts to procure or solicits a person to have illicit sexual intercourse with another person, whether in or out of Canada,
(b) inveigles or entices a person who is not a prostitute or a person of known immoral character to a common bawdy-house or house of assignation for the purpose of illicit intercourse or prostitution,
(c) knowingly conceals a person in a common bawdy-house or house of assignation,
(d) procures or attempts to procure a person to become, whether in or out of Canada, a prostitute,

(e) procures or attempts to procure a person to leave the usual place of abode of that person in Canada, if that place is not a common bawdy-house, with intent that the person may become an inmate or frequenter of a common bawdy-house, whether in or out of Canada,

(f) on the arrival of a person in Canada, directs or causes that person to be directed or takes or causes that person to be taken, to a common bawdy-house or house of assignation,

(g) procures a person to enter or leave Canada, for the purpose of prostitution,

(h) for the purposes of gain, exercises control, direction or influence over the movements of a person in such manner as to show that he is aiding, abetting or compelling that person to engage in or carry on prostitution with any person or generally,

(i) applies or administers to a person or causes that person to take any drug, intoxicating liquor, matter or thing with intent to stupefy or overpower that person in order thereby to enable any person to have illicit sexual intercourse with that person, or

(j) lives wholly or in part on the avails of prostitution of another person,

is guilty of an indictable offence and liable to imprisonment for a term not exceeding ten years.

(2) Notwithstanding paragraph (l)(j), every person who lives wholly or in part on the avails of prostitution of another person who is under the age of eighteen years is guilty of indictable offence and liable to imprisonment for a term exceeding fourteen years.

(3) Evidence that a person lives with or is habitually in the company of a prostitute or lives in a common bawdy-house or in a house of assignation is, in the absence of evidence to the contrary, proof that the person lives on the avails of prostitution, for the purposes of paragraph (l)(j) and subsection (2).

(4) Every person who, in any place, obtains or attempts to obtain, for consideration, the sexual services of a person who is under the age of eighteen years is guilty of an indictable offence and liable to imprisonment for a term not exceeding five years.

Canada Evidence Act Provisions
Section 16, "Witness whose capacity is in question"...

16. (1) Where a proposed witness is a person under fourteen years of age or a person whose mental capacity is challenged, the court shall, before permitting the person to give evidence, conduct an inquiry to determine

a) whether the person understands the nature of an oath or a solemn affirmation; and

b) whether the person is able to communicate the evidence.

(2) A person referred to in subsection (l) who understands the nature of an oath or a solemn affirmation and is able to communicate the evidence shall testify under oath or solemn affirmation.

(3) A person referred to in subsection (l) who does not understand the nature of an oath or a solemn

affirmation but is able to communicate the evidence may testify on promising to tell the truth.

(4) A person referred to in subsection (1) who neither understands the nature of an oath or a solemn affirmation nor is able to communicate the evidence shall not testify.

(5) A party who challenges the mental capacity of a proposed witness of fourteen years of age or more has the burden of satisfying the court that there is an issue as to the capacity of the proposed witness to testify under an oath or a solemn affirmation.

Human Rights For Disabled People

David Baker

For many years, disabled people have been regarded as objects of pity whose needs would be met out of acts of individual charity. While charity remained a pervasive factor in the lives of disabled people, the rise of the modern welfare state led to the introduction of publicly funded health, welfare and social services. The emphasis remained upon the incapacity and dependence of disabled persons.

Most recently, members of disadvantaged groups, such as members of visible minorities, women, and disabled people, have demanded and won legal recognition of their human rights. In practice, this has meant the legally mandated removal of barriers which have the effect of preventing members of these groups from pursuing their ambitions and their potential. Within a pluralistic society, the emphasis shifted to recognizing disabled people's capacity and encouraging their independence.

The shift has been reflected in the growing influence of law on the day to day life of disabled persons. In Canada, this movement is most clearly symbolized by the inclusion of equality guarantees for disabled people in its Constitution: the first country in the world to do so.

Traditional legal analyses have tended to view disabled persons' rights as subsets of generic areas of law, e.g., criminal, tax and family. In order to emphasize the functional impact of the law on the lives of disabled people, I have chosen to cross these boundaries by reviewing how courts in Canada have responded to human rights issues which have been designated "universal".

Canada became a member of the United Nations in 1945. In doing so, Canada pledged to follow article 55(1) of the U.N. Charter whereby "...the U.N. shall promote: universal respect for an observance of human rights and fundamental freedoms for all..." The foundation document for the international protection of human rights is the Universal Declaration of Human Rights (1948). While "disabled" are not specifically listed as a protected class, under Article 2 it states "everyone is entitled to all rights and freedoms set forth in this Declaration without discrimination of any kind, such as race, colour ... birth or other status". The International Commission on Human Rights has interpreted the open ended category of "other status" to include the "disabled". The subsequent passage of the Declaration on the Rights of Mentally Retarded Persons (1971), and the Declaration on the Rights of Disabled Persons (1975) and the appointment of the U.N. Sub-Committee on the Protection of Minorities, (which was specifically to consider the interests of disabled persons) further substantiate this position. The following Articles are contained in the Universal Declaration:

1. Article 2 - Everyone has the right to life, liberty and security of the person.

Life

In Canada, as in other industrialized countries, recent developments in medical technology and the emergence of the welfare state have raised the issue of whether severely handicapped people have the right to live. At this point, the debate appears to be confined to the questions of whether "heroic" medical procedures can be withdrawn or whether life saving medical procedures can be refused. Nevertheless, it is safe to predict that economic downturns resulting in decreased availability of medical or social services, or the rationing of highly expensive new medical technologies will broaden the debate.

In Canada, the leading case on this issue concerns a developmentally handicapped child who resided in an institution in British Columbia. He required the surgical implantation of a shunt in his brain (a routine medical procedure) if he was to survive. His parents refused to give the consent necessary for the operation, and the Public Guardian brought an application in court to allow a substituted consent to be given. The first court to hear the case refused to interfere with the parents' decision. The evidence accepted by the court indicated that the child was in constant pain and lived a vegetative existence. The second court hearing the matter heard evidence which suggested that he was severely handicapped, but happy, and responded in his own way to his environment. This court gave the authority necessary for the operation to be performed.

The case provides guidance on when a court will permit a person to die based on quality of life criteria.

Canada's medicare system ensures that procedures of a life sustaining nature are generally available, irrespective of a person's disability. While there are those who have recommended cost containment by allocating services to those who are most fit, this attitude is not reflected in the law.

Disabled people who are financially unable to support themselves are eligible for a subsistence level of welfare, cost shared by the federal and provincial governments. Since 1970, when high levels of inflation were experienced in Canada, the adequacy of welfare payments has decreased dramatically. Many persons on welfare find it impossible to locate minimally decent housing, and have minimally adequate diets, nevertheless, the current situation cannot yet be characterized as having reached the point of being life threatening.

Liberty

Many disabled people in Canada are institutionalized against their will. This result is achieved through indirect and direct means. Canada has the highest rate of institutional or "total care" of any country in the world. Little support is provided for community living. Thus, many physically disabled people reside in institutions which restrict or eliminate contacts with the outside world, all the while knowing they could be living in the community enjoying their freedom at considerably less cost to the state.

Persons with mental or emotional handicaps have their liberty restricted in an additional way. All provinces have guardianship and mental health legislation. A guardian is someone who makes decisions on behalf of an adult deemed by a court to be incapable of making those decisions. Normally the guardian is the next of kin. A general lack of standards suggests substi-

tute decision making is quite arbitrary.

Mental health legislation is used in acute cases where a period of involuntary institutionalization in a psychiatric facility is deemed necessary by a physician. In contrast to guardianship legislation which has not been fundamentally altered for hundreds of years, changing treatment modalities and an aggressive "inmates rights" movement has led to many recent changes intended to enhance the rights of "involuntary patients".

Security of the Person

A fundamental premise of natural law is the sanctity of the human body from unconsented to interference. In Canada, the violation of this principle constitutes a battery and can result in criminal prosecution and a civil suit for damages. Clearly, exceptions to this rule must be made in the case of communicable diseases where the public interest is at risk. Nevertheless, treatment without consent in the interests of the individual, or alternatively, as a method of social control is widespread in Canada.

Persons with mental handicaps, particularly mental illnesses, are routinely subjected to treatment against their will. The first problem, once again a product of technological developments, is the question of defining procedures for which a consent is required in law. Many psychoanalytic and behaviour modification techniques do not involve either direct or indirect physical touching. Instead, they involve psychological interaction or deprivation techniques which are known to be as potent as surgical or chemical procedures for which consent is acknowledged as a prerequisite. The law in this area requires clarification.

Secondly, there is a mistaken assumption that persons who are confined against their will in psychiatric hospitals are incapable of making treatment decisions on their own behalf. This "wholesale" approach is being replaced by a process of individualized assessments of capacity, backed up by a right to appeal a doctor's decision to treat without consent.

The security of a mentally handicapped person, incapable in law of providing a consent to certain non-therapeutic procedures raises special issues. For example, a medical doctor who instructed at a university medical school used developmentally handicapped adolescents in an institution to teach her students how to perform rectal examinations. A court rejected her contention that the unconsented to procedures served a larger good and convicted her of assault.

The sterilization of developmentally handicapped women was recently reviewed by the Supreme Court of Canada. Not since Alberta's eugenic sterilization laws were repealed in the 1920's has an overt legal authority existed for discriminatory sterilization practices. Nevertheless, a report in Ontario demonstrated that as late as 1978, developmentally handicapped women and girls were being routinely sterilized. In a strongly worded decision, the Supreme Court ruled that a guardian can never give a valid substitute consent to a "non-therapeutic" sterilization.

2. Article 4 - No one shall be held in slavery or servitude; slavery and the slave trade shall be prohibited in all forms.
There exists no political status of slave in Canada. Having said that, it is clear that disabled people in Canada, if they choose to work, are exposed to exploitation.

In many provinces, a disabled person can be paid less than minimum wage. Proponents of this discriminatory provision point to the high rates of unemployment amongst disabled people and suggest this will give them a competitive advantage on the labor market. They overlook the purpose of a minimum wage, i.e., to raise standards of living above the barest level of subsistence and to allow everyone to enjoy a standard of living deemed socially acceptable.

A substantial number of disabled people work in sheltered workshops for which they are paid a pittance. While not forced into workshops, the disabled who wish to supplement their meagre welfare cheques or who seek to enter the competitive labour market (for whom sheltered workshops represent the only "rehabilitation" program available) must accept these conditions. The rehabilitative results of workshops are acknowledged to be very poor. Many people work full-time in workshops for their entire lives. Others are placed by workshops in competitive

businesses for extended periods of time without the benefit of labour law protections.
3. Article 5 - No one shall subjected to torture or to cruel inhuman or degrading treatment or punishment.
The Canadian Bill of Rights (1960) and the Charter of Rights and Freedoms (1981) guarantee Canadians protection against cruel and unusual treatment.

On two occasions, one under the Bill and the second under the Charter, attempts have been made to strike down Canada's Criminal Code provisions governing the treatment of persons found not guilty of a criminal offence by reason of insanity, as violating these guarantees.

In Canada, a person who is found not guilty by reason of insanity is detained for an indeterminate period until they are considered to have "recovered". Thus, for example, a mentally retarded person charged with a trivial offence, such as purse snatching, can spend the rest of his life in an institution for the criminally insane because he will never be "cured" of his handicap.

Under the Bill, this punitive provision was upheld. The case under the Charter is presently before the Supreme Court of Canada.
4. Article 6 - Everyone has the right to recognition everywhere as a person before the law. Everyone in Canada upon reaching the age of majority (the age varies from province to province) is considered a person, in the sense of being able to freely enjoy full rights of citizenship. These rights are to be enjoyed unless removed by process of law.

A major exception to this rule involves residents in various institutions for the care of the disabled. Here, for example, as a condition of receiving the services of a nursing home or home for the aged, a disabled person is required to sign over management of his or her affairs to the administrator of the facility. Thus, the coercive effect of withholding essential services routinely results in the compromising of the individual's rights.

The primary method for removing a person's rights as an adult in a plenary fashion is pursuant to the Mental Incompetency Act. In a case which received international public attention, a non-verbal young man with cerebral palsy battled in court for the right to decide where he would live. His parents, who had placed him in an institution and who had not come to visit him for many years, sought to prevent him from leaving the institution by having him declared mentally incompetent. He testified using a system of picture symbols called blisssymbolics. In the end, the court declared him mentally competent despite his severe physical handicaps and his lack of experience outside the institution.

5. Article 7 - All are equal before the law and are entitled without any discrimination to the equal protection of the law.

Over the last ten years, Canadians have been repeatedly shocked to learn of the widespread abuse of handicapped and elderly persons who were institutionalized for their own protection. Grisly details of torture and abuse of persons in institutions for the mentally handicapped have been revealed and numerous inquests into deaths in nursing homes in Ontario have resulted in widespread calls for reform.

In a rare case where criminal charges were laid against a staff member for physical abuse, the Supreme Court of Canada made important law. The staff member, who admitted striking the resident with a heavy metal spoon on the head, sought the protection of a section of the Criminal Code which permitted a parent or person in loco parentis to use reasonable force to discipline a child. It was argued that the developmentally handicapped adult had the mental age of a child and that the staff member should therefore be given the benefit of this defence. After finding the force used was unreasonable and that the staff member was not in loco parentis, the court went on at length to state that handicapped people should not be denied equal protection of the law by being subjected to perpetual childhood.

6. Article 9 - No one shall be subjected to arbitrary arrest, detention or exile.

Arrest and Detention

In Canada, two medical doctors were authorized to order the detention of persons they believed required psychiatric treatment up until 1967. At that time, the Ontario Mental Health Act was amended to provide criteria based on protecting the "safety of the person or the safety of others". It also created an administrative tribunal to review whether involuntary admission is justifiable in light of the new criteria.

The 1967 Ontario Act was soon duplicated across Canada. Its introduction paralleled the emergence of psychotropic drugs which in turn resulted in shorter periods of hospitalization and a trend towards deinstitutionalization.

In 1978, Ontario again amended its Mental Health Act. Almost simultaneously, a large number of beds in the large provincial psychiatric hospitals were closed. The revised Act further narrowed the criteria for involuntary detention and afforded a due process hearing before a mental health review board. Perhaps sensing the revisions were collateral to the increase of community care for the mentally ill, the amendments were strongly opposed by the medical establishment. Interestingly, the new Ontario model still leaves the power of arrest and detention up to one doctor. The doctor's decision will be overturned if serious and imminent risk of danger to the person or others cannot be demonstrated.

Exile

No one is ejected form Canada because of disability. Nevertheless, disability plays a significant part in Canada's immigration policy, and is the cause of much hardship.

Canada's immigration policy is designed with three objectives in mind: (1) supply of labour otherwise unavailable in Canada; (2) reunification of families; and (3) providing a safe haven for refugees.

Canada's Immigration Act prohibits the admission of persons with communicable diseases with which it is difficult to find fault. It also prohibits potential refugees and relatives from sponsoring for permanent admission to Canada, otherwise eligible disabled persons who might be a drain upon Canada's health or social services. As a result, many families are living in Canada with one disabled family member obliged to remain in the country of origin. This discriminatory policy is being challenged under the equality clause of the Charter of Rights and Freedoms.

7. Article 12 - No one shall be subjected to

arbitrary interference with his privacy, family, home or correspondence, nor to attacks upon his honour and reputation.

Consistent with most jurisdiction's endorsement of deinstitutionalization of disabled people, a patchwork of community support services is slowly emerging. Generally speaking, it can be said that a spectrum of support services is not available, the services are uncoordinated, and demand hopelessly exceeds supply. One mechanism used to deinstitutionalize disabled people is called a group home, where 3-10 disabled people live together in a normal residence, undistinguishable from others in the community.

In all jurisdictions in Canada, there exists zoning legislation designed to prevent socially incompatible uses (i.e. heavy industry and residential housing) from being proximately located.

Despite arguments approved by the Supreme Court of Canada that all people should be treated equally under zoning legislation, group homes have been treated as non-residential uses. As a result, when a group of disabled people wish to live together in order to share common support services, they must apply for a spot-rezoning. This involves notifying all one's neighbours of the proposed use (i.e. as a residence for disabled people) and inviting them to attend before the municipal council to state why no exception to the general zoning rule should be made.

From coast to coast such meeting before municipal councils have resulted in the clearest expressions of hatred and fear of disabled people. Local ratepayers have articulated concerns that group homes will bring dangerous and unsightly people into their neighbourhood which, in turn, will result in reduced property values for their houses.

Some municipalities have decided to avoid the heat of spot rezonings (i.e. dealing with cases on an individual basis) by passing by-laws with permit group homes, provided they are not concentrated in any one area. These "as of right" by-laws have involved lengthy debates and expensive legal challenges. It should also be noted that the end result is far from satisfactory, in that group homes are not treated as normal residential uses but rather as nuisances which must be separated and endured.

Most residential options for disabled people involve far more interference with a person's lifestyle than is necessary. Many institutions following the "medical model" treat disabled people as if they are ill. This involves serious infringements of privacy and little attention being paid to people's dignity. In one case, a disabled man successfully challenged having care of his genital area attended to by a female. Most residential programs for physically disabled people interfere in a paternalistic way with an individual's life style decisions, e.g., dating a member of the opposite sex, consumption of alcohol. There is no separation of the privacy one expects in one's own home from the rehabilitative function over which the disabled person has no control.

8. Article 13 - Everyone has the right to freedom of movement and residence within the borders of each state.

There are no Canadian laws which state that disabled people may not travel or enter buildings freely. Because Canada's architectural and transportation systems were built on the premise that disabled people need not enter, no law was necessary.

Only very recently have there been the first fledgling efforts to make mainline buses, subways and street cars accessible to mobility handicapped people. Instead, municipalities have developed a variety of "parallel" transportation systems, usually built around a fleet of lift and radio equipped vans which provide a "door to door" service. Due to underfunding, it would be fair to characterize these systems as undependable, inflexible and dangerous. Some municipalities provide no service or restrict access very tightly. Others depend upon the services of charities.

There is virtually no accessible regional transportation in Canada. Thus, persons who live in rural areas or satellite communities around larger communities have no means of getting into the larger centres of commerce and government.

In what stands as the most important human rights decision to date involving a disabled Canadian, the Rail Transport Committee of the Canadian Transport Commission decided that it would be in the public interest to require the federally owned passenger rail service to significantly improve its accessibility. The Committee made four major orders:

1. Disabled people were given a right of self-determination, i.e., the right to decide whether or not they required an attendant.

2. The principle of "one-person one-fare" was adopted, i.e., the attendant was perceived alternatively as an extension of the disabled person or of the services provided by the railway, but in either event would be permitted to travel on the disabled person's ticket.

3. Despite being presented with a plan by the railway to install mechanical lifting devices over time in all major rail stations, the railway was required to immediately provide manual boarding assistance at its 52 largest stations, i.e., equality of access.

4. While aware of the additional risks faced by disabled people when travelling, they were not found to be so substantial as to justify denial of carriage, i.e., dignity of risk. Also, the railway was not permitted to extract waivers of liability from such passengers. To allow waivers would have exposed them to undue danger and reduced the incentive for improved safety procedures reflecting the special needs of disabled passengers.

As important as these principles have been, the overall impact of this decision is restricted by the inaccessible design of most of Canada's aging passenger rolling stock. Thus, while the train has become a preferred inter-city transportation system for many disabled people, the environment within most railway cars is quite inhospitable.

Inter-city buses have escaped regulatory attention largely for complex interjurisdictional reasons. While the federal government has legislative, and therefore, human rights jurisdiction over inter-city buses, the regulatory authority over these buses has been transferred to provincial governments. Most private bus companies have implemented the principles of self-determination, one-person one-fare and the dignity of risk; the big problem remains equality of access. Only bus service under direct federal jurisdiction has mechanical lifts and specially designed seating to accommodate the disabled passenger.

Despite the limitations of all the foregoing modes, it is in air travel where the greatest frustration is experienced. This is because most of the high cost renovations allowing accessibility are in place both in airports and on board planes, and yet progress towards full accessibility remains slow. Repeated government reports and complaints by representatives of the disabled have gone unheeded. Hard won gains of the four standards referred to above have been lost by disabled air passengers as a result of deregulation.

Residence

Each province is responsible for prescribing its own building standards, including standards of accessibility for disabled people.

The federal government is responsible for the accessibility of its own buildings. It is justifiably to be praised for the manner in which it has made all federal buildings accessible whether they are old or new, and wherever they are located in the country.

It has also provided that 5% of all units in apartment buildings constructed with mortgage financing from the Canadian Mortgage and Housing Corporation be accessible for mobility handicapped tenants.

Unfortunately, the federal lead has not been followed by the provinces. Most provincial laws apply only to new construction or major renovations, (i.e., no requirement to retrofit) of certain public or quasi-public buildings (i.e., no application to single family housing), are of minimal benefit (i.e., do not deal with design features outside the building such as approaches to the building or major interior features) and can be easily avoided, (i.e., by adjusting level of grade or applying for exemption).

Even with major improvements, the overall progress to be achieved with such laws would be incremental and leave existing buildings permanently inaccessible. For this reason, a recent decision of the Saskatchewan Court of Appeal signals a major shift in judicial attitudes. A young man in a wheelchair entered a movie theatre with a friend. Because there were no spaces available in the body of the theatre from which a person in a wheelchair could view the movie, he was wheeled down to the front of the theatre where he viewed the movie separated from his friend and segregated for all to see. The Court ruled that the Saskatchewan Human Rights Code required the theatre provide several spots from which a person in a wheelchair could view the movie. The decision is the first in Canada in which such renovations to provide accessibility have been ordered.

9. Article 16 - Men and women of full age have the right to marry and found a family. They are entitled to equal rights as to marriage, during marriage, and at its dissolution.
A paternalistic system would deny a disabled person normal healthy sexual outlets and restrict the possibility of marriage and raising a family.

There exist a number of laws which have such a stifling effect on disabled people. For example, until recently, it was a criminal offence to have sexual relations with a "feeble-minded" person. This prohibition made anyone, including a mentally handicapped person who was engaging in healthy, consensual sexual relations with another mentally handicapped person, liable to prosecution. The purpose of the law was clearly to prevent mentally handicapped people form engaging in sexual activity of any type, as well as to protect the person from exploitation.

All provinces in Canada have a variation on the Ontario Marriage Act which prohibits the marriage of "mentally defective or mentally ill" persons. The law treats marriage as a contract requiring a person have the mental capacity to enter a contract. Thus, the property aspects of marriage are emphasized in the law to the detriment of the legitimization of a close personal relationship between people whose mental handicap may be permanent. Again, the purpose of the law is a thinly disguised attempt to deter mentally handicapped people from engaging in sexual activity and having children.

If there are children, Canadian law requires that the child's "best interests" prevail over those of the parent. Obviously, the natural parents enjoy the advantage of the "bonding" which exists between the parent and child. Just as obviously, the courts, when considering whether to remove a child from a disabled parent or parents, considers the degree to which the disability impairs a person's child raising capacity. Until very recently, children were routinely removed from their disabled parents. Discriminatory attitudes have moderated somewhat recently to the point where a court will consider whether the state can assist disabled parents by providing them with the "tools necessary to care for their child".

Another area where society's discriminatory attitudes are apparent is adoption. Governmental agencies interpret their discretion to match orphan children with the best available parents. Physically disabled people have been precluded from adopting on the basis that their disability disqualified them from ever being considered suitable. In a recent case, a woman in a wheelchair successfully challenged her disqualification.

10. Article 21 - Everyone has the right to take part in the government of his country, directly or through freely chosen representatives.
Canada is a multi-party democracy. The most fundamental political right of a citizen is the right to vote. A psychiatric patient successfully challenged the law during the 1988 election. These cases were based on the unqualified right of a citizen to vote contained in the Charter of Rights and Freedoms. As a direct result of these cases, provincial and municipal election legislation was amended, by removing the mental competency standard. At this point it would appear reasonable to predict that most jurisdictions in the country have followed suit or are at risk of having their election legislation challenged in the courts.

11. Article 23 - Everyone has the right to work, to free choice of employment, to just

and favourable conditions of work, and to protection from unemployment.

Remunerative employment is probably the ultimate human right because the salary and status which it provides ensure that other rights are guaranteed.

Canada has the highest rate of unemployment amongst its disabled citizens of any industrialized country. The reasons for this poor record are numerous and complex.

The most readily apparent is that Canada, unlike the rest of the industrialized world, has neither an affirmative action or quota scheme guaranteeing acceptable levels of employment amongst disabled workers. A Royal Commission Report recommended Canada adopt a mandatory affirmative action program, however, the government has introduced a voluntary program. During the first two years of the voluntary program, employment of disabled people actually decreased.

A second reason for the rate of unemployment is the woefully inadequate system of vocational rehabilitation available to disabled people. The small province of Prince Edward Island, for example, has virtually no program at all. In the province of Ontario, the program has undergone massive cuts in recent years to the point where prosthetic devices are no longer available and post-secondary and professional training is no longer subsidized.

Finally, there is a provision in the Income Tax Act prohibiting the deduction of disability related expenses of earning employment income (except for a limited deduction for on-the-job attendant care introduced in 1989). As a result, disabled people must bear the cost of making the accommodations which will make them employable, and yet they are required to pay for these expenditures out of after-tax rather than before-tax income. Many disabled people are financially further ahead remaining on welfare than accepting low paying jobs or jobs that require substantial job related expenditures. It is increasingly being recognized that these disincentives must be removed.

Human rights legislation requires that employers accommodate the special needs of disabled people. Administrative problems have resulted in this obligation being inadequately enforced.

The most important accommodations involve job restructuring. In a recent case, an employer was required to re-allocate heavy lifting from the job description of an employee with a bad back and replace it with additional light duties. Other accommodations would include use of special technologies, support services and modified training. Time will tell whether this ad hoc kind of decision-making is administratively more feasible and effective at securing employment for disabled people than providing quotas or mandatory affirmative action. The two methods are clearly compatible and disabled advocates are seeking reforms which would include both strategies.

12. Article 25 - Everyone has the right to a standard of living adequate for the health and well-being of himself and of his family, including food, clothing, housing, and medical care and necessary social services and the right to security in the event of unemployment, sickness, disability, widowhood, old age or other lack of livelihood in circumstances beyond his control.

Disability is the least well provided for of the catastrophic circumstances enumerated in Article 25. Generally speaking, disabled people who are "unemployable" are eligible for welfare. In fact, disability is a major reason for receiving welfare in Canada. Such payments carry with them the stigma of being labelled "unemployable", together with the intrusive consequence that they will be terminated in the event of cohabitation with another person whose income need be no higher than minimum wage.

Some disabled people do reasonably well. For example, persons injured in the course of their employment are relatively well provided for and are given both a strong financial incentive to return to work and high quality professional assistance in the rehabilitation process. Disabled veterans of the armed services are treated relatively generously.

At the other end of the scale are the minimal payments from Criminal Injuries Compensation Funds, out of which the victims of crime who are injured or disabled may claim benefits. These benefits are allocated according to highly subjective standards and, in any event, they rarely exceed what welfare would provide.

Most other persons who become disabled must look to the courts for compensation which is only available if the disabled person can demonstrate that the other party was negligent (i.e., was at "fault"). A great deal of money is spent on negligence insurance by motor vehicle owners, doctors, property owners and businesses. Unfortunately, a very large percentage of the premiums paid for this insurance never reaches disabled people but instead, goes into the administration and profits of the insurance industry, and to defray the costs of the litigation process. The worker's compensation scheme is far more cost efficient in the sense of translating premiums into payments to disabled people. While a strong lawyers lobby urges that Canada retain "fault" as the basis of compensation, Quebec, and to a more limited extent, Ontario, have recently introduced "no fault" systems.

Another factor in the income redistribution scheme is the Income Tax Act. As stated above, Canada's tax system is basically neutral in terms of its redistributive effect. There are two major provisions in the Act itself dealing with disability.

The first is the handicapped person credit which is available to persons with a severe disability. Secondly, a deduction is provided for "medical expenses" not subsidized by the government or private insurance schemes. It is regressive in the sense that it is of disproportionate benefit to high income earners.

A minority of workers in Canada, primarily those who are members of trade unions, are eligible for private disability insurance benefits. Unfortunately, most workers eligible for these benefits find out after they become disabled that they will have to pay tax on their benefits. The result is that many are only slightly better off than they would have been on welfare. Moreover, most policies terminate the benefits after two years if the recipient is capable of any type of remunerative employment whatsoever.

Canada's largest social program is its fully government funded medicare scheme. At the present time, the last vestiges of two-tier medi-cine have been removed. Thus, while low income people still do not get equal benefit from medicare, the financial deterrents have virtually all been removed. Ironically, 100% funding for all necessary medical services co-exists in many parts of the country with totally unsubsidized dental care, drugs and prosthetics. In some provinces, these are only provided by municipalities to persons on welfare. Even then, these benefits are totally discretionary. Similar discretion is exercised in the case of persons who require special clothing, diets or medical accessories. Thus, many of Canada's lowest income disabled people are dependent upon private charities for these essential services or devices, or go without if charity doesn't meet the need.

Another result of the generous funding of the medical system is that it encourages the medicalization of what would normally be considered non-medical problems. For example, physically handicapped people in many provinces are given the option of having their attendant care needs met in a nursing home where their food and shelter costs are met by the state along with unnecessary medical care, or receiving no support whatsoever. Under such circumstances, it is hardly surprising that people reluctantly accept a life of dependence on the medical system.

13. Article 26 - **Everyone has the right to an education. Education shall be free, at least in the elementary and fundamental stages. Elementary education shall be compulsory. Technical and professional education shall be compulsory. Technical and professional education shall be made generally available and higher education shall be equally accessible to all on the basis of merit. Education shall be directed to the full development of the human personality... Parents have a prior right to choose the kind of education that shall be given to their children.**

Education in Canada is a provincial responsibility, although services are typically delivered by municipally elected school boards.

In no province can it be said that official policy is to meet the individual educational needs of children, whether or not they are disabled. In most provinces, policy has not changed since the Supreme Court of Canada held in 1950 that educators could decide whether or not a child had the mental or physical qualifications for admission to school. Thus, educators were free to refuse to serve children who did not fit the norm. This remains the law to this day, and many disabled children in Canada go without any formal education as a result.

The broad discretion left with school boards to define who will be educated also extends to their right to set standards for the quality of education they provide in general, and more particularly, to the quality of education they provide to disabled children. Not surprisingly, the educational levels achieved by disabled Canadians are far below average.

Some parents have sought integrated placements in regular classrooms. They reason that segregation has the same socially debilitating consequences for mentally or physically handicapped children that it does on racial or ethnic minorities. The results of these cases are not yet conclusive.

Ontario amended its Education Act in 1980 to guarantee every child an "appropriate education". To emphasize this focus on the individual, every parent of an "exceptional child" may appeal the placement of their child in a particular special education program to a Provincial Tribunal. Initial indications are that appropriateness may be subordinated to the availability of programs which the board of education is prepared to offer.

Post-secondary education for disabled students is very uneven. For example, virtually no deaf students attend university in Canada. On the other hand, a group of blind and learning disabled students recently succeeded in a human rights complaint to prompt the government to fund an audio reading service which transcribes books onto tape. This gave the students equal access to materials generally available to non-print handicapped students.

Conclusion

While the initiatives of COPOH, Canada's national cross-disability consumer organization, and other advocacy groups have clearly had an impact in recent years, Canada's poor legislative record stands as a grim reminder of how much more remains to be done by disabled people in the legislatures and the courts. Canada's legislators have been very slow to move from exclusion to equality in their attitudes towards disabled people. It is to be hoped that positive change will accelerate as the consumer movement of disabled persons becomes stronger and more effective.

MEDICAL CONCERNS

In encounters with medical and para-medical professionals, clients are expected to assume the roles of obedient followers. A widely held belief is that care-givers, because of their training, their status, and their expertise have the right to convey unquestioned directives as to the procedures to be followed in attempting to achieve the most positive results. When patients question such diagnosis and procedures they are often viewed by the establishment as individuals who have no understanding and no identity. The disabled and their families are expected to blindly follow the directions of care-givers; after all, it is assumed that they know best.

However well-intentioned the care-givers are, they are prone to misdiagnosis, and/or inappropriate treatments when dealing with members of the disabled community. The disabled often believe that it is not their place to question the analysis of the medical professionals. Consequently, in some cases, the disabled become victims of abuse, since they do not always have advocates who can provide them with loving support in difficult and complex situations.

Douglas Bliken in his article "The Myth of Clinic Judgement" states that problems occur because professionals provide services to the disabled from a clinical perspective when other factors such as, social, economic, and political issues complicate the situation. Further, he indicates that although social prejudice may render a reliance on clinical judgement, it may be little more than a mythology.

The pressures of disabled life frequently precipitate substance abuse among some members of the disabled community. Abuse, as pointed out by Professor Greer, demonstrates that some disabled individuals have too much accessibility to medications, along with other factors, such as health problems, anger, and belligerence which often become their own enemies.

There are many myths that victimize individuals with disabilities and diseases, as illustrated by the current concerns surrounding the recent AIDS awareness in contemporary societies. Patients, family members, and acquaintances are often influenced by myths and false impressions of disability. Thus, Taylor et al. illustrate that cancer patients, AIDS victims, and others find themselves socially isolated from the mainstream of society.

A major trend of the last twenty years has been deinstitutionalization, and it has currently been recognized that many disabled people, including the deaf, blind, and Downs Syndrome patients are capable of making valuable contributions to society. These ideas are exemplified in Von Schneden and Crecco's article.

Caplan in his article and Litton et al. in their article illustrate that the perspectives of professionals towards their clients are crucial in producing positive attitudes in the rehabilitation process. However, it is also noted that the rehabilitation process can be hampered by individuals who perceive disability to mean deviance. The disabled can be labelled involuntary deviants, and as deviants they suffer many stigmatizing experiences which can inhibit their rehabilitative *potentials*. Steven Gold illustrates the above concerns well. Thompson outlines some additional rehabilitation techniques, such as positive confrontation, which can be used by medical and para-medical professionals when dealing with the disabled. Likewise, Brandon directs our attention to the principles of self responsibility, nutritional awareness, fitness, and stress management, as significant factors to address when dealing with the disabled community.

Many of the disabled require personal care attendants who can provide disabled persons with the mobility and support that they require in order to become participating, self-sufficient members of the community. Atkins et al. illustrate that in order for independence to be come a reality to the disabled, personal care attendants are crucial. Sally French notes some of the advantages of disability status according to some health care professionals, who view their own disabilities as advantageous in the work place.

The disabled often discover that the treatment they encounter in society is not a result of their abilities and their potential, but rather it is a consequence of myths, prejudices and discriminations. Thus, the disabled, in addition to "proving themselves", are frequently required to negate the mythologies which impedes and victimizes them.

The Myth of Clinical Judgment

DOUGLAS BIKLEN

Client or Minority?

Deinstitutionalization and community integration for people classified as retarded have been on the national policy agenda for nearly two decades (Blatt & Kaplan, 1966; Kugel & Shearer, 1976; Kugel & Wolfensberger, 1969). Yet over 100,000 retarded people remain institutionalized. After a precipitous drop in the early 1970s, the population of institutions for the retarded now decreases only one or two percent annually (Bruininks & Lakin, 1985). Some states that claim a commitment to community programming appear intent upon accomplishing this goal through the construction of mini-institutions in the community (Taylor, McCord, & Searl, 1981), and at least two states have begun to construct "group homes" on the grounds of old institutions. In education, despite a federal law that requires students with disabilities to be served in the "least restrictive" settings possible, some states excluded more than two-thirds of certain disability groups from regular schools (U.S. Department of Education, 1985). In the area of employment, by nearly any available analysis, two-thirds of all persons with disabilities are unemployed (Bowe, 1978, 1984). Those who seek more independence in their lives often find their efforts stifled by limited physical access, social rejection, and insufficient economic support (Brightman, 1984; Conley, 1985).

Such conditions exemplify the meaning of marginality: People with disabilities are institutionalized, segregated and undereducated, socially rejected, physically excluded from public places, and unemployed. Any other group subjected to these circumstances would most likely be characterized as a minority. Yet the more common tendency has been to view people with disabilities as (a) victimized by a disabling condition and (b) in need of treatment——not of rights.

This perspective keeps the person with a disability from being seen as a minority group member. The notion that people with disabilities suffer at the hands of their disabilities rather than from social ostracism and discrimination sets this group apart from other minority groups. While psychological and physiological differences have certainly been claimed as excuses for sex and race inequality, such claims do not enjoy the apparent face validity and centrality for women and blacks that they historically have had and still have for people with disabilities (*City of Cleburne v. Cleburne Living Center*, 1984a,b; Saraons & Doris, 1969). In other words, people who are at risk for social processing and social control because of their individual, disability-related needs become the captives of a treatment model; they and their lives become medicalized (Bogdan & Taylor, 1976; Gould, 1981; Sarason & Doris, 1969; Szasz, 1961, 1970). The more severe the disability, the greater the likelihood that the person will be regarded more as a "patient" than as an object of discrimination. Indeed, identity as a patient would seem to preclude identification or status as an oppressed minority.

Obviously, people with disabilities, like anyone, may need certain services, such as treatment (e.g., physical therapy, speech-language therapy, medical care) or adaptive help (e.g., prostheses, augmented communication, individualized or adaptive instruction). But to be transformed from a socially valued individual, albeit one needing and receiving some treatment, to the status of perpetual clinical subject, client, or patient is a far more encompassing phenomenon, and one that people with disabilities frequently resist (Bogdan & Taylor, 1982; Karuth, 1985; Kriegel, 1969).

The making of a patient takes numerous forms. It occurs, for example, through diagnosis, classification and labelling, and placement. In education, federal law as well as conventional practice requires classification and placement before students with disabilities can receive specialized or individualized educational

Reprinted from: *Journal of Social Issues, Vol. 44, No. 1, 1988, pp. 127-140*, with permission.

assistance. This fact helps explain why more people are identified and treated as disabled during their school years than at any other time in their lives (Mercer, 1973; Sarason & Doris, 1969). In the areas of jobs and joblessness, medical insurance, and income maintenance, social policies require people with disabilities to prove they are "truly" disabled, "truly" needy, and "truly" worthy of patient or dependent status in order to receive benefits or services. Interestingly, even with such seemingly limiting conditions as mental retardation, many people escape identification upon leaving social-processing institutions (e.g., schools and state asylums; see Mercern 1973; Sarason & Doris, 1969; Bogdan & Taylor, 1982).

Patient status also develops when people's basic individual rights are negated by professionals to whom society grants authority over those judged in need of treatment (Blatt & Kaplan, 1966; Blatt, Ozolins, & McNally, 1979; *Parham v. J.R.*, 1978; Szasz, 1961, 1970; *Youngberg v. Romeo*, 1982). The technical language of treatment typically communicates a quasi-medical mystique, a status difference, and an aura of professional specialization——all of which imply that persons targeted for treatment are patients who must be handled by highly trained experts in specialized locations (Tomlinson, 1982). Because the clinical paradigm so dominates how society defines people with disabilities, it also manifests itself in day-to-day interactions between disabled and nondisabled people. People with disabilities report being seen and treated as "sick" rather than as people whose disability is but one personal quality (Bogdan & Taylor, 1982; Brightman, 1984; Kriegel, 1969; Roth, 1981). Interestingly, while disability rights organizations and other groups have pushed to reduce the medicalization of disability and the unnecessary professionalization of treatment, both phenomena seem to be growing (Szasz, 1970; Tomlinson, 1982; U.S. Department of Education, 1985).

Clinical Treatment/Clinical Judgment in Special Education

Disability treatment professions (e.g., special education, psychology and rehabilitation) operate on a model of individual assessment, diagnosis, and placement. That is, in order to determine the best strategy for educating, rehabilitating, or otherwise serving people with disabilities, professionals must first consider individual needs and the findings of research about the best approaches for meeting such needs. But what is the range of freedom available to professionals' decision making? On a day-to-day basis, professionals do make placement decisions, for example. But what options are available to them? Are the best practices typically among their possible choices? In other words, how does the professional environment frame the professional's work? Do professionals truly have the freedom to exercise professional judgment, or are professionals and consumers alike merely functionaries and pawns in a world of narrowly restricted, love-it-or-leave-it "choices"? As one example, what are the judgment parameters in educational placement?

In mandating the procedure of educating students with disabilities in the least restrictive setting, as articulated in Public Law 94-142, The Education for All Handicapped Children Act of 1975, Congress relied heavily on the language of clinical judgment. Specifically, the law required

procedures to assure that to the maximum extent *appropriate,* handicapped children, including children in public or private institutions or other care facilities, are educated with children who are not handicapped, and that special classes, separate schooling, or other removal of handicapped children from the regular educational environment occurs only when the nature or severity of the handicap is such that education in regular classes with the use of supplementary aids and services cannot be achieved satisfactorily. [Section 612(5) (B)]

The courts have further interpreted legislative intent to indicate that in deciding upon appropriateness of service, the state shall have fulfilled its mandate if it has enlisted qualified professionals to make the decisions (*Board v. Rowley*, 1982). Federal enforcement and state implementation of the "least restrictive environment" provision have similarly relied on clinical judgment. For example, when mechanisms have been designed for monitoring student placements, they have generally increased expectations that case-by-case clinical judgment would insure individualization and neutral decision making in placement recommendations. In the words of the 1985 report to Congress on the implementation of the act (U.S. Department of Education, 1985):

> Typically, these policies establish a placement process that marshals a wide range of professional expertise and involves several levels of professional review, in order to assure that children are placed in appropriate settings. In some States, these more elaborate placement procedures are used only when the normal IEP (individual education plan) process has identified a child for whom (1) no appropriate placement is readily available; (2) an out-of-district placement is recommended; or (3) payment for services is contested. (p. 39)

The presumption of the U.S. government has been that there should be no segregation (e.g., special class placement or separate school placement) in the absence of demonstrable benefits from proposed segregation and evidence that integration in a regular class or in a typical school is not possible:

> Separation or segregation is permissible only when education itself cannot be successful without it, and even then, . . . separation or segregation must be limited by a concept of maximum appropriate integration (e.g., opportunities for peer interaction. (Will, 1985)

Furthermore, segregation could not be justified by administrative excuses, even including the greater availability of special equipment, instructional specialists, or special programs in separate settings (*Roncker v. Walters,* 1983; Will, 1985).

It is not possible to devote more space in this article to the integration/segregation debate (see Bersoff, Kobler, Fiscus, & Ankney, 1972; Biklen,m 1982; Blatt, 1977; Dunn, 1968; Goldstein, Moss, & Jordan, 1965; Garalnick, 1978). However, it is noteworthy that recent research on integration and segregation, particularly in the last five years, suggests substantial support for educating all students, no matter how severely

disabled, in typical schools (Knoblock, 1982; Certo, Haring, & York, 1984; Wilcox & Bellamy, 1982; Stainback & Stainback, 1984; Biklen, 1985). The major research findings can be summarized briefly as follows:

- There appears *no* evidence that segregated schooling produces educational results (e.g., change in intellectual or adaptive behavior) superior to those achieved in integrated schools. Literature reviews on the subject note the difficulties of matching children of like disabilities in different environments and of controlling for variables other than those associated with integration or segregation (Blatt, 1977). Given these problems, however, the literature does not provide evidence for segregated schooling (e.g., separate schools for disabled students only).

- School programs that include disabled and nondisabled students, whether in school-based or community-based settings, minimize the problems that severely retarded students typically experience in generalizing their learning from one setting to another. When they attend typical schools, severely disabled students are constantly exposed to models of the full range of student behavior, in academic as well as social situations (Brinker & Thorpe, 1984; Knoblock, 1982). Particularly where integrated schools utilize community-based nonschool environments, such as shopping centers, public transportation, and work locations for functional training, disabled students can learn from real rather than simulated experiences (Brown et al., 1983a,b, 1986).

- When mildly disabled students have been systematically supported in regular classrooms, they have equalled or outperformed their peers in resource-room programs (Wang & Birch, 1984).

- Integration breeds acceptance by students toward each other. My physical integration leads to greater acceptance (Towfighy-Hooshyar & Zingle, 1984) by nondisabled students toward students who have been classified as disabled. Planned or structured interaction produces even greater tolerance, acceptance, and interaction than mere proximity (Biklen, 1985; Knoblock, 1982; Voeltz, 1982). In return, autobiographical accounts of integrated disabled students and former students suggest that they view themselves as peers of nondisabled students (e.g., Kay, 1981).

- When interaction between disabled and nondisabled students is systematically supported, the resulting increased student-to-student interaction has been shown to predict greater success in achieving IEP goals (Brinker & Thorpe, 1984). In other words, although interaction was once expected to be principally a side benefit of integration, it now appears to constitute a significant factor in skill development.

- Integrated schooling provides expanded options for informal learning and utilization of natural-environment instruction and natural cues (as opposed to highly structured, laboratory-like situations), all of which are now seen as beneficial, particularly when used in conjunction with looser behavioral teaching techniques than were frequently used in the past (Brown et al., 1983a,b, 1986; Coon, Vogelsberg, & Williams, 1981; Halle, 1982; Liberty, Haring, & Martin, 1981).

- Several recent follow-up studies on postschool employment experiences of special education students suggest the benefit of early integrated schooling (Brown et al., 1986; Wehman et al., 1982; Wilcox & Bellamy, 1982). It correlates with successful job placement and job retention.

- Educators' expectations for student performance appear greater for students involved in useful and age-appropriate (and more integrated) rather than non-functional (and potentially more segregated) activities (Bates, Morrow, Pancsofar, & Sedlak, 1984).

- Individual education plans of students in regular schools are more likely to reflect research-based "best practices" than are the IEPs of students in schools for disabled students only (Hunt, Goetz, & Anderson, 1986).

- Certain schools and school districts have demonstrated that they can provide effective educational programs to even the most severely disabled students in regular schools (Taylor & Ferguson, 1985).

- Although this is not an educational *quality* consideration, the cost of educating students of all disability levels is less in regular schools than in disability-only schools (Kakalik, Furry, Thomas, & Carney, 1981).

On the basis of research findings and government policy, it appears that educators should be expected to select typical schools and, to a large extent, regular classes as the placements of choice. In this regard, a recent report to the U.S. Congress indicates the Department of Education's interest in and pleasure with the extent of integrated placement:

> During school year 1982-83, the majority of handicapped students continued to be served in regular education buildings . . . 68 percent of all handicapped children received most of their education in regular classes. . . . . An additional 25 percent received services in separate classes within a regular education building. Taken together, these settings accounted for 93 percent of the handicapped students, who received special education and related services in environments that included non-handicapped peers. *Only* 7 percent of all handicapped children were educated in separate schools or other environments, such as hospitals or homebound instruction. (U.S. Department of Education, 1985, p. 36)

For students aged 6-17, the core school years, less than 5.5% are currently segregated (U.S. Department of Education, 1985, p. 239).

But the summary data obscure the extent of segregation for particular groups of students labelled handicapped, most notably mentally

retarded, emotionally disturbed, and multihandicapped students. If we subtract learning-dis-
abled students and speech-impaired students from
the total numbers of disabled students——two
groups of which only 1.2% and 0.6% respectively
are segregated, but which constitute 67% of all
disabled students——the extent of segregation of
the remaining disabled students jumps from 5.5%
to anywhere from 10 to 55%, depending on the
group considered (U.S. Department of Education,
1985, pp. 239-250).

The state-by-state variation in whether students receive their education in regular schools or
in special disabled-only schools is nothing less
than extraordinary. In certain states, a large
proportion of students labelled retarded attend
special schools for the disabled only: Delaware
and the District of Columbia (37% each), Maryland (40%), Louisiana (23%), New York (30%),
Nevada (29%), New Jersey (23%), and Texas
(20%) (U.S. Department of Education, 1985, p.
242). Yet remarkably, Nebraska segregates none
of its retarded students, and 13 states segregate
less than 3% of students classified as retarded.
In New York State, 10,793 emotionally disturbed
students, 26% of those so labelled are segregated
(U.S. Department of Education, 1985, p. 243).
Other states that educationally segregate substantial proportions of students labelled emotionally
disturbed include California (21%), Delaware
(25%), Illinois (32%), Kentucky (38%), Maryland
(61%), Minnesota (33%), New Jersey (25%),
Ohio (49%), and Pennsylvania (23%) (U.S.
Department of Education, 1985, p. 243). In
sharp contrast, Wisconsin and Nebraska segregate
none of their students classified as emotionally
disturbed.

The group most likely to be segregated is
multihandicapped students. Among states with
more than 1000 multihandicapped students identified, those that segregate the highest proportion
are Maryland and Texas (80%) and New York
(61%) (U.S. Department of Education, 1985, p.
245). Yet California and Massachusetts, two
other states with over 1000 students identified as
multihandicapped, segregate 5 and 4%, respectively.

The foregoing data raise troubling questions.
It appears place of residence, for example,

whether students live in Maryland or in Nebraska, determines whether or not they will attend
regular or special (e.e., separate) schools. Why
is this? Are clinicians in Nebraska of a different
mind about school integration than those in
Maryland? Or are there other, nonclinical factors
that determine the patterns of school placements?
In other words, does the context for professional
decision making allow for the independent exercise of clinical judgement within limits that may
not be supported by research, stated policy, or
clinical judgment?

Second, if the enormous disparities between
states in the proportion of disabled students
educated in regular schools cannot be rationally
explained as a function of differences in professionals' judgment, then what other factors shape
such conditions? Several factors have been
identified as having major influence in school
placement practices. One obvious explanation is
state funding policies. If, for example, a state
provides 100% of the funding for institutional
placements, local school districts will find this an
attractive option for eligible students. Similarly,
if a state provides substantially greater funding
for private school placements of students with
disabilities than it does for placements within
local districts, this too can lead to greater reliance
on segregated placements (Blatt, 1972). Several
of the states having high levels of segregation of
students with moderate and severe retardation and
multiple handicaps are ones in which state funding has been provided to construct regional
separate special schools, for example, Ohio, New
York, New Jersey, and Missouri. Similarly,
where states have established special school
districts to take referrals of students with disabilities from local districts, segregated schooling is
commonplace——for example, in Ohio and New
York.

Third, if one state, Nebraska, can educate all
of its students in regular schools, and more than
a dozen others can achieve nearly complete
integration, does this not suggest the possibility
that all students can be educated in typical
schools? In addition to the national data on
school placements, several studies report schools
and school districts that serve the total population
of school-aged children, disabled and nondisabled

alike (Biklen, 1985; Knoblock, 1982; Taylor & Ferguson, 1985; U.S. Department of Education, 1986). These schools and school districts impose no admission test to establish eligibility. Thus, the question must be asked whether all schools and school districts could not integrate fully, since some have already done so with no negative effects.

Clinical Treatment/Clinical Judgment in Residential Placement and Programs

Policies affecting residential placements and programs for people with retardation and other developmental disabilities, like educational policies, also presume the central importance of clinical judgment. In articulating a goal of adequate treatment, for example, the U.S. Congress charged the states with ensuring *appropriate* services in the "least restrictive" setting:

> Persons with developmental disabilities have a right to appropriate treatment, services and habilitation for such disabilities.
>
> The treatment, services and habilitation for a person with developmental disabilities should be designed to maximize the developmental potential of the person and should be provided in the setting that is least restrictive of the person's liberty. (Developmentally Disabled Assistance and Bill of Rights Act, 1975, Sec. 6010)

As in the field of education, the courts defer to professionals concerning the appropriateness of particular treatments or placements:

> In determining whether the state has met its obligations in these respects, decisions made by the appropriate professionals are entitled to a presumption of correctness. (*Youngber v. Romeo*, 1982, p. 323)

In other words, decisions about residential placement and treatment strategies are in the hands of professionals, even if these treatments of placements limit individual liberty interests (see also Biklen, 1981; *Parham v. J.F.*, 1978).

Research findings on residential programming and policy, as in education, support a high degree of physical as well as social and programmatic integration for people with disabilities and their nondisabled peers. In residential policies this would include, for example, cash support and home services for families to help them maintain a disabled family member at home, support staff to assist people living in apartments, and small, highly personalized group-living situations for people who need assistance in daily living. The research on residential policy and practice for people with retardation can be summarized briefly as follows:

- Even those people whose disabilities include behavior problems have a high rate of success in community placement if they are provided support services (Schalock, Harper, & Genung, 1981).
- When provided "increased training opportunity, increased opportunity to assume responsibility for in-house tasks, more autonomy, clear expectations . . . residents are more likely to perform mastered skills and be satisfied with the residential setting" (Seltzer, 1981, p. 629).
- Even when given little support and when faced with seemingly very difficult life circumstances, people with mild retardation typically retain an optimistic outlook on life (Edgerton, Bollinger, & Herr, 1984).
- People who live in small community residences show greater development in adaptive behavior than do those who reside in large institutions (Sokol-Kessler, Conroy, Feinstein, Lemanowicz, & McCurrin, 1983).
- Community-living arrangements in residential areas and ones that promote "socially integrated vocational, educational, recreational, and social activities" enable people to achieve more socially appropriate behavior than do isolated residences and arrangements that do less to promote social interaction (Hull & Thompson, 1980, p. 26).
- Community-living programs, including family support, are no more expensive and may be less expensive than institu-

tional placements (Intagliata, Wilder, & Cooley, 1979).

- Although public policy specialists originally assumed that people with mild disabilities would benefit the most from community placements and from increased social interaction with non-disabled persons, the benefits are as great for people with severe disabilities. In fact, in terms of improved social circumstances and individual skills, people with severe disabilities show the greatest positive change from access to community living (Hemming, Avender, & Pill, 1981; Raynes, 1980; Conroy, Efthimiou, & Lemanowicz, 1982).

- By definition, institutionalization denies people a range of social experiences (e.g., interaction with people in the community, typical living quarter, participation in work and recreation with people who do not have disabilities). In contrast, while community placement does not guarantee social interaction, it does create the circumstances where interaction becomes possible (Taylor, Biklen, & Knoll, 1987).

- A number of states, municipalities, and service organizations have successfully demonstrated the ability to serve people with the most severe, multiple disabilities, including significant medical complications, in family and small-group settings (Taylor, RAcino, Knoll, & Lutifyya, 1986).

On the basis of these and other similar findings, a number of researchers (Bruininks & Lakin, 1985; Center on Human Policy, 1979; Lakin and Bruininks, 1985; Taylor et al., 1987) have recommended various forms of community integration, typically including family support, supported apartments and homes, and small residences (e.g., three persons).

Interestingly, however, when researchers have explored the reasons behind actual patterns of placements and differences in approaches to residential policy, they have found many nonclinical factors responsible. Why, for example, do some states use community residential programs

for 50 or more people per 100,000 of the general population, while other use them for 5 or fewer (Bruininks, Hauber, & Kudla, 1979)? Why do some states use Medicaid funds to support institutions while others use them only for small community-living programs (Taylor et al., 1981)? Why do some states use institutional placements at a rate seven times greater than other states (Epple, Jacobson, & Janicki, 1985)? Some of the nonclinical factors in such policies include politics, state budgetary agendas, labor interests, past traditions in retardation services, court oversight, public prejudice toward people with disabilities, bureaucratic impediments, and jurisdictional disputes between human service agencies (Rothman & Rothman, 1984; Blatt, 1970; Blatt et al., 1979).

A national survey of institutional closure suggests that states close institutions not simply because professional judgment has resulted in fewer people being institutionalized, but primarily for other nonclinical reasons: increased pressure to convert mental retardation and mental health institutions into prisons, federal funding for new institutional construction; pressure on states to cut costs, availability of alternatives to institutions (although in some cases this means nursing-home or other congregate-care placement), and pressure from advocacy groups (Braddock & Heller, 1985, pp. 172-173). One obvious factor shaping placement decisions has been the federal Medicaid law, which facilitated extensive reconstruction of old, large, state mental retardation institutions, the construction of many smaller nursing homes and other congregate-care facilities ranging in size from 50 to 250 persons, and the emergence of large group homes for 8-15 persons (Taylor et al., 1981).

Conclusion

Society places people with disabilities in the client role, and thus many aspects of their lives become subject to professional authority. Educational experts exercise professional judgment to determine appropriate educational programs and program decisions for them. Residential or other clinical specialists decide who shall live in a group home, who shall be institutionalized, who shall be let out of institutions, and who shall receive assistance to live in apartments or other community settings. Society reinforces such professional authority by establishing it in state and case law.

In fact, however, clinical judgment does not operate in this idealized form. often, in education, in residential policy, and undoubtedly in many other areas of professional practice, clinical judgment is drastically limited by the influence of other nonclinical forces. It may even be mere window dressing for practices that in fact contradict clinical judgment. Certainly, it is mistaken to believe clinical judgment could ever be so influential as to supersede all other social, economic, and political factors that affect people's lives.

The solution to the problem of clinical judgment being overwhelmed by nonclinical forces is not more, better, and therefore more influential clinical judgment. Rather, the problem is in the current model of disability services, which treats questions that are both political *and* professional——such as where and how people shall live or be educated——as if they were purely professional ones. Clinical judgment and assistance surely have a role in people's lives, for example, to explain the effects of different teaching methods, to help people understand their relations with each other, or to enable individuals to develop new skills. But clinical judgment always occurs in a political context and therefore cannot reasonably be viewed as independent of it.

The conditions faced by people with disabilities are those that plague other minorities: social isolation, insufficient and unequal treatment, economic treatment, economic dependency, high unemployment, poor housing, and an unusually high rate of institutionalization. It serves the interests of neither professionals nor their clients——indeed, it perpetuates a myth——to ignore people's need for political and economic changes while offering them only clinical treatment. This seems particularly wrong and harmful when the treatment itself becomes an extension of political and economic disenfranchisement. Put another way, people with disabilities are more likely to achieve increased self-determination, real choice, and power if they cease being defined as clients

whose future rests in the hands of professionals, and are instead recognized as a minority group.

References

Bates, P., Morrow, S., Pancsofar, E., & Sedlak, R. (1984). The effect of functional vs. non-functional activities on attitudes expectations of non-handicapped college students: What they see is what we get. *Journal of the Association for Persons with Severe Handicaps, 9*(2), 73-78.

Bersoff, D., Kobler, M., Fiscus, E., & Ankney, R. (1972). Effectiveness of special class placement for children labeled neurologically handicapped. *Journal of School Psychology, 10,* 157-163.

Biklen, D. (1981). The Supreme Court v. retarded children. *Journal of the Association for Persons with Severe Handicaps, 6*(2), 3-5.

Biklen, D. (1982). The least restrictive environment: Its application to education. In G. Melton (Ed.), *Child and youth services and the law* (pp. 121-144). New York: Haworth Press.

Biklen, D. (1985). *Achieving the complete school: Effective strategies for mainstreaming.* New York: Teachers College Press.

Blatt, B. (1970). *Exodus from pandemonium: Human abuse and a reformation of public policy.* Boston: Allyn & Bacon.

Blatt, B. (1972). Public policy and the education of children with special needs. *Exceptional Children, 38,* 537-545.

Blatt, B. (1977). Issues and values. In B. Blatt, D. Biklen, & R. Bogdan (Eds.), *An alternative textbook in special education* (pp. 3-27). Denver: Love.

Blatt, B., & Kaplan, F. (1966). *Christmas in purgatory.* Boston: Allyn & Bacon.

Blatt, B., Ozolins, A., & McNally, J. (1979). *The family papers: A return to purgatory.* New York: Longman.

Board v. Rowley, 458 U.S. 176, 102 S. Ct. 3034, 73 L. Ed. 2d 690 (1982).

Bogdan, R., & Taylor, S. (1976). The judged, not the judges: An insider's view of mental retardation. *American Psychologist, 31,* 47-52.

Bogdan, R., & Taylor, S. (1982). *Inside out.* Toronto, Canada: University of Toronto Press.

Bowe, F. (1978). *Handicapping America: Barriers to disabled people.* New York: Harper & Row.

Bowe, F. (1984). *Demography and disability: A chartbook for rehabilitation.* Fayetteville: Arkansas Rehabilitation Research and Training Center.

Braddock, D., & Heller, T. (1985). The closure of

mental retardation institutions I: Trends in the United States. *Mental Retardation, 23,* 168-176.

Brightman, A.J. (1984). *Ordinary moments: The disabled experience.* Baltimore, MD: University Park Press.

Brinker, R., & Thorpe, M. (1984). Integration of severely handicapped students and the proportion of IEP objectives achieved. *Exceptional Children, 51,* 168-175.

Brown, L., Ford, A., Nisbet, J., Sweet, M., Donnellan, A., & Gruenewald, L. (1983a). Opportunities available when severely handicapped students attend chronological age appropriate regular schools. *Journal of the Association for Persons with Severe Handicaps, 8*(1), 16-24.

Brown, L., Nisbet, J., Ford, A., Sweet, M., Shiraga, B., York, J., & Loomis, R. (1983b). The critical need for nonschool instruction in educational programs for severely handicapped students. *Journal of the Association for Persons with Severe Handicaps, 8*(3), 71-79.

Brown, L., Shiraga, B., Ford, A., Nisbet, J., VanDeventer, P., Sweet, M., York, J., & Loomis, R. (1986). Teaching severely handicapped students to perform meaningful work in nonsheltered vocational environments. In R.J. Morris & B. Blatt (Eds.), *Special education: Research and trends* (pp. 131-189). New York: Pergamon.

Bruininks, R.H., & Lakin, K.C. (Eds.) (1985). *Living and learning in the least restrictive environment.* Baltimore, MD: Paul Brookes.

Center on Human Policy. (1979). *The community imperative.* Syracuse, NY: Syracuse University, Author.

Certo, N., Haring, N., & York, R. (1984). *Public school integration of severely handicapped students.* Baltimore, MD: Paul Brookes.

City of Cleburne v. Cleburne Living Center, No. 84-468, Amicus Curiae brief, American Association on Mental Deficiency et al., U.S. Supreme Court (1984a).

City of Cleburne v., Cleburne Living Center, No. 84-468, Amicus Curiae brief, Association for Retarded Citizens; United States et al., U.S. Supreme Court (1984b).

Conley, R.W. (1985). Impact of federal programs on employment of mentally retarded persons. In K.C. Lakin & R.H. Bruininks (Eds.), *Strategies for achieving community integration of developmentally disabled citizens* (pp. 193-216). Baltimore, MD: Paul Brookes.

Conroy, J., Efthimiou, J., & Lemanowicz, J. (1982). A matched comparison of the developmental growth of institutionalized and deinstitutionalized mentally retarded clients. *American Journal of Mental Deficiency, 86,* 581-587.

Coon, M., Vogelsberg, R., & Williams, W. (1981). Effects of classroom public transportation instruction on generalization to the natural environment. *Journal of the Association for Persons with Severe Handicaps, 6*(2), 46-53.

Developmentally Disabled Assistance and Bill of Rights Act, 42 U.S.C. (1975).

Dunn, L. (1968). Special education for the mildly retarded: Is much of it justifiable? *Exceptional Children, 35,* 5-22.

Edgerton, R.B., Bollinger, M., & Herr, B. (1984). The cloak of competence: After two decades. *American Journal of Mental Deficiency, 88,* 345-351.

Epple, W.A., Jacobs, J.W., & Janicki, M.P. (1985). Staffing ratios in public institutions for persons with mental retardation in the United States. *Mental Retardation, 23,* 115-124.

Goldstein, H., Moss, J.W., & Jordan, L. (1965). *The efficacy of special class training of the development of mentally retarded children* (U.S.D.E. Cooperative Research Report No. 619). Urbana: University of Illinois.

Gould, S.J. (1981). *The mismeasure of man.* New York: Norton.

Guralnick, M.J. (Ed.) (1978). *Early intervention and the integration of handicapped and nonhandicapped children.* Baltimore, MD: University Park Press.

Halle, J. (1982). Teaching functional language to the handicapped. An integrative model of natural environment teaching techniques. *Journal of the Association for Persons with Severe Handicaps, 7*(4), 29-37.

Hemming, H., Lavender, T., & Pill, R. (1981). Quality of life of mentally retarded adults transferred from large institutions to small units. *American Journal of Mental Deficiency, 86,* 157-169.

Hull, J.T., & Thompson, J.C. (1980). Predicting adaptive functioning of mentally retarded persons in community settings. *American Journal of Mental Deficiency, 85,* 253-261.

Hunt, P., Goetz, L., & Anderson, J. (1986). The quality of IEP objectives associated with placement on integrated versus segregated school sites. *Journal of the Association for Persons with Severe Handicaps, 11*(2), 125-130.

Intagliata, J.C., Wilder, B.S., & Cooley, F.B. (1979). Cost comparison of institutional and community based alternatives for mentally retarded persons. *Mental Retardation, 17,* 154-156.

Kabalik, J.S., Furry, W.S., Thomas, M.A., & Carney, M.F. (1981). *The cost of special education.* Santa Monica, CA: Rand Corporation.

Karuth, D. (1985). If I were a car, I'd be a lemon. In A.J. Brightman (Ed.), *Ordinary moments: The disabled experience* (pp. 9-31). Baltimore, MD: University Park Press.

Kaye, N. (1981). Nancy Kaye. In W. Roth (Ed.), *The handicapped speak* (pp. 49-69). Jefferson, NC: McFarland.

Knoblock, P. (1981). *Teaching and mainstreaming autistic children.* Denver: Love.

Kriegel, L. (1969). Uncle Tom and Tiny Tim: Some reflections on the cripple as Negro. *The American Scholar, 38,* 412-430.

Kugel, R.B., & Shearer, A. (1976). *Changing patterns in residential services for the mentally retarded.* Washington, DC: President's Committee on Mental Retardation.

Kugel, R.B. & Wolfensberger, W. (Eds.) (1969). *Changing patterns in residential services for the mentally retarded.* Washington, DC: President's Committee on Mental Retardation.

Lakin, K.C., & Bruininks, R.H. (Eds.) (1985). *Strategies for achieving community integration of developmentally disabled citizens.* Baltimore, MD: Paul Brookes.

Liberty, K., Haring, N., & Martin, M. (1981). Teaching new skills to the severely handicapped. *Journal of the Association for Persons with Severe Handicaps, 6*(1), 5-13.

Mercer, J. (1973). *Labeling and mentally retarded.* Berkeley: University of California Press.

Parham v. J.R. 442 U.S. 584 (1978).

Raynes, N.V. (1980). The less you've got the less you get: Functional grouping, a cause for concern. *Mental Retardation, 18,* 217-220.

Roncker v. Walters, 70 F. 2d 1058 (6th Cir. 1983).

Roth, W. (1981). *The handicapped speak.* Jefferson, NC: McFarland.

Rothman, D., & Rothman, S.M. (1984). *The Willowbrook wars.* New York: Harper & Row.

Sarason, S., & Doris, J. (1969). *Psychological problems in mental deficiency* (4th ed.). New York: Harper & Row.

Schalock, R.L., Harper, R.S., & Genung, T. (1981). Community integration of mentally retarded adults: Community placement and program success. *American Journal of Mental Deficiency, 85,* 478-488.

Seltzer, G.B. (1981). Community residential adjustment: The relationship among environment, performance, and satisfaction. *American Journal of Mental Deficiency, 85,* 624-630.

Sokol-Kessler, L.E., Conroy, J., Feinstein, C.S., Lemanowicz, J.A., & McCurrin, M. (1983). Developmental progress in institutional and community settings. *Journal of the Association for Persons with Severe Handicaps, 8*(3), 43-48.

Stainback, W., & Stainback, S. (1984). A rationale for the merger of special and regular education. *Exceptional Children 51,* 102-111.

Szasz, T. (1961). *The myth of mental illness.* Garden City, NY: Doubleday Anchor.

Szasz, T. (1970). *The manufacture of madness.* New York: Harper & Row.

Taylor, S.J. & Ferguson, D. (1985). A summary of strategies utilized in model programs and resource materials. In S. Stainback & W. Stainback (Eds.), *Integration of students with severe handicaps into regular schools* (pp. 125-145). Reston, VA: ERIC Clearinghouse on Handicapped and Gifted Children, Council for Exceptional Children.

Taylor, S.J., Biklen, D., & Knoll, J. (1987). *Community integration for people with severe disabilities.* New York: Teachers College Press.

Taylor, S.J., McCord, W., & Searl, S.J. (1981). Medicaid dollars and community homes: The community ICF/MR controversy. *Journal of the Association for Persons with Severe Handicaps, 6*(3), 59-64.

Taylor, S., Racino, J., Knoll, J., & Lutfiyya, Z. (1986). *The nonrestrictive environment: A resource manual on community integration for people with the most severe disabilities.* (Community Integration Project Report). Syracuse, NY: Syracuse University, Center on Human Policy.

Tomlinson, S. (1982). *The sociology of special education.* Boston: Routledge & Kegan Paul.

Towfighy-Hooshyar, N. & Zingle, H. (1984). Regular-class students' attitudes toward integrated multiply handicapped peers. *American Journal of Mental Deficiency, 88,* 630-637.

U.S. Department of Education (1985). *Seventh annual report to Congress on the implementation of Public Law 94-142: The Education for All Handicapped Children Act.* Washington, DC: Author.

U.S. Department of Education (1986). *Eighth annual report to Congress on the implementation of the Education of the Handicapped Act.* Washington, DC: Author.

Voeltz, L. (1982). Effects of structured interactions with severely handicapped peers on children's attitudes. *American Journal of Mental Deficiency, 86,* 180-190.

Wang, M., & Birch, J. (1984). Comparison of a full-time mainstreaming program and a resource room approach. *Exceptional Children, 51,* 33-44.

Wehman, P., Hill, M., Goodall, P., Cleveland, P., Brooks, V., & Pentecost, J. (1982). Job placement and follow-up of moderately and severely handicapped individuals after three years. *Journal of the Association for Persons with Severe Handicaps, 7*(2), 5-16.

Wilcox, B., & Bellamy, G. (1982). *Design of high school programs for severely handicapped students.* Baltimore, MD: Paul Brookes.

Will, M. (1985, January). Least restrictive environment. In *Topical Conference on Least Restrictive Environment.* Washington, DC: U.S. Department of Education.

Youngberg v. Romeo, 457 U.S. 307 (1982).

Substance Abuse Among People with Disabilities: A Problem of Too Much Accessibility

Bobby G. Greer

During the last half of the 1970's and particularly the early part of the 1980's, much was written about the problems faced by disabled people in entering the "mainstream" of society. Problems of architectural, educational, and vocational accessibility were explored in depth by DeLoach and Greer (1981) and Vash (1981). These societal barriers were presented as unjust since they prevented fulfillment of life goals by persons with various types of disabilities. One problem often associated with disabilities, but seldom openly discussed, is the prevalence of, and problems associated with, alcohol and drug abuse among the disabled population.

The reason for overlooking such problems seems clear. Physical or mental disabilities have enough social stigmata attached to them without adding the extra stigma of substance abuse or chemical dependence. Also, the tendency of the public to generalize negative impressions of persons with disabilities discourages professionals from making too much of this issue. Yet, substance abuse among persons with physical or mental disabilities is seriously threatening the rehabilitation potential of a sizeable segment of this population. Recently, an entire issue of **Alcohol Health and Research World** (Winter, 1980-81) was devoted to what was termed the "multidisabled" (i.e., substance abuse problems among persons with physical or mental disabilities). This article will explore the extent of substance abuse among the disabled population, examine some of the possible reasons that such problems exist, and propose some general strategies by which rehabilitation professionals can assist in arresting the increase of such problems.

Prevalence of the Problem

In their survey of American drinking patterns, Cahalan, Cisin, and Crossley (1964) estimate that 12% of American men and 29% of American women used some form of psychotrophic drug. If these two sources are used as baseline use patterns for the general population, then studies to be cited later indicate that such prevalence of alcohol and drug use in some disability groups is significantly higher. Hindman and Widem (1980-81) stated : "The multi-disabled alcoholic——suffering from the disability of alcoholism in combination with at least one other physical or mental disability——is only beginning to emerge as the focus for integrated prevention, outreach, and treatment programming" (p. 5). Although accurate in terms of the need for integrated treatment programs, this statement might lead one to believe that the multidisabled alcoholic is a newly emerging phenomenon. However, Hopkins (1971) cited a source from as early as 1969 which listed alcoholism and drug abuse as one type of suicide. The study in question involved 4.738 Danish war amputees. Of this group, 63 committed suicide, a rate 37.7% greater than the general male population of that country. Of the suicides in this sample, alcohol or drug abuse played a role in 27% of the reported suicides.

Vash (1981) stated that alcoholism is a disorder resulting from the disabled client's need to distort an unpleasant reality. More alarming are figures arising from the empirical studies of clients in a vocational rehabilitation facility, found that 60% of 273 clients had experienced "problems related to alcohol" and 30% of their sample was categorized as "alcoholic." None of this sample had a primary disability relating to alcoholism. O'Donnell, Cooper, Gessner, Shehan, and Ashley (1981-82) reported a study in which alcohol and drug use were factors in 41 of 47 spinal cord injuries. Thirty-two of these spinal cord injured persons resumed alcohol or drug use after leaving the hospital. Hepner, Kirshbaum, and Landes (1980-81), in a study of

Reprinted from: *Journal of Rehabilitation*, Jan/Feb/Mar, 1986, with permission.

physically and mentally disabled clients at a center for independent living, found that 25% of the clients studied were abusing alcohol and/or drugs to the extent that such abuse led to social, mental, or physical dysfunctioning. Hindman and Widem (1980-81) cited a study which reported the incidence of alcohol problems to be 25% among workers at the California Lighthouse for the Blind. DiNitto and Krishef (1983-84), in a study of 214 mentally retarded persons, found a much lower incidence of alcohol-related problems than the previous cited studies of other disability groups. They found that 111 of the mentally retarded subjects (52%) had consumed some type of alcoholic beverage. Of the group reporting to have drunk, only seven (7%) reported drinking daily. But, since daily drinking might not necessarily be abuse, this study did not reveal a significantly greater incidence of abusive drinking among mentally retarded persons. However, 23% of the drinkers reported taking some type of anti-convulsant medication. And, when taken in combination, alcohol and anti-convulsants compound the sedative effect of one another.

O'Farrell, Connors, and Upper (1983) surveyed a psychiatric population of a Veteran's Administration hospital. These investigators found that 32.8% of the patients studied had definite problems with alcohol and 4.6% were abusing drugs. This study specifically excluded patients in wards specializing in the treatment of drug or alcohol problems. They stated, "The prevalence of alcohol abuse problems in this sample is triple the general population and much higher than was found in a previous report on a similar sample" (p. 332).

Thus, alcohol and drug problems appear to be significantly more prevalent among certain types of disability groups. What, then, are the reasons that such problems have a higher incidence among certain disabled groups? Possible reasons for the presence of alcohol and drug abuse among disabled people will be explored in the next section of this article.

Factors Influencing Substance Abuse

"I can't cure paralysis, but I can sure cure pain!" This was a statement made by a dedicated and most competent orthopaedic surgeon to one of the author's classes in **Medical Aspects of Rehabilitation**. It provides some insight into the dynamics by which disabled persons are frequently predisposed to drug abuse. This physician stated that, to some degree, a patient with an amputation or paralysis represented a failure of medical science in his eyes. To compensate for the "guilt" resulting from such "failures", it appeared he would not hesitate to prescribe drugs to "ease their pain."

This rather blatant and candid statement seems to be verified by others in the medical field. Hepner, Kirshbaum, and Landes (1980-81) proposed four levels at which disabled people run a high risk for alcohol or drug abuse. The first "level" listed involves the easy access to prescription drugs due to real medical needs, such as muscle spasms, pain, or excessive spasticity. At a second level, these authors postulated that the excessive amount of frustration experienced by persons with disabilities predisposes them to "choosing an escape" through the use of prescription or illegal drugs or alcohol. The third level proposed by Hepner, Kirshbaum and Landes was that people with disabilities represent "an oppressed minority" and, as such, appear to search for relief from such oppression through chemicals. The last level was that drug and/or alcohol abuse is often the result of medical intervention. Forty-one percent of their sample reported having been prescribed drugs that they did not feel they needed. The author has often heard physicians state that "a glass of wine" is, perhaps, the most effective muscle relaxant for persons with cerebral palsy.

O'Donnel et al (1981-82) also implicate family members, as well as medical personnel and attendants, in enabling persons with disabilities to engage in substance abuse. They stated that: "Guilt also produces placatory behaviors, as family members accede to the patient's request for alcohol so the patient can experience 'something pleasurable'.... hospital personnel, in addition to family members often condone alcohol use. They do this to avoid hostile encounters with patients as well as to cope with their own frustrations" (p. 29).

Glass (1980-81) presented a unique taxonomy of the origins of problem drinking among visually impaired people. He described Type A drinkers and Type B drinkers. In Type A's, problem drinking **predates** visual disability while, Type B's begin problem drinking **after** the onset of disability. Glass conceptualized the major problem of adjustment to disability in general, and visual impairment in particular, as falling within the domain of stress theory. Adapting to the multiple problems of movement and mobility, personal care and hygiene, tool use, and communication all place excessive and stressful demands on the individual. Such stresses eventually result in feelings of frustration, lessened control over one's immediate environment, and helplessness.

One type of reaction that visually impaired people have to such stress, according to Glass (1981), is overidentification with the blind, a form of **positive identification.** In this form, the tasks of adapting to restrictions in mobility, self-care, and reading is readily accepted. On the other hand, having been overly exposed to negative stereotypes of the visually impaired, some individuals, once they become visually disabled, feel stigmatized, helpless, or dependent. Both Type A's and Type B's share a common conceptualization that alcohol use is an acceptable coping tool for adapting to the enhanced stress of visual impairment. However, due to their likelihood of accepting new strategies for skill training and attitude modification, Type B's have a better chance for total rehabilitation than Type A's. That is, Type A's will need rehabilitaiton strategies specifically designed for alcohol abuse.

Recalling the findings of O'Donnell et al (1981-82), Glass's taxonomy could apply to persons with spinal cord injury. That is, since 62% of their clients had abused drugs or alcohol at the time of their initial injury, it is safe to assume that a significant proportion of this sample was experiencing some problems with drugs or alcohol before their injuries, thus falling into Glass's Type A category. It would have been interesting if O'Donnel, et al had ascertained what segment of their sample initiated drug or alcohol abuse **after** their injury. This would have revealed what proportion of their

sample could be classified as Type B's. In a more generic sense, the Type A-Type B classification could apply to any adventitiously disabled person, regardless of the specific nature of the disability. Further research into this area would be wise to include classifying drug or alcohol abusing clients regarding the pre- or post-disability onset of their abuse. For example, Anderson (1980-81) stated:

Another complication to substance abuse treatment is the fact that few of our clients have dealt with their injury, which may have been connected with or caused by substance abuse ... We have found that the people who come to us for substance abuse treatment often were injured while under the influence of alcohol or drugs and had, prior to injury, a very low self esteem. They were using alcohol and drugs before the injury to help themselves feel better about themselves and this pattern has continued or possibly escalated (p. 38).

Wenc (1980-81) discussed the influence of the deinstitutionalization movement on alcohol use and abuse among mildly retarded individuals. This movement has sought to move many such persons from the institution back into the community. Initially, such persons experience isolation and loneliness in the community, particularly if they do not move back into a family situation. In many communities, the local tavern is the center for socialization, and retarded persons discover an acceptance in the tavern lacking in other parts of the community. Wenc cited a series of interviews with mildly retarded individuals who were queried regarding their reason for frequenting taverns. The following are direct quotes from these interviews: "They like me there;" "I'm accepted;" "People know me there;" "When I'm drunk, I'm just like everyone else;" and "In the bar I can be myself."

Before the reader is too quick to get the idea that the majority of deinstitutionalization retarded individuals spend all their time in bars, it should be pointed out that, in their study of drinking patterns of mentally retarded persons, DiNitto and

Krishef (1983-84) found the majority of their sample (52%) drank at home, while only 30% reported they drank primarily in bars.

Proposed Intervention Strategies

Lowenthal and Anderson (1980-81) and Anderson (1980-81) described the general difficulties and barriers encountered in attempting to establish an integrated substance abuse treatment program for disabled people. According to these sources, both architectural and attitudinal barriers exist among substance abuse agencies that are treating physically disabled people. The organizations for persons who are physically disabled, particularly advocacy groups, are reluctant to be too zealous in pursuing needed services for fear of burdening disabled people with an additional stigma of alcoholic or drug addict. Lowenthal and Anderson (1980-81) cited a source which, in speaking of services for the deaf, stated that: "They already have shared the stigma, 'deaf and dumb'; now they shrink from any imposition of the added label of 'deaf and drunk'" (p. 17). Anderson (1980-81) suggested that, in addition to architectural and attitudinal barriers, most alcohol or drug abuse treatment programs are unable to accommodate abusers with spinal cord injuries (SCI) because most such treatment programs begin their day at an hour totally unsuitable for the person who requires two hours to dress and eat. They indicated that: "At the SCI program, the scheduled activities start at 9 A.M., considerably later than in a ambulatory program, because the substance abuse treatment counsellors recognize that a quadriplegic may take between 2 and 4 hours to get out of bed, usually via a lift device, and to accomplish bowel care, showering, grooming and dressing" (p. 38). Both of these sources recommend establishing community networks to promote a close working relationship between the organizations serving people with physical disabilities and those working in the area of substance abuse treatment.

A key ingredient in establishing an integrated approach to serving the multidisabled substance abuser will require the education of professionals from the two fields regarding the nature of the other. Antiquated and inaccurate concepts held by substance abuse personnel regarding persons with disabilities should be dealt with and corrected. The fear of additional stigma and the "such problems don't exist" attitude of many professional personnel in the area of physically disabling conditions should be eradicated through similar educational efforts.

On a much wider scale, a "counter-enabling" effort should be the thrust of awareness programs for all persons directly involved in the rehabilitation of the physically disabled substance abuser. According to Carnes (1983), "Enab-ling ... stems from denial and rationalization. covering up for the addict, protecting him or her from the consequences, and keeping silent about personal concerns are the behavioral ingredients of enabling. It involves a fundamental dishonesty which entails the insane denial of what one knows to be true" (p. 102). Thus, when a rehabilitation counsellor suspects a client has an alcohol or drug problem, but tells himself or herself such an assertion on his or her part would be "too sensitive or personal," the counsellor is engaging in enabling behavior. Each time a physician writes a prescription for a tranquillizer for a disabled client instead of examining closely the client's need for such medication, the physician is an enabler. Milam and Ketchum (1981) quoted a physician who explained why it is so easy to just write a prescription simply in terms of time and economy. The physician stated: "...just before leaving the patient says, 'Oh by the way, Dr. Brown gives me Valium, but he's out of town. Would you write me a prescription for 100?!' She is as uncomfortable about asking as I am about refusing. It takes 30 seconds to write the prescription and 30 minutes not to. Now I have to make a hard choice on a busy afternoon when I'm already behind schedule" (p. 178). The particular physician was speaking in regard to a nondisabled patient. How much more uncomfortable and uncaring would he feel about refusing such a request by a patient who is deaf, quadriplegic, or paraplegic?

Counter-enabling education must then start by introducing members of the rehabilitation team to the basic signs and symptoms of alcohol or drug abuse. Marden (1979) has proposed a formalized measure of alcohol abuse. Although this system concentrates on the abuse of alcohol, if one substituted the phrase, "taking drugs" in the place of "drinking," such criteria apply equally to drug abuse. Marden (1979) listed 11 major problem areas. These areas are:

1. Frequent intoxication (drink or drug induced)
2. Binge drinking (drugging)
3. Symptomatic drinking
4. Psychological dependence
5. Problems with spouse or relatives
6. Problems with friends or neighbors
7. Job problems
8. Problems with law, police, accidents
9. Health problems
10. Financial problems
11. Belligerence (p. 5)

Marden (1979) offered operational definitions of all 11 "signs" in his proposal, and stated that persons receiving a 7+ score have serious problems with alcohol or drugs. Alcoholics Anonymous (1973), in an information pamphlet, lists 12 questions they ask persons to answer honestly regarding themselves. If the person answers any four in an affirmative manner, such a person is experiencing serious difficulties with substance abuse. These questions are:

1. Have you ever decided to stop drinking for a week or so, but only lasted for a couple of days?
2. Do you wish people would mind their own business about your drinking—— stop telling you what to do?
3. Have you ever switched from one kind of drink to another in the hope that this would keep you from getting drunk?
4. Have you had to have an eye-opener upon awakening during the past year?
5. Do you envy people who can drink without getting into trouble?
6. Have you had problems connected with your drinking during the past year?
7. Has your drinking caused trouble at home?
8. Do you ever try to get 'extra' drinks at a party because you do not get enough?
9. Do you tell yourself you can stop drinking any time you want to, even though

you keep getting drunk when you don't mean to?
10. Have you missed days of work or school because of drinking?
11. Do you have "blackouts?"
12. Have you ever felt your life would be better if you did not drink? (Alcoholics Anonymous, 1973).

Again, the term "drug use" or a comparable phrase could be substituted in the questions to ascertain problems with drugs *per se*. Persons in the physical/mental rehabilitation field should be instructed in using these and other similar strategies for determining the severity of substance abuse problems in the client population. Such instruction must be provided by persons knowledgeable in the field of substance abuse. Then, confrontational strategies should be outlined. Such strategies would be designed to cut through the alibi system of the abuser so that he or she has to face the reality of his or her abuse. The alibi system of the true abuser is most formidable and, with multidisabled abusers, their disability and its related stress is at the core of the system. Each team member must be aware of such rationalizing strategy. A sympathetic (enabling) response from any team member might undo much of the progress made in dealing with the substance abuse problem by once more reinforcing the abuser's rationalization.

Finally, effective treatment programs, accessible in every sense of the term, must begin to be established. An ideal facility would not only be architecturally accessible, but have substance abuse reading material that is usable by both the hearing and visually impaired. An example of such material would be the 12 steps of Alcoholics anonymous written for the deaf as presented by Watson, Boros, and Zrimec (1979-80). Some deaf persons, due to deficits in language development, are unable to fully relate to some of the abstract concepts presented in the traditional version of the 12 steps of Alcoholics Anonymous. Therefore, the version presented by Watson et al is more appropriate for such persons. Such programs also need to be staffed with specially trained personnel who can readily deal with the compound problems presented by the physically/mentally disabled abuser.

Conclusion and Recommendations

This article has presented some findings in regard to the possible extent of substance abuse problems among physically and mentally disabled people. Although such problems exist, the reader of this article should not conclude that most disabled persons have problems with alcohol and drugs; such a conclusion would be a grave injustice to both the reader and the disabled citizenry of this country. Many disabled persons must take certain psychotropic medications for valid medical reasons. Many disabled persons go to parties, drink and socialize, and have no particular problems. These persons are not drug addicted or alcoholic! There are physically and mentally disabled individuals who use drugs and/or alcohol, but do not manifest a significant number of the problems outlined above. Others, however, do; and these are the persons toward which this article has attempted to focus attention. Implied throughout this article has been the fact that such problems are very complex and there are no simple answers. The true intent of this article was heuristic to the extent that more research and attention should be focused on this problem area, not to cast doubts on the character of the clients to be served, but only to ensure that they are served in a comprehensive way.

In order to provide such comprehensive services, it is recommended that the following efforts be expanded and or initiated:

1. Conduct further research into the prevalence of substance abuse in the disabled population.
2. Conduct a thorough search for special methods and materials for substance abuser with disabilities.
3. Develop other such methods and materials where needed.
4. If at all possible, develop accessibility for various disability groups to substance abuse programs for the nondisabled so that disabled abusers receive treatment in the "mainstream."
5. Provide training for certain substance abuse personnel in order that they may be more effective with the multidisabled substance abuser.
6. Provide training for general rehabilitation personnel so that they are more sensitive and alert to possible substance abuse problems in their clientele.
7. Establish "counter-enabling" training for rehabilitation personnel.
8. Finally, and most importantly, institute alcohol and drug awareness programs for rehabilitation clients so that they can have more awareness of the choices available to them with regard to alcohol and drug use.

Nineteen eighty-one was designated the International Year of the Disabled. One of the goals was to advance the status of disabled people in the "mainstream" of society. Such a status is now being undermined by the presence of another more tragic disability, and this threat to their status must be met now. Failure to face the problems outlined in this article would negate many of the advances achieved in the last two decades. By implementing the above recommendations, such a threat might be dealt with more effectively.

Concerns of Persons with Cancer as Perceived by Cancer Patients, Physicians, and Rehabilitation Counselors

CELESTE M. TAYLOR AND JACK R. CRISLER

In 1983 an estimated 855,000 people in the United states were diagnosed as having cancer (excluding nonmelanoma skin cancer and carcinoma in situ). Of that number, approximately three of eight will survive the disease and still be living in 1988 (American Cancer Society, 1982). This survival rate notwithstanding, it is a commonly held belief that a diagnosis of cancer is synonymous with death (Burns, 1982).

This spectre of death is only one of many factors the person with cancer must learn to handle in living with this disease. Among other considerations, the loneliness, pain, fatigue, lack of control, loss of independence, and financial drain can be so overwhelming that the person with cancer becomes immobilized by fear and dread. These factors can be compounded by feelings of alienation, even from those closest to the person with cancer.

The stigma associated with having cancer does not seem to apply to people dealing with other life-threatening conditions, such as heart disease. Although the leading cause of death in the United States, heart disease appears to be an acceptable way to live with death, cancer is not. Ironically, almost twice as many people die each year from heart disease as from cancer (Silverberg & Lubera, 1983).

Consider the contrast of reactions to Mr. Smith and Mr. Jones, each of whom faced a life-threatening disease: Mr. Smith received a successful coronary bypass, and for him there was celebration and rejoicing among family, friends, and employer. Mr. Jones, on the other hand, had a bowel resection to remove a malignant tumour of the colon; there was no evidence of metastasis. Yet, for this person with cancer, there was little celebration. In fact, many friends didn't come by at all or, when they did, the conversation was awkward, stilted, and approached with dread. Why was news of the former so much better received than that of the latter? It had nothing to do with facts and everything to do with feelings.

Unfortunately, the subsequent impact of those feelings on the rehabilitation of the person with cancer can be tremendous.

The emotional strain of dealing with cancer has been documented again and again (Kaplan, 1983; Keeling, 1976; Klein, 1971; Moster, 1979; O'Neill, 1975; Rosenbaum, 1975; Sobel & Worden, 1982; Sveinson, 1977). Yet current medical management for cancer typically focuses on the physical aspects of the disease, not the emotional, particularly in the early treatment process. In fact, there appears to be a lack of awareness within the medical and rehabilitation professions of the need for psychosocial intervention in persons with cancer.

Statistically, the survival rate for persons with cancer has risen from on out of three in the 1960s to three out of eight in the 1980s, with 40,000 more persons surviving cancer in 1983 (American Cancer Society, 1982). Although the need for these survivors of cancer to participate in rehabilitation efforts is well-documented, evidence indicates such is not often the case.

Between 1971 and 1979, the number of successful closures on persons with cancer increased in the state/federal rehabilitation program from 1,000 to 1,566, a 55% increase in eight years. However, when viewed in light of the more than 250,000 rehabilitation clients served and closed rehabilitated in each of those years, the state/federal program had a closure rate on clients diagnosed with cancer of less than 1% in its **best** year (Goldberg & Habeck, 1982; Mcaleer & Kluge, 1978). It has been shown that the rehabilitation of persons with cancer compared to that of other disability categories (heart disease, mental disorders, diabetes, tuberculosis, and orthopaedic problems) is cost effective, requiring the lowest expenditures for successful closure than other compared disability groups (McAleer & Kluge, 1978). Yet, time and again the literature indicates that personal bias on the part of the rehabilitation counsellor is a primary

Reprinted from: *Journal of Rehabilitation Jan/Feb/Mar 1988*, with permission.

deterrent to working with the client who has survived cancer (Cromes, 1978; Goldberg & Habeck, 1982; McAleer, 1975; Pinkerton & Nelson, 1978; Sanford, Bluhm, & Glover, 1978).

In light of these facts, the purpose of this study was to first determine whether there was a difference between the overall expressed needs of persons with cancer and the perception of those needs on the part of physicians and state rehabilitation counsellors. The needs of persons with cancer were further delineated into two general categories of (a) need for counselling and (b) expression of emotion. A second purpose of this study was to determine whether there were differences in perceptions among persons with cancer, physicians, and rehabilitaiton counsellors, with regard to those two need categories.

Methodology

Subjects
The subjects participating in this study came from three distinct groups: (a) persons diagnosed with cancer who were receiving medical treatment and/or were under doctor's observation at the time of the survey, (b) physicians who were practising in the same geographical area as that in which the cancer patients' treatment was being provided, and (c) state rehabilitaiton counsellors assigned to the same general geographical area as that in which the cancer patients were residing. The sample of persons with cancer (N = 50) was selected randomly from the patient population of a oncologist. The physician population surveyed (N = 122) was comprised of members of the area medical society. The rehabilitation counsellors sampled (N = 61) were from two districts of the Georgia Division of Rehabilitation Services in the same general geographical area as the persons with cancer and the physicians who were surveyed.

Demographic data collected from the sample populations included the following items: (a) **persons with cancer** - age, sex, living arrangement, marital status, status of cancer, type of cancer, and date of first diagnosis of cancer; (b) **physicians** - age, sex, years in occupation, medical specialty, whether they had dealt professionally with persons with cancer, whether they

or a member of their immediate family had ever had cancer, type of cancer, and date of diagnosis of cancer; (c) **rehabilitation counsellors** - age, sex, years in occupation, area of specialty, whether they or a member of their immediate family had ever had cancer, type of cancer, and date of diagnosis of cancer.

Instruments
The survey of Concerns of Persons with Cancer (SCPC) is a 38-item paper-and-pencil instrument that was constructed specifically for the purposes of this study. Each item is in the form of a statement regarding a possible area of concern or need faced by persons with cancer. The 38 SCPC statements are responded to on a Likert scale format, with five possible response choices: never, not very often, sometimes, often, and most of the time. Completion of the SCPC takes less than 15 minutes.

The SCPC began as a list of 114 statements developed from situations described in personal accounts of individuals with cancer (Moster, 1979; Rosenbaum, 1975; Sveinson, 1977). From the list of 114 statements, duplications were deleted, and the list was reduced to 75. The 75 items were then appraised as to the level of importance by four individuals who had lost a close family member to cancer. The resulting list of 43 items were randomly ordered. The 40-item survey was then submitted to 10 individuals who had personal or professional experiences with cancer for a review of the content of the 40 items. Their responses indicated that the 40 items were indeed areas of concern to persons with cancer. The oncology professionals, however, recommended the deletion of two items concerning the emotional and physical assault caused by medical treatment; their recommendations were heeded, resulting in the final list of 38 items.

The survey of Concerns of Persons with Cancer was made available in two forms, one for persons with cancer (SCPC-I), and one for professionals who dealt with persons that had cancer (SCPC-II). Both surveys were virtually identical in content and format. The primary difference was the personalized nature of the SCPC-I for persons with cancer ("I need counselling") as opposed to the more generic nature of the SCPC-II for professionals dealing with persons who had cancer ("People with cancer need counselling").

Of the 38 items in the two forms of the SCPC, a majority appeared to fall naturally into two content areas: (a) need for counselling and (b) expression of emotion. However, in order to systematically determine category placements, the SCPC was submitted to 10 members of the counselling faculty at the University of Georgia who were asked to categorize each of the 38 items as either "emotional" or "counselling," according to the following guidelines:

> Emotional (E) - Statements in this category were described as expressions of emotions or feelings which were a direct result of having to deal with the disease and effects of cancer;

> Counselling (C) - Statements in this category were described as indications of the need or desire for counselling, guidance, information, or advice on how to deal with the disease and effects of cancer.

This type of categorization was felt to be important since a person with cancer might express emotions associated with the disease, yet not indicate a need or desire for counselling or advice. Conversely, a person with cancer might indicate a need or desire for counselling or information, and yet not be able to freely express the emotions that often accompany the disease. By categorizing the items, it was possible to identify not only particular concerns of persons with cancer but also the concentration of those concerns.

The responses from the counselling faculty regarding more of the faculty members agreed were indicative of a need for counselling, and 23 items that seven or more of the faculty members agreed were expressions of emotions. The remaining six items did not receive the required 70% agreement as to content and, therefore, remained uncategorized.

Procedure

Form I of the SCPC was randomly administered to persons with cancer being seen in the office of a local oncologist. Although one of the authors was available to provide assistance in filling out the instrument, the physician's staff actually handled the distribution and collection of most of the instruments.

Form II of the SCPC was distributed by mail to physician members of the local medical society and to rehabilitation counsellors in the geographical area. All of the mailings were accompanied by stamped, self-addressed envelopes for return. Although all of the data were collected through anonymous responses, the instruments were coded to keep them separate by type of respondent (e.g., physician or rehabilitaiton counsellor).

Method of Analysis

An analysis of variance was used to compare the results of group responses to the survey. The .0001 level of probability was employed as the criterion for determining significant differences among the three groups surveyed for each of the three dependent variables: need for counselling, expression of emotion, and overall expressed concerns. A post hoc comparison was performed on each of the dependent variables using Tukey's Studentized Range (HSD) test to determine between which groups the significance actually existed. An alpha level of .05 was used to determine significance between the mean scores per variable for each of the groups surveyed.

Results

A total of 161 instruments were returned from the sample populations surveyed: 50 persons with cancer, 61 from physicians, and 50 from rehabilitation counsellors. However, 11 of the instruments were incomplete and, therefore, not usable. Of the 150 persons whose responses to the survey instrument were deemed valid, there were 46 cancer patients, 56 physicians, and 48 rehabilitation counsellors.

Demographic Information

Persons with Cancer - The mean age for persons with cancer was 60.02 (two persons listed no age). There were 13 males, 31 females, and 2 persons who did not indicate their sex. Most of the respondents (35) lived with family members, with 8 living alone and 3 persons giving no indication of living arrangements. Two were single, 21 were married, three were divorced, 17 were widowed, and three did not provide their marital status. More than 20 types of cancer were listed, with breast cancer, multiple cancers, colon cancer, and pancreatic cancer being the most prevalent. The dates of cancer diagnosis ranged from the 1980s (32) to 1970 and before (4), with no clear onset date given for the 10 remaining persons.

Physicians - The mean age for physicians was 50.25 years among the 53 males and three females responding. The average length of time in medical practice was 21.3 years. There were 18 specialty areas listed, with Surgery (11), Ob-Gyn (9), and General Practice (6) being the most predominant specialities. Of the 56 physician respondents, a total of 55 had dealt professionally with someone who had cancer (one physician did not respond to this item). Also, 30 of the 56 indicated that they or a member of their immediate family had had cancer, with breast cancer, multiple cancers, lung cancer, and lymphoma being the most prevalent among the 15 types of cancer listed. The dates of cancer diagnosis ranged for the 1980s (10), to the 1970s (9), and before (5). The remaining dates of diagnosis were unclear.

Rehabilitation Counsellors - The mean age for rehabilitation counsellors was 41.33 years (three did not respond regarding age). Of the counsellors, 28 were male, 17 were female, and three gave no indication of gender. The average length of time in rehabilitation counselling was 12.6 years. Seven different specialization areas were listed, with a majority of the counsellors either carrying general caseloads, or giving no indication as to specialty. Of these respondents, 34 had dealt professionally with someone who had cancer, 13 had not, and one person did not respond. Like the physicians, 30 of the 48 respondents indicated that they or a member of their immediate family had had cancer, with 18 indicating no such experience. Among the types of cancer listed by counsellors, the most preva-

lent were lung cancer, multiple cancers, breast cancer, and lymphoma. Dates of diagnosis of cancer were 1980s (8), 1970s (10), and before 1970 (4). Multiple dates of diagnosis were given by four counsellors, and four other counsellors did not indicate a diagnosis date.

Statistical Analysis

A one-way analysis of variance was performed across the three groups (patients, physicians, and counsellors) for each of three dependent variables: Subtest C (23 items indicating Expression of Emotion), and the Total Survey (all 38 items of concern). Each analysis revealed a significant main effect at the .0001 level (see Table 1).

Table 1 Analysis of Variance Summaries			
Dependent Variable	df	MS	F
Subtest C (Need for Counseling)			
Between Ss	2	5.46170512	56.94*
Within Ss	147	0.09591314	
Subtest E (Expression of Emotion)			
Between Ss	2	14.71106107	94.24*
Within Ss	147	0.15610716	
Total Survey (All Concerns Listed)	2	9.44812387	104.24
Between Ss	147	0.09063665	*
* p < .0001			

Since a "significant F ratio by itself does not tell which of the group means are significantly different from the others" (Huck, Cormier, & Bounds, 1974, p. 67), a follow-up comparison was done using Tukey's Studentized Range (HSD) Test. Tukey's HSD is a conservative procedure used to assess the difference between two means. Therefore, if a significant difference is found using this procedure, it indicates there is indeed a significant difference. It should be noted that, in the analysis, any survey item omitted by an individual was not included in the N used to construct the means for those categories. Also, 12 of the 38 SCPC items were reverse coded to assure uniformity in scoring.

To answer the research question, "Is there a significant difference in the expressed and perceived need for counselling among persons with cancer?," comparisons were made between cancer patients, physicians, and state rehabilitation counsellors using Tukey's HSD procedure. The following results were obtained with regard to Subtest C (Need for Counselling):

(1) There was a significant difference, not only between the means of persons with cancer and physicians (p < .05), but also between the means of persons with cancer and state rehabilitation counsellors (p < .05), indicating that both physicians and rehabilitation counsellors perceived a greater need for counselling than cancer patients actually reported.

(2) There was not a significant difference between the means of physicians and state rehabilitation counsellors (p < .05) indicating that physicians and state rehabilitation counsellors were quite similar regarding their perceptions of the need for counselling among persons with cancer. Both groups perceived a greater need for counselling than was actually expressed by cancer patients.

The second research question, "Is there a significant difference in the expressed and perceived emotional state of persons with cancer?," was answered by analyzing responses from cancer patients, physicians, and rehabilitation counsellors using Tukey's HSD for comparison. Results regarding Subtest E (Expression of Emotion) were as follows:

(1) There was a significant difference between the means of cancer patients and physicians (p < .05) and between the means of cancer patients and state rehabilitation counsellors (p < .05) concerning expression of emotion. Both physicians and state rehabilitation counsellors perceived that expression of emotion occurred among cancer patients to a greater degree than what was actually reported by persons with cancer.

(2) The difference between the means of physicians and state rehabilitation counsellors was significant (p < .05), with rehabilitation counsellors perceiving the cancer patient's expression of emotion to occur to a greater degree than did the physicians.

The final research question, "Is there a significant difference between overall expressed concerns of persons with cancer and the perception of those concerns by others?," was addressed by using Tukey's HSD for post hoc comparison of responses from cancer patients, physicians, and state rehabilitation counsellors. The analysis provided the following results with regard to the Total Survey (all 38 items of concern):

(1) The differences between the means of cancer patients and physicians and between the means of cancer patients and state rehabilitation counsellors were significant at the .05 level, with both physicians and rehabilitation counsellors perceiving that overall expressed concerns of persons with cancer occurred to a greater degree than what was actually reported by the cancer patients themselves.

(2) The post hoc comparison on the difference between the means of physicians and state rehabilitation counsellors was significant at the .05 level, with state rehabilitation counsellors perceiving the cancer patient's overall expression of concerns occurring to a greater degree than physicians perceived it to occur.

Table 2 provides differences between the means on the three dependent variables by groups.

Discussion

The results obtained in this study were somewhat surprising, particularly the direction in which the differences actually occurred. Based on the review of literature, the authors thought that the cancer patient's report on overall concerns, as well as on the need for counselling and the expression of emotion, would occur more frequently than what was perceived by physicians or counsellors. However, the results of the data analysis indicate just the opposite.

Two considerations might be offered as possible causes for this occurrence. First, the instrument itself might have been constructed in such a way as to touch too strongly on sensitive areas that some cancer patients might have preferred not to address. On more than one occasion, the cancer patients failed to complete

Table 2
Tukey's Studentized Range (HSD) Test for Variables
Subtest C (Need for Counseling)

Means		Differences Between the Means		
		Patients 2.67	Physicians 3.28	Counselors 3.24
Patients:	2.67		-.60*	-0.56*
Physicians:	3.28	0.60*		0.04
Counselors:	3.24	0.56*	-0.04	

Subtest E (Expression of Emotion)

Means		Differences Between the Means		
		Patients 2.59	Physicians 3.38	Counselors 3.67
Patients:	2.59		-0.79*	-1.08*
Physicians:	3.38	0.79*		-.029*
Counselors:	3.67	1.08*	0.29*	

Total Survey (All Concerns Listed)

Means		Differences Between the Means		
		Patients 2.58	Physicians 3.24	Counselors 3.44
Patients:	2.58		-0.65*	-0.86*
Physicians:	3.24	0.65*		-0.20*
Counselors:	3.44	0.86*	0.20*	

* significant at the .05 level

the survey because it was too emotionally painful for them to do so. This reasoning can also be supported by the fact that more cancer patients omitted responses to items on the survey than either of the other two respondent groups. One might, therefore, question whether all patients who actually did respond to the SCPC-I gave answers that were in accord with their true feelings. It is certainly possible that a denial process might have entered into the responses of some, if not most, of the cancer patients. In the present study the participating oncologist frequently suggested that a more accurate picture could be gathered of his patients' concerns by simply talking with them rather than requesting them to respond to an impersonal survey instrument. In light of the results, his suggestions definitely have merit.

A second possible cause for the cancer patients' self-report on overall concerns (as well as on their need for counselling and their emotional state) being lower than expected might

be that the patients simply were not as distressed by these areas of concern as previously thought. However, one must doubt this line of reasoning when considering the strong argument to the contrary presented in the literature by cancer patients themselves. Indeed, Sobel and Worden (1982) have shown that a large enough percentage of cancer patients do experience sufficient distress with this disease to warrant psychosocial intervention.

The one negative finding in this study ——that there was not a significant difference between the perceptions of physicians and of state rehabilitation counsellors with regard to the cancer patient's need for counselling——is quite encouraging. The authors had thought that physicians would not acknowledge the cancer patient's need for counselling to the degree that state rehabilitaiton counsellors would. However, physicians actually indicated a stronger expectation for the cancer patient's need for counselling than did the counsellors themselves.

Even though studies have shown that physician attitudes have become more positive about the cancer patient's own ability to handle the stresses of cancer (Blanchard, Ruckdeschel, cohen, Shaw, McSharry, & Horton, 1981; Cohen, Ruckdeschel, Blanchard, Rohrbaugh, & Horton, 1982; Haley, Huyng, Paiva, & Juan, 1977; Kaye, Appel, & Joseph, 1981), the above results support the belief that physicians are not totally ignoring the cancer patient's need for support in coping. In fact, in the present study, the physician's positive response to the cancer patient's need for counselling can be interpreted as a willingness on the part of the physician to acknowledge the effects of this disease which go beyond the practice of medicine.

Since 53.5% of physicians responding to the SCPC-II had personal experiences with cancer in addition to professional involvement, it is possible that their responses with regard to the need for counselling were influenced by having had cancer themselves or by having seen it in a member of their immediate family. Likewise, experiences of 63.5% of the state rehabilitation counsellors responding to the survey might have been affected by their also having had cancer or having seen it in a member of their immediate family. Concerns included in both Subtest E (Expression of Emotion) and the Total Survey (all concerns listed) were believed to occur to a greater degree among persons with cancer by state rehabilitation counsellors than by physicians. Since physicians must exclude as much of the emotional as possible in order to cope with the stress of serving persons with cancer (Rosser & Maguire, 1982), these results are not surprising.

Conclusions

Persons with cancer encounter a multitude of problems, not the least of which is the emotional upheaval that seems ever present, particularly in the early stages of diagnosis and treatment. Even if the person with cancer is able to cope with the threat of death from the disease, there is still concern about the cancer patient's ability to continue work while undergoing treatment or return to work once medical treatment has been completed. This study has shown that physicians and rehabilitation counsellors alike are aware of many of the concerns held by persons with cancer. Also, it has been shown that both professions acknowledge the cancer patient's need for assistance in this regard. The question now is, "How can we help?"

Because the treatment of cancer is a highly technical field, it is often conducted in regional or metropolitan medical centers which specialize in the practice of oncology. Likewise, because the provision of rehabilitation services is a specialized profession, it is also often headquartered in regional or district offices. However, it is out of these rehabilitation offices that counsellors are assigned to cover **all** the territory of **every** state. The networking is already in place for rehabilitation to reach the person with cancer. All that is left is for rehabilitation specialists to take those few extra steps to communicate to the medical professionals **who** we are and **what** we are able

to do for their patients. If the results of this study hold any accuracy at all, then the physicians contacted will not only be aware of the need for our services among their patients, they will also be supportive of our efforts to offer those services.

What then are the services we can provide to persons with cancer? Simply enough, they are the same services we offer to any of our other clients: guidance in making appropriate vocational decisions, counselling in learning to cope with their disabling condition, training and/or medical services where needed, and placement services, including intervention with employers who are sceptical of the cancer client's ability to maintain a regular work schedule. Rehabilitation specialists are as qualified to serve persons with cancer as they are to serve persons with diabetes, mental retardation, quadriplegia, depression, dyslexia, or any other condition which is a handicap. We just need to confront and overcome our own fears about cancer and then move ahead to **actively** solicit the medical community for referrals of persons with cancer.

The purpose of rehabilitation has always been to strengthen the positive and diminish the negative in order to provide every opportunity for an individual with a disabling condition to live as nearly normal a life as possible. Properly utilized, rehabilitation services for people with cancer can complement the medical management of this disease and can help provide precious time by freeing the mind, the body, and the spirit from unnecessary fears and concerns. Offering these services is not a simple task, but it is not an impossible one, either. However, it is a task yet to be done.

The question remains: "Are the medical community and the rehabilitation profession ready to meet the challenge?" Many persons with cancer are waiting for an answer.

Role of Orientation and Mobility Specialist in the Deinstitutionalization of Multi-Handicapped Blind Persons

MARGARET VON SCHNEDEN AND STEVEN CRECCO

Abstract
This article describes the role of orientation and mobility specialists employed by the Connecticut State Board of Education and Services for the Blind in the transfer of blind-retarded residents from large state facilities to smaller community homes and workshops. Criteria by which orientation and mobility specialists evaluate independent travel potential are presented, along with the environmental modifications needed to make group homes and workshops more accessible to lower functioning blind persons. The article also examines the responsibilities or orientation and mobility specialists at group homes and workshops during the transition phase.

Over the past several years, a movement has been underway in Connecticut to transfer mentally retarded residents from large state facilities to smaller group homes in local communities. In addition, residents are being placed in sheltered workshops where they are evaluated and trained for competitive employment.

Included in the mentally retarded population are legally blind individuals who, for years, have resided in large state facilities. In this article, this population is defined as blind-retarded, but the term is less than comprehensive because many of these individuals have additional impairments. All, however, do exhibit varying degrees of mental retardation and legal blindness. The degree of visual impairment ranges from the minimum defined standard for legal blindness (ie., 20/200 acuity in the better eye with maximum correction or a peripheral field of 20 degrees or less in the better eye) to total blindness. Other impairments vary significantly throughout the blind-retarded population.

The majority of blind-retarded residents are ambulatory and may travel independently in their living quarters, but this skill has developed over a period of months or years. Often, the adaptation is so specific to one setting that it cannot be easily replicated in another environment without instruction by an orientation and mobility specialist.

Deinstitutionalization requires those who are ambulatory to learn to travel in both new living and work environments. Consequently, orientation and mobility specialists play vital roles in the deinstitutionalization process. This article explains how these specialists, employed by the State of Connecticut, are integrating their expertise into the entire transitional process, from pre-placement evaluations of residents to teaching and consulting at group homes and workshops.

Role of the Orientation and Mobility Specialist

The orientation and mobility specialist teaches legally blind persons to use their remaining senses so they may travel safely and consistently. The specialist may also teach the blind person to use a white cane as a protective aid and a tactile sensor of the immediate environment (Hill & Ponder, 1976). It should be emphasized that cane use is limited to those who possess the necessary sensory-motor skills and spatial concepts to advance beyond hand trailing (ie., the act of using the fingers to follow a wall).

In Connecticut, orientation and mobility specialists are employed by the State Board of Education and Services for the Blind, which serves all legally blind citizens. Their duties are to provide orientation and mobility services to all legally blind children and adults who are referred, with the goal of assisting each blind person to become as independent as his or her capabilities permit.

The potential for independence among blind-retarded people is more difficult to estimate than it is for mentally retarded individuals who are not visually impaired. When visual loss occurs, the

Reprinted From: *Journal of Rehabilitation*, Jan/Feb/Mar 86, with permission.

primary sensory modality for observing, processing, and interacting with environments is destroyed or severely impaired. With additional impairments, such as mental retardation or deafness, the extent of a person's mobility independence will depend on the individual's emotional-intellectual level and the severity of the other physical impairments.

Evaluating Blind-Mentally Retarded Persons

In 1982, orientation and mobility specialists in Connecticut began coordinating their services with the staffs of several large custodial facilities of the Department of Mental Retardation. This coordination was undertaken in anticipation that many blind-retarded persons would eventually be transferred from custodial facilities to small community-based group homes. As part of their involvement in the deinstitutionalization process, orientation and mobility specialists conducted inservice training programs for the Department of Mental Retardation staff, evaluated the travel potential of blind-retarded residents being considered for group home placement, and reported their findings to placement committees.

Bryant and Jansen (1980) stated that when evaluating a mentally retarded blind person who has been institutionalized for many years, the orientation and mobility specialist should consider the specific implications associated with being mentally retarded and blind, as well as the following potential deficits:

1. **Physical-neurological impairments:** These impairments are manifested by posture and gait abnormalities which prevent a person from standing upright or walking normally.
2. **Deficiencies in remaining sensory system:** Perceptual channels for gathering information can be damaged by a hearing loss or by a loss of feeling in the hands or feet. If an individual is deaf-blind, both distance senses are impaired and more reliance must be placed on the sense of touch to gain the necessary sensory information for safe travel. Many persons who became deaf-blind as a result of maternal rubella have little or no expressive language in addition to intellec-

tual, visual, and auditory impairments. With such severe sensory deficits, they require environments that are highly structured and provide consistent tactile guidelines.

3. **Emotional-psychological trauma:** The inability to express feelings verbally and the lack of socially acceptable methods to relieve tension may cause residents to engage in verbal or physical outbursts directed at objects, other people, or themselves. Such behaviors must be taken into consideration during an evaluation because they may interfere with the responsible use of a cane. If medication is used to depress these behaviors, perceptual channels may be affected.
4. **Deficient generalization and skill transfer:** Although a blind-retarded resident may eventually adapt to a ward or wing within the residential facility, he or she may be unable to generalize the skills necessary for safe travel from a known environment to a new location without extensive training.
5. **Functional delay within a custodial setting:** If someone is born visually impaired and mentally retarded, that person often relates passively to the environment. He or she may be carried, fed, and diapered well beyond infancy. As this dependence continues, the mentally-retarded-blind child finds it increasingly difficult to achieve independence. The more custodial the environment remains, the less likely will the child be able to develop other senses, (especially touch and hearing) that are essential to independent functioning.

These diverse physical, emotional, and functional limitations affect an individual's potential for mobility and independence. For example, one person may have the ability to move a short distance by hand trailing a wall or railing, while another may be able to integrate touch with other senses well enough to travel further. One person's limited mobility skills may be due to an inability to relate spatially to the environment and sequence correctly, while another individual may remain spatially oriented and capable of learning several routes without confusion.

All blind-retarded persons do not display identical mobility potential, and each must be evaluated to determine individual aptitude for independent travel. The following questions must be considered by an orientation and mobility specialist when evaluating a blind-retarded person's potential for independent mobility:

1. Is there remaining vision? If so, can its use be considered in designing travel routes? For example, with the use of color or high contrast between object and background, a person may use vision to identify landmarks and destinations.

2. What is the person's understanding of body image? Can the individual identify front, back, left, and right? As shown by Cratty and Sams (1968), for a blind person to achieve effective mobility independence, he or she must first learn how the various body parts interrelate. The more one understands body image, the more that person will comprehend his or her relationship to the outside world and how that relationship varies depending on body movements. If a person cannot distinguish left from right, he or she cannot divide the environment into meaningful components for safe travel.

3. Can the person follow instructions and comprehend them? In this context, comprehension means the ability to repeat a task consistently. If a blind-retarded person is taught to hand trail a surface to locate a particular destination, he or she must eventually demonstrate the ability to maintain contact with the guideline. Otherwise, the individual will be unable to travel safely or consistently in a new environment by using hand trailing skills without supervision.

4. Does an individual, in a familiar environment, use hearing as an aid to travel? Does a totally blind person avoid head-level objects when walking, indication that he or she hears obstacles soon enough to take corrective action? Often, a blind-retarded person cannot explain how sound is used to perceive objects in space. Often, only by observing particular movements, can such a determination be made.

5. Does an individual have difficulties with attention span? A short attention span makes it difficult to concentrate adequately on various tasks. Therefore, those with poor attention spans may be seriously hampered when walking, attending to tactile-auditory clues, and using a cane for protection. Also, those who have difficulty sequencing may have corresponding problems with complex routes.

Evaluation of Group Homes and Workshops

Equally important to the evaluation process is the need for orientation and mobility specialists to examine new living and work areas for possible hazards. Such an evaluation must be done well in advance of the intended placement so that there will be enough time to implement environmental-structural recommendations.

In Connecticut, by initially coordinating services with the Department of Mental Retardation facilities, orientation and mobility specialists were involved in the transition of its source. They met with personnel from group homes and workshops before, rather than after, final placement decisions were made and contributed to the placement process at a time when they could be most effective.

When orientation and mobility specialists evaluate a group home or workshop, they must be particularly concerned with three types of environments. First, workshops often have large open areas in which blind employees cannot travel by trailing tactile guidelines because these guidelines are either nonexistent or segmented. Second, unstable indoor environments (such as large workshops) prevent lower functioning blind persons from learning routes for independent travel. Blind-retarded individuals require environments that have consistent sensory, especially tactile, clues. Finally, lengthy complex routes minimize opportunities for independent travel by blind-retarded persons who have difficulty with spatial orientation and sequencing.

The environment that the person will use is as important to the evaluation process as is his or her skill level. This is especially true if the group home or workshop staff expect the new resident to travel independently. Independence not only enhances a blind individual's self-worth, but also relieves staff members of the responsibility to serve as personal guides. Yet, independence can only be achieved if the environment is properly adapted to meet the mobility needs of the blind-retarded person.

The following suggestions are designed to help make indoor settings more accessible for blind-retarded individuals:

1. Place destinations close to each other with as few turns as possible. Place coat racks and lockers together, either near the door or workplace.

2. Create consistent pathways perhaps by painting them with a yellow line if the floor is dark; this will provide high dark-light contrast. Insist that these walkways be kept clear.

3. Use matte work surfaces to reduce glare and reflections from ceiling lights. Lighting also should accentuate destinations and stairs.

4. Create reference points by using audible sound sources or tactile aids. For example, place a radio in the eating area, or, if preferred, on the lockers. A tactile strip where two pathways intersect may help blind people know where to turn.

5. In a group home, place a tactile strip just before stairs to alert a blind person of an approaching drop-off or step-up. For those with partial sight, the top and bottom steps of a stairway should be identifiable by color contrast. Also, all stairways should have railings on both sides for added safety. Railings should extend one foot beyond the top and bottom of the stairs and their color should contrast the wall (Duncan, Gish, Mulholland, & Townsend, 1977).

6. Arrange for a destination to be located at the beginning or end of a line of objects. For example, the person's locker should be first or last in a row of lockers, or the work seat should be closest to the exit instead of farther away.

7. Implement a labelling system to help a blind-retarded person identify important destinations. This system might use a braille name tag or a piece of material such as felt, terry cloth, or corduroy which is attached to the person's locker, chair, or related object. In this way, the tactile label identifies personal

objects the way a sighted person would use a printed name tag to identify belongings.

Placement in Group Homes or Workshops

Evaluating the blind-retarded person's mobility potential and suggesting environmental modifications for group homes and workshops are important functions to be performed prior to placement. However, the orientation and mobility specialist's primary role occurs during the transition from the residential facility to the community. At that time, the specialist meets with staff members from the new facilities to satisfy the following objectives: (a) to present an inservice training program designed to teach the staff how to guide a blind person, especially in unfamiliar areas; (b) to plan routes for the new resident and teach the person how to travel safely; (c) to review, with staff members, the number and sequence of components for each route; and (d) to write a task analysis for the staff to reinforce training principles when the orientation and mobility specialist is unavailable.

The last point is particularly important because the specialist cannot be available on a daily basis, yet the new blind-retarded resident is usually rote-oriented and weak in skill generalization. For these individuals, learning to transfer previously acquired skills requires constant repetition in the new environment.

By utilizing the task analysis prepared by the orientation and mobility specialist, staff members are equipped with guidelines which enable them to review routes daily and, through constant reinforcement, help the person adjust to the new home and work place. As a consultant, the specialist communicates closely with the staff, monitors the individual's progress by studying the task analysis checklist, and, when necessary, revises task components for the entire route.

Conclusion

By 1990 it is estimated that the majority of residents currently housed in state facilities within Connecticut will have been integrated into the community. Each community group home, both public and private, is classified according to the level of custodial care required for the home to maintain the well-being of its residents.

Due to diversity in group housing, every blind-retarded person must be evaluated for placement in the least restrictive environment commensurate with his or her overall potential, and not based exclusively on the degree of visual loss. Through such evaluations, orientation and mobility specialists are providing suggestions that will make group homes and workshops more accessible to blind people, while encouraging placement committees and group home personnel to consider blindness in its proper context within the entire placement process.

References

Bryant, N.W., & Jansen, W.A. (1980). The mentally retarded visually impaired person. In R. Welsh & B. Blasch (Eds.) **Foundations of orientation and mobility** (pp. 452-459). New York: American Foundation for the Blind.

***, B., & Sams, T. (1968). **Body Image of blind children.** New York: American Foundation for the Blind.

Duncan, J., Gish, C., Mulholland, M.E., & Townsend, E. (1977). Standards, comments, and suggestions on environmental modifications. **Journal of Visual Impairment and Blindness.** 71, 442-455.

Hill, e., & Ponder, P. (1976). **Orientation and mobility techniques: A guide for the practitioner.** New York: American Foundation for the Blind.

Rehabilitation Counselor's Attitudes Toward Their Clients

STEVEN P. KAPLAN

The relationship between counsellor and client has usually been emphasized in the rehabilitation literature as being an important determiner of the eventual success or failure of the client's rehabilitation program (Krauft, Rubin, Cook & Bozarth, 1976; Gellman, 1959; Richman, 1964). Furthermore, the rehabilitation counsellor has traditionally fulfilled several distinct roles: a coordinator of important client services (Ayer & Butler, 1969), an action oriented, goal directed counsellor (Angell, Desau & Havrilla, 1969), a psychological counsellor (Patterson, 1970), a client advocate (Rubin & Roessler, 1978), and a medium to the client for relationships in the outside world (Richman, 1964). All of the above roles cast the counsellor as a helper in the client's rehabilitation adjustment processes and also assumes that the counsellor has the client's best interests at heart. In order to keep a client's interests as foremost and do everything possible to insures the client's optimal rehabilitation adjustment, it would seem necessary for the counsellor to have a positive attitude toward the client. It has been shown that attitudes a person holds toward another affects the interaction between those two people (Triandis, 1971). It has also been reported by Shapiro and Morris (1978) that clients acceptance into treatment, improvement and dropout rates, and successful outcomes are all associated with therapists' attitudes and feelings toward those clients. Therefore, it seems that the attitudes of professional counsellors toward their clients may exert a strong influence on the interaction between the two.

Although the attitude of professional rehabilitation counsellors toward their clients seems to be an important area of study, comprehensive literature reviews on attitudes toward disability have little to report on this important topic (Cook, 1981; Kutner, 1971; McDaniel, 1976; Schneider & Anderson, 1980). The purpose of this article is to review the available literature concerning rehabilitaiton counsellor attitudes toward clients and to discuss the possible effects these attitudes have on counsellors' service delivery functions.

Research on rehabilitaiton counsellor attitudes have generally compared the feelings counsellors hold toward different client groups. For example, Alston and Daniel (1972) found that rehabilitation counsellors' attitudes toward clients varied with the counsellors' perception of the difficulty of rehabilitating the clients. The researchers found that the more difficult the counsellors perceived the client's rehabilitation as being, the more negative the attitude the counsellors tended to have toward the client. Byrd, Byrd, and Emener (1977) compared the attitudes toward twenty different client groups held by practising rehabilitation counsellors, employers and rehabilitation counselling students. Byrd et al. (1977) found that practising counsellors tended to have the least favourable attitudes toward clients and were the least likely to recommend eight of twenty client groups for employment.

The attitudinal differences on the counsellors' part displayed in Alston and Daniel (1972) and Byrd et al. (1977) may well represent a realistic assessment of client needs, but they also seem to represent a potential source of bias that may actually serve to increase the chances that some clients will fail in their rehabilitation programs. This bias may therefore create a self fulfilling prophecy for the counsellor that some types of clients cannot be rehabilitated.

Some additional research studies comparing smaller numbers of client groups have also been conducted. Wicas and Carluccio (1971) found that vocational rehabilitation counsellors showed significant bias and prejudice toward culturally deprived black, exconvict, and expsychiatric patient client groups. Data suggested that counsellor biases affect how counsellors respond to clients with certain handicapping conditions (Wicas & Carluccio, 1971).

Pinkerton and McAleer (1976) found that rehabilitation counsellors had different attitudes toward four different chronic disability groups

Reprinted from: *Journal of Rehabilitation*, Oct/Nov/Dec, 1982, with permission.

(heart disease, renal failure, cancer and paraplegia), and that these attitudes correlated with projected case performance. The researchers correctly hypothesized that counsellors would have the least favourable attitudes toward clients with cancer, and that the counsellors would be willing to do the least for them in terms of case service. A hypothesis generated from this study was that the negative attitudes displayed by these counsellors toward clients with cancer may be a reflection of the counsellors' own fear of contracting cancer (Pinkerton and McAleer, 1976).

Schofield and Kunce (1971) studied rehabilitation counsellors' reactions to different, broadly defined (physically disabled mentally retarded and emotionally disturbed) disability groups. The researchers found that the counsellors tended to stereotype clients in terms of the services they needed as well as in terms of probable personality characteristics. They also found that these stereotypes influenced the counsellor-client interaction.

Kaplan and Thomas (1981) tested 40 rehabilitation counselling graduate students for their attitudes toward an obese client versus the same client when pictured as being of normal weight. Students were asked to gain impressions of a simulated client and then to rate this client on a variety of dimensions. Both groups were presented with the same background information on the client, and the client's present problem in both cases was an accident-induced hearing loss. The experimental group saw a picture of a 35-year-old grossly obese female weighing 340 pounds. The control group saw a picture of the same woman weighing 140 pounds. The pictures were taken from a before-after display in a national weight loss magazine. Results showed that when of normal weight, the client was rated significantly higher on the dimensions of competency, attractiveness, independence, and general evaluation. The authors concluded that the independent variable of client weight significantly influenced the student counsellors' perceptions of the client's personality and rehabilitation potential.

Only one reviewed study has assessed counsellor attitudes toward various disability groups and their relationship to service delivery and client outcome in an actual counselling setting.

Krauft, Rubin, Cook & Bozarth (1976) found that the ability of clients in a rehabilitation center to complete their rehabilitation program was related to counsellor attitudes toward them. These researchers also found that counsellors who held more favourable attitudes toward people with disabilities experienced a greater number of successful closures than counsellors with less favourable attitudes.

Finally, Gottlieb, Kravetz and Thomas (1974) using a semantic differential technique found that rehabilitation counsellors generally held negative attitudes toward people who receive welfare. Other researchers have also found that rehabilitation professionals tend to devalue financial dependence on the government (Janzen, Jorgensen, MacGuffie, Isreal, McPhee & Samuelson, 1968; Thomas & Britton, 1970; Thomas, Greco & Kravetz, 1973). The above results become even more cogent when it is remembered that a large portion of rehabilitation clients receive some type of welfare assistance, and that many of them are in large part supported by the government upon entering the rehabilitation system (McGowen & Porter, 1967; Porter, 1981; Wright, 1980). These facts imply that counsellors have the potential to hold negative attitudes toward many of their clients.

The review of the small body of research was done in an attempt to begin an investigation of the questions of rehabilitation counsellor attitudes toward clients, and the effect (if any) of these attitudes on service delivery to the clients. Collectively, the data seems to indicate that counsellors do in fact have the tendency to hold differing attitudes toward different client groups, and that these attitudes may also effect the type and amount of service the counsellor is willing to provide the client. It is not clear from this research if the counsellors' attitudes are based primarily on the perceived difficulty of successfully rehabilitating a client (see, Alston & Daniel, 1972), or if other variables (e.g., attractiveness) are responsible for the differences. Future research should focus on finding the sources of negative counsellor attitudes toward selected client groups, and on finding ways to foster their improvement.

The research reported in this review were drawn mostly from analogue studies, so definite conclusions are difficult to draw. Still, these data show a tendency for counsellors to display negative attitudes toward some of their clients and also show that these negative attitudes may influence service delivery. The implications for rehabilitation are that some clients may not be receiving optimal service delivery and, therefore, cannot be expected to have optimal rehabilitation outcomes. An exacerbating factor is that clients for the 1980's are expected to be more severely disabled, less able to cope with financial pressures, more likely to have been previous rehabilitation clients, and in general present more difficult rehabilitation challenges than previous clients (DeLoach & Greer, 1979; Kaplan & Questad, 1980). If Alston and Daniel (1972) are correct in their assertion that rehabilitation counsellors' attitudes toward their clients are in large part determined by case difficulty, counsellors in the future can be expected to have negative attitudes toward a greater percentage of their clients. These negative counsellor attitudes toward the more challenging or "difficult" clients may then increase the number of poor client outcomes, which would in turn result in increased financial waste and poorer client adjustment to disability, thereby setting up a cycle that would ultimately harm both clients and the rehabilitation system.

Rehabilitation counsellors are and will remain the profession's most important resource for aiding a client's adjustment to disability, and we need to continually strive to improve our counsellors' ability to provide quality services to clients. Therefore, strategies need to be found to improve potentially negative counsellor attitudes toward their clients. Counsellor awareness of the existence of these negative attitudes may be the first step toward their improvement (Schneider & Anderson, 1980). Furthermore, counsellors should be equipped with the latest rehabilitation technology to aid them in rehabilitating their more challenging clients. Future research focusing on both the improvement of counsellor attitudes (where they are found to be deficient) and improvement of services to difficult rehabilitation clients is necessary if we are to give clients the greatest chance for a successful rehabilitation program.

References

Alston, P. & Daniel, H. Perceived relative impact of disabilities on vocational, educational, and social functioning, **Journal of Applied Rehabilitation Counseling**, 1972, **3**(2), 53-59.

Angell, D., DeSau, G. & Havrilla, A. Rehabilitation counselor versus coordinator ... one of rehabilitation's great straw men. **NRCA Professional Bulletin**, 1969, **9**(1).

Ayer, J. & Butler, A., Rehabilitation counselor professional orientation and role enactment. **Rehabilitation Counseling Bulletin**, 1969, **13**(1), 15-25.

Byrd, E., Byrd, P. & Emener, W. Student, counselor and employer perceptions of the severely disabled. **Rehabilitation Literature**, 1977, **38**, 42-44.

Cook, D. Impact of disability on the individual. In R. Parker & C. Hansen (Eds.), **Rehabilitation counseling.** Boston: Allyn & Bacon, 1981.

DeLoach, C. & Greer, B. Client factors affecting the practice of rehabilitation counseling. **Journal of Applied Rehabilitation Counseling**, 1979, **10**(2), 35-39.

Gellman, W. Roots of prejudice against the handicapped. **Journal of Rehabilitation**, 1959, **25**(1), 4-6, 25.

Janzen, F., Jorgensen, G., MacGuffie, R., Isreal, D., McPhee, W. & Samuelson, C. Interpersonal relationships in rehabilitation. **Rehabilitation Counseling Bulletin**, 1968, **12**(1), 31-35.

Kaplan, S. & Questad, K. Client characteristics in rehabilitation studies. **Journal of Applied Rehabilitation Counseling**, 1980, **11**(4), 165-168.

Kaplan, S. & Thomas, K. Rehabilitation counseling students' perceptions of obese clients. **Rehabilitation Counseling Bulletin**, 1981, **25**(2), 106-109.

Krauft, C., Rubin, S., Cook, D. & Bozarth, J. Counselor attitudes toward disabled persons and client program completion: A pilot study. **Journal of Applied Rehabilitation Counseling**, 1976, **7**, 50-54.

Kutner, B. The social psychology of disability. In W. Neff (Ed.), **Rehabilitation psychology**, Washington, D.C.: American Psychological Association, 1971, pp. 143-167.

McDaniel, J. **Physical disability and human behavior** (2nd ed.). New York: Pergamon Press, 1976.

McGowan, J. & Porter, T. **An introduction to the vocational rehabilitation process.** Washington, D.C.: U.S. Department of HEW-VRA, 1967.

Patterson, C. Power, prestige and the rehabilitation counselor. **Rehabilitation Research and Practice Review**, 1970, **1**(3), 1-7.

Pinkerton, S. & McAleer, C. Influences of client diagnosis of cancer on counseling decisions. **Journal of Counseling Psychology**, 1976, **23**, 575-578.

Porter, T. The extent of disabling conditions. In R. Parker & C. Hansen (Eds.), **Rehabilitation counseling**. Boston: Allyn & Bacon, 1981.

Richman, S. The vocational rehabilitation of the emotionally handicapped in the community. **Rehabilitation Literature**, 1964, **25**(7), 194-202.

Rubin, S., & Roessler, R. **Foundations of the vocational rehabilitation process**. Baltimore: University Park Press, 1978.

Schneider, C. & Anderson, W. Attitudes toward the stigmatized: Some insights from recent research. **Rehabilitation Counseling Bulletin**, 1980, **23**(4), 299-314.

Schofield, L. & Kunce, J. Client disability and counselor behavior. **Rehabilitation Counseling Bulletin**, 1971, **14**(3), 158-167.

Shapiro, A. & Morris, L. Placebo effects in medical and psychological therapies. In S. Garfield & A. Bergin (Eds.), **Handbook of psychotherapy and behavior change** (2nd ed.). New York: Whiley & Sons, 1978.

Thomas, K. & Britton, J. Perceptions of rehabilitation trade instructors and clients: A semantic analysis. **Rehabilitation Counseling Bulletin**. 1970, **14**(1), 27-34.

Thomas, K., Gottlieb, A. & Kravetz, S. Congruence and attributes of meaning: Community mental health center and vocational rehabilitation personnel. **Community Mental Health Journal**, 1974, **10**(4), 204-208.

Thomas, K., Greco, M. & Kravetz, S. Perceptions of work and dependence: A comparison of rehabilitation counselors and social workers. **Rehabilitation Counseling Bulletin**, 1973, **17**(2), 120-128.

Triandis, H. **Attitude and attitude change**. New York: Wiley & Sons, 1971.

Wicas, E. & Carluccio, L. Attitudes of counselors toward three handicapped client groups. **Rehabilitation Counseling Bulletin**, 1971, **15**(1), 25-34.

Wright, G. **Total rehabilitation**. Boston: Little, Brown & Co., 1980.

Occupational Therapists and Physical Therapists: Vital Members in the Rehabilitation and Educational Process of Disabled Students

Freddie W. Litton, Lisa Veron, Harold C. Griffin

In years past, both occupational therapists and physical therapists have been trained primarily to work within a medical model with both adult and paediatric clients. As the result of Public Law 94-142 and its emphasis on meeting the varied and specialized needs of all children, public schools have now become active in employing both physical and occupational therapists. Many special educators are now becoming familiar with the addition of other disciplines within the education of the disabled, most notably the rehabilitation professions of physical and occupational therapy. However, many educators have developed an unclear picture about what services the therapists can provide. This article will illustrate and discuss ways in which an educator can utilize these health-related services as a resource in the programming for disabled students.

The classroom teacher has always been and still is the primary service provider in the educational system. Thus, a responsibility to coordinate and request available professional services often becomes the teacher's responsibility. Public Law 94-142 mandates the provision of services required to meet the specialized instructional needs of handicapped children. Physical and occupational therapy services are among those mandated services. Section 602 of Public Law 94-142, Education for All Handicapped Children Act of 1975 defined related services as:

> Transportation, and such developmental, corrective and supportive services (including speech pathology and audiology, psychological services, physical and occupational therapy, recreation, and medical and counselling services)...as may be required to assist a handicapped child to benefit from special education, and includes the early identification and assessment of handicapping conditions in children.

This interdisciplinary approach to meeting disabled children's needs is a must for providing the optimum educational and rehabilitation services to children as intended by Public Law 94-142. Integrated approaches to servicing children in educational settings have been developed in guidelines established by the American Occupational Therapy Association and the American Physical Therapy Association (Vernon & Poulton, 1980).

General Role of Therapists

Physical and occupational therapists can play a significant role in the education and rehabilitation of disabled children. Their services are valuable at both the consultant and direct level. Teachers of disabled children frequently require the assistance of other professionals in the team approach to work more effectively with handicapped students.

A teacher who notices abnormal characteristics of children such as poor balance, uncoordinated movements, and other motor-related problems may invite an occupational or physical therapist into his or her classroom to provide direct and/or consultative services. Direct services provided by physical therapists are numerous. Some of these include:

1. **Evaluating handicapped students by performing and interpreting tests and measurements of neuromuscular, musculoskeletal, cardiovascular, respiratory, and sensorimotor functions.**
2. **Planning and implementing treatment strategies for students based on evaluation findings.**
3. **Maintaining the motor functions of children in order that they can function in their educational environments.**

Reprinted from: *Journal of Rehabilitation*, Jan/Feb/Mar, 1982, with permission.

providing inservice education to parents and educational personnel (Vernon & Poulton, 1980).

Occupational therapists also provide multifaceted services. Some of these services include:

1. **Improving, developing, and/or restoring functions impaired or lost through illness, injury, or deprivation.**
2. **Improving ability to perform tasks for independent functioning when functions are impaired or lost.**
3. **Preventing, through early intervention, initial or further impairment or loss of function. Specific services include activities of daily living; the design, fabrication, and application of splints; sensorimotor activities; the use of equipment; prevocational evaluation and training; and consultation concerning the adaptation of the physical environment for the disabled (Vernon & Poulton, 1980).**

Teachers may seek information concerning the environmental adjustments for a particular student. An occupational or physical therapist could provide consultative assistance in adaptation necessary for toileting, transportation, and feeding. In addition, therapists could provide assistance in positioning or preferential seating within the classroom (Kinnealey & Morse, 1979). At the school site, therapists can provide consultation for environmental modifications such as architectural barriers of classes on several floors, heavy doors, installation of railings in the toilet area, and modifying the level of cafeteria railings to accommodate wheelchairs (Gulfoyle & Hays, 1979).

Self-Care Skills

Teachers have traditionally incorporated self-care skills as part of the educational programs for disabled students. Therapists can offer additional suggestions for specific self-care skill programs including dressing, feeding, toileting, and grooming. Clothes can often be modified in ways to assist in dressing. Therapists may offer adaptation such as larger buttons and button holes, special attachments for zippers, and models of

shoes and snaps to assist the child in acquiring these skills. The occupational therapists can advise teachers on various feeding techniques to be used with children who are not independent feeders. The teachers and occupational therapists can jointly feed children in the same area of the classroom or cafeteria so that each one can assist and reinforce the other's skills concerning the children's specific needs. In toileting, the occupational therapists and physical therapists can assist the teacher in caring for children with special toileting problems. Spina bifida children may have an ileo-bag which needs to be taken care of by these children. Therapists and teachers can assist spina bifida children in developing such independence in caring for toileting equipment; and being responsible for their own toileting schedules. In addition, therapists can assist in positioning children on the toilet, providing advice about the size of toilets, and stability railings on the toilet. Therapists also can consult with teachers and parents concerning children's physical capabilities. They also can advise teachers and parents concerning children's physical capabilities and potential to develop independence in toilet training. This is particularly helpful in establishing realistic expectations for children in this area of self-help skills.

Motor Developments

Another realm where physical therapists and occupational therapists are critical in assisting classroom teachers is in the formation of motor skills within a developmental and functional framework. Physical therapists' motor activities within a regular classroom may include:

1. **Gait training**
2. **Neurodevelopmental facilitation techniques**
3. **Positioning and handling of children**
4. **Sensory stimulation**
5. **Fitting and monitoring of adaptive equipment**
6. **Joining mobilization techniques (Vernon & Poulton, 1980)**

Occupational therapists' activities in the motor area include:

1. **Improving gross and fine motor function**
2. **Normalization of muscle tone**

3. **Increase of joint range of motion**
4. **Decreasing drooling**
5. **Improving balance**
6. **Improving body image**
7. **Improving the ability to receive and organize stimuli (Vernon & Poulton, 1980)**

Successful performance of functional motor activities helps disabled children develop a better self-image. Services of therapists are critical to disabled children who must maintain muscle strength and joint mobility to be able to move within their classroom. Many disabled children who are motorically impaired depend on the services of therapists to learn such vital skills as crawling, walking, and a perception of their body in space. Classroom teachers can reinforce motor skills introduced by the therapists. This team work between therapists and teachers assists children in making progress in the area of motor development. A traditional distinction of the roles each type of therapist plays in a child's motor development holds that physical therapists are concerned with postural modifications and gross motor development and occupational therapists are concerned perceptual and fine motor development. In recent years these traditional roles have blurred so that both types of professionals are concerned with both types of motor development.

Within any classroom, motor development is an extremely important part of normal maturation. Proper position in desks or wheelchairs assists disabled children in benefiting more from academic instruction. Further, recent work by occupational therapists in sensory-motor integration appears to assist both mildly disabled children and severely disabled students in recognizing their position in space and making them more receptive to "academics" which are presented by classroom teachers (Ayers, 1972). Many of the prelanguage and language programs for multihandicapped children utilize motor development as the basis for further language development (Van Dijk, 1971).

Vocational Skills

Therapists also can assist classroom teachers in the development of vocational skills of disabled students. Both occupational and physical therapists can evaluate which skills children may be capable of developing (Mitchell & Lindsey, 1979). In addition, the therapists aid a student's potential for total independence. Frequently, occupational therapists can assist in making "jigs" or adaptive equipment which will assist individuals in compensating for their disabilities while doing vocational tasks. These pieces of adaptive equipment may assist students in doing such jobs as well as nondisabled individuals. The classroom teacher and occupational therapist can discuss the types of job training which are needed and then the therapist can suggest the methods for adaptation of these tasks for disabled individuals.

Individual Education Plan (IEP) Development

Physical and occupational therapists also work together with classroom teachers in developing individualized educational and rehabilitation plans for students. This requires that physical therapists and occupational therapists be involved in the initial educational evaluations of identified children. They can then participate with an effective data base in the development of goals in motor, self-help and vocational skills, as well as assist in planning for mainstreaming of mildly disabled children. Further, these professionals can advise the entire IEP committee on the necessity of therapy, the level of services required as well as the delivery mode for the related service.

The lack of therapists with specialized paediatric training has caused both the American Occupational Therapy Association and the American Physical Therapy Association to recommend and endorse inservice and continuing education in the area of paediatrics for their members (Hightower, 1973). Many therapists may find that they need assistance in moving from the medical to the educational model as well as in applying evaluation and treatment techniques principally designed for adults to the needs of children. School systems as well as professional organizations should consider assisting therapists in upgrading their competencies by sponsoring appropriate continuing education and/or inservice training to meet the therapists' specialized needs. The paediatric services of physical therapists and occupational therapists are increasingly important to the entire educational process of the disabled child. Public school systems should ensure that these professionals are part of an interdisciplinary effort to meet the needs of their disabled students.

Conclusions

The services of physical therapists and occupational therapists are important to disabled children and their teachers. These therapists can be important resources in the development of gross and fine motor skills, vocational skills and self-help skills. In addition, these therapists can assist teachers in the positioning of students to ensure the most effective environment for learning as well as providing these students with optimum comfort during the educational day. Finally, teachers must invite therapists to be included in the planning process for disabled children. Their expertise can assist teachers to more effectively plan both long and short term goals for their students with disabilities.

The era of classroom teachers essentially working by themselves to educate disabled children must come to a close. In its place must come a team approach to this educational process. Physical therapists and occupational therapists are vital members of such professional teams that are required for the most effective education programs for disabled children.

References

Ayres, A.J. Sensory integration and learning disorders. Los Angeles, CA: Western Psychological Services, 1972.

Gulfoyle, E.M. & Hays, C. Occupational therapy roles and functions in the education of the school-based handicapped student. The American Journal of Occupational Therapy, 1979, 33, 565-576.

Hightower, B. Continuing education in physical therapy. Physical Therapy, 1973, 53, 17-24.

Kinnealey M. & Morse, A. Educational mainstreaming of physically handicapped children. The American Journal of Occupational Therapy, 1979, 33, 365-372.

Mitchell, M. & Lindsey, D. A model for establishing occupational therapy and physical therapy services in the public schools. The American Journal of Occupational Therapy, 1979, 33, 361-364.

Public Law 94-142, Education for All Handicapped Children Act of 1975.

Van Dijk, J. Educational approaches to abnormal development. In Deaf-blind children and their education. Proceedings of the International Conference on the Education of Deaf-Blind Children. Rotterdam: Rotterdam University Press, 1971.

Vernon, L. & Poulton, S. Guidelines: Occupational therapy and physical therapy in the schools. Baton Rouge, LA: Louisiana State Department of Education, 1980.

Getting Well: Impression Management as Stroke Rehabilitation

Steven J. Gold

Illness and Deviance

A shared concern of the many forms of phenomenological sociology is the relation between the individual actors and the values, norms and patterns of behavior of a social group. Phenomenologists argue that individuals learn, adjust to, recreate and change norms and structures by way of social processes. In the process of interacting in groups they adopt the norms of the group and society. Working within this tradition, sociologists have studied marijuana smokers (Becker, 1963), strangers to a society (Schutz, 1944), mental patients (Goffman, 1967) and individuals whose behavior is in some way remote from collective values, and the society which upholds these values.

In all of these studies, the authors describe the process through which actors become aware of their distance from behavioral norms and take special actions because of this awareness. For example, transsexual Agnes (Garfinkel, 1967) creates a flawlessly female self-characterization to counter any challenges to her identity. In a similar vein, Goffman notes that mental inmates recognize and try to support the norm of privacy. Where attendants violate patients' privacy, they embarrass their keepers with intimate comments about dandruff, shaving cuts and style of dress (Goffman, 1967:68). In these studies, bearers of stigma are reported to have a unique understanding of what constitutes being socially normal. Who knows more about acting straight than one who must avoid being detected as stoned (Becker, 1963)? Because they are not normal, deviants must master activities of impression management.

Since Durkheim's *Division of Labor in Society*, social theorists have noted that norms support certain actions while discouraging and punishing others. Drawing on the Durkheimian tradition, Parsons (1951) and Foucault (1965, 1980) have shown that social groups use definitions of health and illness as forms of social control. Recently, students of society have noted a tendency to apply medical definitions to behavior not previously regarded as a matter of health or illness. In Western societies, illness is defined by the highly legitimate and value-neutral institution of medicine. When deviant behavior other than illness is labelled and managed as a medical problem, it is done at least in part, in order to avoid acknowledging the inherently moral issues of identifying and treating deviant individuals (Zola, 1972, Conrad and Schneider, 1980)l. This phenomenon has been labelled the "medicalization of deviance".

Interestingly, a value-free medical definition has been both sought and rejected by "deviant" groups in their attempts to contend with coercive social norms. For example, largely through the efforts of Alcoholics Anonymous, alcoholism is now seen as a sickness and not a crime or personal weakness as it once was (Conrad and Schneider, 1980:108). Whereas gay rights advocates waged a successful campaign to have the American Psychiatric Association remove homosexuality from its list of psychiatric conditions (Conrad and Schneider, 1980:208), Alcoholics Anonymous members sought a medical definition in order to reduce the moral stigma. Gays, by contrast, worked to demedicalize and hence legitimate their lifestyle.

This article explores the response of stroke victims to various competing social definitions of their deviance. A stroke victim is wrenched from his or her original status and must relearn rules of self presentation despite the effects of a physical disability. Stroke victims are treated in an organized, collective manner in hospitals and

* I would like to acknowledge Arlie Hochschild for her assistance in guiding this paper toward publication. For reprint requests, write: Department of Sociology, University of California, Berkeley, Berkeley, CA 94720.

Reprinted from: Qualitative Sociology, 6(3), Fall 1983 by Human Sciences Press, with permission.

rehabilitation centers. Much of their rehabilitation involves learning to display a socially acceptable image of wellness.

Methods

Data were collected during a period of nine months of fieldwork as a volunteer in the Stroke Rehabilitation Center. As one of the few male volunteers, my duties at the center were most often "heavy" jobs such as furniture mover, physical therapy aide, and male attendant. In addition to attending the center, I also visited stroke victims in nursing homes, a local hospital and in their homes to gain access to a diverse sample. Data were gathered through participant observation, formal and informal interviews, examination of the center's files and photography.

Photos (cover, #1, #2) offer a glimpse of the center environment and patient activities. Photography did not commence until I had been at the center for one month in order to avoid my being seen solely as a photographer by the center's members. Because I photographed frequently, little attention was paid to my taking "candid" photos which did not focus on specific individuals (cover, #1, 2). Posed portraits (#3-5) were taken only with the subject's permission. While sociologists are urged to shun reactivity, photographers often make use of their relationship with subjects (Becker, 1974:19). My capacity as a member of the center is reflected in the naturalness of the expressions in the photos.

The General Experience of Stroke

To understand the experience of the stroke victim, one must know a little about strokes. A stroke or "CVA" (cerebral vascular accident) is a blockage in the blood vessels which supply oxygen to the brain. The loss of blood to the brain may cause temporary or permanent brain damage, resulting in impairment of the body part controlled by that portion of the brain. The results of stroke vary in intensity and extent of recovery. The outcomes depend on a number of factors including the area of the brain affected, the physical condition of the afflicted individual

and type of treatment. A stroke victim may lose the use of an arm and leg, the control of facial muscles, the ability to form sentences, or there may be no obvious effects. While stroke is commonly seen as an ailment of the aged, persons of any age can be subject to it. The average age of participants at the stroke center is about 60.[1] Stroke may occur spontaneously or be brought on by physical trauma. When stroke results from non-traumatic causes, it is often painless and usually described as a twinge or numbness, followed by a loss of sensation in the affected area. (American Heart Association, 1981b).

The physical effects of stroke, such as impairment of communication and movement, very more than the emotional reactions. Feelings of depression, isolation and frustration are common. Mood changes are frequent. Self-care and social presentation behaviors, which were previously taken for granted, may become difficult or impossible. Recent stroke victims are often hospitalized. Following examination, surgery is performed on some individuals to aid rehabilitation or reduce the chances of another stoke. Doctors may also prescribe bed rest, physical, speech or psychological therapy, a special diet or anticonvulsive drugs.

As a result of medical treatment, recent stroke victims see themselves as occupying the sick role (Parsons, 1951, 1958, Freidson, 1970). The sick role implies that the stroke victim is exempt from social responsibilities, such as making a living or caring for children, as long as he or she defines being sick as an undesirable and temporary state. The sick role is exemplified by the stroke victim trying to get well and cooperating with the efforts of others to get him or her well. To deviate legitimately, one must avoid forming groups and making claims on the basis of illness as a permanent, legitimate role.

In this way, sick individuals are spared the stigma of social deviance; society also insures that it does not reinforce deviance by too far removing those who are sick. The sick role claims that the concern and supportive care provided by the high status doctor reflect society's concern for the patient. This undercuts alienation and motivates recovery.

While the real condition of stroke victims seldom conforms precisely to the Parsonian ideal type, the sick role does approximate their status during the early stages of the stroke experience. During this time, medical treatment can assure the patient and family that they are well cared for. Exemption from obligations allows the stroke victim to avoid discrediting him or herself because of reduced ability to function. Because the sick role is not a demanding one for a person who feels sick, little effort is required for impression management during this period.

Stroke, however, is a chronic rather than acute ailment, one which cannot be "cured" by the techniques of scientific medicine. As noted by Davis (1963), recent victims of chronic disabilities often have difficulty in understanding the long-term duration of their condition. At first, the sick role is adopted. Later, when it becomes evident that there is no cure, individuals must learn to accept stroke as a life-long condition. Unfortunately, treatment staff are often unwilling or unable to make clear the likelihood and extent of recovery. The sick role is inadequate, yet no new identity is readily available. In this way, stroke victims are prevented from having a clear basis upon which to express an interactional self. Many stroke victims first arrive at the Stroke Rehabilitation Center in this state of identity confusion.

The "Ideology of Therapy"

The Stroke Rehabilitation Center creates and uses an "ideology of therapy." This philosophy is determined by the Center's director, but other staff and participants make significant contributions as well. The director is a charismatic woman in her mid-forties, the wife of a prominent community physician. Trained in physical therapy, Jeannie relies on her effervescent charm as much as her professional knowledge in running the center. She trots about the center addressing the patients, staff and volunteers with cheery greetings and pep talks. She also lends a careful ear to those facing difficulty. Jeannie sometimes flirts with male participants and teases females in order to help spread the high spirits

and good humour. She frequently reminds staff and patients that it is their center.

While the director is vital to the center's "ideology of therapy," other members participate in numerous ways. Special phrases which describe the center, its members and the work of rehabilitation are frequently repeated in casual talk and on ceremonial occasions. Stories of successful rehabilitation are told by staff as testimonials of what stroke victims can and do accomplish.[2] The tales of Mabel's great improvements in speech. Herman's weight loss and positive attitude and Bab's storytelling skills and nine grandchildren are retold, so that all the people in the center can take pride in the group's accomplishments. Participants able to contribute to the center's ideology through their own achievements or suggestions are seen as making progress in rehabilitation. This is especially so for patients who are unable to speak. Their accomplishments are recalled by others, who thus literally speak for a person who cannot speak for him or herself.

The collective orientation of the stroke center contrasts with the traditional hospital, where firmer lines of authority are maintained and patients are seldom encouraged to contribute to the ideology of their rehabilitation. Official information about the center is explicit in defining the central thrust of the rehabilitation process as getting the patient out of the sick role by "mainstreaming" (That is, getting the patient into the mainstream of life).

My interviews indicate that new stroke victims most often see their physical condition as influenced by two events: the physical effects of the stroke itself and the experience of medical treatment.[3] At the center, the sick role, acquired through these two events is rejected through the process of "reframing" (Goffman, 1974). Reframing means teaching stroke victims to project an alert, controlled and responsive self-image. Stroke victims must thereby reject the components of the sick role which employ deviance or absence of wellness.

The stroke center teaches stroke victims that they must fulfill personal obligations and are personally responsible for their own care. They must make a claim of legitimacy by and for stroke victims as a group and they cannot see their condition as a purely negative one. For example, the center's staff consciously uses the active term "participant" instead of the passive term "patient." According to the Parsonian sick role, a patient is supposed to be emotionally attached to his or her doctor. At the stroke center, participants often denigrate their physicians and give credit for their recovery to the center's more attentive physical therapists.

While stroke victims would like to appear and feel well, this is often quite difficult for members of my sample, considering their physical and social position as elderly, disabled and low-income persons. In the stroke center, rehabilitation is accomplished by teaching the participant to redefine stroke from a life-shattering medical ailment to a conquerable inconvenience. For example, one man had a stroke, and for several years before coming to the center claimed to have "given up." During this time, he refused to participate in rehabilitation activities and blamed his stroke on an accident caused by improper care in the hospital: "I stayed in bed and ignored my wife and son." Finally, a neighbour began to visit him, convincing him to *work* towards rehabilitation. When he began to attend the Stroke Rehabilitation Center, he was highly motivated and made rapid progress. "In the center, I used my stubbornness. I am not embarrassed when I talk to people now." According to the center's definition, rehabilitation has occurred when someone who has experienced a stroke is seen and sees him or herself as "a whole, well person" within the center.[4]

According to staff and participants, to accomplish rehabilitation one must rely on inner strength. Inner strength consists of classic Anglo-American character traits such as determination, courage, ability to work hard, concern for others, stoicism, a sense of humour, devotion to family and hope for the future. Inner strength is an excellent tool for accomplishing stroke rehabilitation, because it can be applied to any person, regardless of physical disability. One participant exemplified inner strength when he described his motivations for living alone, even though he was rather severely disabled. (A choice to live alone was made by several par-

ticipants.) "It's the fighting to live alone that keeps me going. I could move in with my daughter, but the soft life is no good. I'd just sit around."

The stroke center emphasizes the therapeutic value of a positive outlook. Displays of cheerfulness, cooperation, outward orientation, and desire to work diligently towards rehabilitation are the means to achieve wellness.

Many seemingly small and mundane actions are treated as expressions of serious progress toward rehabilitation. These include: smiling; giving greetings; making or actively listening to small talk; demonstrating a commitment to difficult, boring or apparently useless therapy activities; expressing gratitude to the center; submitting good-naturedly to teasing; displays of affection; adjustment of clothing; answering personal questions; and being photographed and scrutinized by other participants and staff. These all are heavily rewarded within the center. Such rewards include acceptance by the center's participants and staff, encouragement, personal friendship, favours, gifts and perhaps most important, an institutionally-based image of "I am doing my best and so I am a well person."

To insure success, the ideology-makers of the center maintain that virtually every activity at the stroke center has value in providing participants with therapy and lessons of independence. Even such common activities as scheduling of daily events and the passing of time in itself are therapeutic. Following a schedule teaches punctuality and responsibility.

Criteria of Wellness

In order to explore the way one presents him or herself as a well and interactively competent person, I have developed a list of "criteria of wellness." These include behavior which were specifically encouraged or condemned in the day-to-day life of the Stroke Rehabilitation Center. Participants who were able to display many positive behaviors and few negative ones were seen as exemplary and making excellent progress. The greater the difficulty in displaying such behaviours, the greater the positive evaluation received by that participant. Because many of these behaviors are expressed visually, photographs were helpful in discovering them. Eight categories are included in the list. While there is some overlap among the criteria, each relates to an important area of interactional competence which must be mastered in order to project an image of self which is well. These include: (1) Time orientation, (2) attention span, 930 body control, (4) participation, (5) appearance, (6) knowledge, (7) sharing group values and (8) emotions.

Time Orientation. Time is an important factor in the stroke rehabilitation process (Roth, 1963). To be seen as well in the center, a participant must be able to sense and participate in the daily timing of the center's activities as well as the longer-term flow of the rehabilitation process. The quality and quantity of behavioral displays of alertness, attention and participation require an ability to sense socially appropriate timing. In addition, the ideology of therapy of the center is rooted in a kind of Protestant work ethic, whereby participants are expected to accept the idea that effort expended over a period of time (that is, work) will yield some recovery.

Attention Span. Stroke victims must display sufficient attention to and comprehension of therapy activities, lectures and conversations. Excessive attention, such as focusing on the "hippie" appearance of a volunteer, is frowned upon by staff as "inappropriate" attention.

Body Control. Body control is an important way of demonstrating wellness at the center. Because many of the participants suffer rather severe physical infirmities, standards of body control appropriate to larger society are not applied. However, complete lack of body control is considered inappropriate behavior. For example, limp arms or legs are restrained by slings or braces. In the center, an important issue of body control is the ability to use the bathroom by oneself. Several participants who are unable to do so are accompanied to the center by family members or personal attendants, thus freeing the staff of this responsibility.

Participation. If a stroke patient refuses to participate in several activities at the center over a period of time, he or she will be asked to leave. Generally, participants are permitted to refuse

certain activities, but if they "come around" and begin to take part, they are rewarded.

Appearance. Appearance is an important tool in the management of wellness. This is illustrated by the degree of visual impression management in the posed group of photos (#3-5). Because patients may be limited in their ability to move or speak, their appearance takes on major importance for expressing personal competence. Clothing is a helpful prop for maintaining appearances at the center. Slightly dressy attire is favoured for men, and women participants are complimented for wearing colorful outfits. Jeannie, the director, sets an example by always wearing dresses, make-up and jewellery.

Knowledge. In order to be seen as well, participants are expected to command knowledge of the center's members, ideology and their own daily program. The latter is encouraged by pinning a schedule on their shirtfront. Additional expertise in activities such as table-tennis, crafts or lobbying on behalf of the center is rewarded as an indication of wellness.

Sharing Group Values. The ability to demonstrate that one shares the center's values as well as American middle-class values is vital to appearing well. At the same time, the center's ideology tolerates individualistic coping styles.

Emotions. The display of situationally appropriate emotions is considered vital to the learning of wellness. Emotions of cheeriness, pride and enthusiasm are valued, while excessive displays of depression or anger are discouraged. Emotion work (Hochschild, 1979) training for stroke victims is especially important because the physiological effects of the ailment can alter one's emotional state (Fowler and Fordyce, n.d.:28).

The process by which stroke victims are rewarded with an identity contingent on their display of certain behaviors and outlooks is an illustration of Goffman's (1967) model of society as a system of exchanges of deference and demeanour. Conformity with rules, such as the criteria of wellness, or a commitment to activities of rehabilitation yields not only rehabilitation from stroke, but further confirms a well self. Thus, small pleasantries become infused with much more meaning than they might be given in other settings. "The gestures which we sometimes call empty are perhaps the fullest things of all" (Goffman, 1967:91).

Displays of cheer, effort and cooperation within the center also have an economic motivation, that is, they are criteria of the center's wellness. The center, as a new and marginally funded institution, desires additional support. When local officials visit the center and see the busy and optimistic environment, it is hoped that they will be impressed and provide additional money.

Photographs yield further insight into the way participants display wellness. As noted in the criteria of wellness, because many stroke victims are limited in their ability to move and speak, visual displays are an especially important means of communication in the center. In examining portraits of participants (#3-5), I was struck by the uniformity in style of self-presentation. The participants were from different backgrounds, ages, and sexes. They had a variety of different disabilities from stroke and different opinions of me as a photographer. Yet, their expressions, postures and focus of attention seem quite similar.

The similarity of poses can be seen as a reflection of the values and orientations of the center in which they were taken. Many aspects of the participant's demeanour in photos reveal the "optimistic but firm" outlook which is the theme of rehabilitation activities. For example, in the portraits, backs are straight, chin is forward, corners of the mouth are turned up and there is eye contact. Frowns, avoidance of eye contact or smiles are all absent. In general, the portraits reveal a controlled, focused, energetic and communicative outlook. I call this the "standing tall" posture. Standing tall is the center's motto and appears along with a picture of a tall redwood tree on name tags and other locations throughout the center.

The photos allow participants an ideal medium to show wellness. With the photographer's cooperation, an expression which took only seconds to display is frozen and becomes permanent evidence of the strength of character of its subject. In this way, a photograph becomes a tool of impression management and captures an idealized typification of self, available to be referred to at any time.[5]

Complex Framing

While displays and demeanours such as those shown in the posed portraits might offer conformity to the ideology of the center, it should be noted that such displays might not be felt at all times by those offering them. Or, if sincerely displayed, such actions might be "enriched" with personal as well as institution-defined communication. Such actions yield appropriate demeanour and, at the same time, express personal statements of resentment, irony or autonomy. While individualistic behavior has a potential to disrupt the social organization of the center, it is tolerated and even encouraged, as long as it is not too openly hostile.

Taking a "you rascal you" attitude, the ideology makers of the center deem seemingly antisocial actions wholesome and spirited signs of any well American's character. One example of such behavior is an ironic "shit-eating grin". A participant with this contemptuous smile is seen as making an effort of show a positive outlook, while at the same time expressing disgust toward his or her own situation of disability. One person carried this ironic frame too far. He would often smile and say "shit, shit, it's all bullshit!" On one occasion, this brought a young female volunteer to tears. Staff members comforted the girl, telling her that this man had had a particularly bad life since his stroke.

Another means of displaying both individual and institutional meaning in the center occurs in the choice of clothing. Some persons attend the center regularly attired in garments which violate basic values of rehabilitation. One man wears cowboy boots with heels which make balance training therapy difficult. Another affects mirrored sunglasses which limit eye contact and so hinder the interpersonal communication valued by the center. Like other displays of individual autonomy within the center, these were accepted as allowable transgressions because the "violators" had demonstrated their embrace of the center's ideology in other ways. As mentioned previously, minor violations were tolerated as individual coping styles.

In addition to dealing with the participants' expression of individual as well as institutional meanings, the center also has to adjust to events which have the potential to undermine the center's claims regarding the abilities to stroke victims to become well. Falls, seizures and fits of crying occur unpredictably. These threaten all stroke victims working toward rehabilitation because such events seem to demand sick role treatment. The center counters these occurrences in a manner not unlike the treatment of the physical disabilities of stroke. They are defined as routine, controllable and nonthreatening. Seizures are considered a normal part of the healing process. When a participant is afflicted, the center's physical therapists place him or her in a prone position and calmly observe the patient's condition. This prevents complications from going unnoticed and constitutes a display made by the staff for the participants' benefit. No effort is made to call for outside help and activities within the center go on as usual.

Falls receive similar treatment. The staff ignore the fact that falls can result in injury and that they signify helplessness. Instead, the fallen participant's desire to be active and independent (the cause of the fall) is endorsed. Crying, as a potential threat to the cheery and productive atmosphere of the center, is reframed in several ways. First, crying is often defined as a physiological rather than emotional by-product of stroke in medical literature (Fowler and Fordyce, n.d.:28). Second, according to the center's staff, stroke victims, like all people, become frustrated, depressed and angry. Crying as a means of expressing this. Third, by taking a group therapy approach, crying can be defined as a legitimate form of valued communication. The crying person is then comforted by the staff, so demonstrating the supportive and understanding environment which exists. By reframing potential threats, the center is able to strengthen its ideology of rehabilitation.

Conclusion

The physical event of undergoing a stroke and its medical treatment encourage the stroke victim to see him or herself within the sick role. However, the chronic nature of stroke and the inability of doctors to provide a cure soon make the sick role dysfunctional for both stroke victim and the medical treatment staff. While the sick role is inappropriate, physical disabilities and uncertainty prevent the afflicted individual from presenting him or herself as well.

In offering rehabilitation, the Stroke Rehabilitation Center gives participants an opportunity to alter the relationship between sick role status and the social norms and institutions which define them as sick. The center's socially based, concrete and attainable criteria of wellness, provide individuals with the means to abandon the sick role and make a legitimate claim on the definition of themselves as well persons. By demedicalizing stroke in a social setting, the center allows the participants to claim wellness. Once stroke victims can make a claim on wellness, the physical symptoms which initially implied the existence of a "sick role self" now become inconveniences. At least within the center, these are managed through styles of interaction.

References

American Heart Association
    1981a Strokes: A Guide for the Family.
    1981b An Older Person's Guide to Cardiovascular Health.
Becker, Howard S.
    1963 Outsiders. New York: The Free Press.
    1974 "Photography and sociology." Studies in the Anthropology of Visual Communication 1:3-26.
Conrad, Peter and Joseph Schneider
    1980 Deviance and Medicalization. St. Louis: Mosby.
Davis, Fred
    1963 Passage Through Crisis. Indianapolis: Bobbs-Merrill.
Durkheim, Emile
    1933 The Division of Labor in Society. New York: The Free Press.

Emerson, Joan P.
1970 "Behavior in private places: Sustaining definitions of reality in gynecological examinations." Pp. 74-93 in Hans Peter Drietzel (ed.), Recent Sociology No.2. New York: Macmillan.

Foucault, Michel
1965 Madness and Civilization. New York: Vintage.
1980 History of Sexuality. New York: Vintage.

Fowler, R.S. and Fordyce, W.E.
n. d. Stroke: Why do They Behave That Way. Dallas: American Heart Association.

Freese, Dr. Arthur S.
1980 Stroke: The New Hope and the New Help. New York: Random House.

Freidson, Elliot
1970 The Profession of Medicine. New York: Harper and Row.

Garfinkel, Harold
1967 Studies in Ethnomethodology. Englewood Cliffs, N.J.: Prentice-Hall.

Goffman, Erving
1959 The Presentation of Self in Everyday Life. Garden City: Doubleday Anchor.
1963 Stigma. Englewood Cliffs, N.J.: Prentice Hall.

1967 Interaction Ritual. New York: Harper Colophon.
1974 Frame Analysis. New York: Harper Colophon.
1979 Gender Advertisements. New York: Harper Colophon.

Hochschild, Arlie R.
1979 "Emotion work, feeling rules and social structure." American Journal of Sociology 84: 551-75.

Parsons, Talcott
1951 The Social System. New York: The Free Press.
1958 "Definitions of health and illness in the light of American values and social structure." In E. Gartley Jaco (ed.), Patients, Physicians and Illness. New York: The Free Press.

Roth Julius
1963 Timetables. Indianapolis: Bobbs-Merrill.

Schutz, Alfred
1944 "The stranger: An essay in social psychology." American Journal of Sociology 49: 499-507.

Zola, Irving K.
1972 "Medicine as an institution of social control." Sociological Review 20: 487-504.

References Notes

1. According to the American Heart Association, despite the fact that strokes can occur in persons of any age, six of seven strokes occur in persons over 65 (American Heart Association, 1981:10).
2. Stroke literature often mentions the achievements of stroke victims. Freese (1980:11-12) points out that FDR, Churchill, Walt Whitman, George Frederick Handel and Louis Pasteur all made major accomplishments after their strokes.
3. In addition, stroke victims sometimes mentioned family members' reactions and their own past health history as important in colouring the way they saw their ailment. Patients who experienced stroke through traumatic onset generally do not separate the stroke from the injury which brought it on.
4. Due to less tolerant standards of wellness, even fully rehabilitated stroke victims might be seen as sick in other settings.
5. In *Gender Advertisements*, Goffman (1979) notes how an executive will have a portrait of himself taken at the height of his manly prowess, perhaps having just shot a deer, and will display this photo in his office as evidence of this part of his identity.

Positive Confrontation Techniques for the Rehabilitation Counselor

Richard W. Thoreson

Confrontation is a term that emerged from the Southern California Encounter Group Movement of the 1960's. That movement was responsible for the development of a special kind of experiential group for normal individuals (in contrast to therapy groups for mentally disturbed patients) where group members, through confrontation "with on-the-spot observation of their own behaviour and its effects on others," (Yalom, 1975, p. 470), could learn about their own interpersonal styles and the responses of others to them. The importance of confrontation as a major counseling strategy for stimulating interpersonal learning has been stressed in group-oriented and communication skill training books. For example, its rationale, sub-categories of techniques, and guidelines for use are described in a number of texts in the group therapy, encounter group, family-marital therapy, and counseling communication skill training areas (Berenson & Mitchell, 1974; Carkhuff & Anthony, 1979; Carkhuff & Berenson, 1977; Cormier & Cormier, 1979; Douds, Berenson, Carkhuff & Pierce, 1967; Egan, 1970, 1973, 1976; Eisenberg & Delaney, 1977; Ivey & Authier, 1978; Moustaka, 1959, 1972; Rogers, 1970; Yalom, 1975).

However, despite the recognition given to confrontation in the above-mentioned literature as a promising tool for counseling, it still tends to be looked upon with suspicion and ambivalence by many counseling and rehabilitation professionals. The origins of suspicion and ambivalence may be found in the tendency within counselor training programs either to limit the attention given to confrontation or to treat it as an anathema to a positive empathic relationship, both views limiting its use as a legitimate counseling tool. It might, therefore, be helpful to look at the treatment that has been given to confrontation in the **basic** counseling texts (i.e., those texts that are most widely used in beginning graduate courses in counseling and guid-

ance, rehabilitation counseling, and counseling psychology). With this in mind, the author consulted with University of Missouri-Columbia faculty members who were teaching the basic counseling and rehabilitation courses. A list of 44 texts were generated from these consultations. The total included six rehabilitation counseling texts, ranging in publication dates from 1970 to 1982.

A review of these 44 basic texts revealed the following information: of the 20 counseling texts published prior to 1976, the majority (80 percent) had nothing at all to say about confrontation. Of the 18 counseling texts with publication dates of 1976 or later, 12 (or 67 percent) indexed confrontation. None of the six rehabilitation counseling texts (Bolton & Jaques, 1978; Bozarth & Rubin, 1972; Jaques, 1970; Lasky & Dell Orto, 1979; Moses & Patterson, 1971; Parker & Hansen, 1981) indexed confrontation or had sections devoted to it.

Regarding the amount of coverage devoted to confrontation, it was found that an increase in coverage was given to confrontation since 1976 in the basic counseling texts. However, there was not a comparable increase in the substantive attention given to confrontation. Overall, of the 16 counseling texts that indexed confrontation, seven devoted two pages or less to it. (Blackman, 1977; Blocker, 1966; Boy & Pine, 1982; Brammer, 1968; Corey, 1982; Gazda, 1978; Sahakian, 1976) and four devoted three pages to it (Dyer & Vriends, 1980; Hackney & Nye, 1973; Hansen, Stevic, & Warner, 1978; Ivey, 1980). Only four of the basic counseling texts devoted five or more pages to confrontation (Carkhuff & Anthony, 1979; Carkhuff & Berenson, 1977; Eisenberg & Delaney, 1977; and Ivey & Authier, 1978). Thus, only four (or nine percent) of the total of 44 basic counseling and rehabilitation counseling texts reviewed gave any substantive attention to confrontation.

Reprinted From: *Journal of Rehabilitation*, July/August/Sept, 1982, with permission.

Although this was not a comprehensive or scientific review, the trends seem to be clear. That is, with the exception of Carkhuff and associates, the referencing of confrontation has been given scant attention in basic counseling texts, both pre-1976 and post-1976, and little or no mention has been made of confrontation in basic rehabilitation counseling texts.

After reviewing the literature and searching out views of colleagues, a better understanding of the sources of ambivalence and confusion surrounding the concept of and the use of confrontation began to emerge. First, the ambivalence toward confrontation appears to stem from its origin in the counter culture rebellion and our so-called "depersonalized" society, its identification with the anti-intellectual, anti-scientific, and mystical movements, and its connection with the so-called "third force" or humanistic psychology movement. This latter movement was made popular by respected advocates such as Gordon Allport, Carl Rogers, Erich Fromm, Fritz Perls, and James Bugental, each of whom rejected the mechanistic, behavioral focus of psychology and instead, favored a more broad holistic (and also more vague) view of the individual as a focal point for counseling and therapy (Yalom, 1975).

The ambivalence and resistance to confront may also be related to the middle-class bias in counseling which equates directness and honesty in communication with hostile, aggressive attack. But confrontation is never merely a reaction; it is an act which brings the client into deeper contact with his or her basic strengths, as well as self-destructive behaviors (Douds, Berenson, Carkhuff & Pierce, 1967).

Second, the confusion appears to be found in the tendency for professionals in counseling and rehabilitation to view confrontation in terms of its common dictionary usage of "standing face-to-face with an opponent in hostility or defiance," rahter than in its therapeutic and existential meaning as an intense, direct, deep encounter of a counselor with his or her client toward the objective of helping the client reconcile conflicting views of the self. Counselors often tend to equate confrontation wtih arguing and fall close in their thinking to Faulkner, who stated cynically, "The last sound on the worthless earth will be two human beings trying to launch a homemade space ship and already quarreling about where they are going next" (William Faulkner address, Denver, Colorado, October 2, 1959).

The positive use of confrontation has been touted as a valuable tool for the counselor, while its negative use has been seen as harmful to clients. Unfortunately, the real importance of confrontation as a tool for rehabilitation counseling has been underplayed in the basic counseling literature. It is the intent of this article, therefore, to describe the rationale and the systematic and positive application of confrontation techniques for the rehabilitation counselor. The article consists of the following three secitons: a definition of positive confrontation, a discussion of the scientific study of confrontation, and a description of the effective uses of confrontation by the rehabilitation counselor.

Positive Confrontation: Definitions

Douds, Carkhuff, Berenson, & Pierce (1967) observed that confrontation, with the possible exception of existential approaches, has not been an integral part of any counseling or therapy system. Consistent with the dictionary definition of confrontation as a hostile encounter, its use has been restricted principally to special circumstances and with special client populations (mainly dealing with client aggression, crisis situations, and delinquent or character-disorderd clients where the counselor defensively confronts client aggression). This one-sided approach to confrontation constitutes a fundamental abrogation of true encounter since a true encounter can only occur in the mutuality of a positive, caring confrontation between counselor and client.

Moustakas (1972) futher underscored the critical importance of the counselor-client relationship as a component of positive encounter. He indicated that, as the relationship unfolds into a more personal and meaningful encounter, the client is able to experience a release of feelings and a resolution of issues and conflicts that leads to greater insight, awareness and responsibility. When the counselor allows his or her potential, talent, compassion, and total experience as a human to blend naturally into the relationship, "this unified personal and professional self, meets another peson, a loving or potentially loving person, and through a series of deep encounters" (Moustakas, 1959, p. 151) enables this person to reach his or her own self-fulfillment.

Egan (1970) invoked several rules for positive confrontation. The cardinal rule is to confront only when the counselor is deeply concerned and wishes to involve himself or herself with the client. Secondly, positive confrontation always involves an invitation to the client to self-examination; it is never an act of punishment. Telling a client off, as opposed to self-disclosing feelings in a caring way, may give the counselor some relief, but is punishment and not positive confrontation. Egan pointed to the fine line between therapeutic use of confrontation and punishment. For no matter how sensitively done, confrontation will always have certain punitive side effects. No one wishes to have their cherished misperceptions and rationalizations challenged.

Positive confrontation though it may range from a soft challenge to a major collision between counselor and client, always involves the death of an illusion, an illusion that is successfully keeping a client from becoming what he or she can truly become. Positive confrontation, in this sense, inevitably creates crisis that, in turn, become the psychological catalysts for promoting growth. Growth and change, is made possible by confrontation, in a series of "safe-emergencies," of our illusions (Douds, Carkhuff, Berenson, & Pierce, 1967).

Berenson & Mitchell (1974), summing up the rationale for positive confrontation, stated that confrontation is a part of the more broad objective in counseling of developing a deep level of understanding of the client. It can never by a special gimmick to shock a client to change. For confrontation without the deeper levels of accurate, empathetic understanding becomes cruel, stupid, or psychopathic. Rather, confrontation is an action initiated by the counselor for the sole intent of bringing the client into closer contact with self. The purpose is to enable the client to reconcile conflicting views of self in order that experience and behavior become one in the "here and now" of the counselor-client relationship.

Blocker (1966) summarized confrontation as encounter by stressing the need for a counselor to enter deeply as a person in counseling:

> **The counseling relatinship does not come about by putting on a professional cloak or pulling out a bag of tricks. It is more a product of encounter and confrontation, of interest in and caring about people, than of techniques and abstractions (p. 151).**

The Scientific Study of Confrontation

The work on confrontation that has been reported, sparse as it may be, is very significant. Initiated by Carkhuff, Berensen, and their colleagues in the mid-1960's, their research constitutes the major definitive work on confrontation in the literature of psychotherapy. Berenson, Mitchell, & Laney (1968) and Bereneson, Mitchell, & Moravec (1968) reported that counselors who score high on the core facilitative conditions of concreteness, empathy, positive regard, and genuineness do a considerable amount of confrontation. Thus, being empathic and being confrontive are not mutually exclusive of one another. In fact, empathy demands confrontation. Carkhuff and Berenson (1967) reported that: "The strongest evidence suggests that honest confrontation by high-level functioning therapists of both clients and patients with discrepancies in their expressed behavior elicits constructive therapeutic process movement and ultimately constructive gain or change" (p. 179).

What then of counselors who score low on the core facilitative conditions? Carkhuff, Berenson, and associates reported results that are exactly opposite. Low-level functional counselors do less confrontation and have less satisfactory results. Also, when they do confront, they tend to confront more on client limitations than on client resources. However, counselors who focus on defense mechanisms (i.e., the devices clients use to avoid the deeper understanding of their experience) get moderately good outcomes, even if such counselors are relatively weak in empathy and warmth. For a counselor to be most effective with a client, he or she must be both highly supportive and highly confrontive. It may be comforting for a client to have a counselor who is very patient and understanding, but if that is all the counselor expresses, the client is not apt to make changes.

The Basics of Confrontation

Confrontation flows out of the natural patterns of communication that develop in all kinds of intimate relationships (e.g., marital, friends, or familial). Several natural sources of conflict that have direct applicability to rehabilitation counseling are presented below.

1. One source of conflict is the counselor's idealism regarding what he or she believes should occur in counseling.

For example, many beginning counselors believe that they should always have positive, warm, empathic feelings toward clients, regardless of the clients' behavior in the counseling session. Because this is an irrational belief, such counselors inevitably meet with bitter disappointment. Their subsequent feelings of inadequacy, guilt, and shame over the anger or resentment that they inevitably will feel toward a client serve to complicate the development of positive confrontation.

2. Counselors tend to adopt a "one-person-win" strategy in communication where they win at the expense of the client.

This approach tends to result in a power struggle between the counselor and the client. For example, a client fails to follow through on a rehabilitation plan that both client and counselor had agreed upon. The counselor becomes frustrated and angry and attempts to force the client into following through with the agreed upon plan.

3. Counselors may also engage in person-centered conflict, where they focus on the alleged inadequacies of clients rather than on specific issues.

This strategy is referred to by Stuart (1981) as a "second degree" argument as opposed to a "first-degree" argument. Person-centered conflicts are spawned in bad communication (e.g., using absolutes such as never or always, storing up memories of past mistakes or refusing to take

one another seriously, and in rehabilitation counseling, making "crucializing" statements such as "if you really cared about your plan of recovery..."

Fortunately, there are techniques for avoiding or containing conflict. These techniques are both simple and effective in dealing with conflict through confrontation. They include:

a. Maintain a "here and now" orientation. The counselor's focus is in the present and not the past. When the counselor and client become locked in a bitter argument and look to the past for answers, they are unlikely to agree on what action by whom caused what consequences. They are much more likely to justify or to blame since neither wishes to be viewed as culpable; both hope for vindication. Accusations are followed by counter-accusations and the argument, through thrusts and parries, rapidly intensifies.

b. Adopt a conciliatory set. Get out of the "win-lose" strategy, in which the counselor labels the client's behavior in its most positive light, and aims for an equitable resolution of an issue rather than a one-sided victory. Relabeling involves (a) an honest expression of emotions by the counselor and (b) a firm, direct statement of the problems as the counselor sees it. For example, the counselor might state: "I feel a deep commitment to help you progress in your vocational plan and am very disappointed that you have not followed through with it. I note that this situation resembles what you report is happening to you in your marriage. Your wife is disappointed in you and frustrated when she gives you advice and finds you did not take it. Perhaps it is difficult for you to state what you want to do when it is in opposition to what people close to you want."

c. Arrive at the conflict in small steps. That is, be specific, avoid counter-demands, and take one issue at a time. Remember, the piling of issue upon issue is the stuff of which major conflict is spawned.

Specifics of Confrontation

The best rehabilitation counselors provide both maximum challenge and support for their clients.

Client change is fostered in an atmosphere of warmth and caring coupled with confrontation. Thus, the question is not whether to confront, but **when** and **how** to confront. According to Small (1975), the types of confrontation and when to use them include: (a) **Experiential Confrontation:** Confront when there are discrepancies between what the client says during the counseling session and what the counselor observes. For example, the client says he is doing well, but the counselor notes tears in her eyes. (b) **Action Confrontation:** Confront when there are discrepancies between what the client says in a session and what he or she actually does outside the session. For example, the client tells you that her training in electronics is going along fine, yet the counselor has just received word from the school that she has missed the last two weeks of classes. (c) **Strength Confrontation:** Confront when the client pretends weakness. For example, the client, in tears, says that he cannot continue his social work program because he is too neurotic. The counselor confronts: "Dick, I have seen you not only overcome a severe disability but deal with pain on a daily basis; anguish you doubtless have, but you are a solid, healthy person." (d) **Weakness Confrontation:** Confront when the client plays tough to avoid dealing with the hurt and pain the counselor knows he or she is feeling. For example, the client, with false bravado, insists he does not care whether his co-workers respect him. The counselor confronts by stating: "Sam, I know you are strong, but I can see hurt on your face. I know you must be in pain." A type not mentioned by Small is (e) **Defensive Confrontation:** The counselor should confront when he or she is being attacked or blamed. For example, the client tells the counselor that he or she has failed to help her and that she is certain that her adjustment to disability has become aggravated since she began seeing the counselor. The counselor may reply: "Ann, I feel very distressed by what you are saying, yet I know how much courage it took for you to tell me exactly how you feel." In this form of confrontation, it is important for the counselor to express his or her feelings without guilt or blame, to state the facts simply, and to maintain a present orientation which might serve to contain the conflict.

In addition, Small (1975) specified seven counselor conditions and four client conditions that must be met in order for positive confrontation to take place. The counselor conditions include:

1. **Is the trust between counselor and client high enough?**
2. **Is the counselor willing to become more involved with the client?**
3. **Is the counselor confronting concrete behaviour that the client can do something about?**
4. **Is the counselor confrontation positive and constructive rather than negative and punitive?**
5. **Is the counselor easily understood in his or her confrontation?**
6. **Is the counselor representing fact as fact, feelings as feelings, and inference as inference?**
7. **Has the counselor let the client in on exactly what the motivating factor is for confronting him or her?**

The client conditions are as follows:

1. **Will the client accept the confrontation as an invitation to explore alternatives?**
2. **Is the client open to being told how he or she is regarded?**
3. **Can the client tolerate some of the discomfort and hurt which inevitably will result from the confrontation?**
4. **Does the client believe that the counselor cares about him or her?**

The toughest kind of confrontation and the kinds that is most important for counselors to make is confrontation that results from the pain, frustration, hurt, and anger experienced by counselors when deeply involved in helping a client change. Any change is difficult, and is usually resisted to the fullest. Stuart (1981) suggested several important checkpoints for emotional confrontations with clients who are resisting change. They include:

1. **Qualifying my statement to show acceptance of my anger.** For example, the counselor says to his or her client: "I am feeling very angry about your refusal to do anything for yourself."

2. **Expressing respect for the client while communicating pleasure.** For example, "I know it is difficult for you to deal with partial paralysis. Yet you have shown me that you are a very strong person, and although I know it will be difficult, I see no reason why you cannot begin attending school on a regular basis."

3. **Making a threat that is modest and, therefore, credible.** For example, "I cannot continue to support you in your school plan if you continue to miss as much time as you have been missing."

4. **Asking for a specific, and reasonable change.** For example, "I am asking you for a written plan on how you are going to manage getting to school on a regular basis. Indicate in your plan the problems that are preventing you from attending school and your solutions to them. We will get together one hour each week to talk over your progress. I care for you and want you to be successful. Together we can work out a satisfactory plan."

Confrontation will always exist, be it negative or positive. Much of the ambivalence felt toward confrontation is based upon personally equating it with quarreling. Positive confrontation is, in fact, the exact opposite of quarreling since it requires a careful, compassionate, and conscientious application of good communication skills, and a genuine concern for the client. It requires caring enough about the client to risk his or her anguish or blame. When a counselor cares enough to confront, he or she will touch many painful areas, both in himself or herself as well as the client. But the counselor will offer a true act of caring that will enable the client to replace resistance to change with a deeper, more fulfilling understanding of self (Eisenberg & Delaney, 1977).

The philosophy of rehabilitation stresses restoration of the individual to the highest possible level of physical, economic, social, and emotional self-sufficiency of which he or she is capable (Rusk, 1977). Positive confrontation by the rehabilitation counselor helps to nurture in his or her client the quintessential part of this restoration (i.e., true acceptance and valuing of the totality of self-assets despite disability, acceptance of limitations and unchanging conditions, as well as undreamt of possibilities for growth and change).

References

Berenson, B.G., Mitchell, K.M., & Lancy, R.C. Levels of therapist functioning, type of confrontation and type of patient. **Journal of Clinical Psychology,** 1968 **24,** 111-113.

Berenson, B.G., Mitchell, K.M., & Moravec, J.A. Level of therapist functioning, patient depths of self-exploration and types of confrontation. **Journal of Counseling Psychology,** 1968, **15,** 136-139.

Berenson, B.G., & Mitchell, K.M. **Confrontation for better or worse!** Amherst, Mass.: Human Resource Development Press, 1974.

Blackman, G.J. **Counseling: Theory, process and practice.** Belmont, CA: Wadsworth, 1977.

Blocker, D.H. **Developmental counseling.** New York: Ronald Press, 1966.

Bolton, B., & Jaques, M.E. (Eds.) **Rehabilitation counseling: Theory and practice.** Baltimore, MD: University Park Press, 1978.

Boy, A.V., & Pine, G.J. **Client-centered counseling: A renewal.** Boston, MA: Allyn & Bacon, 1982.

Bozarth, J.D., & Rubin, S.E. **Facilitative management in rehabilitative counseling: A case book.** Champaign, IL: Stipes Publishing Co., 1972.

Brammer, L.M. **Therapeutic psychology: Fundamentals of actualization counseling and psychotherapy.** Englewood Cliffs, NJ: Prentice-Hall, 1968.

Carkhuff, R.R. & Berenson, B.G. **Beyond Counseling and Therapy** (2nd ed.). New York: Rinehart & Winston, 1977.

Carkhuff, R.R. & Anthony, W.A. **The skills of helping: An introduction to counseling skills.** Amherst, MA: Human Resource Development Press, 1979.

Corey, G. **Theory and practice of group counseling.** Monterey, CA: Brooks & Cole, 1982.

Cormier, W.H., & Cormier, L.S. **Interviewing strategies for helpers: A guide to assessment, treatment and evaluation.** Monterey, CA: Brooks & Cole, 1979.

Douds, J., Berenson, B.G., Carkhuff, R.R., & Pierce, R. In search of an honest experience: Confrontation in counseling and life. In R.R. Carkhuff & B.G. Berenson (Eds.). **Beyond counseling and therapy.** (1st ed.). New York: Holt, Rinehart & Winston, 1967.

Dyer, W.W., & Vriends, J. **Group counseling in personal mastery.** New York: Sovereign Books, 1980.

Egan, G. **Encounter process for interpersonal growth.** Belmont, CA: Wadsworth, 1970.

Egan, G. **Face to Face.** Monterey, CA: Brooks & Cole, 1973.

Egan, G. **Interpersonal living.** Monterey, CA: Brooks & Cole, 1976.

Eisenberg, S., & Delaney, D.J. **The counseling process** (2nd ed.). Chicago, IL: Rand McNally, 1977.

Gazda, G.M. **Group counseling: A developmental approach** (2nd ed.). Boston, MA: Allyn Bacon, 1978.

Hackney, H., & Nye, S. **Counseling strategies and objectives.** Englewood Cliffs, NJ: Prentice-Hall, 1973.

Hansen, J.C., Stevic, R.R., & Warner, R.W., Jr. **Counseling theory & process.** Boston, MA: Allyn & Bacon, 1978.

Ivey, A.E., & Authier, J. **Microcounseling. Innovations in interviewing, counseling, psychotherapy and psychoeducation.** Springfield, IL: Charles C. Thomas, 1978.

Ivey, A.E. **Conseling and psychotherapy: Skills, theories and practice.** Englewood Cliffs, NJ: Prentice-Hall, 1980.

Jaques, M.E. **Rehabilitation counseling scope and services.** New York: Houghton Mifflin, 1970.

Lasky, R.G., & Dell Orto, A.E. **Group counseling and physical disability: A rehabilitaiton and health care perspective.** Belmont, CA: Wadsworth, 1979

Moses, H.A., & Patterson, C.H. **Readings in rehabilitation counseling.** (2nd ed.). Champaign, IL: Stipes Publishing Co., 1971.

Moustakas, C.E. **Psychotherapy with children: The living relationship.** New York: Harper & Row, 1959.

Moustakas, C.E. **Loneliness and love.** Englewood Cliffs, NJ: Prentice-Hall, 1972.

Parker, R.M., & Hansen, C.E. **Rehabilitation counseling.** Boston: Allyn & Bacon, 1981.

Rogers, C.R. **Carl Rogers on encounter groups.** New York: Harper & Row, 1970.

Rusk, H.A. **Rehabilitation Medicine** (4th ed.). St. Louis, MO: C.V. Mosby, 1977.

Sahakian, W.S. (Ed.) **Psychotherapy and counseling: Techniques in interventions.** Chicago, IL: Rand McNally, 1976.

Small, J. **Becoming naturally therapeutic.** Austin, TX: Eupsychian Press, 1975.

Stuart, R.B. **Helping couples change: A social learning approach to marital therapy.** New York: Guilford Press, 1981.

Yalom, I.D. **The theory and practice of group psychotherapy** (2nd ed.). New York: Basic Books, 1975.

Health Promotion and Wellness in Rehabilitation Services

Jeffrey E. Brandon

The terms wellness and health promotion are not often associated with the disabled individual or with the rehabilitation process. In fact, wellness and rehabilitation are typically depicted as being near opposite ends of a health continuum (Insel & Roth, 1982). There appears to exist a limited view of wellness that emphasizes the physically fit lifestyle often characterized in the media, while overlooking other important dimensions of health. Also, little thought seems to have been given to the benefits of integrating this new health trend into the rehabilitation process. Before considering the potential for incorporating health promotion philosophy into rehabilitation, it would be helpful to review some definitions of health and wellness.

The traditional medical model views health as the absence of disease or infirmity. Unfortunately, this viewpoint leaves little room for the disabled person to be considered healthy. The more recent definitions of health have a broader focus. Probably the most frequently cited definition of health is from the World Health Organization (WHO). WHO defines health as "a state of complete physical, mental and social well-being and not merely the absence of disease or infirmity" (Mausner & Kramer, 1985, p.4). This definition encompasses the multidimensional nature of health, including the emotional and social areas. Bedworth and Bedworth (1978) defined health as "the quality of a person's physical, psychological, and sociological functioning that enables him or her to deal adequately with self and others in a variety of situations" (p.5). In addition to including the key dimensions of health, their definition emphasized the concept of adaptability, which is important in an everchanging world. Rene Dubos also emphasized this adaptability theme through describing health as a way of life that enables imperfect human beings "to achieve a rewarding and not too painful existence while they cope with an imperfect world" (Insel & Roth, 1982, p.xvii). Wellness is similarly defined by Dunn (1961) as "an integrated method of functioning which is

oriented toward maximizing the potential of which the individual is capable... within the environment where he is functioning" (p.26). These definitions offer an ecological view of health and wellness that is compatible with the goals of the rehabilitation process. Furthermore, these definitions have several qualities that deserve closer consideration.

First, the holistic nature of health is emphasized. Physiological functioning is no longer the single consideration used by the modern health care provider in evaluating the client's health status. This emphasis can be seen in the more comprehensive patient history questionnaires, used by health maintenance organizations and modern clinics, which attempt to address emotional and social functioning as well as specific lifestyle behaviors. The holistic view is also seen in research on stress-related etiology of disease, which emphasizes mind-body interaction as a major variable in health maintenance and illness (Allen, 1983; Antonovsky, 1981; Garfield, 1979; Greenberg, 1983; Pelletier, 1977). This literature suggests that prolonged and intense stress plays a role in many unhealthy conditions, including accidents, common colds, headaches, gastrointestinal ulcers, colitis, and hypertension, as well as contributing to the major causes of death (i.e., cardiovascular disease and cancer). Thus, the role of emotions and social stressors, such as unemployment, disability, poor living conditions, and ineffective interpersonal relationships, are considered to be important contributors to health/disease status.

These definitions also suggest that health is a relative concept since individuals can have different views of what health means because their physical and mental needs, desires, and goals are unique. Regardless of disability, there are always some areas in which individuals can choose to excel. The gourmet chef, for example, may be considerably overweight and openly admits having difficulty performing routine chores without becoming short of breath. Yet,

Reprinted From: *Journal of Rehabilitation*, Oct/Nov/Dec 1985, with permission.

this same person values the stress-reduction, challenge, and social opportunities associated with gourmet cooking. This individual's emphasis in defining health lies in the emotional and social areas.

Finally, the definitions suggest that health is a dynamic, everchanging condition that should be measured in terms of how well individuals live with full use of their available skills or abilities at any point in time. Indeed, the greatest need of all individuals is to function to their fullest in their own unique environment regardless of physical, emotional, or cognitive disabilities. Rehabilitation personnel must recognize that perfect health is a utopian ideal that can never be reached since, as Dubos says, man will never be so perfectly adapted to this environment (Insel & Roth, 1982).

Major content areas for health promotion and wellness applicable to disabled people include the principles of self-responsibility, nutritional awareness, physical fitness, and stress management. Each of these key areas affect the physical, psychological, and social dimensions of health.

Self-Responsibility

Self-responsibility is probably the most important and pervasive area in health promotion and wellness. More individuals are recognizing the tremendous effect that behavior has on their health. This recognition, along with the realization that the medical profession cannot cure chronic, lifestyle-related conditions, has led individuals to assume more responsibility for avoiding major disease/injury risk factors such as driving while intoxicated, smoking tobacco, abusing alcohol and drugs, and being overweight. Based upon an analysis of national morbidity and mortality data, the Centers for Disease Control in Atlanta have estimated that 84 percent of an individual's ability to handle disease is determined by his or her lifestyle, choice of health care providers, and environmental factors. Moreover, lifestyle behaviors specifically accounted for over 50 percent of this ability. Not only could lifestyle behaviors have detrimental

effects on existing disabilities, they could also produce serious complications and additional health problems.

Self-responsibility also extends to knowing the basics of self-treatment. Obviously, disabled individuals may not be completely free of symptoms or pain, yet much can be done to control their condition and prevent additional complications. Basic self-control procedures include complying with the medical regimen and properly using medical treatment facilities and specialists. For example, the diabetic, hypertensive, or heart patient can do much on their own behalf to remain as symptom free as possible by following treatment procedures carefully. The wellness approach, however, goes beyond these basic self-control procedures and includes educating oneself and others about the disabling condition and general health, to the extent that the individual does all that is possible to maximize recovery and prevent further deterioration of his or her health. As noted earlier, wellness is often depicted on a continuum extending from premature death to optimal health. Wellness goes beyond the neutral point to include educational and behavioral enhancement of one's health status. Thus, clients can move in the wellness direction by educating themselves on the specifics of their disabling condition and on health promotion skills which could be applied to other areas of their life. For example, in addition to the basics of insulin management, individuals with diabetes should learn more about the principles of nutrition and exercise.

The concept of self-responsibility is undoubtedly familiar to the rehabilitation specialist. A major goal of the rehabilitation process is to involve the client as co-manager of his or her own rehabilitation program. Wright (1983) described several advantages of co-management, including increased client self-esteem and motivation, and improved potential for learning. These same benefits can also be derived from assuming responsibility for one's own health. The self-responsible individual learns to trust his or her own judgment concerning health behavior and decisions. And with expanded knowledge and improved self-esteem, the individual is better prepared to apply health promotion principles to his or her daily life.

Nutritional Awareness

Whereas self-responsibility is the most important element in health promotion or wellness, nutrition is one of the most discussed and publicized components. Most contemporary Americans are aware of the array of books, articles, and commentary that appear in popular magazines and daily newspapers on special weight-loss diets, natural foods, and the danger of various food additives. Nutritional awareness includes an understanding of the need to consume a properly balanced diet in order to avoid vitamin and mineral deficiencies and toxicities, a preference for consuming food in its more natural or less processed form, and a familiarity with the association between diet and disease. For example, the overweight individual with adequate nutritional information might choose a weight loss approach which includes a balanced eating plan, aerobic exercise, and eating behavior modification. The aim of such a program would be long-term lifestyle change and maintenance of ideal body weight, instead of drastic reducing methods.

Beyond these general principles of nutrition, a more detailed understanding of the various types of drug-food interactions and nutritionally-related side effects of medication would be useful to clients receiving pharmacological treatment so they may adjust their diet appropriately. There are numerous instances of drug-nutrient interactions. Use of anticonvulsant medication has been show to reduce serum levels of vitamin D and several B-complex vitamins (Whitney & Cataldo, 1983). Psychotropic drugs such as tranquilizers may promote appetite and lead to marked weight gain (Williams, 1985). Additionally, Sobsey (1983) discussed special considerations in the diets of severely handicapped children. Proper dietary planning should be obtained through consulting credible nutrition texts and procuring advice from pharmacists, dieticians, or nutritionists.

Physical Fitness

Health-related physical fitness is another important component of health promotion and wellness. High levels of physical fitness enable individuals to carry out their daily responsibilities and have reserve energy for social and recreational pursuits. Physical fitness includes exercises to increase flexibility, cardiovascular endurance, and strength, as well as to maintain ideal body weight. The benefits of exercise include increased range of motion; improved functioning of the circulatory system and lungs; maintenance of normal blood pressure; decreased serum cholesterol and low density lipoproteins (high levels of which are associated with heart disease); increased caloric expenditure which helps to prevent obesity; improved overall muscular strength and endurance; and delayed degenerative changes associated with aging, such as osteoporosis (Dintiman & Greenberg, 1983; Dintiman, Stone, Pennington, & Davis, 1984; Insel & Roth, 1982). Choosing a complete fitness program involves a great deal of planning. Books by Greenberg and Pargman (1986), Hockey (1985), Dintiman et. al. (1984), Getchell (1983), and Mazzeo (1984) are recommended resources for further information. A physician should be consulted prior to commencing a vigorous program for those over age 35, who have cardiovascular disease risk factors (family history, hypertensive, or tobacco smoker), or who are in poor physical condition. The physician may also advise the disabled client on specific aerobic activities that are most adaptable to his or her disability or refer the client to an adapted fitness specialist or specialized fitness program.

Recently, much attention has been devoted to physical and recreational education for disabled people. Research has found reduced fitness levels and increased body fat levels among physically disabled individuals (Lasko, Sucee, & Kinance, 1984; Quirion, Dulacs, & Caron, 1981). Other investigations have demonstrated that significant improvement in physical fitness and recreational pursuits are obtainable by disabled persons (Buettner & Gavron, 1981; French, 1984; Matthews, 1981). Along with physical, occupational, and corrective therapists, specialists in adapted physical education, adult fitness, recreation, and cardiovascular rehabilitation are directly involved in meeting the special exercise needs of disabled individuals. Specific exercise techniques and recreational services for persons with disabilities are available in institutional, community, and private residential settings. These programs include project "HALPE" or Handicapped Adult Leisure-Time P.E. (Daniel, 1981), Home Assisted Recreation (Matthews, 1981), and the Recreation Centre for the Handicapped, Inc. (Pomeroy, 1981). This latter program is one of the largest, having served over 10,000 persons with severe disabilities in the San Francisco area for the past 32 years. The program is comprehensive since it offers supportive services (such as transportation) and provides fitness and recreational programs for adults and children. Two professional journals which reflect the rapid growth in the area of adaptive physical education for disabled persons are the **Adapted Physical Activity Quarterly** and **Challenges: The Journal of Sports and Physical Education for the Disabled.**

In addition to the physical results associated with exercise, there are also psychological benefits. Due to mind-body interaction, improved physical functioning helps optimize emotional health by enabling the individual to feel more alert and able, live with decreased depression and anxiety, improve work productivity, and manage stress (Getchell, 1983; Insel & Roth, 1982).

Stress Management

Exercise is one technique frequently used in comprehensive stress management, the fourth components of health promotion/wellness. The deleterious impact of excessive stress on health has been researched for several decades. Stress related disorders such as chronic anxiety, elevated blood pressure, gastrointestinal ulcers, and colitis are commonplace in our high-tech, urban society. Moreover, evidence is accumulating that implicates stress as a causative agent in infectious disease, traffic accidents, and the development of many chronic conditions such as heart disease, hypertension, and perhaps even cancer (Prager-

Decker & Decker, 1980; Selzer & Vinokur, 1974; Stein, Schiavi, & Camerino, 1976). In addition to the stress commonly associated with interpersonal conflicts, traffic congestion, and demanding schedules, the disabled individual confronts many additional stressors. These may include the physical and emotional suffering associated with an accident or illness, disruption of regular daily routine, loss of income and perhaps family status, and adapting to disability-specific limitations. The impact of stressful life events on future health status has been researched by Holmes and Rahe (1967). They found that greater numbers of stressful life events are associated with increased risk of developing illness in the future. Thus, there may be a need for persons who are disabled to practice stress management in order to reduce the risk of future health problems, as well as to help deal with the emotional and physical difficulties (including pain management) associated with their disabilities.

While comprehensive stress management programs make use of several techniques (i.e., perceptual and life-situation interventions, relaxation training, and exercise), incomplete stress management programs focus solely on relaxation training or physical exercise instruction. Greenberg (1983) proposes setting up multiple "roadblocks" to stress. His stress model of disease, which depicts how chronic stress leads to illness, begins with the occurrence of some life event. This may be receiving a traffic ticket, death of a friend, a job promotion, or any other event requiring adapting to a new situation. Most events require cognitive interpretation before being evaluated as stressful. Thus, Greenberg's second phase of the model involves perceiving the vent as stressful. Obviously whether or not one evaluates the event as stressful depends upon several variables, such as pervious learning history and general cognitive lifestyle. Evaluating the event as stressful leads to one becoming emotionally aroused. Subsequently there follows physiological arousal, which if continued long enough, will eventually lead to disease.

Occasionally, medication such as sedatives and tranquilizers or illegal drugs are used to prevent life situations from being perceived as stressful. Unfortunately, medications are only short-term solutions which may lead to even more stress-producing problems. There are other, more effective techniques that could be used at the early stages of this model to either eliminate or alter one's interpretation of the life event, such as life-situation interventions and perceptual interventions.

Life-situation interventions involve eliminating unnecessary stressors, if at all possible. Some situations can be eliminated through direct intervention. An example could involved individuals with rheumatoid arthritis who find walking difficult and may frequently be unable to find a close parking space for shopping. A life-situation intervention would be to take the steps necessary to obtain a disabled car license certificate so they could use handicapped parking spaces. Another life-situation intervention is assertiveness training, which is applicable to many situations involving interpersonal conflicts. For example, the disabled driver should be encouraged to correct the misinformed, non-disabled individual who parks in the designated handicapped parking spaces. Assertiveness training manuals, such as the one by Bowers and Bowers (1976), are widely available.

People react to stressful events differently; some may catastrophize events, while others may recognize the seriousness of stressful situations, yet focus on the positive elements of the event. For instance, two construction workers are told they have a herniated intervertebral disc that requires immediate surgery and that it will be unlikely that they will be able to return to their construction occupations. One worker may consider such news shattering and become distressed about his potential inability to meet family and financial responsibilities. This individual is likely to have prolonged emotional and physiological reactions which may lead to illness. The second worker, however, views the situation as unfortunate, but perceives it as an opportunity to finish his college education and enter a field that would be more gratifying. He sees the potential for growth in the situation, which is less likely to lead to prolonged

emotional/physiological arousal and subsequent illness. Specific therapy techniques, such as rational emotive therapy and cognitive behavior modification, may be useful in challenging negative thinking/interpretation of the stressor (Rimm & Masters, 1979).

Once the individual perceives an event as stressful and has an emotional reaction to the event, relaxation training is useful in preventing emotional arousal from leading to chronic physiological arousal. Numerous relaxation techniques (such as meditation, autogenic training, progressive muscle relaxation, and biofeedback) are available, and Brandon (1982) has reviewed the research literature on each of these and found them to be generally beneficial in reducing at least some measure of tension.

Once physiological arousal occurs and continues on a prolonged basis, the body must engage in some form of physical activity to use up the extra circulating blood fats and other stress products. This cleansing of dangerous stress by-products may account for the emphasis that some therapists place on physical exercise as an important stress management intervention. Greenberg (1983) proposed a sieve-like model of stress management. Each of the major techniques described can act as a sieve at various phases of the stress model of disease for filtering out portions of the damaging elements of the stress response. Thus, people should rely on all of these approaches to maximize their changes for successful, comprehensive stress management.

Conclusions

In addition to specific suggestions made during the discussion of self-responsibility, nutritional awareness, physical exercise, and stress management, a few other suggestions on the application of health promotion in rehabilitation facilities and programs are presented below. First, the usefulness of health promotion philosophy and activities for all individuals should be apparent. Therefore, in rehabilitation facilities such programming should be made available to the entire staff. This would be beneficial, not only for each participant's health, but also for the facility in that it might improve staff productivity, decrease absenteeism, and reduce staff burnout and subsequent turn-over problems. Moreover, recognizing the staff's active involvement and commitment to health promotion is likely to encourage client participation as well.

Second, the health promotion philosophy should be integrated in the rehabilitation counseling process. Since traditional rehabilitation includes an emphasis on self-responsibility, health promotion could be incorporated as an additional component within this area. Depending upon the needs of the client, specific health promotion activities may also be incorporated into his or her rehabilitation plan. Stress management, for instance, may be recommended for chronic pain sufferers, while exercise may be recommended to increase muscle strength or to help relieve anxiety or depression.

Finally, rehabilitation and residential centers should offer educational experiences and guided practice in the specific areas previously discussed. They could develop programs specifically entitled "health promotion" or offer specific classes on nutrition, exercise, and stress management. A health resource room or library could be developed to provide supporting materials. In some instances, health-related classes could be offered as extensions to comprehensive adjustment services programming.

This article, which addresses only a few of the basic areas of health promotion and wellness, has attempted to encourage rehabilitation specialists to see the usefulness of incorporating a health promotion philosophy into their professional practice. While only a brief overview has been provided, numerous additional resources are available on the general topic of health promotion. These include: **High Level Wellness** (Ardell, 1979); **Holistic Medicine** (Pelletier, 1979); and **Mind as Healer, Mind as Slayer** (Pelletier, 1977). In addition to these books on the topic, several articles appear in publications by the American Public Health Association (**American Journal of Public Health**); Society

for Public Health Education (**Health Education Quarterly**); Society of Behavioral Medicine (**Behavioral Medicine Abstracts**); Society for Prospective Medicine (**An Ounce of Prevention**); and in American Alliance for Health, Physical Education, Recreation, and Dance publications (**Health Education; Journal of Physical Education and Recreation; Research Quarterly**).

References

Allen, R.J. (1983). *Human stress: Its nature and control*. Minneapolis: Burgess.

Antonovsky, A. (1981). *Health, stress, and coping*. San Francisco: Jossey-Bass.

Ardell, D.B. (1979). *High level wellness*. Emmaus, PA: Rodale Press.

Bedworth, D.A., & Bedworth, A.E. (1978). *Health education: A process for human effectiveness*. New York: Harper & Row.

Bowers, S.A., & Bowers, G.H. (1976). *Asserting yourself*. Reading, MA: Addison-Wesley.

Brandon, J.E. (1982). *A comparative evaluation of three relaxation training procedures*. Unpublished doctoral dissertation, Southern Illinois University, Carbondale.

Buettner, L.L., & Garvon, S.J. (1981, November). *Personality changes and physiological effects of a personalized fitness enrichment program for cancer patients*. Paper presented at the meeting of the Third International Symposium on Adapted Physical Activities, New Orleans, LA.

Daniel, C. (1981, November). *Project "HALPE," handicapped adult leisure-time P.E.* Paper presented at the Third International Symposium on Adapted Physical Activities, New Orleans, LA.

Dintiman, G.B., & Greenberg, J.S. (1983). *Health through discovery* (2nd ed.). Reading, MA: Addison-Wesley.

Dintiman, G.B., Stone, S.E., Pennington, J.C., & Davis, R.G. (1984). *Discovering lifetime fitness: Concepts of exercise and weight control*. St. Paul, MN: West.

Dunn, H.L. (1961). *High level wellness*. Arlington, VA: R.W. Beatty Co.

French, R.W. (1984, March). *Effects of a swimming program on children with cystic fibrosis*. Paper presented at the meeting of the American Alliance for Health, Physical Education, Recreation and Dance, Anaheim, CA.

Garfield, C.A. (ed.) (1979). *Stress and survival: The emotional realities of life-threatening illness.* St. Louis, MO: C.V. Mosby.

Getchell, B. (1983). *Physical fitness: A way of life* (3rd ed.). St. Paul, MN: West.

Greenberg, J.S. (1983). *Comprehensive stress management.* Dubuque, IA: Wm. C. Brown.

Greenberg, J.S., & Pargman, D. (1986). *Physical fitness: A wellness approach.* Englewood Cliffs, NJ: Prentice-Hall.

Hockey, R.V. (1985). *Physical fitness: The pathway to healthful living.* St. Louis, MO: C.V. Mosby.

Holmes, T.H., & Rahe, R.H. (1967). The social readjustment rating scale. *Journal of Psychosomatic Research, 11,* 213-218.

Insel, P.M., & Roth, W.T. (1982). *Core concepts in health.* Palo Alto, CA: Mayfield.

Lasko, P., Sucee, A.A., & Kinance, K. (1984, March). *An aerobic threshold and aerobic capacity during arm cranking in quadraplegic and paraplegic adults.* Paper presented at the meeting of the American Alliance for Health, Physical Education, Recreation and Dance, Anaheim, CA.

Matthews, P.R. (1981, November). *Home assisted recreation.* Paper presented at the Third International Symposium on Adapted Physical Activities, New Orleans, LA.

Mausner, J.S. & Kramer, S. (1985). *Mausner & Bhan Epidemiology -- An introductory text.* Philadelphia: W.B. Saunders.

Mazzeo, K.S. (1984). *Shape up through posture, diet, exercise, relaxation.* Englewood, CO: Morton.

Pelletier, K.R. (1977). *Mind as healer, mind as slayer.* New York: Delacorte Press.

Pelletier, K.R. (1979). *Holistic Medicine: From stress to optimum health.* New York: Delacorte Press.

Pomeroy, J. (1981, November). *Recreation unlimited: Responding to persons with severe disabilities.* Paper presented at the Third International Symposium on Adapted Physical Activities, New Orleans, LA.

Prager-Decker, I.J., & Decker, W.A. (1980). The efficacy of muscle relaxation in combating stress. *Health Education, 11,* 40-42.

Quirion, A., Dulacs, S., & Caron, F. (1981, November). *Physical fitness of paraplegics and cerebral palsied subjects.* Paper presented at the Third International Symposium on Adapted Physical Activities, New Orleans, LA.

Rimm, D.C., & Masters, J.C. (1979). *Behavior therapy* (2nd ed.). New York: Academic Press.

Selzer, M.L., & Vinokur, A. (1974). Life events, subjective stress, and traffic accidents. *American Journal of Psychiatry, 131,* 903-906.

Sobsey, R.L. (1983). Nutrition of children with severely handicapping conditions. *The Journal of the Association for Persons with Severe Handicaps, 8,* 14-17.

Stein, M., Schiavi, R.C. & Camerino, M. (1976). Influence of brain and behavior on the immune system. *Science, 191,* 435-440.

Wright, B.A. (1983). *Physical disability: A psychosocial approach* (2nd ed.). New York: Harper & Row.

Whitney, E.N., & Cataldo, C.B. (1983). *Understanding normal and clinical nutrition.* St. Paul, MN: West.

Williams, S.R. (1985). *Nutrition and diet therapy* (5th ed.). St. Louis, MO: Mosby.

Personal Care Attendants:
Attitudes and Factors Contributing to Job Satisfaction

BOBBIE J. ATKINS, ANN B. MEYER, NANCY K. SMITH

Abstract

Quality personal attendant care is imperative to successful independence for physically disabled persons. To help eliminate the existing void in the research literature regarding attendant input, this study was conducted to provide information from the attendant's point of view which could be used to enhance care to physically disabled adults. Data from the 56 current or former attendants were collected via several instruments, e.g., Attitudes Toward Disabled Persons scale, Gordon Personal Profile, Current Attendant Profile. It was found that attendants represented varied backgrounds, were sincerely interested in their work, and felt they needed specific training to be more effective.

As many severely disabled persons cannot attain independent living status without assistance, Fay, Bartels, Corcoran, and McHugh (1977) described personal care attendants (PCAs) as the key to successful independent living. Unfortunately attendant care work frequently is low paying, high demanding, and characterized by high turnover rates (McGwinn, 1977; Thornock, Hutchins, Meyer, Kenyon, & Williams, 1978; Weil, 1979). To improve the chances for success in attaining independent living, development of methods to enhance the role of the attendant are necessary. Reasons for the high turnover rate and identification of factors contributing to job satisfaction should be explored. In an extensive review of the literature on personal care attendants, Smith and Meyer (1981) were able to identify only one study (Hutchins, Thornock, Lindgre, & Parks, 1978) which used PCAs as subjects to determine their perceptions of attendant care. Our literature review found only one study to be added to the Smith and Meyer list, i.e., Stelmach, Postma, Goldstein, and Sheppard (1981). Hence, the purpose of this study

was to determine why the PCA turnover rate is so high and what can be done to make attendant work more appealing. Both currently employed and former PCAs were surveyed to provide information on attendants' attitudes towards their jobs and to ascertain what factors contribute to PCAs decisions to resign from their jobs. It was hoped that a better understanding of attendant care from the PCA point of view would assist disabled persons and the professionals working with them in selecting attendants and fostering harmonious employer-employee relationships.

Methodology

Subjects

The 117-member population for this study consisted of all of the PCAs whom Access to Independence, Inc., referred to its disabled clients between January, 1978, and June, 1980. Access to Independence, Inc., is a center for Independent Living located in Madison, Wisconsin, which offers support services to Dane County residents with physical disabilities.

The total number of participants in this study was 56 representing a response rate of 48%. Of the 56 study participants, 30 (54%) were working attendants at the time, and 26 (46%) were former attendants. Forty-eight (86%) of the subjects were female, and 8 (14%) were male.

Procedure

To maintain the attendants' confidentiality, the initial contact letter was sent by Access to Independence. The letter explained the purpose of the study, asked for participation, explained the time involved (approximately one hour per subject), the financial reward for participating, scheduling information, and emphasized the confidentiality of the study. After a seven-day waiting period, telephone follow-up was

Reprinted From: *Journal of Rehabilitation* July/Aug/Sept 1982, with permission.

undertaken to reach attendants who had not responded to the letter.

Instruments

Three instruments were administered to each subject. The Attitudes Toward Disabled Persons (ATDP) scale was used to examine the effect of attendant attitudes on the attendant-employer relationship and to determine if any particular attitudes toward the disabled correlated with PCA job satisfaction and/or length of employment. The combined Gordon Personal Profile (GPP) and Gordon Personal Inventory (GPI) was administered to provide measures of eight personality traits: ascendancy, responsibility, emotional stability, sociability, cautiousness, original thinking, personal relations, and vigor. Finally, either the Current Attendant Profile (CAP) or the Former Attendant Profile (FAP) were developed and used to obtain subject demographic information, to determine what the PCAs liked and disliked about their work, and to discover reasons for leaving employment.

Statistical Techniques

Relative frequency percentages were determined from absolute frequency totals for responses to questions on the attendant profiles. Ranks were determined for responses to the two questions in which the subjects were asked to rank series of PCA and employer characteristics in order of importance.

A step-wise multiple regression technique was chosen to attempt to predict the length of attendant employment from a series of explanatory variables which could be gathered by disabled employers before hiring, should they be proven to be predictive. The eight quantifiable, independent variables thought to be possible useful predictors, as determined from the review of literature, were the attendants': GPP-I ascendancy scores; GPP-I responsibility scores; GPP-I emotional stability scores; GPP-I personal relations scores; GPP-I vigor scores; ratings of their pay as compared to former jobs; ATDP scores; and perceptions of the proportion of time their employers engaged in social or work activities without them.

Results

Before the study results are presented, two clarifications must be offered. First, many of the subjects answered questions requiring only one answer with multiple responses and all of these responses were recorded. For those questions, the answer percentages totaled more than 100%. Second, all percentages have been rounded off to the nearest whole numbers. Sixty-three percent (35) of the respondents participated via the mail and 38% (21) responded in person.

PCA Demographics

Presented in Table 1 is the attendant demographic profile. The largest percent of attendants was female (86%) working for female employers.

The subjects ages varied with the largest percentage (43%) being less than 27 years old. The majority of PCAs were single (79%) with no dependents (75%). Forty-five percent of the attendants had no previous close contact with the disabled. Eighty-eight percent (49) of the attendants worked for employers whose ethnic heritage was the same as theirs. For 50% of the respondents, their attendant salary was the main source of income.

Job Quality

The elements of attendant work that the subjects liked best are presented in Table 2. Presented in Table 3 are the aspects of their jobs which the attendants liked least.

Examples of the aspects of their jobs which the attendants found most frustrating included: being a live-in attendant and having to change eating and sleeping habits to match employers' (14%).

Reasons for Seeking/Quitting Personal Care Work

The major reasons provided by this sample of PCAs for selecting attendant work focused on one of the following four reasons: wanted to help others (48%); needed to earn money (38%); needed a place to live (9%); and needed work experience related to school work (5%).

Table 1
Attendant Demographic Profile
(n = 56)

Demographic	n	%
Sex		
Female	48	86
Male	8	14
Age		
Less than 27	24	43
27 to 37	15	27
38 to 59	12	22
60 and older	5	9
Marital Status		
Single	30	54
Married	12	21
Separated	2	4
Divorced	8	14
Widowed	4	7
Number of dependents (excluding self)		
None	42	75
One	7	13
Two or more	5	9
Ethnic heritage		
Caucasian	52	93
Afro-American	1	2
Oriental	1	2
Other	2	4
Type of previous close contact with disabled		
Family members	12	21
Work Settings other than longest job	8	14
Spouses	7	13
Other	2	4
None	2	4
	25	45

Table 2
Job Aspects Attendants Liked Best
(n = 56)

Job Aspects	n	%
Being able to help others	21	38
Doing something worthwhile	20	36
Made their own problems seem smaller	6	11
Salary	5	9
Becoming aware of disabled people's needs	2	4
Getting work experience in area they were studying in school	2	4
Having a lot of responsibility	1	2
Other	4	7

The two main reasons the attendants gave for quitting their last attendant positions were change in school schedule (23%) and the employer died or needed more care (20%). It should be noted that low salary was cited by only 7% of the PCAs.

Table 3
Job Aspects Attendants Liked Least
(n = 56)

Job Aspects	n	%
Low salary	15	27
Lack of fringe benefits	10	18
Odd hours	8	14
Boring routine	5	9
Too much responsibility	4	7
Duties such as bowel/bladder programs	3	5
Not enough time off/lack of privacy	3	5
Other	10	18
Like all job aspects	4	7

Job Improvement

Probably the most valuable information obtained in this study can be gleaned from the attendants' responses to questions relating to ways of improving their jobs.

Fringe benefits. Fringe benefits which the subject felt should be given to attendants in addition to their salaries included days off (32%), paid vacation (25%), and paid sick days (13%).

Support groups. If an attendant support group was offered so that interested attendants could get together once or twice a month to discuss mutual problems and give each other support, 86% (48) of the subjects said that they would join such a group.

Attendant training. Seventy-five percent of the attendants felt that it would be helpful if attendants were given more training in personal care work.

Employer training. Seventy percent of the attendants felt that it would be helpful if disabled people were given more training on how to be employers of PCAs.

Table 4
Pearson Product Moment Correlation Coefficients
(n = 56)

Variable	JT	A	R	ES	PR	V	P	ATDP	EI
Job tenure (JT)	1.00	.21	.17	.08	.11	.27	-.03	-.18	.08
Ascendancy (A)	.21	1.00	.61	.68	.56	.63	.04	.01	-.06
Responsibility (R)	.17	.61	1.00	.86	.56	.56	.15	.09	-.15
Emotional stability (ES)	.08	.68	.86	1.00	.61	.52	.16	-.07	-.07
Personal relations (PR)	.11	.56	.56	.61	1.00	.72	.24	.14	-.07
Vigor (V)	.27	.63	.56	.52	.72	1.00	.11	.11	-.09
Pay (P)	-.03	.04	.15	.16	.24	.11	1.00	.01	.20
ATDP (ATDP)	-.18	.01	.09	-.07	.14	.11	.01	1.00	.09
Employer independence (EI)	.08	-.06	-.15	-.07	-.07	-.09	.20	.09	1.00

Predicting Length of PCA Employment

One of the research questions posed by this study was whether or not there seemed to be some specific, measurable traits which correlated with length of PCA employment. It was believed that if such characteristics existed, and could be identified and measured, that disabled employers could use that information to help screen out potential PCAs whose turnover would probably be high. After reviewing the literature, the following characteristics were hypothesized to be the most likely to correlate with employment tenure: ascendancy, responsibility, emotional stability, personal relations, vigor, attitudes toward the disabled, pay compared to previous jobs, and percentages of time employers engaged in independent social or work activities without their attendants.

The Pearson correlation coefficients for all of the dependent and independent variables are presented in Table 4.

A summary of the results of the regression process is presented in Table 5. The characteristic of Vigor was identified as being the most powerful predictor, followed by the ATDP score; together they yielded a combined R^2 of 0.115, a modest but statistically significant proportion of the PCA employment length's variance [Vigor: $F(1, 54)=4.08$; ATDP: $F(2, 53)=3.43$, both $p<.05$]. The remaining variables, listed in descending order of power in Table 5, contributed a combined addition of only 0.103 toward R^2.

Table 5
Multiple Regressoin Summary
(n = 56)

Variable	Multiple r	R^2	Simple r
Vigor	.27	.07	.27*
ATDP	.34	.11	-.18**
Employer independence	.36	.13	.08
Personal relations	.38	.14	.11
Responsibility	.38	.15	.17
Emotional stability	.44	.20	.08
Ascendancy	.46	.21	.21**
Pay	.47	.22	-.03

* Statistically significant, p.05
** Statistically significant, p.20

The high intercorrelations between some of the dependent scores explained why characteristics with lower correlations with the dependent variable were sometimes included in the regression model at a higher priority than those with higher correlations. For example, the trait of Ascendancy was more highly correlated with PCA employment length than ATDP score (r=0.21 and -0.17, respectively). The latter was given a higher priority in the regression model, however, because Ascendancy was highly intercorrelated with Vigor (r=0.63), which had **already** been included in Step 1 of the regression building procedure. Adding Ascendancy at Step 2, instead of the ATDP score, would have contributed little to predicting PCA employment length that Vigor had not already contributed.

Basically, the multiple regression procedure revealed that none of the eight independent variables were practically significant predictors of length of attendance employment, though GPP-Vigor and the ATDP score reach statistical significance. The earlier-reported indications that no one factor seemed to play a major role in attendant turnover, thus were statistically confirmed.

Discussion

Most previous formal and informal discussions about PCAs have focused the "blame" for their high turnover rate either upon the lack of funds allocated to pay PCA salaries, or upon the less than ideal type of person who has been attracted to personal care work (McGwinn, 1977). The results of this study, however, suggest that there was no single reason why PCAs quit their jobs or found them unfulfilling. While low pay was repeatedly mentioned by the subjects as a negative aspect of the job, it was not necessarily the sole reason for the high PCA turnover rate. Obviously, a major improvement in attendant job quality would be salary increases. However, the subjects recognized that this might not be possible, and volunteered some frank, positive suggestions on other actions and attitudes which could be initiated by disabled employers, rehabilitation agencies, and potential attendants, to make PCA work more pleasant and, thus, to encourage longer PCA employment tenure.

Based on the results of this study, the PCAs who participated in this study appeared to be bright, caring, and insightful individuals who were truly concerned about the futures of both their employers and personal care workers, in general. The fact that a majority of the attendants liked/chose PCA work for humanitarian reasons, and were willing to cope with a certain amount of negative job aspects (e.g., boring routines, unusual hours, heavy responsibilities, and low pay), suggested an unusual degree of compassion and dedication in the person choosing personal care work. This generally positive attitude was confirmed by the finding that 95% of the subjects would have recommended PCA work to their best friends.

Since the entire concept of independent living is based upon consumer direction, the attendant-subjects in this study felt that if disabled consumers were responsible enough to hire and direct their own PCAs, they should also be responsible enough to try to resolve some of their employees' job complaints. Rather than continuing to dwell on the problem of attendant turnover as something totally beyond their control, the PCAs felt that disabled employers and rehabilitation agencies could more effectively channel their energies into making job quality improvements. Since the problems of PCA hiring and management will probably remain with severely disabled consumers for their entire lives, it seems advantageous to begin to explore some realistic options for improving the situation, even if there are no total solutions.

Probably the most important job quality recommendation emerging from this study was insightfully summarized by one subject, who urged employers to "make attendant jobs seem as important as they are when one is being hired." Many PCAs felt that more people would be attracted to PCA work and would stay with it longer, if they did not feel that they were just doing manual labor, but rather, a specialized demanding job.

The characteristics/attitudes they look for in potential disabled employers were listed by the PCAs, in order of importance, as: (a) treating employees with kindness, fairness, and respect; (b) knowing their own care needs; (c) ability to offer both praise and criticism, when appropriate; and (d) acting as independently as possible.

Several specific recommendations which could be implemented by agencies for independent living and/or other rehabilitation professions emerged from this study. First, PCAs need more training before beginning PCA work. Second, disabled people need more training on how to be employers of PCAs. Third, 86% (48) of the attendants felt that their jobs could be improved by PCA support programs. Such a group could help to ease job frustration, and hence lengthen the duration of employment.

A fourth effort which the attendants suggested as making their jobs more rewarding and appealing, would be for rehabilitation agencies to launch concerted public information campaigns to educate the public abut the concept of independent living and the importance of PCAs to disabled people. The subjects felt that a more positive image of PCA work would automatically attract more potential attendants, as well as help to keep those who are currently employed working longer.

For the consideration of potential PCAs, as well as disabled employers, the most important characteristics needed by good attendants were listed by the subjects in the following order of importance: dependability/responsibility, patience, understanding/compassion (but not pity), and honesty. Other characteristics which seem to be helpful in PCA work, as seen by people who do it, are flexibility, punctuality, and a sense of humor.

Before they accept PCA positions, potential attendants should be aware that many of the duties performed by a PCA do not directly involve personal care. In this study, for example, the two most often performed PCA tasks were housecleaning and cooking. Thus, if one has strong, negative feelings about cleaning, cooking, running errands, or similar tasks, he/she should seriously reconsider becoming involved in PCA work.

Conclusion

If independence for physically disabled persons is to become a reality, highly qualified PCAs must be employed. The results of this study revealed that a variety of persons became PCAs, that PCAs had a sincere interest in attendant work, and that specific training is needed for both PCAs and disabled employers.

To further examine and expand upon the basic data gathered in this study, future studies could include both PCAs and their disabled employers as subjects, and use both written questionnaire responses and confidential individual interviews as the data gathering mechanisms. Such studies could thus explore the role of the PCA from both the employer's and employee's perspectives.

References

Fay, F.A., Bartels, E.C., Corcoran, P., & McHugh, R. **The BCIL report.** Boston: Regional Medical Rehabilitation Research and Training Center No. 7, 1977.

Hutchins, T.K., Thornock, M., Lindgre, B., & Parks, J. Profile of inhome attendant care workers. **American Rehabilitation,** November-December, 1978, 18-22.

McGwinn, D. Attendant care. **Housing and home services for the disabled--guidelines and experiences in independent living.** Hagerstown: Harper & Row, 1977.

Smith, N.K. & Meyer, A.B. Personal care attendants: Key to living independently. **Rehabilitation Literature,** 1981, **42,** 258-265.

Stelmach, M., Postma, J., Goldstein, S., & Shepard, K.F. Selected factors influencing job satisfaction of attendants of physically disabled adults. **Rehabilitation Literature,** 1981, **42,** 130-137.

Thornock, M., Hutchins, T.K., Meyer, S., Kenyon, A., & Williams, M. Attendant care needs of the physically disabled: Institutional perspectives. **Rehabilitation Literature,** May, 1978, **39,** 147-153.

Weil, N. Living with an attendant. **Rehabilitation Gazette,** 1979, **22,** 19-20.

Experiences of Disabled Health and Caring Professionals

SALLY FRENCH

Introduction

It is frequently argued that having personal experience of an event gives a dimension of knowledge that others cannot fully share. Childbirth is an example, where mothers may assume that neither men nor childless women can fully appreciate the experience. Various self-help groups have been formed because of dissatisfaction with the help that professionals provide or a realisation that such help is limited. Many believe that minority group members have better insight, more commitment and greater rapport with similarly affected people than does the general population (Shearer 1981:177, Finkelstein 1981:34) and that people with extensive professional training do not necessarily help those with disabilities (McKnight 1981:26).

Disabled people are widely discriminated against in most types of employment (McConkey and McCormack 1983:32) which makes it likely that they will find entry to high status professions, such as the health and caring professions, particularly difficult. In a content analysis of the career literature of 26 health and caring professions and occupations (French 1986a:44) it was found that disabled people were never specifically invited to apply, yet ten of these occupations explicitly sought candidates with the ability to empathise and understand ill and disabled people. The radiography profession, for example, was seeking a person having tact and empathy (College of Radiographers 1985) and the audiology technician was required to have, 'a sympathetic and understanding personality.' (British Society of Audiology). These are qualities which disabled people, by virtue of their experience, are likely to possess. Burnfield, a psychiatrist with multiple sclerosis, states:

> I believe that having MS myself has helped me to become more sensitive to the needs of others and that it has enhanced my skills as a healer. I often think of myself as being doubly qualified, firstly as a patient and secondly as a doctor--the order is important. (Burnfield 1983:169).

Perhaps medicine, perceiving itself primarily as a scientific enterprise, does not value personal experience. As Laing states:

> Science finds time for our ordinary world only to find more and more subtle and effective ways to exclude it. Its testimony is not heard in the discourse of science. (Laing 1983:69).

It is unclear whether disabled people are actively discouraged from entering the health and caring professions, but it seems likely that the acceptance of more than a few could seriously challenge the traditional professional/client relationship, where the professional is considered to be the expert and occupies a dominant position over the patient. Sociologists and disabled people alike have written extensively of the conflicts in the doctor/patient relationship which often seem to arise through differing conceptions and definitions of illness and disability (Scott 1969:19, Morgan 1982:60). Many sociologists have commented on the paternalism of medical practice (Faulder 1985:111) and Sutherland (1981:39) notes that professionals base their dealings on a dependency model in which they are the experts and people with disabilities are dependent on them for help. When discussing the issue of disabled people becoming health professionals he states:

> Since the job for which the person is applying would confer a recognition of equality, they tend not to get it, they are judged unsuitable. (Sutherland:1981:40).

Sutherland (1981:127) notes that disabled people are likely to possess skills that able bodied professionals lack or feel insecure in, but in order to improve this situation professionals would need to learn from their clients which in turn

Reprinted from: *Sociology of Health & Illness Vol.10 No.2 1988 ISSN0141-9889*, with permission.

would lead to a reduction in their authority and status.

In a review of the literature concerning disabled people and their employment, there was considerable evidence to show that disabled workers are equally efficient, if not more efficient, than able-bodied workers (Kettle 1981). The research indicates that disabled people are equally as productive as other workers and are less likely to have accidents or be absent from work (Darnbrough and Kinrade 1981:53). This information, however, is largely unknown or ignored and disabled people are frequently assumed to be less capable than other workers, to be absent more often and to be more accident prone (Kettle 1983). Health professionals, being members of society, are likely to view disabled people in a similar way: in fact, their views may be more negative due to the type of relationship they have with disabled people and the fact that they come into contact when the disabled person is deemed to need their help.

Most of the overt justification for the exclusion of disabled people from the health and caring professions is in terms of the disabled person themself: her or his presumed inability to cope, the adverse effect there may be on patients and the assumption of proneness to accidents (Silver 1979:537, Browning 1980:307, Chickadonz et al 1983:333, Libman 1985:2). Others, however, believe that disabled people have unique assets to offer these professions (Hutchins 1976:64, Biehn 1979:1384, Gavin 1980:1086, Bueche 1983:7, Turner 1984:451). Negative attitudes are sometimes rationalised and disguised as concern, emphasizing that the disabled person may damage herself or himself, either psychologically or physically, by undertaking such demanding work (Safilios-Rothschild 1976:69).

There is some evidence to suggest that health and caring professionals are neither particularly positive in their attitudes to disabled people, nor knowledgeable about the implications of disability. For example, in the 1984 career literature of the Chartered Society of Physiotherapy it is stated:

Any form of physical disability or weakness is likely to contra-indicate physiotherapy as a suit-able career, in particular defects in hearing, epilepsy, chest ailments, skin conditions, heart defects, nervous breakdowns. Injuries to backs, knees and hands may also prejudice acceptance for training. (*How to Become a Chartered Physiotherapist.* 1984:2)

Similarly, the Royal College of Nursing (1985:8) believes that candidates with a variety of medical conditions and characteristics, including obesity, eczema and amputation are unsuitable for training. Such statements show the most blatant form of negative discrimination, implying that subtler forms also exist. It should be remembered, however, that the views put forward by professional bodies do not necessarily reflect the views of the membership.

Stetten (1983:27) a visually handicapped physician, is concerned about the narrowness of ophthalmologists' interests. He claims to have learned far more about visual handicap from chance contact with other visually handicapped people than from ophthalmologists and believes that ophthalmologists have 'come to confine their real interests in medicine to events which occur within the globe of the eye.' It is not uncommon for disabled people to complain about the treatment and lack of understanding they receive at the hands of health professionals: a disabled person featured in Sutherland's book recalls her contact with medical personnel as 'a whole series of experiences of being very coldly and formally mauled around ...' (Sutherland 1981:123). Similarly a nurse with epilepsy states:

It seemed to me that the doctors and nurses looking after me had a most appalling lack of insight into the problems of a patient with epilepsy. (Campling 1981:61).

Goffman believes that disabled people have a discredited social identity (Goffman 1968:11) whereby their disability becomes their master status, obscuring all other attributes. He believes that those who associate closely with disabled people are likely to acquire a 'courtesy stigma' whereby they become contaminated with the stigma themselves (Goffman 1968:44). This may be a further reason for not accepting disabled people into the health and caring professions.

Disabled people are often viewed as weak and ineffective which contradicts the popular image of a health professional. Young (1981:153), for example, believes that patients view their doctors as 'God-like figures; strong, powerful, clever and in control of some kind of magic.' Perhaps it is the health professionals, however, who depend on this image more than the patients as a strategy to obscure their real lack of power in the face of illness, disability and death, as well as serving to enhance the placebo effect. These feelings are captured in the Biblical quotation 'Physician heal thyself' (Luke 4 Verse 23), the implication being that physicians who appear powerless to escape disability and illness themselves are unlikely to have the ability to heal or help others.

Many beliefs about disability are irrational and date back to ancient times. Disability and illness have been associated with punishment, evil and sin (Foucault 1967:6, Helman 1984:84). Such images are plentiful in the Bible and in 19th and early 20th century literature. It is possible that some of these perceptions may colour professional attitudes, albeit unconsciously. Others, however, have found that it is disruption to social interaction rather than attribution of responsibility which appears to explain the social distance from individuals with various types of stigma (Albrecht 1982:1319). The need for good communication skills is strongly emphasised by many of the health and caring professions and the belief that disabled people lack these skills may serve as a powerful justification for excluding them.

In contrast, disability is sometimes romanticised and associated with goodness, or disabled people may be perceived as having more insight and greater perception than others. In a questionnaire study of the attitudes of physiotherapists to the recruitment of disabled people into that profession, it was found that seven subjects, 11 per cent, believed that blind physiotherapists have heightened perception, with a further 24,37 per cent, believing them to have greater power of touch or hearing (French 1986:67). These and similar notions may assist disabled people in their quest to become health professionals, although an unfortunate effect of such beliefs is the assumption that disabled people need no special help or consideration. Such attitudes can, in fact, serve to deny disabled people the assistance they require.

Individuals are selected for professional education who are perceived to be similar to those already in the profession. Professionals tend to select recruits 'in their own image', admitting only those who are likely to conform with values considered of importance to the profession. It is likely that the recruitment of disabled people would cause some degree of tension because central beliefs, for example that the professional person is the expert, may be thrown into doubt. Professional etiquette has been described as a body of ritual which preserves before the client the common front of the profession (Hughes 1946:273). Goffman notes that intimate co-operation is required if a given projected definition is to be maintained (Goffman 1969:83) and that teams will only recruit people who can be trusted to perform correctly (Goffman 1969:95).

A further factor which may exclude disabled people from the health and caring professions is that of social class. Health professionals tend to come from middle class backgrounds (Young 1981:145), Scrivens 1982:215) whereas a majority of disabled people come from working class homes (Townsend and Davidson (1982:62). Goffman believes that in order to maintain their status and power professionals need to keep a certain distance between themselves and their clients (Goffman 1969:97), thus a professional member of less power and status may be perceived as a threat. Goffman states:

> If the team is to maintain the impression that it is fostering then there must be some assurance that no individual will be allowed to join both team and audience. (Goffman 1969:97).

Yet by definition a disabled professional would belong to both groups.

Sutherland believes that the stigma of class is added to that of disability and that, conversely, a middle class background may serve to reduce the negativity associated with disability. He explains:

It is much easier to counteract the stereotyped ideas about disability on which discrimination is based if one possesses a middle class background and accent, a university education and the particular type of articulacy and confidence that these factors produce. (Sutherland 1981:35).

To my knowledge there has been no research specifically addressing the experiences and perceptions of people who have become health and caring professionals despite having substantial disabilities themselves. It is hoped that the following study goes a small way to describe their experiences and situation, as well as highlighting what the inclusion of disabled professionals reveals about the orthodox professional/client relationship.

Method

In this study 24 disabled people, currently employed or training in the health and caring professions, were interviewed, and one person, who was working abroad, sent a written account of her experiences using the interview questions as a guide. The sample consisted of nine men and 16 women and represented seven professions and 17 disabilities; two people had dual qualifications. All but two people were accepted for training with their disability, the others acquiring their disabilities during training; ten people had trained within the last five years and 14 within the last ten years. The professions and disabilities represented were:

Professions

Medicine	4
Physiotherapy	7
Occupational therapy	3
Social Work	4
Nurse/Nurse Tutor	1
Prosthetics	3
Counselling	2
Occupational therapy/physiotherapy	1

Disabilities

Visual disability	4
Cerebral palsy	1
Cerebral palsy/visual disability	1
Cerebral palsy/hearing disability	1
Lower limb amputation	4
Tetraplegia	1
Multiple sclerosis	1
Epilepsy	1
Ileostomy	1
Achondroplasia	1
Hearing disability	3
Shoulder/cervical abnormalities	1
Recurrent dislocation of patella	1
Rheumatoid arthritis	1
Ankylosing spondylitis	1
Spina bifida	1
Liver disease	1

Locating these people was difficult and interviewing involved extensive travelling. They were contacted in the following ways: six by publishing letters in the *British Physiotherapy Journal* and *Therapy Weekly* newspaper; seven by the staff of Nottingham University's Disabled Graduate Data Bank; six by word of mouth; three through a charity; two by contacting disabled people, after reading about them in articles; one through a questionnaire sent to physiotherapists, which formed a separate strand of this research.

The interviews were semi-structured but the respondents were encouraged to expand freely. The interviews were all tape recorded and lasted between 15 and 90 minutes. They were then transcribed and the information was categorised subjectively by the researcher. The researcher's own visual disability was disclosed to aid communication and reduce suspicion.

Perceived Advantages and Disadvantages of Disability

All the disabled professionals could see advantages relating to their disability in the work context. The most common response was that they felt better able to empathise with their patients and clients and understand the social and psychological implications of disability.

Some of the professionals believed they had greater patience than their colleagues and others pointed out that the patients and clients had greater confidence in them and were more likely to take their advice. One person said:

> Many clients thought they'd get a slightly better deal through having a blind social worker because they thought I was having to pull out all the stops to prove that I was good and therefore they would get a spin off.

Most people felt they could empathise and understand those with a similar disability best. A partially deaf therapist stated:

> I've got a lot more patience with deaf people and I get more out of them. The doctors say, 'forget it, ask a relative', but I speak to them.

All the deaf people found their ability to lip read helpful. One mentioned her skill at communicating with tracheostomised patients and another found she could lip read patients when nobody else could understand them. One spoke sign language fluently and was sometimes used as an interpreter. Most of the disabled professionals believed that they had more knowledge of disability than the average health professional. A prosthetist, who had a lower limb amputation himself, stated:

> They (patients) want to pick your brain for every bit of knowledge they can get. They're very interested to find out how you coped.

He felt he was able to identify patients' problems, especially the small, less obvious ones which other prosthetists might miss or regard as trivial.

Many reported that their patients and clients frequently commented on the advantage of the disability from their own point of view. A prosthetist with an amputation himself remarked: 'Patients say, 'You've got one, you know what I mean.' Similarly a doctor said:

> Very many people have told me they can talk to me because I know what it feels like to have an illness...Once you get over that hump

of being accepted (for training) in the first place, then you can use your disability.

Many people found that their disability helped to break down professional barriers. A deaf therapist said:

> They don't see me as a health professional who knows it all, who doesn't really understand, they see me as a disabled person.

A doctor found the patients' interest in his electric wheelchair useful in this respect and a social worker found his guide dog helped: 'Even when there's an awful atmosphere he's wagging his tail. He's definitely an ice breaker.'

Several people spoke of the advantage of needing help from their patients or clients. A counsellor explained: 'By me needing help it's actually saying, This is a partnership.' Similarly a blind social worker commented:

> I'm able to say to my clients, 'I'll help you but there are certain ways in which you are going to have to help me', and the client doesn't feel totally taken over or totally worthless.

Some people mentioned that they acted as models to their patients. A counsellor said that many of her clients would say, 'If you can do it, so can I', and a physiotherapist found that the myth that all physiotherapists are very fit helped because her patients assumed this applied to her despite her disability. Several people mentioned that fellow students had learned a great deal about all aspects of disability through having them in the peer group. A therapist with rheumatoid arthritis recalled that when a lecturing doctor spoke of one of his patients as, 'my little R.A. girl', the other students 'fumed'.

Some people pointed out that patients or clients who enjoy being in the sick or disabled role could find the disabled health professional problematic. This can be viewed as a disadvantage from the patients' or clients' point of view but perhaps as an advantage from a professional standpoint in that pressure is put on the patient to comply.

Many people felt that the advantages of their disability not only cancelled out any disadvantages there might be but actually outweighed them. A doctor commented:

MS has been something I've used. Having MS has been an added dimension in my training, in my understanding of people, and in the development of my expertise and skills.

And a prosthetist said:

You have a great understanding of their problems because no matter how good a prosthetist is, if he's got two legs he falls short of really knowing what it's like.

However, two of the disabled professionals firmly believed that their own disability gave them no additional insight into disability, and one congenitally disabled person said she had no special understanding of acquired disability.

Some people pointed out the advantages of their work from a personal point of view. Several physiotherapists mentioned that the active nature of the job benefitted them physically and a number of people with sensory disabilities believed the nature of the work prevented them from becoming isolated. A profoundly deaf therapist said:

I do feel that if I didn't have this type of job where I'm meeting different people every day I would withdraw very quickly into myself.

Many people have been asked to counsel patients or clients with a similar disability to their own or to demonstrate their ability to cope. Many others helped their patients and clients informally, especially if they appeared anxious. Several people said they had been asked to lecture to a wide range of students and colleagues on the subject of their particular disability, or disability in general. A number of the disabled professionals were actively involved in disability issues. Several had written books and articles, and others were involved in voluntary work. Some had given radio talks and one had founded a society for people with his own disability.

In contrast, a few people pointed out the disadvantages that could arise as a result of their disability when interacting with patients or clients. One blind person found lack of non-verbal communication a problem, although others felt able to compensate and even viewed blindness as helpful in some situations. For example, a social worker thought that clients could speak more openly to him because they knew he could not recognise them in other contexts.

A few people found their disabilities had the effect of trivialising patients' problems. This could be a disadvantage but sometimes served as a motivator. A disabled doctor reported that patients would say 'I'm off work with a sore knee and there you are working on your crutches.'

Another doctor found that his severe disability inhibited psychiatric patients from discussing their problems, and a psychiatrist found that some of his patients had a tendency to mother him and could find it difficult in psychoanalysis to express anger or hostility for fear that it would damage him in some way. However, he believed that the working through of such feelings could be an important part of the treatment. An occupational therapist found that elderly, confused patients occasionally lacked confidence in her, but she managed the situation by reassuring them and immediately focusing attention back to them.

The prosthetists with amputations noted that patients could be discouraged by seeing them cope so well. They would sometimes say, 'if only I could walk like you.' They were, however, acutely aware of this problem and were very careful never to compare themselves with their patients.

Access to training

Of the 23 disabled professionals who had been accepted for training with their disability, eight reported that their entry qualifications were better than average, and five thought this was a major factor in their acceptance for training. A further eight people said they had been helped to gain access to training by an influential person. Such people were mainly either doctors of high status, who knew the individual personally, or someone on the selection panel with a particular knowledge or interest in the candidate's disability, for example a person interviewing a blind candidate had a visually handicapped son. Twelve people felt that their acceptance for training had been strongly influenced by one of these two factors. In addition a doctor mentioned the advantage of his privileged background and several people indicated that they came from medical families.

All but one person revealed their disability before interview. Several, especially those with relatively hidden disabilities, were uncertain of the wisdom of this and spoke of being in a dilemma over the issue. A profoundly deaf person felt it was best to reveal her disability after contact had been made because of the 'funny ideas' people have about deafness.

Of the 23 people who were accepted for training with their disabilities, eight experienced difficulty. An occupational therapist stated: 'It didn't matter what I said, they said I couldn't cope,' and a physiotherapist recalled: 'His parting words were, 'Nobody will accept you as a physio, no school's going to accept you.' Interestingly, she was later accepted by the very person who had said this. Several people mentioned that getting as far as the interview was the main problem; a counsellor concluded that professionals 'Have conditioned themselves to believing that the disabled person is the person who should be helped rather than the helper.'

Some people were turned down by one college, on the grounds of disability, but were willingly accepted by another. Several people who were refused entry to physiotherapy training because of disability gained access to occupational therapy without difficulty, and one person who was told by her school career service that every type of work involving patients would be out of the question, was accepted into pharmacy, nursing and physiotherapy.

It must be emphasised, however, that the majority of the disabled professionals interviewed, 15 of the 23, experienced no problems regarding their acceptance for training.

Attitudes of Teachers

Some people experienced negative attidues from their teachers. The most common complaint was a general lack of adaptation to meet their needs. A physiotherapist recalled.:

> They weren't obstructive, but they didn't go out of their way to be helpful either.

And a deaf therapist said:

> I couldn't follow the lectures at all yet I didn't feel I could keep saying 'I'm deaf, will you look at me.'

Some felt they were viewed in terms of their disability, while others mentioned that their teachers lacked confidence in them. Several blind people complained of the excessive concern over their inability to make eye contact with clients and the difficulty they had in convincing teaching staff that they could cope.

A doctor who acquired his illness during training felt unable to confide in the staff. He stated:

> I was very frightened that if I had a disease like that they might suggest that I wasn't able to continue the training and that I wouldn't qualify. I felt if I mentioned the (symptoms) they'd think I was skiving or malingering or being a hypochondriac or neurotic and I wasn't going to be labelled as those things.

Similarly a physiotherapist said:

> I had to try and keep a brave face on it and not let on, I thought it might affect my career, they might just chuck me out.

Only two of the 25 disabled professionals were given substantial concessions during their training, and in both cases they were absolutely essential. Some people were openly informed that there would be no special help. A deaf therapist said:

> They felt that if I wanted to be on the course, I'd got to manage the same as everyone else. The foreign students got more help.

Their feelings about concessions were, however, mixed. A blind person remarked:

> If someone said to me, 'You'd better not do this placement', then I'd rather walk to Australia on my hands than admit that I couldn't.

Despite all the problems only six people failed to complete the course in the minimum possible time.

Twelve of the disabled professionals could recall negative attitudes from their teachers, although they all related instances of positive attitudes too. The remaining 13 regarded the attitudes of their teachers as either neutral or good. A physiotherapist said that she could not recall any aggravation at any level and an occupational therapist stated:

> It didn't seem to matter what problem I had, I just had to go to them and they'd say O.K., there's a way round it.

Employment

The attitudes of colleagues were reported as being overwhelmingly good, although a few people mentioned a certain lack of understanding, saying that their colleagues tended to forget or deny their disability which could create difficulties. For example, a deaf therapist said that people forgot to look at her when speaking and a blind social worker said that certain colleagues felt snubbed when he did not respond to their smiles and waves. A person with epilepsy found that people sometimes did not believe what she said and in one job she was suspected of theft when articles went missing. Some people said they had really to press for what they needed. A visually handicapped social worker had to fight for an office where he could adjust the lighting and get away from colleagues who were so fascinated by his visual aids that he could not get on with his work. Several people said that colleagues failed to realise that to produce the same quantity and quality of work, it was necessary to work both harder and longer.

Both during training and after qualifying some people said they had been encouraged to work with disabled people or in areas of medi-

cine of low prestige. A blind person was accepted for a post on the condition that initially he would work with blind clients. A cousellor commented: 'They always assumed I'd do disability counselling, they were hanging a label round my neck.' A physiotherapist was asked, 'don't you think you should be working with the young chronic sick?' and an occupational therapist was advised to work in psychiatry. After successfully qualifying, two people were advised by members of their own profession to do full time voluntary work.

Some people decided to work with those with the same or similar disabilities to themselves. This could lead to suspicion: two people complained that colleagues thought they might 'over-identify' and therefore lack objectivity. Most people, however, had met with very positive attitudes at work. A deaf therapist commented: 'I depend a little on the staff but they never seem to mind, they never force me into anything.' Only three people reported any instances of negative attitudes from clients or patients.

Just four of the disabled professionals had difficulty finding work. However, a few did meet with negative attitudes in the process. At her first interview in a large London teaching hospital, an occupational therapist was told: 'I must be perfectly honest, I don't see any point in showing you round.'

One problem encountered was the expectation in some of these professions that newly qualified staff would rotate to different medical specialties thereby gaining varied experience, a practice not possible for all the disabled professionals. Some people observed that working in senior posts was easier. A deaf person spoke extensively of the advantages of being in charge. She explained:

> I'm the boss and I delegate what I can't do. I'm in control and I know what's going on, all communication comes through me.

Many people felt that in order to cope, both during training and at work, it was necessary to work harder and be more determined, they spoke of a need to 'prove' themselves. A prosthetist stated:

You've got to keep up with the fellow next to you and be better than him. You've got to work harder at it because there's a weakness there and that's what they'll play on.

Others had come to the conclusion, however, that these feelings originated primarily from within themselves: a blind person had started to ask himself, 'to who am I proving what?'

Where possible people tended to specialise early. They tried to find work where they could function well, for example a deaf therapist said she would avoid a position which involved treating patients in groups and would never work in a very large hospital. However, people with the same type of disability had differing views concerning the suitability or unsuitability of various areas of work; this seemed to be due both to the severity of their disability and to personality factors, so that it is simplistic to generalise.

Fifteen of the disabled professionals were restricted in the type of work they could do. For example, the doctor who used crutches said he would find surgery difficult and could not visit patients at home because of access problems. However, by choosing their specialty and work place carefully most people reported that they could fulfill all of their work obligations.

Conclusion

This research indicates that the majority of the disabled professionals interviewed had, in the main, received positive treatment from colleagues, clients and patients during training and at work. A sizable minority, however, had experienced some degree of negative discrimination either as a result of their colleagues' attitudes or lack of understanding. Most of these problems occurred when attempting to gain access to training and during training. At this time the disabled individuals have no professional status themselves which might serve to reduce the stigma of disability when they qualify. The inequalities inherent in the teacher/student relationship may also create a situation where negative attitudes can be expressed more readily, especially as training in many of these professions has, until recently, been highly authori-

tarian. If, as noted earlier, it is characteristic of professions to maintain both a homogenous membership and social distance from their clients, then those with top positions in the occupational hierarchy, for example the educators, are likely to be key individuals when it comes to putting these strategies into practice.

There is much evidence to suggest that disability may be just one attribute which is considered undesirable in members of the health and caring professions; racial and class discrimination are well documented (Young 1981:145), Watkins (1987:193) and until recently sexual discrimination was also marked (Young 1981:145). In addition French (1986b:5) found that various characteristics which go against the stereotyped image of the physiotherapist are stigmatised by that profession. For example, to be grossly overweight was considered more of a barrier to access than blindness or being wheelchair bound. The social acceptability of a disability may therefore be a more important variable than the limitations it may give rise to.

Not all professionals subscribe to the view that disabled people are unsuitable as health professionals. Turner notes the hypocrisy of excluding disabled people from these professions.

How can we tell patients they can lead normal lives when we don't allow their peers to become our colleagues? Though not yet illegal to discriminate on health grounds there can be no doubt it is immoral and unethical to do so. (Turner 1984:451).

The assertion that disabled health and caring professionals are better able to understand their patients and clients than their colleagues and empathise more readily with them does, however, need further investigation. Although disabled people are likely to share some common experiences, the disabled population is an unusually heterogenous one; on the surface at least there seems little in common between a blind person and a mentally handicapped person, or someone who is deaf and someone who is wheelchair bound. Some researchers have noted that many disabled adults avoid contact with similarly disabled people (Shakespeare 1975:20). It is likely too that the 'able' disabled have had to remove themselves from the disabled community in order to succeed in a society which views disability in negative terms (Safilios-Rothschild 1976:71). This lack of contact amongst disabled people would hardly seem to favour the development of empathy and understanding amongst them.

Shearer (1981:182) believes that disabled people have no more or less sense of common political identity than individuals who make up any other group sharing a common characteristic, and Oliver (1984:29) notes the conflicts which occur in various organisations of and for disabled people and how the differential treatment they receive from the state fosters divisions amongst them (Oliver 1984:27). It is also possible that the negative labels applied to disabled people lead to a poor self image which in turn predisposes them to low acceptance of each other.

The degree of discrimination against disabled people wishing to become health and caring professionals cannot be fully answered by this research. Dissimilar professional ideologies might suggest that there would be different levels of discrimination amongst the professions. This was not found to be the case, although the numbers of people in each profession was far too small for this finding to carry much weight. It also remains unclear whether disabled people do have a better understanding of illness and disability than their able-bodied colleagues, although it can be argued that this is not a central issue as disabled people should not be expected to perform better than other people in order to be accepted.

It is evident that further research is needed in this little researched area. This small study does, however, suggest that disabled professionals are no less capable than their able-bodied colleagues and may have unique assets to bring to these professions, although their presence might well undermine traditional professional values and beliefs.

References

Albrecht, G. *et al* (1982) Social Distance from the Stigmatised: A Test of Two Theories, *Social Science and Medicine* 16, 1319-27.

Biehn, J. (1979) Psychiatric Illness in Physicians, *Canadian Medical Association Journal* 2, 1342.

Browning, H.K.E. (1980) Careers for Diabetic Girls in Nursing, *British Medical Journal* 255, 307.

Bueche, M.N. (1983) The Student with a Hearing Loss: Coping Strategies, *Nurse Education* 3(4), 7-11.

Burnfield, A. (1983) *Multiple Sclerosis: A Personal Exploration*. London: Souvenir Press.

Campling, J. (1981) *Images of Ourselves*. London: Routledge and Kegan Paul.

Darnbrough, A. and Kinrade, D. (1981) The Disabled Person and Employment, In Guthrie, d. (ed) *Disability Legislation and Practice*. London: Macmillan Press Limited.

Chickadonz, G.H. *et al* (1983) Educating a Deaf Nursing Student, *Nursing and Health Care*, 4(6) 327-33.

Employment and Training of Audiology Technicians, British Society of Audiology.

Faulder, C. (1985) *Whose Body Is It?* London: Virago Press.

Finkelstein, V. (1981) "To Deny or not to Deny Disability". In Brechin A., *et al* (eds) *Handicap in a Social World*. Sevenoaks: Hodder and Stoughton.

Foucault, M. (1967) *Madness and Civilisation*. London: Tavistock Publications.

French, S.A. (1986a) *Handicapped People in the Health and Caring Professions: Attitudes, Practices and Experiences*, M.Sc. Dissertation. London: South Bank Polytechnic.

French, S.A. (1986b) Obesity - A Greater Stigma than Disability, *Therapy Weekly*, 13(17) 5-6.

Gavin, A. (1980) Meeting the Challenge of Professional Social Work: Education of the Hearing Impaired, *American Annals of the Deaf*, 125, 1086-90.

Goffman, I. (1968) *Stigma*, London: Penguin Books.

Goffman, I. (1969) *The Presentation of Self in Everyday Life*. London: Penguin Books.

Health Screening of Entrants to Nurse Training (1985), The Royal College of Nursing.

Helman, C. (1984) *Culture, Health and Illness*. Bristol: John Wright and Sons.

How to Become a Chartered Physiotherapist (1984). The Chartered Society of Physiotherapy.

Hughes, E.C. (1946) "Institutions". In Lee A.M. (ed) *New Outline of the Principles of Sociology*, New York: Barnes and Noble.

Hutchins, T.V. (1978) "Affirmative Action for the Physically Disabled in Social Work", *Journal of Education for Social Work*, 14(3) 64-70.

Johnson, T.J. (1972) *Professions and Power*, London: Macmillan.

Kettle, M. (1983) *Disabled People and Their Employment*. Banstead: Association of Disabled Professionals.

Laing, R.D. (1983) *The Voice of Experience*. London: Penguin Books.

Libman, G. (1985) Doctor Who Overcomes Deafness, *Synapse*, 4(5) 2-3.

McConkey, R. and McCormick, B. (1983) *Breaking Barriers*. London: Souvenir Press.

McKnight, J. (1981) "Professionalised Service and Disabling Help". In Brechin A. *et al* (eds) *Handicap in a Social World*. Sevenoaks: Hodder and Stoughton.

Morgan, M. (1982) "The Doctor-Patient Relationship". In Patrick, L. and Scambler, G. (eds) *Sociology as Applied to Medicine*. London: Bailliere Tindal.

Oliver, M. (1984) "The Politics of Disability", *Critical Social Policy*, Winter, 21-32.

Radiology - Your Career? (1985), The College of Radiographers.

Safilios-Rothschild, C. (1976) Disabled Persons Self-definitions and their Implications for Rehabilitation (extracts). In Finkelstein, V. (1985) *Rehabilitation: Supplementary Readings*, Milton Keynes: The Open University Press.

Scott, R. (1969) *The Making of Blind Men*. New York: Russell Sage Foundation.

Scrivens, E. (1982) "The National Health Service: Origins and Issues". In Patrick, D.L. and Scambler, G. *Sociology as Applied to Medicine*. London: Bailliere Tindall.

Shakespeare, R. (1975) *The Psychology of Handicap*. London: Methuen.

Shearer, A. (1981) *Disability: Whose Handicap?* London: Basil Blackwell.

Silver, L.B. *et al* (1979) "Mental Health of Medical School Applicants: The Role of the Admissions Committee", *Journal of Medical Education*, 54(7) 234-8.

Stetten, D. (1983) "Tomorrow's Physician", *Pharos*, 46(3) 36-41.

Sutherland, A.T. (1981) *Disabled We Stand*. London: Souvenir Press.

Townsend, P. and Davidson, N. (eds) (1982) *Inequalities in Health*. London: Penguin Books.

Turner, C. (1984) "Who Cares?" *Journal of Occupational Health*, October, 149-53.

Watkins, S. (1987) *Medicine and Labour*. London: Lawrence Wishart.

Young, G. (1981) "A Woman in Medicine: Reflections from the Inside". In Roberts, H. (ed) *Women, Health and Reproduction*. London: Routledge and Kegan Paul.

10 WHAT IT MEANS TO BE DIFFERENT: PERSPECTIVES OF THE DISABLED

Our society stresses the values of conformity and acceptance. Hence, the disabled, especially the handicapped are often labelled involuntary deviants as a consequence of their disabling conditions. In being defined deviant, they are subject to the stress of being different and to the stigma imposed by society on people who violate the norm. The disabled are frequently required by the problems imposed by their conditions to counter the values and norms of an unsympathetic society. In all relations, the disabled encounter barriers and they often perceive themselves as outsiders in their communities. Attitudes towards the disabled are often ones of compassion and pity, rather than involvement and participation. Large segments of the disabled community encounter situations where they are treated with pity and compassion and not with equality and acceptance. This widespread societal stance makes integration and participation difficult, but not impossible. Perhaps, we can only understand the legitimate meaning of what it is like to be disabled by studying the lives of those who have lived with disabling conditions. Unfortunately, throughout their lives, many of the disabled have discovered that "it is not what they are that is important, but rather it is how they are seen by others."

Those who experience stuttering and those who are deaf are often seen by others as stupid, and those with long term terminal conditions are often viewed as recluses and as not wanting to be part of society. Likewise those with Cerebral Palsy and other nervous disorders are often seen as drunks and inept. The list of disabilities and the perceptions of these conditions is endless. Perhaps it will suffice to refer to an early 1980's movie titled "Who's Life Is It Anyway". The story line for this movie deals with an artist who becomes a quadriplegic as a result of a tragic car accident; the artist was portrayed as having dignity because he refused to face his disability and rather he starved himself to death, becoming a hero. The implications of this Hollywood catastrophe are that quadriplegics are perceived as being invaluable and as having nothing worthwhile to offer to society; further they are not able to have a quality life; they are a useless burden who would be better off dead. As a result, those with dignity should opt for suicide. What a tragic message! This sounds like a philosophy out of the Nazi era, which promoted the idea that those who do not fit the social image or standard should be removed from society. This movie overlooks a crucial question about disability and that is "what is the reality beyond the image?" In reality there are many quadriplegic who live positive, fulfilling, contributing, and meaningful lives, many as professionals, spouses, and parents. Some are even intellectuals and most can be deemed "normal" in every sense of the word except for the fact that they are challenged by a disabling condition which most others will never confront. Unfortunately, images and labels take away the reality; there are many myths and stereotypes of the disabled generated by the media which perpetuate archaic misrepresentations of the disabled. The consequence of these damaging images is that they often impede the progress of the disabled person in many facets of their life.

This meaning of being different is addressed in the final section of this work which deals with the personal experiences and intimate thoughts of the disabled about their conditions and about the experiences they have encountered in their communities. For instance, Geoffrion et al. explores some of the restrictions imposed on the disabled and learned by them, like exclusion, isolation, and learned passivity and helplessness. Another way to appreciate the consequences of being disabled would be to read Christie Brown's autobiography or to view the movies "Elephant Man" or "Mask". These portrayals adequately present the compassion, sexuality, and identity of disabled persons. They also demonstrate the socially-erected barriers which frequently impede the disabled in the pursuit of their goals and ambitions. The concerns are further expanded upon by Pat Worth's presentation.

As illustrated, the disabled are victims of images and attitudes; this idea is addressed by Kent et al. As these authors demonstrate, many of the negative effects and the feelings of discomfort stem from uncertainty when able bodied people interact with the disabled. One instance of this uncertainty is evident in the perceptions of role expectations. Studies of all disabled categories reveal that large segments of society often ascribe the role of deviance to people with disabilities, and as we know, normals, in the best situations, are very reluctant to become involved with deviants. However, the emergent tragedy is that the disabled are involuntary deviants, yet being deviant whether voluntary or involuntary is of no concern to a society plagued by a reliance on conformity and well being. Being different, by virtue of being disabled often allows many normals to distance themselves and remain uninvolved with the disabled. Acceptance and rejection is a process, and often the disabled are initially rejected in all cases until they are able to "prove themselves" worthy of normal treatment. The significance of many of these experiences is outlined by Frank.

Some disabled individuals are able to closet their abnormalities. This ability is crucial since we are living in an era where gays, ex-mental patients, racial minorities, and a host of others are counselled to come out of the closet and expose their uniqueness. Consequently a general openness has occurred with respect to the rights and privileges of these minorities. For some there are many rights and privileges to be gained from leaving the closet while others when exposed merely suffer a more severe stigma. Hence, coming out of the closet will never be a universal process because there will always be a friend, parent, spouse, or employer that will reject the "deviant trait". Journeys out of the closet are segmented because they are dependent on the reactions of others which are indecisive and often unpredictable. These concerns are clearly addressed by Ozer in her study of hidden disabilities.

Indeed the title of the last article is appropriate: "How Shall We See Them?" Perhaps, a clear metaphor can be illustrated between the plight of the disabled and the plight of other minorities in the human rights movement. We are aware of the goals to be achieved, yet significant barriers remain in our society. These impediments can be overcome but it will require persistence, hard work and suffering especially by those victimized during this transition by social attitudes and impressions.

Autobiographical Perspectives: Severe Communication Handicaps

LEO D. GEOFFRION AND RINA ESHEL

What would it be like to be unable to converse with anyone? It is difficult to imagine a life without speech or other convenient means of expressing oneself in spite of apparently normal receptive skills. While abundant literature exists describing communication handicaps as seen by clinicians or parents, few accounts document reactions from the personal perspective of the handicapped individual.

Autobiographies by communication-handicapped persons provide valuable insights into the strengths and weaknesses of current practices as seen by the recipient of these services. This paper summarizes the communication experiences of nonvocal individuals. Recent work on the development of nonmoral communication aids has opened a large variety of communication alternatives. As these devices develop it is important to examine their use, not just in clinics and schools, but in everyday life. These autobiographies provide a potent window into the daily use of communication.

The Autobiographies Studied

Among the many autobiographies by handicapped individuals, five have been located which describe the life experiences of individuals with severe expressive communication disorders. When one considers the great personal effort to produce each of these it is hardly surprising that they are so rare. The autobiographers are:

Joseph Deacon: Deacon was born in England with severe cerebral palsy. From early childhood he lived in a residential institution and received little formal education. His speech was unintelligible until age 22 when he became friends with Ernie Roberts, another handicapped resident. Roberts miraculously understood Deacon's speech and has served as his companion ever since. So far they have produced two works: *Joey* (Deacon, 1974), his autobio-

graphy; and *I Will* (Deacon & Roberts, 1977), a fictional account of a handicapped couple who marry and raise a family.

June Van Lint: Van Lint (1975) was the mother of four adopted children and an active person who enjoyed camping and other outdoor sports until complications following a traffic accident left her paralysed and without speech. Her autobiography recounts the early years of adjustment with particular attention to the many problems of communication and personal care.

Bill Kiser: Kiser was born with quadriplegic cerebral palsy. His parents educated him at home, and he eventually earned a high school diploma and attended occasional courses at a local college. As he matured he gained sufficient motor control to produce understandable speech. In hopes of improving his coordination he elected for ultrasonic brain surgery. Instead the surgery destroyed whatever motor coordination and speech skills he had developed, leaving him totally helpless and frustrated. He slowly retaught himself the needed motor and communication skills in spite of having been judged hopeless by many clinicians. Kiser currently works as a journalist producing a column for handicapped persons.

Christy Brown: Brown was born with cerebral palsy in 1932 to a large working-class Irish family. He showed no expressive skills until age five when he began to print letters using chalk between the toes of his left foot. He became very proficient in both writing and drawing with his foot, even winning a local painting contest. For him, both physiotherapy and formal education began at about age 17 with the opening of a new cerebral palsy center in Ireland. One of the first steps in his therapy was the demand that he cease to write or paint using his left foot since the unnatural position placed great strain on the rest of his body. This advice was followed carefully for about two years even though he was

Reprinted from: *Journal of Rehabilitation*, April/May/June 1982, with permission never able to write successfully with his hands. By the end of the book (age 20) he reports that he occasionally resorts to writing with his foot when the creative urge is too strong for the tedium of dictating to others (Brown, 1955). In addition to his autobiography, Brown has written several novels and collections of poems.

Tim Hartwig: Hartwig's unpublished autobiography is the most recent. It recounts his school experiences during the 60's and 70's. Unlike the others he received special services early in life and is the only one to have used special adaptive equipment for communication. His autobiography focuses more on some of the people who affected his development than on a chronological account of life experiences.[1]

Communication Techniques

While these five authors represent a diversity of backgrounds and handicaps all share the problem of severely limited speech. This section examines their experiences with different communication techniques. Particular attention is devoted to their use of communication aids and problems associated with them.

Typing and Writing

All developed good typing and writing skills although most used unusual methods. Deacon's typing system was the most complex in that it required several distinct steps. Deacon dictated his thoughts to Ernie who was illiterate and whose CP precluded typing. Ernie in turn announced each word to a third person, Tom, who could write. After the nurses checked them for spelling and grammatical errors, Deacon reread each letter to Ernie who announced them to Tom who typed.

Deacon's unusual typing system suggests an overlooked dimension for many handicapped individuals. Most communication aids assume dyadic interaction between the handicapped person and a caretaker, teacher, or parent. While helpful in tutorial or therapy sessions, their usefulness elsewhere is often limited by the amount of time the caretaker can devote to each handicapped person. Perhaps communication can

be greatly increased by opportunities to communicate with and through other handicapped individuals.

Kiser was the most proficient typist and relied heavily on it in his career as a journalist. One innovation he developed was to anticipate the questions people might ask and then type the answers onto cards for later use. This allowed him to take long trips unescorted:

> **Since I had learned to get around town on my own by typing notes for people who could not understand my speech, I told Hugh Blackstone and the others that I would be alright travelling alone, using my method of communication...My notes served me well, although they did not permit me to talk to the cute stewardesses as the other men were doing. (pp. 101-102)**

As Van Lint regained enough control of one hand to type, it soon became her major means of communication although she reports many problems with it:

> **At home a lot of my typing was not understandable when I was through with it. I started a word; the person looking over my shoulder would talk much faster than I could type, and often guess the word before I finished the first. The person might not guess the next word, etc. So I ended up with a conglomeration of letters and words that made no sense except to the person who had witnessed the typing. (p. 125)**

> **Being unable to roll the platen back can be another problem. I may be typing merrily along on a certain subject when someone comes along and wants to talk to me. I can't change the paper so I space a few spaces and start talking by typewriter, indicating to the other to read...Then they leave and I space a few spaces and start talking by typewriter, indicating to the other to**

read...Then they leave and I space a few more spaces and go on with what I was typing...Then sometime later individuals...read what I've written and it doesn't make any sense. I want very badly to tell them to skip that portion but they don't have a chance of understanding me, so it's better just to leave them confused and thinking I've flipped my lid. (p. 127)

These comments illustrate some of the modification that may be needed in designing typing aids. Ideally the system should provide the equivalent of a scratch pad where one can generate brief messages without disturbing the main text. Such features are becoming available in word processors. Van Lint currently uses AP-PLEWRITER, a commercial word processor program for the APPLE II computer and is much more pleased with it than with her typewriter.[2]

Hartwig is the only typist whose machine was specifically designed for handicapped individuals. His Auto-Com (Vanderheiden & Grilley, 1977) allows him to compose complete messages before sending them to an attached printer. Furthermore, common words and phrases can be stored in its memory and later retyped with a single motor act. Hartwig was most enthusiastic about this aid:

I was so excited about this new machine that I couldn't believe it. My thought could quickly and accurately be transcribed on a television screen for all to see! I would be able to communicate with anyone, not just the few people who had a lot of contact with me. I would be able to complete my homework assignments without the teacher helping me every single minute....(p. 32)

I was moved up two grades in one year after I was able to do my school work on the Auto Com...(p. 38)

Brown did not type but instead taught himself to write using his left foot. Both writing and painting became passionate fixations to which he devoted many hours. By age seventeen he had developed considerable skill with this system as illustrated in the following incident:

I was asleep when we reached Dublin. I awoke when a hand touched my shoulder and shook it lightly. I looked up lazily and saw it was [the stewardess]. She was standing in front of me, smiling. Somehow she had heard I painted with my left foot and asked me if I would paint her a picture when I got home, if I had the time. I nodded my head vigorously meaning to assure her that I had all the time in the world. She then asked me for my address so that she might call for the painting. I tried to tell her. But all that came out of my mouth was a queer sort of noise. I tried again. I tried again. I got desperate. Then wildly I scraped off my left shoe and sock, and leaning backward, I raised my left foot over my head, plucked the pencil from her breast pocket and wrote the address on the fly-leaf of her prayer book. (pp. 90-91)

Gesture and Pointing

Deacon is the only one who reports much use of pointing or gesturing to communicate. This approach was used whenever his companion Ernie was unavailable:

I was taken to the psychologist and asked the difference between a triangle, oval shape and round ring. They were on paper. I pointed to the figures with my nose and I got them all right. Also she asked me how many pennies in a shilling. I answered by blinking my eyes twelve times. (Deacon, 1974, p. 15) I wanted to know how Uncle Fred was but I could not make them understand me. He had a gold tooth but I could not see anything that looked like gold to point at. Then suddenly I saw

Grandma's gold wedding...and I pointed to the ring and my teeth and Annie put two and two together and came up with the right question. (Deacon, 1974, pp. 46-47)
Alfie pointed to his eye and his watch and said: Darling we'll see them when the time comes. (Deacon & Roberts, 1977, p.58)

These three examples demonstrate the range of messages attempted in gestural communication. While concrete messages like the first one are universally understood, the abstractness of the third makes it uncertain that most would comprehend its intended meaning. In clinical practice one often observes gestures which appear to make no sense to the observer. Perhaps some of these represent attempts to express thoughts too complex for the simple gestures available. Those who work with such individuals need to remain alert to this possibility.

Scanning Communication

Scanning further reduces the motor coordination demands needed for communication. In this approach the companion scans through the available menu of messages watching for a preset signal from the handicapped person. Thus with only one motoric movement the handicapped individual can indicate his or her desires.

In her early months of recovery, Van Lint blinked to select letters as others scanned through the alphabet letter by letter. The use of eyeblinks proved to be awkward since it forced her to suppress her normal reflexes with painful results. Van Lint found this system the least satisfactory and reports many difficulties with it:

To communicate by the slow spelling method I was forced to become very patient, and to develop a good memory. I had to remember both the sentence, which took forever to get across, plus the letter of which word was understood last. Sometimes I knew where I was, but was mistaken about what other people had understood...(p. 21)

Perhaps the most interesting phenomenon reported by Van Lint is the way that scanning forced substantial changes in her expressive language. She often found herself using unusual syntax structures:

People come to what they think is the logical stopping place in my sentence and stop before I am finished. This usually completely changes the meaning of what I am saying. No matter what I did, I couldn't make them understand that I wasn't finished. So after much frustration I learned to construct sentences so that the subject is the last word. I had to pick and choose my words very carefully to use the least number of words possible. (p. 21)

Individuals with severe communication handicaps often show peculiar deviations from standard English, which are frequently interpreted as indications that neural damage has also affected the brain's language centers. Van Lint's experiences suggest a plausible alternate hypothesis: that some deviations represent a normal adaptation to a very abnormal communication setting.

The slow communication rates inherent in scanning were another frustrating problem for Van Lint. She expresses complaints of messages left unfinished because there was not enough time, confusions caused by the conversation shifting topic before she could express herself, and the inability to qualify a response. She often found herself saying "no" to her children's requests because of the hazards inherent in an unconditional "yes."

Van Lint also recommends devising a signal to indicate when one is changing the topic of conversation. Since she was totally dependent on others for the scanning, she used these opportunities not only to answer their questions but also to express her own concerns. If the other person failed to detect the shift of topic, confusion was sure to follow.

Discussion

Rehabilitaiton therapy for persons with severe communication handicaps is broadening from concern for accurate speech production alone to an acceptance of total communication. The term total communication (TC) has its origins in the education of the deaf and advocates the use of all available modes including speech, writing, typing, pointing, gestures and signs. TC emphasizes that the development of good communication skills is more important than the development of any one modality. Indeed the various modes are seen as complementary rather than competitive.

The shift toward TC comes at a time when the breakthroughs in computer electronics make possible the development of a wide variety of communication systems capable of accommodating diverse motor handicaps. Devices already allow nonvocal quadriplegics to draw pictures, write letters, compose music, or speak using a synthetic speech generator (Goldenberg, 1979). These can expand dramatically the communication opportunities for the handicapped provided one understands their role in everyday life.

A communication system for the handicapped is very different from a language therapy tool. The ideal communication system is one which is usable throughout the day for diverse purposes in varied settings to interact with different people. It should permit fluent conversation with little personal effort. Most current aids fall short of this goal as illustrated by the experiences of these handicapped authors.

Speech is clearly the communication system which best fits this ideal. Its primacy as a communication channel is demonstrated by the way that it remains the preferred mode of communication even when it is severely impaired. Van Lint was the only truly nonvocal writer in this group.

The other communication modes are used mainly to supplement speech. Writing and typing were the most common alternatives used. Traditional typing aids have consisted of keyboard guards placed over the conventional machine. VanLint's frustration with typing contrasted to Hartwig's unqualified enthusiasm for the Auto-Com suggests that electronic typing aids which provide better editing control are preferred.

Communication techniques such as gestures and pointing require less fine motor control than typing or writing, but introduce severe problems. The producer must possess the ingenuity to invent gestures as needed, while the receiver must infer complex meanings from simple signs. Deacon's experiences suggest that many gestures by handicapped individuals may be misunderstood by others.

Scanning was the least satisfactory system for these authors. Its slow speed, severe memory load, and extreme dependence on the cooperation of others makes it very awkward. Modern electronic scanning aids can help but delays are inevitable. Informal experiments by the senior author show that even a physically normal individual cannot easily scan at a rate faster than 0.7 seconds per choice. Using standard data on word length and letter frequency, this transforms to a maximum rate of about four words per minute. Unless one resorts to abbreviated spellings for words and highly compressed syntax, communication in the scanning mode is too slow for fluent conversation.

Another issue unexplored in the present literature on communication is the interaction between an aid and the user's language. Tedious communication systems like scanning forced Van Lint to resort to unusual syntactic forms to express her thoughts. Since Van Lint had been unimpaired until her accident she was very aware of these changes. In the case of a physically handicapped child, how will a communication system change that child's language patterns? This and other questions need to be addressed in developing communication systems for the handicapped.

One final concern arising from these autobiographies is that of learned passivity, as demonstrated in the following excerpt:

> **There came a light tapping at the closed door. I heard it, but the others didn't. I couldn't answer the door. I couldn't tell the other people to answer the door. By this time I could squeak, but if I did the people construed it to**

mean something was wrong with me. So I had learn to be more patient and wait for a louder knock. It took a long time to face the fact that if I did anything the situation became more difficult. (Van Lint, 1975, p. 22-23)

While passivity may be an annoyance for Van Lint, its developmental implications are critical since a passive attitude toward communication may be linked to poor social and language development (Goldenberg, 1979; Geoffrion, 1982). The passive communicator gets far less practice using the language which in turn leads to greater reluctance to use the language. Rehabilitaiton therapy must encourage active use of the language even if one is not fluent in its correct forms.

References

Brown, C. My left foot. New York: Simon & Shuster, 1955.

Deacon, J.J. Joey. New York: Scribner, 1974.

Deacon, J.J. & Roberts, E. I will. Special Children, 1977, 3, 44-68.

Geoffrion, L.D. The ability of hearing impaired students to communicate using a teletype system. The Volta Review, 1982, 84, 96-108.

Goldenberg, E.P. Special technology for special children: computers to serve communication and autonomy in the education of handicapped children. Baltimore, MD: University Park Press. 1979.

Kiser, B. New light of hope. New Canaan, CT: Keats Publishing, 1974.

McDonald, E.T. & Schultz, A.R. Communication boards for cerebral palsied children. Journal of Speech and Hearing Disorders, 1973, 38, 73-88.

Vanderheiden, G.C. & Grilley, K. (Eds.) Nonvocal communication techniques and aids for the severely physically handicapped. Baltimore, MD: University Park Press, 1977.

Van Lint, J. My new life. San Diego, CA: Neyenesch Printers, 1975.

References Notes

1. Hartwig, T.J. My Life in a Wheelchair, Unpublished manuscript.
2. Van Lint, J. Personal correspondence, Jan. 5, 1981.

A Self-Advocate's Perspective
A Conversation with Pat Worth

People have many impressions of what intrusive or aversive procedures are. When you're forced to go to an institution, that's painful and intrusive. When you're forced to live in an environment that the average person could never live in, that's painful and aversive. I wonder how some of the professionals would feel if something like the cattle prod was used on them. Or if they were forced to go into a time-out room because people thought they were bad. Or if they had to walk the hallways in an institution and smell the scent of urine or have no privacy of their own in their own rooms. I think they use intrusives because the alternatives scare them. When we think of alternatives, that puts them out of a job.

I was once at a conference that presented intrusive procedures and alternatives. One of the presenters actually said that some of the people he was working with told him they "like being in restraints free from self-injurious behaviour." I was angry at that. First of all, I'm not hearing this from people with a mental handicap so I'm not going to take this professional's word for it. I believe that people can be taught to say things they don't want to say. Even scare them to death to make them say something. I know that because they scared me to death when I was in a group home. They said you stop talking about living out on your own or we'll admit you into an institution. They hung that threat over my head. One of the people from the group home was actually sent back to an institution. He said he was fed up with the group home. He didn't want to live there any more. So they said his only alternative was to move back to the institution. He went back, not of his own free will. he was thinking about running away. I don't know what stopped him. I think he should have. I took off. Others may not be as courageous because they don't have anywhere to run to. The ones who speak up learn not to because they know what they are going to get.

But when you talk about punishment, I'll give you an example. It's when a person with a mental handicap goes to a workshop and thinks she's not worth anything.

Tom used to be a pretty good friend of mine. He was my buddy in the sheltered workshop and in the group home. He decided one day that he wasn't going to do the jobs they gave him. His job was twist-tying dolls. That's' what he was doing for something like seven years, longer than me. He just got bored of it and decided he was just going to sit there until they gave him something to make it worth his while being there. The supervisor told him to do his job or they were going to dock his pay. Big deal, it's not much anyway. He didn't do it so she went to the manager. The manager decided to act like the big tough guy and tried to pick him up off the chair and throw him behind the shipping door. So Tom goes back home after they tell him to get out of the workshop, expecting the staff to take his side and advocate for him. They didn't do that at all. They didn't even believe that he hit the manager in self-defence. The management got away with it and Tom got kicked out of the group home. Tom's back home living with his mom now.

If you try to speak out for yourself and the system doesn't listen to you, there's no more advocacy. All you see are walls. That's what the group home was. If the staff didn't hear, you'd talk to the walls. They'd think you were crazy for talking to the walls, but if they wouldn't talk to you or listen to you what are you supposed to do? If you had to live the kind of life that people in group homes had, you'd probably knock your head on tables and walls just like them.

To make workshop staff and professionals using intrusives see the alternative we have to make them listen to self-advocates more. You've got to go to the people who have been through that punishment, people with mental handicaps from institutions or from workshops. Why don't they go to them and find out how they like being

Reprinted with permission of Pat Worth from the book *The Language of Pain —— Perspectives on Behaviour Management* in the workshop? How did they like being in an institution? Did they think it was necessary?

There is a method called "gentle teaching" that is fairly simple and should have been taught a long time ago instead of building institutions. It is an alternative that shows what happens when the walls aren't there. The alternatives to walls are communication and patience. I mean, if you don't act the way I want you to act, does that mean I have the right to haul off and hit you? You'd get pretty mad if I did. If people don't act the way some professionals want them to act, the professionals think they've got the right to use some sort of shock treatment.

Some people argue that the alternatives require too many people to work with the person who has a handicap. It only takes one person to listen. It only takes one person to advocate. It only takes one person to feel kindness. So it doesn't take all that many people. It just takes one person to start it all off. If you're living in an institution and a staff person walks by you, you want to talk to that person, but they walk by you like you're dirt or something. That hurts. What are you going to do? Are you just going to stand there and not do anything about it? Individuals with mental handicaps are defenceless people. If somebody doesn't talk to them, they hit their heads, because that's the way they get a reaction. I'll bet you that none of this would have gone this far if positive alternatives would have been in focus in the first place instead of building institutions. Society builds walls when it builds institutions. It builds walls to keep people with handicaps in and away from society. But if it can build walls, it can tear them down.

And there are other things like being forced to earn tokens, food and outings that don't seem harmful but they are still intrusive because they're still a punishment. I shouldn't have to earn the right to have food. Why should I have to behave to get that? You're talking about behaving and you're talking about the way they want you to behave. That kind of treatment is a power trip. People use these simple little power trips to say: "If you don't behave you don't get these candies today." That's what they say to people in jail: "If you don't behave you won't get your bread and water." This is even worse

because people with a mental handicap in institutions haven't committed a crime. Nobody's telling staff that if they don't behave, they shouldn't be working there. They're a risk to people in institutions. The staff consider people with a mental handicap a risk to society, but actually the staff are a risk to us. Just by saying if you don't behave you don't get this food —— we'll eventually starve to death. We're innocent inmates in institutions.

In my job, I visit institutions and help people there. Although I know what's going on there, people are too scared to talk about it. Not too long ago I went to a meeting at a regional centre. At the group meeting, there was this one very scared person sitting there with a black eye. I asked him, "Who did this to you?" He looked at me as if he was going to say something, then I said, "Was it a staff person?" And he absolutely froze. He was scared to death.

So far, I haven't been able to get close enough to these people to hear their stories. Why should they talk to me anyway? I get to go home at night, I don't have to stay there. They know if they talk to me, chances are they'll get into a lot of trouble. The punishment gets worse if you tell somebody else about it. It's not that they don't trust me, the problem is I'm never left alone with them. There is a staff person there all the time.

One person dared. He didn't talk about the procedures used against him, although you could see it. His name was James. He talked about missing his mom and his dad —— he's been there for seventeen years. He said he's about thirty-five. James wants to get out. He knows the terrible things the system is doing to him. A lot of people with mental handicaps don't know. He's scared every day of his life. And I know he's in trouble because he's losing weight. He's dying. He's in a wheelchair so he can't exactly walk out. He's a person who they said was low functioning and had a learning problem. But he can talk the same way I can. Do I have a learning problem?

In fact, the silent treatment is another intrusive procedure. One of the staff people (this was before she found out I was involved with People First) was sitting with me during a coffee break and she was telling me a story about a person with a handicap who had attacked her in the institution. She walked by him on her way to the office and he was upset about something and wanted to talk to her but she didn't have the time. So he just walked into the office, grabbed her by the arm and he pushed her into the corner. She hurt her back. Apparently, they sent this person off to be cattle prodded. You're not talking about somebody who was banging his head or abusing himself. You're talking about somebody who pushed a staff person. Her way of pushing him back was giving him shock treatment.

He pushed her because she ignored him. When I go to the institution the first thing I see is people who have been labelled retarded waling all around the place with nothing to do. People are just walking the halls like zombies.

If I were one of those people who couldn't speak but was suffering I would be saying, "Help me, I'm dying." That's all that should be needed to say. When I first met James, from the first minute he saw me, he knew I was not a staff person. That was the first thing he said to me just before a staff person came in. It's so hard to build up their trust. I've only been on this job for two years and although I've gained some trust I understand why others don't trust me. They've been treated like dirt by everyone they've come into contact with. Why should they trust me? I'm going to continue building their trust, I think I can. But it's going to take a long time. That's the damage the system has done.

Unfortunately, I don't think many people who are institutionalized are aware that it's not done to everyone. I think they really believe they have to have it done to them. They probably think that a lot of it's done to people in the community. They don't realize that only they are being treated this way.

And the government isn't helping matters. The Ontario Research Council spent $90,000 on improving the cattle prod. I would have spent that money building accessible homes. The minister made a big announcement about the multi-year plan to reduce the number of institutions and then he turns around and gives the Research Council $90,000 to develop another

stinking new prod. I call it the people prod. What a backwards government.

Those people are going to die before they can get out if this keeps up. It's going to be too late to build homes for them. They're going to be dead. Never mind what it means when they come out —— will they go into boarding homes or group homes that continue using those treatments? They're going to build their own institutions in the community —— make the whole community an institution.

Of course we now have the *Charter*. But what's in the Canadian *Charter of Rights and Freedoms* is nice words. It sort of reminds me of the American Declaration of Independence. They read out these fancy words in black and white and decided what independence meant. But then they still went around killing people. The *Charter of Rights* you know, the words are nice, but the words are just on paper. Where does the paper go? The paper goes in the garbage.

What we need is a strategy. If just one person goes to the minister, he doesn't have to listen to that person. If two people go, he may listen. If three people go, there's a better chance. If an organization goes, what chance does the minister have? He can't walk away. If the organizations around here that support people with a mental handicap would just stop taking single stands and put some joint action behind those stands, we would have positive results. Why should you have to make an appointment to see someone like the minister? If an organization decides to go into his office, I don't think he would stop you. He fights force with force to keep us away. Organizations have got to fight force with force to tear the walls down. People like that are the reason why the walls are still standing. It is people like us who have taken the stand against the walls. You've got to do something to tear them down.

People First is taking action against the multi-year plan in Ontario because we have to be involved. We've got to have our say in that. The multi-year plan is supposed to be a plan designed by the ministry to close institutions, I think, within twenty-five years. I think that's too long. They'll all be dead by then.

598 What It Means To Be Different

Time is important in another sense. I think time is something that we have to give to other people. But in the institution, all they have time for is walking the hallway. That's not time actually: that's death. They're waiting to die. Some professionals have time to inflict unnecessary pain but they don't have time to listen. They are the jury: they sentence them. In a court of law, when criminals are convicted they are sentenced and the jury decides what the punishment will be. So I believe that in cases where people have a mental handicap, society is the jury and they're saying too bad, your sentence is a life in an institution or a group home. Their only crime is that they have some kind of handicap. If that's true, why aren't some professionals locked up? Their handicap is that they have a closed mind. They've been getting away free.

And it's not just doctors and professionals who have to change, it's ordinary citizens. If they've never lived that kind of life and they don't know what it's like, they should darn well listen to experienced people like Peter Park who lived in an institution for eighteen years. He speaks about the institutional life and everything he says is fact. When he goes out to the public though, they're always questioning whether this is true or not and if they have doubts, then that's the time for hearing them. That's the time when they should be pushing the government to go inside institutions. If they want to see it for themselves I think that's great, that erases doubt. The community hasn't pushed the government hard enough yet to open the doors.

And I don't think ordinary citizens know anything about institutions and intrusive procedures yet. I think they believe that institutions are a good place. I think that's what a lot of parents think. You know these days parents are even told by doctors before-hand if their child will be born retarded. The doctor's word is as good as gold, doctors can't be wrong. It's hard for a mother to accept that a doctor is wrong. A lot of mothers over the years have been putting their sons and daughters in institutions.

It takes a lot of listening because there are horrible stories, they're unbelievable stories. But even if you have any doubt, it is reason enough to push the government.

Another challenge is convincing parents. It's very difficult but you have to take their blindfolds off. I've actually done it, I've actually convinced some parents that that kind of treatment is not necessary because I've talked about my job and my life. A lot of people think that people with a mental handicap can't talk to people in the community and here I am in the community talking to people. The alternative is simply listening. I think to teach people like that, you have to rebound against what they're going to say. You take away their argument and you're really powerful with your own argument. I would say to a parent like that, look at the results in my friend when someone listened. My friend didn't bang his head any more. My friend stopped hitting himself.

Actually Peter once told me that there was a person with a mental handicap he knew who would bang himself all the time and he wouldn't stop. He saw this staff person walk by and ignore him, so Peter came over, held his hands in a gentle way, and said, "What did you want to say?" He told him plain and simple. I would still say to the parent, the alternative is to have feelings and to listen and care. Just listen to that person and he or she will tell you what they want.

I know it's hard for one staff person to care for five or six people who are banging their heads. So then it's time to have advocates. Each person should have an advocate. If one staff person is trying to listen to six people all the time, then there's no way he or she can do it. The part that makes People First members so vulnerable in institutions, group homes or sheltered workshops is that they're put away in a place they can't be heard. They have nobody speaking out for them. One good staff person can't walk around to 923 people and listen to all their problems. But I can't see any reason why you can't have 923 advocates walking around listening to all their problems. I'm talking about volunteer advocates——people free from the system. It all goes back to answering how you get the community involved in institutions——by forcing the government to open the doors. Step

A Self-Advocate's Perspective 599

two——after you get the doors open, you let them inside to see what goes on. It automatically becomes clear why you should advocate. I'm a self-advocate and I also advocate for people with mental handicaps in genera. But I can't be there to stop the punishment all the time. I'm not there all the time to say——Aw no, this is wrong. I can't do it all by myself. I'm only one person. Having an advocate there, at least a lot of the time, will allow him or her to become a part of the person's life, a real friend, who could become the person's closest friend. An advocate is somebody who goes inside the walls and listens to a person behind those walls even though the walls are there. The advocate should be right there with the person who has a mental handicap.

There are other ways to help knock down those walls. I'm going to suggest to people with all good intentions, stop using paperwork. It doesn't work. Paperwork amounts to filing things away. Fine, let's do that, but we have to go beyond there. The paperwork isn't the mouth. The mouth is what creates the action. Start going into colleges and universities, start hitting the politicians —— you can push them to support you.

Peter Park talks to everyone about his experiences to educate them. Barry Smith talks about his experiences at the Edgar Institution and the time-out room. I don't know what his crime was —— probably being a nice guy. A lot of people, and not just People First members, will tell you about their experiences at conferences because that's really the only time that they get a chance to speak up. I can't get around to all of them. There are too many. They'll say, when I was in an institution, I had nothing to do. I was walking the hallway because there was nothing better to do. When I was in the institution, they used to put me into this dark room because I got into too many fights. Or I was sterilized, which up until the *Eve* case was general practice in institutions.

I tell people about my life too. I was in a group home that was like a mini-institution. There were thirty-five people living in that home. You had to share your room with five other people, line up for your meals. I wasn't very big

then, I only about 55 kilos but they had me on diet foods. You see, I am more than 183 cm. tall and now weigh about 120 kilos. It seems the staff are only concerned about getting the job done. They get paid whether we eat, sleep or whatever. You're talking about people in the system who are well trained not to care. If they put slop on the table and you're faced with either eating it or not eating it and starving, what are you going to do? Most of them are too afraid to talk because they'll lose their jobs if they show some sign of care and the good ones leave the system all the time. They can't stand looking at the treatment. If you're a good-hearted person who really shows feelings towards people who are vulnerable, how can you go into a sheltered workshop and watch them sit there twist-tying dolls or packaging diapers? How can you go into a group home and be caring while they share their room with five other people? Or to be lectured by staff when you say you want to move out? Or to be threatened that we'll send you to an institution if you don't stop talking bad about this place. How can you stand watching that if you really care?

And staff get tired of hearing complaints. The people don't want to eat steamed food. They want to eat real food. All they hear is the ministry says this, the ministry says that. All staff do is come out with excuses why they can't get an oven in for Pete's sake. What bothers me is that institutions have a lot of money. One institution's budget is $65,000,000 per year. What are they using it on? Certainly not on recreation. They have nothing to do there during the day. They're just using that money on a cafeteria full of steamed food and the time-out room, wards after wards after wards after wards. They're not using it on privacy. They're using it on making people feel angry when they have to line up to go to the washroom, making them feel angry because they have no privacy, making them scream out because they have nothing else to do, making them die because they can't survive.

It's the attitude that does it, and the way people think. The first institution was built on attitude.

It's time to change those attitudes. If I were a staff person and someone was being self-abusive, I would ask if that person wanted to be touched. She's hitting herself to be touched. Nobody else touches people who are forced to live in these places. So what's wrong with coming along and holding their hands with care and saying, "Did you want to say something?"; just listening to what they had to say.

If I were a staff person in an institution and someone was trying to harm me, I would put up my arms like I'm almost surrendering and say, "Did I do something wrong?" If you struggle enough, one of you is going to give in. But during the struggle you're going to be communicating. That person's not going to hurt you because during that time you're going to be listening to that person because you're going to be touching that person.

And if the person was throwing objects across the room, I'd have the same attitude. Throwing chairs across the room is not harming me. Sometimes at night when I'm really angry I pick up my pillow and I throw it across the room. The message is: they want to get the hell out. I say, I'm willing to listen.

At one institution, I have this friend whose name is Derek. Derek's an interesting guy. Sometimes he's nice, sometimes he can be hard to get along with, sometimes he's temperamental. Sometimes six people are needed to hold him down. They're not doing it with love, they're doing it as their job. But if those six people were hugging him to make him feel secure, it would be the difference.

These restraining procedures of other intrusives are not being used on people like you who haven't been labelled. I was speaking at a conference once and I told everyone in the room, if you could all close your eyes for five minutes and imagine what it would be like for you without community living and you were all living in an institution or a group home and it was so crowded you felt like screaming, no privacy, no job, nothing, just institutional behaviour, you would wake up and say I have the right to be treated as an equal. I have the right to go out and make my own life. I have the right to get the support that I need. If everybody in the world was living in an institution, you'd all die one by one. That's how it's violating their rights. It's because you're saying to people who have been labelled, you've got to die.

A lot of people ask me, what would be the final victory for all people with a mental handicap? It's when the last wall comes tumbling down and we all get to go home, raising our head in victory saying: "We've got a home now. We're going home." And there will actually be a home there. Just a natural way of life without all the things that were in the institutions. In my lifetime, I want to see that day. I'm going to do everything to make sure I see it. I saw it for me, I saw it for Peter, I want to see it for everyone until the last wall comes down, then I want to lead the march to freedom. I have this wild dream where I imagine the last wall coming down and all people with a mental handicap in the province marching with a flag of freedom to the provincial government buildings in Ontario and saying to the Premier, "Too bad you lost." Then they'd all go home and have a real supper.

Attitudes of Peer Groups Toward Paraplegic Individuals

JAYLENE KENT, DESMOND CARTWRIGHT, PETER OSSORIO

In the past, the majority of research and clinical emphasis in the rehabilitation of spinal cord injured persons has focused on the physical parameters of the disability; for example, an emphasis has been placed on relearning the skills of daily living, mobility training, and vocational training. However, psychological and social dimensions also play a critical role in the rehabilitation process, and successful rehabilitation should, therefore, include the psychosocial integration of the paraplegic with the community. A review of the literature suggests that critical gaps in our knowledge of the psychosocial adjustment to spinal cord injury still exist (Trieschmann, 1978). Perhaps the most powerful testimony of the need for further research in this area is found in the high suicide rate among members of this population (Trieschmann, 1980).

Some psychological research that may be pertinent to the problem of psychosocial adjustment comes from social psychology. For example, the concepts of difference and physical attractiveness are learned at a very early age, and we learn to evaluate people on these two dimensions (Berschied & Walster, 1974). As a consequence, spinal cord injured persons may devalue themselves according to these internalized standards and believe that others devalue them accordingly. The result may be withdrawal from social situations upon being released from the rehabilitation hospital (Cogswell, 1968). The degree to which these individuals are capable of coping with the world and managing social situations through a process of self-socialization seems to vary greatly. It does appear, however, that a variety of social skills may be critical to the successful rehabilitation of individuals with spinal cord injuries (Dunn, Van Horn, & Herman, 1977; Romano, 1976; Trieshmann, 1980).

One social skill that seems important to the rehabilitation and interpersonal adjustment of paraplegic individuals is the ability to make friends in their peer groups. However, the effectiveness with which a paraplegic is able to interact socially is reflated to the attitudes held by the peers with whom the paraplegic is reacting. Therefore, it was in the interest of learning about the attitudes held by the peers of paraplegics that the present research was undertaken. More precisely, the desire was to explore the specific dynamics affecting the friendship formation process between the paraplegics and an ablebodied peer group.

A plausible way to begin such an investigation was to measure attitudes held by the ablebodied peer group toward the paraplegic. Because the peak ages of spinal cord injury are 18, 19, and 20, with a modal age of 20 years, a college population provided a convenient peer group sample (Young & Northrup, 1979). Initially, the hope was to employ the widely used attitudinal scale developed by Yuker, Block, and Young (1966), the **Attitudes Towards Disabled Persons Scale**, more commonly known as the ATDP Scale. Upon close examination of this instrument, however, it became clear that the ATDP was too general for the purposes of this study, not only in the content of its questions, but also in viewing the disabled collectively. In fact, there was very little information available of any kind that addressed the interpersonal adjustment of paraplegics, specifically in regard to forming friendships with their ablebodied peers.

Due to the lack of an acceptable instrument, the researchers decided that the simplest way to identify feelings and attitudes held by the ablebodied peers of paraplegics was to ask them. Once this information was obtained, an attitudinal scale could be developed that would focus on the issues relevant to the friendship formation process between the two groups. Two experiments were required to elucidate the friendship formation process. In the first experiment, interviews were conducted to identify some issues of concern to the ablebodied peer group regarding paraplegics. In the second experiment, attitudinal scale items were generated from the content of the interviews. These experiments and their results are described below.

Reprinted from: *Journal of Rehabilitation*, July/Aug/Sep 1984, with permission.

Experiment 1

Pervious studies in the area of attitudinal assessment have shown that few people publicly report negative feelings about the disabled, whether it be in response to a questionnaire or a structured interview (Yuker & Block, 1979). Nevertheless, there is a good reason to suspect that negative feelings toward paraplegic individuals do exist. Such reactions are countered by the cultural climate of the United States which says that public statements toward the handicapped will be positive or at least neutral (Yuker & Block, 1979). The decision to utilize an unstructured interview technique was made in the hope of circumventing or at least minimizing this effect.

Method

Sample

The sample included 10 ablebodied undergraduate students (5 female, 5 male) from a 200 level Psychology of Adjustment class who volunteered to be interviewed in exchange for extra credit in the course. They were unaware of what the topic of the interview would be until they arrived at the designated interview area. All subjects were between the ages of 19 and 24 and were Caucasian, with the exception of one Asian male.

Procedure

Students were interviewed singly in a private office by the first author. An unstructured interview technique that focused on clarifying feelings, concerns, and beliefs toward paraplegics was utilized. Some common trends and content redundancy appeared in the information uncovered during the 10 interviews. All interviews were recorded and their contents catalogued using a frequency tally.

Results

The issues occurring with the greatest frequency in the interviews are presented below under the following two major categories: factors discouraging friendships with paraplegics and factors encouraging friendships with paraplegics.

Factors Discouraging Friendships with Paraplegics

1. Such a friendship requires **extra effort and sacrifice.**
   a. Ablebodied peers anticipate and fear that such a friendship would be a burden because they see paraplegic individuals as having dependency needs. Individuals who are paraplegic require special procedures when getting in and out of cars, and when going up and down stairs. In addition, they require special equipment.
   b. Activities that friends of this age typically pursue together would be constrained if a paraplegic individual was included; for example, playing a casual game of football or frisbee, or going to a restaurant, concert, or movie.
   c. The paraplegic person has lost his or her ability to be spontaneous in joining activities; therefore, he or she is a likely candidate to be excluded from impromptu social activities.
   d. There is a belief that the life styles of an ablebodied and a paraplegic person are so different that they have very little in common. Therefore, there is little incentive to include a paraplegic person in social activities.
2. Most ablebodied people feel a **sense of discomfort** when in the immediate presence of individuals who are paraplegic. This feeling is due to many factors, most of which are associated with fear of some kind.
   a. They are afraid of their pity or sorrow showing.
   b. They are afraid of saying the wrong thing and/or not knowing what to say.
   c. They want to ask questions regarding the nature of the disability and what life is like on a daily basis, but fear that such questions are too personal.
   d. They do not know how the paraplegic person is feeling, and are afraid that gestures of friendship will not be seen as sincere.

e. There is a fear of staring and over-emphasizing the disability.

f. People are afraid that paraplegics are fragile individuals and fear injuring them physically.

g. People tend not to be open and on the level during their interactions with paraplegic persons.

h. People experience a sense of helplessness, a feeling that the situation is out of one's control

i. One of the greatest contributions to discomfort in the interaction is the problem of eye contact. Various interpretations of this experience were offered by different students. For example:

(1) Because one is forced to look down at paraplegic individuals, there is a tendency to speak to them as if they were children, in spite of cognitions that this person in an wheelchair is an adult.

(2) There was a tendency for the uneasiness felt in interactions to be expressed by making no eye contact and instead to look around the room.

(3) Some students pointed out that it is disturbing to look at people who are not altogether normal, and if one does look at the disability (as forced to do when having a conversation with a paraplegic individual), it becomes staring.

(4) Still another version of the eye contact problem is the concern that paraplegic individuals themselves will feel uncomfortable if they notice eye contact being made. Surely, this would make them feel they are being stared at. This, in turn, leads to the avoidance of eye contact.

j. Physical disability is equated with mental impairment.

3. Some people **shun the paraplegic**. This behaviour is attributed to an inability to accept the paraplegic person perhaps because acceptance would force the individual to think about paraplegia happening to them or to someone they love.

4. Some people are **concerned about what their other friends would think** if they were seen with an individual who is a paraplegic.

5. Some peers feel **guilty**.

6. An issue of particular relevance to the peers of paraplegic university students is that of **proximity**. Paraplegic students are typically forced to sit in either the front or the back of classrooms, and ablebodied students who wish to socialize with them are obliged to sit accordingly. In addition, paraplegic students are forced to take accessible routes to and from classes. In some cases, they may be identical to the route used by the ablebodied students; but if not, paraplegic students are removed from the mainstream of their ablebodied peers.

Factors Encouraging Friendships with Paraplegics

1. **Curiosity** would be a motivating factor for some.

2. Some peers believe that they could **learn more form a paraplegic** friend than from an ablebodied friend. The paraplegic person would have different things to offer because his or her lifestyle is perceived to be so different that conversations would center around different topics. For these reasons, some felt that such an association would be a unique and good experience.

3. Some felt that the **friendship would be more highly valued by the paraplegic** person because he or she would not have very many friends to appreciate.

4. **Paraplegic individuals are admired and respected,** and consequently, valued persons.

5. Both parties would **open up** and **put more** into the friendship.

Most peers seemed to think that it **would not** be more difficult to develop a friendship with a person who is paraplegic, once the "ice" was broken. The "ice" however, was expected to be more difficult to break with a paraplegic person than with another ablebodied peer.

After having the opportunity to hear some common concerns regarding paraplegic individuals, it became important to identify some procedures that would serve to allay common misgivings of their ablebodied peers and therefore, encourage a friendship with this particular disabled population. These procedures were explored during the interviews, and may be summarized as relaxation through exposure and education. Some of the specific procedures suggested by the interviewees included:

1. Being able to observe a paraplegic person in a relaxed setting with fiends or family and learn how people who know that individual interact with him or her.
2. Learning specific ways in which one can be helpful (i.e., how to assist paraplegic persons in and out of cars and in maneuvering stairs). In general, learning the easiest way to make the individual with paraplegia comfortable.
3. Learning to relax around persons who are paraplegic.
4. Learning that paraplegic persons have adjusted to their situation by hearing them talk about their activities, making jokes, and seeing them have a good time.
5. By becoming close friends with a paraplegic person.
6. Seeing them protrayed on TV, in movies, or comic strips.
7. Being able to talk about their feelings and reactions toward paraplegic individuals.
8. Seeing persons with paraplegia in their place of work.

Discussion of Experiment I

Perhaps one of the most striking features that characterized the majority of the interviews was the initial denial on the part of the student of having had any direct contact with a paraplegic individual. This denial was interesting in that the initial recollection differed from reality. It was not until after envisioning a hypothetical interaction with a paraplegic person or talking about their general feelings toward such a person, that the students would typically have an "aha" experience and recall that, in fact, there had been some direct contact.

Another interesting contradiction was clearly evident in the content of the interviews. In many cases, the factors that encourage a friendship with a paraplegic person were also cited as factors that discourage such a friendship. For example, being different in life-style from an ablebodied person may be unique, and therefore, attractive to an ablebodied individual, and may simultaneously be unattractive and provide the basis for discouraging friendship with a paraplegic person.

Probably the most encouraging and consistent feeling that was expressed by all students was an admiration and respect for the individual who is paraplegic. However, caution should temper one's optimism regarding this finding since many of the emotions associated with paraplegia are mixed and contradictory.

Experiment II

The interview contents for the first experiment supported the notion that issues relevant to the friendship formation process between the ablebodied peer group and individuals with paraplegia were not addressed in traditional attitudinal scales such as the ATDP. Devising an appropriate attitudinal instrument, guided by the interview contents of the first experiment, was one of the aims of the second study. Another goal was to determine if learning about disability through viewing a film about the disabled, would change attitudes toward them. Previous research has shown that exposure to, and education about, the handicapped encourages more favourable attitudes toward that group (Antonak, 1981; Bozza & Lindberg, 1979; Dailey & Halpin, 1981; Grosse & Sheppard, 1979). It was expected that after viewing a film, improved attitudes toward paraplegic individuals would be reflected in increased ATDP scores.

Method

Sample

The sample consisted of 30 undergraduate students in a 200 level Psychology of Adjustment class. The experimental procedure was incorporated into the lecture for that one hour class presentation.

Procedure

Answer forms and pencils for the attitudinal survey were distributed. The 6-point Likert Scale, with responses ranging from +3 (I agree very much) to -3 (I disagree very much), was displayed on the overhead projector. All items on the A form of the ATDP and the 12 items generated for the interviews were then administered orally. The questions were structured so that the same Lickert Scale was utilized in answering all items to either attitudinal survey. All of the 12 items on the newly developed survey had the common stem: "Meeting or seeing a person in a wheelchair..."

1. Makes you feel uncomfortable.
2. Makes you curious about him and his daily routine.
3. Makes you unsure how to react.
4. Makes you feel lucky.
5. Makes you afraid of saying the wrong thing or not knowing what to say.
6. Makes you feel grateful.
7. Makes you want to help him.
8. Makes you afraid your pity will show.
9. Makes you feel afraid.
10. Makes you respond to him as if he were a child.
11. Makes you feel that he is helpless.
12. Makes you afraid of staring at him.

Upon completing these 12 items, a 28 minute film entitled, "The Toughest Barrier," was viewed[1]. This film portrayed:

> A candid and penetrating look into the world of the handicapped. In counterpoint to the commonly accepted attitude that disabled people should be pitied and helped, an amazing group of handicapped individuals tells a very different story...the toughest barrier for any disabled person is the attitudes of the society. (Centron Films, 1983, p. 36).

Immediately after viewing the film, the B form of the ATDP was orally administered to the class.

Results and Discussion of Experiment II

Mean scores were 101.19 on the ATDP-A form and 110.41 on the B form. The increase in the means following the film viewing was statistically significant ($p < .01$) and reflects the expected improvement in attitudes toward the disabled.

The twelve items on the new experimental instrument items fell into two factors, one consisting of eight items and the other of four. Alpha coefficients of .835 and .595 respectively, indicate good internal consistency for the two factors. As shown in Table 1, low correlations with the ATDP (.426 and .066 respectively) indicate that the experimental instrument was measuring different attitudes than the ATDP.

Table 1
Correlation Coefficients Between ATDP Scales and Two New Scales (N = 300)

	Scales			
	1 ATDP-A	2 ATDP-B	3 NEW-1	4 NEW-2
1	(.81)	.71	.42	.15
2		(.90)	.43	.07
3			(.84)	.17
4				(.60)

a. Values in parentheses are alpha-coefficients of internal consistency. For $r > .12$, $p < .05$; for $r > .15$, $p < .01$.

When viewing the respective items that fell into the two factors, two themes immediately appear. One factor seemed to be "grateful curiosity." The four items that composed this factor were related to "curiosity," "luck," and "being grateful." The other factor appeared to reflect the "sense of discomfort" that was expressed in the interviews. These items dealt with being "uncomfortable," "unsure," "afraid," and "helpless."

General Discussion

The data presented in this study and noted elsewhere support the view that much of the negative affect and feeling of discomfort that have been observed in the interaction between the paraplegic and ablebodied groups may be partially ascribed to uncertainty about appropriate role expectations and role enactments. This premise is supported by data indicating that one of the best ways to overcome discomfort, fear, and prejudice toward disabled people is through direct and frequent contact with disabled people on a peer level (Bozza & Lindberg, 1979). Experience and education allow for the formulation of reasonable role expectations.

Given that the disabled population is a growing one, and one that is becoming more forceful in seeing that its constitutional rights of equality are being met, it seems inevitable that a more integrated society will evolve. For many, this "natural" integration will provide the educational opportunity needed to overcome ignorance and prejudice.

However, as has already been shown by the suicide rate in the paraplegic population alone, this is far too high a price to pay for education and open mindedness. Some strategies to minimize the psychological casualties of physical disability have been found such as exposing and educating ablebodied people in regard to paraplegia. The next step is to refine and implement them. Clearly ablebodied peers with different patterns of attitudes toward paraplegic persons will need different strategies to help change those attitudes. The ATDP scales measure attitudes of sharing a common humanity versus feeling that disabled people are entirely different. The small sample of new items tested in the present research has shown that at least two more important dimensions of attitudes toward paraplegics must be considered; namely, **sense of discomfort** and **grateful curiosity.** The interview results, of course, have generated far more items than the sample of twelve studied so far. The authors plan to continue their research, using longer samples of these new items.

References

Antonak, R. (1981). Prediction of attitudes toward disabled persons: A multivariate analysis. **Journal of General Psychology, 104,** 119-123.

Berscheid, E., & Walster, E. (1974). In **Advances in Experimental Social Psychology.** New York: Academic Press, **1,** 157-215.

Bozza, L., & Lindberg, C. (Eds.) (1979). **Ready, willing and able! What you should know about workers with disabilities.** Albertson, NY: Human Resources Center.

Cogswell, B. (1968). Self-socialization: Readjustment of paraplegics in the community. **Journal of Rehabilitation, 34,** 11-13.

Dailey, J., & Halpin, G. (1981). Modifying undergraduates' attitudes toward the handicapped by videotapes. **Journal of Special Education, 15,** 333-339.

Dunn, M., Van Horn, E., & Herman, S. (1977, November). A comparison of three training procedures for spinal cord injury social skills. Paper presented at American Congress of Rehabilitation Medicine, Miami Beach.

Grosse, V., & Sheppard, G. (1979). Attitudes toward physically disabled persons: Do education and personal contact make a difference? **Canadian Counsellor, 13,** 131-135.

Romano, M. (1976). Social skills training with the newly handicapped. **Archives of Physical Medicine and Rehabilitation, 57,** 302-303.

Trieschmann, R. (1980). The psychological, social, and vocational adjustment to spinal cord injury. **Annual Review of Rehabilitation,** Vol.I. New York: Springer Publishing Co.

Trieschmann, R. (1978). **The psychological social and vocational adjustment to spinal cord injury: A strategy for future research.** Final report of RSA grant 13-P-59011/9-01. Los Angeles: Easter Seal Society of Los Angeles County.

Young, J.S., & Northrup, N.E. (1979). **Statistical information pertaining to some of the most commonly asked questions abut SCI.** Baltimore: National Spinal Cord Injury Data Research Center.

Yuker, H.E., & Block, J.R. (1979). **Challenging barriers to change: Attitudes toward the**

disabled. Albertson, NY: Human Resources Center.

Yuker, H.E., Block, J.R., & Young, J.H. (1966). **The measurement of attitudes toward disabled person**. Albertson, NY: Human Resources Center.

Footnotes

1.   Produced by ISURF Film Production Unit, Iowa State University.

Life History Model of Adaptation to Disability: The Case of a 'Congenital Amputee'

GELYA FRANK

Introduction

The concept of 'adaptation' in cultural anthropology has been used to refer to behavior that, for the individual or for the group, results in survival[1]. Life histories provide a means to understand behaviors that result in the survival of persons with physical disabilities in society. All cultures presume a standard body-type, on which normative roles are organized; age and gender provide the key physiological variable in such a scheme. Individuals whose bodies vary form the norm due to congenital or acquired disabilities may find that their culture has a niche available to them; the blind or crippled mendicant, for example, is a stock figure in the imagery of the pre-industrial and industrial societies [2].

In post-Industrial Western societies, access to the roles associated with normal adulthood has been increased, for the physically disabled, by medical procedures which prolong life, correct organic dysfunctions and reconstruct cosmetic "defects". Also, the shift in the national economy away from occupations requiring physical labor, to ones providing services and the processing of information, creates a climate relatively favourable to the lifestyle of some individuals with limitations of physical function. Most important, the policies of the welfare state, which began by extending benevolent support to workers who could no longer remain in the work force due to medical conditions acquired on the job, have been expanded to include support for those who, for reasons construed as medical, could never enter the work force at all [3].

The stigma of physiological variance is like a gatekeeper, making questionable the attempts of the disabled to pass into normal roles, and through those roles, to survive as social beings. Stigma interferes with the routine, face-to-face interactions [4], provoking crises of self-concept [5] that can be more disabling than limitation in physical function itself. Adaptation to a disability requires the individual's vigilant response to a procession of special environmental challenges, in which encounters with stigma frequently appear. The outcomes of such encounters are significant, since, over time, they shape that combination of feeling and belief called 'attitude', with which an individual faces new situations. Daily living presents the individual with opportunities and with challenges to functioning in the full array of domains characterizing the adaptation of the human species. Whatever the given mode of production, these domains include the family, technology, religion and ideology, voluntary association, and work. The life history of a person with a physical disability attends, therefore, not only to stigma, but to behaviors in those roles behind the gates that stigma guards.

This paper presents a summary of the life history of Diane DeVries [6], a woman with quadrilateral limb deficiencies, whom I first met in 1976, as a teaching assistant in the Department of Anthropology, at UCLA. From my vantage in the upper tier of the lecture hall, I could see Diane enter the classroom in an electric wheelchair with lever arm control, face the lectern, and take notes with a pen held between her arm and cheek, leaning her notebook on a homemade wood desk top that slid over the arms of her chair. As I observed this woman, who lacked legs and had above elbow stumps of about equal length, I imagined that she lived at home with her parents and would probably never marry or have sexual experiences. In other words, the question arose, "what kind of life could such an individual have in our society?"

The life history of Diane DeVries represents a collaborative effort, between the subject and researcher, to produce a holistic, qualitative account that would bear on theoretical issues, but that primarily and essentially would convey a

Reprinted from: *Soc. Sci. Med.* Vol. 19, No. 6, pp. 639–645, 1984, with permission. Printed in Great Britain. All rights reserved, Pergamon Press Ltd.

sense of the personal experience of severe congenital disability. The life history, conceived in this way, emerged from a humanistic interest in presenting the voices of people often unheard [7], yet whose lives were otherwise studied, and acted upon, based on data that are decontextualized and fragmented from the standpoint of the individual [8]. From a clinical standpoint, there is a need for such documents. In medicine and in the allied health fields, such as occupational therapy, despite the probabilities that might bear on a given case, the goal of rehabilitation is to achieve a result that is actual, against an indeterminate field of possibility. Clinical reasoning invokes not only the formal procedures of rehabilitaiton, but the professional's past experiences and knowledge of cases [9]. The life history method can offer images of the lives over time of persons with disabilities in their natural circumstances and settings, against which clinical practice can be reflected.

In a larger sense, life histories contribute images to the on-going critique of our society's "culture of disability", providing realistic expectations for both the disabled, and those ablebodied with whom they come in contact, concerning the possible roles that disabled persons can perform and the lives they can lead. Substantively, the life of Diane DeVries represents an adaptation to a severe congenital disability based on an orientation to her own cultural normalcy as a member of American society, the positive valuation of independent performance of daily tasks to the extent of her own abilities, and a reliance on a mix of institutional supports for the disabled and for the population at large. An important finding is that this individual's own account of her life downplays her extensive medical history, and that here encounters with stigma are reported in a way that highlights the positive image she holds of her body and its capabilities.

Diane DeVries: Brief Case History

Diane DeVries [10] was the first child born to her parents, Kenneth and Irene Fields, in the town of Denison, Texas, in 1950. Both parents were 20 years old and white. They came form working

class homes and were married in the Nazarene church. The child was born without lower limbs and with above-elbow stumps. The etiology was unknown, as is the precise incidence and prevalence of this particular configuration of limb deficiency [11].

Diane's birth was received with shock and rejection by the maternal grandmother, who had a kind of exorcism performed in the house when Irene came home to stay with the infant. She was accused of fornicating with Satan and bearing "the Devil's daughter". Within the year, the family left for Long Beach, California, where they settled with the help of one of the mother's sisters. The father, who had gone into the air force after high school, began to work in the construction trades as a carpenter. The family lived in a succession of single-family homes around southern California. Diane's developmental achievements engaged the proud and doting attention of her parents, as their first child.

Another daughter, Debbie, was born 2 years later. As soon as Debbie could walk and talk, she became responsible for assisting with the caretaking of her older sister. An attempt was made to preserve the normal birth order roles. From the very beginning, Diane was incorporated into the family's activities, including outdoor trips with another family, to a lakeside spot in their campers. Diane was able to swim in an inner tube rigged with a gunny sack by her father and tied to the shore with a rope. Two other children, a boy and a girl, were born after a period of several years, when the family was more settled. With them, Diane was clearly an older sibling, who could be relied on for babysitting and other responsibilities.

At age 5, Diane was referred to UCLA's Child Amputee Prosthetics Project (CAPP) for training in upper and lower extremity prosthese. Advances in the technology of artificial arms and legs for amputees were made in the wake of World War II and soon applied to the paediatric population [12]. Diane was fitted with a series of bilateral upper extremity prostheses, with harnesses and cables. She experienced irritations due to heat and bone growth, requiring surgical revisions of her stumps. An all-day wearing pattern was prescribed. It was enforced by her mother, but with difficulty. Diane did become proficient at such tasks as removing the wax paper from sandwiches, managing her milk container and using utensils, with assistance in pre-positioning her terminal devices.

Diane was also fitted with a lower extremity bucket with rocker feet, which she operated by shifting her weight from side to side, similar to the way she "walked" naturally. Very shortly after, she received a three-wheeled cart which she could operate by pushing herself along with a crutch. Later, she received an electric wheelchair. It was the reasoning of her rehabilitation team of CAPP that use of upper extremity prostheses would lead to independence for Diane, with possible self-support through a vocation, versus a life of dependence, or even institutionalization. It was also judged that Diane would not be able to use functional artificial legs because she lacked stumps.

Diane stopped using her artificial arms at the age of 12 or 13, while living for a time at Rancho Los Amigos Hospital, a county rehabilitation facility. She has continued to develop idiosyncratic, but, for her, maximally self-sufficient ways to perform her activities of daily living. Because these ways vary from the usual, I was sometimes not able to accurately observe even simple aspects of her ability to function. In 1977, I wrote my impressions of some of her self-care activities:

> She can feed herself, if someone cooks the food and places it before her in manageable pieces. She can undress by wriggling against a stationary object, but needs to be dressed. She can drive her own wheelchair both forward and back, but needs someone to plug the batteries in. She can get off her chair and onto the couch by herself, and off the couch to the floor, but not the reverse. She can take herself to the toilet, but needs to be wiped, and consequently urinates only twice a day.

> Her bed is on the floor, so she can put herself to bed. She can handle a glass by balancing it between her face and shoulder, if someone places it there. She can swim, and has done so since she was a child. Once a year, she goes to the dentist to have her teeth cleaned. She cannot brush or floss. She can

open sliding doors, if they are left ajar, but not doors with handles.

After reading this description, Diane wrote me a note pointing out the inaccuracies of my observations. Her response follows:

> Just a few technical corrections. I have a stool which enables me to get from the floor back up to my chair.

> At that time, my bed just happened to have been on the floor. I can get in and out of any bed——from w/c (wheelchair) to bed and reverse——from bed to floor (not falling out! HA) but not the reverse.

> I balance a glass between my face and arm-——if it were my shoulder I would die of thirst. Picture that, and you'll see what I mean. No one needs to place it there. I can pick up a glass, cup, or can, and drink it myself.

> I DO and CAN brush my teeth. I place the brush in my mouth and move it with both arms——for the uppers——with my right arm and tongue for everywhere else. No. I can not floss.

> Doors. I can OPEN any door as long as I can get to the doorknob, which I turn with my arm and chin. I can not close a door behind me (except, of course, for a sliding door).

Life History Methods: "Turnings"

The life history in anthropology is a highly qualitative method that relies on interpretation. One of the problems raised again and again is how to describe and compare lives without imposing an overly 'etic' framework [13]. Dollard [14] proposed a set of criteria for evaluating the adequacy of life histories in elaborating the relationship between individual and culture. More recently, Mandelbaum [15] suggested looking for critical junctures in a life, in which the individual "takes on a new set of roles, enters into fresh relations with a new set of people, and acquires a new self-conception". These junctures, called "turnings", mark off the principal periods of the person's life.

The "dimensions" of lives, into which the "turnings" introduce change, mandelbaum describes very broadly. They include cultural role expectations for the achievements of a life plan, interactions undertaken by the individual in the social identity. Mandelbaum next suggests examining the "adaptations" that each turning brings. These, following Kluckhohn, can be thought of as behaviors that contribute to the survival of the individual or the group. Concerning this concept of adaptation, Mandelbaum writes that each person changes in order to maintain continuity; so it follows that one might look at each "turning" to see how and why the person adapted his, or her, behavior and what the person tried to change and to maintain.

Mandelbaum illustrated the use of his model for analyzing life histories through the concepts of 'turnings', 'dimensions', and 'adaptations' by applying it to the life of Gandhi, who was no longer alive; this made his task in some ways easier. He makes the point that "a person's own view of the watersheds in his life may not exactly coincide with the significant turnings that an observer may notice, but that the view may nonetheless be important in the way in which he directs his life". In the interest of preserving an "emic" or phenomenological, approach in the life history of Diane DeVries, I asked her, early in 1983, to chart the significant events in her life and to point out the 'turnings', after having defined this term. In response, Diane prepared a handwritten chart of about 125 events, for which she indicated the emotional valence by writing in colored inks [16]. Of these events, she identified eleven 'turnings' (Fig. 1).

Figure 1. Diane DeVries life chart.

Key:	+	=	'nice, pleasant, good things'
	0	=	'neutral'
	-	=	'emotional, terrible things, not really nice'

1950	0	Birth
1953	+	Sister Debbie born
1955	0	Entered kindergarten at Benjamin F. Tucker school for handicapped children
1956	0	Met lifelong friend Gimmie Mae
	0	Met friend Dr Hall. Surgeon for many years at Child Amputee Prosthetics Project
		TURNING 1:
-		WAS WEARING BOTH UPPER AND LOWER LIMBS
1957	+	First of many summers spent at Camp Paivika, for crippled children
	+	First summer 'crush' over Mike S.
	0	'Went steady' for first time with Chuck N.
	0	Met, and began swimming for Evelyn Dupont
1961	-	Received great mobility with new tri-wheeled bucket
1962		TURNING 2:
-		WAS SENT TO RANCHO TO RECEIVE ARTIFICIAL LEGS
	+	Met lifelong friend Christie
	0	Began to menstruate
	0	Smoked first cigarette & continued on
	+	Met, & fell-in-love with Tim H.
	+	Stopped using my artificial arms
1964	0	Entered first 'normal' jr high (Hoover)
	0	Back at home for short time
	-	Began drinking a little, & eating a lot of pills
	-	Received an ugly pair of cosmetic legs from Rancho
	+	Became good, lifelong friends with Steve Hicks, who eventually introduced me to Jim
1965	+	Sister Becky was born

	−	Sent Norwalk convalescent home
	+	Saw Tim H. again
	−	Saw two of my roommates die in same week
	+	Back to Rancho
1966	0	Dated Johnny S., who soon died of cancer
	+	Met good friend Joyce S.

TURNING 3:

	−	**BEGAN DRINKING HEAVILY, ALONG WITH EATING PILLS & WEED**
	−	Joyce & I busted, and confined to our ward for 14 days

TURNING 4:

1968	+	**GRADUATE FROM JORDAN HIGH SCHOOL**
	0	Attend senior prom with Rancho therapist aid, Wayne, and have sex for first time
	+	Met, & fell-in-love with first black man, Eric. We plan on marriage but gets killed on motorcycle
	0	Met good friend, & soon to be next affair, Ray
	−	Last summer at Camp Paivika
	+	Got my first apartment with first attendant Linda
	−	Met & dated 'creep' Ron
	+	Had Thanksgiving with Linda's family. Become part of their family
	−	Began BUYING my dope
1969	0	Ray moves in my apartment while I'm still dating Ron. We then have an affair
	+	Meet lifelong friend Alice at Ron's party
	+	Alice moves in——Ray moves out
	0	Steve H. is dating Alice; I'm dating Steve's roomy D.
	+	One night I couldn't come over so Steve brings friend, Jim DeVries. Two days later he moves in
1970	−	Notice Mom's future roommate at Mom & Dad's house

1971	−	Jim's head is run over & nearly dies
	−	I have nervous breakdown
	−	Jim and I split up
	−	I go live in convalescent home & he goes to Iowa
	0	I begin dating my doctor, Mike B.
	−	Mike gets me into Buddhism Chuck & Audrey & 3 yr old Wendy living with us
1972	+	Alice and I fly to Iowa for a month
	−	Found out about Dad's cancer
	−	Mom & Dad divorce
	0	Left convalescent home to live with friends Georgeanne and Ladonna
	0	Returned to convalescent home because of nerves
	0	Lived with Debbie for short time
	+	Debbie's daughter, Brandy born
	−	Danny——Debbie's husband dies in auto accident
	0	Leave Deb's for convalescent home in Gardena

TURNING 5:

1973	+	**MET, & FELL-IN-LOVE WITH PAQUAL FLORES**
	+	Moved in with Ladonna
	−	Found out Jim had married
	+	Return to Pasqual & live together
	+	Began UCLA and on the news to get van
	+	Went to Rancho and had an affair there with Mike
	+	Returned to Pasqual
	0	Met & dated another black man, Rico
1975	−	Dad died
	−	Had three miscarriages with Pasqual
	0	Pasqual & I split up
	+	Moved to W.L.A. with Alice for UCLA

TURNING 6:

	+	**MET LIFELONG FRIEND MICHAEL FARKAS & BEGAN WORK ON HIS DREAM——A FILM**

1976 - Vicki died (suicide) & because of
          it, I come into a lot of money
       + Met lifelong friend, & T.A. in
          Anthropology Gelya Frank
       - Jim comes back with alcohol
          problem, & wife trouble!
       0 Alice leaves; Jim & I move to
          Westwood
1977 - Begin seeing a psychologist
       - Have severe asthma attack which
          puts me in UCLA Med. Center
       - Christie and I have fight & never
          talk again until Christmas 1982!

          TURNING 7:
       0 I TRANSFER TO BERKELEY,
          THUS JIM & I MOVE TO
          BERKELEY

       + Jim & I get married in an Oak-
          land courthouse
       + For our honey moon we take
          amtrak across U.S.
       - Michael very upset over my
          marriage
       0 Meet Jim's family for first time
          since his accident
1978 - Jim is busted for drunk driving &
          goes to jail
       + His sister Jan comes to visit me
          while he's in jail
1979 0 We move back to L.A.
       0 Find Chuck & Audrey again
       - Jim & I split up again. He goes
          to Pennsylvania & I go to a
          convalescent home for 3 days
       + Mom helps me get a place, & out
          of that convalescent home
       + I get to have Wendy a lot
       - I start seeing Mike W. again
       - Chuck & Audrey split up
1980 0 File for divorce

          TURNING 8:
       0 MOVE TO ANOTHER CON-
          VALESCENT HOME

       + Pasqual is there and we see each
          other before he dies

          TURNING 9:
       + I GET SAVED AT CHRIS-
          TIANS IN ACTION

       + Jim back in Calif for short time
       - Had 2 last affairs before getting
          saved
       + Stopped smoking (both) & drink-
          ing
       + Met spiritual parents Jana &
          Leonard
       + Met good friend & spiritual big
          sister Charlotte
       + Introduced, & began attending
          Community Chapel
       + Healed of asthma!
       - Debbie tries to kill herself &
          ALMOST makes it
       + First time I had seen power of
          God move by my laying on of
          hands!

          TURNING 10:
1981 - BAD CAR ACCIDENT WITH
          ROOMY

       + Jim calls & hears about my ac-
          cident & comes back
       + When I'm able to sit, I get Jim to
          Community Chapel
       + Jim then repents & serves Jesus

          TURNING 11
       + JIM GETS WATER BAPTIZED
          & DELIVERED OF ALCOHOL
          IN THE WATER

       0 Brother's daughter, Teresa Jen-
          nifer born
       + Jim & I went on trip to Iowa and
          Grand Canyon
1982 + Jim enters Bible College
       + I enter Bible College
       + Lead Alice in the sinner's prayer
       + Christie calls me!

Overview Interpretation of Diane's Life

Cultural normality

An apparent feature of Diane's account of her life is how closely it falls within the normal cultural and developmental expectations of her age, gender and social background. There are the childhood years at home and at school, playing with siblings and friends, involvement in teenage drug culture, graduation from high school, initiation to sex, falling in love and living with a partner, going to college, making a more stable relationship with a spouse and a turn toward Christian spirituality and community. The chart indicates a rich set of relationships over time with friends, of whom there are many. The extensive medical history, of which I am aware, is downplayed. It is not as prominent in Diane's review of her life as it is in my account of it. Rather than note, for example, any of the numerous surgeries on her stumps during childhood for revision of bone spurs, Diane only mentions meeting Dr Cameron Hall, her surgeon at CAPP, whom she identifies as a friend.

This adaptation was made with a certain confidence that Diane is fundamentally normal. Whenever discussing the unknown etiology of her limb deficiencies, Diane has relied on her father's account: "It's just something that happened". In her own view, "The only thing that's wrong with me, is just that I don't have arms and legs...they're nice and neat, too...I can dress how I want and look how I want". The feeling of looking essentially normal was reinforced in the teenage sub-culture of disability, at Rancho (Turning 2), where Diane's friend Christie, a paraplegic, introduced her to the notion of 'looking together' and not like 'a crip'. Diane explains what 'looking together' means to her:

> Any crip's going to be looked at. But at least they'll say : "Wow, look at that person in the wheelchair. Hey, but you know, not too bad!" Because after they get over the fact that you're in a wheelchair, then they look at you. And as long as you're not hanging over your wheelchair and drooling out of your mouth, not doing something you don't have to do, that to me is "looking together".

> Like, when I was a kid, I hated wearing skirts and dresses, because with a skirt you could notice even more that there are legs missing than when you wore shorts and a top. Shorts and a top fitted your body and that made the fact that no legs were

there not look so bad. You didn't have loose material hanging around.

> And whatever I did, like feed myself, drink, I was able to do it without any sloppiness...Vicki, this friend of mine, one of the nicest things I ever heard anyone tell me...one time, we were still at Rancho, and we were eating dinner, and she once told me: "For someone with no hands, you sure are neat". I said, "Oh!" It made me feel good, because I hate dropping things and all this, so you have to be super careful in the beginning, when you're learning, how to do it. And then it gets to be very natural, if you can do it good.

Institutional niche

Also apparent in this life history is the mix of institutional supports, including ones that have to do specifically with disability and ones that do not. In Diane's account, her experiences with institutions that have no necessary connection with her disability are given more positive evaluations, and they are mentioned more frequently as time passes, than her experiences with institutions related to her disability. Diane's orientation is toward the mainstream rather than toward a sub-culture of the disabled, but she has lived in both.

In a sense, she is bi-cultural, growing up in the family in which she was the only disabled member, but attending a school for handicapped children, undergoing rigorous training in the use of prostheses and numerous hospitalizations for orthopaedic surgery, living for a time as a teenager at a county rehabilitation facility (Turning 2), living with an attendant in an apartment which she paid for using her SSI (Supplemental Security Income) check, and so on. Her first sexual experience was with an able-bodied man (Turning 4). Her first serious love relationship was with a man who was a quadriplegic (Turning 5). Her marriage is to an able-bodied man, who has had to struggle to overcome alcohol dependence (Turning 7).

At the present time, she and her husband are living in an apartment not far from the place where she grew up and her family still lives.

Her husband is her attendant, and they use his check as part of their income. She lives across the street form her church, where both are enroled in Bible college, and about a mile from Rancho, where she is still eligible for orthopaedic services, which were necessary for her this year when she underwent an anterior cervical fusion of the fifth and sixth vertebrae.

The church community is, for Diane, another primary institution of adaptation. She is there most weekdays, three nights a week and on Sundays. During the day, she replaces the receptionist if someone is needed, types envelopes, corrects catechism tests, runs to the post office and 'does things people don't have the time to do'. She and her husband together have the hospital ministry, and visit sick members of the congregation. Diane feels that she is now in the right place at the right time:

> Where we are now, it is perfect. I don't have to have the fear of what am I going to do if Jim's not around. The people I know now are different. I know I can call and they'll come over no matter what they're doing. The Lord brought me to this point.

> If Jim's not around, people pitch in. It's like a big family. No one is embarrassed about helping me. I've been here three years now and they all know me. It's real easy, real nice. If anything happened to me, I'd just pick up the phone. They'd be there to help me. If I got real sick with asthma, or had to go to the bathroom, or couldn't get off the couch, they'd be over.

Orientation toward independent living
Another feature that calls for attention in Diane's life chart is her orientation toward independent living. In DeJong's [17] definition, 'independent living' refers to severely disabled persons having access to those medical and social services that enable them to live in the community, short of being gainfully employed. Diane's choices with respect to using the technology for the disabled reflect this orientation. Artificial arms were awkward to use and uncomfortable. In addition, Diane judged them to be more stigmatizing than

her unencumbered body. In them, she felt she looked like 'a little Frandie' (a Frankenstein monster). Without them, she felt more natural: "I've always been really in tune with my body...I always liked my body when I had nothing connected with it". Mobility, however, is at an absolute premium. With adolescence approaching, the three-wheeled cart and crutches, which Diane had used enthusiastically, and without impediment, were traded for an electric wheelchair with lever controls.

The wheelchair is part of Diane's standard 'tool kit'. Another feature of her folk technology is a wooden lap board that fits over the arms of her wheelchair, of which the prototype was built by her father. She has a curved fork on a metal arm clip, also designed by her father, which she carries in an all-purpose book bag that hangs on her chair. She carries a plastic backscratcher for reach, which her occupational therapist at CAPP first supplied her. Her husband has made her a desk that is open in front, so she can drive up to it, with a shelf on the bottom, in reach, and with the lamp switch built into a place where she can turn it on and off. They have a van, formerly from the State Department of Rehabilitation, but now their own, bought with the insurance from a serious car accident in which Diane was involved (Turning 10). Also essential for Diane's independence is a push button telephone which she can manipulate without assistance between face and arm.

Diane and Jim live at a minimal level of support, in which their expenses equal or exceed their income in any given month [18]. Income is based on Diane's SSI check, $426.00 per month, plus the California State IHSS (In-Home Supportive Services) payment for attendant care, $244.00. Jim has begun to work as a carpenter and in other capacities, as he has become successful in his struggle with alcohol. Diane answered the question, 'How would you define independence?'

> Independence is being able to function in society without having to rely on a whole stream of people and places. I see myself as independent because I don't have to depend on my family anymore, on Mom, or on hospital care,

always running to the emergency room. I'm independent of Rancho and my family, and even of attendants, because I'm married. I'm dependent on Jim basically, but most women are dependent on their husbands. Even in a convalescent home, I still was independent. I didn't need a lot of help from the nurses. But I am dependent on the government, financially, for what I can get and can't get. So there's a fine line between the two.

Conclusion

Diane DeVries is a 33-year old woman who likes images of unicorns, photographs of dancers and posters of Barbra Streisand's funny face. When I once suggested that her body reminded me of the Venus de Milo, she vigorously agree. She has made choices throughout her life that orient her to the mainstream of her culture rather than to a subculture of disability. Despite the fact that she was born without legs and with above-elbow stumps, she sees her body, and herself, as natural and normal.

Her adaptation to independent living in the community has been made stable by her marriage to an individual who earns his income as her attendant. Their engagement with an intentional community, in this case, the institution of the church, provides additional support services of a magnitude and quality that could not be bought directly, and which Diane and Jim are able to reciprocate through their own good works. Given a substructure of government subsidy, this represents an institutional niche in which Diane DeVries experiences her life at this time as 'independent'.

References

1. Kluckhohn C. The limitations of adaptation and adjustment as concepts for understanding cultural behavior. In *Culture and Behavior: Collected Essays of Clyde Kluckhohn* (Edited by Kluckhohn R.), pp. 225-264. The Free Press of Glencoe, New York, 1962.
2. See, for example, Gwaltney J. *The Thrice Shy: Cultural Accommodation to Blindness and Other Disasters in a Mexican Community*. Columbia University Press, New York, 1970. Gwaltney describes the traditional status and prestige reserved for travelling blind beggars in a Mexican village near Oaxaca.
3. I am focusing here on the adaptive aspect of contemporary Western society for the physically disabled, but a dialectic would reveal, of course, a list of corresponding challenges to survival, including the iatrogenic potential of high technology medicine, fragmentation in professional responsibility for medical care and follow-up, the isolation and immobilization of the physically disabled due to architectural barriers and inaccessible transportation, and such contradictions in public policy as the withdrawal of stipends from those who are able to earn more than a poverty-level income. See Bowe F. *Rehabilitation America: Toward Independence for Disabled and Elderly People*. Harper & Row, New York, 1980.
4. Goffman E. *Stigma*. Prentice-Hall, Englewood Cliffs, NJ, 1963.
5. Wright B. *Physical disability——A Psychological Approach*. Harper & Row, New York, 1960.
6. Frank G. Venus on wheels: the life history of a congenital amputee. Doctoral dissertation, Department of Anthropology, University of California, Los Angeles, 1981. (Copies available from UMI, 300 N. Zeeb Road, Ann Arbor, MI 48106, U.S.A.)
7. Langness L.L. and Frank G. *Lives: An Anthropological Approach to Biography*. Chandler & Sharp, Novato, CA, 1981.
8. In this case, see, for example, Sharples G.E. Ned. *Child Amputees: Disability Outcomes and Antecedents*. Initial Follow-up Study of Selected Patients of an In-Patient Service. School of Public Health, University of Michigan, Grant No. PC-1003, Children's Bureau, Social and Rehabilitation Service, U.S. Department of Health, Education and Welfare. The sample for Sharples' study of physical and social performance of child amputees, based on medical records and home interview data, is comprised mainly of unilateral, below-elbow, congenital and acquired amputees, and addresses the subjects' degree of success in prosthesis use. To apply the findings of such a study to a bilateral, above-elbow, congenitally limb deficient child, also missing lower extremities, would require considerable interpretation, and would entail a low degree of predictive power.

Other studies, such as of thalidomide births, include other inapplicable variables, such as the presence of useful appendages such as 'flippers'. The point is not so much that Diane DeVries represents a unique case, as that sample-based studies fail to predict for all the features of a medical situation. Clinical judgments by professional, as well as value judgments by patients themselves, will have to be made on the basis of other kinds of information, such as the images a life history might offer.

9. Rogers J.C. Clinical reasoning: the ethics, science, and art. Eleanor Clarke Slagle Lectureship——1983. *Am. J. Occup. Ther.* **37**, 601-616, 1983.

10. This is the subject's real name. We decided early in the study to not employ pseudonyms or other disidentifying devices. We felt equally that disguises might dull our passionate impulse to present things that were both true and real: true in their essential meaning and real because they actually happened.

11. The exact incidence of congenital limb deficiencies like Diane's is impossible to specify, partly because such terms as *hemimelia* ('half-limb') and *amelia* ('lacking limb'), for which statistics appear, cover a wide variety of malformations. In 1973, in the United States, the Commission on Professional and Hospital Activities, reported that reduction deformities of the upper limb numbered about 225 births; reduction deformities of the lower limb numbered 118. My source for these figures was R.P. Leavitt, Science Information Division, the National Foundation, March of Dimes.

12. CAPP was established in 1955 by a contract with Crippled Children Services of the California Department of Public Health, with funds from the United States Children's Bureau. See Blakeslee B. *The Limb-Deficient Child*. Child Amputee Prosthetics Project, University of California Press, Berkeley, 1963.

13. The 'emic'/'etic' distinction was borrowed by anthropology from linguistics to refer to the difference between the way a member of a culture will perceive sense data, as compared to the way such data will be construed by an outside observer, and, especially, by a social scientist.

14. Dollard J. *Criteria for the Life History: With Analyses of Six Notable Documents*. Institute for Human Relations, Yale University Press, New Haven, CT, 1935.

15. Mandelbaum D.G. The study of life history: Gandhi. *Curr. Anthrop.* **14**, 177-206, 1973.

16. The identification of the 'turnings' was done collaboratively, discussing and critiquing Diane's initial choices by subjecting them to the definition of her term. In indicating the emotional valence of these events. Diane attempted to represent her feelings at the time the events took place, since she is aware that her values have changed.

17.   DeJong G. Independent living: from social movement to analytic paradigm. *Archs phys. med. Rehab.* **60**, 435-446, 1979.

18.   The combined base income for Diane and Jim DeVries is approx. $700.00 per month. Working part-time at telephone jobs, Diane has in the past brought in an additional $50.00 per week or $200.00 per month. These jobs are erratic, and if she is laid off, she is not necessarily eligible for unemployment benefits. The monthly expenses for the DeVries household include $325.00 for rent, an estimated $17.00 for utilities, $40.00 for the phone, $80.00 for groceries and $40.00 for insurance on the van. Given the size of their income, their church-related expenses are substantial. Between November 1981 and June 1983, Jim used his attendant check to pay for a foundation stone in the church building fund, an obligation of $200.00 per month. Of the income remaining each month, 20 percent, or $100.00, is tithed to the church. Finally, both Diane and Jim pay a nominal amount for their classes at Bible school. They receive occasional gifts of cash and loans from friends and family, and accept invitations to eat elsewhere, without expense, about twice weekly. A most significant expense for Diane is that of medical care and related costs, including wheelchair repairs, which she receives free of charge, through Medi-Cal.

Disability as Moral Experience: Epilepsy and Self in Routine Relationships

JOSEPH W. SCHNEIDER *DRAKE UNIVERSITY*

This paper draws on depth interview data from an availability sample of 80 people with epilepsy to examine the moral experience of disability (cf. E. Goffman, 1959, "The Moral Career of the Mental Patient," Psychiatry, 22, 123-135). This concept directs attention to how those who live in the social world of epilepsy, and of disability more generally, define themselves and others in both positive and negative ways. Most discussions of the moral aspects of disability turn on the concept of stigma, and epilepsy certainly is a prime area for such study. This paper, however, focuses on the consequences of disability for the distribution of work and responsibility in routine, everyday relationships and how, in turn, this affects the way people see, think about, and feel about themselves. Particular attention is given to family, parental, and employment relationships. The paper raises the question, If disability is a social construction and has such costs, how can we best construct it for all concerned?

In their introduction to this special issue, Fine and Asch identify several gaps in social science research on disability and suggest how we might address these neglected questions. The research for this paper grew out of one such gap: the virtual absence of studies that reported, in people's own words, the routine experience of living with chronic illness and disability. This paper is based on in depth interviews that provide an insider's view of what it is like to be a person with epilepsy in our society. In other forums, Peter Conrad and I have presented a sociological analysis of "illness experience" (Conrad, 1987; Roth & Conrad, 1987; Schneider & Conrad, 1983). Here I want to focus on the "moral experience" of epilepsy and disability, to distinguish between this idea and stigma, and to argue for a perspective on disability as rooted in social interaction and culture rather than in the bodies and minds of those we call "handicapped" and "disabled."

The Experience of Disability

Detailed and systematic knowledge about the *experience* of disability——what it is like to *be* disabled——is central to a deeper understanding of disability in social life (Herzlich, 1973). Research has only begun to accumulate that examines these experiences of people with multiple sclerosis (Davis, 1973; Stewart & Sullivan, 1982), rheumatoid arthritis (Locker, 1984), cystic fibrosis (Waddell, 1982), diabetes (Benoliel, 1975; Maines, 1983, 1984), heart disease (Cowie, 1976; Speedling, 1982), cancer (Bluebond-Langner, 1978; Comaroff & Maguire, 1981; Gyllenskold, 1982), of people who are deaf (Groce, 1984; Higgins, 1979), and of those with epilepsy and diverse other physical conditions (Fisher & Galler, 1986; Fitzpatrick, Hinton, Newmar, Scambler, & Thompson, 1984; Locker, 1981; Shearer, 1981; Thomas, 1982; Zola, 1982). Most of what professionals know about living with disability is a product of research done from perspectives outside this experience——research by able-bodied experts who often give priority to their scientific theories and research techniques rather than to the words and perceptions of the people they study. The most common outsider perspectives are medical, namely, clinical and therapeutic viewpoints. However, even social scientists have studied disability and illness

Thanks to Adrienne Asch, Peter Conrad, and anonymous reviewers for helpful comments on earlier drafts of this paper, which was initially presented at the 1983 meetings of the American Sociological Association in Detroit. This research was supported by grants from the National Institute of Mental Health (MH 30818-01) and the Epilepsy Foundation of America.

Correspondence should be addressed to Joseph W. Schneider, Department of Sociology, Drake University, Des Moines, IA 50311.

Reprinted from: *Journal of Social Issues,* Vol. 44, No. 1, 1988, pp. 63-78, with permission.

almost entirely as defined by *their* concepts and theories, rather than those of the people involved.

While "outsider" research surely has contributed to the improvement of medical and surgical treatment, it tells us little, if anything, about the details and the nature of disability as a lived social psychological phenomenon (cf. Matza, 1969). In fact, such research can be misleading or simply wrong about these questions (Asch, 1984; Bynder & New, 1976; New, 1984). For instance, it is apparent that many people find coping with the *social* meanings and practices surrounding disability considerably more difficult than coping with the physical or biological limitations they have (Task Force on psychology and the Handicapped, 1984).

Most disability research defines the problem as something in individuals' bodies and/or minds rather than in the social situation (but for exceptions, see DeJong, 1979; Goffman, 1969; Resenhan, 1973). This is part of the dominant medical view of epilepsy and other physical impairments (Conrad & Schneider, 1980; Freidson, 1970; zola, 1972). When we have wanted to know what epilepsy is, and how to respond to it we typically have gone to medical experts. Their current view of epilepsy is "a convulsive disorder [that] is the expression of a sudden, excessive, disorderly discharge of neurons in either a structurally normal or diseased cortex. The discharge results in an almost instantaneous disturbance of sensation, loss of consciousness, convulsive movement, or some combination thereof" (Harrison, 1980, p. 131). Medical experts divide these seizures into various diagnostic and descriptive categories based on how much they are generalized, partial and focused, in body involvement. People with more generalized seizures are usually expected to suffer greater disability than those whose seizures are more focused and partial.

Physicians believe the causes of epilepsy are varied and often unclear. Perinatal conditions, early childhood infection, and head trauma are identified as known causative factors. Research suggests that in some cases, heredity plays an important role. The most common medical treatment of epilepsy is anticonvulsant and tranquillizing drugs. These drugs usually control but do not eliminate seizures. Neurosurgery is used to control seizures in some extreme cases. Physicians routinely serve as "gatekeepers" by documenting that a patient is either "seizure free" or is have seizures, and thus is able or not able to drive a car safely, work around machinery, and so on. The definitions, theories, practices, and social institutions that maintain this medical "ownership" of epilepsy constitute an important part of the "objective reality" with which people so labelled must deal.

In our research, we avoided taking a medical perspective on epilepsy (Schneider & Conrad, 1981). Instead, we adopted a sociological point of view by interviewing the people who themselves live with and experience this world. Categories such as epilepsy, illness, disease, and disability are not "givens" in nature (Conrad & Schneider, 1980; Fabrega, 1972a,b; Freidson, 1970; Sedgwick, 1973), but rather "socially constructed" categories that emerge from the interpretive activities of people acting together in social situations (Berger & Luckmann, 1966; Blumer, 1969; Cooley, 1922; Mead, 1943). The "experts" on what disability is, then, include the disabled, their families, friends, and associates.

Disability, Stigma, and Moral Experience

Sociologists have pointed out that chronic illness and disability can become grounds for a "spoiled" identity, i.e., one of lesser social value (Freidson, 1966, 1970; Goffman, 1963; Zola, 1972). While most cultures discourage holding disabled people responsible for their conditions (see Dingwall, 1976; McHugh, 1970; Parsons, 1951), the negative evaluation of illness and disability in our culture is nevertheless associated with the ill or disabled person in many social settings.

Epilepsy is a stigmatized condition. Meanings associated with it have historically gone well beyond the general undesirability of illness. They convey highly negative personal qualities——spirit possession, uncleanness, pollution, divine punishment, madness, uncontrolled violence, and "criminal tendencies." As a current public service announcement reminds us, "Epilepsy——It's not what you think." People with epilepsy have much experience with these stig-matizing definitions (Dell, 1986; Ryan, Kempner, & Emlen, 1980; schneider & Conrad, 1980, 1983; West, 1979b, 1986; but see Caveness & Gallup, 1980).

I believe there are subtleties of this experi-ence that affect the selves of those involved but that are missed by the concept of stigma. For instance, in our society most of us assume that people with disabilities need and want others' help and care. They "lack" something (ability? competence?) and thus must rely on various "able" others. This assumption obscures the fact that we all——able-bodied and disabled alike——sometimes want and need such help. It en-courages us to see, to think of, ill and disabled people as "receivers," and of the well as "givers." Using these categories, we thus create and nur-ture an incomplete understanding of the relation-ships and people involved, one that surely influences how we see and feel about ourselves.

I use the concept "moral exper-ience"——suggested by Goffman's (1959) dis-cussion of the moral career of mental patients——to help us think further about this aspect of the disability experience. Goffman says the *moral* aspect of this career refers to "the regular se-quence of changes that career entails in the person's self and in his framework of imagery for judging himself and others" (p. 123). Moral experience thus focuses attention on how people transform *lived* social life into positive or nega-tive meanings about self. Both Goffman's and Hughes's (1958) work remind us that such transformations involve not only the disabled but also the various others with whom they interact. While I follow Goffman in focusing on relation-ships as an important crucible of the self, I am concerned less with how the label "epilepsy" spoils identity than with the impact of the percep-tions that grow out of and guide routine "role-directed" interactions. The key role relationship here is between the disabled and the able-bodied, and a major issue is how social definitions of disability affect the division of labor and respon-sibility between those involved (cf. Davis, 1961).

Data and Sample

Our sample was based on the availability and cooperation of volunteers who said they had epilepsy. We interviewed 80 people between 1976 and 1979. The interviews lasted from one to three hours, were guided by roughly 50 open-ended questions, and were tape recorded (see Schneider & Conrad, 1983). Because of the stigma of epilepsy, many people are hesitant or refuse to disclose their diagnosis. No complete population list of people with epilepsy exists and private physicians, of course, protect the iden-tities of their patients. This self-selection may have produced a sample of people more likely to tell their stories, and perhaps also to mention negative experiences, although there were both positive and negative themes in virtually all interviews.

Volunteers came from a local epilepsy self-help group, a vocational rehabilitation program, from responses to classified advertisements in local newspapers and posters in public places, and through referrals from other respondents. Those interviewed ranged in age form 14 to 54 years (average age 28: median age 27); there were 44 women and 36 men. Of our respon-dents, 25% said they were diagnosed prior to adolescence, 44% during adolescence, and 7% as young adults. Over half were single; 65% had some college work or beyond, yet about 65% said their total family incomes were less than $16,000. About one-third said they were employed in white-collar jobs, but fully one-fourth of the sample were students, many of whom said they were on their way to profes-sional and managerial occupations. Fifteen percent said they were unemployed and looking for work at the time of the interview. Interviews with 68 respondents were done in a metropolitan area in the Midwest; 12 came from a major city on the East Coast. The people and stories from these two segments of the sample did not seem to vary in important ways.

Our study was independent of medical or institutional settings. None of our respondents had been institutionalized in any long-term care facility because of epilepsy; none was interviewed in a hospital, clinic, or physician's office. This is unusual for research on epilepsy and on other kinds of disability (other exceptions include Trostle, Hanser, & Susser, 1983; West, 1979a,b, Whitman et al., 1984; and a small number of epidemiological studies). We avoided medical seizure nomenclature in our interviews. Moreover, we did not make the common assumption, based on these categories, that people with generalized seizures (tonic-clonic, "grand mal") necessarily "suffer" more from, or have a more difficult time with, epilepsy than those whose seizures are focused and less visually drastic (e.g., absence, focal motor, temporal lobe, "petit mal"). Our respondents' reports described the full range of seizures found in standard medical classifications (Commission for the Control of Epilepsy and its Consequences, 1978, Vol. 2, Part1, p. 164).

In our analysis we followed the inductive "grounded theory" approach of Glaser and Strauss (1967). Thus we attempted to stay close to the meanings of respondents' words and stories while searching for similar kinds of experience. The categories in the following analysis——"family relationships," "parents," "seizure in public," "at work," and "self"——are topics and issues that were central to much of our respondents' talk.

Epilepsy and Self in Everyday Relationships

Routine relationships are a good place to study moral experience. From them we shape our sense of who we are, based in part on our perceptions of how others see and behave toward us. This is true both for people who are disabled and for those who are well and able-bodied. When one party to the interaction is categorized as disabled, however, many givens of routine interaction become problematic.

Parson's (1951) influential conception of the "sick role" posits willing support from others and cooperation by the ill/disabled as part of this culturally specified pattern. The familiar role prescriptions that define disability can encourage

able-bodied intimates to see their already diffuse obligations to the disabled or ill person as even more open-ended (Corbin & Strauss, 1985; Fisher & Galler, 1986). If called upon, they are expected to respond. Better yet, they should *anticipate* the needs of the disabled, and so avoid putting the latter in a position of having to routinely ask for help. In fact, disabled people may provide others an opportunity to *demonstrate* what "good," "caring," and "responsible" people they are.

Stories from our respondents and other people with disabilities about being "helped" against their will illustrate the strength of these presumptions. Those with disabilities (and, indeed, perhaps all of us) can find it difficult to control and direct the help they get. At the same time, these expectations, when applied, can push people with disabilities further into dependence. This seemed clear in respondents' comments about care given by family members, and especially by parents (cf. Strauss, Fagerhaugh, Suczek, & wiener, 1982a,b; Suczek, Fagerhaugh, Strauss, & wiener, 1981).

Family Relationships

One common way intimates interact with people who have disabilities is through direct care giving. many research reports have shown that such care often involves a good deal of work (Burton, 1975; Corbin & Strauss, 1982, 1985; Featherstone, 1980; locker, 1984; Voysey, 1975). With epilepsy, however, family members and intimates can do little direct, specialized care work. Patients typically see physicians every six months to a year for routine evaluations, unless they experience unusual symptoms such as more, and/or more generalized, seizures or drug "side effects." Unlike the complex work surrounding end stage renal disease, or the simple but still important routine care for people with ostomies, epilepsy involves little direct treatment.

There is, however, considerable family care given other than managing treatment regimens. Respondents described, for example, how parents and spouses regularly reminded them of what to do or not to do in case of seizures. They would also drive to the doctor, the pharmacy, or other places, especially for a child or for an adult who could not obtain a driver's license. They would sometimes carry medications, in case they were needed during an outing, and they helped to keep epilepsy and seizures secret from outsiders.

While our respondents appreciated and even expected some of this care, parents' good intentions often weighed heavily on them and carried subtle meaning about their self. One man, diagnosed at age 6, recalled his mother's protective work:

> My mother . . . put a lot of, uh, barriers up there. "Bill, you can't do this," "Bill, you can't do that," "Bill, take your pills three times a day," or "If you don't take your pills. . . ." She gave me too much loving, which is no good. She'd try to compensate or something for [my epilepsy]. And I believe she overcompensated.

Another man said his father would talk to him about his epilepsy when he was growing up:

> Mostly he told me I'd never be able to do things like everybody else could. Couldn't drive, shouldn't swim, couldn't be alone. . . One main thing that really stuck in my head was my father always told me, and my mother [did] too . . . I'd never be able to live a normal life, y'know. I couldn't get a job where any tools were around, or machinery; couldn't drive, couldn't go out climbin' hills or something. Couldn't be in the boat.

Often these and similar parental lessons set the direction for how children thought about themselves: as people who were *not* able. In other cases, such as the latter one, they became ideas to challenge, in part as a test of one's competence as normal. The man quoted above said he went against these parental directives to see if "I could do things without . . . somethin' happenin' . . . [like] if I ran around the block I wouldn't have a seizure." He found that he could. This sense of overcoming the actual or supposed limitations of epilepsy became a source of pride and success, even a badge of normality. It was a resource for a strengthened sense of self (see Charmaz, 1982, on how chronically ill people develop a "supernormal identity").

Other respondents described very different family lessons: that epilepsy was "not important" for their lives, selves and futures; that it could be controlled by medication and was, in any case, a "medical problem just like diabetes and other things." They were told that epilepsy never should be "used as an excuse" for failure or reduced effort, and that it should not diminish them in others' eyes.

Many respondents spoke how parents or spouses "worried a lot" about them. Such worry, like advice and admonition, was described as requiring the family's time and energy, and leading them to do their work. Risk associated with seizures was a paramount concern, because of the possibility of physical harm, but parents who saw epilepsy as highly stigmatizing (to themselves as well as to their children) also worried a good deal about the risk of disclosure.

Women respondents especially told elaborate and intensely felt stories about both kinds of parental worry. Mothers were most commonly recalled as the prime worriers. One 29-year-old woman who had epilepsy since childhood said of their mother,

> Well, I'm sure it aged her because she worries [still] so damn much about people finding out. Well, she worries about her kids all the time; that we weren't home, you know, if we weren't home at a certain time or didn't take our medication [she and her sister both had epilepsy] that you were going to have a seizure, or she could be called at work, or if somebody would find out.

One 19-year-old woman who had epilepsy since she was an infant said her mother worried about her all the time, whether she was in the house, out shopping, and even when she was asleep:

> When I go out shopping by myself, my mom worries about me. When I'm home late, my mom worries about me. When I'm taking my bath, my mom pounds on the door——"Are you all right?" "Are you all right"——you know, to make sure . . . and that bothers me.

Knowing of such worry seemed to contribute to a definition of self as less than fully able. A Parent's worry easily became a child's belief. If a parent worried *that* much, perhaps there were "good reasons." For instance, we asked the woman described about her plans for the future, whether she would be able to live alone, apart from her parents. She said, with some hesitation, "I would probably drive my parents up the roof, [but] I think I would . . . I think I would probably have to be extra careful, but I think I can." It was an appealing idea, but she had specific reservations:

> The only thing that bothers me now is I have my convulsions mostly in my sleep, and I'm afraid of . . . what if I swallow my tongue? What if I can't get out of this? . . . I'll die. And I feel like when my parents try to wake me up and I wouldn't wake up, you know, that would be really scary. It scares my mom, but she checks up on me.

She had learned the comfort of watchful, protective parental care. Despite her hopeful anticipations, she was wary of a move and of independence.

If we consider conventional gender roles, it seems likely that women may experience these moral aspects of epilepsy and disability as considerably more constraining and debilitating than men do because they simultaneously occupy the culturally limited positions of "child" and "woman" (see Fine and Asch, 1981). Respondents said this protection sometimes made them feel like "little children" others had to "watch out for" and "take care of." One 27-year-old woman said,

> They [parents] tried to baby me. I think they wanted me to live with them the rest of my life. They still do. They still treat me like I'm 10 years old. They come up to my place and tell me how to take care of my kids, and how to do this and how to do that. . . . They don't think I can take care of the kids.

In contrast, she believed she *could* give proper care to her children and she *was* doing so.

Another woman, 35, who had epilepsy since she was 19, said of her relationship with her parents,

> Oh, I think it would be better if I moved to a different town and was completely away from them. They kind of treat you like you are still real young. They live [here]. They think they still have to be very protective.

This parental worry and attention was perhaps *her* most abiding worry about having epilepsy.

Parents' worry, advice, and protection thus often magnified the significance of epilepsy in children's lives and could become a kind of control that isolated, restricted, and further disabled the children. Because their time together was spent on talk and action about epilepsy, medication, seizures, secrecy, precautions, instructions, reminders, and the like, there was less time for other topics and activities. The social and cultural realities of epilepsy could extend into more and more of routine social experience, quite aside from its stigma and official restrictions. As one 35-year-old woman said of her well-intentioned parents.

> They don't let you forget you have it. If they could only just forget about it, you know? I think they are very well-intentioned, but it's just that it's always in the back of their mind "Well, you have epilepsy, and I'll do this for you and I'll do that for you."

Having someone so willing to "do" for you can subtly disable, especially when coupled with a definition of self implied in the disabled role. How much dependence is desirable and how much is "too much" are important but difficult questions. Many said they did not "like" accepting this help, but most said they tolerated it, even as adults. In such conformity they appeared to make it more difficult to be seen, and to see themselves, as "normal" people.

Our research demonstrates that help and care not only vary in form, but that their content can be very consequential for how recipients cope with their condition. Our data do not show that parents should "do nothing," but they do imply that doing less, within a context of general support, may be preferable to doing more (cf. Lemert, 1951, 1972; Tannenbaum, 1938).

Seizures in Public Places

Our respondents believed seizures in social settings greatly impose on others, who suddenly see a person "out of control," "not responsible," behaving in a bizarre fashion, convulsing, unconscious, having difficulty breathing.   Our respondents thought these others felt "uncomfortable" because they neither knew what they were seeing nor what to do.   To do nothing in such situations is both counterintuitive (relatives and close friends had to *learn* to "do nothing") and opens the possibility of subsequently having to give an account for one's inaction.

The most common reaction of naive witnesses was to medicalize the event (Conrad & Schneider, 1980) by calling an ambulance. One woman used the term "sickness" in describing these reactions to seizures——even by friends who knew of her epilepsy:

> I think they panic. More than anything else, it's the idea, "I don't want to be around you if you have one 'cuz I don't know what to do." I think I can say that about a neighbour guy. I think he's like my husband. As long as a sickness is over there, fine and dandy . . . even if it's someone getting sick to their stomach. "Just stay over ther because I don't know what to do with you if you are sick."

She said of her friends, "they think I'm fine, as long as I don't have one [seizure] in front of them."

These comments raise the question of how seizures and sickness or disability are alike. This woman said that as a child she learned, "If you are sick, go in the corner and come out when you're feeling better." This suggests not only that people with sickness and disability should be segregated, but that seizures, as a kind of disability, become grounds for a shift in responsibility from the ill person to well others. The collective work of carrying on interaction is suddenly stopped; new definitions of the situation are made——often without the presence of any knowledgeable "interpreters" for the unconscious person——and a reorganized division of labor

and responsibility emerge. Those at hand take over the control that earlier resided with the individual.

One answer to the above question, then, is that both seizures and sickness involve social situations in which well others are called upon to act on behalf of the disabled person. Such work may have important costs for the disabled person's self-concept. Once such a shift occurs, it is as though the person who had the seizure becomes generally rather than situationally disabled. Except for the few minutes, even seconds, during a seizure, the person *is* able and able-bodied.   However, standard medical-administrative categories reinforce, if not create, these general definitions by banning people with epilepsy from various "high-risk" activities and situations, even though they are fully able, most of the time, to perform competently in them.

Many of the stories about seizures and others' responses came from work settings, where issues of responsibility are more explicit. Once work supervisors and peers had been called upon to "take over" during a seizure, they were thereafter felt to be wary and watchful. Respondents said others sometimes treated them as people who could not be "counted on to handle" routine situations. One man who suffered a severe head injury from a fall due to a seizure on the job told of attempting to return to work:

> When I tried to go back to work, we played all kind of hell trying to get me back. My doctor said I was ready physically, able to go back to work. The company insisted I go see their doctor. He said, "What did your doctor say?" I told him and he says, "I don't know what the hell you're doin' her then." I says, "I don't either." Finally, they said, "Okay, you can come back to work next week." Then they put it off for another week. The typical excuse was they couldn't decide back in the main office. Then, when I cam back they wanted me to wear my hardhat . . . in the office!   My boss, my immediate supervisor . . . I don't think he really understood the whole thing. Pure ignorance on his part.

He said he had the feeling "they were keeping an eye on" him for almost two years after he did return to work. Even then, his full responsi-bilities——travelling through the state as a technical expert——were restricted because his supervisors feared they "might be too much" for him.

A woman described surreptitious surveillance by co-workers after she had a seizure at work:

> Like after I fall on the job, I've got people coming up and checking on me all night to see if I'm okay. You get to feel like a little baby after a while and you don't get treated the same. Every once in awhile you'll see somebody coming in like to go to the bath-room on my floor, or the guard comes up and he says, "Hummm, I thought I smelled smoke up here." In a way it makes you feel kind of bad you can't operate on your own two feet.

Quite aside from whether these others' stated reasons were true, this woman and other respon-dents *felt*, after a seizure at work, others didn't trust them and never acted quite the same. "It's almost as if," one woman said, "they were expec-ting me to have another seizure."

Comments about interactional competence after a seizure were not limited to work settings, but covered a variety of situations, from informal friendship groups to bureaucratic organizations, including schools and rehabilitaiton agencies. In a particularly ironic incident, one man told of being banned from a vocational rehabilitation program because program personnel believed he had a seizure while at the program workshop:

> They asked me what I wanted to do. At the time I had a cane, so I said, "I wanna refinish it." So, I had some stripper in a great big pan and I tripped and fell, face forward, into the stripper and passed out. So they said, "Well, he had a seizure." But I don't think I did. I ingested so much of that stuff into my sys-tem . . . I don't think it was a seizure. But they kicked me out and told me I couldn't come back. I said, "Man, I thought that's what you guys were here for." He says, "Well, we can't have you on our property as long as there's a possibility of you having a seizure, because you could sue the state."

He had become, due to his "seizure," a liability to an organization dedicated to removing precisely such limiting definitions. The rehabilit-ation people told this man that as long as he "had seizures," he was too much of a risk to be given responsibility. Here we see agency personnel defining the disabled person as possible trouble for the agency and state. They used the categor-ies "epileptic" and "seizures" to "make sense" of *their* experience in the presence of "such people," even though such definitions might not be shared by those so categorized.

Restrictions on driving were one of the most keenly felt limitations based on epilepsy (in actuality, based on the application of standard medical-administrative definitions of it). Our respondents described how difficult it was not to be allowed to drive due to state driver's license laws. Beyond the significance of car or license as a symbol of their social competence, these restrictions enormously increased their sense of dependency on family members and friends. In consequence, they became more disabled and caused more work for able-bodied others, further tilting these already asymmetric relationships. Our respondents decried the injustice of such restrictions and often simply lied about epilepsy when applying for a driver's license.

Implications and Discussion

While we may sometimes feel the social expec-tations about disability as constraining, most of us see them simply as "the way things are." It is, however, important to appreciate that these meanings and expectations of disability are created and perpetuated by us all, and that disab-ility is not a given in social life. Unlike a leg that does not work well or a neuromuscular system that produces unexpected and unwelcome seizures, the social category of disability can be done away with, or at least changed dramatically. Since we create these social constructions, we can also demolish them, or at least tame those we find to be undesirable.

But this is too sanguine a view. Social construction work is always political work. The diverse people who make up the world of disab-ility have various investments——in the status quo as well as in other arrangements and definitions of disability, and from the behavior that accompanies them? The present data suggest some quite subtle aspects of disability. Our respondents' stories make it clear that to understand disability as a social phenomenon we must carefully examine *relationships* between the so-called disabled and able-bodied others, and in particular, ask ourselves what these relationships *could be.*

Being defined as a disabled person, whether because of the possibility of seizures or of heart attack, or because of the appearance and shape of one's body, commonly becomes grounds for receiving others' attention, care, and help. However, disabled people also invest much emotional energy to make workable relationships with able-bodied others, as Fisher and Galler (1986) pointed out in a recent paper on relationships between pairs of able-bodied and disabled women had to work harder——"go more than half way"——to break through the wall their bodies seemed to throw up against others' "normal" behavior toward them (cf. Davis, 1961).

Moreover, our respondents found it difficult to ignore or refuse overtures of help offered. Sometimes, of course, they *wanted* this help. But for people with disabilities, such "normal" dependence may come at an extraordinary cost. To act normally and accept such care and concern can become a warrant for their abnormality——evidence that they in fact need and deserve such help as not fully competent players in the routine dramas of social life (cf. Bogdan & Biklin, 1977; Thomas, 1982). Moreover, it threatens to make their own giving to and helping of others invisible.

On the other side are the so-called able-bodied, who are likely to see such help as their responsibility. In exchange for such giving, they can receive the comforts of a satisfied conscience and kind words from observers. They are "good people" because they do this "good" but often difficult work. Finally, they can all but ignore the many routine ways that disabled people help their able-bodied intimates and associates.

Our respondents were well aware how much work and worry parents and others did for them. Other research on disability has documented the amount and variety of this work that parents and spouses do for disabled children and family members (Burton, 1975; Locker, 1981; speedling, 1982; Voysey, 1975). How do these able-bodied people see themselves and their situations? While they appear not to blame the disabled other, do they resent the time, energy, and work involved? Do they ask themselves what are *their* payoffs (see Kidder, Fagan, & Cohn, 1981)? If they do, how are their feelings of resentment and devotions balanced?

"To do away with disability"——what might that mean in terms of the social definition of disability? It would certainly not mean that all bodies would be free of unwanted changes and forms. Given the existence of impaired bodies, then, what optimum cultural practices and social definitions can we bring to them? This is the central and most challenging question for future action and social policy on disability.

References

Asch, A. (1984). The experience of disability: A challenge for psychology. *American Psychologist, 39,* 529-536.

Benoliel, J.Q. (1975). Childhood diabetes: The commonplace in living becomes uncommon. In A.L. Strauss & B.G. Glaser (Eds.), *Chronic illness and the quality of life* (pp. 89-98). St. Louis, MO: Mosby.

Berger, P.L. , & Luckmann, T. (1966). *The social construction of reality.* New York: Doubleday.

Bluebond-Langner, M. (1978). *The private worlds of dying children.* Princeton, NJ: Princeton University Press.

Blumer, H. (1969). *Symbolic interactionism.* Englewood Cliffs, NJ: Prentice-Hall.

Bogdan, R., & Biklin, D. (1977). Handicapism. *Social Policy, 7,* 14-19.

Burton, L. (1975). *The family life of sick children.* London: Routledge & Kegan Paul.

Bynder, H., & New, P.K. (1976). Time for change: From micro- to macro-sociological concepts in disability research. *Journal of Health and Social Behavior, 17,* 45-52.

Caveness, W.F., & Gallup, G.H. (1980). A survey of attitudes toward epilepsy in 1979 with an indication of trends over the last thirty years. *Epilepsia, 21,* 509-518.

Charmaz, K. (1982). *The development of a supernormal identity in the chronically ill.* Unpublished manuscript, Department of Sociology, Sonoma State University, Rohnert Park, CA.

Comaroff, J., & Maguire, P. (1981). Ambiguity and the search for meaning: Childhood leukaemia in the modern clinical context. *Social Science and Medicine, 15B,* 115-123.

Commission for the Control of Epilepsy and its Consequences. (1978). *Plan for nationwide action on epilepsy* [Volumes I-IV; Pub. No. (NIH) 78-276]. Washington, D.C.:U.S. Department of Health, Education and Welfare.

Conrad, P. (1987). The experience of illness: Recent and new directions. In J.A. Roth & P. Conrad (Eds.), *The experience and management of chronic illness* (Vol. 6, pp. 1-31). Greenwich, CT:JAI Press.

Conrad, P., & Schneider, J.W. (1980). *Deviance and medicalization.* St. Louis, MO: Mosby.

Cooley, C.H. (1922). *Human nature and the social order.* New York: Scribner.

Corbin, J., & Strauss, A.L. (1982). *Trajectory and work and biography.* Unpublished manuscript. Department of Social and Behavioral Sciences, School of Nursing, University of California, San Francisco.

Corbin, J., & Strauss, A.L. (1985). Managing illness at home: Three lines of work. *Qualitative Sociology, 8,* 224-247.

Cowie, B. (1976). The cardiac patient's perception of his heart attack. *Social Science and Medicine, 10,* 87-96.

Davis, F. (1961). Deviance disavowal: The management of strained interaction by the visibly handicapped. *Social Problems, 9,* 120-132.

Davis, M. (1973). *Living with multiple sclerosis.* Springfield, IL: Thomas.

DeJong, G. (1979). *The movement for independent living: Origins, ideology, and implications for disability research.* Unpublished manuscript. East Lansing: Michigan State University Center for International Rehabilitation.

Dell, J. (1986). Social dimensions of epilepsy: Stigma and response. In S. Whitman & B.P. Hermann (Eds.), *The social dimensions of psychopathology in epilepsy* (pp. 185-210). New York: Oxford.

Dingwall, R. (1976). *Aspects of illness.* New York: St. Martin's Press.

Fabrega, H., Jr. (1972a). The study of disease in relation to culture. *Behavioral Science, 17,* 183-200.

Fabrega, H., Jr. (1972b). Concepts of disease: Logical features and social implications. *Perspectives in Biology and Medicine, 15,* 583-616.

Featherstone, H. (1980). *A difference in the family.* New York: Penguin.

Fine, M., & Asch, A. (1981). Disabled women: Sexism without the pedestal. *Journal of Sociology and Social Welfare, 8,* 233-248.

Fisher, B., & Galler, R. (1988). Friendship and fairness: How disability affects friendship between women. In M. Fine & A. Asch (Eds.), *Women with disabilities: Essays in Psychology, Culture, and Politics.* Philadelphia: Temple University Press.

Fitzpatrick, R., Hinton, J., Newman, S., Scambler, G., & Thompson, J. (1984). *The experience of illness.* London: Tavistock.

Freidson, E. (1966). Disability as social deviance. In M.B. Sussman (Ed.), *Sociology and rehabilitation* (pp. 71-99). Washington, D.C.: American Sociological Association.

Freidson, E. (1970). *The profession of medicine.* New York: Dodd, Mead.

Glaser, B.G., & Strauss, A.L. (1967). *The discovery of grounded theory.* Chicago: Aldine.

Goffman, E. (1959). The moral career of the mental patient. *Psychiatry, 22,* 123-135.

Goffman, E. (1963). *Stigma.* Englewood Cliffs, NJ: Prentice-Hall.

Goffman, E. (1969). The insanity of place. *Psychiatry, 32,* 357-388.

Groce, N. (1984). Anthropology and the handicapped: The need for a cross-cultural perspective. In S.C. Hey, G. Kiger, & J. Sidel (Eds.), *Social aspects of chronic illness, impairment and disability* (pp. 197-203). Salem, OR: Willamette University Press.

Gyllenskold, K. (1982). *Breast cancer: The psychological effects of the disese and its treatment.* London: Tavistock.

Harrison, T.R. (1980). *Harrison's principles of internal medicine* (9th ed.). New York: McGraw-Hill.

Herzlich, C. (1973). *Health and illness: A social psychological analysis.* London: Academic Press.

Higgins, P.C. (1979). Outsiders in a hearing world: The deaf community. *Urban Life, 8,* 3-22.

Hughes, E.C. (1958). *Men and their work.* New York: Free Press.

Kidder, L.H., Fagan, M.A., & Cohn, E.S. (1981). Giving and receiving: Social justice in close relationships. In M.J. Lerner & S.C. Lerner (Eds.), *The justice motive in social behavior* (pp. 235-259), New York: Plenum.

Lemert, E.M. (1951). *Social pathology.* New York: McGraw-Hill.

Lemert, E.M. (1972). *Human deviance, social prob-*

lems, and social control (2nd ed.). Englewood Cliffs, NJ: Prentice-Hall.

Locker, D. (1981). Symptoms and illness: The cognitive organization of disorder. London: Tavistock.

Locker, D. (1984). Disability and disadvantage: The consequences of chronic illness. London: Tavistock.

Maines, D. (1983). Time and biography in diabetic experience. Mid-American Review of Sociology, 8, 103-117.

Maines, D. (1984). The social arrangements of diabetic self-help groups. In A.L. Strauss & B.G. Glaser (Eds.), Chronic illness and the quality of life (2nd ed. pp. 111-123). St. Louis, MO: Mosby.

Matza, D. (1969). Becoming deviant. Englewood Cliffs, NJ: Prentice-Hall.

McHugh, P. (1970). A common-sense conception of deviance. In J.D. Douglas (Ed.), Deviance and respectability (pp. 61-88). New York: Basic.

Mead, G.H. (1943). Mind, self, and society. Chicago, University of Chicago Press.

New, P.K. (1984). Disability research and policy. Social Science and Medicine, 19, 585-586.

Parsons, T. (1951). The social system. Glencoe, IL: Free Press.

Rosenhan, D.L. (1973). On being sane in insane places. Science, 179, 250-258.

Roth, J.A., & Conrad, P. (Eds.) (1987). The experience and management of chronic illness (Vol. 6). Greenwich, CT:JAI Press.

Ryan, R., Kempner, K., & Emlen, A.C. (1980). The stigma of epilepsy as a self-concept. Epilepsia, 21, 433-443.

Schneider, J.W., & Conrad, P. (1980). In the closet with illness: Epilepsy, stigma potential, and information control. Social Problems, 28, 32-44.

Schneider, J.W., & Conrad, P. (1981). Medical and sociological typologies: The case of epilepsy. Social Science and Medicine, 15A, 211-219.

Schneider, J.W., & Conrad, P. (1983). Having epilepsy: The experience and control of illness. Philadelphia: Temple University Press.

Sedgwick, P. (1973, Summer/fall). Mental illness is illness. Salmagundi, pp. 196-224.

Shearer, A. (1981). Disability: Whose handicap? Oxford: Blackwell.

Speedling, E.J. (1982). Heart attack: The family response at home and in the hospital. New York: Tavistock.

Stewart, D.C., & Sullivan, T.J. (1982). Illness behavior and the sick role in chronic disease: The case of multiple sclerosis. Social Science and Medic-

ine, 16, 1307-1404.

Strauss, A.L., Fagerhaugh, S., Suczek, B., & Wiener, C. (1982a). The work of hospitalized patients. Social Science and Medicine, 16, 977-986.

Strauss, A.L., Fagerhaugh, S., Suczek, B., & Wiener, C. (1982b). Sentimental work in the technologized hospital. Sociology of Health and Illness, 4, 254-278.

Suczek, B., Fagerhaugh, S., Strauss, A.L., & Wiener, C. (1981). Kin work in a technologized hospital. Unpublished manuscript, Department of Social and Behavioral Sciences, School of Nursing, University of California, San Francisco.

Tannenbaum, F. (1938). Crime and the community. New York: Columbia University Press.

Task Force on Psychology and the Handicapped. (1984). Final report of the Task Force on Psychology and the Handicapped. American Psychologist, 39, 545-550.

Thomas, D. (1982). The experience of handicap. London: Methuen.

Trostle, J.A., Hauser, W.A., & Susser, I.S. (1983). The logic of noncompliance: Management of epilepsy from the patient's point of view. Culture, Medicine and Psychiatry, 7, 35-56.

Voysey, M. (1975). A constant burden: The reconstruction of family life. London: Routledge & Kegan Paul.

Waddell, C. (1982). The process of neutralization and the uncertainties of cystic fibrosis. Sociology of Health and Illness, 4, 210-220.

West, P.B. (1979a). Making sense of epilepsy. In D.J. Osborne, M.M. Gruneberg, & J.R. Eiser (Eds.), Research in psychology and medicine (pp. 162-169). New York: Academic Press.

West, P.B. (1979b). An investigation into the social construction and consequences of the label epilepsy. Sociological Review, 27, 719-741.

West, P.B. (1986). The social meaning of epilepsy: Stigma as a potential explanation for psychopathology in children. In S. Whitman & B.P. Hermann (Eds.), The social dimensions of psychopathology in epilepsy (pp. 245-266). New York: Oxford.

Whitman, S., Coleman, T., Patmon, C., Desai, B., Cohen, R., & King, L. (1984). Epilepsy in prison: Elevated prevalence and no relation to violence. Neurology, 34, 775-782.

Zola, I.K. (1972). Medicine as an institution of social control. Sociological Review, 20, 487-504.

Zola, I.K. (1982). Missing pieces: A chronicle of living with a disability. Philadelphia: Temple University Press.

Hidden Disability

Lynnie Ozer

February 23, 1986

This is a special evening for reflection and gratitude. Tomorrow I will be graduated from New York University with a doctorate in German literature - the culmination of eight years of dedication. A momentous occasion in anyone's life, it is a miracle in mine because I was born retarded.

_____

When I was sixteen months old I was diagnosed by a team of endocrinologists at Duke University as a cretin dwarf or a child born without a functioning thyroid gland. Desiccated thyroid was orally administered and after one month I was transformed from a jaundiced, bloated blob with a protruding tongue to a normal looking infant. One of the doctors told my mother that I would most likely be physically normal but - due to the lateness of the diagnosis - that permanent mental retardation was highly probable. Then he added: "It is ultimately in the hands of the mother and God."

My parents brought me back home to New York and began their determined battle for my normalcy. They became my therapists, making me walk when I crawled, reading to me day and evening until a spark was ignited in my dim awareness. At the age of four I began to read and devoured every book I found. The mental retardation was completely gone! It was fortunate that I had books and the companionship of my parents because the neighbourhood children would have nothing to do with me. Despite the doctor's prognosis, my physical development was severely retarded. When I was five years old I could not walk without falling and was still incontinent. Fairy-tale figures became my friends and I erected a fortress of a fantasy to ease the loneliness. Moreover, my parents gave me the autobiography of Helen Keller which strengthened my own determination to be able to function independently. I fought to learn to ride a bicycle even though I fell off it constantly. My mother sent me to dancing school to develop my coordination. I was never exempted from standards set for my peers. High grades and good manners were expected and my parents were strict with me regarding all infractions.

When I was nine, my father took a position as a rabbi in a small Long Island town. I was the "new girl" at school and that in itself posed difficulty. During physical education classes the competitive upper middle-class girls discovered my inability to perform at their level. I became as a result the outcast and scapegoat for my classmates who would follow me out of the locker room screaming "creep" and "freak" at me. After school they would walk beside me as I headed for home, imitating my awkward gait. To avoid the taunts, I would hide behind the trees until the children were gone. Summers were worse.My parents sent me to camp, believing that the fresh air and sports would be beneficial to me. That should have been the case, but the girls at camp could not comprehend why an ostensibly normal child could not pitch a ball straight or swim a lap as they could. I wasn't even able to run to first base in a ball game without falling. After the games the little girls would wait until no adult was present in our cabin and then pounce upon me, hitting, scratching and biting. "You told us you never had polio," they screamed. "Then why can't you be like us, you freak?" How could I have explained cretinism to them when I myself didn't understand my condition? I only knew that I **had** to take my pills every day of my life. My mother constantly emphasized the urgency of this. It is important to mention that I tried my best to be good at the sports at camp and at school because I never felt that I had the right **not** to do my best. My upbringing ensured that sense of duty in me. No matter how I tried, the children saw the results and not the efforts. Because there were no crutches to excuse my lack of ability, my peers perceived my failure as laziness or spite. I grew to hate the children who tormented me. However, I hated myself even more, certain that I was repulsive and inferior. I never fought back or

Reprinted From: _Journal of Rehabilitation_, Jan/Feb/Mar, 1987, with permission.

retaliated verbally. instead, I sat in my room and prayed that harm would befall my persecutors. Corroded with resentment, I was on the way to becoming mentally as well as physically ill.

My parents had no idea of what was happening to me. I was so ashamed of the constant rejections that I kept silent. It was only when the drama teacher at camp told my mother how the girls were abusing me that the truth began to come out. I was never sent back to summer camp. Then, a fifth-grade teacher called my mother in to tell her that I was severely disturbed. At this point, my mother sought the advice of a psychiatrist who told her to let me express verbally all my rage against the children who humiliated me. Otherwise, he warned, I might become psychotic. She took his suggestion seriously. I will never forget the night after a dance recital when my cousin told me I had moved like a cripple and ruined the show. On the way home I was hanging half way out of the car window, screaming at the top of my lungs: "I hate Judy! God, make her a cripple, too!" My father blanched, but my mother whispered: "Charlie, let her get it out of her system. This may save her."

When I was about eleven years old, my mother explained my condition to me and stressed that the constant rejection I suffered at the hands of my peer was not my fault. Both my parents increased their efforts to be companions to me. When it was discovered that I could sing very well, I was promptly given voice and piano lessons. By the time I was in my early teens I had some status at school because of the leading roles I was given in the musicals. I began to dream of being a great star. My mother, with her usual realism, saw the obstacles that my still faulty coordination would present on a stage and discouraged my ambition. My father, however, nurtured my dreams, constantly telling me how beautiful and gifted I was. This compensated somewhat for the brutalization my self-esteem had undergone at school and at camp.

My father deserves a great deal of credit for my survival during the childhood and teen years. If my mother gave me grit, he healed the wounds dealt me by the other children. My mother set me on the firm ground of reality, which prepared me for life's hardships later on. My father gave me the wings of fantasy I can don at all times. The anchor in reality and the ability to dream thus complement each other. Rather than preach at me, my father lived the decency he expected of me. For example, he found a wallet on the street and promptly brought it to the police station. Although he suffered severe depressions periodically, he never yielded to them and became dysfunctional. My father, and my mother as well, were always motivated by a strong sense of obligation to others. A breakdown would have meant, for my father, reneging on his obligations. He willed himself to weather the storms when they struck. A week before I entered college my father died of leukaemia. During the last year of his life I had an example before me of courage and simple dignity. He promised me he would always be with me, and he was and is. I draw to this day from the wellspring of his legacy. On his gravestone the epitaph stands: "Noble spirit sweet and strong. Wild heart full of dreams." My mother wrote it and expressed therewith the very essence of the man she had loved for twenty-five years. When life seemed least worth living for me, my father would say: "Darling, it takes a realist to believe in miracles." I often use that phrase to encourage myself and others. There is no doubt that I am indebted for whatever I have achieved and surmounted to my valiant and loving parents.

Before I turn to an account of my adult years, I feel it is vital to try to objectify the cruelty I experienced from my peers. That cruelty, I have come to understand, was not levelled at me personally. The girl next door to me had epilepsy. After a seizure she was kicked by a child in our neighbourhood until she bled. The treatment accorded to me and the epileptic girl must be viewed against the background of the times. Those years were the 1950s, a decade of rigid conformity. Any manifestations of differentness, whether physical or mental, were viewed with distrust and hostility. My condition falls into the category of "hidden disability." Diabetics, epileptics and others with illnesses that are not immediately apparent are expected to be like everybody else. When our illness reveals itself, it is usually uncomprehended and hence condemned. Children in my generation were not taught compassion for abnormality. We who had hidden disabilities did not fit into the world of the able-bodied and were not really a part of the world of the visibly disabled. Thus, we straddled both worlds, trying to maintain our balance. The marches of the 1960s, the Women's Movement and the Gay Liberation Movement all paved the way for a new consciousness for the disabled. First, we were called handicapped, then disabled. Now we like to refer to ourselves as physically or mentally challenged. The media have done a great deal to change the image of those who suffer from any form of disability. Beginning with the play and the ensuing film "The Elephant Man," there have been such films as "Mask" and countless television documentaries as well as episodes in popular series depicting the handicaps created by society for the disabled person. The television series "Highway to Heaven" recently showed a story in which a paraplegic lawyer defends a young man with a misshapen face against the charge of assaulting a blind girl. An episode like this one and many other television movies act in the service of enlightenment, changing the disabled person's self-image and also societal attitudes toward disability.

To return to my own story, adulthood has been far better than childhood or adolescence. When I entered the University of Indiana in Bloomington I found caring friends who knew nothing of my past. I was careful to gout the fact of my illness from everybody. Since I did not have to engage in sports, there was no problem. However, despite my happiness at college, the depressions which had plagued my father began to attack me. They occurred from the time I was nineteen and usually lasted a few weeks or even months. With maturity, I find the depressions becoming easier to control. When they come - these tidal waves washing over me - I fight them, refusing to be overwhelmed. Like my father, I have never allowed myself to reach the point of dysfunctionality. In the musical "The Fantastics" the narrator says:

Who understands why spring is born
out of winter's labouring pain
or why we must all die a bit
before we grow again?

After these bouts of depression I emerge from the tunnel of the mind stronger each time.

When I completed my undergraduate work in singing and drama with high honours, I spent seven years abroad teaching, translating and singing concerts. Although my performing career was only part-time, it brought me an enormous sense of worth. Admiration healed - and still heals - the wounds as nothing else can. Out of a sense of obligation toward the medical profession which had made it possible for me to lead a productive life, I took a graduate degree in medical translation and worked during my sojourn in Munich as a translator for a psychiatric research institute. When I returned to New York I found that there were no jobs to utilize my talents as a teacher or translator. Thus, I took a job as a bilingual administrative assistant in a music publishing company where I sank into a massive depression because office work did not strengthen my ego. Again, I pulled myself out of the despondency and worked fanatically until I was promoted to the level of assistant director of the rights clearance department and German language Specialist. Still, I was unfulfilled creatively.

One evening my mother came to my apartment and told me that she had the solution to my problem. She would pay my tuition toward a doctorate in German literature. She believed that the involvement in reaching such a goal would be more therapeutic than lying on a psychiatrists's couch. When I said that I felt like a nobody because I had failed to attain the recognition I had envisioned for myself, my mother took a crumpled piece of paper from her purse and quietly told me: "You have not had the success you wanted and certainly even deserved. That is true. But you have achieved something rarer than most successful people. Don't ever underestimate your accomplishment in overcoming your illness and all the problems in your childhood. You were privileged to triumph." Then she read me the poem that was on the piece of paper. The last verse is:

The way of all fulfilment goes
through darkness to achieve the light.
The root whose daughter is the rose
was nourished in the utter night.
(From "Flowerings" by Olivia Hale)

Thus, my path toward the goal of a doctorate began.

During the years in which I attended classes I distinguished myself and earned the respect of my colleagues and professors. Again, being admired soother the hurt that always lurks beneath the surface. Then, in the spring of 1982 classes ended and I had difficulty in absorbing what I read. A sudden weight gain convinced me that I needed more medication, but my doctor refused to consider this because she thought I would go into a state of thyroid toxicity (which results from an overdose of medication and leads to high blood pressure and even a stroke). At night I would try to study and think that if my dosage was indeed correct, as the doctor maintained, the medication was no longer working and I would become retarded again. I would drink myself to sleep, sobbing in terror. Soon I could not sleep without a bottle of wine. Then it became a pint of vodka. Finally, my mother saw my state and demanded that I increase my medication, which I did. I got slimmer and was able to absorb the literature again. However, the drinking continued. I passed the orals with distinction and then faced the problem of my alcohol dependency. When I saw that I could stop at one glass of wine, I stopped cold and have never had another drink since. Strangely enough, living with my thyroid condition made it easy to face my drinking problem. I think that the reason for recidivism among alcoholics is that they usually have not be acquainted with the limitations imposed by a disability **other** than alcoholism - and alcoholism is a form of disability. I had the advantage in this case because I **already** knew how to cope with the restrictions of illness and with the feeling of being different.

During the next three years I worked on my doctoral dissertation and continued at my job where I enjoyed the support of both colleagues and superiors in my endeavour. In addition, I began to sing at night clubs from time to time. My mother found a new doctor for me and he discovered that I had indeed been underdosed. I go for blood tests regularly now to avoid the consequences of incorrect dosage. The experience with my former thyroid specialist was an object lesson: We disabled people cannot blindly trust anyone simply by virtue of his or her position as "Specialist." The patient can often sense something wrong before it shows up on tests. I know that I have to look out for sudden weight gain or weight loss, lassitude or excessive energy, inability to absorb information or steel-trap apprehension. Above all, I must have my blood tests every few months even though I find the experience unpleasant. In the course of the last two years I have also found a voice to express my situation as a woman with a hidden disability. Writing about it transforms the pain from a prison into poetry.

———

It is already eleven o'clock. I have written steadily for two hours. Yes, I've come a long way, but there is still a great deal to change. Even if I don't live in the past, it lives in me. A humiliation or rejection opens up the scars and leaves the wounds exposed. But I cannot indulge myself in such vulnerability any longer. I am happier than I have ever been and I am loved by many people. My vindictiveness does me more harm than those whom I wish ill. I resent the past and fear the future rather than cherishing the present. Many people suffer far more from their disabilities than I do - in their adulthood as well as in their childhood. The gratitude I should feel at all times is not always there. Like a fearful horse, I stand before the hurdle of the past, wading in the quagmire of old injuries. Will I be able to rise above this, too? Will I be able to transcend it and make it meaningful instead of destructive? I look at my father's picture and recall how he loved to sing with me the freedom song "We Shall Overcome." He would want me to try - at least to try.

Tomorrow I will have my Ph.D.! The road was long and sometimes rough, but I did it! I ask myself sleepily: Would I want to have been spared my disability? No, I wouldn't change anything. My mother's words come back to me: "You were privileged to triumph."

How Shall We See Them? Perspectives for Research with Disabled Organizations

J. THOMAS MAY AND ROBERT F. HILL

Introduction

The broad interest in disability and rehabilitation in the United States during the past decade has resulted in significant achievements in legislation, resource allocation, and a heightened sense of awareness in the general public. These long-overdue developments are laudatory, as is the emerging dialogue among social scientists seeking a broad theoretical framework which permits a more precise understanding of these phenomena.[1]

The Movement for Independent Living (ILM) is a principal context for the dialogue over macro-theoretical constructions of disability.[1-3] This is hardly fortuitous inasmuch as the ILM proposes fundamental revision in traditional institutions and relationships. For example, it is perceived for purposes of analysis as a social movement. Furthermore, it presumes a fundamental shift in the nature of the relationship between disabled and able-bodied societies (ostensibly from toward segregation integration) and it encourages the definition of issues and questions in the context of political economy (resource allocation). Finally, the ILM has promoted a reconsideration of the role of rehabilitation specialists, and in so doing, questioned the efficacy of professional dominance.

Obviously, this dialogue holds profound meaning for future research. At the same time, it has limited meaning for social scientists engaged by other, less-dramatic aspects of disabled life, particularly those investigations with an applied orientation or action programs jointly coordinated with disabled people. These activities are better informed by studies which sort out and test mid-range theory, and particularly by reports which analyze strategies for cooperation between able-bodied social investigators and action groups composed of disabled citizens [4]. Such information is essential to exchange and

negotiation as both groups articulate and negotiate a new set of relationships.

Given the current literary context, this paper will argue for a continuation of a two-tiered research strategy with the exchange over macro-theoretical constructions proceeding simultaneously with a vigorous dialogue around immediate issues which focus on cooperative strategies between disabled and able-bodied groups.

Employing a case analysis, the paper focuses on a documentary film project administered by a group of disabled people and analyzes the theoretical assumptions and positions of two social scientists (able-bodied) who served as consultants to the project. The paper first summarizes the positions of the social scientists (the authors) at the beginning of the project: what they expected to find, which previous theoretical notions would be pertinent and resonant and how expectations and theory would influence their strategy. Next, it contrasts the preliminary assumptions and positions with the realities of the project. A concluding section assesses the 'before/after' contrast and notes the implications which may be useful to other investigators involved in collaborative research endeavors involving disabled people. There are pitfalls to any collaborative endeavour, the most obvious of which have been discussed at length in the exchange of the emic and etic perspectives. The description of our experience can contribute to an expanded discussion of 'outsider-insider' relationships.

The Project

During a 4-year period (1978-1982), the authors served as consultants in the research, production and programming of a documentary film on disability entitled "Breaking Through" [5]. The project was coordinated through a state-wide organization, the Coalition of Citizens, with

Reprinted from *Soc. Sci. Med. Vol. 19, No. 6, pp. 603-608, 1984*, with permission. Printed in Great Britain. All rights Reserved. Pergamon Press, Ltd.

Disabilities (CCD). A committee of the CCD composed exclusively of women was responsible for the administration of the project. This group had conceived and promoted the idea initially, and retained a dominant role throughout the period of the project.

The authors were responsible for a number of different project tasks during this period. Initially, they were commissioned to prepare background papers which would identify salient issues pertinent to disability in American society. In turn, these papers would provide the context within which the film script would be written and the shooting scenes devised. Later, the consultants participated in discussion panels composed of representatives from the CCD, soliciting personal experiences related to these broader issues. Following the completion of the film, the consultants coordinated a series of forums which combined for public audiences throughout the State a screening of the film and a discussion period.

The consultants were further charged with a wider and less tangible responsibility: moderating the adversarial posture of the CCD and insuring a degree of objectivity in the film content and direction. This charge emanated from the primary funding agency [6] which was apprehensive that the film might become one-sided and polemical. This added role did not cause problems with the CCD committee during the period of the film preparation.

The consultant's entree to the disabled group was facilitated initially by the mandate in the grant award requiring the participation of academic consultants in all stages of the project. While such a 'forced' entree might have caused resentment at the outset, it was ameliorated by a positive factor: the consultants provided a buffer and a legitimation to the granting agency.

The formal justification became unnecessary as rapport developed. The second stage of the project called for group discussions focusing on the content of the consultant's position papers. These meetings served in large measure as instructional forums as the CCD representatives described their lives and aspirations. Most were arranged around a social event, such as a luncheon, thereby insuring informality and maximizing

exchange. With the onset of these discussions, the CCD members completely welcomed the consultants, perhaps seeing this as a prime opportunity to 'educate' them. Subsequently, the consultants were included on a regular basis in the social activities of the CCD committee members.

The analysis which follows is based on a variety of types of data. The position papers prepared at the beginning of the project form a reliable point of departure. The field notes accumulated by the authors document the development of the collaborative relationship. In addition, the authors obtained access to the pertinent files of the granting agency which permitted another perspective on the project. Finally, the authors met on a regular basis throughout this period. Their discussions focused on the progress of the project, the preparation of formal papers [7, 8], and a review of pertinent literature. These materials were also used in the preparation of this paper.

The Preliminary Framework and Strategy

The authors were required to prepare position papers at the outset of the project. These papers sought to define in broad fashion the context within which the movie script would be drafted. The papers focused on disability from three perspectives——cultural anthropology, medical sociology and social history. Quite apart from their role in the project, these papers articulated the authors' assumptions regarding disability. As such, they provided an explicit framework for the strategies which the authors would employ in working with the disabled group. A brief summary of these positions will provide a basis for contrasting subsequent actions.

Disability form the outside

In its broadest terms, we conceived of disability as a socially-conferred identity with varying manifestations across cultural lines and historical periods. The classic work of Goffman [9] provided the obvious foundation and a point of departure. Specifically, we anticipated that our response and that of other able-bodied persons would vary according to the extent and visibility of the disability. The authors further expected that there would be a differential response based on their perceptions of the cause, or source of the disability. The public esteem accorded paraplegics presumed by gender, age and setting to be military veterans was obvious. This would have meaning particularly at the outset when relationships were impersonal and fleeting. Closely related was the assumption that our response would vary according to our perceptions regarding the individual's degree of control over the disability.

The authors fixed these perceptions in the context of historical patterns of popular values and images. Vital themes of American ideology were at issue——the efficacy of work, rugged individualism and personal self-sufficiency. The attitudes of able-bodied people toward the disabled would be influenced by their historical themes. We were impressed with the extraordinary burden imposed on disabled persons by these ideologies; the image of rugged individualism, for example, was in sharp contrast to the realities of disabled life. Among historical images, we noted, there appeared to emerge two key themes in the mind of the non-disabled: disability conferred extraordinary prowess on other senses, and the vacillation in the popular mind between pity and ostracism. The former theme found expression in images ranging from Beethoven to Franklin Roosevelt; it presumed that the loss of one attribute or sense somehow enhanced the others. The latter theme, we felt, was typified best by Gill's description of the response to a co-worker at the *New Yorker*:

> He was lame. One had to feel sympathy for him because of that inescapable burden.... It became plain early in his stay with us that...he trafficked in his lameness.... He was a writer of little talent, but...how did he continue to trick us into feeling that if we didn't admire his work, we were despising him as a cripple?[10]

Within the disabled community

From their previous research, the authors anticipated that the socially-prescribed roles defined by the able-bodied society would be met in varying ways by the members of the CCD. Earlier work by Hill and Stein [11-13], for example, prompted us to anticipate a certain degree of stigma 'disavowal' or 'passing'; the evidence of these phenomena within ethnic/racial groups, we reasoned, was sufficient to suspect it among the disabled. We further anticipated that the project might provide the vehicle for a 'revival' movement not unlike the earlier white, ethnic movement in the United States [11]. Such a development, stressing the positive aspects of disability and the need for social and political cohesion, might be deemed essential for the interests of nascent leaders among the disabled.

The concept of culture was the keystone for our expectations of intergroup dynamics. We presumed that shared sentiments and values, common experiences of rejection and inequitable access to resources would crystallize into some form of social cohesion. At one extreme, there could be a 'culture of disability', not unlike the 'culture of poverty' formulated by Lewis [14, 15]. This postulation assumed that disabled persons adapted to their way of life and devised strategies to achieve maintenance. Following Valentine [16] we gave little currency to such a dubious notion. However, we did anticipate that the able-bodied public might employ such an ideology to explain individual and group behavior among disabled persons. It was possible, we thought, that a variation of this concept could be used to explain group cohesion among individuals with different forms of disability.

A more reasonable use of the culture concept, we anticipated, might follow the logic and direction of ethnic studies. A genre of polemical literature from disabled organizations was being published and circulated. Much of this literature depicted the disabled as 'the last minority', linking with singular clarity the disability movement in the popular mind with the revered, historical movements. We doubted that this literature could coalesce a population with vast diversities of disabilities. Instead, we hypothesized a somewhat different possibility——the evolution of a pluralist, cultural mosaic, uniting common concerns of a diverse group into something akin to a 'panethic' movement. Such a concept appeared pertinent for the analysis of CCD groups.

The Project Experience

The world that we found differed in significant ways from what we had anticipated. We will present our observations in the context of what we expected and address three general categories: (a) the social organization of a disabled community; (b) relations with the able-bodied world; (c) the viability of culture as a tool for analysis.

The social organization of a disabled group
The consultants approached the project anticipating that the very substance of disability would provide the basis of social organization, clique formation and power relationships. We reasoned that disability was all pervasive and that factors such as severity, date of onset and similarity of appliances would explain behavior patterns; that the experiences common to individuals with multiple sclerosis, for example, would dominate all aspects of their lives. Similarly, it seemed logical to assume that individuals with early-childhood onset or congenital limitations would have experiences vastly different from those with 'acquired' or adult-onset disabilities. While the paraplegic experience is profound in our society, we anticipated that victims of accidents in adulthood had led a life vastly different from a person paralysed from childhood, and therefore, would have a much different world view.

We quickly realized, however, that the force of the disability factors was moderated to a significant degree by variables more reflective of the able-bodied society. Specifically, the primary basis of social organization within this population was education, gender, marital status, age and local-cosmopolitan orientation.

The traditional notion of gender roles, so obvious in the broader society, was reflected clearly within the disabled community, particularly in terms of power and resource allocation. The consultant became aware of the pervasiveness of traditional role expectations early in the project. Women informants on the film committee depicted the state organization as 'chauvinist' and 'male-dominated'. Both in structure and organization, respondents argued, the organization reflected the attitude that men should exercise political power and organizational leadership. At the onset of the project, there were no women serving as officers of the state CCD; there was only one exception to this organizational pattern 4 years later. The committee which assumed responsibility for the production of the film was composed entirely of women. While several disabled males participated in this activity, particulary in the discussion groups, their involvement was unenthusiastic.

The evidence of male dominance became more visible and palpable as the stakes increased. Midway through the project, the CCD mandated the formation of a committee to develop a consulting arm of the organization. The purpose of this committee was to advertise and coordinate professional consulting services to those public and private agencies seeking to implement Section 504 (Rehabilitation Act of 1973). The discussions around this and similar entrepreneurial efforts were always couched in economic terms; consulting jobs would be well paid. At no point in the deliberations or the subsequent activities of this committee were women brought into participation.

Variations in levels of formal education provided another useful indicator of clique formation within the disabled group community. The core members of the film committee had developed alliances in graduate school; to a significant degree, they revolved as satellites around a particularly dynamic and sympathetic faculty member. The graduate school experience and orientation imparted a level of cosmopolitanism significantly different from the majority of women associated with CCD, most of whom were from the rural-small town settings with considerably less formal education.

Finally, all of the women on the film committee were single at the time of the project. This obviously permitted a relative level of freedom beyond that of their peers who had family responsibilities. More significant, perhaps, it allowed them to anticipate a professional career at some future point.

Relations with the able-bodied world

The respondent's relations with the non-disabled world were based in large measure on a fundamental conviction: the traditional image of disabled people ('stereotypes') was demeaning to both groups and had to be changed; some new form for interpersonal relationships had to be substituted. The respondents pursued this goal with near-crusade fervour. It dominated their conversations and was in fact a fundamental rationale for the preparation of the film. There was no clear consensus as to the form that the new relationship should take; equity, independence and mutual respect were general characteristics mentioned.

In the absence of a clear model of the 'idealized' new relationship, the respondents spent considerable time and energy documenting the prevalence of the traditional 'stereotypes'. The behavior of peers was scrutinized with the same care afforded able-bodied individuals and groups. A demeaning image existed for each disability and when peers exhibited behaviors approaching this image, they became the focus of opprobrium. The blind pencil salesperson ('rattling cups') was one prominent example; wheel-chair-bound persons accepting unessential assistance was another. Above all else, the 'stereotype' was characterized by dependence and passivity.

The attempt to recast this traditional image forced the respondents to identify and attach institutions which perpetuated these images in contemporary life. The telethons were a source of particular concern. They were seen as a reinforcement in the public mind of the abject dependence of disabled persons. The respondents viewed the telethons as no more than one small step beyond the image of the begging cripple; they were sanitized, impersonal appeals to emotion based on a presentation which emphasized dependence. The telethons not only failed to address the question of inequity, they reinforced it. Perhaps of equal significance, the telethons commanded a larger viewing audience and thus, influenced a significant part of the population. To disclaim publicly the telethons was almost a cardinal requirement for participation within the CCD group.

This attitude found expression in the film. The concluding section contained a lengthy sequence which summarized and restated in visual form all of these objections. A television set tuned to one of the telethons provided the audio background as the camera presented the visual image of a disabled person (cerebral palsy) in the process of preparing a complicated meal in her own apartment. This was followed by a film sequence which captured the cook and her friends (most of whom were able-bodied) at the table preparing to eat. The image of a wheel-chair-bound person manipulating kitchen appliances, exhibiting culinary skills and entertaining a 'mixed' (disabled and non-disabled) party of friends contrasted starkly with the presentation of disabled life on the telethon.

The attempts to devise a new set of relationships was confounded by the absence of functional models to emulate. There existed in the popular literature few examples which depicted for the average disabled person equitable relationships with the able-bodied world. The increased publicity devoted to disability in the 1970s had focused on the achievements of disabled individuals in 'normal' activities: paraplegics who bowled or played basket ball; sight-impaired students with reading appliances. Little attention was devoted to the perceptions of those achievements by able-bodied persons, and more importantly, how these perceptions would find expression in specific relationships. The contemporary media presentations offered no real alternative. Nor were models available within the CCD group. Among the respondents, there were no examples known to the investigators of successful 'mixed' marriages or long-term relationships.

In their attempt to develop and propagate a model of an 'idealized' relationship, the respondents focused attention on their ability to perform routine but essential daily-living activities. The fact that disabled persons could have a normal sexual life was an important issue. The inability of the able-bodied world to understand this was evidence for the respondents of their existence of the traditional 'stereotype'. Discussions on this topic were punctuated with humorous anecdotes describing the naivete of non-disabled persons. More privately, some informants were not guarded in describing prior sexual affairs or liaisons. The film broached this theme through the description of a paraplegic mother who had delivered two children through natural childbirth methods.

Occupational status and achievement was another daily-living activity essential to the contemporary image of disability, and therefore, the new relationship with the able-bodied world. A regular job was highly prized and those with careers widely esteemed. Above all, a job or career held the promise of regular income and thereby, relief from dependence on family or meagre disability payments. A job, therefore, promised to provide the basis for bridging the able-bodied and disabled worlds. While these views were regular topics in conversations with the respondents, they were explored in detail in the film. Each disabled person featured in the film was identified in terms of a career or occupation. Each person selected for inclusion in the film had an occupation and regular income, achievements not common among the general disabled population. In the minds of the respondents, occupational status represented one of the credentials essential to acceptance on an equitable basis by the majority society.

The respondents felt they could best pursue the mission of changing the traditional stereotypes of disabled people through education of the able-bodied public. The overall project (film and public forums) was structured with this in mind. Their choice of this strategy was facilitated by the marginal status they held within the CCD power structure. From this marginal position and with their more cosmopolitan contacts, the respondents felt equipped to function as gatekeepers to the disabled world.

The consultants fit well into this scheme. As faculty members with doctoral degree, they were presumed to have a certain level of expertise which would legitimize the mission and strategy. The association of the consultants with health and medical education provided an additional measure of status.

Given this mission and strategy, the type of leader who evolved among our respondents was significantly different from what had been anticipated. We had presumed that gatekeeping and leadership functions would be allocated to those with skills and characteristics which most approximated the able-bodied society. The earlier civil rights and white ethnic movements provided a basis for this assumption; in the initial stages of those movements, leadership had been assumed by individuals with social backgrounds (education and occupation) and physical characteristics (skin color, physical appearance) most closely approximating leadership in the majority society. The assumption, however, proved only partly correct. While education and occupation clearly were significant predictors, physical characteristics and limitations were not.

The individual who assumed the principle leadership role had cerebral palsy. She served as the project director for the film grant. Of all our respondents, several of whom served in equally-important positions this person had the most severe disability; she had neural, motor, and aural limitations. Yet, the film committee insisted throughout the project that she function as the leader and represent the group in all dealings with able-bodied groups. One official (able-bodied) at the granting agency recalled:

It was almost as if they (the disabled group) were rubbing disability in our face. It was much more than simply legitimizing themselves, because all of them had disabilities. It was a conscious thing; she was the most disabled [17].

While interpersonal relations with the able-bodied world reflected this mission of education, the disabled respondents approached medical professionals and institutions in a somewhat different fashion. To a large extent, this was based on their prior personal experiences most of which had been unfavourable. One particularly dramatic sequence in the film summarized a widely-held attitude. A paraplegic woman spoke with considerable emotion of the impersonal treatment by physicians:

They treated my body as if I were not there. They controlled my body. It was only after I got away from them that I regained control of my body [18].

Yet these and other unsavoury experiences had to be balanced against the necessary dependence on medicine and medical care professionals. Periodic check-ups and therapy routines were essential for most respondents. Moreover, there was the dilemma prompted by vague promises in the media of eminent scientific 'breakthoughs' which could achieve 'cures'.

This genre of information ('the magic cure') presented a profound dilemma to the disabled group. It was discussed only on rare occasions; it was ignored completely in the film script. While the respondents were genuinely pleased for those individuals who might be potential benefactors of the new technology, they were also aware of the negative effects on the group. such innovations promised to exempt or 'relieve' a person of the fundamental element of identity with the disabled community. Furthermore, the fact that a condition might be 'cured' or altered to a 'normal' stage was a subtle and unwelcome reminder to the respondents that disability was not the identity of choice when alternatives were available.

The resulting ambivalence in the minds of the respondents was highlighted in the course of the project. One person featured in the film had impaired hearing. He had been featured prominently as a model of occupational achievement. A cooperating employer had arranged a simple and inexpensive device to permit him to perform a job that customarily required hearing; he had become a model employee. After the filming and prior to distribution, this person received successfully a cochlear implant which corrected the disability. Subsequently, his participation in the CCD group declined, and there was little or no mention of him in subsequent conversations.

Implications

There are lessons from this case analysis which have implications for future research with disabled groups. We will summarize these points in two categories: (1) theoretical frameworks for understanding the disabled community and (2) strategies for cooperative, action research.

The use of culture as an operational framework for research with groups similar in com-position to the CCD is limited. The diversity of the disability experience negated any sense of shared values and behaviors. The conventional mechanisms for identity maintenance within an organization——familial, political, residential, consanguineal——were absent in the CCD. Instead, shared values and sentiments were derived largely from the common experiences of stigma and rejection by the able-bodied society. Within that set of experiences, power and clique formation was associated with factors reflective of the values of the broader society, such as gender roles, education and occupation.

To the extent that diversity effects organizational cohesion and member identity, the disability-specific organizations may exhibit a greater sense of 'community'. Though their focus was on stigma, this is one of the key findings in the seminal research of Ablon [4] and Becker [19]. These organizations, therefore, are more able to articulate and pursue specific programs which seek to meet the needs of the membership.

Coalitions of disabled individuals attempt, through enlarged membership and organizational efficiency, to represent more effectively the broad interests of their constituents. In this process, specific goals are replaced by ones more universal in nature. At the same time, these organization exhibit less of the sense of 'community' apparent in disability-specific groups. We have suggested that these umbrella or coalition groups may be approached as diluted, panethnic organizations. However, we have reservations about the veracity of a theoretical framework which relies heavily on the model of ethnicity.

The degree of homogeneity of an organization of disabled persons may influence decisively cooperative research ventures with interested social investigators who are able-bodied. As a hearing person, for example, Becker [19] found some initial 'reticence' on the part of her respondents in an organization of hearing-impaired persons.

Our experience with entry to a coalition group was much less difficult. The respondents had not dealt with their disability (coping) through a set of experiences which were common to all—— the 'normalizing' process that Davis [20] noted. We believe this contributed to the lack of clear and rigid boundaries for the coalition group, thereby facilitating our access. Perhaps equally important, the respondents had defined as a mission the need to change the traditional roles and relationships. With such an agenda, it is plausible that they considered efforts directed toward boundary definition and group unity within the disabled community as 'traditional' and counter-productive.

References

1. Williams G.H. The movement for independent living: an evaluation and critique. *Soc. Sci. Med.* **15**, 1003-1010, 1983.
2. DeJong G. *The Movement for Independent Living: Origin, Ideology and Implications for Disability Research*. University Center for International Rehabilitation, U.S.A./Michigan State University, 1979.
3. Ben-Sira Z. Societal integration of the disabled: power struggle or enhancement of individual coping capacities. *Soc. Sci. Med.* **15**, 1011-1014, 1983.
4. Ablon J. Dwarfism and social identity; self-help group participation. *Soc. Sci. Med.* **15B**, 25-30, 1981.
5. Breaking Through: A Documentary Film on Disability (16mm, 30 minutes). Sponsored by the State Coalition of Citizens with Disabilities, 1980.
6. Major funding for the film was provided by the State Humanities Committee, a state-based program sponsored in part by the National Endowment for the Humanities.
7. May J.T. and Hill R.F. Consorting with the disabled: problems and prospects. Paper presented at the meetings of the Society for Applied Anthropology, Denver, CO, 1980.
8. May J.T. and Hill R.F. The humanist consultant in social issue media projects: problems of role and structure. Unpublished paper, 1981.
9. Goffman E. *Stigma: Notes on the Management of Spoiled Identity*. Prentice-Hall, Englewood Cliffs, NJ, 1963.
10. Gill B. *Here at the New Yorker,* p.19, Random House, New York, 1975.
11. Stein H.F. and Hill R.F. *The Ethnic Imperative: Examining the New White Ethnic Movement*. The Pennsylvania State University Press, University Park, 1977.
12. Stein H.F. and Hill R.F. Adaptive modalities among Polish and Slovak Americans. *Anthropology* **3**, 95-107, 1979.
13. Hill R.F. *Exploring the Dimensions of Ethnicity*. Arno Press, New York, 1980.
14. Lewis O. *Five Families: Mexican Case Studies in the Culture of Poverty*. Basic Books, New York, 1959.
15. Lewis O. *La Vida: A Puerto Rican Family in the Culture of Poverty*. Random House, New York, 1966.
16. Valentine, C.C. *Culture and Poverty: Critique and Counter-proposals*. The University of Chicago Press, Chicago, 1968.
17. Interview, Assistant Director, State-based Humanities program.
18. Film Script, Breaking Through: A Documentary film on Disability.
19. Becker G. Coping with stigma: lifelong adaptation of deaf people. *Soc. Sci. Med.* **15B**, 21-24, 1981.
20. Davis F. *Passage Through Crisis*. Bobbs Merrill, Indianapolis, 1963.

APPENDIX A

Bibliography of Organizations for the Disabled
- American and Canadian

This work has attempted to identify and analyse many of the crucial concerns that effect the disabled and those who come into contact with them in various domains. Specific information on particular disabilities may be obtained by contacting the national organizations which service the individual disabilities, in both Canada and the United States. Some of these organizations are outlined on the following pages. In larger communities there are often local organizations, many of which are affiliated with national groups; these organizations constitute an excellent resource base for information and, in many instances, counseling.

If you are uncertain as to which organization you should contact for specific concerns and problems please write the author at the following address: Dr. Mark Nagler, Department of Sociology, Renison College, University of Waterloo, Waterloo, Ontario, Canada, N2L 3G4. Telephone (519) 884-4400.

AMERICAN ORGANIZATIONS FOR DISABLED PEOPLE

Accent on Information
P.O. Box 700
Bloomington, Il 61702
(309) 378-2961

Access for the Handicapped
5014 42nd Street, N.W.
Washington, D.C. 20016
(202) 966-5500

American Amputee Foundation
Box 55218, Hillcrest Station
Little Rock, AR 72225
(501) 666-2523

American Society of Handicapped
Physicians
105 Morris Dr.
Bastrop, LA, 71220
(318) 281-4436

Amputee Shoe and Glove Exchange
P.O. Box 27067
Houston, Texas 77227

Amputees in Motion
P.O. Box 2703
Escondido, CA 92025
(619) 454-9300

Association for Children and Adults
with Learning Disabilities
4156 Library Road
Pittsburgh, PA 15234
(412) 341-1515

Association for Hispanic Handicapped
of New Jersey
Ten Jackson St.
Patterson, NJ, 07501
(201) 742-7500

Association of Learning Disabled Adults
P.O. Box 9722, Friendship Station
Washington, DC 20016
(202) 593-1035

Association of Rehabilitation Programs
in Data Processing
P.O. Box 2392
Gaithsburg, MD 20879
(301) 640-5444

Canine Companions for Independence
P.O. Box 446
Santa Rosa, CA 95402
(707) 528-0830

Center on Human Policy
724 Comstock Ave.
Syracuse University
Syracuse, NY 12344
(315) 443-3851

Congress of Organizations of the
Physically Handicapped
16630 Beverly
Tinly Park, IL 60477

Council of Citizens with Low Vision
1400 N Drake Rd., #218
Kalamazoo, MI 49007
(616) 381-9566

Council For Learning Disabilities
P.O. Box 40303
Overland Park, KS 66204
(913) 492-8755

Disability Rights Center
2500 Q St., N.W., Suite 121
Washington, DC 20007
(202) 337-4119

Disability Rights Education
and Defense Fund
2212 Sixth Street
Berkeley, CA 94710
(415) 664-2555

Disabled People's International (U.S.A.)
1720 Oregon St., Suite 4
Berkeley, CA 94703
(415) 486-8314

Easter Seal Research Foundation of the
National Easter Seal Society
c/o National Easter Seal Society
70 E. Lake Street
Chicago, Il 60601
(312) 726-6200

Extensions for Independence
757 Emroy St., #514
Imperial Beach, CA 92032
(619) 423-7709

Foundation for Children With
Learning Disabilities
99 Park Avenue, 6th Floor
New York, NY 10016
(212) 687-7211

Foundation for Science and the
Handicapped
236 Grand Street
Morgantown, WY 26505
(307) 293-5201

Gazette International Networking Institute
4502 Maryland Ave.
St. Louis, MO 63108
(314) 361-0475

Goodwill Industries of America
9200 Wisconsin Ave.
Bethesda, MD 20814
(301) 530-6500

Goodwill Industries Volunteer Services
9200 Wisconsin Ave.
Bethesda, MD 20814
(301) 530-6500

Handicap Introductions
22N Main Street, #1
P.O. Box 232
Coopersburg, PA 18036
(215) 282-1577

Human Resources Center
I.U. Willets Road
Albertson, NY 11507
(516) 747-5400

Indoor Sports Club
145 Highland St.
Napoleon, OH 43545
(419) 592-5756

Information Center for Individuals
With Handicaps
Ft. Point Place
17-43 Wormwood Street
Boston, MA 02210
(617) 727-5540

International Association of
Laryngectomees
c/o American Cancer Society
Tower Place
3340 Peachtree Road, N.E.
Atlanta, GA 30026
(404) 320-3333

International Council on Disability
25 E. 21st Street
New York, NY 10010
(212) 420-1500

International Mailbag Club
c/o Mrs. James Sheppard
130 Center St.
Findlay, OH 45840
(419) 422-2362

Just One Break
373 Park Ave. S.
New York, NY 10016
(212) 725-2500

Job Accommodation Network
809 Allen
P.O. Box 6122
West Virginia University
Morgantown, WV 26500

Learning How
P.O. Box 35481
Charlotte, NC 28235
(704) 376-4735

Lost Cords Club
c/o American Cancer Society
International Association of
Laryngectomees
1599 Cliffton Road N.E.
Atlanta, GA 30329
(404) 898-1400

Medical, Educational, Social Service
Association
476 Main Street
West Chicago, Il 60185
(312) 393-2930

Mobility International (U.S.A.)
P.O. Box 3551
Eugene, OR 97403
(503) 343-1284

Multidisciplinary Institute for
Neuropsychological Development
48 Garden Street
Cambridge, MA 02138
(617) 547-9845

International Amputation Foundation
12-45 150th St.
Whitestone, NY 11357
(718) 767-0596

National Association of the
Physically Handicapped
76 Elm Street
London, OH 43140
(614) 852-1664

National Association of the
Protection and Advocacy Systems
220 I Street, N.E., Suite 150
Washington, DC 20001
(202) 546-8202

National Council on Independent Living
c/o Access Living
310 S. Petoria Street, Suite 210
Chicago, IL 60607
(312) 226-5900

National Easter Seal Society
70 E. Lake Street
Chicago, IL 60601
(312) 726-6200

National Industries for the
Severely Handicapped
2235 Cedar Ln.
Vienna, VA 22180
(703) 560-6800

National Information Center for
Children and Youth with Handicaps
P.O. Box 1492
Washington, DC 20013
(202) 893-6061

National Institute for
Rehabilitation Engineering
P.O. Box T
Hewitt, NJ 07421
(201) 853-6585

National Network of Learning
Disabled Adults
c/o Jay Brill
808 N. 82nd Street, Suite F2
Scottsdale, AZ 85257
(602) 941-5112

National Odd Shoe Exchange
P.O. Box 56845
Phoenix, AZ 85079
(602) 246-8725

Networking Project for Disabled
Women and Girls
c/o YWCA of the City of New York
610 Lexington Ave. 9th Floor
New York, NY 10022
(212) 755-4500

Para-Amps
P.O. Box 515
South Beliot, IL 61080
(815) 362-3627

People to People Committee
for the Handicapped
P.O. Box 18131
Washington, DC 20036
(202) 774-7446

Perceptions Inc.
P.O. Box 142
Millburn, NJ 07041
(201) 376-3766

PRIDE Foundation - Promote Real
Independence for the Disabled and Elderly
71 Plaza Ct.
Gorton, CT 06340
(203) 445-1448

Resna
1101 Connecticut Ave., N.W.,
Suite 700
Washington, D.C. 20036
(202) 857-1199

Responsible Hospitality Institute
11 Pearl Street
Springfield, MA 01103
(413) 732-7780

Siblings for Significant Change
105 E. 22nd St., 7th Floor
New York, NY 10010
(212) 420-0776

Special Recreation Inc.
362 Koser Ave.
Iowa City, IA 52246
(319) 337-7578

Support Dogs for the Handicapped
P.O. Box 966
St. Louis, MO 63044
(314) 487-2004

TASH: The Association for Persons with
Severe Handicaps
7010 Roosevelt Way N.E.
Seattle, WA 98115
(206) 523-8446

Time Out To Enjoy
P.O. Box 1084
Evanston, IL 60204
(312) 940-9633

United Together
3111 Haworth
University of Kansas
Lawrence, KS 66045
(913) 864-4950

Very Special Arts
J.F. Kennedy Center for the Performing
Arts
Education Office
Washington, DC 20566
(202) 662-8899

World Institute on Disability
1720 Oregon Street, Suite 4
Berkeley, CA 94703
(415) 486-8314

World Rehabilitation Fund
400 E. 34th Street
New York, NY 10016
(212) 340-6062

CANADIAN ORGANIZATIONS FOR DISABLED PEOPLE

Toronto Organizations:

Canadian Anaesthetists Society
187 Gerrard Street East
Toronto, Ontario M5B 2K8
(416) 923-1449

Canadian Association for Narcolepsy
1947 Avenue Road
Toronto, Ontario M5R 2G1
(416) 782-5930

Canadian Association
for Rehabilitation
234 Eglinton East
Toronto, Ontario M4O 1K5
(416) 481-9111

Canadian Association of
Speech - Language
Pathologists and Audiologists
44 Eglinton West
Toronto, Ontario M4R 1A1
(416) 440-0641

Canadian Association of the Deaf
271 Spadina Road
Toronto, Ontario M5R 2V3
(416) 928-1350

Canadian Cancer Society
2 Carlton
Toronto, Ontario M5B 1J3
(416) 593-7533

Canadian Cystic Fibrosis
Foundation
2221 Yonge Street
Toronto, Ontario M4S 2B4
(416) 485-9149

Canadian Deaf, Blind and
Rubella Association
Meaford, Ontario
(519) 538-3431

Canadian Diabetes Association
National Office:
78 Bond
Toronto, Ontario M5B 2J8
(416) 362-4440
Toronto Branch:
562 Eglinton Street East
Toronto, Ontario M4P 1B9
(416) 488-8871

Canadian Rehabilitation Council for the
Disabled
1 Yonge Street
Toronto, Ontario M5E 1N4
(416) 862-0340

Canadian Rehabilitative Consultants
64 Melrose Avenue
Toronto, Ontario M5M 1Y5
(416) 482-5047

Canadian Rett Syndrome Association
7 Snowcrest
Toronto, Ontario M2K 2K5
(416) 226-0559

Canadian Sickle Cell Society
1801 Eglinton West
Toronto, Ontario M6E 2M8
(416) 789-7615

Canadian Trauma Consultants Limited
65 Queen Street West
Toronto, Ontario M5M 2M5
(416) 863-1581

Canadian Dietetic Association
480 University Avenue
Toronto, Ontario M5G 1W8
(416) 596-0857

Canadian Friends of Schizophrenics
95 Barber Greene
Toronto, Ontario M3C 2A2
(416) 455-8204

Canadian Geriatrics Research Society
21 Dundas Square
Toronto, Ontario M5B 1B6
(416) 363-3218

Canadian Group Psychotherapy Association
27 Renova Drive
Toronto, Ontario M9C 3E8
(416) 621-8413

Canadian Hearing Society
271 Spadina Road
Toronto, Ontario M5R 2V3
(416) 964-9595
(Also Ontario Deafness Research Fund)

Canadian Heart Foundation
477 Mount Pleasant
Toronto, Ontario M4S 2L9
(416) 489-7100

Canadian Hemophilia Society
1300 Yonge Street
Toronto, Ontaro M4T 1W6
(416) 972-0641

Canadian Institute of Health Care
1886 Eglinton Avenue West
Toronto, Ontario M6E 2J5
(416) 785-5572

Canadian Mental Health Association
3101 Bathurst
Toronto, Ontario M6A 2A6
(416) 789-9757

Canadian National Institute
for the Blind
1931 Bayview Avenue
Toronto, Ontario M4G 4C8
(416) 480-7580

Canadian Occupational Therapy Foundation
110 Eglinton Avenue West
Toronto, Ontario M4R 2G5
(416) 487-5404

Canadian Paraplegic Association
520 Sutherland Drive
Toronto, Ontario M4G 1C1
(416) 422-5640

Canadian Phlebitis Society
275 MacPherson
Toronto, Ontario M4V 1A4
(416) 920-3067

Canadian Physiotherapy Association
44 Eglinton Avenue West
Toronto, Ontaro M4R 1A1
(416) 485-1139

Canadian Psychiatric Research Foundation
220 Yonge Street
Toronto, Ontario M5B 2M1
(416) 591-9289

Canadian Red Cross Society
6725 Airport Road
Toronto, Ontario
(416) 678-8000
(613) 739-3000

Canadian Patients Rights Association
40 Homewood Avenue
Toronto, Ontario M4Y 2K2
(416) 923-9629

Canadian Spina Bifida & Hydrocephalus
Association
55 Queen Street East, Suite 300
Toronto, Ontario M5C 1R6
(416) 364-1871

Easter Seal Society
24 Ferrand Drive
Toronto, Ontario M3C 3N2
(416) 421-8377

Multiple Sclerosis Society
P.O. Box 144, Station D
Scarborough, Ontario
(416) 281-1211

Muscular Dystrophy Association
150 Eglinton Avenue East
Toronto, Ontario M4P 1J3
(416) 488-0030

Low Vision Association of Ontario
145 Adelaide West
Toronto, Ontario M5M 3W9
(416) 868-1001

Freedom in Travelling
65 Tromley Drive
Etobicoke, Ontario M9B 5X7
(416) 234-8511

Epilepsy Association
80 Richmond Street West, Suite 804
Toronto, Ontario M5M 2A4
(416) 363-4011

Ontario Society for Autistic Citizens
5468 Dundas Street West
Toronto, Ontario M9B 1B5
(416) 231-2426

Ottawa Organizations:

Canadian AIDS Society
11-170 Laurier Avenue West
Ottawa, Ontario K1P 6J6
(613) 230-3580

Canadian Blind Sports Association
1600 James Naismith Drive
Ottawa, Ontario K1B 5N8
(613) 748-5609

Canadian Cancer Society
268 Bd Street - Joseph Mi
Ottawa, Ontario
(613) 777-4428

Canadian Cerebral Palsy Association
880 Wellington
Ottawa, Ontaro K1R 6K7
(613) 235-4048

Canadian Council on Smoking and Health
1565 Carling Avenue
Ottawa, Ontario K1Z 8R1
(613) 722-3419

Canadian Deaf Sports Association
427 Preston
Ottawa, Ontario K1S 4N3
(613) 235-7880

Canadian Diabetes Association
205-251 Bank Street
Ottawa, Ontario K2P 1X2
(613) 235-9154

Canadian Downs Syndrome Society
2685 Iris
Ottawa, Ontrio K2C 1E4
(613) 596-1399

Canadian Federation of Sport
Organizations for the Disabled
1600 Naismith Place
Ottawa, Ontario K1B 5N8
(613) 748-5630

Canadian Foundation for Ileitis and
Colitis (Crohn's Disease)
12 Parkmount Crescent
Nepean, Ontario K2M 5T4
(613) 596-9635

Canadian National Institute
for the Blind
320 McLeod
Ottawa, Ontario K2P 1A2
(613) 563-4021

Canadian Paraplegic Association
703-200 Elgin
Ottawa, Ontario K2P 2K6
(613) 235-8305

Canadian Pediatric Kidney Disease
Reference Center
451 Smythe Road
Ottawa, Ontario K1H 8M5
(613) 737-4098

Canadian Psoriasis Foundation
1565 Carling Avenue
Ottawa, Ontario K1Z 8R1
(613) 728-4000